THE OXFORD HANDBOOK OF

LATIN AMERICAN ECONOMICS

THE OXFORD HANDBOOK OF

LATIN AMERICAN ECONOMICS

Edited by

JOSÉ ANTONIO OCAMPO

and

JAIME ROS

OXFORD
UNIVERSITY PRESS

OXFORD
UNIVERSITY PRESS

Great Clarendon Street, Oxford OX2 6DP

Oxford University Press is a department of the University of Oxford.
It furthers the University's objective of excellence in research, scholarship,
and education by publishing worldwide in

Oxford New York

Auckland Cape Town Dar es Salaam Hong Kong Karachi
Kuala Lumpur Madrid Melbourne Mexico City Nairobi
New Delhi Shanghai Taipei Toronto

With offices in

Argentina Austria Brazil Chile Czech Republic France Greece
Guatemala Hungary Italy Japan Poland Portugal Singapore
South Korea Switzerland Thailand Turkey Ukraine Vietnam

Oxford is a registered trade mark of Oxford University Press
in the UK and in certain other countries

Published in the United States
by Oxford University Press Inc., New York

British Library Cataloguing in Publication Data
Data available

Library of Congress Cataloging in Publication Data
Data available

Typeset by SPI Publisher Services, Pondicherry, India
Printed in Great Britain by
on acid-free paper by
CPI Antony Rowe, Chippenham, Wiltshire

ISBN 978-0-19-957104-8

1 3 5 7 9 10 8 6 4 2

Preface

Latin America has been central to the main debates in development economics. Given the region's traditionally high levels of inequality in the distribution of income in comparison to other developing regions and the developed nations, this includes, first of all, the relationships between income inequality and economic growth. The debates on the importance of geography vs. institutions in development have often concentrated on Latin America's colonial legacy. The region's experiences with import substitution industrialization in the post war period and more recently with market reforms have been the focus of attention in the debates on the effects of trade, trade openness and protection on growth and income distribution.

Similarly, the abundance of natural resources in the region and the resulting specialization of many countries in primary exports have, for many, illustrated the importance of the "Dutch disease" and the "resource curse" in development as well as the effects of the pattern of trade specialization on economic growth. The experience with State-led industrialization and the market reforms of the "Washington consensus" era have also been an important input in the debates on the appropriate balance of State and markets in different stages of economic development.

Despite the interest in the region, which has increased over time, there is no handbook on Latin American economics and there are only a few general textbooks on Latin American economics available in the English language, notably Eliana Cardoso and Ann Helwedge, *Latin America's Economies: Diversity, Trends, and Conflicts*, which is more than a decade old, and Patrice Franko's *The Puzzle of Latin American Economic Development*.

As a result of all this, the most readily available general books on the economics of the region are the institutional reports published by multilateral organizations—the United Nations Economic Commission for Latin America and the Caribbean, the Inter-American Development Bank, and the World Bank—which tend to have a short life span and do not have broad academic use.

Furthermore, most of the literature on Latin American economics is generally published in Spanish and Portuguese, not English, and the literature available in English is biased towards certain conceptual frameworks, and therefore tends to leave aside analyses by the school that is broadly known as Latin American structuralism (and neostructuralism).

Interestingly, and in contrast to this lacuna, there are two handbooks on Latin American economic history: *An Economic History of Twentieth Century Latin America*, a three-volume collection edited by Enrique Cárdenas, José Antonio Ocampo and Rosemary Thorp, and the two-volume *Cambridge Economic History of Latin America*, edited by Victor Bulmer-Thomas, John Coatsworth and Roberto Cortés Conde.

This Handbook aims at filling that significant gap. It has three additional features that make it particularly attractive. First, it covers a fairly complete set of relevant issues. Second, it includes contributions from economists who belong to different schools of economic thought. So, the reader will find a range of perspectives from orthodox to heterodox. Third, we have also taken care of guaranteeing that the contributors come from throughout Latin America, recognizing the diversity of the region.

The Handbook is organized into five parts. The first looks at long-term and cross-cutting issues, including shifting ideas on development and the economic performance of the region under different development strategies, the institutional roots of Latin America's underdevelopment, the political economy of economic policy making, the rise, decline and reemergence of alternative paradigms from the Washington consensus to new developmentalism, and the environmental sustainability of the development pattern.

The second part considers macroeconomic topics, including the management of capital account booms and busts, the evolution and performance of exchange rate regimes, the advances and challenges of monetary policies and financial development, and the major fiscal policy issues confronting the region, including a comparison of Latin American fiscal policies with those of the OECD.

The third part analyzes the different facets of insertion of the region's economies into the global economic system. First, it addresses the role of Latin America in the world trade system, the attempts at regional and hemispheric integration, and the effects of trade liberalization on growth, employment and wages. Second, it looks at the effects of dependence on natural resources, characteristic of many countries of the region, on growth and human development. Finally, it reviews the trends of foreign direct investment, the opportunities and challenges raised by the emergence of China as buyer of the region's commodities and competitor in the world market, and the transformation of Latin America from a region of immigration to one of massive emigration.

The fourth part deals with matters of productive development. At the aggregate level it analyzes issues of technological catching up and divergence as well as different perspectives on the poor productivity and growth performance of the region during recent decades. At the sectoral level, it looks at agricultural policies and performance, the problems and prospects of the energy sector, and the effects on growth of lagging infrastructure development.

The last part looks at the social dimensions of development. First, it analyzes the evolution of income inequality, poverty and economic insecurity in the region, particularly the rise and fall of inequality and poverty over the past decades. Second, it looks at the evolution of labor markets including the expansion of the informal sector and issues of labor market regulation. Finally, it examines the performance of and policies towards the educational sector, as well as the evolution of social assistance programs and social security reforms in the region.

We want to thank Oxford University Press for having asked us to lead this effort, and to the authors, who had to bear our repeated requests for revision of their chapters. We also want to thank Juliana Vallejo, who provided invaluable help in this editorial effort, as well as James Giganti and Farah Siddique, who helped us in the processing of the manuscript, and Anthony Tillet, who translated three of the chapters.

We have the firm conviction that this Handbook is a significant contribution to the academic and policy community, those interested in Latin America and those interested in how the region fits into exercises in comparative development.

José Antonio Ocampo and Jaime Ros

Contents

List of Figures (and Map)   xiii
List of Tables   xix
Contributors   xxiii

PART I DEVELOPMENT PARADIGMS AND LONG-TERM GROWTH PERFORMANCE

1 Shifting Paradigms in Latin America's Economic Development   3
   José Antonio Ocampo and Jaime Ros

2 Institutions and the Historical Roots of Latin American Divergence   26
   Luis Bértola

3 Political Institutions, Policymaking, and Economic Policy in
   Latin America   50
   Martín Ardanaz, Carlos Scartascini, and Mariano Tommasi

4 The Washington Consensus: Assessing a "Damaged Brand"   79
   Nancy Birdsall, Augusto de la Torre, and Felipe Valencia Caicedo

5 From Old to New Developmentalism in Latin America   108
   Luiz Carlos Bresser-Pereira

6 Environmental Sustainability   130
   Carlos J. de Miguel and Osvaldo Sunkel

PART II MACROECONOMICS AND FINANCE

7 Taming Capital Account Shocks: Managing Booms and Busts   161
   Ricardo Ffrench-Davis and Stephany Griffith-Jones

8 Exchange Rate Regimes in Latin America   187
   Roberto Frenkel and Martín Rapetti

9 Monetary Policy in Latin America: Performance under Crisis
and the Challenges of Exuberance   214
PABLO GARCÍA-SILVA AND MANUEL MARFÁN

10 Domestic Financial Development in Latin America   241
JOSÉ MARÍA FANELLI

11 Fiscal Policy in Latin America   266
MAURICIO CÁRDENAS AND GUILLERMO PERRY

12 Fiscal Legitimacy, Inequalities, and Democratic Consolidation
in Latin America   293
JAVIER SANTISO AND PABLO ZOIDO

PART III INTEGRATION INTO THE WORLD ECONOMY

13 Latin America in the World Trade System   317
DIANA TUSSIE

14 Regional Integration   341
PAOLO GIORDANO AND ROBERT DEVLIN

15 The Effects of Trade Liberalization on Growth, Employment,
and Wages   368
EDUARDO LORA

16 The Recent Commodity Price Boom and Latin American Growth:
More than New Bottles for an Old Wine?   394
EDMAR L. BACHA AND ALBERT FISHLOW

17 Curse or Blessing? Natural Resources and Human Development   411
JOSÉ GREGORIO PINEDA AND FRANCISCO RODRÍGUEZ

18 Foreign Direct Investment in Latin America   438
JOÃO CARLOS FERRAZ, MICHAEL MORTIMORE, AND MÁRCIA TAVARES

19 China and the Future of Latin American Economic Development   461
KEVIN P. GALLAGHER AND ROBERTO PORZECANSKI

20 Latin America in the Recent Wave of International Migration   488
ALEJANDRO I. CANALES

PART IV   PRODUCTIVE SECTOR DEVELOPMENT

21 Structural Transformation and Economic Growth in Latin America   519
    RICARDO HAUSMANN

22 Learning, Technological Capabilities, and Structural Dynamics   546
    MARIO CIMOLI AND GABRIEL PORCILE

23 Why Has Productivity Growth Stagnated in Most Latin
    American Countries Since the Neo-Liberal Reforms?   568
    JOSÉ GABRIEL PALMA

24 Agricultural and Rural Development   608
    SALOMÓN SALCEDO, FERNANDO SOTO-BAQUERO, JOSÉ GRAZIANO DA SILVA,
    RODRIGO CASTAÑEDA SEPÚLVEDA, AND SERGIO GÓMEZ ECHENIQUE

25 An Energy Panorama of Latin America   636
    HUMBERTO CAMPODÓNICO

26 Infrastructure in Latin America   659
    CÉSAR CALDERÓN AND LUIS SERVÉN

PART V   SOCIAL DEVELOPMENT

27 The Rise and Fall of Income Inequality in Latin America   691
    LEONARDO GASPARINI AND NORA LUSTIG

28 Multidimensional Poverty in Latin America: Concept,
    Measurement, and Policy   715
    REBECA GRYNSPAN AND LUIS F. LÓPEZ-CALVA

29 Economic Insecurity and Development in Latin America
    and the Caribbean   741
    ROB VOS

30 Employment: The Dominance of the Informal Economy   767
    VICTOR E. TOKMAN

31 Latin American Labor Reforms: Evaluating Risk and Security   790
    MARÍA VICTORIA MURILLO, LUCAS RONCONI, AND ANDREW SCHRANK

32 Education   813
    MIGUEL URQUIOLA

33 Social Protection in Latin America: Achievements and Limitations   836
    FRANCISCO H. G. FERREIRA AND DAVID A. ROBALINO

34 Social Security Reforms in Latin America   863
    ANDRAS UTHOFF

Index   887

Figures (and map)

FIGURES

1.1	Latin America's relative per capita GDP	9
1.2	Latin America's poverty	22
2.1	Growth rates of population and per capita GDP, 1500–1820 and 1820–2001, by region	30
3.1	Policy Index across countries	62
3.2	Civil Service Development Index	69
3.3	Party system institutionalization, programmatic orientation, and the quality of policies	71
4.1	Latin American structural reform index average (1985–2002)	84
4.2(a)	Latin American inflation, 1990–2000	85
4.2(b)	Latin American inflation, selected countries, 1990–2000	85
4.3(a)	Latin American budget balance, selected countries, 1990–9	86
4.3(b)	Latin American public debt, selected countries, 1990–9	86
4.4	International financial liberalization index, 1973–2002	88
4.5	Latin America and East Asia: Gross Domestic Savings, 1970–2008	89
4.6	Latin American capital markets reform implementation, 1990–2002	90
4.7	Latin American advance of reforms, 1989–99	91
4.8	Latin America and East Asia: relative GDP per capita, 1980–2006	92
4.9	International education expenditure vs. PISA scores, 2006	102
5.1	Tendency towards the overvaluation of the exchange rate	115
6.1	Latin America and the Caribbean: changes in soil usage	133
6.2	Select countries: evolution of energy intensity and GDP per capita (1990–2005)	136
6.3	Latin America and the Caribbean: proportion of land areas covered by forest	138
6.4	Gross Savings and Adjusted Net Savings	144
6.5	Latin America and the Caribbean: frequency of hydro-meteorological events, 1970–2009	149
6.6	Latin America and the Caribbean: coupling among GDP, energy, and CO_2 emissions	151

7.1	Latin America: country risk and stock exchange prices, 1990–2004	169
7.2	Latin America (19): GDP growth instability, 1990–2009	174
7.3	Latin America (19): external shocks and growth of aggregate demand, 1990–2009	175
7.4	Latin America (19): GDP and aggregate demand, 1990–2009	176
7.5	Latin America (19): net capital inflows and real exchange rate, 1980–2009	177
8.1	Argentina: bilateral RER with the US, deflated by CPI indexes	207
8.2	Brazil: Bilateral RER with the US, deflated by CPI indexes	208
8.3	Chile: Bilateral RER with the US, deflated by CPI indexes	208
8.4	Colombia: bilateral RER with the US, deflated by CPI indexes	209
8.5	Mexico: bilateral RER with the US, deflated by CPI indexes	209
8.6	Peru: bilateral RER with the US, deflated by CPI indexes	210
9.1	Average inflation and volatility	215
9.2	Quarterly year-on-year GDP growth rates in crisis periods	217
9.3	Interest rates in crisis periods	218
9.4	Nominal exchange rates in crisis periods	219
9.5	Exchange rate regimes	221
9.6	Deposit dollarization in select economies	225
9.7	External and fiscal vulnerabilities	227
9.8	External accounts and the real exchange rate in Mexico	234
10.1	Credit/GDP ratio and per capita GDP	249
10.2	Stock market capitalization/GDP ratio and per capita GDP	249
10.3	Stock market capitalization/GDP ratio and private credit/GDP ratio	250
10.4	Corporate bonds/GDP ratio and private credit/GDP ratio	251
10.5	The functional approach to financial development	260
10.6	Financial structure, dysfunctions, and regulations	262
11.1	Tax rates: value-added tax, individual income tax, corporation income tax	270
11.2	Latin America: initial primary spending levels (1995) and increases (1995–2008)	272
11.3	Social spending as a share of GDP	273
11.4	Discretionary fiscal policy response to cyclical conditions	276
11.5	The stabilizing role of government size	277
11.6	Country correlations between the cyclical components of net capital inflows and real GDP, 1960–2003	279
11.7	Subnational over general government's expenditure	282
11.8	Measures of sustainability: required vs. observed primary fiscal surpluses	286
11.9	Public debt and sovereign rating (1995–2005)	288

11.10	Share of domestic debt over total debt and GDP per capita, average for 2000–4	288
12.1	Fiscal policy measures, Latin American and OECD countries	296
12.2	Composition of revenue and expenditure in Latin American and OECD countries, regional averages, 1990–2006	299
12.3	Redistribution of income by means of taxes and transfers in Europe and Latin America, in selected countries	306
12.4	Education: spending and results in OECD countries and selected emerging countries	308
14.1	Date of implementation of Latin American trading agreements	348
14.2	Trade flows and openness in postwar Latin America	354
14.3	Structure of the FTAA negotiations	360
14.4	The proliferation of trade agreements in the Americas	365
15.1	Wage gap between workers with high education vs. medium education	385
17.1	Relationship between GDP growth, HDI changes, and natural resources	426
17.2	Relationship between HDI components' growth and natural resources	426
18.1	FDI inflows to and outflows from Latin American countries, 1990–2008	439
18.2	Origin of FDI flows to Latin America, 1999–2003 and 2004–8	443
18.3	Sectoral distribution of inward FDI, 1998, 2007	444
18.4	OFDI by investor countries, 1994–2008	453
19.1	Latin American exports to China	463
19.2	Manufacturing exports	470
19.3	Share of total manufacturing export growth, 2000–6	471
20.1	Latin America: gross annual migration flow to USA and Spain, 1997–2007	497
20.2	Age structure by sex of Latin American migrants: USA and Spain, 2008	501
20.3	Population growth of 20–49-year-olds by migratory status: USA and Spain, 2002–7	502
20.4	Sex ratio of Latin American immigrants in USA and Spain, 1996–2008	505
20.5	Latin American immigrants by level of education and region of origin: USA and Spain, 2007	506
20.6	Economic activity rates by sex: USA and Spain, 2007	509
20.7	Latin American immigrants by employment sector and sex: USA and Spain, 2007	510

20.8	Latin American immigrants in selected occupations by sex: USA and Spain, 2007	511
21.1	Relationship between export sophistication and GDP per capita, 2005	526
21.2	Visual representation of the product space	532
21.3	The "open forest" at different GDP levels	534
21.4	Distance to the quality frontier in existing export products	535
22.1	Traverse in development process and hysteresis	550
22.2	Productivity gap between Latin America and the technological frontier	560
22.3	Productivity and structural change: Latin America and the USA, 1990–2007	561
23.1	Brazil's GDP per capita as a multiple of India's GDP per capita, and Mexico's as a multiple of Vietnam's, 1950–2008	572
23.2	Latin America and other regions: GDP growth, 1950–80 and 1980–2008	573
23.3	Mexico and Thailand: Output, employment, and productivity, 1950–2008	574
23.4	Productivity growth: Argentina, Brazil, Chile, and Peru vs. China, Indonesia, and Taiwan, 1950–2008	576
23.5	Latin America and five Asian economies: TFP, 1960–2004	577
23.6	Investment patterns in Latin America and Asia, 1950–2008	580
23.7	Latin America and other developing regions: public investment as a share of GDP, 1970–2008	582
23.8	Brazil and Chile: growth of non-residential investment per worker and of productivity per hour, 1950–2008	583
23.9	Latin America and Asia: growth rate of investment per worker and of labor productivity, 1950–80 and 1990–2008	584
23.10	Latin America: the contrasting fortunes of employment and labor productivity in the post-reform period, 1990–2008	586
23.11	Latin America's "flexible" labor markets, 1990–2008	588
23.12	Brazil, Mexico, Colombia, and Chile: relative productivity gaps with the US	593
23.13	Exports and GDP growth in four developing regions, 1990–2008	595
23.14	"Anti-clockwise" export trajectories between the 1960s and 1990s	596
23.15	Latin America: the neglect of manufacturing and the post-1980 process of de-industrialization	600
24.1	Average annual rate of growth in agricultural added value and total GDP, 1979/81–2005/7	627
25.1	Latin America and the Caribbean: energy demand, 2007	637
25.2	Latin America and the Caribbean, 1971 and 2005: total fuel consumption by sector	638
25.3(a)	Oil reserves by country, 2000 and 2008	639

25.3(b)	Gas reserves by country, 2000 and 2008	640
25.4	Latin America: state enterprise and foreign direct investments, 2000–8	646
25.5	Latin America and the Caribbean: FDI in the oil sector	647
26.1	Survey measures of infrastructure quality	667
26.2	Infrastructure quantity, quality, growth, and inequality	671
26.3	Growth changes across regions due to infrastructure development	673
26.4	Total infrastructure investment in Latin America	676
26.5	Private sector participation in infrastructure	680
27.1	Gini coefficients: countries around the world	693
27.2	Latin American excess inequality	694
27.3	Inequality in Latin America and the world	695
27.4	Gini coefficients: Latin America, 1980–2008	696
27.5	Inequality Argentina	701
27.6	Inequality in Brazil: Gini coefficient, 1981–2007	704
27.7	Inequality in Mexico: Gini coefficient, 1984–2006	707
28.1	Human Development Index value trends in LAC, 1990, 2000, and 2006	728
28.2	Evolution of multidimensional poverty in Latin America	732
28.3	Multidimensional poverty in Latin America: urban vs. rural	733
28.4	Evolution of poverty in Latin America by dimension, 1992–2006	734
28.5	Multidimensional and income poverty	737
29.1(a)	Growth of GDP per capita in developing countries, excluding China and India, 1970–2009	747
29.1(b)	Growth of GDP per capita in Latin America and the Caribbean, 1970–2009	747
29.2	Latin America: trade shocks of countries grouped by sector of export specialization, 2001–10	749
29.3	Latin America: primary deficit and public infrastructure investment, 1980–2001	751
29.4	Poverty–growth relationship in Latin America and the Caribbean, 1990 to mid-2000s	752
29.5	Latin America: urban employed population with health and/or pension coverage in selected Latin American countries	754
29.6	Latin America and Caribbean: relationship between share of own account and contributing family workers in employment and GDP per capita, mid-2000s	754
30.1	Unemployment rate and growth of GNP: Latin America and the Caribbean, 1980–2009	771
30.2	Informal economy by country, 2008	777
30.3	Informal economy: employment structure in Latin America, 2008	779
30.4	Social security coverage by sector and contract	780
31.1	Number of reforms: Latin America, 1985–2009	799

31.2   Number of countries implementing reforms: Latin America,
          1985–2009   799
31.3   External flexibility by executive ideology   801
31.4   Personal security by executive ideology   803
32.1   Average years of schooling for 1938–40 and 1968–70 birth cohorts   814
32.2   Age-enrollment profiles for Chile and Honduras   815
32.3   Maximum schooling, average years in school, and average years
          of schooling in Chile and Honduras   821
32.4   Percentage of students who attain given levels of reading proficiency   827
32.5   Latin American performance in international tests   828
33.1   Chronology of major innovations in social protection in LAC   840
33.2   Old age pension coverage: contributory and non-contributory   843
34.1   Number of dependents per formal worker   870
34.2   Employed persons registered with social security:
          Latin America, c. 2006   872

MAP

20.1   Gender composition of gross emigration flow to Spain and
          the USA by countries of origin, 2006–8   504

TABLES

....

1.1	Weighted average growth rates	11
1.2	Indicators of human development	12
1.3	GDP per capita in richest Latin American countries vs. southern Europe and Japan	13
1.4	Relative growth performance, 1990–2008	21
2.1	Per capita GDP, population, and GDP 1500–2003 by region and relative to world average	28
2.2	Per capita GDP of some Latin American countries, 1820–2003	32
3.1	Features of public policies and economic development	60
3.2	Features of public policies in Latin American countries	61
3.3	Summary of some measures of legislature capabilities	66
3.4	Relative judicial independence, selected Latin American and Caribbean countries, 1975 and 2005	68
4.1	The decalogue of Washington Consensus policies (1989)	81
5.1	Growth of per capita income in selected countries, 1950–2006	112
5.2	Old and new developmentalism	119
5.3	Conventional orthodoxy and new developmentalism (growth)	123
5.4	Conventional orthodoxy and new developmentalism (macro)	123
6.1	Physical indicators for Latin America and the Caribbean: average annual growth rates	132
6.2	Latin America and the Caribbean: trade composition by category, 1990–2006	135
6.3	Under-5 mortality	141
6.4	PM10 emissions in select cities	141
6.A1	Multilateral environmental agreements	153
6.A2	Multilateral environmental agreements	154
6.A3	Multilateral environmental agreements	155
7.1	Latin America (19): composition of capital flows, 1977–2008	170
8.1	RER volatility	201
10.1	Size of the financial system in Latin America	245
10.2	Stock market turnover ratios	254
11.1	Tax revenue as a percentage of GDP	269
11.2	Public balance as a percentage of GDP	280
12.1	The size of government, Latin American and OECD countries	297
12.2	Analysis of government revenue, Latin American and OECD countries	300

12.3   Analysis of government expenditure, Latin American and
       OECD countries   302
13.1   Trends in average applied tariff rates, 1985–2007   321
13.2   Latin American weight in world merchandise exports, selected periods 322
13.3   Latin America and the Caribbean: total exports by subregional
       integration scheme, 1990–2007   325
13.4   Preferential trade agreements notified to the GATT/WTO   329
13.5   Export shares by main destination, 2000 and 2007   332
14.1   Old and new regionalism: objectives and stylized facts   350
14.2   Old and new regionalism: policy instruments   351
14.3   Product structure of Latin American trade flows   356
14.4   Intra-industry trade in Latin American regional
       integration agreements   357
14.5   Geographical structure of Latin American trade flows   357
15.1   Average tariffs   369
15.2   Imports and exports of goods and services   370
15.3   A summary of Latin Americans' opinions about trade liberalization 373
15.4   The growth effect of Latin American trade reforms: summary of
       econometric estimates   375
15.5   Sectoral employment in Latin America, 1980s–2000s   379
17.1(a) Summary statistics: mean of variables (all countries, 1980–2005) 413
17.1(b) Summary statistics: mean of variables (high net exporters/importers,
       1980–2005)   413
17.2(a) OLS results: determinants of HDI change   427
17.2(b) OLS results: determinants of GDP per capita growth   428
17.2(c) OLS results: determinants of change in literacy ratio   429
17.2(d) OLS results: determinants of gross enrollment ratio   430
17.2(e) OLS results: determinants of life expectancy   431
17.3   Latin American interaction results: determinants of HDI change   432
18.1   Distribution of FDI in Latin America, 1994–2003 and 2004–8   442
19.1   Five countries, ten sectors, dominate LAC trade to China   464
19.2   Share of Chinese exports in selected countries and sectors, 2008   465
19.3   Latin America's top commodity exports in context   466
19.4   Chinese export market shares   473
19.5   China: taking away the (manufacturing) ladder?   476
19.6   Threatened exports to the world   479
19.7   Exports to Latin America: share of total   481
19.8   Threatened exports to Latin America, 2006   482
19.9   Characteristics and dynamism of top 20 LAC manufacturing
       imports from China   483
20.1   Characteristics and composition of migrant population by
       major world region   493

20.2	Latin America: immigrants, emigrants, and net migration, by major international region	495
20.3	Major intraregional gross migration flows in Latin America	496
20.4	Gross immigration from Latin America, stock and flow by country of birth: USA and Spain	499
20.5	Latin American immigrants in USA and Spain, by sex and sex ratio	503
20.6	Characteristics of employment by migratory condition: USA and Spain, 2007	512
21.1	Growth in GDP per capita and GDP per worker and workers per capita, 1997–2007	521
21.2	GDP per worker and contribution of increased schooling	522
21.3	Centrality of goods in the product space	533
21.4	Growth regressions controlling for the product space	537
21.5	Typology of development policies	539
22.1	Phases of economic growth in Latin America	551
22.2	Specialization, productive structure, TCs, and growth	556
22.3	Productive structure and technology: selected countries	558
23.1	TFP growth: Latin America, Asia, South Africa, and OECD, 1960–2004	579
24.1	Changes to the agro-productive structure of Latin America, 1979/81–2005/7	619
24.2	Variations in the stock and production value of the livestock sector, 1980–2005	622
24.3	Latin American trade in agro-food products, 1979/81–2004/6	625
24.4	Destination of farm exports by subregion, 1982/4–2004/6	626
24.5	Share of agricultural added value in total GDP: average per decade, 1980–2007	628
24.6	Population and employment in Latin America	629
24.7	Poverty and extreme poverty in Latin America, 1980–2007	630
25.1	Latin America and the Caribbean: trade balance, 2007	639
25.2	Importance of the hydrocarbon sector in the economy, 2007	640
25.3	Investment by state-owned and mixed oil enterprises, 2000–8	647
25.4	Latin America: export capacity by gas pipeline, 2008	650
25.5	Regasification terminal capacity	651
25.6	Latin America: biofuel mix for gasoline and diesel	654
26.1	Infrastructure quantity and quality: LAC vis-à-vis other regions	662
26.2	Access to infrastructure	669
26.3	Investment in infrastructure in Latin America, 1981–2006	677
28.1	Evolution of income poverty in Latin America	717
28.2	Evolution of the Human Development Index in LAC countries	727
28.3	Multidimensional poverty index in Latin America and the Caribbean	735

29.1	Macroeconomic volatility	744
29.2	Incidence of recessions	746
29.3	Managing risks and vulnerabilities	757
30.1	Informal economy in Latin America, 1990–2008	776
31.1	Reforms to procedures affecting external flexibility, 1985–99	794
31.2	Reforms to procedures affecting external flexibility, 2000–10	795
31.3	Enforcement resources in Latin America, 1985–2009	806
31.4	Enforcement resources by RBTA negotiating status	807
32.1	Country rankings by urban enrollment rates in specific age ranges	817
32.2	Net enrollment rate, years of school, and years of schooling: Chile and Honduras	820
32.3	Ranking by average years of schooling accumulated in the formal '1–12' system	822
32.4	Ranking by effectiveness gap	824
32.5	A "bottom line" ordering of countries by attendance and effectiveness	825
33.1	Social expenditures in LAC	844
33.2	Trends in social assistance expenditures in LAC countries	845
33.3	The impact of CCT programs on national poverty indices	853
34.1	Social security coverage: Latin America, c. 1990, 2002, and 2006	873

CONTRIBUTORS

Martín Ardanaz PhD candidate, Department of Political Science, Columbia University, New York

Edmar L. Bacha Director or the Institute of Economic Policy Studies Casa das Garças, Rio de Janeiro

Luis Bértola Professor of the Economic and Social History Program, Faculty of Social Sciences at Universidad de la República, Montevideo

Nancy Birdsall President of the Center for Global Development (CGD), Washington, DC

Luiz Carlos Bresser-Pereira Emeritus Professor of the Getulio Vargas Foundation, São Paulo

César Calderón Senior Economist at the Office of the Chief Economist of the Latin America and the Caribbean Region at the World Bank, Washington, DC

Humberto Campodónico Professor at the Economics Department of the Universidad Nacional Mayor de San Marcos, Lima

Alejandro I. Canales Researcher, Department of Regional Studies, University of Guadalajara

Mauricio Cárdenas Senior Fellow and Director of the Latin America Initiative at the Brookings Institution, Washington, DC

Rodrigo Castañeda Sepúlveda Consultant at FAO Regional Office for Latin America and the Caribbean, Santiago

Mario Cimoli Director of the Division of Production, Productivity, and Management of the United Nations Economic Commission for Latin America and the Caribbean (ECLAC), Santiago, and Professor of Economics, University of Venice

José Graziano da Silva FAO Regional Representative for Latin America and the Caribbean, Santiago, and Professor at UNICAMP (Universidade Estadual de Campinas), Brasil

Augusto de la Torre Chief Economist for Latin America and the Caribbean of the World Bank, Washington, DC

Carlos J. de Miguel Environmental Affairs Officer in the Sustainable Development and Human Settlements Division at the United Nations Economic Commission for Latin America and the Caribbean (ECLAC), Santiago

Robert Devlin Director of the Department for Effective Public Management, Organization of American States, Washington, DC

José María Fanelli Senior Researcher at CEDES (Center for the Study of State and Society), Buenos Aires and former Director of the Economics Department at the University of Buenos Aires

João Carlos Ferraz Director of Banco Nacional de Desenvolvimento Econômico e Social (BNDES), Brasilia

Francisco H. G. Ferreira Deputy Chief Economist for Latin America and the Caribbean, World Bank, Washington, DC

Ricardo Ffrench-Davis Professor of the Department of Economics at University of Chile, Santiago

Albert Fishlow Professor Emeritus of University of California, Berkeley, and Columbia University, New York

Roberto Frenkel Principal Reasearch Associate at CEDES (Center for the Study of State and Society), Buenos Aires, and Professor at the University of Buenos Aires

Kevin P. Gallagher Associate Professor of International Relations at Boston University, Boston and Senior Researcher at the Global Development and Environment Institute, Tufts University, Medford/Somerville

Pablo García-Silva Alternate Executive Director, Southern Cone, International Monetary Fund

Leonardo Gasparini Director of the Center for Distributional, Labor and Social Studies (CEDLAS) at Universidad Nacional de La Plata

Paolo Giordano Senior Trade Economist in the Integration and Trade Sector of the Inter-American Development Bank, Washington, DC

Sergio Gómez Echenique Consultant at the FAO (Food and Agriculture Organization of the United Nations) Regional Office for Latin America and the Caribbean, Santiago

Stephany Griffith-Jones Head of Financial Research of the Initiative for Policy Dialogue at Columbia University, New York

Rebeca Grynspan Associate Administrator of the United Nations Development Programme (UNDP), New York

Ricardo Hausmann Professor of the Practice of Economic Development in Harvard Kennedy School and Director of the Center for International Development at Harvard University, Cambridge, MA

Luis F. López-Calva Chief Economist of the Regional Bureau for Latin America and the Caribbean, United Nations Development Programme (UNDP), New York

Eduardo Lora Manager of the Research Department of the Inter-American Development Bank, Washington, DC

Nora Lustig Samuel Z. Stone Professor of Latin American Economics at Tulane University, New Orleans and nonresident fellow of the Center for Global Development, Washington, DC, and the Inter-American Dialogue, Washington, DC

Manuel Marfán Vice-Governor, Central Bank of Chile, Santiago

Michael Mortimore Former Head of the Unit on Investment and Corporate Strategies at the Economic Commission for Latin America and the Caribbean (ECLAC), Santiago

María Victoria Murillo Associate Professor of the Department of Political Science and the School of International Affairs at Columbia University, New York

José Antonio Ocampo Professor at the School of International and Public Affairs (SIPA) and Member of the Committee on Global Thought at Columbia University, New York

José Gabriel Palma Senior Lecturer at the Faculty of Economics, Cambridge University

Guillermo Perry Research Associate, Fedesarrollo, Bogotá; and Non Resident Fellow, Center For Global Development, Washington, DC

José Gregorio Pineda Senior Policy Researcher at the Human Development Report Office of the United Nations Development Programme (UNDP), New York

Gabriel Porcile Professor of Economics at Federal University of Paraná and Researcher of the Conselho Nacional de Desenvolvimento Científico e Tecnológico (CNPQ), Brasilia

Roberto Porzecanski Associate at McKinsey & Company and researcher at the Global Development and Environment Institute at Tufts University, Medford/Somerville

Martín Rapetti Adjunt Researcher at Centro de Estudios de Estado y Sociedad (CEDES), Buenos Aires

David A. Robalino Leader Labor Team, Social Protection and Labor, The World Bank, Washington, DC

Francisco Rodríguez Head of Research of the Human Development Report Office in the United Nations Development Programme (UNDP), New York

Lucas Ronconi Associate researcher at the Center for the Implementation of Public Policies Promoting Equity and Growth (CIPPEC), Buenos Aires

Jaime Ros is Professor of Economics at the Universidad Nacional Autónama de México

Salomón Salcedo Senior Policy Officer, FAO (Food and Agriculture Organization of the United Nations), New York

Javier Santiso Professor of Economics, ESADE Business School, Barcelona and Chair of the OECD Emerging Markets Network (EmNet), Paris

Carlos Scartascini Lead Economist of the Research Department at the Inter-American Development Bank, Washington, DC

Andrew Schrank Associate Professor of the Department of Sociology at University of New Mexico, Albuquerque

Luis Servén Senior Advisor in the World Bank, Washington, DC

Fernando Soto-Baquero Coordinator of the Policy Group of the FAO (Food and Agriculture Organization of the United Nations) Regional Office for Latin America and the Caribbean, Santiago

Osvaldo Sunkel Chairman of the Editorial Council of CEPAL Review at the United Nations Economic Commission for Latin America and the Caribbean (ECLAC), Santiago

Márcia Tavares Economic Affairs Officer of the United Nations Economic Commission for Latin America and the Caribbean (ECLAC), Santiago

Victor E. Tokman Former ILO Regional Director for Latin America and the Caribbean, Santiago, and Professor at the Department of Economics of the University of Chile and Facultad Latinoamericana de Estudios Sociales (FLACSO), Santiago.

Mariano Tommasi Professor, Department of Economics, Universidad de San Andres, Buenos Aires and Visiting Scholar, Research Department, Inter-American Development Bank, Washington, DC

Diana Tussie Convenor of the International Relations Department at Facultad Latinoamericana de Estudios Sociales (FLACSO), Buenos Aires, and Director of the Latin American Trade Network, Buenos Aires

Miguel Urquiola Associate Professor of the School of International and Public Affairs and Economics Department at Columbia University, New York

Andras Uthoff Member, Pension System Consultative Committee, Chile, Santiago, and Lecturer, Department of Economics, Universidad de Chile, Santiago, and Independent Consultant

Felipe Valencia Caicedo Consultant, The World Bank, Washington, DC

Rob Vos Director of Development Policy and Analysis at the United Nations Department of Economic and Social Affairs, New York

Pablo Zoido Economist in the OECD Education Directorate, Paris

PART I

DEVELOPMENT PARADIGMS AND LONG-TERM GROWTH PERFORMANCE

CHAPTER 1

....

SHIFTING PARADIGMS IN LATIN AMERICA'S ECONOMIC DEVELOPMENT

....

JOSÉ ANTONIO OCAMPO AND JAIME ROS

1.1 INTRODUCTION

....

Latin America has experienced in recent decades a major shift in the paradigms that oriented its development patterns. In the first decades after World War II ("postwar period", for short), the region had embraced a paradigm that placed the developmental state at the center of the strategy, with industrialization as the major objective, which was regarded at the time as critical to increase living standards. We will characterize this paradigm as state-led industrialization, a concept that—following Cárdenas, Ocampo, and Thorp (2000)—expands upon the more traditional concept of Import Substitution Industrialization (ISI), because import substitution was only one of its features and not the central feature in all countries during all time periods. This strategy had taken root in the postwar years, but it had precedents in the long protectionist past of many Latin American countries (Coatsworth and Williamson 2003) and in the responses to the external shocks experienced during World War I and, particularly, the Great Depression of the 1930s, which will be the point of departure for our analysis. This paradigm was replaced during the 1970s in a few countries and the mid-1980s in the rest of the region by another which placed markets and integration into the world economy at the center.

This chapter analyzes the central features of both paradigms and presents an overall evaluation of its development outcomes. The economic literature is full of caricatures of both paradigms—of state-led industrialization in the more orthodox literature, and of market-led development in the more critical literature in recent years. Caricatures have the advantage that they are easy to demolish, and the obvious disadvantage that they do not reflect what was actually thought or done in economic policy. We provide here a more balanced view of both paradigms. Following terminology that was common in Latin American structuralism in the past but has actually become quite fashionable in other schools of thought in recent years, we will refer to the industrial countries as the "center" and developing countries as the "periphery" of the world economy.

1.2 STATE-LED INDUSTRIALIZATION

The collapse of Latin America's terms of trade and export revenues in the 1930s, together with increased protectionism in the center of the world economy, suggested to many that excessive reliance on foreign trade and primary exports as engines of growth could be detrimental to economic development, and thus had a major role in the paradigm shift that took place in those years. While the break with the previous phase of economic development—the classic period of primary export-led growth—may have been less clear-cut than implied by much writing on the subject, both because industrialization was not new in the region and because the primary export sectors continued to have an important role in the development process, the collapse of the primary export-led growth process led to the emergence of a new development strategy that combined industrialization and enhanced state intervention.

The collapse of the primary export-led growth process was not, however, the only "big fact" that contributed to a paradigm shift. The collapse of the world financial system was another, as the financing boom that many Latin American countries experienced in the 1920s was followed by a bust and default in the early 1930s. Furthermore, this collapse had long-term implications, since an alternative world financial system would not emerge until the 1960s. Also, as noted by Lindauer and Pritchett (2002), the Great Depression of the 1930s had shown that an activist government was needed to bring stability to the economy, whereas the world war effort and the rapid industrialization of the Soviet Union had suggested that governments could plan and direct successfully rapid expansions of economic activity and radical transformations of the economic structure. The successful reconstruction of Europe under the Marshall Plan showed, finally, that large inflows of aid could greatly contribute to development.

What were the main components of the new development strategy that emerged in Latin America? Following Fishlow (1985), we can say that there were three elements which manifested themselves very clearly in the new conceptions: macroeconomic policies centered on the management of the balance of payments, industrialization as the engine of growth, and a strong state intervention in various areas of the economy.

1.2.1 Macroeconomic policies in the periphery

The previous phase of export-led growth had been characterized by recurrent balance of payments crises, as cyclical collapses in commodity prices were generally accompanied by sharp reversals of capital flows. In response to these crises, an important group of

Latin American countries had shown a tendency to abandon the gold or silver standard for more or less prolonged periods of time. However, this proclivity was always accompanied by the aspiration to restore those standards, implying that there was never an attempt to permanently abandon macroeconomic orthodoxy. All this changed radically with the crisis of the 1930s, as the foundations of orthodoxy were undermined by the collapse of the gold standard in the central countries themselves. The abandonment of the gold standard by its architect, Great Britain, in September 1931 was a landmark which was followed (and in some cases anticipated) by pragmatic attempts in various industrialized countries to face the crisis through public spending and expansionary monetary policies.

Economic theory itself experienced a radical change with the publication of John Maynard Keynes' *The General Theory of Employment, Interest and Money*, which led to an unprecedented macroeconomic activism aimed at stabilizing the business cycle. Counter-cyclical macroeconomic policies also emerged in Latin America as a result of the crisis of the 1930s, but their major features were different from those in industrialized countries, reflecting the different nature of the determinants of the business cycle in the periphery of the world economy. Indeed, while Keynesian thinking focused on the stabilization of aggregate demand through active fiscal and monetary policies, the predominance of external shocks—on raw material prices as well as volatile capital flows—explains why the focus of macroeconomic management in Latin America leant towards the management of balance of payments shocks, both negative and positive.

With time, government intervention in this area became more complex, and included (with a variety of national experiences) exchange controls, tariffs and direct import controls, taxes on traditional exports, and multiple exchange rates—which were often used as instruments of trade policy rather than exchange rate policy and, later in the process, incentives for new exports. Many of these instruments had parallels in industrialized countries, particularly Western Europe, where multiple exchange rates were common in several countries and exchange controls were only fully dismantled as late as 1990. The management of these instruments responded to aggregate supply shocks of external origin and, by trying to shift demand towards domestic goods, had a more important counter-cyclical role than aggregate demand management as such.

1.2.2 The industrialization strategy

Balance of payments interventions were intimately linked, in turn, to the second component of the development strategy, industrialization, whose focus was nonetheless on long-term growth. The industrialization strategy did not emerge suddenly, in practice or in theory, but arose rather gradually as the mistrust in the possibility of a return to primary export-led growth took hold. Fundamental landmarks in this process were the collapse of raw material prices after World War I and again in the 1930s. Moreover, as noted by Diaz-Alejandro (2000), the emergence of protectionist policies in the industrialized countries multiplied these direct negative impacts. The passage of the Smoot–Hawley tariff in the US in 1930, the British Commonwealth preferences of 1932, the reinforced protectionism by France, Germany, and Japan—and discriminatory trade arrangements for areas under their political hegemony—contributed to the feeling in Latin America that the era of export-led growth had come to an end. As a result, even if prosperity returned in the industrialized economies, the outlook for Latin America's exports that competed with production in industrial countries or their colonies and commonwealths was pessimistic.

The idea of industrialization also gained strength in world economic thinking, and in the 1940s became the basis of the new economic development theories. Industrialization and development became synonymous for several decades. Nonetheless, just as in the case of macroeconomic management centered on the balance of payments, it was facts that forced the shift to industrialization policies and, at least in the initial stages, more as a result of experimentation than an articulated theory. As brilliantly expressed by Love (1994): "Industrialization in Latin America was fact before it was policy, and policy before it was theory" (p. 395).

The idea of industrialization emerged from the facts to the point that it was adopted in Latin America at a time when—with a few exceptions such as Mexico—the interests of commodity exporters continued to be dominant. Moreover, those interests continued to play an important role during the whole industrial development phase, among other reasons because industrialization continued to depend on the foreign exchange generated by commodity exports. Indeed, in Hirschman's (1971) interpretation, a distinctive characteristic of Latin America's industrialization, in contrast to the experience of "late industrialization" in Europe examined by Gerschenkron (1962), was precisely the weakness of industrial interests in relation to those of primary product exporters.

The theory, which in the Latin American case was provided by the United Nations Economic Commission for Latin America (CEPAL being its Spanish acronym),[1] arrived in an advanced stage to rationalize a process that was proceeding at full strength almost everywhere. It is worth noting that in this vision, embodied above all in CEPAL's 1949 report, which Hirschman baptized as the "Latin American Manifesto," the solution to Latin America's development problems was not to isolate itself from the international economy but to redefine its insertion into the international division of labor. This was essential, in CEPAL's view, for the Latin American countries to benefit from technological change which was viewed as intimately linked to industrialization. Moreover, industrialization policies varied through time in order to correct their own excesses, to respond to new opportunities that the world economy started to offer in the 1960s, and to adapt to the opportunities open to countries of different sizes. As emphasized in various histories of CEPAL's thinking (Bielschowsky 1998; ECLAC 1998; Rosenthal 2004), from the 1960s CEPAL became persistently critical of the excesses of import substitution, and advocated a "mixed model" that combined import substitution with export diversification and regional integration. This strategy helped rationalize import substi-

[1] United Nations Economic Commission for Latin America and the Caribbean, after the Caribbean joined.

tution and exploit the opportunities that were increasingly available to developing countries in world markets. It also helped adapt the strategy to the possibilities for small countries. Such mixed model became the dominant pattern in the region during the mid-1960s, and was reflected in the generalization of export promotion policies, the partial rationalization of the complex structure of tariff and non-tariff protection, the elimination and simplification of multiple exchange rate regimes, and the adoption of gradual devaluation policies in countries with an inflationary tradition (Ffrench-Davis, Muñoz, and Palma 1998; Ocampo 2004a).

In particular, the small economies returned early in the postwar period to reliance on primary exports, which they mixed with the promotion of light manufacturing and, in the case of Central America, with the launch of its common market in 1960. Even in some larger economies, like Peru and Venezuela, primary exports continued to be central to the development strategy. In those larger economies where industrialization was the core of the development strategy (i.e. Argentina, Brazil, Chile, Colombia, and Mexico), export promotion policies, geared to the development of new export sectors, became common in the mid-1960s. These policies included export subsidies (tax rebates and subsidized export credit), import duty drawbacks for exporting firms, and export processing zones.[2] As already mentioned, gradual devaluation ("crawling pegs"), to compensate for the inflation differential between the domestic economy and its main trading partners, also became an important export promotion instrument in several major South American countries, notably Argentina, Brazil, Chile, and Colombia, from the mid-1960s onwards.

1.2.3 State intervention

The first two components of the development strategy produced an unprecedented degree of state intervention in the economy. But state intervention also involved a wider array of policy instruments in addition to interventions in the management of the balance of payments and the use of protection as a development policy instrument. The state intervened actively in providing fiscal incentives to new industries and in financing productive activities through state development banks such as BNDES in Brazil, CORFO in Chile, IFI in Colombia, and NAFINSA in Mexico, and the establishment of directed credit to strategic sectors. It also developed a complex intervention apparatus in the agricultural sector (technological development centers, price regulations, distribution of agricultural products, irrigation, and in some cases agrarian reform). The process was also accompanied by an expansion of public expenditures, with priority

---

[2] The first and major example is the maquiladora plants in Mexico's northern border, which in 1965 began processing textiles and later assembling electronic components for export to the US. Similar free trade zones were later introduced in many other countries, notably in Central American and Caribbean countries (Dominican Republic and Haiti being the first) to exploit locational advantages (low transport costs due to proximity to the US market) and labor cost advantages.

given to economic development spending on infrastructure and social services, financed by the development of a new tax base that relied much more on incomes and indirect taxes on domestic economic activities than on import tariffs. The development of infrastructure services (water and sewage, electricity and telecommunications) as well as, in several countries, financial services, also relied heavily on state-owned banks.

The development strategy also led to greater activism in social policy. Some developments were common to the region in the postwar period, in particular the establishment of public education and health systems. The more developed schemes followed a tendency to create social security systems based on wage employment and to actively regulate the labor market. In the more developed countries of the region, these systems had started to be developed in the last phases of the primary export-led phase. To the extent that access to wage employment in the modern sectors was limited—particularly in the less developed countries—the results were "segmented welfare states," in which wage earners in the formal sector had a wide array of benefits to which the urban informal sector and most of the rural population did not have access. The poorer sectors of the population remained subject to the laws of economies which worked with an "unlimited labor supply" *à la* W. Arthur Lewis. On the other hand, under the initial leadership of Mexico and in a wider set of countries from the 1960s, different agrarian reform models were applied. In general their results were limited, except in the case of Cuba, and thus only partially changed the extremely high concentration of rural property inherited from the past. In most cases, therefore, the weight of dominant agrarian interests continued to prevail.

State intervention and industrialization thus became distinctive features of a whole era. It is worth noting, however, that among the different models of state intervention that were typical in the immediate postwar period, Latin America opted for a *lesser* rather than a greater degree of state intervention—that is, for a model of economic organization in which private enterprise continued to have a major role. Indeed, in the early postwar years, and with very few exceptions (the US being the most important one), the real choice was not between state vs. free market economies but rather among different variants of state intervention and economic planning. In this spectrum, Latin America opted for a mixed economy model, which resembled more that of Western Europe than the different variants of socialist systems that proliferated at the time, including in Asia and Africa. In Latin America, only Cuba adopted a socialist model at a later stage (in the 1960s); there were also failed attempts in that direction by Chile and Nicaragua in the 1970s and 1980s respectively. It is also worth noting that foreign investment was welcome to the extent that it contributed to the industrialization process. While in many countries its access was certainly restricted in some sectors—natural resources, infrastructure, and financial services, in particular—it is also true that overall, these restrictions were less stringent than in the "Japanese model" followed at the time in Japan and some East Asian tigers (notably in South Korea).

The preference for a mixed economy, with a large presence of domestic and foreign private-sector firms, is likely to have its historical roots in the fact that Latin America had experienced, unlike other regions, a relatively fast process of economic growth in the period preceding state-led industrialization. Indeed, from 1913 to 1950 Latin America

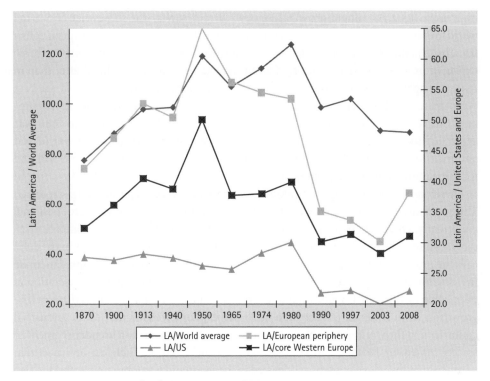

FIGURE 1.1 Latin America's relative per capita GDP

Source: Maddison (2006) and online updates of his series. Core Western Europe refers to Maddison's Europe 12, and European periphery to Maddison's 14 small Western European countries.

had been, together with the United States, the region of fastest growth in the world (Figure 1.1). Relative success thus contributed to curtailing the "statist excesses" in the subsequent phase of development.

1.2.4 The development performance of the region under state-led industrialization

Latin America's development performance during the period of state-led industrialization has been a controversial issue. For some, the postwar period should be seen as a golden age of unprecedented prosperity and increase in living standards. For others, the postwar period witnessed a dismal performance in which Latin America squandered opportunities for rapid growth and catching up.

A first reason for the disagreement has to do with the perspective adopted. The 1950–80 period was one of unprecedented prosperity for the world economy as a whole. In this context, Latin America's average comparative performance was not particularly impressive. Its 2.7% annual growth rate of GDP per capita was somewhat above the world average and that of the US but lower than that of the core Western European countries. In the latter case, however, the war collapse and later reconstruction are the basic explanation, as the relative position of Latin America in 1980 was slightly better than in 1940 (see again Figure 1.1). The region's average performance did fall short of the best performances in Southern Europe, Japan and the East Asia tigers. But, again, if we compare this with the European periphery, Latin America's relative position in 1980 was again slightly better than in 1940. Furthermore, if we leave out the early post-war period and focus on 1965-1980, Latin America grew faster than the average for the world and for the leading industrial countries.

Therefore, a positive view of economic performance is a more appropriate perspective. This was indeed a period of acceleration of growth with respect to a successful past and, particularly, a period of major economic and social transformations which compare favorably with what happened in Latin America before 1950 and after 1980. Hirschman (1987) calls the 1950–80 period "les trente glorieuses" precisely because of the substantial increase in living standards. Performance is particularly remarkable given the rapid acceleration in population growth and urbanization that took place during these years. Indeed, total GDP growth in Latin America (rather than GDP per capita) exceeded that of the industrial countries and the world (see Table 1.1). Progress started to permeate a broader segment of society. Based on Bértola, Hernández, and Siniscalchi (2010), Table 1.2 indicates that advance in human development accelerated in the 1940s and was rapid until 1980 (see also the analysis in Astorga, Bergés, and FitzGerald 2003). Prados de la Escosura (2007) also estimates that the bulk of the reduction in poverty achieved during the 20th century took place between 1950 and 1980. Nonetheless, income inequality remained very high by world standards, and increased in several countries over different time periods.

An additional reason for the disagreement concerning the growth record during the period of state-led industrialization is the high heterogeneity of performances across the region. Take, for example, the richest economies in 1950, Venezuela and, particularly, the Southern Cone countries (Chile, Argentina, and Uruguay). These countries had an income per capita well above that of southern Europe or Japan in 1950. Compared to the performance of these countries after 1950, the growth performance of the Latin American richer economies looks dismal indeed (Table 1.3). By 1980, Greece, Portugal, and Spain had caught up with Argentina and surpassed Uruguay and Chile, while Italy and Japan had incomes per capita that were more than twice those of Chile and Uruguay and well above those of Argentina.

Yet now look at Brazil and Mexico and other fast-growing countries in Latin America (which also include Costa Rica, Ecuador and Panama with growth rates of over 3% per capita; Colombia, the Dominican Republic, Guatemala, and Paraguay can be added to that list since the mid-1960s). Although not as good as the best performers in East Asia, these economies' rates of growth of GDP implied a process of catching up with several developed economies, certainly including the United States (see Table 1.1). Brazil was the star performer with GDP per capita growth of 4.1% per year from 1950 to 1980, while Mexico also had a rather high growth rate of 3.4%—in both cases despite rapid

Table 1.1 Weighted average growth rates (%)

	GDP		GDP per worker		GDP per capita	
	1950–80	1990–2008	1950–80	1990–2008	1950–80	1990–2008
Argentina	3.3	4.2	2.0	1.8	1.6	3.0
Bolivia	3.2	3.8	2.4	0.4	0.9	1.5
Brazil	7.0	3.0	3.4	0.6	4.1	1.5
Chile	3.5	5.4	1.9	3.7	1.4	4.0
Colombia	5.1	3.5	2.3	0.5	2.3	1.9
Costa Rica	6.3	5.1	2.9	1.5	3.2	2.8
Dominican Republic	5.8	5.7	2.6	3.0	2.7	3.9
Ecuador	6.1	3.2	4.1	−0.3	3.2	1.5
El Salvador	4.1	3.8	1.4	1.5	1.2	1.8
Guatemala	5.0	4.0	2.7	1.5	2.2	1.5
Honduras	4.3	4.1	1.9	−0.4	1.3	1.8
Mexico	6.6	3.0	3.4	0.5	3.4	1.6
Nicaragua	4.1	3.3	0.7	0.1	1.0	1.5
Panama	6.1	5.6	3.6	2.5	3.2	3.6
Paraguay	5.5	2.6	3.0	−1.1	2.8	0.5
Peru	4.9	4.9	2.4	1.8	2.1	3.4
Uruguay	2.2	3.2	1.2	1.6	1.3	2.8
Venezuela	6.0	3.2	2.4	−0.7	2.2	1.2
Latin America	5.5	3.4	2.7	0.7	2.7	1.8
United States	3.6	2.8			2.2	1.7
Core Western Europe	4.1	1.9			3.5	1.6
European periphery	4.3	2.2			3.4	1.3
World	4.5	3.7			2.6	2.4

Source: Latin America according to ECLAC database. Non-Latin America according to Maddison (2003) and online updates of his series.

Table 1.2 Indicators of human development

	Education Index[a]		Life Expectancy Index[b]		Human Development[c]	
	LA20	LA7[d]	LA20[e]	LA7	LA20	LA7
A. Latin American index						
1900		0.101		0.141		0.074
1910		0.113		0.185		0.092
1920		0.129		0.233		0.106
1930		0.150		0.265		0.123
1940		0.175		0.321		0.142
1950		0.206	0.420	0.435		0.183
1960	0.227	0.236	0.555	0.576	0.214	0.227
1970	0.275	0.286	0.618	0.633	0.257	0.271
1980	0.327	0.334	0.689	0.702	0.311	0.326
1990	0.401	0.414	0.743	0.751	0.334	0.354
2000	0.446	0.461	0.770	0.780	0.367	0.390
B. Relative to industrial economies						
1900		0.255		0.343		0.305
1910		0.264		0.382		0.335
1920		0.283		0.425		0.356
1930		0.310		0.437		0.364
1940		0.343		0.505		0.388
1950		0.380		0.591		0.439
1960	0.393	0.410	0.717	0.744	0.452	0.479
1970	0.424	0.441	0.783	0.802	0.466	0.492
1980	0.462	0.472	0.828	0.844	0.499	0.524
1990	0.532	0.549	0.866	0.876	0.485	0.513
2000	0.570	0.589	0.869	0.880	0.486	0.516

[a] The Education Index refers to years of schooling, with a ceiling of 16 years.
[b] The Life Expectancy Index has a minimum standard of 20 years and a maximum of 85 years.
[c] The Human Development Index is a geometric average of the first two and per capita GDP.
[d] LA7 includes Argentina, Brazil, Chile, Colombia, Mexico, Uruguay, and Venezuela.
[e] LA20 includes also Bolivia, Costa Rica, Cuba, Dominican Republic, Ecuador, El Salvador, Guatemala, Haiti, Honduras, Nicaragua, Panama, Paraguay, and Peru.

Source: Bértola, Hernández, and Siniscalchi (2010).

population growth, which implied that GDP growth was very fast (7.0 and 6.6% respectively).

What factors explain these differences in growth performance? The first one has to do with the size of the economy. It cannot be a coincidence that Brazil and Mexico, the two

Table 1.3 GDP per capita in richest Latin American countries vs. southern Europe and Japan

	1950	1980
Venezuela	7,462	10,139
Argentina	4,987	8,206
Uruguay	4,659	6,577
Chile	3,670	5,680
Italy	3,502	13,149
Spain	2,189	9,203
Portugal	2,086	8,044
Japan	1,921	13,428
Greece	1,915	8,971

Source: Maddison (2006).

most populous countries, were those able to sustain the highest rates of growth during the second, more difficult phase of industrialization, in which manufacturing expanded into heavy intermediates (steel and petrochemicals), consumer durables, and some capital goods. The size of their domestic markets is probably a major factor here, since it allowed industrial sectors with high fixed costs (associated with their capital intensity), and, as a result, strong economies of scale, to be established while it attracted the foreign investment required to set up these capital and technologically intensive industries. For these reasons, it also facilitated the transition to the "mixed model" in which non-traditional exports played an increasing role in the expansion of manufacturing industries. In other countries, the opportunities for industrialization were concentrated in light consumer goods and intermediate goods with low capital and technology intensity, and attempts to enter the "difficult phase" could have resulted in highly inefficient manufacturing sectors.

A second factor has to do with the structural features of the domestic economy—a fact that differentiates the Southern Cone countries from the rest of Latin America. Díaz-Alejandro (1988: ch. 12) highlights this factor in his comparison of the economic histories of Argentina and Brazil. Brazil had a Lewis-type economy with a surplus of labor that generated an elastic supply of labor to the modern sector of the economy. The expansion of the industrial sector meant that the process of industrialization caused labor to move from low- to high-productivity sectors (from the "subsistence" to the industrial sector). These productivity gains were behind the rapid increases in GDP per capita. Argentina, by contrast, was a mature economy in which more sectors were modern, and there was not a large subsistence sector. This meant that the economy would benefit less from the reallocation of labor from low- to high-productivity sectors. Rather, the expansion of the industrial sector caused labor to be taken away from the modern export sector. Because industrialization crowded out labor in the export sector, the anti-export bias was higher in Argentina. It was implied that formal labor markets were more developed and unionization was more important (see below).

A third factor relates to the role of export promotion policies and exchange rate policy, and the degree of success of the transition to the "mixed model" of import substitution-cum-export promotion. It is worth noting that most of the fast-growing economies are among those that started experimenting with export promotion policies some time in the 1960s or early 1970s; two of them (Brazil and Colombia) also adopted crawling pegs. By contrast, the slow-growing economies, with few exceptions such as Argentina and Chile, were not early adopters of export-promotion policies. In the case of the countries with large domestic markets (Brazil, Mexico, and to a lesser extent Colombia), the success of export promotion policies was facilitated by the smaller anti-export bias generated by more moderate protection of intermediate and capital goods. All this suggests some role in growth outcomes for the type of industrialization policy adopted.

In relation to economic performance, it must be pointed out, finally, that despite Latin America's reputation for high inflation, this was not a general feature of the region before the 1970s. Indeed, as noted by Sheahan (1987), in the 1950s and 1960s only four countries (Argentina, Brazil, Chile, and Uruguay) could be characterized as having had high rates of inflation relative to the rest of the world. In the 1960s the other 14 countries had rates of inflation lower than the average inflation rate in Asia (which has a reputation for low inflation), and ten countries (in Central America and the Caribbean plus Mexico, Paraguay, and Venezuela) had lower inflation than the average for the world economy (4.0%). One factor behind the inflationary trends of the Southern Cone countries was the strength of the labor unions. With indexation systems (of the exchange rate, in particular), Brazil and Colombia were able, from the mid-1960s, to avoid the overvaluation and unstable real exchange rates affecting their export competitiveness, and the uncertainty and stimulus to speculative activity with its discouraging effects on long-term investments. This can also be said of Chile after its 1970s traumas (high inflation under the Allende years, followed by massive macroeconomic imbalances during the first phase of the Pinochet regime).

1.3 THE ERA OF MARKET REFORMS

State-led industrialization started to be criticized in the 1960s both by the political left and by economic orthodoxy.[3] From the left, the criticism focused on the inability to overcome external dependency and, above all, to transform the dependent and unequal social structures inherited from the past. In particular, as already pointed out, the industrialization experience had done little to eliminate the very unequal income distribution and, in some cases, was thought to have led to growing social marginalization. Moreover,

---

[3] See e.g. the reviews of the debate at different points in time by Hirschman (1971), Fishlow (1985), and Love (1994).

the initial dependence on primary exports had been compounded with new forms of dependence on foreign capital and technology. Without necessarily sharing the point of view of the political left, Hirschman (1971) expressed brilliantly the underlying idea: "Industrialization was expected to change the social order and all it did was to supply manufactures" (p. 123).

The criticism from economic orthodoxy, located at the time in some US universities and the International Monetary Fund—though not yet at the World Bank[4]—centered on high inflation and associated lack of macroeconomic discipline—which, as discussed above, was relevant only for a few countries—and on the allocative inefficiencies that were generated in particular by trade protection and resulting anti-export bias (negative effective rates of protection for exporting sectors), as well as by anti-agricultural (net taxing of the agricultural sectors, largely through price regulation) and anti-employment biases (on the assumption that Latin America's comparative advantages were in labor-intensive sectors). Major texts in this line of criticism included Little, Scitovsky, and Scott (1970), based on a comparative study of seven developing countries in Asia and Latin America, and the major NBER research project led by Krueger (1978), which emphasized the superior growth and productivity performance of "outward oriented" industrialization vis-à-vis import substitution strategies.

Eventually, the viewpoint of economic orthodoxy, extended to encompass the criticism of a wider range of state interventions, became the dominant paradigm. According to Lindauer and Pritchett (2002), a number of "big facts" contributed to this new paradigm shift in Latin America and elsewhere in the developing world. The rapid growth of East Asia, based on manufacturing exports and outward orientation, led to a reassessment of the role of trade as well as of the role of government, given the mainstream (incorrect) interpretation of the East Asian development experience in the 1970s and 1980s as supposedly less state-led. The shortcomings of central planning were by the early 1980s also becoming clear, both in its strong form (the Soviet Union and Eastern Europe in general, as well as China, which would adopt a major shift in the late 1970s) and in its soft form (India with its disappointing growth performance). In the late 1980s, the fall of the Soviet Union and the end of communism in Central and Eastern Europe did much to further undermine the support for state-led development.

For Latin America, however, the debt crisis of the 1980s was by far the most important "big fact" determining the shift in the paradigm. The critics of state-led industrialization saw this event as the crisis of the whole development model followed until then. Independently of the problems that that model was facing in several countries, this is an incorrect interpretation. More than structural problems, the debt crisis was the result of the risky macroeconomic policies of the 1970s and, particularly, the second half of that decade: high external indebtedness, in the context of low real interest rates at the international level, and high commodity prices, combined with a huge external shock

[4] The Bank was, at least until the 1970s, part of the industrialist consensus, and contributed with its projects to the industrialization process and to building modern apparatus of state intervention, notably in the areas of infrastructure.

generated by the strong and unexpected increase of interest rates in the US in 1979–80 and the collapse, also largely unexpected, of commodity prices (Díaz-Alejandro 1988: ch. 15; Ocampo 2004a). The predominance of these macroeconomic factors over structural factors is reflected in the fact that the crisis hit large debtors, such as Brazil and Mexico, that continued to pursue state-led industrialization, but also affected with equal or even greater severity those countries that had engaged in the 1970s in market liberalization experiments (Argentina, Chile, and Uruguay). In contrast, the country that better managed the boom of the second half of the 1970s (Colombia) was hit by the contagion generated by the debt crisis, but did relatively well.

In any case, this event led to a reversal of the previous consensus on the development strategy and to a new conventional wisdom which viewed government as an obstacle to development, the private sector as the leading actor, trade as the engine of growth, and foreign direct investment as a priority.

1.3.1 The new paradigm

An essential difference between the rise of the new and the old paradigms lies in the relationship between ideas and practice. As we have seen, the old paradigm, articulated by CEPAL, arrived at an advanced stage in order to rationalize a process that was already in place. In the new paradigm shift, ideas came first as an intellectual and even openly ideological attack that acquired full force in the 1970s. The most paradigmatic case was, of course, the Chicago school offensive in Chile, which started in the 1950s and whose main results arrived with the Pinochet regime, giving a distinctive feature to a regime that initially lacked an economic model (Valdés 1995). Some texts, especially Balassa et al. (1986), had an important role in this process.

The World Bank and the IMF also had an important role in the diffusion of the reform agenda, through their policy conditionality. This gave the shift an appearance of an external imposition. This is in contrast with the previous paradigm, which, although conditioned by external influences, clearly emerged from within. Thus, while the document that best synthesized the vision of the previous period was CEPAL's "Latin American Manifesto," the one that more clearly articulates the new paradigm is the ten policy recommendations of the "Washington Consensus" formulated by Williamson (1990) to summarize what he perceived to be the reform agenda being pushed by the Washington institutions. The center of gravity had clearly shifted towards the economic thought generated in industrial economies and especially in the United States. To use CEPAL's terminology, the "center–periphery" model now dominated the realm of economic ideas prevailing in Latin America. Although these external influences were important, the view of the reform agenda as a mere external imposition is incorrect, as we will see below.

If industrialization and state intervention had been at the core of the previous development phase, the liberalization of market forces took that role under the new paradigm. In the area of macroeconomics, the idea that became popular in the 1970s, and especially in the 1980s, was that of "getting the prices right"—an expression that made reference to achieving an equilibrium exchange rate and letting interest rates be determined by market forces. The expression was also used to highlight the need for eliminating the discrimination against agricultural goods that resulted from price regulation by the state, as well as the need to set the price of public utilities in such a way as to cover costs. Later, the emphasis shifted in the macroeconomic area to low inflation rates guaranteed by autonomous central banks. In more than a few cases, however, inflation targets were achieved through the overvaluation of the exchange rate, thus contradicting the objective of "getting the prices right."

Low inflation in turn entailed the need to maintain healthy public-sector finances—an objective that proved harder to achieve. In the 1980s, the task was synonymous with reducing public spending, and thus rearranging government priorities, as well as changing the tax structure by increasing value added tax and reducing direct tax rates. Towards the end of the 1990s, public finance restructuring involved in addition the formulation of explicit fiscal targets of different kinds (primary surplus or budget balance, but also restrictions on the growth of government spending), as part of a broader set of fiscal responsibility rules which also affected the regional or local fiscal authorities in federal or decentralized systems.

With respect to changes in the economic structure, the early and prominent components of the reform agenda were trade liberalization and deeper integration into the world economy based on comparative advantages, as well as a broad opening up to foreign direct investment. Although only a few countries imitated the Chilean model, adopted in the 1970s, of establishing a uniform tariff, tariffs were sharply reduced and the tariff structure radically simplified as non-tariff barriers were largely eliminated. The objective of setting low tariffs was thus achieved to a much greater extent than in the classical period of primary export-led growth. Moreover, under the leadership of Mexico and Chile, a wave of free trade agreements was launched.

Trade liberalization was accompanied also by the dismantling of state intervention in productive development that characterized the previous period, not only in the manufacturing sector but also in agricultural development. This vision was succinctly summarized by a lemma that was repeated in several contexts: "the best industrial policy is *not* to have an industrial policy." In the application of this precept, technology policy, on which little progress had been made in the previous development phase (except, perhaps, in some agricultural research institutions), was also set aside, despite the fact that this is an element of intervention around which there is greater consensus. Trade liberalization and the dismantling of productive development policies was based on a number of arguments: the negative effects of protection on static efficiency (by moving the economy away from specialization according to comparative advantage and closing it off from external competition) as well as the encouragement of rent-seeking behavior as firms devoted resources to gaining advantages rather than increasing their efficiency.

Trade liberalization was accompanied, in addition, by the elimination of exchange controls and domestic financial liberalization. The latter included the liberalization of interest rates, the elimination of most forms of directed credit, and the reduction and simplification of reserve requirements on bank deposits. In this case, advocates of reform argued that the previous system of "financial repression" discouraged savings, as deposits frequently received negative real interest rates on their funds. This led, in their view, to limited access to credit, especially for small and medium-size enterprises, and in several instances to lending based on political connections rather than the profitability of the projects.

Another element in this agenda of structural reforms was the privatization of a large set of public enterprises together with the opening up to private investment of public services and utilities sectors. In this case, however, the process was more gradual, and a number of countries kept public-sector banks and a number of other firms, notably in oil and infrastructure services (water and sewage more than electricity and telecommunications). The more general deregulation of private economic activities was also part of the agenda, although it was recognized from the beginning that there should be some regulation of monopolistic practices and unfair competition, including those that could present themselves in privatized utilities. It was also accepted that financial liberalization required regulation to avoid the accumulation of excessive risks in the financial system, though the full acceptance of the need for regulation only came after a fair number of domestic financial crises.

Social development was not prominent in the initial market reform agenda. In Williamson's original decalogue, for example, spending on education and health was only mentioned as a priority in the task of reducing and restructuring public sector expenditures. However, in the reform proposals that the World Bank promoted, there were three ideas amply disseminated: decentralization, targeting of public social spending towards the poor, and the introduction of private-sector participation in the provision of social services. There was, in any case, recognition of the essential role of the state in this area. A topic where there was an overlap between this agenda and fiscal retrenchment was the pensions regime. The introduction of a new individual savings scheme, adopted by Chile in the 1980s to replace the old pay-as-you-go system, was disseminated as a panacea in the region and beyond, especially in post-communist Central Europe, even though not all reformers followed this trend. There was, finally, an agenda of at least partial liberalization of labor markets, but here political factors largely blocked the reform proposals (Chapter 31 in this volume, by Murillo, Ronconi, and Schrank).

1.3.2 Policy diversity

As the implementation of the new paradigm made major strides, alternative policy proposals were advanced from other quarters. CEPAL's *Changing Production Patterns with Social Equity* (ECLAC 1990) was an important contribution in this regard, to which other contributions from this institution were added in subsequent years. Outside CEPAL, the alternative paradigm took the form of "neo-structuralism"

(Sunkel 1993; Bielschowsky 2009). These alternative proposals focused on four predominant themes:

(i) the adoption of more active and counter-cyclical macroeconomic policies in order to avoid, in particular, the disequilibria generated by boom-bust cycles in external financing;

(ii) the combination of trade liberalization with open regionalism;

(iii) the promotion of innovation through active technology and productive development policies adjusted to the new open economies; and

(iv) the adoption of equity at the center of development policy (see esp. Ocampo 2004b; Ffrench-Davis 2005).

Over time, this last objective would eventually obtain an important place in the agenda of those institutions that promoted reforms, in particular the World Bank, and the first would be brought into the agenda during the 2008–9 global financial crisis.

Reflecting these and other alternative views, the map of structural reforms shows a diversity of national responses, even during the years of greater activism (see e.g. Stallings and Peres 2000). This diversity indicates, furthermore, that the transformation cannot be simply understood as an external imposition: it was really the outcome of national decisions adopted since the mid-1980s by democratic political regimes, in sharp contrast with the initial neo-liberal experiments in the 1970s in the Southern Cone. Diversity was evident both in the models of macroeconomic management and in the speed and scope of some structural reforms—trade opening, financial liberalization, and the privatization process. There were, in addition, relatively common elements that were not part of the initial reform agenda and that responded more to domestic political pressures. Chief among them is the generalized increase in social spending that took off in the 1990s (ECLAC 2009). Greater social activism, together with the very limited scope for labor market deregulation, are probably the most important contributions to the revision of the reform agenda that came with the democratic wave that simultaneously swept the region. Another element that emerged from the political realm was support for regional economic integration, which was in opposition to the more orthodox visions that promoted unilateral trade liberalization.

Diversity became broader over time as a reflection of the poor results of reforms in several countries, as well as of the open political rejection of market reforms in some countries. The "lost half-decade" that followed the Asian crisis of 1997 and the Russian crisis of 1998 was a turning point in this regard. From then on, a greater pragmatism was accompanied by the incorporation of new issues into the agenda, especially those relating to equity and institutional development. The excessively positive assessments of the reforms, which curiously were drafted as the new crisis hit the region (IDB 1997; World Bank 1997), were followed by much more subtle views that emphasized the need to make progress in overcoming the severe problems of poverty and inequality in the region, as well as on institutional development (see esp. Kuczynski and Williamson 2003; World Bank 2006).

1.3.3 Economic and social performance

The economic and social performance of Latin America since the 1980s has been weaker than that of the previous development phase. This is true even if we leave aside the "lost decade" of the 1980s. For the period 1990–2008, the average of Latin America's per capita GDP growth rate has been 1.8% per year, well below the growth rate of the period 1950–80 (2.7%) and less than the average growth rate of the world economy (see again Table 1.1). The growth performance of GDP per worker, a gross measure of productivity, is even worse: 0.7% per year for 1990–2008 vs. 2.7% in 1950–80. This means that most of the increase in GDP per capita since 1990 has been the result of the demographic bonus resulting from the slowdown of population growth (from 2.7% to 1.5%) in the face of a still relatively fast growth of the labor force (2.6% per year, a rate similar to the 2.8% of 1950–80) (see Ros 2009).

Table 1.1 indicates that only two countries have experienced a dynamic growth of productivity since 1990 (Chile and the Dominican Republic); two countries show fairly similar though relatively low productivity growth in both periods (El Salvador and Uruguay); the rest show a much poorer performance in 1990–2008 than in 1950–80. This poor overall productivity performance is not due to the absence of new dynamic and highly productive activities; rather, it reflects the rising share of low-productivity informal activities, as the dynamic highly productive sectors were unable to absorb a larger share of the labor force.

Despite the significant demographic bonus, the mixed growth performance during the reform period is illustrated in Table 1.4. There are seven countries that have grown since 1990 at a per capita rate above the world average, six of which have improved in this respect relative to their own past performance, while eleven countries have experienced performance below the world average, and seven of them also with respect to their past record. Across countries there is no apparent relationship between the degree and timing of market liberalization and growth performance. The countries in the upper left corner of the table include Chile, an early reformer, the Dominican Republic, a late reformer, turbulent Argentina, with a heterodox exchange rate policy since 2002, and relatively more orthodox Peru. Interestingly, all the fast-growing economies under state-led industrialization, most of which have thoroughly liberalized their economies, have now underperformed in relation to past and world trends, with the major exceptions of the Dominican Republic and Panama. In contrast, the poor performers under state-led industrialization have done better under the new paradigm.

This economic performance was affected not only by the poor results of the market reforms but also by worldwide macroeconomic turbulence. The collapse of growth during the lost decade of the 1980s was followed by a recovery in 1990–97, although at a slower pace than during the years of state-led industrialization, and then by the "lost half decade" of 1998–2003. As a result, the relative position of Latin America in the world economy went back in 2003 to the levels of 1900 (Figure 1.1)! The combination of a new surge in external financing and the increase in commodity prices, which had been absent since the 1970s, generated a new boom in 2004–7, at a pace that was then more similar to

Table 1.4 Relative growth performance, 1990–2008

		Relative to 1950–80	
		Above	Below
	Above	Chile (4.0%)	Costa Rica (2.8%)
		Dominican Rep. (3.9%)	
		Panama (3.6%)	
		Peru (3.4%)	
		Argentina (3.0%)	
		Uruguay (2.8%)	
Relative to world average	Below	El Salvador (1.8%)	Colombia (1.9%)
		Honduras (1.8%)	Mexico (1.6%)
		Bolivia (1.5%)	Brazil (1.5%)
		Nicaragua (1.5%)	Ecuador (1.5%)
			Guatemala (1.5%)
			Venezuela (1.2%)
			Paraguay (0.5%)

Source: See Table 1.1 (average per capita GDP growth in 1990–2008 in parentheses).

that of the 1970s. But if the slow pace of economic growth since 1990 cannot solely be attributed to market reforms, neither can reformers claim for themselves the success of the recent period, which had also been remarkable in countries now embracing more heterodox views. In any case, the global crisis in 2008–9 suddenly interrupted the recovery after 2003, bringing about a deep recession in 2009 which was second only, among emerging and developing countries, to that of Central and Eastern Europe.

In the social development area there was really no "lost decade," as revealed by the continuous progress made in education and health in the 1980s (see Table 1.2), though with a slowdown in the 1990s that, together with the fall in relative per capita income, led to a lag in human development vis-à-vis the industrial countries. The lost decade led to a significant increase in income poverty, but this was followed by progress in this area during the two periods of economic expansion in the 1990s and the new century, with a partial reversal during the "lost half-decade." However, it was only in 2005 that poverty rates returned to their 1980 levels, so that in this area Latin America lost a quarter of a century rather than a decade (Figure 1.2)! Reduction in poverty rates was significantly helped—and in countries with young populations in 1980 greatly so—by the near-completion of the demographic transition since, as already mentioned, most of the increase in average per capita incomes for the region was the result of the demographic bonus—i.e. the increase in the labor force rather than the increase in GDP per worker (Ros 2009).

The significant reduction in poverty levels during the first decade of the 21st century also reflects the effects of an improvement in income distribution in several countries,

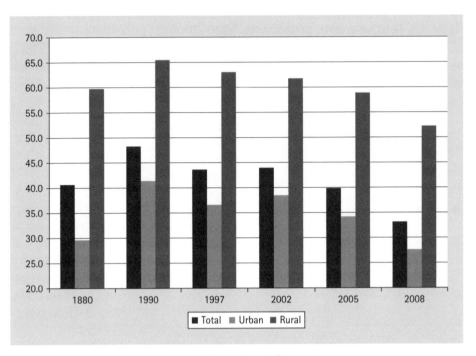

FIGURE 1.2 Latin America's poverty

Source: ECLAC (2009).

which reversed the moderate deterioration that had taken place on average from the early 1990s to the early 2000s (and in some cases, in the 1970s or 1980s). The factors behind the recent improvement in income distribution are still subject to debate. Rising social spending has played an important role, both transfers to poor households and, even more so, improved educational opportunities, which is a major factor behind the reduction in the skill premia, in sharp contrast to the opposite trend that was experienced in most Latin American countries during the 1990s. Improved distribution was facilitated by more conjunctural factors, such as the reduction in the rural–urban gap, thanks to booming agricultural prices, and increased formal employment during the 2003–8 boom, in the context of a significant reduction in the growth of the labor force. In any case, these improvements have only made a small dent in the large inequalities that still characterize the region (Gasparini et al. 2009; Cornia 2010).

1.4 Looking forward

The mixed outcomes of market reforms led to a heated debate and the reopening of many issues in the development agenda (Birdsall, de la Torre, and Valencia Caicedo, Chapter 4 below). If we look back at the neo-structuralist views set out by CEPAL since the 1990s, counter-cyclical macroeconomic policies and more active social policies are now clearly on the regional agenda. As we have seen, economic integration was introduced by politics rather than economics, though its success has been mixed. There is also broader agreement on the need for active technology policies, accompanied now by growing interest in production sector policies, under the leadership of Brazil, but action is still marginal in both areas in most countries. As in the past, regional differences in responses are already evident, in some cases backed by strong ideologies.

Major external shocks have always led to significant changes in Latin America. The 2008–9 world financial crisis was a shock of this type, and one which has already led to broader state activism throughout the world. An equally significant event is the collapse of international trade that took place during the recent crisis, and its still insufficient recovery as this chapter is written. Whatever happens in this area will be crucial, given the emphasis of market reforms on integration into the world economy. The crisis will also speed up the shift away from Western hegemony in economic affairs. These processes may lead to new changes, which could be major or even epochal ones. The immediate future will thus be full of news about global development patterns.

References

Astorga, P., Bergés, A. R., and FitzGerald, V. (2003). 'The Standard of Living in Latin America During the Twentieth Century', Working Paper Series No. 103, Oxford: University of Oxford, Latin American Centre.

Balassa, B., Bueno, G. M., Kuczynski, P. P., and Simonsen, M. H. (1986). *Towards Renewed Economic Growth in Latin America*, Washington, DC: Institute for International Economics.

Bértola, L., Hernández, M., and Siniscalchi, S. (2010). 'Un índice histórico de desarrollo humano de América Latina en perspectiva comparada', Documento de Trabajo, Universidad de la República, Montevideo.

Bielschowsky, R. (1998). 'Cincuenta años de pensamiento de la CEPAL: una reseña', in *Cincuenta años de pensamiento de la CEPAL*, Santiago, Chile: Fondo de Cultura Económica and ECLAC.

—— (2009). 'Sixty Years of ECLAC: Structuralism and Neo-Structuralism', *CEPAL Review* 97 (December).

Cárdenas, E., Ocampo, J. A., and Thorp, R. (eds) (2000). *Industrialization and the State in Latin America: The Post War Years* (An Economic History of Twentieth-Century Latin America, vol. 3), Basingstoke and New York: Palgrave Press and St. Martin's.

Coatsworth, J. H., and Williamson, J. (2003). 'Always Protectionist? Latin American Tariffs from Independence to Great Depression', *Journal of Latin American Studies* 36.

Cornia, G. A. (2010). 'Income Distribution under Latin America's Center-Left Regimes', *Journal of Human Development and Capabilities* 11.1.

DÍAZ-ALEJANDRO, C. F. (1988). *Trade, Development and the World Economy: Selected Essays of Carlos F. Díaz-Alejandro*, ed. A. Velasco, Oxford: Blackwell.

—— (2000). 'Latin America in the 1930s', in R. Thorp (ed.), *The Role of the Periphery in World Crisis* (An Economic History of Twentieth-Century Latin America, vol. 2), Basingstoke and New York: Palgrave Press and St. Martin's.

ECLAC (United Nations Economic Commission for Latin America and the Caribbean) (1990). *Changing Production Patterns with Social Equity*, Santiago.

—— (1998). *Economic Survey of Latin America and the Caribbean*, Santiago.

—— (2009). *Social Panorama of Latin America*, Santiago.

FFRENCH-DAVIS, R. (2005). *Reformas para América Latina: después del fundamentalismo neoliberal*, Buenos Aires: Siglo XXI Editores.

—— MUÑOZ, O., and PALMA, G. (1998). 'The Latin American Economies, 1959–1990', in L. Bethell (ed.), *Latin America: Economy and Society Since 1930*, Cambridge: Cambridge University Press.

FISHLOW, A. (1985). 'El estado de la ciencia económica en América Latina', in *Progreso Económico y Social en América Latina, Informe 1985*, Washington, DC: Inter-American Development Bank.

GASPARINI, L., CRUCES, G., TORNAROLLI, L., and MARCHIONNI, M. (2009). 'A Turning Point? Recent Developments on Inequality in Latin America and the Caribbean', paper presented at UNDP-RBLAC, New York, January.

GERSCHENKRON, A. (1962). *Economic Backwardness in Historical Perspective*, Cambridge, Mass.: Belknap and Harvard University Press.

HIRSCHMAN, A. O. (ed.) (1971). 'The Political Economy of Import-Substituting Industrialization in Latin America', in *A Bias for Hope: Essays on Development and Latin America*, New Haven, Conn.: Yale University Press.

—— (1987). 'The Political Economy of Latin American Development: Seven Exercises in Retrospection', *Latin American Research Review* 22.3.

IDB (Inter-American Development Bank) (1997). *América Latina tras una década de reformas: progreso económico y social en América Latina*, Washington, DC.

KRUEGER, A. O. (1978). *Liberalization Attempts and Consequences*, New York: National Bureau of Economic Research.

KUCZYNSKI, P. P., and WILLIAMSON, J. (eds) (2003). *After the Washington Consensus: Restarting Growth and Reform in Latin America*, Washington, DC: Institute for International Economics.

LINDAUER, D., and PRITCHETT, L. (2002). 'What's the Big Idea? The Third Generation of Policies for Economic Growth', *Economia* 3.1.

LITTLE, I., SCITOVSKY, T., and SCOTT, M. (1970). *Industry and Trade in Some Developing Countries*, London: Oxford University Press.

LOVE, J. L. (1994). 'Economic Ideas and Ideologies in Latin America Since 1930', in L. Bethel (ed.), *The Cambridge History of Latin America*, vol. 6, Cambridge: Cambridge University Press.

MADDISON, ANGUS (2003). *The World Economy: Historical Statistics*, Paris, OECD.

—— (2006). *The World Economy*, vol. 2: *Historical Statistics*, Paris: OECD.

OCAMPO, J. A. (2004a). 'La América Latina y la economía mundial en el largo siglo XX', *El Trimestre Económico* 71.4, No. 284.

—— (2004b). *Reconstruir el futuro: globalización, desarrollo y democracia en América Latina*, Bogotá: Norma and CEPAL.

PRADOS DE LA ESCOSURA, L. (2007). 'Inequality and Poverty in Latin America: A Long-Run Exploration', in T. Hatton, K. O'Rourke, and A. Taylor (eds), *The New Comparative Economic History: Essays in Honor of Jeffrey G. Williamson*, Cambridge, Mass.: MIT Press.

ROS, J. (2009). 'Poverty Reduction in Latin America: The Role of Demographic, Social and Economic Factors', *CEPAL Review* 98.

ROSENTHAL, G. (2004). 'ECLAC: A Commitment to a Latin American Way Toward Development' in Yves Berthelot (ed.), *Unity and Diversity in Development Ideas: Perspectives from the UN Regional Commissions*, United Nations Intellectual History Project Series, Bloomington: Indiana University Press.

SHEAHAN, J. (1987). *Patterns of Development in Latin America: Poverty, Repression, and Economic Strategy*, Princeton, NJ: Princeton University Press.

STALLINGS, B., and PERES, W. (2000). *Growth, Employment and Equity: The Impact of the Economic Reforms in Latin America and the Caribbean*, Washington, DC: The Brookings Institution and ECLAC.

SUNKEL, O. (ed.) (1993). *Development from Within: Toward a Neostructuralist Approach for Latin America*, Boulder, Colo.: Lynne Rienner.

VALDÉS, J. G. (1995). *Pinochet's Economists: The Chicago School in Chile*, Cambridge: Cambridge University Press.

WILLIAMSON, J. (ed.) (1990). 'What Washington Means By Policy Reform', in *Latin American Adjustment: How Much Has Happened?* Washington, DC: Institute for International Economics.

World Bank (1997). *The Long March: A Reform Agenda for Latin America and the Caribbean in the Next Decade*, Washington, DC.

—— (2006). *Poverty Reduction and Growth: Virtuous and Vicious Circles*, Washington, DC.

CHAPTER 2

INSTITUTIONS AND THE
HISTORICAL ROOTS OF
LATIN AMERICAN
DIVERGENCE

LUIS BÉRTOLA

2.1 INTRODUCTION[1]

There is no doubt that Latin America has fallen behind the more developed countries as regards per capita income, but there is still much debate about when and why this happened.

In this chapter, I analyze the relation between long-term growth and institutional development in Latin America. My motivation is a certain dissatisfaction with the state of the art concerning general theories on Latin American development, as expressed both by today's very widespread neo-institutional approach, which considers that institutions created during colonial times were responsible for backwardness, and by most of the reactions against that approach. I propose some guidelines to interpreting long-run Latin American development that try to capture the contributions of recent research, but also find some inspiration in previous structuralist and Marxist writings on Latin America.

In the first part of this chapter I will present a few stylized facts about Latin American relative performance, to which the institutional discussion is related. The second section starts with a conceptual discussion of institutions and relations of production and discusses different applications to the Latin American context. I finish by summarizing my conclusions.

[1] This chapter is part of a research project financed by the Fondo Clemente Estable, Ministerio de Educación y Cultura, Uruguay. I am grateful for most valuable comments by the editors of this volume, and by Jorge Álvarez, Reto Bertoni, Daniele Bonfanti, Javier Rodríguez Weber, Jeffrey Williamson, and participants at the 5th Annual Research Meeting of the Uruguayan Economic History Association.

2.2 WHEN DID LATIN AMERICA FALL BEHIND?

2.2.1 Latin America, the West, and the Rest

Since 1500, Latin America's per capita GDP has fluctuated within a range of +/– 20% of average world per capita income (Table 2.1). However, differences of per capita GDP between countries and regions has been steadily increasing. Thus, while the gap between Latin America and the West has continuously widened, so has the gap between Latin America and Africa until now, and likewise the gap between Latin America and Asia until the 1950s.

International relative growth rates have been increasingly discussed in terms of the "little divergence" and the "great divergence". The Western countries moved from a relatively slow growth path dominated by population expansion in 1500–1820, to a fast and intensive growth path since the 1820s, in which per capita GDP growth clearly dominated over population growth (Figure 2.1). During the first period, the rest of the world only grew extensively, and at slower rates than the West, giving rise to the so-called "little divergence." During the second period, GDP growth rates accelerated, but population growth remained high and accounted for half of total growth. World productivity, as measured by per capita GDP, grew at only 60% of the growth rate of the West, giving rise to the so-called "great divergence."

After independence, Latin America (LA) followed a path similar to the Rest of the world: it showed slightly higher growth rates but with the same structure, which is that population growth explained 60% of total growth. Latin America's per capita GDP growth was only 70% of that of the West. Relative growth, however, may blur the size of the gap. Between 1820 and 2008 the absolute size of the gap increased by a factor of 40, and in relative terms it became 2.9 times higher than average LA per capita income. As regards colonial times, it is very difficult to estimate GDP and population. Based on very fragile assumptions such as those of Maddison, we might guess that there really was a non-negligible gap between Latin America and the West, but it did not widen significantly during this period.

To sum up, while the West was growing extensively and somewhat slowly, the gap between the West and the Rest (Latin America included) was not negligible, but increased moderately. When the West shifted to an intensive growth pattern LA lagged further and further behind and the gap became huge, in spite of LA having continued and even accelerating growth. Therefore, while the original gap and colonial heritage deserve considerable attention, new growth patterns emerged and the scene changed dramatically after the Industrial Revolution.

We can identify different periods in the life of the independent Latin American countries.

The "cost of independence" seems to have been huge in terms of relative development. This is a traditional view, represented for example by Halperin Donghi (1985). This point is also implied in Bates, Coatsworth, and Williamson's (2007) descriptive name "Lost

Table 2.1 Per capita GDP, population, and GDP 1500–2003 by region (1990 international dollars) and relative to world average

	1500	1820	1870	1913	1950	1973	2001
Per capita GDP ($)							
West	702	1,109	1,882	3,672	5,649	13,082	22,509
Rest	538	578	606	860	1,091	2,072	3,372
LA	416	648	813	1,481	2,506	4,504	5,811
Rest without LA	545	576	597	821	960	1,809	3,105
World	566	667	875	1,525	2,111	4,091	6,049
West–LA gap	286	461	1,069	2,191	3,143	8,578	16,698
West–LA gap/LA	0.69	0.71	1.31	1.48	1.25	1.90	2.87
Per capita GDP (world average = 1)							
West	1.24	1.66	2.15	2.41	2.68	3.20	3.72
Rest	0.95	0.87	0.69	0.56	0.52	0.51	0.56
LA	0.73	0.97	0.93	0.97	1.19	1.10	0.96
Rest without LA	0.96	0.86	0.68	0.54	0.45	0.44	0.51
World	1.00	1.00	1.00	1.00	1.00	1.00	1.00

Table 2.1 (contd.)

	1500	1820	1870	1913	1950	1973	2001
Population (millions)							
West	75	175	268	424	565	718	859
Rest	363	867	1004	1367	1959	3198	5290
LA	18	22	40	81	166	308	531
Rest without LA	345	845	964	1286	1793	2890	4759
World	438	1,042	1,272	1,791	2,524	3,916	6,149
GDP (thousand millions)							
West	53	194.4	504.5	1,556.9	3,193	9,398	19,331
Rest	195.3	501	608.2	1,175.2	2,137	6,626	17,862
LA	7.3	14	33	119.9	416	1,398	3,087
Rest without LA	188	487	575.68	1,055.3	1,721	5,228	14,775
World	248.3	695.4	1112.7	2,732.1	5,330	16,024	37,193

Source: Maddison (2007: tables 1a–c); for Latin America 1820 and 1870, Prados de la Escosura (2009: table 6).

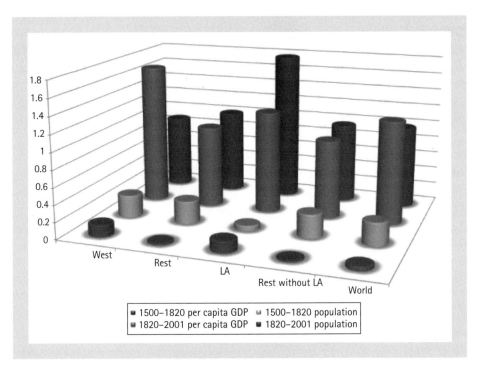

FIGURE 2.1 Growth rates of population and per capita GDP, 1500–1820 and 1820–2001, by region

Source: Table 2.1.

Decades." However, more recently Prados de la Escosura (2009: 306) concluded that between 1820 and 1870 Latin America grew "at a similar rate to the global average, matching that of the European periphery and proving far higher than that occurring in Asia and Africa. 'Lost decades' seems to be an inadequate description of aggregate performance in post-independence Latin America."

We find it difficult to agree with this author. First, while world average annual growth was 0.6%, 12 Western European countries (Europe 12) were growing at 1% and the US at 1.3%, the Latin American rate was only 0.4%. Secondly, the gap between Latin America and Europe 12 increased from 0.9 to 1.6 of Latin America's per capita GDP; the gap between the US and Latin America increased from 0.9 to 2.0 of Latin America's per capita GDP. Some countries were growing fast, and many former colonies were taking advantage of that. Even if Latin America was not a stagnant or sclerotic society, the decades following independence were lost in terms of relative performance and potential growth. Gelman (forthcoming) states that during this period disparities increased significantly in Latin America, as the commodity lottery allowed some regions to grow fast while others remained stagnant, thus making it difficult to generalize. Even if true, this statement does not change the general view: diverse performance is not a special feature of this period in Latin America.

Within two quite different environments Latin American performance in 1870-1950 seems, at first glance, to have been reasonably good. While the gap between the West and the Rest increased from 2.3 in 1870 to 4.5 in 1913 and to 5.6 in 1950, Latin America went up from 0.9 of the world average to 1 in 1913 and 1.4 in 1950. The gap between LA and both Africa and Asia increased considerably. However, there is no reason to be complacent about this performance: the absolute gap between per capita income in the West and that of Latin America increased by 81% in 1870–1913 and by a further 52% in 1913–50 (it widened by 176% in 1870–1950). It increased from 131% to 148% of LA's GDP between 1870 and 1913, but narrowed to 125% in 1950.

The trend has changed since the 1950s. During the Golden Age (when the West grew as never before) and after (when Asia started to grow faster and the communist world was still doing well), Latin America lagged behind, although the gap between it and Africa continued to widen. Latin America's performance after the 1970s was relatively poorer, in spite of a slower growth rate in the West.

2.2.2 Latin American diversity

Latin America is diverse, and its development and growth have been uneven. As can be seen in Table 2.2, in 1820 the combined per capita GDP of Argentina and Uruguay may have been double that of the rest of the continent combined. The trend until the 1950s was of increasing disparities between countries, probably since the early years of independence (Gelman forthcoming), with Chile and Cuba already in the-high income group in the 1870s, and Venezuela joining in the 1950s.

However, starting in the 1910s, the Latin American economies began to converge. This was due to sluggish growth in the relatively high-income countries and fast growth in Brazil, Mexico, and Colombia, for example. Today no Latin American country rates as a developed country, but this does not mean that some of them, at certain points in time and under special circumstances (often related to the so called "commodity lottery"), have not had high income levels and high growth rates. However, Latin American countries have not been able to sustain high growth rates over time. Instead of steadily approaching the levels of the world's leading economies, they have tended to experience "truncated convergence" (Ocampo and Parra 2007) and have shifted between "convergence and divergence regimes" (Bértola and Porcile 2006).

Relative backwardness, however, is not stagnation or total inertia. Since the time of the conquest, per capita income in the region has grown by a factor of 17, and since independence it has grown tenfold. If we add population growth to these figures, since Independence total GDP has grown by a factor of 283 while GDP in the West increased by a factor of 117 in the same period. This kind of growth must mean that far-reaching structural and institutional changes have taken place. No doubt the kinds of growth mechanism have changed over time, and so the institutional determinants of growth and the impact of growth on institutions probably changed as well. In both cases, these changes affected both the domestic and the international arena.

Table 2.2 Per capita GDP of some Latin American countries, 1820–2003 (1990 international dollars)

	1820	1870	1913	1950	1973	1990	2003
Argentina	1,249	1,837	3,797	4,987	7,962	6,436	7,666
Brazil	652	680	811	1,672	3,882	4,924	5,563
Chile	607	1,295	2,988	3,670	5,034	6,402	10,951
Colombia	423	539	1,236	2,153	3,499	4,840	5,228
Mexico	693	720	1,732	2,365	4,853	6,085	7,137
Uruguay	1,004	1,880	3,310	4,659	4,974	6,474	6,805
Venezuela	347	529	1,104	7,462	10,625	8,313	6,988
Average	648	813	1,618	2,696	4,875	5,465	6,278

Source: Maddison (2007); Latin America 1820 and 1870, de la Escosura (2009: table 6).

2.3 INSTITUTIONS IN THE LATIN AMERICAN CONTEXT

In the last decade, the Latin American experience has been re-examined with neo-institutional approaches including work by Engerman and Sokoloff (1997), Landes (1999), North, Weingast, and Summerhill (2000), Acemoglu, Johnson, and Robinson (2005), Lange, Mahoney, and Vom Hau (2006), Robinson (2006), and Sokoloff and Zolt (2007). With some nuances, even Coatsworth (2008) can be included in this group. These studies involve the basic idea that the fundamental causes of Latin America's long-run backwardness are to be found in the institutions that were set up shortly after the Spanish conquest, which promoted a high concentration of wealth and political power. Regardless of their disagreement about the factors that ultimately determined the nature of these institutions, or even the timing, these authors all seem to trace Latin American backwardness to its colonial roots. This is a traditional subject in Latin American historiography, and an issue that the new literature generally ignores (see Stein and Stein 1970; Furtado 1974; Cardoso and Pérez Brignoli 1979; Sunkel and Paz 1982; and many others).

Nevertheless, this is a very important development: when this new line of research re-emerged in the 1990s, the dominant approach to Latin American backwardness centered on the idea that these countries developed in a negative way in the middle decades of the 20th century largely because the scene was dominated by state-led growth and import-substitution strategies. Neo-institutional approaches also had important policy implications: as institutions are path-dependent and very prone to inertia, no policy recommendation imposed from the outside can easily change long-run trends unless considerable domestic changes also take place. The development prospects implied by this view are not particularly optimistic.

2.3.1 Institutions: new institutional economics and Marxism

Institutional analysis is not new, and it is worth recapitulating what is new in neo-institutional approaches so as to grasp their contributions and eventual shortcomings. Many of the previous theories about Latin American economic history have some kind of Marxist inspiration. In order to compare the new contributions with previous ones, it would be interesting to compare New Institutional Economics with Marxism.

New Institutional Economics is the result of three decades of refining definitions and formal approaches. This movement combines two complementary sets of ideas (Dye 2006: 170): North's contributions (1990; 1994), which define institutions as rules of the game, and Acemoglu and Robinson's approach (2006), which conceptualizes institutions as producers of sustained or equilibrium behavior.

According to North (1994), "Institutions are the humanly devised constraints that structure human interaction. They are made up of formal constraints (e.g. rules, laws, constitutions), informal constraints (e.g. norms of behavior, conventions, self-imposed codes of conduct), and their enforcement mechanisms. Together they define the incentive structure of societies and specifically economies" (p. 360).

Informal institutions are awarded an important role in the theory. Formal institutions may be imposed on different societies or different formal settings and may be adopted in enthusiastic response to what has been applied in other societies. Unless these institutions are also embedded in informal institutions, ways of behavior, and beliefs, however, the probable outcome could be quite different than what was expected (Dye 2006).

The New Institutional Economics approach to institutions mainly boils down to two distinct sets of institutions, which are almost sufficient to explain modern economic growth. One set has to do with property rights, and there are two dimensions to this: the economic and the political. The economic dimension is the defense of property rights. The political dimension involves attaining and defending civil rights, i.e. the right to a political voice to defend the interests of the people of the country, and in particular the right to defend property and income from abuses by wealthy and politically powerful elites and dictators. What matters here is capital accumulation. The second set of institutions has to do with inequality. When power and wealth are highly concentrated, this makes for a context in which it is easier for elites to expropriate wealth and income and abuse power, but this kind of situation hampers the accumulation of human capital. A skewed distribution of income and wealth will probably impose limits on the accumulation of education and knowledge by the great mass of the population and thus impede growth.

Most New Institutional Economists have in mind the Solow-type growth model extended with human capital. The institutions considered by New Institutional Economists are concentrated at the macro-level. However, there is no clear consideration of the institutions that regulate the micro-level or all the different institutions that regulate the innovation process. Innovation seems to be seen as an outcome of human and physical capital accumulation. Based on the concepts of scarcity and competition, good institutions are those that foster fair competition. As in the Solow-type model, productivity growth is obviously important, but no clear explanation of it is proposed.

It seems paradoxical that New Institutional Economics should focus so much on domestic relations and avoid too many references to international relations, because in neo-classical economics the main focus in development economics has been to promote free trade, globalization, and integration into international factor and commodity markets. It seems that New Institutional Economists share with neo-classical approaches the idea that international integration naturally has a positive impact on development. However, the main idea is that, no matter how powerful global forces might be, their contribution to development largely depends on the domestic institutions each country has, since it is institutions that can cause slow-growth equilibrium even when international conditions are supposedly favorable.

The Marxian view is that economies develop as the result of the interaction between the productive forces (people, techniques, knowledge, physical capital, land, particular geographical and climatic conditions) and the social relations of production, i.e. relations between different social groups involving power and ownership of natural resources, physical capital, knowledge, and labor. Marx differentiates between the structure and the super-structure. The structure is composed of relations of production and productive forces (endowments). The relations of production are themselves institutional arrangements, i.e. relations between individuals and groups of individuals who have different positions with respect to the ownership of land, capital, and labor. Formal institutions (the super-structure) are based on informal, pre-existing relations of forces, social relations, and they constitute the legal apparatus and its enforcement mechanisms, the state or other organizations that play this role, and also ideology, religion, and culture.

What is the connection between the relations of production and institutions? Is it possible to produce a conceptual interface? These concepts have many similarities. What North calls "institutions" are what Marx calls "social relations of production." The relations of production exist at both the informal and the formal level. In the latter case, they become part of the super-structure of society.

What is probably more important is to see how these different levels of analysis interact with each other, and what their hierarchies are. The comparison between the two groups of theories is made difficult by the variety of approaches within each school of thought. In order to make the discussion easier, we will focus on how these different views appear in the Latin American context.

2.3.2 The colonial heritage

2.3.2.1 Neo-institutionalism and the colonial heritage

Most New Institutionalists seem to agree that colonial institutions are the fundamental cause of Latin America's backwardness. However, they do not agree on the origin of these institutions.

Landes (1999) and North et al. (2000) state that Latin American institutions are mainly the result of some kind of cultural and political transfer from the colonizing power. On a list of alternative features, Latin America (unlike North America) is always on the wrong side: federalism vs. centralism, democracy vs. monarchy, transparency and accountability vs. privileges and arbitrary decisions, free trade vs. monopolistic policies, religious freedom vs. official doctrine, cultural pluralism vs. monoculturalism and racism. This point was recently reformulated by Lange, Mahoney, and vom Hau (2006), who maintain that the differences arise from two different economic doctrines, the liberal view and the mercantilist stance. In a joint article, Sokoloff and Robinson (de Ferranti et al. 2004: ch. 4) agree in their opposition to this view:

> Following Engerman and Sokoloff (1997, 2000, 2002) and Acemoglu, Johnson, and Robinson (2001, 2002), the authors of this chapter argue that the contemporary situation cannot be understood without recognizing that extreme inequality emerged soon after the Europeans began to colonize the Americas half a millennium ago, and has been reflected in the institutions they put in place. Both this initial inequality and institutions were shaped largely by the factor endowments that the Europeans found in Central and South America, rather than the nature of the colonial powers themselves. Although these colonies ultimately gained independence and the development of technology and the world economy brought about important changes, extreme inequality persisted into the nineteenth and twentieth centuries because the evolution of political and economic institutions tended to reproduce and reinforce highly unequal distributions of wealth, human capital, and political influence. (World Bank 2003: ch. 4)

But these two authors later disagree. The Engerman and Sokoloff argument may be labeled as endowment deterministic:

> ...various features of the factor endowments of the three categories of New World Economies, including soils, climates, and the size or density of the native population, may have predisposed those colonies toward paths of development associated with different degrees of inequality in wealth, human capital, and political power, as well as with different potentials for economic growth. Even if, later on, institutions may ultimately affect the evolution of factor endowments, the initial conditions with respect to factor endowment had long, lingering effects. (Engerman and Sokoloff 1997: 275–6)[2]

In subsequent papers, Sokoloff with other co-authors make further studies of institutional architecture, but now with reference to education, political participation and suffrage, fiscal policy, local government, etc. However, the basic idea remains: poor institutions rely on the features of domestic resource endowments.

---

[2] The three categories here are (1) tropical crops like sugar that yield increasing returns to scale and promote the concentration of property. This was reinforced by the introduction of slave labor; (2) corn production, which never had increasing returns to scale and which led to a farmer society; (3) the Andean and Mesoamerican societies, with their high concentration of land, natural resources, and domestic labor, i.e. a similar structure of incentives to those prevailing in the tropical regions (Engerman and Sokoloff 1997).

Acemoglu and Robinson's approach differs from this. Rather than emphasizing natural resources in the different regions or dwelling on the supposedly different technical features of the different kinds of production with respect to increasing returns to scale, they mainly focus on one kind of endowment, labor. Their arguments boil down to quite a simple idea: in places where the native population is numerous or immigration is hampered by a fear of diseases, there are incentives for the colonial elite to develop coercive labor relations. This leads them to set up "bad" institutions that further foster the concentration of wealth and political power. The opposite scenario pertains when colonists form the majority of the population: they create "good" institutions for themselves, thus promoting the accumulation of physical, human and "political" capital. The origin of the colonists does not really matter, and nor do the geographical determinants of technical aspects of society, but the environment in which colonists settle is significant. To support the notion that institutions rather than geography or natural endowments play a decisive role, Acemoglu and Robinson use the "reversal of fortune" argument. This is the idea that regions with high development levels in 1500 had lower per capita income at the end of the 20th century, and what was probably explained by geography in 1500 institutions reversed as time went by.

According to Acemoglu and Robinson (2006), the distribution of wealth and the political regime at a certain point of departure is the *de jure* and tacit political framework which determines the prevailing formal and informal economic and political institutions.

In short, two assertions feature Neo-institutionalist thinking on Latin America: that early colonial institutions are the main explanation of Latin American backwardness; and that these institutions were inert to a large extent and tended to reproduce themselves over time. However, there are still considerable disagreements about the origin of institutions, between a resource determinism that can be said to be exogenous, a cultural or political determinism that is also exogenous and is dependent on the kind of colonial power, and an endogenous sociopolitical determinism.

2.3.2.2 *Marxist and structuralist approaches to the colonial heritage*

Marx considers the distributional outcomes of previous processes to be the starting point for prevailing social relations. The Marxist emphasis is probably on the fact that, logically, the real tacit relations of production emanating from power relations are the ultimate determinants of the shape that formal institutions take. In the Marxian approach, social relations are embedded in power relations and wealth distribution, which according to Acemoglu and Robinson constitute the given equilibrium variables at time zero.

Differences between Marx and North may be more important. When North's institutions ultimately rely on culture, North turns Marx upside down. If North's institutions are more related to daily experience and particular local conditions, then the gap gets smaller.

However, even within Marxism different approaches may be found. One widespread view is to see development as the unrestricted unfolding of productive forces, which use social relations as a vehicle for progress. Once the social relations that previously powered growth start hampering it, progressive social forces introduce revolutionary changes to power relations and new social relations of production appear, and this frees productive forces so that they can develop and clear the way for further progress (Lange 1980). While for North, performance is the result of institutions (institutions are the ultimate causes of growth; the accumulation of physical capital, labor, and human capital are the proximate causes of growth), according to this deterministic Marxist view we might conclude that the development of productive forces is the ultimate cause of growth.

Marx's own studies of capitalism can be read as meaning that capitalist social relations are the real forces that, through their economic reproduction, have the power to produce the unprecedented development of productive forces. This is what happened during the Industrial Revolution, a specific product of capitalism. It might be said that in Marx the relations of production determine the rate and direction of the development of productive forces. Other Marxist approaches, such as those of Robert Brenner (1990), emphasize the role played by social and political power relations to explain the different paths of capitalist development and economic performance in Europe. Acemoglu and Robinson can be placed close to this point of view.

Let us take a look at one example of the Marxist approach to Latin American growth and "institutions." Ciro Flamarión Santana Cardoso and Héctor Pérez Brignoli's *Historia Económica de América Latina* (1979, henceforth referred to as C&PB) is a book that has been almost completely ignored by New Institutional Economics, as it was neither translated into English nor presented in New Institutional language. The reason to choose this work as an example, among many others, is that it is a very good synthesis of varied earlier contributions from many.

In short, C&PB's argument is as follows. Latin American colonial societies are based on three components: the European economy, African pre-colonial societies, and obviously the pre-Columbian civilizations. These components combined in different ways in different parts of the region in response to local environmental and social conditions. Societies developed as a part or extension of the European economy, but they also developed structures and dynamics of their own. For example, the fact that there was no second agrarian revolution in Latin America can hardly be explained by the dominance of Spain or Portugal alone, as no colony of any other colonial power had such a revolution either (p. 150). The different regions are identified by four different criteria:

(a) the colonial power (weak explanatory power, as compared to North);
(b) the degree of linkage with world markets (export centers, subsidiary economies, and marginal regions often overlap in the same space);
(c) the kind of product, highly dependent on geography (mining centers, tropical products, the production of foodstuffs and consumer goods for domestic markets), with big impacts on techniques and social organization; and
(d) labor relations and the character of the colonization process.

In this last type, authors distinguish, first, Euro-Indian regions, which were the core areas of the pre-Columbian civilizations and where colonization meant a redistribution of productive factors and the imposition of forced labor on reorganized peasant communities in many different and heterogeneous forms. Second, there were Euro-African societies, i.e. more homogeneous slave societies in regions suitable for tropical crops. Third, there were Euro-American societies in temperate regions with low native population densities and increasing European immigration. The various combinations of all these factors gave rise to a wide variety of regional cases.

The land was owned by the crown and was bestowed on individuals to promote conquest and colonization. Occupied land could be bought from the crown, and the Indian communities had to have enough land to live on, reproduce, and pay taxes. In the wake of the demographic catastrophe and the decline in silver production, the hacienda system came into being. This was based on large tracts of land owned by the church or other landlords, mine owners, merchants, and bureaucrats. The *mestizos* were not allowed to own land.

A hacienda might be more or less market-oriented, but the hacienda system seems not to have been particularly prosperous. Most fortunes were made in mining and trade. Colonial Latin America was technologically backward. In spite of technology transfers from Europe, production was quite primitive, and the technological path was more oriented to the extensive use of land based on exploiting unskilled forced labor than to the intensive use of land as such. Colonizers adapted to the prevailing local conditions instead of making use of up-to-date European technology. Thus the Indian–European mix led to technological stagnation or even involution.

The more market-oriented plantations combined two agrarian sectors: production by slaves for their own consumption, and the production of goods for the market. Even though the division of labor was more advanced, the technological pattern was equally backward, as it was based on the extensive use of labor and land. Technical change was not impossible, but slave economies were not a particularly susceptible environment in this respect. Plantations were firmly inserted into trade flows and closely linked to European markets. Profits depended on the cost of labor (partly thanks to the existence of high levels of self-sufficiency) and international commodity prices. Plantations were also highly dependent on the supply of labor through the slave trade, and on the severe application of enforcement mechanisms. As regards land, the Spanish, Portuguese, and French colonies preserved the patrimonial character of land ownership, unlike the system in the British and Dutch colonies, where land markets came into being quite early.

In short, C&PB gather into a single view many of the nuances that would later appear in the varied range of new institutionalist approaches. However, while in neo-institutional approaches most of the story is already written, this is not the case with C&PB. As we will see, other writers, such as John Coatsworth, also share this view.

2.3.3 Latin America, the Industrial Revolution, and the national state

C&PB consider that the period 1750–1870 was when the relation between Latin America and the world economy was reformulated, a process that can also be viewed as a transition to peripheral capitalism, i.e. a kind of capitalism lacking the structural and technological dynamics that feature in the central economies. These authors concentrate their analysis on the late colonial period and on the second half of the 19th century, when a process with three components took place: the abolition of slavery, the liberal reforms (which involved the expropriation of church land, the control and privatization of public land, and the control of the labor and land of indigenous peasant communities), and expansion into new areas. The C&PB study is particularly weak when it deals with the role of independence. It seems as though one volume of the book is missing. The "great delay," as it was called by Halperin Donghi (1985), is a vacuum. According to most studies this was a period of disorder and of sluggish and discontinuous economic growth. This period was also neglected by the main body of neo-institutional writing because the most important part of the story had already been written.

According to C&PB, in the context of the independence of the British colonies, the Industrial Revolution, and the Napoleonic Wars, Latin America enjoyed relatively fast economic growth and institutional reorganization which, following Lynch (1991), has been called "the second conquest." The Bourbon and Pombalian reforms were aimed at extracting as much profit as possible from the colonial system, and in this process the previous inward-looking trend was reversed and the Latin American economy became more closely linked to the international economy. Thus, the colonial heritage is not mainly a matter of what happened during the early years of colonization. These international links, formal and informal, were not an original sin at time zero but an ongoing determinant of economic, social, and political developments. While in New Institutional writing the colonial powers and the colonizers play the role of initiators, and afterwards domestic institutions keep on reproducing themselves, in C&PB's approach the colonial powers remain an important and dynamic factor. It is worth noticing that C&PB's approach constituted a frontal attack on the extreme versions of dependency approaches, which saw external links as the main source of underdevelopment and the exploitation of the periphery as the main explanation of capitalism's development at the core. Domestic relations are seen to play a key role in the explanation of European development and also in that of Latin America. However, external relations do not disappear.

This is an important point. New Institutional Economics mainly developed in the US, and it seems to export to Latin American studies some features of the North American experience and to reproduce that pattern of analysis. Most of the successful development experience of the US is that of a large, independent nation (see introduction to Haber 1997). Most studies of US development assign the decisive and outstanding role to domestic forces. It seems that when studying Latin America, New Institutional Economics is prone to some kind of path dependence. The shift towards the study of domestic forces is not exclusive to neo-institutionalists. The so-called dependency school (Hettne 1990) started by focusing almost completely on external forces, but slowly moved to consideration of domestic barriers to growth. ECLAC's pioneering works from the 1950s mainly focused on the so-called centre–periphery system, and had some kind of naive view about the underlying potential of Latin American society and the capacities of the state; but in the 1960s domestic structural barriers to growth and development (agrarian structures, trade mechanisms, patterns of consumption, etc.)

came to the forefront of the analysis, although the center–periphery approach was not neglected (Rodríguez 2007). New Institutional approaches are another example of this movement. However, New Institutional Economics seems to have focused too much on domestic circumstances and to have forgotten the role played by the changing dynamics of international relations. The recent book by North, Wallis, and Weingast (2009) is almost completely about the creation of "open-access economies" but in a closed-economy framework.

John Coatsworth is an experienced Latin America specialist. His view (2008) differs from others and is full of insights. He shares with C&PB the idea that 1750–1870 was an important period of missed opportunities. He seems to take the side of the branch of New Institutional tradition that believes Latin American backwardness is closely linked to Iberian institutions. Coatsworth's view is similar to that of North et al. (2009), insofar as the Industrial Revolution is seen as the result of previous institutional changes in Holland and England.

> … the Portuguese and Spanish empires had failed to adapt to the revolution in property rights that produced a Commercial Revolution and sustained economic advance in Britain and the Netherlands at least a century earlier. The Iberian failure to modernize property rights and other institutions affected elites as well as commoners. As generations of Spanish and Portuguese policymakers understood, the survival of their empires depended crucially on the maintenance of a fragile equilibrium in which the authority of weak and distant monarchs depended as much on keeping settler elites insecure in their rights and properties as it did on keeping the lid on discontent from below. By clinging to absolutist principles and colonial hierarchies of race and caste, the Iberian World had already lost the opportunity to make an Industrial Revolution on its own. (Coatsworth 2008: 558)

According to Coatsworth, Latin American elites were not as powerful as North American ones because the peasant communities were able to keep control of their land, which contrasts with the drastic land expropriations implemented in North America and in Australia and New Zealand, for example. This weakness in Latin America made local elites dependent on the protection of the colonial power, and this in turn meant that colonial power in Latin America was longer-lived than in North America. The elite were taxed by the colonial power in many different ways, which differs from what happened in North America. The colonial powers were partly responsible for the weakness of the local elites, as the Iberian colonial powers were careful not to give local elites sufficient autonomy or property rights over land or even over labor.

Coatsworth goes even further with a highly controversial statement: economic growth did not require institutions that encouraged the poor to invent and invest, but rather institutions that made it possible for people of means to do so. Latin America was not unequal enough to promote accumulation by the local elites.

This point is interesting for two different reasons. First, it tacitly confronts the idea that the institutions that are good for growth are always the same. I firmly share this view. Capitalist development is not always a story about increasing equality. Industrialization led to an increase in inequality, the so-called first phase of the Kuznets curve. However, there is a second aspect with which I disagree: the fact that peasants kept part of the land does not necessarily mean that elites lacked a degree of control. Quite the contrary: the presence of large numbers of peasants is what makes it possible to extract labor from them and to maintain an unequal social structure. Peasants were assured a piece of land because they worked it for their own subsistence, and the existence of this peasant community made it possible to generate a workforce that paid taxes to the haciendas, the church, and the crown. We are not talking about free peasants who were able to accumulate, get richer, buy new land, and so on, but about people who lived close to subsistence levels and produced surplus labor for the elite, both domestic and colonial, and were dominated by an oppressive class, race, and caste system. We are still not in a position to say how severe inequality was by modern standards. However, a great deal of work would have to be done before the idea of a not-too-unequal colonial society could be acceptable. What really matters is not merely inequality measures such as the Gini-coefficient, but the kind of inequality that prevailed and the underlying social relations and their dynamic implications. And in this discussion of inequality, international relations have to be included since it was not only the domestic elite that were involved.

Coatsworth also emphasizes that the efforts of the Iberian empires were mainly devoted to defending their territories, repressing internal rebellions, and extracting tax revenues to do both; they did not have enough energy to invest in public services, physical infrastructure or human capital. The weak national states in Latin America that had to cope with these tasks were faced with a much harder situation because the Industrial Revolution had already changed the international arena, and what was expected from peripheral regions was that they would produce raw materials. In every field of industrial production there was now tougher competition from the industrialized world and easier access to world markets thanks to the transport revolution.

> To resist such pressures, Latin America would have needed strong and effective governments committed to promoting modern industry, that is, not less inequality and exploitation, but perhaps much more of both, including subsidies to business and efforts to keep wages down. Until late in the nineteenth century or later, any country or colony that had not already made its own industrial revolution faced insuperable difficulties trying to import one from elsewhere. (Coatsworth 2008: 560)

Instead of strong national states, Latin American societies had highly volatile formal institutions. What really matters are the underlying informal institutions and not the successive formal constitutions that were introduced from time to time and later on changed. A self-reinforcing institutional process repeatedly restored political power to the conservative elite, as governments were not expected to last for long and as informal institutions interacted with the formal ones—and in fact changed the original aims of the latter (Dye 2006).

A similar point was made by C&PB (pp. 92–3) with reference to liberal reforms. Constitutions were designed to extend rights to the broad mass of the population, but ultimately they were limited and constrained by underlying forces, and in the end they gave political rights only to the white elites. On a more abstract level, this is a good example of the particular way in which existing, real, and informal social relations have an impact on the form taken by formal institutions.

According to Coatsworth, "The pace of nineteenth century institutional modernization, with its socio-economic correlates, performs better as a predictor of long term economic performance than colonial extraction and exploitation, as is proposed by Acemoglu, et al." (2008: 565). Coatsworth further states that the pace was quickest in the temperate zone colonies populated mainly by European settlers and their descendants (i.e. the expansion of the frontier), and that the areas that were slowest to modernize their institutions included Brazil and the centers of pre-Columbian civilizations: "The duration and depth of the post-independence civil conflicts depended on the nature of colonial social conditions: conflicts tended to deepen and last longer in places where the power and status of settler elites was most challenged from below. International competition often exacerbated the persistent internal conflicts."

Two comments are in order here, following what was said above. First, what Coatsworth is saying about the 19th century is not very different from the C&PB argument about the way in which economic reforms advanced in different areas in Latin America. Secondly, however, it is striking that Coatsworth makes an attempt to disconnect 19th-century processes from colonial institutions, given the fact that his own reasoning makes it clear that the socio-institutional context he mentions is described precisely according to the features these institutions adopted during the colonial period. Once again, what we see is an artificial attempt to isolate forces and causes in limited time and conceptual frameworks, while what we have in front of us is a process in which new domestic and external forces transform and maintain features of the past. It is impossible to disconnect the pace at which reforms advanced in the 19th century from the ways in which the different socioeconomic structures and institutions evolved during the colonial period.

2.3.4 Institutions and the first globalization boom

Some general features of economic performance in different Latin American regions have been described elsewhere (Furtado 1974; Cardoso and Faletto 1979; Sunkel and Paz 1982; Bulmer-Thomas 1994; Bértola and Williamson 2006). Latin American growth performance improved, but growth was unequally distributed. The regions that expanded their frontiers in temperate zones with high shares of immigrant labor had higher growth rates and higher levels of foreign investment, literacy, exports per capita, etc. Plantation economies, especially those on the Atlantic coast, were further behind in all these respects, and the core colonial regions come at the bottom of the performance list, but not too far behind the tropical regions.

This ranking clearly reflects what was mentioned above concerning the pace at which institutional modernization took place in the different regions. However, as we have noted, the causal chains are not simple. Institutional modernization had to do with previous economic and institutional developments in a process with deep historical roots, closely linked to colonial structures that were based on extracting a surplus from the native population, where this population was large enough, and from slave plantations in areas where native labor was not available and where free immigration was not attracted.

There is general agreement about the broad institutional features of the period of export-led growth. This period ended the *larga espera* (long wait), and authoritarian, exclusive, elitist regimes succeeded in imposing order and stimulating progress. In spite of the high institutional volatility described by Dye, this period was different from the 50 years following independence in that the central power of the states was really strengthened and the property rights of the elite were more efficiently preserved.

The provocative arguments put forward by Coatsworth (2008) are again a good starting point for our discussion:

> The nineteenth century ended...by committing the sins that much of the new political economy erroneously attributed to the colonial era: relatively high economic inequality, dominance of government by narrow economic elites, exclusion of competing interests and groups from political influence, and "bad" institutions that fail to protect the property and human rights of majorities. Unfortunately for our theorists, and for the region, the nature and timing of Latin America's sinning clearly indicates that it was good for economic growth, not bad. The conditions that Engerman-Sokoloff and Acemoglu, Johnson, and Robinson saw as blocking economic growth were in fact the conditions that made it possible.

Let us consider some of these interesting assertions one by one.

These "bad" institutions were good for growth. Latin America grew somewhat faster than world averages, and improved its position relative to Asia and Africa. However, as mentioned previously, the gap between the per capita income of the West and that of Latin America increased by 81% in 1870–1913 and from 131% to 148% of LA's per capita GDP in the same period. This gap may be used as a proxy for the technological gap, and reflects the ability to compete in world markets with skill-intensive products. It follows that in the wake of the first globalization boom Latin America's prospects of catching up were worse. As Coatsworth correctly stresses, the Industrial Revolution led to a new institutional order based on exchanging raw materials for manufactured goods. As the Latin American structuralist tradition repeatedly stressed, export-led growth itself was never a guarantee that the golden road to growth and development would be found.

What was supposed to happen in terms of inequality in the 18th century really happened in the late 19th century. At the present time there is an interesting debate about this subject. Most people agree that Latin America had relatively fast growth in the second half of the 18th century. This process was not particularly egalitarian: the majority of the population was not given property or political rights. It is undeniable that the late 19th century had its own characteristics. A transport revolution made new regions economically competitive and prosperous, labor systems were transformed, investment in infrastructure produced many changes in relative productivity, and there was a redistribution of land in favor of the elites and at the expense of peasant communities, the church, and the state. However, there is a big gap between these phenomena and the assertion that colonial society was not unequal and that inequality was a late 19th-century process. Both Williamson (2009) and Coatsworth (2008) think that inequality in Latin America was not particularly high when compared to Europe at the same time. Williamson bases his arguments on the Milanovic, Lindert, and Williamson (2007) idea that inequality cannot be so great if per capita GDP is low, because there will not be a sufficiently large surplus for the elite to appropriate. However, there seems to be agreement that inequality was high in Latin America at the end of the colonial period (not only and not principally in terms of income), and some new estimates show that inequality was already high on the eve of the first globalization boom. The evolution of inequality during the first globalization is also a matter of debate (Bértola et al. 2010).

Inequality was good for growth. All classical authors assumed that capital accumulation meant the concentration of income and wealth in the hands of "Schumpeterian" capitalists (not rent-earners *à la* Ricardo). The Lewis model also meant there was a first phase of increasing inequality linked to growth, and this paralleled the idea of the Kuznets curve. This is a good point against the universal neo-institutionalist growth model. And this is also compatible with world history, as it presents industrialization as going hand in hand with increasing domestic *and* international inequality, adopting the form of uneven development and even imperialism, plunder, invasions, expropriation. and so forth. While the first globalization boom increased growth rates in Latin America, the kind of growth that took place conditioned future patterns. Modern economic growth is characterized by the systematic use of knowledge to transform nature and society. The first globalization boom was made possible not by a sudden reduction in transport costs, but by a steady, continuous, cumulative increase in technical capabilities, which strongly affected international competitiveness. Latin American growth was based on the exploitation of natural resources. Technical change was often quite limited. Contrary to what pro-global theorists have believed, the first globalization boom was not strong enough to break with the informal and formal institutions that had evolved so slowly and were so deeply rooted in the Latin American social network. Quite the contrary, in fact: as the structuralist tradition and C&PB have correctly stressed, the first globalization boom often ended up interacting with or even strengthening the power of landed, commercial, and political elites. And in the process, the kind of development and the kind of inequality produced was a long way from the inequality trends that tended to empower a technologically dynamic industrial sector. The colonial heritage, based on the exploitation of natural resources using large numbers of dependent and slave labor, was almost ubiquitous; economic development during the first globalization boom was path-dependent to a high extent. The elitist societies and the patterns of development imposed by colonial rule constrained the transformation of these societies, leading to what C&BP correctly characterize as peripheral capitalism, where land was highly concentrated and labor relations did not evolve into free labor relations but towards a continuum of very varied forms of dependent labor, in a context characterized by sluggish technological change.

These kinds of societies are able to grow, but in most cases not to converge. And if convergence happened to be possible, as in the countries of the Rio de la Plata, it seems that it did not happen on a sustained basis but only as long as some positive impacts of globalization lasted.

The Latin American settler economies, such as those of Argentina and Uruguay, were the most successful. There, many positive situations combined: the production of goods competing with European producers on the basis of free labor and with a good location close to the coast, and the relative weakness of colonial institutions due partly to low population density. However, even in these cases the pattern of land appropriation differed significantly from other apparently similar settler societies such as Australia and New Zealand. The way in which land was appropriated is due to the combination of new forces and patterns of behavior and institutional features that clearly show the colonial heritage, more in informal relations than in formal ones. The result made for big differences in the innovative capacities of the two groups of economies, and in the way the factorial distribution of income took place between landowners, capitalists, and workers, favoring land rents in the Rio de la Plata (Alvarez, Bértola, and Porcile 2007). Besides, it is difficult to neglect the role played by close links to a dynamic central economy, as was the case with the former British colonies.

2.4 CONCLUDING REMARKS

Relative backwardness has been a constant feature of the history of Latin America. In spite of the important technological transfers consequent upon the conquest and of not-negligible growth during the colonial times, in the wake of independence the gap between Latin America and the industrializing world was already wide. The gap widened during the first decades after independence, due to the diffusion of the Industrial Revolution from Britain to the European continent, increasing growth rates in the West, and institutional volatility in the new Latin American Republics. While Latin America resumed growth after the 1870s, the gap was not reduced. In the last decades of the 20th century, the Latin American economies diverged even more from those of the West. Throughout this process there were far-reaching domestic and international changes. New actors appeared, technological revolutions took place, and social relations as well as formal institutions were transformed.

I have argued in favor of the Neo-institutionalist approach to Latin American economic history in the sense that the colonial institutional setting had a long-lasting impact on Latin American development. I stressed, however, that most of the varying and even contradictory assertions made by different Neo-institutionalist writers had already been advanced, in Marxist language, in works such as that of C. F. S. Cardoso and H. Pérez Brignoli.

We have criticized Neo-institutionalist writings for being excessively focused on original colonial institutions and their lasting effects, and for neglecting to some extent how these institutions changed in relation to a profound transformation in international relations and technological environments. The Industrial Revolution symbolizes these far-reaching transformations, which radically affected the way in which the Latin American countries were integrated into the world economy. The Bourbon and Pombalian reforms, Independence, the Liberal Reforms, the abolition of slavery, and the expansion to new areas were followed by radical changes in social relations, political institutions, and international relations. The pace at which these changes came about depended on several particular circumstances and to a large extent on the previous development path in colonial times in what came to be different independent Latin America states, and this had a huge impact on the increased disparity in economic performance among these new republics.

We have also argued that many reactions against New Institutional approaches seem to be exaggerated. The idea that some contemporary features of Latin America such as high income inequality are products of the late 19th century, and not of colonial times, makes a similar mistake to the idea attributed to neo-institutionalist writings: instead of omitting important historical changes that were continuous in the historical process, an artificial break in this process is introduced, negating the almost obvious institutional inertia that was present in many aspects of Latin American economic life. In this respect I have argued that Latin American inequality was at a high level by the end of the colonial period, and that this kind of inequality can hardly be estimated merely in terms of a Gini-coefficient. What really matters is the kind of social and power relations underlying economic life and the distributional and technological dynamics they involved. I have further argued that the kind of inequality produced during the First Globalization boom could hardly be considered good for growth. While the idea that growth prospects were not always linked to diminishing inequality constitutes a good and frontal criticism of some Neo-institutional writings, the kind of inequality produced in Latin America was not necessarily good for growth. By then the world economy had gone through not one but two industrial revolutions. International trade was increasingly moving towards skill-intensive products, inequality gave rise to serious shortcomings in terms of human capital accumulation, and the pattern of specialization reinforced a path of slow rates of technical change and social relations not particularly conducive to technical change.

Globalization studies—which almost completely focus on resource allocation, factor movements and price convergence—usually underestimate the institutional context in which globalization forces expand, and underestimate the negative impact of globalization on the domestic economy in terms of institutional development, patterns of specialization, and technical change.

State-led growth led to many mistakes, but most current analyses of this period ignore the problems the Latin American economies were facing at the end of the first globalization boom, and the deep historical roots of these problems. The search for structural change, associated with radical institutional and social changes and the enhanced capacity of the national state, first appeared as a spontaneous reaction to negative external demand shocks. When this was developed as a more explicit theory, its reach was clearly conditioned by several economic, social, political, and institutional constraints, which widened the gap between theory and practice. Thus, excessive protectionism, biased structural change towards light industry, a lack of policies aimed at deepening technological spillovers from foreign investment, and autarkic nationalism were all features that hampered technological and structural change. However, a good assessment of the achievements and limits of state-led growth can only be accurately made in the light of the historical roots of Latin American divergence.

REFERENCES

ACEMOGLU, D., JOHNSON, S., and ROBINSON, J. (2005). 'Institutions as a Fundamental Cause of Long-Run Growth', in P. Aghion and S. Durlauf (eds), *Handbook of Economic Growth*, Amsterdam: Elsevier.

—— and ROBINSON, J. (2006). *Economic Origins of Dictatorship and Democracy*, New York: Cambridge University Press.

ÁLVAREZ, J., BÉRTOLA, L., and PORCILE, G. (eds) (2007). *Primos ricos y empobrecidos: crecimiento, distribución del ingreso e instituciones en Australia-Nueva Zelanda vs. Argentina-Uruguay*, Montevideo: Fin de Siglo.

BATES, R. H., COATSWORTH, J. H., and WILLIAMSON, J. G. (2007). 'Lost Decades: Postindependence Performance in Latin America and Africa', *Journal of Economic History* 67.4.

BÉRTOLA, L., and PORCILE, G. (2006). 'Convergence, Trade and Industrial Policy: Argentina, Brazil and Uruguay in the International Economy, 1900–1980', *Revista de historia económica/Journal of Iberian and Latin American Economic History* 1.

—— and WILLIAMSON, J. (2006). 'Globalization in Latin America before 1940', in V. Bulmer-Thomas, J. Coatsworth, and R. Cortés Conde (eds), *The Cambridge Economic History of Latin America*, vol. 2, New York: Cambridge University Press.

BÉRTOLA, L., CASTELNOVO, C., RODRÍGUEZ WEBER, J., and WILLEBALD, H. (2010). 'Between the Colonial Heritage and the First Globalization Boom: On Income Inequality in the Southern Cone', *Revista de historia económica/Journal of Iberian and Latin American Economic History* 28.2.

BRENNER, R. (1990). 'Agrarian Class Structure and Economic Development in Pre-Industrial Europe', in T. H. Aston and C. H. E. Philpin (eds), *The Brenner Debate: Agrarian Class Structure and Economic Development in Pre-Industrial Europe*, Cambridge: Cambridge University Press.

BULMER-THOMAS, V. (1994). *The Economic History of Latin America Since Independence*, Cambridge: Cambridge University Press.

CARDOSO, F. H., and FALETTO, E. (1979). *Dependency and Development in Latin America*, Berkeley: University of California Press.

CARDOSO, C. F. S., and PÉREZ BRIGNOLI, H. (1979). *Historia económica de América Latina*, Barcelona: Critica.

COATSWORTH, J. (2008). 'Inequality, Institutions and Economic Growth in Latin America', *Journal of Latin American Studies* 40.3.

DE FERRANTI, D., PERRY, G., FERREIRA, F., and WALTON, M. (2004). *Inequality in Latin America and the Caribbean: Breaking with History?* Washington, DC: World Bank.

DONGHI, T. H. (1985). 'Economy and Society in Post-Independence Spanish America', in L. Bethell (ed.), *The Cambridge History of Latin America*, vol. 3: *From Independence to c. 1870*, Cambridge: Cambridge University Press.

DYE, A. (2006). 'The Institutional Framework', in V. Bulmer-Thomas, J. Coatsworth, and R. Cortés Conde (eds), *The Cambridge Economic History of Latin America*, vol. 2, New York: Cambridge University Press.

ENGERMAN, S., and SOKOLOFF, K. (1997). 'Factor Endowments, Institutions and Differential Paths of Growth Among New World Economies: A View from Economic Historians of the United States', in S. Haber (ed.), *How Latin America Fell Behind*, Stanford, Calif.: Stanford University Press.

FURTADO, C. (1974). *La économía Latinoamericana desde la Conquista Ibérica hasta la Revolución Cubana*, México: Siglo XXI.

GELMAN, J. (forthcoming). 'Dimensión económica de la Independencia', in *Las Indepedencias latinoamericanas y el persistente sueño de la Gran Patria Nuestra*, Servicio de Relaciones Exteriores de México.

HABER, S. (ed.) (1997). *How Latin America Fell Behind. Essays on the Economic History of Brazil and México, 1800–1914*, Stanford, Calif.: Stanford University Press.

HETTNE, B. (1990). Development Theory and the Three Worlds, Harlow: Longman.

LANDES, D. (1999). *The Wealth and Poverty of Nations: Why Some Are So Rich and Some So Poor*, New York: Norton.

LANGE, O. (1980). *Economía política*. (Originally published in Poland as *Ekonomia Polityczna*, Pantswowe Wydawnictwo Naukowe, 1969.)

LANGE, M., MAHONEY, J., and VOM HAU, M. (2006). 'Colonialism and Development: A Comparative Analysis of Spanish and British Colonies', *American Journal of Sociology* 11.5.

LYNCH, J. (1991). 'Las repúblicas del Río de la Plata', in L. Bethell (ed.), *Historia de América Latina*, vol. 6 (*América latina independiente, 1820–1870*), Barcelona: Critica.

MADDISON, A. (2007).*Contours of the World Economy, 1–2030 AD: Essays in Macro-economic History*, Oxford: Oxford University Press.

MILANOVIC, B., LINDERT, P., and WILLIAMSON, J. (2007). 'Measuring Ancient Inequality', World Bank Policy Research Working Paper No. 4412, Washington, DC.

NORTH, D. (1990). *Institutions, Institutional Change and Economic Performance*, Cambridge: Cambridge University Press.

—— (1994). 'Economic Performance Through Time', *American Economic Review*, 84.3.

—— WALLIS, J. J., and SUMMERHILL, W. (2000). 'Order, Disorder and Economic Change: Latin America versus North America', in B. B. de Mesquita and H. L. Root (eds), *Governing for Prosperity*, New Haven, Conn.: Yale University Press.

—— —— and WEINGAST, B. R. (2009). *Violence and Social Orders: A Conceptual Framework for Understanding Recorded Human History*, Cambridge: Cambridge University Press.

OCAMPO, J. A., and PARRA, M. (2007) 'The Dual Divergence: Growth Successes and Collapses in the Developing World Since 1980', in R. Ffrench-Davis and José Luis Machinea (eds), *Economic Growth with Equity: Challenges for Latin America*, Basingstoke: Palgrave Macmillan and ECLAC.

PRADOS DE LA ESCOSURA, L. (2009). 'Lost Decades? Economic Performance in Post-Independence Latin America', *Journal of Latin American Studies* 41.2.

ROBINSON, J. (2006). 'El equilibrio de América Latina', in F. Fukuyama (ed.), *La brecha entre América Latina y Estados Unidos*, Argentina: Fondo de Cultura Económica.

RODRÍGUEZ, O. (2007). *El estructuralismo latinoamericano*, Mexico: Siglo XXI.

SOKOLOFF, K., and ZOLT, E. (2007). 'Inequality and the Evolution of Institutions of Taxation: Evidence from the Economic History of the Americas', in S. Edwards, G. Esquivel, and G. Márquez (eds), *The Decline of the Latin American Economies: Growth, Institutions and Crisis*, Chicago: University of Chicago Press.

STEIN, S., and STEIN, B. (1970). *The Colonial Heritage of Latin America: Essays on Economic Dependence in Perspective*, New York: Oxford University Press.

SUNKEL, O., and PAZ, P. (1982). *El Subdesarrollo Latinoamericano y la Teoría del Desarrollo*, México: Siglo XXI.

WILLIAMSON, J. (2009). 'Five Centuries of Latin American Inequality', NBER Working Paper No. 15305, Cambridge, Mass.

World Bank (2003). *Inequality in Latin America and the Caribbean: Breaking with History?* Washington, DC.

CHAPTER 3

....

POLITICAL INSTITUTIONS, POLICYMAKING, AND ECONOMIC POLICY IN LATIN AMERICA

....

MARTÍN ARDANAZ, CARLOS SCARTASCINI,
AND MARIANO TOMMASI

3.1 INTRODUCTION[1]

....

Economists have been traditionally interested in understanding which policies work best for increasing welfare and providing adequate policy recommendations. In their quest, they have generally studied policymaking using models in which economic policies are chosen by a benevolent social planner. The point of departure of this chapter is that policies are not chosen by benevolent planners (or similar constructs), but are instead the outcome of strategic interactions among a number of key participants (voters, economic interest groups, politicians, technocrats), each with its own motivations and incentives. Moreover, it is also necessary to consider that policy decisions have an intertemporal component (i.e. policies usually have an impact beyond the period in which they are discussed, and political actors usually interact over time). Thus to understand policies—and the features of those policies relevant for their impact on behavior and welfare—it is necessary to study strategic political interactions over time. By doing so it is possible to understand better what aspects of the functioning of the institutions of democracy are relevant for explaining the features of policies, and hence for explaining patterns of development.

[1] We received valuable comments and suggestions from José Antonio Ocampo and Jaime Ros. We are grateful to Melisa Iorianni for her assistance during the production of this chapter.

This chapter presents a brief and selective overview of some themes in the *political economy* of policymaking Latin America. The first section selectively reviews some of the key contributions to the study of political economy of Latin America during its major phases of economic and institutional development. It briefly covers stop-go cycles, bureaucratic authoritarianism, dependency theory, the political economy of import-substituting industrialization, and the political economy of market-oriented reforms. It roughly follows a timeline of actual events and of academic understanding and methodological vintages in attempting to explain those events. It focuses on major economic policies (such as macro, trade regime, state or private ownership) and macro political outcomes (such as the switches between dictatorship and democracy).[2]

The rest of the chapter focuses more narrowly on a strand of recent research that concentrates on actual decision and implementation processes, and on the political institutions and state and social actors involved in those processes. The motivation for such an emphasis is twofold, relating to a timeline of events and academic vintages. On the one hand, in relation to the usual concerns of development economists, it is important to emphasize the importance of home-grown development strategies adapted (among other things) to each country's institutional capabilities. On the other, after two decades of democratic practice, it is plausible to rely on deeper knowledge about the inner workings of democratic institutions to understand the actual functioning of the policymaking process in each country. This way, this chapter complements and "piggybacks" on a wealth of new research in political science.

3.2 BIG THEMES IN THE POLITICAL ECONOMY OF LATIN AMERICA

During much of the 20th century two facts shaped the research agenda of political economy scholars in Latin America. The political fact was that democracies were unstable regime types, with military rule as the often substitute. The economic fact was the prevalence among policymakers of a growth strategy, known as Import Substitution Industrialization (ISI), characterized by a variety of macro and micro policies consisting of high levels of trade restrictions coupled with active state involvement in the productive process (Hirschman 1968).

These facts gave rise to research questions or puzzles among political economy scholars such as (1) why are democracies in Latin America unstable? and (2) what

[2] An earlier version of this chapter (Ardanaz, Scartascini, and Tommasi 2009) provides a slightly longer review of that earlier literature on the political economy of Latin America. In choosing to follow a virtual timeline of events and research, we have left out some important recent work in political economy, such as the economic theories of dictatorship and democracy of Acemoglu and Robinson, and Engerman and Sokoloff's work on path dependence, inequality and development across the Americas (see e.g. Engerman and Sokoloff 2002; Acemoglu and Robinson 2006).

types of coalitions and economic interests support different regime types and economic policies? The theoretical frameworks of the time (modernization theory, structuralism, or the dependency school) provided clues for solving those puzzles. While each of these frameworks differ along important dimensions, the three have in common a focus on deep *structural socioeconomic* factors (such as level of development, class or sectoral structure, the international division of labor) that are outside the immediate control of individuals but that affect group behavior and thus political and economic outcomes.

For example, in trying to explain the instability of democracy among Southern Cone countries, Guillermo O'Donnell looked at the impact of economic cycles ("stop–go") and distributive conflicts between interest groups (urban vs. rural sectors, "popular" sectors vs. the "elite") on the political system. Basically, in each cycle, different coalitions are formed and the interests of those coalitions determine policies. During the "go" phase, the internal market alliance—made up of the working class and organized middle-class workers along with the "local" national urban bourgeoisie, encompassing the smaller, less efficient domestic firms—pursued their preferred economic policies. Thus, export restrictions and trade taxes made possible the transfer of resources from the rural to the "popular" ISI sector through real wage increases and industrial subsidies. However, balance of payments crises marked the end of the expansive phase of the cycle and thus created the opportunity for a different type of coalition to shift the course of economic policy: a coalition made up of rural interests, and internationally oriented businesses, that benefited from exchange rate devaluations. In terms of political regime dynamics, this coalition provided the social base of support for the inauguration of military governments which O'Donnell (1973) dubbed "bureaucratic authoritarian."

At the same time as political scientists were trying to explain political regime instability in Latin America, economists and other social scientists were debating the roots of Latin America's economic underdevelopment. Many intellectual strands came together (economists working at ECLAC, sociologists, economic historians, etc.) in the 1960s with the elaboration of a more general and comprehensive theoretical framework that came to be known as the "dependency school." While there is some heterogeneity in the depth and logic of the arguments stressed by different scholars within this perspective, a common assumption made by *dependentistas* is that the underdevelopment of Latin America can only be understood in connection with the region's historical insertion into the international division of labor. Contrary to comparative advantage assumptions common in neoclassical economics, dependentistas claimed that the distribution of the gains from trade between developed (the "center") and developing (the "periphery") nations consistently disadvantaged developing economies, such as those in Latin America (Cardoso and Falleto 1969). In particular, the region's insertion into the international economy as producer and exporter of raw materials and foodstuffs for the industrial center and importer of manufactured goods made it vulnerable to declines in foreign trade and terms of trade deterioration, and undermined local capital accumulation, thus contributing to its underdevelopment.

The severity of the external constraint on the economies of the region reached a peak during the 1930s, provoking a switch in development strategy that led to the inauguration of ISI. During this period, governments such as those in Argentina, Brazil, Chile, and Peru engaged in fiscal and monetary expansion and exchange rate appreciation intended to shift income to "popular" groups in the service and ISI sectors. All of them discounted the risks of inflation posed by expansive fiscal and monetary policies, and relied instead on extensive price controls and foreign exchange rationing to subsidize ISI industries. Most important, as foreign exchange reserves were depleted and fiscal pressures mounted, the policies in each of these cases ended in inflationary disasters and economic collapse.

In order to understand this "macroeconomic populism" (Dornbusch and Edwards 1991) or "*facilismo macroeconómico*" (Ocampo 2004), the crucial point from a political economy perspective is to understand the political support base and incentives of populist leaders, whose origin can be traced in part to class and sectoral divisions in the economy. For example, Sachs (1989) argues that high income inequality in Latin America contributes to intense political pressures for populist macroeconomic policies that raise the incomes of lower-income groups. However, because there is little or no intraregional correlation between populist policy cycles and income distribution, a focus on sectoral divisions that emerged within the context of ISI and the primary export sector seemed to provide a better explanation for the persistence of populist cycles across Latin America (Kaufman and Stallings 1991).[3]

While Latin America grew at an annual average rate of almost 6% between 1950 and 1980, certain features of ISI steadily undermined the long-term sustainability of this growth strategy. By the 1980s, most Latin American economies were in disarray, weighed down by accumulated external debt, delayed adjustment to negative external shocks, and a desperate need for reserves. As a result of the debt crisis, economic policy views in the region began to converge on a different set of fundamentals based on market forces, international competition, and a more limited role for the government in economic affairs. These views were connected to a climate of ideas which had a focal point in the so-called "Washington Consensus," a list of policy prescriptions considered capable of restoring growth in Latin America. The combination of economic reform with democratization shaped the research agenda of subsequent political economy scholarship.[4]

For example, during the 1980s and 1990s, economists and other social scientists working on the political economy of Latin America were involved in creating a literature

---

[3] Similarly, Frieden (1991) presents an analytical framework based on class (capital vs. labor) and sectoral cleavages within the business community (asset-specific vs. liquid asset holders) to explain variation in economic policy reactions to fluctuations in the supply of foreign credit in five major LAC countries (Argentina, Brazil, Chile, Mexico, and Venezuela).

[4] See Geddes (2002) for a more general overview on the impact of such changes to the study of politics in developing countries.

known as the "political economy of reform," an attempt to understand the strategies and conditions leading to different reform sequences and outcomes in the various countries.[5] A large portion of the reform literature, at least on the side of economics, worked on the premise that the reforms that countries needed to undertake were technically obvious; reform was therefore a matter of figuring out the way to implement those reforms in the context of a collective action problem due to the fact that losers from reform are concentrated, whereas beneficiaries are diffused. Following this logic, several Latin American scholars focused on the role of key socioeconomic interest groups (e.g. business, labor unions) and "distributional" coalitions in shaping the reform process and its outcomes.[6]

However, the transformations in the political economy of Latin America during the 1980s and 1990s were not only economic. In the political realm, as transitions to democracy encompassed nearly the whole region, political science scholars began to debate the promise and peril of alternative institutional designs for consolidating democratic regimes. In particular, one of the main issues on the agenda was whether Latin America should switch to parliamentary forms of government or stick with presidential constitutions. The facts informing the debate were by then clear: presidential democracies were unstable in comparison to parliamentary ones. Latin America, a region historically characterized by the preponderance of presidential constitutions, offered the highest level of regime instability, understood as shifts between democracy and dictatorship (Cheibub 2007). The question then was whether presidentialism was to blame for that record.

Starting with the seminal contribution of Juan Linz (1990), a lively debate in both academic and political circles emerged around the relative merits and perils of presidentialism in Latin America. Linz argued that presidentialism is inherently prone to regime breakdown, given that this form of government does not provide incentives for cooperation between president and legislatures. While some authors offered responses to Linz in defense of presidentialism,[7] the Linzian view remained popular among academics: they recommended the adoption of parliamentary systems in particular countries of the region, and soon some of these proposals even reached the policy agenda.[8] Both the literature on the market reform period by economists and the analysis of alternative institutional arrangements by political scientists provides a nice background for the line of research to be presented in the next section.

---

[5] See Rodrik (1996) and Tommasi and Velasco (1996).

[6] See Schneider (2004a) for a review of this literature.

[7] Shugart and Carey (1992) and Mainwaring and Shugart (1997).

[8] In Argentina, a presidentially appointed commission in the 1980s studied the issue of regime type and recommended a move toward parliamentarism, but the proposal did not make headway among politicians. Similar proposals were debated, but not adopted, in Chile. In Brazil, politicians put the question before voters in a 1993 referendum that offered not only parliamentarism, but also the option for returning to a monarchy, as alternatives to presidentialism (Carey 2005).

3.3 POLITICAL INSTITUTIONS, POLICYMAKING, POLICIES, AND OUTCOMES IN LATIN AMERICAN DEMOCRACIES

Economists have tended to focus on uncovering which are the best policies that countries should adopt in order to develop. The last "universal recipe" recommended and adopted throughout Latin America were the market-oriented reforms of the 1990s. The varied and less-than-stellar outcomes of that effort have redirected intellectual attention. This chapter reports on one particular line of inquiry which emphasizes that economic and social outcomes are the results not so much of the specific contents of policies and titles of institutions (whether utility companies are public or private) as of several characteristics of these policies. As will be shown later, countries able to generate policies with such attributes will reap the benefits of specific economic reforms more than others. If the policies adopted do not have such attributes—no matter how good they look on paper—they are unlikely to achieve good development outcomes.

Rodrik (1995), for instance, analyzed six countries that implemented a set of policies that shared the same generic title—"export subsidization"—but had widely different degrees of success. He relates their success to such features as the consistency with which the policy was implemented, which office was in charge, how the policy was bundled (or not) with other policy objectives, and how predictable the future of the policy was. Rodrik's insights resonate well in the context of Latin America, a region that during the last couple of decades embarked on a process of market-oriented reforms which, despite a similar orientation and content of policy packages, have had very diverse results in practice (Forteza and Tommasi 2006).

This example illustrates that public policies are more than their titles. More important for performance and outcomes are fundamental state capabilities, such as the ability to commit to not expropriating, or the ability to enforce compliance. However, such capabilities do not fall from the sky, nor are they provided by benevolent social planners. They are instead derived from the process by which policies are discussed, decided, implemented, evaluated, and modified. In a nutshell, policies are endogenous to the *policymaking process* (PMP), which by definition is a political process that involves a multiplicity of actors (such as professional politicians, economic interest groups, and common citizens) who interact in a variety of formal and informal arenas (such as Congress or the street), which can in turn be more or less transparent.

As noted above, development outcomes depend on the features of public policies more than on their titles. But what are these features specifically? This study focuses on several dimensions that seem to capture the necessary conditions for policies to have a positive impact on welfare. Those conditions include the *stability* or credibility of policy, *adaptability* of policies to changing economic conditions, *coordination and coherence* of policies across areas and levels of government, *quality of implementation and enforcement, public-regardedness* (see below), and *efficiency.*[9] What explains variation in such policy features? It has been argued in previous work that the extent to which some desirable policy characteristics are attained depends on the behavior of political and socioeconomic actors in the policymaking process in general, and in particular on their capacity to *cooperate*, i.e. to reach and enforce intertemporal agreements.[10] The PMP is viewed as a series of bargains and exchanges among political actors whose behavior depends on their interests, incentives, and constraints, and on their expectations about the behavior of other actors. These interactive patterns of behavior constitute equilibria of the policymaking game, which are conditioned by the rules of the policymaking process and by some characteristics of the players. In democratic polities, these rules of the game relate to the workings of *political institutions* such as the legislature, executive–legislative relations, the political party system, the judiciary, and the civil service. Thus, political institutions play a key explanatory role in understanding the determinants of political cooperation and, therefore, its effects on policy features and socioeconomic outcomes.

Political institutions have occupied center stage in explaining both economic policy[11] and development outcomes[12] across the political economy research field. In the context of Latin America, the study of democratic political institutions lagged behind much of the developed world for an obvious reason: for much of the 20th century, democracies in the region were the exception rather than the rule. For example, as late as the 1970s only around a third of Latin American countries could be considered democracies, following standard definitions in political science.[13]

The late 1970s and 1980s were the time of democratization in Latin America. With the 1989 democratic elections in Brazil and Chile, all Latin American countries, with the exception of Cuba, had elected constitutional governments, marking a significant transformation in the region away from long periods dominated by military authoritarianism. As countries in the region started to experience more or less stable democratic rule, the study of political institutions expanded dramatically. Thus, a new breed of researchers has been deploying some of the tools originally developed to study American politics (and later European politics) to study the details of the workings of political institutions in Latin America.[14] In this chapter we draw on this scholarly work to show how political institutions work in shaping the incentives of politicians and other players in the PMP,

---

[9] The next section provides definitions and empirical counterparts to each of these dimensions.

[10] See e.g. Spiller, Stein, and Tommasi (2003); Spiller and Tommasi (2007); and Scartascini, Stein, and Tommasi (2009).

[11] See Persson and Tabellini (2000; 2003) for surveys.

[12] Rodrik, Subramanian, and Trebbi (2004).

[13] Such as the criteria of Przeworski et al. (2000).

[14] Some excellent books focusing on institutional features of Latin American polities are Mainwaring and Scully (1995) on party systems, Mainwaring and Shugart (1997) on constitutional and partisan powers of the president, Carey and Shugart (1998) on the executive decree authority, Morgenstern and Nacif (2002) on legislative politics, and Gibson (2004) on federalism. A recent report by UNDP (2005) brings together parts of this rich literature to explore the functioning of democracy in Latin America.

thereby affecting economic policy in the region. Below we sketch the main insights of a framework developed to explore the institutional determinants of policy outcomes.[15]

3.3.1 Modeling the policymaking process as an intertemporal game

The policymaking process in modern-day democracies can be understood as a process of bargains and exchanges among various political and socioeconomic actors. Some of these exchanges are consummated instantly (spot transactions), while in many other cases current actions or resources are exchanged for promises of future actions or resources (intertemporal transactions). Issues of credibility and the capacity to enforce political and policy agreements are crucial for political actors to be able to engage in intertemporal transactions.[16]

A number of features, amenable to analysis from a transaction cost perspective, characterize the political transactions surrounding public policies:

(1) Politics and policymaking take place over time.
(2) The relative political power of various actors changes over time.
(3) There are elements of both conflict and commonality of interests in almost any relevant policy issue.
(4) The socioeconomic reality in which policies operate changes over time.
(5) Most policies could be characterized by two decision frequencies: moments of major institutional definition and regular policymaking under those rules.
(6) Many of the changing realities in (4) are such that it would be impossible for political or policy agreements to cover every feasible future circumstance.

Models capturing those features have been developed, using the logic of repeated games to analyze policymaking (Spiller and Tommasi 2007: ch. 2). As a result of such analysis it is possible to explain the characteristics of policies and ultimately certain patterns of development. The ability of a polity to cooperate determines whether certain characteristics of policies are attainable. For example, in less-cooperative policymaking environments, policies might be too volatile and/or too rigid, poorly coordinated, and in general of low quality due to insufficient investment.[17] These properties of policies are among the dependent variables explored below.

---

[15] See Spiller et al. (2003) and Spiller and Tommasi (2007) for a more detailed account and formalization of this framework.

[16] In addition to the key *time* dimension, there is a *spatial* element to these bargains, as these can take place in arenas with varying levels of "institutionalization": while on one extreme, formal institutions such as Congress and parties are the central locus of demands by socioeconomic actors, at the other end of the spectrum, the "street" can provide the space for interest groups to deploy alternative political technologies (e.g. road blockades) to influence economic policy (Scartascini and Tommasi 2009).

[17] See Spiller and Tommasi (2007) for proper formalization.

3.3.2 The characteristics of policies

As previously mentioned, several characteristics of policies condition whether they deliver the expected welfare impacts. Among them are the six discussed immediately below.

- *Policy stability*. Having stable policies does not mean that policies cannot change at all, but rather that changes tend to respond to changing economic conditions or to failure of previous policies, rather than to slight shifts in political winds. Some countries seem capable of sustaining most policies over time (such as Chile). In other countries, policies are frequently reversed, often at each minor change of political winds, leading to a highly volatile policy environment.
- *Policy adaptability*. It is desirable for countries to be able to adapt policies to changing economic conditions and to change policies when they are clearly failing. Policy adaptability can be hindered either by a policymaking process prone to gridlock or by rigidities introduced explicitly to avoid opportunistic manipulation of policy. That is, in order to limit opportunism by the government of the day, some countries may choose to resort to fixed policy rules that are difficult to change (as in the case of Argentina's Convertibility Rule). This, of course, would limit policy volatility, but at the cost of reducing adaptability. As shown in the experience of Argentina, it may prove to be a costly trade-off.
- *Policy coordination and coherence*. Public policies are the outcome of actions taken by multiple actors in the policymaking process. Ideally, different agents acting in the same policy domain should coordinate their actions to produce coherent policies. In some cases coordination across policy areas is crucial (fiscal and monetary policy, health and education, and so on.) If agencies do not coordinate, even the best individual policies might not deliver to their full potential. The ability to coordinate is strongly related to the ability of actors to cooperate and to invest in their capabilities.
- *Policy implementation and enforcement*. A policy could be well thought out and pass through the appropriate legislative debate yet be completely ineffective if it is not well implemented and enforced. In many countries, the quality of policy implementation and enforcement is quite poor. This is associated in part with the lack of capable and independent bureaucracies, as well as the lack of strong judiciaries. To an important degree, the quality of policy implementation and enforcement in a given country will depend on the extent to which policymakers in that country have incentives and resources to invest in such policy capabilities.
- *Policy efficiency*. Whatever policy direction a government decides to follow (redistribute to the poor, clean the environment, promote non-traditional exports), it can do so with varying degrees of efficiency—i.e. by making better or worse use of its human and economic resources. Efficient policies imply, for example, that public spending is not wasteful. Efficient policies, however, might not necessarily be

public-regarded (the government could be very efficient in targeting a very small subset of the population).

- *Public-regardedness of policies.* "Public-regardedness" refers to the extent to which policies produced by a given system promote the general welfare and resemble public goods (i.e. are "public-regarding") or tend instead to funnel private benefits to certain individuals, factions, or regions (Cox and McCubbins 2001).[18]

We have created various empirical measures of these policy characteristics for most countries in Latin America, originally using opinion survey data encompassing more than 150 experts in 18 Latin American countries, and later expanding the analysis to a larger cross-section by drawing from available international data sources.[19] As expected, these policy features have a positive association with some measures of economic development (Table 3.1).

Table 3.2 summarizes how each country of Latin America fares in each one of the indices and in a composite index we call "Policy Index."[20] Countries have been ordered according to this composite index.

Figure 3.1 puts these values in international context. Latin American countries as a group do not rank very highly in indices of policy quality, but there is substantial intra-regional variation. Chile ranks high in the international comparison; a few countries (Uruguay, Costa Rica, Mexico, El Salvador, and Brazil) appear around the median of the world, a set of countries including Colombia is in the second quintile from the bottom, and then there is a group of countries at the low end of the distribution.

3.3.3 Political institutions, cooperation, and policy outcomes

We have argued that the ability of political and socioeconomic actors to cooperate is an important determinant of the characteristics of policies. The next question, then, is: what conditions make policy cooperation more likely? Drawing insights from the theory of repeated games, some of the factors that affect the degree of cooperation in equilibrium outcomes are the following:

---

[18] With the partial exception of the sixth policy characteristic (public-regardedness), the reader might be puzzled by the absence of equity or distributional aspects of public policy in this list. This omission does not mean that we are not aware of or concerned by the obvious fact that inequality is a major issue in Latin America, one of the most unequal regions in the world. We have tried to focus on characteristics of policies independently of their distributional content (and of other "contents") to highlight the importance of these policy qualities in attaining the desired societal objectives, including equity concerns. For instance, in Machado, Scartascini, and Tommasi (forthcoming), it is shown that countries with stronger policymaking capabilities, such as those highlighted here, are better able to achieve coverage objectives in policy areas such as education and health.

[19] Such as the World Economic Forum's Global Competitiveness Report, Columbia University State Capacity Survey, the Profils Institutionnels database, the Bertelsmann Transformation Index (BTI), and the Economic Freedom of the World Project (Fraser Institute).

[20] The specific components of each index can be found in Berkman et al. (2009).

Table 3.1 Features of public policies and economic development

	Stability	Adaptability	Coordination and coherence	Implementation and enforcement	Public regardedness	Efficiency	Obs.
Latin American countries							
GDP per capita growth 1990–2007	0.443*	0.46**	0.465*	0.536*	0.695***	0.537**	18
	0.257	0.307	0.345	0.400	0.555**	0.404*	18
Human Development Index (change) 1990–2005	0.581***	0.684***	0.71***	0.607***	0.594***	0.748***	18
	0.532**	0.5912***	0.678***	0.546**	0.544**	0.708***	18
Developing countries							
GDP per capita growth 1990–2007	0.392***	0.304***	0.328***	0.173*	0.197**	0.238***	113
	0.296***	0.333***	0.341***	0.199**	0.243***	0.248***	107
Human Development Index (change) 1990–2005	0.379***	0.401***	0.458***	0.312***	0.418***	0.446***	97
	0.192*	0.291***	0.301***	0.11	0.217**	0.253***	97

Note: Simple correlations between policy qualities and political variables are shown in the first row of each subgroup.
Partial-out correlations (controlling for GDP per capita of 1990) are shown in the second row of each subgroup.
* Significant at 10%; ** Significant at 5%; *** Significant at 1%.

Source: Authors' calculations using data from World Development Indicators and Berkman et al. (2009).

Table 3.2 Features of public policies in Latin American countries

Country	Stability	Adaptability	Implementation and enforcement	Coordination and Coherence	Public-regardedness	Efficiency	Policy Index
Chile	3.3	3.2	3.1	2.1	2.8	3.0	3.0
Uruguay	3.1	2.8	2.2	n.a	2.3	1.7	2.3
Brazil	3.0	2.6	2.3	2.0	1.5	1.5	2.2
Mexico	2.8	1.9	1.9	1.5	1.7	1.8	1.9
Costa Rica	2.8	2.0	2.2	1.3	1.9	1.0	1.9
Colombia	2.7	2.4	2.1	1.5	1.2	1.5	1.9
El Salvador	2.6	1.5	2.1	0.7	2.0	1.7	1.9
Peru	2.6	1.9	1.5	0.8	1.8	1.1	1.6
Panama	2.2	1.7	1.7	1.8	1.3	1.4	1.6
Argentina	2.7	1.8	1.3	1.4	1.1	1.4	1.5
Honduras	2.4	1.3	1.6	0.0	0.9	0.8	1.3
Bolivia	1.7	1.5	1.6	1.0	0.9	1.0	1.2
Nicaragua	2.1	1.3	1.4	1.3	0.7	1.1	1.2
Dominican Republic	1.9	1.4	1.5	1.3	1.3	0.6	1.2
Venezuela	2.0	1.1	1.4	1.0	1.2	0.5	1.1
Ecuador	1.7	1.6	1.3	1.3	1.2	0.6	1.1
Guatemala	1.9	1.0	0.8	0.9	1.0	1.0	1.0
Paraguay	1.8	1.3	1.0	0.4	0.3	0.6	0.8

Source: Author's calculation using data from Berkman et al. (2009).

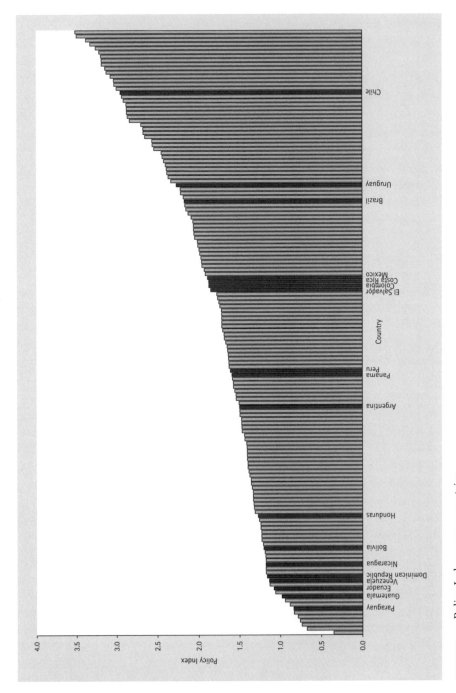

FIGURE 3.1 Policy Index across countries

Source: Author's calculation using data from Berkman et al. (2009).

- *Number of political players.* The larger the number of players, the smaller the set of other parameters for which cooperation is obtained. In a complex modern polity, the empirical counterpart of this abstract concept might relate to the capacity for aggregation of institutions such as the political party system, or of other structures of political participation of socioeconomic interests.
- *Intertemporal linkages among key actors.* The intertemporal pattern of interactions among specific individuals in formal political positions (such as legislators, governors, bureaucrats, and business or union leaders) matters for developing cooperative outcomes. It is not the same to have a legislature in which the same individuals interact over extended periods of time as to have a legislature where individuals change frequently. Cooperation is less likely in the latter.
- *Delegation.* Other than self-enforcement through repeated interaction, certain forms of cooperation could be achieved by alternative institutional means. Delegating policy to an independent bureaucracy is one such alternative. Similarly, societal actors such as business interests are more likely to enter the policymaking process in a non-particularistic and long-term way if they have invested in building more permanent structures of interaction with policymakers such as business associations and think tanks.
- *Availability of enforcement technologies.* As in transaction cost economics, intertemporal cooperation is easier to achieve if there is good third-party enforcement. The presence and characteristics of a potentially impartial umpire and enforcer of political agreements, such as an independent judiciary, will vary from country to country, providing variance in the degree of enforcement of intertemporal political cooperation.
- *Characteristics of the arenas where key political actors undertake their exchange.* The complex intertemporal exchanges required for the implementation of effective public policies could be facilitated by the existence of exchange arenas that are organized in ways that make cooperation easier to enforce. For example, it might be easier if transactions were part of legislative debate than if they were the outcome of closed backroom negotiations. Seminal work on the US Congress debates the role that different institutional arrangements have in facilitating legislative bargaining. While these studies suggest that most of the policy "action" takes place in institutionalized arenas such as Congress, the legislature certainly does not exhaust the possible locus of exchange among socioeconomic and political actors, especially in developing countries such as those of Latin America. Whether the legislature is the arena where these transactions take place is adequately institutionalized depends on several factors, including legislators' incentives and capabilities.

To sum up, political cooperation leading to effective public policies is more likely if: (1) the level of aggregation at which political actors enter the policy process is high; (2) those actors have long horizons and/or strong intertemporal linkages; (3) good delegation technologies are available; (4) good enforcement technologies (such as a strong court to arbitrate) are available; and (5) the key political exchanges take place in arenas where properties (1)–(4) tend to be satisfied.

What are the actual characteristics of political institutions and of the organization of actors that make political cooperation (and hence good public policies) more or less likely? The theoretical elements of the game listed above could be mapped to observable features of policymaking environments. For example, judicial independence seems to be a natural proxy—though not necessarily the only one—for the existence of enforcement technologies. Similarly, the quality of the civil service seems to approximate the existence of delegation mechanisms.[21]

We have shown elsewhere (Stein and Tommasi 2007 for Latin America; Scartascini, Stein, and Tommasi 2009 for a broad cross-section of countries) that proxies for these characteristics of institutions are highly significant for explaining the features of policies emphasized before. Below we describe some of these characteristics of institutions in the Latin American context.

3.3.3.1 *Congressional policymaking capabilities*

Congress is the democratic arena *par excellence* for the negotiation and enforcement of intertemporal policy agreements. Legislatures are critical to the functioning of democracy and act as an important arena for discussing and negotiating policy. A legislature made of up professional legislators (with technical capabilities for discussing and overseeing policies) and adequate organizational structures can facilitate the development of relatively consensual and consistent policies over time.

During the last decades, important contributions in political science have advanced the understanding of legislatures in Latin America.[22] Against the backdrop of earlier stylized views of the functioning of presidential systems in the region,[23] and by drawing on seminal studies of the US Congress, this new scholarship suggests that, while legislatures in Latin America in general may not be heavily involved in formulating and advocating policy change, they are nonetheless relevant to policy outcomes. Although it is true that in executive–legislative interactions legislatures are usually

---

[21] Interestingly, some of these concepts also embody qualities that are the result of the intertemporal equilibrium in which the polity happens to be at a given point in time. That is, having a highly skilled and professionalized civil service is by no means the result of a random drawing by nature or the result of a de jure institution imported from abroad. On the contrary, it is the result of years of investments in the capabilities of the civil service and self-restraint by a government that does not use the bureaucracy as a political instrument for patronage and clientelism. These behaviors are only possible in polities interested in long-run welfare, and they would seldom occur in polities where taking short-term advantage of political power is a higher priority.

[22] See Morgenstern and Nacif (2002) and references therein for details, especially the chapters by Morgenstern and Cox.

[23] That stylized view of political systems in the region, associated with the notion of *hyperpresidentialism*, emphasizes personalization of power, disdain for institutions, and confrontational political style. In that view, Latin America legislatures are no checks to presidential powers, and "delegative democracies" (O'Donnell 1994) are the norm. According to some views, when the president enjoys a governing majority, then the legislature is simply a rubber stamp to executive decisions and plays a subservient role; in contrast, in situations of divided or minority governments, the legislature solely plays an obstructionist role, which leads to impasse or deadlock. In our view, that is a mode of interaction that obtains *in equilibrium* in some countries, but not in others.

relegated to play a "reactive" role and presidents a more "proactive" one, the image of a recalcitrant assembly vis-à-vis an imperial president is by no means the only pattern of legislative politics in Latin America. Legislatures in some countries are in fact *active* in policymaking not only by performing the role of veto players blocking legislation proposed by the executive, but also by negotiating policy issues behind the scenes with the executive or in amending or reformulating executive legislative initiatives.

What factors affect whether legislatures play an active role in policymaking? Among other institutional features, *electoral rules* are key determinants of legislators' career prospects, and hence can contribute to or undermine investment in the development of legislature's policymaking capacities (Morgenstern and Nacif 2002). In other words, if legislators do not intend to remain in the legislature, they are unlikely to take an interest in institutionalizing the body so that it can develop a collective interest in policy and oversight responsibilities. In contrast to the US Congress, in which the "electoral connection" works in the direction of long legislative careers and a strong committee system, the rates of immediate re-election to the Congress in Latin America are low on average, although there is some important variation within the region (Saiegh 2010). In some countries, low re-election rates have conspired against the development of policymaking capacities of legislatures. In these countries, legislators typically have an incentive to work toward advancing a career outside the legislature (such as in national, state, or local government) and are also less experienced. Their career objectives are often furthered by satisfying (in some cases, provincial) party leaders rather than centering their attention on satisfying constituents' interests and demands (Coppedge 1997; Jones et al. 2002). As a result, the technical expertise and strength of committee systems in these legislatures tends to be lower than in countries with higher re-election rates (e.g. Chile or Uruguay).

Following these insights, IDB (2005) developed an index that attempts to capture the policymaking capabilities of Latin American legislatures with reference to some aspects of Congress as an organization, as well as to some characteristics of legislators. The index includes both objective and subjective variables, such as the strength and specialization of congressional committees, the confidence that the public has in Congress as an institution, the level of education and legislative experience of legislators, their technical expertise, and the extent to which Congress is a desirable career place for politicians (see Table 3.3).

Saiegh (2010) examines the robustness of such characterization when only the quantitative indicators are included, using multidimensional scaling (MDS) techniques. Comparing 18 Latin American legislatures to identify the main differences in their organizational structures, institutional features, and membership characteristics, Saiegh confirms that those legislatures with greater capabilities are the ones that play more constructive roles in the PMP, enabling intertemporal agreements and-long time horizon policies.[24]

---

[24] Some of these measures on legislative capabilities, capturing opinion about the effectiveness of lawmaking bodies and confidence in Parliament are available for a large sample of countries. Berkman et al. (2009) and Scartascini et al. (2009) show that these measures seem to be a good predictor of the policy features introduced in the previous section.

Table 3.3 Summary of some measures of legislature capabilities

Country	Confidence in Congress, average 1996–2004[a]	Effectiveness of lawmaking bodies[b]	Average experience of legislators (years)	% of legislators with university education[c]	Average no. of committee memberships per legislator	Strength of committees	Place to build career	Technical expertise	Congress Capability Index
Argentina	20.5	1.6	2.9	69.6	4.50	Medium	Low	Low	Low
Bolivia	19.9	1.8	3.3	78.4	1.66	Medium	Medium	Medium	Medium
Brazil	24.9	3.1	5.5	54.0	0.92	Medium	High	High	High
Chile	36.0	3.7	8.0	79.4	1.95	High	High	High	High
Colombia	20.3	2.7	4.0	91.6	0.86	High	High	Medium	High
Costa Rica	29.9	2.2	2.6	80.4	2.09	High	Medium	Low	Medium
Dominican Republic[d]	n.a.	2.0	3.1	49.6	3.54	Low	High	Low	Low
Ecuador	13.3	1.7	3.5	83.1	1.26	High	Medium	Low	Medium
El Salvador	27.7	2.1	3.9	64.0	2.44	Medium	High	Low	Medium
Guatemala	19.9	1.8	3.2	68.4	3.24	Low	Medium	Low	Low
Honduras	30.8	2.6	3.0	73.1	2.34	Low	Low	Low	Low
Mexico	27.4	2.0	1.9	89.5	2.43	High	Medium	Medium	Medium
Nicaragua	23.1	1.6	3.5	85.6	1.96	Low	Medium	Medium	Medium
Panama	22.5	1.8	5.8	81.3	1.86	Medium	High	Low	Medium
Paraguay	25.0	2.2	5.5	75.4	3.15	Low	High	Low	Medium
Peru	22.1	1.7	5.2	92.9	2.44	Low	Low	Low	Low
Uruguay	38.2	2.7	8.8	68.4	0.98	High	High	Low	High
Venezuela	27.8	1.4	4.9	74.6	0.97	Medium	Medium	Low	Medium

Note: [a] Latinobarometer;   [b] World Economic Forum (2005).   [c] PELA (2002);
[d] the Dominican Republic was included only in the 2004 survey; no average is shown.

Source: IDB (2005) (based on PELA, various years, and Saiegh 2010).

3.3.3.2 *Judicial independence*

The Judiciary, especially the Supreme Court or Constitutional Tribunal is a natural candidate for the enforcement of those political or policy agreements reflected in constitutions and laws. In its role as an independent referee, the judiciary can provide a "durability mechanism" that can increase the probability of reaching intertemporal agreements. A judiciary that effectively plays its role may contribute to better public policy outcomes, such as enhanced policy stability, and policy implementation and enforcement.

Magaldi de Sousa (2010) provides a typological framework for categorizing and comparatively assessing the scope of *judicial activism*, that is, the extent of courts' involvement in the PMP across Latin America. The extent to which the judiciary can veto new legislation, shape legislative content, enforce the implementation of existing rules as an impartial referee, and act as an alternative representative of society in the PMP defines the four main characteristics and roles discussed by the author. However, the extent of judicial activism is a function, among other things, of the level of judicial independence. Although judicial independence has various interrelated dimensions, a de facto independent judiciary is one that issues rulings that are respected and enforced by the legislative and executive branch; that receives an adequate appropriation of resources; and that is not compromised by political attempts to undermine its impartiality. Without institutions that guarantee budgetary autonomy, a uniform, transparent, and merit-based appointment system, stable tenure for judges, and promotion procedures based on evaluation of performance, Latin American courts simply would not be able to veto policies, shape their content, or act as a referee and a societal representative. To put it differently, judicial independence is a necessary (although not sufficient) condition for judicial activism.

Table 3.4 shows the relative rankings of judicial independence for selected Latin American countries in 1975 and 2005. Chile, Brazil, and Uruguay achieved considerable higher levels of judicial independence, while Venezuela and Argentina seem to have moved in the opposite direction.

The evidence presented by Magaldi de Souza supports the argument that courts are increasing their impact on the PMP in Latin America. Furthermore, while countries with broad judicial activism seem to present rather stable and adaptable public policies, the democracies with narrower levels of judicial activism show more volatility and rigidity in their policies. In line with this argument, Scartascini, Stein, and Tommasi (2009) show that a proxy of judicial independence, which captures whether the judiciary is subject to interference by the government or other political actors, correlates well with policy features such as stability, adaptability, coherence and coordination, implementation and enforcement in a large sample of countries.

3.3.3.3 *Civil service capacity*

A strong, independent, and professional bureaucracy seems the most natural vehicle for the flexible enforcement of political agreements via delegation. An effective and capable bureaucracy is likely to improve the quality of implementation of public policies, as well as their coordination across ministries. The competence and independence of the

Table 3.4 Relative judicial independence, selected Latin American and Caribbean countries, 1975 and 2005

Ranking	1975	2005[a]
1 More judicial independence	Costa Rica	Uruguay (15)
2	Venezuela	Costa Rica (1)
3	Colombia	Chile (16)
4	Argentina	Brazil (12)
5	Mexico	Dominican Republic (7)
6	El Salvador	Mexico (5)
7	Dominican Republic	El Salvador (6)
8	Peru	Colombia (3)
9	Panama	Guatemala (11)
10	Ecuador	Bolivia (14)
11	Guatemala	Honduras (13)
12	Brazil	Peru (8)
13	Honduras	Argentina (4)
14	Bolivia	Panama (9)
15	Uruguay	Paraguay (18)
16	Chile	Ecuador (10)
17	Nicaragua	Venezuela (2)
18 Less judicial independence	Paraguay	Nicaragua (17)

[a] 1975 rankings are in parentheses.

Source: Magaldi de Sousa (2010) (based on Verner 1984 and World Economic Forum 2005).

bureaucracy may decrease the susceptibility of likelihood that policy will be prone to politicization and political opportunism, and could increase policy adaptability to changing circumstances by relying on technical expertise.

Zuvanic and Iacoviello (2010) discuss some characteristics of Latin American bureaucracies, their role in the PMP, and their capacity to put into practice long-lasting agreements. Their characterization is based on a model where two dimensions—autonomy of political power and technical capacity—are considered. They group bureaucracies into four types: patronage, administrative, meritocratic, and parallel. On the basis of this typology, they present evidence that characterizes Chile, Brazil, and Costa Rica as cases that stand out in the region because of the higher level of development of their civil services. At the other extreme, the most critical situation occurs in Bolivia, Peru, Paraguay, Ecuador, and various Central American countries. Considering both dimensions simultaneously, Figure 3.2 groups Latin American countries according to their levels of bureaucratic development.[25]

---

[25] Scartascini et al. (2009) use cross country regressions to show that a similar proxy for the degree of professionalism of the bureaucracy has a significant positive effect on the overall quality of public policies.

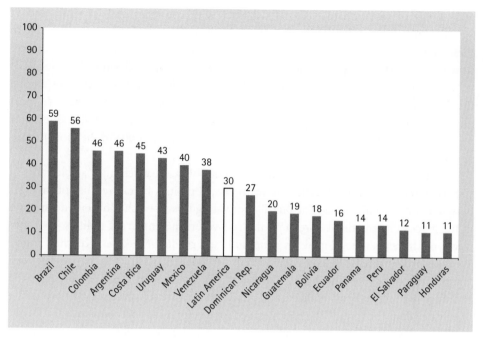

FIGURE 3.2 Civil Service Development Index

Source: Zuvanic and Iacoviello (2010).

3.3.3.4 *Party system characteristics*

Mainwaring and Scully (1995) introduced a central concept into the study of Latin American party systems: *party system institutionalization* (PSI).[26] An institutionalized party system is a natural aggregator that reduces the effective number of players at the bargaining table and increases the horizons of individual political actors. The structure and organization of political parties and party systems can have an important influence on the policymaking process, both by playing a direct role and through interactions with other institutions. Political parties can influence policy debates, affect executive–legislative relations, enhance or constrict the possibilities for coordination in Congress, or manage the incentives of politicians at both the national and local level. In sum, institutionalized party systems serve as facilitators of intertemporal policy compromise.

Several indicators have been developed to measure the different dimensions of PSI in Latin America. For example, the stability of inter-party competition is usually measured using the level of vote or seat volatility in different elections. Latin America presents a

---

[26] Party systems can be considered institutionalized when four conditions are present: the patterns of interparty competition are relatively stable; parties have fairly stable and deep bases of societal support; parties and elections are viewed as legitimate and as the sole instruments for determining who governs; and party organizations are characterized by stable rules and structures (Mainwaring and Scully 1995).

wide range of variation in electoral volatility, with countries such as Chile and El Salvador possessing volatility levels comparable to those found in Western Europe. In these democracies, the same parties tend to win comparable vote and seat shares over time. In contrast, the region is home to other countries with extremely high levels of volatility, such as Peru, Guatemala, and Venezuela. Here, parties that were among the most relevant in the country either ceased to exist or saw their popular support plummet over a very short period. At the same time, parties that either did not exist or were inconsequential players only a few years earlier became some of the most prominent in the country (Jones 2010).

The dimension of PSI that refers to the extent political parties enjoy stable roots in society is related to a broader theme in the party politics literature: that of linkages between citizens and parties. The puzzle motivating this research is observed variation in the types of interaction between parties and voters in democratic polities. Two stylized types have been developed: *programmatic* and *clientelist linkages* (Kitschelt 2000). Whereas programmatic linkages deal with impersonal and indirect exchanges between voters and politicians who trade vote for public policies, in clientelist linkages the exchange is direct and personalized, and public policies are substituted by the proffering of private goods for votes.[27] The goods traded for electoral support come in many forms: public employment, selective incentives such as cash or minor consumption goods, and public programs.

Figure 3.3 shows the values of the quality of policies index for different combinations of measures of party system institutionalization and the extent to which parties are programmatic, developed by Jones (2010). Two important points emerge from this figure. First, there are no countries with programmatic parties that are not institutionalized (i.e. the left quadrant of the figure is empty). Secondly, party system institutionalization *per se* does not tend to correlate with high-quality policies.[28] Policies only seem to get better when party systems are both institutionalized *and* programmatic.

This last point on interactions can be made more general. One of the key lessons that we have learned from the study of the institutional determinants of policymaking is that political institutions tend to work interactively (Tsebelis 2002). Previous literature on political institutions tended to use a single criterion to identify the main characteristics of a polity.[29] The relations and interactions among all those dimensions were underdeveloped. However, to understand the policymaking process of a given country, it is not enough to simply aggregate the generic effects induced by each of its institutional features. As the case studies in IDB (2005) and country chapters in Stein et al. (2008) show, these interactions are *non-additive*, in the sense that the effect of one particular institutional characteristic depends on the whole array of institutions in the system.

---

[27] Of course, no political party system falls exclusively into a "pure" programmatic or "pure" clientelist category. Even in the most programmatic party systems, parties employ some forms of clientelistic practice.

[28] Scartascini et al. (2009) confirm this point using a larger sample of countries.

[29] Using dichotomies such as presidential/parliamentary, majoritarian/proportional, two-party/multiparty, federal/unitary institutions.

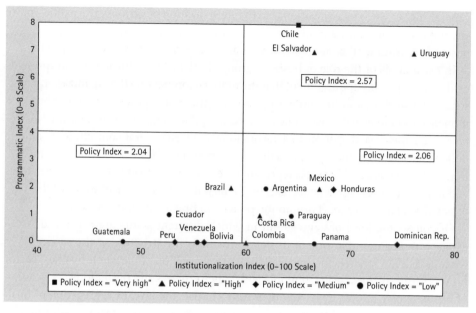

FIGURE 3.3 Party system institutionalization, programmatic orientation, and the quality of policies

Notes: Boxes show the average value of the Policy Index for the countries in each quadrant.

Source: IDB (2005) (based on Stein and Tommasi 2005 and Jones 2010).

3.3.3.5 *Socioeconomic interest groups and the PMP*

No matter how important a role political institutions play in affecting the level of cooperation in the PMP and the quality of policies, they are only one among a range of factors that help explain this variation. While so far we have concentrated on the incentives of professional politicians and state actors to cooperate and hence produce policies of high quality, the nature of policymaking and the characteristics of resulting policies are also affected by some characteristics and organization of key socioeconomic actors in each polity.[30] These include players such as business groups and labor unions whose diverse constituencies make leaders pursue different types of policies. For space reasons, in this section we focus on business. What characteristics of business groups affect whether cooperation in the PMP obtains in equilibrium?

One important determinant is the *level of aggregation* and form of articulation of economic interests. The types of demand pursued in the political arena will be different depending on whether, say, business actors enter that arena individually (as firms), at the industry level (textile, metallurgic), at the sectoral level (industry, agriculture), or as economy-wide associations. Even though the relationship is not strictly monotonic, in

---

[30] In incorporating these groups into the analysis, we follow the rich tradition of political economy scholarship reviewed previously, which focused on the collective action capacity of socioeconomic interest groups, the level of aggregation of their demands, and the links between these interest groups and policymakers.

general, higher levels of association lead to internalization of various externalities, more encompassing interests, and demands more oriented towards improving the general business environment (better judicial system, more infrastructure, more credit, etc.).

In his analysis of the role of business groups in the PMP, Schneider (2010) presents evidence supporting the argument that the more encompassing the organization representing business is, and the more transparent is the policy process, the more business influence in politics will push policy toward the public-regarding continuum.[31] A feature of business participation that favors longer intertemporal commitments among policymakers and business people is the representation of business on policy councils.[32] Both policymakers and business representatives have incentives to develop reputations and not to renege on agreements reached in the policy council. An example of this type of policies is found in export promotion policies in Brazil, Chile, and Mexico.

Of course, the level of aggregation in which different actors are organized is not exogenous. For example, one of its determinants is the structure of the economy; in some cases a few large sectors can lead the collective action of the whole business sector (as was formerly the case in Colombia with coffee growers and the national association of businessmen, known by its acronym ANDI). Also, the level of aggregation of business participation in politics depends on past state action organizing such interests (Schneider 2004b).

In some countries, policymaking is highly concentrated and decisions related to productivity are handled by a small and cohesive group of public officials. In that context, groups may benefit by organizing themselves in a similarly concentrated fashion. When decision-making is more fragmented, either because more people have a say in policy matters or because decisions are made at a more decentralized level of government (locality instead of central government), groups may choose to influence policies in a more fragmented way (as is the case in Colombia nowadays, where business groups have fragmented) or to concentrate efforts on trying to affect policies at the local level (which seems to be the case in Brazil, where businesses are more prone to individually seek tax exemptions at the state level than to collectively negotiate for lower taxes).

3.3.3.6 *The arenas of policymaking: institutionalized or not?*

As noted above, the arenas where exchanges among political and socioeconomic groups interact to make policy matters for the resulting policy outcomes. While in developed democracies most of the policy action can be observed through the workings of formal political institutions (Congress, the judiciary) and stylized forms of participation (voting, lobbying), to study policymaking in developing countries one needs to incorporate additional arenas of interaction, with varying levels of institutionalization. Within this

---

[31] On the other hand, business influences that favor the private-regarding end of the continuum are likely to arise in instances of narrow policies, and when business representation occurs predominantly through channels that are less transparent and that involve small numbers of firms or individuals.

[32] Of course, having policy councils is not always enough. In some cases, they may serve no purpose if business organization is highly fragmented. For additional information on this, see Scartascini and Tommasi (2010). Eslava and Meléndez (2009) discuss this issue in the context of Colombia.

"extra" space, socioeconomic groups in turn can deploy a variety of participation mechanisms, which can be referred to as "alternative political technologies," including activities such as protests, road blockades, disruption of economic activity, and the like.[33]

While political actions such as voting or lobbying according to the rules of the game, and participating in blockades or bribing, may be complementary, one can think of examples in which certain socioeconomic groups will take different roads depending on what the institutional environment has to offer (making such decisions *substitutes* in practice). For instance, there will be circumstances in which business interests will invest more resources in strengthening right-wing political parties and think tanks that defend their general interests (as they do in Chile) than in bribing politicians, judges, or bureaucrats to get special privileges for their firm or sector (as they do in other countries of the region). These different types of decisions have an important investment component, and are likely to reinforce the degree of institutionalization or lack thereof over time.

One of the implications of this line of argument is that particular institutional equilibria will affect the investment decisions of players towards different types of political participation, thus reinforcing the prevalent form of institutionalization (or lack thereof). For example, Scartascini and Tommasi (2009) provide empirical evidence that proxies for institutional quality (say of Congress) as those described above tend to be negatively correlated with various measures of conflict among a large sample of countries.[34]

3.3.3.7 *Putting things together at the country level*

The previous sections have looked into some of the main arenas and actors of Latin American policymaking, trying to gain some general comparative insights into the effects of various characteristics of those actors and arenas on policymaking and on policies. But each country has a unique configuration and a unique mode of interaction: the total is more than the sum of the parts. Space constraints prevent us from describing the policymaking processes of specific countries in its entirety. For that, we refer readers to the country chapters in the edited volume *Policymaking in Latin America* (Stein et al. 2008).

3.4 CONCLUDING THOUGHTS

One of the main points advocated in this chapter is that analysts should beware of naive economic recommendations that ignore political and institutional considerations. If economists are to offer effective policy recommendations, they need to have a solid

---

[33] This section draws on Scartascini and Tommasi (2009).

[34] Furthermore, Machado et al. (2009) use multilevel modeling techniques to show that countries with poor quality of the institutional environment present patterns of individual protest participation different from countries with "better" institutions across Latin America.

understanding of the institutional capabilities and political realities of the polities under consideration. This chapter has presented some perspectives on how to approach such analysis, with a particular focus on how political rules work for or against intertemporal cooperation among political actors.

We have argued that certain key features of economic policy may be as important in achieving development goals as their content or orientation, the latter being the traditional focus of economists. As shown by the recent experience of Latin America with the market reform process, the impact of policies on growth depends not only on a particular orientation but also on some generic features of the policies. An "ideal" policy that lacks credibility and is poorly implemented and enforced may be more distorting than a "suboptimal" policy that is stable and well implemented. Countries able to generate policies with such attributes will reap the benefits of specific economic reforms more than others. If policies adopted do not have such attributes, no matter how good they look on paper, it is unlikely they will achieve good development outcomes.

This chapter has shown that the extent to which polities obtain key policy features depends on the workings of political institutions (which define *how* the policymaking game is played), on the characteristics of the arenas of interaction (which define *where* the policymaking game is played), and on certain characteristics of key socioeconomic groups (which define *who* interacts with professional politicians in pursuing different policy preferences).

Fortunately, economists have started to move away from the conviction that there are recipes of universal applicability to all countries. A universal set of "right" policies does not exist. What might work at one point in time in a given country might not work in a different place or in the same place at another time. The political economy approach presented here offers a lens through which to shed light on these key issues.

REFERENCES

ACEMOGLU, D., and ROBINSON, J. (2006). *Economic Origins of Dictatorship and Democracy*, New York: Cambridge University Press.

ARDANAZ, M., SCARTASCINI, C., and TOMMASI, M. (2009). 'Political Institutions, Policymaking, and Economic Policy in Latin America: A Survey', Washington, DC: Inter-American Development Bank.

BERKMAN, H., SCARTASCINI, C., STEIN, E., and TOMMASI, M. (2009). 'Policies, State Capabilities, and Political Institutions: An International Dataset', Washington, DC: Inter-American Development Bank.

CARDOSO, F. H., and FALLETO, E. (1969). *Dependency and Development in Latin America*, Berkeley: University of California Press.

CAREY, J., and SHUGART, M. (eds) (1998). *Executive Decree Authority*, New York: Cambridge University Press.

—— (2005). 'Presidential Versus Parliamentary Goverment', in C. Menard and M. Shirley (eds), *Handbook of New Institutional Economics*, Boston: Kluwer Academic Press.

CHEIBUB, J. (2007). *Presidentialism, Parliamentarism, and Democracy*, New York: Cambridge University Press.

COPPEDGE, M. (1997). *Strong Parties and Lame Ducks: Presidential Partyarchy and Factionalism in. Venezuela*, Stanford: Stanford University Press.

—— (1998). 'The Dynamic Diversity of Latin American Party Systems', *Party Politics* 4.4.

COX, G., and McCUBBINS, M. D. (2001). 'The Institutional Determinants of Economic Policy Outcomes', in S. Haggard and M. D. McCubbins (eds), *Presidents, Parliaments and Policy*, New York: Cambridge University Press.

DORNBUSCH, R., and EDWARDS, S. (eds) (1991). *The Macroeconomics of Populism in Latin America*, Chicago: University of Chicago Press.

ENGERMAN, S. L., and SOKOLOFF, K. L. (2002). 'Factor Endowments, Inequality, and Paths of Development among New World Economies', *Economia* 3.1.

ESLAVA, M., and MELÉNDEZ, M. (2009). 'Cómo los grupos de interés influyen sobre la productividad', in E. Lora and C. Scartascini (eds), *Consecuencias Imprevistas de la Constitución de 1991*, Bogotá: Alfaomega.

FORTEZA, Á., and TOMMASI, M. (2006). 'On the Political Economy of Pro-Market Reform in Latin America', in J. Fanelli and G. McMahon (eds), *Understanding Market Reforms*, vol. 2: *Motivation, Implementation and Sustainability*, New York: Palgrave Macmillan.

FRIEDEN, J. (1991). *Debt, Development and Democracy*, Princeton, NJ: Princeton University Press.

GEDDES, B. (2002). 'The Great Transformation in the Study of Politics in Developing Countries', in I. Katznelson and H. Milner (eds), *Political Science: The State of the Discipline*, vol. 3, New York: Norton and American Political Science Association.

GIBSON, E. (ed.) (2004). *Federalism and Democracy in Latin America*, Baltimore: Johns Hopkins University Press.

HIRSCHMAN, A. O. (1968). 'The Political Economy of Import Substituting Industrialization in Latin America', *Quarterly Journal of Economics* 82.1.

Inter-American Development Bank (IDB) (2005). *The Politics of Policies: Economic and Social Progress in Latin America and the Caribbean 2006 Report*, Washington, DC: Inter-American Development Bank and David Rockefeller Center for Latin American Studies, Harvard University.

JONES, M. P. (2010). 'Beyond the Electoral Connection: Political Parties' Effect on the Policymaking Process', in C. Scartascini, E. Stein, and M. Tommasi (eds), *How Democracy Works: Political Institutions, Actors and Arenas in Latin America Policymaking*, Washington, DC: Inter-American Development Bank and David Rockefeller Center for Latin American Studies, Harvard University.

—— SAIEGH, S., SPILLER, P., and TOMMASI, M. (2002). 'Amateur Legislators, Professional Politicians: The Consequences of Party-Centered Electoral Rules in Federal Systems', *American Journal of Political Science* 46.3.

KAUFMAN, R., and STALLINGS, B. (1991). 'The Political Economy of Latin American Populism', in R. Dornbusch and S. Edwards (eds), *The Macroeconomics of Populism in Latin America*, Chicago: University of Chicago Press.

KITSCHELT, H. (2000). 'Linkages between Citizens and Politicians in Democratic Polities', *Comparative Political Studies* 33.6–7.

LINZ, J. (1990). 'The Perils of Presidentialism', *Journal of Democracy* 1.1.

MACHADO, F., SCARTASCINI, C., and TOMMASI, M. (2009). 'Political Institutions and Street Protests in Latin America', Inter-American Development Bank Working Paper No. 110, Washington, DC: Inter-American Development Bank.

——— ——— ——— (forthcoming). 'Political Institutions and Policy Outcomes around the World: How Intertemporal Transactions Matter for the Quality of Public Policies', Washington, DC: Inter-American Development Bank.

MAGALDI DE SOUSA, M. (2010). 'Courts Engagement: The Different Functions of the Judiciary in Policymaking', in C. Scartascini, E. Stein, and M. Tommasi (eds), *How Democracy Works: Political Institutions, Actors and Arenas in Latin America Policymaking*, Washington, DC: Inter-American Development Bank and David Rockefeller Center for Latin American Studies, Harvard University.

MAINWARING, S., and SCULLY, T. R. (1995). *Building Democratic Institutions: Party Systems in Latin America*, Stanford, Calif.: Stanford University Press.

——— and SHUGART, M. (eds) (1997). *Presidentialism and Democracy in Latin America*, New York: Cambridge University Press.

MORGENSTERN, S., and NACIF, B. (2002). *Legislative Politics in Latin America*, Cambridge: Cambridge University Press.

OCAMPO, J. A. (2004). *Reconstruir el futuro: globalizacion, desarrollo y democracia en América Latina*, Bogota: CEPAL and Norma.

O'DONNELL, G. (1973). *Modernization and Bureaucratic Authoritarianism*, Berkeley: University of California Press.

——— (1994). 'Delegative Democracy', *Journal of Democracy* 5.1.

PELA (Proyecto de Elites Latinoamericanas) (2002). *Proyecto de Elites LatinoAmericanas, 1994–2005*, Salamanca: Universidad de Salamanca.

PERSSON, T., and TABELLINI, G. (2000). *Political Economics: Explaining Economic Policy*, Cambridge, Mass.: Massachusetts Institute of Technology Press.

——— (2003). *The Economic Effects of Constitutions*, Cambridge, Mass.: Massachusetts Institute of Technology Press.

PRZEWORSKI, A., ALVAREZ, M., CHEIBUB, J., and LIMONGI, F. (2000). *Democracy and Development: Political Regimes and Material Well-being in the World, 1950–1990*, New York: Cambridge University Press.

RODRIK, D. (1995). 'Political Economy of Trade Policy', in G. M. Grossman and K. Rogoff (eds), *Handbook of International Economics 3*, Amsterdam: Elsevier and North-Holland.

——— (1996). 'Understanding Economic Policy Reform', *Journal of Economic Literature* 34.1.

——— SUBRAMANIAN, A., and TREBBI, F. (2004). 'Institutions Rule: The Primacy of Institutions Over Geography and Integration in Economic Development', *Journal of Economic Growth* 9.2.

SACHS, J. D. (1989). 'Social Conflict and Populist Policies in Latin America', National Bureau of Economic Research Working Paper No. 2897, Cambridge, Mass.: National Bureau of Economic Research.

SAIEGH, S. M. (2010). 'Active Players or Rubber-Stamps? An Evaluation of the Policymaking Role of Latin American Legislatures', in C. Scartascini, E. Stein, and M. Tommasi (eds), *How Democracy Works: Political Institutions, Actors and Arenas in Latin America Policymaking*, Washington, DC: Inter-American Development Bank and David Rockefeller Center for Latin American Studies, Harvard University.

SAMUELS, D. (2003). *Ambition, Federalism, and Legislative Politics in Brazil*, Cambridge: Cambridge University Press.

SCARTASCINI, C. and TOMMASI, M. (2009). 'The Making of Policy: Institutionalized or Not?', Inter-American Development Bank Working Paper No. 108, Washington, DC: Inter-American Development Bank.

—— —— (2010). 'The Politics of Productivity' in *The Age of Productivity*, Washington, DC: Inter-American Development Bank and Palgrave Macmillan.

—— STEIN, E., and TOMMASI, M. (2009). 'Political Institutions, Intertemporal Cooperation, and the Quality of Policies', Research Department Working Paper No. 676, Washington, DC: Inter-American Development Bank.

—— —— —— (eds) (2010). *How Democracy Works: Political Institutions, Actors and Arenas in Latin American Policymaking*, Washington, DC: Inter-American Development Bank and David Rockefeller Center for Latin American Studies, Harvard University.

SCHNEIDER, B. R. (2004a). 'Organizing Interests and Coalitions in the Politics of Market Reform in Latin America', *World Politics* 56.3.

—— (2004b). *Business Politics and the State in Twentieth-Century Latin America*, New York: Cambridge University Press.

—— (2010). 'Business Politics and Policy Making in Contemporary Latin America', in C. Scartascini, E. Stein, and M. Tommasi (eds), *How Democracy Works: Political Institutions, Actors and Arenas in Latin America Policymaking*, Washington, DC: Inter-American Development Bank and David Rockefeller Center for Latin American Studies, Harvard University.

SHUGART, M., and CAREY, J. (1992). *Presidents and Assemblies: Constitutional Design and Electoral Dynamics*, New York: Cambridge University Press.

SPILLER, P. T., STEIN, E., and TOMMASI, M. (2003). 'Political Institutions, Policymaking Processes and Policy Outcomes: An Intertemporal Transactions Framework', Department of Economics Working Paper No. 59, Universidad de San Andres.

—— and TOMMASI, M. (2007). *The Institutional Foundations of Public Policy in Argentina*, New York: Cambridge University Press.

STEIN, E., and TOMMASI, M. (2005). 'Democratic Institutions, Policymaking Processes and the Quality of Policies in Latin America', paper presented at the seminar 'A New Development Agenda for Latin America', Universidad de Salamanca (October).

—— —— (2007). 'The Institutional Determinants of State Capability in Latin America', in F. Bourguignon and B. Pleskovic (eds), *Beyond Transition (Annual World Bank Conference on Development Economics)*, Washington, DC: World Bank.

—— —— (eds) (2008). *Policymaking in Latin America: How Politics Shapes Policies*, Washington, DC: Inter-American Development Bank and David Rockefeller Center for Latin American Studies, Harvard University.

—— SCARTASCINI, C., SPILLER, P., and TOMMASI, M. (eds.) (2008) *Policymaking in Latin America: How Politics Shapes Policies*, Washington, DC: Inter-American Development Bank and David Rockefeller Center for Latin American Studies, Harvard University.

TOMMASI, M., and VELASCO, A. (1996). 'Where Are We in the Political Economy of Reform?', *Journal of Policy Reform* 1.2.

TSEBELIS, G. (2002). *Veto Players: How Political Institutions Work*, Princeton, NJ: Princeton University Press.

UNDP (United Nations Development Programme) (2005). *Democracy in Latin America: Towards a Citizens' Democracy*, New York: United Nations Development Programme.

VERNER, J. (1984). 'The Independence of Supreme Courts in Latin America: A Review of the
    Literature', *Journal of Latin American Studies* 16.2.
World Economic Forum (2005). *The Global Competitiveness Report 2004–2005.*
ZUVANIC, L., and IACOVIELLO, M. (2010). 'The Weakest Link: The Bureaucracy and Civil
    Service Systems in Latin America', in C. Scartascini, E. Stein, and M. Tommasi (eds), *How
    Democracy Works: Political Institutions, Actors and Arenas in Latin America Policymaking,*
    Washington, DC: Inter-American Development Bank and David Rockefeller Center for
    Latin American Studies, Harvard University.

CHAPTER 4

....

THE WASHINGTON CONSENSUS: ASSESSING A "DAMAGED BRAND"

....

NANCY BIRDSALL, AUGUSTO DE LA TORRE,
AND FELIPE VALENCIA CAICEDO

4.1 INTRODUCTION[1]

....

It is hard to overemphasize the practical and ideological importance of the so-called "Washington Consensus" in Latin America. The Decalogue of Consensus policies laid out by John Williamson in 1989, at a Conference organized by the Institute for International Finance (Williamson 1990), took on a life of its own in subsequent decades, becoming in the minds of advocates and pundits alike a manifesto for capitalist economic development. For its advocates, the Consensus reflected a doctrine of economic freedom that was best suited for the political democracies to which many Latin countries had returned after a long spell of military dictatorships (Williamson 1993). For its opponents, as Williamson (2002) himself noted, the Consensus was an unjust "set of neoliberal policies...imposed on hapless countries by the Washington-based international financial institutions." Regardless of the view, there is no denying that overall the Consensus became, in Moisés Naím's (2002) epigrammatic expression, a "damaged brand."

The social and economic philosophy implicit in the Consensus was not created by Williamson. It was, so to speak, "in the air"—a robust intellectual and ideological current

    [1] We thank Mauricio Cárdenas, Alan Gelb, Rudolf Hommes, Santiago Levy, José Antonio Ocampo, Jaime Ros, Sergio Schmukler, and John Williamson for very helpful comments. For a more extensive discussion of some of the issues and specific references, see Birdsall, de la Torre, and Valencia (2010). The views expressed in this chaper are entirely those of the authors and do not necessarily represent the views of the Center for Global Development or the World Bank Group.

of the times which emphasized the virtuous combination of political democracy and free markets. Williamson's article rode on a global wave that transformed the conventional wisdom in favor of free market economics—which included the rise of neoclassical economics and the rational expectations revolution among academic macroeconomists. It is no coincidence that the appearance in 1989 of the Washington Consensus coincided with the fall of the Berlin Wall, which marked symbolically the burial of centrally planned economies.

4.2 THE WASHINGTON CONSENSUS

Around the time that Williamson's article was published, the intellectual effervescence had been sufficient to move the dominant economic development policy paradigm away from a model of state dirigisme focused on inwardly orientated import substitution industrialization—which had prevailed in Latin America and the Caribbean (LAC) during the 1960s and 1970s—towards greater reliance on markets, openness, and export orientation. This mutation started in the 1970s, gained momentum during the 1980s—when a corrosive and generalized debt crisis sunk the region into a "lost decade"—and reached its heights during the 1990s—arguably the glorious years for the Washington Consensus.

The ability of import substitution to promote growth showed signs of exhaustion by the late 1970s as macroeconomic imbalances mounted. But if there is one common economic episode that helped synchronize the shift away from import substitution throughout the region it was the debt crisis. Its beginnings were marked by a fateful meeting in 1982, when Mexican officials announced their payment difficulties to the US Secretary of the Treasury.[2] The painful adjustment process turned the 1980s into a lost decade. As capital inflows abruptly stopped and terms of trade deteriorated sharply, countries were forced into deep and highly disruptive fiscal expenditure cuts, major currency devaluations, and severe restrictions on imports, including on vital capital and intermediate goods. This brought about a dramatic erosion of real wages and living standards. Per capita income collapsed, unemployment rose, and in some countries inflation exploded. Politically, the economic hardships tested the recently restored democracies (which followed the military dictatorships of the 1960s and 1970s in Argentina, Brazil, Bolivia, Ecuador, Guatemala, Haiti, Honduras, Nicaragua, Panama, Paraguay, and Uruguay). Against this background, by 1989 the shift away from "state-led industrialization" (as Ocampo and Ros aptly name it in their contribution to this Handbook) or "import-substitution industrialization" (as it is more commonly called) towards a more market-led model gained momentum.

Williamson's article was thus published when the region was already on the road of change. What Williamson did was to summarize in a Decalogue of 10 policies (Table 4.1)

---

[2] While triggered by an external shock—the sharp rise in dollar interest rates engineered by the US Fed to fight inflation—the severity of the debt crisis reflected a dangerous accumulation of domestic vulnerabilities associated with a benign external environment. Low global interest rates and high commodity prices invited or at least allowed what came to be judged as an unaffordable and inefficient intrusion of the state into the economy.

the converging views that had clearly emerged among the participants (which included prominent Latin American scholars and policymakers) in an 1989 Institute of International Economics Conference organized in Washington, DC by John Williamson himself entitled *Latin American Adjustment: How Much Has Happened?* (Williamson 1990). While reflecting his own views, his article constitutes a synthesis of policies already in vogue at the time—in the region as well as in Washington. Indeed, Williamson is better portrayed as a recorder than as a creator of the new paradigm; the real actors in

Table 4.1 The decalogue of Washington Consensus policies (1989)

1. Fiscal discipline	Budget deficits—properly measured to include local governments, state enterprises, and the Central Bank—should be small enough to be financed without recourse to the inflation tax.
2. Public expenditure re-prioritization	Public spending should move away from politically popular but economically unwarranted projects (bloated bureaucracies, indiscriminate subsidies, white elephants) and towards neglected fields with high economic returns and the potential to improve income distribution (primary health and education, infrastructure).
3. Tax reform	To improve incentives and horizontal equity, the tax base should be broad and marginal tax rates moderate. Taxing interest on assets held abroad ("flight capital") should become a priority in the medium term.
4. Positive real interest rates	Ultimately, interest rates should be market-determined. As this could be destabilizing in an environment of weak confidence, policy should have more modest objectives for the transition, mainly to abolish preferential interest rates for privileged borrowers and achieve a moderately positive real interest rate.
5. Competitive exchange rates	Countries need a unified (at least for trade transactions) exchange rate set at a level sufficiently competitive to induce a rapid growth in non-traditional exports, and managed so as to assure exporters that this competitiveness will be maintained in the future.
6. Trade liberalization	Quantitative trade restrictions should be replaced by tariffs, and these should be progressively reduced until a uniform low tariff in the range of 10 % is achieved.
7. Foreign direct investment	Barriers impeding foreign direct investment and the entry of foreign firms should be abolished; foreign and domestic firms should be allowed to compete on equal terms.
8. Privatization	State enterprises should be privatized.
9. Deregulation	Governments should abolish regulations that impede the entry of new firms or restrict competition, and ensure that all regulations are justified by such criteria as safety, environmental protection, or prudential supervision of financial institutions.
10. Property rights	The legal system should provide secure property rights without excessive costs, and make these available to the informal sector.

Sources: Williamson (1990; 1993).

the drama of the decade that followed were the technocrats and political leaders in the region itself.[3]

These winds of change were reflected not just in Williamson's piece but in other writings of the time, urging export-orientation, increased savings along with efficient investment, and a simplification and streamlining of a hitherto all-too-present role of government (e.g. Balassa et al. 1986). Even ECLAC—still viewed as the intellectual home of a more state-led approach to development—supplemented the shift away from inward orientation (Bianchi, Devlin, and Ramos 1987).

The Washington Consensus was a Latin American version of what had in fact become a worldwide consensus by the 1990s. It had in common with the international version the conviction that economic prosperity could only be obtained by *harnessing the power of markets*. This was associated with a view of government interventionism as a fountainhead of distortions that represses creativity and causes resources to be misallocated. The new paradigm called for allowing the free play of market forces to coordinate through price signals myriads of decentralized decisions of firms and individuals, thus enabling efficient resource allocation and fostering creative entrepreneurship.[4] But there were two other key features in the Latin version of the new paradigm that were captured in the Washington Consensus. The first was the *quest for macroeconomic stabilization*; the second a *marked shift towards an outward oriented growth strategy*. The shift to sound macro management was understood as a precondition for market-based development. The shift to an outwardly orientated growth strategy was propelled by the exhaustion of import substitution and the success in East Asia of export-led growth.

A careful review of Table 4.1 shows clearly that Williamson's actual formulation of the Consensus emphasized the technical dimensions of economic policy, and is measured and balanced in its overall prescriptions. Its Latin American flavor comes through policy prescriptions geared to addressing Latin-specific maladies: macroeconomic stabilization (e.g. fiscal discipline to avoid high inflation, tax reform to broaden the tax base, and positive real interest rates to overcome financial repression) and outward orientation (e.g. the elimination of import quotas and low and uniform import tariffs and a competitive exchange rate to induce non-traditional export growth; and the removal of barriers to FDI). The pro-market agenda was embodied in policies aimed at: removing the entrepreneurial function of the state (e.g. privatization of state enterprises); freeing and enabling markets (via deregulation, the strengthening of property rights, moderate marginal tax rates, low and uniform import tariffs, and a level playing field for foreign and domestic firms); and complementing markets (via the reorientation of public expenditures to primary education, health and infrastructure, both for growth and to improve the distribution of income).

In contrast to the popular perception, Williamson's Decalogue is a far cry from market fundamentalism. He does not even mention the liberalization of the (non-FDI)

---

[3] The role of the international financial institutions, which pushed for the reforms, often conditioning their loans on reform progress, remains a matter of debate. Reforms would not have been implemented only in response to outside pressure—but the pressure was probably not irrelevant to their timing and depth, and in some cases to the backlash that they created.

[4] Official World Bank and Inter-American Development Bank (IDB) documents that appeared during the 1980s heralded the coming of this new age for development thinking, signaling that the view had left academic circles and was being mainstreamed into practical policy. See also Edwards (1995).

capital account—which became increasingly controversial in the policy debate as the 1990s unfolded. On the liberalization of domestic financial markets, moreover, Williamson is restrained, calling only for gradually allowing interest rates to be market determined. Similarly, he steers away from the polar choices in exchange rate policy—a hard peg or a fully free floating rate—which are arguably most consistent with the unfettered play of market forces. Instead, he advocates keeping a "competitive exchange rate" which in practice requires discretional intervention by the Central Bank.

Williamson's formulation is also a far cry from a radical view in favor of a minimalist state that is commonly attributed to the Consensus. There is no supply-side economics calling for a reduction in tax burdens or a major shrinking of the size of the state. To be sure, the privatization of state enterprises is a central policy in Williamson's Decalogue, but it is not justified as a means to reduce the size of the state but to achieve economic efficiency and *reorient* government spending in favor of health, education, and infrastructure, much of this in order for the state to play a greater redistributive role. In this respect, Williamson's article subsumed some of the equity considerations that had appeared, for instance, in UNICEF's (1987) report on *Adjustment with a Human Face*.

Later on, Williamson (2000) characterized his ten policy items as summarizing the "lowest common denominator of policy advice being addressed by the Washington-based institutions to Latin American countries as of 1989." But this narrow characterization was a late and unsuccessful effort to keep the Washington Consensus term from being dragged into an excessively ideological realm. By then it was already seen as a synonym of market fundamentalism and neo-liberalism. The induction of the appealing "Washington Consensus" term into the ideological sphere is now a fact of history. And this helps explain why such renowned economists as Nobel Prize winner Joseph Stiglitz criticize the Consensus sharply even as they warn about the dangers of unrestrained financial liberalization and recommend measured trade liberalization, along the same lines of Williamson's initial formulation. It is therefore more appropriate to characterize the Consensus—as is done in this chapter—as an expression of a broader change in economic development policy, a paradigmatic shift in favor of macroeconomic stabilization and market-based development.

4.3 CONSENSUS-STYLE REFORMS: IMPLEMENTATION

During the 1990s, most Latin American countries embraced Consensus-style reforms, with strong support from international institutions, particularly in the context of IMF stabilization programs and policy-based lending programs of multilateral development banks. While the record is mixed and there was significant variation across countries, the vigor of reform implementation in the region was higher than at any time in memory. Lora (2001) detects a "great wave" of Consensus-style structural reforms during the 1990s, with particular intensity and concentration in the first half of the 1990s (Figure 4.1). His structural reform index—which is measured on a scale from 0 to 1 and combines policy

actions in the areas of trade, foreign exchange, taxation, financial liberalization, privatization, labor, and pensions—rose steeply from about 0.4 in 1989 to almost 0.6 in 1995. As
the structural reform process lost momentum in the region since 2000, it is fair to say that
the 1990s constituted the "glorious years" of the Washington Consensus.

The 1990s saw copious policy action with respect to macroeconomic stabilization. In
that decade Latin America finally conquered inflation—bringing it down from hyperinflation or chronically high levels to single digit rates in most countries (Figure 4.2).
Behind this achievement were important reforms to central banking that virtually eliminated the monetary financing of fiscal deficits. While progress on the fiscal front was
less impressive than in the monetary area, things generally moved in the direction of
greater viability, a process that was aided in several countries (such as Argentina, Costa
Rica, Dominican Republic, Ecuador, Mexico, Peru, and Venezuela) by sovereign debt
reduction agreements reached with external creditors under the Brady Initiative. The
average public-sector deficit in the region declined from minus 2.4% of GDP in 1980–9
to almost zero during the mid-1990s, while public sector external debt fell on average
from 60% to 40% of GDP during the 1990s, even if the total (external and internal) public debt did not decrease much (Figure 4.3).

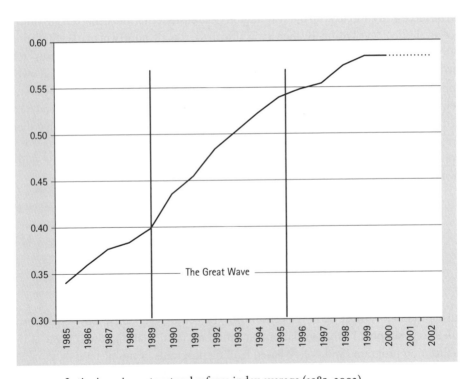

FIGURE 4.1 Latin American structural reform index average (1985–2002)

Source: Lora (2001).

Note: The advance of the reforms is measured as the margin for reform existing in 1985 that has been utilized in
subsequent years. It includes measures of trade, finance, tax, and privatization policies.

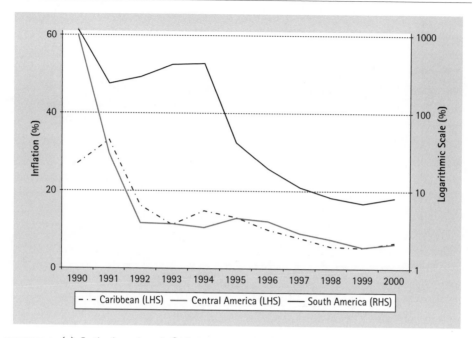

FIGURE 4.2(a) Latin American inflation, 1990–2000

Source: World Economic Outlook and International Financial Statistics, IMF.

Note: Weighted regional averages.

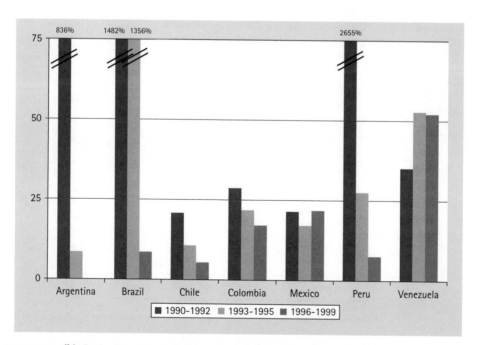

FIGURE 4.2(b) Latin American inflation, selected countries, 1990–2000 (%)

Source: World Economic Outlook and International Financial Statistics, IMF.

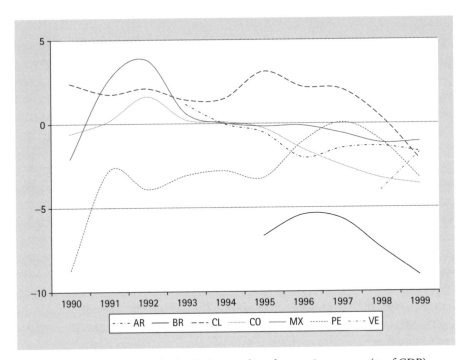

FIGURE 4.3(a) Latin American budget balance, selected countries, 1990–9 (% of GDP)

Source: Economist Intelligence Unit.

Note: Central government budget.

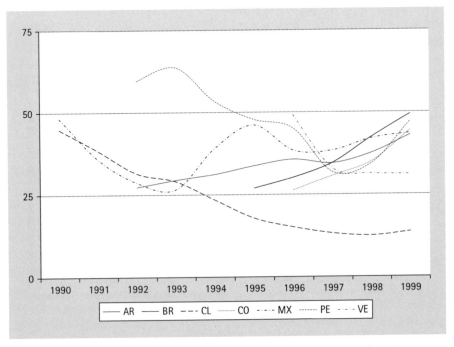

FIGURE 4.3(b) Latin American public debt, selected countries, 1990–9 (% of GDP)

Source: Economist Intelligence Unit.

Note: Central government debt.

Considering specific components of structural reform, action was clearly most intense in the area of liberalization, both in trade and finance. With respect to trade, the 1990s saw a confirmation of a liberalization trend that had started in the mid-1980s, involving mainly the removal of import quotas and the reduction of average import tariffs. The average tariff rate for the region, which had fallen from nearly 50% in the early 1980s to around 33% in 1990, declined further during the 1990s to around 10% by 1999. The 1990s added to this trend a new feature—a significant reduction in the variance of import tariffs to only one fourth by the end of the 1990s of what it was at the beginning of the decade (Lora 2001).

But it was arguably in finance where—departing from Williamson's cautious formulation—Latin America's liberalization-oriented reforms were most aggressively implemented. While the region had lagged considerably behind the global wave of financial liberalization of the 1980s, it embraced it with vengeance during the 1990s. The financial liberalization index developed by Kaminsky and Schmukler (2003) shows that it took only the first half of the 1990s for the region to bring the relatively closed and repressed financial systems to a level of liberalization comparable to that of developed countries (Figure 4.4). Financial liberalization was carried out on the domestic and external fronts. Direct credit controls were abandoned and interest rates deregulated. Restrictions on foreign investment were lifted, and most other controls on foreign exchange and capital account transactions were dismantled. Foreign banks were allowed and encouraged to establish local presences.

Liberalization on the external front may have been attractive for many countries—despite its potential effects on exchange rates and financial systems—because of the region's low domestic savings. Private domestic savings were low (partly because the wealthy minority tended to save and invest abroad, including in their children's education, and the poor majority saved little) while public savings were constrained by high public debt service (see Figure 4.5, comparing Latin American and East Asian savings). Perhaps this is why Williamson included taxing "flight capital" as a priority in the medium term. The reliance on foreign capital inflows was in turn associated with constant appreciation pressures on the exchange rates, which undermined competitiveness in non-commodity exports. Again the comparison with East Asia is apt.

While it is well known that the reform and modernization of the regulatory and supervisory arrangements for financial markets lagged their liberalization (which, as noted below, constituted a source of systemic vulnerability), the 1990s did see important, if insufficient, improvements in legal, regulatory, trading, and informational infrastructures that are germane to financial markets. These included the revamping of Central Bank charters as well as the upgrading of banking and capital markets legislation (Figure 4.6).

The 1990s also registered a wave of privatizations (of public banks and enterprises) and significant, albeit one-dimensional, pension reforms. More than 800 public enterprises were privatized between 1988 and 1997 (Birdsall, de la Torre, and Menezes 2008) and the cumulative amount of funds raised through privatizations during the 1990s was

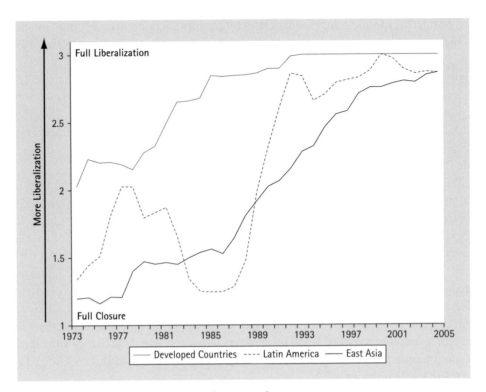

FIGURE 4.4 International financial liberalization index, 1973–2002

Source: De la Torre and Schmukler (2007).

Note: The liberalization index is calculated as the simple average of three indices (liberalization of the capital account, domestic financial sector, and stock market) that range between 1 and 3, where 1 means no liberalization and 3 means full liberalization. The regional averages are simple country averages.

in the order of US$200 billion (de la Torre and Schmukler 2007).[5] In pensions, Chile's pioneering reform of 1981 had a major demonstration effect throughout Latin America. Similar systems were adopted during the 1990s by Argentina, Bolivia, Colombia, Costa Rica, El Salvador, Mexico, Peru, and Uruguay. These reforms consisted basically of a shift away from government-administered, pay-as-you-go, defined-benefit pension systems for private sector employees towards systems that rely mainly on a so-called "second pillar" of mandatory, defined, and privately administered pension funds. The market orientation herein is clear, as these pension reforms shifted from the state to the capital markets the dominant role in administering retirement-related savings.

Structural reform intensity was more modest in tax reform and nonexistent in labor markets (Figure 4.7). Lora's index of labor market reforms barely rose during the 1990s. Lastly, Williamson's inclusion of "public expenditure reprioritization" has not been

---

[5] The actual motives for privatization ranged from the search for efficiency gains to the need for fiscal revenues to pure rent-seeking.

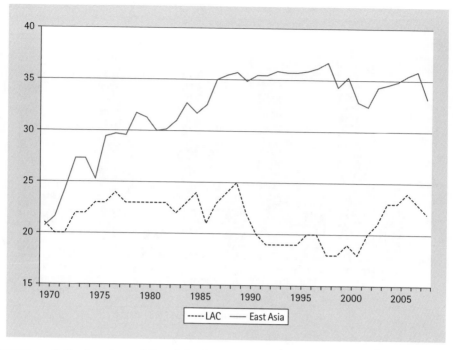

FIGURE 4.5 Latin America and East Asia: Gross Domestic Savings, 1970–2008 (% of GDP)

Source: World Development Indicators, World Bank.

Note: East Asia is the un-weighted average of Hong Kong, Singapore, South Korea, Taiwan, Indonesia, Thailand, and Malaysia, while LAC covers the whole Latin American and Caribbean region.

viewed by students of the Consensus as a structural reform and is not included in Lora 95 or other indices—which is itself a commentary on the tendency even in scholarly work to overlook aspects of the Consensus that are not associated with market liberalization.[6]

4.4 CONSENSUS-STYLE REFORMS: OUTCOMES

While Latin America championed the Washington Consensus in the 1990s, the observed outcomes were disheartening and puzzling. Disheartening because of what was arguably too meager a payoff relative to the intensity of the reform effort. Puzzling because of the lack of clarity on what went wrong. This section discusses the disheartening side of the equation. The next addresses the puzzles.

---

[6] Other important reforms were implemented during the 1990s which arguably lie outside the scope of the Consensus. Several countries e.g. adopted new constitutions and moved decidedly towards fiscal decentralization.

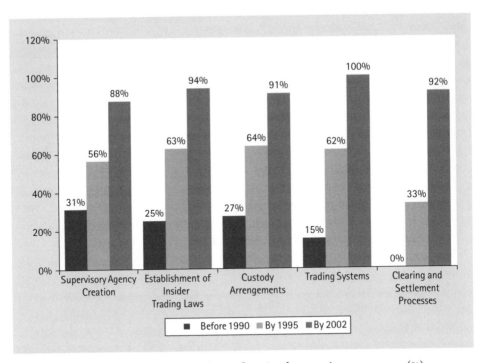

FIGURE 4.6 Latin American capital markets reform implementation, 1990–2002 (%)

Source: de la Torre and Schmukler (2007).

As noted, inflation reduction and macroeconomic stabilization were an undeniable achievement of the 1990s. In addition, the optimism inspired by the convergence of views around Consensus-style reforms contributed to a major surge in net private capital inflows to the region. These inflows rose from US$14 billion in 1990 to US$86 billion in 1997, before declining to US$47 billion in 1999 in the wake of the Asian financial crisis (Birdsall et al. 2008). Whether these inflows led to higher investment is a different question, and it seems that in general they did not (Ffrench-Davis and Reisen 1998).

But when the attention is focused on the outcome variables that really matter for economic development—per capita income, poverty, and income distribution—the Washington Consensus yielded little progress during the 1990s relative to expectations in most of Latin America, with the notable exception of Chile (and even there excluding income distribution).[7]

---

[7] The Dominican Republic was another notable exception during the 1990s, especially in terms of robust economic growth.

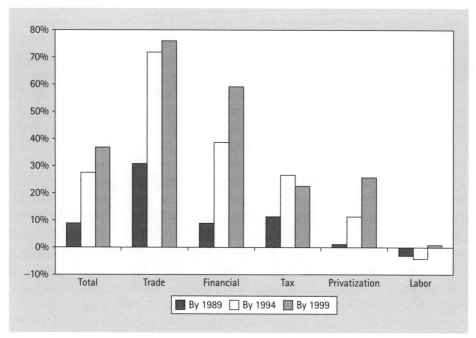

FIGURE 4.7 Latin American advance of reforms, 1989–99

Source: Lora (2001).

Note: The advance of the reforms is measured as the margin for reform existing in 1985 that has been utilized by 1989, 1995, and 1999.

4.4.1 Factual overview

Consider first GDP growth and per capita income. Regional growth did recover modestly—from 1.1% per year in 1980–90 to 3.6% in 1990–7 and 3% average for the 1990s as a whole. But this hardly involved productivity growth and was not sufficient to reduce the convergence gap in per capita income between the region and rich economies.[8] Instead, the ratio of per capita income in Latin America relative to the United States, which had already fallen precipitously during the "lost decade" of the 1980s, continued to decline, albeit marginally, throughout the 1990s (Figure 4.8). This stands in sharp contrast with the experience of the East Asian "Tigers," whose per capita income gap with the US narrowed significantly, while countries pursued

---

[8] On the generally low total factor productivity growth in Latin America during the 1990s, see Loayza, Fajnzylber, and Calderón (2005). While overall productivity in the region was relatively low, except in the case of Chile, major productivity gains were realized in many countries at the sector level, especially in agriculture.

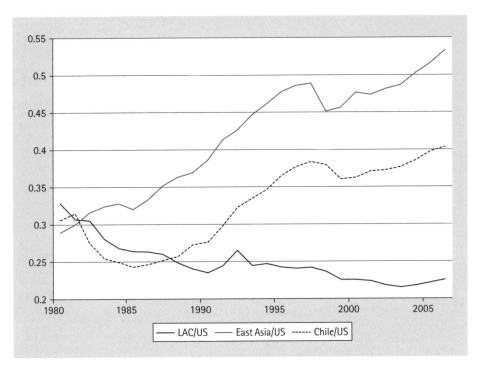

FIGURE 4.8 Latin America and East Asia: relative GDP per capita, 1980–2006 (ratio to US GDP per capita, in constant 1990 US$)

Source: Historical Statistics of the World Economy.

Note: GDP PPP figures, LAC is the weighted average of Argentina, Brazil, Chile, Colombia, Mexico, Peru, Uruguay, and Venezuela.

policies that were not framed in the Washington Consensus spirit of liberalization, privatization, and macroeconomic stabilization. The exception in the disappointing growth picture for Latin America was Chile, which became the poster child of the Washington Consensus policy agenda. Real GDP growth in Chile rose to an average of 6.4% per annum during the 1990s from 4.5% per annum in the 1980s, so that the ratio of Chilean to US per capita income increased significantly over the decade (Figure 4.8).

Outcomes in the social arena were even more disappointing. Consider first poverty. The expectation was that the pickup of growth in the 1990s, modest though it was, would lead to a proportional reduction in poverty. That expectation was not realized. While the region's per capita GDP increased by a cumulative 12% from 1990 to 2000, the regional poverty rate (measured at $4 a day in PPP terms), according to World Bank estimates, did not decrease. Moreover, the absolute number of poor in the region (calculated on the basis of countries' own definitions of the poverty line) remained roughly constant, at around 200 million people throughout the 1990s. Only in Chile did the poverty rate fall sharply, from 38.6% in 1990 to 20.2% in 2000 (see Chapter 28 by Grysnpan and López-Calva in this Handbook).[9]

The distributional outcome was equally frustrating as income inequality remained stubbornly high throughout the 1990s. The non-weighted average Gini coefficient for income distribution in the region increased somewhat, from 50.5 in the early 1990s to 51.4 in 2000, while the weighted average remained virtually unchanged (World Bank 2004). Even Chile's Gini coefficient was stuck at around 55 during the 1990s. The fact is that income inequality is stickier than poverty everywhere and has remained stubbornly high in the region for decades (declining later on for the first time, and only modestly, in several countries during the 2002–7 period of faster growth—see Chapter 27 by Gasparini and Lustig in this Handbook).

From a strictly technical point of view, the limited progress on social outcomes might have been foreseen. The Washington Consensus reforms were mainly meant to liberalize and stabilize the economies and allow for growth, not reduce inequality. But to the extent that the 1990s became in the public consciousness the decade of the Washington Consensus reforms, and those reforms became synonymous with expectations of social as well as growth outcomes, expectations were disappointed.

4.4.2 Counterfactual overview

There is then little doubt that outcomes during the 1990s in terms of growth, poverty, and inequality were disheartening relative to the expectations of the reformers. But would the assessment change if the focus is placed on reform impacts not relative to expectations but compared to the counterfactual—i.e. what would have happened in the absence of Consensus-style policies? This line of inquiry—evidently of greater interest to academics than to the average citizen—has given rise to copious empirical research. When all is said and done, the preponderance of the econometric evidence arising from this research suggests that Latin America would have been worse off without the reforms. Per capita income and output in the 1990s would have been lower and poverty deeper. Moreover, the relatively strong performance of Latin America during the global crisis of 2008–9 can be attributed to a significant extent to improvements in macroeconomic and financial fundamentals resulting in part from the reforms of the 1990s and early 2000s.

The results from econometric studies have to be taken with a large grain of salt, of course, considering the numerous and thorny technical complications with the associated empirical tests.[10] While they differ in terms of evidence and methodology and their

---

[9] The situation in the unemployment front was varied, but job creation was generally weak during the 1990s and informality tended to increase (Stallings and Peres 2000).

[10] These include: small sample sizes; the potential presence of global trends that may affect both reforms and outcomes; difficulties in quantitatively isolating impacts; complications in establishing a causal relationships; problems with adequately measuring reforms, their degree of implementation and, even more, their quality; and the dependency of results on time periods under investigation.

results are difficult to compare, a general pattern emerges: earlier research that focuses on the first half of the 1990s tends to produce results that are more favorable to Consensus-style reforms than later research focusing on the second half of the 1990s.

Lora and Barrera (1997), comparing 1987–9 with 1993–5, find that structural reforms and macro stabilization policies spurred growth by 2.2 percentage points relative to the growth rate that would have been obtained in the absence of reforms. Easterly, Loayza, and Montiel (1997) find that reforms allowed the region to return to a 2% per capita growth rate from 1991 to 1993, a rate that was higher than predicted by their model. Similarly, Fernández-Arias and Montiel (1997) find a contribution of stabilization and structural reforms to long-run growth of 1.84 percentage points, and argue that Latin American growth during the 1990s was greater than otherwise predicted.

While the generation of early research converges on the view that reforms boosted growth in the first half of the 1990s by about 2 percentage points,[11] later studies have a much less favorable assessment. Lora and Panizza (2002) compare 1985–7 with 1997–9 and find that the reforms lifted growth in the latter period by only 0.6 percentage points. They conclude that the beneficial impact of reforms decreased as the 1990s unfolded and that their effects were largely transitory, raising the level of income but not the rate of growth. A series of studies spearheaded by ECLAC also yielded very modest results. Escaith and Morley (2001) find a minimal and non-robust effect of the reforms taken as a whole. Stallings and Peres (2000) conclude that a 10% increase in the overall reform index boosted growth by a meager 0.2 of a percentage point, and that the effects of individual reforms were ambiguous. While import liberalization, privatization and capital account opening had a positive effect, the same is not true for the tax or the financial reform indexes. In a review article, Ocampo (2004) notes that the positive post-reform performance in the first part of the 1990s stands in contrast with the low growth of the "lost-half decade" of 1998–2002, emphasizing that growth during the decade was sluggish and volatile.

Studies on the effects of Consensus-style reforms on poverty and inequality, independent of their growth effects, are rarer, with the notable exceptions of Morley (2000) and Behrman, Birdsall, and Székely (2007). The latter conclude that financial sector liberalization was associated with an increase in income inequality, though with diminishing effects over time. Other reforms, including privatization, seem to have reduced inequality. The privatization of water and other services, in particular, actually improved access for the poor and reduced the prices they paid (see studies in Nellis and Birdsall 2005). But the overall effect of the reforms was at best neutral and at worst harmful in terms of income inequality outcomes.

---

[11] This result was confirmed later on by Loayza et al. (2005), who, comparing 1986–90 with 1996–9, estimated that structural reforms and accompanying macro stabilization policies had a 1.9 percentage point average impact on growth for Latin America for the decade as a whole—but this is an exception among the studies that appeared after 1997.

4.4.3 Bottom line

The conclusion is inescapable that, with the exception of Chile, outcomes during the 1990s generally fell significantly short of the reformers' expectations. Even if inequality is not considered—on the grounds that, barring a revolution, it is likely to take generations to significantly decline—the growth and poverty reduction outcomes were disheartening when compared to the intensity of the reform effort. There is reasonable support for the technical counterfactual argument that growth in the first part of the 1990s would have been lower and poverty higher in the absence of Consensus-type reforms. But even this view loses force when: the years beyond 1997 are taken into account, individual reforms are examined separately, and growth volatility (not just the growth rate) is also considered. Moreover, the counterfactual reasoning—that without reforms things would have been worse—provides little consolation to the region's many poor and chronically unemployed citizens.

The sense of disenchantment with the Washington Consensus deepened dramatically in the late 1990s and early 2000s when the region was hit by a wave of financial turbulence that pushed several countries into crippling twin (banking and currency) crises, including Ecuador (1999–2000), Argentina (2001–2), Uruguay (2002), and the Dominican Republic (2003). Not surprisingly, during 2001–3 per capita income growth in the region was negative even as other regions in the world enjoyed positive growth.

As the region entered the new millennium, not only did the Washington Consensus lose support but it also generated vibrant opposition in many quarters. With societies disappointed by the outcomes, policymakers found little or no ground to mobilize the political coalitions needed for additional doses of Consensus-style reforms.[12] Not surprisingly, the region entered into a period of structural reform fatigue, and economic reforms stalled in most Latin American countries after 1997 (Lora 2001).

So, what went wrong with the Washington Consensus? To this puzzle we turn next.

4.5 WHAT WENT WRONG?

Setting ideological differences aside, there is a wide range of economic views on what went wrong with the Washington Consensus-inspired program. The same evidence examined from different perspectives has led to different diagnoses, which we classify into three categories:

---

[12] Public opinion polls (*Latinobarómetro*) of early 2000 found Latin Americans resentful of market-oriented reforms, especially privatization, and tired of high unemployment and stagnant wages.

- There was nothing wrong with the Consensus reform program itself. The problem was the faulty implementation of the reforms (including due to political economy constraints) combined with impatience regarding their effects.
- The Consensus reform program was fundamentally flawed. Variant one: the Consensus failed to consider sequencing issues and threshold effects. Variant two: the Consensus was based on a simplistic and ultimately wrong understanding of the linkages between policy reform and economic outcomes.
- The Consensus reform program was incomplete. It was based on too narrow a view of what matters for economic development and left out essential areas for reform.

Each of these contrasting views captures a relevant aspect of the debate, bringing out points that are mostly complementary but sometimes fundamentally at odds with each other. The reader should not to make too much of this taxonomy of views, as there is no presumption that it represents a complete set or that it is necessarily superior to potential alternative taxonomies. It should be seen essentially as a framework constructed from hindsight to help organize and discuss in an orderly fashion the salient aspects of, and discrepancies in, the assessment of the Washington Consensus.

4.5.1 Faulty implementation and impatience

According to this view, the Washington Consensus was fundamentally right in its principles, content, and overall design. The set of Consensus-inspired reforms is fairly complete and reflects international "best practices" that are, by and large, of general applicability across developing countries and for a broad range of development stages. Moreover, as noted earlier, econometric studies suggest that Consensus-style reforms were part of the solution and not the problem.

Supporters of this view argue that the shortfall in the outcomes relative to expectations was not due to flaws with the Consensus reform package itself but to the deficient manner in which it was implemented (IMF 2005). Reforms were unevenly implemented across countries, hence the uneven outcomes. Reform reversals were not infrequent. Where reforms were implemented more deeply and consistently (i.e. Chile), they were associated with impressive growth and poverty reduction outcomes. In the majority of countries, however, reforms, even when initiated, were insufficiently implemented. In many cases, for instance, laws were passed but regulatory changes, institutional adaptations, and capacity-building did not follow, and/or were not adequately enforced. In other cases, key reforms were not even initiated (as in the labor area).

Moreover—this view contends—reformers were too impatient, unreasonably expecting results to materialize sooner than warranted. While the expectation of a rapid payoff was justified with respect to some types of first-generation reforms—especially in the macroeconomic stabilization arena—it was unrealistic for the more complex structural reforms that typically require long implementation and gestation periods. Looking back from 2010, a case can be made that the payoff of sustained reform did come for Latin

America in this millennium, when the global crisis of 2008–9 hit. Countries that had persevered in implementing sound macroeconomic policies over the past fifteen years and that reacted with appropriate reforms to the crises of the late 1990s—e.g. by introducing greater exchange rate flexibility, developing local-currency debt markets, reducing currency mismatches, and modernizing financial regulation and supervision—came out of the recent global crisis without systemic damage. Those reforms helped reduce systemic vulnerability, prepared the countries to better face financial globalization, and enabled them to undertake countercyclical policies to cushion the effects of the external shock and avoid a systemic crises at home (Rojas-Suarez 2009; World Bank 2010). Their experience illustrates that patience and sustained implementation of Consensus-style reforms pays off in the long run.

This view does not ignore the costs of reforms, including those arising from transitory instability. But it notes that this is as it should be, since teething pains and even crises are part of the market-oriented development process. The opening and competition that result from liberalization may increase instability in the short run but will also help expose weaknesses and foster a cleansing process that ultimately strengthens defenses and stimulates further reform. Over time, through pain and success, learning takes place and incentives are eventually set right, yielding durable results. Chile's strengths owe in no small part to a constructive reaction to the painful crises of the late 1970s and early 1980s.

The message that naturally arises from this view is the need to persevere. Reform must be sustained and consistent. The emphasis going forward should thus be on overcoming political resistance to reform implementation. Politics mattered much more than reformers anticipated, and thus more attention should be directed to the political economy of reform implementation. This is an essential complement to the technical soundness of reform design. And along the path to economic development a premium should be placed on letting market discipline work, recognizing that it sets in motion a process that involves short-term pain and long-term gain—a process of creative destruction.

4.5.2 Fundamental flaws

This view, in sharp contrast with the previous one, finds the Washington Consensus agenda to be seriously wrong in some fundamental sense. It involves two variants that are very different in nature.

The first variant is the sequencing critique. The original formulation of the Consensus was mostly silent on sequencing. It left open the question whether the outcomes would be similar, independently of whether reforms were implemented simultaneously or separately and, in the latter case, regardless of the order of implementation. A key focus—though by no means the only one—of this critique is on premature financial market liberalization—the deregulation of the domestic financial system and opening of the external capital account ahead of adequate regulatory strengthening. A wrong sequencing of reforms in this field can turn the normal pains of growing up into unnecessary suffering, as financial crises can rapidly wipe out gains achieved over several decades.[13]

Sequencing arguments can also involve a reference to threshold effects—i.e. the notion that positive outcomes cannot be attained unless a minimum degree of implementation of an appropriate combination of complementary reforms is achieved. This perspective leads to the recommendation that reforms should be ordered so as to ensure, for example, that certain preconditions are put in place first to enhance the likelihood of success of subsequent reforms. Thus, the best-designed fiscal rules would not work well in the absence of institutional preconditions that prevent, say, populist governments from arbitrarily breaking rules and contracts. This perspective also leads to the warning that there may be little or no gain (and maybe even significant losses) if a critical mass of complementary reforms is not implemented in a coordinated fashion (Rojas-Suarez 2009).

The sequencing critique could also be applied to other reforms. Trade liberalization in the absence of a safety net can undermine poverty reduction, and privatization short of an adequate regulatory framework may lead to monopoly pricing. In some cases, the resulting political backlash can short-circuit the reform process itself. Initial uncorrected flaws may compromise implementation. In that sense, the "right" sequence is easier to define on paper than in the real world, where reformers usually had to make do with second-best approaches in the face of political constraints.

Consider now the second variant of the view that the Washington Consensus incurred fundamental flaws. It contends that the main error was the Consensus's apparent assumption that a one-to-one mapping exists always and everywhere between reforms and economic outcomes. The reality is, however, much more complex and elusive. As noted by Hausmann, Rodrik, and Velasco (2008), reforms that "work wonders in some places may have weak, unintended, or negative effects in others." The empirical evidence that specific reform packages have predictable, robust, and systematic effects on national growth rates is quite weak (Rodrik 2005a). Moreover, much of the variance that explains the difference in countries' growth rates is random, which implies that imitating the successful reform experiences of other countries is not in general a good strategy for a given country (Easterly et al. 1993). In all, contrary to the implicit understanding of the Washington Consensus as generally applicable, effective reform agendas have to be carefully tailored to individual country circumstances, in both their design and their implementation sequence. The expectation that certain reforms would promise certain good outcomes relatively automatically was simply wrong.

---

[13] In the second half of the 1990s, emphasis was placed on the capacity of weak banking systems to operate prudently in freer financial markets. Some analysts counsel emerging economies to roll back capital account opening and "throw sand in the wheels," including through Chilean-style disincentives on short-term inflows. Some even suggest that capital flows should be managed on a permanent basis. Others advocate delaying liberalization until markets for domestic currency denominated debt are developed.

It does not necessarily follow from this variant that anything goes when it comes to growth determinants and the design of reform packages. A constructive but nuanced way forward is feasible under this view, as illustrated in Dani Rodrik's (2005b) "Growth Strategies" chapter in the *Handbook of Economic Growth*. While specific reform packages must be tailor-made, good economics highlights the crucial relevance of growth "foundations" or "first principles," notably the role of technological innovation and institutions such as property rights, sound money, fiscal viability, and contestable markets (Growth Commission 2008; Rojas-Suarez 2009). Although the mapping of first principles to specific reform packages is elusive and country-specific, the former can be adequately served by diverse policy packages.

Moreover, growth strategies must be informed by the critical distinction between *igniting* and *sustaining* economic growth (Hausmann, Pritchett, and Rodrik 2005). Igniting growth in a particular country typically requires a few (often unconventional) reforms that need not unduly tax the country's limited institutional capacity. But the exact composition of these few reforms and how they can successfully be combined with "first principles" cannot be predicted easily—it varies from country to country. Sustaining growth is a different matter—it requires the cumulative building of functional institutions to maintain productive dynamism and endow the economy with resilience to shocks over the long term. A sensible growth strategy would search for the tailor-made agenda of few reforms that can ignite a growth process. Once ignited, growth itself can help align incentives in the polity in favor of reforms that strengthen the growth foundations, thus setting in motion a virtuous circle that sustains growth over the long haul.

Putting together growth-oriented reform programs that are adequately adapted to a given country is, then, a much more difficult and complex task than the Washington Consensus led people to believe. But it is not an impossible task. To avoid getting things wrong, there is no substitute for deep country knowledge and experience. To use an analogy often mentioned by the late Rudy Dornbusch, good reformers are like good "country doctors" than can develop "good diagnoses" and "suitable cures" for individual patients whom they know well. Thus, adequately designed and appropriately implemented reforms are more likely to be developed by well-trained, practically minded, and experienced economists that collectively have not only a good grasp of international reform practices but also experience in and strong knowledge of the circumstances of the country in question. These packages will, by definition, stay away from mechanical application of "best practices" and from unprioritized "laundry list" reform agendas. They will also stay away from the pessimistic belief that nothing can be done where institutions are weak. And much help can be gotten in this process from a finer "growth diagnostics" method, one that focuses on the binding constraints to growth, rather than on the distance to "best practices," along the lines of the method proposed by Hausmann, Rodrik, and Velasco (2008). While not a silver bullet, this method can greatly complement the task of reform prioritization and design (see also IDB 2009).

4.5.3 Incomplete agenda

This third view agrees with the first one in stating that the Consensus reform program was not wrong in what it included. But it differs from it in claiming that the Consensus was patently incomplete—that it did not include all the relevant reforms needed to achieve sustainable and equitable growth. The Consensus simply had too narrow an understanding of what matters for growth and development.

Trying to assemble a comprehensive list of important reform areas left out by the Consensus is a rather futile exercise, for the components chosen for inclusion are not independent of the perspective adopted and the preferences of the researcher—and one that in any case lies beyond the scope of this chapter. In what follows, therefore, we simply illustrate this view using as guidance key flagship reports published by multilateral development agencies (World Bank, IDB, ECLAC, and CAF) in the new millennium. Using headline publications from some of the institutions that supported (and at times actively championed) the Consensus during the 1990s helps highlight the growing acceptance of this third view.

Among the many reform areas left out by the Washington Consensus are: (a) volatility; (b) institutions; (c) knowledge and technological innovation; and (d) equity.[14] What these areas have in common is the presence of significant market failures (due to externalities, coordination problems, and imperfect information) which markets themselves cannot repair and that thus require active policy. They were not seen as part of a Consensus-style reform agenda basically because the Consensus relied on well-functioning markets to solve the relevant development challenges, and viewed any state interference in the economy with suspicion.[15]

Consider first *volatility*. By focusing on the first moment—the expected value of reform effects—Washington Consensus-style policies ignored the crucial relevance of the second moment: the volatility of such effects. The fact is that volatility has an independent, first-order impact on economic development. This argument was forcibly put forward in the 1995 annual report of the IDB on *Overcoming Volatility* (IDB 1995). It discussed Latin America's proneness to volatility, driven by a high incidence of external shocks whose effects are magnified by shallow financial markets and inconsistent macro policies. Volatility is estimated to have reduced the region's historical growth rate by one percentage point, with particularly strong negative impacts on investment in infrastructure and human capital and especially detrimental impacts on poverty and inequality. To overcome volatility, reforms need to put a premium on export diversification, financial market deepening, and stable macroeconomic—particularly fiscal—policy.

---

[14] A key area that was completely ignored by the Washington Consensus is environmental sustainability, particularly climate change. This topic is not developed here, as it is as much about global as domestic policy. See, however, Stern (2008) and World Bank (2009).

[15] Many successful reformers, like Chile, also implemented important reforms in these other areas, thus supplementing the Washington Consensus.

Subsequent reports of the World Bank and ECLAC drove home similar arguments and worries. The 2000 flagship publication of the Latin America region of the World Bank, *Securing our Future in the Global Economy*, raised key policy issues from the macroeconomic, social, financial, labor, and poverty dimensions. At ECLAC, Ffrench-Davis and Ocampo (2001) argued that financial liberalization brought with it the globalization of volatility and a new variety of crises, linked to shocks to the newly deregulated emerging capital markets. Indiscriminate opening of the capital account led to macroeconomic disequilibria, including exchange rate and asset price overshooting, which placed countries in a "financierist trap" of high vulnerability. To escape the trap, a relatively flexible exchange rate and comprehensive macroeconomic regulation is thus recommended.

Consider next *institutions*. The Consensus overlooked the institutional underpinnings of its proposed policies, with one key exception: establishing secure property rights which, in the spirit of De Soto (1989), should also be available to the informal sector. However, quoting Rodrik (2006), property rights "was the last item on the list and came almost as an afterthought." Williamson himself noted (see Birdsall et al. 2008) that property rights were added "mostly to get to a total of 10 items." In general, the Consensus was largely blind to institutions. It came at the end of the 1980s before what amounted to an institutional revolution in the development economics literature in the 1990s.

Multilateral agencies jumped onto the institutional bandwagon starting in the late 1990s, as the realization grew stronger that the efficiency of markets and durability of reform effects need appropriate institutional frameworks to avoid such problems as rent-seeking and policy reversals. With respect to Latin America, this was illustrated in the 1998 World Bank's regional flagship entitled *Beyond the Washington Consensus: Institutions Matter* as well as in the IDB's 1997 report *Latin America after a Decade of Reforms*. The former summarizes the evidence on the role of institutions in long-run economic development, makes a case in favor of the feasibility of institutional reform, and offers a policy-oriented analysis of institutional reform issues in the financial sector, education, judicial systems, and public administration. The latter develops an analytical framework and uses case studies to explain why policy reform processes that work in certain institutional environments may not work in others. The institutional literature also influenced the 2008 Growth Commission Report chaired by Michael Spence, which concludes that there can be no simple recipe for growth and sustainable development, implying that too much is country-specific to define any general policy consensus.

Consider now *knowledge and technological innovation*. If the Washington Consensus touched on this area, it did so indirectly—when it advocated the reorientation of public expenditure towards education and emphasized the need to remove barriers to FDI. The latter was intended not just to enhance competition but also to facilitate technological transfer. That the Consensus did not delve more into policies related to technological innovation is somewhat surprising. After all, technological progress is at the heart of market-based growth and has been regarded as the main driver of productivity growth in economic theory since the times of Robert Solow's papers in the 1950s and 1960s. The implicit assumption in Consensus-style reform agendas seems to have been that policies to promote export orientation and the opening to FDI would be sufficient to achieve the adoption and adaptation of new technologies as well as to eventually foster the capacity to innovate.

While the theme of knowledge and innovation was never absent from the academic literature, multilateral agencies sought to bring it squarely into Latin American development policy thinking during the early 2000s. The Latin American region of the World Bank devoted its 2002 flagship publication to the issues associated in connecting *Natural Resources to the Knowledge Economy* and its 2003 flagship to *Closing the Gap in Education and Technology*. These reports were later complemented by ECLAC's 2008 Report on *Structural Change and Productivity Growth*. This body of research argued that the region's growth has not lagged behind due to a natural-resource curse but rather due to a major shortfall in technological adoption and innovation. The regional deficiency in "national learning capacity" is not independent of its gap in the quality of its education (Figure 4.9), which along with entrepreneurship constitutes a key ingredient for innovation. A premium should then be placed on policies to diversify international trade and foreign direct investment flows, improve education (particularly secondary and tertiary), deepen the links between universities and the private sector, and foster the development of innovation networks.

Around the same time, the IDB and the Andean Development Corporation (CAF) focused on the role of knowledge and technology in growth from the perspective of

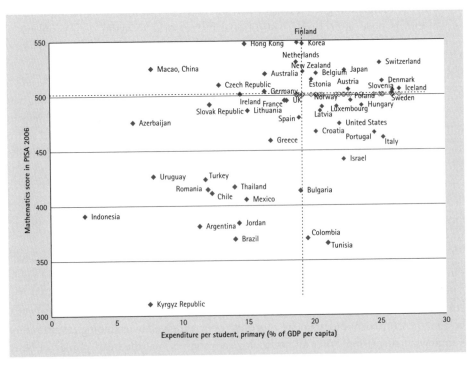

FIGURE 4.9 International education expenditure vs. PISA scores, 2006

Source: PISA and World Development Indicators.

Note: Public expenditure per student is the public current spending on education divided by the total number of students in the primary level.

competitiveness. They did so through their annual reports entitled, respectively, *Competitiveness* (IDB 2001) and *Competiveness and Growth* (Sachs and Vial 2002). To correct the low levels of factor accumulation and productivity in Latin America, policies should aim at alleviating credit constraints, modernizing labor markets, boosting human capital investment, easing infrastructure bottlenecks, and fostering the development of clusters and supply chains.

Consider finally *equity*, the social arena where, as noted, the disenchantment with the Washington Consensus was the greatest. Williamson himself later noted (see Birdsall et al. 2008) that the Consensus policies he compiled were oriented towards achieving efficiency, not equity, and that he "deliberately excluded from the list anything which was primarily redistributive [because he] felt that the Washington of the 1980s…was essentially contemptuous of equity concerns."

When it comes to economic development, equity considerations are not simply a helpful corollary, but an essential ingredient, especially in unequal Latin America. For one thing, equity is in itself as important a developmental objective as growth—not least considering that excessive inequality of outcomes and high inequality of opportunity constitute an insult to our basic sense of justice. To the extent that reform efforts' uneven outcomes reflect unequal opportunities—across racial or ethnic groups and between those born poor and those born rich—their sense of unfairness also undermines the legitimacy of those reforms. Moreover, by failing to more explicitly deal with equity, the Washington Consensus neglected what is in effect a key impediment to growth. High income inequality not only hinders the impact of growth on poverty reduction but can itself contribute to low growth, which in turn makes it difficult to reduce inequality. Institutions and policies in contexts with high poverty and top-heavy concentration of income may themselves be a source of growth-impairing inefficiency (Aghion, Caroli, and Garcia-Peñalosa 1999; Demirguc-Kunt and Levine 2009; Levy and Walton 2009). Under those conditions, for example, the interplay among political parties, business organizations, and powerful, large labor unions can result in rent-seeking and monopoly behavior that undermines the growth gains the reforms were meant to capture. And imperfect credit markets combined with unequal endowments (of financial and human capital) typical of Latin America are widely acknowledged as a constraint on growth, implying that inequality itself is worth addressing explicitly to minimize that perverse combination.

It was in this failure to include an explicit concern with equity that Birdsall et al. (2008) find the most notable shortcoming of Washington Consensus-inspired reform packages. The omission undermined the benefits of and enthusiasm for market-oriented reforms. These authors discuss win-win policies that would serve the interests of greater equity while enhancing growth directly and indirectly. They reaffirm the relevance of fiscal discipline and countercyclical macroeconomic and financial policies. But they also emphasize new areas for policy action, including the establishment of automatic social safety nets; improving schooling for the poor; making income taxes progressive in practice; building a more supportive environment for small businesses; protecting worker rights and labor mobility; launching a head-on attack on corruption and discrimination; repairing land markets and establishing consumer-driven public services.

The equity theme was also bought to the center stage of the development policy debate through official publications by multilateral agencies. ECLAC focused on this issue in *Productive Transformation with Equity* (1990) and *Equity, Development and Citizenship* (2000). In its 1998 annual report, *Facing up to Inequality in Latin America*, the IDB studied the resilience of the region's high inequality, attributing the gap mainly to wage differentials in a segmented labor market and underlying educational disparity. Inequality was also tackled in the World Bank's 2004 regional flagship *Inequality in Latin America*. The report emphasizes the deep historical roots of inequality and its multidimensionality, affecting not just income but also the distribution of education, health, water, sanitation, electricity, and telecommunication provision. It recommends using the redistributive power of the state through progressive taxation, basic service provision, and transfers. It also advocates policies aimed at broadening asset ownership by democratizing education, improving land distribution, investing in public infrastructure, and making the labor market truly inclusive.

4.6 CONCLUDING REMARKS

For all of its faults, the policies set out in Williamson's original Washington Consensus hold enduring messages. Countries that ignore them do so at their peril. If there is any consensus about the Consensus, it is especially with respect to sound macroeconomic policy, including not only fiscal discipline (still a challenge in most of the region) and transparent and steady monetary policy but also, arguably, flexible exchange rates with a small dose of management. On these the Consensus aptly reflected the direction taken since the late 1980s by most Latin policymakers, by then already deeply allergic to the region's periodic and destructive bouts of inflation. That this allergy was shared by citizens and voters virtually everywhere, and that the relevant macroeconomic stabilization policies could be relatively easily implemented by a small technically adept cadre, no doubt made it more likely that the macroeconomic discipline espoused in the Consensus would take hold in the polity (Naím 2000). However, much of the controversy has focused not on the merits of the policies themselves but on the role of the IMF and the World Bank in conditioning their lending to policy changes that not only included reasonable fixes to macro problems but also privatization, trade and capital market liberalization, and other structural policies, without due attention to the supportive institutional matrix and to an extent that in many countries was politically toxic.

While the Consensus is typically criticized for its dogmatic adherence to market fundamentalism, in fact the view that development must be market-based has also endured—not only in Latin America, the original home of the Consensus, but throughout the developing world (Birdsall 2011). The reliance on markets to foster development is in effect a New Consensus among emerging market and other developing countries, and it has survived well the crises of the second half of the 1990s and early 2000s as well as the global crisis of 2008–9, including in Africa (Radelet 2010). To be sure, warring parties have engaged over the past quarter-century in heated debates about the merits and shortcomings of the Consensus (defined variously as the original ten points, as market fundamentalism, neo-liberalism, or multiple variations of those). Yet, beyond the differences, the great majority of developing countries—across the ideological spectrum from China to Chile—in fact adhere to a market orientation and indeed to a quest for safe integration into global markets.

So, on the one hand, the love-and-hate affair with the 1989 Washington Consensus is probably over. On the other, the relationship with markets has resulted in many marriages. But if we are to see in this century a more complex challenge that will test any consensus, and one that was brutally highlighted by the subprime crisis turned global, it will be on the interactions between the market and the state, and on how to best manage that marriage in a shock-prone global economy.

REFERENCES

AGHION, P., CAROLI, E., and GARCIA-PEÑALOSA, C. (1999). 'Inequality and Economic Growth: The Perspective of the New Growth Theories', *Journal of Economic Literature* 37.4.

BALASSA, B., BUENO, G., KUCZYNSKI, P.-P., and SIMONSEN, M. H. (1986). *Toward Renewed Growth in Latin America*, Washington, DC: Institute for International Economics.

BEHRMAN, J., BIRDSALL, N., and SZÉKELY, M. (2007). 'Economic Policy Changes and Wage Differentials in Latin America', *Economic Development and Cultural Change* 56.1.

BIANCHI, A., DEVLIN, R., and RAMOS, J. (1987). 'The Adjustment Process in Latin America: 1981–1986', presented at the IMF and World Bank Symposium on Growth-Oriented Adjustment Programs, Washington, DC.

BIRDSALL, N. (2011). 'The Global Financial Crisis: The Beginning of the End of the "Development" Agenda?', in F. Fukuyama and N. Birdsall (eds), *New Ideas for Development after the Financial Crisis*, Baltimore: Johns Hopkins University Press.

—— DE LA TORRE, A., and MENEZES, R. (2008). *Fair Growth: Economic Policies for Latin America's Poor and Middle-Income Majority*, Washington, DC: Center for Global Development.

—— —— and VALENCIA, C. F. (2010). 'The Washington Consensus: Assessing a Damaged Brand', World Bank Policy Research Working Paper 5316, Washington, DC.

DE LA TORRE, A., and SCHMUKLER, S. (2007). *Emerging Capital Markets and Globalization*, Washington, DC: World Bank and Stanford University Press.

DEMIRGUC-KUNT, A., and LEVINE, R. (2009). 'Finance and Inequality: Theory and Evidence', World Bank Policy Research Working Paper Series No. 4967, Washington, DC.

DE SOTO, H. (1989). *The Other Path: The Invisible Revolution in the Third World*, New York: Harper & Row.

EASTERLY, W., KREMER, M., PRITCHETT, L., and SUMMERS, L. (1993). 'Good Policy or Good Luck? Country Growth Performance and Temporary Shocks', *Journal of Monetary Economics* 32.3.

EASTERLY, W., LOAYZA, N., and MONTIEL, P. (1997). 'Has Latin America's Post-Reform Growth Been Disappointing?', *Journal of International Economics* 43.3–4.

ECLAC (UN Economic Commission for Latin America and the Caribbean) (1990). *Productive Transformation with Equity*, Santiago, Chile.

—— (2000). *Equity, Development and Citizenship*, Santiago, Chile.

—— (2008). *Structural Change and Productivity Growth: 20 Years Later, Old Problems, New Opportunities*, Santiago, Chile.

EDWARDS, S. (1995). *Crisis and Reform in Latin America: From Despair to Hope*, Washington, DC: World Bank and Oxford University Press.

ESCAITH, H., and MORLEY, S. (2001). 'The Effect of Structural Reforms on Growth in Latin America and the Caribbean: An Empirical Approach', *El trimestre económico* 68.4.

FERNÁNDEZ-ARIAS, E., and MONTIEL, P. (1997). 'Reform and Growth in Latin America: All Pain, No Gain?', IDB Working Paper No. 351, Washington, DC.

FFRENCH-DAVIS, R., and OCAMPO, J. A. (2001). 'The Globalization of Financial Volatility: Challenges for Emerging Economies', in R. Ffrench-Davis (ed.), *Financial Crises in "Successful" Emerging Economies*, Washington, DC: Brookings Institution Press and ECLAC.

—— and REISEN, H. (1998). *Capital Flows and Investment Performance: Lessons from Latin America*, Paris: OECD and ECLAC.

Growth Commission (2008). *The Growth Report: Strategies for Sustained Growth and Inclusive Development*, Washington, DC: World Bank.

HAUSMANN, R., PRITCHETT, L., and RODRIK, D. (2005).'Growth Accelerations', *Journal of Economic Growth* 10.4.

—— RODRIK, D., and VELASCO, A. (2008). 'Growth Diagnostics', in N. Serra and J. Stiglitz (eds), *The Washington Consensus Reconsidered*, New York: Oxford University Press.

IDB (Inter-American Development Bank) (1995). *Overcoming Volatility*, Washington, DC.

—— (1997). *Latin America After a Decade of Reforms*, Washington, DC.

—— (1998). *Facing Up to Inequality in Latin America*, Washington, DC.

—— (2001). *Competitiveness: The Business of Growth*, Washington, DC.

—— (2009). *Growing Pains: Binding Constraints to Productive Investment in Latin America*, Washington, DC.

IMF (International Monetary Fund) (2005). 'Stabilization and Reform in Latin America: A Macroeconomic Perspective on the Experience Since the Early 1990s', Occasional Paper No. 238, Washington, DC.

KAMINSKY, G., and SCHMUKLER, S. (2003). 'Short-Run Pain, Long-Run Gain: The Effects of Financial Liberalization', NBER Working Paper No. 9787, Cambridge, Mass.

LEVY, S., and WALTON, M. (2009). *No Growth Without Equity? Inequality, Interests and Competition in Mexico*, Washington, DC: World Bank and Palgrave Macmillan.

LOAYZA, N., FAJNZYLBER, P., and CALDERÓN, C. (2005). *Economic Growth in Latin America and the Caribbean: Stylized Facts, Explanations, and Forecasts*, Washington, DC: World Bank.

LORA, E. (2001). 'Structural Reforms in Latin America: What Has Been Reformed and How to Measure It', IDB Working Paper No. 466, Washington, DC.

—— and BARRERA, F. (1997). *Una década de reformas estructurales en América Latina: el crecimiento, la productividad y la inversión ya no son como antes*, Washington, DC: IDB.

—— and PANIZZA, U. (2002). 'Structural Reforms in Latin America Under Scrutiny', IDB Working Paper No. 470, Washington, DC.

MORLEY, S. (2000). *The Impact of Reforms on Equity in Latin America*, Washington, DC: World Bank.

NAÍM, M. (2000). 'Fads and Fashion in Economic Reforms: Washington Consensus or Washington Confusion?', *Third World Quarterly* 21.3.

—— (2002). 'Washington Consensus: A Damaged Brand', *Financial Times*, October 28.

NELLIS, J., and BIRDSALL, N. (eds) (2005). *Reality Check: The Distributional Impact of Privatization in Developing Countries*, Washington, DC: Center for Global Development.

OCAMPO, J. A. (2004). 'Latin America's Growth and Equity Frustrations During Structural Reforms', *Journal of Economic Perspectives* 18.2.

RADELET, S. (2010). *Emerging Africa: How 17 Countries Are Leading the Way*, Washington, DC: Center for Global Development.

RODRIK, D. (2005a). 'Why We Learn Nothing from Regressing Economic Growth on Policies', Harvard University, mimeograph.

—— (2005b). 'Growth Strategies', in P. Aghion and S. Durlauf (eds), *Handbook of Economic Growth*, Amsterdam: Elsevier.

—— (2006). 'Goodbye Washington Consensus, Hello Washington Confusion?', *Journal of Economic Literature* 44.4.

ROJAS-SUAREZ, L. (ed.) (2009). *Growing Pains in Latin America: An Economic Growth Framework as Applied to Brazil, Colombia, Costa Rica, Mexico, and Peru*, Washington, DC: Center for Global Development.

SACHS, J., and VIAL, J. (2002). 'Competitividad y crecimiento en los países andinos y en América Latina', Andean Competitiveness Project Working Papers, Harvard University.

STALLINGS, B., and PERES, W. (2000). *Growth Employment and Equity: The Impact of the Economic Reforms in Latin America and the Caribbean*, Washington, DC: ECLAC and Brookings Institution.

STERN, N. (2008). 'The Economics of Climate Change', *American Economic Review: Papers and Proceedings* 98.2.

UNICEF (United Nations Children's Fund) (1987). *Adjustment with a Human Face*, New York: Oxford University Press.

WILLIAMSON, J. (ed.) (1990). *Latin American Adjustment: How Much Has Happened?* Washington, DC: Institute for International Economics.

—— (1993). 'Democracy and the Washington Consensus', *World Development* 21.8.

—— (2000). 'What Should the World Bank Think about the Washington Consensus?', *World Bank Research Observer* 15.2.

—— (2002). *Did the Washington Consensus Fail?* Washington, DC: Peterson Institute for International Economics.

World Bank (1998). *Beyond the Washington Consensus: Institutions Matter*, Washington, DC.

—— (2000). *Securing our Future in the Global Economy*, Washington, DC.

—— (2002). *From Natural Resources to the Knowledge Economy*, Washington, DC.

—— (2003). *Closing the Gap in Education and Technology*, Washington, DC.

—— (2004). *Inequality in Latin America: Breaking with History?* Washington, DC.

—— (2009). *Low Carbon, High Growth: Latin American Responses to Climate Change*, Washington, DC.

—— (2010). *From Global Collapse to Recovery*, Washington, DC.

CHAPTER 5

....

FROM OLD TO NEW DEVELOPMENTALISM IN LATIN AMERICA

....

LUIZ CARLOS BRESSER-PEREIRA

5.1 INTRODUCTION

....

From the 1930s, or at least from the 1950s, Latin American countries adopted a successful national development strategy, national developmentalism, based on development economics and Latin American structuralist economic theory. In the late 1980s, after ten years of foreign debt crisis combined with high rates of inflation, this strategy required redefinition. It was thus replaced by the Washington Consensus or conventional orthodoxy—an imported strategy based on the deregulation of markets, growth with foreign savings, high interest rates, and overvalued exchange rates. Ten years later, after the 1994 Mexican, the 1998 Brazilian, and the 2001 Argentinean financial crises, the failure of this strategy became evident from the repeated balance of payment crises and the failure to improve living standards.

The results of orthodox policies are contrary to middle-income developing countries' objective of catching up with industrial countries—not commercial globalization that eventually proved to be an opportunity, as the Asian experience shows, but financial globalization or financial liberalization that made each developing country unable to control its exchange rate. Since the early 2000s, Latin American countries have once again been seeking a national development strategy. In the political realm, this search has been evident in the successive elections of center-left and nationalist political leaders. Yet the success of this search is not assured. What are the alternative theory and economic policy to conventional orthodoxy? What institutional reforms and economic policies would such a strategy entail?

To respond to these questions we must make a realistic assessment of the different realities and levels of development existing in Latin America. The poorer a country, the more unequal and poorly educated will be its people, and the more difficult it will be to govern and to formulate appropriate economic policies. The challenges that all developing countries faced in the 1950s, when this question was first asked by the pioneers of development economics,[1] varied according to the stage of development of each country. Countries are, first, supposed to undertake primitive accumulation and create minimal capitalist class; second, they must complete their modernization or capitalist revolution, which involves industrialization and the formation of an autonomous or truly national state; and third, after being equipped with a modern business class, a large professional middle class, and a large wage-earning class, and with the basic institutions required for economic growth, countries must prove themselves capable of continuing to grow fast and of gradually catching up with the growth levels of rich countries. In Latin America I would say that all countries, except for Haiti and perhaps Nicaragua, have completed primitive accumulation, and that a group of countries, including at least Argentina, Brazil, Mexico, Chile, Uruguay, and Costa Rica, have completed their capitalist revolutions and may be considered middle-income countries. This being so, it is not sufficient simply to ask what the alternative to conventional orthodoxy is; in defining this alternative it is also necessary to distinguish middle-income countries from poor countries in the region, as they face different challenges. In this chapter, I will discuss new developmentalism in middle-income countries.

Considering the questions and the caveats set out above, I will adopt an historical method to compare the two competing strategies that Latin America faces today: conventional orthodoxy and new developmentalism. The chaper is divided into five sections. In 5.2, I discuss briefly old or national developmentalism, its relation to the Latin American structuralist school of thought, and its success in promoting economic growth between 1930 and 1980. In 5.3, I briefly discuss the causes for the demise of national-developmentalism and its substitution by the Washington consensus or conventional orthodoxy. Given the failure of this alternative to promote stability and growth, in section 5.4 I discuss the rise of structuralist development macroeconomics and new developmentalism. In 5.5, I compare new developmentalism with old developmentalism, and in 5.6, new developmentalism with conventional orthodoxy. My objective in these two sections is to demonstrate that there is a sensible alternative to conventional orthodoxy—an alternative based on Latin American structuralism and on the successful experience of fast-growing Asian countries.

---

[1] I refer to economists like Albert Hirschman, Arthur Lewis, Celso Furtado, Gunnar Myrdal, Hans Singer, Michel Kalecki, Ragnar Nurse, Raul Presbisch, and Paul Rosenstein-Rodan.

5.2 NATIONAL DEVELOPMENTALISM
AND STRUCTURALISM

Between the 1930s and the 1970s, Latin American countries grew at an extraordinary pace. They took advantage of the weakness of the center in the 1930s in order to formulate national development strategies that, in essence, implied protection of the infant national industry (or import-substitution industrialization) and the promotion of enforced savings by the state.[2] Additionally, the state was supposed to make direct investments in infrastructure and in certain basic industries whose capital requirements and risks were large. This strategy was called "national developmentalism." Such a name was designed to emphasize that, first, the policy's basic objective was to promote economic development, and, second, in order for this to happen, the nation—i.e. businessmen, the state bureaucracy, the middle classes, and the workers united in international competition—had to define the means of reaching this objective within the framework of the capitalist system, having the state as the principal instrument of collective action.

The first statesman who devised national developmentalism in Latin America was Getúlio Vargas, who governed Brazil from 1930–45 and 1950–4. On the other hand, the notable Latin American economists, sociologists, political scientists, and philosophers who formulated this strategy in the 1950s came together in the Economic Commission for Latin America and Caribbean (ECLAC) in Santiago, Chile, and in Instituto Superior de Estudos Brasileiros (ISEB) in Rio de Janeiro, Brazil. They developed a theory of underdevelopment and a nationalist view of economic development based on the critique of imperialism or of "the center–periphery relation"—a euphemism suited to public intellectuals associated with an organization of the United Nations. Latin American economists, among them Raul Prebisch, Celso Furtado, Osvaldo Sunkel, Anibal Pinto, and Ignacio Rangel, drew on the classical political economy of Adam Smith and Karl Marx, the macroeconomics of John Maynard Keynes and Michał Kalecki, and the new ideas of the development economics school (of which they were part) to form the Latin American structuralist school.

The central elements of structuralism were the critique of the law of comparative advantage in international trade, the dualist character of underdeveloped economies, the existence of unlimited supply of labor, economic development as a structural change or as industrialization, the role of the state in producing forced savings and directly investing in key industries, the existence of structural inflation, the proposal of a national-developmentalist strategy based on import substitution industrialization, and,

---

[2] I use "state" to mean the law system and the organization that guarantees it; it is what in the US is called "government." On the other hand, I use "national state" or "nation-state" to mean the country, the sovereign territorial political entity formed by a nation, a state, and a territory.

in the advanced stages, export promotion of manufactured goods (Cardenas, Ocampo, and Thorp 2001). Whereas the structuralist thinking was a Latin American version of development economics, national developmentalism was the corresponding national development strategy. As a state-led strategy, it understood that markets are effective in resource allocation provided that they are combined with economic planning and the constitution of state-owned enterprises. National developmentalism was a strategy supported in one way or another by industrialists, the public bureaucracies, and urban workers. It faced intellectual opposition from neoclassical or monetarist economists, and political opposition from the liberal middle classes and the old oligarchy whose interests were based on the export of primary goods.

5.3 CONVENTIONAL ORTHODOXY

Although the demise of national developmentalism and its replacement by conventional orthodoxy would happen only in the late 1980s, its origins are in the mid-1960s—after the military coups in Brazil (1964), Argentina (1967), and Uruguay (1968). The following historical factors contributed to this outcome: (a) the exhaustion of the state-led import-substitution strategy; (b) the major foreign debt crisis of the 1980s; (c) the intellectual dominance of the associated-dependency interpretation of Latin America since the early 1970s—an interpretation that dismissed the dualist and peripheral character of Latin American societies;[3] (d) the success of the US policy (beginning in the late 1960s) of training Latin American economists in doctoral programs in the United States; and (e) the neoliberal wave and, in the academic world, the rise of neoclassical economics, public choice theory, and new institutionalism—three sophisticated attempts to ground neoliberalism scientifically.

To replace developmentalism, Washington proposed a "consensus" formed from a cluster of orthodox macroeconomic policies and market-oriented institutional reforms including the most debatable policy of all, financial liberalization—the extension of financial globalization to developing countries.[4] The failure of conventional orthodoxy to promote Latin America's economic development is widely acknowledged today. This is demonstrated in Table 5.1, which shows the per capita rates of growth of the main Latin American countries during 1950–80, 1981–2006, and 1990–2006. While between 1950 and 1980 the average annual growth rate of Latin American countries listed in the table was 3.11%, after 1981 it was 0.77%, and after 1990 1.6%. The low rate since 1981 was also caused by the great debt crisis of the 1980s, which reflected the mistaken policy of growth with foreign savings of the 1970s. The poor 1.6% rate since 1990—practically half the rate

---

[3] See Bresser-Pereira (2011).

[4] Note that John Williamson's original 1990 document on the Washington consensus did not include financial liberalization, because he viewed it as risky. This reform was added later, in the early 1990s.

Table 5.1 Growth of per capita income in selected countries, 1950–2006 (constant 2000 dollars)

Country	1950–80 Annual growth rate (%)	1981–2006 Annual growth rate (%)	1990–2006 Annual growth rate (%)	2006 income per capita([a])
Argentina	1.60	0.54	2.55	8,733.4
Mexico	3.37	0.93	1.61	6,951.5
Uruguay	1.30	1.23	2.17	6,770.2
Chile	1.38	3.01	4.13	5,889.1
Costa Rica	3.16	1.56	2.75	4,819.8
Panama	3.24	1.55	3.03	4,743.6
Brazil	4.12	0.53	1.18	4,043.1
Venezuela	2.20	− 0.01	0.74	5,429.6
Colombia	2.28	1.50	1.64	2,673.9
Peru	2.08	0.36	2.77	2,555.8
Ecuador	3.16	0.63	1.35	1,608.0
Paraguay	2.67	0.07	−0.01	1,397.9
Bolivia	0.92	0.00	1.27	1,064.4
Cuba	−	1.22	0.98	3,890.4
Average	3.11	0.77	1.60	−

Source: www.eclac.org Observation: average annual growth rate weighted by population.

([a]) Per capita income (constant $2,000).

achieved between 1950 and 1980—is a consequence of the neoliberal policies of the Washington Consensus in the region. The well-known exception is Chile, whose growth between 1990 and 2006 was substantially superior to the 1950–1980 periods. After ten years of radical neoliberal policies, the military regime adopted a competent liberal and export-led strategy that was pursued and improved by the democratic strategy after 1990. Argentina also presented a slightly better performance from 1990 on, but the major 2001 crisis showed how fragile was the prosperity derived from the convertibility plan.

The failure of conventional orthodoxy would not be so clearly demonstrated by these contrasting growth figures if the Asian countries that rejected the Washington Consensus and retained control over their economies, principally their control on the exchange rate, had also experienced falling growth rates since 1981 or 1990; it was just the opposite in China, India, or Indonesia. Their growth rates in the second period greatly increased. Thus, while convergence was taking place in the fast-growing Asian countries, Latin American countries lagged behind, clearly demonstrating what Ocampo and Parra (2008: 101–11) call the "dual divergence: between developing countries and the industrial world, on one hand, and among developing countries, on the other."

Conventional orthodoxy may be summarily defined by four propositions:

(1) Middle-income countries' major problem is the lack of microeconomic reforms capable of enabling the market to operate freely.

(2) Controlling inflation is the main purpose of macroeconomic policy.

(3) This is so even if achieving the control of inflation means that interest rates are high and the exchange rate correspondingly appreciated.

(4) Economic development is a competition among countries to obtain foreign savings (current account deficits), and therefore the foreign exchange appreciation caused by capital inflows required to finance the deficits is no cause for concern because the returns on the increased investment rate pay for it.[5]

5.4 New developmentalism and development macroeconomics

When it became manifest that the Washington Consensus was not causing growth but rather financial instability and increasing inequality, the reaction in Latin America was not surprising. It began at the political level with the election of a succession of nationalist and left-wing leaders, creating room for national policies. Yet, because most of these countries are poor, they are very difficult to govern. Their new administrations are searching for an alternative economic strategy, but the probability of success is low. At the knowledge level, however, principally in the more developed countries of the region, economists and other social scientists are observing the success of the fast-growing Asian countries and are persuaded that, despite cultural and economic differences, such experiences may be helpful in devising a Latin American development alternative. The name that I have given to this proposed alternative strategy is "new developmentalism."

New developmentalism is a set of values, ideas, institutions, and economic policies through which, in the early 21st century, middle-income countries sought to catch up with developed countries. It is not an economic theory but a strategy; it is a national development strategy, based mainly on Keynesian macroeconomics and structuralist development macroeconomics. It is the set of ideas that enables developing nations to reject rich nations' proposals and pressures for reform and economic policy, like capital account liberalization and growth with foreign savings. It is the means by which businessmen, government officials, workers, and intellectuals can stand together as a nation to promote economic development. New developmentalism is suitable for middle-income countries rather than for poor countries, not because poor countries do not require a national development strategy, but because their strategies involve accomplishing primitive accumulation and industrial revolution—in other words, because the challenges they face are different from those faced by middle-income countries.

---

[5] See Frenkel (2003), Bresser-Pereira and Nakano (2003), Bresser-Pereira and Gala (2007), Bresser-Pereira (2010).

The basic propositions behind new developmentalism are macroeconomic; they derive from a structuralist development macroeconomics being defined by critical Latin American economists who have as a parameter the macroeconomic policies of fast-growing Asian countries based on fiscal responsibility, exchange rate responsibility, and the assignation of a strategic role for the state.[6] The supply aspects of economic growth including industrial policy are naturally considered in this approach, but, given its Keynesian and Kaleckian foundation, two tendencies that suppress demand—the tendency of wages to increase below the productivity rate and the tendency towards the overvaluation of the exchange rate—are crucial. The first derives from the definition of a developing country as a dual economy, and from the classic work of Arthur Lewis (1954) showing that developing countries face an unlimited supply of labor—representing a major impediment to the creation of mass consumption economies in the region along the lines discussed mainly by Ricardo Bielschowsky (2008).[7] This fact implies a rise in wages when the worker migrates from the traditional sector to the modern sector, but thereafter it suppresses wages in the modern sector—which causes increasing inequality and a chronic insufficiency of demand. In the 1970s, in Latin America, this problem was classically "solved" by the production of luxury goods to be consumed by the middle class and the rich, or by exporting wage goods and importing luxury goods and capital goods.[8]

The second structural tendency—towards the overvaluation of the exchange rate—explains why the exchange rate is not eventually controlled by the market, but by balance of payment crises. As conventional economics presupposes that wages are well equilibrated by the labor market, it supposes that the same happens with the exchange rate. Yet, if the exchange rate is left fully free in a developing country, a series of structural and policy factors will lead it to appreciate, causing the country to incur a current account deficit, in turn causing the country to become indebted, suffer from chronic financial fragility, and, finally, when foreign creditors lose confidence, face a "sudden stop"—a balance of payment or currency crisis and a sharp devaluation.

This tendency derives from two structural factors: from the "Dutch disease" originated in Ricardian rents that drives down (appreciates) the exchange rate from the "industrial equilibrium" to the "current account equilibrium," and from the higher profit and interest rates prevailing in developing countries, which attract foreign capital, appreciate the

---

[6] My own contribution to structuralist development macroeconomics—the one that I am in some way resuming in this chapter—is in Bresser-Pereira (2010); an earlier attempt was Bresser-Pereira (1977). Lance Taylor (1983; 1991) has long been developing a structural macroeconomics. In the same line we have the major contributions of Jaime Ros (2003), Roberto Frenkel (2003; 2008), and Ricardo Ffrench-Davis (2003).

[7] Ricardo Bielschowsky has been discussing this theme since 2003, when he coordinated with Guido Mantega the Lula administration's *Plano Plurianual 2004–2007*, in which there is a section on the long-term growth strategy in which mass consumption is emphasized. This was always an assumption for the work of Celso Furtado and Antonio Barros de Castro.

[8] See Bresser-Pereira (1970; 1977), Tavares and Serra (1972), and Bacha (1973).

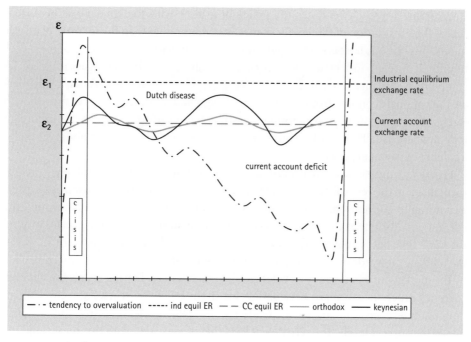

FIGURE 5.1 Tendency towards the overvaluation of the exchange rate

exchange rate below the current account equilibrium, and cause current account deficits. Yet this second structural factor is not sufficient to explain why, after reaching the current equilibrium, the exchange rate continues to appreciate, as we can see in Figure 5.1, and both current account deficits and foreign debt continue to increase. To understand that, it is necessary to take into account some economic policies mostly inspired by conventional orthodoxy that further appreciate the national currency: (1) by the policy of growth with foreign savings, (2) by the use of inflation targeting to justify high interest rates, (3) by the use of the exchange rate as a nominal anchor to fight inflation and increase wages artificially, (4) by the policy of capital deepening aiming to increase the interest rate to attract foreign capital. It is also amplified by (5) "exchange rate populism"—the populist practice originally discussed by Adolfo Canitrot (1975) of appreciating the currency to control inflation, increase real wages—and thus securing re-election.

Given these two tendencies, new developmentalism asserts the importance of an income policy that keeps wages growing with productivity and an exchange rate policy that neutralizes the overvaluation tendency. Both create investment opportunities that increase the investment rate and, in consequence, the savings rate.[9] When this

---

[9] The two-gap model asserted that besides the savings constraint, developing countries face a foreign currencies constraint, thus needing loans or investments from rich countries.

structuralist approach criticizes the policy of growth with foreign savings because it causes the substitution of foreign for domestic savings rather than the increase of investments, this critique is not only of conventional economics but also of development economics if foreign indebtedness is used as a solution to the two-gap problem. A competitive exchange rate will avoid the two-gap problem—in other words, it will liberate the national economy from the need for foreign finance or the policy of growth with foreign savings. Instead of promoting investment and savings, the increase in foreign indebtedness usually promotes consumption, causes financial fragility, and, eventually, a balance of payment crisis.

Figure 5.1 summarizes structuralist development macroeconomics and new developmentalism. In the vertical axis we have the exchange rate and in the horizontal axis, time. According to conventional economics, the exchange rate fluctuates nicely around the current equilibrium exchange rate; according to Keynesians, it also fluctuates around the same line, but is volatile; according to the ideas briefly summarized here, however, the tendency towards overvaluation of the exchange rate means that it is not controlled by the market but by currency or balance of payment crises. During crises, the national currency experiences a sharp devaluation, but in the following years, if the government does not intervene to neutralize the tendency, the "Dutch disease" brings the exchange rate to the current level—the zero deficit level that is consistent with this market failure. Yet the national currency continues to appreciate, or (as shown in Figure 5.1) to move downwards. This additional appreciation is caused by the inflow of foreign capital attracted by high structural and policy-defined interest rates, by the policy of growth with foreign savings, by the use of nominal anchors, by the use of inflation targeting as a substitute for a nominal anchor, by capital-deepening policies, and by exchange rate populism.

As this downward movement takes place, wages, artificially increased by the appreciation of the currency, cause increase in consumption; the current account deficit appears and increases steadily; foreign indebtedness increases; and eventually foreign creditors, concerned with the high current account deficit and the high foreign debt, suspend the rollover of the foreign debt and cause a sudden stop: the balance of payment crisis that again depreciates the currency.

5.5 OLD AND NEW DEVELOPMENTALISM

I will briefly compare new developmentalism with the other two strategies—old national developmentalism and conventional orthodoxy—beginning with the former. I see five main differences between national developmentalism and new developmentalism, all related to the fact that many countries remain developing but have ceased to be poor, are no longer characterized by infant industries, and are now middle-income countries. This fact has a first and major consequence: while old developmentalism was relatively protectionist, new developmentalism is not; whereas old developmentalism was based on import substitution, new developmentalism is export-led. In the thirty golden years after World War II, middle-income countries did not represent competition or a threat to rich nations. Yet, since the 1970s, with the NICs (newly industrialized countries) and, since the 1990s, with China and finally India, they have become much more competitive. In this context, manufacturing industry has moved forward from infancy and thus does not require generalized protection. Between the 1930s and the 1950s, the import-substitution model was effective in establishing the industrial bases of Latin American countries. The tariffs were a way to protect infant industry and also to neutralize the Dutch disease on the import side. After the mid-1960s, however, governments should have begun dropping some of their tax barriers to imports and adopting an export-led model combined with the development of the domestic market. Some countries, principally Brazil and Mexico, did orient their exports to manufacturing, but retained high import taxes. It was only in the late 1980s and early 1990s that trade liberalization took place, in the midst of a major economic crisis, and often hurriedly and haphazardly. This was a mistake: in countries like Brazil and Argentina, import taxes were not just a response to the infant industry problem, but a way of neutralizing, on the import side, the Dutch disease caused by the highly favorable natural conditions that these countries offer for cattle breeding and agricultural exports.

New developmentalism is not protectionist: it simply emphasizes the need for a competitive exchange rate, i.e. an exchange rate that renders viable other tradable industries utilizing state-of-the-art technology, in addition to the one that originates or causes the Dutch disease. It assumes that middle-income countries have already passed through the infant-industry stage but still face the Dutch disease and, for that reason, experience long-term appreciation of their exchange rate that is consistent with equilibrium in the current account balance, but renders economically non-viable other tradable industries using state-of-the-art technology. The larger the gap between the current equilibrium and the industrial equilibrium exchange rate, the more "serious" will be the disease—the higher will be the obstacle preventing other tradable industries from prosperity. The more serious the disease, the more the country will be impeded in transferring labor from the production of lower to higher per capita valued-added goods or from simple to sophisticated industries—a key structural condition for economic growth.[10] In order to neutralize the Dutch disease, the basic policy is to impose a tax or a retention on exports of the commodities that cause it. Such a tax will shift upwards the supply curve of these goods; if the tax is sufficient, exports of that good that were viable at the current equilibrium exchange rate will now be only viable at the industrial equilibrium—the exchange rate level that makes viable all other tradable industries utilizing state-of-the-art technology. Tariff protection does this job only partially, limited to the import side. To

---

[10] As José Antonio Ocampo and Rob Vos (2008: 34) observe, "productivity growth in developed countries mainly relies on technological innovation. For developing countries, however, growth and development are much less about pushing the technology frontier and much more about changing the structure of production towards activities with higher levels of productivity."

include the export side and enable industries utilizing modern technology to export, a tax is required on exports of goods.[11]

Unlike old developmentalism, which embraced the export pessimism of development economics, new developmentalism bets on the ability of developing countries to export medium value-added manufactured goods or high value-added primary products. The experience of the past thirty years has clearly shown that export pessimism was one of the great theoretical mistakes of development economics. In the late 1960s, Latin American countries should have begun shifting decisively from the import-substitution model to the export-led model, as Korea and Taiwan did. In Latin America, Chile was the first to effect such a change and, as a result, is often pointed to as an example of a successful neo-liberal strategy of development. In fact, neoliberalism was fully practiced in Chile only between 1973 and 1981, coming to an end with a major balance-of-payments crisis in 1982.[12] The export-led model is not neoliberal if it is combined with an expanding domestic market and with the neutralization of the Dutch disease (which Chileans accomplish by taxing copper exports). The fast-growing Asian countries originally adopted an import-substitution strategy but soon changed to an export-led model, which has two main advantages over the import-substitution model. First, the industries are not limited to the domestic market. This is important for small countries but equally fundamental to a country with a relatively large domestic market. Second, if a country adopts this strategy, the economic authorities will frame an industrial policy to benefit their national firms, automatically establishing an efficiency criterion to guide them: only efficient firms will benefit from the industrial policy. In the case of the import-substitution model, very inefficient firms may be enjoying the benefits of protection; in the case of the export-led model, the likelihood of this happening is substantially smaller.

A second difference between old and new developmentalism concerns the role of the state. In the 1950s, under national developmentalism, countries were poor, and the state was supposed to play a leading role in achieving forced savings and in investing not only in monopolistic industries but also in industries characterized by large economies of scale and thus requiring huge sums of capital. Fifty years later, most of the Latin American nation-states are middle-income countries; they have already completed or are involved in their own capitalist revolutions; they are equipped with a stock of capital that did not exist before, and able to finance investment; they are equipped with entrepreneurial, professional, and working classes able to industrialize and modernize their countries. The state continues to play a key role, but a normative, enabling, and encouraging role rather than a direct role in production. Both forms of developmentalism cast the state in a leading role in terms of ensuring the proper operation of the market and providing the general conditions for capital accumulation, such as education, health, transportation, communications, and power infrastructures. In addition, however, under the developmentalism of the 1950s, the state also played a crucial role in promot-

---

[11] Bresser-Pereira (2008; 2010).
[12] See Alejandro (1981) and Ffrench-Davis (2003).

Table 5.2 Old and new developmentalism

Old developmentalism	New developmentalism
1. Industrialization is state-led and based on import substitution.	1. Export-led industrialization combined with strong domestic market.
2. Leading role for the state in obtaining forced savings and in making investments.	2. The state is supposed to create investment opportunities and reduce economic inequalities.
3. Industrial policy is central.	3. Industrial policy is subsidiary; what is essential is a competitive exchange rate.
4. Mixed attitude in relation to budget deficits.	4. Rejection of fiscal deficits. If the country suffers from the Dutch disease it should have current account and fiscal surpluses.
5. Relative complacency towards inflation.	5. No complacency towards inflation.

ing forced savings, thereby contributing to countries' primitive accumulation processes; furthermore, the state made direct investments in infrastructure and heavy industry where the sums required exceeded the private sector's savings.

This has changed since the 1980s. With new developmentalism, the state still can and must promote forced savings and invest in certain strategic industries, but the national private sector now has the resources and managerial ability to provide a sizable portion of the necessary investment. New developmentalism rejects the neoliberal thesis that "the state no longer has resources to invest in the infrastructure." Whether the state has or does not have resources depends on how its citizens behave and on how the state is managed. But new developmentalism understands that in all sectors where reasonable competition exists, the state must not be an investor; instead, it must concentrate on defending and ensuring competition. Even after these investments have been excluded, there are many left to the state to finance with public savings rather than debt.

Third, new developmentalism supports industrial policy but rejects the pre-eminent role played in national developmentalism. More important than an industrial policy is a competent macroeconomic policy based on fiscal balance, moderate interest rates, and a competitive exchange rate—an exchange rate that makes industries viable or competitive using the best technology available in the world. The state may, and is supposed to, support business enterprises, but only strategically, and not permanently. And it is supposed to make this support conditional on businesses achieving international competitiveness.

Fourth, new developmentalism rejects misleading notions of growth based chiefly on chronic public deficits—an equivocal idea that became popular in Latin America, but was not shared by the main economists who originally defined it. This was one of the most severe distortions that national developmentalism endured in the 1980s in the hands of its latter-day populist advocates. Keynes, in whose name economic populism was promoted, pointed out the importance of aggregate demand and legitimized resorting to public deficits in recessions, but he never advocated chronic public deficits. He always assumed that a fiscally balanced national economy might, for a brief while, give up this balance to re-establish employment levels. The notable economists who formulated the developmentalist strategy, such as Furtado, Prebisch, and Rangel, were Keynesians, and regarded aggregate demand management as an important tool for promoting development. But they never defended the economic populism of chronic deficits. Those who came in their wake, however, did so. When Celso Furtado, faced with the severe crisis of the early 1960s, proposed his *Plano Trienal* (1963b), these second-rate propagandists accused him of having an "orthodox rebound."

New developmentalism defends fiscal equilibrium, not in the name of "orthodoxy" but because it realizes that the state is the nation's instrument for collective action *par excellence*. If the state is so strategic, its apparatus must be strong, sound, and capacious; and for this very reason, its finances must be in balance. More than this, its debt must be small and long in maturity. The worst thing that can happen to a state as an organization (the state also stands for the rule of law) is to be in thrall to creditors, be they domestic or foreign. Foreign creditors are particularly dangerous, because they and their capital may at any time leave the country. However, domestic creditors, transformed into rentiers and supported by the financial system, can impose disastrous economic policies on the country. If the country suffers the Dutch disease and is able to neutralize it, it will shift from the current to the industrial equilibrium exchange rate, and will experience current account surpluses. The best practice, in this case, is to build a sovereign fund abroad in order to avoid the inflow of capitals and the re-evaluation of the currency; this fund should be financed by a corresponding fiscal surplus.

Fifth and last, new developmentalism is different from national developmentalism because, while the latter was relatively complacent about inflation, new developmentalism is not. Old developmentalism had good reason to be relatively complacent: the structural theory of inflation asserted that, due to the imperfections of domestic markets, developing countries should live with moderate rates of inflation. In middle-income countries, markets are not so imperfect, and experience has shown that inflation may turn into a curse.

In sum, because middle-income countries are at a different stage, new developmentalism is more favorable to the market as an efficient institution to coordinate the economic system than was old developmentalism, although its perspective is far removed from the irrational faith in the market evinced by conventional orthodoxy.

5.6 NEW DEVELOPMENTALISM AND CONVENTIONAL ORTHODOXY

In this chapter I am supporting new developmentalism, but conventional orthodoxy is still dominant, principally in defining macroeconomic policy in Latin America. Let us now examine the differences between these two competing strategies. Conventional economic orthodoxy is made up of a set of theories, diagnoses, and policy proposals that rich nations offer to developing countries. It is based on neoclassical economics but it should not be confused with it, because it is not theoretical but openly ideological and oriented toward institutional reforms and economic policies. While neoclassical economics is based in universities, particularly in the United States, conventional orthodoxy springs mainly from Washington, DC, home of the US Treasury Department and of the two agencies that are supposedly international but in fact are subordinate to the US Treasury: the International Monetary Fund and the World Bank. The former is charged with macroeconomic policy and the latter with development. Second, conventional orthodoxy originated in New York, the headquarters or point of convergence of major international banks and multinational corporations. Conventional orthodoxy changes over time. Since the 1980s, it has become identified with the "Washington Consensus," which cannot be understood simply as the list of ten reforms or adjustments set out by John Williamson (1990). His list included reforms and adjustments that were and still are necessary. The problem is not in the reforms, but in the radical, laissez-faire way in which they were understood, and in the inclusion of a reform that Williamson deliberately did not include in his list because he was aware of the risks involved: financial liberalization.

Inasmuch as conventional orthodoxy is the practical expression of neoliberal ideology, it is the ideology of the market vs. the state. While new developmentalism requires a strong state and a strong market, and believes there is no contradiction between them, conventional orthodoxy wishes to strengthen the market by weakening the state, as if the two institutions were parties in a zero-sum game. In the 20th century the state has grown in terms of tax burden and the level of market regulation as a result of the increased dimensions and complexity of modern societies—in other words, as an outcome of the fact that a strong and relatively large state is a requirement for a strong and competitive market. Nevertheless, conventional orthodoxy sees this growth as just the consequence of populist politicians and of a state friendly bureaucracy. Certainly, the state has also grown as a result of clientelism and of pressures of the bureaucracy to have more positions to occupy in the state organization, but conventional orthodoxy does not distinguish legitimate state growth from the illegitimate variety.

The central difference between conventional orthodoxy and new developmentalism lies in the fact that conventional orthodoxy believes that the market is an institution that coordinates production optimally if it is free of interference, whereas new developmentalism views the market as an efficient institution to coordinate economic systems, but knows its limitations and the need for regulation. Factor allocation is the task that it performs best, but even here it faces problems. In stimulating investment and innovation, it is insufficient, because it fails to neutralize the two structural tendencies existing in developing countries that we have already briefly discussed: the tendency of the exchange rate to overvaluation and the tendency of wages to increase less than productivity. Besides, markets are a clearly unsatisfactory mechanism for distributing income, favoring the stronger and more capable participants. While conventional orthodoxy acknowledges market failures but asserts that state failures are worse, new developmentalism rejects such pessimism about the possibilities of collective action and demands a capable state—not as a trade-off for a weak market but combined with a strong market. If human beings are able to build institutions to regulate human actions, including the market itself, there is no reason why they should not be able to strengthen the state organization or apparatus (making its administration more legitimate, its finances more solid, and its management more efficient) or to strengthen the constitutional or legal system (increasingly adjusting its institutions to social needs). Politics and democracy exist precisely for that purpose; and the more advanced democracies have been making major advances in this area in the last century.

Insofar as one of the foundations of new developmentalism is classical political economy, which was essentially a theory of the "wealth of nations" (Smith) and of capital accumulation (Marx), social structures and institutions are fundamental to its reasoning. Besides, as it adopts a historical approach to economic development, the teachings of Keynes and Kalecki (whose method was essentially historical-deductive instead of hypothetical-deductive), of the German Historical School, and of the American Institutionalist School are an essential part of this vision.[13] Institutions are fundamental, and to reform them is a permanent requirement insofar as, in the complex and dynamic societies, economic activities must be constantly re-regulated. In contrast, conventional orthodoxy, based on neoclassical economics, only recently acknowledged the role of institutions, in the context of "new institutionalism." Unlike historical institutionalism, which sees pre-capitalist institutions as obstacles to economic growth, and actively seeks to develop a set or cluster of institutions (a national growth strategy) to create investment opportunities for business entrepreneurs, new institutionalism offers a simplistic answer to the problem: it is sufficient that institutions guarantee property rights and contracts or, more broadly, the good working of markets, which will automatically promote growth.

In comparing new developmentalism and conventional orthodoxy, it is difficult to distinguish macroeconomic policies from growth strategies because, in the context of a structuralist development macroeconomics, these two levels are closely intertwined. Growth is impossible without stability. The macroeconomic prices—the profit rate, the interest rate, the wage rate, the inflation rate, and the exchange rate—are not just determinants of macroeconomic stability: policies in relation to them are crucial for economic growth.

Following Tables 5.3 and 5.4 that resume mostly growth and macro policies, let us compare the two strategies.

First, whereas conventional orthodoxy gives no economic role to nations, new developmentalism emphasizes their existence, and underlines the fact that in globalization they became more interdependent and more strategic because economic competition is not restricted to business enterprises, but also applies to nations.

---

[13] The German Historical School is the school of Gustav Schmoller, Otto Rank, Max Weber, and, in a different tradition, of Friedrich List; the American Institutionalist School is the school of Thorstein Veblen, Wesley Mitchell, and John R. Commons.

Table 5.3 Conventional orthodoxy and new developmentalism (growth)

Conventional orthodoxy	New developmentalism
1. No economic role for the nation.	1. The nation is the agent defining the national development strategy.
2. The fundamental institutions to promote growth are property rights and contracts.	2. The key institution to promote growth is a national development strategy.
3. Reforms reducing the size of state and deregulating markets.	3. Reforms strengthening the state and markets—the latter by being regulated, not deregulated.
4. Minimal role of the state in investing and in industrial policy.	4. Moderate role in investing and in industrial policy; large role in redistribution.
5. No structural tendencies.	5. Tendency to the overvaluation of the exchange rate and of wages to increase less than productivity.
6. Growth financed with foreign savings.	6. Growth with domestic savings. Foreign savings appreciate the exchange rate and cause substitution of foreign for domestic savings.

Table 5.4 Conventional orthodoxy and new developmentalism (macro)

Conventional orthodoxy	New developmentalism
7. The central bank has a single mandate target: inflation. Other objectives are to be pursued by the government.	7. The central bank and the government have three mandate targets: inflation, exchange rate, and employment.
8. The primary surplus is the central fiscal standard.	8. The budget deficit and public savings are the central fiscal standards.
9. Fully floating exchange rate; no exchange rate objective, nor related policy.	9. Floating but administered exchange rate; the competitive exchange rate corresponds to "industrial equilibrium" exchange rate.
10. The central bank uses a single instrument: the short-term interest rate; the government keeps public deficit under control.	10. The central bank may also buy reserves, and the government besides controlling the budget may impose controls on capital inflows.
11. No income policy necessary.	11. A minimum wage and a minimum income policy are required to keep wages increasing with productivity.

Second, whereas conventional orthodoxy sees property rights and contracts as the key institutions for growth, new developmentalism asserts that a national development strategy plays this role insofar as it is a cluster of laws, policies, understandings, and values that create investment opportunities for business entrepreneurs.

Third, conventional orthodoxy supports institutional reforms that reduce the size of the state and strengthen the market, and ascribes a minimal role to the state in investment and industrial policy, whereas new developmentalism supports reforms strengthening markets and enabling the state to perform its regulatory and investment stimulating role. For new developmentalism, the state is the main instrument of collective action of the nation—of a national society with a sense of common destiny and of reasonable solidarity when competing internationally.

Fourth, conventional orthodoxy sees no role for the state in investment and in industrial policy, whereas new developmentalism aims at a capable and efficient state able to make public investments that are not attractive to the private sector or that are monopolist, or that involve huge rents (as in the case of the oil industry), and believes that a strategic industrial policy remains necessary. New developmentalism gives priority to export industries and to high per capita value-added industries, i.e. industries with a high technological or knowledge content.

Fifth, conventional orthodoxy sees no structural tendencies to tackle, whereas new developmentalism identifies the two major tendencies already discussed: the tendency of wages to increase below the productivity rate, and of the exchange rate to become overvalued and be "controlled" by balance of payment crises instead of by the market.

Sixth, conventional orthodoxy believes and strongly asserts that growth of middle-income countries should be financed with foreign savings, because they could not count on domestic savings to finance their growth, whereas new developmentalism rejects this assertion. Foreign savings do not need to be rejected, but they involve a high rate of substitution for domestic savings. This rate of substitution tends to be high even when foreign direct investments finance the current account deficit. Thus, the country should aim at current account balance and grow with domestic savings. Foreign investments oriented to the domestic market are welcome provided that they have as counterpart the opening of the rich countries to investments of the middle-income countries. New developmentalism believes that it is not only necessary but possible to increase domestic saving; but for that to happen, the first condition is to have a competitive instead of a chronically overvalued currency that increases artificially wages and consumption.

Seventh, now entering the realm of macroeconomic policy, the central bank has a single mandate: to control inflation; other objectives are to be pursued by the government. In contrast, for conventional orthodoxy the central bank should have a triple mandate: in association with the finance ministry, the central bank should control inflation, keep the exchange rate competitive (compatible with the current account balance and the gradual transfer of manpower to more knowledge-intensive or high per capita value-added industries), and achieve reasonably full employment. Thus, the central bank does not have full independence, insofar as this role should be performed together with the government.

Contrary to what neoclassical macroeconomics asserts, the central bank does not have at its disposal a single instrument but several instruments besides the interest rate: it may accumulate foreign exchange reserves and establish capital inflow controls to avoid the tendency of the exchange rate to relative appreciation—a common tendency among middle-income countries. The interest rate is an instrument to control inflation, but its average level may be considerably lower than conventional orthodoxy assumes for developing countries.

Eighth, for conventional orthodoxy the primary surplus is the central fiscal objective, whereas new developmentalism is more demanding in this matter: it wants most public investments to be financed by public savings, and considers the convenience of budget surplus if, in consequence of the neutralization of the Dutch disease, current account surplus materializes. I have already mentioned that the country should neutralize the Dutch disease with the help of a tax or retention on sales or exports that shifts the supply curve of the "Dutch disease" goods to the competitive equilibrium—the industrial one. In consequence, it should represent a fiscal surplus insofar as the revenues from the tax or "retention" on the goods originating the disease should not be expended, but used to build a sovereign fund.

According to structuralist development macroeconomics, the exchange rate is not only a macroeconomic price. It is also a major instrument of growth, as recent research has demonstrated.[14] Before the 1990s, conventional orthodoxy was concerned with foreign exchange rates and, during balance-of-payments crises, always demanded foreign-exchange depreciations in addition to fiscal adjustments. Since the 1990s, however, this policy has been abandoned. Instead, the IMF has practically forgotten current account deficits (they were foreign savings) and limited its recommendations to exchange rate depreciation. The twin-deficit hypothesis exempted it from worrying about current account deficits: all it had to do was to concern itself with the primary surplus. For a while, it chose to support foreign exchange-rate anchors and dollarization; after the failure of that strategy in Mexico, Brazil, and above all Argentina, the IMF turned to fully floating exchange rates combined with inflation targeting—another and more indirect way of imposing a nominal anchor on the economy insofar as the appreciation of the currency caused by high interest rates represented the main outcome of the inflation-targeting policy.

Thus, ninth, conventional orthodoxy supports a fully floating exchange rate, defines no exchange rate objectives, and rejects the possibility of an exchange rate policy, whereas new developmentalism wants a floating but managed exchange rate, and aims at a competitive exchange rate that corresponds to the industrial equilibrium, i.e. to the rate that produces economically viable and tradable industries utilizing the best technology. Conventional orthodoxy insists that it is "impossible" to manage the long-term exchange rate, but historical evidence shows the contrary; this may be true for the United States, where the dollar is the international reserve currency, but it is not true for other countries.

Tenth, for conventional orthodoxy the central bank uses a single instrument—the short-term interest rate—while the government keeps public deficit under control. In contrast, in new developmentalism the central bank may also buy reserves, and the government besides controlling the budget may impose control on capital inflows. The argument that capital controls are not viable is not empirically correct; the inference

---

[14] There is a growing literature relating the exchange rate to investments, savings, and growth (Razin and Collins 1997; Bresser-Pereira and Nakano 2003; Gala 2006; Bresser-Pereira and Gala 2007; Rodrik 2007; Eichengreen 2008; Williamson 2008; Bresser-Pereira 2010).

that, given Mundell's triangle of impossibility, countries are supposed to renounce capital controls to have autonomy in monetary policy and guarantee capital mobility starts from the assumption that capital mobility is preferable to control of the exchange rate—which is at least debatable.

Finally, since developing countries are dualistic countries that face the problem of an unlimited supply of labor, there is the tendency of wages to increase more slowly than productivity. Thus, there is a tendency towards the concentration of income that must be checked by economic policy—particularly by a minimum wage policy and a large program of social expenditures in education, health care, social assistance, and social security—not only for distributive reasons, but also because inequality is a source of political instability that is eventually a major obstacle to growth (Przeworski and Curvale 2006).

5.7 CONCLUSION

New developmentalism draws on the experience of fast-growing Asian countries and on a structuralist development macroeconomics. This approach is based on two structural tendencies that grow on the demand side: the tendency to overvalue the exchange rate and the tendency of wages to grow below the increase of productivity. The first tendency calls principally for the neutralization of the Dutch disease and growth with domestic savings, and the second calls for incomes policy, particularly for minimum wage and social expenditures policy. Short-term macroeconomic policies must be oriented to responsible fiscal practices, a moderate average interest rate, and a competitive exchange rate; this is the policy tripod of new developmentalism, whereas conventional orthodoxy usually supports high interest rates and overvalued exchange rates. Both strategies support fiscal discipline, but only new developmentalism asks for a balanced current account.

Can new developmentalism become hegemonic in Latin America, as developmentalism was in the past? I believe so, since Keynesian-structuralist economists demonstrate to the business and political elites of the region that they offer a practical and responsible cluster of policies—policies that will increase financial stability and make economic growth substantially higher. Since the early 2000s it has become clear that the time of Washington Consensus is over; the present global financial crisis has put a definitive end to it. New perspectives are opening up for Latin America. In the framework of new developmentalism, each individual country now has the possibility of adopting effectively national development strategies—strategies that widen the role of the state in regulating markets, that create profit opportunities stimulating private investment and innovation, and that increase the country's international competitiveness while protecting labor, the poor, and the environment.

REFERENCES

ALEJANDRO, C. D. (1981). 'Southern Cone stabilization plans', in W. Cline and S. Weintraub (eds), *Economic Stabilization in Developing Countries*, Washington, DC: Brookings Institution.

BACHA, E. L. (1973). 'Sobre a dinâmica de crescimento da economía industrial subdesenvolvida', *Pesquisa e planejamento econômico* 3.4.

—— and TAYLOR, E. (1976). 'The unequalizing spiral: a first growth model for Belindia', *Quarterly Journal of Economics* 90.2: 197–218.

BIELSCHOWSKY, R. (2008). 'Desenvolvimento econômico, inclusão social e a dinâmica de consumo de massa', presented to the Escola de Administração Fazendária do Ministério da Fazenda, Brazil, September.

BRESSER-PEREIRA, L. C. (1970). 'Dividir ou multiplicar? A distribuição da renda e a recuperação da economia brasileira' [Divide or multiply? Income distribution and the recovery of the Brazilian economy], *Visão*, November 21. Reprinted in *Development and Crisis in Brazil*, Boulder, Colo.: Westview Press,1984. Available at: www.bresserpereira.org.br

—— (1974). 'El nuevo modelo brasileño de desarrollo' [The new Brazilian development model], *Desarrollo económico* 14.55: 569–88.

—— (1977). *Estado e subdesenvolvimento industrializado* [State and industrialized underdevelopment], São Paulo: Brasiliense.

—— (ed.) (1984). 'Divide or multiply? Income distribution and the recovery of the Brazilian economy', in *Development and Crisis in Brazil*, Boulder, Colo.: Westview Press.

—— (2006). 'De la CEPAL y del ISEB a la teoría de la dependencia' [From ECLAC and ISEB to dependency theory], *Desarrollo económico* 46.183: 419–40.

—— (2008). 'Dutch disease and its neutralization: a Ricardian approach', *Brazilian Journal of Political Economy* 28.1: 47–71.

—— (2010). *Globalization and Competition: Why Some Emergent Countries Succeed while Others Fall Behind*, New York: Cambridge University Press.

—— (2011). 'From the national-bourgeois to the associated dependency interpretation of Latin-America', *Latin American Perspectives*: 178, 38.3: 40–58.

—— and GALA, P. (2007). 'Why foreign savings fail to cause growth', *Brazilian Journal of Political Economy* 27.1: 3–19.

—— and NAKANO, Y. (1987). *The Theory of Inertial Inflation: The Foundation of Economic Reform in Brazil and Argentina*, Boulder, Colo.: Rienner.

—— —— (2003). 'Economic growth with foreign savings?', *Brazilian Journal of Political Economy* 23.2: 3–27.

CANITROT, A. (1975). 'La experiencia populista de distribución de renta' [The populist experience of income distribution], *Desarrollo económico* 15.59: 331–51.

CARDENAS, H., OCAMPO, J. A., and THORP, R. (eds) (2001). *The Export Age: The Latin American Economies in the Late Nineteenth and Early Twentieth Centuries* (An Economic History of Twentieth-Century Latin America 1), Basingstoke and New York: Palgrave and St. Martin's.

CARDOSO, F. H., and FALETTO, E. (1979). *Dependency and Development in Latin America*, Berkeley: University of California Press.

CHANG, H.-J. (2003). *Kicking Away the Ladder: Development Strategy in Historical Perspective*, London: Anthem Press.

DUTT, A. K., and Ros, J. (eds) (2003). 'Development economics and political economy', in *Development Economics and Structuralist Macroeconomics*, Cheltenham: Elgar.

EICHENGREEN, B. (2008). 'The real exchange rate and economic growth', prepared for the Commission on Growth and Development, Washington, DC: World Bank.

FFRENCH-DAVIS, R. (2003). *Entre el neoliberalismo y el crecimiento con equidad* [Between neoliberalism and growth with equity], 3rd edn, Santiago, Chile: Sáes.

FRANK, A. G. (1966). 'The development of underdevelopment', *Monthly Review* 18.4: 17–31.

FRENKEL, R. (2003). 'Globalización y crisis financieras en América Latina' [Globalization and financial crises in Latin America], *Revista de economia política* 23.3: 94–111.

——(2008). 'Tipo de cambio real competitivo, inflación y política monetaria', *Revista de la CEPAL* 96: 189–99.

FURTADO, C. (1963a). *The Economic Growth of Brazil*, Los Angeles: University of California Press.

——(1963b). *Plano trienal de desenvolvimento econômico e social (1963–1965)* [The three-year plan of economic and social development], Rio de Janeiro: Síntese.

——(1970). *Obstacles to Development in Latin America*, New York: Anchor Books.

GALA, P. (2006). 'Política cambial e macroeconomia do desenvolvimento' [Exchange rate policy and development macroeconomics], São Paulo: São Paulo School of Economics of Getulio Vargas Foundation, Ph.D dissertation.

GELLNER, E. (1983). *Nations and Nationalism*, Ithaca, NY: Cornell University Press.

——(1996). 'The coming of nationalism and its interpretation: the myths of nation and class', in G. Balakrishnan (ed.), *Mapping the Nation*, London: Verso.

LEWIS, A. W. (1954). 'Economic development with unlimited supply of labor', *The Manchester School* 22.2: 139–91.

MANKIW, N. G. (2006). 'The macroeconomist as scientist and engineer', *Journal of Economic Perspectives* 20.4: 29–46.

OCAMPO, J. A., and PARRA, M. A. (2008). 'The Dual Divergence: Successes and Collapses in the Developing World Since 1980', in J. A. Ocampo, K. S. Jomo, and R. Vos (eds), *Growth Divergences*, London: Zed Books.

——and Vos, R. (2008). *Uneven Economic Development*, London: Zed Books, in association with the United Nations.

——— and JOMO, K. S. (eds) (2008). *Growth Divergences*, London: Zed Books, in association with the United Nations.

PAZOS, F. (1972). *Chronic Inflation in Latin America*, New York: Praeger.

PRZEWORSKI, A., and CURVALE, C. (2006). 'Explica la política la brecha económica entre Estados Unidos y América Latina?' [Does politics explain the economic gap between the United States and Latin America?], in F. Fukuyama (ed.), *La brecha entre América Latina y Estados Unidos*, Buenos Aires: Fondo de Cultura Económica.

RAZIN, O., and COLLINS, S. (1997). 'Real exchange rate misalignments and growth', NBER Working Paper No. 6147, Cambridge, Mass.

RODRIK, D. (2007). 'The real exchange rate and economic growth: theory and evidence', WCFIA Working Paper No. 141, Harvard University.

ROS, JAIME (2003). 'Inflation, stabilization and growth: multiple equilibria in a structuralist model', in A. Dutt and J. Ros (eds), *Development Economics and Structuralist Macroeconomics*, Cheltenham: Elgar.

SACHS, JEFFREY D. (1990). 'Social conflict and populist policies in Latin America', in R. Brunetta and C. Dell-Arringa (eds), *Labor Relations and Economic Performance*, New York: Macmillan.

TAVARES, M., and SERRA, J. (1972). 'Além da estagnação' [Beyond stagnation], in M. Tavares (ed.), *Da substituição de importações ao capitalismo financeiro* [From imports substitution to finance capitalism], Rio de Janeiro: Zahar.

TAYLOR, L. (1983). *Structuralist Macroeconomics: Applicable Models for the Third World*, New York: Basic Books.

—— (1991). *Income Distribution, Inflation, and Growth*, Cambridge, Mass.: MIT Press.

WILLIAMSON, J. (ed.) (1990) 'The progress of policy reform in Latin America', in *Latin American Adjustment: How Much Has Happened?* Washington, DC: Institute for International Economics.

—— (2008). 'Exchange rate economics', Working Paper No. 3, Washington, DC: Peterson Institute for International Economics.

....

CHAPTER 6

ENVIRONMENTAL
SUSTAINABILITY

....

CARLOS J. DE MIGUEL AND OSVALDO SUNKEL

6.1 INTRODUCTION

....

> The exceptional (economic) impetus gained over the last few decades, until recent times, is the consequence not only of impressive technical progress but also of irrational exploitation of natural resources-above all, of energy—which, in its turn, has had a marked influence on the orientation of technique...Until recent times technological research had not concerned itself with the adverse effects of technique on the environment...Thus, the repercussions of development on the biosphere are very serious.

These prescient words were written by Raul Prebisch in 1980 in a context of oil crisis, thus incorporating environmental issues in his characterization of the structure of peripheral capitalism. He also noted that the ambivalence of technology—its enormous contribution to human welfare, thanks to the steady upward trend of productivity, in opposition to its damaging repercussions on the biosphere—was considered to be an exogenous element by economists, and required deliberate action to resolve these contradictions which escaped the regulatory operation of market laws.

There has been progress since then: on the one hand there has been the development of the environmental economy; on the other, governments in the region are more conscious of the state's role, so that either from conviction or from a variety of national and international pressures, action has been taken not to achieve the "major adjustments in the operation of the system" (Prebisch 1980), but rather to mitigate the most adverse or contentious environmental effects. The question is whether this has contributed or will contribute to progress in the development of peripheral economies—Latin America and the Caribbean—resolving the problems of the biosphere, or whether new forms of development must be devised. To find an answer, we analyze, first, the relationship between styles of development and the environment; second, the state of the environment and natural resources arising from this relationship; and third, whether existing policies and current international challenges might provide the region with a new opportunity for more sustainable development.

6.2 THE DEPENDENCE OF LATIN AMERICA AND THE CARIBBEAN'S DEVELOPMENT STYLE ON ITS NATURAL ASSETS

The development style that dominated the world in the 1980s and increasingly in Latin American countries was the "transnational" (Sunkel 1980), characterized by the dominant role of transnational corporations; significant limitations on national governments to choose alternative development paths; homogenization of patterns of production and consumption on a world scale; internationalization of industrial production and promotion of the formation of global value chains; intensive and continuing technological innovation; and also the intensified exploitation of natural resources and growing dependence on hydrocarbons, and the generation of wastes and pollutants on a large scale. What we now call "globalization" has accentuated the interdependence of countries. The links between international trade and the environment and between developed and developing countries (Ocampo and Martin 2004), are examples of dual interdependence. Above all, what is now a part of the problem will undoubtedly become part of the solution.

In a region marked by structural, social, and ecological heterogeneity, this style of development arose by exploiting comparative advantages which reinforced a preexisting production structure, based on the exploitation of natural resources, which benefits from a bias towards investment, innovation, and technological development. On the other hand, with slow (and volatile) economic growth the region's serious poverty and inequality problems encouraged short-term priorities, further placing the environment at a disadvantage.

While the region has shown a sectoral shift to services from primary and industrial activities, the reduced weight of the latter does not mean less pressure on the environment. On the contrary, a growth strategy based on greater international integration encourages the expansion of the agricultural frontier, increasing mineral, forestry, and fisheries resources extraction, and an intensification of pollutant emissions (Table 6.1).

From the 1970s to the present day, more than 150 million hectares have been incorporated into agricultural production, although the intensity of change has declined considerably in recent years (Table 6.1 and Figure 6.1). Between 1990 and 2005, 4.5 million hectares per year of forest area was lost, representing around 7% of the region's area recorded in 1990 (FAO 2007). The principal generator of change has been livestock production, particularly in humid tropical zones. Mexico's and Central America's

Table 6.1 Physical indicators for Latin America and the Caribbean: average annual growth rates (%)

	Units	1980–84	1985–9	1990–94	1995–9	2000	2005–9
Agricultural area	000 hectares	0.40	0.50	0.50	0.20	0.1[a]	—
Volume of agricultural production	000 metric tons	3.30	–3.00	4.70	–1.10	6.1[b]	—
Fertilizer consumption	Tonnes	–0.40	2.40	4.30	7.60	9.00	4.0[c]
Cattle stocks	000 head	1.00	1.60	1.20	0.5[d]	–	—
Volume of production of industrial roundwood	000 m^3	1.30	4.00	3.40	2.00	2.4[b]	—
Firewood production	000 m^3	1.50	1.20	1.50	1.20	0.4[b]	—
Fish production (marine catch)	Metric tonnes	5.90	6.90	11.10	–4.10	–15.9[e]	—
Fish production (aquaculture)	Metric tonnes	38.70	23.80	18.20	11.40	38.1[e]	—
Mining production (volume) including petroleum	000 tons	1.30	3.50	3.20	2.40	2.60	–0.4[f]
Mining production (volume) excluding petroleum	000 tons	–1.80	7.20	3.30	1.20	4.90	1.4[f]
Carbon Dioxide (CO$_2$) emissions	Tonnes	0.80	3.10	3.10	3.60	2.8[a]	—
Population growth (%)	000	2.10	1.90	1.80	1.60	1.30	1.30
Gross Domestic Product: accumulated increase	Million $US at constant prices of year 2000	0.20	2.10	4.10	3.00	2.00	5.2[g]

[a] 2000–5   [b] 2000–2   [c] 2005–6   [d] 1995–8   [e] 2000–1   [f] 2005–7   [g] 2005–8.

Source: Authors, based on Environmental Statistics and Indicators (BADEIMA); Sustainable Development Indicators (BADESALC); Economic Statistics and Indicators (BADECON) and Annual Statistical Yearbook for Latin America and the Caribbean, 2008, ECLAC.

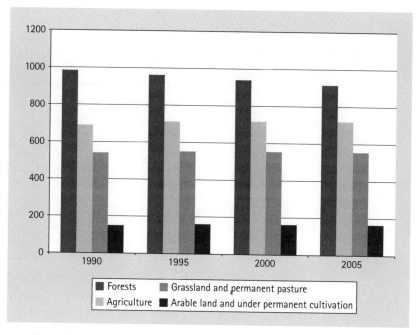

FIGURE 6.1 Latin America and the Caribbean: changes in soil usage (000 hectares)

Source: FAO (2007).

production structure has shifted toward 'in-bond' (*maquila*) manufacture to the detriment of natural resources, which contrasts with the fact that Central America is the subregion that has experienced the greatest pressure on forests. The intensification and modernization of agriculture, particularly in South America, and the push by the forest products industry based on plantations, partly explains this reduced pressure. Flourishing monoculture agriculture for export, for example soya, is linked to the expansion of the agricultural frontier, greater use of fertilizers and pesticides, and greater concentration of landownership, with severe social and ecological impacts. Besides, once the most productive lands have been occupied, changes in soil usage occur over more fragile eco-systems and with greater biological diversity.

Around 12% of the forest areas of Latin America and the Caribbean is used for production. However, while in Central America and the Caribbean the principal use is firewood, in South America exploitation is principally industrial. In 2005, industrial usage was greater than that for firewood. Forestry has experienced an extraordinary boom since the 1990s, principally in South America. The leading exporters of forest products are Guyana, Chile, Brazil, and Uruguay. The Caribbean, Central America, and Mexico are net importers. All the littoral countries of Latin America and the Caribbean are net exporters of fish products; they represent more than 8% of Guyana's GDP, almost 5% of Surinam, 4% of Ecuador, and 3% of Panama and Chile (FAO 2006). Mining is the other sector that is fundamental to the regional economy, as a net exporter of metals and hydrocarbons. The continent's production of zinc, aluminium, and copper represents 28, 22, and 19% respectively of world production.

In summary, primary products represent around 35% of regional exports, a proportion which climbs to 47% if Mexico is excluded. If manufactures based on natural resources are also included, such as petrol refining, processed forest, and agricultural products and metals, the percentage of exports increases to 54% with Mexico included, and jumps to 72% if it is excluded (Table 6.2). In countries like Venezuela, Jamaica or Ecuador it reaches 90%, while Chile, Bolivia, and Trinidad and Tobago easily exceed 80%. It might be thought that higher prices for raw materials favor the stability of the quantum, which would relieve environmental pressures, but its growth has been maintained within its trend.

It is now clear that it is possible to talk of two regional patterns of specialization. First, that of South America, based on natural resources as the driving force of development; second, that of Mexico, Central America, and the Caribbean, where low- and medium-level technology-based manufactures, using cheap labor, have gained ground vis-à-vis the previous dependence on the natural assets. For this last group, tourism is a growing component in the development model. Both development patterns have their environmental consequences. The first, as well as the possible exhaustion of natural resources (e.g. several fish stocks), generates important environmental liabilities. It also produces important environmental externalities like air, water, and soil contamination, and, no less importantly, it can provoke a loss of a region's natural heritage. The second of these patterns itself has both direct and indirect externalities, the latter associated with the process of precarious urbanization to accommodate the workforce. Finally, massive tourism has had important consequences for the sustainability of the coast and the very fragile marine and territorial ecosystems that exist in that environment.

The environmental consequences of foreign direct investment (FDI) are difficult to evaluate. On the one hand it has had a crucial role in helping define huge export projects which exploit natural resources, and in the increasingly competitive trajectory of environmentally sensitive industries (Romo Murillo 2007). On the other, it can bring better environmental practices, and has facilitated the development of public service enterprises, particularly water and sanitation, in many countries that have granted concessions to private transnational firms. Finally, there is no clear evidence that Latin America has encouraged environmental havens; specific studies show that when investing in the region, it is legal security, the rules about investment protection, country risk, quality of the labor force, etc. that are the key issues, well above a concern with environmental norms and their laxity. Also, the presence of foreign capital and the importance of exports in total firm sales notably increase the likelihood of environmental investments, together with the larger size of firms, their age, the strictness of the environmental controls, and local social pressures (Ferraz and Seroa da Motta 2001).

The fundamental origin of the energy that feeds this development model and contributes to its pressures is petroleum. Although its role has diminished since the 1970s, it still represents 45% of energy supply. In 2005 fossil fuels provided around 70% of regional energy, and they will gain ground as a component of the energy matrix in coming years

Table 6.2 Latin America and the Caribbean: trade composition by category, 1990–2006 (%)

	1990		2000		2006	
	Including Mexico	Excluding Mexico	Including Mexico	Excluding Mexico	Including Mexico	Excluding Mexico
Exports						
Primary products	**49.1**	**49.7**	**27.5**	**41.1**	**35.9**	**47.0**
Industrialized goods	**49.8**	**49.1**	**70.9**	**56.2**	**61.6**	**49.5**
Based on natural resources	22.0	24.5	17.3	27.6	18.3	24.6
Low technology	9.6	10.3	11.8	8.6	8.1	6.2
Medium technology	15.6	12.2	25.3	14.0	23.1	14.8
High technology	2.6	2.0	16.6	6.0	12.1	3.9
Other transactions	**1.2**	**1.3**	**1.5**	**2.6**	**2.6**	**3.5**
Total	**100.0**	**100.0**	**100.0**	**100.0**	**100.0**	**100.0**
Imports						
Primary products	**18.6**	**21.1**	**9.6**	**13.5**	**10.9**	**14.2**
Industrialized goods	**76.8**	**77.4**	**88.0**	**85.2**	**85.9**	**81.7**
Based on natural resources	19.8	20.3	15.9	20.1	17.4	18.9
Low technology	10.0	9.0	14.9	12.2	12.6	10.9
Medium technology	34.1	35.5	35.6	33.9	35.4	34.3
High technology	12.9	12.7	21.6	19.0	20.5	17.5
Other transactions	**4.6**	**1.5**	**2.4**	**1.3**	**3.1**	**4.1**
Total	**100.0**	**100.0**	**100.0**	**100.0**	**100.0**	**100.0**

Source: Based on ECLAC (2008b).

because of the growth of gas and coal. Hydro-energy represented only a small part of the energy supply at the beginning of the 1970s, thereafter increasing progressively and stabilizing at around 9%. The reform process and investment dynamics, together with the greater availability of gas, advanced the development of combined thermal cycle to the detriment of hydroelectricity (Acquatella 2008; Altomonte 2008). Above all, the region continues to be (relatively) one of the cleanest in terms of energy supply. Hydroelectricity is four times greater than the world average. Renewable energy, principally biomass, while reducing its proportion, continues to represent around 18% of supply, and biofuels are notably being developed under Brazil's leadership. Other sources of renewable energy such as solar, wind, geothermal, and tidal, while at an early stage, show great potential.

The growth of the region's energy intensity has been practically stagnant since the 1970s, in contrast to the reductions achieved in other areas of the world; it is higher than the OECD countries, but substantially less than China. Total energy consumption (in thousands of barrels of oil equivalent) per million dollars (constant 2000 prices) was 1.59 in 1971, declining to 1.47 in 1980, following the petroleum crisis—a figure similar to the 2007 calculation of 1.46. The stagnation of the energy intensity of Latin America and the Caribbean is related to its productive and export structure, and—with the increase in per capita electricity use and fuel consumption for transport—a product

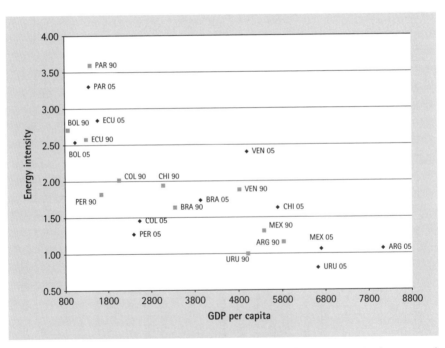

FIGURE 6.2 Select countries: evolution of energy intensity and GDP per capita (1990–2005)

Source: From statistics and economic indicators (BADECON) and Annual Statistical Yearbook for Latin America and the Caribbean (ECLAC 2008).

Note: The Energy Intensity Index is expressed in millions of barrels of petroleum equivalent per million US $ of GDP at constant prices of year 2000. GDP per capita is calculated in US constant $2,000.

of the population's greater acquisitive power. However, there are notable differences among subregions and countries, in terms both of energy intensity and of its evolution. So Central America, and particularly Mexico, show reduced energy intensity, while in South America it remains stable. Ecuador and Venezuela, petroleum exporters, have increased their intensity, as has Brazil (although by less), while the remaining countries have reduced it (Figure 6.2).

Total energy consumption per capita across the region is very dissimilar. While the average for Latin America and the Caribbean was 40 gigajoules in 2005, around 50% more than at the beginning of the 1970s, Central America reached 23. Trinidad and Tobago, Mexico and Venezuela consume most (159, 64, and 63 gigajoules respectively), while Haiti, Bolivia, Honduras, and Nicaragua experience the greatest shortages (under 20).

6.3 The state of the environmental and the natural resources in Latin America and the Caribbean

Latin America and the Caribbean is a region rich in natural resources and biodiversity, and contains almost a quarter of the world's forest area. In relative terms it can be regarded as an environmentally privileged region. Nevertheless, it is a region that continues to face pressures caused by antiquated production processes and territorial settlements, which have been magnified by the predominant development model. In spite of the strategies and specific policies that have reversed some deterioration and encouraged systems and technologies that minimize environmental impacts, as we will see, the balance has been negative (Gligo 1995).

6.3.1 The rural environment: biodiversity, deforestation, soil degradation, and desertification

Latin America and the Caribbean, with its climatic and physiological diversity, is the greatest source of genetic biodiversity in the world. There are more "megadiverse" countries than in other regions—Bolivia, Brazil, Colombia, Costa Rica, Ecuador, Mexico, Peru, and Venezuela. The Amazon is considered to be the planet's lungs, and is home to 50% of the world's biodiversity. The existence of endemic species in the region is a great responsibility; their disappearance would also result in their extinction from the planet (ECLAC/UNEP 2002); moreover, numerous animal and vegetable species have an economic potential that would be lost if they disappeared. According to the *Global Environmental Outlook* "GEO-4" (UNEP 2007), the threat to biodiversity and ecosystems constitutes one of the four great environmental priorities for the region.

Many of the environmental problems are linked to changes in land use. In particular, deforestation to increase cultivated land and grassland is the principal cause of biodiversity loss as well as of soil degradation and desertification, and seriously affects the availability and regulation of water resources. The region is dedicating almost half its natural ecosystems to agriculture and cattle (ECLAC/UNEP 2002), and 66% of the loss of the world's forest cover, between 2000 and 2005 (GEO-4), is occurring in Latin America, principally Brazil. Soil degradation affects around 16% of the territory, being particularly severe in Central America; the erosion of the Andean and Central American mountain zones, the desertification that affects 25% of the surface, and the contamination of water resources have a very negative impact on the genetic heritage.

The countries of the region have made a notable effort to conserve their natural inheritance by organizing protected areas (the majority on land, although the number of marine reserves are growing). This force is principally funded from the national budget. The creation of the Meso-American Biological Corridor and the program for the conservation of the tropical humid forest in Brazil are some of the experiments that have encouraged a strong increase in the number of protected areas in the region. The government of Ecuador, for example, has developed the initiative Yasuni-ITT, which hopes

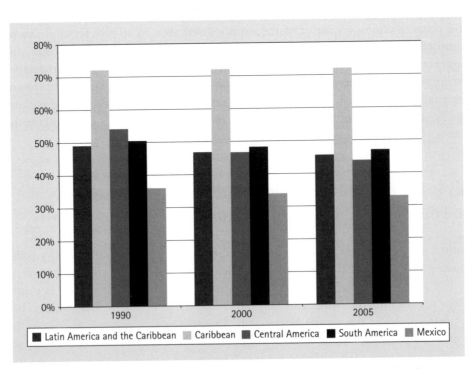

FIGURE 6.3 Latin America and the Caribbean: proportion of land areas covered by forest

Source: Based on the *Statistical Yearbook for Latin America and the Caribbean* (ECLAC 2008).

to pay Ecuador to stop exploitation in perpetuity of untapped underground oil reserves in one of the most biologically diverse regions in the world. From 1990, depending on the subregion, protected areas have grown by between 50% and 100%, with South America showing the greatest increase. In 2007 Venezuela had 70% of its territory under protection, with Belize, Colombia, and Guatemala having around 30% and Brazil tripling its 1990 figure. There have been notable increases in protected areas since that date in Ecuador, Mexico, Nicaragua, and Surinam, with figures of around 7% to 15%.

Furthermore, changing land use is the main source of emissions of greenhouse gases in the region. The Latin American and Caribbean forests store an average of 138 tonnes of carbon per hectare from vegetation and another 128 tonnes from soils (ECLAC 2008a). The tropical forests hold most of the reserves. The 2007 report of the International Group of Experts on Climate Change ran simulations using the value of 109 tonnes per hectare as a base; assuming that the region would loose 68.7 million hectares of forest between 1990 and 2005, then almost 7,500 million tonnes of carbon, equivalent to 27,500 tonnes of CO_2, would have entered the atmosphere; with a conservative estimate of US$10 per tonne, this would have amounted to US$ 75,000 million over the period, or an annual loss of US$5,000 million— a substantial sum, which could amount to between 3% and 4% of agricultural value added. Further, one would have to assume that a good part of this forest cover would be replaced by cattle, with a consequent increase in methane emissions. The loss for the region is clear enough, even though the analysis did not consider the costs and benefits associated with projects or policies that affect deforestation.

About 25% of Latin American and Caribbean land is dry, and it is estimated that over 75% of the land area, like cultivated land, show evidence of soil degradation. The figures are few and divergent; nevertheless, all countries in the region face some sort of soil degradation, making numerous ecosystems highly vulnerable. In Central America, the pine and oak forests, the dry forests of the Pacific Coast, and the thorn forests in Guatemala are very vulnerable, principally because the poor live on and cultivate inadequate slopes, which become degraded, which obliges them to expand cultivation to even more vulnerable zones (ECLAC 2008a). In the Caribbean, the extreme meteorological events and marked seasonal variations of rainfall alternate with prolonged droughts and torrential rain, which aggravate soil degradation, particularly on islands of volcanic origin, and exhaust the coastal areas. The island of La Espanola, Haitian territory, is an example of extreme degradation. In South America, as well as the severe degradation of the high plateau (*altiplano*), there are the well-known cases of the Brazilian North East and the Chaco. According to different studies, the costs of degradation are very high, and can fluctuate between 3% and 13% of agricultural value added. Estimating the costs of biodiversity loss is very complicated, for while it is a fundamental asset that contributes to human welfare by providing various ecosystem goods and services, it also has an intrinsic value (Millennium Ecosystem Assessment 2005), without market values.

Other factors to consider in this balance are the contributions of fertilizers and pesticides to the intensification and extension of agricultural production, deforestation, and soil erosion; their abuse creates negative externalities for aquifers and biodiversity. Fertilizer consumption has been increasing at accelerating rates since 1980, to an average annual rate of 9% for the first five years of the 2000s; from then the rate appears to have moderated. Information about recent herbicides and pesticides use is limited, as the FAO has stopped updating this series. As both toxic and bio-accumulative substances, they can cause serious human and animal health problems.

6.3.2 The urban environment: atmospheric and hydraulic contamination, garbage, dangerous residues, and congestion

Latin America and the Caribbean is a highly urban region. Seventy-seven per cent of the 550 million population live in cities, which increases to almost 90% in the Southern Cone. Mega cities are commonplace—almost all capitals are in this category. Mexico City, São Paulo, Buenos Aires, and Lima have 20, 18, 3, and 9 million inhabitants respectively. The dominant paradigm is associated with a high level of industrial concentration and intense migrations from the countryside to the city, encouraged by greater opportunities. In fact, with the exceptions of Chile and Uruguay, the rate of poverty is always higher in rural than urban areas (ECLAC 2009a). Soil degradation and natural disasters are factors that contribute to this migration.

One regional priority must be to face the irrational growth of cities and the consequences of this for the environment. The lack of urban planning has been well documented (Jordán and Martínez 2009; Samaniego, Jordán, and Rehner 2009,) with multiple environmental consequences: increases in solid waste as well as liquid residues, atmospheric contamination,[1] access to clean water and sanitation, pressure on surrounding ecosystems, among others; but in turn, the loss of urban environmental quality directly affects the health and welfare of citizens. In addition, urban sprawl and the preference for automobiles over public transport has created congestion, more and longer journeys, and greater energy consumption that increases air contamination, so making urban transport another regional challenge. The automobile fleet continues to grow; between 1980 and 2000 the number of automobiles practically doubled, although the ratio per 100 inhabitants remains low at fewe4r than 20. The number of light vehicles is expected to double between 2000 and 2030, and by 2050 to be triple the 2000 number (Samaniego 2009). Some governments are making efforts to improve public transport; noteworthy are Bogota (*Transmilenio*), Curitiba, Mexico City (*Metrobús*), and Santiago, Chile (*TranSantiago, Chile*). However, most incentives encourage private transport, pedestrian infrastructure is deficient, and bicycle paths are nonexistent.

---

[1] Intra-household pollution is an important factor for morbidity and mortality from respiratory diseases in the region, but it also occurs in rural areas and is associated with burning biomass for heating and cooking food. In the region, its impact on health is higher than pollution from particulates and other gases in the cities themselves, but this often goes unnoticed. The countries most affected are in the Andes (Bolivia, Ecuador, and Peru), part of Central America, and Haiti.

Table 6.3 Under-5 mortality

Countries and sub-regions	Under 5 mortality (by 1,000 live births)	Deaths recorded as due to serious respiratory infection (%)
Latin America and the Caribbean	40	9
Brazil	45	7
Mexico	34	10
Andean region	40	11
Southern Cone	23	6
Central America	45	21
Latin Caribbean	46	7
English Caribbean	28	6

Source: PAHO (2004).

Table 6.4 PM10 emissions in select cities (%)

City	Mobile	Fixed	Area
Bogota	33.3	66.6	
Buenos Aires	63.6	4.0	32.4
Lima	66.3	33.0	0.7
Mexico city	61.4	32.7	5.9
Sao Paulo[a]	44.8	55.2	0.0
Santiago	56.4	31.4	12.2

Source: PAHO (2005).

Notes: [a] For São Paulo the figures refer to total suspended solids.

More than 100 million people are exposed to atmospheric contamination that exceed WHO guidelines in the region, creating serious health problems (Cifuentes et al. 2005). Over 35, 000 deaths—principally the elderly, children, and asthmatics—are attributed to air contamination (PAHO 2002).

Emissions of particulate matter, including its precursors such as sulfur dioxide and nitrogen oxides, have different origins. Transport is the main source of direct and indirect pollution drag and lift (Table 6.4). The paving of streets, reducing the sulfur content of fuels, and improved technical reviews and modernization of the automobile fleet are valuable steps, but need to be reinforced. For example, Brazil's diesel sulfur content is around 1,000 ppm, compared to 500 ppm in Mexico City, while in Santiago, Chile it has been reduced to 50 ppm. Most European countries insist of a maximum of 50 ppm, and for Scandinavian countries the limit is 15 ppm (Walsh 2005). Bus and truck ppm values are extremely high and fleets are poorly maintained, while automobile replacement is very low (many are 10 and even 20 years old). Growing congestion contributes to emission increases.

Fixed or industrial emissions are the second most important source of pollution, although most affected cities have imposed norms and standards for their control. The geographical location of some cities like Santiago, Chile and Mexico City have special climatic and topographical conditions, with inverted thermal episodes that reduce their natural dispersion and result in critical situations and greater population exposure.

Cifuentes et al. (2005) show that 26 Latin American cities, with a combined population of 81 million people, are exposed to particulates at a level far higher than the accepted international limits. A reduction to North American standards could avoid 10,500–13,500 premature deaths as well as the associated social costs. This number is the equivalent of between 2% and 2.6% of annual deaths in the cities studied.

The region's urban population face a dual challenge, with threats associated with access to safe water and garbage disposal and the recent and growing risks of contamination. While the region is providing more drinking water and better sanitation, especially in urban centers, more than 130 million people remain without these services, and a similar number live in slums. Only 14% of water supply is treated, which compares to 23% for garbage. Over the last 30 years, the quantity of residual solids has doubled in the region, and the share of organic and toxic wastes has increased. These conditions, in the context of poverty and poor hygiene behavior, have a strong impact on health. Intestinal illnesses are one of the principal causes of under-5 mortality, which is an indicator that varies directly and significantly with poverty levels and inversely with sanitation coverage and access to drinking water (ECLAC 2005). Countries where there has been an increase in sewage treatment show notable reductions in hepatitis, cholera, and typhoid fever.

It should not be forgotten that an important number of cities are located on or near the coast, with channels that discharge contaminated water into the sea. Half the region's population lives within 100 km of the coast. Thus, coastal degradation and the contamination of the sea are great environmental challenges to the region. The coastal and marine ecosystems have been strongly affected by population pressures, infrastructure development, and tourism. Aquaculture—principally for the development of shrimp farms—has caused losses to the mangrove swamp of 67% in Panama, 36% in Mexico, and 25% in Peru (UNEP 2007). Coral reefs are also threatened: in the Caribbean, around 61% of the reefs are under threat because of tourism and contamination, among other factors. In turn, the loss of these natural barriers increases the vulnerability of coastal human settlements to natural events. In general, the region's oceans are affected by water pollution, which stems from urban and rural inland activities increasing the nutrients that cause eutrophication problems, urban expansion, lack of sewage treatment (86% without treatment), lack of control of vessel discharges and oil spills, and minor water flows into rivers that increase the level of salinity.

6.4 Toward sustainable development— opportunity or traumatic adjustment?

6.4.1 The basis of natural resources; sustainability and "artificialization"

Any human activity brings associated impacts, but the problem occurs when the limits of the natural environment is exceeded according to their assimilation capacity and their ability to restore balance. The growing process of artificial transformation[2] (Sunkel 1980) should be channeled into a sustainable style of development, for it is necessary to account for natural capital (natural resources and environmental services).[3] Unfortunately the balance in the region is not encouraging; apart from the meager savings and investment rates (necessary to increase physical capital) and the performance in education (necessary to increase human capital), which have room for improvement, natural capital seems doomed to continuous decline. There is little regional information, as countries do not undertake integrated economic and environmental accounts. What is available is a calculation of the ecological net domestic product (PINE)[4] in Mexico, or an adjusted saving measure calculated by the World Bank.[5] For Mexico, the total cost of the exhaustion of natural resources and environmental degradation is around 10% of GDP/GNI, equivalent to that of fixed capital consumption, although there is a steady and slight downward trend in these costs. On the other hand, in Latin America and the Caribbean, gross saving has recently increased from 20% of GDP in 1990 to around 23%, while adjusted savings have scarcely varied from values a little above 5% of GDP, showing that there has been less and less saving owing to the exhaustion of natural and environmental resources (adjustments from 13% to 17%). In China, with higher savings rates, the "environmental adjustment" is similar, although it has been decreasing over time, while that of the OECD is much lower—around 10%, but stable over time (see Figure 6.4). In the Latin American and Caribbean region, many countries have negative net adjusted savings rates, which show their strong dependence on natural resources—for example Bolivia, Chile, Ecuador, Venezuela, and Peru. On the contrary, Honduras, Costa Rica, and Panama experienced positive

---

[2] Constructed or artificial environment.

[3] There are two ways to view sustainability: weak sustainability, which assumes that different forms of capital are substitutable, so that a reduction in natural capital could be compensated by an increase in other kinds of capital in such a way as to maintain the balance; and strong sustainability, which sees capital as complementary, so that it is necessary to ensure that natural capital itself is sustainable.

[4] PINE: Net Domestic Product—Total Exhaustion and Environmental Degradation Cost.

[5] Net adjusted savings discounts from gross national savings fixed capital consumption, the exhaustion of mineral, energy and forest resources, damage caused by CO_2 and PM10 and increases according to educational expenditures, to provide an idea of long-term savings.

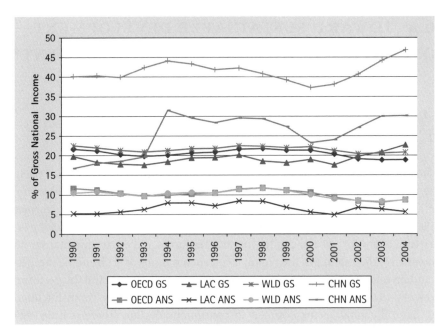

FIGURE 6.4 Gross Savings (GS) and Adjusted Net Savings (ANS)

Source: Authors' own construction from World Bank information.

Notes: LAC: Latin America and the Caribbean; WLD: world; CHN: China.

adjustments. This regional assessment shows that when these adjustments are taken into account, saving rates are much less substantial.

States have the power to charge royalties to recover for their citizens the extraordinary Ricardian rents obtained by exploiting natural assets, and to compensate for loss. Indeed, the tax revenue in the region from fees and royalties for the extraction and export of natural resources account for 28% of tax collected, much higher than OECD countries (15%). There are substantial variations between countries; in Argentina, Brazil, the Dominican Republic, Guatemala, Peru, and Uruguay, they do not reach 15%, while in Bolivia, Colombia, Panama, and Venezuela they are more than 40% (OECD 2008). However, its allocation for the maintenance of the stock of capital, understood in its broadest sense, is doubtful. The region can report only few examples of this approach such as Chile, which legislated for an Innovation Fund for competitiveness as the recipient for the collected funds.

6.4.2 Institutionality and environmental policies

Latin America and the Caribbean's environmental management has evolved in recent years. Environmental issues have come to the forefront as responses to the United Nations Conference on Human Environment (Stockholm, 1972) and especially after the

Earth Summit (Rio, 1992), which formulated Agenda 21, the Framework Convention on Climate Change, the Convention on Biological Diversity, and Convention to Combat Desertification (see Annex 6.1). Gradually, and with differences, the region has achieved a modern institutionality, with the creation of ministries as the highest environmental authorities (Bárcena et al. 2002), the consolidation of the standards that make up framework laws for the environment, and the inclusion of environmental rights and obligations as part of constitutions. Environmental regulations and market instruments have come to complement each other in environmental management, together with examples of the successful use of tax instruments to resolve environmental problems (Acquatella and Bárcena 2005).

As well as the large conferences that have stimulated environmental institutionality and standards, there are endogenous factors—the magnitude of the problems, their impact on the health and welfare of citizens—together with exogenous pressures, particularly opening up regional trade with partners that insist on environmental standards which otherwise would have been delayed.

Over the last few years, however, this positive trend appears to have lost its impetus, as the marginal cost of additional policies has increased and the opportunity costs in terms of resources for effective environmental policy have risen. There are many reasons for this change, in particular:

(i) The small environmental budget contrasts with the level of the problems and the overall costs of their resolution. Environmental expenditures hardly exceed 1% of GDP and rarely more than 3% of total public expenditure. In addition, environmental budgets are subject to strong volatility that vitiates stable and continuous environmental policies, with major cuts during periods of economic recession (Bárcena and de Miguel 2003). International funding for the environment is elusive and, in a region of middle-income countries, will probably decrease over time.

(ii) While legislative development is important, monitoring implementation and performance is poor. The assigned financial and human resources are in contrast to the magnitude of the challenges, and have resulted in a progressive increase in environmental conflicts. So too the preparation of legal personnel, conversant with these issues, is in its infancy.

(iii) There are many serious failures of coordination, coherence, and integration among different public policies that directly and indirectly impact environmental issues (Lerda, Acquatella, and Gómez 2003); this causes contradictory actions, thus making efficient and effective policymaking more difficult. So too the so-called implicit policies—i.e. sectoral and economic policies with environmental implications—often reduce the effectiveness of explicit environmental policies, leading to complete annulment (Gligo 2006).

(iv) Environmental policies are allowed only a peripheral role, and little effective power is granted to environmental authorities, which are often obliged to negotiate with economic authorities in a disadvantageous situation (Ocampo 1999).

(v) The other environmental protagonists—civil society and business—tend to be reactive. Apart from the exception of some environmental NGOs, firms associated with business councils for sustainable development, signatories of the Global Pact, or other socially responsible business initiatives, as well as citizen reactions to big environmental conflicts, environmental issues constitute little more than anecdotes for ordinary mortals. The lack of environmental education and information, and obstacles to greater participation, limit changes to environmental consciousness.

Nevertheless, it is important to reiterate that environmental policy is totally justified and should be central to government actions. Environmental issues reflect the differences between private and public interests (or between private and social costs). The presence of externalities and the nature of public goods exhibited by many environmental goods and services require governments to act, and make the state responsible for its lack of action.

Among the most urgent activities are: integration between ecosystem and land use managements; encouraging policies to supply drinking water and sanitation; combining environmental policies with urban and land use planning; and developing policies to improve energy efficiency (ECLAC 2005). To these one might add: the need to strengthen policies that protect biodiversity and ecosystems, without forgetting marine and coastal zones; encouraging science and technology, where the region appears to be very backward, to support sustainable development; and better use of the natural heritage and any existing ancestral knowledge.

Neither do implicit policies help. Take energy as an example. The great regional potential for renewable energy is not being taken advantage of because environmental benefits, which would justify altering relative prices by subsidies or taxes on polluting alternatives, have not been considered. So too it is necessary seriously to examine alternative sources of renewable and non-conventional energy that might significantly replace hydrocarbons. The lack of policy priorities for energy efficiency, although encouraged by rising hydrocarbon prices, impedes the utilization of one of the region's greatest potential source of emission reduction. To alter one of the bases of the transnational development style—dependence on hydrocarbons—requires a reduction in their use or at least a decoupling between energy use and economic production for which price signals are essential. However, these are going in the opposite direction. The price of diesel in all OECD countries was US$1.10 per liter in 2006, and US$1.40 per liter among European countries, while the average for Latin America it was US$ 0.60 cents, lower than the US price of US$ 0.70 cents, although in petroleum exporter countries the price was even lower. Faced with the continuous increase of the international price of petroleum and fuel, the general response has been to reduce the tax rate. In the OECD, the tax on premium petroleum, used mainly for personal vehicles, was reduced by 5 points (from 59% to 54% of the price); in Latin America and the Caribbean it was reduced by 13 points, from 47% to 34%. The tax proportion for diesel is lower, but it was also reduced like petroleum, and these reductions were overall greater in the Central American isthmus.

What could have been a great opportunity for technological innovation, for policies which promote energy efficiency, for changing production patterns based almost exclusively on petroleum and consumption that mirrors the 'American style of life', was regarded as a risk to development and an attack on citizens' purchasing power; thus the response is to maintain prices at the expense of tax receipts. When prices become more tolerable, oil taxes will not be recouped, leading to a new change of relative prices in their favor and a smaller tax take to cover the large social and environmental needs facing countries in the region.

In any case, greater changes require substantial transformations to development styles that countries are apparently unwilling to make, and which public policies are unlikely to achieve unless all of society is involved. Restrictions or outside pressure can force countries to create the appearance of solutions, but maybe only the shock of a global economic or climatic crisis could generate the necessary environment for a drastic change.

6.4.3 The new global green pact

In mid-2008 the world and the region were preparing themselves for a new petroleum crisis—which fortunately, as a consequence, reignited interest in energy efficiency and security (many countries in the region began or intensified policies), and in renewable and alternative energy. By the end of 2008 all these concerns had given way to the threat of a new world economic crisis, but now energy had a lower priority because of more reasonable prices. However, the situation continued, and when the world began to organize itself to face the crisis with stimulus policies, the idea of the 'Global Green New Deal' was born (Barbier 2009). The Initiative for a Green Economy was launched by the United Nations in support of smart investment. In the short term this might help reactivate the world economy and in the medium term reduce carbon footprints and help achieve the Millennium Development Goals—in other words, help to move to a more sustainable development model.

The range of policies adopted by the countries of the American continent can be analyzed as a function of environmental effects using the action–impact matrix (Munasinghe et al. 2006). Tax and sector policies have the most direct impact on changes in patterns of production and consumption. Most countries in the region use expansive fiscal policies to stimulate infrastructure and housing construction. But these policies have not brought about sustainable architecture, energy efficient construction, improved urban public transport infrastructure, or alternatives to road transport. However, there are some positive features: paving streets in a city saturated with air pollution permits reduction of particulate airborne matter (Chile); the improvement of urban road infrastructure improves transport efficiency and thereby reduces CO_2 emissions; and potable water supply, sewerage, and sanitation (Argentina, Colombia, Nicaragua) have health benefits and improve the quality of water resources.

Tax stimuli in the energy sector—supply as well as demand—have been notably negative as incentives to encourage low carbon intensity economies. To favor fuel, electricity, water, etc. by not incorporating environmental externalities may have short-term benefits by reducing consumer costs, but inefficient incentives can be more expensive in the medium term. Many countries have reduced taxes, granted subsidies, set maximum prices, or applied other measures to fuels without considering their environmental implications. There are alternatives, for example the targeting of subsidies to buy fuel for collective urban transport (Nicaragua), supporting mass use of this type of transport (El Salvador), or tariff revisions to ensure that a reduction in petroleum prices is quickly transferred to help reduce public transport prices (Costa Rica). Uruguay's support for the production of renewable energy equipment and science and technology is another example that should be promoted in the region, together with the consolidation and development of efficiency energy measures. Additionally, traditional policies to reactivate the automobile industry allow environmental benefits when focusing on more fuel-efficient and less polluting fleet renewal instead of its expansion.

Methods of financing the stimuli package have not taken the opportunity to implement environmental taxation, i.e. to tax bads. Furthermore, transfers and subsidies conditionality, commonly used in social policies, could inspire fiscal and sectoral policies according to their environmental implications.

6.4.4 Climate change

The global climate is a public good, and therefore climate change, from the economist's point of view, represents its greatest negative externality (Stern 2007). Given its magnitude, climate change will principally determine the characteristics and conditions of economic development in this century. On the one hand, the impacts and adaptation processes will be, without question, impressive and increasing throughout the century in various economic activities, such as agriculture, hydrology, land use, biodiversity, tourism, the infrastructure, and public health. On the other hand, the development of new technological options that promote lower carbon intensities and the economic costs of mitigation will certainly be significant in areas like, energy, transportation, or forest conservation, and will alter current patterns of economic development (Galindo 2009).

The undeniable warming of the climate, reported by the IPCC, is already affecting Latin America and the Caribbean's climate. Temperatures have increased by 1 C during the 20th century, while sea levels have risen by 2–3 mm annually since the 1980s and there have been changes to precipitation patterns (de la Torre et al. 2009). Extreme hydro-meteorological events have become more common and intense (Figure 6.5), causing damages valued at US$ 2,100 million annually. Climate change is having an increasing impact on various countries and regions; this region's vulnerability is one of its principal environmental, social, and economic challenges (UNEP 2007; de la Torre et al. 2009; Samaniego 2009).

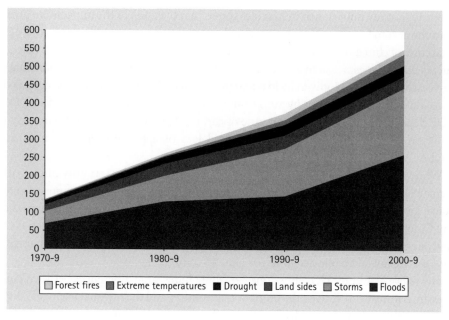

FIGURE 6.5 Latin America and the Caribbean: frequency of hydro-meteorological events, 1970–2009

Source: ECLAC, based on "EM-DAT: Emergency Events Database", at: http://www.em-dat.net

The key issues, in terms of the impact of climate change on ecosystems (likely to increase during this century), are:

(i) warming and eventual deterioration of the Andean mountain ecosystems including the retreat of Andean glaciers;

(ii) bleaching of coral reefs and the possible ecological collapse of the Caribbean Basin;

(iii) damage to large tracts of wetlands and associated coastal systems in the Gulf of Mexico; and

(iv) the risk of continuing death of forest in the Amazon basin.

If global measures are not taken to reduce emissions, then the socioeconomic damage will be very serious and adaptation will require considerable effort. As yet there are few studies that quantify costs for the region, which cover the loss of agricultural productivity and water scarcity, together with hydro-meteorological phenomena, discussed above, as well as increases in sea levels, the increasing possibility of plagues and illnesses, and the loss of biodiversity and ecosystems (which are difficult to cost). It has been estimated using a time horizon to 2100, annual losses which amount to between 0.23% and 0.56% of GDP, depending on the scenario (Tol 2002). Medvedev and van der Mensbrugghe (2010) project a loss of 1% of GDP by 2050 if the temperatures increase by two degrees (at present value an impact of 18% of GDP, using a 5.5% discount rate). The exhaustive

'Stern' type study undertaken in Mexico[6] shows that the costs of the impacts are greater than those associated with an international mitigation agreement for the country. The total costs of climate change will reach by 2100 around 6.2% of GDP, using a 4% discount rate, excluding livestock activities, extreme events, increasing sea levels, and non-market costs associated with biodiversity loss and human lives. Mitigation costs associated with a 50% reduction in emissions by 2100 from 2002 would range between 0.7% and 2.2% of GDP depending on the value of a tonne of carbon (Galindo 2009). A similar study for Chile on climate change suggests an annual loss of approximately 1.1% until 2100 (ECLAC 2009b). In both studies poverty levels increase.

While Latin America and the Caribbean is being and will be seriously impacted by climate change, the region contributes no more than 12% of global emissions of greenhouse gases, 70% of which are concentrated in Mexico, Brazil, Argentina, Venezuela, and Colombia. Average per capita emissions of these gases are 9.9 tCO_2e (tonnes of CO_2 equivalent), which could be reduced to 5.4tCO_2e if emissions coming from changes in land use are not taken into account (Samaniego 2009).

The regional average CO_2 emissions per capita hides large differences between countries. In Trinidad and Tobago the number is around 25, and the regional average is duplicated by Venezuela and exceeded by Mexico, Argentina, and Chile.

The main emitters of greenhouse gases are agriculture and forestry, together with changes in land use, transport, and energy. Industry and wastes contribute much less in relative terms.

In general the region is a low emitter and an important carbon sink (given its large forest areas). However, the downshift trend of emissions from land use change has been steadily countered by increasing energy use. The major challenge is to decouple GDP from energy consumption, and to decouple both from CO_2 emissions (Figure 6.6). As shown, while trends in Mexico appear positive, those in the Caribbean and Central America are distinctly negative.

The region does have important mitigation opportunities which bring important economic benefits, as reflected by the curves of marginal abatement costs calculated for several countries. In the case of Chile, for example, this corresponds to profiting from the high potential for energy efficiency in specific activities such as transport, industry, mining, and the sector of public, household, and commercial services. In most cases their application costs are very low (promotion, regulation, certification, small-scale improved technologies, etc.) and the benefits from fuel savings are high. Furthermore, these measures are the most effective way to reduce greenhouse gases. There are also opportunities in the transport sector and hydropower options that should not be dismissed (O'Ryan, Díaz, and Clerc 2009).

On the other hand, the international community has implemented financial mechanisms to support both mitigation and adaptation in a region that for now has

---

[6] ECLAC/CEPAL is leading this type of study for the nations of Central America, the Caribbean. and in Argentina, Bolivia, Chile, Colombia, Ecuador, Paraguay, Peru, and Uruguay.

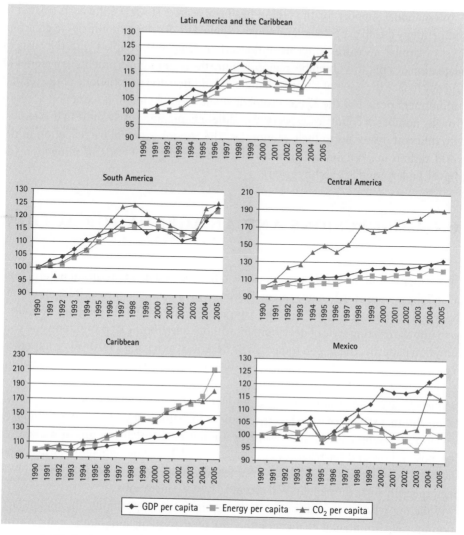

FIGURE 6.6 Latin America and the Caribbean: coupling among GDP, energy, and CO_2 emissions

Source: Based on statistics and economic indicators (BADECON), Annual Statistical Yearbook for Latin America and the Caribbean, (2008) and Population Estimates and Projections (CELADE), ECLAC/CEPAL.

no obligation to reduce emissions but does have numerous adaptation costs. However, these are small in relation to needs. Official development assistance received by the region is 8.6% of the world total, and of this figure only 5.3% is for general environmental protection and for the objectives of the conventions agreed at the World Summit. The region has received $544 million from the Global Environment Facility, primarily for mitigation actions. In addition, the CDM's funds are slight when compared to mitigation needs. The Adaptation Fund, agreed as part of the Kyoto Protocol, is a potential source of funding.

International support for the region has been scarce. However, the costs related to competitivity due to expected requirements applied by developed countries (e.g. carbon taxes or similar measures in terms of the carbon footprint), coupled with the costs of adaptation of a highly vulnerable region, require the region's governments as a matter of urgency to face the issue of climate change.[7] In addition, the negotiations of the second commitment period of the Kyoto Protocol would require emission reduction across a growing number of countries, especially middle-income, and surely some in this region, with different outcomes to their economies. The region's eventual participation in the world carbon market should allow a reduction in the global costs of mitigation (de Miguel, Ludena, and Schuschny 2009).

6.5 CONCLUSIONS AND AN AGENDA FOR ACTION

Latin America and the Caribbean continue to have advantages in terms of natural capital and the quality of the environment. However, the region's pattern of integration into the world economy combine with the aspirations of its citizens to join and be assimilated into the existing style of development without questioning its production and consumption patterns. The region today can be described as having a relatively competitive export structure, dependent on industries that make intensive use of energy and natural resources and generate high pollution.

The natural resource base affects the production structure and the pattern of specialization, but that structure is no less the result of the efforts of each country to build its model of development. Natural resources are not in themselves a gift or a curse—it depends on how and for what reason they are used. It will be difficult to switch to an alternative development model, environmentally more sustainable, from the present one, especially since the benefits will accrue to future generations.

While the reliance on natural assets is a competitive opportunity, the region faces enormous environmental challenges: the loss of ecosystems and biodiversity, uncontrolled urban expansion, vulnerability in terms of climate change, etc. which requires a rejuvenated State to play a role. The management of externalities and public goods urgently require that states take the lead in many areas, if not to change the development style, at least to make it sustainable in the medium term. The first step is to strengthen institutional capacities, including greater efforts in education, participation, and environmental justice for citizens. Greater financial resources are needed for sustainability, but it should be a joint action between the region and developed countries, especially in those areas that encompass global public goods or bads. That is, the principle of common but differentiated responsibilities should be applied both in financing and in technology

---

[7] There are already impacts and behaviors originating with climate change that lead to different adaptation and mitigation processes which are not always efficient from an economic perspective and less so for sustainable development (Galindo 2009).

transfer. On the other hand, the region can take its own actions to reduce environmental pressures—in areas such as energy efficiency, materials use, and water resources—while generating economic benefits.

The challenge of climate change cannot be avoided. The region is highly vulnerable to natural disasters, which will only intensify. The costs of adaptation will be high; therefore, an active role in pursuing a global agreement to mitigate emissions, taking into account the different degrees of development of participants, can be beneficial for the region. To reduce global CO_2 emissions to levels that avoid a climate crisis of unknown consequences for human life and ecosystems will require radical changes to production, transportation, consumption, energy use, land use, and urban planning patterns. Rapid action can generate long-term comparative advantage; if not, it will be the future requirements of developed countries, linked to the concept of the carbon footprint, that will impose more costly and reactive measures. Current actions to exit the global economic crisis offer a clear opportunity to adopt a long-term view and push the region towards a more dynamic and non-traumatic sustainable development model. For Latin American and Caribbean countries, we are talking about applying the old idea of sustainable development—no more, no less than growth with equity and environmental protection.

ANNEX 6.1

MULTILATERAL ENVIRONMENTAL AGREEMENTS

Year of signature and year that the country became party to the agreement (through ratification, acceptance, approval or adhesion). P: party; F: signature; EV: entry into force.

Table 6.A1 Multilateral environmental agreements

Country	Ramsar[ap]	Heritage[bp]	CITES[cq]	CMS[dr]	Law of the Sea[e]	
	P	P	P	EV	F	P
Argentina	1992	1978	1981	1992	1984	1995
Belize	1998	1990	1986	–	1982	1983
Bolivia	1990	1976	1979	2003	1984	1995
Brazil	1993	1977	1975	–	1982	1988
Chile	1981	1980	1975	1983	1982	1997
Colombia	1998	1983	1981	–	1982	–
Costa Rica	1991	1977	1975	2007	1982	1992
Cuba	2001	1981	1990	2008	1982	1984
Ecuador	1990	1975	1975	2004	–	–

Table 6.A1 (contd.)

Country	Ramsar[ap]	Heritage[bp]	CITES[cq]	CMS[dr]	Law of the Sea[e]	
	P	P	P	EV	F	P
El Salvador	1999	1991	1987	–	1984	–
Guatemala	1990	1979	1979	–	1983	1997
Guyana	–	1977	1976	–	1982	1993
Haiti	–	1980	–	–	1982	1996
Honduras	1993	1979	1985	2007	1982	1993
Mexico	1986	1984	1991	–	1982	1983
Nicaragua	1997	1979	1977	–	1984	2000
Panama	1990	1978	1978	1989	1982	1996
Paraguay	1995	1988	1976	1999	1982	1986
Peru	1992	1982	1975	1997	–	–
Dominican Republic	2002	1985	1986	–	1982	–
Suriname	1985	1997	1980	–	1982	1998
Uruguay	1984	1989	1975	1990	1982	1992
Venezuela (Bolivarian Republic of)	1988	1990	1977	–	–	–

Year of signature and year that the country became party to the agreement (through ratification, acceptance, approval or adhesion) P: party, F: signature, EV: entry into force.

Table 6.A2 Multilateral environmental agreements

Country	Vienna[f]		Montreal[g]		Basel[h]		Diversity[i]		UNFCCC[j]	
	F	P	F	P	F	P	F	P	F	P
Argentina	1985	1990	1988	1990	1989	1991	1992	1994	1992	1994
Belize	–	1997	–	1998	–	1997	1992	1993	1992	1994
Bolivia	–	1994	–	1994	1989	1996	1992	1994	1992	1994
Brazil	–	1990	–	1990	–	1992	1992	1994	1992	1994
Chile	1985	1990	1988	1990	1990	1992	1992	1994	1992	1994
Colombia	–	1990	–	1993	1989	1996	1992	1994	1992	1995
Costa Rica	–	1991	–	1991	–	1995	1992	1994	1992	1994
Cuba	–	1992	–	1992	–	1994	1992	1994	1992	1994
Ecuador	–	1990	–	1990	1989	1993	1992	1993	1992	1993
El Salvador	–	1992	–	1992	1990	1991	1992	1994	1992	1995
Guatemala	–	1987	–	1989	1989	1995	1992	1995	1992	1995
Guyana	–	1993	–	1993	–	2001	1992	1994	1992	1994

(continued)

Table 6.A2 (contd.)

Country	Vienna[f]		Montreal[g]		Basel[h]		Diversity[i]		UNFCCC[j]	
	F	P	F	P	F	P	F	P	F	P
Haiti	–	2000	–	2000	1989	–	1992	1996	1992	1996
Honduras	–	1993	–	1993	–	1995	1992	1995	1992	1995
Mexico	1985	1987	1987	1988	1989	1991	1992	1993	1992	1993
Nicaragua	–	1993	–	1993	–	1997	1992	1995	1992	1995
Panama	–	1989	1987	1989	1989	1991	1992	1995	1993	1995
Paraguay	–	1992	–	1992	–	1995	1992	1994	1992	1994
Peru	1985	1989	–	1993	–	1993	1992	1993	1992	1993
Dominican Republic	–	1993	–	1993	–	1999	1992	1996	1992	1998
Suriname	–	1997	–	1997	–	–	1992	1996	1992	1997
Uruguay	–	1989	–	1991	–	1991	1992	1993	1992	1994
Venezuela (Bolivarian Republic of)	–	1988	1987	1989	1989	1998	1992	1994	1992	1994

Year of signature and year that the country became party to the agreement (through ratification, acceptance, approval or adhesion) P: party, F: signature, EV: entry into force.

Table 6.A3 Multilateral environmental agreements

Country	UNCCD[k]		Kyoto[l]		Rotterdam[m]		Cartagena[n]		Stockholm[o]	
	F	P	F	P	F	P	F	P	F	P
Argentina	1994	1997	1998	2001	1998	2004	2000	–	2001	2005
Belize	–	1998	–	2003	–	2005	–	2004	2002	–
Bolivia	1994	1996	1998	1999	–	2003	2000	2002	2001	2003
Brazil	1994	1997	1998	2002	1998	2004	–	2003	2001	2004
Chile	1995	1997	1998	2002	1998	2005	2000	–	2001	2005
Colombia	1994	1999	–	2001	1998	–	2000	2003	2001	2008
Costa Rica	1994	1998	1998	2002	1999	–	2000	2007	2002	2007
Cuba	1994	1997	1999	2002	1998	2008	2000	2002	2001	2007
Ecuador	1995	1995	1999	2000	1998	2004	2000	2003	2001	2004
El Salvador	–	1997	1998	1998	1999	1999	2000	2003	2001	2008
Guatemala	–	1998	1998	1999	–	–	–	2004	2002	2008
Guyana	–	1997	–	2003	–	2007	–	2008	–	2007
Haiti	1994	1996	–	2005	–	–	2000	–	2001	–
Honduras	1995	1997	1999	2000	–	–	2000	–	2002	2005

Table 6.A3 (contd.)

Country	UNCCD[k]		Kyoto[l]		Rotterdam[m]		Cartagena[n]		Stockholm[o]	
	F	P	F	P	F	P	F	P	F	P
Mexico	1994	1995	1998	2000	–	2005	2000	2002	2001	2003
Nicaragua	1994	1998	1998	1999	–	2008	2000	2002	2001	2005
Panama	1995	1996	1998	1999	1998	2000	2001	2002	2001	2003
Paraguay	1994	1997	1998	1999	1998	2003	2001	2004	2001	2004
Peru	1994	1995	1998	2002	1998	2005	2000	2004	2001	2005
Dominican Republic	–	1997	–	2002	–	2006	–	2006	2001	2007
Suriname	–	2000	–	2006	–	2000	–	2008	2002	–
Uruguay	–	1999	1998	2001	1998	2003	2001	–	2001	2004
Venezuela (Bolivarian Republic of)	–	1998	–	2005	–	2005	2000	2002	2001	2005

Source: Statistical Yearbook 2008, ECLAC.

[a] The Ramsar Convention on Wetlands of International Importance especially as Waterfowl Habitat, 1971.

[b] The Convention Concerning the Protection of the World Cultural and Natural Heritage, 1972.

[c] The Convention on the International Trade in Endangered Species of Wild Fauna and Flora, 1973.

[d] The Convention on the Conservation of Migratory Species of Wild Animals, 1979.

[e] The United Nations Convention on the Law of the Sea, 1982.

[f] The Vienna Convention for the Protection of the Ozone Layer, 1985.

[g] The Montreal Protocol on Substances that Deplete the Ozone Layer, 1987.

[h] The Basel Convention on the Control of Transboundary Movements of Hazardous Wastes and their Disposal, 1989.

[i] The United Nations Convention on Biological Diversity, 1992.

[j] The United Nations Framework Convention on Climate Change, 1992.

[k] The United Nations Convention to Combat Desertification in Those Countries Experiencing Serious Drought and/or Desertification, 1994.

[l] The Kyoto Protocol to the United Nations Framework Convention on Climate Change, 1997.

[m] The Rotterdam Convention on the Prior Informed Consent Procedure for Certain Hazardous Chemicals and Pesticides in International Trade, 1998.

[n] The Cartagena Protocol on Biosafety to the Convention on Biological Diversity, 2000.

[o] The Stockholm Convention on Persistent Organic Pollutants, 2001.

[p] The year that the countries signed the agreement is not available.

[q] All the countries that are party to this convention signed it between 1973 and 1974, the period in which the convention was open for signature.

[r] Year that the convention went into force in the country.

References

ACQUATELLA, J. (2008). *Energía y cambio climático: oportunidades para una política energética integrada en América Latina y el Caribe*, Santiago, Chile: ECLAC.

——and BÁRCENA, A. (eds) (2005). *Política fiscal y medio ambiente: bases para una agenda común*, Santiago, Chile: ECLAC.

ALTOMONTE, H. (ed.) (2008). 'América Latina y el Caribe frente a la coyuntura energética internacional: oportunidades para una nueva agenda de políticas', presented at the Seminario Crisis Alimentaria y Energética, Santiago, Chile: ASDI and GTZ, September.

BARBIER, E. (2009). 'A Global Green New Deal', report prepared for the Green Economy Initiative, UNEP.

BÁRCENA, A., and DE MIGUEL, C. (eds) (2003). *Financing for Sustainable Development: Visions and Proposals for Action from a Latin American and Caribbean Perspective*, Santiago, Chile: United Nations.

—— et al. (2002). 'Financing for Sustainable Development in Latin America and the Caribbean: From Monterrey to Johannesburg', Santiago, Chile: ECLAC.

CIFUENTES, L., KRUPNICK, A., O'RYAN, R., and TOMAN, M. (2005). *Urban Air Quality and Human Health in Latin America and the Caribbean*, Washington, DC: IDB.

DE LA TORRE, A., FAJNZYLBER, P., and NASH, J. (2009). *Low Carbon, High Growth: Latin American Responses to Climate Change*, Washington, DC: World Bank.

DE MIGUEL, C., LUDENA, C., and SCHUSCHNY, A. (2009). 'Climate Change and Reduction of CO_2 Emissions: The Role of Developing Countries in Carbon Trade Markets', presented at the 12th Annual GTAP Conference on Global Economic Analysis, Santiago, Chile, June. Serie medio ambiente y desarrollo, forthcoming, CEPAL, Santiago, Chile.

ECLAC (UN Economic Commission for Latin America and the Caribbean) (2005). *The Millennium Development Goals: A Latin American and Caribbean Perspective*, Santiago, Chile.

—— (2008a). 'Agricultura, desarrollo rural, tierra, sequía y desertificación: resultados, tendencias y desafíos para el desarrollo sostenible de América Latina y el Caribe', project document from the Regional Implementation Forum on Sustainable Development, Santiago, Chile, November 2007.

—— (2008b). *Latin America and the Caribbean in the World Economy 2007: 2008 Trends*, Santiago, Chile.

—— (2009a). *Social Panorama of Latin America, 2008*, Santiago, Chile.

—— (2009b). *La economía del cambio climático en Chile: síntesis*, Santiago, Chile.

—— (2009c). *Statistical Yearbook for Latin America and the Caribbean, 2008*, Santiago, Chile.

ECLAC/UNEP (UN Environment Programme) (2002). *The Sustainability of Development in Latin America and the Caribbean: Challenges and Opportunities*, Santiago, Chile.

FAO (Food and Agriculture Organization) (2006). *FAO Statistical Yearbook, 2005–2006 1*, Rome.

—— (2007). *State of the World's Forests 2007*, Rome.

FERRAZ, C., and SEROA DA MOTTA, R. (2001). 'Regulação, mercado ou pressão social? Os determinantes do investimento ambiental na industria', Rio de Janeiro, Instituto de Investigación Económica Aplicada.

GALINDO, L. M. (ed.) (2009). *La economía del cambio climático en México: síntesis*, Mexico City: SEMARNAT.

GLIGO, N. (1995). 'The present state and future prospects of the environment in Latin America and the Caribbean', *CEPAL Review 55*.

—— (2006). *Estilos de desarrollo y medio ambiente en América Latina, un cuarto de siglo después* (Serie medioambiente y desarrollo), Santiago, Chile: ECLAC.

JORDÁN, R., and MARTINEZ, R. (2009). *Pobreza y precariedad urbana en América Latina y el Caribe: situación actual y financiamiento de políticas y programas*, Santiago, Chile: ECLAC.

LERDA, J. C., ACQUATELLA, J., and GÓMEZ, J. J. (2003). *Integración, coherencia y coordinación de políticas públicas sectoriales: reflexiones para el caso de las políticas fiscal y ambiental* (Serie medioambiente y desarrollo), Santiago, Chile: ECLAC.

MEDVEDEV, D., and VAN DER MENSBRUGGHE, D. (2010). 'Climate Change in Latin America: Impacts and Mitigation Policy Options', in de Miguel et al. (eds), in *Modeling Public Policies in Latin America and the Caribbean*, Santiago, Chile Libros de la CEPAL 109.

Millennium Ecosystem Assessment (2005). *Ecosystems and Human Well-Being: Synthesis*, Washington, DC: Island Press.

MUNASINGHE, M., et al. (eds) (2006). *Macroeconomic Policies for Sustainable Growth: Analytical Framework and Policy Studies of Brazil and Chile*, Cheltenham: Elgar.

OCAMPO, J. A. (1999). *Políticas e instituciones para el desarrollo sostenible en América Latina y el Caribe* (Serie medio ambiente y desarrollo), Santiago, Chile: ECLAC.

—— and MARTIN, J. (eds) (2004). *América Latina y el Caribe en la era global*, Bogotá: Alfaomega and ECLAC.

OECD (Organisation for Economic Co-operation and Development) (2008). *Latin American Economic Outlook 2009*, Paris.

O'RYAN, R., DÍAZ, M., and CLERC, J. (2009). *Consumo de energía y emisiones de gases de efecto invernadero en Chile 2007–2030 y opciones de mitigación*, PROGEA, Universidad de Chile.

PAHO (Pan American Health Organization) (2002). *Health Situation in the Americas: Basic Indicators 2002*, Washington, DC.

—— (2004). *Health Situation in the Americas: Basic Indicators 2004*, Washington, DC.

—— (2005). *An Assessment of Health Effects of Ambient Air Pollution in Latin America and the Caribbean*, Washington, DC.

PREBISCH, R. (1980). 'Biosphere and development', *CEPAL Review* 12.

QUEZADA, F. (2007). *Status and Potential of Commercial Bioprospecting Activities in Latin America and the Caribbean* (Serie medio ambiente y desarrollo), Santiago, Chile, ECLAC.

ROMO MURILLO, D. (2007). *La competitividad exportadora de los sectores ambientalmente sensibles y la construcción de un patrón exportador sostenible en América Latina y el Caribe*, Santiago, Chile: ECLAC.

SAMANIEGO, J. (ed.) (2009). *Economics of Climate Change and Development in Latin America and the Caribbean, Summary 2009*, Santiago, Chile: ECLAC.

—— JORDÁN, R., and REHNER, J. (2009). *Metropolitan Cities Sustainability: Regional Panorama, Latin America*, Santiago, Chile: ECLAC.

STERN, N. (2007). *The Economics of Climate Change: The Stern Review*, Cambridge: Cambridge University Press.

SUNKEL, O. (1980). 'The Interaction between Styles of Development and the Environment in Latin America', *CEPAL Review* 12.

TOL, R. S. J. (2002). 'Estimates of the Damage Cost of Climate Change', *Environmental and Resource Economics, European Association of Environmental and Resource Economists* 21.1.

UNEP (United Nations Environmental Programme) (2007). *Global Environmental Outlook: Environment for Development (GEO-4)*, Valletta: Progress Press.

WALSH, M. P. (2005). 'Status Report: Low Sulfur Diesel Fuel Trends Worldwide', memo, June 13.

PART II

MACROECONOMICS AND FINANCE

CHAPTER 7

....

TAMING CAPITAL ACCOUNT SHOCKS: MANAGING BOOMS AND BUSTS

....

RICARDO FFRENCH-DAVIS AND
STEPHANY GRIFFITH-JONES

7.1 INTRODUCTION

....

A paradox and weakness of the triumph of the market economy in recent decades was the fact that liberalization was the strongest in the area—finance—where market imperfections are in fact the largest. Indeed, as a result of rapid and widespread liberalization of both domestic and international financial systems, as well as capital accounts, currency and financial sector crises became increasingly frequent, and developmentally as well as fiscally, costly. This has culminated in the global financial crisis, that started in 2007 in the developed countries and which was, to a large degree, also a result of extreme financial liberalization, accompanied by insufficient and inappropriate regulation.

Latin America, especially in the Southern Cone, had followed this pattern of liberalization and crises since the late 1970s. Díaz Alejandro (1985) had then very perceptively synthesized this as "Good-bye financial repression, hello financial crisis." Domestic financial crises interacted with the 1980s major Latin American debt crisis, to lead to a lost decade for growth and equity (see e.g. Griffith-Jones and Sunkel 1989).

In particular, the liberalization of the capital accounts of Latin American economies led to sharp surges and then reversals of capital flows, which posed both severe difficulties for macro-economic management (Ffrench-Davis and Griffith-Jones 2003) and led to very costly crises.

As the Latin American debt crisis of the 1980s was followed by the Mexican peso crisis and the East Asian crisis, a major discussion arose internationally about the urgent need to reform the international financial architecture. Griffith-Jones and Ocampo (2003;

2009) have long emphasized the need for strengthening countercyclical elements in this international architecture, to allow greater space for countercyclical macroeconomic policies at the national level. This approach has gained further relevance and support with the 2007–9 global financial crisis, and the ensuing discussion and reforms on countercyclical as well as comprehensive regulation and international liquidity provision. Particularly, if the attempts at international financial reform fail or are insufficient to curb excessive boom–bust patterns of capital flows, as well as their severe costs, the issue of slowing down capital account liberalization is again of great policy relevance; where this liberalization has already largely taken place, as in Latin America, reintroducing capital account regulations is again becoming relevant.

International capital markets have grown dramatically since the mid-1960s. Although international capital movements partly reflect expanding economies, increasing world trade, and the globalization of production, they also involve purely financial factors that rose notably faster. The revolutionary innovations that have taken place in telecommunications technology, and the emergence of increasingly "sophisticated" financial techniques, contributed to a boom in international financial flows. Increasingly, these capital movements used opaque instruments, that were totally non-transparent and unregulated, such as the Over the Counter (OTC) derivatives. Booming domestic and international financial flows occurred in a framework of lax or incomplete regulations and supervision, and in which existing regulations, such as the Basel II banking regulation, were in fact pro-cyclical, which reinforced the inherent pro-cyclicality of financial and banking markets.[1] More recently, since the 2007–8 global financial crisis there is growing agreement over the significant shortage of macroeconomic and financial governance in the present stage of unbalanced globalization (Griffith-Jones and Ocampo 2009).

This critical problem has had crucial relevance for Latin American countries (LACs) in the last decades. In the 1980s, the links with international capital markets were largely severed as a result of the debt crisis. However, the region enjoyed a booming expansion of capital flows during 1991–4, from mid-1995 to 1997, in the mid-2000s, and again from mid-2009. At the beginning, these surges, especially in the early 1990s, were most welcome because they overcame a binding external constraint that was contributing to low investment levels and to a severe economic recession in the region; but they later became excessive, and contributed to the vulnerability that was revealed when the Asian crisis hit LACs. On the four occasions, these increasing inflows generated an unwelcome and distorting effect on real macroeconomic balances.

We have observed that emerging economies, frequently led by capital surges, penetrate into *vulnerability zones*, which is contrary to conventional economic views that capital flows provide discipline for governments to follow better macroeconomic policies. The vulnerabilities generated include:

---

[1] For early discussion of these issues, see United Nations (1999); Griffith-Jones (2001); Ocampo (2003).

   (i) high external liabilities, with a large short-term share;
  (ii) significant current account deficits;
 (iii) appreciated exchange rates and currency mismatches;
 (iv) high prices of domestic financial assets and real estate;
  (v) sizable increases in money supply as counterpart of the accumulation of international reserves.

The longer and deeper the economy's penetration into those vulnerability zones, the more severe the *financieristic trap* in which authorities could get caught, and the lower the probability of leaving it without undergoing a crisis and long-lasting economic and social costs. The absence or weakness of policies moderating the boom—leaning against the wind through macroeconomic and regulatory policies during overheating and/or curbing excessive capital inflows—endangers the feasibility of adopting a strong reactivating policy under the frequently recessive environment following the bust (see Ffrench-Davis 2006).

7.2 LIBERALIZATION OF THE CAPITAL ACCOUNT

Most general equilibrium frameworks take no account of important real-world conditions in capital flows, such as informational gaps and asymmetries, that contribute to problems such as herding, the incompleteness of the market within which investors operate, and the allocation implications of the volatility of financing. These factors frequently do not allow countries spontaneously to tap the benefits of foreign savings. Indeed, systemic market failure does occur. Frequent reminders of this feature are the major financial crises, mostly accompanied by macroeconomic collapse, that have taken place in recent economic history, including the debt crisis in Latin America in the 1980s and the Mexican, Asian, Argentinian, and Brazilian crises, as well as the recent global crisis that started in the US.

7.2.1 The case for regulation: sequencing, selectivity, and volatility

Reforms were inclined toward rapid liberalization of the capital account. Particularly, in the mid-1970s three Southern Cone countries—Argentina, Chile, and Uruguay— underwent radical economic liberalization processes, inspired partly by the financial repression hypothesis. The Southern Cone experiment collapsed in the early 1980s after speculative bubbles on asset prices, low domestic savings and investment, with a huge external debt. The history was repeated to a significant extent during the 1990s, when the reforms *à la* Washington Consensus were implemented in several LACs, *pari passu* with the two capital surges present in that decade.

As far as sequencing is concerned, there is now consensus that the capital account opening was premature and should have been postponed until other major reforms had been consolidated and equilibrium prices established. The lesson is that during adjustment, open capital accounts (especially in periods of elastic supply of international finance) can induce capital surges, with destabilizing macroeconomic and sectoral effects.

First, if productive investment capacity reacts slowly and/or with a lag and domestic financial markets remain incomplete and poorly supervised, additional external resources cannot be absorbed efficiently in the domestic economy, thereby threatening the future stability of flows themselves. Second, fiscal parameters need to be consolidated, tax evasion must be placed under control, and policy must be flexible, for without a sound tax base and flexible fiscal instruments, authorities must rely excessively on monetary policy to regulate aggregate demand. Third, under capital surges, financial markets adjust faster than economic structures; this usually leads to the emergence of bubbles in financial assets and real estate markets, together with exchange rate appreciation (and/or inflation).

The policy response to avoid all those sources of vulnerability is to impose a gradual adjustment in financial flows, accommodating its speed to that at which productive structures can adjust. In brief, if it is decided to liberalize the capital account, the speed at which it should be done must be tailored to the economy's capacity to absorb and allocate efficiently external resources, as it may take many years before conditions emerge (such as a deep and institutionally diversified domestic financial market; a broad, consolidated tax base; a diversified, internationally competitive export sector; and a wide range of available macroeconomic policy instruments) that will allow their economies to absorb unregulated capital flows in ways that are consistent with sustained growth and social equity.

The gradual approach also stems from the belief that macroeconomic stability also requires a certain sequence in capital account opening itself. A clear distinction can be drawn between inflows and outflows, and it is suggested that countries should liberalize the former before the latter, partly because the benefits that can be derived from outflows are more evident after accumulating substantial net assets (Williamson 1993; Rodrik 1998). There could also be sequencing within the components of inflows and outflows: for instance, long-term inflows could be liberalized before short-term transactions, while in the case of outflows, priority might be given to direct export-oriented investments and trade credit.

The proponents of sequencing usually question only the order and timing of liberalization, not the ultimate objective of an open capital account. Yet the overriding importance of real macroeconomic stability, coupled with the overwhelming size of international capital markets compared with the much smaller Latin American economies and the severe imperfections existing in such markets that lead to very high volatility of such flows, may render highly undesirable an inflexible commitment in all circumstances to an across-the-board open capital account. Indeed, the increasing volatility of international capital flows, and their huge size—as well as the high cost of crises—have for some time given rise to renewed discussion in industrialized countries on the potentially destabilizing behavior of capital markets and the possible need for capital account regulations (Financial Stability Forum 2000; Stiglitz et al. 2006).

A somewhat different issue to sequencing and selectivity refers to the cyclicality of flows. It is not identical to have a given form of opening under stable or under volatile flows. Given the acknowledged volatility of financial flows, countercyclical devices should complement gradual reforms. In periods when resources are scarce, there would be justification for seeking ways of attracting capital inflows, especially trade credit and long term flows, and erecting certain barriers to discourage capital outflows. The reverse would apply when there was an abundance of capital in the markets, as in 1990–4, 1996–7, and 2004–7—or even since mid-2009 for many LACs. For the sake of macroeconomic stability, in these circumstances short-term and liquid inflows should be transitorily restricted or discouraged and some channels for outflows promoted.

7.2.2 The objectives, nature, and experience with capital account regulations

Obviously, sequencing and countercyclicality imply the presence of either price-based or quantitative regulations. The more pressing the need for management, and the more underdeveloped fiscal and monetary policies are, the more likely it is that the use of direct regulations, such as quantitative controls, on certain types of capital flow will be warranted, even if only temporarily (Ocampo 2003). Often, controls of any type are considered inefficient and capable of being circumvented by ever more sophisticated capital market operations. But, as Williamson (2000) has pointed out, "assertions about the ineffectiveness of capital controls are vastly exaggerated."

In developing countries, these regulations should have three policy aims: (i) reduce currency mismatches; (ii) improve maturity structure of external debt; and (iii) increase the room for maneuver of macroeconomic policies. In any case, capital account regulations are a complement for sound real macroeconomic policies, not a substitute for them.

Specific regulations should be put in place to control currency mismatches, including those associated with derivative operations. The strict prohibition of currency mismatches in the portfolios of financial intermediaries is probably the best rule. Authorities should also closely monitor the currency risk of non-financial firms operating in non-tradable sectors, which may eventually become credit risks for banks. Regulations can be used to establish more stringent provisions and/or risk weighting (and therefore higher capital requirements) for these operations (Ocampo 2003).

Capital account regulations should also aim at improving debt profiles, and in this way reducing the risks associated with liability structures that are biased towards short-term capital flows. This is a severe cause of vulnerability, as evidenced in several currency crises in emerging economies (Rodrik and Velasco 2000; see Ocampo 2003). They can also be used as a complementary tool of macroeconomic policy. If effective, they provide room for action during periods of financial euphoria, through the adoption of a contractionary monetary policy and reduced appreciation pressures; they will also reduce or eliminate the usual quasi-fiscal costs of sterilized foreign exchange accumulation. In the other phase of the cycle, of binding external constraints, they may provide space for expansionary monetary and fiscal policies.[2]

Overall innovative experiences in the 1990s indicate that price-based regulations, particularly unremunerated reserve requirements (URR) on capital inflows, can provide useful instruments, in terms of improving debt profiles, facilitating the adoption of counter-cyclical macroeconomic policies during the boom, and minimizing the costly adjustment during downturns following overheated disequilibria. URRs are thus aimed at deterring macro policies and ratios from penetrating into vulnerability zones. Following the positive experience of Chile in the first half of the 1990s (see Agosin and Ffrench-Davis 2001; Ffrench-Davis 2010, ch. VIII), these regulations were also usefully applied in Colombia (Ocampo and Tovar 2003). These regulations also (i) provide a more market-friendly environment for irreversible investment decisions; (ii) help avoid significant output gaps between actual and potential GDP; (iii) avoid outlier macro prices (exchange and interest rates); and (iv) discourage outlier macro ratios (deficit on current account/GDP, price/earnings ratios of equity stocks, and net short-term and liquid external liabilities/international reserves).

On the other hand, the experience with quantitative type regulations includes the well-known action of Malaysia in 1998 of imposing tough non-price regulations on outflows. Data supports the view that they were effective in contributing to the sharp GDP recovery in 1999, by making feasible the active fiscal and monetary policies implemented by Malaysia to face the crisis (Kaplan and Rodrik 2001). They also include the traditional controls, such as quantitative restrictions on short-term financial borrowing and regulations on outflows by domestic agents. Experience indicates that these regulations have worked quite efficiently for the objective of macroeconomic policy to significantly reduce the domestic macroeconomic sensitivity to international financial volatility, as in China and India.

Despite their advantages and the improved understanding of the causes of "modern" financial crisis in emerging economies, capital account regulations were not widely used during the boom of the mid-2000s. Even more, the moves to introduce URRs by Argentina, Colombia, and Thailand led to serious rejection by financial markets, and their lead was not followed by others. Some countries did introduce other regulations, particularly on the purchase of domestic currency government bonds by international institutional investors.

In 2009, there was again a perception of increased need to discourage excessive inflows, as the carry trade linked to loose monetary policy in the developed countries

---

[2] The market rewards *prudently balanced* external debt structures, because, during times of uncertainty, the market usually responds to *gross* financing requirements, which means that the rollover of short-term liabilities is not financially neutral (see Ocampo 2003).

creates very large short-term inflows to countries, leading to excessive appreciation of their currencies. This has resulted in Brazil taxing portfolio inflows in October 2009—a form of capital regulation similar in its economic effects to URRs. Asian countries like Taiwan have followed similar policies.

7.3 ORIGINS AND COMPOSITION OF PRIVATE CAPITAL SURGES IN THE 1990S AND 2000S

There is well-documented evidence that the initial surge of private flows, in the early 1990s, was originated to a large extent in the supply side of capital flows rather than in the demand side.[3] It was associated with technological innovation in financial markets, as well as institutional and monetary policy changes in developed economies, and was encouraged by some economic authorities and powerful lobbying forces (see Bhagwati 2004 for a strong criticism of that lobbyist activity). The financial surge toward the emerging economies (EEs) originated mainly in the US liberalization of financial out-flows in the US; its domestic recession in the early 1990s—with a limited local demand for funds, and very low real interest rates, due to loose monetary policy—led investors to search for yields in other markets. *Pari passu*, there was a fast opening in the capital accounts of EEs, first in Latin America; consequently, this opening was implemented under abundant supply. Latin America was a receptive market, with the binding external constraint still prevailing in 1990, and offered the expectation of high rates of return.

7.3.1 Surges and falls of inflows and diversification toward volatility

There was a massive scale-up of private capital flows to Latin America in the early 1990s. Net capital inflows climbed in 1992–4, to 3.6% of GDP and an average of US$52 billion. Furthermore, after the drop in 1995, they jumped to US$79 billion (4.5%) in 1996–7 (See Table 7.1 below).

The sharp increase of international financial flows from the early 1990s was notably more diversified than in the 1970s. The trend was a shift from medium-term bank credit, which was the predominant source of financing in the 1970s, to more portfolio flows (equity and bonds), short-term time deposits, and acquisitions of domestic firms by for-eign investors. Overall, these changes in the composition of finance were seen by many observers as positive, since they involved a greater diversification of capital flows; flows

---

[3] The classical paper is Calvo, Leiderman, and Reinhart (1993). Diverse approaches and emphasis are found in Griffith-Jones (1998); Rodrik (1998); Krugman (2000); Stiglitz (2000); Eichengreen (2004).

with variable interest rates (particularly dangerous for funding long-term development, as shown by the 1980s debt crisis) represented a small share of total inflows.

However, there were crucial dangerous features, stressed by some observers (for our own work, see Ffrench-Davis and Griffith-Jones 1995). One perceived source of vulnerability was that current account deficits grew too sharply, as occurred in previous booms. Second, associated with that fact, real exchange rates had generally been strongly associated with the net capital flows: they appreciated significantly during the surge and depreciated sharply during the bust (see Figure 7.4 below). Indeed, the evolution of real exchange rates has responded, to a large degree, to financial flows (rather than to the real forces behind the current account). Third, the domestic investment ratio did not grow *pari passu* with capital inflows; actually, capital formation has been notably low in the region during all the period of reforms *à la* Washington Consensus (see Ffrench-Davis 2006: ch. 3).

Paradoxically, this diversification seemed to have potentially brought more instability, in as much, as since the 1990s there has tended to be a *diversification toward highly reversible sources of funding*. If each component tended to respond to different causes of fluctuations, diversification would likely imply that the fluctuations of the diverse flows compensate each other, leading to more stable total flows. However, the new components not only were more unstable but were prone to be subject to common contagions; they have frequently shared similar bouts of over-optimism and over-pessimism. The potential reversibility of flows is not observed during the expansive-boom stage of the cycles, but explodes abruptly with the contagion of negative changes of mood common to diverse financial markets.[4] For instance, Figure 7.1 shows the sharp cyclical fluctuations of stock prices, just taking an average of the indexes of Latin America; its fluctuations are strongly correlated with the country risk grading of LACs. It is a fact, that risk rating has been quite pro-cyclical, as discussed below.

One of the most dynamic and comparatively stable flows to LAC is foreign direct investment (FDI), which has risen sharply since the Tequila crisis, from about 1% of GDP in the early 1990s to almost 3% between 1996 and 2003, though falling to 1.9% in 2004–8. FDI includes, however, two components: traditional greenfield investment and more novel M&A, which have been more pro-cyclical (see Table 7.1).

The traditional FDI experienced a sharp rise since the mid-1990s. It expanded fast in the world, and in particular to LACs, as an important agent of globalization. Greenfield FDI inflows are, by their own nature, reflected directly in capital formation, and continue to be more stable (it is a persistent variable, with a unitary root).[5] On the contrary, mergers and acquisitions (M&A) is an inflow not linked with the direct generation of productive capacity. Private domestic sales of firms to FDI are frequently followed by financial outflows, especially under recessive gaps; this depicts a clearly pro-cyclical

---

[4] The accelerated growth of derivatives markets contributed to soften "micro-instability" but has tended to increase "macro-instability" and to reduce transparency. See Dodd and Griffith-Jones (2006).

[5] Prasad et al. (2003: table 1 and fig. 3) report data on volatility of total inward FDI, bank loans and portfolio investment. The authors confirm the conclusion from other abundant research that FDI is less volatile, even though they did not control for M&A.

behavior. For example, about one-half of FDI inflows into Latin America in 1996–2003 corresponded to M&A (UNCTAD 2005).

On the whole, only greenfield FDI flows seem to be a fairly stable and rather irreversible capital inflow, and flows of FDI that are already well into the investment process tend to continue until projects are completed. However, it should be stressed that the same multinationals that carry out FDI often hedge their exposure pro-cyclically, or even speculate; these latter transactions are often destabilizing.

The foundations of a broad liquid market for portfolio investment that were laid down with the Brady bonds in the late 1980s developed vigorously in the 1990s and 2000s, with Latin America as a major destination for both bond and stock financing.

The advantage of bonds is that they are often at fixed interest rates until maturity. However, spreads are highly volatile through the cycle, as indicated in Figure 7.1. The average maturity for bonds is also highly sensitive to the cycle.

Equity investment was a new form of external private funding for LACs. This has the advantage of a cyclical sensitivity of dividends. However, equity flows carry very important volatility risks for recipient countries. Foreign financiers can, suddenly, not only stop investing in equities but try to sell their stocks quickly, if they fear a worsening

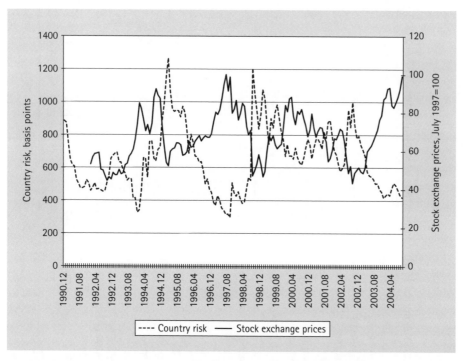

FIGURE 7.1 Latin America: country risk and stock exchange prices, 1990–2004 (basis points, indices)

Source: Country risk (measured by the sovereign spread over the U.S. zero coupon curve): JP Morgan, Emerging Market Bond Index (EMBI). Stock exchange prices: IFC, Standard and Poor's. Dollar denominated.

Table 7.1 Latin America (19): composition of capital flows, 1977–2008 (US$ billions and percentage of trend GDP)

	US$ billions	1977–81	1982–90	1991	1992–4	1995	1996–7	1998–2003	2004–6	2007	2008	2004–8
1	Current account	−24.3	−10.3	−17.0	−43.5	−37.8	−51.5	−40.9	35.6	16.1	−27.5	19.1
2	Trade balance	−9.4	20.3	4.5	−22.0	−12.3	−21.4	−12.3	63.2	47.0	14.3	50.2
3	Rents	−16.1	−35.3	−31.4	−33.5	−40.7	−45.1	−53.1	−79.7	−95.1	−105.7	−88.0
4	Unrequited transfers	1.2	4.8	10.0	12.0	15.3	15.1	24.5	52.1	64.2	64.0	56.9
5	Net capital inflows	27.8	−12.9	23.2	52.4	28.5	79.4	31.8	4.4	98.8	56.9	33.8
6	Net FDI	5.1	5.5	11.0	15.7	25.8	48.9	60.4	42.3	83.6	88.9	59.9
7	M&A inflows	0.0	1.3	2.9	5.7	7.4	26.3	32.8	23.8	23.8	24.8	24.0
8	Greenfield FDI inflows	5.4	4.6	9.5	12.7	22.4	28.0	34.1	44.6	83.2	98.5	63.1
9	Outflows	0.3	−0.4	−1.3	−2.7	−4.0	−5.4	−6.6	−26.1	−23.5	−34.4	−27.2
10	Portfolio	1.3	0.6	16.4	57.6	2.6	37.0	2.1	−2.1	59.5	−10.1	8.6
11	Other capital	21.4	−16.0	−4.8	−17.7	6.0	−2.2	−23.5	−31.7	−34.1	−21.8	−30.2
12	Special flows	0.5	23.6	11.8	3.9	31.7	−7.9	10.7	−8.5	1.9	3.9	−3.9
13	Reserves accumulation	4.1	0.4	18.1	12.9	22.4	20.0	1.6	31.5	116.9	33.3	49.0
14	Net transfer of funds	13.5	−19.9	13.6	34.8	34.7	41.4	13.9	−31.7	69.9	19.1	−1.2
15	Trend GDP	598	862	1252	1454	1644	1767	2113	2835	3333	3599	3088
16	GDP	622	795	1244	1507	1794	2032	1971	2648	3614	4086	3128

	Percentage of trend GDP	1977–81	1982–90	1991	1992–4	1995	1996–7	1998–2003	2004–6	2007	2008	2004–8
1	Current account	-3.9	-1.3	-1.4	-3.0	-2.3	-2.9	-2.1	1.2	0.5	-0.8	0.7
2	Trade balance	-1.5	2.4	0.4	-1.5	-0.7	-1.2	-0.7	2.2	1.4	0.4	1.7
3	Rents	-2.6	-4.3	-2.5	-2.3	-2.5	-2.6	-2.5	-2.8	-2.9	-2.9	-2.8
4	Unrequited transfers	0.2	0.5	0.8	0.8	0.9	0.9	1.1	1.8	1.9	1.8	1.8
5	Net capital inflows	4.6	-1.5	1.9	3.6	1.7	4.5	1.6	0.1	3.0	1.6	1.0
6	Net FDI	0.8	0.6	0.9	1.1	1.6	2.8	2.9	1.5	2.5	2.5	1.9
7	MtA inflows	0.0	0.1	0.2	0.4	0.4	1.5	1.6	0.8	0.7	0.7	0.8
8	Greenfield FDI inflows	0.9	0.6	0.8	0.9	1.4	1.6	1.6	1.6	2.5	2.7	2.0
9	Outflows	0.0	0.0	-0.1	-0.2	-0.2	-0.3	-0.3	-0.9	-0.7	-1.0	-0.9
10	Portfolio	0.2	0.0	1.3	3.9	0.2	2.1	0.1	-0.1	1.8	-0.3	0.3
11	Other capital	3.5	-1.8	-0.4	-1.2	0.4	-0.1	-1.1	-1.1	-1.0	-0.6	-1.0
12	Special flows	0.1	2.8	0.9	0.3	1.9	-0.4	0.5	-0.3	0.1	0.1	-0.1
13	Reserves accumulation	0.7	0.0	1.4	0.9	1.4	1.1	0.0	1.1	3.5	0.9	1.5
14	Net transfer of funds	2.3	-2.4	1.1	2.4	2.1	2.3	0.7	-1.1	2.1	0.5	-0.1

Source: Based on official data from ECLAC and UNCTAD for MtA. Trend GDP was calculated by filtering nominal GDP in US dollars (Hodrick-Prescott filter, lambda=100).

prospect. This leads to pressure on the exchange rate and/or to price drops in the domestic stock exchange. This latter could have a negative impact on aggregate demand—via wealth and panic effects. As long as markets are led by players who specialize in short-term yields, the risks of great volatility are inherent to external financing (Eatwell 1997).

7.3.2 Global factors affecting Latin America

Amongst important institutional changes affecting capital flows to developing countries that occurred in the 2000s, we underline two. The first is the introduction of collective action clauses into bond issues of many EEs, which facilitates future debt restructuring. It is important to highlight that these changes have not increased the cost of borrowing for countries that introduced these clauses. The second is the approval of Basel II, without participation of developing countries, and thus without taking account of their interests. Basel II tends to restrict the supply of bank flows to developing countries, and to increase their cost. Perhaps most worrying, as has been increasingly recognized in the wake of the global financial crisis, is that it will increase pro-cyclicality of international and domestic bank lending (Griffith-Jones and Persaud 2008).

The great regulatory debate that followed the recent global financial crisis will also have important implications for developing countries, but as this process was ongoing at the time of writing, we cannot yet extract definitive lessons. It does, however, seem clear that there will be a more general trend to greater countercyclicality and comprehensiveness in regulation, which should be beneficial for ensuring greater stability in flows towards Latin America (Griffith-Jones and Ocampo with Ortiz 2009).

One outstanding feature behind the supply of funds to EEs is that institutional investors, especially pension funds and insurance companies, saw their total assets increase dramatically in recent decades. At the same time, there has been a clear trend towards an increase of the share of foreign assets in total assets. This led to the development of specialized markets, such as the bonds and shares issued by EEs. A result of the development of these markets is that the role of credit rating agencies has broadened considerably, as they provide information to investors. However, there has been widespread criticism of the markedly pro-cyclical behavior of ratings during the gestation and explosion of the Asian crisis (see Reisen 2003) and in the build-up of the global financial crisis (Goodhart 2010).

As pointed out, the large expansion of liquidity by developed countries' central banks in the wake of the global financial crisis has led to a major surge in short term flows to Latin America and much of emerging economies, in 2009, in search of higher yields, contributing to significant appreciation of exchange rates and sharply rising stock markets. Evidently, stock prices became inconsistent with the slow recovery of economic activity, and exchange rates also inconsistent with the need to progress toward sustainable macroeconomic balances suited for development. These trends are suggesting that new bubbles are being created.

7.3.3 The financial risks of the newer capital flows

The benefits of interaction with private capital flows for the development of LAC economies depend, to a great extent, on stable and predictable access to financial markets, especially valuable for long-term investment. The risk of abrupt stops in supply and/or sharp increases in cost and shortening of the maturity terms of external liabilities are partly determined by perceptions of risk and hence host country policies. But, as pointed out, access also can be heavily conditioned by exogenously determined supply-side dynamics, related to industrialized country policies in the areas of macroeconomics and prudential regulation, as well as developments in financial markets themselves.

One new source of a growing potential for market instability are derivatives, which have become increasingly important in financial activity. These transactions are unregulated, often with no margin or capital standards. Furthermore, information on derivative transactions continues to be extremely incomplete, especially when they are on the over-the-counter market (Dodd and Griffith-Jones 2006). The role of derivatives in the carry trade was very negative both during the surge of inflows to Latin America in 2004–7, which contributed to appreciating exchange rates, and in the reversal of flows in the wake of the global crisis; it implied a major reversal of the carry trade for a brief period in 2008, leading to sharp depreciations and significant losses by companies in countries like Mexico.

Given the increase in global systemic risk, central banks, and governments in LACs should seek to participate actively in global discussions of regulation, especially those that affect their countries. The fact that three Latin American countries, Brazil, Mexico, and Argentina, since 2009 have participated in the global regulatory forums, like the Financial Stability Board and the Basel Banking Committee, should facilitate such a task somewhat.

7.3.4 New policy strength and challenges

It should however be emphasized that LAC governments have made efforts to reduce their vulnerability to financial crises, and have recently in the good times, such as the mid-2000s, accumulated large levels of foreign exchange reserves, as well as both reducing the level of external public debt and improving its structure (longer maturities, higher proportion in local currency). Indeed, as can be seen in Table 7.1, Latin American countries accumulated annually on average $49 billion of foreign exchange reserves during the 2004–8 period, i.e. around 1.5% of GDP every year. Net foreign exchange reserves for the seven largest LAC countries in late 2007 reached 12.3% of GDP, almost double their level in 2001; even more important, as percentage of foreign debt, net reserves for those seven major countries reached 58% in 2007, compared with 20% in 2001 (Ocampo 2009). This implies that LACs were somewhat less vulnerable through the financial channel to the global financial crisis, though they were badly hit via the trade and remittances channel, and initially suffered a major, albeit brief, reversal of capital flows. Indeed, governments were more able than in the past to pursue somewhat countercyclical fiscal policies; where necessary, too, governments could use part of their reserves to provide trade credit to their exporters, and working capital to other private companies, whose external sources had dried up.

The reversal of flows during the worst of the global crisis affected all credit flows, including trade credit; it also implied major selling of Latin American shares and other paper, to provide liquidity to US mutual and hedge funds; as pointed out, it also implied major reversals of the carry trade. These trends led to a brief but costly period of sharply falling stock markets. Large currency depreciations and losses by companies involved in derivatives markets also took place, followed by a significant recession. In 2009, average GDP of Latin America decreased by nearly 2%.

7.4 THE LINKS BETWEEN ECONOMIC GROWTH AND CAPITAL FLOWS

One outstanding feature of the economies of the region is the high instability exhibited by GDP, as shown by Figure 7.2. The volatility of capital flows has generated serious negative effects on the real economies of recipient countries. Economic downturn—and particularly financial crises, which often result from, or are aggravated by, volatile financial flows—have a negative impact on economic growth and employment; they often result in

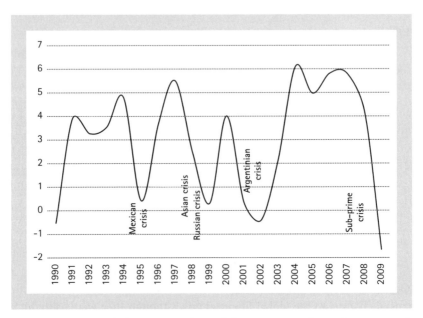

FIGURE 7.2 Latin America (19): GDP growth instability, 1990–2009 (annual percentage change)

Source: Based on ECLAC figures.

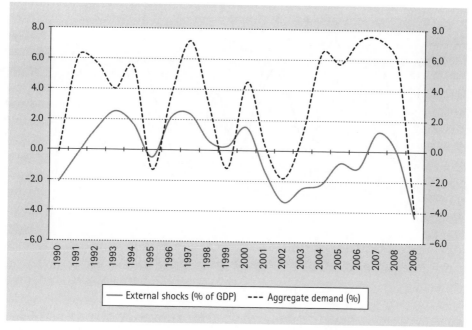

FIGURE 7.3 Latin America (19): external shocks and growth of aggregate demand, 1990–2009 (% of GDP; annual average growth rate)

Source: Ffrench-Davis (2008), and updated figures, based on data from ECLAC.

Note: External Shocks include net transfers of resources from abroad plus the terms-of-trade effect, both measured as percentages of GDP.

reduced investment in both physical and human capital. Figure 7.3 shows the systematic association between swings in external shocks and their impact on aggregate demand. In other words, in recent decades, generally, real volatility has had an external origin: external shocks have been notably stronger than domestically originated shocks.

In a situation with unemployment of productive factors, the positive shock has positive Keynesian-type effects: it eliminates the binding external constraint, making possible an economic recovery with higher use of productive capacity, and thus leading to rising output, income, employment, and investment ratio. However, the behavior of some macro variables during economic recovery is most significant. It happens that most crises since the 1980s have been the result of badly managed booms (Ocampo 2003). During the boom is when degrees of freedom to choose policies are broader and when future imbalances may be generated. To move toward a macroeconomics-for-growth, we need a systematic differentiation between what is economic recovery and what is generation of additional capacity. Disregarding this crucial feature not only leads to neglect of the relevance of investment from the point of view of public policies, but also stimulates the private sector to run a *destabilizing inter-temporal adjustment*. Thus, a sharp distinction between creating capacity and using existing capacity should be guiding domestic macroeconomic policy.

Figure 7.4 shows that changes of actual GDP have been sharply associated with fluctuations in aggregate demand. In the last four decades, aggregate demand changes have led GDP changes in both booms and recessions that have affected the region.

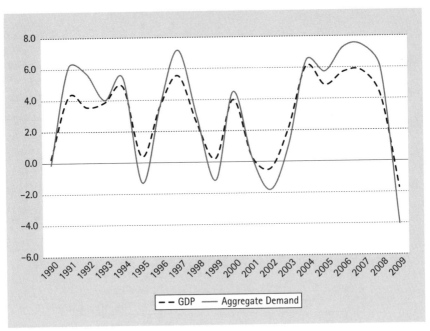

FIGURE 7.4 Latin America (19): GDP and aggregate demand, 1990–2009 (annual average growth rates)

Sources: Ffrench-Davis (2006) and ECLAC (2010: fig. 11.5).

Inflows, under a binding external constraint, tend to be extremely efficient initially, since idle labor and capital are utilized; but it never must be forgotten that if there is such a constraint, this implies that there is a macroeconomic disequilibrium in the real economy: actual GDP is lower than potential GDP, with implications for growth and equity, and for employment and capital formation (see Ffrench-Davis 2006: ch. 2). In fact, when the external constraint disappears as a result of inflows, this implies aggregate demand increases. Given that there is an output gap, actual GDP can also rise. For the region as a whole, 2004 is an outstanding case. For six years Latin America had averaged a meager 1.4% GDP growth, less than the rise in population. In 2004 GDP jumped over 6%, thanks to a change in the macroeconomic environment, brought by the acute improvement in external conditions.

In the case of all the general cycles experienced by the region since the late 1980s, trends initially reflected the recovery toward 'normal' levels of aggregate demand, imports, and the real exchange rate, all of which were determined by the external constraint during the previous period. After a while, however, the continuing abundance of capital generated an over-shooting in those macro variables, leading in several cases to unsustainable macroeconomic imbalances, and inviting a recession.

In fact, if capital inflows or improved terms of trade stimulate processes of recovery in economies with unemployment of productive factors, actual productivity rises because of an increase in the rate of utilization of potential GDP. Then agents, authorities, and many researchers may confuse the jump in actual productivity, which is based on the utilization of previously idle labor and capital, with a structural increase in the sustainable speed of productivity improvements and in permanent income. Consequently, the market response would tend to be an inter-temporal upward adjustment in consumption, with the external gap covered with capital inflows, as long as the supply of foreign savings is available. That implies a crowding-out of domestic savings. The inter-temporal adjustment ends up being destabilizing.

The increased availability of funds tends to generate a process of exchange rate appreciation; in fact, the RER has been influenced to a large degree by capital flows, as shown in Figure 7.5. Then the expectations of continued, persistent appreciation encourage additional inflows from dealers operating with maturity horizons located within the expected appreciation of the domestic currency. For allocation efficiency and for export-oriented development strategies, a macro price—as significant as the exchange rate—led by capital inflows conducted by short-termist agents reveals a severe policy inconsistency. The increase in aggregate demand, pushed up by inflows and appreciation, and by a rising share of the domestic demand for tradables, artificially augments the absorptive capacity and the demand for foreign savings. Thus, exogenous changes (like fluctuations in the supply of funds) are converted into an endogenous process, leading to domestic vulnerability, given the potential reversibility of flows.

When actual output is reaching the production frontier, with the recessive gap elapsing, more active policies are needed to regulate the expansion of aggregate demand. It is essential to keep the rate of expansion of demand in line with the growth of productive

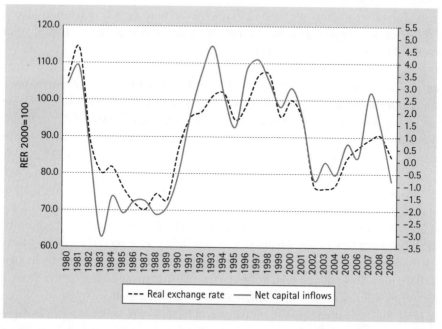

FIGURE 7.5 Latin America (19): net capital inflows and real exchange rate, 1980–2009 (RER in 2000=100; flows in % of GDP)

Source: Average figures for 19 countries based an ECLAC data.

capacity (and also with sustainable external financing). Otherwise, if passive macroeconomic policies are adopted in situations of positive external shocks (such as lower international interest rates or increased supply of capital inflows), then the economy will be subject to inflationary pressures and/or a growing gap between expenditure and output. In all events, a future adjustment in the opposite direction will usually be built up.

In brief, an effective pro-growth countercyclical policy mix is needed. As documented by Kaminsky, Reinhart, and Végh (2004) for a sample of 104 countries, the opposite has tended to occur in the past. Both monetary and fiscal policies (as well as the exchange rate) have behaved pro-cyclically and have multiplied the effects of financial shocks. Consequently, there is need for counter-cyclical intervention.

Intervention is based on two assumptions: (i) the monetary and fiscal authority has a better idea of future macroeconomic trends in the balance of payments and their long-term effects on the economy; and (ii) more fundamentally, its objectives are longer term than those of agents operating in short-term markets whose training and rewards are associated to earnings in the short term (Zahler 1998). An outstanding feature of most recent macroeconomic crises in East Asia and Latin America is that currency and financial crises have been suffered by EEs that usually were considered to be highly "successful" by IFIs and financial agents. EEs were "rewarded" with large private capital flows, and falling spreads, in parallel with accumulating rising stocks of external liabilities, over-appreciation of exchange rates, and unsustainable prices of stocks and of expensive real estate. As explained in Ffrench-Davis (2006: ch. 6), given all these signals of macroeconomic disequilibria, why did neither agent act in due time to curb flows well before a crisis? It has been agents specialized in microeconomic aspects of finance, placed in the short-term or liquid segments of capital markets, who acquire a dominant voice in the generation of macroeconomic expectations.

During all the expansive processes there has been an evident contagion of over-optimism among creditors. Rather than appetite for risk, in those episodes agents supplying funding underestimate or ignore risk. Borrowers are also victims of the syndrome of financial euphoria during the boom periods. The agents predominant in the financial markets are specialized in short-term liquid investment, operate within short-term horizons, are highly mobile geographically, and seek returns in the short run. This explains, from the supply-side, why the surges of flows to LACs—in 1977–81, 1991–4, and mid-1995–8—have been *processes* that went on for several years rather than one-shot changes in supply. In this sense, the relevance for policy design of making a distinction between two different types of volatility of capital flows—short- and medium-term instability—must be stressed. Medium-term instability leads several variables—like the stock market, real estate prices, and the exchange rate—to move persistently in a given direction, providing "wrong certainties" to the market, encouraging capital flows, and *seeking economic rents* rather than differences in real productivity.

In brief, the interaction between the two sets of factors—*the nature of agents* and *a process of adjustment*—explains the dynamics of capital flows over time, and explains why suppliers keep pouring-in funds while real macroeconomic fundamentals gradually worsen. The accumulation of stocks of assets abroad by financial suppliers until the boom stage of the cycle is well advanced, and a subsequent sudden reversal of flows, can both be considered to be *rational* responses on the part of individual agents with short-term horizons. This is because it is of little concern to these investors whether (long-term) fundamentals are being improved or worsened while they continue to raise profits from additional inflows. Thus, they will continue to supply net inflows until expectations of an imminent reversal build-up. Indeed, for many influential financial operators, the more relevant variables are related not to the long-term fundamentals but to short-term profitability. In conclusion, economic agents specialized in the allocation of financial funding, who operate with short-horizons "by training and by reward," have played the leading role in determining macroeconomic conditions and policy design in LACs. It implies that a financieristic approach becomes predominant rather than a productivistic approach.

As Ffrench-Davis and Griffith-Jones (1995) argued, several preconditions need to be met for capital flows to produce sustained growth—i.e. to create a virtuous "debt cycle." These include:

(a) a high proportion of the inflows should go into investment;
(b) the additional investment should be efficient;
(c) a large proportion of the increased investment should go into tradeables, so as to help generate the foreign currency required for servicing the debt;
(d) creditors and investors must be willing to provide stable and predictable capital flows on reasonable terms.

Unfortunately, it is both difficult and rare, at least in recent Latin American economic history, for large surges of capital flows to lead to sustained growth. A serious source of concern is that in 2009, capital flows to LAC increased sharply, leading again to increased prices of stock markets and strengthened exchange rates, while investment as percentage of GDP was falling. This may relate to the fact that the above-listed preconditions are not being met.

Large surges of capital flows tend to contribute to overvalued exchange rates. Overvaluation, and the instability that brings, discourages investment in tradables, and especially in exports, which are meant to be one of the most dynamic sectors in a market economy. More broadly, volatility in key macroeconomic variables—not only exchange rates but also domestic credit levels, asset values, interest rates, and the rate of growth itself—have a negative effect on investment levels via business expectations, as they increase uncertainty about future profitability of investment. As investors have the option of delaying investment until more information arrives, there exists an opportunity cost of investing now rather than waiting. Therefore, increased volatility in macroeconomic variables, which augments uncertainty, reduces the level of private investment, as various empirical studies have shown.[6]

---

[6] In a complementary line, Ffrench-Davis (2006: ch. 3) has shown that the gap between actual and potential GDP has been a determinant variable explaining the low investment ratio since the 1980s.

For obvious reasons, overvalued exchange rates encourage growth of current account deficits. As this trend continues, and as foreign exchange liabilities (especially short-term) increase, the likelihood increases of a reversal of capital flows and a currency crisis. Such a currency crisis can increase the risk of a banking crisis.

Another negative interaction between capital flows and sustainable growth operates via the impact on the fiscal balance and public investment. With a surge of short-term capital inflows, there is a change in market perceptions about what they will accept as a sustainable level of public expenditure. As this increases, the "permitted" fiscal deficit can rise quite sharply for a transition period, given the space opened by the higher expected GDP growth. Once foreign creditors and lenders see the cumulative effect of their individual decisions, however, sentiment can change suddenly, possibly even to a lower public debt ratio than before the initial favorable change of perception. The financial market then requires a sharp adjustment in the fiscal balance. As taxes are difficult to increase rapidly and current spending is difficult to cut, public investment tends to the main adjustment mechanism. Sharp fluctuations in public investment are very negative, as efficiency is lost both when projects are started too rapidly and when ongoing ones are frozen or delayed once started. Also the volatility and resulting inefficiency of public investment negatively affects private investment because there often are strong complementarities between them.

A final, external reason that makes it difficult for surges of short-term capital to contribute to sustained growth is related to the volatile nature of capital flows themselves. Rather than faithful companions, capital flows are fair-weather friends. Their "friendliness" for a country or of emerging countries as an "asset class" may quickly change, due to a deterioration in key national variables (such as current account deficits, fiscal deficits, or the ratio of short-term foreign liabilities to reserves) that they themselves partly contributed to, or because of external factors, such as variations in developed countries' interest rates (Mexico, late 1994) or contagion from currency crises in other emerging markets (Brazil, early 1999) or even in developed markets (late 2008 to early 2009).

7.5 POLICY CHALLENGES FOR LATIN AMERICA

7.5.1 Capital account liberalization and foreign exchange policy

In a number of LAC countries, trade liberalization was accompanied by a broad opening of the capital account. For example, in the capital surges prevailing from the early 1990s up to 1998, the liberalization of the capital account prompted considerable exchange rate appreciation just when trade reforms urgently required the opposite: a compensatory real depreciation.

The mix of import liberalization and RER appreciation, which became feasible only due to net inflows of funding, implied a sharp destruction of import substituting sectors, including not only inefficient firms that had been over-protected but also producers which would be efficient under "normal" (non-outlier) relative prices and a more gradual movement to a new equilibrium. The exchange rate has a strong impact on the allocation of resources between tradables and non-tradables. This role has been strengthened by the sharp reduction of protectionism in LACs (Bouzas and Keifman 2003).

Exchange rate instability tends to reduce the capacity to identify comparative advantages, a trend that undermines capital formation. On the export side, it often has a negative and stronger impact on new exports, on those undertaken by companies with less diversified markets, and on those with more limited access to capital markets; in the import side, it tends to crowd out the production of import substituters, particularly by small and medium enterprises (SMEs). Consequently, exchange rate instability, caused often by capital flow volatility is biased against non-traditional producers.

Instability usually reduces the average rate of use of resources, and biases the market toward the short-term and financial rent-seeking. A policy that avoids extreme ups and downs in the real exchange rate allows for a sustainable higher average level of effective demand and economic activity. Therefore, it tends to encourage a greater utilization of capacity and to encourage productive investment.

Exchange rate stability and competitiveness is especially important in a developing economy undergoing structural transformation, exhibiting sharp heterogeneity, and with crucial incomplete factors markets; even more than in homogeneous and diversified developed economies, redeployment of resources across sectors is hard and costly. Hence, it is essential for the exchange rate to be guided by the trend shown by the current account of the balance of payments projections (at full employment), seeking to attenuate the transmission of short-term fluctuations of the capital flows into the domestic economy. Capital controls are crucial to moderate destabilizing capital flows and their negative effects on the domestic financial sector and macroeconomic balances. Thus capital controls can be seen both as a prudential tool—to avoid systemic risk in the financial sector, distortions in the production of tradables—and as a tool to avoid macroeconomic imbalances. Capital controls should however always be seen as a complement, and not as a substitute, for good macroeconomic policies.

7.5.2 Financial and capital account reforms

During the 1990s an extended liberalization was carried out in LACs relating both to domestic capital markets and to the capital account. The predominant pattern followed the more naive orthodoxy, repeating to a large degree the 1970s inefficient reform experience of the Southern Cone. There was widespread disregard for the high risk of generating speculative bubbles. It is interesting to note that a "financieristic" bias assigned a strategic role to the sector's sharp liberalization, without considering in the reform design the characteristics of the market failures in question (see Díaz-Alejandro 1985; Stiglitz 2000).[7]

A distinctive feature of macroeconomic management, in the transition toward development of the most successful newly industrialized countries, has been the predominance of productive over financial dimensions, with financial aspects serving the "real" side. On the contrary, in many LACs there prevailed the phenomenon of "financierism"— i.e. the dominance (or strong influence and powerful lobbying) of short-termist financial agents in macroeconomic decisions. The growing link with the international financial system facilitated the dissociation from the needs of domestic productive systems, encouraged capital outflows during periods of domestic crises, and allowed the predominance of a short-termist bias at the expense of concerns for productivity and additions to productive capacity. In short, total openness to the international financial markets, in developing economies, tends to imply integration into more speculative segments of developed world markets.

From the mid-1990s, campaigning and elected Latin American presidents became regular visitors to Wall Street. International mass media, in turn, began to talk about the "market's candidate," actually just referring to financial markets. The strengthening of this dimension has provoked a growing duality, worrisome for democracy, in the constituencies taken into account by authorities in EEs. Thus, an outcome of the specific road taken by globalization has been that experts in financial intermediation—a microeconomic training—have become determinant, in too many cases, for the evolution of the domestic macroeconomic balances and their volatility (Ffrench-Davis 2006: ch. 8).

7.5.3 A positive agenda for managing the capital account for development

As we discussed, international finance has played a leading role in defining business cycles in Latin America. The high costs generated by business cycles are thus evidently related to the strong and growing connections between domestic and international capital markets. This implies that an essential objective of public policies must be to reap the benefits from external savings, while reducing the intensity of capital account cycles and their negative effects on domestic economic and social variables.

The common assertion in the mainstream economic literature that efficiency requires an open capital account is based on assumptions that are often unrealistic regarding the functioning of international capital markets and their interaction with EEs. These con-

---

[7] In a brilliant analysis of financial reforms implemented, in the Southern Cone in the 1970s, Carlos Díaz-Alejandro (1985) concludes that "financial reforms...yielded by 1983 domestic financial sectors characterized by widespread bankruptcies, massive government interventions to rescue private institutions, and low domestic savings. The clearest example of this is Chile."

ventional arguments are far more strongly challenged after numerous and costly crises, both in emerging and—more recently—in developed countries. Therefore, it is increasingly evident that across-the-board capital account liberalization, resulting in large flows intensive in financial capital (loosely linked to gross capital formation, GCF) rather than in long-term capital and greenfield FDI (directly linked to GCF), can be a destabilizing source of shocks, rather than providing additional resources for long-term development.

From an analytical point of view, recent crises have shed light on a number of mistaken hypotheses that had become part of the "conventional wisdom." They are based on three wrong assumptions: (i) recovery from crises is rapid; (ii) open capital accounts discourage macroeconomic disequilibria; (iii) short-term inflows complement domestic savings. These beliefs have misleadingly prescribed a passive approach in the management of macroeconomic policies.

As an alternative approach, we propose a set of active macro policies for open economies. In all of them, the underlying principle is that usually crises are the consequence of badly managed booms; consequently, the main aim of macroeconomic policies should be of a prudential nature, by controlling booms before they become unsustainable. In particular, since international capital markets give rise to frequent cycles of abundance and scarcity of funding and systemic crises, policymakers should exercise active capital account management (including capital controls, both for financial prudential and for macroeconomic reasons) and exchange rate management, in order to ensure that capital inflows are consistent with real macroeconomic stability, investment, and growth based on systemic competitiveness. Indeed, in the last decades we have learnt that, in spite of the new challenges imposed by globalization of financial volatility, there remains significant room for successful domestic policies. The accumulation of reserves in LAC countries during the 2000s is an example of such policies.

Evidence shows that capital surges, and their intrinsic volatility, are costly both for growth and for equity. It is true that several crises, especially in the past, were caused by irresponsible or populist policies. But, in the normal or boom stages of the business cycle, it has been quite common in successful emerging economies that a capital surge flowing into foreign exchange and stock markets and credit increases has been the leading variable behind an excessive increase in aggregate demand, associated with exchange rate appreciation and bubbles in the stock market. The consequence has been a growing trade deficit, led by the capital surge, with a deficit generated in the private sector. These "wrong" policies have been supported by suppliers of international financing and encouraged by financial analysts, risk rating agencies, and IFIs: recall the enthusiastic praise for Argentina in the 1990s, or for Mexico in the first half of the 1990s, or the fashionable assertion that Latin America has "learnt how to do macroeconomics" (see Ffrench-Davis 2008 for the counterargument).

A better understanding of the working of domestic and international financial markets is at the core of integrating successfully with the world economy. More systematic efforts should be at work in order to bring pragmatism into the highly ideological approach to capital account liberalization that has often prevailed.

REFERENCES

AGOSIN, M., and FFRENCH-DAVIS, R. (2001). 'Managing Capital Inflows in Chile', in S. Griffith-Jones, M. Montes, and A. Nasution (eds), *Short-Term Capital Flows and Economic Crises*, New York: Oxford University Press and United Nations University.

BHAGWATI, J. (2004). *In Defense of Globalization*, New York: Oxford University Press.

BOUZAS, R., and KEIFMAN, S. (2003). 'Making Trade Liberalization Work', in P. P. Kuczynski and J. Williamson (eds), *After the Washington Consensus: Restarting Growth and Reform in Latin America*, Washington, DC: Institute for International Economics.

CALVO, G. (1997). 'Varieties of Capital-Market Crises', in G. Calvo and M. King (eds), *The Debt Burden and its Consequences for Monetary Policy*, London: Macmillan.

—— LEIDERMAN, E., and REINHART, C. (1993). 'Capital Inflows and Real Exchange Rate Appreciation in Latin America: The Role of External Factors', *IMF Staff Papers* 401.

—— and MENDOZA, E. (2000). 'Rational Contagion and the Globalization of Securities Markets', *Journal of International Economics* 51.1.

D'ARISTA, J., and GRIFFITH-JONES, S. (2008). 'Agenda and Criteria for Financial Regulatory Reform', working paper, New York: Initiative for Policy Dialogue. Available online at: http://www.gsb.columbia.edu/ipd/programs/item.cfm?prid=133&iyid=13&itid=1486

DÍAZ-ALEJANDRO, C. (1985). 'Good-Bye Financial Repression, Hello Financial Crash', *Journal of Development Economics* 191.2.

DODD, R., and GRIFFITH-JONES, S. (2006). *Report on Derivatives Markets: Stabilizing or Speculative Impact on Chile and a Comparison with Brazil*, Santiago, Chile, Chile: ECLAC.

EATWELL, J. (1997). 'International Capital Liberalization: The Impact on World Development', *Estudios de economía* 24.2.

ECLAC (UN Economic Commission for Latin America and the Caribbean) (1994). *Latin America and the Caribbean: Policies to Improve Linkages with the Global Economy*, Santiago, Chile.

—— (2002). *Growth with Stability: Financing for Development in the New International Context*, Santiago, Chile.

—— (2010). *Time for Equality: Closing Gaps, Opening Trails*, May, Santiago, Chile: ECLAC.

EICHENGREEN, B. (2004). *Capital Flows and Crises*, Cambridge, Mass.: MIT Press.

FFRENCH-DAVIS, R. (2006). *Reforming Latin America's Economies after Market Fundamentalism*, New York: Palgrave Macmillan.

—— (2008). 'From Financieristic to Real Macroeconomics: Seeking Development Convergence in Emerging Economies', Commission on Growth and Development Working Paper No. 44, Washington, DC: World Bank.

—— (2010). *Economic Reforms in Chile: From Dictatorship to Democracy*, 2nd edn, London: Palgrave Macmillan.

—— and GRIFFITH-JONES, S. (eds) (1995). *Coping With Capital Surges: The Return of Finance to Latin America*, Boulder, Colo.: Rienner.

—— —— (eds) (2003). *From Capital Surges to Drought: Seeking Stability from Emerging Economies*. London: Palgrave Macmillan.

Financial Stability Forum (2000). 'Report of the Working Group on Capital Flows', Basel: Bank for International Settlements.

GOODHART, C. A. E. (2010). 'How, If At All, Should Credit Rating Agencies (CRAs) be Regulated?', in S. Griffith-Jones, J. A. Ocampo, and J. E. Stiglitz (eds), *Time for a Visible Hand: Lessons from the 2008 World Financial Crisis*, New York: Oxford University Press.

GRIFFITH-JONES, S. (1998). *Global Capital Flows: Should They Be Regulated?* London: Macmillan.

—— (2001). 'An International Financial Architecture for Crisis Prevention', in R. Ffrench-Davis (ed.), *Financial Crises in 'Successful' Emerging Economies*, Washington, DC: Brookings Institution Press and ECLAC.

—— and OCAMPO, J. A. (2003). 'What Progress on International Financial Reform? Why So Limited?', report prepared for EGDI, Sweden.

—— —— (2009). 'Global Governance for Financial Stability and Development', prepared for the Development Dimensions of Global Economic Governance Series, New York: Initiative for Policy Dialogue and UNDP.

—— with ORTIZ, A. (2009). 'Building on the Counter-cyclical Consensus', prepared for IPD-FEPS Conference, Brussels, October.

—— and PERSAUD, A. (2008) 'The Pro-cyclical Impact of Basel II on Emerging Markets and its Political Economy', in J. A. Ocampo and J. E. Stiglitz (eds), *Capital Market Liberalization and Development*, New York: Oxford University Press.

—— and SUNKEL, O. (1989). *Debt and Development Crises in Latin America: The End of an Illusion*, New York: Oxford University Press.

KAMINSKY, G., REINHART, C., and VÉGH, C. (2004). 'When It Rains, It Pours: Pro-cyclical Capital Flows and Macroeconomic Policies', NBER Working Paper No. 10780.

KAPLAN, E., and D. RODRIK (2001). 'Did the Malaysian Capital Controls Work?', NBER Working Paper No. 8142, Cambridge, Mass.

KRUGMAN, P. (2000). 'Crises: The Price of Globalization?', *Proceedings*, Federal Reserve Bank of Kansas City.

—— (2005). 'Is Fiscal Policy Poised for a Comeback?', *Oxford Review of Economic Policy* 21.4.

OCAMPO, J. A. (2003). 'Capital Account and Counter-cyclical Prudential Regulations in Developing Countries', in Ffrench-Davis and Griffith-Jones (2003).

—— (2009). 'Latin America and the Global Financial Crisis', *Cambridge Journal of Economics* 33.4.

—— and TOVAR, C. (2003). 'Colombia's Experience with Reserve Requirements on Capital Inflows', *CEPAL Review* 8.1.

PRASAD, E., ROGOFF, K., WEI, S., and KOSE, M. (2003). 'Effects of Financial Globalization on Developing Countries: Some Empirical Evidence', IMF Occasional Paper No. 220.

REINHART, C., and ROGOFF, K. (2009). 'The Aftermath of Financial Crises', NBER Working Paper No. 14656.

REISEN, H. (2003). 'Ratings Since the Asian Crisis', in Ffrench-Davis and Griffith-Jones (2003).

RODRIK, D. (1998). 'Who Needs Capital Account Convertibility?', in S. Fischer et al. (ed.). *Should the IMF Pursue Capital Account Convertibility? Princeton Essays in International Finance207*, Princeton, NJ: Princeton University Press.

—— (2007). 'The Real Exchange Rate and Economic Growth: Theory and Evidence', WCFIA Working Paper.

—— and VELASCO, A. (2000). 'Short-Term Capital Flows', in B. Pleskovic and J. Stiglitz (eds), *Annual World Bank Conference on Development Economics 1999*, Washington, DC: World Bank.

STIGLITZ, J. (2000). 'Capital Market Liberalization, Economic Growth and Instability', *World Development* 28.6.

—— (2002). *Globalization and its Discontents*, New York: Norton.

——OCAMPO, J. A., FFRENCH-DAVIS, R., SPIEGEL, S., and NAYYAR, D. (2006). *Stability with Growth: Macroeconomics, Liberalization, and Development*, Oxford and New York: Oxford University Press and IPD.

UNCTAD (UN Conference on Trade and Development) (2005). *World Investment Report 2005*, Geneva.

United Nations (1999). *Towards a New International Financial Architecture*, Report of the Task Force of the Executive Committee on Economic and Social Affairs.

WILLIAMSON, J. (1993). 'A Cost–Benefit Analysis of Capital Account Liberalization' in H. Reisen and B. Fischer (eds), *Financial Opening: Policy Issues and Experiences in Developing Countries*, Paris: OECD.

——(2000). 'Exchange Rate Regimes for Emerging Markets: Reviving the Intermediate Option', in *Policy Analysis in International Economics* 60, Washington, DC: Institute for International Economics.

——(2003). 'Overview: An Agenda for Restarting Growth and Reform', in Kuczynski and Williamson (2003).

ZAHLER, R. (1998). 'The Central Bank and Chilean Macroeconomic Policy in the 1990s', *CEPAL Review* 64.

CHAPTER 8

EXCHANGE RATE REGIMES IN LATIN AMERICA

ROBERTO FRENKEL AND MARTÍN RAPETTI

8.1 INTRODUCTION[1]

Latin American (LA) economic history is rich in cases of interest for macroeconomists. The region has provided substantial material for the study of inflation, unemployment, financial and balance of payment crises, and, to a lesser extent, episodes of rapid growth. A central goal of this chapter is to present a persuasive argument showing that exchange rate policies and regimes have played a significant role in shaping many of these macroeconomic outcomes. We develop a historical narrative of the economic performance and exchange rate arrangements of LA countries since the Second World War.

In a small open economy the nominal exchange rate (NER) is a key macroeconomic variable. Its relevance derives from its effects on both nominal and real variables, including the inflation rate, the balance of payments, output and employment levels, and the rate of economic growth. An exchange rate regime is defined by the rules followed by the central bank regarding the degree of intervention in the foreign exchange (FX) market and therefore by the degree of official commitment in the determination of the NER.[2] Thus, through its effect on the NER, an exchange rate regime can have a decisive influence on five key economic policy objectives: price stability, domestic financial stability, external balance, internal balance, and economic growth. In our narrative, we look at how LA governments, trying to attain one or some of these goals, chose their exchange rate regimes given specific domestic and external conditions.

[1] We thank Oscar Dancourt, José Antonio Ocampo, and Jaime Ros for valuable comments. We also thank the SECyT (Argentina) and the Ford Foundation for financial support.
[2] Our classification of regimes essentially coincides with that of IMF's *Annual Report on Exchange Rate Arrangements and Exchange Rate Restrictions*.

The chapter is organized as follows. After this introduction, section 8.2 provides a historical overview of the main trends of exchange rate arrangements in LA, focusing on Argentina, Brazil, Chile, Colombia, Mexico, and Peru. This narrative goes from the post world war period up until the unfolding of the subprime crisis in the US and its effects on LA. Section 8.3 closes with the main conclusions derived from our analysis. Figures showing the real exchange rate in Argentina, Brazil, Chile, Colombia, Mexico, and Peru between 1980 and 2008 are provided as an Appendix to the chapter.[3] We follow the LA convention defining the exchange rate as the domestic price of a foreign currency (i.e. units of domestic currency per unit of US dollar). A rise in the NER implies a nominal depreciation and a fall an appreciation. The same logic applies for the real exchange rate (RER). In this regard, we refer to more competitive or undervalued RER to higher values of the RER.

8.2 A HISTORICAL OVERVIEW

In each period the exchange rate regime choice in LA has been designed to orient macroeconomic policy towards the objectives considered most urgent or demanding. Changes in the international context were crucial in these choices. Most of the changes in the external conditions have affected the countries in the region simultaneously. However, the policy reaction has not been uniform. These strategies were determined to a great extent by countries' economic policy agendas—namely, the problems perceived as demanding immediate attention and the elements of the economic performance that were deemed necessary to preserve. Therefore, national policy agendas have had a component of path dependency.

8.2.1 The 1950s and 1960s

The main characteristics of the international conditions that LA faced during the postwar period remained virtually unchanged up until the late 1960s. The international monetary system followed the Bretton Woods rules, which established that countries had to maintain fixed exchange rates against the US dollar. These parities could be adjusted in the presence of fundamental disequilibrium. Given the virtual absence of private sources of international finance, the only substantial source of external finance for the region came from official development financing (including the World Bank and USAID) and the IMF. In order to get financial assistance, countries had to negotiate their exchange rate policy with the latter institution.

---

[3] These series use the CPI as a deflator. Each one has a base equal to 1 for the average RER between 1980 and 2008.

By the end of the period of high commodity prices associated with the Korean War, many LA countries started to experience balance of payments problems and had to rely on exchange rate adjustments agreed on with the IMF.[4] This was the beginning of a period characterized by stop-and-go dynamics resulting from the inconsistency between the adjustable pegs regimes and inflation rates. Shortages in FX reserves required adjustment of the fixed exchange rate. Devaluations, in turn, transitorily alleviated the balance of payment problems due to the fall in the demand for imports caused by the contractionary effect on aggregate demand. However, they also led to the acceleration of the inflation rate due to wage indexation and real wage resistance. Real exchange rate (RER) appreciation resulting from inflation led again to balance of payment difficulties. This cyclical stop-and-go dynamic was a stylized fact among many countries in the region since mid-1950s and during the 1960s.

In order to deal with high inflation and avoid stop-and-go dynamics, by the mid-1960s an innovative solution was found: the passive crawling peg. Under this regime, Argentina, Brazil, Chile, and Colombia managed to relax the balance of payment constraint and experienced an acceleration of economic growth. The crawling peg had been proposed by academic economists as a solution to the problem faced by the Bretton Woods system given the different rates of (low) inflation experienced by developed countries during the mid-1960s. However, the IMF rejected the proposal, even when the system was on the edge of its collapse (Williamson 1981). In a more pragmatic fashion, the crawling peg was simultaneously invented and adopted in LA around the same period. The adoption of this regime was certainly not universal. Other countries, most notably Mexico, Peru and Venezuela, did not experience high levels of inflation, and maintained fixed regimes up to the 1970s or beyond.

It has been commonly indicated that Chile in 1965 was the first country to adopt a crawling peg. In fact, Argentina had implemented such a regime in early 1964 (García Vázquez 1994). The crawling peg was then adopted by Chile in April 1965, Colombia in early 1967, and Brazil in August 1968, reaching a respectable status among developing countries during and after the 1970s. In these four countries, economic authorities adjusted the NER periodically without predetermined rules. The frequency of adjustments varied from country to country. In the three years that the crawling peg lasted in Argentina, the NER was devalued on average once every other month. During the first years of its implementation in Colombia, on the other hand, authorities adjusted the NER almost every week. In Chile and Brazil, devaluations were essentially carried out on a monthly basis.

In all four countries, the purpose of implementing crawling pegs was to achieve RER stability and thus stimulate export growth and diversification. In Chile and especially Colombia, authorities believed that export dynamism required not only RER stability but also competitiveness; for that purpose they pursued rates of devaluation that tended

---

[4] Peru was the first LA country to sign an agreement with the IMF in 1954. Then Mexico, Chile, Paraguay, Nicaragua, Cuba, Bolivia, Colombia, Honduras, Nicaragua, El Salvador, Argentina, Brazil, and Haiti signed agreements with the IMF during the 1950s—some of them more than once.

to outpace past inflation rates. In the four countries, economic performance exhibited a significant improvement after the adoption of the crawling pegs. Between 1965 and 1970, Chile's economy grew at 4% per year and non-copper exports expanded substantially (Ffrench-Davis 1981; 2002). The exchange rate policy shifted to a fixed regime in 1970, when the government of Salvador Allende initiated its socialist attempt. During the first seven-year period since the implementation of the crawling peg focused on a competitive and stable RER (1967–74), Colombia experienced the period of highest economic growth in its post-World War II history: GDP grew at 6.6% annually and the value of non-traditional exports multiplied by a factor of seven (Urrutia 1981; Ocampo 1994). The implementation of the crawling peg in Brazil also coincided with the initiation of a period of high growth, popularly known as *o milagre econômico* (economic miracle). Between 1968 and 1973, the economy grew at an average rate of about 11% per year and exports more than tripled, stimulated by the expansion of non-traditional items (Bacha 1979). Argentina initiated a period of growth acceleration and export diversification with the implementation of the crawling peg. Although the regime was abandoned in mid-1967, the authorities managed to keep a stable and competitive real exchange rate (SCRER) in the subsequent period through a sharp devaluation in 1968 followed by a NER fixation. A second round of devaluations began in mid-1970, but in this case inflation accelerated and the RER gradually appreciated, prompting a massive balance of payments crisis in 1975. Overall, between 1964 and 1974, GDP grew at a yearly rate of 5%, non-traditional exports passed from representing less than 5% of total exports to about 25%, and the trade balance remained always positive (Gerchunoff and Llach 2003).

A negative aspect associated with these experiences was the behavior of inflation. In Argentina, the NER adjustments maintained RER stability during the three years that the crawling peg lasted, but they also contributed to high inflation, around 30% per year. In Colombia, the inflation rate gradually moved from figures around 5-10% before the implementation of the crawling peg to around 25% by the late 1970s. In Brazil the implementation of the crawling peg did not change inflationary dynamics substantially; the inflation rate remained around 20% and only accelerated after the first oil shock in 1973. Chile was the only case in which inflation was actually reduced. Although the path of NER depreciation tended to outpace past inflation, inflationary expectations did not accelerate. The inflation rate averaged 26% between 1965 and 1970, which—despite being still high—was significantly lower than the one prevailing when the crawling peg was implemented (about 50%).

8.2.2 The 1970s

Between the late 1960s and the early 1970s, LA countries began to face a significantly different international context: the gradual emergence of the second wave of financial globalization. Two key events in this process occurred during the first half of the 1970s. First, there was a shift in developed countries from fixed to floating exchange rates, which strongly stimulated the development of FX markets and their derivatives. Second, OPEC countries generated the first coordinated rise in the price of oil. The shock rapidly caused large current account imbalances in oil-importing countries, and at the same time supplied the incipient Eurodollar market with abundant liquidity. Beginning in that period, international capital flows have grown concurrently with a progressive deregulation of capital accounts and liberalization of domestic financial systems. Both trends shaped the second wave of financial globalization. LA was part of that process from its very beginning. Brazil started to tap the Eurodollar market in the late 1960s. Argentina, Chile, Mexico, Peru, Uruguay, and Venezuela jumped in as recipients of capital flows in different moments of the 1970s. Since then, the financial integration with global markets has become a very important factor in the performance of LA economies and their macroeconomic policies.

The new global scenario was one of high liquidity and high inflation. The international interest rate was low; in some periods the real interest rate was even negative. In this context, two polar cases of international financial integration and macroeconomic policy formulation can be identified in LA. This is revealed in the contrast between Brazil and the Southern Cone countries (Argentina, Chile, and Uruguay).

As mentioned above, Brazil had been growing at very high rates since 1968, with a level of inflation that was high according to current standards, but controlled according to the prevalent view at that time. The oil shock of 1973 generated a large trade deficit. In such a context, the Brazilian authorities decided to continue stimulating growth and take advantage of the international financial conditions to finance not only the increased value of imports but also an additional program of public and private investment, aimed at deepening the process of import substitution. The government was the main recipient and intermediary of the international credits, which were used for financing both public and private investment. There was no significant modification of the exchange rate regime—a passive crawling peg intended to preserve a SCRER—or the monetary policy that had been in practice since the late 1960s. Both the current account deficit and the foreign debt followed rising trends.

During the first half of the 1970s, Argentina, Chile, and Uruguay had suffered severe economic and political crises that resulted in persistently high inflation rates. The military coups that took power immediately afterwards tried to take advantage of the international financial conditions to induce radical changes in the economic structures and fight inflation at the same time. They liberalized the domestic financial systems, reduced taxes on trade, tackled with different intensity fiscal imbalances, and opened the capital account. In the second half of the 1970s, all three countries oriented their exchange rate policies towards stabilizing prices, adopting active crawling peg regimes. The so-called *tablitas* were schedules of pre-announced rates of devaluation, which were meant to function as nominal anchors for inflation. The theoretical support of these policies—the recently formulated monetary approach to the balance of payments—posited that the size of the current account deficit was irrelevant, since capital inflows would automatically and passively compensate for it. The only variable that needed to be controlled was the expansion of domestic credit by the central bank. If the source of money creation (i.e. fiscal deficits) was under control, the exchange rate policy could be oriented to an exclusive inflation target, disregarding its effects on the balance of payments and other aspects of economic performance. In all three cases, the private sector was the main recipient of external credits. The experiences led to substantial RER appreciation and a rapid increase in current account deficits and foreign debts. This macroeconomic configuration finally ended up in dramatic balance of payments and financial crises.[5]

Other countries also opened their capital accounts and borrowed from the international capital markets, but did not abandon their traditional pegged exchange rates regimes. This was, for instance, the case for Mexico. Due to an excessively expansive fiscal policy during the early 1970s, Mexico suffered a severe balance of payment crisis in 1976, forcing the authorities to devalue for the first time in more than 20 years. After a year of sequential adjustments, the NER was fixed again in early 1977. About that time, the discovery of voluminous oil reserves changed economic perspectives. The perception that the increase in oil prices represented a permanent change encouraged the government to initiate an ambitious industrialization program borrowing from the international capital markets. The economy expanded at rates of 8–9% between 1978 and 1981, inducing an acceleration of the inflation rate, which remained about 20% yearly. Given the fixed NER, the RER appreciated and current account deficit soared. The oil shock had a similar impact on Venezuela's economic performance. Public expenditure soared, the RER appreciated substantially, and foreign debt increased significantly.[6]

The next important change in the external context occurred in late 1979, when the Federal Reserve modified the orientation of monetary policy, thus, prompting a rise in international interest rates. To this event, a further increase in oil prices was added in 1979. These changes did not initially trigger drastic changes in the macroeconomic policies in the region. However, all the economies that had been involved in the process of financial globalization shared one important feature: they maintained large current account deficits and accumulated foreign debts. The persistent current account deficits and the accumulation of foreign debt thus left the economies vulnerable to changes in the external financial conditions.

8.2.3 The 1980s

The rise in international interest rates and the interruption in access to foreign finance in the early 1980s triggered massive balance of payments (and in some cases domestic financial) crises in almost all LA countries. The immediate reaction of national authorities to this new external scenario was to reorient macroeconomic policies to cope with

---

[5] For a detailed description of the stabilization program in Argentina see Frenkel (1983) and Fernandez (1985); for the Chilean case, see Ffrench-Davis (1983) and Corbo (1985); and for the Uruguayan case, see Hanson and de Melo (1985).

[6] For the Mexican case, see Moreno-Brid and Ros (2009); for the Venezuelan case, see Rodríguez (1985).

the effects of the debt crisis. All countries relied on significant devaluations, and oriented their monetary and fiscal policies towards the management of fiscal and external disequilibria and their repercussions. Colombia was an exception. Since it had had a more cautious approach to external borrowing during the booming period (i.e. it only contracted foreign debt during 1979–82 and in smaller doses), the change in the external financial conditions had not such a perverse impact on its economy. In fact, Colombia was the only major LA country that surfed the early 1980s with positive GDP growth rates.

Between 1982 and 1990, the interaction of LA countries with international financial markets was limited to a series of negotiations of the foreign debt inherited from the crisis. During this period, international credit was rationed and subject to negotiations with the creditor banks and the IMF. The countries had to make substantial payments to honor at least part of their external obligations. However, not all major countries in the region performed the same during the period. Two main elements help explain the differences in their performances: first, the gap between the external financial needs and financial support provided by the international financial institutions; second, the inflationary processes that followed the devaluations of the early 1980s. Both factors were substantially more favorable for Chile and Colombia compared to Argentina, Brazil, and Mexico.

The external finance needs were relatively manageable in Colombia. Chile, on the contrary, was the country with the highest debt/GDP ratio in the region, and its needs for external credit were bulky. However, it managed to receive the largest proportion of the disposable resources for the region from the international institutions and also to engineer a favorable debt restructuring. On the other hand, in both Chile and Colombia the inflation rate —although accelerated after the crises—never surpassed 35% a year. For these reasons, both countries managed to balanced their external accounts and avoid sharp devaluations after the first round of external adjustment. In the context of a manageable inflation rate, both countries used exchange rate regimes oriented towards preserving a stable RER. Colombia continued with the passive crawling peg regime that had been launched in the late 1960s, and sustained a modest economic performance. Chile put into practice an innovative crawling bands regime in 1984, targeting a SCRER aimed at generating a significant trade surplus to compensate for the lack of external finance. Given that the initial fluctuation bands were too small, the system initially resembled a standard passive crawling peg. Later, in the second half of the 1980s, the fluctuation bands were gradually increased and then substantially sharpened in the early 1990s. The implementation of crawling bands targeting a SCRER coincides with the beginning of the period of the highest and most sustained growth in Chile's history.

The size of the external gap and the acceleration of inflation following the crises intensely affected the economic performance of Argentina, Brazil, and Mexico. For these countries, the 1980s were a lost decade. In Mexico the inflation rate passed from being around 30% annually to above 100% after the crisis. Between 1984 and 1986 it oscillated around annual figures of 60–70%, and then accelerated again in late 1986, reaching rates above three digits up until mid-1988, when a successful stabilization program managed to bring down inflation. In Argentina and Brazil, inflation rates never fell below three digits, except immediately after launching the heterodox stabilization plans in the mid-1980s, when inflation rates transitorily descended to two-digit figures. None of these three countries managed to close the external financial gap and reach a lasting restructuring agreement with their creditors. In order to induce external adjustments, they continually relied on sharp devaluations.

By the mid-1980s, the inflationary process tended to accelerate in both Argentina and Brazil. In order to stop these developments, Argentina in 1985 and Brazil in 1986 launched the so-called heterodox stabilization programs. These were shock-therapy plans in which the fixation of the NER was used as the main nominal anchor. One special characteristic of these programs was that the authorities substantially devalued the domestic currencies before the fixation. The Southern Cone programs have demonstrated that stabilization plans are typically followed by real appreciation due to inertial inflation after the fixation. The ex-ante devaluation was meant to compensate for such an expected appreciation, but also because the authorities wanted to reach an ex-post competitive RER. Given the lack of foreign credit, external balance could only be achieved by substantial trade surpluses, for which a competitive RER would be crucial. The initial conditions of the programs also required external and fiscal equilibria compatible with the fixed exchange rate. To that end, agreement with the external creditors and the international financial institutions aiming to soften the credit constraint was also essential. The heterodox component of the plans was the use of incomes polices (price and wage controls) to coordinate the dynamics of the labor and goods markets with the fixed exchange rate, and to stop the widespread use of indexation mechanisms. Another innovative element of these programs was the monetary reforms that included the introduction of new currencies (the Austral in Argentina and the Cruzado in Brazil). The plans were initially successful both in reducing inflation significantly and in fostering economic recovery. However, the difficulties involved in preserving the external and fiscal balance led to new devaluations and fiscal adjustments that resulted in recessions and the acceleration of inflation.[7]

After reaching an inflation rate of 165% in 1987, Mexico launched a stabilization program in 1988, which shared some similarities with those previously implemented in Argentina and Brazil. The *Pacto de Solidaridad Económica* (Economic Solidary Pact) was a plan that combined fiscal adjustment, fixation of the NER, and incomes policies. The program was successful in bringing inflation down. One year later, it was reformulated. The exchange rate regime was replaced by a crawling peg following a small rate of devaluation. In November 1991, the crawling peg was substituted with a band within which the NER was allowed to fluctuate. The ceiling of the band was increased by small daily adjustments, while the floor remained constant. Since the stabilization program was launched, the RER tended to appreciate and the economy started to register increas-

---

[7] Analyses of the Argentine Austral Plan can be found in Frenkel (1987) and Heymann (1987), and of the Brazilian Cruzado Plan in Bacha (1987).

ing current account deficits. But, contrary to the experience of Argentina and Brazil with the heterodox plans, Mexico was not forced to give up the exchange rate regime and devalue its currency to achieve external balance. The change in international financial conditions during the late 1980s helped the country maintain the macroeconomic policies. The highly liquid environment, low international interest rates, and especially the restructuring of its external debt in 1989 under the Brady Plan made Mexico a very attractive destination for international investors. Thus, Mexico began the 1990s with a macroeconomic configuration characterized by an (asymmetric) crawling band within which the NER remained virtually fixed, rapid liberalization of trade and finance, RER appreciation, and both increasing current account deficits and increasing capital inflows. This configuration persisted until 1994, when foreign investors' fear concerning the sustainability of the (virtually) fixed exchange rate triggered a reversal of capital flows and a balance of payments crisis (Dornbusch and Werner 1994).

8.2.4 The 1990s

The change in the international financial conditions beginning around 1989 represented another turning point. As in the second half of the 1970s, this new period was also characterized by high liquidity and low interest rates in international financial markets. In such a context, in 1989 the US government launched the Brady Plan, which aimed to help highly indebted countries relieve their debt burden with international banks. The increased deregulation of domestic financial systems in developed economies also contributed to this process by widening the group of institutions demanding assets from these new emerging market countries. Overall, these changes in the international context "pushed" capital from developed countries into the developing world (Calvo, Leiderman, and Reinhart 1993). For LA countries, this new international context meant the end of the external credit rationing they had faced during the 1980s. Capital inflows to the region peaked in 1993, fell in 1995 as a consequence of the Mexican crisis, and grew again until the eruption of the Asian and Russian crises in 1997–8.

Once again, national macroeconomic policies adapted to the new international context according to the previous evolution of the economies and national policy agendas. Two polar strategies can also be identified for this period. Argentina, Brazil, and Mexico, which had unsuccessfully fought high inflation and remained stagnant during the 1980s, welcomed the novel international financial context because it made viable to carry exchange rate-based stabilization programs without facing the external credit constraint that prevailed in the previous decade.

As mentioned above, Mexico launched the *Pacto de Solidaridad Económica* based on an almost fixed exchange rate. Argentina did so even more aggressively, launching the so-called "convertibility" regime in early 1991, which was characterized by the fixation of the domestic currency against the US dollar (AR$/$1) and the establishment of a currency board system by law. The convertibility was implemented concurrently with liberalizing measures including an almost complete liberalization of trade flows and full deregulation of the capital account. There was also an impressive process of privatization. The stabilization program also involved price negotiations between the government and several productive sectors, aimed at reinforcing the effect of the exchange rate peg as a nominal anchor on inflation. The program was very successful at curbing high inflation. However, as occurred in Mexico, stabilization came together with RER appreciation, large current account deficits, and growing external debt.

Brazil had received significant capital inflows during the early 1990s, but at that time the authorities found them problematic as they hindered the conduction of monetary and the exchange rate policies based on a passive crawling peg regime. The new international context became functional to macroeconomic policy only in 1994, when the Real Plan was launched. The stabilization program was implemented in three steps. First, a comprehensive adjustment of fiscal accounts was implemented. The second stage included a monetary reform, in which a new unit of account (the Unit of Real Value, URV) pegged to the US dollar was introduced. The goal of this second stage was to facilitate the gradual re-denomination of existing contracts—with overlapping indexing mechanisms—in the new URV. Since the value of the URV was fixed in terms of US dollars, the conversion of the contractual system into UVR helped eradicate indexation mechanisms from the economy.[8] Finally, in July 1994, once the process of re-denomination of the contractual system into the new unit of account was concluded, the central bank started to issue the URV, which, renamed Real, began to operate as the new currency. Under the new exchange rate regime, the monetary authority was committed to selling FX reserves once the price of the Real reached US$1, but was not obliged to intervene when it was below that parity. As in the cases of Mexico and Argentina, the purpose of this virtually fixed regime was to provide an anchor for inflation. The effects of the Real Plan on the RER, the external accounts and debt accumulation were similar to those observed in Mexico and Argentina, and the process finally led to an exchange rate crisis in early 1999 (Bacha 2003).

The other polar strategy during the 1990s was that followed by Chile and Colombia. They also adapted their macroeconomic policies to the new international financial conditions, but trying to maintain a cautious orientation regarding capital inflows and their effects on the real economy. Given that inflation was not as severe a problem as in Argentina, Brazil, and Mexico, these countries oriented their macroeconomic policy so as to preserve a SCRER (especially Chile), while providing at the same time enough monetary autonomy to achieve a gradual deceleration in the inflation rate. To that end, macroeconomic policy was configured around two key elements. First, a crawling band regime, which was meant to maintain a SCRER in the medium run while generating NER volatility in the short run. Second, since the degree of NER volatility was not enough to guarantee monetary policy autonomy, both countries also adopted regulations on the capital account. This gave monetary policy enough room to target a gradual decrease in inflation rates. Thus, without using the NER as a nominal anchor, both Chile

---

[8] The intellectual roots of the monetary reform are due to a paper by Arida and Lara-Resende (1985), popularized by Dornbusch (1985) as the "Larida proposal."

and Colombia achieved a gradual deceleration of inflation during the first half of the 1990s and maintained relatively high rates of economic growth. The experience of Chile with the crawling bands targeting a SCRER was especially successful. Between 1984 to 1997, Chile experienced the most successful period in its modern economic history: GDP and exports grew at about 7% per year, unemployment fell from 20% to 6%, and poverty from 50% to 22%.[9]

Peru represents a singular and interesting case in this narrative. During the 1980s, the country had followed a similar path to those of Argentina, Brazil, and Mexico, including the implementation and failure of a heterodox stabilization program and the acceleration of inflation, which ended in a hyperinflationary episode in 1989–90. Thus, Peru also began the decade with high inflation and a stagnant economy. However, as occurred in Chile and Colombia, the macroeconomic policy followed during the early 1990s managed to reduce inflation significantly without fixing the NER. In 1990, the central bank of Peru stopped targeting the NER and adopted a system of monetary targets and managed floating. The restrictive monetary policy between 1990 and 1992 led to a substantial RER overvaluation, which helped decelerate the inflation rate. For almost a decade the central bank maintained this policy mix, relying on interventions in the FX market as the main mechanism to control the quantity of money and manage the NER. The strategy was successful in reducing inflation without generating recessionary trends. Between 1994 and 2002, the economy expanded at about 4% annually and the inflation rate fell from about 40% to less than 3% (Dancourt 1999).

The rise of international interest rates in early 1994 was an important factor causing the Mexican currency crisis. Speculation against the peso during that year finally forced the authorities to let it float in December 1994. The economy contracted by 6.2% in 1995 and many domestic banks went bankrupt (Ros 2001). The "tequila effect" spread to Argentina, which also suffered a sudden stop of capital inflows. Granted a voluminous financial assistance package led by the IMF, the Argentine authorities managed to preserve the convertibility regime in 1995. That did not prevent, however, the recessive impact of capital outflows on the activity level (–2.8%) or the severe financial crisis that led many domestic banks to bankruptcy.

The Asian and Russian crises in 1997–8 affected Brazil, whose external account was showing signs of vulnerability. In 1998, the current account deficit had reached 4.5% of GDP and the RER a level 30% lower than the average of the 1980s. In January 1999, after several months of resisting persistent speculation against its FX reserves, the Brazilian central bank decided to let the Real float. The financial contagion of the Asian and Russian crises and the currency crisis in Brazil triggered a prolonged depression in Argentina beginning in the second half of 1998 and ending in a financial and external crisis in 2001–2. The consequent economic collapse resulted in a 21% contraction in GDP with respect to the peak of mid-1998 and up to a 21.5% rise in the

---

[9] For Chile's experience with the crawling bands, see Vergara (1994), Williamson (1996), Zahler (1998), and Ffrench-Davis (2002). The Colombian experience with the crawling-bands-cum-capital-controls is analyzed in Williamson (1996), Villar and Rincón (2000), and Ocampo and Tovar (2003).

unemployment rate, leaving half the population below the poverty line. The government also declared a massive default on its external debt (Damil, Frenkel, and Rapetti 2010).

Chile, Colombia, and Peru did not suffer external crises during the 1990s. Certainly, the RER in both Chile and Colombia followed appreciating trends between the mid-1990s and the unfolding of the Asian and Russian crises in 1997–8. These trends were in fact facilitated by the monetary authorities of these countries, who decided to drive the bands downwards in the mid-1990s. The fact that the Mexican crisis had not significantly affected capital inflows to these economies, combined with a widespread belief during that time that capital flows to emerging markets were a permanent (and stable) phenomenon, strengthened monetary authorities' conviction that RER appreciations were required. Their resulting appreciation was, however, moderate and short-lived compared to those in Argentina, Brazil, and Mexico. This difference helps to explain their relatively more robust external conditions and their greater degrees of freedom to control the exchange rate when the crises hit their economies. Nonetheless, the Asian and Russian crises had a negative impact on Chile, Colombia, and Peru. The greater flexibility of the exchange rate regimes in Colombia and Peru did not prevent the negative effects of NER depreciation and capital outflows on their financial systems, and both Colombia and Peru suffered financial crises in 1999.

8.2.5 The 2000s

The Mexican crisis of 1994, but more markedly the Asian and Russian crises of 1997–8, induced important changes in the views of policy makers and economists concerning the choice of exchange rate regimes in developing countries. A number of authors began to argue that in a world of high capital mobility, intermediate regimes were highly prone to currency crises. A notion gradually started to emerge suggesting that developing countries should have either a pure floating exchange rate or a hard peg regime—such as a currency board or full official dollarization (Fischer 2001). The prevalent opinion actually favored pure floating regimes as a better institutional setting to deal with the admitted volatility of capital flows. However, since Argentina's convertibility—and other hard pegs in a few small countries like Hong Kong—had survived these crises, the prevalent view reserved a status for hard pegs as a corner solution for a few special cases.

Most LA countries opted for "pure" floating and inflation targeting (FIT) for their exchange rate and monetary regimes.[10] After the crisis, Mexico let the peso float while using a monetary policy of monetary aggregates to control inflation. In 1999 the country

---

[10] The movement toward greater exchange rate flexibility during the 2000s was not unanimous. Ecuador and El Salvador followed the opposite direction and adopted the US dollar as main currency in January 2000 and January 2001, respectively. For analyses of these dollarization experiences, see Beckerman and Solimano (2002) and Quispe-Agnoli and Whisler (2006). Panama is, of course, the earliest country adopting dollarization in LA (Goldfajn and Olivares 2001).

switched to an inflation targeting regime, with a monetary instrument to determine the interest rate that later evolved into the formal utilization of an overnight interest rate. Also in 1999, Brazil, Colombia, and Chile joined the club of LA FIT countries. Brazil did so after its currency crisis at the beginning of that year. Both Chile and Colombia had already been utilizing annual targets of inflation since 1990 and 1991 respectively. Although they were not labeled as inflation targeters at that time, these countries can be considered pioneers in the implementation of such a regime in the region. Peru had been using managed floating jointly with a monetary regime based on quantitative monetary targets since the early 1990s. In 2002 the central bank formally adopted a "pure" floating and an inflation targeting regime. Initially, the authorities kept monetary aggregates as main policy instrument, but in 2003 they switched to overnight interest rate, coupled with sterilized interventions.

Despite their public statements about their exchange rate regime choice, none of the LA FIT countries has let its currency float the way assumed under a conventional FIT arrangement (Chang 2008). Central banks in LA FIT countries have not had a passive role in the determination of the NER. Evidence shows that central banks in these countries have set their reference interest rate in reaction to NER movements. A priori, this is not inconsistent with a pure FIT regime. Given that the NER is an important transmission mechanism for monetary policy and that its level and changes have important effects on inflation and aggregate demand, FIT central banks can use the interest rate to influence inflation through its effects on the NER (Mishkin and Schmidt-Hebbel 2002). However, the behavior of the central banks in LA FIT countries has gone beyond influencing the NER via interest movements. Intervention in the FX market has been very common, and therefore their exchange rate regimes are better classified as managed floating.

Between the late 1990s and the early 2000s, intervention in the FX market appeared to be motivated by the attempt to avoid substantial NER depreciations. Some analysts have interpreted their behavior as a case of "fear of floating." According to Calvo and Reinhart (2002), there are two main reasons why countries may fear to float. First, nominal depreciations are likely to accelerate inflation. In this regard, FX interventions appear to be a policy instrument that complements overnight interest rates in curbing inflation. For instance, De Gregorio, Tokman, and Valdés (2005) explain that the Central Bank of Chile decided to intervene in the FX market to contain the depreciation pressures during 2001 and 2002 generated by the 9/11 attack, the convertibility collapse in Argentina, and turbulence in Brazil due to the presidential elections. According to the authors, the authorities believed that in these episodes the NER overreacted and that a monetary tightening would have unnecessarily deepened the cycle. Chang (2008) cites memorandums from the central bank of Brazil invoking similar arguments for their FX interventions during the turmoil before the presidential elections in 2002. Second, sudden upward movements in the NER can have undesired balance sheet effects in dollarized economies. With this motivation, interventions are meant to target financial stability as a policy objective in its own right. Peru, the country with the most dollarized financial system among the LA floaters, is probably the best example of this case.[11] As some analysts have observed, given the high degree of financial dollarization, the Peruvian version of the FIT policy has had an explicit focus on ameliorating NER fluctuations that can affect the normal behavior of the financial system (Dancourt 2009). Moreover, the central bank has purposely accumulated FX reserves so that it can serve as lender of last resort in dollars in case of a bank run (Armas and Grippa 2006).

Between 2004 and 2008, international financial markets increased their appetite for risk leading to an unprecedented surge in capital flows to developing countries. The policy reaction in many of these countries was to actively intervene in the FX market; but contrary to what is expected under the fear of floating hypothesis, central banks purchased FX instead of selling. Two main explanations have been offered for this behavior. One suggests that countries accumulate reserves to reduce NER volatility and to prevent large swings of the NER due to international capital volatility (Aizenman and Lee 2007). The other indicates that it is the consequence of a development strategy based on an exchange rate policy aimed at preserving a SCRER (Dooley, Garber, and Folkerts-Landau 2007). This latter strategy has sometimes been labeled as neo-mercantilism; although we prefer to call it neo-developmentalist.

During this period, central banks in LA FIT countries accumulated a substantial volume of FX reserves. The process of reserve accumulation, however, was not homogeneous across countries. Between 2004 and 2008, Brazil quadrupled its stock of FX reserves, Peru more than tripled it and Colombia doubled it. Mexico, although increasing the stock of FX reserves during this period (+50%), had a less systematic strategy. The Central Bank of Chile had a more passive role in the FX market: it only began to accumulate reserves persistently in mid-2007, increasing its stock of foreign exchange reserves by 50% between that period and Lehman Brothers' collapse. However, the accumulation of FX by the fiscal stabilization funds during the copper price boom since 2004 helped substantially to avoid a massive appreciation without requiring the intervention of the central bank. Many analysts interpret this recent trend as an effort to prevent excessive appreciations of the RER.[12] It is important to notice, however, that the latter does not mean that these countries followed a SCRER or neo-developmentalist strategy: preventing excessive RER appreciations markedly differs from pursuing a SCRER. In our view, recent trends of exchange rate policies in LA FIT countries are better interpreted as an example of precautionary motive, rather than as the result of pursuing a SCRER or neo-developmentalist strategy.[13]

Several reasons make it inappropriate to include the LA FIT countries within the neo-developmentalist group. First, as documented by Chang (2008), all central banks from

---

[11] In December 1999, 82% of credit in Peru's financial system was denominated in dollars. Since then there has been an explicit policy to de-dollarize the economy. By December 2008, the level fell to 52%. Other dollarized countries, like Argentina, Bolivia, and Uruguay, have also taken explicit measures to reduce financial dollarization in their economies during the 2000s.

[12] See Chang (2008) for the cases of Brazil, Colombia, and Peru, Agosin (2009) for Chile, and Dancourt (2009) for Peru.

[13] See Frenkel and Rapetti (2010) for an elaboration of this point.

Table 8.1 RER volatility

	Coefficient of variation	Variation (%) against Argentina (2003–8)	Variation (%) against Chile (1985–95)
Argentina (2003–8)	0.068	–	–
Chile (1985–95)	0.079	–	–
Brazil (2000–8)	0.244	259	209
Chile (2000–8)	0.130	91	65
Colombia (2000–8)	0.153	125	94
Mexico (2000–8)	0.050	−26	−37
Peru (2003–8)	0.066	−3	−16

these countries have made explicit statements that they do not pursue exchange rate targets. They claim that, under their regimes, exchange rates are determined by fundamentals and interventions are only meant to avoid excessive deviations from fundamental levels. Certainly, claims may contradict actual actions. However, they seem to be backed by the actual behavior of their RERs. In none of these countries does the behavior of the RER resemble that observed in other countries where authorities explicitly asserted that they were following SCRER strategies, as in Chile with the crawling bands (1985–95), or Argentina with the managed floating after the convertibility crisis (2003–8), which is commented on below.

First, the RERs in the FIT countries have tended to be substantially more volatile. Table 8.1 reports the coefficient of variation of the RER as an indicator of volatility.[14] With the exception of Mexico and Peru, the RER has been substantially more volatile in the FIT countries than in the experiences with SCRER (Argentina 2003–8 and Chile 1985–95). The RER has been particularly volatile under the Brazilian FIT. It is also interesting to notice that the switch from the crawling bands to the FIT has resulted in more volatility in the RER of Chile.

Mexico and Peru preserved stable RER, but at substantially appreciated levels. Mexico followed a persistent real appreciation trend from late 1996, which ended in early 2002 with a RER even more appreciated (about 8% lower) than the year before the tequila crisis (1994). Between early 2002 and the fall of Lehman Brothers in September 2008, the RER remained slightly more depreciated than during the pre-tequila crisis, but more appreciated than the 1980–2001 average. In Peru, the RER was kept relatively competitive during 2002–7 compared to the average prevailing during the 1990s. However, it remained substantially appreciated if comparison is made with the average during the 1980s.

---

[14] The reported RER are the bilateral RER against the US, deflated by CPI indexes. The periods utilized for each experience exclude the year in which each regime was implemented.

In the other LA FIT countries, significant appreciation trends were also observed. When the inflation targets were threatened, central banks did not hesitate to induce NER appreciation to meet them. This was clearly observed in the wake of rising inflation fuelled by the surge in food and energy prices beginning in 2004. All central banks raised interest rates and allowed the NER to appreciate with the aim of limiting the pass-through from imported inflation. In Brazil, the RER depreciated between its currency crisis in early 1999 and late 2002 due to a succession of adverse shocks. Beginning in late 2002, the RER followed a systematic appreciation trend, which has been substantially exacerbated since 2004. This trend lasted until Lehman Brothers' bankruptcy. At that moment, the RER had reached a minimum about 8% lower than the pre-1999 crisis and about 30% lower than the 1980–2008 average. The trajectory of the RER in Colombia was similar to that in Brazil. After a period of sustained depreciation resulting from similar adverse shocks, the RER followed a persistent appreciation trend. By mid-2008, its level reached the lowest level in 24 years, 27% lower than the 1980–2008 average. The post-2002 appreciation in Chile was softer, although it also accelerated since 2004. By mid-2008 the RER reached a level about 18% lower than the average of the 1980–2008 period.

Several authors have emphasized the greater volatility and the appreciation bias that have characterized the behavior of the RER in the LA FIT countries. Galindo and Ros (2008) show that the FIT arrangement in Mexico has had an appreciation bias. Using VAR econometrics, they find that this has resulted from an asymmetric monetary policy, which has been tightened when the NER depreciates, but not loosened when it appreciates. Barbosa-Filho (2008) claims that the Brazilian central bank has also followed an asymmetric monetary policy, which has been responsible for the RER appreciation. He observes that, between 2000 and 2006, inflation targets were met only in the years in which the RER experienced substantial appreciation. Agosin (2009) estimates a Markov-switching model for the behavior of the RER in Chile. He finds that the shift from the crawling bands to the FIT arrangement coincides with a regime switch in the model. Similar to the evidence in Table 8.1, Agosin finds that the volatility of the RER corresponding to the first regime (crawling bands) is substantially lower to the one in the second regime (FIT).

In its search for greater flexibility, Argentina followed a somewhat different path than that of the FIT countries. After the 2001–2 crisis the authorities tried to recreate a macroeconomic regime similar to that in Chile during the crawling bands period. However, instead of adopting such a regime, the central bank followed a pragmatic managed floating arrangement, which implicitly aimed to combine a certain degree of short-run NER volatility with the preservation of a SCRER in the medium run. The exchange rate policy has also had an explicit goal of FX reserve accumulation meant to protect against volatility in international financial flows. The SCRER combined with fiscal surplus (to which the public debt restructuring in 2005 contributed substantially) provided the economy a sound macroeconomic configuration. It was the first time in its modern history that Argentina maintained external and fiscal surpluses for such a long period (2002–8), while growing at a 8.5% average annual rate. The favorable external conditions—especially the high international prices of the agricultural commodities that the country exports—were important, but explained only part of the economic performance. It was the expansion of the whole tradable sector (exportable and import substitutive activities) that pulled the economy up and put it on a rapid growth path. Analysts tend to agree that the dynamic behavior of output, employment, and investment has been associated with the positive effects of the SCRER on tradable activities and its multiplier effects on the rest of the economy.

Rapid growth was interrupted in the second quarter of 2008, before the US financial crisis spread to the rest of the world, due to a series of political conflicts. By that time, the official strategy had shown signs of exhaustion. The RER had started to appreciate significantly due to the acceleration of inflation that began to be noticeable by 2006, due to both domestic and international factors (rising commodity prices in the latter case). As in Chile in the second half of the 1980s, the initial phase of rapid growth (from mid-2002 to mid-2004) occurred in a context of highly under-utilized capacity and high unemployment and underemployment in the labor market. As the economy recuperated, aggregate investment increased but rising employment contributed to the rise of nominal wages. One element that also contributed to the acceleration of the inflation rate was the lack of coordination in macroeconomic policy. Monetary and exchange rate policies focused on preserving a SCRER—which was intended to put the economy on a high growth path—but the government could not develop any additional instrument to manage aggregate demand. Contrarily to the Chilean case, the low interest rate policy and the pro-cyclical fiscal policy operated as additional expansionary impulses to an already fast-growing aggregate demand. The acceleration of inflation was thus a self-aborting result of Argentine SCRER strategy (Frenkel and Rapetti 2008; Damill and Frenkel 2009).

8.3 AN ANALYTICAL INTERPRETATION

Probably the most important conclusion that can be drawn from our historical analysis is that the *level* of the RER has had a significant influence in the macroeconomic performance of LA countries. In particular, the experiences reviewed suggest that an excessively appreciated RER can lead to negative outcomes affecting short- and medium-term growth. The experience in the region corroborates the consolidated view that overvalued RER have detrimental effects on economic growth (Easterly 2005). The exchange rate regime choice may not be neutral in that regard. Our historical narrative illustrates how fixed and semi-fixed exchange rate regimes focused on price stabilization can lead to excessive RER appreciation, current account deficits, and balance of payment and financial crises. The experiences with the *tablitas* in the late 1970s and that of Argentina during the 1990s attest that crises can reach the dimension of great depressions.

Certainly, pegs have been shown to be essential in providing a nominal anchor in contexts of high inflation or hyperinflation. As our narrative shows, a stylized fact of exchange-rate-based stabilization programs in the region is that they have been typically followed by RER appreciations and current account deficits. Given that under these regimes a NER correction is not an option, all the burden tends to rely on labor productivity gains and other non-price supply-side improvements. These typically take time, and might not be enough to correct excessive RER misalignments. In that case, a significant deflation of domestic non-tradable goods prices is required to correct the lack of competitiveness in the tradable sector. If prices are downward inflexible, it may also impinge a painful contraction and high unemployment. Even if this adjustment mechanism is feasible, the well known debt deflation effect tends to undermine it.

These complications make clear a trade-off that policymakers face when implementing exchange rate-based stabilization programs. Given that the RER will appreciate after its implementation, they would like to depreciate the NER before fixing it, as attempted in the heterodox programs in Argentina and Brazil in the mid-1980s. However, given that the pass-through of NER movements to domestic prices is high in high-inflation environments, a substantial depreciation of the NER before fixing may fail to stabilize prices and might even accelerate inflation. This trade-off suggests that policymakers should carefully consider not only how to implement an exchange rate-based stabilization program but also what potential exit options they have in case a correction of a RER misalignment is needed.

In more general terms, LA experience with exchange rate-based stabilization programs highlights the important role that exchange rate regimes have in keeping track of the behavior of the RER and avoiding RER misalignments. In conditions of moderately high inflation (say 30% per year), LA experience has shown that it is possible to reduce inflation gradually without using the exchange rate as an anchor. Chile beginning in the mid-1980s and Colombia and Peru in the early 1990s are clear examples of this.

These experiences have led LA countries to gradually converge—through different national paths—towards the adoption of more flexible exchange rate regimes. Under conditions of low inflation, as has been the case for all major economies since the late 1990s, flexibility has shown to be highly valuable. The lack of commitment to the level of the NER provides the economy flexibility to adjust to external shocks without resulting in reputational costs for the monetary authorities. The lack of commitment also eliminates the incentives of one-way bets in the FX market by speculators. In their portfolio choices between domestic and foreign assets (and liabilities), private agents have to assume the exchange rate risk. Therefore, a lower exposure to NER variations and lower financial fragility to external shocks is likely to be observed.

But this transition has not lead to pure floating. In both pure and managed floating, the monetary authority has no commitment regarding the level of the NER. However, in the former the central bank commits itself not to intervene in the FX market. A managed floating regime is more flexible because it allows the monetary authority to intervene whenever it considers necessary. The degree of discretion is highest. This regime provides the same flexibility to absorb unexpected shocks as a pure floating, while also entitling the monetary authority to influence the NER with FX interventions. This extra degree of freedom has been highly valued among LA central banks, since in their search for greater flexibility none of them adopted a pure floating regime. By the early 2000s, all central banks of the major countries in the region had switched to managed floating regimes. These include not only the self-declared Argentinean managed floating but also those of the FIT countries.

Another important lesson that emerges from our analyses is that managed floating in a context of high integration to international financial markets requires a significant degree of intervention in the FX market. By its own definition, managed floating is a regime in which the monetary authority "guides" the behavior of the NER without committing to any specific value. The motivation behind that guidance varies: it could be intended to preserve the RER within certain more or less specific range as in the SCRER strategy, or simply within a wider range avoiding excessive appreciation or undervaluation. Given the relative small size of domestic FX markets in LA, capital flows have a substantial impact on the exchange rate. To minimize such an impact, central banks intervene in the FX markets. To avoid undesired depreciation trends they need to dispose a sizeable stock of FX reserves to persuade the public they can satisfy the private demand for FX at the current NER. On the other hand, to avoid undesired appreciation trends, central banks need to intervene in the market, buying the excess supply of FX. As a result of both buying interventions and the need of a sizeable stock for the selling interventions, central banks in developing countries highly exposed to international capital flows need to accumulate FX reserves.

As described in our narrative, managed floating regimes in LA have been accompanied by a systematic and massive accumulation of FX reserves. This strategy has proven to be useful. There is little doubt that the large stocks of FX reserves—together with the greater NER flexibility—were essential to help central banks handle the financial impact of the international financial crisis of 2007–8 (Ocampo 2009). Despite the skeptical assessment by many analysts, it would be a hard task to persuade central banks in LA of the inefficiencies of accumulating FX reserves after this experience.

Recent managed floating in LA has been used either to avoid excessive appreciating or depreciating long swings in the RER, as occurred with the FIT countries or to preserve a SCRER, as happened in Argentina. Conventional wisdom seems to favor the choice of a FIT strategy for central banks in developing countries. International financial institutions and academic centers tend to support this view. On the other hand, the poor macroeconomic management in Argentina since 2007 has not contributed either to the marketing of the SCRER policy. Nevertheless, the analysis in this chapter suggests that the rejection of the SCRER policy should not be so straightforward. Our historical narrative has presented evidence suggesting that LA economies have tended to perform better when the exchange rate policy managed to preserve a SCRER.

Some successful experiences of growth acceleration in the region have coincided with periods in which the exchange rate policy was purposely oriented towards that goal. For instance, the arguably two most successful growth experiences in LA during the post-World War II period have occurred in parallel with the implementation of exchange rate regimes targeting a SCRER. These experiences are the "Brazilian miracle" starting in the late 1960s simultaneous with the implementation of the crawling peg, and Chile's experience with the crawling bands between the mid-1980s and mid-1990s.

There are also other important cases in which this correlation between the exchange rate policy and economic performance has been observed: the crawling pegs in Argentina and Colombia between the mid-1960s and mid-1970s and the managed floating in Argentina since 2002.[15] Certainly, this observation should not be interpreted as indicating that exchange rate regimes targeting a SCRER are *the* explanation behind the success of these experiences. Economic growth and development are complex processes that involve the combination of many social, political, and economic factors. In any case, our historical narrative supports the conclusion reached by a recent body of empirical studies indicating that undervalued RER tend to foster economic growth in developing countries.[16] The analysis here thus suggests that the exchange rate policy can make an important contribution to economic development by preserving a SCRER.

Certainly, policies oriented towards preserving a SCRER are not free from risks. Experience has shown that it is not unusual to find cases of policies that, while trying to preserve a SCRER, end up accelerating inflation. For instance, during the years that the crawling peg was introduced in Colombia (1967–74), the inflation rate experienced an upward trend, followed by persistent inflation for two additional decades. Argentina's recent performance with the managed floating regime is another eloquent example.

It would be wrong, however, to conclude that this is an unavoidable result of any exchange rate policy focused on a SCRER. Inflation in Chile under the crawling bands regime decreased substantially. The experience of Chile between the mid-1980s and mid-1990s is an example of the macroeconomic coordination required to manage a SCRER policy. It combined a relatively flexible exchange regime (i.e. crawling bands), capital controls, countercyclical fiscal policy, and an autonomous monetary policy with a reference interest rate as a policy tool. The combination of crawling bands, sterilized interventions, and capital controls allowed the central bank to avoid the policy "trilemma" and simultaneously set the interest rate and the NER. Fiscal policy was used (although not always) to moderate aggregate demand pressures. With these policies— coupled with others focused on microeconomic aspects—the authorities managed to preserve a SCRER, reduce inflation, promote rapid growth of both exports and GDP, and avoid external and financial crises during turbulent periods. This successful trajectory lasted more than a decade.

The strategy was abandoned because the authorities understood that the policy simultaneously targeting the NER and setting the interest rate was incompatible with financial integration. They interpreted that the quasi-fiscal cost due to sterilized interventions

---

[15] It is interesting to note that the first four of these cases are among the few experiences of growth accelerations identified by Haussmann et al. (2005) in the LA region. The case of Argentina in the post-convertibility period is not included in the authors' sample, but still meets their criteria to be labeled as an episode of growth acceleration.

[16] See e.g. Razin and Collins (1999), Hausmann et al. (2005), Aguirre and Calderon (2005), Gala (2008), Rodrik (2008), and Razmi, Rapetti, and Scott (2009).

of about 0.5% of GDP was an indication that the policy would not be sustainable over time.[17] The shift to a FIT regime was a voluntary decision to provide macroeconomic policy flexibility to deal with international capital movements. With this new orientation, the preservation of the SCRER and capital controls were sacrificed. Another option would have been to shift to a managed floating regime and preserve the focus on the SCRER.

APPENDIX

REAL EXCHANGE RATES OF SELECTED LATIN AMERICAN COUNTRIES

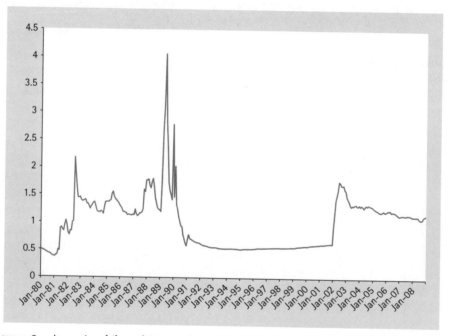

FIGURE 8.1 Argentina: bilateral RER with the US, deflated by CPI indexes (Index 1 = average 1980–2008)

Source: International Financial Statistics, IMF.

[17] A common view among economists is that sterilized interventions can only be used in the short-run and are unsustainable for longer periods. Frenkel (2007) analyzes the conditions under which they are sustainable in the long run. A pragmatic view is offered by John Williamson (1996: 30) who assessing the cost of sterilization in Chile in the mid-1990s pointed out that: "[if paying 1%–1.5% of GDP] is the price of preserving a model that works, it would be cheap." For recent optimistic view of the role of sterilized interventions in macroeconomic policy in developing countries, see Blanchard, Dell'Ariccia, and Mauro (2010).

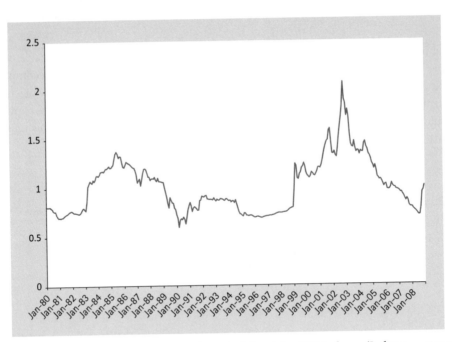

FIGURE 8.2 Brazil: Bilateral RER with the US, deflated by CPI indexes (Index 1 = average 1980–2008)

Source: International Financial Statistics, IMF.

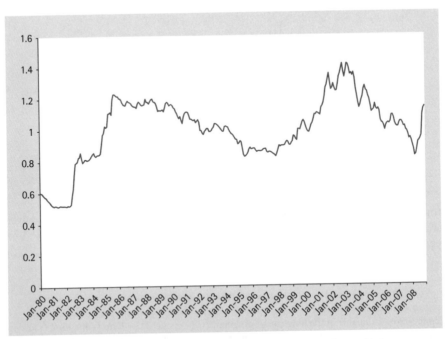

FIGURE 8.3 Chile: Bilateral RER with the US, deflated by CPI indexes (Index 1 = average 1980–2008)

Source: International Financial Statistics, IMF.

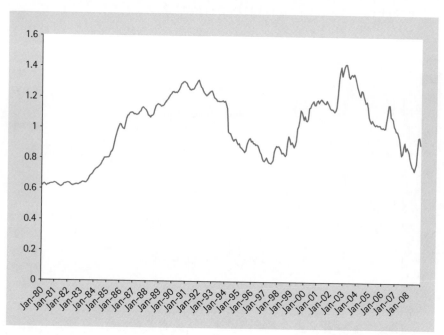

FIGURE 8.4 Colombia: bilateral RER with the US, deflated by CPI indexes (Index 1 = average 1980–2008)

Source: International Financial Statistics, IMF.

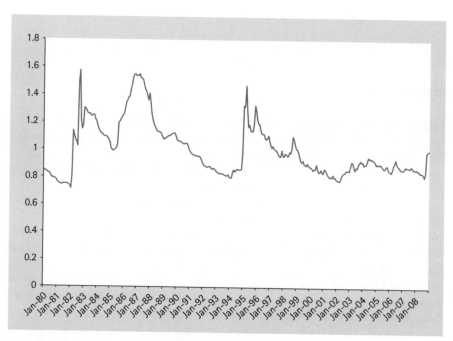

FIGURE 8.5 Mexico: bilateral RER with the US, deflated by CPI indexes (Index 1 = average 1980–2008)

Source: International Financial Statistics, IMF.

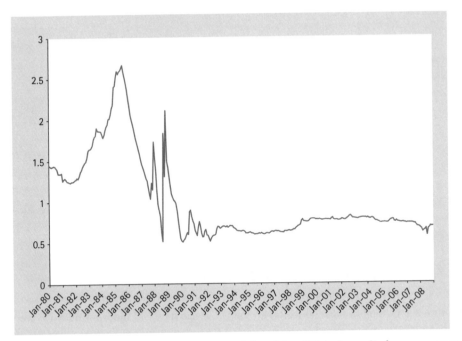

FIGURE 8.6 Peru: bilateral RER with the US, deflated by CPI indexes (Index 1 = average 1980–2008)

Source: International Financial Statistics, IMF.

REFERENCES

AGOSIN, M. (2009). 'Evolución macroeconómica y financiera de Chile en la última década', Documento Técnico 68, Iniciativa para la Transparencia Financiera', available online at: http://www.itf.org.ar/pdf/documentos/68-2010.pdf

AGUIRRE, Á., and CALDERON, C. (2005). 'Real Exchange Rate Misalignments and Economic Performance', Working Paper No. 315, Central Bank of Chile.

AIZENMAN, J., and LEE, J. (2007). 'International Reserves: Precautionary vs. Mercantilist Views, Theory and Evidence', *Open Economic Review* 18.2.

ARIDA, P., and LARA-RESENDE, A. (1985). 'Inertial Inflation and Monetary Reform in Brazil', in John Williamson (ed.), *Inflation and Indexation: Argentina, Brazil, and Israel*, Cambridge, Mass.: MIT Press.

ARMAS, A., and GRIPPA, F. (2006). 'Inflation Targeting in a Dollarized Economy: The Peruvian Experience', in A. Armas, A. Ize, and E. Levy-Yeyati (eds), *Financial Dollarization: The Policy Agenda*, New York: Palgrave Macmillan.

BACHA, E. (1979). 'Notes on the Brazilian Experience with Minidevaluations, 1968–1976', *Journal of Development Economics* 6.4.

——(1987). 'La inercia y el conflicto: el Plan Cruzado y sus desafíos', *Estudios económicos*, número extraordinario.

—— (2003). 'Brazil's Plano Real: A View from the Inside', in A. Dutt and J. Ros (eds), *Development Economics and Structuralist Macroeconomics: Essays in Honor of Lance Taylor*, Cheltenham: Elgar.

BARBOSA-FILHO, N. (2008). 'Inflation Targeting in Brasil: 1999–2006', *International Review of Applied Economics* 22.2.

BECKERMAN, P., and SOLIMANO, A. (2002). *Crisis and Dollarization in Ecuador: Stability, Growth, and Social Equity*, Washington, DC: World Bank.

BLANCHARD, O., DELL'ARICCIA, G., and MAURO, P. (2010). 'Rethinking Macroeconomic Policy', IMF Staff Position Note.

CALVO, G., LEIDERMAN, L., and REINHART, C. (1993). 'Capital Inflows and Real Exchange Rate Appreciation in Latin America: The Role of External Factors', *IMF Staff Papers* 40.1.

—— and REINHART, C. (2002). 'Fear of Floating', *Quarterly Journal of Economics* 107.2.

CHANG, R. (2008). 'Inflation Targeting, Reserve Accumulation, and Exchange Rate Management in Latin America', Borradores de Economía No. 487, Banco de la República de Colombia.

CORBO, V. (1985). 'Reforms and Macroeconomic Adjustments in Chile during 1974–1984', *World Development* 13.8.

DAMILL, M., and FRENKEL, R. (2009). 'Las políticas macroeconómicas en la evolución reciente de la economía argentina', CEDES, mimeo.

—— —— and RAPETTI, M. (2010). 'The Argentine Debt: History, Default and Restructuring', in B. Herman, J. A. Ocampo, and S. Spiegel (eds), *Overcoming Developing Country Debt Crises*, New York: Oxford University Press.

DANCOURT, O. (1999). 'Structural Reforms and Macroeconomic Policy in Peru, 1990–1996', in L. Taylor (ed.), *After Neoliberalism: What Next for Latin America?* Ann Arbor: University of Michigan Press.

—— (2009). 'Perú: la recesión del 2008-09 en perspective', Documento Técnico 67, Iniciativa para la Transparencia Financiera', available online at: http://www.itf.org.ar/pdf/documentos /67-2010.pdf

DE GREGORIO, J., TOKMAN, A., and VALDÉS, R. (2005). 'Flexible Exchange Rate with Inflation Targeting in Chile: Experience and Issues', Economic Policy Paper No. 14, Central Bank of Chile.

DÍAZ-ALEJANDRO, C. (1985). 'Good-Bye Financial Repression, Hello Financial Crash', *Journal of Development Economics* 19.1, 2.

DOOLEY, M., GARBER, P., and FOLKERTS-LANDAU, D. (2007). 'Direct Investment, Rising Real Wages and the Absorption of Excess Labor in the Periphery', in R. Clarida (ed.), *G7 Current Account Imbalances: Sustainability and Adjustment*, Chicago: University of Chicago Press.

DORNBUSCH, R. (1985). 'Comment', in J. Williamson (ed.), *Inflation and Indexation: Argentina, Brazil, and Israel*, Cambridge, Mass.: MIT Press.

—— and WERNER, A. (1994). 'Mexico: Stabilization, Reform and No Growth', *Brookings Papers on Economic Activity* 25.1.

EASTERLY, W. (2005). 'National Policies and Economic Growth: A Reappraisal', in P. Aghion and S. Durlauf (eds), *Handbook of Economic Growth*, Amsterdam: Elsevier.

FERNÁNDEZ, R. (1985). 'The Expectation Management Approach to Stabilization in Argentina during 1976-82', *World Development* 13.8.

FFRENCH-DAVIS, R. (1981). 'Exchange Rate Policies in Chile: The Experience with the Crawling Peg', in J. Williamson (ed.), *Exchange Rate Rules: The Theory, Performance, and Prospects of the Crawling Peg*, New York: Macmillan and St. Martin's Press.

FFRENCH-DAVIS, R. (1983). 'The Monetarist Experiment in Chile: A Critical Survey', *World Development* 11.11.

—— (2002). *Chile entre el neoliberalismo y el crecimiento con equidad: reformas y políticas desde 1973*, Buenos Aires: Siglo XXI.

FISCHER, S. (2001). 'Exchange Rate Regimes: Is the Bipolar-View Correct?', *Journal of Economic Perspectives* 15.2.

FRENKEL, R. (1983). 'La apertura financiera externa: el caso argentino', in R. Ffrench-Davis (ed.), *Relaciones financieras externas y su efecto en la economía latinoamericana*, México: Fondo de Cultura Económica.

—— (1987). 'Heterodox Theory and Policy: The Austral Plan in Argentina', *Journal of Development Economics* 27.1 and 2.

—— (2007). 'The Sustainability of Monetary Sterilization Policies', *CEPAL Review* 93.

—— and RAPETTI, M. (2008). 'Five Years of Competitive and Stable Real Exchange Rate in Argentina, 2002–2007', *International Review of Applied Economics* 22.2.

—— —— (2010). 'A Concise History of Exchange Rate Regimes in Latin America', Working Paper No. 1, Department of Economics, University of Massachusetts.

GALA, P. (2008). 'Real Exchange Rate Levels and Economic Development: Theoretical Analysis and Econometric Evidence', *Cambridge Journal of Economics* 32.2.

GALINDO, L., and ROS, J. (2008). 'Alternatives to Inflation Targeting in Mexico', *International Review of Applied Economics* 22.2.

GARCÍA VÁZQUEZ, E. (1994). 'La economía durante la presidencia de Illia', *Desarrollo económico* 34.134.

GERCHUNOFF, P., and LLACH, L. (2003). *El ciclo de la ilusión y el desencanto*, Buenos Aires: Ariel Sociedad Economica.

GOLDFAJN, I., and OLIVARES, G. (2001). 'Full Dollarization: The Case of Panama', *Economía* 1.2.

HANSON, J., and DE MELO, J. (1985). 'External Shocks, Financial Reforms, and Stabilization Attempts in Uruguay During 1974–83', *World Development* 13.8.

HAUSMANN, R., PRITCHETT, L., and RODRIK, D. (2005). 'Growth Accelerations', *Journal of Economic Growth* 10.4.

HEYMANN, D. (1987). 'The Austral Plan', *American Economic Review* 77.2.

MISHKIN, F., and SCHMIDT-HEBBEL, K. (2002). 'One Decade of Inflation Targeting in the World: What Do We Know and What Do We Need to Know?', in N. Loayza and R. Soto (eds), *Inflation Targeting: Design, Performance, Challenges*, Santiago, Chile: Central Bank of Chile.

MORENO-BRID, J. C., and ROS, J. (2009). *Development and Growth in the Mexican Economy*, New York: Oxford University Press.

OCAMPO, J. A. (1994). 'Trade Policy and Industrialization in Colombia, 1967–91', in G. Helleiner (ed.), *Trade Policy and Industrialization in Turbulent Times*, London: Routledge.

—— (2009). 'Latin America and the Global Financial Crisis', *Cambridge Journal of Economics* 33.4.

—— and TOVAR, C. (2003). 'Colombia's Experience with Reserve Requirements on Capital Inflows', *CEPAL Review* 81.

QUISPE-AGNOLI, M., and WHISLER, E. (2006). 'Official Dollarization and the Banking System in Ecuador and El Salvador', *Economic Review*, Federal Reserve Bank of Atlanta Q3.

RAZIN, A., and COLLINS, S. (1999). 'Real-Exchange-Rate Misalignments and Growth', in A. Razin and E. Sadka (eds), *The Economics of Globalization: Policy Perspectives from Public Economics*, New York: Cambridge University Press.

RAZMI, A., RAPETTI, M., and SKOTT, P. (2009). 'The Real Exchange Rate as a Development Policy Tool', Working Paper No. 7, Department of Economics, University of Massachusetts.

RODRÍGUEZ, M. (1985). 'Auge petrolero, estancamiento y políticas de ajuste en Venezuela', *Coyuntura económica Andina*, Fedesarrollo Bogotá.

RODRIK, D. (2008). 'The Real Exchange Rate and Economic Growth', *Brookings Papers on Economic Activity*, Fall.

ROS, J. (2001). 'From the Capital Surge to the Financial Crisis and Beyond: Mexico in the 1990s', in R. Ffrench-Davis (ed.), *Financial Crises in 'Successful' Emerging Economies*, Washington, DC: Brookings Institution Press and ECLAC.

URRUTIA, M. (1981). 'Experience with the Crawling Peg in Colombia', in J. Williamson (ed.), *Exchange Rate Rules: The Theory, Performance, and Prospects of the Crawling Peg*, New York: Macmillan and St. Martin's Press.

VERGARA, R. (1994). 'Política cambiaria en Chile: la experiencia de una década (1984–1994)', *Estudios públicos 56*.

VILLAR, L., and RINCÓN, H. (2000). 'The Colombian Economy in the Nineties: Capital Flows and Foreign Exchange Regimes', Borradores de Economía No. 149, Banco de la República de Colombia.

WILLIAMSON, J. (ed.) (1981). 'The Crawling Peg in Historical Perspective', in *Exchange Rate Rules: The Theory, Performance, and Prospects of the Crawling Peg*, New York: Macmillan and St. Martin's Press.

—— (1996). *The Crawling Band as an Exchange Rate Regime: Lessons from Chile, Colombia and Israel*, Washington, DC: Institute for International Economics.

ZAHLER, R. (1998). 'The Central Bank and Chilean Macroeconomic Policy in the 1990s', *CEPAL Review 64*.

CHAPTER 9

··

MONETARY POLICY IN LATIN AMERICA: PERFORMANCE UNDER CRISIS AND THE CHALLENGES OF EXUBERANCE

··

PABLO GARCÍA-SILVA AND MANUEL MARFÁN

9.1 INTRODUCTION[1]

··

The performance of emerging economies relative to developed ones has been an important issue in the run-up to, unfolding of, and aftermath of the 2008–9 financial turmoil and the Great Recession. Specifically, in the case of Latin America, in sharp contrast to periods of turbulence in previous decades, we first argue that financial and price stability has been preserved, with impacts on growth that have been less dramatic than in the early 1980s, while monetary policy has reacted more flexibly. This is presented in sections 9.2 and 9.3. Then, we discuss in section 9.4 a number of aspects that we believe have contributed to this improved performance during the recent crisis, such as initial economic conditions, especially the fiscal and external positions of the economies in the run-up to the crisis; the evolution of monetary/ exchange rate regimes, particularly the shift to inflation targeting and flexible exchange rate regimes; and structural and institutional aspects such as central bank independence, reduced domestic financial dollarization, and the strength of fiscal institutions. We discuss also the implications of fiscal and monetary policy interactions.

[1] This chapter does not represent the views of the Central Bank of Chile, or those of the Board of the International Monetary Fund, its management, staff, or any of the IMF member countries. We thank Mauricio Calani for excellent research assistantship.

Section 9.5 develops some thoughts on the implications for monetary policy of exuberant periods. Section 9.6 concludes.

9.2 MACROECONOMIC PERFORMANCE DURING CRISIS PERIODS

We begin by analyzing the macroeconomic performance in terms of inflation and growth of the seven largest Latin American economies during crisis periods. Inflation has been the scourge of the region for decades, becoming the symbol of macroeconomic mismanagement and instability. With this in mind, the maintenance of low inflation in the region is noteworthy, particularly in a context of major global turmoil and financial dislocation. Not only has average inflation remained stable, but it has also become less volatile, both over time and across economies (Figure 9.1).

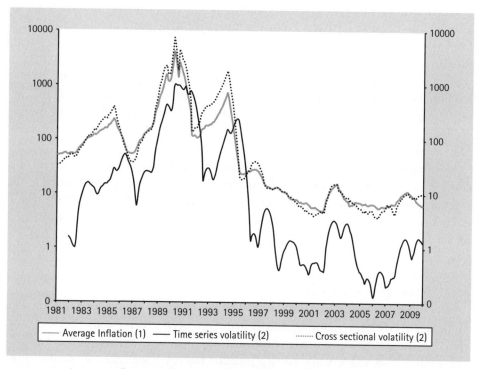

FIGURE 9.1 Average inflation and volatility (logarithmic scales)

Source: Authors' calculations using data from National Statistical Office and Central Bank.

Notes: (1) Calculated as the simple average of official annual inflation figures for Argentina, Brazil, Chile, Colombia, Mexico, Peru, and Venezuela. (2) Rolling 12 month standard deviation of average annual inflation. (3) Cross-sectional (across selected economies) standard deviation of annual inflation.

These are not completely new phenomena, as in the first half of the past decade inflation did not become rampant, in spite of severe local turbulences during both the "tequila crisis" in 1994–5 and the Asian crisis/Russian default episodes in 1997–8. Since then, the region has managed to sail through the large Brazilian devaluation of 1999, the high turbulences in the run-up to the Argentinean default in 2001, and the uncertainty and volatility that surrounded the Brazilian presidential election in 2002.

Indeed, the region has withstood the bouts of financial turmoil that started in late 2008, maintaining the achievement of low inflation initiated in the previous period. Of course, this assessment does not imply that from an absolute perspective the current inflationary environment in Latin America is desirable, or that no challenges remain. A high inflation environment has persisted in Argentina and Venezuela, while the stickiness of price dynamics in Mexico and Brazil has prevented a sustained path towards lower inflation. Volatility of inflation in Chile has also remained significant, as the rate of inflation has moved from an undesirably high level to an equally undesirable low one. But from a historical standpoint, the achievements in terms of higher price stability experienced in the first part of this decade do not seem to have been materially challenged by the current bout of global turbulences.

With respect to growth outcomes the picture is more mixed. Average GDP growth of the seven large economies was above 5% between mid-2004 and mid-2008, followed by a slump into negative territory. From a comparative standpoint, average growth performance during this crisis has not been that different from the outcomes of the Asian/Russian crisis and the slump of 2002. However, in contrast to the depression of 1982–3, when a relatively comparable global recession occurred, the performance on average has been better, and the cross-sectional variation has been lower. Moreover, in the current circumstances, aggregate output performance has been more driven by the specific economic situation of some economies. For instance, in the current environment, Mexico stands as a large outlier (Figure 9.2).

More important, in relation to the size of the global slump in growth, the current outcome in Latin America on average shows a marked improvement as compared to the reaction during past global growth patterns during crisis periods. Although the region did not remain unscathed, it avoided the prototypical financial crisis that, for instance, hit some Central European and Eastern European economies. In the case of Chile, De Gregorio (2009) has noted that in all previous local recessions, growth was significantly below global average, but in 2009 growth was similar to the average. This can also be noted for the region as a whole.

Hence, from an overall perspective, the macroeconomic outcome for Latin America in the recent crisis has been significantly better on average than during previous crisis episodes. The growth slowdown has been relatively modest, given the significant magnitude of the global shock, while average inflation has remained relatively stable, maintaining the achievement of price stability of the early part of the last decade.

The next section presents the monetary policy and exchange rate response during the recent crisis, before moving to the underlying structural or institutional aspects that have been behind this enhanced countercyclical role played by monetary policy.

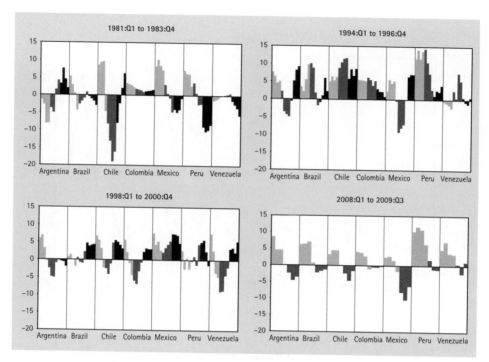

FIGURE 9.2 Quarterly year-o-year GDP growth rates in crisis periods

Source: CEPAL, Cuaderno Estadistico 37, when available. Otherwise, International Financial Statistics, Central Banks.

Notes: (1) Linear interpolation of the case of Venezuela 1980–83. (2) Light gray: first year of given period. Dark gray: second year of given period. Black: third year of given period.

9.3 THE MONETARY POLICY AND EXCHANGE RATE RESPONSE

Figure 9.3 shows the path of short terms interest rates of the seven large Latin American economies during the chosen crises periods, and Figure 9.4 depicts the nominal exchange rate movements. The differences between the current monetary and exchange rate movements are striking. After 1981, nominal interest rates stayed at high levels, and even increased significantly in some cases. During the tequila crisis, several economies were still attempting to consolidate disinflation or tackle very high inflation processes. Over 1997–8, monetary policy reacted with a tightening to the outbreak of turbulences during the Russian default, and only entered a period of easing after most of the financial turmoil had lapsed by mid-1999. In sharp contrast, from late 2008 and early 2009, still within the window of rough gyrations in global markets, a monetary policy easing process clearly occurred across almost all selected economies, bringing the policy interest rates to lows seldom or never experienced before. In Chile, in particular, the policy rate hit the zero lower bound, and non-conventional policies were used. The only two

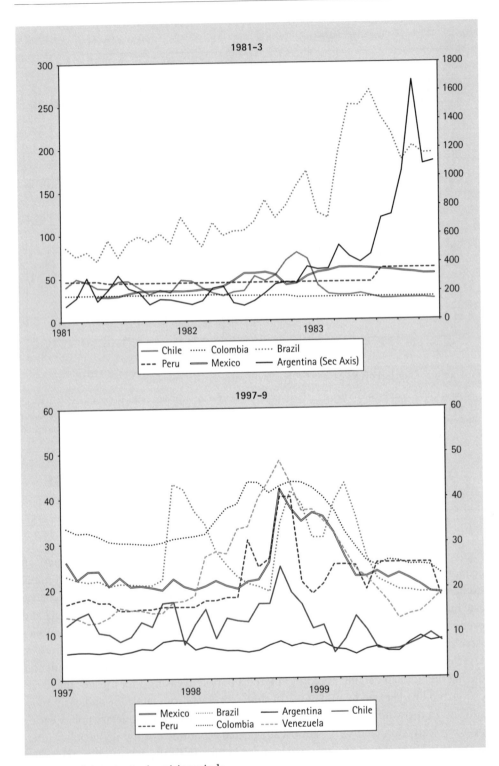

FIGURE 9.3 Interest rates in crisis periods

Source: Bloomberg. 90- or 30-day interest rates used in the cases when monetary policy rates were not available.

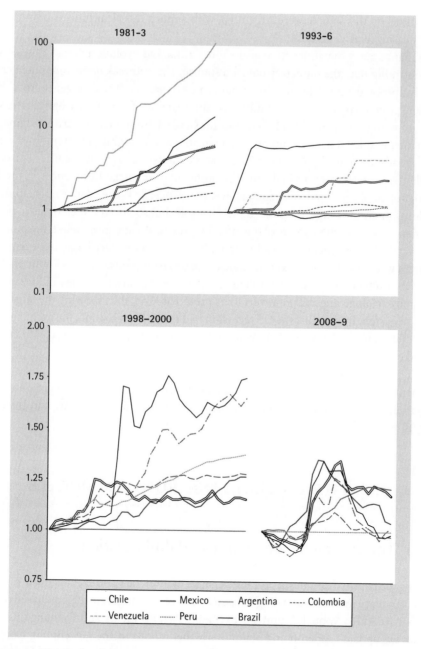

FIGURE 9.4 Nominal exchange rates in crisis periods (1981–3 and 1994–6 shown in logarithmic scale, scaled to January of starting year=100)

Source: Bloomberg.

exceptions on this sample were Argentina, with a much less clear process of monetary policy easing, and Venezuela.

Exchange rates dynamics have also shown a marked evolution across crises, even more striking than the monetary policy response. The outbreak of the 1980s debt crisis clearly uprooted any anchoring for exchange rate dynamics. The divergence from their starting point is apparent. By the mid-1990s, this reaction of nominal exchange rates was still occurring, most notably of course in Mexico, where the tequila crisis originated. Even during the Asian crisis, nominal depreciations were highly persistent. In the current situation, the evolution of exchange rates contrasts sharply with earlier episodes. While the initial depreciation during the outbreak of financial turbulences in the last quarter of 2008 was rapid, over 2009 a reversion proceeded. The relative normalization of global financial conditions indeed played a role, but so also did the domestic policy reaction. Thanks to the stability of the inflation process documented above, the nominal exchange rate movements allowed for an adjustment to the very large, but eventually transitory, real and financial external shock with no lasting consequences for the anchoring of the exchange rate path and of concomitant expectations. In the case of Mexico, the nominal exchange rate did not revert to its pre-crisis level, thus showing the larger and more persistent impact that the US recession had there. In Argentina, the exchange rate depreciation was delayed, while in Venezuela a very large exchange rate adjustment did not take place until 2010.

What are the underlying factors behind this improvement in monetary policy management? The next section surveys a number of those: the exchange rate regime and dollarization, external and fiscal vulnerability, and central bank autonomy and inflation targets.

9.4 THE UNDERLYING FUNDAMENTALS

9.4.1 The exchange rate regime and dollarization

During the past two decades, a profound change of monetary and exchange rate regimes has taken place in the world. Using a classification of exchange rate regimes based on the IMF's AREAER (Annual Report on Exchange Arrangements and Exchange Restrictions), we update Calderón and Schmidt-Hebbel (2008) to 2008, excluding from the sample the low income countries group. The classifications used are those of Calderón and Schmidt-Hebbel (2008), where exchange rate regimes are distinguished between hard peg, intermediate, flexible, and free fall (i.e. where extremely high inflation or a hyperinflation process prevailed). Figure 9.5 presents the breakdown for all the economies in the sample from 1975 to 2008. Intermediate regimes (which represented about 50% of total cases in 1975) shrank significantly, while flexible exchange rates, admittedly in several cases with active reserve accumulation, and hard pegs became prevalent. The

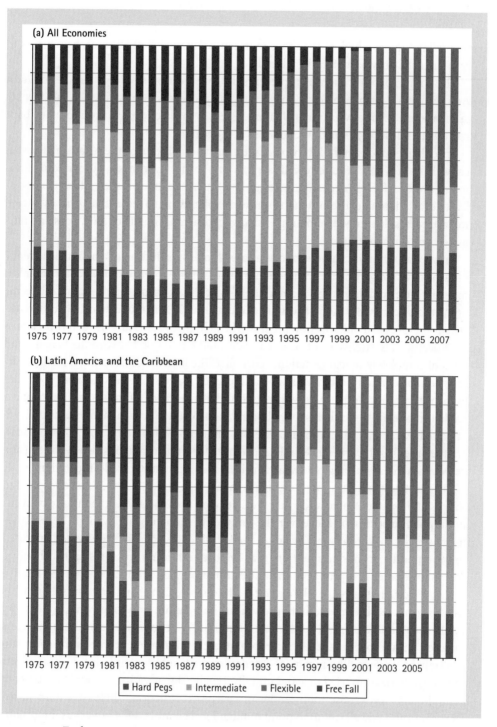

FIGURE 9.5 Exchange rate regimes

Source: Calderón and Schmidt-Hebbel (2008) and IMF AREAER (2007; 2008).

Notes: LAC comprises Argentina, Bolivia, Brazil, Chile, Colombia, Costa Rica, Dominican Republic, Ecuador, El Salvador, Guatemala, Honduras, Jamaica, Mexico, Nicaragua, Panama, Paraguay, Peru, Trinidad and Tobago, Uruguay, and Venezuela.

free-fall grouping, which in the 1990s represented up to 20% of all cases, has shrunk to zero since the early part of the last decade.

The bottom panel of Figure 9.5 presents the classification of a large number of Latin American and Caribbean economies. Here, the process is even starker. While flexible exchange rate regimes were virtually nonexistent in the late 1970s, since 2000 they have represented close to 50% of the economies in the region.

Speculative attacks in the last two decades, most notably during the Asian and Russian crisis, have provided ground to validate this two-corner hypothesis, but without eliminating a role for foreign exchange interventions. Intermediate exchange rate schemes—at least de facto if not de jure and in the sense of explicitly managed exchange rates—seem to have been substituted by floating exchange rate arrangements or hard pegs and ultimately, full dollarization.

Full dollarization is characterized as a case of total substitution of a national currency in favor of a foreign one for transaction motives, in the absence of full factor mobility. Indeed, factor mobility is the main although not the exclusive feature of an economic union that goes beyond monetary unification, such as the euro zone, which we differentiate with respect to a dollarization process. The literature examining the determinants of such decisions is extensive but relies basically on the trade-off between the benefits and costs of completely reneging national currency. The benefits of adopting a foreign currency can be derived from both financial and trade aspects. On the one hand, a smaller exchange rate risk—especially with regard to balance sheet effects— and importing a credible monetary policy helps to anchor inflation expectations when monetary policy is impaired by reputational problems (see Bayoumi and Eichengreen 1997; Corbo 2002). On the other hand, particularly in Europe, monetary integration has also been seen as a vehicle to stabilize interregional relative prices, and thus to foster trade integration.

The main cost is the loss of monetary exchange rate policy instruments to respond to shocks and/or to nominal and real cycles, leaving fiscal policy as the unique conventional policy instrument. Moreover, the "imported" monetary policy might be responding to shocks and/or business cycles in the US which, if not synchronized or mirrored in the domestic economic situation, may impose additional pressures on fiscal policy. Also, shocks and their propagation on inflation imply concomitant impacts on relative prices, especially the real exchange rate. Although real exchange rate misalignments can be corrected by productivity growth in the medium and long run, productivity rarely accommodates macroeconomic disequilibria in the short run. Rather, excess inflation with respect to the US may accumulate a misalignment that in the short run can only be corrected by means of a deflation, with subsequent balance sheet effects that the dollarization tried to avoid initially. Finally, dollarization impairs the ability of central banks to exercise their lender-of-last-resort function. This last argument led Haussman and Powell (1999) to point out that local central banks can act as intermediaries with the main liquidity provider (e.g. the Federal Reserve), or international organizations in times of financial distress, and would therefore still have a worst-case-scenario insurance role. The international liquidity provision by the Federal Reserve in 2008–9 through currency swaps to major central banks may validate such a possibility, although that provision was not available for dollarized economies.

On the other extreme, full-fledged inflation targeting with a monetary policy rule and clean exchange rate floating has shown a gap between the theoretical recommendation and actual practice in Latin America. Schmidt-Hebbel and Werner (2002) estimated rolling coefficients of Taylor Rules for Brazil, Chile, and Mexico using moving samples. Their main finding is that Taylor-type monetary policy rules show episodic shifts in the three economies. Indeed, for normal periods and long periods of time there is no evidence of systematic policy reaction to exchange rates, but in periods of financial distress the exchange rate becomes a significant factor in the monetary policy reaction. This again shows that the selection of more flexible regimes has not been to the detriment of disqualifying the relevance of foreign exchange intervention if needed.

There may be a number of reasons for such a behavior. The one that seems common to all cases is when a trade-off between price stability and financial stability appears. This trade-off can be immediate, for instance when presented with tight liquidity conditions in local USD markets, or more preventive, so as to pre-empt the unfolding of what are perceived as excessive real appreciations or real depreciation. Perhaps the most pure case of inflation targeting is the Chilean one, but since 2000 there have been three episodes of intervention in foreign currency justified by exceptional circumstances that led to overshooting in the exchange rate (see De Gregorio, Tokman, and Valdés 2005; García 2009). Intervention in the foreign exchange market is frequent in Brazil, Colombia, Mexico (after the 2008 turmoil), and Peru. In the last two countries, an additional argument is the presence of domestic dollarization (see next section), so exchange rate volatility is linked to domestic redistribution of wealth. The fear to float in those cases seems justified.

Colombia combines inflation targeting with non-conventional policies affecting currency arbitrage, such as unremunerated reserve requirements on capital inflows (commonly referred to as *encaje*). In effect, the *encaje* on foreign financial inflows is a means to partially avoid excess appreciation of the peso arising from monetary stabilization. Recently, Brazil also introduced a tax on cross-border financial transactions to avoid financial pressure on the real. Moreover, the transmission mechanisms of the monetary policy rule in Brazil are different from the standard theoretical case, since development banking controlled either by the federal government or by state authorities fulfill a large portion of corporate financial needs.

9.4.2 Domestic dollarization and indexation

In addition to full dollarization or partial currency pegs, there is another form of "living with the dollar"—partial financial dollarization or the dual-currency phenomenon which is present in several countries of the region. Unlike full dollarization, the main foreign currency demand motive relies on its role of store of value, and is a financial policy issue countries have to struggle against. Dollarization in such countries has imposed a challenge for national monetary authorities who operate under conditions of narrow monetary base and potentially reduced effectiveness of monetary policy. Dollarization also entails non-trivial financial stability issues. Financial systems which face high foreign currency demand deposits relative to total deposits are exposed to currency risk. Banks then optimally hedge such risk by holding dollar-denominated assets. This, however, only replaces foreign currency risk with dollar loan default risk. Moreover, the currency mismatch does not disappear but is transferred to firms. Dollar-denominated liabilities at the firm level have non-trivial consequences, as sketched by Céspedes, Chang, and Velasco (2004), who model the balance sheet effect. Currency mismatches, via depreciation, result in expanding the firms' liability burden after the monetary policy response to (negative) external shocks, amplifying them.

Dollarization can always be avoided by law, and this has been indeed the case. However, restricting financial dollarization may come at the cost of overseas liquidity management by domestic agents, which ultimately prevents the deepening of the financial system with the direct consequences on long-run growth and welfare such underdevelopment entails.

In Latin America in particular (for those countries with available data), there is vast heterogeneity in the level of dollarization. On the one hand countries such as Peru, Bolivia and Uruguay exhibit very high ratios of foreign denominated deposits to total deposits in the banking system, mainly due to their sinful hyperinflationary history. In Argentina, onshore foreign currency deposits, which used to be very significant, almost disappeared as a result of its 2001–2 crisis. Still, a significant portion of domestic long-term contracts, although paid in domestic currency, use the exchange rate as the unit of account. This indexation to the dollar, although part of dollarization as we understand it, is not captured by the size of foreign currency deposits, and neither are offshore deposits. Countries such as Brazil, Colombia, and Venezuela exhibit close to zero ratios of the same metric because of the restrictions on dollar deposits in the local financial system. These trends, however, also leave offshore deposits unaccounted for. On the other hand, countries such as Chile and Mexico have devised ways to enjoy low dollar-denominated demand deposits. It is intriguing to observe such differences across economies which are not drastically different (Figure 9.6).

In the rest of the world, the picture is a hybrid of these two country clusters. Honohan (2009) reports that between 1994 and 2004, in 76 countries for which there is available data, deposit dollarization has remained between 25% and 32%. Furthermore, he shows that its peak occurred during 2002, followed by a smooth reversal to 1999 levels by 2004. Nevertheless, one distinctive feature arises. Highly dollarized economies, which are not tax havens, carry the hyperinflation history burden. The naturally low credibility of monetary policy (MP), in turn, would be further reinforced by the degree of dollarization (Cowan and Do 2003; Duffy, Nikitin, and Smith 2004), resulting in something like a dollarization trap. Dollarization, then, is perhaps simply a symptom of a more deep-rooted, well-known policy failure: irresponsible policy actions.[2]

The theoretical support for such stylized facts is presented by Ize and Levy-Yeyati (2003) and IDB (2005). These authors highlight the fact that dollarization may actually

---

[2] An alternative to dollarization is the recourse to domestic indexation. See Herrera and Valdés (2005) for a review of the Chilean experience on indexation and dollarization.

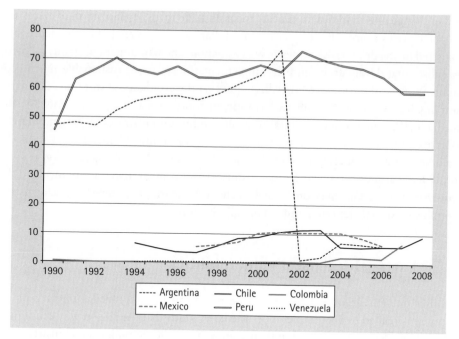

FIGURE 9.6 Deposit dollarization in select economies

Source: Authors' Elaboration on data from Honohan (2009).

be an optimal response of depositors who choose a minimum variance portfolio composed of a dollar-denominated and a local-currency-denominated asset. Thus, exchange
rate variability for the former, and inflation variability (and therefore its level) for the
latter, are key determinants in agents' decision of dollar and peso liquid asset demand.
Under this rational behavior, one should expect agents in countries with high and, more
importantly, variable inflation history to be reluctant to store wealth in local currency.

Although the consequences of "original sin," in the sense of liability dollarization
(Eichengreen and Hausmann 1999), seem to be dire, the evolution of the degree of dollarization over the past two decades does not seem to show a marked trend. Moreover,
heavily dollarized economies, such as Peru, have performed extremely well in the current circumstances. Hence, although it is quite clear that a professional consensus is not
forthcoming with respect to the type of monetary and exchange rate combination
towards which economies should converge, the adoption of flexible exchange rate
regimes, even in the presence of heavy dollarization, have not apparently disrupted the
ability of economies to adjust to significant external shocks. This is consistent with the
view that de-dollarization in Peru has been more of a consequence than a cause of macroeconomic stability (García-Escribano 2010). The forced de-dollarization of Argentina
is also an argument in this direction.

The experiences of dollarization and de-dollarization in Chile also confirm this view.
Herrera and Valdés (2005) document how in periods of capital account liberalization

and exchange rate rigidities, in the late 1950s and late 1970s, dollarization of credit and property prices soared. By the mid-1980s, dollarization retreated after the depression triggered by the debt crisis, domestic overvaluation, and banking fragility was followed by substantial devaluations and the implementation of more sustainable macroeconomic frameworks. Moreover, they highlight that the avoidance of sustained dollarization in Chile was related to initial institutional conditions and developments. On the one hand, the long history of capital controls and the administrative, legal, and judicial tools to enforce them surely limited the extent of onshore and offshore dollarization. On the other hand, the development of CPI indexation, aided by a strong legal framework, sound fiscal accounts (at least from a historical and comparative standpoint), and the growth of institutional investors helped create a large market of indexed financial instruments as a more efficient substitute than dollarization.

9.4.3 External and fiscal vulnerabilities

Another possible argument that could be related to the improved monetary policy response is related to debt intolerance. The latter holds that the reason why economies cannot issue debt denominated in their own currency lies in political and institutional weaknesses that increase excessively the risks of default. The argument is that the economies that repudiate or default regularly in their financial commitments are not capable of contracting additional debt on the international markets, developing "intolerance." Borio and Packer (2004) show that the countries that suffer debt intolerance tend to experience worse sovereign risk assessment by rating agencies.

The policy implication of this hypothesis is that either credible institutional progress that reduces the risk of default or very conservative macroeconomic management reduce the prevalence of this intolerance, and hence the broad vulnerability of the economies to external shocks. Furthermore, this enhanced robustness allows for a more aggressive countercyclical reaction by monetary policy. Figure 9.8 displays a number of indicators of external and fiscal vulnerabilities. The level of external debt, international reserves, and the current account deficit are usual indicators of external vulnerabilities, while the fiscal deficit is also a broad indicator of the scope public policy has for engaging in countercyclical macroeconomic policies. The picture that emerges is suggestive of an improved position both on the external and the fiscal side (Figure 9.7).

A distinct feature of the situation previous to the recent crisis is the drastic improvement in Chile, Peru, and Argentina. Indeed, international reserves do show a more marked increase with respect to the level observed in 1981, previous to the debt crisis, with higher levels of reserves over GDP in Argentina, Brazil, Mexico, and Peru. In Chile it would also be the case if the sovereign wealth fund is added to international reserves. External debt is lower than in previous episodes in all cases except Argentina, and the current accounts have displayed either lower deficits or actual surpluses.

How far the improved external and fiscal accounts in the run-up to the 2008 crises showed a more robust structural situation or rather a cyclical reflection of high com-

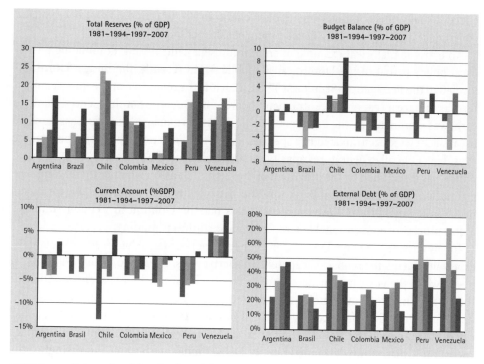

FIGURE 9.7 External and fiscal vulnerabilities

Note: Bars represent pre-crisis levels.

modity prices has been a matter of debate. Izquierdo and Talvi (2008) and Ocampo (2007), for instance, have argued that the current account and fiscal surpluses in Latin America by late 2007 and early 2008 did not reflect—apart from some specific cases, such as Chile and some Central American economies—a clear structural shift in the way fiscal policy had been conducted, but simply the effect of the commodity price boom. This entails a challenge in the pattern that commodity prices do not persist in their high levels of the past few years.

9.4.4 Monetary policy and fiscal policy interactions

Some summarized examples help illustrate the importance for the performance of monetary policy of the concomitant behavior of fiscal policy as well as the strength of fiscal institutions. Marfán (1986) argues about the historical relevance in the region of struggling fiscal vs. monetary authorities in cases of a non-deep financial system, and not integrated to external markets. In that context, one of the two authorities must be subordinated, as fiscal policy may be independent of monetary policy as long as fiscal deficits can be financed in a conventional way. Otherwise, either fiscal policy must adjust to a binding cash constraint imposed by the Central Bank, or the fiscal deficit must be monetized. Usually, this combination has been characteristic of economies with weak fiscal governance, thus affecting the development of a deeper financial system.

An extreme historical example of an omnipresent central bank dominating a weak fiscal policy is that of the Dominican Republic. Until recently, the Budget Office was located in the Presidency (Secretaría Técnica), while the main role of the finance minister was to have a seat at the central bank board. The Governor of the Central Bank, in turn, was nominated by the President. Fiscal policy was managed on a cash basis, where fiscal slacks were accumulated in a special account for discretionary expenditures of the President. Overall expenditure capacity was dependent on the availability of cash. Fiscal policy was disciplined by the judgment of the Central Bank on whether there was financial slack or not. The Central Bank was thus the sole institution accountable for macroeconomic equilibrium. Only in recent years has the Dominican Republic initiated a slow process of conventional macroeconomic institution-building.

In any case, the average Dominican economic performance has been respectable—especially during the 1990s—except for two sharp cycles. The first one, in the late 1980s, began when the government started to borrow from abroad, breaking the rationale of the system. In effect, fiscal policy, conducted on the basis of a cash constraint, could develop large deficits financed by financial inflows. The Central Bank, in turn, could not sterilize enough the monetization of excess foreign reserves, and symptoms of macroeconomic disruption developed rapidly. Debt compliance became increasingly difficult for the government, and default was finally declared. As a consequence, the Dominican Republic was rationed out of international financial markets throughout all the 1990s, while the central bank recovered its ability to discipline fiscal policy. Macroeconomic equilibrium and growth was rapidly restored, but the main institutional reforms were postponed. The second episode was in the early 2000s, when the government decided to issue sovereign bonds, generating a boom–bust cycle with many analogies with the first episode. Technical assistance to the Dominican Republic has correctly emphasized the need to develop more robust institutions, a process already initiated.

A historical example of a dominant fiscal policy and a subordinated central bank is the case of Argentina. For reasons beyond the scope of this chapter, Argentina has suffered from fiscal and financial federalism, along with rigidities that have developed especially in the form of significant fiscal earmarking. In this context, fiscal adjustment in periods of distress has faced abysmal difficulties. In the 1980s, two episodes of monetization of fiscal deficits ended up in classical cases of hyperinflation and default, with a monetary reform in between ("Plan Austral"). In 1991 a new monetary reform with constitutional backing was installed. A hard peg regime in the form of a currency board was the staple component of a plan aiming at two main purposes: to introduce a credible nominal anchor in the fixed exchange rate, and to block future monetization of fiscal deficits. In 1992 the independence of the Banco Central de la República Argentina obtained legal status.

The rest is a well-known story. The initial years of the currency board exhibited fiscal discipline, although excess private-sector spending introduced some stress to the new regime. In the mid-1990s the Argentinean government started a sequence of sovereign bonds issuances, and fiscal deficits reappeared. The policy regime forced the Central Bank to monetize the concomitant accumulation of foreign reserves, with no relevant sterilization mechanisms available, and inflation reappeared as well. With a hard-peg exchange rate, excess inflation generated an increasing real exchange rate misalignment.[3] The overall macroeconomic rationale rested on a policy regime where convergence could not be granted by monetary authorities. The President of the Central Bank was sacked after he was sued by the government, jeopardizing the institutional independence of the Bank. A sequence of adjustment programs with the IMF could not recover fiscal discipline. The attempt of the management of the IMF to institutionalize a device for sovereign bankruptcy (SDRM) did not prosper, Argentina was left to itself, and the political crisis escalated. The abandonment of the currency board developed into a collapse of the Argentinean payments system. The economic and social crisis that followed is amongst the most painful catastrophes registered in modern economic history in the region. At the same time, it also marked the starting point of a fast recovery.

In the aftermath, Argentina has followed a policy regime with a managed exchange rate. The high degree of domestic dollarization, however, makes exchange rate volatility too costly to bear, and intervention is the rule rather than the exception. Recently, a struggle between the Central Bank and the government ended in the resignation of the governor.

Brazil, on the contrary, is a success story of a monetary reform ("Plan Real") with initially weak fiscal institutions. As in Argentina in the 1980s, Brazil had suffered the consequences of unmanageable fiscal federalism and fiscal deficit monetization that also ended up in episodes of hyperinflation, with a monetary reform in between as well ("Plan Cruzado"). A failed attempt of fiscal restraint also took place in the early 1990s ("Plan Collor"). In the last year of President Itamar Franco's administration (1994) a new monetary reform was introduced ("Plan Real"). The initial political backing of this plan transformed the minister of finance, Fernando Henrique Cardoso, into a national political figure. Cardoso became President of Brazil as of 1995, and governed for two successive periods. Itamar Franco, in turn, maintained a high political stature, and took office as the Governor of the state of Minas Gerais. As in the previous stabilization programs, the initial fiscal efforts started to fade, along with the credibility of the plan. During the "tequila" and Asian crises, but especially during the Russian sovereign debt default of 1998, Brazil was evaluated as a less resilient case than Argentina, according to the sovereign spreads of the time.

It was during the upheaval of 1998 that Brazil accelerated its reforms—backed by IMF programs—aimed at structurally improving fiscal and financial governance. The per-

---

[3] The debate on the underlying roots of the Argentinean debacle of 2001–2 is still going on (what was first: the real exchange rate misalignment or excess overall expenditure?). Whatever the position, it is a truism that a policy regime aimed at reducing the degrees of freedom of fiscal policy ended up with a degree of freedom of monetary policy while fiscal policy continued being discretionary.

sonal commitment of President Cardoso to the passing of laws and constitutional reforms in the Parliament, along with the political backing that he gave to the ministry of finance and the central bank, are crucial to the success that followed. The two macroeconomic staples of these renewed efforts were the introduction of an inflation targeting monetary regime with exchange rate floating, on the one hand, and the setting of a primary fiscal surplus target of 3.5% of GDP, on the other.

Among the many other actions of this period, two reflect the authorities' boldness and ownership of the process. First, the federal government issued dollar-denominated public bonds in the domestic market with the explicit purpose of transferring the exchange rate financial risk from the private to the public sector. Thus, the balance-sheet effects of the real devaluation that accompanied this process were concentrated in the federal government. Second, there was an epic struggle between the federal government (led by Cardoso) and the states' authorities (led by Itamar Franco, Cardoso's former boss) during the legislative discussions for reforming fiscal and financial federalism. The signals of political backing and technical audacity of the whole process implied a paramount improvement in the Brazilian economic outlook. A credibility shock on the eve of President Lula's election, in 2002, introduced enormous stress. The commitment of the future authorities to raise the fiscal primary surplus target to 4.25% of GDP—even beyond the recommendation of the IMF at the time—allowed the restoration of credibility. It also paved the way to strengthening economic institutions during the next administration.

9.4.5 Central bank autonomy and inflation-targeting regimes

We have seen how key the practical links between fiscal institutions and monetary policy performance are. On a theoretical basis, the link between better monetary performance and central bank autonomy is clear from the traditional problem of dynamic inconsistency pioneered by Phelps, in his criticism of the Phillips curve, or by Barro and Gordon (1983). In those economies with unstable political systems or absence of governance and accountability mechanisms for macroeconomic policy, central banks will be subject to the discretion of the current political administration, and hence agents will end up expecting that monetary policy (among other things) will abuse any available "trade-off" between inflation and unemployment.

During the 1990s the central banks of Latin America substantially increased their degrees of legal independence.[4] This is of course relevant. The traditional evidence (e.g. Grilli, Masciandario, and Tabellini 1991; Cukierman, Webb, and Neyapti 1992; Alesina and Summers 1993) shows that there is a significant negative relation between the degree of Central Bank autonomy (measured using the Cukierman index) and inflation, but that this interrelation disappears in the case of the emerging economies. Cukierman (2006) argues that this difference can be due to the large discrepancies between the legal defini-

---

[4] Indexes of central bank autonomy can be found in Cukierman (2006). For Latin American countries, see Jâcome and Vásquez (2006). See also Schmidt-Hebbel (2006).

tions of independence and the effective degree of independence. However, Céspedes and Valdés (2006) show a strong link between the degree of autonomy and the pass-through of exchange rate fluctuations to inflation. Diana and Sidiropoulos (2004) show how economies with independent central banks display lower sacrifice ratios. Jácome and Vásquez (2006) find a negative relationship between the inflation rate and central bank independence in Latin America, even after controlling for a number of other variables.

This enhanced autonomy of central banks has coincided with an increased importance of inflation targeting. While IMF (2004) reports that in 1999 there were eight economies with inflation targeting regimes, by 2004 this number had increased to 21. Schmidt-Hebbel (2006) shows how this change has also occurred in a significant way in Latin American, towards both inflation targeting and more flexible exchange rate regimes. According to Hammond (2010), as of 2010, Brazil, Chile, Colombia, Guatemala, Mexico, and Peru had implemented full-fledged inflation targeting regimes. Their differing practical approaches to foreign exchange intervention, as mentioned in previous sections, shows that inflation targeting does not require an absolute discarding of interventions as a useful tool. In fact, Hammond (2010), in his "state-of-the-art" assessment of inflation targeting in the world, does not consider as a necessary condition for inflation targeting the lack of intervention in the foreign exchange market. In this view of inflation targeting, price stability is explicitly recognized as the main goal of monetary policy; there is a public announcement of a quantitative target for inflation. Moreover, monetary policy is based on a wide set of information, explicitly encompassing the forecasting of inflation, including an inflation forecast. There are transparency and accountability mechanisms for the monetary authority.

As has been recognized, a major advantage of inflation targeting is that it combines elements of both rules and discretion in monetary policy, and it has been therefore characterized as "constrained discretion." Thus, it can be argued that as long as foreign exchange intervention is conducted without contradicting the main characteristics of inflation targeting (namely the role for rules and discretion, the fact that inflation stability remains the main medium turn objective for monetary policy, and transparency and accountability in policymaking), it clearly can be part of the toolbox of inflation targeting central banks.

9.5 Exuberance, off-equilibrium paths, and monetary policy

Mainstream monetary theory assumes that long-run equilibrium is determined by real variables, including relative prices, while monetary policy provides a necessary anchor to set nominal prices. Any macroeconomic real variable exhibiting a deviation from its stationary value would be located in a "saddle path" which converges to the stationary equilibrium through time. Monetary policy would affect real variables in the short run only, and can therefore accelerate that convergence to the steady state equilibrium but without affecting it. To enhance a monetary policy targeting one or more long-run real variables would lead to a failure and, at its worst, can influence the stationary equilibrium in the wrong direction.

However, most Latin American economies have faced off equilibrium episodes with exploding "convergence" achieved through domestic crises. The financially seismic nature of the region has led to an important discussion beyond the orthodox monetary theory view. The literature on this aspect has had as a main focus the multiple-equilibrium approach developed initially by Guillermo Calvo (Landerretche and Marfán 2007). The financial stress faced by Brazil prior to the first election of President Lula da Silva is a notable example of multiple equilibria. International financial investors worried that the probable new authorities of Brazil were not committed to the fiscal rule in place, targeting a primary surplus. The episode could have had disruptive effects, as convergence of public and private debt was not guaranteed. The adherence of the incoming authorities to a harder fiscal rule immediately calmed investors, and control over the economic situation was restored.

Economic models trying to deal with the multiple-equilibrium approach are simple in their economics, sophisticated in their mathematics, and intractable when trying to adjust to actual data. The extensions to monetary policy, however, are clear. First, credibility and reputation are essential to its actual efficacy; second, there is no such thing as *the* stationary equilibrium; third, policymakers' good judgment cannot be replaced by modeling.

As we discussed above, partially dollarized economies of the region intervene continuously in the exchange rate market, regardless of their monetary policy regime. Inflation targeters such as Peru, for instance, use as a measure of success a low volatility of the exchange rate, even in periods of financial distress (e.g. Lago 2009). The new authorities of the Central Bank of Argentina define their regime as a quantitative monetary targeting with exchange rate administration. Even in Chile—a non-dollarized economy and perhaps with the most polar inflation targeting regime of the region—the institutional statement is that the exchange rate is determined by free floating, but the Central Bank of Chile reserves its right to intervene whenever the board considers it necessary. In fact, the CBC has actively intervened in the foreign exchange market four times since 2001, always with an underlying argument related to financial stability rather than to inflation targeting.

In effect, financial stability concerns have repeatedly moved monetary authorities out of simple policy schemes in the region. The main point for consideration arises when imprudent behavior jeopardizes solvency and/or the soundness of the payments system—meaning that financial stability is not granted under likely pessimistic scenarios. The experience of the region has been that if monetary authorities do nothing other than make verbal interventions, the outcome can be excessively costly. The problem that remains, however, is that there is no consensus among economists as to what should be done.

A recent promising approach is that of Christiano et al. (2007). The argument is that future productivity gains are difficult to forecast, and thus the long-run stationary equilibrium is difficult to assess as well. If agents expect a future positive shock on productivity, the immediate economic response would be a rise in asset prices and an increase in expenditure, and the overall short-run equilibrium would be consistent with a "saddle path" leading to the new steady state with higher productivity. But if future productivity does not keep up with expectations, eventually the economy will fall into a slump.

What is attractive about this argument is that it is compatible with three features that are part of Latin America's wisdom: first, nobody can prove that a bubble is a bubble before it bursts; second, most busts are preceded by a boom; third, even if there is a consensus on the diagnostic, there is no consensus on which are the instruments to be used.

Marfán, Medina, and Soto (2009) use the Christiano et al. (2007) argument in a micro-founded DSGE model, calibrated to the Chilean experience of the 1990s. The main initial argument is that future effects on productivity arising from structural reforms and/or technical innovation cannot be predicted accurately, since there is no previous history on which to base the forecasts. To wait and see could be a bad microeconomic strategy if others change their decisions as soon as institutional or productive innovations are announced. But if economic agents act according to a notional increase in future productivity growth that is not entirely fulfilled, the outcome will be a boom–bust cycle. They try a number of conventional combinations in the monetary policy reaction function, but there is no clear-cut conventional monetary policy scheme that can prevent either the boom or the bust.

Marfán (2005) also explores excess private expenditure arising from over-optimism, but using a sort of a Mundell–Fleming approach amplified with a Phillips curve based on rational expectations. The rationale is based on the accounting identity where excess private expenditure plus excess public expenditure is equal to the deficit of the current account of the balance of payments. The argument states that a combination of private-sector exuberance and fiscal discipline may lead to exchange rate misalignment and to current account deficits that cannot be sustained under reasonable, non-optimistic scenarios. This combination has been repeated several times in Latin America and, more recently, in other emerging and developed economies. We illustrate the problem with a couple of figures for Mexico in 1990–2002 (Figure 9.8).

In the early 1990s, after years of public-sector indiscipline, Mexico exhibited a significant improvement in its fiscal accounts, while a deterioration of the current account balance was signaling an excess domestic expenditure problem. The accounting leads to a diagnostic of excess private expenditure, as shown by the left-hand side of Figure 9.8 (i.e. a widening gap between private investment and private savings). In a concomitant way, the real exchange rate followed an appreciating pace that could not be sustained without a significant productivity gain. A likely explanation could be that Mexico was in transition to a new and better stationary equilibrium associated with NAFTA negotiations. At the end of the day, Mexico became "addicted" to good news in order to postpone adjustment. When the good news ceased, the bust of the "tequila crisis" could not be avoided.

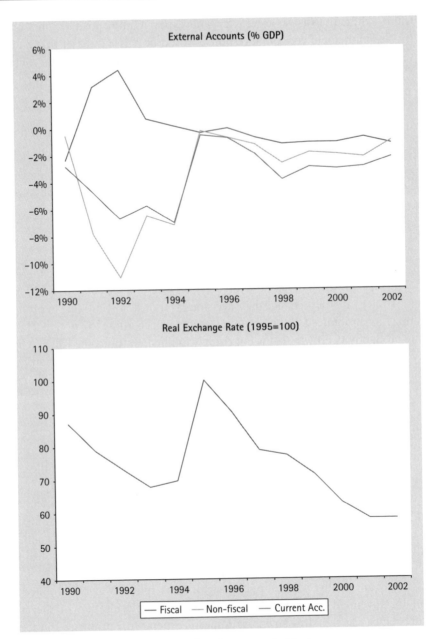

FIGURE 9.8 External accounts and the real exchange rate in Mexico

Source: Marfán (2005).

Chile showed the same symptoms in the late 1970s and the 1990s, along with the Southeast Asian economies (Thailand, Indonesia, the Philippines, Malaysia, and South Korea) that went into crisis in 1997: disciplined fiscal policy, increasing exchange rate misalignment, and current account deterioration. The UK in the late 1980s and, more recently, the US in the late 1990s and early 2000s are additional examples of the same combination in developed economies.

These cases have in common that private-sector exuberance was based on the idea of future prosperity. We have already mentioned the case of Mexico and the NAFTA negotiations. In the case of Chile 1979–82, over-optimism was based on the presumption that structural reforms would soon be reflected in higher rates of potential growth, as in Southeast Asia prior to the 1997 crisis, and in the UK in the late 1980s. The US over-optimism of the late 1990s was grounded in the mix of future benefits derived from technological breakthroughs and the credibility of the Treasury and Fed's authorities.

These cases also have in common that the cycle ended up either in economic recessions or in profound crises.

Marfán (2005) showed that monetary policy cannot perform a prudential strategy by means of conventional instruments. Although fiscal policy can theoretically tackle vulnerability by generating a sufficiently large fiscal surplus to attain a sustainable current account, the political economy of such a policy scheme is unsustainable. With an already disciplined fiscal policy, there is no way in which the authority can convince society to either increase taxes or cut government programs to prevent the side effects of over-optimism concerning future prospects. Marfán (2005) also shows that a tax on financial inflows, like the one Chile introduced in 1991, could theoretically tackle the vulnerability enhanced by private-sector exuberance as well. The transmission mechanism in this case would be that a strict monetary policy can reduce expenditure, while the tax on financial inflows would prevent further misalignment of the exchange rate. In short, two independent policy instruments can tackle two policy objectives. The costs of such a prudential device are immediate, while its benefits and efficacy are notional both ex-ante and ex-post, given the impossibility to construct a counterfactual scenario. A sufficiently wide consensus among economists on how to tackle excess private expenditure is still to be constructed. The Colombian experience, where prudential financial regulation is an intrinsic part of monetary policy, is more the exception than the rule.

We end this section in the same way that we started it. Monetary policy theory is constructed under the assumption that there exists a stationary equilibrium that monetary policy cannot affect. The multiplicity of possible stationary equilibria would need the introduction of prudential policy safeguards to prevent costly adjustments under likely pessimistic scenarios. This is a matter that has received attention, but the academic discussion is still polarized.[5] A wider consensus on the issue is still pending.[6]

---

[5] See Griffith-Jones and Ocampo with Ortiz (2009) for a recent review on the issue. See also Persaud (2009) for a contrasting view and Ostry et al. (2010) for a recent IMF staff perspective.

[6] The experience of the authors of this chapter is that central bank practitioners are open to practical solutions for macro-prudential action. In the 2007 Annual Conference of the Central Bank of Chile,

9.6 CONCLUSIONS AND CHALLENGES

The improvement in the monetary and exchange rate policies management since the late 1990s, along with a bolstering of external and fiscal accounts, has gone a long way towards making the region less vulnerable to global financial turmoil. The modest and seemingly transient growth impact of world recession in 2009, the lack of an unhinging of the inflation process, and a healthy adjustment in the exchange rates—all in spite of the major financial dislocations suffered by the world economy—is proof of this. However, challenges remain. This section will address a few of them.

The first challenge the region faces going forward is the consolidation of the commitment to price stability. Although important achievements have been made, stable and low inflation remains elusive. A high-inflation environment has persisted in Argentina and Venezuela, while the stickiness of price dynamics in Mexico and Brazil has prevented a sustained disinflation in spite of the growth slowdown. The volatility of inflation in Chile has also remained very high, moving from undesirably high levels to very low inflation rates. Consolidating past achievements and moving forwards will result in complementary effects in other dimensions, such as lower-liability dollarization and increased potency of countercyclical policies. Edwards (1998) for the case of Mexico and Chile, Gurtner (2004) for the case of Argentina, and Rocha (1997) for the case of Brazil have emphasized the dangers of implementing aggressive stabilizations in the absence of credible macroeconomic management. A consolidation of the policy credibility in the current circumstances of economic recovery will help reduce the costs of future stabilization efforts.

The second, related challenge is the management of booms led by private-sector exuberance that show simultaneously an increasing deficit of the balance of payments current account and a strengthening of the real exchange rate. A real appreciation with an increasing deficit of the current account can lead to inconsistencies if the steady state of the economy has not actually shifted, while leading authorities to complacency thanks to the muted inflationary response to the boom on account of the pressures towards appreciation. Although stories abound regarding the structural changes that validate this exuberance, policymakers need to be keenly aware of the risks of misidentifying the underlying processes. Mexico, in the run-up to the tequila crisis, or Chile in 1980–1 and, with less intensity, in 1998–9, are examples of these types of dynamics. The recent crisis has shown that this combination is not exclusive to emerging economies. Several

---

attended by worldwide central bankers and academicians, a related issue was discussed after one of those attending stated that if he saw a housing bubble, he would raise interest rates and explain. In an e-mail exchange of the authors of this chapter with Stanley Fischer, we asked him what he would do if he saw a bubble (not necessarily in housing prices). His answer was: "I would consider whether there are any regulatory measures that can deal with the problem, and if so use them; and in addition consider whether an increase in the interest rate would also be appropriate" (quoted with permission).

developed economies have suffered from this phenomenon, usually fueled by policy-makers' lack of concern about the possibility of inconsistency in the current account and asset prices. It has been shown that the realization that the underlying process has not changed can lead to hard landings and deep crises (Marfán et al. 2009).

The policy response to these types of dynamics is not by any means a resolved issue. The unresolved debate in the developed world regarding the way regulatory policy, monetary policy, and asset prices should interact is one example. The understanding of the drivers of global imbalances and real exchange rates, and the role of unorthodox instruments such as capital controls, is another. It is agreed, however, that proper regulation and supervision of the banking system is an important institutional insurance in the face of credit cycles, particularly if multiple equilibria and runs are possible (see Krugman 1979; Diamond and Dybvig 1983; Obstfeld 1986; 1996; Velasco 1996).

Thus, as Angeletos and Werning (2006) have pointed out, there are two approaches taken by economists when they analyze crisis. One is reflected in the literature of models of multiple equilibria, which present crises as sudden changes from one equilibrium to another. These changes are usually triggered by shifts in expectations or Keynesian animal spirits. In these models, coordination failures play a large role, and thus a framework of institutions and policies that help agents choose the most socially efficient equilibrium is key. Rules, such as flexibility in the exchange rate and inflation targeting, managed by an autonomous central bank, can contribute to solve this coordination problem. The other approach is based on models of fundamental misalignments and misguided policies, such as the traditional first-generation currency crises. In these cases too, making a clear choice on the exchange rate and monetary policy framework can go a long way towards minimizing the risk of inconsistent policies.

The challenges of exuberance and crisis are not easily handled by monetary policy. In practice and in some circumstances, asset prices do not seem to follow the fundamental developments of the variables that determine them. This creates tensions in aggregate demand and supply, making sometimes contradictory demands for the conduct of monetary policy. The role of additional instruments, such as foreign exchange intervention and capital controls, is again under debate, but unfortunately consensus on their relative importance, the ways of implementation, and their coordination with other standard policy instruments remains elusive.

The macroeconomic history of Latin America is not only about the loss and recovery of credibility during crises but also about the daily difficulties countries face in maintaining their institutional frameworks during tranquil times. Calderón and Schmidt-Hebbel (2003) and Calderón, Duncan, and Schmidt-Hebbel (2004) propose that credibility is a prerequisite for the adoption of anti-cyclical macroeconomic policies during crises. This credibility needs to be built up during normal times, where the temptation for excesses is larger and the macroeconomic constraints looser.

According to Céspedes and Soto (2005), the history of Chilean disinflation is one of a meticulous construction of credibility over two decades, during periods of high and slow growth. It is clear that the current management of monetary policy in several Latin American economies shows that this path is becoming more widely trodden. But challenges will remain, and how these are faced will only be known when the inevitable future bout of global financial turbulence affects the region. Maintaining sound fiscal management and a proper design of the institutional relationships between monetary and fiscal policies will remain critical, as well as a flexible and pragmatic approach to exchange rate flexibility.

References

ALESINA, A., and SUMMERS, L. (1993). 'Central Bank Independence and Macroeconomic Performance: Some Comparative Evidence', *Journal of Money, Credit and Banking* 25.2.

ANGELETOS, G. M., and WERNING, I. (2006). 'Crises and Prices: Information Aggregation, Multiplicity, and Volatility', *American Economic Review*, American Economic Association 96.5.

BARRO, R. J., and GORDON, D. B. (1983). 'Rules, Discretion and Reputation in a Model of Monetary Policy', *Journal of Monetary Economics* 12.1.

BAYOUMI, T., and EICHENGREEN, B. (1997). 'Ever Closer to Heaven? An Optimum-Currency-Area Index for European Countries', *European Economic Review* 41.3–5.

BORIO, C., and PACKER, F. (2004). 'Assessing New Perspectives on Country Risk', *BIS Quarterly Review*, December.

CALDERÓN, C., SCHMIDT-HEBBEL, K. (2003). 'Macroeconomic Policies and Performance in Latin America', *Journal of International Money and Finance* 22.7.

—— —— (2008). 'Choosing an Exchange Rate Regime', Working Paper No. 494, Central Bank of Chile, Santiago, Chile.

——. DUNCAN, R., and SCHMIDT-HEBBEL, K. (2004). 'Institutions and Cyclical Proper-ties of Macroeconomic Policies', Working Paper No. 285, Central Bank of Chile, Santiago, Chile.

CÉSPEDES, L. F., and SOTO, C. (2005). 'Credibility and Inflation Targeting in an Emerging Market: Lessons from the Chilean Experience', *International Finance* 8.3.

—— and VALDÉS, R. (2006). 'Autonomía de bancos centrales: la experiencia Chilena', *Revista de Economía Chilena* 9.1.

—— CHANG, R., and VELASCO, A. (2004). 'Balance Sheets and Exchange Rate Policy', *American Economic Review* 94.4.

CHRISTIANO, L. J., ILUT, C., MOTTO, R., and ROSTAGNO, M. (2007). 'Monetary Policy and Stock Market Boom–Bust Cycle', working paper, Northwestern University.

CORBO, V. (2002). 'Monetary Policy in Latin America in the 90s', Working Paper No. 78, Central Bank of Chile, Santiago, Chile.

COWAN, K., and DO, Q.-T. (2003). 'Financial Dollarization and Central Bank Credibility', Working Paper No. 3082, World Bank, Washington, DC.

CUKIERMAN, A. (2006). 'Central Bank Independence and Monetary Policymaking Institutions: Past, Present, and Future', Working Paper No. 360, Central Bank of Chile, Santiago, Chile.

—— WEBB, S., and NEYAPTI, B. (1992). 'Measuring the Independence of Central Banks and Its Effect on Policy Outcomes', *World Bank Economic Review* 6.3.

DE GREGORIO, J. (2009). 'La macroeconómia, los macroeconomistas y la crisis', *Latin American Journal of Economics* 46.134.

—— TOKMAN, A., and VALDÉS, R. (2005). 'Tipo de cambio flexible con metas de inflación en Chile: experiencia y temas de interés', Economic Policy Paper No. 14, Central Bank of Chile, Santiago, Chile.

DIAMOND, D., and DYBVIG, P. (1983). 'Bank Runs, Deposit Insurance and Liquidity', *Journal of Political Economy* 91.3.

DIANA, G., and SIDIROPOULOS, M. (2004). 'Central Bank Independence, Speed of Disinflation and the Sacrifice Ratio', *Open Economies Review* 15.4.

DUFFY, J., NIKITIN, M., and SMITH, R. T. (2004). 'Dollarization Traps', University of Alberta, mimeograph.

EDWARDS, S. (1998). 'Interest Rate Volatility, Capital Controls, and Contagion', NBER Working Paper No. 6756, Cambridge, Mass.

EICHENGREEN, B., and HAUSMANN, R. (1999). 'Exchange Rate Regimes and Financial Fragility', NBER Working Paper No. 7418, Cambridge, Mass.

GARCÍA, P. (2009). 'Financial Turmoil, Illiquidity and the Policy Response: the Case of Chile', Economic Policy Paper No. 19, Central Bank of Chile, Santiago, Chile.

GARCÍA-ESCRIBANO, M. (2010). 'Peru: Drivers of De-dollarization', IMF Working Paper 10/169, Washington, DC.

GRIFFITH-JONES, S., and OCAMPO, J. A., with ORTIZ, A. (2009). 'Building on Counter-Cyclical Consensus: A Policy Agenda', Prepared for IPD-FEPS Conference, Brussels, October.

GRILLI, V., MASCIANDARO, D., and TABELLINI, G. (1991). 'Political and Monetary Institutions and Public Financial Policies in the Industrial Countries', *Economic Policy* 6.13.

GURTNER, F. J. (2004). 'Why did Argentina's Currency Board Collapse?', *World Economy* 27.5.

HAMMOND, G. (2010). 'State of the Art of Inflation Targeting', Centre for Central Banking Studies Handbook No. 29, Bank of England, London.

HAUSSMAN, R., and POWELL, A. (1999). 'Dollarization: Issues of Implementation', IDB, mimeograph.

HERRERA, L. O., and VALDÉS, R. (2005). 'Dedollarization, Indexation and Nominalization: The Chilean Experience', *Journal of Policy Reform* 8.4.

HONOHAN, P. (2009). 'The Retreat of International Dollarization', *International Finance* 11.3.

IDB (Inter-American Development Bank) (2005). *Unlocking Credit: The Quest for Deep and Stable Bank Lending*, Washington, DC.

IMF (International Monetary Fund) (2004). 'Advancing Structural Reforms', *IMF World Economic and Financial Surveys*, Washington, DC: IMF.

—— 'Annual Report on Exchange Arrangements and Exchange Restrictions', various issues.

IZE, A., and LEVY-YEYATI, E. (2003). 'Financial Dollarization', *Journal of International Economics* 59.2.

IZQUIERDO, A., and TALVI, E. (2008). *All That Glitters May Not Be Gold: Assessing Latin America's Recent Macroeconomic Performance*, Washington, DC: IDB.

JÁCOME, L., and VÁSQUEZ, F. (2006). 'Is There Any Link between Legal Central Bank Independence and Inflation? Evidence from Latin America and the Caribbean', Paolo Baffi Centre Research Paper No. 2008-07, Milan.

KRUGMAN, P. (1979). 'A Model of Balance of Payments Crises', *Journal of Money, Credit and Banking* 11.3.

LAGO, R. (2009). 'Perú frente a la debacle: punto de partida, políticas y resultados', XVII Encuentro de Economistas BCRP, Lima.

LANDERRETCHE, O., and M. MARFÁN (2007). 'Gobernabilidad macro económica, una reflexión desde América Latina', mimeo, Corporación de Investigaciones Económicas para América Latina.

MARFÁN, M. (1986). 'La política fiscal macroeconómica', in R. Cortázar (ed.), *Políticas macr-oeconómicas: una perspectiva Latinoamericana*, Santiago, Chile: CIEPLAN.

—— (2005). 'Fiscal policy efficacy and private deficits: a macroeconomic approach', in J. A. Ocampo (ed.), *Beyond Reforms: Structural Dynamic and Macroeconomic Vulnerability*, Washington, DC, and Stanford, Calif.: World Bank and Stanford University Press.

—— MEDINA, J. P., and SOTO, C. (2009). 'Overoptimism, Boom–Bust Cycles and Monetary Policy in Small Open Economies', in K. Schmidt-Hebbel and C. E. Walsh (eds), *Monetary Policy under Uncertainty and Learning*, Santiago, Chile: Central Bank of Chile.

OBSTFELD, M. (1986). 'Speculative Attacks and the External Constraint in a Maximizing Model of the Balance of Payments', *Canadian Journal of Economics* 19.1.

—— (1996). 'Models of Currency Crisis with Self-Fulfilling Features', *European Economic Review* 40.3–5.

OCAMPO, J. A. (2007). 'The Macroeconomics of the Latin American Economic Boom', *CEPAL Review* 93.

OSTRY, J., et al. (2010). 'Capital Inflows: The Role of Controls', IMF Staff Position Note, Washington, DC.

PERSAUD, A. (2009). 'Macro-Prudential Regulation: Fixing Fundamental Market (and Regulatory) Failures', Crisis Response Note No. 6, World Bank, Washington, DC.

ROCHA, F. (1997). 'Long-Run Limits on the Brazilian Government Debt', *Revista Brasileira de Economia* 51.4.

SCHMIDT-HEBBEL, K. (2006). 'La gran transición de regímenes cambiarios y monetarios en América Latina', Economic Policy Paper No. 17, Central Bank of Chile, Santiago, Chile.

—— and WERNER, A. (2002). 'Inflation Targeting in Brazil, Chile, and Mexico: Performance, Credibility, and the Exchange Rate', Working Paper 171, Central Bank of Chile, Santiago.

VELASCO, A. (1996). 'When Are Fixed Exchange Rates Really Fixed?', NBER Working Paper No. 5842, Cambridge, Mass.

CHAPTER 10

DOMESTIC FINANCIAL DEVELOPMENT IN LATIN AMERICA

JOSÉ MARÍA FANELLI

10.1 INTRODUCTION[1]

In two seminal books, McKinnon (1973) and Shaw (1973) called attention to the linkages between financial development and economic growth. According to these authors, the lack of financial deepening harms growth because it discourages savings and distorts investment allocation. They attributed the lack of financial deepening to financial "repression" originating in government intervention in the form of government-determined interest rates and credit allocation, as well as a strict control of the capital account. The policy implication of this diagnosis was clear: "liberalize" the economy from financial repression. Although deregulation would likely cause interest rates to increase, growth would accelerate hand in hand with higher savings and the productivity gains that better investment allocation would bring about.

Given the low financial deepening in Latin America (LA) in the 1970s, these ideas were very influential, and contributed to placing financial development on the post-Bretton Woods policy agenda. The implementation of the liberalization agenda, however, was far more difficult than had been expected. The first liberalization attempts in the Southern Cone of Latin America in the late 1970s resulted in financial crises and the collapse of investment and output (Fanelli and Frenkel 1993; Fanelli and Medhora 1998). The advocates of liberalization, nonetheless, diagnosed that the failures were caused by an incorrect sequencing of policies rather than by theoretical flaws, and deemed it critical that macroeconomic stability be secured before liberalizing, and that

[1] The author is grateful to Ramiro Albrieu for research assistance and extensive discussions on the topics of this chapter.

deregulation of the domestic financial system precede the decontrolling of the capital account (McKinnon 1991).

In light of the difficulties, the theoretical foundations of financial liberalization policies were put under severe scrutiny. Díaz Alejandro (1985) provocatively entitled a paper assessing the liberalization experiences "Good-Bye Financial Repression, Hello Financial Crash." Using new research results about the role of information in economics and finance, other researchers pointed out that the state has an important function in financial markets (see Stiglitz 1994).

Despite the theoretical and practical problems, domestic financial systems and the capital account continued to be deregulated into the 1990s. Two major factors fostered the process: the increasing globalization of finance—the Brady Plan played a critical role in creating a liquid market for LA bonds—and the intellectual and political influence of the Washington Consensus.

Although some cases were successful, such as Chile's implementation of stricter regulations and supervision in the 1980s, the results of the financial (and other structural) reforms in the 1990s contributed weakly to growth and financial development (see de la Torre, Gozzi, and Schmukler 2006). The largest economies in the region experienced deep financial stress, most notably Mexico (1994) and Argentina (2002), or severe capital account reversals (e.g. Brazil, 1998). Not even successful reformers escaped the risk of crises: in 2003 the Dominican Republic, which had been as successful as Chile after implementing structural reforms in the 1990s, suffered a "classic" LA financial crisis. Ecuador, in turn, had to abandon its domestic currency after suffering a financial collapse.

In fact, severe financial disequilibria became so pervasive in Latin America—and other emerging economies—that the specialized researchers coined a new set of terms: "contagion," "sudden stop," "twin crises," "original sin," and "fear of floating." In essence, these phenomena were manifestations of the old, unsolved, liberalization/sequencing/domestic financial development problems under different circumstances and regions. To be sure, knowledge about these phenomena has improved, but we lack a consistent, unified analytical framework to analyze them and identify policies that could promote domestic financial deepening or, at least, secure financial stability. In light of this, it is not surprising that at the beginning of the 2000s, some researchers perceived "reform fatigue" in LA (Lora et al. 2003; Fanelli 2007).

Reform fatigue gave way to policy pragmatism in the 2000s, and several countries in the region opted for a strategy of self-insurance (Medhora 2007; Ocampo 2007). The strategy has been instrumental in reducing the impact of the financial crises in advanced economies on the region. In contrast with the experience of the late 1990s, there were no financial crises in the region. Contagion, nonetheless, was far from absent. When financial turmoil deepened in the American economy and Europe in 2008, the region showed symptoms of a sudden stop.

Pragmatism and self-insurance may be a sensible response in a world with imperfect capital markets and a flawed international financial architecture. But LA is still in need of a strategy for domestic financial development, given that the factors that made it necessary in the past are still prevalent: the vast majority of the population is segregated from the formal financial system, and investment and entrepreneurial capacity is still credit-constrained (see de la Torre et al. 2006).

This brief reference to the Latin American experience suggests that the following three questions are central when assessing the role of domestic financial development in the region:

1. What are the specific linkages between growth and financial development?
2. What are the determinants of domestic financial development?
3. What is the relationship between domestic financial development, crises, and international financial integration?

Research concerning these three questions has been quite dynamic, although progress has not been uniform. A good deal of the effort has targeted the first question. The linkages between growth and finance are now much clearer from the theoretical point of view than they were when McKinnon and Shaw raised the question. What has become the standard view—which we will call "functional"—places market frictions at center stage and accounts for the growth–finance relationship in terms of the *functions* that financial intermediation performs. The role of finance is to reduce transaction, information, and enforcing costs, increasing the efficiency with which the economy fulfills a set of five fundamental financial functions: (i) the production of ex ante information about possible investments, (ii) the monitoring of investments and implementation of corporate governance, (iii) the trading, diversification, and management of risk, (iv) the mobilization and pooling of savings, and (v) the easing of the exchange of goods and services (Levine 2005; 2008). Concerning empirical evidence, the functional approach has mostly relied on econometric studies involving cross-country data. The studies demonstrated that there is a positive association between growth and financial development, although they faced two obstacles. First, the operationalization of concepts is difficult. The functional view defines financial development in terms of the functions that the financial system must perform, but the available indicators used in the regressions, such as private credit/GDP, do not directly measure such functions (Levine 2005). Second, it is difficult to identify the direction of causality (see Beck 2008). In an overall assessment of the research results, Levine (2005) concluded that it has been reasonably proved that countries with better functioning banks and securities markets grow faster.

The attainments of the functional approach with regard to question (2) are less encouraging. This is not a minor problem: it might be of little help to know that financial development boosts growth if it is unclear how to promote it. Levine (2005) points to a number of conceptual and empirical difficulties. One main conceptual obstacle is that financial development involves the analysis of the institutions that affect finance and the context (political, cultural, and geographical). In fact, these elements also play a role with respect to question (3): in certain contexts, financial transactions may give rise to financial instability and crisis episodes that may have deleterious effects on domestic financial development. The research concerning the problems associated with question (3), however, was not necessarily motivated by the issue of financial development. Neither did it follow the guidelines of a unified research agenda or conceptual framework. Indeed, the findings were generated by studies that focused on specific issues, such as the design of prudential regulations or the study of financial crises and sudden stops. Although important findings exist concerning, say, the interactions between micro regulations and systemic risk, or the effects of sudden stops on domestic financial stability, a deeper analysis of the implications for financial development is still pending. Indeed, one of the main purposes of the following sections is to elaborate on such implications.

The goal of this chapter is to discuss the problems of domestic financial development in Latin America. This means that I will focus on issues related with questions (2) and (3). Section 10.2 presents and analyzes a set of stylized facts concerning the Latin American financial system and its evolution during the "second globalization" period. Section 10.3 discusses the dynamics of financial development. I emphasize three issues: the role of crises and reforms as drivers of change; the links between liquidity generation and financial stability; and the coordination failures associated with low financial deepening. I conclude by analyzing the challenges associated with growth-friendly financial development, focusing on systemic factors, institution-building, and volatility.

10.2 STYLIZED FACTS ABOUT THE LATIN AMERICAN FINANCIAL SYSTEM

In this section I discuss a number of stylized facts about LA financial systems. I examine the size, structure, and changes in the regulatory framework, and focus on those aspects that are relevant to the two questions on financial development posed above.[2]

10.2.1 Size

The size (relative to GDP) of LA financial systems is significantly smaller in Latin America than in developed countries. This is true of all segments: the banking system and the stock and bond markets.

Private bank credit as a percentage of GDP in LA and the Caribbean is smaller than in OECD countries and other emerging regions, such as East Asia (see Table 10.1). This is true, as a rule, for the seven largest countries (LAC-7), with the exception of Chile, and for other smaller countries, with the exception of Panama, which is a dollarized international financial center. Nevertheless, banks are key suppliers of domestic financing

---

[2] I do not intend to present a full description of the region's financial system. For a thorough analysis of LA banking systems, see IDB (2005); for capital markets, Schmukler and de la Torre (2007); and for bond markets, Borenztein et al. (2008) and Jeanneau and Tovar (2008a; 2008b).

Table 10.1 Size of the financial system in Latin America (%)

	Credit to private sector/GDP[a]	Private bonds capitalization/ GDP[a]	Public bonds capitalization/ GDP[a]	Stock market capitalization/ GDP[a]	Credit volatility[b]
High-income countries					
OECD	66.8	17.3	23.8	124.3	15.4
Non-OECD	114.9	50.2	43.6	95.7	23.5
Developing countries					
Latin America and Caribbean	30.9	n.d.	n.d.	37.5	28.1
Largest countries (LAC-7)					
Argentina	10.9	7.6	27.6	33.3	32.4
Brazil	31.1	14.9	44.0	56.0	15.5
Chile	61.9	16.5	11.8	107.3	11.4
Colombia	30.9	0.5	31.2	38.1	13.7
Mexico	14.8	16.3	18.6	35.3	29.6
Peru	17.2	3.7	9.5	51.8	20.4
Venezuela	12.8	0.6	77.7	3.6	28.7
Other selected LA countries					
Dominican Republic	18.6	n.d.	n.d.	n.d.	11.7
Uruguay	22.5	n.d.	n.d.	0.6	40.2
Ecuador	22.1	n.d.	n.d.	8.9	11.9
Costa Rica	33.6	n.d.	n.d.	7.8	6.2
Guatemala	29.0	n.d.	n.d.	n.d.	17.4
Panama	76.7	n.d.	n.d.	31.9	11.7
El Salvador	41.3	n.d.	n.d.	24.6	21.7
East Asia and Pacific	39.7	17.4	29.7	49.4	25.5
Europe and Central Asia	30.1	n.d.	22.6	26.6	45.1
Middle East and North Africa	28.4	n.d.	n.d.	42.4	18.5
South Asia	31.1	0.9	29.6	31.9	19.5
Sub-Saharan Africa	16.2	14.3	28.8	38.6	21.3

[a] Year 2006. [b] Average 1995–2007.

Source: Beck et al. (2006) and WDI data.

because the markets for corporate bonds are thin and, although market capitalization is comparable to other developing regions, stock markets are not dynamic sources of investment financing. Note, however, that there are important disparities. The Chilean level of financial development stands out: market capitalization has grown substantially and is approaching the level corresponding to OECD countries. Brazil and Peru, in turn, show above-average market capitalization, although the level is well below the Chilean.

The high frequency of financial crises has unquestionably harmed financial development in LA. Argentina and Mexico are good examples (note the high volatility of the credit supply). The banking sectors of these two countries were severely hit by crises, and banks have not yet been able to rebuild the banking system's ability to generate an adequate supply of credit. The case of Mexico is striking for its low credit/GDP ratio because the crisis took place more than a decade ago and the Mexican government has been engaged in an active program to increase credit to business firms and households in recent years (Haber 2009). Argentina's post-crisis financial policies have been somewhat erratic, even though the financial position of both the private and the public sectors improved substantially. The counterpart of disintermediation in Argentina has been an increasing demand for foreign assets. The Argentine and Mexican post-crisis experiences suggest that, under certain circumstances, crises can induce path dependency.

10.2.2 Regulatory changes

The regulatory framework of the banking sector has been substantially reformed in the last two decades in line with the BIS standards and other best-practice guidelines pushed by the international financial institutions (IFIs). The process embraced the entire region and resulted in a Copernican change in the situation of financial repression that McKinnon had described in the 1970s. According to the IDB (2005), all LA countries claim to follow a Basel methodology and to have established capital requirements equal to or stricter than the 8% minimum. Likewise, on paper, supervisory powers are similar to those in developed and developing countries.

There are, however, a number of pending issues concerning the implementation of regulations and supervisory practices. First, differences exist between de jure and de facto supervisory powers. In practice, there still are problems of related lending, the lack of diversification, and delayed remedial actions. For example, flawed supervision was an important cause of the crisis in the Dominican Republic in the 2000s. Second, the IDB report finds that the average Latin American and Caribbean countries are compliant with only half of the 30 Basel Core Principles for Effective Banking Supervision. This impinges on the correct valuation of assets and on the appropriate treatment of non-performing loans and the banks' provisions for loan losses. Third, despite the frequent occurrence of aggregate financial stress, prudential regulations do not take into account, as a rule, systemic features, such as the degree of overall currency and maturity mismatches in the system. In addition, the treatment of lending to the sovereign has been a source of instability. In calculating capital requirements, government loans are typically given a zero risk weight. When negative shocks hit the economy, banks tend to increase the holdings of government debt, and this often results in the under-capitalization of banks, which are unable to face situations of stress, as was the case in Argentina in 2001.

The flaws in bank regulations and supervisory practices have played a central role in explaining some of the observed crises. However, as Ocampo (2003) forcefully argues, we should not overlook the fact that it was the deregulation of the capital account that played a role in the generation of crises. Capital inflows contribute to exacerbating credit booms, and in most cases crises are the result of poorly managed booms. In this regard, after evaluating the empirical evidence, Aizenman (2002) concludes that there is solid evidence that financial opening increases the chance of financial crises. Reinhart and Rogoff (2009) find that the frequency of banking crises increased after the break-up of the Bretton Woods system and after financial international capital account liberalization took root. Periods of high international capital mobility have repeatedly produced international banking crises. They also corroborate previous findings that systemic banking crises are typically preceded by asset price bubbles, large capital inflows, and credit booms. The evidence shown in their paper indicates that the LA performance after the 1980s is consistent with this fact. IDB (2005) and Calvo et al. (2008) emphasize the linkage between sudden stops and banking crises. According to IDB (2005), countries facing different macro fundamentals were hit at the same time in the LAC-7 by external shocks, and this was accompanied by a de-leveraging of domestic debt and a real depreciation of the currency. About 56% of sudden stops have materialized together with banking crises and this percentage is much higher in cases in which the country is dollarized or has a fixed exchange rate regime.

Two other important consequences of privatization and deregulation have been the increase in the participation of foreign banks and the reduction in the market share of public banks. Despite this, state-owned banks still play an important role in the region. Neither foreign nor public banks, however, have played their expected role. State-owned banks as well as foreign banks have faced difficulties in expanding credit or directing credit toward small firms or sectors, while foreign banks did not behave differently in times of crisis. Likewise, bank spreads tend to move in a pro-cyclical way. The IDB report highlights that public banks reduce borrowing costs due to lower funding costs, although they also have higher overhead costs. Another important fact is that public banks react less to macroeconomic shocks and public credit is less pro-cyclical (IDB 2005).

Development banks have undergone important transformations but are still important, as is the case in other developing regions, notably South Asia and Sub-Saharan Africa. ALIDE, the association of LA development banks, has some 120 members. There has been an increment in the number of banks that operate as second-tier institutions and an increasing emphasis on co-financing and the involvement of private agents. The largest bank operates in Brazil (BNDES), and the most important institutions are located in this country, Mexico, and Argentina. Development banks may have a critical role in market *creation* within a context in which deregulation has not been successful at generating a robust market for long-term credit, venture capital, and supplying services to small debtors (Calderón Alcas 2005).

Equity markets gained momentum in the 1990s thanks to privatizations, which increased the supply and fostered the demand for domestic shares while attracting a large amount of foreign investment. A consolidation process followed the first wave of the divestiture of public enterprises and many firms were acquired by foreign corporations, which in some cases de-listed the firm. Indeed, corporate issuers have tended to migrate to international financial centers, the main vehicle being the ADR (American Depositary Receipts). Another element that negatively influenced equity markets was the 1998 crisis and the subsequent fall in equity issuance.

In most recent years there has been a larger reliance on bond issuance by private firms. The size of private bond markets increased, especially in Mexico and Chile and also in Colombia and Brazil. The shift in favor of bond financing was favored by the demand for fixed-income by institutional investors, which have become more important along with the reform of the pension system. Derivatives markets, in turn, are thin and account for a tiny fraction of world markets. The largest markets are in Argentina, Mexico, and, particularly, Brazil—where liquidity is high. OTC transactions are important but are more opaque, and this harms the price revelation function of capital markets (see Schmukler and de la Torre 2007; Borensztein et al. 2008).

10.2.3 Banks and markets

Figures 10.1 and 10.2 illustrate a well-known fact: the supply of credit to the private sector and market capitalization as percentage of GDP are positively correlated with GDP per capita. The credit ratios corresponding to the LAC-7 economies fall below the ratio that would be predicted based on the region's per capita GDP, with the exception of Chile. The graph corresponding to stock market capitalization confirms that Chile leads the region followed by Brazil and Peru.

The public bonds/GDP ratio is comparable to the ratios observed in other regions. Although debt markets were geared toward international markets in the 1990s, in the 2000s the share of domestic public debt has risen and most domestic public debt is now in local currency or indexed to the CPI (Cowan et al. 2006). In addition, the maturity of domestic public debt has lengthened. Domestic public and corporate bond markets have developed further, notably in Brazil but also in Mexico, Colombia, and Chile. The access of SMEs to the bond market nonetheless remains highly restricted (see Schmukler and de la Torre 2007; Borenztein et al. 2008).

Using a cluster analysis, García Herrero et al. (2002) show that there are important disparities within LA and distinguish four different levels of development. Chile and Panama are in the most advanced cluster. Panama is a small dollarized economy. Chile, in contrast, has a domestic currency, conducts an independent monetary policy, and has instituted an inflation targeting regime. Financial depth in Chile is well above the region's average. With regard to the three largest LA economies, financial depth in Brazil is higher than in Mexico and Argentina, which lag behind. A good number of LA countries, in turn, are classified in the two least developed clusters (see García Herrero et al. 2002).

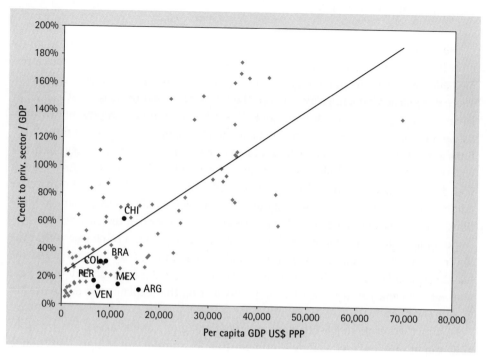

FIGURE 10.1 Credit/GDP ratio and per capita GDP

Source: Beck et al. (2006) and UN data.

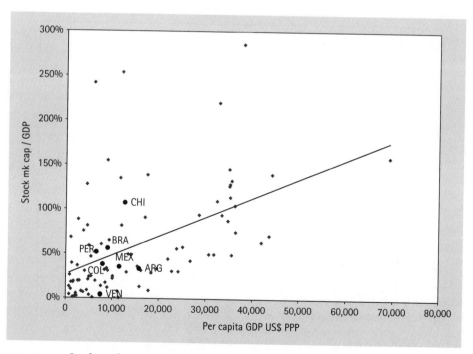

FIGURE 10.2 Stock market capitalization/GDP ratio and per capita GDP

Source: Beck et al. (2006) and UN data.

The LA financial system is often said to be bank-based. and in fact banks are relatively more important than in emerging Asia. However, given the small scale of financial intermediation and markets in the region, this classification may be a source of confusion. There is no structural similarity between the LA systems and the classical German or Japanese prototypes. The bank-based and market-based prototypes represent two alternative ways of performing the same financial functions, but in LA some of these functions are not fulfilled by intermediaries or markets and are internalized within firms, governments, and households, or are simply not fulfilled. The LA structures are not scaled-down versions of the full-scale bank-based prototype, and have not shown a clear tendency to develop and improve the way in which they fulfill the basic financial functions, with the exception of Chile. Figures 10.3 and 10.4 show that the observations corresponding to all segments of the LAC-7 financial systems tend to cluster within the lower left-hand rectangle below international averages; that is, both markets and the banking system are small. This is in line with the finding that it is financial development and not the bank-based vs. market-based distinction that explains the differences in growth (Levine 2002).

In sum, these facts suggest that a number of the region's financial systems are probably caught in a low financial development trap. It is important to note that though banks and markets may be substitutes at the micro level, important systemic complementarities exist between the different segments of the financial system,

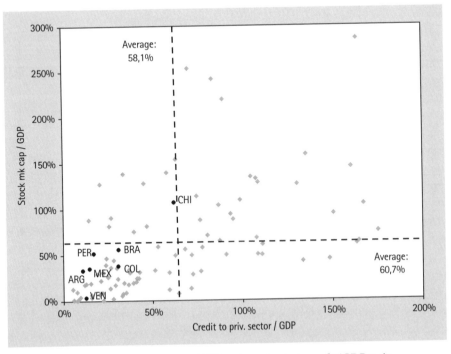

FIGURE 10.3 Stock market capitalization/GDP ratio and private credit/GDP ratio

Source: Beck et al. (2006).

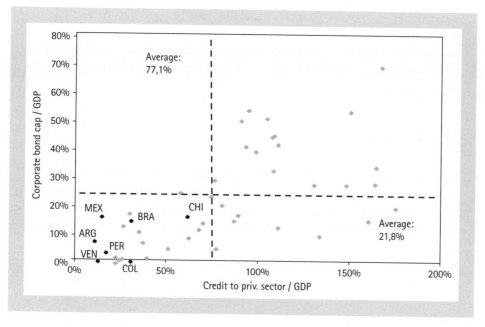

FIGURE 10.4 Corporate bonds/GDP ratio and private credit/GDP ratio

Source: Beck et al. (2006).

which cannot be exploited when both banks and markets are small. As is well known, systemic complementarities lead to externalities. Complementarities can be generated by many sources: Schmukler and de la Torre (2007) call attention to the fact that there is a bank at the end of any transaction in the capital markets, and additionally, banks frequently act as market makers; therefore, weak banks mean low tradability of securities and low market liquidity because there can be important agglomeration and networking effects. Deepthi et al. (2003) argue that mutual funds and other segments of capital markets are complementarities because they contribute to increasing transactions, and hence induce positive transaction externalities. In the next section, I will elaborate on the role that the structural features that we have identified may have in potentially generating a low financial development trap.

10.3 FINANCIAL STRUCTURE AND DYSFUNCTIONS

The stylized facts that we have discussed indicate that LA financial systems present important structural imbalances. In addition to hindering the system's performance of the five functions identified in the literature, these imbalances may also produce dysfunctionalities, such as financial instability. We believe that the analysis of the dysfunctions and the process of their creation may contribute to understanding the impediments to financial development and to improving the design of financial regulations. We will now analyze five features of LA financial systems that will be useful in clarifying these points.

10.3.1 Small size

The small size of the banking system makes it difficult to exploit scale economies, which are important in the business of financial intermediation. García Herrero et al. (2002) find evidence that bank efficiency—measured by the net interest margin—broadly goes hand in hand with bank size, and that the efficiency of the region does not rank well internationally.

When the size of the banking system is small, interest rate spreads (the gap between the interest rates charged on loans and the return on deposits) tend to be higher. According to the IDB (2005), spreads are effectively high in the region, as are real interest rates. Of course, high spreads and interest rates may also reflect market power, but García Herrero et al. (2002) and IDB (2005) find that there is still a low level of bank concentration compared with other regions of the world, despite bank consolidation and the entry of foreign banks. The degree of market power is nonetheless difficult to assess and highly idiosyncratic.[3] The work of Haber (2009) on Mexico is a good illustration. The charge for interest margins at the largest banks is no higher than their smaller competitors; however, they earn rents from market power through subtle oligopolistic pricing strategies. The banks charge fees and commissions above those that would prevail in a more competitive market to maintain accounts and process payments. To obtain a loan, the borrower must have an account at the bank that is extending the loan. He argues that an efficient way to increase credit is to facilitate market entry.

Beyond the static effects on the cost of credit, a small-scale banking system has long-run effects on financial development because, as was mentioned above, strategic complementarities exist between banks and markets. More specifically, the size of the banking system has a bearing on this because banks usually act as market makers and LA is no exception. Since banks have access to cheap liquidity sources of funds, they are usually tempted to act as market makers to profit from the high spreads that are typical of illiquid markets. They will also find it profitable to invest in information to profit from possible misalignments in security prices.[4] Indeed, banks enjoy a competitive advantage

[3] Other idiosyncratic variables that affect spreads and show a large degree of cross-country variation are the risk of defaults on loans, underlying regulations, and bank taxation. Soundness indicators, such as asset quality and risk-weighted capital nevertheless fare relatively well (García Herrero et al. 2002).
[4] Note that banks have incentives to invest in information despite information externalities because high market risk acts as a barrier to entry (which reduces the external effects). In any case, it is also true that over-the-counter operations explain a good part of the transactions in LA, and they are more opaque.

because of the combination of better information *and* access to cheap liquidity. However, the smaller the size of the banking system, the weaker market-making activity will be, and under these conditions, markets will be thinner and the existence of significant gaps between prices and fundamental values will be more probable. In this way, the small size of the banking sector becomes an obstacle to improving market liquidity in LA.

10.3.2 Market liquidity

We must take into account, nonetheless, that overall liquidity conditions depend not only on *market* liquidity but also on *funding* liquidity. Montes-Negret (2009) defines market liquidity as the ability to trade an asset at short notice, at low cost and with little impact on price; and funding liquidity as the ability of banks to meet their liabilities, or unwind or settle their positions as they come due.

The level of *market liquidity* in LA tends to be deficient. A number of structural features contribute to this fact. One main obstacle is the small size of security markets and the reduced value traded, which makes prices volatile and may give rise to huge increases in the bid–ask spread when uncertainty increases. Although stock market capitalization and value traded have increased since the 1980s and have substantially increased in the case of Brazil, value traded is still much lower than in East Asia, where value traded hovers around 100% of GDP. Another negative feature is that the market turnover ratio is not only low but highly unstable and pro-cyclical (see Table 10.2).

Trading in bond markets is higher, but is dominated by public sector debt and repo operations. In Brazil, for example, repo transactions exceed the value traded of the underlying assets, and the market is more liquid (Schmukler and de la Torre 2007). A second structural obstacle is related with the characteristics of investors, which do not help to increase the volume of transactions. Institutional investors are less important than in developed countries, although pension funds have helped to increase the size of the markets along with the privatization of social security. Chile has led this process. The effect of pension funds on liquidity, however, is lower because they privilege buy-and-hold strategies. Owing to regulations, their portfolio composition is biased in favor of the highest rated securities. Retail investors are not significant; a large proportion of the population is poor, and wealthy individuals have direct access to sophisticated portfolio managers from abroad. In addition, the mutual fund industry is small and access to capital markets is difficult for small savers (Deepthi et al. 2003). Some recent developments concerning internationalization and mergers and acquisitions constitute a third obstacle to the increase in market liquidity. Larger corporations are using ADRs more and more as vehicles to participate in international markets. As part of the trading activity has moved abroad, the trading activity in domestic markets tends to fall. This process has had the collateral benefit of improving corporate governance to the extent that good governance is a prerequisite to cross-listing the shares in global markets. But it has also contributed to deepening market segmentation: smaller firms can only access a domestic market in which value traded has weakened. The participation of domestic bond-issuers

Table 10.2 Stock market turnover ratios (%)

	1995	2002	2007
Argentina	12.24	0.91	9.85
Brazil	46.72	30.83	56.1
Chile	15.51	5.96	22.82
Colombia	7.83	2.37	13.04
Mexico	30.92	24	30.78
Peru	39.28	9.21	8.75
Venezuela	13.06	2.07	9.98

Source: Beck et al. (2006), updated May 2009.

in foreign bond markets has also grown, although the largest proportion of the instruments traded corresponds to government bonds. In sum, migration to international markets might increase segmentation because well-known firms have better access (Schmukler and de la Torre 2007).

10.3.3 Funding liquidity

Beyond their role concerning market liquidity, banks are key suppliers of funding liquidity to the rest of the system. As Tirole (2009) highlights, banks affect both types of liquidity as part of the process of liquidity and asset-liability management. One main obstacle for LA banks is that the average maturity of bank deposits tends to be short and money markets are limited—although there are exceptions concerning the latter, notably Brazil. It is no wonder, then, that banks privilege short-term lending as a way to control the degree of maturity mismatch between credit and deposits. Indeed, the low capacity to generate funding liquidity associated with the short-term maturity of deposits and credits is common within the LAC-7 group (see García Herrero et al. 2002; Tovar 2007). This harms the system's ability to generate liquidity, giving rise to potential aggregate liquidity problems.

The banks' decision not to generate higher funding liquidity because they believe that their own access to future funding liquidity may be difficult creates a low-funding-liquidity equilibrium in which both deposits and credits will be short-term and funding liquidity will be scarce. This is why a key indicator that financial development is effectively materializing is the lengthening of the term-to-maturity of deposits and lending. The increase in bonds' maturity is also a positive indicator. This has occurred in Chile and also in Mexico and Brazil (see Jeanneau and Tovar 2008a). The case of Chile, where bank credit and capital markets have grown alongside each other, also suggests that there are strong complementarities between improved funding and market liquidity.

10.3.4 Systemic risk

A low-liquidity-equilibrium financial system, in which both market and funding liquidity are low, is prone to induce sizable expectational errors and to bear a substantial amount of systemic risk. In effect, low market liquidity is associated with higher volatility and more frequent and significant misalignments between prices and fundamentals. Under these conditions, unmet expectations can easily push the agent from a speculative to a Ponzi situation. These risks create a demand for hedging instruments as well as for flexible access to funding liquidity to reshape the balance sheets after the occurrence of a shock. But markets and liquidity-generating intermediaries do not develop, or are very weak, in a low-liquidity equilibrium; consequently, liquidity squeezes and solvency problems are likely to be more frequent. This latter fact will probably increase systemic risk to the extent that payment failures may induce negative externalities. Tirole (2009) calls attention to the influence of cross-exposure in the financial system: if there is cross-exposure, a small shock to one institution or the economy may propagate quickly, generating contagion, panics, and aggregate liquidity shortages.

The central banks are in a privileged position to deal with aggregate liquidity and systemic risk to the extent that they have the instruments to help banks manage funding liquidity. The LA experience, however, suggests that their room to maneuver is very limited. For example, to ensure the liquidity of banks and debtors during the financial stress episodes of the 1980s, the central banks from a number of LA countries allocated rediscount loans to banks, but the associated increase in the money supply fueled inflation and destabilized the nominal anchor. Argentina, for example, suffered a hyperinflationary episode in the late 1980s, and four other countries experienced similar episodes. This means that the close link between aggregate liquidity and the stability of the economy's nominal anchor sets strict limits on the ability to allocate rediscount loans to illiquid or distressed banks. The central bank must preserve the value of the central bank money, which provides a generally accepted means of exchange and a means for the denomination and settlement of contracts. Deposit insurance mechanisms are alternatives for providing liquidity under stress. However, the experience in the region indicates that weak supervision can be a source of moral hazard and, therefore, of systemic risk.

Many countries in the region instituted inflation targeting regimes and have made significant progress in securing a credible anchor for nominal contracts. This is the case, for example, of Chile, Colombia, Peru, Brazil, and Mexico (see Chang 2007). If this effort is not accompanied by a framework to ensure banking stability, however, a problem of time inconsistency could arise. If the central bank does not act as a lender of last resort to control for inflation, market participants may expect banks to be directly or indirectly bailed out by the treasury and they may fear that the treasury will be unable to repay its debts. Reinhart and Rogoff (2009) highlight that past financial crises have resulted in large increases in the public debt and, frequently, in defaults. Hence, the central bank's low-inflation commitment may be time-inconsistent. To avoid this problem, the government must guarantee the sustainability of the public debt. This indicates that the ability of the central bank to generate aggregate liquidity during a period of financial stress, the monetary regime, and public debt sustainability are inextricably related because of the possibility of policy-dominance effects (Togo 2007).

Dollarization also has a bearing on the central bank's ability to deal with aggregate liquidity problems. If the country is fully dollarized, the central bank cannot act as lender of last resort. In those countries in which the banking system is dollarized and banks are exposed to exchange rate risks because they have a mismatch between foreign liabilities and domestic assets, the central bank will probably not generate excessive liquidity out of a "fear of floating": the authorities fear that if they let the currency float and there is a large depreciation, the banks might go bankrupt. This strategy typically results in high and volatile interest rates that may harm financial stability and the sustainability of the public debt, as Blanchard (2004) emphasized in analyzing the case of Brazil.

International markets can be a source of liquidity. However, abundant evidence shows that capital flows behave pro-cyclically. This fact has been intensively researched (see Ocampo 2003; Stiglitz and Ocampo 2008; Kose et al. 2009). For our discussion, it suffices to highlight that when domestic liquidity conditions worsen and foreign investors risk losing capital or having it frozen during a bankruptcy or public debt restructuring, they withdraw capital and unwind positions.

Finally, the institutions of the international financial architecture (IFA) could act as the "spare wheel" concerning liquidity generation. However, the resources that IFIs provided to counterbalance capital outflows and ease the credit crunch in the past did not suffice to significantly smooth aggregate fluctuations. More often than not, the conditionality attached to the funds did not help, either. In the context of the 2008 crisis, nonetheless, we can see some progress toward a more flexible approach. The IMF has approved changes in its lending framework, the most important being the creation of the Flexible Credit Line for crisis prevention and the "modernization" of the conditionality. Also highly relevant were the liquidity swap facilities that the Fed set up with the central banks of Brazil and Mexico as part of the anti-crisis efforts in 2008.

10.3.5 Crises

The factors that feed systemic risk also have a bearing on financial crisis. This is not surprising, since crises are systemic phenomena. Note that the crises that occurred in LA during the second globalization have been closely associated with capital flows. On the one hand, the seeds of financial collapses are typically planted during credit booms associated with surges in capital inflows. On the other, when the bust occurs, the belief that the government will monetize the debt or will fall into financial default triggers flight to quality episodes. Since quality is associated with foreign assets, episodes of financial stress usually give rise to currency runs and large currency depreciations. In analyzing the occurrence of "twin" banking and credit crises of the type that occurred in Mexico, Kaminsky and Reinhart (1999) find that problems in the banking sector typically precede a currency crisis, and that the currency crisis deepens the banking crisis, activating a vicious spiral. They also find that financial liberalization often precedes banking crises.

Crises in the region have other important characteristics that should be taken into account when analyzing dysfunctionalities and traps. First, they frequently embrace various segments of the financial system (see Tovar 2007). Laeven and Valencia (2008) identify different types: banking, currency, and sovereign debt. In total, they counted 124 banking crises and found that several countries experienced multiple crises. In the case of the LAC-7 countries it is possible to identify 14 banking crises, 22 currency crises, and 7 debt crises. The period 2003–7 is exceptionally good, given that there were no crises in LAC-7 countries.

Second, financial crises have multiple causes. Laeven and Valencia's (2008) dataset confirms previous findings. The causes may be unsustainable macroeconomic policies (current account deficits and unsustainable public debt), excessive credit booms, large capital inflows, and balance sheet fragilities, combined with policy paralysis due to a variety of political and economic constraints. Currency and maturity mismatches were a salient feature of many financial crises, while off-balance-sheet operations of the banking sector were prominent in others. In various instances the crises were triggered by depositor runs on banks. It was very frequently observed that systemically important financial institutions were in distress.

Third, financial crises affect the public sector balance sheet. Reinhart and Rogoff (2009) analyze the evidence about banking crises from a very long-run perspective, and find that banking crises weaken fiscal positions, with government revenues invariably contracting, and fiscal expenditures often expanding sharply. The fiscal burden of banking crisis extends far beyond the commonly cited cost of the bailouts (see Roubini 2008). Three years after a financial crisis, central government debt increased on average by about 86%. Indeed, a high incidence of global banking crises has historically been associated with a high incidence of sovereign defaults and the restructuring of external debt, although many now-advanced economies have graduated from a history of serial default. This is not the case for LA.

Fourth, financial crises may involve a large-scale redefinition of property rights. Fanelli (2008a) emphasizes this point for the case of emerging countries and, particularly, Latin America. Laeven and Valencia (2008) find that policy responses reallocate wealth toward banks and debtors and away from taxpayers to help restart productive investment. Aizenman (2002) argues that, on the darker side of globalization, financial crises increase the scope for conflicts, and that the key issue is not only the ultimate distribution of the burden of adjustment between the debtors and creditors but also the length of time it would take to settle the dispute. Fanelli (2008a) states that the conflicts involving property rights increase uncertainty and feed macroeconomic volatility, and that under such conditions, the functioning of institutions will worsen. This may give rise to a vicious circle because crises and distributional conflicts simultaneously harm and call for better regulations and conflict-management institutions. Fanelli (2008b) and Magendzo and Titelmann (2008) analyze the way in which Argentina (a failed reform) and Chile (a successful reform) faced this problem.

In sum, although it is true that progress has been made in creating markets, instruments, and institutions, as well as in managing monetary policy, the dysfunctionalities that remain are important. It seems sensible that any attempt at accounting for financial development in Latin America will have to take into account these facts.

10.4 CONCLUSIONS

Three questions stand out concerning LA financial development: first, can the financial system develop endogenously departing from the existent initial conditions, which include dysfunctional elements? Second, who/what are the drivers of change? Third, under what conditions do the changes necessary to release the pro-development forces lead to stable dynamics? The functional approach provides specific answers to the first two questions; but the answers to the third are far less clear-cut and so, therefore, are the policy and regulatory prescriptions.

The four boxes in Figure 10.5 summarize the logic of the functional approach to financial development.

The upper rectangle of Figure 10.5 shows the drivers of change according to the functional view. The drivers are associated with financial innovations that seek to minimize transaction costs and promote institutional change: technology, learning, market competition, and deregulation. Rajan (2005) argues that there is circular causation: technology helps spur deregulation, which in turn creates a larger market in which technologies can be utilized, creating further technological advances. Within this process, products offered initially by intermediaries will ultimately move to markets because markets are more efficient than intermediaries when the products have standardized terms, can serve a large number of customers, and are well-enough understood by transactors. All these changes will improve the financial functions listed in the right-hand rectangle of Figure 10.5. Furthermore, increased volume reduces marginal transaction costs, and in this way the process pushes the economy toward the theoretically limiting case of zero marginal transactions costs and dynamically complete markets. Market frictions appear at the center of Figure 10.5 because, according to Levine (2005; 2008), financial development occurs when financial instruments, markets, and intermediaries ameliorate—although they do not necessarily eliminate—the effects of information, enforcement, and transactions costs.

This view provides a rudimentary theory of institutional change. The basic intuition is that the particular institutions and organizational forms that arise within the financial system, at a given place and moment, represent an endogenous response to minimize the costs of transaction frictions and behavioral distortions in executing the financial functions common to every economy (Merton and Bodie 2005).

If the functional view about the change drivers and endogenous institutional change were correct, we should see an endogenous increase in the supply of securitized instruments, higher market liquidity, and increasing risk-absorbing capacity in the system after liberalization. Although some of these developments have been observed, there are important features of the LA experience that are difficult to account for in terms of this view.

First, with few exceptions, the size of the system and market liquidity did not increase substantially. Under these conditions, the process of financial deregulation has been prone to generate instability because of the difficulties to manage liquidity, solvency, and systemic risks. Large fluctuations in aggregate liquidity and boom–bust credit cycles associated with volatile capital flows were frequently observed. Beyond these effects on short-run stability, the long-run evolution of the overwhelming majority of the region's financial systems did not result in the weakening of negative structural features, such as the lack of scale, short-termism, and the exclusion of a good part of the population from financial markets. Some countries, however, have shown progress concerning de-dollarization and the lengthening of maturity (Jeanneau and Tovar 2008a).

Second, while deregulation was a driver of change in LA, the process differed substantially from the one envisaged by the functional theory. On the one hand, deregulation was not primarily pushed by private-sector-led endogenous innovations and technical change, but rather by conscious government efforts to promote financial development and adapt to exogenous changes in the global economy. On the other, crises have been a prime driver of changes in the LA financial structure, an more often than not, the changes have harmed rather than fostered financial development. The functional view considers that crises are part and parcel of the learning process, and hence of development; crises are generated by incidents of faulty engineering, whose consequences will be subsequently corrected as part of the learning process (Merton and Bodie 2005). The effects of errors, and therefore crises, are fully reversible. The cases of Argentina and Mexico indicate, however, that this is not the case in LA. Indeed, the two drivers of change, reforms and crises, have been closely intertwined: financial and capital-account liberalization often resulted in severe financial stress, while regulatory reforms were often triggered by crises.

These facts suggest that the functional approach has not paid enough attention to the role of dysfunctionalities in financial development, nor to the constraints posed by instability and a volatile environment on the government's ability to impose institutional change ("reforms"). This explains the difficulties in addressing the third question, concerning financial stability and the design of regulations. Figure 10.6 will be useful in briefly analyzing the policy implications of these conclusions.

On the basis of our earlier discussion, Figure 10.6 shows the relationships between structural features and dysfunctions. The four hexagons correspond to the structural features (thin markets, dollarization, etc.), while the dashed rectangles represent the associated dysfunctions (weak market liquidity, deficient supervision, and so on). The circles represent the rules of the game that impinge on the functioning of the financial system. They identify "nodes" for policy action. Since policy actions involve changes in laws and regulations, it is only natural to conclude that institutional change is inherent to financial development.

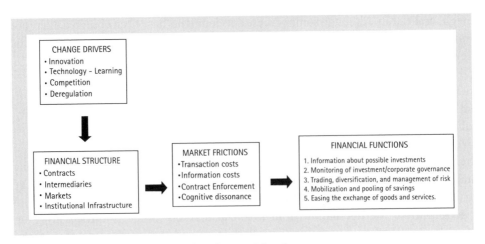

FIGURE 10.5 The functional approach to financial development

The "prudential regulations" node is critical for any attempt to increase financial deepening, improve liquidity (market and funding), and control undue mismatches (term and currency). We have seen that LA countries have made important efforts to improve the regulatory framework, but there is still much to be done, not only because of the important remaining structural weaknesses but also because LA will have to adapt to the regulatory reforms to be implemented in the rest of the world.

The evidence reviewed indicates that, in designing the prudential framework, it is crucial to consider both solvency and liquidity generation and mismatches. The LA countries have adopted the guidelines of Basel I, but it is now widely recognized that these regulations induce pro-cyclicality. Many practical questions nonetheless remain concerning what instruments would best be used to achieve regulatory counter-cyclicality (see Ocampo and Griffith-Jones 2009). Among the instruments that can be used are counter-cyclical capital requirements, specific provisions for latent risks of new lending (in line with the system implemented in Spain), counter-cyclical leverage, and limits on loan-to-collateral value ratios to reflect long-term trends rather than cyclical variations (although identifying the trend in LA can be daunting). To avoid crises, it is central to monitor currency and maturity mismatches (particularly for non-tradable sectors). In the case of LA, however, excessive complexity should be avoided. In some cases it may be preferable to use simpler instruments like limits on the growth of bank credit and liquidity requirements based on imbalances in the maturities of assets and liabilities in the banks' balance sheets. Nonetheless, there may be a trade-off between the goal of minimizing systemic risks and the goal of accelerating financial development. To strike a balance between the two goals is no easy task.

From our analysis it follows that the "macroeconomic regime" node deserves particular attention. It is necessary to ensure the coordination between monetary, fiscal, and financial policies to avoid dominance effects. The sustainability of public debt is vital to the credibility of prudential regulations and the central bank. To be sure, we are not overlooking the progress concerning the policies that have improved the authorities' ability to manage systemic risk. Inflation has fallen in the region, public debt sustainability has been strengthened, and the LA countries have invested heavily in self-insurance via reserve accumulation.

Indeed, it may be argued that self-insurance policies may harm domestic financial development. Self-insurance, supported by current account surpluses, means that a good part of domestic savings will be allocated to finance reserve accumulation rather than to investment, and this means less productivity-enhancing financial intermediation. This is why policy initiatives involving the IFA node can make a contribution. The design of better mechanisms to manage international liquidity in line with the "new" approach of the IMF as well as regional efforts—like the Chiang Mai Initiative and the FLAR—and swaps agreements between central banks can help reduce the costs of and incentives for self-insurance.

One important task for financial development policies is to design institutional mechanisms to internalize systemic effects. One key challenge is to exploit the strategic complementarities between banks and markets and create suitable conditions for intermediaries and institutions to create sufficient liquidity. In this regard the state and development banks have a natural role in promoting market-making activities and widening access to credit to those segments of the population that are currently excluded from financial markets.

Figure 10.6 is useful in emphasizing that financial-friendly initiatives must take into account the interactions between different segments of the legal and regulatory framework. Two facts are worth mentioning in light of the LA experience. First, there are several nodes of rules involved and these nodes have connections with other social and economic spheres. For example, there is a consensus in the literature that the quality of the legal and judicial framework has an important bearing on financial efficiency, and LA is no exception (IDB 2005). However, the financial policy initiatives that target this node should be designed taking into account that the legal framework must be functional to a diversity of social and political goals—from political stability to the protection of consumers. If this fact is overlooked, the space for reform will be overestimated. In Paraguay, for instance, some capital market reforms faced significant difficulties because they were based on legal norms pertaining to a different legal tradition.

Second, beyond extra-financial effects, the initiatives that target one specific node are likely to affect several parts of the financial system itself, and will thus call for suitable changes in the norms corresponding to other regulatory nodes. Ocampo (2003) emphasizes that macroeconomic policies, capital account, and prudential regulations must be coordinated. For example, changes in the prudential regulation node without taking into account pro-cyclical effects of capital adequacy can result in an increment in systemic risk. Likewise, isolated changes will invite regulatory arbitrage and may foster non-financial firms' leverage. Hence, prudential regulations must be complemented with work on the node of macroeconomic policies,

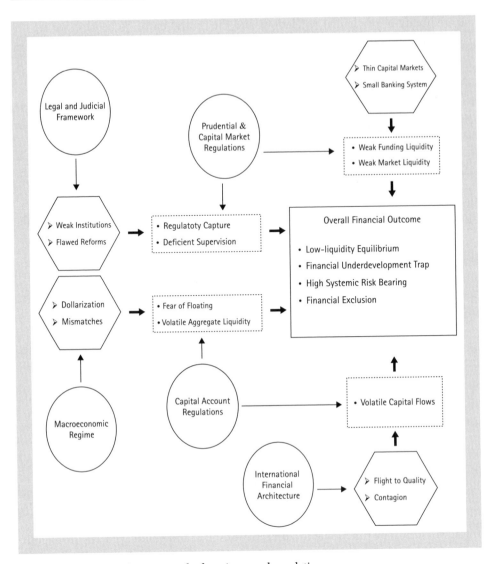

FIGURE 10.6 Financial structure, dysfunctions, and regulations

capital account regulations, and the IFA. The newly created Financial Stability Board can potentially play a key role in achieving a higher degree of consistency between the IFA and national prudential regulation frameworks. The shock-absorbing ability of the system can be substantially strengthened by giving more importance to these coordination problems.

In sum, this evidence suggests that financial development is not a matter of corner solutions. It seems that the institutional changes that are relevant to finance are neither fully endogenous nor fully exogenous. More specifically, the Chilean case—as well as the more recent developments in Brazil—indicates that it is possible to build the rules of the game "from within" the institutions that were inherited. Mexico and Argentina, on the other hand, illustrate the role of endogenous dysfunctionalities: the effects of the dysfunctionalities were stronger than the beneficial effects of reforms in terms of financial development. Furthermore, all these experiences indicate that institution-building is a process rather than an act. The distributive conflicts associated with crises affect the polity's ability to build the regulatory framework that is necessary to strengthen financial development (Fanelli 2008a). This said, we should not overlook that the theory of financial institution building is still rudimentary. Three critical points are: (a) how to build in a volatile environment; (b) how to build in the context of globalized financial markets; and (c) how to build if building capacity is low. Promoting financial deepening has much more to do with market *creation* than with market liberalization, and the task of market creation involves intensive institution-building.

REFERENCES

AIZENMAN, J. (2002). 'Financial Opening: Evidence and Policy Options', NBER Working Paper No. 8900, Cambridge, Mass.

BECK, T. (2008). 'The Econometrics of Finance and Growth', World Bank, mimeograph, Washington, DC.

—— DEMIRGUC-KUNT, A., and LEVINE, R. (2006). 'A New Database on Financial Development and Structure', World Bank Policy Research Working Paper, Washington, DC.

BLANCHARD, O. (2004). 'Fiscal Dominance and Inflation Targeting: Lessons from Brazil', NBER Working Paper No. 10389, Cambridge, Mass.

BORENSZTEIN, E., COWAN, K., EICHENGREEN, B., and PANIZZA, U. (2008). *Bond Markets In Latin America: On The Verge Of A Big Bang?* Cambridge, Mass.: MIT Press.

CALDERÓN ALCAS, R. (2005). *La banca de desarrollo en América Latina y el Caribe*, Santiago, Chile: CEPAL.

CALVO, G., IZQUIERDO, A., and MEJÍA, L. (2008). 'Systemic Sudden Stops: The Relevance of Balance-Sheet Effects and Financial Integration', NBER Working Paper No. 14406, Cambridge, Mass.

CHANG, R. (2007). 'Inflation Targeting, Reserves Accumulation, and Exchange Rate Management in Latin America', FLAR and Banco de la República de Colombia, mimeograph, Bogotá.

COWAN, K., LEVY-YEYATI, E., PANIZZA, U., and STURZENEGGER, F. (2006). 'Public Debt in the Americas', IDB, mimeograph, Washington, DC.

DEEPTHI, F., KLAPPER, L., SULLA, V., and VITTAS, D. (2003). 'The Global Growth of Mutual Funds', World Bank Policy Research Working Paper No. 3055, Washington, DC.

DE LA TORRE, A., GOZZI, J. C., and SCHMUKLER, S. L. (2006). 'Financial Development in Latin America: Big Emerging Issues, Limited Policy Answers', World Bank Policy Research Working Paper No. 3963, Washington, DC.

DÍAZ-ALEJANDRO, C. (1985). 'Good-Bye Financial Repression, Hello Financial Crash', *Journal of Development Economics* 19.1–2.

FANELLI, J. M. (ed.) (2007). *Understanding Market Reform in Latin America. Similar Reforms, Diverse Constituencies, Varied Results*, New York: Palgrave Macmillan.

FANELLI J. M. (ed.) (2008a). *Macroeconomic Volatility, Institutions, and Financial Architectures: The Developing World Experience*, New York: Palgrave Macmillan.

—— (2008b). 'Argentina', in Fanelli (2008a).

—— and FRENKEL, R. (1993). 'On Gradualism, Shock Treatment and Sequencing', in *International Monetary and Financial Issues for the 1990s: Research Papers for The Group of Twenty-Four*, vol. 2, New York: United Nations.

—— and MEDHORA, R. (eds) (1998). *Financial Liberalization in Developing Countries*, London: Macmillan.

GARCÍA HERRERO, A., et al. (2002). 'Latin American Financial Development in Perspective', Working Paper No. 0216, Banco de España, Madrid.

HABER, S. (2009). 'Why Banks Do Not Lend: the Mexican Financial System', in M. Walton and S. Levy (eds), *No Growth without Equity? Inequality, Interests, and Competition in Mexico*, Washington, DC: World Bank.

IDB (Inter-American Development Bank) (2005). *Unlocking Credit: The Quest for Deep and Stable Bank lending*, Baltimore: Johns Hopkins University Press.

JEANNEAU, S., and TOVAR, C. (2008a). 'Latin America's Local Currency Bond Market: An Overview', *BIS Papers* 36 (Department of Business, Innovation and Skills, London).

—— —— (2008b). 'Financial stability implications of local currency bond markets: an overview of the risks', *BIS Papers* 36 (Department of Business, Innovation and Skills, London).

KAMINSKY, G. L., and REINHART, C. M. (1999). 'The Twin Crises: The Causes of Banking and Balance-of-Payments Problems', *American Economic Review* 89.3.

KOSE, M. A., PRASAD, E. S., ROGOFF, K., and WEI, S. (2009). 'Financial Globalization and Economic Policies', IZA (Institute for the Study of Labor) Discussion Paper No. 4037.

LAEVEN, L., and VALENCIA, F. (2008). 'Systemic Banking Crises: A New Database', IMF Working Paper No. 08224, Washington, DC.

LEVINE, R. (2002). 'Bank-Based or Market-Based Financial Systems: Which is Better?' NBER Working Paper No. W9138, Cambridge, Mass.

—— (2005). 'Finance and Growth: Theory and Evidence', in P. Aghion and S. Durlauf (eds), *The Handbook of Economic Growth*, Amsterdam: Elsevier.

—— (2008). 'Finance, Growth, and the Poor', in *The Financial Development Report 2008*, World Economic Forum, Geneva.

LORA, E., PANIZZA, U., and QUISPE-AGNOLI, M. (2003). 'Reform Fatigue: Symptoms, Reasons, Implications', presented at Rethinking Structural Reform in Latin America, Sponsored by the Federal Reserve Bank of Atlanta and the IDB, Georgia, October.

MAGENDZO, I., and TITELMAN, D. (2008). 'Chile', in Fanelli (2008a).

McKINNON, R. I. (1973). *Money and Capital in Economic Development*, Washington, DC: Brookings Institution.

—— (1991). *The Order of Economic Liberalization: Financial Control in the Transition to a Market Economy*, Baltimore: Johns Hopkins University Press.

MEDHORA, R. (2007). 'The Uneven Build Up of Global Reserves', *World Economics* 8.4.

MERTON, R. C., and BODIE, Z. (2005). 'The Design of Financial Systems: Towards a Synthesis of Function and Structure', *Journal of Investment Management* 3.1.

MONTES-NEGRET, F. (2009). 'The Heavenly Liquidity Twin: The Increasing Importance of Liquidity Risk', World Bank Policy Research Working Paper No. 5139, Washington, DC.

OCAMPO, J. A. (2003). 'Capital-Account and Counter-cyclical Prudential Regulations in Developing Countries', in R. Ffrench-Davis and S. Griffith-Jones (eds), *From Capital Surges to Drought: Seeking Stability for Emerging Markets*, London: Palgrave Macillan.

—— (2007). 'The Macroeconomics of the Latin American Boom', *CEPAL Review* 93.

—— and GRIFFITH-JONES, S. (2009). 'Building on the Counter-cyclical Consensus: A Policy Agenda', presented at 'Toward Basel III?', Brussels, October 12.

RAJAN, R. (2005). 'Has Financial Development Made the World Riskier?', NBER Working Paper No. 11728, Cambridge, Mass.

REINHART, C., and ROGOFF, K. (2009). 'Banking Crises: An Equal Opportunity Menace', Centre for Economic Policy Research Discussion Paper No. 7131, London.

ROUBINI, N. (2008). 'Financial Crises, Financial Stability, and Reform: Supervision and Regulation of Financial Systems in a World of Financial Globalization', in *The World Economic Forum Financial Development Report 2008*.

SCHMUKLER, S., and DE LA TORRE, A. (2007). *Emerging Capital Markets and Globalization: The Latin American Experience*, Washington, DC: World Bank.

SHAW, E. (1973). *Financial Deepening in Economic Development*, New York: Oxford University Press.

STIGLITZ, JOSEPH E. (1994). 'The Role of the State in Financial Markets', in *Proceedings of the World Bank Annual Conference on Development Economics, 1993*, Washington, DC: World Bank.

—— and OCAMPO, J. A. (eds) (2008). *Capital Market Liberalization and Development*, New York: Oxford University Press.

TIROLE, J. (2009). 'Illiquidity and All Its Friends', presented at the 8th Annual BIS Conference, Basel, June 25–6.

TOGO, E. (2007). 'Coordinating Public Debt Management with Fiscal and Monetary Policies: An Analytical Framework', World Bank Policy Research Working Paper No. 4369, Washington, DC.

TOVAR, C. (2007). 'Banks and the Changing Nature of Risk in Latin America and the Caribbean', *BIS Papers* No. 33 (Department of Business, Innovation and Skills, London).

CHAPTER 11

....

FISCAL POLICY IN LATIN AMERICA

....

MAURICIO CÁRDENAS AND GUILLERMO PERRY

11.1 INTRODUCTION[1]

....

Fiscal policy is a broad subject. Entire volumes can be written about the performance of each one of its main components—public revenues, expenditures, and debt—in Latin America. The same can be said about fiscal policy in each of the countries of the region. Therefore, this chapter narrows the subject to a few tractable topics of special relevance and impact for overall economic development in the region.

Fiscal policy plays a central role in at least three key areas. First, the provision of public goods is determined by the capacity of the state to collect taxes and spend effectively and efficiently. Second, fiscal instruments can be used to engage in redistribution, by taxing some groups and targeting expenditures to others. Thirdly, fiscal policy can offset or amplify shocks that affect the business cycle. Although in theory fiscal policy should contribute to the delivery of public goods, redistribution, and macroeconomic stability, in practice this has not always been the case in Latin America. In fact, many analysts argue that the failure to achieve the goals of fiscal policy is an esential factor in why the region has performed poorly in terms of growth and equity.

We are aware that much of what we observe today in terms of fiscal policy outcomes has deep and fundamental determinants—such as the institutions inherited from colonial times—but we leave that for other chapters in this Handbook to discuss. Focusing on current issues, the chapter is organized around four topics where we present the key stylized facts that distinguish Latin America from other regions, and discuss the most compelling explanations provided in the analytical literature. We start with the broad topic of fiscal state capacity in Latin America. With the exception of a few countries, such

[1] The authors would like to thank Victor Saavedra for excellent research assistance and the editors of this volume for comments and suggestions.

as Brazil, low tax revenues have been a distinctive feature in Latin America. Of course, low fiscal capacity translates into inadequate provision of public goods and limited ability to engage in effective redistribution (Cárdenas 2010).

The second topic is the well-documented pro-cyclical nature of fiscal policy in Latin America. This is a critical issue because fiscal policies should allow countries to achieve macroeconomic stability, rather than exacerbating economic fluctuations. Although countercyclical fiscal policies were adopted in a few Latin American countries in response to the 2008–9 global recession, procyclical policies are still deeply ingrained in the region.

The third topic is fiscal decentralization. Despite very low tax revenue generation at the subnational level, government expenditures are increasingly decentralized in Latin America. Most countries have complex systems of fiscal transfers from the central government to subnational governments that often lead to overspending, low local tax efforts, local capture, and wide regional divergence in the quantity and quality of public service provision. But, here too, progress has been made in some countries which have been able to combine regional and local development with sound fiscal management.

The last section deals with sustainability issues. The main point is that very few countries in the region issue sovereign debt internationally rated as "investment grade." This means that there is a non-negligible risk of fiscal crises involving public debt defaults and rescheduling. In line with recent research on the topic, we argue that in addition to fiscal deficits—due to the lack of expenditure restraint and the low tax revenues—public debt *management* has been the cause of frequent fiscal crises. For example, a depreciation can lead to a fiscal crisis when the public debt is denominated in foreign currency, even if the fiscal deficit is small. The same can happen when much of the public debt is short-term and cannot be rolled over due to a change in financial markets. These are areas of high relevance, where progress has also been made: some countries are developing deeper markets for domestic currency-denominated long-term public debt. Furthermore, many countries have adopted fiscal responsibility laws that require governments to improve transparency and reveal contingencies in the balance sheet, reducing the likelihood of defaults.

11.2 Fiscal capacity in Latin America

11.2.1 Taxation

Taxation is a good starting point for the analysis of fiscal policies. To a large extent, tax revenues determine the capacity of governments to provide public goods and redistribute resources. The size of the state, the amount of redistribution from the rich to the poor—or from one region to another—and the allocation of resources across sectors and time are all fundamentally related to tax policy. Tax revenues also reflect previous decisions that shape the capacity of governments to collect taxes, and thus are very revealing of how economic policies are designed, approved, and implemented in a particular society. In general, actors that play key roles in the broader policymaking process tend to be also active players in the process of discussing, enacting, and implementing tax policies. For all these reasons, it is hard to think of a more relevant area of policy with ramifications over almost every aspect of the economy and society.

Although Latin America is far from homogeneous in this regard, tax revenues of central governments in the average country in the region were barely 14.7% of GDP in 2005, in contrast to 27.1% in developed countries. Using data from the IMF for 127 countries, and regressing tax revenues over GDP on a Latin American and Caribbean dummy, yields a highly significant coefficient of −8.8, implying that the region is nearly a full one standard deviation below the world's average. Of all the countries in the region, only Brazil can be considered to have a level of tax revenues comparable to that of the OECD countries. The composition of tax revenues is also quite different relative to developed counties: on average income taxes represent 12.4% of GDP in OECD countries and only 4.6% of GDP in Latin America. But the most remarkable feature of the tax system in Latin America is related to the role of personal income taxes: nearly 75% of the total income tax revenue is collected through personal income taxes in OECD countries, in contrast to only 39% in Latin America. With the exception of Brazil, Colombia, and Peru, virtually every country in the region collects less than 2% of GDP in personal income taxes (which are practically nonexistent in countries like Bolivia and Guatemala), compared to 9% of GDP in the average OECD country.

Although lower per capita incomes reduce the personal income tax base, in practice the number of exemptions and deductions has gone beyond what can be justified on economic grounds. For example, in Colombia individuals earning less than 3.5 times the national per capita income level are not subject to this tax (meaning that individuals with relatively high incomes do not pay income taxes). The corresponding figures are 2.6 times in Argentina and Peru, and 2 times in Brazil. The fact that the incomes of individuals at the very top end of the distribution are not taxed results in very low personal income tax revenues. Goni, López, and Servén (2008) argue that this feature explains why taxes play a very limited redistributive role in Latin America than in Europe.

Underscoring the fundamental forces that explain why fiscal state capacities in Latin America are relatively weak is a daunting task. Sokoloff and Zolt (2006) argue that, historically, tax policy has been a mechanism for the reproduction of inequality. Elites favor low vat tax collections (and more regressive taxes such as the sales and VAT taxes) as well as the private provision of education, health, and other services such as security. Limited access to these services—or outright exclusion—is one of the mechanisms explaining why economic and social inequality has been Latin America's most distinctive feature.

Although fiscal capacities remained unambiguously weak during most of the 20th century, the region has experienced a significant transformation in recent years. The wave of democratization, which has taken place since the late 1980s, has made political systems more pluralistic and inclusive. As a consequence of the greater degree of participation and representation, demands on the Latin American state have been extensive. Countries have tried to respond to those demands by raising tax revenues and increasing the coverage of basic services.

Table 11.1 shows how tax revenues as a percentage of GDP have performed in the region since 1990. While there is some disparity, the general point is that there has been an increase in tax revenues in most countries. Moreover, there is evidence of some convergence in tax efforts: countries with the greatest increases in tax revenues between 1990 and 2005 are precisely those with lower tax efforts in 1990. This is the case, for example, of Venezuela, Bolivia, Nicaragua, Colombia, and the Dominican Republic. Change has been lower (in percentage terms) in countries where tax revenues were already relatively high in 1990 (such as Uruguay and Brazil). Tax revenues fell between 1990 and 2005 in Mexico and Panama, providing two remarkable exceptions to this norm.

Tax revenues have increased in spite of globalization: every country in the region has faced a generalized reduction in tariffs that, on average, were slashed from 46% in 1985 to 12% in 1999 (the sharpest declines took place in earlier part of the 1990s). In addition to the reduction in tariffs, greater capital mobility forced countries to trim tax rates on

Table 11.1 Tax revenue as a percentage of GDP

	1990	1995	2000	2005	Absolute change 1990/2005
Brazil	20.2	20.6	23.3	25.5	5.3
Uruguay	14.6	14.6	15.2	19.7	5.1
Argentina	12.1	15.5	18.1	23.6	11.5
Chile	13.8	15.5	16.3	16.8	3.0
Honduras	14.7	16.3	16.5	16.9	2.2
Nicaragua	8.1	12.2	14.5	16.8	8.7
Panama	10.3	10.9	9.6	8.9	−1.4
Bolivia	7.0	10.6	12.3	17.8	10.8
Colombia	7.8	9.7	11.2	14.8	7.0
Peru	10.7	13.6	12.2	13.6	2.9
El Salvador	7.5	12.0	10.8	12.6	5.1
Paraguay	9.4	12.5	10.8	11.8	2.4
Costa Rica	10.8	11.9	13.3	13.6	2.8
Dominican Republic	8.2	10.7	12.5	14.1	5.9
Ecuador	7.8	7.1	10.2	10.3	2.5
Mexico	10.7	9.3	10.6	9.7	−1.0
Guatemala	7.6	8.9	10.6	11.2	3.6
Venezuela	3.5	8.2	8.6	11.6	8.1

Source: Cetrángolo and Gómez Sabaini (2007).

business and individuals (see Figure 11.1). The loss of revenues from the reduction of import tariffs has been largely offset with revenues from value added taxes (VAT), introduced in most countries between the mid-1980s and the mid-1990s, that now generate 37% of all tax revenues (equivalent to 5.5% of GDP). These changes imply that tax policy has been a very active area of reform. As documented in Lora and Cárdenas (2006), every country has undertaken 2.5 important tax reforms since 1990, on average, and 11 countries have overhauled their tax systems radically.

Brazil, Colombia, and Guatemala provide contrasting examples of the recent trends. Colombia has been a very active tax reformer, mainly as a result of the 1991 Constitution which mandated additional expenditures in multiple areas, including larger fiscal transfers to subnational governments. Much of the additional tax effort has been achieved by increasing the reliance on the VAT, through an increase in the tax rate from 10% to 16% during the 1990s but with limited success in terms of widening the tax base. As in other countries, a 0.2% temporary tax on financial transactions was adopted in 1998, and was made permanent in 2003 while the tax rate was raised to 0.4 percent. In the same vein, a transitory net wealth tax was established in 2002 to strengthen the defense forces. Congress extended this tax for three additional years in 2003, four years in 2006, and until 2014 in a law passed in 2009. The general message is that revenue needs have led to decisions to introduce new forms of taxation, rather than increasing

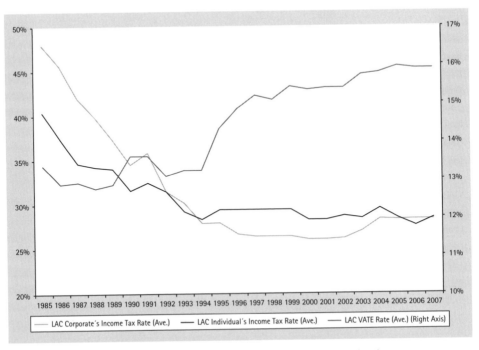

FIGURE 11.1 Tax rates: value-added tax, individual income tax, corporation income tax

Source: Price Waterhouse Cooper: individual taxes and corporation taxes. Worldwide summaries. Several years. ECLAC.

the effectiveness of the VAT or income taxes. Quite the contrary, tax policy has been used as a substitute for industrial policy by providing a generous treatment of investment and lowering effective rates of taxation through the use of special economic zones and other tax breaks. This experience sharply contrasts with that of Chile, where the tax system is horizontally more neutral, meaning that corporations face the same effective tax rate regardless of the size, location, economic sector, or any other characteristic.

The ability of the political system to deliver revenues through complex and improvised taxes is not specific to Colombia. In Brazil, tax revenues as a proportion of GDP have increased significantly over the last two decades and are now the highest in Latin America. Gross federal government tax revenues increased from 20.2% of GDP in 1990 to 25.5% in 2005. One third of the revues come from a version of the VAT, which is collected by the states. The power of the executive has been instrumental in strengthening the tax enforcement capabilities of the tax administration office. However, the federal government has not been able to implement comprehensive tax reform. In late 1997, and not for the first time, the government considered some proposals that were quite radical. The main proposal was to discard turnover and cascading taxes, as well as the state VAT taxes, and replace them with three new taxes: a consistent broad-based nationally managed VAT; a new federal excise tax on a small number of goods and services; and a local retail sales tax. Since then, governments have made unsuccessful efforts to arrive at a consensus about tax reform.

Tax revenues in Guatemala have traditionally been among the lowest in Latin America. The tax burden was 7.6% of GDP in 1990. Following the stabilization of the economy and the partial compliance with the peace accord, tax revenues increased to 11.2% of GDP in 2005. Much of the increase is attributable to the VAT, while efforts to raise income taxation have been systematically overturned by the Constitutional Court in response to legal action by the private sector. The effectiveness of the business sector in influencing policies essentially rests on the institutional weakness of the executive and the Guatemalan political parties.

In sum, tax revenues have increased in the majority of Latin American countries reflecting significant action in terms of tax reform. However, personal income taxation remains underdeveloped in contrast to progress with the VAT and some economically inefficient taxes (though effective in terms of tax collections) such as the financial transactions tax. Although politically difficult, increasing effective taxation on personal income is a crucial issue in Latin America's pending development agenda. The same applies to tax administration, which needs to be able to effectively audit a much larger number of taxpayers.

11.2.2 Expenditures

Although finding consistent and comparable measures of government expenditures is difficult, the general pattern is that central government outlays have increased

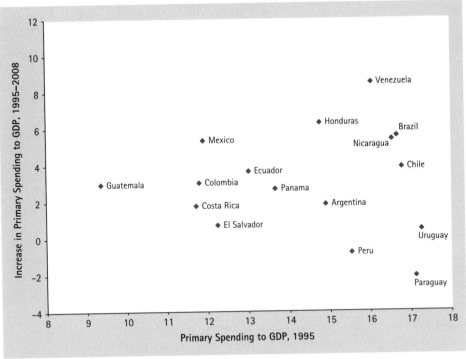

FIGURE 11.2 Latin America: initial primary spending levels (1995) and increases (1995–2008)

Source: ECLAC.

significantly in the majority of countries in the region. As shown in Figure 11.2, the countries with the largest increases since 1995 are Bolivia and Venezuela. This trend has been weaker in countries with fewer revenues from natural resources, such as those in Central America, resulting in more disparity in the size of the governments in the region than was the case a few decades ago. While most countries have moved in the direction of having larger governments, Peru and Paraguay have gone in the opposite direction.

While fiscal populism cannot be ruled out as an explanation in countries which have increased expenditures in unsustainable ways, greater expenditures to reduce poverty and exclusion have been a direct consequence of political democratization since the mid-1980s. Also, greater use of budget rigidities and entitlements, often embodied in constitutions, has made increases in expenditures hard to reverse posing problems for macroeconomic stabilization which we will discuss in the next section.

Expenditures in the social sectors (e.g. education, health, water, sanitation, housing subsidies, social security) have been the main force behind the increase in government spending. According to Figure 11.3, which includes social security, social expenditures increased in almost every country in the region between 1990 and 2004. However, there is great dispersion as social spending ranges from 6.1% of GDP in Guatemala to 19.6% of GDP in Uruguay.

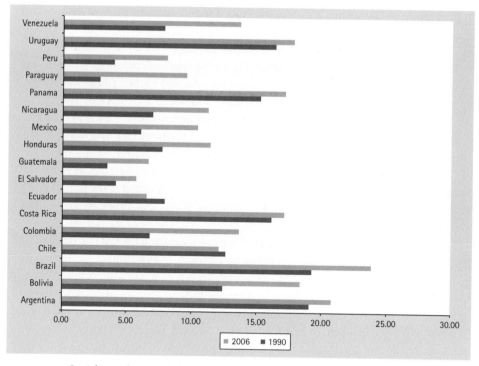

FIGURE 11.3 Social spending as a share of GDP

Source: ECLAC. When data for 2006 were missing, data from 2004–5 have been used.

These trends have made social spending in Latin America higher than in Emerging Asia (but still lower than in the OECD countries). One positive consequence has been the improvement in some social indicators. This is the case in primary and secondary enrollment rates and various measures of health outcomes such as access to clean water, immunization rates, and infant mortality rates. This is perhaps Latin America's major development achievement in recent decades.

But gaps relative to advanced countries remain high and, as documented elsewhere in this Handbook, Latin America continues to underperform in many aspects, including educational quality, repetition rates, and access to early age development programs. The very few Latin American countries that have participated in international standardized tests assessing educational quality in science and mathematics have tended to rank very low.

Despite increased social spending, poverty and inequality remain high, suggesting that social expenditures have been poorly targeted. Again, there are important differences: social expenditures are progressive in Chile, Costa Rica, and Uruguay, while very regressive in Bolivia, Peru, and Nicaragua (ECLAC 2006). But in general it is accurate to say that the distributive effect of this spending has been modest in most Latin American countries. Breceda, Rigolini, and Saavedra (2009) look at the distributional effects of social spending (separating pensions from spending in education, health, and direct transfers) and compare the results for Latin America to those of the UK and the US. According to their results, in their group of Latin American countries social spending to the poorest quintile corresponds to 92% of social spending to the richest quintile, against 233% for the UK. This means that it is often the better off that benefit the most from social expenditures.

The analysis also differs greatly depending on the types of spending. It is well established that a high proportion of outlays in pensions and higher education accrue to upper-income groups, while primary education and social assistance benefit the poor (de Ferranti et al. 2004; ECLAC 2006). Targeted social programs—such as conditional cash transfers—have overall improved the welfare of the poor (see World Bank 2009). However, spending on these and other social assistance programs remains low in terms of GDP and as a share of total social spending. In fact, in countries such as El Salvador, Honduras, Bolivia, Ecuador, and Guatemala, only a small fraction of the population has access to social protection, in contrast to Argentina, Chile, and Uruguay, where there is universal or near universal coverage.

Finally, greater social expenditures in Latin America during the last two decades have tended to crowd out expenditures in public infrastructure affecting longer-term output growth. According to Calderón, Easterly, and Serven (2002a; 2002b), infrastructure spending as a share of GDP has fallen in most Latin American countries since the mid-1980s for two reasons. First, privatization in the 1990s did not deliver the expected results in terms of private investment in infrastructure. Second, social expenditures have been constitutionally and legally protected, leaving investment in infrastructure as the more flexible and adaptable component of the budget. In other words, emphasis on the social sectors has reduced the ability of governments to invest in infrastructure, and the private sector has not been able to offset that trend.

Underinvestment in infrastructure has resulted in low public capital per person in Latin America compared with the fast-growing East Asian economies. According to the IMF (2004), this has lowered long-run GDP growth by an estimated one percentage point per year, but results vary from 3 percentage points in Argentina, Bolivia, and Brazil to 1.5–2 percentage points in Mexico, Chile, and Peru.

11.3 STABILIZATION

Latin America has traditionally exhibited high levels of output and consumption volatility, largely as a consequence of its high exposure to shocks to terms of trade, demand for exports, and capital flows.[2] Rather than mitigating these shocks, Latin American fiscal policies have been highly pro-cyclical, according to a large number of empirical studies.[3]

---

[2] See Perry (2009).
[3] Gavin and Perotti (1997), Mailhos and Sosa (2000), Kaminsky, Reinhart, and Végh (2004), Alesina and Tabellini (2005), Talvi and Végh (2005), Sturzenegger and Wernek (2006), Suescún (2007), Strawczynski and Zeira (2009), Ilzetski and Végh (2008).

In determining the degree of pro-cyclicality of fiscal policies, it is important to distinguish between the effect of automatic stabilizers (variations in fiscal balances that are directly due to the business cycle and exogenous shocks) and discretionary fiscal policies. Most available studies argue that the variation in real public expenditures (excluding debt service) is largely due to discretionary policies, as the region does not have major automatic expenditure stabilizers, such as broad unemployment insurance programs. In contrast, most of the variations in real fiscal revenues are automatic (determined by terms of trade volatility and the business cycle) because tax policy is rarely used as a discretionary countercyclical tool in the region, given that statutory tax changes require lengthy congressional approvals and their revenue consequences take place with important lags.

Available estimates of the procyclicality of public expenditures may suffer from endogeneity problems, as results may rather reflect reverse causality due to the expansionary effect of increases in public spending.[4] Ilzetski and Végh (2008) deal with the endogeneity problem with different methods (instrumental variables, Arellano-Bond GMM techniques, simultaneous equations, and VAR models) and find robust results indicating that causality runs both ways (i.e. that public expenditure decisions indeed behave strongly pro-cyclically in developing countries and that they also have significant expansionary effects). In other words, real public expenditures are significantly increased in good times, and decreased in bad times, and through this pro-cyclical behavior they do significantly augment the amplitude of the business cycle.[5]

Suescún (2007) estimates a "structural fiscal balance" by subtracting the effects of the business cycle and cycles in commodity prices on tax revenues. The resulting balance gives a good approximation of how pro-cyclical or countercyclical are discretionary fiscal policies. Focusing on the revenue side only, he finds that automatic stabilizers have a lower effect in Latin America as compared to OECD countries. This is a consequence of both low effective tax collections and low estimated income elasticities of tax revenues, which suggest deficiencies in design and administration of the tax system. Adjusted by the effects of automatic stabilizers, he further finds that most Latin American countries have run significant pro-cyclical discretionary fiscal policies in contrast with many, though not all, industrial countries (see Figure 11.4).

As a consequence of both these results, the overall net effect of fiscal balances is destabilizing in the region. Thus, surprisingly, countries with larger public sectors in Latin America tend to have more volatile economies, contrary to what happens among industrialized countries (see Figure 11.5). Of course, a complete analysis of macroeconomic instability has to include other dimensions, such as the magnitude of external shocks and the monetary and exchange rate frameworks.

[4] Exceptions include Ilzetski and Végh (2008).
[5] Ilzetski and Végh (2008) also find some evidence (not always robust) that public expenditures also behave procyclically in developed countries (in contrast with most previous estimates), though less so than in developing countries, and that their effect on the economic cycle is not significant.

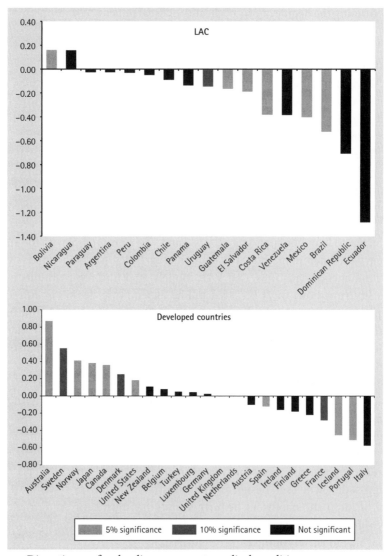

FIGURE 11.4 Discretionary fiscal policy response to cyclical conditions

Source: Suescún (2007).

Notes: A positive sign is countercyclical. The coefficient of the output gap in a regression with a cyclical adjusted primary balance (a proxy for discretionary policy) as the dependent variable.

In addition to augmenting, instead of mitigating, the effects of commodity price shocks and business cycles, the pro-cyclicality of fiscal policies in Latin America often has two other pernicious effects. First, it contributes to the previously mentioned bias against public investment in Latin America, especially during fiscal adjustment periods, which has led to severe lags in infrastructure investment. Indeed, boom periods normally lead to increases in both public investment and current expenditures. Later on, when governments are forced to cut expenditures for lack of financing during busts, such cuts fall basically on public investment, as reducing public wages or

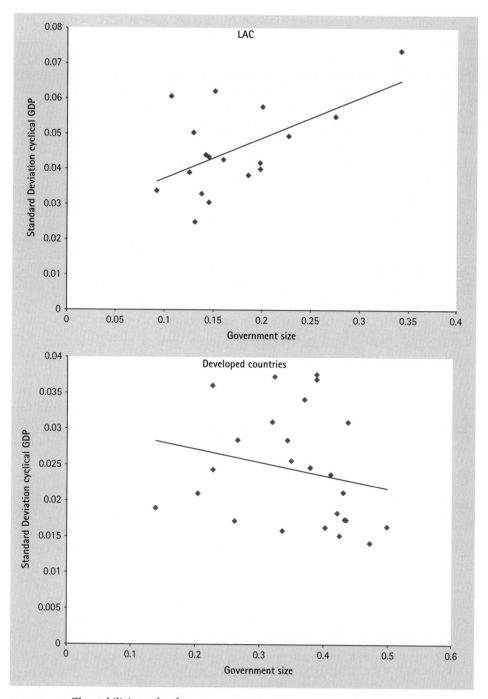

FIGURE 11.5 The stabilizing role of government size

Source: Suescún (2007).

firing public servants usually carry higher political costs. Such an effect of pro-cyclical fiscal policies has been documented in some recent studies.[6]

Second, pro-cyclical fiscal policies often lead to fiscal crises and default on public debt. This is either because the required expenditure cuts during recessions may become politically unviable or because actual cuts may deepen recessions and financial markets shut down as they respond procyclically. The latter situation was observed in 1999–2001, when Argentina experienced a protracted recession as a consequence of the strong real exchange rate appreciation (after the Euro and Real depreciations vis-à-vis the dollar to which the Argentinean peso was fixed). The government, facing severe financing constraints, undertook a sharp pro-cyclical contraction of public expenditures. This was seen by the markets as aggravating the recessionary forces, leading to perceptions of fiscal unsustainability in the short term and resulting in even higher spreads (contrary to what the authorities and the IMF expected).

Why are discretionary fiscal policies so procyclical in Latin America? Explanations have typically underscored either political incentives and/or the pro-cyclicality of financial markets. Most analysts of budgetary processes find that, unless there are strong institutional constraints, political incentives normally lead to greater spending during booms.[7] Such political incentives exist as long as voters and supporters value the immediate provision of additional goods and services (and campaign financiers value additional contracts), and do not fully understand or punish the potential future effects of such actions. Furthermore, governments may find difficult to impose austerity during a boom after a cut in expenditures during the previous bust. In addition, due to distributional concerns, some governments may find it politically hard to reduce public expenditures to compensate for booming private expenditures (see Marfán 2005). When a slowdown or recession arrives, revenues fall sharply and governments often find themselves without access to either credit or previously saved resources, so they have no option but to cut public expenditures.

The fact that governments normally see their access to credit reduced during slowdowns and recessions (and enhanced during booms) is usually attributed to an inherent pro-cyclicality of capital flows (see Figure 11.6) and, more generally, of financial markets.[8] It should be noted, however, that when governments act pro-cyclically in booms, increasing expenditures to unsustainable levels, it makes eminent sense for creditors not to finance deficits in busts, as doing so might lead to unsustainable debt levels and eventual defaults. In other words, why should creditors believe that next time governments will behave differently and limit expenditure growth in booms in order to repay debt that was incurred in busts? Even when a new government, facing a slowdown or recession, promises and intends to act countercyclically also in the next boom, such promises will not be credible, as there could be an intertemporal consistency problem: it would be in

---

[6]   See Perry, Servén, and Suescún (2008).

[7]   Tornell and Lane (1999), Talvi and Végh (2005), and Alesina and Tabellini (2005).

[8]   See Gavin and Perotti (1997), Prasad et al. (2003), Riascos and Végh (2003), Kaminsky, Reinhart, and Végh (2004), Mendoza and Oviedo (2006), Perry (2009).

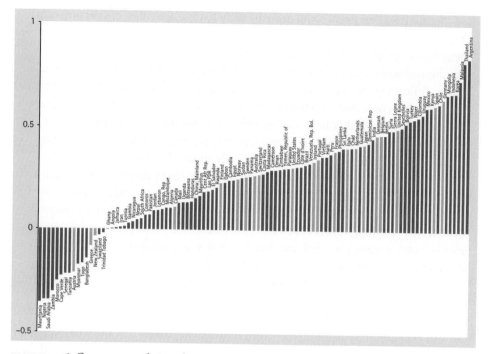

FIGURE 11.6 Country correlations between the cyclical components of net capital inflows and real GDP, 1960–2003

Source: Kamisky, Reinhart, and Végh (2004).

Notes: (i) Dark bars are OECD countries and light ones are non-OECD countries. (ii) The cyclical components have been estimated using the Hodrick–Prescott Filter. (iii) A positive correlation indicates pro-cyclical capital flows.

its interest, or in the next government's interest, to default on such a promise, unless the government can find a credible way of making commitments on its future actions.

If political incentives are behind the observed pro-cyclicality of fiscal policies in Latin America, as these hypotheses suggest, avoiding such an outcome would require institutional changes that constrain expenditure growth in good times. Several countries fiscally dependent on commodity revenues, for which the degree of pro-cyclicality of fiscal policies tends to be higher, have attempted in the past to establish "stabilization funds" that require compulsory savings when commodity prices reach a threshold, in an attempt to smooth public expenditures and limit their high procyclicality.[9] Early examples were the National Coffee Fund in Colombia (created in 1940) and Chile's Copper Stabilization Fund, operative since 1985. Venezuela, Colombia, and Ecuador have also enacted oil stabilization funds with similar purposes in different periods. The experience with such funds is mixed. In the case of Venezuela and Ecuador, governments were able to change the rules as soon as they found them too binding. In the case of Colombia,

---

[9] They have also been justified as attempting to mitigate abrupt variations in real exchange rates in order to reduce the risk of Dutch Disease effects.

the coffee fund was very successful until the early 1990, when coffee ceased to be a driver of the business cycle, and the oil fund was not successful in stabilizing government expenditures during the 1990s, when oil became Colombia's leading export, as overall expenditures increased, in spite of the savings in the oil fund, financed through increased debt. In Chile, the fund was instrumental in avoiding overspending during the copper price boom that coincided with the return to democracy, but it failed to allow the application of countercyclical policies during the 1999 slowdown, given that it did not have clear dis-saving rules, and that the attempt by the government to use part of its resources to increase expenditures was contested politically and by the markets.[10]

The design and enactment of the Chilean Structural Surplus Rule (SSR) came as an answer to these limitations. This rule requires estimating a "structural balance" by subtracting (or adding) revenues in excess (or deficit) of those estimated on the basis of potential GDP and long-term expected copper prices, and putting aside from the budget (or using) such excesses (or deficits). Further, it demands that such structural balance should equal a surplus of 0.5% of GDP (until recently 1% of GDP), to permit coverage of the central bank quasi-fiscal deficit arising from the high levels of debt incurred during the bank rescue of 1982. Recently, the SSR became a law providing clear saving and dis-saving rules, overcoming the problems experienced in 1999, and covering overall revenues and expenditures, avoiding the shortcomings encountered in the Colombian Oil Fund experience. Actually, Chile was the only Latin American country that maintained significant surpluses during the 2004–7 boom (see Table 11.2), and was able to implement a strongly countercyclical fiscal policy during the 2008–9 crisis.[11]

Table 11.2 Public balance as a percentage of GDP

Country	GDP Growth 2004	General government fiscal balance, 2004–7	Central government fiscal balance, 2004–7	Central government primary balance, 2003–7
Argentina	8.8	1.7	1	2.76
Brazil	4.5	−2.83	−2.56	2.34
Chile	5.3	5.92	5.8	6.58
Colombia	6.2	−0.43	−3.76	−0.33
Mexico	3.8	−0.05	−1.5	0
Perú	7.1	0.98	0.34	2.12
Venezuela	11.8	0.7	0.7	3.24

Source: IMF and ECLAC.

[10] See Perry and Leipziger (1999), Kumhof and Laxton (2009).
[11] The IMF (2009) estimates the Chilean fiscal stimulus package in 2.9% of GDP, while other packages in the region were smaller.

It is unclear to what extent other countries in the region could imitate this success. The SSR requires credible potential GDP, tax elasticities, and long-term copper prices estimates (through independent panels of experts). More importantly, it requires a broad political backing. Otherwise a government will be able to scrap it when it becomes binding (as happened in the Venezuelan and Ecuadorian cases, and more recently in Colombia in 2003, when the oil stabilization law was changed to allow the government additional spending during a boom period) without facing significant opposition and political costs.

In addition to perverse political economy incentives, IMF lending during crises, which has normally been conditioned to fiscal adjustment, has contributed to the pro-cyclical pattern in fiscal policies. More generally, the excessive focus of fiscal policy on current debt and balances has been another contributor to the pro-cyclicality of fiscal policies in Latin America and in the rest of the developing world. This has been to a large extent a consequence of the excessive focus of the IMF and the markets on such indicators, under the erroneous assumption that they are adequate indicators of intertemporal sustainability of fiscal policies. In fact they do not take into account either cyclical effects or intertemporal effects of public investment (thus reinforcing anti-investment biases.)[12] Thus, IMF and country programs, as well as fiscal responsibility laws promoted by the IMF in the early 2000s, usually set rigid short-term goals (in terms of deficit and debt levels), without correcting for cyclical effects of economic activity and commodity prices, leading to (or reinforcing the incentives in favor of) pro-cyclical fiscal policies. It has been suggested that the IMF should instead apply to developing countries a structural balance approach (as is already the case for developed countries), and help design and apply adequate rules, like the Chilean SSR.[13]

11.4 DECENTRALIZATION

The last decades of the 20th century witnessed a major move towards decentralization of political power and/or public expenditures in many if not most Latin American countries. This trend was associated to the return to democracy (Argentina, Brazil, and Chile) or the consolidation and deepening of democracy (Colombia, Bolivia, Mexico after the end of PRI hegemony, and Peru after Fujimori). Decentralization of political power and public expenditures is presently deeper in some federal countries (Argentina and Brazil), but it has become quite significant also in some unitary republics, through elections of governors and mayors and significant decentralization of public expenditures, as in the case of Colombia and Bolivia (see Figure 11.7).

---

[12] See Perry, Servén, and Suescún (2008).
[13] See ECLAC (1998).

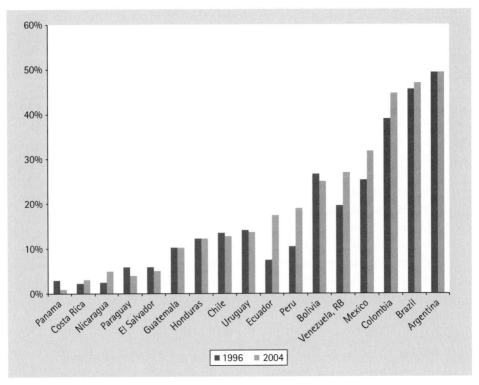

FIGURE 11.7 Subnational over general government's expenditure

Source: Daughters and Harper (2007).

With the exception of Brazil and Uruguay, and to a lesser extent Argentina and Bolivia, this trend was not accompanied by a significant reallocation of taxes to subnational entities but rather by increased transfers of federal or national government tax collections.[14] Still, in most countries there was an increase in autonomy in managing traditional subnational taxes (e.g. in Colombia municipalities can fix, within limits, the rates for property, industry and trade, and gasoline taxes).

It is generally expected that decentralization improves service delivery, by bringing authorities closer and more responsive to citizens needs. However, while some subnational governments—usually among the largest and with higher income per capita—have shown widely improved results, in many others growth of coverage has been dismal and quality has often suffered. For example, in Colombia there have been widely publicized successes, such as those of Bogotá and Medellin and the Department of Antioquia, along with many cases of major corruption and even capture of public funds by local politicians or even illegal groups.

Such ambivalent results have been a reflection of differences in local taxation, administrative capabilities, and local institutional and political development, which were not properly taken into account in the speed with which decentralization drives normally

---

[14] Burki, Perry, and Dillinger (1999), Dillinger, Perry, and Webb (2003).

took place. But they also reflect more generally the high dependence on poorly designed fiscal transfers from the center (which erode accountability links between authorities and citizens) and severe mismatches in the allocation of responsibilities and authority over resources (human or financial) in specific services.

The high dependence on transfers is partially a reflection of the fact that the major revenue-producing taxes can be more effectively administered centrally. Though in some mature federal countries, states effectively administer personal income taxes or VAT surtaxes, such experiences have been rare in Latin America. Only Brazil has at present a state-level VAT, which as mentioned above has given rise to repeated unsuccessful attempts to reform, as it is imposing severe economic efficiency costs according to most available studies.[15] Mexico also experimented with a decentralized state VAT in the 1980s and recentralized it afterwards. No Latin American country has experimented with decentralized income taxes. But even taxes that can be efficiently decentralized, such as property, transit (vehicle permits and taxes), and specific consumption levies (on fuels, alcoholic beverages, tobacco, etc.), are relatively underdeveloped in most countries in the region, in some cases due to rigid central law statutes and in others because of poor local incentives or political capture. There is a generalized opinion in favor of the need of strengthening regional and local taxation, but no clear agreement on how best to proceed.

The design of transfers to subnational governments has suffered from many drawbacks, arising partly from conflicting objectives. On the one hand, transfers should "equalize" capabilities among subnational entities. On the other, transfers should reflect local tax effort in order to avoid substituting local sources of funds. In practice, neither of these goals is achieved and the final design of the transfer system has been an outcome of complex political transactions. The richer and most powerful states or provinces usually oppose equalization effectively. At the other extreme, small states and municipalities, often get a fraction of transfers to be distributed evenly among jurisdictions, excessively benefiting low-density regions with low development capacities, thus stimulating inefficient subdivisions and creation of new provinces and municipalities in order to maximize received transfers.

Furthermore, earmarking has been pervasive—a practice which reflects the central government mistrust of subnational capabilities and which, though it effectively protects allocations to priority sectors (such as education and health), often results in excessive expenditure rigidities and inefficiencies. In addition, transfers have been initially set, in many cases, to respond to historical expenditures and existing capacities in specific services, with no incentives for improved performance. Changes towards allocations proportional to the population being served, and/or to be served (e.g. children actually in school or to be enrolled: the so called "capitation" criteria), as in Brazil and Colombia, have resulted in important increases in efficiency.[16] In some cases transfers have been too discretionary, limiting subnational entities, autonomy and planning capacity.

Automatic transfers linked to specific central revenues have often generated distortions (as governments favor those taxes that are not shared) and volatility, while at the

---

[15] Ebrill et al. (2002) and Bird and Gendron (2007).
[16] Bonet (2006), Lora (2007), and Townsend (2007).

same time contributing to the overall procyclicality of public expenditures. Problems encountered have led towards delinking automatic transfers from national revenue, as in the case of Colombia and Argentina.

The frequent allocation of a fraction of oil and mineral royalties to producing regions and localities deserve a special mention. Although a case could be made in favor of such a practice (compensating regions for negative externality effects), in practice royalties have exacerbated regional and local disparities, creating serious waste during revenue booms and painful fiscal adjustments during busts. This is an area for urgent reform in several countries, as the recent experience with Brazilian municipalities receiving oil royalties testifies.

Mismatches in the allocation of responsibilities and authority over resources have also often led to a serious problem of accountability and efficiency. Thus, for example, subnational entities have frequently been assigned responsibilities over primary and secondary education, but key decisions on teacher's wages, hiring, firing, allocation to schools, and/ or promotions have remained centralized, responding to pressures from powerful centralized unions. Leaving subnational entities with a theoretical responsibility, but without any meaningful control over the most important inputs for educational outcomes, cannot produce effective or efficient results. Further, in such a case neither the central government nor subnational governments can be held accountable. Further, decentralization of decisions rarely reaches the schools, where it has been found that it really matters.

Optimal decentralization of service provision depends on many factors that vary from one service to another: the presence of economies of scale and network effects (trunk roads, railroads and power transmission cannot be efficiently decentralized); the degree of heterogeneity of the service and the intensity of interactions with citizens (health and education require effective decentralization to hospitals and schools, though with proper accountability procedures); the degree of participation of private providers (it is normally inefficient to decentralize regulation of water supply provision); technological and administrative complexities and capabilities (poor and backward municipalities cannot be expected to organize and run efficient water supply companies). Getting the balance right requires some flexibility and capacity to adapt, which "one size fits all" constitutional and legal statutes rarely permit.

In addition to a wide variation in results in service delivery, rapid decentralization has often led to financial bankruptcies and debt defaults by subnational governments. Examples include infamous default episodes of major states and provinces in Brazil and Argentina which led countries to impose debt and expenditure controls to subnational agencies. Thus, at present most countries in the region require ex ante authorizations for subnational indebtedness (at least when debt/revenue indicators surpass certain thresholds) and some countries limit the ratio of current expenditures to revenues (as is the case in Colombia). As local governments often need access to long-term financing for major investment projects, getting the right balance between flexibility and precautionary controls is difficult. Some experiments, such as Mexico's required ratings, and Colombia's differential treatments according to the level of indebtedness (excessive, moderate, and low), combined with differential capital requirements through prudential banking regulation, seem to achieve a reasonable balance.

Concerns over public finances stability, and ambivalent results in service delivery, have often led (as indicated in the case of Colombia and Brazil) to significant revisions of original decentralization laws. Some observers interpret these episodes as required fine tunings to guarantee the long-term sustainability of an essentially irreversible long-term political decentralization process. Others see them as part of a "re-centralization" trend, associated in some countries with the presence of increasingly centralizing governments (e.g. Venezuela).

Finally, while there is wide agreement on the need to actively build capacities and promote transparency and accountability at regional and local levels, there is no clear agreement on how to proceed, and most initiatives have been rather timid, disintegrated, and eventually ineffective. A key institutional weakness of decentralization processes in Latin America has been the lack of a central agency that effectively supports capacity building at the local level. While this is a serious shortcoming, transparency and accountability at the local level can be partially supported from above: success ultimately depends on political competition, strong leadership, and the strength of the local civil society.

11.5 SUSTAINABILITY

This last section looks at the issue of public finance sustainability, mainly because the frequency of defaults and fiscal crises in Latin America deserves an explanation. In part, lack of public finance sustainability is the mirror image of the pervasiveness of fiscal deficits. In the previous sections we alluded to the causes of high fiscal deficits such as the existence of a narrow tax base, the tendency to overspend, the separation of taxation and expenditure decisions, and the limited expenditure flexibility.

But fiscal crises are not just a consequence of the accumulation of fiscal deficits. The Latin American experience shows that the composition and management of public debt matters a great deal. Questions related to whether public debt is issued in local or foreign currency, whether it is in the hands of external or internal creditors, or whether it has short or long-term maturities are critical in order to assess the fiscal vulnerability of a given country. It has been argued that these features are more relevant in explaining why countries experience severe fiscal crises than a cursory look at the level of public debt would imply.[17] In other words, the analysis of sustainability has to go beyond the causes of fiscal imbalances.

Sustainability is a somewhat elusive concept. However, most analysts would agree that the long run-fiscal position of a country is financially viable when the future flow of primary surpluses (adequately discounted) is high enough to cover the existing level of public debt. In more formal terms, for public debt to be sustainable the following condition has to be satisfied in the long run:

$$s = (r - g) d$$

[17] See IDB (2007).

where d is level of public debt as a proportion of GDP, r is the real interest rate, g is the economy's growth rate, and s is the government's primary surplus as a percentage of GDP. The equation provides a simple way of calculating the primary surplus that the government would need to generate to stabilize its debt (given the historical averages of the interest rate and GDP growth).

The estimated primary surplus can then be compared with its observed value. Countries are more likely to default on their debts when the primary surplus required to assure sustainability is much greater than its actual value. The IDB recently estimated these values using the average return on Latin America's debt between 1992 and 2004 (7.5%) and each country's own long-run growth rate. The results of this calculation indicate that the primary surpluses observed were too low given the value of public debt for a large number of countries in the region (see Figure 11.8).

But these measures of sustainability suffer some limitations. Contrary to what happens in the industrial countries, where the change in the stock of debt (Δd) is simply equal to the fiscal deficit plus a small accounting residual (called errors and omissions), in developing countries the unexplained residual can be quite large for at least three reasons. First, as mentioned above, a portion of public debt is denominated in foreign currency, so variations in the exchange rate have an impact. (The effect is more complex

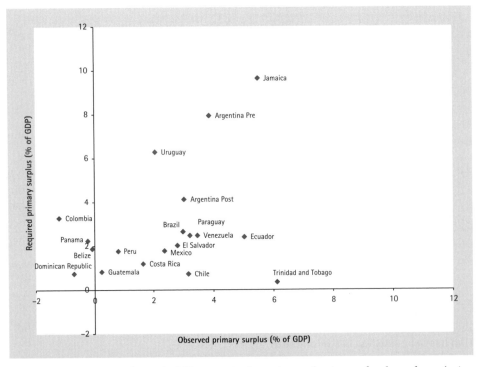

FIGURE 11.8 Measures of sustainability: required vs. observed primary fiscal surpluses (using median real interest rate from Latin Eurobond Index Yield)

Source: IDB (2007).

Notes: Heavily Indebted and Poor Countries (HIPC) (Bolivia, Honduras, and Nicaragua) are not included, given that the effective real interest rate is lower than the average GDP growth rate.

because a depreciation can reduce the deficit if the government is a net exporter.) Public debt can also be indexed to the inflation rate, which can change for reasons that in principle have no relation to the fiscal position of the country.

Second, increases in outstanding debt often result from government interventions that are not expected and, in some cases, not even reflected in the standard fiscal accounts. During banking crises—which provide the canonical example—governments issue large amounts of debt to rescue financial institutions. In fact, government exposure to financial-sector crises has been one of the most important sources of debt burdens. The cost of these hidden exposures is estimated to have been 19% of GDP in Mexico (1995–7), 14.5% of GDP in Argentina (1999–2002), and 8.5% of GDP in Brazil (1996–2000). This is also the case of contingent liabilities and the recognition of fiscal "skeletons" that have the power to explode public debt. The general point is that if governments do not really know the details about future contingencies, it is virtually impossible to determine what constitutes sustainable fiscal policy.

The third reason for unexplained changes in the stock of debt has to do with defaults and write-offs. As the recent experiences of Argentina and Ecuador suggest, this is not a minor issue in a region where defaults have been frequent. The unexplained residuals can sometimes be significantly large. For example, in Argentina public debt/GDP increased from 50% in 2001 to 140% in 2004 (mostly due to a currency depreciation), then fell to 80% in 2005 as a result of a write-off. But even after leaving aside extreme values like these (excluding the top and bottom 2% of the distribution of the unexplained residuals), the value of public debt in developing countries increases 3 percentage points of GDP faster on average per year than the fiscal deficit would predict.

Another key dimension from the viewpoint of risk is the debt's maturity structure. Naturally, shorter maturities imply a higher refinancing risk, exacerbating the transmission between overall macroeconomic instability and public finances. A sudden increase in the value of public debt imposes a much harder problem when it needs to be refinanced in the short run, in comparison to when amortizations are spread over a large number of years. There are many examples of this problem, such as Mexico's experience with the rollover of its short term public bonds (CETES) during the 1994 "tequila crisis."

One way of incorporating the uncertainty associated with variables such as interest rates, exchange rates, and the stock of debt is to compute the maximum value debt-to-GDP ratio that would be sustainable under stressed scenarios. This is what credit rating agencies do, as illustrated by the fact that a country's credit rating is not necessarily related the debt/gdp level (see Figure 11.9), but to measures of uncertainty such as the exposure associated with a currency mismatch, the volatility in the cyclical component of GDP and the maximum interest that allows debt to remain sustainable.

Governments in Latin America have been trying to reduce their dependence on external financing, and hence their exposure to external risks, by increasing the domestic component of public debt. In fact, on average in Latin America the share of domestic bonds in total public debt increased to 36% in 2000–4 from 26% in 1990–4. But there is large heterogeneity in this dimension. Differences in the size of the domestic market (measured by per capita GDP) seem to play a role (although it is not the only factor). According to Figure 11.10, domestic public debt is more than 50% of public debt in

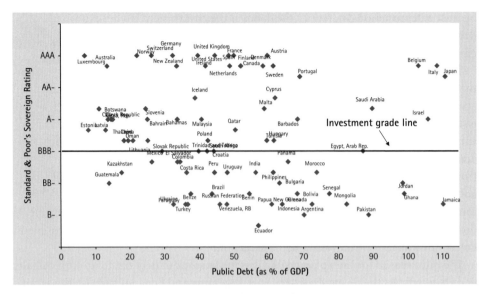

FIGURE 11.9 Public debt and sovereign rating (1995–2005)

Source: IDB (2007).

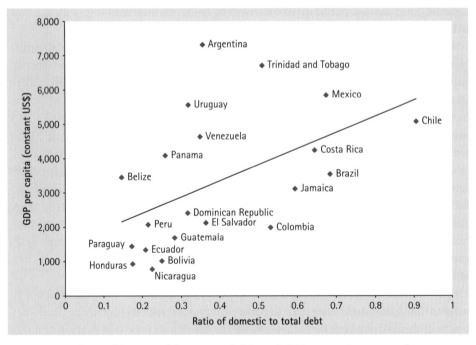

FIGURE 11.10 Share of domestic debt over total debt and GDP per capita, average for 2000–4

Source: IDB (2007).

counties like Brazil, Chile, and Costa Rica that have relatively high income per capita. But it is also high in Colombia, where reducing the debt's exposure to external shocks has been a clear policy goal.

11.6 FINAL REMARKS

Rather than summarizing the main messages of this chapter, we conclude with a positive note by highlighting the significant improvement in the quality of fiscal management in some key economies in the region during the last decade. Greater fiscal discipline brought down public debt levels, while debt-management policies resulted in the development of a market for long-term public debt denominated in domestic currency. Chile adopted, and other countries are in the process of adopting, well-defined fiscal rules that provide greater macroeconomic stability. As a result of this transformation, and in contrast to what happened during the crisis episode of the late 1990s, some countries were able to implement sizeable fiscal stimulus packages in response to the global recession of 2008–9 with a positive impact on growth and employment.

But progress should not lead to complacency. On the one hand, fiscal frameworks remain relatively weak. A large number of countries still lack the political consensus and the institutions necessary to support sound fiscal policies. On the other hand, more progress needs to be done in the other aspects of fiscal policy discussed in this chapter. Widening the tax bases, making the tax system simpler and more neutral, increasing tax revenues, and improving the efficiency of expenditures are pending issues in the fiscal reform agenda. The decentralization drive of expenditures show some successes but also many failures: further fine tuning is required to achieve the potential promises of fiscal decentralization while reducing potential adverse impacts in terms of increased regional inequality and local capture and waste. But few goals are as important as enhancing the redistributive capacity of fiscal policies. The last two decades have witnessed a stellar increase in social spending. What the evidence suggests is that much more has to be done in the design of these interventions (including better targeting) in order to reduce inequality in a significant and enduring way.

REFERENCES

ALESINA, A., and TABELLINI, G. (2005). 'Why is Fiscal Policy Often Procyclical?', *Journal of the European Economic Association* 6.5.

BIRD, R., and GENDRON, P. (2007). *VAT in Developing and Transitional Countries*, New York: Cambridge University Press.

BONET, J. (2006). 'Desequilibrios regionales en la política de descentralización en Colombia', Regional Working Paper No. 77, Banco de la República de Colombia, Bogotá.

BRAMI-CELENTANO, A. (2008). 'Fiscal Federalism, Democracy and Trade Integration: The Case of the Brazilian VAT', presented at the 8th Arnoldshain Seminar, São Paolo, March 31 – April 4.

BRECEDA, K., RIGOLINI, J., and SAAVEDRA, J. (2009). 'Latin America and the Social Contract: Patterns of Social Spending and Taxation', Population and Development Review 35.4.

BURKI, S., PERRY, G., and DILLINGER, W. (1999). Beyond the Center: Decentralizing the State, Washington, DC: World Bank.

CABALLERO, R., and KRISHNAMURTHY, A. (2005). 'Fiscal Policy and Financial Depth', NBER Working Paper No. 10532, Cambridge, Mass.

CALDERÓN, C., and SERVÉN, L. (2002). 'The Output Cost of Latin America's Infrastructure Gap', Working Paper No. 186, Central Bank of Chile, Santiago.

—— EASTERLY, W., and SERVÉN, L. (2002a). 'Infrastructure Compression and Public Sector Solvency in Latin America', Working Paper No. 187, Central Bank of Chile, Santiago.

—— —— —— (2002b). 'How Did Latin America's Infrastructure Fare in the Era of Macroeconomic Crisis?', Working Paper No. 185, Central Bank of Chile, Santiago.

CÁRDENAS, M. (2010). 'State Capacity in Latin America', Economia, 10.2: 1–45.

—— and LORA, E. (2007). 'La reforma de las instituciones fiscales en América Latina', in J. L. Machinea and N. Serra (eds), Visiones del desarrollo de América Latina CEPAL y Fundación CIDOB, Santiago, Chile: CEPAL.

CETRÁNGOLO, O., and GÓMEZ SABAINI, J. C. (2007). La tributación directa en América Latina y los desafíos de la imposición a la renta, Santiago, Chile: CEPAL.

CORTÉS, F., PERRY, G., and ROZO, S. (2008). Temas de economía política e inversión en infraestructura en América Latina, Caracas: Corporación Andina de Fomento.

DAUGHTERS, R., and HARPER, L. (2007). 'Fiscal and Political Decentralization Reforms', in E. Lora (ed.), The State of State Reform in Latin America, Washington, DC: Inter-American Development Bank.

DE FERRANTI, D., PERRY, G., FERREIRA, F., and WALTON, M. (2004). Inequality in Latin America: Breaking with History? Washington, DC: World Bank.

DILLINGER, W., PERRY, G., and WEBB, S. B. (2003). Can Fiscal Stability Coexist with Decentralization? The Case of LAC, Washington, DC: World Bank.

ECLAC (UN Economic Commission for Latin America and the Caribbean) (1998). The Fiscal Covenant, Santiago.

—— (2006). Social Panorama of the Americas, Santiago.

EBRILL, L., KEEN, M., BODIN, J., and SUMMERS, V. (2002). The Modern VAT, Washington, DC: IMF.

GAVIN, M., and PEROTTI, R. (1997). 'Fiscal Policy in Latin America', NBER Macroeconomics Annual 12.

—— HAUSMAN, R., and LEIDERMAN, L. (1995). The Macroeconmics of Capital Flows to Latin America: Experience and Policy Issues, Washington, DC: IDB.

—— —— PEROTTI, R., and TALVI, E. (1996). Managing Fiscal Policy in Latin America: Volatility, Procyclicality and limited Creditworthiness, Washington, DC: IDB.

GONI, E., LÓPEZ, H., and SERVÉN, L. (2008). 'Fiscal Redistribution and Income Inequality in Latin America', World Bank Policy Research Working Paper No. 4487, Washington, DC.

IDB (Inter-American Development Bank) (2007). *Living with Debt: How to Limit Risks of Sovereign Finance*, Economic and Social Progress Report (IPES), Washington, DC.

ILZETZKI, E., and VÉGH, C. (2008). 'Procyclical Fiscal Policy in Developing Countries: Truth or Fiction?', NBER Working Paper No. 14191, Cambridge, Mass.

IMF (2004). 'Stabilization and Reforms in Latin America: A Macroeconomic Perspective of the Experience Since the Early 1990s', Mimeo, Washington, DC.

KAMINSKY, G. L. REINHART, C. M., and VÉGH, C. A. (2004). *When It Rains, It Pours: Procyclical Capital Flows and Macroeconomic Policies*, Cambridge, Mass.: NBER.

KUMHOF, M., and LAXTON, D. (2009). 'Chile's Structural Fiscal Policy Rule: A Model Based Evaluation', IMF Working Paper No. 88, Washington, DC.

LANE, P., and TORNELL, A. (1998). 'Why Aren't Savings Rates in Latin America Procyclical?', *Journal of Development Economics* 57.1.

LORA, E. (2007). *The State of State Reform in Latin America*, Washington, DC: IDB.

——and CÁRDENAS, M. (2006). 'The Reform of Fiscal Institutions in Latin America', RES Working Paper No. 4457, Washington, DC: IDB.

MAILHOS, J., and SOSA, S. (2000). *El comportamiento cíclico de la política fiscal en Uruguay*, CERES, Banco Central de Uruguay, Montevideo.

MARFÁN, M. (2005). 'Fiscal Policy Efficacy and Private Deficits: A Macroeconomic Approach', in J. A. Ocampo (ed.), *Beyond Reforms: Structural Dynamics and Macroeconomic Vulnerability*, Palo Alto, Calif.: Stanford University Press and ECLAC.

MENDOZA, E., and OVIEDO, M. (2006). 'Fiscal Policy and Macroeconomic Uncertainty in Emerging Markets: The Tale of the Tormented Insurer', NBER Working Paper No. 12586, Cambridge, Mass.

PERRY, G. (2009). *Beyond Lending: How MDBs Can Help Developing Countries Reduce Volatility*, Washington, DC: Center for Global Development.

——and LEIPZIGER, D. (1999). *Chile: Recent Policy Lessons and Emerging Challenges*, Washington, DC: World Bank.

——and SERVÉN, L. (2003). *The Anatomy of a Multiple Crisis: Why Was Argentina Special and What Can We Learn From It?* Washington, DC: World Bank.

————and SUESCÚN, R. (2008). *Fiscal Policy, Stabilization and Growth: Prudence or Abstinence?* Washington, DC: International Bank for Reconstruction and Development.

PRASAD, E., ROGOFF, K., WEI, S.-J., and KOSE, M. A. (2003). 'Effects of Financial Globalization on Developing Countries: Some Empirical Evidence', IMF Occasional Paper No. 220, Washington, DC.

RIASCOS, A., and VÉGH, C. (2003). 'Procyclical Fiscal Policy in Developing Countries: The Role of Incomplete Markets', mimeograph, University of California, Los Angeles.

SCHICK, A. (1998). *A Contemporary Approach to Public Expenditure Management*, Washington, DC: World Bank.

SOKOLOFF, K., and ZOLT, E. (2006). 'Inequality and the Evolution of Institutions of Taxation: Evidence from the Economic History of the Americas', mimeograph, University of California, Los Angeles.

SUESCÚN, R. (2007). 'The Size and Effectiveness of Automatic Fiscal Stabilizers in Latin America', World Bank Policy Research Working Paper No. 4244, Washington, DC.

STRAWCZYNSKI, M., and ZEIRA, J. (2009). 'Cyclicality of Fiscal Policy: Permanent and Transitory Shocks', CEPR Discussion Paper No. 7271, London: Centre for Economic Policy Research.

STURZENEGGER, F., and WERNEK, R. (2006). 'Fiscal Federalism and Procyclical Spending: The Cases of Argentina and Brazil', *Economica* 52.1–2.

TALVI, E., and VÉGH, C. (2005). 'Tax Base Variability and Procyclical Fiscal Policy in Developing Countries', *Journal of Development Economics* 78.1.

TORNELL, A., and LANE, P. (1999). 'The Voracity Effect', *American Economic Review* 89.1.

TOWNSEND, J. (2007). *International Handbook of School Effectiveness and Improvement*, Dordrecht: Springer.

World Bank (2009). 'Conditional Cash Transfers: Reducing Present and Future Poverty', World Bank Policy Research Report, Washington, DC.

CHAPTER 12

FISCAL LEGITIMACY, INEQUALITIES, AND DEMOCRATIC CONSOLIDATION IN LATIN AMERICA

JAVIER SANTISO AND PABLO ZOIDO

12.1 THE NEW FISCAL TRANSITION IN LATIN AMERICA

Midway through the 2000s, the macroeconomic situation in Latin America has been generally analyzed as positive. Inflation control is perhaps one of the most important achievements in this respect. The return to sustained growth starting in 2003 is also worth noting. Since that time, the region has grown by an average of nearly 5% per year until the recession of the year 2009. Although still far from that of other emerging economies such as China and India, it is the best growth rate posted by the region in decades, and when the 2008 global crisis happened, Latin America weathered the storm surprisingly well, some countries like Chile or Peru even showing fiscal countercyclical capacities. The economic crisis has hit the entire world economy, with governments stepping in to rescue financial systems and kick-start economic growth. This adds up to a triumph for government fiscal policy, though this must be used audaciously. One of the unexpected by-products of the current global financial crisis is that it has placed fiscal policy back at the center of the public policy debate.

The fiscal comeback argument is, if anything, more relevant for emerging and developing economies. Consider the example of Latin America, where governments have taken enormous strides in putting their fiscal houses in order. The OECD's *Latin American Economic Outlook 2009* (OECD 2008) shows that, since the end of the debt crisis of the 1980s, governments have experienced exceptional revenues and fiscal policy showed in general a pro-cyclical pattern during the recent bonanza of the decade of the 2000s (see Ocampo 2009), before the global crisis of the years 2008–9. Fiscal deficits have fallen from 11% of public revenues in the 1970s and 1980s, to only 8% since 2000. The year-to-year volatility of taxes, spending and deficits—long a feature of fiscal policy-making in the region with harmful effects for economic performance—has likewise fallen: an index of deficit volatility calculated for the 2009 Outlook shows a fall of a third from 1990–4 to 2000–6, with Latin America standing just 6% above the volatility levels in OECD countries in the latter period.

This focus on growth (or avoiding recessions in the case of the 2008–9 global crisis and its Latin American developments), however, must not blind anyone to the other policy objectives for which fiscal tools are useful. Fiscal systems can provide the resources needed to carry out pro-growth investments and structural transformations, which are so essential for long-term growth in developing and emerging economies. Moreover, taxes and public spending can directly attack poverty and inequality, twin problems that continue to beset the region. In a word, fiscal policy has a powerful potential to promote development.

In recent years, the vast majority of Latin American countries have made a firm commitment to a pragmatic political economy combining market economy and trade and financial openness with social programs and policies (see Santiso 2006). The region has also made a political and institutional commitment to democracy. Never before have there been so many democracies in the region as a whole. The health of these market democracies is strong, as evidenced by the 2006–7 electoral cycle. Most of the elections were held in a fair and open environment. They were competitive, there was a handover in power, and the groups that lost gained a significant share of power and electoral support. They also took place without major financial disruption, contrary to previous cycles (Nieto and Santiso 2008; 2009).

Of all emerging regions, Latin America has made the firmest commitment to democracy and the market economy as fundamental values on which to build its development. In this regard, it shares the background values of OECD countries. A growing sense of pragmatism in the institutional reform and public policy processes is increasingly apparent in the region, in contrast to the messianic solutions of the past that wrought so much harm (Santiso 2006).

Yet much remains to be done: there is still ample room for macroeconomic improvement, not to mention the significant challenge of reducing poverty levels and inequality. At the same time, despite the success of the 2006–7 electoral cycle, which brought about changes in government and smooth transitions of power, democratic consolidation has a long road ahead. *Impossibilism* (Santiso 2006) is far from banished from the Latin American political scene. Peru and Mexico in 2006, where radical breakaway candidates made a strong showing in the latest elections, as well as the political collapse of Honduras in 2009, offer a clear warning in this respect. In the same line, the victories in the past of Chávez in Venezuela, Morales in Bolivia, or Correa in Ecuador are all wake-up calls for clear action against poverty and inequality in the region. An ongoing distrust of the institutions is in most cases due not only to acts of corruption or bad government, but also to the need for the macroeconomic optimism of the 2000s to translate into concrete economic and social reforms for the majority of citizens and the most vulnerable groups.

Seen in this light, the capacity of fiscal policy to do good is substantially unrealized in Latin America. Fiscal policy has done little or nothing to reduce vast income inequality in the region (see Bárcena and Serra 2009). While taxes and transfers reduce inequality by 19 Gini points in Europe, the difference is less than 2 Gini points in Latin America (the Gini index is a commonly used measure of income inequality that ranges from zero—everyone has the same income—to 100—one person has all the income). Clearly, more money is needed to meet development deficits: in Latin America, despite impressive economic performance in recent years, nearly 200 million people live in poverty. More money has been mobilized in the domestic economy to address these challenges, but the gap with OECD countries is still big. Government expenditures averaged 25% of GDP in Latin America versus 44% in OECD countries over the period 1990–2006. For a fiscal policy that serves development, however, quality matters as much as, if not more than, quantity, as we will argue in this chapter. The comparison between Latin American and OECD countries, which we will develop later in the first section, allows us to contrast the achievements and pending progress of the region, focusing in particular on the need for more progressive spending in the region—something achieved by OECD countries, even ones like Spain or Italy. This is a recurrent theme that the OECD Development Centre has been arguing since the very first LEOs (OECD's *Latin American Economic Outlook*) and also argued by the OECD in the case of Chile (which joined the organization in 2010), in its *Chile Economic Survey* of 2010 (OECD 2010).[1]

In this chapter, after a comparative analysis of OECD and Latin American fiscal magnitudes (section 12.2), we will stress this development dimension of fiscal policies, focusing in particular on the Latin American context (12.3 and 12.4). We develop later some conclusions and policy proposals (12.5).

12.2 FISCAL SYSTEMS IN LATIN AMERICA AND OECD COUNTRIES

This section briefly reviews the structure, characteristics, and performance of the fiscal system in Latin America. The period examined covers the transition from the boom years (for a macroeconomic overview of this period see Izquierdo and Talvi 2008). It provides a solid foundation for understanding where Latin America has been, and where it is going, in matters of fiscal performance. In this section we focus on both revenues

---

[1] For comments from key Latin American leaders on these pledges for more progressivity on fiscal spending, in order to boost fiscal legitimacy and democracy in the region, see the comment from former Chilean presidents Michèle Bachelet: http://www.youtube.com/watch?v=locL-LvwbX4; and Ricardo Lagos: http://www.youtube.com/watch?v=2cFEJOLyKCQ and also from Secretary General of the Organization of American States (OAS): http://www.youtube.com/watch?v=YH1XQv-KOPM

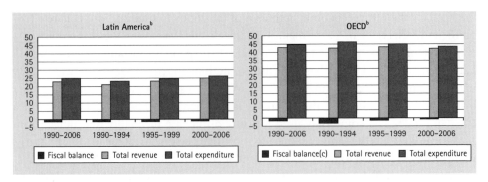

FIGURE 12.1 Fiscal policy measures, Latin American and OECD countries[a] (regional averages, % of GDP)

Source: OECD Development Centre calculations based on the ECLAC ILPES Public Finance database for Latin America, and OECD General Government Accounts data for OECD countries.

[a]OECD data refer to the consolidated general government sector. In Latin America, coverage corresponds to the non-financial public sector where possible, otherwise uses the widest measure available.   [b]Mexico is included in both groups.   [c]In OECD countries the fiscal balance corresponds to net lending/borrowing.

and expenditures and less on fiscal volatility issues, traditionally a common feature in Latin America.

These country-by-country data demonstrate that fiscal performance in Latin America is anything but homogeneous. It presents a variety of experiences that can only be partially captured by summary statistics. Nevertheless, it is possible to distinguish between two broad groups of countries: the relatively more prosperous (Argentina, Brazil, Chile, Costa Rica, Mexico, Panama, Uruguay, and Venezuela) and the relatively less prosperous (Bolivia, Colombia, Dominican Republic, Ecuador, El Salvador, Guatemala, Honduras, Nicaragua, Paraguay, and Peru), as measured by income per head.

Both OECD and Latin American economies have run budget deficits during the last decade and a half and, as shown in Figure 12.1, their deficits have been proportionally similar (1.9% and 1.6% of GDP respectively). However, while the typical Latin American deficit remained around this level throughout the entire period, those in OECD countries fell from 3.5% of GDP in the early 1990s to 0.7% in the 21st century. In the future, with OECD fiscal deficits ballooning, we should see more convergence.

This figure also highlights the significant differences between the two regions in terms of fiscal revenue and expenditure. Throughout the period, expenditures accounted for 25% of GDP in Latin America, against 44% in OECD countries (see Figure 12.1). Similarly, fiscal revenues exhibit a marked gap: 42% in OECD countries but only 23% in Latin America. Table 12.1 provides additional information.

As a share of government revenues—which may be a better measure of a country's capacity to meet its debt obligations—Latin America's deficits have been larger than those in OECD countries: 8.3% versus 4.5%. Upper-middle-income Latin American countries had deficit-to-revenue ratios in the OECD range, at 5.3% but in lower middle-income countries the ratio reached 10.5%. The gap between industrial and Latin

Table 12.1 The size of government, Latin American and OECD countries[a] (regional averages, %)

	Region[b]	1990–2006	1990–4	1995–9	2000–6
Fiscal balance/GDP[d]	Latin America	−1.55	−1.67	−1.58	−1.44
	Upper middle income[c]	−1.14	−1.32	−1.19	−0.97
	Lower middle income[c]	−1.84	−1.90	−1.84	−1.81
	OECD	−1.86	−3.52	−1.83	−0.69
Fiscal balance/Total revenue[d]	Latin America	−8.34	−9.83	−7.90	−7.59
	Upper middle income[c]	−5.32	−5.84	−5.51	−4.80
	Lower middle income[c]	−10.51	−12.41	−9.62	−9.78
	OECD	−4.51	−7.74	−4.35	−2.30
Primary balance/GDP[e]	Latin America	1.12	1.12	0.90	1.28
	Upper middle income[c]	2.16	1.77	1.84	2.68
	Lower middle income[c]	0.34	0.70	0.22	0.18
	OECD	1.87	1.43	2.07	2.05
Primary balance/Total revenue[e]	Latin America	3.98	4.53	3.57	3.89
	Upper middle income[c]	8.18	7.53	7.28	9.29
	Lower middle income[c]	0.87	2.64	0.86	−0.38
	OECD	4.38	3.98	4.86	4.33
Total revenue/GDP	Latin America	23.24	21.69	22.65	24.78
	Upper middle income[c]	25.80	24.01	25.09	27.59
	Lower middle income[c]	21.34	20.09	20.87	22.57
	OECD	42.16	42.03	42.50	42.01
Total expenditure/GDP	Latin America	24.78	23.35	24.24	26.18
	Upper middle income[c]	26.94	25.32	26.28	28.57
	Lower middle income[c]	23.15	21.99	22.72	24.30
	OECD	44.02	45.55	44.32	42.70
Primary expenditure/GDP[e]	Latin America	22.09	20.52	21.72	23.47
	Upper middle income[c]	23.64	22.23	23.25	24.92
	Lower middle income[c]	20.93	19.31	20.59	22.33
	OECD	39.84	39.88	39.91	39.77

Source: OECD Development Centre calculations based on the ECLAC ILPES Public Finance database for Latin America, and OECD General Government Accounts data for OECD countries.

[a] OECD data refer to the consolidated general government sector. In Latin America coverage corresponds to the non-financial public sector where possible, otherwise uses the widest measure available.

[b] Mexico is included in both groups.

[c] Following the World Bank categorization, the upper-middle-income countries are Argentina, Brazil, Chile, Costa Rica, Mexico, Panama, Uruguay, and Venezuela. The lower-middle-income group comprises Bolivia, Colombia, Dominican Republic, Ecuador, El Salvador, Guatemala, Honduras, Nicaragua and Paraguay.

[d] For OECD countries the fiscal balance corresponds to net lending/borrowing.

[e] OECD primary balance and primary expenditure exclude the impact of gross interest payments. The OECD Economic Outlook, however, reports these measures excluding the impact of net interest.

American countries remains marked, though it has narrowed considerably since the 1970–95 period analyzed by Gavin and Perotti (1997), who reported Latin American deficits of around 11% of total revenues. To support the debt that these deficits imply, Latin American governments have run a consistently positive primary surplus (i.e. the difference between revenue and expenditure before debt service costs). In upper-middle-income Latin American countries this surplus has been larger than in OECD countries, both relative to the size of the economy and as a share of government revenue.

Government revenues were substantially higher as a share of GDP in OECD countries (at 42%) than in Latin America (23%). Within Latin America, the ratios for upper-middle-income and lower-middle-income countries were separated by five percentage points, with greater revenue raised in the higher income countries. The relative stability of these ratios over time in OECD countries and Latin America is notable. Fiscal revenues include non-tax revenues, which for many Latin American countries can be sizeable. Pure tax revenues, however, represented only 16% of GDP in Latin America, vs. 35% in OECD countries (although there is considerable variation in Latin America, with a country like Brazil, for example, reaching OECD levels and tripling those of a country like Guatemala). Analyzing this further, tax revenues amounted to only 13% of GDP in lower-middle-income countries in Latin America, compared to 20% in the region's upper-middle-income countries.

As already underlined, the Latin American average masks considerable variation among countries. In a typical year, revenues were over 30% of GDP in Brazil, Chile, Bolivia, Paraguay, and Venezuela, but under 20% in El Salvador, Honduras, Peru, Panama, and the Dominican Republic. In Guatemala, government revenues were consistently a little over 11% of GDP. Not surprisingly, the classification of Latin American countries into high-revenue and low-revenue categories yields essentially the same groups as a division of countries into high-expenditure and low-expenditure governments.

Expenditures have grown slightly more rapidly than revenues in Latin America but only just. Expenditures stood at 26% of GDP in 2000–6, against 23% in 1990–4. As with revenues, the gap between OECD and Latin American countries is substantial: 44% in the OECD against 25% in Latin America, measured as average share of GDP over the entire period. Compared with the 1970–95 figures reported by Gavin and Perotti, Table 12.1 suggests that expenditures, as a proportion of GDP, has been growing over time in Latin America but stayed broadly constant in OECD countries; they report total expenditure of 23% of GDP and 45% respectively.

Figure 12.2 looks more closely at the composition of revenues and expenditures in Latin American and OECD countries. It reveals striking differences. In Latin America, indirect taxes and non-tax revenues make up most of government revenues, whereas OECD countries rely much more heavily on direct taxes and social security contributions (SSC). On the other side of the ledger, capital expenditure and interest payments account for 33% of Latin American expenditure, while in the OECD social transfers play a major role.

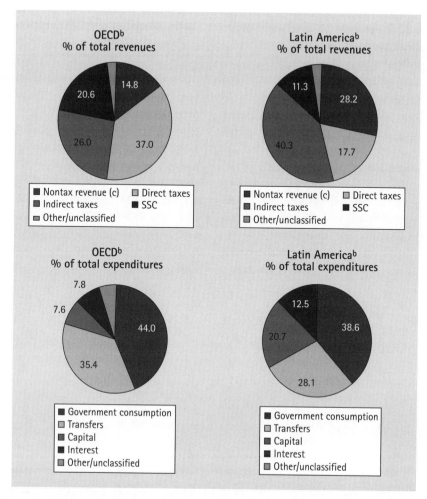

FIGURE 12.2 Composition of revenue and expenditure in Latin America and OECD countries,[a] regional averages, 1990–2006

Source: OECD Development Centre calculations based on the ECLAC ILPES Public Finance database, the OECD Development Centre Latin American Revenue Statistics database, the OECD Revenue Statistics database, and OECD General Government Accounts data.
[a]OECD data refer to the consolidated general government sector. In Latin America, coverage corresponds to the non-financial public sector where possible, otherwise uses the widest measure available.   [b]Mexico is included in both groups.   [c]ECLAC ILPES data on non-tax revenues in Mexico has been adjusted to reclassify the fees levied on hydrocarbon production as taxes, in accordance with OECD revenue statistics guidelines.

A look at the detailed data in Figure 12.2 provides additional information about the former issues. On the revenue side, three critical distinctions stand out. First, Latin American countries rely far more on indirect taxes than OECD countries. Between 1990 and 2006, indirect taxes made up 58% of tax revenues in Latin America but only 33% in OECD countries—with notable stability over time in these proportions (see Table 12.2). The distinction between upper-middle-income and lower-middle-income

Table 12.2 Analysis of government revenue, Latin American and OECD countries[a] (regional averages, %)

	Region[b]	1990–2006	1990–4	1995–9	2000–6
Non-tax revenue/GDP[d]	Latin America	5.94	6.44	5.68	6.07
	Upper middle income[c]	6.90	7.21	6.53	7.20
	Lower middle income[c]	5.16	5.84	5.01	5.16
	OECD	5.79	6.17	5.83	5.59
Tax revenue/GDP	Latin America	16.18	14.69	15.98	17.39
	Upper middle income[c]	19.69	18.91	19.25	20.57
	Lower middle income[c]	13.37	11.32	13.36	14.84
	OECD	35.05	34.37	35.33	35.47
Direct taxes/GDP	Latin America	4.04	3.65	3.77	4.52
	Upper middle income[c]	5.42	5.25	5.01	5.85
	Lower middle income[c]	2.94	2.37	2.77	3.46
	OECD	14.71	14.57	14.82	15.00
Individual income tax/GDP	Latin America	0.75	0.31	0.69	0.70
	Upper middle income[c]	0.61	0.14	0.74	0.85
	Lower middle income[c]	0.89	0.63	0.61	0.56
	OECD	9.51	9.81	9.66	9.37
Indirect taxes/GDP	Latin America	9.17	8.18	9.15	9.89
	Upper middle income[c]	9.96	9.28	9.85	10.51
	Lower middle income[c]	8.54	7.29	8.60	9.39
	OECD	11.30	10.96	11.43	11.37
International trade taxes/GDP	Latin America	1.64	1.87	1.78	1.37
	Upper middle income[c]	1.31	1.56	1.28	1.15
	Lower middle income[c]	1.90	2.12	2.17	1.55
	OECD	0.42	0.67	0.44	0.24

Source: OECD Development Centre calculations based upon Chapter Four of this volume, the ECLAC ILPES Public Finance Database and the OECD Revenue Statistics Database (OECD 2007a).

[a] OECD data refer to the consolidated general government sector. In Latin America coverage corresponds to the non-financial public sector where possible, otherwise uses the widest measure available.

[b] Mexico is included in both groups.

[c] Following the World Bank categorization, the upper-middle-income countries are Argentina, Brazil, Chile, Costa Rica, Mexico, Panama, Uruguay, and Venezuela. The lower-middle-income group comprises Bolivia, Colombia, Dominican Republic, Ecuador, El Salvador, Guatemala, Honduras, Nicaragua, and Paraguay.

[d] ECLAC ILPES data on non-tax revenues in Mexico has been adjusted to reclassify the fees levied on hydrocarbon production as taxes, in accordance with OECD revenue statistics guidelines.

[e] In Latin America, data for individual income tax covers Argentina, Bolivia, Brazil, Chile, Costa Rica, Dominican Republic, Guatemala, Honduras, Panama, Peru, and Uruguay.

Latin American countries, on the other hand, is sizeable: respectively they raise 50% and 64% of their tax revenues from indirect taxes. Direct taxes, meanwhile, contributed only 25% of Latin America's tax revenue (a proportion which grew slightly over the period) compared with 42% in OECD countries. In only four Latin American countries—Colombia, Mexico, Panama and Venezuela—do direct taxes exceed 30% of tax revenues.

The contribution of individual income taxes, the most visible and most personal of the direct taxes, reveals a stark disparity: such taxes contribute 27% of tax revenue in OECD countries but only 4% in Latin America. This means that only about a quarter of the income tax take in Latin America is paid by individuals (rather than corporations), in comparison to about 70% in OECD countries. In practice, taxes on corporations are a more volatile revenue source than taxes on individual income, which has corresponding consequences for the stability of revenues in Latin America.

When Gavin and Perotti conducted their study, direct taxes were falling as a share of total tax revenue. That trend has been reversed. The share of direct taxes rose slightly in Latin America, from 25% of tax revenues in the first half of the 1990s to 26% in the first six years of the new millennium. Latin America is therefore continuing to rely heavily on indirect taxes for fiscal policy.

A second striking feature of revenue composition in Latin America is that countries in the region rely to a far greater degree on non-tax revenues than do their counterparts in the OECD. Non-tax revenues, such as fees and royalties from natural resource extraction and exports, constituted 28% of total revenues in Latin America but only 15% in OECD countries. The Latin American average masks considerable variations. At one end of the scale, the proportion was 15% or less in Argentina, Brazil, the Dominican Republic, Guatemala, Peru, and Uruguay, as against 40% or more in Bolivia, Colombia, Panama, and Venezuela.

A third feature of government revenues is the comparative importance of trade taxes in Latin America. Such taxes tend to be higher in developing countries, reflecting their relative ease of collection and enforceability. Trade taxes are more important to the lower-middle-income countries in the region (15% of tax revenues) than to the upper-middle-income countries (7%), compared with less than 1% in the OECD. Among Latin American countries, the Dominican Republic relies most on trade taxes, with 28% of its tax revenues coming from this source. Overall, the period under review saw a decline in the importance of trade taxes in most countries in Latin America, even if their absolute share remained well above OECD levels. From making up 15% of tax revenue in the first half of the 1990s, the share of trade taxes declined to 9% in 2000–6.

On the expenditure side, the clearest distinction between OECD and Latin American countries emerges from the relative importance of capital expenditure and interest payments on public debt (see Table 12.3). Capital expenditure averaged 21% of total expenditure over the period 1990–2006 in Latin America, and only 8% in the OECD. Within this, the share of capital expenditure was substantially higher in lower-middle-income countries (25%) than in upper-middle-income countries (16%). Interest, meanwhile, consumed 12% of government expenditure in Latin America and only 8% in the

Table 12.3 Analysis of government expenditure, Latin American and OECD countries[a] (regional averages, %)

	Region[b]	1990–2006	1990–1994	1995–1999	2000–2006
Government consumption/ GDP[d]	Latin America	9.11	8.79	8.78	9.37
	Upper middle income[c]	9.31	8.53	9.16	9.55
	Lower middle income[c]	8.95	9.02	8.45	9.22
	OECD	19.22	19.34	18.83	19.25
Transfers/GDP	Latin America	6.39	5.43	6.37	7.50
	Upper middle income[c]	9.03	8.28	8.72	9.87
	Lower middle income[c]	4.27	2.94	4.28	5.60
	OECD	15.99	16.41	15.96	15.73
Capital expenditure/GDP	Latin America	5.01	4.90	5.43	4.82
	Upper middle income[c]	4.17	4.35	4.24	4.03
	Lower middle income[c]	5.60	5.34	6.25	5.36
	OECD	3.03	2.82	3.06	2.90
Interest/GDP[e]	Latin America	2.84	2.83	2.70	2.82
	Upper middle income[c]	3.54	2.88	3.33	3.73
	Lower middle income[c]	2.28	2.79	2.19	2.09
	OECD	3.55	4.87	3.90	2.75

Source: OECD Development Centre calculations based on the ECLAC ILPES Public Finance database for Latin America, and OECD General Government Accounts data for OECD countries.

[a] OECD data refer to the consolidated general government sector. In Latin America, coverage corresponds to the non-financial public sector where possible, otherwise uses the widest measure available.

[b] Mexico is included in both groups.

[c] Following the World Bank categorization, the upper-middle-income countries are Argentina, Brazil, Chile, Costa Rica, Mexico, Panama, Uruguay, and Venezuela. The lower-middle-income group comprises Bolivia, Colombia, Dominican Republic, Ecuador, El Salvador, Guatemala, Honduras, Nicaragua, and Paraguay.

[d] Government consumption for Latin America is calculated as the sum of wages and salaries and purchases of goods and services.

[e] For OECD countries, interest payments on public debt are taken as the interest payable in the primary distribution-of-income account for general government.

OECD. Moreover, as Table 12.3 shows, in the OECD this share has been steadily falling, while it has remained more or less constant in Latin America over the last decade.

Table 12.3 also shows that government consumption as a share of expenditure has changed little, falling from 41% in 1990–4 to 40% in 2000–6 in Latin America, while rising slightly from 42% to 45% in the OECD. Transfers constitute a larger share of expenditure in the OECD than in Latin America, but the two have strongly converged over the last decade and a half. Transfers as a share of total expenditures in Latin America grew from 24% in 1990–4 to 30% in 2000–6, while the corresponding figures for the OECD were 34 and 37%.

The image of Latin America as a region of fiscal irresponsibility, whether deliberate or accidental, is out of date. By any measure, a new maturity emerged in the 2000s, revealing itself in improved fiscal discipline more or less throughout the region. Deficits are falling, and difficult—often long-delayed—fiscal reforms are starting to get under way. Perhaps the strongest, and certainly the most topical, is the reaction to the macroeconomic bonanza of recent years, which has been accompanied by policies less pro-cyclical than might have been expected on historical evidence. Chile, which joined the OECD in early 2010, demonstrates best practice not only in the region but in the world in terms of fiscal policies and reforms, providing a benchmark for both emerging and developed countries. Other countries have also been showing major innovations in terms of fiscal policies, processes, or institutions. In particular, the experiences of participatory budgeting processes, developed first in the city of Porto Alegre, Brazil, and later in other parts of the continent, deserve attention, as do the audit and controlling institutions built up around the region over the past decades (see OEA/PNUD 2009: 36–40, 53–56, 70–4; and also the complete study on government auditing in Latin America by Carlos Santiso, 2009).

12.3 FISCAL POLICY AND DEMOCRATIC LEGITIMACY: A CLOSE RELATIONSHIP

In Latin America, academics and policymakers have been concerned with fiscal policy at least since the beginning of the 1960s. "Social pressure in Latin America is fostering a preoccupation for income distribution," wrote the Chilean economist Aníbal Pinto. "Even among the few countries with relatively dynamic growth a conscience is maturing that extreme inequality in the distribution of the fruits of progress constitutes a social and economic problem of the utmost importance" (Pinto 1962).

From that time on, issues of taxation and public expenditure have been a recurrent item on the Latin American agenda. Who should pay taxes—and how much—often appears as a highly technical matter for the attention of professional economists. Yet at a deeper level, fiscal policy is also an expression of the very soul of a society. "The spirit of a people," wrote the economist Joseph Schumpeter in 1918, "its cultural level, its social structure, the deeds its policy may prepare—all this and more is written in its fiscal history, stripped of all phrases" (cited in Moore 2004).

Fiscal policy is linked to economic development (Easterly and Rebelo 1993) but its impact is also very important democratic governance. In fact, historians trace the development of democracy in Europe and even the very origin of the United States of America back to the development of a fiscal state with broader representation and a more inclusive voting franchise (Moore 2004; 2007; Moore and Schneider 2004). The debate on fiscal policy in Latin America is moving away from being seen as a trade-off between efficiency and equity.

Fiscal policy is hence also linked to democratic development. This raises the question of fiscal legitimacy. Democratic governance is characterized by democratic legitimacy, the confidence that people grant to democracy over all other forms of government, and by their acceptance of the way it works. In the same way, fiscal legitimacy is a reflection of the confidence people grant to their governments' performance in spending the revenue they collect in taxes.

As described in greater detail in recent reports by the OECD (2007; 2008), fiscal reform, and in particular improvement of the redistributive capacities of fiscal policies, can play a key role in strengthening citizens' trust in democratic institutions. Other institutions in the region have also been devoting major efforts to bringing fiscal issues back onto the agenda and relating them to the so-called "fiscal pacts", i.e. the need to deepen the legitimacy of fiscal policies (see in particular the previous report from other international organizations, in particular ECLAC/CEPAL 1998; World Bank 2006).

It is precisely in democracy that fiscal policy can more fully play its stabilizing and redistributive role. The region reflects global trends that emphasize the importance of fiscal policy. But a sound fiscal policy also requires fiscal legitimacy—in other words, trust on the part of citizens that the authorities collect taxes and spend public revenues appropriately. Taxes and fiscal policies are at the very heart of democracy, voted by parliaments, trusted by citizens. This trust can only be achieved through more and better tax collection, but also by making government spending fairer and more efficient (for a special focus on Brazil and Mexico, see e.g. Elizondo and Santiso 2007). In Latin American, however, the aversion towards paying taxes, the inefficiencies of fiscal spending, and the low quality of public goods generated undermine fiscal legitimacy.

This lack of fiscal legitimacy is the key to understanding why Latin American countries have failed to support functioning welfare systems. Fiscal legitimacy is intimately related to what economists call "tax morale," or "the moral principles or values individuals hold about paying their tax" (Torgler 2005). It is approximated by the proportion of survey respondents who think tax avoidance can never be justified. Higher fiscal legitimacy provides higher motivation to pay taxes. A growing literature shows the importance of tax morale in tax compliance and in the size of the informal economy (Cummings et al. 2006; Braun 2007; Torgler and Schneider 2007). As so neatly put by the Swiss economist Benno Torgler (2005), "Taxpayers are more inclined to comply with the law if the exchange between the paid tax and the performed government services are found to be equitable." Micro empirical studies show that tax morale is also closely intertwined with democratic legitimacy. Higher tax morale is associated with democratic attitudes, in particular support for government officials and the Head of State, and the belief that others respect the rule of law (Torgler, Schneider, and Schaltegger 2007). Fiscal legitimacy is therefore among the factors that determine people's readiness to pay taxes (or the lengths to which they will go to avoid them).

This literature inherits the notion of applying the principle of *quid pro quo* to public finance, first defended by Swedish economist Knut Wicksel (1986):

No one can complain if he secures a benefit which he himself considers to be (greater or at least) as great as the price he has to pay. But when individuals or groups find or believe they find that for them the marginal utility of a given public service does not equal the marginal utility of the private goods they have to contribute, then these individuals or groups will, without fail, feel overburdened. It will be no consolation to them to be assured that the utility of public services as a whole far exceeds the total value of the individual sacrifices.

Fiscal legitimacy is linked with high fiscal performance and good democratic governance. Higher fiscal legitimacy will lead to higher tax morale and reduce the incentive to avoid taxes or join the informal economy. Thus, to increase tax revenue, governments can work on improving fiscal legitimacy because of its impact on the willingness to pay taxes and the informal economy. For individual Latin American countries, there is a significant correlation between the proportion of the population trusting that taxes are well spent and the proportion satisfied with democracy. Improving fiscal performance will thus also strengthen democratic governance, although the relationship between fiscal legitimacy and democratic governance is a complex one and deserves further analysis.

It is recurrently observed that Latin American countries have some of the highest levels of inequality in the world. Moreover, nearly 40% of the region's population lives in conditions of poverty. This population of nearly 200 million cannot be ignored. Up to now, one of the main weaknesses of Latin America's tax systems has in fact been their inability to significantly bridge the gap between rich and poor. Unlike in many OECD countries, fiscal policy plays little or no redistributive role in Latin America (Goñi, López, and Servén 2006).

As Figure 12.3 demonstrates, fiscal policy in Latin America is inefficient in terms of redistribution, particularly in comparison to Europe (Goñi et al. 2006). Despite slight differences among some countries, the findings are irrefutable: when measured using Gini coefficients, inequality is less dissimilar in Europe and Latin America before taxes and transfers. However, where as fiscal policy in Europe helps to reduce inequality by 15% (and in some countries by 20%), it is reduced by only 2% in Latin America on average for the Latin American countries for which we computed the data. If we incorporate the social programs like *Fame Zero* in Brazil or *Oportunidades* in Mexico, the numbers look a little less severe, but they remain roughly along the same lines.

Although part of the explanation is quantitative, the qualitative aspect is also important: Europe's taxes and transfers are better oriented and more progressive. These weaknesses are no secret to Latin America's citizens. One indication of structural problems in the quality of fiscal policy in the region is Latin Americans' obvious distrust of their systems. According to data from Latinobarómetro, less than 25% of the region's population believe that their taxes are spent properly (Latinobarómetro 2003; 2005). When fiscal policy fails to bridge the gap between rich and poor, the system's credibility is adversely affected. The low level of fiscal legitimacy in Latin America helps to explain why many countries in the region do not have functional social welfare systems:

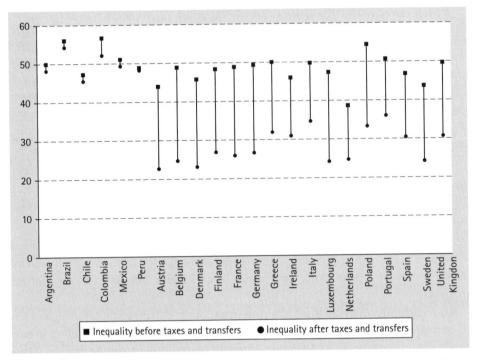

FIGURE 12.3 Redistribution of income by means of taxes and transfers in Europe and Latin America, in selected countries

Source: OECD Development Centre (2007); based on data from Goñi, López, and Servén et al. (2006).

the poor quality of fiscal policies makes it difficult to generate income, which impedes government spending and ends up undermining trust in the tax system.

12.4 KEYS TO IMPROVING THE QUALITY OF FISCAL POLICY IN LATIN AMERICA: MORE, BETTER, AND FAIRER TAX COLLECTION AND SPENDING

The key to promoting fiscal legitimacy in Latin America lies in improving the social impact of spending. The regressivity of fiscal policies has a negative effect on the legitimacy of the tax system. The more regressive these policies, the smaller the percentage of the population that trusts their taxes are being used properly.

Although it is true that these data are based on perceptions, these perceptions constitute a significant part of the "objective" reality for governments when they consider the possibility of developing sustainable social welfare systems. Latin American countries have been introducing important reforms to their tax systems since the 1980s, many of which have yielded positive results. In particular, over the past 25 years significant progress has been made in strengthening the fiscal institutions, and new rules to control the public deficit and measures designed to encourage fiscal responsibility and improve transparency have been introduced. One of the positive outcomes of these reforms has been the growing fiscal discipline that we see in the region, although it is true that a favorable international climate has also helped.

Even so, many reforms still need to be introduced to create more sound and progressive tax systems that can allow more effective tax collection and government spending, thereby helping to reduce excessive inequality. Just as the motto *citius, altius, fortius* (faster, higher, stronger) has long inspired athletes who compete in the Olympic Games, today's Latin American governments should draw inspiration from the motto "more, better, and fairer" when implementing their fiscal reforms. The debate over fiscal policy in the region requires transcending the traditional dichotomy between efficiency and fairness in favor of a better understanding of the need for extensive reforms on both fronts, and this is slowly happening.

On the one hand, Latin American countries need more tax collection in order to be able to invest more in public services. The architects of the fiscal reforms of the 1990s strengthened the budget rules from a revenue standpoint, for instance, by approving fiscal responsibility laws and developing multi-year budgets, while at the same time setting legal limits on government spending in order to control debt and the deficit. Nevertheless, 92% of Latin Americans believe that their government should spend more on health care, 57% feel that spending on basic education should be increased, and 75% maintain that more money should be spent on social welfare (Latinobarómetro 2006). The quality of public schools and governments' effectiveness in reducing poverty and inequality receive the lowest scores (Lora 2006). These opinions are corroborated by data which show that government spending is more pro-cyclical, public investment is lower—especially in infrastructure—and the quality of government bureaucracy is worse than in other emerging countries with similar labor costs (Clements, Faircloth, and Verhoeven 2007).

Mexico offers a good example of the need to spend more which is apparent in many Latin American countries. With the amount of taxes collected representing less than 12% of GDP and social security contributions close to only 2%, Mexico's tax collection capacity is among the lowest in Latin America. Although the introduction of important fiscal reforms starting in 1996 has led to significant progress in terms of the budget preparation process, greater transparency, and control of oil revenue volatility, it has not brought about a substantial increase in government revenues (OECD 2007). It remains to be seen whether the recent fiscal reforms introduced by President Felipe Calderón's government in 2009—the aim of which is precisely to increase tax collection by more than 2% of GDP through new taxes on bank deposits and hydrocarbons, while at the same time introducing a flat-rate business tax and reducing fiscal pressure on Pemex, the state-owned oil company—will succeed not only in increasing government revenues but also in improving the

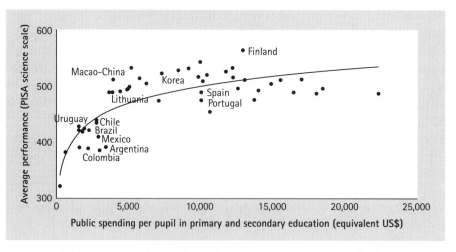

FIGURE 12.4 Education: spending and results in OECD countries and selected emerging countries

Source: OECD Development Centre (2007); based on data from the Programme for International Student Assessment (PISA) (OECD 2005b).

quality of public services. In any case, it is an important first step towards the goal of spending more and better.

Despite the need to generate revenues that can be used to finance government spending, the quality of the tax system is defined more by its ability to produce results. In this respect, spending better is even more important than spending more. The poor quality of spending, often combined with insufficient levels of investment, largely explains why Latin American citizens' access to basic services continues to be inadequate, especially for the poorest segments of the population. For example, Mexican students have significantly lower levels and results than Lithuanian students, despite the fact that the educational expenditures of this country's government are similar to those of Mexico (see Figure 12.4). The quality of government spending in Mexico may explain a large portion of these relatively inferior results, as revealed by an exhaustive OECD study of Mexico's educational sector conducted in 2005. The study showed that 90% of educational spending was allocated to salaries (80% for teachers and 10% for other staff), 60% of primary school teachers did not have a university degree, and 70% of secondary school teachers had no teacher training (OECD 2005a).

Brazil is another good example of the importance of spending quality. With collection levels near 35% of GDP, the country's volume of tax collection is close to the average of OECD countries and far higher than the average of Latin America in general (17%). However, social indicators that reflect the quality and efficiency of Brazilian government spending are far below the average of OECD countries. Despite the imposition of a healthy fiscal discipline, Brazil's reforms have made the tax system more complex and spending more rigid, which has led to greater inefficiency and made the introduction of additional reforms more difficult (OECD 2006).

The words of Chilean President Bachelet during the opening of the forum on social cohesion between the European Union and Latin America are significant: "Our democracies have not been efficient … they have not succeeded in quickly improving the living conditions of citizens, especially the most vulnerable, and the political consequences are visible today." In fact, social spending in Latin America has increased. A big part of the problem then is its poor quality, as evidenced by the fact that much of the social spending that exists has little impact. This is mainly because these increases have benefited special-interest groups and not the majority of the population or its most vulnerable elements. It is also important that spending be geared toward policies that actually reduce poverty and inequality. The region needs government spending that is not only more and better, but also fairer. It is surprising that in many Latin American countries the fiscal policy is regressive, with most of the benefits and transfers going to the wealthiest households. Except for conditional cash transfer programs like *Bolsa Familia* in Brazil and *Oportunidades* in Mexico, many social welfare programs in the region tend to be regressive (Goñi et al. 2006).

For example, the proportion of poor households with access to public sewage services, bathroom facilities, and secondary education is generally one-half of that of wealthy households, with even greater differences in terms of access to telephones, another topic discussed at length in OECD (2007). The poorest quintile of the population receives 16% of social spending, mostly in the form of education spending; the wealthiest quintile receives nearly twice this volume, generally in the form of government spending on social security. While in many OECD countries transfers represent more than two-thirds of the funds made available by the tax system to reduce inequality, their positive impact is much lower in Latin America because of their smaller volume and problems in allocation. Pension funds and unemployment insurance are two of the principal examples of regressivity in Latin American public transfers. There is also ample evidence that government spending on health care and education is, in the best of cases, only slightly progressive and can even be extremely regressive in sectors such as higher education.

12.5 TOWARD GREATER FISCAL AND DEMOCRATIC LEGITIMACY: SOME CONCLUSIONS AND PROPOSALS

Democracy puts fiscal policy at the heart of the relationship between citizens and the state. Fiscal policy will continue to be a major development issue for Latin America, as it is in OECD countries, posing one of the main challenges for the region. Latin America is the most unequal region of the world. Governments cannot ignore the challenges of fighting poverty and inequality while promoting stable and sustainable economic growth and development.

Latin America suffers from low fiscal legitimacy. In many Latin American countries, fiscal performance and democratic governance are damaged by citizens' lack of trust and confidence in democratic fiscal institutions. One explanation for this distrust of the government's fiscal responsibility is that, in contrast to most OECD countries, taxes and transfers play little or no redistributive role in most Latin America states. When taxation fails to deliver and help bridge the gap between the richer and the poorer, the credibility of the fiscal system suffers: poor quality fiscal policy hinders tax revenue, frustrates public expenditure, and undermines fiscal and democratic legitimacy.

Many governments are already trying to do a better job in terms of improving fiscal efficiency and promoting socioeconomic equity. Fiscal reform in the region has made some progress, producing positive results. Successful reforms to strengthen fiscal institutions includes the introduction of new rules to control public deficits, new fiscal responsibility laws, and measures to enhance transparency. Partly as a result of these reforms, much of the region offers the word a new face: stable and predictable macroeconomic environments, thanks to lower inflation levels, sounder public finances, more reasonable debt management, and lower risk premiums.

The region needs better, fairer, and more public spending, not only on health and education but also on infrastructure and innovation. In many countries fiscal policy is regressive because wealthier households receive most of the benefits. Social insurance programs, in particular, are notably regressive throughout the region. Conditional cash transfer programs, such as *Bolsa Familia* in Brazil or *Oportunidades* in Mexico, on the contrary, are very progressive but they are still relatively modest. In terms of tax reform, one major pending challenge is the elimination of special exemptions in direct and indirect taxes, making the tax systems fairer and more balanced and avoiding fiscal and rent captures by segments of the society and polity (Elizondo and Santiso 2007).

Such fiscal legitimacy is not only an issue of capacity. Strengthening administrative capabilities can only take tax administration half-way. It is commonly argued that in developing countries tax administration is part of tax policy. That may be true, but tax administration is not tax politics. The political economy of fiscal reforms, the engineering and trade-offs needed to achieve fiscal reforms, are at the very core of fiscal issues. Bringing politics back into tax policy could improve tax policy and democratic legitimacy throughout the region. Tax reform in the 1990s, for instance in Peru during the Fujimori administration, introduced a reform program that completely overhauled the tax administration. The new tax administration was more meritocratic, more flexible. and more effective. But even the most capable administration can be manipulated and misused, as the Peruvian case showed.

Fiscal reform should aim at broadening benefits across the population and bringing people closer to the politics of fiscal policy. To do so, they have to bring about an informed political debate. This will only happen if there is more transparency in the system, more access to information, and independent actors with the capacity and the financial independence to carry out a critical evaluation of policies and proposed reforms. In the process, democratic legitimacy would be strengthened.

Fiscal reforms can and must help to consolidate democratic legitimacy in Latin American. An open, constructive debate on fiscal policies in Latin America will be instrumental not only in expanding the process of approving new tax mechanisms but also in facilitating their implementation. The introduction of measures aimed at strengthening tax collection and spending allocation mechanisms in sectors such as health care, education, infrastructure, and innovation will make it possible to bridge the gap between public policies and the population. At the same time, transparency should improve public perception that a fair benefit is received in exchange for taxes paid, since scrutiny of government spending and fiscal policy makes citizens feel that they are more a part of the democratic process.

As pointed out throughout this chapter, encouraging more, better, and fairer government spending should be the cornerstone of this effort to improve fiscal legitimacy, which will in turn have a positive impact on democratic legitimacy. There are also other measures that would help to strengthen citizens' trust in the tax systems. For example, having third parties involved in scrutinizing and evaluating public policies would help to improve transparency and accountability of the public authorities with respect to taxes, in terms both of how efficiently they are collected and of how appropriately they are spent. In many Latin American countries, research centers and economic think-tanks are already playing an important role in this regard, even though low funding levels and a scarcity of human resources limit their activity. More financial resources would need to be created to give them the necessary means to analyze and evaluate public policies, while protecting and guaranteeing their independence at all times (Santiso and Whitehead 2006).

Of equal importance is the need to increase the tax base so that the tax systems are fairer and more balanced. One of the main tax-related challenges that remains unresolved is to make collection systems more balanced by eliminating special exemptions on direct and indirect taxes which benefit certain segments of the population. These reforms will help to discourage tax evasion by increasing collection and expanding the tax base. The example of Spain illustrates the importance of building a broad consensus that allows these measures to be carried through, since implementation is even more important than policy development itself. The close link between the democratic and fiscal reforms introduced in Spain 30 years ago—the Moncloa Pacts—shows that democracy allows a country not only to approve measures but also to adapt, based on a pragmatic approach, the reform process itself to changes in the context as they occur (OECD 2007).

In their efforts to improve fiscal legitimacy and strengthen democratic governance, Latin American countries must restore the political dimension to tax and fiscal activity in an explicit, transparent manner. Democracy is the political system in which fiscal policy can achieve its potential as a tool for allocating resources, redistributing revenue, and ensuring macroeconomic stability. Fiscal reform should seek to increase benefits for the entire population and bridge the gap between citizens and the state. An open, informed political debate, which can only take place if the system is more transparent and the public has greater access to information, is an excellent way of achieving this goal. Developing and strengthening the ability of government bodies and the various administrations to provide this information through periodic reports and statistical tools must be made a priority. This will make it possible to achieve higher levels of public scrutiny, which will not only result in improved fiscal policy but will also strengthen public trust in the democratic system, the cornerstone of Latin American development.

References

Bárcena, A., and Serra, N. (eds) (2009). *Reformas para la cohesion social en América Latina: panorama antes de la crisis*, Santiago, Chile, and Barcelona: CEPAL and CIDOB.

Braun, M. (2007). 'Fiscal Reform in Latin America: The Silent Revolution That Is Pinning Populism', *Americas Quarterly*, Spring.

CEPAL (Comisión Económica para Améerica Latina) (1998). *El pacto fiscal: fortalezas, debilidades, desafíos*, Santiago, Chile.

Clements, B., Faircloth, C., and Verhoeven, M. (2007). 'Public Expenditure in Latin America: Trends and Key Policy Issues', IMF Working Paper No. 07/21.

Cummings, R. G., Martinez-Vàzquez, J., McKee, M., and Torgler, B. (2006). 'Effects of Tax Morale on Tax Compliance: Experimental and Survey Evidence', Working Paper Series No. 197, Program in Law and Economics, University of California, Berkeley.

Easterly, W., and Rebelo, S. (1993). 'Fiscal Policy and Economic Growth: An Empirical Investigation', *Journal of Monetary Economics* 32.3.

ECLAC (UN Economic Commission for Latin America and the Caribbean)/CEPAL (1998). *El pacto fiscal: fortalezas, debilidades y desafíos*, Santiago, Chile.

—— (2005). *Social Panorama of Latin America*, Santiago, Chile.

Elizondo, C., and Santiso, J. (2007). 'Devórame otra vez: violencia fiscal en América Latina', mimeograph, Paris: OECD.

Gavin, M., and Perotti, R. (1997). 'Fiscal Policy in Latin America', *NBER Macroeconomics Annual* 12.

Goñi, E., López, H., and Servén, L. (2006). 'Fiscal Reform for Social Equity in Latin America', mimeograph, Washington, DC: World Bank.

Izquierdo, A., and Talvi, E. (eds) (2008). *All that Glitters May Not Be Gold: Assessing Latin America's Recent Macroeconomic Performance*, Washington, DC: IDB.

—— —— (2009). *Policy Trade-offs for Unprecedented Times: Confronting the Global Crisis in Latin America and the Caribbean*, Washington, DC: IDB.

Latinobarómetro (2003). *Summary Report*, available online at: www.latinobarometro.org

—— (2005). *Summary Report*, available online at: www.latinobarometro.org

—— (2006). *Summary Report*, available online at: www.latinobarometro.org

Lora, E. (2006). 'The Future of Fiscal Pacts in Latin America', presented at the Economic Forum of the Ibero-American Summit: Economic Policies for a New Social Pact in Latin America, CIDOB Foundation, Barcelona, October 6–7.

Moore, M. (2004). 'Revenues, State Formation and the Quality of Governance in Developing Countries', *International Political Science Review* 25.3.

—— (2007). 'How Does Taxation Affect the Quality of Governance?', Institute of Development Studies Working Paper No. 280, Brighton.

—— and SCHNEIDER, A. (2004). 'Taxation, Governance and Poverty: Where Do the Middle Income Countries Fit?', Institute of Development Studies Working Paper No. 230, Brighton.

NIETO, S., and SANTISO, J. (2008). 'Wall Street and Elections in Latin American Emerging Economies', OECD Development Centre Working Paper No. 272.

—— —— (2009). 'Revisiting Political Budget Cycles in Latin America', OECD Development Centre Working Paper No. 281.

OCAMPO, J. A. (2009). 'Latin American and the Global Financial Crisis', *Cambridge Journal of Economics* 33.4.

OEA/PNUD (Organización de los Estados Americanos/Programa de las Naciones Unidas para el Desarrollo) (2009). *La democracia de ciudadania: una agenda para la construccion de la democracia en América latina*, Washington, DC and New York.

OECD (Organisation for Economic Co-operation and Development) (2004). *Learning for Tomorrow's World: First Results from PISA 2003*, Paris.

—— (2005a). *Economic Survey of Mexico*, Paris.

—— (2005b). *Education at a Glance*, Paris.

—— (2006). *Economic Survey of Brazil*, Paris.

—— (2007). *Latin American Economic Outlook 2008*, Paris.

—— (2008). *Latin American Economic Outlook 2009*, Paris.

—— (2010). *Chile: OECD Economic Survey*, Paris.

PINTO, A. (1962). 'Notes on Income Distribution and Redistribution Strategy', *El trimestre económico* 115.

SANTISO, C. (2009). *The Political Economy of Government Auditing: Financial Governance and the Rule of Law in Latin America*, London: Routledge.

SANTISO, J. (2006). *Latin America's Political Economy of the Possible*, Cambridge, Mass.: MIT Press.

—— and WHITEHEAD, L. (2006). 'Ulysses, the Sirens and the Art of Navigation: Political and Technical Rationality in Latin America', OECD Development Centre Working Paper No. 256, Paris.

TORGLER, B. (2005). 'Tax Morale in Latin America', *Public Choice* 122.1–2.

—— and SCHNEIDER, F. (2007). 'Shadow Economy, Tax Morale, Governance and Institutional Quality: A Panel Analysis', CREMA Working Paper No. 2007-2, Basel.

—— —— and SCHALTEGGER, C. (2007). 'With or Against the People?', CREMA Working Paper No. 2007-04, Basel.

WICKSEL, K. (1986) 'A new principle of just taxation', in R. A. Musgrave and A. T. Peacock (eds) and J. M. Buchanan (trans.), *Classics in the Theory of Public Finance*, New York: Macmillan and St. Martin's Press.

World Bank (2006). *Poverty Reduction and Growth: Virtuous and Vicious Cycles*, Washington, DC.

PART III

INTEGRATION INTO THE WORLD ECONOMY

CHAPTER 13

....

LATIN AMERICA IN THE
WORLD TRADE SYSTEM

....

DIANA TUSSIE

13.1 INTRODUCTION[1]

....

Twenty countries, large and small, share the fortunes and misfortunes of this continent
of contrasts. The region covers a vast variety of people, places, interests, and resources,
from single crop dependence in Honduras to the industrial prowess of Brazil and
Mexico. Despite the sharp differences, the purpose of this chapter is to draw a picture
of trade policy trends. Indeed, policy trends have come in tides. After the Great
Depression and throughout the rest of the 20th century, countries have basically
approached trade following two successive and opposed strategies. The first approach
was inward-looking industrialization. While this development path was initially a mere
defensive response to two major events, World War I and the 1930s crisis, that put an
end to the gold-standard regime and reduced multilateral trade to minimum levels, it
later became a fully fledged strategy, known as import substitution industrialization
(ISI) after the Second World War.

The LA version of the ISI model showed strains and bottlenecks in several countries
from the early 1970s. But the death-stroke to this strategy came in the wake of the debt
crisis of the early 1980s that destroyed some of the underpinnings of the model. The
mid-1980s ushered in a paradigm shift, an empowered flux of policies leading to the
final crumbling of the high protection that had shaped and inspired policy for half a
century. The region was seen as the test-bed for the Washington-consensus version of
the neoliberal agenda. In many countries these ideas fell on fertile ground, given the
policy space that had been opened up by hyperinflation, political instability, and the

[1] As always, the generous and diligent research assistance of Pablo Trucco for the completion of this
piece is most gratefully acknowledged.

generalized economic crisis of the 1980s. The trade policy mix therein applied combinations of three elements: trade liberalization, regional trade agreements, and full absorption into the multilateral system. Regionalism shifted from traditional intraregional agreements to north–south trade agreements and an attempted US-sponsored megabloc, the Free Trade Area of the Americas. Subsequent reaction to the disastrous results of the neoliberal agenda was predictably varied, but a rethinking of the dominant policy agenda took place across the board. As a result, at the turn of the century, rather than the neat convergence under the megabloc, what we see is elastic bundling and rebundling, which in turn have together reshaped stances in systemic issues. Activism in the World Trade Organization acquired an unprecedented intensity, accompanied and followed by criss-crossing bilateral agreements. Pushed by the changing dynamics of global demand and supply, and especially the rise of powerhouses in Asia, trans-continental agreements have made an entry.

A strong focus of the development literature has been on the role of the trade policy regime in growth, and more broadly on the link between liberalization and growth. Country performance in relation to these issues has been the subject of controversy for well over a century. The debate on whether trade was a handmaiden or an engine of growth was an analytical one before it became increasingly fact-based from the late 1960s onwards, when developing countries were first subjected to intensive scrutiny in the heat of the center–periphery debates. This chapter will not touch on the debate, but instead will review the path taken in a stylized fashion. The aim here is not to elaborate on any of these vast and complex topics, but rather to show interconnectedness as well as the most significant ways in which the region participates in the trade system. The exercise draws attention to the broad similarities and inevitably leaves out a great diversity and variability.

13.2 FROM IMPORT SUBSTITUTION TO LIBERALIZATION: AN ANALYTICAL NARRATIVE

The inward-looking phase in LA has acquired "an almost mythical status" (Bulmer Thomas 2003: 398) as a result of the controversies over the role of trade in development and the missionary zeal to contrast it unfavorably with export-led growth. Much of this criticism overlooked the fact that the inward-looking phase saw the emergence of modern industry, which in turn was able to provide decent work to growing populations. The international turmoil of the 1930s was a major determinant that drove the Latin American turn towards import substitution, attempting to shift demand from imports to domestic sources. Ever since then, and even after the postwar recovery, there has been a sharp reduction in the weight of LA in the world economy as measured by its share in global trade and capital flows. LA remained all the same extremely vulnerable to fluctuations in the world economy, and especially to the fortunes of commodity exports.

As the world economy recovered from war, Latin American exports began again to reach their usual destinations. In the early 1960s the United States and Europe each shared about a third of the region's exports. Intra-Latin American trade increased from 10% in 1950 to 15% in 1963. A marked feature of LA development in this period was that the share of commodity exports in total exports remained quite high even when the share of industry in GDP was growing fast.

From the peak of 13% of world exports in 1950, mostly explained by the boom in global demand for commodities, the share of LA fell below 6% in 1960 and to a 4% range in the 1970s and early 1980s (see Table 13.2). While Brazil's share fell to 1%, Argentina stands out as the largest loser. Its share in world exports decreased in the same period: from 3% to 0.4% of world exports in 1980. Exports were generally concentrated in a small number of commodities which often accounted for more than half of total exports. Gradually some diversification efforts bore fruit. The shift away from primary commodities exports has often been regarded as a way to achieve more effective participation in the international division of labor. Manufactures are expected to allow for a more rapid productivity growth and expansion of employment; they also offer better prospects for stable export earnings, thereby avoiding the declining terms of trade that have frustrated the development of many commodity-dependent economies (UNCTAD 2002).

Mixing import substitution with export promotion (Cárdenas, Ocampo, and Thorp 2000), manufactured exports showed good results, not only in some of the bigger non-oil exporting economies but also in some of the smaller Central American and Caribbean countries, especially Costa Rica, Haiti, and Guatemala as a result of intraregional trade and offshore processing for the US market. By 1980 they were a third of total exports in Brazil and Mexico, and a fifth in Argentina and Colombia. As a reflection of the increased share of manufactures in total exports, over the 1970s intra- LA trade increased from 18% to 21% and to the other developing countries from 4% to 7%. The United States absorbed over a third of Latin American exports while the European share continued to decline to a fifth.

In Brazil, the arsenal of export tax credits, income tax reduction, and import duty rebates related to export performance reached a peak in the late 1970s and were called into question by competing countries. Total subsidies comfortably exceeded 25% of the value of exports (Abreu 1993). Manufactured exports to the US grew 9 times from a low $63 million in the early 1970s. The pressure to induce Brazil to conform to an agreement limiting the use of export subsidies became a US policy priority through the Tokyo Round of the General Agreement on Tariffs and Trade (GATT) which ended in 1979. The US succeeded in extracting a tacit commitment to phase out the leading subsidy programs and to sign the subsidy code of the Tokyo Round. On the other hand, after the oil discoveries in 1976 Mexico resisted similar pressures and decided against signing the code and joining GATT altogether; while Colombia despite joining GATT, delayed signing the code, as did Argentina.

The other above-average performer among the larger Latin American economies in the decade after the first oil price hike was Mexico, which also opened the 1970s with a strategy based on export promotion. Mexico encouraged assembly operations through its *maquiladora* industry on the northern border, which enjoyed tariff-free access to the

US. In view of its ample industrial base. Mexico also promoted other kinds of manufactured exports.

From the mid-1960s, export promotion policies became a pillar of foreign economic policy not only in most of the larger Latin American economies, but also in some of the smaller economies such as Honduras, Haiti, El Salvador, Guatemala, and the Dominican Republic through incentives for foreign companies (mostly from the US) that assembled manufactured goods in export-processing zones.

When oil prices quadrupled in 1973–4 and then trebled in 1978–9, oil importers confronted rising import bills, trade deficits, and payments imbalances. The impact on the balance of payments was harsh after the first oil shock but devastating after the second one. It came hand in hand with the 1979 interest rate hikes, a sudden reversal of capital flows, and a steep fall in the demand for commodities, amounting to a triple external shock. Sugar exporters were particularly badly hit by the additional support of the US government to domestic production, which led to a sharp decline over the 1980s in the US sugar-import quota. International commodity agreements ran into difficulties: the tin agreement, for example, collapsed, pushing world prices down to very low levels. In despair the repeated reaction was import suppression, despite its heavy social and economic costs. The typical situation was one of immediate and severe balance-of-payments and fiscal crises, since debt service impinged heavily on the national budget. Countries devalued and adopted varieties of sharply orthodox policies, seeking import suppression by cutting demand (Thorp 1998).

Between 1983 and 1990 growth was nil in most countries, and average per capita GDP at the end of the period was 11% lower than at the beginning of the decade. The period became known as the lost decade. The struggle to survive produced widely varying strategies. Some countries changed to a higher gear and pushed on with the promotion of exports. Such was the case of the larger ones such as Argentina, Colombia, Brazil, and Mexico, as well as some of the smaller economies as Haiti and the Dominican Republic, which moved also into a mix of ISI with export promotion. Most governments viewed access to the US market as *the* key to export diversification.

As the economic crisis deepened, governments were forced to restrain fiscal and credit instruments to promote industry and export diversification, even before the tighter rules on export subsidies were enforced in the World Trade Organization (WTO). Increasingly they turned to the Bretton Woods Institutions for a financial lifeline, which was offered with a package of policy-based lending including widespread deregulation. Trade liberalization was typically set as a condition. The policymaking process as much as the bargaining power of these countries were directly affected by the drying up of financial markets. The resort to lending from the World Bank and the International Monetary Fund increased their leverage on policymaking and made room for policy-based loans that had a direct impact on the characteristics of Latin American trade regimes[2] (see Glover and Tussie 1993). Mexico, a long-time adherent of protection, opted

---

[2] Chile stands apart as an early starter; it initiated the reforms in 1975 under Pinochet, about a decade before the rest.

for trade liberalization in 1984 in the hope of moderating inflation, but also as a response to creditor pressure. In the following year, Mexico joined GATT, a momentous decision given the policy stance till that point.

Driven by expediency and lack of options, by the 1990s most Latin American countries had undertaken substantial trade liberalization to include the elimination of tariffs and non-tariff barriers. The commonality of the advice and similarity in policy instruments has led to describe this set of policy prescriptions as "the Washington Consensus" (Williamson 1994). A broad set of macroeconomic reforms was ushered in along with revamped trade policies: virtual elimination of non-tariff barriers, the adoption of lower average tariffs, and a greater uniformity of tariff structures, as shown in Table 13.1. Average levels of protection were shed dramatically in the decade running from the mid-1980s until the mid-1990s, at which point they continued to fall, but at a much slower pace. Average applied tariffs went from 29% in 1985 to 11.8% in 1995, but only reached 8.1% twelve years later, in 2007.[3] In parallel, and consistently with the liberaliza-

Table 13.1 Trends in average applied tariff rates, 1985–2007 (unweighted %)

Country	1985	1990	1995	2000	2005	2007
Argentina	35.0	20.5	12.7	15.2	10.6	10.7
Bolivia	12.1	16.0	9.7	9.2	7.2	6.2
Brazil	51.0	32.2	13.2	16.6	12.3	12.1
Chile	20.0	15.0	10.7	9.0	4.9	1.9
Colombia	61.0	27.0	13.8	12.4	11.9	10.7
Costa Rica	21.1	15.0	9.7	5.0	7.0	6.2
Dominican Rep.	18.0	17.8	17.8	20.2	9.2	8.5
Ecuador	37.7	28.0	12.5	12.1	11.8	9.8
El Salvador	23.0	21.1	10.0	7.2	6.4	5.2
Guatemala	23.0	22.8	9.7	6.9	6.7	5.4
Honduras	21.0	15.4	9.6	8.1	6.7	5.2
Mexico	25.2	11.1	12.4	18.2	9.2	11.9
Nicaragua	23.0	20.6	7.7	3.0	6.8	5.4
Paraguay	10.9	12.6	9.7	13.4	8.4	7.8
Peru	46.0	26.0	16.2	13.2	9.2	8.5
Uruguay	38.0	23.0	12.7	12.9	9.9	9.4
Venezuela	28.0	19.0	12.8	13.2	12.8	12.3
Average	29.1	20.2	11.8	11.5	8.9	8.1

Source: Heidrich (2009).

[3] Despite the pace, tariffs have certainly not converged with the developed world; moreover, many Latin American countries have also not gone as quickly in the last decade as East Asian countries, such as China, Indonesia, or even Middle Eastern ones such as Turkey (Heidrich 2009).

tion trend, nearly all Latin American and Caribbean countries became members of GATT, and later of the WTO, abiding by all obligations. Yet the steepest cuts were carried out under the network of preferential trade agreements, either regional (the bastion of all trade policies) or the new brand of growing extraregional agreements.

Despite this striking reduction of tariffs, the share of exports share in world trade remained remarkably stable, swaying between 3.9% and 5.3% (on average) from the 1970s to the 2000s, as Table 13.2 shows.

The general upshot of trade liberalization was a weakened balance of payments. After a sharp cutback in imports necessitated by the debt crisis of the 1980s, both exports and imports accelerated during the 1990s in most developing countries, but spending on imports generally rose faster than export earnings. This gap between import and export growth rates was particularly large for Latin America, where trade liberalization was coupled with the opening of the capital account and, given the liquidity in global markets, resulted in a strong appreciation of the real exchange rate by the mid-1990s that continued unabated until the turn of the century. The Argentine crash in 2001 was a paradigmatic case of the problems raised by the simultaneous implementation of both a stabilization and a liberalization program.

Latin America has been an outstanding example of a region where economic liberalization has been disappointing, and even considerably poorer than in the ISI phase (Ocampo 2004). Being politically organized, the large exporters capture policy and push for the opening of sectors where they are apt to enjoy the benefits of intra-industry trade liberalization which, while upsizing the pro-trade big firms, downsizes import competing small firms.

The traditional approach to economic integration became an initial casualty of adjustment. In real terms, the 1985–6 level of intra-Latin American exports was less than two-thirds of the 1981 level ($7.5 billion and $11.9 billion, respectively) (Thorp 1998). Intraregional imports declined even more rapidly than extraregional imports. When the debt overhang was left behind in the early 1990s, regional integration regained an unprecedented momentum (Table 13.3).

Table 13.2 Latin American weight in world merchandise exports, selected periods

	Average for the period %	Standard Deviation %
1960–9	5.3	0.5
1970–9	3.9	0.3
1980–9	4.3	0.5
1990–9	4.3	0.5
2000–8	5.2	0.2

Source: World Trade Organization.

The shift toward new trade strategies also resulted in a flurry of trade negotiations at all levels. Demands from developed countries often transformed them into institutional negotiations to target regulatory policies as distortions to trade, much like IMF or World Bank structural adjustment packages. Although such structural adjustment considerably reduced their bargaining power, many countries found solace in associations with fellow travelers—the increased number of countries that were now knocking at the door of the WTO.

13.3 THE OMNIPRESENCE OF REGIONAL INTEGRATION

The bastion of trade policy in Latin America has been regional integration: the formation of closer economic links between countries that are geographically near each other, especially by preferential trade agreements, whereby goods produced inside the region are subject to lower trade barriers than goods produced outside. A strengthening of regional economic ties encapsulated a development strategy of export diversification with long run externalities. Manufactures total more than 80% of their intraregional trade, whereas the share of manufactures drops noticeably in trade with the rest of the world.

The creation of the European Economic Community in 1958 was a true catalyzer of LA regionalism. A first generation of integration initiatives emerged in the early 1960s. On the whole they were lackluster. The emphasis was on market enlargement aiming for expanded import substitution. In 1960, a Latin American Free Trade Association (LAFTA) was formed, including all of South America and Mexico with a free trade area as a target for 1972. There was some reduction of trade barriers in the early 1960s in LAFTA, but liberalization stalled after 1964. In 1968, the deadline to establish a free trade area was extended to 1980. While not an outstanding success, LAFTA was one of the factors that explained the expansion of regional trade from a low of 6% to 12% of total trade in its first six years, after which intraregional trade plateaued.

Due to the disappointment with the narrow step-by-step trade focus of LAFTA, the Andean Pact (currently Community of Andean Nations) was established as a subregional agreement by Colombia, Peru, Bolivia, Chile, and Ecuador with the Cartagena Agreement in 1969. The Andean Pact as initially conceived was a customs union supported by common industrial policies. A Central American Common Market (1960) and a Caribbean Free Trade Area (CARIFTA, later CARICOM, 1973) were also created. In 1980, the LAFTA framework was replaced by the Latin American Integration Association (LAIA) and the initial ambitions of across the board free trade were buried, allowing a system of intraregional preferences. Regional agreements continued to be seen as a means to overcome the inherent scale limitations in each country, assist industries to become competitive on a regional level, and encourage industrial development within a cooperative framework.

The Caribbean Basin Initiative (1983) was a stepping stone in trade relations with the United States. It was conceived by the Reagan administration as a way of isolating pro-Soviet Nicaragua and Cuba. This agreement, covering Costa Rica, Honduras, El Salvador, Guatemala, Panama, and the Caribbean region (except Guyana and Cuba) provided duty-free access to the US market (with some exceptions) for twelve years. Sugar, however, a major commodity export from the Caribbean, remained subject to import quotas. And since 80% of the region's exports were already covered by previous preferences, the new facility increased the list by only 15%.

The outstanding agreement of the 1980s was the Argentina–Brazil accord of July 1986, which was the platform for the Southern Cone Common Market, MERCOSUR. In newly democratic Brazil and Argentina, a longstanding idea of a common market was revived. This was already a breakthrough in integration, since it recognized the need for negotiations at the firm level and appropriate institutional support. This had been lacking in LAFTA. The treaty was signed in 1991 by Argentina, Brazil, Paraguay, and Uruguay. In a world of agricultural protectionism MERCOSUR was the first regional agreement to grant agricultural duty free except for sugar.

Nevertheless, the turning point came at the end of the 1980s with a change of systemic implications in US policy. In 1987 the United States signed its first major free trade area with Canada, signaling a policy U-turn from the single-track multilateral stance.[4] From that point on the US would move in multiple tracks, no longer giving pre-eminence to multilateralism. In 1990 the North American Free Trade Area (NAFTA) negotiations were opened between Canada, Mexico, and the US: NAFTA was the first free-trade area linking a developing country to developed ones.

The irony of the George H.W. Bush administration's proposal was that it represented a reversal of the initial motivation for integration in the 1950s. Economic integration was then envisaged both as an essential stimulus to import substituting industrialization and as a creative defense against US economic superiority, and was therefore opposed by the United States (with the exception of the Alliance for Progress period). Adherence to a trade agreement now became a way of locking a country into a new set of rules, and of expressing a commitment to those rules in the eyes of investors. The interest of the United States in a free trade area with Mexico and Canada was also more explicitly a byproduct of the enthusiasm for "disciplinary neo-liberalism," since at the heart of the project was leveling the playing field, i.e. the harmonization of rules so that US investment might flow smoothly into Mexico and facilitate trade and growth. Other countries, fearing trade diversion, immediately began to make moves to be granted parity status with NAFTA—or outright membership. A chain reaction based on the "fear of exclusion" ensued.

In fact, in 1990 the region's four subregional agreements represented a minor share of total exports of the region, while the bulk of commodity exports took place outside of the framework of regional integration (see Table 13.3). This situation changed significantly in the course of the 1990s. Regional economic integration, which had waned in

---

[4] Two years earlier a first free trade agreement was signed with Israel. Although an omen of things to come, it did not have systemic implications.

Table 13.3 Latin America and the Caribbean: total exports by subregional integration scheme, 1990–2007 (millions of current dollars and %)

	1990	1995	1998	2002	2003	2004	2005	2006	2007	Jan.–Mar. 2007	Jan.–Mar. 2008
Latin American Integration Association (LAIA)											
Total exports	112,694	204,170	251,345	319,807	346,145	427,835	506,557	602,803	675,139	154,001	189,416
Exports to LAIA	13,589	35,471	43,118	36,164	40,872	56,777	72,979	91,757	107,586	22,664	29,678
% intrasubregional exports	12.1	17.4	17.2	11.3	11.8	13.3	14.4	15.2	15.9	14.7	15.7
Andean Community											
Total exports	31,751	39,134	38,896	52,177	54,716	74,140	100,089	126,112	139,102	29,596	44,213
Exports to Andean Community	1,312	4,812	5,504	5,227	4,900	7,604	10,313	12,719	12,909	2,622	4,012
% intrasubregional exports	4.1	12.3	14.2	10.0	9.0	10.5	10.3	10.1	9.3	8.9	9.1
Southern Common Market (MERCOSUR)											
Total exports	46,403	70,129	80,227	89,500	106,674	134,196	162,512	188,188	221,498	46,749	56,718
Exports to MERCOSUR	4,127	14,199	20,322	10,197	12,709	17,319	21,134	26,626	33,051	6,807	9,415
% intrasubregional exports	8.9	20.2	25.3	11.4	11.9	12.9	13.0	14.1	14.9	14.6	16.6
Central American Common Market (CACM)											
Total exports (1)	4,480	8,745	14,987	17,006	18,117	19,767	21,849	24,493	26,036	6,795	7,257
Exports to CACM (2)	624	1,451	2,754	2,871	3,110	3,506	3,912	4,429	5,217	1,218	1,305

Table 13.3 (contd.)

	1990	1995	1998	2002	2003	2004	2005	2006	2007	Jan.–Mar. 2007	Jan.–Mar. 2008
% intrasubregional exports	13.9	16.6	18.4	16.9	17.2	17.7	17.9	18.1	20.0	17.9	18.0
Caribbean Community (CARICOM)											
Total exports (1)	4,118	5,598	4,790	5,732	6,712	7,880	15,949	18,709	19,872	5,734.3	5,666
Exports to CARICOM (2)	509	843	1,031	1,220	1,419	1,810	2,091	2,427	2,793	693.9	775.2
Percentage intrasubregional exports	10.3	14.2	18.6	17.2	16.5	17.4	13.1	13.0	14.1	12.1	13.7
Latin America and the Caribbean											
Total exports (1)	130,214	227,922	280,065	347,610	376,590	472,444	568,798	679,713	761,959	167,356	203,061
Exports to Latin America and the Caribbean (2)	18,727	45,180	56,644	53,424	59,635	79,952	99,839	121,923	144,211	30,600	39,063
Percentage intraregional exports	13.9	19.8	20.2	15.4	15.8	16.9	17.6	17.9	18.9	18.3	19.2

Source: ECLAC (2008).

the aftermath of the debt crisis, made a comeback. LA energized intraregional agreements in an unprecedented manner by creating and revamping intraregional customs unions formed (or reformed) in the early 1990s—the Andean Community, the Caribbean Community (CARICOM), the Central American Common Market (CACM), and the Southern Common Market (MERCOSUR).

Trade expansion within each of the four customs unions was impressive. Over the 1990s, LA became increasingly important for the export strategy of other Latin American countries. At the end of the century, the United States became a major trading partner for Mexico and Central American countries, whereas the more distant Southern Cone countries were exporting most of their goods and services to either Europe or neighboring countries.

MERCOSUR was given a boost. Chile and Bolivia became associates of the group in 1996 and 1997 respectively. MERCOSUR subsequently signed a free trade agreement with the Andean Community of Nations (ACN). This agreement also went through a period of resurgence, with bilateral trade links flourishing (Colombia–Venezuela, Ecuador–Colombia). Even in Central America, where continued political tension made it particularly difficult to breathe new life into integration, a presidential summit in 1990 launched a new agreement. One of the main features of most of the trade agreements of the time was that liberalization was front-loaded, and schedules proceeded quickly and across the board. This was a sharp contrast with the cumbersome step-by-step positive lists of the first-generation agreements (Devlin and Ffrench-Davis 1998).

In 1994 President Clinton convened the first Summit of the Americas and launched the 34-country negotiations for the Free Trade Area of the Americas (FTAA), which was to merge the aspiring customs unions and NAFTA under a single umbrella. The proposed FTAA was meant to lock in liberalization and use the hemisphere as a foundation that could discipline resistance on contested issues in the WTO. In fact, Latin America is the only region where American influence had remained largely uncontested after the end of the Cold War.

Yet its many roadblocks took the project down a winding road; the grand objective of the enterprise dissolved. Ten years after inception, the FTAA fell into a de facto suspension: the January 1, 2005 completion deadline was never reached. The US, under George W. Bush, frustrated both domestically and internationally with the FTAA process, changed course and turned to the pursuit of bilateral pacts, inducing a race between countries to gain access to its market. The change of course was not merely a means of favoring loyal allies and punishing hesitant friends. The thrust of the new deals was towards implanting a range of disciplines in the region which reflect a set of extraregional and global interests at least as much as they respond to regional priorities (Phillips 2003: 6). The promotion of its interests in a more docile environment appeared more tempting than a continued uphill struggle against a host of reluctant players. As the politics of the queue ensued, intra-Latin American relations became dominated by the configuration and reconfiguration of "porous regions" meant to simultaneously engage and offset US power (Tussie 2009a).

The trend to bilateralization was first paralleled by the bilateral agreements between Mexico and Chile, and then replicated to numerous other countries of the region. The major goal was to take advantage of first mover gains. Rather than promoting the enlargement of NAFTA, Mexico took the early decision to pursue a series of bilateral and subregional overlapping free trade agreements with other countries: Chile, Colombia, Costa Rica, Venezuela, Bolivia, Nicaragua, Guatemala, Honduras, El Salvador, Belize, Panama, Trinidad and Tobago, Peru, Brazil, and then across the oceans. Nevertheless, Mexico's dependence on the US remained very high. The United States accounted for nearly 80% of Mexican exports and imports before the global financial crisis erupted in 2008.

By 2003 resistance to American-led regional trade integration gained momentum. After the invasion of Iraq and the sloppy coup attempt against the President of Venezuela Hugo Chavez in 2002, a mood of anti-Americanism swept the continent, with the good fortune of high commodity prices providing an enabling environment. MERCOSUR's disagreement with a good part of the FTAA agenda in the 2004 ministerial, and the final opposition at the Summit of the Americas in Mar del Plata, Argentina, in 2005, led to the foundering of the grand strategy. To overcome these obstacles the US offered bilateral FTAs; a web of bilateral agreements was cast over the region. Central American countries have negotiated an FTA with the US (CAFTA, later extended to the Dominican Republic, and known as the DR-CAFTA). Peru and Colombia moved with a free hand to sign their respective free trade agreements with the US (and moved on to extraregional partners, such as the EU and Asian countries). The ACN was hence hollowed out. In 2006 Venezuela moved out of the Andean Community and became poised to join MERCOSUR, indicating stronger cooperation ties with countries that have not signed bilateral agreements with the United States than with its previous partners.

In contrast to the Andean Community, CARICOM, CACM, and MERCOSUR engaged in external negotiations but still acting as customs unions—leaving little room for individual members' trade outreach—though on different grounds. Caribbean countries have a great need for developing and maintaining a cohesive and effective framework to overcome the intrinsic difficulties of small-scale countries with multi-layered trade schemes. As for MERCOSUR, its regulations allegedly contend incompatibility with commitments involving third countries. However, its two bigger members, Brazil and Argentina, appear to have softened their stances to consent some freedom of action to individual members.[5]

Today, there are about 50 regional agreements (either customs unions, FTAs, or PTAs into force involving LA countries (23% of RTA in force in the world) (Table 13.4) and an ever-growing pipeline of over 30 under negotiation. Central America has concluded FTAs with CARICOM countries, and a number of them are already negotiating with the Andean countries and exploring the prospect of an accord with the European Union (EU), Canada, Singapore, South Korea, China, etc. CARICOM signed a free trade agreement with the

---

[5] Uruguay e.g. signed a Trade and Investment Framework Agreement with the United States without breaking away from the strictures of the common external tariff.

Table 13.4 Preferential trade agreements (PTAs) notified to the GATT/WTO (including free trade areas (FTAs), customs unions (CU), and economic integration agreements (EIA))

Members	Coverage	Type	Date of entry into force
Canada–Peru	Goods & Services	FTA & EIA	1-Aug-2009
Peru–Singapore	Goods & Services	FTA & EIA	1-Aug-2009
Chile–Colombia	Goods & Services	FTA & EIA	8-May-2009
Australia–Chile	Goods & Services	FTA & EIA	6-Mar-2009
US–Peru	Goods & Services	FTA & EIA	1-Feb-2009
Panama–Honduras (Central America)	Goods & Services	FTA & EIA	9-Jan-2009
Panama–Costa Rica (Central America)	Goods & Services	FTA & EIA	23-Nov-2008
Panama–Chile	Goods & Services	FTA & EIA	7-Mar-2008
Nicaragua and the Separate Customs Territory of Taiwan, Penghu, Kinmen and Matsu	Goods & Services	FTA & EIA	1-Jan-2008
Chile–Japan	Goods & Services	FTA & EIA	3-Sep-2007
Chile–India	Goods	PTA	17-Aug-2007
Chile–China	Goods	FTA	1-Oct-2006
Panama–Singapore	Goods & Services	FTA & EIA	24-Jul-2006
Dominican Republic–Central America–United States Free Trade Agreement (CAFTA-DR)	Goods & Services	FTA & EIA	1-Mar-2006
Japan–Mexico	Goods & Services	FTA & EIA	1-Apr-2005
EFTA–Chile	Goods & Services	FTA & EIA	1-Dec-2004
Korea, Republic of–Chile	Goods & Services	FTA & EIA	1-Apr-2004
Panama and the Separate Customs Territory of Taiwan, Penghu, Kinmen and Matsu	Goods & Services	FTA & EIA	1-Jan-2004
US–Chile	Goods & Services	FTA & EIA	1-Jan-2004
Panama–El Salvador (Central America)	Goods & Services	FTA & EIA	11-Apr-2003
EC–Chile	Goods & Services	FTA & EIA	1-Feb-2003(G) 1-Mar-2005(S)
Canada–Costa Rica	Goods	FTA	1-Nov-2002
Chile–El Salvador (Central America)	Goods & Services	FTA & EIA	1-Jun-2002
Chile–Costa Rica (Central America)	Goods & Services	FTA & EIA	15-Feb-2002
EFTA–Mexico	Goods & Services	FTA & EIA	1-Jul-2001
Honduras–Mexico	Goods & Services	FTA & EIA	1-Jun-2001
El Salvador–Mexico	Goods & Services	FTA & EIA	15-Mar-2001
Guatemala–Mexico	Goods & Services	FTA & EIA	15-Mar-2001
EC–Mexico	Goods & Services	FTA & EIA	1-Jul-2000(G) 1-Oct-2000(S)

(cont.)

Table 13.4 (contd.)

Members	Coverage	Type	Date of entry into force
Israel–Mexico	Goods	FTA	1-Jul-2000
Chile–Mexico	Goods & Services	FTA & EIA	1-Aug-1999
Mexico–Nicaragua	Goods & Services	FTA & EIA	1-Jul-1998
Canada–Chile	Goods & Services	FTA & EIA	5-Jul-1997
Costa Rica–Mexico	Goods & Services	FTA & EIA	1-Jan-1995
North American Free Trade Agreement (NAFTA)	Goods & Services	FTA & EIA	1-Jan-1994
MERCOSUR	Goods	CU	29-Nov-1991
Andean Community (CAN)	Goods	CU	25-May-1988
Latin American Integration Association (LAIA)	Goods	PTA	18-Mar-1981
CARICOM	Goods	CU	1-Aug-1973
Central American Common Market (CACM)	Goods	CU	12-Oct-1961
CARICOM	Services	EIA	1-Jul-1997
MERCOSUR	Services	EIA	7-Dec-2005

Source: WTO, available online at: http://www.wto.org/english/tratop_e/region_e/region_e.htm (last visited January 2010).

Dominican Republic in 2001, and has announced the start of free trade negotiations with MERCOSUR.

The proliferation of FTAs has continued, spiralling out to extraregional countries as well. For most countries in South America, Europe is as important a trading partner as the United States and Canada combined. A number of subregions would stand to benefit as much from trade and investment liberalization in the European Union as from the FTAA. One of the reasons why Mexico took up an agreement with the European Union despite its already strong dependence on the United States markets was precisely to minimize any residue of trade diversion, diversify export markets, and attract European FDI. For Chile, the European Union represented roughly a fifth of its total exports at the time of the FTA; the agreement was meant to enhance market diversification.

While since 1990 trade flows have gained relevance in regional output, so has the relevance of RTAs. Before the eruption of the international crisis in 2008, almost three-quarters of the region's exports came under some type of intraregional or extraregional preferential arrangement. The trend was most marked for Mexico and Central America. In the process, Chile and Mexico have become genuine "semi-hubs" for FTAs in the hemisphere. Chile chose to keep a low, flat tariff while engaging in a multi-track market access strategy, with an ever-expanding network of free trade agreements. While Chilean exports remain mainly based on natural resources, market destination has diversified considerably.

The multiplication of trade agreements has been accompanied by a less drastic fall in external tariffs than had been the case at the start of trade reform in the 1990s when downward pressure reached a maximum. Mexico and Chile are outliers, with the lowest MFN tariffs. All in all, today, trade flows in LA are freer than ever before. Trade is almost fully liberalized among members of the various subregional groups such as Caricom, the CACM, MERCOSUR, and NAFTA. The stagnation of the FTAA talks in 2003 triggered a further quest for bilateral intraregional FTAs. Among the most recent highlights are the MERCOSUR–Andean Community FTA of 2004, the US–Central America–Dominican Republic FTA (DR-CAFTA) of 2005, and the culmination of the US–Colombia, US–Peru, US–Panama, Chile–Peru, and Chile–Colombia FTA negotiations in 2007.

The proliferation of FTAs makes it impossible to draw sharp lines around trade blocs. As the worldwide trend shows, these boundaries are "fuzzy" (Baldwin 2006). Snowballing bilateral agreements make boundaries indeterminate and in constant reconfiguration. Traditional blocs once envisaged as fixed are now in a state of flux, and come under varying degrees of stress as newcomers join and old members defect.[6] To sum up, we are no longer in the presence of a fixed one-stop shop. Paraphrasing Baldwin, trade blocs are fuzzy since the geographical boundaries shift constantly due to FTAs proliferation. They are also "leaky" in the sense that the bloc's tariff wall has several holes due to associations with other blocs across the world. The days of Latin America-only integration are over.

13.3.1 Cross-bloc associations: trans-continentalism

If the 1990s denoted a revealed preference for agreements within the hemisphere, the 21st century revealed a preference for reaching outside the region, whether it implied negotiating with European Union or further afield with Asian partners. Mexico and Chile have become hubs in themselves as a result of their particularly intense activity in the negotiation of bilateral agreements.

Intraregionalism is today yielding to "trans-continentalism" (Estevadeordal, Shearer, and Suominen 2007). Countries have sought to establish an early foothold in Asia. In 2003 Chile and South Korea signed the Asian country's first comprehensive bilateral FTA, and in 2005 Chile concluded negotiations for a four-part FTA with Brunei Darussalam, New Zealand, and Singapore. An FTA between Chile and China—the East Asian economy's first extraregional FTA—came into effect in October 2006, and in November 2006 Chile became the second country in the region to reach an FTA with Japan. The Mexico–Japan Economic Partnership Agreement, Japan's first extraregional free trade agreement, also took effect in 2005. The same year, Peru and Thailand signed a bilateral FTA, while FTAs between Taipei, China, on the one hand, and Panama and Guatemala, on the other, took effect in 2004 and 2006 respectively. Panama also concluded FTA negotiations with

---

[6] This process of reconfiguration is not peculiar to Latin America; it is similar to the process that Britain triggered when it defected from the European Free Trade Area to join the European Economic Community. The countries linked to sterling followed suit and EFTA was gradually hollowed out.

Singapore in 2006; while Costa Rica did likewise in 2010. The steps reaching out to the Pacific agreements are poised to continue their expansion. Chile, Mexico, Costa Rica, and Peru are pursuing closer ties with Asia in the context of the Asia-Pacific Economic Cooperation (APEC) forum inaugurated in 1989.

Across the Atlantic, agreements with the European Union (EU) keep marching on. Five years after NAFTA, Mexico signed an FTA with the EU in 2000, as did Chile in 2003. In May 2006, the EU and CACM countries announced the launch of negotiations for a comprehensive Association Agreement; while Ecuador, Colombia, and Peru remain engaged in negotiations with the EU and the EU–CARICOM talks were close to their final phase at the time of writing. Besides the trans-Pacific and trans-Atlantic fronts, MERCOSUR has concluded an agreement with India. MERCOSUR has not abandoned hope of building up an interregional association with the EU, and there are initiatives to cover South Africa, India, South Korea, China, and the Gulf, among others.

Marching in step with this activity, the geographical composition of trade flows has changed (see Table 13.5). The most notable shift is the drop of the United States as an export destination and the rising relevance of Asia. The dynamism of the Asian markets in the 2000s was translated into the increase above 10% in the share of exports to the region, while the weight of the US as an export market moved in the opposite direction. To be sure, there are wide intraregional differences; countries such as Argentina, Brazil,

Table 13.5 Export shares by main destination, 2000 and 2007 (% of total exports)

	Latin America and the Caribbean		China		Asia-Pacific		United States		European Union (27 countries)	
	2000	2007	2000	2007	2000	2007	2000	2007	2000	2007
South America										
Argentina	48	39	3	10	8	16	12	8	18	19
Bolivia	47	61	0	1	1	12	24	9	17	6
Brazil	25	25	2	10	12	18	24	15	28	24
Chile	22	16	5	15	29	36	18	13	25	24
Colombia	29	36	0	3	3	6	51	31	14	18
Ecuador	32	32	1	1	12	3	40	43	16	16
Paraguay	75	72	0	1	4	4	3	3	11	21
Peru	22	18	7	12	20	24	28	19	21	18
Uruguay	55	37	4	6	10	12	8	10	16	22
Venezuela (Bol. Rep. Of)	20	15	0	4	1	5	55	52	5	9
Central America										
Costa Rica	19	25	0	14	3	24	38	25	21	24
El Salvador	28	39	0	0	1	3	24	48	11	6

Table 13.5 (contd.)

	Latin America and the Caribbean		China		Asia-Pacific		United States		European Union (27 countries)	
Guatemala	36	41	0	1	3	4	59	42	10	6
Honduras	6	21	0	0	4	2	77	69	10	10
Nicaragua	23	22	0	0	1	2	41	63	20	7
Panama	20	19	0	0	3	6	50	21	19	50
Mexico	3	6	0	1	1	3	89	78	3	6
Caribbean										
Bahamas			-	1	4	17	29	21	52	44
Barbados			0	0	2	2	5	12	20	17
Belize			-	-	3	8	52	28	38	35
Cuba	8	11	5	28	8	29	0	0	39	21
Dominican Republic	4	5	0	2	1	6	87	67	6	17
Dominica			-	27	7	31	7	2	31	18
Grenada			-	0	0	1	51	21	31	14
Guyana			1	2	4	5	25	17	30	33
Haiti			0	1	0	4	87	75	5	5
Jamaica			1	3	3	5	38	35	32	31
Saint Kitts and Nevis			0	0	1	0	68	61	23	20
Saint Lucia			0	0	1	0	18	26	55	48
Saint Vincent and the Grenadines			-	-	2	0	3	1	46	69
Suriname			0	0	5	1	25	9	29	21
Trinidad and Tobago			0	0	1	2	47	59	14	9
Latin America and the Caribbean	16	18	1	6	6	12	60	42	12	15

Source: ECLAC (2008).

Chile, and Peru have seen their commodity exports to China surge in their export baskets. Even in the 21st century it seems that LA's insertion in world markets may still be shaped by its distinctive resource base, this time with China as the new outlet for oil, agricultural, and mineral commodities such as copper and iron ore.

Trade with Asia gained dynamism for the region as a whole and for each subcontinent separately—the same applies to each of the subregional integration schemes. In the 2000s, extraregional trade was a much stronger factor than intraregional trade. As Table 13.5 shows, this pattern is clearer in the cases of South American countries.

The new century thus opened with the imprint of elastic bundling and rebundling, rather than neat convergence. This issue has a sharper edge since the demise of the FTAA and the slackened impetus of the US. Nonetheless, the EU and the US, each vying to gain a competitive edge, are striving to obtain economic liberalization in the region beyond the levels established by the WTO. The processes currently ongoing with the EU seem to provide incentives for convergence, since the latter requests customs unions to set a common baseline for negotiations. This procedure may provide incentives for countries to harmonize and coordinate their norms (LATN 2006). However, after the FTAA was cut short, agreements with the US were signed on a one-to-one basis, with strong differences in rules of origin; all matters being equal, they will not necessarily lead to convergence. Alternative projects continually jostle and overlap, without achieving completion or consensus, littering the landscape with agreements that contain specific incentives for specific interests.

13.4 IN THE GLOBAL TRADE REGIME: FROM PASSIVE BYSTANDERS TO ACTIVE DRIVERS

A country's trade chances depend on a mix of conditions and circumstances based on endowments, internal structures, and the world market context. Policies and internal dynamics matter, but they are formulated and implemented within the context of a facilitating or inhibiting global regime. This context was first marked by GATT and then by its successor, the WTO, which sets limits and crystallizes trends. As such, what is possible for national policy is set by the trade regime, itself continuously redefined by the negotiating process and the right to litigate. For that reason the trade regime retains heavy overtones of a North–South struggle.

Based on liberal economic theories that assert a connection between open trade and growth, the regime has sought to promote the liberalization of trade, has enforced a set of rules and regulations, and has served as a forum to settle disputes. The system was originally conceived at the end of World War II. Its first expression was GATT, adopted in 1947 by 23 founding members. Between 1947 and 1994, GATT held a total of eight rounds of tariff reductions, leading to substantial liberalization of the trade in manufactures of developed countries. The premises underlying import-substitution policies were so widely accepted in the postwar period that they were incorporated when the charter of GATT was drafted. Article XVIII explicitly excluded developing countries from the "full obligations" of industrialized countries, and permitted them to adopt tariff and quantitative restrictions. They were also entitled to "special and differential treatment" in other areas (Krueger 1997: 5).

For most developing economies, GATT was "a rich men's club." Amongst the LA countries, only Brazil, Chile, and Cuba (where some of the pre-negotiations had taken place) were present at inception. Haiti, Nicaragua, Peru, the Dominican Republic, and Uruguay followed soon after signing the charter. Large LA economies only became contracting parties later on. Argentina, Jamaica, Guyana, Trinidad and Tobago, and Barbados joined in the 1960s. Colombia joined in 1981 after the Tokyo round (1973–9) and became a key player in the preparatory phase of the Uruguay Round (UR). Mexico joined in 1985 in the run-up to the UR (1986–94). Global protectionism affected Latin American exports, especially for temperate agricultural commodities, processed tropical goods, textiles, and apparel. Tariff lines of Latin American economies were mostly "unbound,"[7] i.e. there were no undertakings on tariff ceilings. Quantitative import restrictions justified on balance-of-payments grounds (GATT Article XVIII: B) were commonly used, and afforded considerable protection.

The rounds of negotiation delivered meager benefits for developing countries. Liberalization remained largely restricted to intra-industry, intra-firm trade, where the shedding of tariffs opened opportunities for the large-scale operations in industrial countries (Tussie 1988). Whereas as late as 1955 the trade in manufactured products among developed countries had accounted for a third of world trade, this had risen to nearly half by the end of the 1960s. No efforts were made to tackle the issues of trade in primary products, which was excluded from its orbit, so that it was unable to tackle the panoply of tariffs and non-tariff barriers on primary products (posing severe obstacles for other countries to develop downstream processing) or the subsidies that grew unabated after the Common Agricultural Policy (CAP) of the European Economic Community (EEC) came into being in the 1960s.

As subsidies grew, the developed countries also surpassed the developing countries in the value of primary product exports, so their total contribution to world trade had reached over 80% by 1969. The Tokyo Round did not dent agricultural protectionism, nor did it halt tight-fisted regulation of steel, textile, and apparel products. The imposition of a code of conduct to restrict export subsidies made the use of trade interventions increasingly out of bounds. Claiming "unfair competition" from developing countries, fiscal rebates of the sort that many countries applied to promote manufactures were outlawed, and successive exports came under the purview of anti-dumping and countervailing duty reprisals. The UR was launched in 1986 while most countries were still in the throes of the debt crisis. The LA countries that joined GATT at that time seized the multilateral agenda as a means to lock in freshly acquired preferences within trade policies or as an element to throw into their "package of concessions."

To accompany the integrationist thrust there came an acceptance both of rules and of tariff reductions for the first time. Certainly, in former rounds, countries that had already joined GATT had either stood on the sidelines or had pressed to be released from rules. But when the UR closed in 1995, all countries extended their "bindings" to almost all tariff items. The LA average applied external tariff was drastically reduced to 11.8% (Table 13.1), and the maximum tariff fell from the peak of more than 80% to 40%. Only Chile and Peru applied uniform tariffs, with minor exceptions.

Overwhelmed at the time by depressed commodity prices, Latin American foodstuff exporting countries joined the Australian-led coalition of countries, the Cairns Group of Fair Traders, to press for the reduction of trade barriers and rampant subsidies affecting

---

[7] "Bindings" in the WTO jargon means that tariffs, once set, cannot be raised unless they are renegotiated with partners. New concessions must be offered for a tariff item to become unbound.

agricultural trade. The goal was a direct response to the subsidy war that kept pushing by then gravely depressed commodity prices towards a continued free fall—a factor leading to the debt crises of the 1980s. The members jointly accounted for a significant portion of world agricultural exports, but were all victims of the subsidy wars between Europe and the US. Besides Australia, the group comprised Argentina, Brazil, Canada, Chile, Colombia, Hungary, Indonesia, Malaysia, New Zealand, the Philippines, Thailand, and Uruguay. Brushing aside the historical dividing line between developed and developing countries, it allowed countries to participate proactively as empowered insiders to the negotiations. The Cairns Group was a mighty learning experience: not only did it turn out to be a relevant coalition holding the balance through the UR (Tussie 1993), but it also marked a fundamental break from the earlier "passivism" in trade negotiations.

Despite the cumulative efforts, countries came out sorely disappointed. They soon learnt that acceptance of the rules of the game (including their own liberalization) did not translate automatically into leverage, as they found it difficult to decisively influence the process of agenda-setting and to shape the final outcome of negotiations. The outcome of the UR was severely imbalanced. While developing countries reduced tariffs, increased bindings, accepted tighter rules on intellectual property, and agreed to get rid of export subsidies, not much was gained in terms of improved market access.

In agriculture, even after reduction by 36%, which was the set obligation, in order to retain room to maneuver, many products ended up with higher levels of protection than applied before the UR. For example, the following *ad valorem* tariffs were notified by the EU as base rates: rice 361%, wheat 156%, sugar 297%, meat 125%, and dairy products 288% (Hathaway and Ingco 1996). Subsidies on agricultural products were "bound," i.e. could not be increased beyond the level notified, but binding levels were strikingly generous in the amount of water included over and above the leeway to change from restricted to unrestricted categories (the notorious "blue box"[8]) and other such loopholes. Estimation of public support to farmers provides the following figures: In Japan, US$23,000/ farmer; in EU US$20,000/ farmer, and in USA US$16,000/ farmer.

Prior to the commodity bonanza of 2003–8, in Japan agricultural subsidies represented 58% of the total value of production, and in the EU and the US 35% and 21% respectively. In short, there was meager agricultural liberalization and in many cases there was room for retrogression (Meller 2003). Tariff escalation by industrial countries retained substantial loading against imports from developing countries. Much more important for development strategy were the provisions on intellectual property rights (TRIPs). All members had to recognize minimum rights for owners of intellectual property, and to establish national enforcement mechanisms. Under these provisions the pharmaceutical industry was able to hold back on making valuable drugs available to developing countries. In the case of Argentina, it has been estimated that rents of $425 million per year may have been transferred from domestic to international pharmaceu-

---

[8] "The blue box" refers to government support payments which limit production by imposing production quotas or requiring farmers to set aside part of their land. Blue box measures were excepted from the general rule that all subsidies linked to production must be reduced or kept within defined minimal (*de minimis*) levels.

tical industries (Nogues 2005). The right to other policy instruments was also narrowed down, and challenged in WTO committees and the dispute settlement mechanism: price bands[9] and simplified drawback schemes (in Chile), price reference system for imports (in Uruguay), export credits (in Brazil), regional subsidies for tobacco and port development (in Argentina), among others. An underlying reason for the imbalanced outcome was that negotiations were not used to open foreign markets, but as a means of locking in reforms. In this context of enfeebled bargaining power, the world of ever-growing continuous negotiations strengthened essential asymmetries, bringing developing countries under disciplines from which they had previously been exempt. Negotiations often turned out to be opportunities for a combination of structural adjustment packages along comparative advantage patterns.

When the costs of new obligations hit the raw nerve of policy, especially after the so-called Battle of Seattle, the 1999 Ministerial Conference, asymmetries in the WTO became a matter of concern for business and civil society alike. A new awareness and the power of numbers (i.e. the jump in WTO membership) gradually gave way to a new negotiating dynamic based on the formation of multiple negotiating coalitions. Pent-up dissatisfaction re-emerged at the subsequent Ministerial Conference in Cancun in 2003. This time governments prepared beforehand, showing their ability to act in pursuit of collective interests and in favor of leveling the playing field. Brazil took the lead and joined forces with other emerging powers—China, India, South Africa—as well as with leading agricultural exporters in LA.

A remarkable development was the rise of a powerful negotiating voice with the formation of the G-20, a group centered on Brazil and India.[10] Following in the footsteps of the Cairns Group, the G-20 was set up just before the Cancun Ministerial Conference, in order to coordinate pressure on the EU and the US to reduce their import tariffs, export subsidies, and domestic support in agriculture. By then China was "dictating global prices for nearly everything from copper to microchips," since its share of world trade had jumped from 1% to more than 6% over the previous 20 years (Blázquez-Lidoy, Rodríguez, and Santiso 2006: 32). Leaning on commodity power as the new engine of growth, countries flexed their muscles against the historical rigidities in the trade regime, and especially against the subsidies of developed countries which, if not brought under control, could now gain the race for access to the prized Chinese markets. After the Ministerial meeting in Cancun, Brazil in conjunction with India begun to play an innovative role, showing a greater interest in and capacity to coordinate and lead positions.[11]

---

[9] The use of price bands provides a buffer from lower world than domestic prices. It consists of setting a band of upper and lower prices for imports so as to trigger the application of an offsetting tariff when the international price of a product falls below the lower band level.

[10] The G-20 comprises the following LA countries: Argentina, Bolivia, Brazil, Cuba, Chile, Colombia, Costa Rica, Ecuador, El Salvador, Guatemala, Mexico, Paraguay, Peru, Uruguay, and Venezuela.

[11] The newfound commodity power was also a factor that enabled countries to hedge their bets and decide whether or not to plunge into the FTAA. A few months after Cancun, the FTAA was cut short. The US perceived the G-20 to be such a serious challenge to its agenda that Colombia, Costa Rica, Guatemala, Peru, Ecuador, and El Salvador, at that point in time negotiating free trade areas with the US, were asked not to participate in the G-20 if they were interested in access to the US market. Once the agreements were signed, these countries rejoined the G20.

Learning from the experience of the G-20, tropical exporters in the Andean and Central American countries have followed suit and come together as the G-11, upholding the liberalization of tropical products. Interestingly, this coalition so far comprises solely LA members of the Andean Community and the Central American Common Market (Bolivia, Colombia, Costa Rica, Ecuador, El Salvador, Guatemala, Honduras, Panama, Peru, Nicaragua, and Venezuela). Another bargaining coalition where LA countries are active with a mostly defensive attitude is the G-33,[12] consisting mainly of net food-importing developing countries concerned about the prospects of premature liberalization at home.

These new coalitions have a proactive agenda, typified in technically substantive proposals at each stage of the negotiations, and which is increasingly covering issues other than agriculture, particularly the so-called non-agricultural market access chapters. Each one relies on considerable research to support its agenda and looks for windows of opportunity to move. As such, the strategy is a stark contrast against the ideological battles that countries had put up in their call for the new international economic order of the 1970s. Even more interesting is the permanent interaction between the coalitions. Due to the differing priorities (and sometimes directly conflicting interests) of some of these coalitions, rifts are bound to appear from time to time. "Alliances of sympathy" between coalitions build bridges and attempt to coordinate positions and share information with other developing countries, and at the very least minimize overt contradictions when fuller coordination is not possible. Facilitated by overlapping membership, the bridges between the G-20 and the G-33—the former representing offensive agricultural interests and the latter arguing for the respect of food security—serve as a case in point.

In the world of negotiations, coalitions continue their tasks. But coalitions are not a matter of principle. They are formed for specific contextual reasons, in this case the need to open up and to an extent democratize the WTO decisionmaking process. In such settings, coalitions play a major regulating role through movement as much as through existence. But framing and defining problems, questions, and issues does not translate neatly into a full development strategy. Such issue-specific trade alliances are restricted to the liberalization of certain products or, alternatively, to the concern not to give away policy space in exchange for market access—a necessary but insufficient condition for development, as witnessed by the 2001 Doha Declaration on Public Health. In view of the massive transfer of rents from developing countries to multinational drug companies, awareness that patent protection may now be too strong has increased. At the same time as countries accept intrusive disciplines over an ever-widening scope of development policy areas by virtue of the North–South free trade agreements, they use the WTO to resist the continuous un-leveling of the playing field, and are bent on obtaining a more balanced treatment of domestic needs than was admitted in the UR. This proactive posture has been also present in a number of areas. Paraguay and Bolivia have been active in

[12] The G-33 comprises the following LA countries: Antigua and Barbuda, Barbados, Belize, Cuba, China, Grenada, Guyana, Haiti, Honduras, Jamaica, Nicaragua, Panama, Peru, Dominican Republic, Saint Kitts and Nevis, Saint Vicent and Granadines, Saint Lucia, Surinam, Trinidad and Tobago, and Venezuela.

raising the special needs of landlocked countries. Chile, Colombia, Mexico, Argentina, and Brazil form part of the group to promote tighter practices on the use of antidumping, either of a free trade or defensive variety. Whatever the eventual outcomes of the Doha Round, coalitions have introduced a semblance of limited pluralism in the WTO.

Certainly, the entry of China into the WTO has shaken policies as well as beliefs. While China's low labor costs and strong competitiveness pose risks to manufactured exports, its appetite for raw materials and foodstuffs has favored LA's commodity endowments. In 2003 China became the world's largest importer of cotton, copper, and soybean, and the fourth largest importer of oil. It has become the region's fastest-growing export market. Given this vigorous demand, the region went through a period of unprecedented bonanza. The new engine of growth had centrifugal effects on the loose stitching of regional agreements, displacing the role that neighboring countries had held. Trade with China is, however, very much concentrated on a small basket of commodities, copper, oil, iron ore, soybeans, and wood. The new engine of growth may deepen the historical trade specialization toward commodities—goods usually characterized by strong price volatility. Unless an effort to deepen specializations is mustered, and over-reliance on a single engine of growth is tempered, dependence on a few commodities will intensify; countries will remain overexposed to trade shocks, and the inequality-generating forces of international asymmetries will not be tamed.

REFERENCES

ABREU, M. (1993). 'Latin America in the World Trading System', Working Paper No. 295, Pontificia Universidad Catolica de Rio de Janeiro.

BALDWIN, R. (2006). 'Multilateralizing Regionalism: Spaghetti Bowls as Building Blocs on the Path to Global Free Trade', NBER Working Paper No. 12545, Cambridge, Mass.

BLÁZQUEZ-LIDOY, J., RODRÍGUEZ, J., and SANTISO, J. (2006). 'Angel or Demon? China's Trade Impact on Latin American countries', *CEPAL Review* 90.

BULMER-THOMAS, V. (2003). *The Economic History of Latin America Since Independence*, 2nd edn, New York: Cambridge University Press.

—— and PAGE, S. (1999). 'Trade Relations in the Americas: Mercosur, the Free Trade Area of the Americas and the European Union', in J. Dunkerley and V. Bulmer-Thomas (eds), *The United States and Latin America: The New Agenda*, Cambridge, Mass.: Harvard University Press.

CÁRDENAS, E., OCAMPO, J. A., and THORP, R. (2000). *An Economic History of 20th-Century Latin America*, Vol. 3: *Industrialization and the State in Latin America*, Basingstoke and New York: Palgrave and St. Martins Press.

DEVLIN, R., and ESTEVADEORDAL, A. (2001). 'What is new in the new regionalism in the Americas?', INTAL Working Paper No. 6, Washington, DC.

—— and FFRENCH-DAVIS, R. (1998). 'Towards an Evaluation of Regional Integration in Latin America in the 1990s', INTAL Working Paper No. 2.

ECLAC (UN Economic Committee for Latin America and the Caribbean) (2008). *Latin America and the Caribbean in the World Economy 2007: Trends 2008*, Santiago, Chile.

ESTEVADEORDAL, A., SHEARER, M., and SUOMINEN, K. (2007). 'Multilateralizing RTAs in the Americas: State of Play and Ways Forward', presented at the Conference on Multilateralising Regionalism, WTO and CEPR, Geneva, September 10–12.

FINGER, M., and NOGUES, J. (2002). 'The Unbalanced Uruguay Outcome: The New Areas in Future WTO Negotiations', *World Economy* 25.3.

GLOVER, D. J., and TUSSIE, D. (1993). *Developing Countries and World Trade: Policies and Bargaining Strategies*, Boulder, Colo.: Rienner.

HATHAWAY, D., and INGCO, M. (1996). 'Agricultural Liberalization and the Uruguay Round', in W. Martin and L. A. Winters (eds), *The Uruguay Round and the Developing Countries*, Cambridge: Cambridge University Press.

HEIDRICH, P. (2009). 'Latin America and the WTO: Current and Future Scenarios', presented at the Geneva Trade and Development Symposium, LATN and COPLA, Geneva, November 30 – December 2.

—— and TUSSIE, D. (2010). 'Regional Trade Agreements and the WTO: The Gyrating Gears of Interdependence', in D. Steger (ed.), *Redesigning the WTO for the Twenty First Century*, Ottawa: Wilfried Laurier University Press, CIGI, and IDRC.

KRUEGER, A. (1997). 'Trade Policy and Economic Development: How We Learn', *American Economic Review* 87.1.

KUWAYAMA, M., DURÁN LIMA, J., and SILVA, V. (2005). 'Bilateralism and Regionalism: Re-establishing the Primacy of Multilateralism—a Latin American and Caribbean Perspective', ECLAC International Trade Series Paper No. 58, Santiago, Chile.

LATN (Latin America Training Network) (2006). *Meeting Report on Global Governance and Regionalism*, Buenos Aires.

MELLER, P. (2003). 'A Developing Country View on Liberalization of Tariff and Trade Barriers', LATN Working Paper No. 19, Buenos Aires.

NOGUES, J. (2005). *Argentina*, International Trade 0502009, EconWPA.

OCAMPO, J. A. (2004). 'Latin America's Growth and Equity Frustrations During Structural Reforms', *Journal of Economic Perspectives* 18.2.

PHILLIPS, N. (2003). 'Hemispheric Integration and Subregionalism in the Americas', *International Affairs* 79.2.

THORP, R. (1998). *Poverty, Progress and Exclusion: An Economic History of Latin America in the Twentieth Century*, Washington, DC: IDB.

TUSSIE, D. (1988). *The LDCs and the World Trading System: A Challenge to the GATT*, London and New York: Pinter and St. Martin's Press.

—— (1993). 'Holding the Balance: The Cairns Group in the Uruguay Round', in D. Tussie and D. Glover (eds), *Developing Countries and World Trade: Policies and Bargaining Strategies*, Boulder, Colo.: Rienner.

—— (2009a). 'Latin America: Contrasting Motivations for Regional Projects', *Review of International Studies* 35.

—— (2009b). 'Process Drivers in Trade Negotiations: The Role of Research on the Path to Grounding and Contextualizing', *Global Governance* 15.3.

UNCTAD (UN Conference on Trade and Development) (2002). *Trade and Development Report*, New York and Geneva.

VENTURA-DIAS, V. (2004). 'Introduction: Juggling with WTO Rules in Latin America', in M. F. Lengyel and V. Ventura-Dias (eds), *Trade Policy Reform in Latin America: Multilateral Rules and Domestic Institutions*, Basingstoke: Palgrave Macmillan.

WILLIAMSON, J. (ed.) (1994). *The Political Economy of Policy Reform*, Washington, DC: Institute for International Economics.

WTO (World Trade Organization) (2001). 'Declaration on the TRIPS Agreement and Public Health', available online at: http://www.wto.org/english/thewto_e/minist_e/min01_e/mindecl_trips_e.htm

CHAPTER 14

REGIONAL INTEGRATION

PAOLO GIORDANO AND ROBERT DEVLIN

14.1 INTRODUCTION[1]

In Latin America, the drive for regional integration goes back to the postcolonial era and is rooted in the ideals of the founding fathers known as the *libertadores*. Regional integration has been a recurrent theme that has inspired many generations of intellectuals and political leaders irrespective of their political persuasion. The aspiration was to integrate with economic instruments vast territories segmented by daunting geographical barriers, and to overcome the legacy of a colonial infrastructure system planned to extract rents from the periphery and strategically prevent communication among provinces and colonies, rather than stimulating shared prosperity and independence. More recently, integration policies have been seen as additional tools to better navigate the uncharted waters of globalization.

In the postwar period, regional integration, or wider preferential trade agreements, developed in three waves: the "old" regionalism of the 1950s and 1960s, which was an attempt to rationalize the Depression-era import substitution policies at a moment when they were displaying diminishing returns; the "new" regionalism of the 1990s and early 2000s, which was an attempt to strengthen the foundations of outward-oriented policies at a moment when the nature of globalization was changing dramatically; and the current phase, in which proliferating bilateral North–South agreements seem to prevail over ailing subregional projects and there is a growing consensus on the need to promote the convergence of partially overlapping initiatives.

The objective of this chapter is to schematically present the origin, development, and future perspectives of regional integration in Latin America. Emphasis will be placed on regional integration agreements (RIA), mainly free trade areas and customs unions involving regional partners, as opposed to other forms of preferential trade agreements.

[1] The opinions expressed herein are those of the authors and do not reflect in any way the official position of their respective institutions or their member countries.

Section 14.2 presents the main driving forces that explain the continued quest for regional integration in the region, with emphasis on their transformation over time. Section 14.3 describes the main initiatives at play under the old regionalism. Section 14.4 highlights the many novelties of the new regionalism, with emphasis on the policy background, the strategic objectives, and the policy instruments. Section 14.5 compares the performance of the old and the new regionalism. Section 14.6 presents the state of play of integration today after a failed attempt at hemispheric integration and the proliferation of bilateralism. Section 14.7 concludes.

14.2 THE RATIONALE FOR ECONOMIC INTEGRATION

Through formal or informal agreements, regional integration initiatives allow policymakers to realize a number of economic and political objectives. The effects of regional integration sought by policymakers are the object of a vast body of literature (see e.g. Panagariya 2000). Simplifying, it is possible to summarize them in three broad categories analyzed in turn below. These motivations have been present in all Latin American integration efforts. Nevertheless, their relative weight has shifted over time.

14.2.1 Economic welfare

Economic integration generates static economic benefits and costs. Integration agreements involving substantial lowering of tariff and non-tariff barriers are likely to unleash new trade and investment flows. Particularly when they are coupled with objectives of external liberalization, they help to "create"—rather than "divert"—trade and investment. As a result, static efficiency in the allocation of factors of production across productive sectors is enhanced, and national welfare available for redistribution increases. Terms of trade can also improve and generate benefits at the expenses of the excluded parties, but this effect is not very relevant for economies that are small in global terms such as those of Latin America. Finally, integration policies that expand the size of the domestic market allow firms to tap into economies of scale and intra-firm cost reduction effects.

In the longer run, RIA may also create dynamic effects and contribute to the accumulation of capital, including attracting foreign direct investment to the larger market, thereby generating higher growth rates. Albeit hard to measure and admittedly difficult to isolate from other variables, dynamic gains from integration may materialize either when domestic firms that are exposed to foreign competition are induced to increase productivity, or when regional integration favors in any way the accumulation of capital and "learning," as when it provides incentives to produce and export goods with a higher content of technology or value added.

14.2.2 Policy signaling

The participation in RIA has been frequently used to signal the commitment to certain policies using peer pressure and legal commitments of like-minded neighbors as a lock-in instrument. Through RIAs, member countries may upgrade their regulatory frameworks and meet the standards of more advanced partners. Similarly, in an era when market-oriented structural reforms are a priority, a RIA can be used to signal "good" policies and stigmatize "bad" ones, thereby helping countries to maintain domestic reforms on track.

Economic integration is also an endogenous self-propelling policy driver. Deeper integration provides a useful infrastructure and incentives for further cooperation, including investments in regional public goods such as regional road networks, energy transmission lines, or, more generally, cooperation in a wide array of cross-border matters (Devlin and Estevadeordal 2004). By creating political economy incentives for shared prosperity, regional integration is a self-reinforcing additional policy tool to promote structural transformation among like-minded countries.

Finally, RIAs can help to uphold democratic values. Particularly in more recent agreements, embracing democracy has been a prerequisite for entering the club. Therefore the risk of exclusion can inspire common efforts to enhance the quality of democratic governance in the member states.

With different timing and intensity, all these factors have played a role in Latin American integration. However, the old integration schemes of the early postwar period that were mainly grounded in defensive objectives of member countries at the expense of excluded countries, entailed relatively high domestic efficiency costs, and in certain cases displayed internal contradictions. In contrast, the newer agreements have been more effective in promoting efficient static and dynamic benefits, as well as the non-traditional gains from integration (Devlin and Giordano 2004).

14.2.3 Systemic strategies

By the turn of this century, trade integration initiatives had begun to proliferate in the Americas and elsewhere. Thus strategic rationales related to the systemic interconnection of partially overlapping agreements became increasingly important. Indeed, Latin American countries started to use trade integration, both South–South and North–South, as a strategic instrument to enhance the preparedness for wider hemispheric and multilateral trade liberalization.

In a world of competitive trade liberalization, one in which preferences built through the negotiation of bilateral or regional agreements are eroded rapidly, first-movers have an advantage. Early integration can enable countries to gain an edge in new markets and to attract foreign investments. Conversely, failure in the integration race may result in remaining outside the web of agreements and forgoing the benefits they confer. Signing agreements with as many partners as possible, both with neighbors and with distant countries, has been viewed as a way to seize commercial opportunities emerging around the world.

The regional component of the integration strategy is therefore increasingly perceived as less important, and North–South agreements have emerged as desirable policy options.

Preferential and multilateral trade rules are in most cases very similar. Thus, preparing for, negotiating, and implementing agreements on either front often yields cross-fertilization effects. As an example, accumulating experience with the WTO dispute settlement mechanism undoubtedly improves governments' capacity to negotiate similar mechanisms in a bilateral context. Similarly, implementing the provisions included in the services chapter of a preferential agreement facilitates further negotiations at the multilateral level. For Latin America, the simultaneous implementation of unilateral trade reforms, the active participation in the Uruguay and Doha rounds of multilateral talks, and the multiplication of new RIAs were therefore self-reinforcing policy propositions.

Likewise, but on the defensive side, preferential agreements can function as fallback solutions when "first-best" options are not available. Multilateral trade talks may become too protracted or result in shallow scenarios. Preferential trade polices can therefore be used as an insurance policy against the failure of generating market access through other means. Likewise, in mercantilist terms, countries that have already negotiated market access with major trading partners have less to lose in global talks and have strong incentives to "multilateralize" concessions in exchange for reciprocal market access on a preferential base.

But integration is not an end in itself. It is rather one, out of many, policy instruments through which governments can facilitate domestic firms' global competitiveness. In a world of increasingly fragmented global production value chains, trade patterns have evolved at an unprecedented speed. The variety of tradable products and services has grown exponentially, technological change has promoted new forms of international division of labor, and transportation costs have dropped dramatically. Integration agreements are therefore used to position national firms in strategic high-value-added segments of global value chains.

Motivated by such a wide array of dynamically changing drivers, the objectives, outcomes, and policy instruments of the Latin American RIAs have evolved notably through time. Their analysis is the object of the following sections.

14.3 THE OLD REGIONALISM

The period 1930–50 saw Latin America's industrialization and growth sustained to a large degree by protection of domestic markets and proactive state economic policy. This style of development, while a natural reaction to the effects of the Great Depression, collapse of international markets, and widespread protectionism in the world economy, was in fact a consolidation of characteristics that had been gradually building up in the region during earlier decades (Ocampo 2006). Moreover, the economic performance was quite good in comparison to the depressed economies of the North during most of that period (Díaz-Alejandro 1985).

Given this relative success, the pattern of state-led industrialization via import substitution *cum* protection had a strong domestic constituency after World War I. Moreover, there was a sense of export pessimism in the region, given slipping commodity prices and the failure of the GATT to reduce high levels of protection on products where the region had a comparative advantage (Ocampo 2006). In addition, the reality of the region was given a highly influential conceptual framework and economic justification through the work of Raúl Prebisch and the UN Economic Commission for Latin America and the Caribbean[2] (ECLAC, or CEPAL in Spanish). It also received technical and financial support from the Inter-American Development Bank (IDB), as eloquently stated by its first President, Felipe Herrera, who declared: "We will be the Bank of integration."

But growth in Latin America began to flag in the second half of the 1950s. The diagnosis was that the process of industrialization through the deepening of import substitution beyond consumer goods was constrained by inadequate market size, i.e. capital and intermediate goods could not achieve cost-effective economies of scale. The solution that gained traction in the region—and which was strongly promoted by CEPAL, IDB, and other regional institutions—was regional integration. It was seen as a vehicle to rationalize domestic protection, induce competition, expand market size, and provide an environment to nurture diversification into manufactured exports which have more knowledge content, are more income-elastic than commodities and hence are less susceptible to volatile prices (see e.g. Prebisch 1959).

Three major initiatives emerged in the 1960s: the Central American Common Market (CACM) (1960),[3] the Latin American Free Trade Area (LAFTA) (1961),[4] and the Andean Pact (1969).[5] The CACM and the Andean Pact were modeled after the European common market, while LAFTA was a less ambitious free trade area.

14.3.1 The Central American Common Market

The CACM agreement was the earliest and most successful initiative, and one in which CEPAL provided substantial technical support. Ninety-five per cent of tariff lines were liberalized at the start, and by 1966 almost all were freed among the partners. There was an agreement for a CET, a development bank, a secretariat, and groundwork for a monetary authority.

Intraregional trade reached 28% of total trade by 1970, of which 96% was in manufactures. The agreement was indeed a major tool of industrialization (Ocampo 2006).

---

[2] Moreover, the Prebisch state-led framework laid out in ECLAC (1949) shared characteristics with other mainstream development theories of the era such as those of Rodenstein-Rodan, Nurske, Myrdal, and Hirschman.

[3] The agreement included Guatemala, El Salvador, Honduras, Nicaragua, and Costa Rica.

[4] The agreement included the South American countries and Mexico.

[5] The agreement included Chile, Peru, Bolivia, Ecuador, Colombia, and Venezuela, which joined the agreement in 1973.

Unfortunately, the agreement fell into crisis in the 1970s due to political and economic tension among some of the partners

14.3.2 The Latin American Free Trade Area

The LAFTA initiative had been driven originally by the concept of a common market, but what actually emerged was an agreement for a free trade area. The goal was to achieve free trade in twelve years through liberalization in annual product-by-product negotiation rounds. The focus was on regional multilateral liberalization, but LAFTA also had ambitions of sectoral industrial programming, basically aimed at regulating investments by multinational corporations (MNCs) and at nurturing home-grown industrialization, including in public sector firms. The institutional framework was "light," consisting of intergovernmental committees.

However, liberalization momentum was lost after the first three rounds. In 1980 the treaty was revised into a flexible framework of negotiation of full or partial bilateral trade preferences (called Economic Complementarity Agreements) in specific products. The new agreement was called the Latin American Integration Association (ALADI in Spanish).

14.3.3 The Andean Pact

The origin of the Andean Pact, formally known as the Cartagena Agreement, was dissatisfaction of the smaller and medium-sized Andean economies in LAFTA at what was perceived to be disproportionate benefits for the larger economies.[6] The Pact was also paradigmatic of the fullest thinking about regional integration in this period.

While the ratio between the smaller and bigger economies was 50 to 1 in LAFTA, in the Andean Pact it was just 19 to 1. The objective was liberalization of most products by 1980 and elimination of all exceptions by 1990. While liberalization through agreed lists was automatic, the lists themselves were extremely complex and maybe for that reason less than effective in terms of implementation. About one-third of the tariff lines were reserved for sectoral programming, and goods not produced in the subregion were reserved for the two poorest economies, Bolivia and Ecuador. There was an agreement to establish a common external tariff (CET) by 1980 that would begin by immediate establishment of a transitional "minimum" common external tariff (MCET), at first averaging 40% and later revised to 29% in 1975. Bolivia and Ecuador received substantial special and differential treatment: exclusive rights to sectors for which there was no production in the region, accelerated liberalization by other Andean partners, and more rights to exemptions. The members also agreed to Decision 24, which put restrictions on ownership and profit remittances of foreign firms. As for institutional setting, it was

---

[6] The complaint is well reviewed by Salgado (1979).

"heavy:" a Commission with supranational powers, and an independent three- person board (Junta) that made recommendations to the Commission and was supported by a large corps of highly qualified technocrats. The Pact also gave birth to a development bank and a tribunal.

The Pact's liberalization stalled in the 1970s, although it did bring the average tariff within the subregion down by about a third. Trade among the partners rose from 2% in 1970 to just 4% in 1980. Sectoral programming remained limited, and did not get beyond the petrochemical sector. The CET was never established. Finally, Chile withdrew in 1976 in the name of the ultra-liberal, market-based economic philosophy of the Pinochet government.

This round of experiences in regional integration, while not without its merits, was frustrated by the very phenomenon it aimed to rationalize: the domestic inclination towards protection which, with the exception of Central America, blocked advances once the easy phases of liberalization were completed. Another major obstacle was political tension over perceived imbalances of benefits and costs. Moreover, there may have been an imbalance in institutional architectures: LAFTA being too light and the Andean Pact and the CACM too heavy, at least for the initial required steps.

14.4 THE NEW REGIONALISM

The three aforementioned agreements had already lost their dynamism in the 1970s, and the debt crisis of the 1980s appeared to be a death-blow to regional integration as intraregional trade plummeted.

But in the late 1980s, under the aegis of LAIA, Argentina and Brazil entered into sectoral agreements that eventually gave birth to MERCOSUR in 1991. The creation of a common market between Brazil, Argentina, Uruguay, and Paraguay was to begin in stages with rapid preferential trade liberalization and a process of forming a customs union. Meanwhile the Andean Pact revived, freeing trade under presidential leadership, agreeing to construct a customs union among three of the members (Colombia, Venezuela, and Ecuador), and "rebranding" with a new name, the Andean Community, expressing the ambition to be a common market by 2005 and a community some time later. A similar initiative relaunched integration in Central America. Finally, the decision of Mexico to sign a North American Free Trade Area (NAFTA) with the United States and Canada marked the start of a new era for regional integration policies.

14.4.1 Integration as a complement to structural reforms

This rebirth of regional integration emerged during the period of structural reforms aiming to cure Latin America of its "bad habits" of protectionism. The region had by the 1990s already initiated substantial unilateral trade liberalization and was committed to the GATT's Uruguay Round. Free-traders in the Vinerian tradition were disturbed by the emergence of renewed interest in preferential trade because of concern for welfare losses from trade diversion and the undermining of the multilateral trading system. MERCOSUR, given its size and ambition, stimulated a major debate about the pros and cons of RIAs (Devlin 1997; Yeats 1997), much of which continues today, albeit in more muted tones.

This new wave of regional integration received strong intellectual and institutional support from regional bodies such as CEPAL (ECLAC 1994) and the IDB (2002). In a seminal academic contribution, Ethier (1998) highlighted the new features of this wave of integration: he coined the expression "new regionalism" and argued that rather than being a retrogressive step to old bad habits, the regionalism of the 1990s was part and parcel of opening up of the region's economies. He pointed out that when tariffs are relatively low the risks of Vinerian trade diversion are also low, and argued that much of the growth of interregional trade that worried Vinerian free traders was an outgrowth of previous unilateral liberalization, because it reduced "distance"

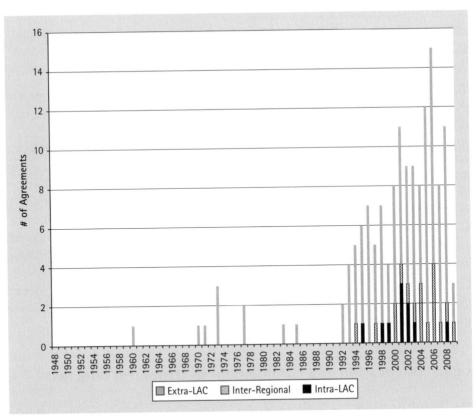

FIGURE 14.1 Date of implementation of Latin American trading agreements

Source: IDB, Integration and Trade Sector (INT).

between neighbors and allowed the pull of geography to take hold. Likewise, in a context of genuine structural reforms, he showed that the importance of non-traditional motives, such as signaling liberalizing intentions to the private sector, notably increased. Indeed, when for whatever reason unilateral liberalization was not politically palatable, "locking-in" liberalization commitments through a formal trade treaty, and promoting peace and democracy in a region, were important motivations for the creation of MERCOSUR as well as the revamping of older initiatives (Devlin and Estevadeordal 2001).

The new regionalism also manifested itself in the unprecedented phenomenon of Latin American countries pursuing free trade areas with northern industrialized countries. Figure 14.1 shows the number of trade agreements implemented between Latin American countries and their partners during the postwar period.

The figure clearly shows the proliferation of agreements in the last decades, and the increasing incidence of North–South agreements with extra-regional partners. This new vintage of integration agreements began with Mexico joining NAFTA in 1994, the launch of the Free Trade Area of the Americas (FTAA) initiative in 1995, and the accumulation of more bilateral FTAs with the developed OECD countries, starting with Mexico's Association Agreement with the EU (AA) (2000), and Chile's FTA with the US and AA with the EU in 2003.[7] More recently, the march for FTA partners has even gone on to highly competitive Asian countries such as Singapore and China as well.

14.4.2 Renewed policy objectives

To better understand the new regionalism as a new product and not a rehash of the old regionalism of the 1960s, first observe Table 14.1, which compares the objectives and some salient stylized facts in the two episodes of regional integration. As illustrated, there are many more differences than similarities between the two periods.

What made the new regionalism fundamentally different from the old was the policy framework it was supporting. In the old regionalism, deepening import substitution was really the only major goal. Defensive trade diversion was indeed explicitly sought after to promote industrialization. The agreements aimed to offset costs with special and differential treatment, financing, and planning. There was indifference as to negotiating with democratic or authoritarian regimes, and it was inconceivable to do a free trade deal with the United States, or any other industrialized country.

The new regionalism turned the old regionalism on its head (Devlin and Estevadeordal 2001). It was an integral part of the structural reform process designed to make the economies more open, outward-looking, and internationally competitive, all in a democratic setting. Essentially, regional integration became the third tier in a three-tiered liberalization process, combined with unilateral and multilateral opening.

---

[7] The EU is also negotiating AAs, which include a free trade agreement, with MERCOSUR, the Andean Community, and the CACM.

Table 14.1 Old and new regionalism: objectives and stylized facts

OLD	NEW	Similar	Different
Policy framework			
Support import substitution Industrialization	Support structural reforms		•
Support authoritarian or democratic regimes	Support democratic regimes only		•
Static issues			
Create a preferential regional market	Create preferential regional market	•	
Create home market-like access	Create home market-like access	•	
Improve terms of trade	Improve terms of trade	•	
Maintain/increase external protection	Reduce external protection		•
Promote trade diversion	Minimize trade diversion		•
Scope: goods only	Scope: goods, services, investment, intellectual property, etc.		•
Dynamic issues			
Rationalize protected industries and achieve economies of scale	Rationalize protected industries and achieve economies of scale	•	
Promote investment	Promote investment	•	
Control/limit FDI	Attract FDI		•
Absorb unemployed/underemployed resources	More efficiency criteria		•
Limit regional competition	Promote regional competition		•
Limited concern for competitiveness and exports	Promote competitiveness and exports		•
Non-traditional effects			
Non-traditional effects: none	Lock-in; signaling; non-trade cooperation		•
Improve regional bargaining power	Improve international bargaining power		•
Systemic issues			
Respond to regional blocs	Respond to regional blocs	•	
GATT consistency (enabling clause)	GATT/WTO consistency (Article XXIV and GATS V)	•	
South–South exclusively	South–South and North–South		•
Marginal role in GATT	Strong role in GATT/WTO		•
Institutional Issues			
Bureaucracy-led process	Politically led process		•
Heavy institutional structure	Light institutional structure		•
Industrial planning	Market-based		•
Structural balance among partners	Avoid radical imbalance		•

Source: Devlin and Giordano (2004).

14.4.3 Innovative integration instruments

The policy instruments chosen to implement the new integration policies were also quite different from those of the past (Table 14.2).

14.4.3.1 *Coverage*

The old regionalism only focused on goods trade. In contrast, most of the new regionalism covers a broad range of trade disciplines, many going beyond regulations of border trade to domestic policy parameters. Indeed, some of the agreed disciplines are even deeper than WTO commitments, such as competition policy.

Table 14.2 Old and new regionalism: policy instruments

Old	New
Trade coverage	
Focus on goods liberalization	Goods and new second generation issues (services, intellectual property rights, government procurement, etc.)
Trade liberalization in goods	
Positive lists or limited automatic schedules[a,b]	Negative lists and automatic schedules
Extensive exceptions (>10%)[a,b]	Very limited exceptions (<10%)[c]
Rules of origin	
Simple rules across tariff universe	Complex rules and families of rules of origin
Common external tariffs	
Average > 40% and high Standard Deviation[b,e]	Average < 15%[d] and moderate standard deviation
Industrial planning	
Extensive[a,b,e]	None (market-based)
Special and differentiated treatment	
Extensive[a,b,e]	Minimalist
Restrictions on participation of foreign direct investment in integration	
Important (formal or informal)[a,b,e]	National treatment
Dispute settlement	
None[a,b,e]	Incipient
Institutions	
Extensive (European model)[a,e]	Scaled down or nonexistent

[a] Latin American Free Trade Area (LAFTA);   [b] Andean Community (former Andean Pact);
[c] Tariff lines;   [d] Tariff level;   [e] Central American Common Market (CACM).

14.4.3.2 *Trade liberalization*

In the past, intraregional liberalization was generally achieved by means of laborious liberalization exercises: for example, LAFTA and the Andean Pact essentially proceeded in "small steps" and *de facto* or *de jure* excluded very sizeable amounts of actual or potential trade. In the new regionalism, liberalization schedules have been relatively universal, automatic, and irreversible as they sought to liberalize the bulk of regional or bilateral trade over ten years. An extreme example is MERCOSUR, under which 95% of the tariff lines were liberalized in four years.

14.4.3.3 *Rules of origin*

In the old regionalism, rules of origin were nonexistent or extremely simple. In the new regionalism, they tend to be more complex, influenced by the NAFTA model.[8] However, the rules of origin are one of the more controversial aspects of the new agreements since they are not very transparent, can be difficult to administer, and can serve protectionist interests.[9]

14.4.3.4 *Common external tariffs*

As was seen in the Andean Pact, the level of the CETs could be high, and could involve generally increased protection. Dispersion, and thereby the scope for lack of predictability and inefficiencies, could be high as well; for example, in Central America the CET ranged from 12% to 80%. In the new regionalism the establishment of CETs has been integrated into general unilateral liberalization. Therefore the average external tariff of Latin American countries fell from 40% to 12% between 1985 and 1995. In such a context, agreed CETs typically range between 0% and 20%. But, as will be clearer later, implementation has been elusive.

14.4.3.5 *Industrial planning*

Planning and industrial programming was an integral part of the old regionalism, while the new version appeals much more to free market forces.

14.4.3.6 *Special and differential treatment (S&D)*

This was ubiquitous in the old schemes and intensely argued for by the smaller economies. In the new regionalism there have been minimal demands for S&D; asymmetric capacities have been dealt with through more favorable liberalization schedules and technical assistance in the case of the North–South configurations. However, requests for the creation of compensatory mechanisms have increased, as

---

[8] They are based on combinations of change in tariff heading, technical specifications, and regional content.

[9] For a comprehensive analytical view of rules of orgin and their effects, see Cadot et al. (2006).

some members judged that the benefits of integration were not equally distributed. As an example, recently MERCOSUR has established a special fund to deal with asymmetries, but all members are eligible to access it (Blyde, Fernández-Arias, and Giordano 2008).

14.4.3.7 *Foreign direct investment*

The old regionalism was skeptical of MNC behavior. It aimed to channel foreign direct investments into preferred activities, and to tame some unwanted behaviors. The Andean Pact's Decision 24 was the highest expression of these concerns.

14.4.3.8 *Dispute settlement*

None of the old agreements had formal settlement procedures, although the Andean Pact did eventually set up a tribunal, but this acquired teeth only after 1990. In those days diplomacy was the principal tool for dispute settlement. The new agreements tend to have mechanisms to resolve disputes, but application can be patchy in the South–South version.

14.4.3.9 *Institutions*

We saw that the CACM and Andean Pact were institutionally heavy. The new regionalism has generally been more parsimonious. The former agreements kept, but reformed, their institutional structure. MERCOSUR only had intergovernmental committees until it later established a small secretariat. NAFTA and the other FTAs rely on intergovernmental committees. It could be argued that "light" structures of the new regionalism made sense at the outset. But the deepening of ambitious and complex agreements like MERCOSUR and NAFTA may have suffered because of slow institutional development vis-à-vis increasing economic ties.

14.5 MEASURING THE PERFORMANCE OF THE OLD AND NEW REGIONALISM

The two waves of RIAs outlined so far had a very different impact on the trade performance of their member countries.

14.5.1 Trade openness

Figure 14.2 displays the value of total merchandise trade of Latin American and Caribbean countries (left hand) and the openness coefficient, measured as the value of

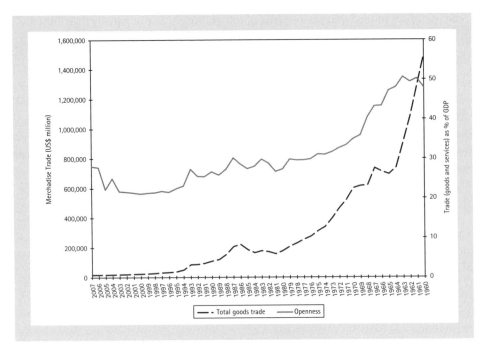

FIGURE 14.2 Trade flows and openness in postwar Latin America

Source: Authors' calculations based on COMTRADE.

trade in goods and services as a percentage of the gross domestic product (right hand). The difference between the two periods is striking.

As hinted earlier, under the old regionalism, trade performance was generally lackluster. In the two decades that separate 1960 and the peak achieved in 1981, Latin American merchandise trade increased from 17 to 220 million dollars. However, this moderate trade expansion associated with rather high, albeit declining, growth rates caused a virtual stability of the openness coefficient, which stood below 30% throughout the whole period. In other words, regional integration failed to prompt a process of substantial trade expansion and economic opening. It is certainly possible to point out differences among countries and some impact on manufacturing sectors, but in general terms this outcome is hardly surprising if one considers that regional integration was embedded in an import-substitution policy framework.

This state of affairs changed radically in the late 1980s, after the virtual stagnation of trade witnessed during the "lost decade" that followed the debt crisis of 1982. During the era of the new regionalism, Latin American trade grew exponentially. In two decades, between 1988 and 2008, merchandise trade grew from 200 million dollars to 1.5 billion dollars, and the openness coefficient jumped from 30% to almost 50%. This deep structural change clearly supports the notion that the new generation of RIAs was part of a new economic paradigm in which trade openness is considered a fundamental ingredient of economic development strategies.

14.5.2 Structure of trade flows

A deeper analysis of the sectoral and geographical composition of trade flows reveals other essential features of this structural transformation process. Tables 14.3 and 14.4 show, respectively, a remarkable qualitative transformation of Latin American and Caribbean import and export flows in three benchmark years.

The region is moving away from a traditional North–South specialization pattern under which it exports commodities in exchange for manufactures products. As an example, the share of manufactures in total exports climbed from 16% in 1965 to 32% in 1985 and 56% in 2006. Preferential trade agreements have been supportive of this diversification process.

The fact that RIAs supported the process of industrialization through the quantitative expansion of intraregional flows of manufactures is well documented (see e.g. IDB 2002). More to the point, Devlin and Giordano (2004) show that under the new regionalism, RIAs also promoted a qualitative transformation of trade in manufactures. Table 14.4 shows that, when compared with extraregional (XR) trade with non-RIA partners, intraregional (IR) trade is characterized by a high intensity of intra-industry trade in sophisticated differentiated goods. In other words, particularly in South America, regional agreements provided markets for industrial goods not exported elsewhere and functioned as a platform for export diversification.

The intense trade diplomacy of the 1990s also had an impact on the geographical composition of trade, which shifted markedly over time (Table 14.5). On the export front, exports directed to intra-LAC markets inched up from 12% in 1965 to 17% in 2006. The small but not negligible increase of this indicator in the last period shows the greater effectiveness of the second generation of agreements in promoting trade flows when compared to the previous one. Likewise, the surge in regional exports to the United States and Canada, up from 27% in 1965 to 50% in 2006, show the growing significance of North–South agreements. On the extraregional front, the figures reveal an increasing penetration of Asian markets, which have been the object of recent agreements, and the continuous and steep erosion of the market share of European countries, which have lagged behind in the conclusion of trade agreements with the region. The same pattern is evident on the import side, although with one conspicuous difference: the recent impressive expansion of the Asian market share, which grew from less than 10% in 1985 to 25% in 2006 at the expense of European and North American countries.

14.5.3 Coverage of preferential trade agreements

As a result, for certain countries of the region, trade relations exist these days predominantly in the context of preferential trading schemes. This is the case for countries such as Chile, for which 85% of total imports originate in RTA partners, Mexico (70%), El Salvador (60%), Costa Rica (50%), Argentina (40%), or Colombia (30%),

Table 14.3 Product structure of Latin American trade flows

		(US$000)			(%)		
		1965	1985	2006	1965	1985	2006
Exports	Total	10,019,797	92,181,394	626,032,515	100	100	100
	Food and live animals	3,878,923	20,323,417	75,380,073	39	22	12
	Beverages and tobacco	54,040	802,442	6,914,208	1	1	1
	Crude materials	1,627,818	7,970,498	58,327,921	16	9	9
	Mineral fuels	2,862,924	33,249,020	135,007,417	29	36	22
	Animal and vegetable oils and fats	170,954	1,910,140	6,180,964	2	2	1
	Chemicals	194,062	3,691,248	30,154,564	2	4	5
	Manufactured goods	1,072,711	12,423,364	86,613,510	11	13	14
	Machinery and transport equipment	74,166	8,514,275	182,261,989	1	9	29
	Miscellaneous manufactured articles	65,603	2,896,391	40,023,883	1	3	6
	Commodities and transactions not otherwise classified	18,596	400,598	5,167,988	0	0	1
Imports	Total	8,507,696	60,176,588	547,182,044	100	100	100
	Food and live animals	870,036	4,787,045	27,627,607	10	8	5
	Beverages and tobacco	49,378	237,046	1,862,629	1	0	0
	Crude materials	578,123	3,731,984	15,548,822	7	6	3
	Mineral fuels	568,089	11,189,318	55,588,994	7	19	10
	Animal and vegetable oils and fats	77,422	764,017	2,227,178	1	1	0
	Chemicals	1,126,191	9,199,758	73,711,507	13	15	13
	Manufactured goods	1,672,244	7,279,618	79,431,286	20	12	15
	Machinery and transport equipment	3,073,586	19,283,569	228,362,586	36	32	42
	Miscellaneous manufactured articles	447,298	3,452,528	52,670,704	5	6	10
	Commodities and transactsions not otherwise classified	45,329	251,704	10,150,730	1	0	2

Source: authors' calculations based on COMTRADE.

Note: The data include the following Latin American reporting countries: Argentina, Bolivia, Brazil, Chile, Colombia, Costa Rica, Ecuador, El Salvador, Guatemala, Honduras, Mexico, Nicaragua, Panama, Paraguay, Peru, and Venezuela.

Table 14.4 Intra–industry trade in Latin American regional integration agreements

RIA	Flow	1980	1985	1990	1995
Central American Common Market	IR	31.0	36.7	25.7	33.9
	XR	2.9	3.8	7.2	6.8
Andean Community	IR	7.2	7.0	11.3	28.7
	XR	2.8	3.9	7.6	8.4
NAFTA*	IR	14.4	50.2	34.4	56.8
	XR	6.4	8.8	14.6	16.5
MERCOSUR	IR	17.0	21.1	36.7	47.9
	XR	10.7	15.7	18.8	15.5

Source: Adapted from Devlin and Giordano (2004).
Notes: IR (Intra-regional): flows to RIA partners; XR (Extra-regional): flows to non-RIA partners; *NAFTA indicator shows Mexico's intra-industry trade inside and outside of NAFTA.

Table 14.5 Geographical structure of Latin American trade flows

		(US$000)			(%)		
		1965	1985	2006	1965	1985	2006
Exports	World	10,019,797	92,181,394	626,032,515	100	100	100
	LAC	1,259,495	9,642,482	105,069,035	13	10	17
	Canada & US	3,727,353	39,059,067	316,079,721	37	42	50
	EU-27	3,381,413	22,844,767	83,717,407	34	25	13
	Asia-Pacific	568,823	8,663,073	58,068,682	6	9	9
Imports	World	8,507,696	60,176,588	547,182,044	100	100	100
	LAC	1,204,298	10,417,149	104,048,059	14	17	19
	Canada & US	3,911,557	24,893,208	200,775,203	46	41	37
	EU-27	2,407,270	11,477,305	74,277,307	28	19	14
	Asia-Pacific	502,357	5,497,536	125,550,021	6	9	23

Source: authors' calculations based on COMTRADE.

Notes: The data include the following Latin American reporting countries: Argentina, Bolivia, Brazil, Chile, Colombia, Costa Rica, Ecuador, El Salvador, Guatemala, Honduras, Mexico, Nicaragua, Panama, Paraguay, Peru, and Venezuela. The LAC partner region includes all Latin American and Caribbean countries for which data are available.

just to name a few. By 2020 virtually all agreements currently in force will have reached maturity and deployed all their liberalization potential. In other words, for Latin America, trading with preferred partners is already one of the most salient components of the global integration strategy, and its importance is expected to grow rapidly in the next decade.

14.5.4 Efficiency and welfare effects

The renaissance of RIAs prompted a debate on the efficiency and welfare effects of preferential trade policies. Devlin and Giordano (2004) carefully surveyed the available evidence for Latin America, and concluded that while the first-generation agreements might have generated trade diversion and thereby welfare losses, the bulk of the empirical studies on the newer agreements support the conclusion that trade creation outweighed trade diversion.

Estevadeordal, Freund, and Ornelas (2008) seem to have settled this debate. They use a unique database covering tariffs and trade in a panel of the ten major regional economies over the period 1990–2001 to assess whether RIAs are building or stumbling blocks for global free trade. They uncover strong and statistically significant evidence that preferences induce a faster decline in external tariffs, at least in free trade areas as opposed to customs unions.

These findings lead to the conclusion that the concerns relating to the trade-diverting effects of the new generation of Latin American preferential trade liberalization agreements seem to have been overstated. The question, however, remains as to whether RIAs accentuate the pro-cyclicality of trade flows and, more generally, whether this new wave of integration agreement is headed towards convergence or further fragmentation. This will be the subject of the next section.

14.6 REGIONAL INTEGRATION IN THE 21ST CENTURY: CONVERGENCE OR FRAGMENTATION?

The perspectives for the future of Latin American integration are deeply connected with the transformation of the global economy at the outset of the 21st century. Global competition is more multipolar, as major developing economies such as China or India become key global players. The United States departed from its historic preference for trade multilateralism and developed a web of preferential trading agreements. The European Union enlarged its membership, seems to have abandoned its preference for biregional preferential negotiations, and is leaning towards bilateralism. The Doha Round is being protracted beyond all expectation, and there is an emerging debate on the effectiveness of the WTO as a regulator of the world trading system. Popular skepticism about globalization is rising. The global financial crisis, the deep economic recession, the volatility of economic indicators, coupled with some questioning of the viability of export-led growth in a possibly less externally benign post-crisis environment, are some of the factors that lie behind the redefinition of the integration strategy of Latin American countries.

Likewise, the region is undergoing a number of deep economic and political processes, which will impact on regional and global integration strategies. After more than a decade of enthusiasm for liberal economic reforms, there is mounting anxiety as to the fair distribution of the benefits of globalization (Giordano 2009). Major concerns over energy security are redesigning a web of geopolitical alliances. And the structure of leadership is changing rapidly, notably in South America, where Brazil is now a key global player.

The question is therefore whether we are in the wake of a new phase of Latin American integration. In order to answer the question, it is crucial to assess the trajectory of hemispheric integration, the state of the subregional initiatives, and the new web of bilateral free trade areas and other integration initiatives.

14.6.1 Hemispheric integration in the FTAA: so close yet so far

One of the major manifestations of the spirit of the new regionalism was the willingness of Latin American countries to enter into free trade agreements with Northern industrialized countries. This was a radical departure from the old regionalism seen earlier, in which protection and rules implicitly kept major industrialized economies at arm's length.

The precursor of the new North–South approach to economic integration was NAFTA, which joined the US, Canada, and Mexico in what was in its day a very advanced and comprehensive free trade area involving many trade-related disciplines well beyond the region's traditional scope of market access and even the rules of the multilateral trading system (Hufbauer and Schott 2005).

The FTAA initiative emerged out of the Summit of the Americas held in Miami in December 1994. This meeting, conceived by the Clinton administration, was the first heads of state meeting of the countries of the hemisphere (less Cuba) since 1967. Notably, trade was not part of the discussions until just several months before the Summit: it was at the insistence of many Latin American countries that the topic finally did enter the draft agenda and Declaration (Hayes 1996). The heads of state of the 34 governments called for a hemispheric free trade agreement by 2005. A Preparatory Process began in June 1995 with meetings of working groups paralleling many of the NAFTA-type disciplines. In September 1998 negotiations were formally launched in nine areas, as shown in Figure 14.3. The IDB/ECLAC/OAS Tripartite Committee deployed staff and financial resources to support the process.

All along, the discussion was about achieving an ambitious free trade area in which all would share the same obligations under the principle of "a single undertaking," not withstanding the possibility of asymmetric schedules for implementation of disciplines "according to the capacity" of each country.

As negotiations proceeded, however, progress became increasingly difficult. A heavily bracketed draft text of an agreement was produced. Approaching the deadline of 2005, ministers, in a meeting in Miami in November 2003, agreed to a two-tiered FTAA,[10] a

---

[10] "We instruct the Trade Negotiations Committee to develop a common and balanced set of rights and obligations applicable to all countries. The negotiations on the common set of rights and obligations will include provisions in each of the following negotiating areas: market access; agriculture; services; investment; government procurement; intellectual property; competition policy; subsidies, antidumping, and countervailing duties; and dispute settlement. *On a plurilateral basis* [emphasis added], interested parties may choose to develop additional liberalization and disciplines" (FTAA 2003).

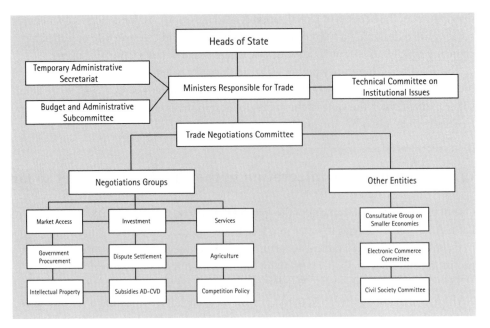

FIGURE 14.3 Structure of the FTAA negotiations

Source: IDB (2002).

basic tier of obligations and a top tier for those countries that wanted to agree to more "ambition" in their obligations. The objective of the single undertaking was abandoned in the interests of promoting a consensus agreement in the face of the approach of the closing deadline. This was followed by a meeting of vice-ministers in Puebla, Mexico, in February 2004 to implement the ministerial guidelines in order to arrive at an agreement by the deadline of January 2005. But after that meeting negotiations were suspended, and trade became a contentious issue at the fourth Summit of the Americas held in November 2005.

What happened? First, it has to be admitted that arriving at an agreement was an inherently very difficult challenge (Blanco and Zabuldovsky 2003). The countries had already liberalized a large part of their trade. Hence, the remaining serious barriers that were the targets of offensives by some countries tended to be politically sensitive defensive measures for others. This dynamic manifested itself everywhere, and was particularly evident in the two biggest economies, with Brazil targeting US barriers (especially subsidies) in agriculture, and the US targeting Brazil's barriers in domestic industry.

Second, by the 2000s some of the liberalization fervor that had given impulse to the FTAA may have waned in some parts of Latin America. In the early 1990s countries were at an enthusiastic stage of signaling their commitment to structural reforms through RIAs. Supporting the FTAA was a big signal in that regard. But by 2003 there was some fatigue with the Washington Consensus and the reform process itself. Even in the US, foreign trade competition became a hotly debated political issue. There was also the onset of a cycle of high commodity prices, offering prospects of better times in Latin America even without an agreement.

Third, governments and negotiators changed over time and with that perhaps the commitments to the original project. In this sense it may be that the ten-year schedule for the FTAA process was too long and hence failed to capture the opportune moment of reform sentiments in the region.

Fourth, the FTAA lacked a sufficient political dimension. This was probably a good way to start in order to avoid excessive politicization of the process. But as the negotiation moved into the "moment of truth," there was need for political intervention at the highest level. However, the governments basically kept separate the politics of the Summit process and the FTAA negotiations. The prevailing notion of the times was that an ambitious free trade agreement was good for development in the region in any event. Further developments proved that that view was too simplistic.

Fifth, in the face of resistance by MERCOSUR to its propositions in the negotiations for an agreement, the US began a strategy of parallel negotiations of "NAFTA-plus" agreements termed "competitive liberalization." However, it may have had the effect of carving out the constituency for an FTAA. Indeed, the incentive for a bilateral agreement with the US was there for many of the countries in the Caribbean and the Andean Community because maintenance of US trade preferences was linked in the respective treaties to concluding an FTAA, or in its absence, a bilateral FTA. When MERCOSUR was perceived by some of drifting from legitimate hard negotiations for its own interests in an FTAA to perhaps having second thoughts about the FTAA project itself, many countries bolted to negotiate a bilateral with the US.[11]

As Central America and other countries started to focus on bilateral agreements with the US, the urgency of an FTAA waned for them.[12] MERCOSUR tended to become isolated as a consequence, as evidenced in the irritation among a sizeable number of countries about the Miami ministerial two-tiered agreement, called derogatorily "FTAA lite." This was ironic, because when the negotiations began in 1998 most countries shared MERCOSUR's offensive targets for the US, i.e. elimination of agricultural protection and subsidies, elimination of anti-dumping actions, suspicion of disciplines on intellectual property, and resistance to labor and environmental standards. Once the US was able to negotiate bilateral agreements with the countries, it essentially was much easier to protect its defensive interests and exercise its offensive objectives.

Finally, the decision in 1995 to close the FTAA negotiations with a US–Brazil co-Chair, while looking brilliant then, in retrospect may have been a stumbling block. When the two big economies were not able to resolve their differences in the Puebla Vice-Ministerial, the authority to attempt to broker a deal between them was lacking. The process simply drifted into silence.

---

[11] Costa Rica was the first to make the request, and this expanded first to other Central American Countries and then to the Dominican Republic to constitute what was know then as the CAFTA-DR agreement.

[12] As well as for Mexico and Chile, which had already concluded bilateral agreements with the US.

14.6.2 Subregional integration: some achievements and many challenges ahead

After the initial successes reported in the first years of the new regionalism, subregional agreements are under pressure to deliver on early promises. As a result, the state of regional agreements in the region is currently not so rosy.

14.6.2.1 *MERCOSUR*

MERCOSUR, an earlier icon of the new regionalism, is struggling between the ambition of its original architecture and the dissatisfaction of the smaller members. The original novelty of the agreement had been the negotiation of a very ambitious roadmap of deepening via innovative economic integration instruments. However, there is a growing gap between the diplomatic dimension of the agreement and the economic incentives for economic cooperation. The expectation that access to the Brazilian market would serve as a springboard for other parties' export development did not materialize. Meanwhile, on the external front joint negotiations have not resulted in access to major export markets.

In order to advance towards a new phase, MERCOSUR members therefore need to address a number of key strategic issues related to the choice of:

(i) the format of the integration agreement, notably whether to pursue the deepening of the customs union or to revert to a free trade agreement which allows more degrees of freedom in external trade policy and negotiations;

(ii) the institutional structure of the agreement, particularly assessing the effectiveness of inter-government bodies and the need of supra-national common executive institutions;

(iii) mechanisms to deal with economic asymmetries and a widespread perception of unbalanced distribution of benefits and costs of integration; and

(iv) effective dispute settlement and complementary mechanisms that can curb unilateral actions and discourage resurgent protectionist pressure, originating particularly in sectors traditionally reluctant to economic opening.

14.6.2.2 *The Andean community*

The bloc needs to face a number of issues related to the very essence of the integration process, some of which stand out as major priorities. Political cohesion among members needs to be strengthened after the decision of Venezuela to withdraw from the bloc in 2006 and the new associate status of Chile in 2007. The extended body of integration instruments needs to be modernized, as Andean provisions run the risk of being eroded by deeper commitments of individual countries to extraregional partners, notably the United States. The bloc-to-bloc negotiations with the European Union are exposing some tensions among the members, and are signaling the increasing ineffectiveness of the integration scheme.

14.6.2.3 *Central American Common Market*

With the exception of periods of major turmoil, regional integration in Central America has generally met expectations and delivered positive outcomes. In the last decades there have been several breakthroughs, but the process is still at a halfway stage despite the strong political commitment to deeper integration.

The intraregional free trade area is virtually complete, but the residual tariff and non-tariff barriers are concentrated in politically sensitive sectors which have proved to be hard to liberalize. Completion of the CET is stumbling in a small number of sectors, and there is an urgent need to promote the full free circulation of goods. The negotiation and ratification of the DR-CAFTA may have mixed impacts on the deepening of the integration process: the implementation of domestic complementary agendas may provide a deeper base for the harmonization of regional regulatory standards, but the implementation of asymmetric tariff phase-out schedules will delay the adoption of a CET. Finally, negotiations with the European Union may strengthen the RIA, provided however that emerging political discrepancies among member countries do not jeopardize the process. On balance, Central American integration is quite promising and seems to be well positioned to meet future challenges.

14.6.2.4 *Other cooperation initiatives*

More recently there has been an emergence of new regional cooperation initiatives in which trade liberalization is not considered the central building bloc. The Bolivarian Alternative for the People of the Americas (ALBA) is an agreement that was initiated by Venezuela and Cuba at the end of 2004 and joined subsequently by Nicaragua, Bolivia, Honduras, Dominica, and St Vincent and the Grenadines. The agreement's stated aim is to go beyond free trade in giving high priority to improved social welfare and mutual aid. In South America, the Union of South American Nations (UNASUR) was formally created in 2008 at a summit held in Brasilia (Brazil). UNASUR is composed of the twelve South American nations. The initiative's objectives are modeled after the European Union: they include the creation of a single market by 2019 and cooperation in diverse areas, including infrastructure, migration, and policy dialogue.

Meanwhile, there is an increasing proliferation of initiatives that coexist—sometimes with minimal institutional connections—with subregional agreements. Their purpose is to promote policy and functional cooperation in specific projects, notably in infrastructure. The most salient examples are the Initiative for the Integration of the Regional Infrastructure of South America and the Mesoamerican Integration and Development Project, respectively known by their Latino acronyms of IIRSA and PM.

IIRSA is an unprecedented development plan to link South American economies through infrastructure investment projects. IIRSA regional investments are expected to integrate highway networks, river ways, hydroelectric dams, and telecommunications links throughout the subcontinent, particularly in remote and isolated regions, to allow greater trade and to contribute to the consolidation of the South American Community of Nations. The initiative was launched in late 2000 with the participation of the twelve South American countries. It is being supported by the Inter-American Development Bank (IDB), the Corporación Andina de Fomento (CAF), and the River Plate Basin Financial Development Fund (Fonplata), which together form a Technical Coordination Committee that provides technical and financial support to the initiative.

The Mesoamerican Integration and Development Project, formerly known as the Puebla–Panama Plan, is a development plan formally initiated in 2001 to articulate cooperation, development, and integration efforts of the countries of the Mesoamerican region (Central America plus Mexico, Belize, and, more recently, Colombia). The initiative is intended to remedy a lack of investment and to stimulate trade in the region by building or improving large infrastructure projects such as highways, air and sea ports, and electric and telecommunications grids.

It is certainly too early to assess the record of these geopolitical or project-based initiatives. Strategic policy dialogs on global issues and innovative cooperation initiatives have materialized in ALBA and UNASUR. Meanwhile, IIRSA and PM have laid the ground for multi-billion investment plans in the region. The nature of the political agreements means that their development is very much dependent on how strong the political commitment and solidarity will be among the partners. On the other hand, the record of project-based initiatives will depend on the technical, financial, and political viability of priority projects. In any event the materialization of this latest vintage of cooperation agreements is a novelty that deserves careful consideration.

14.6.3 North–South free trade agreements: variable geometry and convergence initiatives

Against a backdrop of slow multilateral negotiations, the lack, or incipient nature, of a defined common framework for regional cooperation such as the FTAA or UNASUR, and subregional schemes struggling to meet expectations, the most dynamic dimension of the integration agenda is therefore the bilateral one. After almost a decade of intense negotiations, more than thirty bilateral agreements are already in force in the region (see Figure 14.4).

An optimistic view of this state of affairs leads to the conclusion that policymakers are practicing the "art of the possible." It is possible that in the long run the accumulation of bilateral agreements will lead to the convergence of trade disciplines and ultimately to reach the goal of trade liberalization in the region. In other words, the original objective of LAFTA would be achieved gradually and naturally by means of bilateral agreements coexisting with arrangements that have deeper objectives such as MERCOSUR or other common market projects in the Andean and Central American subregions. A more skeptical view would instead point out the many differences and inconsistencies among bilateral agreements. According to this view, asymmetric tariff liberalization chronograms and sectoral patterns of exclusions, differences in the definition of rules of origin,

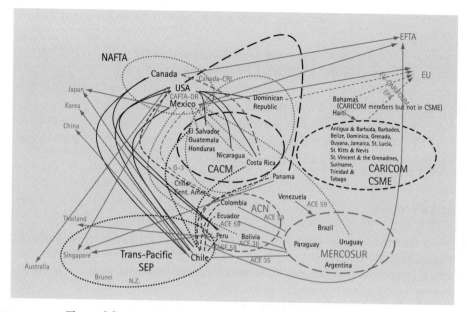

FIGURE 14.4 The proliferation of trade agreements in the Americas

Source: IDB, Integration and Trade Sector (INT).

and incompatibilities in trade rules will have the effect of postponing indefinitely the goal of Latin American integration.

14.7 CONCLUSION

Latin American integration is an unfinished business. Overall, three generations of intense negotiations, alternated with periods of stalling and regressions, contributed to deepen economic interdependence, strengthen market-based reforms, and more recently cement functional cooperation initiatives among like-minded countries. However, the rapid changes occurring in globalization and the still imponderable effects of the global financial crisis will be a litmus test for the capacity of regional integration initiatives to contribute to development and poverty reduction.

It is worth noting that interest in Latin American integration tends to revive when the region is under creeping threat. This happened in the 1960s with the eroding effectiveness of national import substitution industrialization for growth, and in the 1990s with the challenge to adapt to a new phase of globalization and the clear emergence of regional blocks in the world economy. If the international economy recovers only very slowly, if protectionism becomes more prevalent and possibilities for postwar type of export-led growth becomes less feasible, "getting together" in deep regional integration may become much more compelling than it was in the boom years leading up to the crisis of 2008.

As far as hemispheric integration is concerned, it could begin if the United States and Brazil ever advance towards a bilateral FTA in the context of a new shared hemispheric agenda. That would not overcome the challenges of inconsistencies among agreements, but it might provide the political catalyst to overcome them at the hemispheric level.

It is certainly too early to have a definitive view on the subject. However, what seems very likely is that, as a result of the developments mentioned above, we are witnessing the beginning of a new era for Latin American regional integration.

REFERENCES

BLANCO, H., and ZABULDOVSKY, J. (2003). 'Free Trade Area of the Americas: The Scope of the Negotiation', INTAL-ITD-STA Working Paper SITI-01, Washington, DC: IDB.

BLYDE, J., FERNÁNDEZ-ARIAS, E., and GIORDANO, P. (2008). *Deepening Integration in Mercosur: Dealing with Disparities*, Washington, DC: IDB.

CADOT, O., ESTEVADEORDAL, A., EISENMANN, A. S., and VERDIER, T. (2006). *The Origin of Goods: Rules of Origin in Regional Trade Agreements*, Oxford: Oxford University Press.

DEVLIN, R. (1997). 'En defensa del Mercosur', *Archivos del Presente* 7.

—— and ESTEVADEORDAL, A. (2001). 'What's New in the New Regionalism in the Americas?', in V. Bulmer-Thomas (ed.), *Regional Integration in Latin America and the Caribbean: The Political Economy of Open Regionalism*, London: ILAS and University of London.

—— —— (2004). 'Trade and Cooperation: A Regional Goods Approach', in A. Estevadeordal et al. (eds), *Regional Public Goods: From Theory to Practice*, Washington, DC: IDB.

—— and GIORDANO, P. (2004). 'The Old and New Regionalism: Benefits, Costs and Implications for the Free Trade Area of the Americas', in A. Estevadeordal, D. Rodrik, A. Taylor, and A. Velasco (eds), *FTAA and Beyond: Prospects for Integration in the Americas*, Cambridge, Mass.: Harvard University Press.

DÍAZ-ALEJANDRO, C. (1985). 'The Early 1980s in Latin America: 1930s One More Time?', presented at the Expert Meeting on Crisis and Development in Latin America, ECLAC, Santiago, Chile, April 29 – May 3.

ECLAC (UN Economic Commission for Latin America and the Caribbean) (1994). *Economic Survey of Latin America*, Santiago, Chile.

—— (1994). *Open Regionalism in Latin America and the Caribbean*, Santiago, Chile.

ESTEVADEORDAL, A., FREUND, C., and ORNELAS, E. (2008). 'Does Regionalism Affect Trade Liberalization toward Non Members?', *Quarterly Journal of Economics* 123.4.

ETHIER, W. (1998). 'The New Regionalism', *Economic Journal* 108.449.

FTAA (Free Trade Area of the Americas) (2003). Ministerial Declaration, Miami, November 20.

GIORDANO, P. (2009). *Trade and Poverty in Latin America*, Washington, DC: IDB.

HAYES, M. (1996). *Building the Hemispheric Community: Lessons from the Summit of the Americas Process*, Washington, DC: Inter-American Dialogue.

HUFBAUER, G., and SCHOTT, J. (2005). *NAFTA Revisited: Achievements and Challenges*, Washington, DC: Peterson Institute for International Economics.

IDB (Inter-American Development Bank) (2002). *Beyond Borders: The New Regionalism in Latin America. Economic and Social Progress in Latin America 2002 Report*, Washington, DC

OCAMPO, J. A. (2006). 'Latin America and the World Economy in the Long 20th Century', in K. S. Jomo (ed.), *The Long 20th Century, The Great Divergence: Hegemony, Uneven Development and Global Inequality*, New Delhi: Oxford University Press.

PANAGARIYA, A. (2000). 'Preferential Trade Liberalization: The Traditional Theory and New Developments', *Journal of Economic Literature* 38.2.

PREBISCH, R. (1959). 'Commercial Policy in the Underdeveloped Countries', *American Economic Review* 49.2.

SALGADO, G. (1979). 'El mercado regional Latinamericano: el proyecto y la realidad', *CEPAL Review* 7.

YEATS, A. (1997). 'Does Mercosur's Trade Performance Raise Concerns about the Effects of Regional Trade Arrangements?', World Bank Policy Research Working Paper No. 1729, Washington, DC.

CHAPTER 15

....

THE EFFECTS OF TRADE LIBERALIZATION ON GROWTH, EMPLOYMENT, AND WAGES

....

EDUARDO LORA

15.1 INTRODUCTION[1]

....

This chapter examines the effects on growth, employment, and wages of the trade liberalization policies pursued in Latin America between the late 1980s and the late 1990s. The chapter starts with a short description of trade liberalization measures, followed by a discussion of their expected results, both by the reformers and their opponents. The two central sections of the chapter present a survey of the empirical literature that has assessed the effects of trade liberalization on growth and employment, with an emphasis (but not exclusively) on Latin America. The three main conclusions of the chapter, which are presented in the final section, are:

1. Trade liberalization did increase productivity and economic growth, but modestly and perhaps temporarily, conceivably because it did not reallocate productive resources, including labor, as may have been predicted on the basis of theory.
2. While trade liberalization did increase productivity, it did not have the expected effect on wages, which fell in the sectors most subject to competition, especially those of lower-skilled workers.
3. Trade liberalization may have contributed to widening wage gaps, although to a lesser extent than is generally believed.

[1] The author acknowledges valuable assistantship from Lucas Higuera and Myriam Escobar Genes. This chapter draws partially from work by the author for IDB (2003: ch. 5). Valuable comments by José Antonio Ocampo are also acknowledged.

15.2 TRADE LIBERALIZATION IN LATIN AMERICA AND THE CARIBBEAN

The 1990s witnessed major changes in economic policies in Latin America, largely following the set of prescriptions of the Washington Consensus. A key component was trade liberalization. The core of trade liberalization was the lowering of tariff and non-tariff barriers to imports that formerly sought to protect domestic production, especially in the manufacturing sectors. Since the early 1980s, every country in Latin America and the Caribbean (LAC) undertook trade liberalization, with a reduction of at least 10 percentage points in the average tariff rate. For the region as a whole, the average tariff rate declined from 58.9 % in 1985 to 23.9 five years later and 13.9 in 1995. In the second half of the 1990s only five countries had an average tariff rate of more than 15%, and in the early 2000s only one had (see Table 15.1, which presents tariff data by five-year periods starting 1985). The tariff dispersion was also significantly reduced, although in most countries tariffs remained higher for consumer goods than for intermediate and capital goods, and for agricultural goods than for industrial goods.

Table 15.1 Average tariffs (% of GDP)

	Average Import Tariffs[a]			
	1985[b]–9	1990–4	1995–9	2000–4[c]
Argentina	47.7	16.4	14.1	12.7
Bolivia	21.2	11.5	10.4	9.6
Brazil	64.1	22.3	13.8	12.5
Chile	19.0	10.5	9.8	8.0
Colombia	53.3	12.8	11.8	11.7
Costa Rica	53.8	30.9	19.0	6.0
Dominican Republic	n.a.	25.1	19.4	11.0
Ecuador	38.2	17.7	10.7	11.3
El Salvador	24.6	17.2	10.2	7.3
Guatemala	33.2	15.0	10.2	7.0
Honduras	39.3	n.a.	8.8	6.6
Jamaica	12.6	9.9	10.1	8.9
Mexico	30.3	20.9	20.0	16.4
Nicaragua	14.4	4.9	3.4	4.9
Paraguay	46.0	14.6	11.8	10.6
Peru	68.7	20.0	15.2	13.5
Trinidad and Tobago	25.8	9.6	9.6	9.6

(continued)

Table 15.1 (contd.)

	Average Import Tariffs[a]			
	1985[b]–9	1990–4	1995–9	2000–4[c]
Uruguay	92.2	57.5	27.9	12.1
Venezuela	30.1	14.9	12.1	12.1
Latin America and the Caribbean[d]	39.7	18.4	13.1	10.1

Source: Author's elaboration based on Lora (2001) and IDB (2009).

[a] Values obtained by splicing two overlapping series;   [b] Or first year available;
[c] Or most recent year available;   [d] Simple average.

Table 15.2 Imports and exports of goods and services (% of GDP)

	Imports			Exports		
	1980–4	1990–4	2005–8	1980–4	1990–4	2005–8
Argentina	6.2	7.8	19.6	7.6	7.8	24.8
Bolivia	24.9	27.1	32.4	25.8	21.0	41.3
Brazil	9.3	8.3	12.3	10.2	9.6	14.4
Chile	24.3	28.3	32.3	21.4	30.2	44.7
Colombia	14.4	16.8	20.6	12.3	18.2	17.4
Costa Rica	37.4	39.3	54.6	34.8	34.1	48.1
Dominican Republic	24.9	42.9	37.2	19.4	36.9	29.4
Ecuador	25.0	29.6	34.4	23.6	30.8	33.3
El Salvador	30.7	32.7	48.0	26.0	18.2	26.9
Guatemala	19.4	24.9	40.7	16.0	18.5	23.7
Honduras	34.2	41.5	77.6	29.5	35.7	53.6
Jamaica	52.0	55.9	n.a	45.5	51.8	n.a
Mexico	11.0	20.0	29.6	14.6	16.4	28.0
Nicaragua	34.1	46.4	62.3	19.7	20.0	31.1
Paraguay	21.4	46.3	56.2	13.6	36.5	53.9
Peru	18.7	15.1	22.0	18.8	13.1	27.9
Trinidad and Tobago	38.3	33.3	38.4	38.8	43.6	64.3
Uruguay	20.4	19.1	30.1	19.4	20.7	28.9
Venezuela	19.7	25.0	21.8	24.8	31.0	35.4
Latin America and the Caribbean[a]	24.5	29.5	37.2	22.2	26.0	34.8

Source: Author's elaboration based on World Bank (2009).

[a] Simple averages.

Non-tariff trade restrictions, which were applied to 37.6% of imports in the pre-reform period, affected only 6.3% of imports by the mid-1990s (IDB 1996). Lower tariff and non-tariff restrictions enabled merchandise imports to rise as a percentage of gross domestic product (GDP) in most countries. For the whole region, average (goods and services) import coefficients increased from 24.5% of GDP in 1980–4 to 29.5% in 1990–4, and to 37.2% in 2005–8. Exports showed similar patterns, as export coefficients increased from 22.2 to 26% of GDP between 1980–4 and 1990–4, and then to 34.8 in 2005–8 (Table 15.2).[2] However, in a longer-term perspective, part of the export coefficient increases during the 1980s and 1990s was the result of reduced GDP growth rather than faster export growth, which only took place in the 2000s (Ocampo 2004; 2009).

15.3 EXPECTED RESULTS OF TRADE LIBERALIZATION

Trade liberalization was considered the central piece of the reform agenda of the late 1980s and 1990s in LAC because of its expected impact on productivity and growth, which would eventually translate into better work opportunities and higher wages. Two main reasons were given for that expectation. First, trade liberalization, as well as other liberalization reforms, would eliminate market distortions and government interference, which were obscuring price signals, lessening efficiency, and hindering the use of productive resources, including labor. Second, liberalization of international trade would stimulate the demand for unskilled labor as a factor of production assumed to be relatively abundant in the LAC countries, and hence it would increase wages. Even so, the reformers were aware that in the short run these steps could increase unemployment and reduce wages in the sectors most heavily protected by the trade barriers before the reforms.

The optimistic prospects for the medium-run effects of trade liberalization stand in contrast to the adverse judgments they received from labor organizations and some non-governmental organizations. A common opinion was that "domestic manufacturing sectors and employment have been hit hard by indiscriminate import liberalization...while increased exports have failed to generate significant domestic economic activity and employment." (SAPRIN 2002: 174–6).

In general, public opinion on trade liberalization has not been as negative as is often assumed (Fernández and Rodrik 1990). Over 78% of Latin Americans surveyed in 1998 believed that the impact of free trade on their countries was very good or somewhat

---

[2] Unless otherwise noted, all the data on trade come from World Bank, *World Development Indicators*, 2009. The data on tariffs come from Lora (2001) and the FTAA (Free Trade Area of the Americas) Hemispheric Database.

good (Table 15.3). When asked in 2001 about the effect on the economic development of their countries of the proposed Free Trade Area of the Americas, 62% of those interviewed said that it would help a lot or some. In 2004, a survey asked about the effect of free trade agreements on labor opportunities, and found that just 20% of respondents expected a negative or very negative effect, while over 43% expected a positive or very positive effect (tellingly, a full 30% declared they did not know).[3] But although public opinion in general may not be opposed to free trade, empirical evidence indicates that trade liberalization was politically costly for the LAC governments that undertook such measures between the mid-1980s and the mid-1990s (Lora and Olivera 2005).

15.4 DID TRADE LIBERALIZATION ACHIEVE HIGHER PRODUCTIVITY AND GROWTH?

The fact that economic growth in Latin America has been disappointing, and improved only slightly after the period of intense market reforms, is often taken as an indicator that trade liberalization failed to achieve its central objective of speeding up economic growth through more efficient use of productive resources. However, given the multiplicity of factors that can influence growth and productivity, this conclusion is not warranted. Careful empirical studies are required to isolate the effects of the trade liberalization from the possible effects arising from other circumstances—from factors external to the economies, such as world economic growth, the availability of external financing, or international prices, to a host of internal factors, such as macroeconomic stabilization policies or the institutional or political environment.

Table 15.4 summarizes the results of six studies that have evaluated the effects of trade liberalization on growth using econometric methods. The first three studies analyze growth effects up to the mid-1990s and have consistent results (Easterly, Loayza, and Montiel 1997; Fernández-Arias and Montiel 1997; Lora and Barrera 1998). According to these studies, the effects were positive and substantial. For example, Lora and Barrera find that trade liberalization, measured as an index of average tariffs and tariff dispersion, had a significant and permanent impact on growth and productivity. According to their estimates, until the mid-1990s, trade liberalization raised Latin America's growth rate between 1.2 and 1.5 percentage points (the combined effect of all the structural reforms and macroeconomic stabilization policies undertaken in Latin America was 2.8–2.9 percentage points of additional growth).

More recent studies point to less encouraging effects. Escaith and Morley (2001), using data for 1970–95, find a negative but not significant effect of trade liberalization; they list as possible explanations for this the destructive impact of foreign competition

---

[3] In a novel study, Baker (2009) explores the reasons for the high popularity of free trade in Latin America which, in his view, is due to its beneficial effects on consumption choices and prices.

Table 15.3 A summary of Latin Americans' opinions about trade liberalization

	%
Beliefs about the impact of free trade (1998)[a]	
Very good	37.3
Somewhat good	40.9
Somewhat bad	9.4
Very bad	4.6
No response	7.9
Expected effect of an hemispheric free trade area on the economy (2001)[b]	
Would help a lot	29.0
Would help some	36.3
Would help little	16.5
Would not help	5.5
No response	12.8
Expected effect of free trade agreements on labor opportunities (2004)[c]	
Very positive	6.6
Positive	36.1
Negative	15.9
Very negative	4.2
None whatsoever	5.6
Does not know enough to give an opinion	14.6
Does not know	15.4
No response	1.7
How much free trade agreements improve the economy (2008)[d]	
Nil	15.3
2	8.5
3	13.6
4	19.7
5	19.0
6	12.4
A lot	11.5

Source: [a] Baker (2003), from the *Wall Street Journal* Americas survey (1998), which covered 14 Latin American countries.
[b] Latinobarometro (2001), covering 17 countries ("As you may know, it has been agreed that by 2005 there will be a free trade zone covering Latin America, the US and Canada. Do you believe that a free trade area in the Americas would help a lot, some, little or not all the economic development of your country?").
[c] Latinobarómetro (2004), covering 18 countries ("Do international free trade agreements have a very positive, positive, negative, very negative or no impact on labor opportunities, or do you not know enough to give an opinion?").
[d] LAPOP (2008), covering 17 countries ("To what extent do you believe the free trade agreements will help improve the economy?").

on import substitution industries and the deleterious effects on investment of the uncertainty caused by the reforms. With data for 1985–99, Lora and Panizza (2002) make new estimates of the effects of the reforms on growth, including trade liberalization. They find that the effects were more modest and of a transitory nature because they seemed to be diluted after the reforms were in place for some time. Loayza, Fajnzylber, and Calderón (2005) also find more modest effects of the reforms in general, and trade liberalization in particular, in their update of the estimates of Easterly et al. (1997).

The effects of trade liberalization on growth have been the subject of intense debate, not only in LAC but worldwide.[4] According to most cross-country studies, there is a clear and positive correlation (controlling for a host of other variables that may affect growth) between opening to international trade and subsequent economic growth (Dollar 1992; Sachs and Warner 1995; Edwards 1998; Frankel and Romer 1999; Dollar and Kraay 2000; Greenaway, Morgan, and Wright 2002). While there is wide consensus that deeper trade openness is strongly associated with faster growth, evidence on the relationship between trade liberalization *policies* and growth is less robust. In fact, severe criticisms have been raised concerning the validity of some of these studies: "the strong results in this literature arise either from obvious misspecification or from the use of measures of openness that are proxies for other policy or institutional variables that have an independent detrimental effect on growth" (Rodriguez and Rodrik 2001: 315).

In an attempt to understand the differences in the previous literature, some recent work has explored whether or not trade liberalization on its own guarantees faster growth. The conclusion is that policies that foster investment or human capital accumulation are key to making permanent the growth effect of trade liberalization, as well as a stable exchange rate system, coherent fiscal and monetary policies, and uncorrupt policy makers (Baldwin 2003; Winters, McCulloch, and McKay 2004).

It is important to keep in mind that a modest (or even negative) effect of trade liberalization on GDP growth may be consistent with a positive effect on firm-level or sector-level productivity if the resources displaced from the trade competing sectors are left idle or underemployed. In fact, several studies that have focused on productivity at the industry or firm level have found positive effects of trade liberalization.[5] A study of 27 industries in seven LAC countries finds a strong positive correlation between trade reform, export and import growth, and productivity growth (Paus, Reinhardt, and Robinson 2003). Several other studies using firm-level data for Brazil (Ferreira and Rossi 2003; López-Córdova and Mesquita 2004; Muendler 2004), Chile (Pavcnik 2002),

---

[4] For more extensive literature surveys, see Freeman (2004) and Winters, McCulloch, and McKay (2004).

[5] Trade liberalization may increase productivity in the manufacturing sectors through the following channels: (i) increasing productivity at the firm-level (of existing firms), (ii) facilitating the faster growth of more productive firms (e.g. by increasing exports), (iii) inducing the entry of firms more productive than the existing ones, and (iv) increasing the probability of exit of the less productive firms (with respect to that of the more productive firms), which tend to be relatively small firms. The second and fourth channels seem vastly more important than the others. See Bernard, Redding, and Schott (2007) and Pagés (2010).

Table 15.4 The growth effect of Latin American trade reforms: summary of econometric estimates

	Periods of comparison	Growth effect of trade reform (% points, annual)	Of which, permanent	Period analyzed	Trade reform measure	Estimation technique
Easterly, Loayza, and Montiel (1997)	1991–3 vs. 1986–90	1.9	1.9	1960–93	Trade depth	Generalized method of moments
Lora and Barrera (1998)	1993–5 vs. 1985–7	1.2–1.5	0.8–1.1	1986–95	Index of tariffs and tariff dispersion	Panel data with random effects
Fernández-Arias and Montiel (1997)	1991–5 vs. 1986–90	1.8	1.8	1961–95	Trade depth and index of tariffs and tariff dispersion	Generalized method of moments
Escaith and Morley (2001)	1991–6 vs. 1986–90	Not significant	Not significant	1971–96	Index of tariffs and tariff dispersion	Panel data with random effects
Lora and Panizza (2002)	1991–3 vs 1985–7 1997–9 vs. 1985–7	1.3 0.6	Nil Nil	1986–99	Index of tariffs and tariff dispersion	Panel data with fixed effects
Loayza, Fajnzylber, and Calderón (2005)	1991–5 vs. 1986–90 1996–9 vs. 1986–90	0.18 0.35	0.18 0.35	1960–2000	Trade depth	Generalized method of moments

Note: All growth effects are simple averages of country estimates as reported in the studies cited, except in Loayza et al. (2005), which does not report an average. In this case the average effect was calculated from the country estimates reported by the authors in an appendix.

Colombia (Eslava et al. 2004; Fernándes 2007), México (López-Córdova and Mesquita 2004), and Uruguay (Casacuberta, Fachola, and Gandelman 2004) show that trade liberalization increased industry-level productivity. Focusing on 318 large manufacturing firms in Brazil, Hay (2001) found large productivity effects; while focusing on micro-enterprises in Brazil and Mexico, Tybout and Erdem (2003) have found that productivity increases in the import-competing sectors as a result of trade liberalization.

In short, despite the differences between the various studies, the conclusion that can be drawn is that, contrary to the expectations created by the reformers and some of the early empirical literature, trade liberalization had an effect on growth which, although probably positive, was modest and transitory. Productivity effects, though important in some sectors or groups of firms did not have a major effect on the overall economy.

15.5 EFFECTS OF TRADE LIBERALIZATION ON LABOR

The aim of trade liberalization (along with other liberalization measures) was to reallocate resources from previously protected sectors toward more efficient sectors, especially export sectors. In almost all countries in the region, exports actually grew substantially between the early 1980s and the mid-2000s, as shown in Table 15.2. Nevertheless, the prevailing opinion is that the export sector did not manage to make up for the destruction of employment in the previously protected sectors, and that the jobs created have been inferior in terms of pay, stability, and other labor conditions, (Stallings and Peres 2000: 200–1; SAPRIN 2002: 55–6).

The second issue of concern is the effect that the trade liberalization had on pay for labor. The reformers expected that at least in the medium run liberalization would raise wages because of its expected effect on investment and productivity, and by leading to the reallocation of employment toward the more efficient sectors. But this does not seem to have happened. On the contrary, it is widely held that liberalization lowered wages, especially for lower-skilled workers, thereby helping to widen pay inequality (SAPRIN 2002: 55–6).

Many opinions on the effects of trade liberalization on labor are based on comparisons between the situation before and after the reforms, and often point to specific sectors, regions, or groups of workers or companies. These comparisons are a good starting point for identifying the problems, but they do not provide sufficiently general proof of the effects of the reforms because they do not allow for isolating the influence of other factors that may affect the impact on labor. And they do not make it possible to know whether these observations are representative of what may have happened to a larger number of workers or companies. This type of analysis requires econometric methods available only to specialists, and extensive databases that exist only in some countries. Hence the debate is inevitably inconclusive because in many cases it is impossible to verify (or reject) whether the problems identified by observers are the result of trade liberalization (or other reforms) and whether they are a common phenomenon. Even when data exist, the results of econometric studies may be inconclusive for technical or interpretation reasons. Despite these limitations, some conclusions on the labor effects of liberalization may be advanced on the basis of available evidence.[6]

15.5.1 Trade liberalization and unemployment

It is possible that the impact of liberalization on employment was initially—and still is—the main reason for political and public opposition by some groups to this reform. In the short run, the main possible reason for expecting higher unemployment after opening the economy is that during the process of reallocating resources from sectors that are no longer viable toward those that may be so, more workers will be looking for jobs. Thus, while increased imports following liberalization may displace domestic production, prompting companies to lay off workers, exports may respond with a lag. In the longer run, unemployment may remain above its initial level if wage rigidities prevent the absorption of labor, especially in countries whose exports are natural resource-intensive and not labor-intensive (since trade liberalization induces the expansion of the sectors intensive in the relatively abundant factor).

Given the attention that the issue attracts in the media and in public discussion, it is surprising how few academic studies have assessed the influence of trade liberalization on unemployment. Márquez and Pagés (1998) studied the relationship between unemployment and liberalization in 18 LAC countries since the 1970s. In their analysis they tested whether variations in unemployment rates had a relationship with liberalization over time, isolating the influence of other variables. They concluded that liberalization has no effect on unemployment. This finding does not rule out the possibility that in specific cases changes in trade policy may have produced unemployment. In a few countries around the world, unemployment rates have increased by about 10 points starting from the time when the economy opened up and lasting for a period of more than a decade before falling back to levels similar to and lower than initial unemployment (Rama 2003). But this pattern does not seem to have occurred in the wave of reforms during the 1990s in LAC, nor does this pattern seem to have been common in the past, as shown by a set of studies on episodes of trade liberalization in the postwar period up to the mid-1980s. Based on the experiences of 19 countries, including 6 in LAC (Argentina, Brazil,

---

[6] Useful literature surveys are Freeman (2004), Goldberg and Pavcnik (2004), and Hoekman and Winters (2005). In what follows, our focus is on ex post empirical evidence as opposed to ex ante, or simulation models that attempt to predict the effects of trade reforms. For a survey of the latter, see Bouet (2006). Ganuza et al. (2001) is an ambitious attempt to use micro-simulations to assess the effects of trade liberalization on poverty and inequality through the labor market in 17 LAC countries. Although the method assures consistency and provides a very rich description of the changes in the labor market, it is entirely based on a before-and-after analysis, whereas no attempt is made to connect the changes in the labor market variables with those in trade variables or policies.

Chile, Colombia, Peru, and Uruguay), the authors note: "based on the data and analysis of country studies it can be concluded that on the whole attempts at liberalization have not had significant transition costs in terms of unemployment" (Michaely, Papageorgiou, and Choksi 1991: 80).

15.5.2 Liberalization and aggregate employment

Although there are no empirical grounds for attributing unemployment to liberalization, there may have been adverse effects on aggregate employment, which would not be reflected in unemployment if (numbers similar to) the workers affected opted to leave the labor market. A few studies have established that *controlling for product level* (and other macro variables), the lowering of tariffs reduced aggregate employment levels (IDB 1997; Stallings and Peres 2000). Another study concludes that trade liberalization, measured with trade openness, reduced the labor intensity of growth in LAC (Weller 2001). Strictly speaking, however, these studies do not provide a basis for claiming that trade liberalization reduced employment. The only thing that can be said based on them is that liberalization increased labor productivity because it reduced employment *for each product unit*. Márquez and Pagés (1998) is the only study that analyzes this issue, and the results are quite revealing. When *controlling for the product level*, the finding is the same as in the other studies: that liberalization had negative effects on total employment. It is estimated that an increase of 1% of GDP in trade flows with the rest of the world leads to a reduction of 0.06% in aggregate employment—a modest effect, albeit statistically significant. Inasmuch as trade deepening increased 20% in the average LAC country between the beginning of the 1980s and the mid-2000s, employment would have fallen a total of 1.2% during this period as a result of liberalization, which would be a modest effect. However, if production levels are not controlled for, this effect is reduced even further and ceases to be significant, suggesting that the effects of increased productivity and the level of production have opposite implications on employment and that, on the whole, they cancel one another out. The conclusion that liberalization has scant effects on employment is consistent with the conclusion of the studies on episodes of trade liberalization in the post-war period: "The overwhelming impression . . . is that import ratios and employment were correlated either very weakly or not at all" (Michaely et al. 1991: 76).

In short, statistical evidence does not provide a basis for stating that liberalization processes have lowered total levels of employment or raised unemployment rates. The explanation for the high unemployment rates observed in Argentina, Colombia, Uruguay, and Venezuela should be sought in macroeconomic factors or labor legislation factors (IDB 2003). Trade liberalization did have a short-term unemployment cost in Brazil, but it faded away as factor intensities adjusted to absorb the excess of labor (Mesquita and Najberg 2000).

Although trade liberalization may have had very limited, if any, effects on aggregate employment or unemployment, this conclusion does not eliminate the possibility that it may have had other effects on labor. Rather, if liberalization did not cause changes in total employment or unemployment, it may have been because the adjustment to the changes in the level and composition of demand for labor has taken place through the sector composition of employment, wage levels, or quality of jobs.

15.5.3 Liberalization and sector composition of employment

The bulk of (net) additional employment in LAC in the 1990s and early 2000s was created in the service sectors, while in several countries manufacturing shed jobs in large numbers. As a result, the share of manufacturing in total employment fell on average from 19.6% in the end 1980s to 17.6% in the mid-1990s and to 15.6 in the mid-2000s. Commerce and the modern service sectors (transportation and financial services) gained importance at a faster pace than other services (personal, communal, and government), which actually lost weight in total employment (Table 15.5). Were these changes in the composition of employment the result of liberalization or other factors (such as exchange rate or technological changes)?

Several studies conclude that trade liberalization does seem to have affected industrial employment, albeit in some cases by a surprisingly small amount in view of the extent of reductions in tariffs and other mechanisms for protecting industry. Consider the case of Mexico, where, as in most countries in the region, tariffs and import controls were cut sharply. The average tariff fell from 23.5% in 1985 to 12.5% in 1990, and the maximum tariff dropped from 100% to 20% during the same period, while import licenses, which were formerly applied to 92% of imports, covered only 20% in 1990 and have covered even less since then. These major changes in protection had little effect on sector employment: based on data from industrial

Table 15.5 Sectoral employment in Latin America, 1980s–2000s (%)

	Late 1980s	Mid-1990s	Mid-2000s
Agriculture and mining	6.4	6.3	6.9
Manufacturing	19.6	17.6	15.6
Electricity, gas, and water	1.0	0.8	0.6
Construction	6.7	6.7	7.1
Commerce	21.7	25.9	28.1
Transportation	6.0	6.5	6.9
Financial services	5.1	5.8	6.3
Other services	33.3	30.2	28.3
Total	100.0	100.0	100.0

Source: ECLAC (2009).

Note: Simple averages of 18 countries. Data for urban areas only. Non-specified sectors are excluded.

establishments, for every percentage point decline in tariffs, employment through-out manufacturing fell by an estimated 0.02 to 0.03%, and hence declines in employ-ment were minimal (Revenga 1997). Other studies have found equally modest effects, which were concentrated among factory workers, since employment in administra-tive activities showed practically no change (Hanson and Harrison 1999; Feliciano 2001). The explanation lies partly in the fact that the adjustment took place through wages and partly in the fact that tariff reductions had little impact on production in the affected sectors.

In Colombia, the liberalization of the 1990s also seems to have had little effect on industrial employment. It dropped markedly during the 1980s, despite tariff and non-tariff protection, and deepened only marginally after the tariff reduction in the early 1990s. This phenomenon was partly the result of the trade opening that helped lower the price of capital in relation to labor. Other factors operating in the same direction were the rise in the exchange rate and increased payroll taxes (Cárdenas and Gutiérrez 1997).

By contrast, in Uruguay, tariff reductions seem to have had a strong effect on indus-trial employment, which is reasonable considering the small size of the economy. It has been estimated that in Uruguay, for every percentage point that protection was reduced, industrial employment fell between 0.4% and 0.5% in the same year (Rama 1994). With a reduction of some 20 points in tariffs from the mid-1980s until the end of the 1990s, lib-eralization may have caused a 10% drop in industrial employment. According to a more recent study, trade liberalization in Uruguay resulted in higher job creation, but much higher job destruction in the manufacturing sector between 1982 and 1995 (Casacuberta et al. 2004).

Although each case may have been different, the effects of liberalization on indus-trial employment seem to have been small for the average of the 18 countries analyzed by Márquez and Pagés (1998). According to their calculations, for every percentage point decline in the average tariff, industrial employment fell between 0.2% and 0.3%. With a 40-point decline in tariffs since the beginning of the trade liberalization proc-ess, as was the average in LAC, tariff reductions would be responsible for between 6% and 9% decline in industrial employment. Alternatively, for every 1 percentage point increase in trade flows, employment in industry declined between 0.1% and 0.14%. These calculations do not take into account the indirect effect of trade or tariffs on the level of industrial production. If this effect were also adverse, the result would be a greater decline in employment. However, when this effect is incorporated, declines in industrial production are found to be less, again suggesting that liberalization did not have the destructive effects on industrial production (and thereby on employment) that are often attributed to it.

A similar conclusion is drawn from a study of six LAC countries between 1980 and 2000 based on firm and plant level data (Haltiwanger et al. 2004). Exploiting variations in country, sector, and year, they find that decreases in tariffs do not result in any net reductions in employment (in some specifications, they result in *increases* in net employment).

Liberalization may have had greater effects on agricultural employment. However, as noted in a study by the Economic Commission for Latin America and the Caribbean (ECLAC) based on the experience of nine countries,

> the most important transformations in the agricultural sector resulted not only from the reforms, but also from processes that began at least a decade earlier. The most significant were the incorporation of new technologies, reduction of cultivated land, increase of land dedicated to livestock and forest plantations, and employment decline. (Stallings and Peres 2000: 179)

Consequently, although liberalization may have caused significant labor displacement in some agricultural operations that were exposed to competition, it would be a mistake to think that this was the main cause of the decline of employment in agriculture. Unfortunately, no econometric studies have attempted to calculate the effects of liberalization on the agricultural sector because for this sector, unlike manufacturing, the information on production and employment needed for such measurements is not available.

What is known for certain, however, is that the catastrophic predictions of displacement of employment, which were based on calculating the labor requirements for agricultural goods that could not compete internationally, have not come true. For instance, it was feared that the North American Free Trade Agreement (NAFTA), which forced Mexico to sharply reduce protection for corn and other farm products, would cause the displacement of up to 15 million workers (de Janvry, Sadoulet, and Davis 1997). Actually, what happened was unexpected: the areas devoted to corn, the product most affected, expanded, and although productivity declined, there was only moderate displacement of labor. However, income from production declined and environmental sustainability may have declined in some areas (Nadal 2000).

In short, although some sectors suffered loss of employment as a result of a reduction in tariffs and other import protection, the changes in employment levels were limited, both in the aggregate and in the sectors in which protection was reduced. However, these conclusions refer to net changes in employment, behind which are concealed large flows of employment creation and destruction. Although it has not had a major impact on levels of aggregate or sector employment, liberalization may have affected the flows of employment creation and destruction, and hence employment stability.

15.5.4 Trade liberalization, employment mobility, stability, and informality

Liberalization seems to have had a modest effect on the extent of reallocation of employment between sectors of production. In their analysis of the experiences of 25 countries at different stages of development (13 of them in LAC), Seddon and Wacziarg (2004) find that the extent of changes in the composition of employment between the major sectors *declined* after trade liberalization measures. In their examination of subsectors of manufacturing industry, they find that the recomposition of employment did increase after liberalization, but the estimated effects were small and statistically weak. Several other studies for Mexico and Colombia confirm the lack of sectoral job reallocation related with trade liberalization (Attanasio, Goldberg, and Pavcnik 2004 for Colombia; Hanson and Harrison 1999 for Mexico). Therefore, although the empirical evidence is inconclusive, trade liberalization seems to have produced very little, if any, labor reallocation between industrial subsectors.

In the presence of heterogeneous firms, the reallocation can be possible *within* sectors, as the demand may shift towards more productive firms within the same sector. This hypothesis is tested by Haltiwanger et al. (2004) for six LAC countries between 1980 and 2000 with firm-level data. They conclude that trade liberalization does increase job reallocation within sectors. Their conclusion holds irrespective of the job legislation differences across countries and its changes through time. Therefore labor reallocation within sectors contributed to productivity increases at the sector level. However, several studies led by ECLAC suggest that trade liberalization may have increased firm heterogeneity within sectors, as the larger firms, which tend to be more productive and to export a larger share of their production, adopted better technologies and became more productive in the wake of trade liberalization (for a survey, see Ocampo 2009).

The fear that liberalization and globalization in general are making employment permanently more unstable finds support in the positions of noted academics, like Rodrik (1997), who argues that globalization has made the demand for labor more unstable because of increased competition between domestic and foreign markets and because companies can turn to imported inputs as a way of lowering production costs. Because companies now find it easier to substitute imported for domestic inputs and can even go outside the firm to contract a major portion of the production process, production tends to be more unstable, and this greater instability tends to fall on workers, especially those with lower skills who are easily replaceable.

The empirical evidence does not sustain the claim that liberalization has had such a destabilizing effect. In Chile, Colombia, and Mexico, where Rodrik's hypothesis has been studied explicitly, no coherent evidence has been found that trade liberalization policies or various measures of trade deepening have an impact on the elasticities of employment demand (which, however, have shifted sharply in both directions). According to the authors of the study, "if globalization is making the life of workers more unstable, it is probably through other mechanisms" (Fajnzylber and Maloney 2005).

The relationship between trade liberalization and informal employment has not been extensively addressed in the literature. Despite the claims of the "race to the bottom," where countries lower their labor market standards to increase competitive advantages, one of the few studies on the topic finds no relationship between trade policy and informality in Brazil, whereas in Colombia it does find such negative association between tariffs and the probability of working in the informal sector, but only for the period before the labor market reform that reduced the restrictions to hiring and firing of workers (Goldberg and Pavcnik 2003; Attanasio et al. 2004).

15.5.5 Liberalization and wage levels

There is no empirical basis for claiming that greater openness to trade permanently worsens the wages of all workers in a country. However, as this section will show, international evidence suggests that wages drop initially with liberalization and that some groups suffer significant losses of income.

If increased openness to trade does increase the productivity and income levels of countries (a contentious claim, as we have seen), wages should be expected to rise more rapidly in countries that are more integrated internationally. According to Rama (2003), the growth pattern of wages in a sample of 70 countries from all regions of the world supports that presumption: in those developing countries that were more open to world trade, average real wages in the 1990s were 30% higher than in the 1980s; in those that were less open, the increase was only 13%; and the percentage for developed countries was around 20%.

However, although openness to trade may help increase wages, the effect is not instantaneous. According to Rama (2003), a trade increase of 1% of GDP tends to be associated with an initial 0.3% decline in wages. It is only after the third year that, on average for the 70 countries considered, wages increase. These estimates imply that an increase of 20 percentage points of GDP in trade penetration, which was the average in LAC, could explain an initial 6% drop in real wages if it happened all at once. It is important to note that these calculations have to do with changes in the degree of penetration of imports and exports, and hence they do not necessarily reflect the effects of tariff reductions. Moreover, these results should be treated with caution: they may be skewed by the presence of reverse causality because an initial drop in wages may facilitate greater trade.

Some studies of individual countries have focused on analyzing the (short-term) effects of lower tariffs on wages in the manufacturing sectors (rather than the entire economy). In the case of Mexico, it has been estimated that in the companies that were affected by a 40-point drop in tariffs, real wages fell between 8% and 10%. For the manufacturing sector as a whole, it is calculated that the tariff reductions in the late 1980s caused a 3–4% drop in wages. The elimination of quantitative controls on imports may have had an even greater effect, but it is difficult to quantify with precision (Revenga 1997). In Colombia, where the average tariff fell from 50% in 1984 to 13% in 1998, the effect on the average wage in manufacturing was also 3–4%. In the industrial sectors that were initially protected, the effect may have been as much as 7%. In addition, increases in import penetration may have had some additional effect on industrial wages (Goldberg and Pavcnik 2001). Due to their short time horizon, the studies do not provide a basis for saying whether these wage drops were permanent. It is perhaps surprising that the effects of liberalization on wages have been relatively pronounced in comparison with the modest changes in employment and its composition. There is no definitive explanation for this phenomenon, but one possible hypothesis is that workers were sharing in the rents (and inefficiencies) that protection afforded companies. The lowering of tariffs could be accommodated without major changes in employment by improved productivity and elimination of those rents. Another hypothesis states that the more unskilled labor-intensive sectors experienced the higher tariff reductions. Given the lack of inter-industry job reallocations, the returns on the more protected intensive factor were reduced (Goldberg and Pavcnic 2004). A third hypothesis suggests that wage declines were partly due to labor rigidities, which limited the possibility of labor reallocation across sectors, or to the existence of imperfect product markets. The contrast with the US is revealing, given its greater labor mobility compared to the LAC countries: in the US, trade shocks are absorbed mainly by employment adjustments than by wage changes (Revenga 1992).

15.5.6 Wage gaps

The impact of trade liberalization measures on wage gaps has been one of the most studied aspects of the structural reforms of the 1990s in LAC. The issue arouses interest because the increase in wage gaps between skilled and unskilled workers has been striking in some countries and was unexpected by many economists, who had predicted that lowering tariffs would increase the demand for unskilled labor, and hence would help narrow wage gaps. Although, in principle, this prediction is consistent with a very simplified model of comparative advantages, it rests on a series of unrealistic assumptions, from constant returns to scale and full employment, to having skilled and unskilled labor as the only two factors of production involved in the production of two tradable goods. Using simulation models that are more realistic representations of the economies, Vos et al. (2006) found that a uniform import tariff reduction could be expected to increase wage gaps in some countries (Brazil, Cuba, Costa Rica, Ecuador) and to reduce it in others (Argentina, Mexico, Uruguay).

The widening of wage gaps by education level has been significant, although less pronounced than is sometimes claimed. Comparing the wage incomes of workers with high education (defined as more than 13 years of education) with those with medium education (between 9 and 13 years), the gap increased by 6.2% in the 1990s (average for 17 countries in the region), which is a modest increase. Between the end of the 1990s and mid-2000s, the gap increased only 4.3% (18 countries). Similarly, if workers with high education are compared with those with fewer than 9 years of education, the increase in their wage gap was 10.1% by in the 1990s, and just 1.1% between the end of the 1990s and mid-2000s. Besides, there are substantial differences between countries (Figure 15.1). In a few countries, the trend toward wider gaps that were observed at the beginning of liberalization has halted or reversed in recent years. In Mexico, the trend stopped after 1994, when NAFTA came into effect, and in Argentina, the increase throughout the 1990s was halted after the crisis of 2001.

Many studies have examined the relationship between the wage gap and the process of opening up to international trade in the past few decades. Although various studies find a significant relationship between the two variables, there is consensus that the influence of liberalization on the wage gap has been modest and indirect, possibly reflecting the influence of technological change.

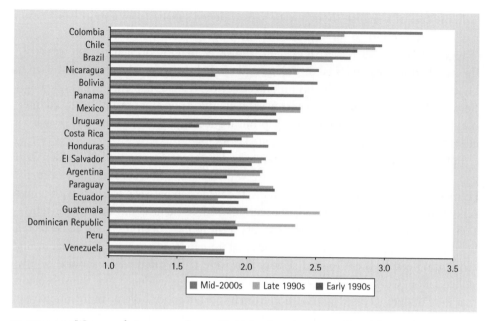

FIGURE 15.1 Wage gap between workers with high education vs. medium education

Source: Socio-Economic Database for Latin America and the Caribbean (CEDLAS) and World Bank (2009).

Notes: Medium education comprises 9–13 years of education, and high education comprises more than 13 years.

The case of Argentina is revealing, because the increase in the wage gaps between university-educated workers and those with a high school education or less during the 1990s took place when the relative supply of university-educated workers was increasing fast, which means that there was considerable demand pressure for workers with this level of education. Economic studies are in agreement that greater import penetration influenced this trend, although in a rather limited way. Greater import penetration of industrial goods explains only 10% of the increase in the wage gap favoring workers with a university education between 1992 and 1999 (see Galiani and Sanguinetti 2000; Sanguinetti, Arim, and Pantano 2001). Although these studies have established that in sectors where import penetration was greater, the wage gap increased more, they do not clearly show why. The most common explanation is that greater competition from imports induced companies to adopt more sophisticated technologies that require relatively more skilled labor.

In the cases of Colombia and Costa Rica, there is also evidence that liberalization helped widen the wage gap in industry by increasing relative demand for more skilled workers, apparently due to increased investment and the adoption of technologies skewed toward such workers (Robbins and Gindling 1999 for Costa Rica; and Cárdenas and Gutiérrez 1997, Attanasio et al. 2004, and Goldberg and Pavcnik 2005 for Colombia). However, there could be other mechanisms behind such processes, such as the increase in sector wage premia (due to increases in returns of education) and increased informality (Attanasio et al. 2004; Goldberg and Pavcnik 2005).

In the case of Uruguay, though wage gaps widened substantially, import penetration has not been found to directly impact the wage gap in the manufacturing sectors (Sanguinetti et al. 2001). There is evidence, however, that import penetration weakened the negotiating capacity of labor unions and eroded the wage advantages that used to benefit workers in the more highly unionized sectors (Cassoni, Allen, and Labadie 1999). Because the wage gap tends to be narrower when union power is greater, increased international trade may widen the wage gap not for technological reasons, but because it alters the negotiating power of less educated workers.

But greater openness to international trade does not necessary lead to a wider wage gap. Brazil is an interesting case, because with the trade liberalization that occurred between the late 1980s and the mid-1990s, the wage gap between workers with a high school education or more fell vis-à-vis workers with less education, and the concentration of all wages was reduced. Lower tariffs seem to have been the main cause of this behavior by decreasing the prices of goods that were more intensive in skilled labor, and reorienting employment toward sectors that were more intensive in the use of low-skilled labor (Gonzaga, Filho, and Terra 2006). There is evidence that the subsectors that were under increased competition from imported goods became more intensive in the use of skilled labor, but that did not bring about an appreciable increase in wage inequality (Green, Dickerson, and Arbache 2001; Pavcnik, Blom, and Schady 2002; Carneiro and Arbache 2003). A similar conclusion applies to industry wage premia (Pavcnik et al. 2004).

Finally, the case of Mexico is illuminating because it combines two well-defined phases of trade liberalization since 1985: first, the unilateral decision to implement a sharp reduction in tariffs and more uniform tariffs, and second, integration with the United States and Canada, starting with NAFTA in January 1994. During the first phase, the wage gap increased, but in the second phase it tended to decrease slightly (Robertson 2000; 2004). A portion of the initial increase in the wage gap may have been due to tariff reduction because the most protected sectors tended to use low-skilled and highly unionized workers (Revenga 1997; Hanson and Harrison 1999; Harrison and Hanson 1999). However, there are few indications that this was the predominant effect. There is little relationship between the extent of the changes in tariffs and the changes in product prices or in the wage gap between high and low-skilled workers in companies in the affected sectors. However, there is a relationship between the wage gap in different companies and the weight of exports in their sales or indicators of the adoption of new technologies (Hanson and Harrison 1999; Harrison and Hanson 1999). The expansion of the *maquila* plants accounted for more than 50% of the widening of the wage gap between skilled and unskilled workers at the end of the 1980s, and it has continued to exert substantial pressure because the foreign-owned *maquila* plants—like other enterprises with investment from the same source—demand higher-skilled workers and pay better than domestic companies in the same sectors (Hanson 2003).

In the second phase, the relative price increased for goods that were intensive in low-skilled labor, which is consistent with the slight narrowing of wage inequality. This could be explained by the fact that in this phase, tariffs on such goods were lowered further, and because of Mexico's exports to the United States and Canada requiring lower-skilled labor than those it imports from those countries (Robertson 2000). Nevertheless, another possible explanation for the slight reduction in wage inequality in Mexico is that liberalization has different short- and long-term effects. The increased inequality that may occur in the initial phases is not necessarily a permanent effect, as suggested by Chile's somewhat longer experience. Chile's liberalization began in 1973 and deepened during the 1980s. Wage inequality—measured by the ratio of pay between the highest-wage 10% and the lowest-wage 10%—increased from around three-to-one in the early 1970s to almost five-to-one in 1988, but from that point it began to decline until it returned to close to the starting point (de Ferranti et al. 2002: 143). This suggests that changes in labor remuneration are an economic signal to which producers respond by introducing technologies that allow for more efficient use of costly human resources, and to which individuals respond by investing in those types of education that are best rewarded by the market.

Regardless of whether the effects of liberalization on wage gaps are permanent (about which there is still little evidence), the most important conclusion of all these studies is that liberalization and inequality do not necessarily go hand in hand. This is the conclusion also reached by the few examinations of common patterns in the influence of liberalization in various countries. An econometric study based on a panel of household surveys for 18 countries in the past two decades finds no evidence that liberalization processes have had a discernible effect on the wage gap between education levels (Behrman, Birdsall, and Székely 2000). The authors observe the effects of both tariffs and trade penetration on the wage gap, without distinguishing between industries. By contrast, a study that includes Argentina (1986–99), Brazil (1982–99), Chile (1966–99), Colombia (1982–99), and Mexico (1987–99) finds that the wage gap by subsector of the manufacturing industry has common patterns of behavior that are associated with changes in the demand for labor, possibly for technological reasons. First, increases in the wage gap occurred within sectors and in the same sectors in all countries. Second, the intensity of this phenomenon was related to the import penetration of inputs and capital goods of those industries. Third, the increase in the wage gap proved to be more sensitive to the technological content of those imports than to their penetration (Sánchez-Páramo and Schady 2003). This evidence notwithstanding, the extent of these effects is modest, and could even be consistent with phenomena other than technological change.

These conclusions about LAC are not surprising in light of world experience. Indeed, although wage inequality has increased in many countries over the past three decades, this phenomenon has not been shown to be explicable by changes in trade liberalization policies or by the volume of trade flows. Although evidence available for previous periods is limited, an analysis of import liberalization experiences up to the mid-1980s concluded: "No clear patterns emerge. The presumption that liberalization is bound to worsen income distribution, making the poor poorer, is not borne out" (Michaely et al. 1991: 103).

15.6 CONCLUSION: THE SURPRISES OF TRADE LIBERALIZATION

Trade liberalization was one of the major reforms of the 1990s in LAC. Tariff and non-tariff barriers to imports were slashed and a substantial increase in import and export ratios took place, as expected. Overall, however, trade liberalization was a source of big surprises that defy the views of both its advocates and its critics.

It did increase productivity and economic growth, but modestly and perhaps temporarily, and certainly much less than its advocates had expected—conceivably because it did not reallocate productive resources, including labor, as may have been predicted on the basis of theory. Although those sectors more exposed to trade competition did experience efficiency improvements, trade liberalization did not have much effect on employment composition. This is a surprise to those economic analysts who, on the basis of the theory of comparative advantage, expected resources to move massively toward activities that were potentially more efficient and more intensive in the use of the most abundant resources. It is also a surprise for those who imagined that increased imports would produce massive worker dismissals in the import competing sectors. Against all fears, trade liberalization did not have noticeable effects on unemployment. This is also a surprise for many economists, who expected that the unemployment associated with the transition of workers from some sectors to others would increase, at least initially. The fact that little employment was reallocated between sectors does not mean that companies or workers did not suffer traumas due to liberalization, or that the labor market lacked the vitality to respond to such an important policy change.

Furthermore, while trade liberalization did increase productivity, it did not have the expected effect on wages, which fell in the sectors most subject to competition, especially those of lower-skilled workers. This is a surprise for economists trained in neoclassical analysis, who usually assume that wages correspond to workers' marginal productivity, and that liberalization should lead to more productive use of all resources, including labor, elimination of rents that favor capitalists, and lower prices for agricultural and industrial goods consumed by workers. What seems to have happened (although there is no direct evidence supporting it) is that workers were sharing in these rents and were forced to give them up in order to hold onto their jobs. The fact that in many countries tariffs (and import controls) were higher for those sectors that were more labor-intensive (especially in unskilled labor) also helps explain this paradox. Liberalization may have lowered wages in industry by allowing entry into domestic markets of goods from countries with lower production costs.

Finally, and possibly the most debated aspect of trade liberalization in public and academic circles in LAC, is that it helped widen the wage gap between skilled and unskilled workers. While this effect of trade liberalization is inconsistent with a standard comparative advantage model with two goods and where the only two factors of production are unskilled and skilled labor, it does not necessarily hold under less restrictive assumptions. The explanation for the widening wage gap may be found more in the area of technology and other little-understood mechanisms than in the mechanics of relative prices directly associated with international trade.

The lesson from this series of surprises is one of modesty for economists and moderation for critics. At the same time, evidence is limited by lack of information, the shortness of the time period for observing some of the effects of liberalization, and conceptual and technical barriers to interpreting the results. Moreover, the evidence is restricted by the inclinations of academic research, which do not necessarily coincide with the concerns and fears of the public. Finally, none of the foregoing surprises constitutes a rule because there are many variations among country experiences.

REFERENCES

ATTANASIO, O., GOLDBERG, P., and PAVCNIK, N. (2004). 'Trade Reforms and Wage Inequality in Colombia', *Journal of Development Economics* 74.

BAKER, A. (2003). 'Why Is Trade Reform so Popular in Latin America? A Consumption-Based Theory of Trade Policy Preferences', *World Politics* 55.3.

—— (2009). *The Market and the Masses in Latin America: Policy Reform and Consumption in Liberalizing Economies*, Cambridge: Cambridge University Press.

BALDWIN, R. (2003). 'Openness and Growth: What's The Empirical Relationship?', NBER Working Paper No. 9578, Cambridge, Mass.

BEHRMAN, J., BIRDSALL, N., and SZÉKELY, M. (2000). 'Economic Reform and Wage Differentials in Latin America', IDB Working Paper No. 435, Washington, DC.

BERNARD, A., REDDING, S., and SCHOTT, P. (2007). 'Comparative Advantage and Heterogeneous Firms', *Review of Economic Studies* 74.1.

BOUET, A. (2006). 'What can the Poor Expect from Trade Liberalization? Opening the "Black Box" of Trade Modeling', MTID Discussion Paper No. 93, International Food Policy Research Institute, Washington, DC.

CÁRDENAS, M., and GUTIÉRREZ, C. (1997). 'Impacto de las reformas estructurales sobre la eficiencia y la equidad', in M. Cárdenas (ed.), *Empleo y distribución del ingreso en Latin America. ¿Hemos avanzado?* Bogotá: TM Editores.

CARNEIRO, F., and ARBACHE, J. (2003). 'The Impacts of Trade on the Brazilian Labor Market: A CGE Model Approach', *World Development* 31.9.

CASACUBERTA, C., FACHOLA, G., and GANDELMAN, N. (2004). 'The Impact of Trade Liberalization on Employment, Capital, and Productivity Dynamics: Evidence from the Uruguayan Manufacturing Sector', *Journal of Economic Policy Reform* 7.4.

CASSONI, A., ALLEN, S., and LABADIE, G. (1999). 'Union, Labor Market Regulation, and Employment in Uruguay', mimeograph, IDB, Washington, DC.

CEDLAS (Centro de Estudios Distributivos, Laborales y Sociales) and World Bank (2009). 'Socio-economic Database for Latin America and the Caribbean', available online at: http://www.depeco.econo.unlp.edu.ar/sedlac/ eng/statistics.php

DE FERRANTI, D. et al. (2002). 'From Natural Resources to the Knowledge Economy: Trade and Job Equality', Washington, DC: World Bank.

DE JANVRY, A., SADOULET, E., and DAVIS, B. (1997). 'NAFTA and Agriculture: An Early Assessment', Working Paper No. 807, Department of Agriculture and Resource Economics, University of California at Berkeley.

DOLLAR, D. (1992). 'Outward Oriented Developing Economies Really Do Grow More Rapidly: Evidence from 95 LDCs 1976–85', *Economic Development and Cultural Change* 40.

—— and KRAAY, A. (2000). 'Trade Growth and Poverty', Washington, DC: World Bank.

EASTERLY, W., LOAYZA, N., and MONTIEL, P. (1997). 'Has Latin America's Post Reform Growth Been Disappointing?', *Journal of International Economics* 43.

ECLAC (UN EconomicCommission for Latin America and the Caribbean) (2009). 'CEPAL Stat Online: Data Bases and Statistical Publications', available online at: http://websie.eclac.cl/infest/ajax/cepalstat.asp?carpeta=estadisticas

EDWARDS, S. (1998). 'Openness, Productivity and Growth: What Do We Really Know?', *Economic Journal* 108.

ESCAITH, H., and MORLEY, S. (2001). 'El efecto de las reformas estructurales en el crecimiento económico de Latin America y el Caribe: una estimación empírica', *El trimestre económico* 68.

ESLAVA, M., HALTIWANGER, J., KUGLER, A., and KUGLER, M. (2004). 'The Effects of Structural Reforms on Productivity and Profitability Enhancing Reallocation: Evidence from Colombia', *Journal of Development Economics* 75.

FAJNZYLBER, P., and MALONEY, W. (2005). 'Labor Demand and Trade Reform in Latin America', *Journal of International Economics* 66.2.

FELICIANO, Z. (2001). 'Workers and Trade Liberalization: The Impact of Trade Reforms in Mexico on Wages and Unemployment', *Industrial and Labor Relations Review* 55.1.

FERNÁNDES, A. (2007). 'Trade Policy, Trade Volumes and Plant-Level Productivity in Colombian Manufacturing Industries', *Journal of International Economics* 71.

FERNÁNDEZ, R., and RODRIK, D. (1990). 'Why is Trade Reform so Unpopular? On Status Quo Bias in Policy Reforms', NBER Working Paper No. 3269, Cambridge, Mass.

FERNÁNDEZ-ARIAS, E., and MONTIEL, P. (1997). 'Reform and Growth in Latin America: All Pain, No Gain?', Working Paper No. 351, IDB, Washington, DC.

FERREIRA, P. C., and ROSSI, J. L. (2003). 'New Evidence from Brazil on Trade Liberalization And Productivity Growth', *International Economic Review* 44.4.

FRANKEL, J., and ROMER, D. (1999). 'Does Trade Cause Growth?', *American Economic Review* 89.

FREEMAN, R. (2004). 'Trade Wars: The Exaggerated Impact of Trade in Economic Debate', *World Economy* 27.1.

GALIANI, S., and SANGUINETTI, P. (2000). *Wage Inequality and Trade Liberalization: Evidence from Argentina*, Buenos Aires: Universidad Torcuato Di Tella.

GANUZA, E., PAES DE BARROS, R., TAYLOR, L., and VOS, R. (2001). *Liberalización, desigualdad y pobreza: América Latina en los 90*, Buenos Aires: Eudeba.

GOLDBERG, P. K., and PAVCNIK, N. (2001). 'Trade Protection and Wages: Evidence from the Colombian Trade Reforms', NBER Working Paper No. 8575, Cambridge, Mass.

—— —— (2003). 'The Response of the Informal Sector to Trade Liberalization', NBER Working Paper No. 9443, Cambridge, Mass.

—— —— (2004). 'Trade, Inequality and Poverty: What Do We Know? Evidence from Recent Trade Liberalization Episodes in Developing Countries', NBER Working Paper No. 10593, Cambridge, Mass.

—— —— (2005). 'Trade, Wages, and The Political Economy of Trade Protection: Evidence from the Colombia Trade Reforms', *Journal of International Economics* 66.1.

GONZAGA, G., FILHO, N. M., and TERRA, C. (2006). 'Trade Liberalization and the Evolution of Skill Earnings Differentials in Brazil', *Journal of International Economics* 68.2.

GREEN, F., DICKERSON, A., and ARBACHE, J.S. (2001). 'A Picture of Wage Inequality and the Allocation of Labor Through the Period of Trade Liberalization: The Case of Brazil', *World Development* 29.

GREENAWAY, D., MORGAN, W., and WRIGHT, P. (2002). 'Trade Liberalisation and Growth in Developing Countries', *Journal of Development Economics* 67.

HALTIWANGER, J., et al. (2004). 'Effects of Tariffs and Real Exchange Rates on Job Reallocation: Evidence from Latin America', *Journal of Economic Policy Reform* 7.4.

HANSON, G. (2003). 'What Has Happened to Wages in Mexico since NAFTA? Implications for Hemispheric Free Trade', NBER Working Paper No. W9563, Cambridge, Mass.

—— and HARRISON, A. (1999). 'Trade and Wage Inequality in Mexico', *Industrial and Labor Relations Review* 52.2.

HARRISON, A., and HANSON, G. (1999). 'Who Gains from Trade Reform? Some Remaining Puzzles', *Journal of Development Economics* 59.

HAY, D. (2001). 'The Post-1990 Brazilian Trade Liberalization and the Performance of Large Manufacturing Firms: Productivity, Market Shares and Profits', *Economic Journal* 111.

HOEKMAN, B., and WINTERS, A. (2005). 'Trade and Employment: Stylized Factors and Research Findings', World Bank Policy Research Working Paper No. 3676, Washington, DC.

IDB (Inter-American Development Bank) (1996). *Making Social Services Work: Economic and Social Progress in Latin America, 1996 Report*, Washington, DC.

—— (1997). *Latin America After a Decade of Reforms: Economic and Social Progress in Latin America, 1997 Report*, Washington, DC.

—— (2003). *Good Jobs Wanted: Labor Markets in Latin America. Economic and Social Progress in Latin America, 2004 Report*, Washington, DC.

—— (2009). 'Hemispheric Trade and Tariff Database', available online at: http://www .ftaa-alca.org/NGROUPS/NGMADB_e.asp

LAPOP (2008). 'The Americas Barometer', Latin American Public Opinion Project, available online at: http://www.vanderbilt.edu/lapop/datasets

Latinobarómetro (2001). 'Latinobarómetro database', available online at: http://www .latinobarometro.org/

—— (2004). 'Latinobarómetro database', available online at: http://www.latinobarometro.org/

LOAYZA, N., FAJNZYLBER, P., and CALDERÓN, C. (2005). 'Economic Growth in Latin America and The Caribbean: Stylized Facts, Explanations, and Forecasts', Working Paper No. 265, Central Bank of Chile, Santiago.

LÓPEZ-CÓRDOVA, E., and MESQUITA, M. (2004). 'Regional Integration and Productivity: The Experiences of Brazil and Mexico', INTAL-ITD Working Paper No. 14, Washington, DC.

LORA, E. (2001). 'Structural Reforms in Latin America: What Has Been Reformed and How to Measure it', IDB Working Paper No. 466, Washington, DC.

—— and BARRERA, F. (1998). 'El crecimiento económico en América Latina después de una década de reformas estructurales', *Pensamiento Iberoamericano–Revista de economía política*, special issue.

—— and OLIVERA, M. (2005). 'The Electoral Consequences of the Washington Consensus', IDB Working Paper No. 530, Washington, DC.

—— and PANIZZA, U. (2002). 'Structural Reforms in Latin America Under Scrutiny', IDB Working Paper No. 470, Washington, DC.

MÁRQUEZ, G., and PAGÉS, C. (1998). 'Trade and Employment: Evidence from Latin America and the Caribbean', IDB Working Paper No. 366, Washington, DC.

MESQUITA, M., and NAJBERG, S. (2000). 'Trade Liberalisation in Brazil: Creating or Exporting Jobs?', *Journal of Development Studies* 36.3.

MICHAELY, M., PAPAGEORGIOU, D., and CHOKSI, A. (1991). *Liberalizing Foreign Trade. Lessons of Experience in the Developing World 7*, Cambridge, Mass.: Blackwell.

MUENDLER, M. (2004). 'Trade, Technology, and Productivity: A Study of Brazilian Manufacturers, 1986–1998', University of California and CESifo.

NADAL, A. (2000). *The Environmental and Social Impacts of Economic Liberalization on Corn Production in Mexico*, London: Oxfam and WWF International.

OCAMPO, J. A. (2004). 'La América Latina y la economía mundial en el largo siglo XX', *El trimestre económico* 284.

—— (2009). 'Comercio y crecimiento incluyente', Flacso Working Paper No. 106, Latin American Trade Network, Buenos Aires.

PAGÉS, C. (ed.) (2010). *The Age of Productivity: Transforming Economies from the Bottom Up, Development in the Americas*, Washington, DC: IDB.

PAUS, E., REINHARDT, N., and ROBINSON, M. (2003). 'Trade Liberalization and Productivity Growth in Latin American Manufacturing, 1970–98', *Journal of Policy Reform* 6.1.

PAVCNIK, N. (2002). 'Trade Liberalization, Exit, and Productivity Improvements: Evidence from Chilean Plants', *Review of Economic Studies* 69.1.

—— BLOM, A., and SCHADY, N. (2002). 'Trade Liberalization and Labor Market Adjustment in Brazil', World Bank Policy Research Working Paper No. 2982, Washington, DC.

—— —— —— and GOLDBERG, P. (2004). 'Trade Liberalization and Industry Wage Structure: Evidence from Brazil', *World Bank Economic Review* 18.3.

RAMA, M. (1994). 'The Labor Market and Trade Reform in Manufacturing', in M. Connolly and J. de Melo (eds), *The Effects of Protectionism on a Small Country: The Case of Uruguay*, Washington, DC: World Bank.

—— (2003). 'Globalization and Workers in Developing Countries', World Bank Policy Research Working Paper No. 2858, Washington, DC.

REVENGA, A. (1992). 'Exporting Jobs? The Impact of Import Competition on Employment and Wages in US Manufacturing', *Quarterly Journal of Economics* 107.1.

—— (1997). 'Employment and Wage Effects of Trade Liberalization: The Case of Mexican Manufacturing', *Journal of Labor Economics* 107.1.

ROBBINS, D., and GINDLING, T. H. (1999). 'Trade Liberalization and the Relative Wages for More-Skilled Workers in Costa Rica', *Review of Development Economics* 3.2.

ROBERTSON, R. (2000). 'Trade Liberalisation and Wage Inequality: Lessons from the Mexican Experience', *World Economy* 23.6.

—— (2004). 'Relative Prices and Wage Inequality: Evidence from Mexico', *Journal of International Economics* 64.2.

RODRÍGUEZ, F., and RODRIK, D. (2001). 'Trade Policy and Economic Growth: A Skeptic's Guide to the Cross-National Evidence', *NBER Macroeconomics Annual* 15.

RODRIK, D. (1997). *Has Globalization Gone Too Far?* Washington, DC: Institute for International Economics.

SACHS, J., and WARNER, A. (1995). 'Economic Reforms and the Process of Global Integration', *Brookings Papers on Economic Activity* 1.

SÁNCHEZ-PÁRAMO, C., and SCHADY, N. (2003). 'Off and Running? Technology, Trade and the Rising Demand for Skilled Workers in Latin America', World Bank Policy Research Working Paper No. 3015, Washington, DC.

SANGUINETTI, P., ARIM, R., and PANTANO, J. (2001). *Changes in Production and Employment Structure and Relative Wages in Argentina and Uruguay*, Buenos Aires: Universidad Torcuato Di Tella.

SAPRIN (Structural Adjustment Participatory Review International Network) (2002). 'The Policy Roots of Economic Crisis And Poverty', Washington, DC.

SEDDON, J., and WACZIARG, R. (2004). 'Trade Liberalization and Intersectoral Labor Movements', *Journal of International Economics* 64.2.

STALLINGS, B., and PERES, W. (2000). *Growth, Employment, and Equity: The Impact of the Economic Reforms in Latin America and the Caribbean*, Washington, DC: Brookings Institution.

TYBOUT, J., and ERDEM, E. (2003). 'Trade Policy and Industrial Sector Responses: Using Evolutionary Models to Interpret the Evidence', NBER Working Paper No. W9947, Cambride, Mass.

VOS, R., GANUZA, E., MORLEY, S., and ROBINSON, S. (2006). *Who Gains From Free Trade? Export-Led Growth, Inequality and Poverty in Latin America*, London: Routledge.

WELLER, J. (2001). *Economic Reforms, Growth and Employment: Labour Markets in Latin America and the Caribbean*, Santiago, Chile: CEPAL.

WINTERS, A., MCCULLOCH, N., and MCKAY, A. (2004). 'Trade Liberalization and Poverty: The Evidence So Far', *Journal of Economic Literature* 42.

World Bank (2009). 'World Development Indicators', available online at: http://ddp-ext. worldbank.org/ext/DDPQQ/member.do?method=getMembers&userid=1&queryId=135

CHAPTER 16

THE RECENT COMMODITY PRICE BOOM AND LATIN AMERICAN GROWTH: MORE THAN NEW BOTTLES FOR AN OLD WINE?

EDMAR L. BACHA AND ALBERT FISHLOW

16.1 INTRODUCTION

After a twenty-five-year decline starting in the early 1980s, commodity prices surged in the early 21st century, only to collapse as a result of the 2008–9 financial crisis—thus seeming to confirm that the previous surge was just only one more example of the traditional stop/go long-term commodity price pattern. However, powered by the rapid recovery of the commodity-hungry Asian nations (and perhaps also by very low worldwide interest rates), commodity prices recovered their strength from mid-2009. At the point of writing, April 2010, every indication was that this upward price trend would continue—perhaps with less impetus than in the 2002–7 period, because of the weaker economic recovery in industrial nations.

Resource-rich Latin America benefited from this surge of commodity prices, and per capita GDP growth rates reached levels last seen in the 1970s. Rising commodity prices led to improved current account balances and induced large foreign capital inflows. Real exchange rates appreciated as a consequence, but the novelty of the cycle was a sizeable accumulation of foreign reserves and a marked reduction in foreign indebtedness. Thus, when the international crisis hit in mid-2008, the region's policy-makers had the means to soften the impact of the external shocks through appropriate countercyclical macro policies.

In 2010, Latin America was growing again and commodity prices were strengthening. The combination is a fortunate one, but it is not without its contradictions. The main tension is an old one, and it goes by the name of "deindustrialization" or "Dutch Disease": as domestic resources are attracted to commodity-related sectors, there is a tendency for the real exchange rate to appreciate and, as a consequence, for non-commodity-related manufactures to lose competitiveness and risk being crowded out both from international and domestic markets. Rather than exiting, the negatively impacted manufacturing sectors often make their voices heard—demanding government intervention to maintain them in business.

This is not the only tension raised by the recent commodity price boom, for the exchange rate may appreciate not as a direct consequence of commodity exports, but rather because of capital inflows that are attracted by the region's improved economic prospects. Hence, at stake is not only an old controversy on industrialization patterns but also a new one on capital inflows and concurrent current account deficits. Involved as well is a question of domestic interest rates, and their appropriate level.

We will delve more deeply into this question of appropriate policy instruments—domestic and international—to offset the regular volatility of commodity prices. In this process, it is essential to disaggregate. Agricultural, mineral, and petroleum prices do not necessarily move in conjunction, let alone all the products in the first two categories. Indexes can sometimes deceive.

But first, we wish to comment briefly upon the extensive literature devoted to this subject. Few other subjects in economics have as lengthy a tradition. Mercantilism and protectionism date far back. We begin with the post-World War II contributions of Raul Prebisch and Hans Singer. It is hardly an accident that Latin America—unengaged directly in the war and an initial supplier of exports to war-torn Europe—should become the focus of import substitution industrialization in the 1950s. Some countries in the region had achieved economic growth in the Great Depression, and sought to sustain it; others were motivated to try.

Then, we focus briefly upon four different country experiences within the region. Their selection relates back to their type of exports, as well as the distinctive policies being pursued. All had embarked upon import substitution in the 1950s. All benefited from gains in the terms of trade in the 2000s. But the results greatly diverged.

We start with Argentina, the only historic case of descent from a ranking in the top ten per capita incomes in 1900 to much lower placement more than a century later. Reliance upon exports of agricultural products—and their cyclical price variability—have much to do with this result, but so does policy choice. Argentina moved from export of meat and wheat to concentration upon soybeans in the last two decades. But export taxes and import restrictions have continued as central features.

We follow with Chile, where copper production has dominated since 1945. Subject to greater price volatility owing to the commodity concentration of its exports, Chile impresses by its polarization of policy. Despite size limitations, it first committed itself to industrialization behind high protective barriers. Then an attempt to accommodate fully to the market in the Pinochet period proved equally mistaken. Finally, there has been success under the Concertación. Natural resource exports, and rising copper prices, have greatly helped in this transformation.

Venezuela is our third case, a classic petroleum exporter with the highest Latin American per capita income in the 1950s, and a failure to achieve sustained, and more diversified, economic development well before the arrival upon the scene of Hugo Chávez in the 1990s. In this instance, domestic and international policies clearly interact, beginning with entry into OPEC in the 1970s. In more recent times, there has been the great increase in oil prices from 2003 to 2008, replicated again in 2010, but accompanied by increasingly inadequate policy interventions that cannot help but remind one of early responses to sudden export wealth that ended in the Lost Decade of the 1980s.

Brazil is the last example we consider. What differentiates this experience is the combination of agricultural, mineral, and petroleum exports—including ethanol and biodiesel fuels—in recent years. At the same time, its industrial sector has been large and, since the 1990s, without the great tariff protection characterizing earlier rapid expansion. The public sector has much expanded, and inflation has been tamed since the Plan Real in 1994. Moreover, the economy fully survived the Great Recession and registered an impressive recovery in 2010. Here the central issue becomes the magnitude and form of intervention compatible with resource wealth.

On the basis of this diverse history, we return in the final section to reconsider the appropriate policy mix to avert the negative consequences of commodity price volatility and to proceed to sustainable development.

16.2 THE CURSE AND THE DISEASE

Several strands in the development economics literature discuss natural resources and economic growth. Perhaps David Landes (1998) first coined the term "natural resource curse," meaning that countries well endowed with natural resources would tend to grow less rapidly than countries not so well endowed. In the region, the Prebisch–Singer thesis (Prebisch 1950; Singer 1950) on the long-run trend for declining terms of trade of primary products was prominent in the years immediately following World War II: it would be as a result of this trend that countries specializing in primary products exports would be condemned to grow more slowly.

Much ink has been spent on the logic and the empirics of this terms-of-trade proposition, but the final verdict of recent studies is that downward structural price-breaks are present but no long-run trend is discernible in the secular data (Cuddington, Ludeman, and Jayasuriya 2007; Brahmbhatt and Canuto 2010; Ocampo and Parra 2010). This result is nonetheless consistent with cyclical swings of great magnitude, such as that in 1919, in the 1970s, and almost certainly after 2004. Moreover, there are some individual commodities whose longer-term experience may show a trend. Taken together, the relevant policy problem is the response to such volatility.

This earlier had taken two forms: international producer efforts to control supply like OPEC and others, and national stockpiles to dampen price swings.[1] Only in recent years has another appeared: sovereign wealth funds. These have been accumulated during the upward phase of the cycle, with the intention of expenditure during the downward phase. As a consequence, governments can avoid the excesses of prosperity and the depths of depression. For some petroleum exporters with limited reserves, the intent is also to establish an endowment. Presently, such holdings constitute $3.8 trillion—Chile is the only country in the region represented (IFSL Research 2010).

Another popular strand of the natural resource curse argues that primary production is not as "dynamic" as industry, both because of lower total productivity growth and becaue of lower income-elasticity of final demand. Empirical results do not confirm the first proposition: productivity in agriculture or mining tends to grow as fast as or faster than in industry among efficient producers (Martin and Mitra 2001; Wright and Czelusta 2007).[2] It is however a well-known fact of development economics since Kuznets (1966) that, as income grows, population and income shares shift out of primary products into industry and then into services. But production structure does not need to be replicated in trade patterns. If a country is well endowed with natural resources, its exports can continue to be dominated by them, even as it develops and most of its population shifts into industry and then into services.

Norway has the highest income per capita in the world, and oil dominates its exports. Other countries that developed on the basis of primary-product exports include Australia, Canada, Finland, and New Zealand, not to mention Sweden and the United States well into the 20th century. Clearly, what characterizes (or historically character-ized) these countries are high primary-product endowments per capita. As population grows, the relative abundance of natural resources decline and, as a consequence, export patterns tend to replicate domestic production patterns more closely, i.e. the share of industry and services in exports grow.

The example of the Nordic "old world" and Anglo-Saxon "new world" countries not-withstanding, the fact remains that a very large number of primary-product exporters—notably in Africa and Latin America—display a very poor growth performance.[3] If the export share of primary products either in total exports or in GDP is used as a criterion, innumerable cross-section regressions since the well-known study of Sachs and Warner

[1] There had been earlier attempts to incorporate consumers as well, such as the International Coffee Agreement involving Brazil and Colombia.

[2] Prebisch and Singer were concerned not with relative productivity growth rates, but with the proposition that technical progress would be appropriated as higher wages in the manufacturing center and be dispersed as lower prices in the primary-producing periphery. Their argument presumes that labor is fully employed in the center and in unlimited supply in the periphery (Lewis 1954). But in this case, it can be argued that what should matter to the periphery is the growth of employment rather than the terms-of-trade trend (Bacha 1983).

[3] Notable exceptions from the natural resource curse in the developing world include Malaysia, Thailand, Oman, Botswana, and Chile.

(1995) would seem to confirm the "resource curse:" developing countries rich in natural resources tend to grow less than those exporting manufactured products.

However, in a series of recent studies, Lederman and Maloney (2007; 2008) take issue with such a conclusion. They argue that the resource curse—apparent in the simple correlation between specialization and growth[4]—disappears when a measure of export concentration is introduced in the regressions. They thus suggest that the curse is one of lack of diversification, not resources. This finding is consistent with the view of a resource drag on growth arising from the limited possibilities of variation among commodities—but then, as de Ferranti et al. (2002) and Lederman and Xu (2007) argue, diversification into non-resource sectors from a strong resource base is feasible, as illustrated by the Nordic and New World Anglo-nations that are now well-developed countries.

From this perspective, the curse would derive not from the nature of the export good but from excessive export concentration and lack of flexibility to shift out of sectors as required by the evolution of world demand and the country's comparative advantage. Specialization in commodities, however, would seem to have a definitive drawback, as their prices tend to be much more volatile than manufacturing prices, making it difficult to disentangle temporary from permanent price changes, and thus reducing fixed investment and growth. Some authors have thus suggested that it is exactly the volatility of natural resource prices, rather than the trend, that is bad for economic growth (Hausmann and Rigobon 2003; Blattman, Hwang, and Williamson 2007; Poelhekke and van der Ploeg 2007).

Furthermore, the volatility of prices and the relative magnitude of the natural-resource sector for many countries imply huge swings in fiscal revenues, invoking all the attendant complexities of public decisionmaking. In the upswing, the question is whether these revenues will be put to good use, wasted, or allowed to become actively detrimental. Tornell and Lane (1999) document what they call a voracity effect, whereby a sudden influx of riches leads to a more than one-for-one increase in spending as interest groups demand their share of the windfall.[5] Because the process exhibits hysteresis, any ebb in the bonanza can lead to fiscal crises as expenditures remain high while revenues collapse.

Thus, of the various possible channels through which natural resources could be a curse to long-run development, the quality of institutions and governance is perhaps the most widely hypothesized. Isham et al. (2005) find that the commodities that are damaging to institutional development, which they call "point source" resources, are (in addition to oil): other minerals, plantation crops, and coffee and cocoa. Sala-i-Martin and Subramanian (2003) and Bulte, Damania, and Deacon (2005) also find that point

---

[4] See the recent book of Ocampo, Rada, and Taylor (2009: ch. 4), demonstrating this proposition.

[5] Contemplating with some despair the dispute in Brazil's Congress for a share of future oil-revenues, President Lula aptly synthesized the voracity effect with the observation: "they are fighting for the chips (*pirão* in Portuguese) before catching the fish" (interview for the newspaper *A Tarde* on March 26, 2010).

source resources such as oil and some particular minerals undermine institutional quality and thereby growth, but not agricultural resources. According to Collier and Goderis (2007), negative long-run growth effects are mostly related to oil and minerals, while there is little evidence of negative growth effects related to high prices for agricultural commodities, which are generally more open to competitive entry. But Collier and Goderis also find that high oil and mineral prices mostly have a negative impact on long-run growth in exporting countries with bad governance. They have a significant positive impact on growth in exporters with good governance.

This last finding, according to Brahmbhatt and Canuto (2010), suggests that continued high commodity prices in the next few years could provide valuable resources to accelerate economic and social development in commodity-exporting countries with good policies and governance. Lederman and Maloney (2008) argue that with new data, new econometric analyses provide (for them) definite evidence that there is no curse, not even indirectly through the political institutions that would most likely be affected by the curse-via-politics effects, which has been central in the literature on the point source nature of natural resources.[6] Nonetheless, despite what they consider to be the unreliable evidence concerning the curse-through-politics hypothesis, they grant that institutional arrangements to smooth out the economic consequences of natural resource windfalls make a lot of sense.

Perhaps the main focus of such policy interventions relates to the so-called Dutch Disease.[7] The phenomenon arises when a strong, but perhaps temporary, upward swing in the world price of the export commodity causes a large appreciation of the currency, an increase in spending especially by the government, an increase in the price of non-traded goods, a resultant shift of inputs out of non-export-commodity traded goods, and a current account deficit (Frankel 2010). When crowded-out non-commodity tradable goods are in the manufacturing sector, the feared effect is de-industrialization.

But what would make this movement a "disease"? One argument, particularly relevant if the complete cycle is not adequately foreseen, is that it is all painfully reversed when the world price of the export commodity goes back down. Capital outflows may occur, accelerating the need for devaluation in the midst of a balance-of-payments crisis. A second interpretation is that the crowding-out of non-commodity exports is judged undesirable, perhaps because the manufacturing sector has greater externalities for long-run growth. The second view is just another way of describing the natural-

[6] Lerderman and Maloney's claim of a "resource blessing" is based on the measurement of a country's natural resource abundance by its per capita net natural resource exports. This is equal to a country's per capita income times its net natural resources exports over GDP. The latter is a frequent measure of natural resource abundance in previous studies that claimed to have identified a "resource curse" in the data. Lederman and Maloney's abundance measure gives more weight to countries with higher per capita income, and this may bias their results towards showing that resources are a blessing rather than a curse.

[7] The name "Dutch Disease" was coined by the *Economist* magazine in 1977 and was originally inspired by side-effects of natural gas discoveries by the Netherlands in the late 1950s.

resource curse previously discussed; it would thus seem appropriate to reserve the term "Dutch Disease" for the cyclical phenomenon.

When viewed from this cyclical perspective, the term applies as well to temporary surges in capital inflows leading to real appreciation and a shift into non-tradables, and away from non-booming tradables. Naturally, large capital inflows may result from a commodity boom itself, thus helping to magnify its Dutch Disease impacts. The sharpness of the commodity boom, on the other hand, may be magnified by destabilizing speculative demand in futures commodity markets, which have gained much prominence in recent years.

At stake here are a series of cumulative foreign shocks that generate volatility and hence lower growth in commodity-producing developing countries. These may be compounded by domestic macroeconomic and political instability: most developing countries are still subject to monetary and fiscal policies that are pro-cyclical rather than countercyclical: they tend to be expansionary in booms and contractionary in recessions, thus exacerbating the magnitude of the swings.

We return to consideration of such matters in our concluding section. Before we do, it is necessary to examine in greater, if brief, detail the contrasting experiences of our four country cases.

16.2.1 Argentina

Argentina is perhaps the world's best case of the presumed natural resource curse: a rich and fertile country that went astray in the post-World War II period. Already by that time, the country had deviated from its previous participation in world trade. In the boom before 1914, the sum of imports and exports represented about 80% of national income; by 1950 that ratio was down to 20%. Import substitution had already been substantially under way during the Great Depression, where much of that decline was concentrated.

Slow then to devalue, the country had to rely instead upon direct currency controls, and other limits to trade, but the special relationship with Britain through the Roca Runciman Treaty produced a lesser response than shown by other large economies in the region. Argentina continued its debt payment; "a less well-behaved policy...would have freed resources for the adoption of expansionary domestic policies by the federal government and for further consolidation of Argentine industry through the expansion of capital goods imports" (Thorp 1998: 116)

After the war, politics entered powerfully, and has remained as the dominant element in Argentine economics since. Perón's ascent was significant as the basis for a new economics. That involved conscious redistribution of income from both agricultural and industrial interests—who had managed their differences in the midst of rising tariff protection—to the urban labor force. The extent of the shift is impressive. Union affiliation was only 10% of non-agricultural employment in 1936; by 1950, that ratio had increased to 49%. The consequence is equally impressive. Labor's share in national income went up by eight percentage points until the mid-1950s. Thereafter, while this gain was reversed, the struggle implicitly continued (Della Paolera and Taylor 2003: 135).

Perón was overthrown by the military in the mid-1950s, but they ceded control to a civilian successor in 1958; in 1962 the military returned, but briefly. Finally in 1966, as had already happened elsewhere in the region, the military returned more permanent-ly—except for a brief elected interlude of Perón and his second wife, Isabela, until Alfonsin was elected at the end of 1983. Despite the macroeconomic problems associ-ated with his term, and the failure of the Austral Plan, peaceful succession by Menem averted arbitrary intervention once again. A similar crisis occurred with the end of the fixed exchange rate and the forced resignation of de la Rua at the end of 2001.

Argentina continues with political fragility and weak institutions down to the present. Menem's two terms, rooted in expansive foreign investment and favorable access to the Brazilian market, did not change the country as definitively as some expected. The sub-sequent succession of the Presidents Kirschner, and their attempt to define a different, non-IMF structuralist strategy, suggests a vain search. Policy has been a short-term stra-tegic accommodation rather than a set of permanent rules enabling sustained produc-tivity advance.

Over much of the period, external trade had remained at low levels, and tariffs high, along with other periodic interventions like export duties, until the 1990s. Thereafter, trade has taken on greater importance. Now exports and imports again account for something like 45% of income. There has been a dual role. On the one side, MERCOSUR opened new possibilities for exports of manufactured products to Brazil, especially of automobiles. On the other, Argentina remained an agricultural exporter to the rest of the world, but specialized increasingly in soybeans, as Chinese demand rapidly expanded. Unlike the case of Brazil until recently, there has been open commitment to new genetic varieties with consequent cost reductions.

Nonetheless, and in spite of more rapid growth of exports than product over the last two decades, few would choose Argentina as a case where natural-resource richness has finally translated into a basis for successful development. Historically, while terms of trade have shown high volatility, government trade policy has managed to avert a corre-sponding impact upon income receipts of farmers. When foreign prices were high, they were taxed; when low, subsidies were implicitly granted. But seeming stabilization did not avoid internal struggles with industry, and a relative disadvantage that still persists in political terms (Della Paolera and Taylor 2003: 107).

Import substitution again intensified in Argentina, after the crisis of 2001. There is a strong belief that domestic manufactures can become more productive, and a better source for development than reliance upon agriculture and free markets. Yet real invest-ment has fallen short, in no small part owing to the restrictions placed upon imports of capital goods elevating their cost, while savings continues relatively high. Foreign invest-ment is cautious about commitment, given its past experience, and a present where offi-cial price indexes report only half the inflation rate.

In sum, despite the favorable external environment for commodities that again has evolved, Argentina has not yet managed to resolve its fundamental internal problems.

These weigh much more heavily upon satisfactory economic growth than variations in the terms of trade. Volatility there has been, but its origins are much more in "the insta-bility of the 'rules of the game' (policy regimes, regulatory norms, property rights enforcement, and so on)" (Chudnofsky and Lopez 2007: 27). There is scope to take advantage of a favorable resource base, and at the same time to achieve the needed com-petitiveness and efficiency within the industrial sector. Continuity is a virtue that has been lacking.

16.2.2 Chile

Chile's long democratic tradition came to a violent turning point in 1973 with the advent of the Pinochet dictatorship. Economic conditions, seemingly so positive in the 1960s when the Frei government had benefited from Alliance for Progress resources and undertaken far-reaching reforms, had equally turned negative in the early 1970s. Inflation was at the rate of 900% a year, and fiscal and balance-of-payments deficits were beyond salvation. Populist policies put into place by the Allende government were no solution.

The 'Chicago Boys' who led the economic ministries for the next decade sought to reverse entirely the previous commitment to import substitution industrialization and large state presence. Their efforts were only partially successful. Monetarism, with its attendant Law of One Price, did not work as a strategy to enforce an end to continuing inflation. Inflation fell, but with a considerable lag. A large current account deficit and a domestic financial boom were not precursors of restored economic growth. The econ-omy soon came crashing down again in 1982, following the plunge in copper prices and US recession. The Chilean government guaranteed, rather than abandoned, the private debt that had been incurred, and the "free market" experiment was effectively over.

New macroeconomic policies followed, less orthodox in character, and with variable exchange rates. Modest expansion resumed, but it was too late to save the dictatorship. Fundamental changes had occurred within the economy, however. Future tariffs were to remain low. Privatization, but not of the copper facilities, was to recur. So were signifi-cant institutional changes involving government pensions, the role of the Central Bank, and of private initiative more generally.

The Concertación took office in 1990. Subsequent Chilean growth became endemic. Inflation continuously fell, and along with it, real interest rates. Domestic industry, reas-sured, dramatically increased its savings rates and began to invest. New activities eschewed dependence on tariff protection. Firmer governmental rules were established to assure continuing fiscal regularity. Foreign investment returned. Copper production that had been 80% public reversed to 70% private by 2000, as facilities came online. As income continuously rose, domestic poverty rapidly fell, although income distribution inequality persisted at preceding high levels. Policies respected the primacy of the mar-ket for production signals, while insisting upon the legitimacy and importance of inter-vention for social ends.

Public expenditure contributed to better health, housing, and education. Revisions were made in the pension system, increasing coverage and benefits for the poorest. Collective bargaining rules were modernized. Research and development outlays increased.

Policy has continued to look outward from the region. Chile has been the most active country in the world in achieving free trade agreements. It has entered into NAFTA, and eschewed the higher tariffs and problematic features of MERCOSUR. Its principal exports, beyond copper, include fruit and vegetables, forest products, fish, and wine. More than 40% of GDP consists of exports, of which copper represents about half. The reciprocal is access to a range of imported manufactured products of higher quality and lower price than could be produced domestically. While the United States has long yielded its position as the prime recipient of exports, it retains its leadership in Chilean imports.

In recent years, as the price of copper soared upwards after 2003, Chile has demonstrated the effectiveness of compensatory fiscal policy. The gain of an increased export surplus—equivalent to more than 5% of national product as the price went up to $4 a pound—has been encapsulated within a sovereign wealth fund, and invested in domestic (and up to 30%, foreign) instruments. These resources—now involving more than $15 billion dollars—were accessible to compensate for the dramatic fall in price back to $1.40 in 2009. A fiscal deficit replaced the previous surplus. As a result, Chilean income fell only modestly in 2009, and avoided the rapid decline suffered by many other countries in the fourth quarter of 2008. Those funds are now available as Chile seeks to compensate for the earthquake of 2010 by undertaking a massive rebuilding effort.

More fundamentally, Chile has become the poster example for the very absence of a natural resource curse. That was hardly always so. The country has traversed an exceptional course from initial complete commitment to the Prebisch doctrine of an inevitable decline in the terms of trade in the 1950s to a sovereign wealth fund, used to good advantage, in the 21st century. Domestic manufactures account for a relatively small percentage of national income. Mining is virtually comparable. The public sector remains relatively small, but efficient.

In the process, Chile has modernized politically as well. The election of conservative candidate Sebastian Piñera in 2010 epitomizes the trend. He replaced President Bachelet of the Concertación, who ended her term with popularity in the range of 70%. There is now a powerful political center in Chile, rejecting the magical irrealism of the far left and the far right, both of which held sway in the past. That maturity is important for the economic policies to be pursued in the future.

16.2.3 Venezuela

This is the classic post-World War II Latin American case of natural resource wealth and its eventual accompanying curse. There was initially only great gain.

Petroleum exploitation began in the 1920s. By 1950, Venezuela stood next to Argentina in regional per capita income, and by 1970 surpassed it. With the rapid rise in oil price of the 1970s, orchestrated by OPEC, of which Venezuela was a member, gains expanded further.[8] The country co-chaired the 1975 Paris meeting on International Economic Cooperation which sought—unsuccessfully—a North–South agreement.

Political advance occurred simultaneously. In 1958, through a power-sharing agreement, Acción Democratica (AD) and the Christian Democrats (COPEI) agreed upon presidential alternation to replace the military government. That process continued unhindered until the 1990s, even while much of the rest of the region fell into military dictatorship. Immigrants became an important part of the rapidly growing population.

Import substitution industrialization was pursued during this interval, and tariff and quota limitations were imposed. New industries were started. Imports grew only half as fast as total product. But a much larger percentage of them continued to consist of consumer goods, unlike the experience of other countries. Another difference was the importance of the state: the public sector dominated, receiving abundant revenues from petroleum exports, and expending some of them as subsidies. Some 20% of total employment was found in state-run activities. Not least, gasoline prices were kept low, providing gain to the middle- and upper-income groups

This happy situation dramatically altered in the 1980s. Venezuela too experienced a lost decade, less because of accumulated past indebtedness than because of the rapid decline of the international petroleum price. In such circumstances, devaluation became necessary, and occurred in 1983. Debt service began to absorb a large share of lesser export earnings. Government revenues, tied to oil, fell dramatically. By 1989, income per capita had returned to its 1973 level.

All of the many beneficiaries of the state suddenly were in an unusual competitive relationship: more for some translated into less for others. The civil service was corrupt and unwieldy. The military was bought off. Political power was centralized. The urban poor were largely excluded, and their benefits circumscribed. More than half had fallen below the poverty line (Reid 2007: 162).

Carlos Andrés Pérez was elected a second time in 1988. This time—as was the case elsewhere in the region—there was no alternative to internal reform. It never really happened. Instead, an early effort to raise the gasoline price resulted in a popular uprising, the *Caracazo*, with the deaths of more than 400. Although the administration continued with its policies, Congress, and the Accion Democrática party, was no longer amenable. Hugo Chávez attempted a coup in February 1993, but failed; in the same year, Pérez was impeached.

In 1998, Chávez was elected as President. That event, and the constituent assembly that followed, initiated the new Bolivarian Republic. It has continued and extended until today. Chávez remains as president until 2012, and perhaps beyond. The Venezuelan economy is still dependent upon oil, which represent almost 90% of its export revenues, and much of its fiscal receipts. In between, there is more than a decade about which there are two very radically different, and irreconcilable, interpretations.

---

[8] Between 1920 and 1980, its economy grew faster than any other, according to data assembled by Angus Maddison.

Partisans of the regime stress its high rate of expansion of close to 10% annually begin-ning in 2003, i.e. after the failure of the coup in the previous April assured control over PDVSA, the national oil company of Venezuela. Most of the growth is attributed by them to the non-oil sector, and indeed, to private activity. During the expansion, social spending went up, inequality dramatically declined, and education improved. Moreover, they see an intent to diversify away from oil, and thus fully escape from the adverse incentives of the Dutch disease (Weisbrot, Ray, and Sandoval 2009).

Opponents contest virtually all of these consequences of what was undeniably a highly profitable increase in petroleum prices between 2002 and 2008, and which began to surge once again in the second half of 2009. In early 2011, with the beginning of popu-lar uprisings in North Africa, oil prices rose rapidly once more. They deny commitment to a pro-poor policy, and emphasize the limited advances attained in a variety of human development indicators. The results attained, moreover, are less than they should be, given the great rise in income that occurred (Rodriguez 2008).

What is evident is intent. Chávez is committed to a new style of governance, and not merely within Venezuela itself. His bold ambitions, like those of Bolivar, are continent-wide, and even go beyond. New institutions like the Missions are mechanisms for trying to reach out to the poor, not very different from what had been attempted in earlier pop-ulist ventures in the region. Nor are the results—despite the abundance forthcoming from the enormous rise in petroleum prices—entirely at variance. There has been pro-gressively greater reliance upon rationing, rather than the market.

Much increased expenditures have resulted in persistent fiscal deficits, despite a great rise in governmental revenues. Inflation has threatened to get out of hand. An overval-ued fixed exchange rate has had to be devalued, more than once. Multiple exchange rates have returned. Despite curbs on capital outflows, accumulated foreign exchange reserves are seemingly fewer than they should be. A presumed sovereign wealth fund has been utilized elsewhere, in part for non-budgeted outlays, and resources are not available for compensatory fiscal policy.[9]

The full extent of the problem has been alleviated by a return to higher petroleum prices in the market. Chávez has recently agreed to participation of foreign oil firms, including Chevron of the United States, in developing the extensive shale oil deposits in the Orinoco river basin. There will even be a reduction of the royalty charge from 33.3% to 20%. Much greater publicity has been given to agreements with China and Russia, whose starting dates are much more distant.

How Venezuela will eventually emerge remains unknown. But natural resources have not been an unmixed gift. Indeed, recent reports indicate that the country now is ranked—by the price of credit default swaps—as most likely to default within the next

---

[9] The real extent of Venezuelan reserves is complicated by the inclusion of domestic resources, at the official exchange rate, in the accounting of some. But domestic money can be created without cost, as the past decade reveals. An implicit inflationary tax imposes costs on the poor that have not generally been part of the discussion.

five years. Venezuela's probability was 48.5%, while Greece was classified with a chance of 25.4%. Norway, on the other hand, led the list of the safest sovereign borrowers.[10]

16.2.4 Brazil

From the late 16th century through the 1930s, Brazil was coffee and coffee was Brazil. The country has since successfully industrialized, on the basis of its large and growing domestic market, and has diversified its exports—coffee now is only a tiny fraction of its exports. Brazil took perhaps too long to move away from an import substitution strategy, but thanks to market-oriented reforms implemented since the early 1990s, it became an active participant in the world economy.[11] The country is an agriculture powerhouse (being a major world exporter not only of coffee, but of sugar, orange juice, tobacco, soybeans, corn, beef, poultry, and pork). Its two biggest companies, Petrobras and Vale, are leading players in the international oil and iron-ore markets. It is a testimony to the abundance of Brazil's natural resources that commodities and commodity-related products constitute two-thirds of the country's product exports. The recent discovery of very large deep-sea oil deposits in Brazil's southeastern offshore will certainly solidify both the country's importance in world commodities markets and that of commodities in Brazil's export bill.

Brazil has been one of the main beneficiaries of the commodity price boom in the early 21st century. The country's total exports grew to $197 billion in 2008 from $72 billion in 2003, and its GDP growth rate averaged 4.8% in the period, a considerable feat not only in comparison with the meager results in the previous decade, but also considering Brazil's low saving and investment rates. In this period, Brazil benefited not only from high commodity prices but also from large inflows of foreign capital. The consequence was a significant appreciation of the *real* even while the Central Bank accumulated record-high levels of international reserves. As the share of commodities and commodity-related products in Brazil's exports increased, the worry arose in several parts of the country whether Brazil was catching the Dutch disease or, worse still, becoming de-industrialized. But the academic studies that have looked into this question failed to find evidence either for the Dutch Disease or for the de-industrialization thesis (see Puga 2007; Barros and Pereira 2008; Jank et al. 2008; Nassif 2008; Souza 2009; Bonelli and Pessoa 2010). Non-commodity-related industries are finding it harder than before to maintain growth in their exports, but they have plenty of room for expansion in a rapidly growing and still well-protected domestic market.

This evidence has not dissipated concerns about the valorization of the *real*, because at least part of it is being led by (short-term) capital inflows, attracted by high interest rates, rather than by commodity prices. The price-induced surge in imports and

---

[10] *Financial Times*, April 8, 2010.
[11] See Fishlow (2011) for an analysis of Brazil's evolution since the end of authoritarian rule in 1985.

slowdown of non-commodity exports contribute to an enlarging current account deficit, which may not be so easily financeable in the future. The immediate issue here is Brazil's macroeconomic policy mix: floating exchange rates in the context of an open capital account, and domestic interest rates maintained higher than abroad to keep inflation under control.

Academics point to the obvious, beyond the immediate policy-mix issue—Brazil's low savings rates and persistent government budget deficits. Were savings higher and deficits lower, interest rates could be reduced without risking higher inflation and providing room for a more competitive exchange rate. Without such austerity, however, the country seems condemned to a below-par potential GDP growth rate that may lead to increasing discomfort with current macroeconomic policies, and an increase in the appeal of long-abandoned populist policies. Strong recovery in 2009, after all, was enabled by expansionary fiscal and monetary policies. But persistently high interest rates and exchange rate volatility hamper growth.

The recently discovered of apparently very large deep-sea oil deposits in Brazil's southeastern offshore may offer some relief. In fact, the main test whether Brazil will fall prey to a "resource curse" or will instead benefit from a "resource blessing" may occur in the next few years, when the country starts drilling oil out of its sub-salt deposits. Recent events give little reason for hope. To deal with the new oil riches, President Lula sent to Congress a proposal for major changes in the rules for oil exploration—a shift from a successful concessions-based regime to a still unproven profit-sharing regime, with the obligatory participation of the state-owned oil company Petrobras as the sole driller in all new oil consortia. In addition, a new state-owned entity would have exclusive commercialization rights over the new oil finds. The government majority approved such changes in the Lower House, but sent to the Senate a bill with a totally new distribution of oil revenues between the union, states, and municipalities—and this has paralyzed deliberations on the new oil-exploration regime.

Industrial policy has emerged as another contentious issue. The Brazilian Development Bank, BNDES, played a central role in the rapid recovery of 2009, and its role in financing investment has been enhanced. The government's Programa de Aceleração do Crescimento, although only partially completed, has already been supplemented with another to take effect beginning in 2011, featuring Petrobras. Politics again is much involved, as the presidential election nears. Afterwards, the same rationality that has enabled Brazilian success in recent years should return.

16.3 CONCLUDING REMARKS

This essay's title gives hint of our conclusion. Commodity exports have been a continuing subject of attention and concern well before the contributions of Raul Prebisch and Hans Singer in the postwar period. The rise of commodity-hungry China and India, and Asia more generally, as well as the growing importance of internationally based finance for price determination, are new arrivals on the scene. "Encouragingly, during the course of the recent commodity boom, fiscal spending in resource-dependent developing nations has been much more prudent than during earlier booms" (World Bank 2009: 9).

For Latin America's economies, the question is whether the wine has now finally reached maturity—and whether it can be fully appreciated in the new bottles without provoking inebriation.

None of the earlier generalizations offered as a guide to practical policies has held up over the last years. More sophisticated econometrics has substituted for the earlier attempts to establish a basis for policy decisions. Whereas the earlier danger was a conviction of inevitably falling terms of trade, now it seems increasingly to project rising gains that can finance all kinds of public interventions.

Countries will have to design their trade policies in accordance with a changing pattern of comparative advantage. Massive intervention designed to modify that reality runs the risk of repeating past import-substituting industrialization all over again. International trade can be a powerful instrument underwriting economic growth, but not without domestic efforts to assure innovation and technological change over the longer run.

The four Latin American cases considered reinforce this conclusion.

Argentina has been unable to translate its resource richness into a source of continuous advance over the last 50 years. Advance and change has occurred within the export sector, without being able to stimulate parallel alteration in the rest of the economy. Policies have been even more volatile than product prices.

Chile has achieved impressive gains over the last two decades. Per capita income has increased quite steadily, as the external market has driven a transformation doubling the share of exports over this period. New primary exports have emerged, although copper has retained its central role within them. The private sector has become innovative. Compensatory fiscal policy has made its positive effects felt, even in the midst of price increases much greater than in the past. Such price volatility has been dampened by effective public intervention.

Venezuela is our third case. Petroleum has not served to underwrite sustained economic growth. Instead, the cyclical heights and depths have reflected themselves in domestic economic instability. This was increasingly manifest over the last decade. Interventionist public policy has not learned very much from the errors of the past; and there has been an inability to take full advantage of the present cycle of price advance.

Brazil has managed a remarkable transition over this same period. Import substitution has worked to develop a domestic industrial base of significant magnitude and one capable of international competition. Agricultural productivity has increased, enabling a premier market position. Mineral exploration has consolidated a growing role— marked by Brazilian foreign investment abroad. Most recently, discovery of petroleum resources below the salt layer represents a source of potential wealth.

In all of these cases, the dominating feature is domestic politics and its transformation over time. Resource wealth inevitably brings with it a greater susceptibility to volatility. The question is how to cope. That internal response determines whether natural resources translate into a virtue or a curse.

REFERENCES

BACHA, E. (1983). 'An Interpretation of Unequal Exchange from Prebisch–Singer to Emmanuel', *Journal of Development Economics* 13.1–2.

BARROS, O., and PEREIRA, R. (2008). 'Desmitificando a tese de desindustrializacao: reestruturação da industria brasileira em uma época de transformações globais', in O. Barros and F. Giambiagi (eds), *Brasil globalizado: o Brasil em um mundo surpreendente*, Rio de Janeiro: Campus.

BLATTMAN, C., HWANG, J., and WILLIAMSON, J. (2007). 'Winners and Losers in the Commodity Lottery: The Impact of the Terms of Trade Growth and Volatility in the Periphery, 1870–1939', *Journal of Development Economics* 82.1.

BONELLI, R., and PESSOA, S. (2010). 'Desindustrializaçao no Brasil: resumo da evidencia', Texto para Discussao 7, Centro de Desenvolvimento Economico, Instituto Brasileiro de Economía, Fundacao Getulio Vargas, Rio de Janeiro, March.

BRAHMBHATT, M., and CANUTO, O. (2010). 'Natural Resources and Development Strategy After the Crisis', World Bank Economic Premise No. 1, Washington, DC.

BULTE, E., DAMANIA, R., and DEACON, R. (2005). 'Resource Intensity, Institutions and Development', *World Development* 33.7.

CHUDNOFSKY, D., and LOPEZ, A. (2007). *The Elusive Quest for Growth in Argentina*, New York: Palgrave.

COLLIER, P., and GODERIS, B. (2007). 'Commodity Prices, Growth and Natural Resources Curse: Reconciling a Conundrum', Working Paper No. 276, Centre for the Study of African Economies, Oxford.

CUDDINGTON, J., LUDEMAN, R., and JAYASURIYA, S. (2007). 'Prebisch–Singer Redux', in Lederman and Maloney (2007).

DE FERRANTI, D. et al. (2002). *From Natural Resources to the Knowledge Economy: Trade and Job Quality*, Washington, DC: World Bank.

DELLA PAOLERA, G., and TAYLOR, A. (2003). *A New Economic History of Argentina*, New York: Cambridge University Press.

FISHLOW, A. (2011). *O novo Brasil*, São Paulo: Saint Paul.

FRANKEL, J. (2010). 'The Natural Resource Curse: A Survey', Harvard University Center for International Development Working Paper 195 (May). Forthcoming in B. Schaffer (ed.), *Export Perils*, University of Pennsylvania Press.

HAUSMANN, R., and RIGOBON, R. (2003). 'An Alternative Interpretation of the Resource Curse: Theory and Policy Implications', in J. Davis (ed.), *Fiscal Policy Formulation and Implementation in Oil-Producing Countries*, Washington, DC: IMF.

IFSL (International Financial Services London) Research (2010). *Sovereign Wealth Funds 2010*, March.

ISHAM, J. et al. (2005). 'The Varieties of Resource Experience: Natural Resource Export Structures and the Political Economy of Economic Growth', *World Bank Economic Review* 19.2.

JANK, M. et al. (2008). 'Exportacoes: existe uma doenca holandesa', in O. Barros and F. Giambiagi (eds), *Brasil globalizado: o Brasil em um mundo surpreendente*, Rio de Janeiro: Campus.

KUZNETS, S. (1966). *Modern Economic Growth*, New Haven, Conn.: Yale University Press.

LANDES, D. (1998). *The Wealth and Poverty of Nations: Why Some Are So Rich and Some So Poor*, New York: Norton.

LEDERMAN, D., and MALONEY, W. (eds) (2007). *Natural Resources: Neither Curse nor Destiny*, Palo Alto, Calif., and Washington, DC: Stanford University Press and World Bank.

———— (2008). 'In Search of the Missing Resource Curse', *Economía* 9.1.

——and XU, L. (2007). 'Comparative Advantage and Trade Intensity: Are Traditional Endowments Destiny?', in Lederman and Maloney (2007).

LEWIS, A. (1954). 'Economic Development with Unlimited Supplies of Labor', *Manchester School of Economics and Social Studies* 22.2.

MADDISON, A. (2003). *The World Economy: A Millennial Perspective*, Paris: OECD.

MARTIN, W., and MITRA, D. (2001). 'Productivity Growth and Convergence in Agriculture and Manufacturing', *Economic Development and Cultural Change* 49.2.

NASSIF, A. (2008). 'Ha evidencia de desindustrialização no Brasil?', *Revista de Economía politica* 28.1.

OCAMPO, J. A., and PARRA, M. (2010). 'The Terms of Trade for Commodities since the Mid-19th Century', *Journal of Iberian and Latin American Economic History* 28.1.

——RADA, C., and TAYLOR, L. (2009). *Growth and Policy in Developing Countries: A Structuralist Approach*, New York: Columbia University Press.

POELHEKKE, S., and VAN DER PLOEG, F. (2007). 'Volatility, Financial Development and the Natural Resource Curse', CEPR Discussion Paper No. 6513, London.

PREBISCH, R. (1950). *The Economic Development of Latin America and its Principal Problems*, New York: ECLAC.

PUGA, F. (2007). 'Aumento das importacoes nao geram desindustrializacao', BNDES Visao do Desenvolvimento No. 26, Rio de Janeiro.

REID, M. (2007). *Forgotten Continent: The Battle for Latin America's Soul*, New Haven, Conn.: Yale University Press.

RODRÍGUEZ, F. (2008). 'An Empty Revolution: The Unfulfilled Promises of Hugo Chávez', *Foreign Affairs* 87.2.

SACHS, J. D., and WARNER, A. M. (1995). 'Natural Resource Abundance and Economic Growth', Harvard Institute for International Development, Development Discussion Paper 517a (October).

SALA-I-MARTIN, X., and SUBRAMANIAN, A. (2003). 'Addressing the Natural Resource Curse: An Illustration from Nigeria', IMF Working Paper No. 03/139, Washington, DC.

SINGER, H. (1950). 'The Distribution of Gains Between Investing and Borrowing Countries', *American Economic Review* 40.2.

SOUZA, C. (2009). 'O Brasil Pegou a Doenca Holandesa?', PhD thesis, Economics Department, University of São Paulo.

THORP, R. (1998). *Progress, Poverty and Exclusion*, Washington, DC: IDB.

TORNELL, A., and LANE, P. (1999). 'The Voracity Effect', *American Economic Review* 89.1.

WEISBROT, M., RAY, R., and SANDOVAL, L. (2009). 'The Chávez Administration at 10 Years: The Economy and Social Indicators', *CEPR Reports and Issue Briefs* 2009-04.

World Bank (2009). *Global Economic Prospects and the Developing Countries*, Washington, DC.

WRIGHT, G., and CZELUSTA, J.W. (2007). 'Resource-Based Growth Past and Present', in Lederman and Maloney (2007).

CHAPTER 17

···

CURSE OR BLESSING? NATURAL RESOURCES AND HUMAN DEVELOPMENT

···

JOSÉ GREGORIO PINEDA
AND FRANCISCO RODRÍGUEZ

17.1 INTRODUCTION[1]

···

It is paradoxical to think that natural resource riches hurt rather than help an endowed country. Yet this is precisely the argument that has permeated academic and policy circles for decades. A plethora of papers containing empirical analyses, game-theoretic models, and case studies has appeared, attempting to explain why natural resources could be bad for economic growth and development. Some of the more popular explanations involve the Dutch Disease, economic volatility, rent-seeking, and weak institutions, all of which are argued to negatively impact growth.

However, with new empirical evidence and deeper probing into the causes of growth collapse, doubt has begun to build regarding a causal relationship between natural resources and economic growth. A growing literature has arisen involving those who do not subscribe to the theory of a natural resource curse or who believe in a conditional curse. Many success stories have arisen from natural resource wealth. Norway has long utilized its Petroleum Fund to stabilize its oil wealth, providing economic security for the country. More recently, Chile's Copper Stabilization Fund has proven to be a successful element in the country's economic recovery since the mid-1980s. In both cases, resource

[1] This chapter has benefited from previous discussions with Daniel Lederman, Ricardo Hausmann, Jeni Klugman, Jose Antonio Ocampo, and Jaime Ros, as well as seminar participants at HDRO. We are grateful to Daniel Lederman and Bill Maloney for kindly providing us access to their data. The chapter also benefited from excellent research assistance provided by Zachary Gidwitz, Martin Philipp Heger, and Mark Purser. All errors remain our responsibility.

dependence presented challenges that were properly managed, resulting in economic prosperity. Key challenges in the literature involve disentangling the effect of natural resources from those of other factors which may be correlated with resource abundance but independently affect growth, distinguishing between the direct role that natural resources may play in affecting progress and the way in which it may interact with other determinants, and identifying exogenous sources of variation in resource abundance.

Recent studies have highlighted major differences between performance as measured by the yardstick of economic growth and human development.[2] In particular, there is no significant correlation between per capita income growth and changes in the non-income components of human development, even over relatively long periods of time (up to four decades). While growth was stagnant for the poorest regions like Africa, adult literacy more than doubled and enrolment rates increased by 72% over the same period. If countries' performance in growth and human development can be so disparate, one might also expect there to be differences in their correlates.

Building on the empirical and theoretical work done by Daniel Lederman and William F. Maloney (2008), this chapter argues against a natural resource curse not only with respect to GDP growth but most importantly for other dimensions of human development. We show that changes of human development from 1970 to 2005, proxied by changes in the Human Development Index, are positively and significantly correlated with natural resource abundance. While our results are consistent with those of Lederman and Maloney, who find natural resources to be possibly positive for growth, we find strong evidence that natural resources are even better for the human development. This is particularly true for the non-income elements of human development.

This chapter also takes a close look at the Latin American case. Resource abundance has often been singled out as one of the culprits for the region's poor development. On the other hand, as we will discuss in the next section, there are quite a few cases in which resources have coexisted with strong performance in the region. Are natural resources harming Latin America's development prospects? Anticipating our results, we find evidence that the human development-enhancing effect of natural resources is lower in Latin America than in the rest of the world, suggesting that Latin America may not be fully taking advantage of the possibilities deriving from its factor endowments.

In Tables 17.1(a) and (b), we present selected summary statistics of the main data we use here, subdivided by countries that are net exporters and net importers of natural resources.[3] Table 17.1(a) shows that, compared with all countries, net importers have higher levels in HDI as well as in all of its components. However, looking at changes in variables reveals a somewhat different scenario. Changes in life expectancy are roughly the same across all country groupings. GDP growth has been smaller for net exporter countries, which is at the heart of the natural curse hypothesis. However, changes in the non-income component of HDI, primarily associated with literacy and gross enroll-

[2] See Rodríguez (2009), Binder and Georgiadis (2010), and Gray and Purser (2010). Some of these points were raised earlier by Easterly (1999).
[3] These are countries that export (import) more than the average.

Table 17.1(a) Summary statistics: mean of variables (all countries, 1980–2005)

	Levels			Changes		
	All countries	Net exporters	Net importers	All countries	Net exporter	Net importer
HDI	0.7337	0.7102	0.7685	0.0045	0.0043	0.0047
	108	*57*	*51*	*108*	*57*	*51*
Non-income HDI	0.7594	0.7321	0.7899	0.0054	0.0056	0.0052
	110	*58*	*52*	*110*	*58*	*52*
GDP per capita	8.67	8.5141	8.8282	0.0153	0.0097	0.021
	141	*71*	*70*	*141*	*71*	*70*
Life expectancy	67.9206	65.5284	70.3446	0.3059	0.3033	0.3085
	151	*76*	*75*	*151*	*76*	*75*
Gross enrollment	0.7143	0.6935	0.7377	0.0066	0.007	0.0063
	115	*61*	*54*	*115*	*61*	*54*
Literacy	0.8269	0.8142	0.8397	0.0062	0.0068	0.0057
	140	*70*	*70*	*140*	*70*	*70*

Table 17.1(b) Summary statistics: mean of variables (high net exporters/ importers, 1980–2005)

	Levels			Changes		
	All countries	High net exporters	High net importers	All countries	High net exporters	High net importers
HDI	0.7337	0.8371	0.8869	0.0045	0.0043	0.0042
	108	*29*	*25*	*108*	*29*	*25*
Non-income HDI	0.7594	0.844	0.8904	0.0054	0.0055	0.0042
	110	*29*	*25*	*110*	*29*	*25*
GDP per capita	8.67	9.427	9.6968	0.0153	0.0107	0.0254
	141	*37*	*35*	*141*	*37*	*35*
Life expectancy	67.9206	72.4482	75.4347	0.3059	0.3203	0.2858
	151	*38*	*38*	*151*	*38*	*38*
Gross enrollment	0.7143	0.8045	0.8379	0.0066	0.007	0.0059
	115	*30*	*26*	*115*	*30*	*26*
Literacy	0.8269	0.8992	0.948	0.0062	0.0059	0.0035
	140	*36*	*34*	*140*	*36*	*34*

Source: Authors' calculations.
Note: "High net exporters/importers" refers to countries that are exporting/importing more than the average.

ment, are on average larger for net exporting countries. Results are even stronger, in the comparison of changes, if we focus on the high net exporters and high net importers. As we can see from Table 17.1(b), all changes are greater for net exporters than net importers except for per capita GDP growth. This potentially indicates that natural resources affect human development primarily through channels other than income.

The remainder of the chapter is organized as follows. Section 17.2 presents a literature review of the effect of natural resources on development: the theoretical arguments, different channels of impact, and why natural resources might not be a curse after all. Section 17.2.1 contains a special discussion that focuses on a comparative analysis of different growth experiences of Latin America and the rest of the world with respect to natural resources. Section 17.3 presents our data and empirical methodology. Section 17.4 discusses our results, which find natural resources to be positively correlated with human development. Section 17.5 concludes.

17.2 LITERATURE REVIEW

Broadly speaking, the resource curse literature has highlighted five channels through which natural resource abundance may affect human development: Dutch Disease, deterioration of the terms of trade and commodity price volatility, trade structure, depletion, and rent-seeking, all of which are complicated by institutional weakness. We discuss each of these in turn.

The term "Dutch Disease" was initially coined to describe the observed collapse of the Dutch manufacturing sector following the discovery of natural gas in 1959.[4] Corden (1984) first modeled this effect. His basic model shows how capital moves away from non-oil tradables as oil booms, weakening the overall economy. An influx of foreign capital to the booming resource sector causes an appreciation in the exchange rate. A higher exchange rate raises economy-wide prices, leading the non-resource tradable sectors to lose competitiveness abroad.

One traditional argument about why natural resources abundance could not necessarily be good for development is that over time the terms of trade of countries exporting commodities will deteriorate compared to those of countries exporting manufacture goods (see Singer 1950; Prebisch 1950). Ocampo and Parra (2003) analyzed the relative price series for 24 commodities and found empirical evidence of a significant deterioration in the terms of trade over the course of the 20th century, although this was not a secular declining trend of the terms of trade.

Sachs and Warner's (1995b) empirical work showed that countries with a high ratio of natural resources to GDP in their base year 1970, grew more slowly over the next two decades than their resource-scarce counterparts. Their analysis is cross-sectional, using the share of GNP in 1970 consisting of primary products to define natural resource

---

[4] 'The Dutch Disease,' *The Economist*, November 26, 1977.

abundance, and controlling for other potential growth determinants such as economic openness, rule of law, and growth of external terms of trade, and found a negative relationship between natural resources and growth.

Humphreys, Sachs, and Stiglitz (2007) describe a related challenge of natural resource abundance and dependence: volatility. They view natural resources as assets with exceptional volatility.[5] World natural resource prices are historically volatile due to varying rates of extraction, and the nature of contracts with multi-national companies. Stiglitz (2007)[6] and Shaxson (2005) argue that the latter effect arises from multinationals coercing countries into bearing the brunt of the income variability. Volatility has many adverse effects, including making development planning difficult, social spending sporadic, and foreign investors wary.

The problems of volatility are exacerbated when an economy is overly dependent on the natural resource industry. Lederman and Maloney (2007b)[7] argue that a trade structure lacking export diversification hurts growth, not natural resources. To test this theory, they redo the Sachs and Warner analysis with the inclusion of variables for export concentration and intra-industry trade. Their findings demonstrate that any negative effect of natural resources on growth disappears in the presence of a variable capturing export concentration.

Rodríguez and Sachs (1999) introduce a different channel through which natural resources can appear to damage growth: depletion. Their model shows an underdeveloped country overshooting its steady state during a resource boom. After the initial rise in income, the growth rate turns negative, and the country converges to its steady state from above. Resource revenues consumed by the domestic economy will naturally decrease over time, tending to zero. In this way, after a country enjoys the resource boom, it negatively converges to its overshot steady state. Sachs and Warner's (2005) empirical evidence support this model by finding a negative growth rate associated with natural resource abundance only after an increase in initial wealth. One important implication is that the observed negative growth is simply the reversion of the positive growth occurring immediately after the boom. Therefore it is a depletion effect, rather than natural resources, that is responsible for the negative growth rates. Rodríguez and Sachs show that if an economy instead invests its windfall in foreign assets that generate a steady stream of revenue, a negative growth rate can be averted.

Another channel of particular relevance for natural resource abundant countries is the vulnerability to external shocks and the different productive linkages that an economy has. Hausmann, Rodríguez, and Wagner (2007) show that countries with lower export flexibility—which they measure using an indicator of the density of the product space developed by Hausmann and Klinger (2006)—have a harder time recovering from crises caused by export collapses, as it is more difficult for them to move productive

---

[5] The book suggests that non-renewable natural resource should be viewed as assets rather than production.

[6] Humphreys, Sachs, and Stiglitz (2007: ch. 2).

[7] Lederman and Maloney (2007c: ch. 2).

resources to a new sector. This is particularly relevant for resource-abundant countries, as many natural resources, such as oil, are found to occupy areas of low density in the product space.

Jaime Ros (2000) illustrates a contrary case of resources enriching a country when sufficient industrial linkages exists. In these cases, the spending of resource rents can actually have an anti-Dutch Disease effect. Two pieces of evidence supporting this thesis are the fact that in countries where natural resources are scarce, one observes stunted industrial development in areas that thrive in resource rich countries, and the fact that Latin America's "primary export phase" was fueled by resource abundance. When proper returns to scale existed in complementary industrial sectors, resource booms fueled major economic expansions.

In the last decade, however, most of the blame for poor growth rates in resource dependent states has been put on institutional weaknesses. A number of these explanations actually emphasize institutional interactions: many have observed (Karl 1997; Lederman and Maloney 2007b; Wright and Czelusta 2007) that natural resources have been huge economic boons for many countries while appearing not to have helped, or even possibly to have hurt, other countries, suggesting the existence of conditional factors which may be amplifying any effect of natural resources. One logical suspect is institutions.

Tornell and Lane (1999) note that under certain circumstances, point-source resources such as fuels and minerals intensify rent-seeking behavior. Rent-seeking, by nature, leads to perverse fiscal redistribution, inefficient capital projects, and corruption. Tornell and Lane identify two main exacerbating traits. The first is the absence of strong legal and political institutions. The second is the presence of multiple power groups, such as parasitic provincial governments, protection-seeking industrial centers and labor unions, and political patronage networks. These two situations create what Tornell and Lane call a "voracity effect," where a large resource windfall will generate an increase in fiscal redistribution that is more than proportionate, thereby reducing growth. Guerrilla uprisings in Colombia, Nicaragua, El Salvador, Guatemala, and Peru, as well as Native American riots in Ecuador, Bolivia, Mexico, and Brazil, are examples. Di John (2009) explains that these are all the result of rival political groups using non-market methods to capture resource rents, another manifestation of the voracity effect.

Karl (1997) examines the nature of petro-state institutions in detail. She finds parallel institutions among rent-centered states, whether they be Venezuela, Nigeria, Saudi-Arabia, or even 16th-century Spain. In almost all cases, the state is the direct recipient of the rent wealth, which diminishes the need for taxation. Without taxation, the nature of the social contract between the government and citizens is eroded, while the state can expand its own jurisdiction. The state's primary purpose becomes spending. Success for businesses, labor organizations, and the middle class is redefined as the ability to gain or curry political influence.

A significant finding unique to Karl's analysis is that the major failed petro-states, Nigeria, Algeria, Iran, and Venezuela, all had one defining characteristic: they developed their institutions at the same time that petroleum was discovered and multinational oil companies entered the picture. In many cases, the oil companies helped write the tax laws, and countries' institutions formed around patronage and oil politics. In almost all cases, the state was the direct recipient of the rent wealth. Maloney (2007) shows that this led to a lack of interest in developing other industries, as demonstrated even in gold- and silver-rich 16th-century Spain. What resulted in Spain's case similarly developed for these other petro-states: a type of "cultural Dutch Disease."

Further work by Sala-i-Martin and Subramanian (2003) shows a direct causal relationship between natural resources and weak institutions. They theorize that natural resources influence growth indirectly through institutions. This would account for the lack of significance of the natural resource variable found in many analyses. Regressing natural resources directly on institutions produced surprisingly strong results. Even when a dummy for oil is included, the impact on institutions is still significantly negative. In fact, they find that once institutions have been controlled for, oil actually has a beneficial effect on growth.

Wantchekon (1999) empirically demonstrates a causal relationship between natural resources and authoritarianism, finding that natural resources negatively impact democracy. He postulates that authoritarianism arises due to one-party dominance combined with weak rule of law. This incites the opposition to use non-constitutional means to compete for political power. In response, the incumbent pre-empts this move by repressing or banning the opposition party. However, when the rule of law is strong and political power is less concentrated, and distribution of resource rents is properly monitored by an independent agency, the incumbent's advantage is largely mitigated. This can be seen in Norway's case.[8] Wantchekon's empirical results show no impact on democracy from natural resources in countries where resource dependence is low (10% or less). However, when resource dependence is high (90% or more), a 1 percentage point increase in resource dependence leads to democracy index dropping 2.15%.[9] Nevertheless, the literature has failed to uncover a significant effect of democracy on growth, so that this is unlikely to be a major channel of transmission.

There are some cases where countries with weak institutions have enjoyed strong growth. Haber, Razo, and Maurer (2003) investigate one such case. From 1876 to 1911, Mexican dictator Porfirio Díaz employed a system of selective property rights that were quite effective. The scheme secured protection for the economic elites but not for the masses. In fact, this system survived the eighteen years of bloody civil war following Díaz's demise, allowing for healthy growth despite the existence of a failed state. Haber et al. argue that an oil-exporting country's government need not secure credible commitments to everyone. As long as government can make credible commitments to the privileged elites and companies responsible for the majority of economic activity, it is not necessarily imperative for property rights and beneficial institutions to extend to the population as a whole. While securing rights for the entire population is often viewed as a prerequisite for full development, the authors show that substantial growth can be

---

[8] Haber and Menaldo (2009) reject Wantchekon's findings.

[9] This uses 1998 data.

obtained simply by securing property rights for the major oil companies, which requires "neither rule of law nor a stable polity."

A number of policies have been suggested to help alleviate any negative effects associated with natural resources. Van Wijnbergen (1984) shows that government investment in human capital and industries intense in learning-by-doing spillovers will adequately protect a non-resource sector from Dutch Disease effects. Karl (1997) argues that resource dollars must be isolated from the domestic economy by such means as investing internationally, accumulating foreign reserves, and paying off foreign debts. Wantchekon (1999) similarly recommends a "resource fund," modeled on Norway's stabilization fund, as a way to keep resource money from negatively impacting an economy. Collier and Gunning (1996) recommend distributing the revenue directly to the citizenry. Revenue would then be obtained through taxing the citizenry rather than directly through resource rents. This, the authors argue, ensures greater wealth distribution while making the government more accountable to its taxpayers. Martin (2007)[10] states that policies moving away from concentration in primary resource exports should be taken *only* if there are clear market failures arising from the overconcentration *and* if feasible alternative policies are actually available. Assuming a country would not choose to ignore its natural resource wealth, four options remain for diversifying exports: raising levels of physical and human capital; increasing the competitiveness of other industries; lowering barriers to trade; and reducing transportation and communication costs.

With more data available and more sophisticated econometric techniques, it has become easier to tease out the true causes of economic collapse. Lederman and Maloney (2007b) examine and critique the previous literature. They criticize Sachs and Warner's proxy for resource abundance: exports as a share of GDP. For countries such as Singapore, this proxy shows bloated natural resource endowments, as large quantities of resources move through their ports. Sachs and Warner recognize this, and for two countries they used a different proxy: net resource exports as a share of GDP. Lederman and Maloney question why this metric wasn't used for all countries in their sample instead of just for these two countries. To some degree, resources move through all countries and therefore are incorrectly counted toward the proxy.

Lederman and Maloney (2007b) show that when either proxy is used for all countries, the negative effect of natural resources found by Sachs and Warner vanishes. Additionally, Sala-i-Martin, Doppelhofer, and Miller (2004) find that the Sachs and Warner proxy lacks sufficient robustness to be considered as a core explanatory variable.[11] Lederman and Maloney show that after controlling for fixed effects in a panel context, the negative effect of natural resources disappears. Finally, they find that adding an export concentration variable (the Herfindahl index) also eliminates the resource curse.[12] The general conclusion that Lederman and Maloney (2007b) draw from their

[10] Lederman and Maloney (2007c: ch. 11).

[11] The variable "fraction GDP in mining" ranked as the 12th most robust explanatory variable (Lederman and Maloney 2007b).

[12] Due to our econometric analysis being closely based on the work by Lederman and Maloney, further discussion of their variables and technique is in a later section.

analysis is that natural resources are assets for development that necessitate appropriate policies and adequate human and physical capital. They argue that countries can properly employ natural resources to create sustainable economic growth and development through proper export diversification, human and physical capital investment, volatility, and real exchange rate control.

17.2.1 Latin America: a regional comparison

Venezuela's case is arguably the best researched in Latin America, with numerous studies and extensive available data. Venezuela's experience with rent-rich resources began with strong growth but was followed by economic deterioration. Venezuela's economy performed strongly in the first half of the 20th century, boasting the highest growth rate in Latin America. After 1980, however, the country's economy deteriorated, with its non-oil sector growing one-fourth the amount of Indonesia's and one-sixth that of Mexico's. Rodríguez and Hausmann (2009) show that Venezuela's non-oil economic activity is primarily confined to energy-intensive industries, which exploit the same comparative advantage in oil, doing little to protect the economy from its over-reliance on petroleum products. Hausmann and Rodríguez (2009) use the export flexibility measure of Hausmann and Klinger (2006)—which these authors term "open forests"—to look for traits in Latin America's petro-states, specifically Venezuela. They observe that Venezuela has a strikingly low open forest level, even compared to its neighbors. In 1980, at the start of Venezuela's growth collapse, its open forest was 13.8% of the world average and 15.7% of the South American average. A comparison with Mexico's higher level might help to explain Mexico's partial resilience to falling oil prices in the 1980s.

Hausmann and Rodríguez point out that while Venezuela has a remarkably low open forest, this appears to be a common trait of oil-exporting countries. Even after controlling for income, fuel exporters—those countries for which fuel constitutes over 80% of total exports—have an average open forest that is 2.17 log points lower than non-fuel exporters. This implies that those inputs necessary for oil production have little value for producing other high-value exports.

But Venezuela did not always do poorly with oil. Rodríguez and Gomolin (2009) describe Venezuela's turn-of-the-century consolidation of economic, military, and political power, arguing that this was key to the country's success in developing the institutions for properly utilizing future oil revenue. At the turn of the century, before the discovery of oil, Venezuelan dictator Cipriano Castro had modernized the army, centralizing command and suppressing dissent. An intricately woven web of political patronage backed this authority under Castro's successor, Juan Vicente Gómez, when incentives for political support were increased and expanded. Thus Venezuela receives oil under a consolidated and centralized state.

In stark contrast, Mexico failed to centralize and consolidate its national public finances in the early 20th century. The armed forces remained unmodernized as well.

Total municipal revenues almost equalled federal revenues, which stood at 4% of GDP. Wealthy municipalities had access to military resources and posed the first challenges to the central government in the early 20th century. With no set of centralized political and economic institutions in place, the influx of oil revenue following 1910 did not generate the growth spurt in Mexico that occurred in Venezuela.

Di John (2009) studies the Venezuelan case from a political economy perspective. Venezuela has enjoyed large oil revenues since 1920. Di John divides this 85-year span into two periods, each with its own polity type. From 1920 to 1968, Venezuela is described as a consolidated state with a centralized political organization. According to Di John, this type of polity could handle a big-push import substitution industrialization (ISI) development plan backed by resource rents, since patronage can be deployed through a one-party state backed by an organized military. After 1968, however, the polity turned into what Di John calls a consolidated state with a fragmented political organization. This type of polity can handle only small-scale ISI, for the high level of coordination necessary for big-push ISI is not possible with such political friction. Therefore, Di John concludes, Venezuela began its economic decline due to the incompatibility of its development strategy with its changing polity type after 1968.

At the turn of the 20th century, Argentina and Scandinavia enjoyed similar levels of wealth as well as similar levels of natural resources. Maloney (2007) puts forward evidence that Argentina's weak performance throughout the 20th century stemmed from poor national learning and innovation systems, hindrances to technological adoption, and backward incentive structures arising from the protectionist era of ISI. This description could probably be extended to Latin America as a whole. Scandinavian countries, on the other hand, successfully developed with primary commodities. They used their natural resources as catalysts for learning and technological innovation, as did countries like the United States and Australia. These countries combined an early emphasis on literacy and education with investments in positive spillover-yielding, dynamic firms. These same firms developed into the high-tech companies that lead their respective industries today. Even when Scandinavian countries had the same level of income as Latin America, their literacy rates were two times greater. By 1842, a mere decade after a mandatory school system was introduced; Sweden's literacy rate was nearly 100%. The mixture of advanced education, knowledge clusters, industry-financed research, and open economies are what distinguished Scandinavia from Latin America. As a result, Sweden and Finland have become case studies for successful development through natural resources (Blomström and Kokko 2007).

Bravo-Ortega and de Gregorio (2007) further explain the growth of disparity between different regions of the world through the 20th century. They look at kilometers of railway, primary enrollment, and literacy rates from 1870 to 1910 as signs of differing levels of physical and human capital. Latin America lagged in all three categories behind Europe, Canada, the United States, and Australia. Using the Sachs and Warner (1995b) proxy for natural resources, they find that when the average level of education for a country reaches just three years, natural resources become positively correlated with growth.

Latin American countries have had widely varying experiences with natural resources. Chile's copper industry dominated the country's economy for over 150 years, but a price boom from 1965 to 1977 did little for the Chilean economy. Instead, Chile's economic acceleration began in 1982 with currency devaluation, financial reform, pension reform, and privatization (Collier and Sater 1996). In a similar vein, Caselli and Michaels (2009) employ an intra-country study of Brazil to show that resource-rich municipalities enjoyed little to no social benefit from their oil windfalls. Caselli and Michaels argue that this was primarily due to corruption and inefficient distribution. Aragón and Rud (2009), on the other hand, demonstrate a positive effect of natural resources on the local population. They find that Yanacocha, a Peruvian gold mine, improved local incomes and standards of living. They argued that these improvements were not the result of an increase in social spending. Instead, they said that the effects resulted from an increase in demand for local inputs.

The oil boom of the 1970s resulted in the greatest reworking of the international economic landscape since the gold rush of the Americas in the 16th century (Karl 1997). The record influx of cash to petro-states led to oversized government ambition and public spending. Benefits of this spending included a massive expansion of public welfare, an increase in employment, and a rise in the standard of living. Middle Eastern countries offered free healthcare, education, and extensive pensions. Latin American countries invested in job creation and subsidized housing and fuel. Petro-governments in both regions took advantage of their newly unrestricted capital immediately. They embarked on massive spending campaigns, primarily involving capital-intensive projects. Viewing their oil as an exhaustible commodity, the governments spent rapidly.

Issues emerged immediately. Bottlenecks in production and limited capacity in management and infrastructure led to delays, inefficiencies, and rising domestic prices. The appreciating currency and unprecedented levels of state spending produced Dutch Disease effects. Local industry deteriorated, making the state even more dependent on petroleum. State expenditures quickly outpaced the massive oil revenues even while income remained high. Foreign capital was easily accessible for the first time due to countries' rent-derived collateral, but this led to a huge debt overhang. When prices dropped, petro-states were broke and unable to repay their loans.

However, not all countries experienced the same difficulties with their natural resources: certain countries were able to employ natural resources to fuel unprecedented growth and development. Wright and Czelusta (2007) examine the 19th-century United States and its success with natural resources. Based on resource-fueled development, the United States overtook the United Kingdom in GDP per worker hour by 1890 and led the world in productivity by 1913. In arguments parallel to those of Karl (1997) and Maloney (2007), Wright and Czelusta contrast the US with former Spanish colonies who lived passively off of their resource rents. The US developed an accommodating legal environment, undertook massive investments in infrastructure and knowledge, and promoted resource focused education. In doing so, it was able to produce more metals more efficiently than many countries with far larger resource endowments. Australia and Botswana provide further examples of successful resource-based growth. Australia created a knowledge-intensive mineral sector that produces billions of dollars in intellectual property alone. Acemoglu, Johnson, and Robinson (2003) showcase Botswana as one of sub-Saharan Africa's few successes, a feat accomplished by combining good institutions with a thriving diamond-mining sector.

In general, the literature suggests that natural resources can be an important part of the country's pain or prosperity. However, it would be wrong to unequivocally state that natural resources are *the* reason for a country's woes. Instead, what the case studies suggest is that weak institutions and poor policies make countries vulnerable to the pitfalls presented by natural resources. Natural resources can also be a blessing, and some countries have used natural resources to fuel unprecedented growth and development.

17.3 DATA AND EMPIRICAL METHODOLOGY

Our empirical strategy is similar to that of Lederman and Maloney (2007b), extended in two directions. First, we analyze the effect of natural resource abundance not only on per capita GDP growth but also on human development. Second, our sample goes from 1970 to 2005, given the newly available dataset of human development developed by Gray and Purser (2010).

For measuring the natural resource wealth of countries, our primary explanatory variable, there are many possible proxies in the literature. None is perfectly suited to the purpose of estimating coefficients in human development equations. Most scholars measure natural resources as the share of one or more of primary product exports, including agricultural raw materials, food, fuel, ores, and metals to GDP (e.g. Leamer et al. 1999; Sala-i-Martin et al. 2004; Nunn 2008). However, most of the measures are not necessarily measures of resource abundance, but rather measures of dependence on natural resources. We use Lederman and Maloney's measure of net exports, which applies the primary goods groups of Leamer et al. (1999). Natural resource exports per worker is our indicator of resource abundance, to which we will refer as the direct effect of natural resources on human development.[13] A key advantage of this strategy is that this proxy, unlike other proxies, is positively correlated with natural resource endowment per worker. Additionally, it has the advantage of being a multi-commodity trade-based proxy, which allows for a larger coverage of countries.

However, as Lederman and Maloney recognize, there could be two flaws with this proxy, both related to consumption. First, income growth increases consumption, which could lead to a bias when estimating the relationship between net exports per labor and income. There is clear empirical evidence of this, demonstrated by a positive correlation of exports and income among net exporters. There is even greater bias when

---

[13] Lederman and Maloney define net exports of natural resources as "exports minus imports of natural-resource-related goods, based on Leamer's commodity clusters." See Appendix 17A for a full description of all variables.

non-resource-related sectors cause this increase in income, resulting in a negative correlation of growth and exports. Second, an increase in imports and decrease in exports of natural resources is associated with a rise in capital endowments.[14] To help solve these problems, they use an additional covariate: imports of natural resources per worker, which will measure the indirect effect on natural resources on human development. While the coefficient of interest remains that of the export variable, the sum of the two coefficients (the sum of the direct and indirect effect) measures the total effect of natural resources on human development.

The following analysis centers on two types of regressions. Our baseline results are generated by running a typical OLS cross-country growth regression, which includes a convergence term, a proxy for the abundance of natural resources, a set of conditional variables, and regional dummies. While with the linear regression we can address the question "On average, are natural resources good for human development?", it cannot answer the other important question: "Do natural resources influence human development differently for countries in Latin America?" For this purpose, we also add to the previous regressions a set of regional dummy interactions and check for any differential effect of natural resources among regions, particularly among Latin American countries.

One issue that frequently arises with least-squares estimations is the role of outliers, posing the question of how to treat some countries' values that differ substantially from other countries' observations. These deviations can tilt the regression line upwards or downwards, and consequently, the results can be driven by them (see e.g. Easterly 2005; Rodríguez 2007). We thus estimate all our regressions eliminating these outliers. In order to do this, we use the DFBETA measure proposed by Belsley, Kuh, and Welsch (2004), an influence measure which identifies those observations with a significant impact on the results.[15] The DFBETA for a predictor and for a particular observation is the difference between the regression coefficient calculated for all the data and the regression coefficient calculated with the observation deleted, scaled by the standard error calculated with the observation deleted.

17.4 RESULTS

Tables 17.2(a)–(e) show the results of our panel regressions with HDI and its subcomponents changes as the dependent variable and natural resource abundance as the key variables of interest. All tables include three specifications that contain a convergence variable in addition to the resource variables along with regional dummies. The second set of specifications, in column two, also include terms of trade growth. We also have another set of specifications, in column three, which include the institutional variable.

---

[14] This relationship is extracted from the Rybczynski Theorem.
[15] See also Cook and Weisberg (1982). We restrict our estimations to the cut-off value for the absolute value of DFBETAs being smaller than 2/sqrt(N), where N is the number of observations.

17.4.1 OLS (main results)

In addition to the reported coefficients, significance levels, standard errors, and test statistics, we also calculated standardized regression coefficients in order to examine the relative importance of each variable for determining the growth (changes) in HDI. These so-called beta-coefficients make the magnitude of each individual exogenous variable's impact comparable by being unit-free.

Our OLS results indicate that natural resource abundance has a positive effect on human development, since the coefficients for the net exporters of natural resources are positive and statistically significant for all specifications. In analyzing the total effect of natural resources (the sum of the coefficients of net exports and total imports), we found that its effect is positive for both net resource-exporting and importing countries, with the effect being stronger for net exporters, as shown by about twice as large standardized (beta) coefficients. Furthermore the statistical significance is more robust for the net exporters, as the total effect of natural resources in determining HDI is statistically significant across all three specifications. Such a consistent result across models was not found for net importers, for whom natural resources are significant only after the inclusion of terms of trade growth. It is important to note that the coefficient for the net imports of natural resources is not significant in any regression. Also, for net importers, the indirect effect of natural resources (measured by the total imports per worker, M/L) is stronger than the direct effect (measured by the absolute value of their net exports of natural resources, NX/L), while for exporters the inverse holds true, indicating that the impacts of natural resources are mostly relevant in those countries where they are abundant.

All three specifications include the initial HDI level of 1970 to test for convergence. The negative and statistically significant coefficients of the initial HDI values of 1970 indicate that there is indeed convergence in human development. In fact the convergence term exerts more impact on human development and all its subcomponents than any other explanatory variable, as we can see by comparing the absolute value of the beta coefficient.

After convergence, net exports of natural resources is the second most important variable in explaining changes in HDI. An increase of the natural resources exported by net exporters by a factor equivalent to one standard deviation leads to a 0.34 to 0.38 standard deviations increase in the change in HDI, depending on the model. This boost in HDI changes is only about one-ninth that of an equivalent increases by net importers, which implies that the effect of direct resource endowments is important only for net exporters. The reverse applies for indirect effects of natural resources, where only net natural resource-importers demonstrate a significant response that is more than twice as strong as the insignificant beta coefficient for net exporters.

The inclusion of the terms of trade growth and institutional variables did not change the joint significance or magnitude of the two natural resource variables for net exporters and net importers, as reflected by the F test for the sum of coefficients.

We now turn to discussing the effects of natural resources on the components of the HDI. Natural resource abundance measures played a significant and positive role in all literacy models. In fact, both net export and net import as composite measures of the natural resources played a positive and significant role in the determination of literacy. The two other non-income HDI composites, gross enrollment and life expectancy, show positive and significant relationships only for some specifications. For life expectancy, the joint effect is positive and mostly significant. Gross Enrollment was negatively and significantly affected by the indirect effect of natural resource endowments for exporters, an effect that is captured in the aggregation of the sum of both exporting coefficients. Both direct and indirect resource variables were negative for almost all specifications for importers. Only in one specification did natural resource abundance show a positive association with gross enrollment on a 10% significance level, and all but one sum of coefficients for either net exporters or importers showed a negative sign.

Regarding the income HDI component, GDP per capita growth shows that natural resource abundance could be a blessing for growth.[16] In comparing the GDP to the HDI results, we find that the latter is more conclusive in terms or the statistical significance of the direct effect of natural resource abundance. For both the HDI and GDP we find that resource abundance is more important for exporters than importers. However, in the case of GDP, the effect of natural resources through total imports (the indirect effect) is stronger than the direct effect (through net export of natural resources). The standardized coefficients further show that the direct effect of natural resources (NX/L) is important for HDI (by a factor of almost two), while the indirect effect (M/L) is more important for GDP/capita (by a factor of around nine times more).

The previous discussion is illustrated with Figures 17.1 and 17.2, which show a less significant effect of natural resource abundance on GDP growth than on HDI, particularly on the non-income components.

17.4.2 OLS (regional interactions results)

Table 17.3 replicates our main results, and similarly includes HDI and its subcomponents changes as the dependent variable and natural resource abundance as the key variables of interest, but includes a set of regional interaction effects for Latin America. Like our previous set of results, all tables include a convergence variable in addition to the resource variables along with regional dummies.

These new set of regressions confirm our main results that natural resource abundance has a positive effect on human development, since the coefficients for the net exporters of natural resources are positive and statistically significant for all specifications. Similarly, in analyzing the total effect of natural resources (the sum of the coefficients of net exports and total imports) on human development, we also found that its effect is positive for net resource exporting countries. However, the Latin America interaction effect shows that the impact of natural resources on human development is

---

[16] This result is similar to that reported by Lederman and Maloney (2007b), with the difference that our sample goes from 1970 to 2005.

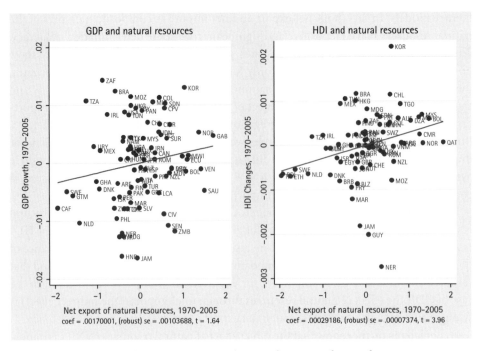

FIGURE 17.1 Relationship between GDP growth, HDI changes, and natural resources

Source: Authors' calculations.

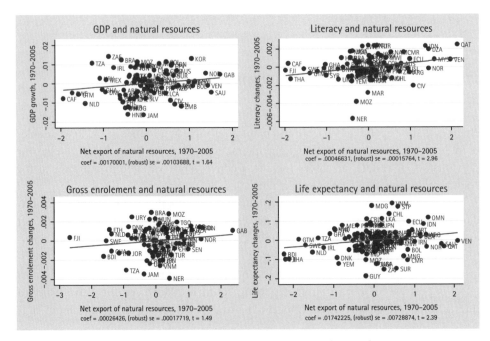

FIGURE 17.2 Relationship between HDI components' growth and natural resources

Source: Authors' calculations.

Table 17.2(a) OLS results: determinants of HDI change

Explanatory variable:	Coeff.	Beta	Coeff.	Beta	Coeff.	Beta
Net Natural Resource Exports (pos NX/L)	0.000292[a] [7.37e−05]	0.33981	0.000393[b] [7.59e−05]	0.35913	0.000394[a] [7.63e−05]	0.37969
Net Natural Resource Imports (neg NX/L)	0.00006 [0.000134]	0.05156	0.00014 [0.000117]	0.09365	0.00006 [0.000108]	0.04509
Total Imports of Net Natural Resource Exporters (pos M/L)	0.00006 [0.000115]	0.05358	0.000225[c] [0.000135]	0.18589	0.00010 [0.000105]	0.08394
Total Imports of Net Natural Resource Importers (neg M/L)	0.00022 [0.000167]	0.12004	0.00035 [0.000221]	0.15518	0.000373[b] [0.000177]	0.18974
HDI in 1970	−0.0134[a] [0.00236]	−1.71018	−0.0159[a] [0.00149]	−1.78169	−0.0146[a] [0.00161]	−1.78237
Terms of Trade Growth			−0.00071 [0.00735]	−0.00646	−0.0100* [0.00593]	−0.09460
Executive Constraint					0.00062 [0.000455]	0.17232
Sum of coefficients:						
pos NX/L + pos M/L	0.00035	0.39339	0.00062	0.54502	0.00049	0.4636242
F test	6.63000		16.80000		15.90000	
p value	0.01250		0.00010		0.00020	
neg NX/L + neg M/L	0.000287	0.17159	0.00049	0.24883	0.00043	0.2348335
F test	2.29000		6.70000		7.06000	
p value	0.13520		0.01240		0.01070	
Observations	73		66		61	
R-squared	0.79		0.865		0.888	

1. Robust standard errors in Square brackets. 2. Growth refers to annual average growth in the period 1970–2005. 3. Regional dummies are included in all specifications.
[a] p<0.01, [b] p<0.05, [c] p<0.1.

Table 17.2(b) OLS results: determinants of GDP per capita growth

Explanatory variable:	Coeff.	Beta	Coeff.	Beta	Coeff.	Beta
Net Natural Resource Exports (pos NX/L)	0.00170 [0.00104]	0.16956	0.00198[b] [0.000959]	0.18609	0.00093 [0.00111]	0.10190
Net Natural Resource Imports (neg NX/L)	0.00064 [0.00135]	0.04772	0.00036 [0.00112]	0.02928	0.00011 [0.00144]	0.00989
Total Imports of Net Natural Resource Exporters (pos M/L)	0.00769[a] [0.00138]	0.66068	0.00751[a] [0.00139]	0.63625	0.00581[a] [0.00192]	0.58137
Total Imports of Net Natural Resource Importers (neg M/L)	0.00934[a] [0.00158]	0.53767	0.0101[a] [0.00164]	0.60918	0.00659[b] [0.00266]	0.44100
ln GDP per capita in 1970	−0.0158[a] [0.00214]	−1.01210	−0.0136[a] [0.00245]	−0.91855	−0.0102[a] [0.00280]	−0.78807
Terms of Trade Growth			−0.129[a] [0.0479]	−0.16614	−0.08490 [0.0541]	−0.13258
ln Executive Constraint					0.00406 [0.00383]	0.15532
Sum of coefficients:						
pos NX/L + pos M/L	0.00939	0.83024	0.00949	0.82234	0.00674	0.68327
F test	45.92000		39.75000		7.77000	
p value	0.00000		0.00000		0.00740	
neg NX/L + neg M/L	0.009976	0.58538	0.01046	0.63846	0.00670	0.45089
F test	50.68000		62.29000		5.68000	
p value	0.00000		0.00000		0.02070	
Observations	85		78		68	
R-squared	0.78		0.802		0.753	

1. Robust standard errors in Square brackets. 2. Growth refers to annual average growth in the period 1970–2005. 3. Regional dummies are included in all specifications.
[a] $p<0.01$, [b] $p<0.05$, [c] $p<0.1$.

Table 17.2(c) OLS results: determinants of change in literacy ratio

Explanatory variables	Coeff.	Beta	Coeff.	Beta	Coeff.	Beta
Net Natural Resource Exports (pos NX/L)	0.000466[a] [0.000158]	0.17814	0.000521[a] [0.000179]	0.16870	0.000634[a] [0.000198]	0.20423
Net Natural Resource Imports (neg NX/L)	0.00011 [0.000214]	0.02773	0.00006 [0.000222]	0.01604	0.00012 [0.000210]	0.02780
Total Imports of Net Natural Resource Exporters (pos M/L)	0.00021 [0.000224]	0.06877	0.000438[b] [0.000212]	0.13132	0.000705[a] [0.000237]	0.21182
Total Imports of Net Natural Resource Importers (neg M/L)	0.00112[a] [0.000282]	0.22469	0.00128[a] [0.000354]	0.22706	0.00151[a] [0.000394]	0.25711
Literacy in 1970	−0.0137[a] [0.00156]	−0.94903	−0.0161[a] [0.00132]	−1.02477	−0.0167[a] [0.00136]	−1.03237
Terms of Trade Growth			0.00351 [0.00984]	0.01442	−0.01330 [0.0108]	−0.05828
Executive Constraint					−0.00108 [0.000680]	−0.11603
Sum of coefficients:						
pos NX/L + pos M/L	0.00068	0.24691	0.00096	0.30002	0.00134	0.41605
F test	6.53000		10.40000		14.43000	
p value	0.01270		0.00200		0.00040	
neg NX/L + neg M/L	0.00123	0.25243	0.00134	0.24311	0.00163	0.28492
F test	25.71000		20.11000		21.62000	
p value	0.00000		0.00000		0.00000	
Observations	84		80		70	
R-squared	0.892		0.912		0.93	

1. Robust standard errors in Square brackets. 2. Growth refers to annual average growth in the period 1970–2005. 3. Regional dummies are included in all specifications.
[a] p<0.01, [b] p<0.05, [c] p<0.1.

Table 17.2(d) OLS results: determinants of gross enrollment ratio

Explanatory variables	Coeff.	Beta	Coeff.	Beta	Coeff.	Beta
Net Natural Resource Exports (pos NX/L)	0.00026 [0.000177]	0.18679	0.00012 [0.000194]	0.07226	0.000320[a] [0.000188]	0.18069
Net Natural Resource Imports (neg NX/L)	−0.00007 [0.000310]	−0.02960	0.00000 [0.000336]	−0.00186	−0.00004 [0.000277]	−0.01891
Total Imports of Net Natural Resource Exporters (pos M/L)	−0.000618[b] [0.000305]	−0.35604	−0.000797[b] [0.000336]	−0.45089	−0.00033 [0.000275]	−0.17626
Total Imports of Net Natural Resource Importers (neg M/L)	−0.00042 [0.000444]	−0.12466	−0.00060 [0.000499]	−0.17468	0.00016 [0.000556]	0.04365
Gros Enrolment in 1970	−0.0136[a] [0.00206]	−0.94458	−0.0146[a] [0.00159]	−0.99961	−0.0175[a] [0.00156]	−1.07918
Terms of Trade Growth			−0.0376[a] [0.0134]	−0.20804	−0.0375[a] [0.0122]	−0.19903
Executive Constraint					0.00222[a] [0.000566]	0.35130
Sum of coefficients:						
pos NX/L + pos M/L	−0.00035	−0.16925	−0.00068	−0.37864	−0.00001	0.00443
F test	1.69000		4.93000		0.00000	
p value	0.19810		0.03070		0.94950	
neg NX/L + neg M/L	−0.00049	−0.15426	−0.00061	−0.17654	0.00012	0.02474
F test	1.51000		2.33000		0.08000	
p value	0.22460		0.13310		0.77420	
Observations	73		66		65	
R-squared	0.651		0.728		0.786	

1. Robust standard errors in Square brackets. 2. Growth refers to annual average growth in the period 1970–2005. 3. Regional dummies are included in all specifications.

[a] $p<0.01$, [b] $p<0.05$, [c] $p<0.1$.

Table 17.2(e) OLS results: determinants of life expectancy

Explanatory variables	Coeff.	Beta	Coeff.	Beta	Coeff.	Beta
Net Natural Resource Exports (pos NX/L)	0.0174[b] [0.00729]	0.19841	0.01100 [0.00977]	0.09235	0.01380 [0.00993]	0.11097
Net Natural Resource Imports (neg NX/L)	0.00027 [0.00748]	0.02433	−0.00275 [0.00898]	−0.02185	−0.00069 [0.00947]	−0.00532
Total Imports of Net Natural Resource Exporters (pos M/L)	0.00356 [0.0114]	−0.00948	0.00987 [0.0134]	0.07540	0.0266[b] [0.0119]	0.19638
Total Imports of Net Natural Resource Importers (neg M/L)	0.00127 [0.00966]	−0.03744	0.00874 [0.0144]	0.05095	0.0289[c] [0.0172]	0.15890
Life Expectancy in 1970	−0.0189[a] [0.00164]	−1.05483	−0.0189[a] [0.00181]	−1.20715	−0.0197[a] [0.00176]	−1.23390
Terms of Trade Growth			0.23800 [0.504]	0.02821	−0.50100 [0.510]	−0.05742
Executive Constraint					−0.03150 [0.0440]	−0.08682
Sum of coefficients:						
pos NX/L + pos M/L	0.02096	0.18893	0.02087	0.16775	0.04040	0.30735
F test	3.98000		2.12000		8.28000	
p value	0.04910		0.14960		0.00540	
neg NX/L + neg M/L	0.00154	−0.01310	0.00599	0.02910	0.02821	0.15358
F test	0.02000		0.18000		3.48000	
p value	0.88160		0.67490		0.06660	
Observations	102		90		79	
R-squared	0.803		0.788		0.865	

1. Robust standard errors in Square brackets. 2. Growth refers to annual average growth in the period 1970–2005. 3. Regional dummies are included in all specifications.

[a] $p<0.01$, [b] $p<0.05$, [c] $p<0.1$.

Table 17.3 Latin American interaction results: determinants of HDI change

Explanatory variables	HDI	GDP	Literacy	Gross Enrollment	Life Expectancy
	Coeff.	Coeff.	Coeff.	Coeff.	Coeff.
Net Natural Resource Exports (pos NX/L)	0.234ᵃ [0.0214]	0.256ᵃ [0.0391]	0.00102ᵃ [0.000290]	0.00370ᶜ [0.00198]	0.0379ᵃ [0.00512]
Net Natural Resource Imports (neg NX/L)	0.000187 [0.000221]	0.00134 [0.00153]	−0.000139 [0.000316]	−0.000849ᵃ [0.000296]	0.0135 [0.0106]
Total Imports of Net Natural Resource Exporters (pos M/L)	−0.199ᵃ [0.0182]	−0.218ᵃ [0.0313]	0.000709 [0.000728]	−0.00218ᵃ [0.000789]	−0.106 [0.109]
Total Imports of Net Natural Resource Importers (neg M/L)	6.20E−06 [0.000249]	0.00761ᵃ [0.00214]	0.00124ᵇ [0.000574]	−0.00022 [0.000428]	−0.0188 [0.0137]
Value in 1970	−0.0141ᵃ [0.00275]	−0.0168ᵃ [0.00262]	−0.0128ᵃ [0.00195]	−0.0143ᵃ [0.00331]	−0.0185ᵃ [0.00176]
Dummy Latin America and the Caribbean	0.000773 [0.000609]	−0.0152ᵃ [0.00401]	−0.000822 [0.000736]	−0.00186 [0.00126]	0.300ᵃ [0.0494]
Interaction Latin America and Net Natural Resources Exports	−0.234ᵃ [0.0217]	−0.253ᵃ [0.0395]	−0.000807ᶜ [0.000408]	−0.00419ᶜ [0.00218]	−0.0469ᵃ [0.0166]
Interaction Latin America and Total Imports of Net Natural Resources Exporters	0.199ᵃ [0.0181]	0.223ᵃ [0.0315]	−0.00118 [0.000843]	0.000821 [0.000994]	0.129 [0.110]
Observations	70	78	85	77	100
R-squared	0.814	0.802	0.888	0.711	0.817

1. Robust standard errors in brackets. 2. Growth refers to annual average growth in the period 1970–2005. 3. Regional dummies are included in all specifications.
ᵃ p<0.01, ᵇ p<0.05, ᶜ p<0.1.

Appendix 17A Data variable definitions, and sources

Variable	Definition	Source
Natural resources by labor force	Net exports of natural resources, defined as exports minus imports, divided by the labor force. The labor force is defined as the population between the ages of 15 and 64.	WDI and UN COMTRADE
Growth of GDP per capita, 1970–2005	Average annual growth of real GDP per capita (constant prices: chain series).	Authors' calculations based on Penn World Table (Heston, Summers, and Aten 2002)
Log GDP per capita	Real GDP per capita (constant prices: chain series) divided by total population.	Penn World Table (Heston et al. 2002)
Openness	Percentage of years with open economic policies as defined by Sachs and Warner (1995a).	Sachs and Warner (1995a)
Terms-of-trade growth	The growth of external terms of trade is defined as the ratio of export to import price indices of goods and services.	World Development Indicators
HDI	A composite index measuring average achievement in three basic dimensions of human development—a long and healthy life, access to knowledge, and a decent standard of living.	Gray and Purser (2009)
Literacy rate, adult	The proportion of the adult population aged 15 years and older that is literate.	Gray and Purser (2009)
Life expectancy at birth	The number of years a newborn infant could expect to live if prevailing patters of age-specific mortality rates at the time of birth were to stay the same throughout the child's life.	Gray and Purser (2009)
Enrollment ratio, gross combined, for primary, secondary, and tertiary education	The number of students enrolled in primary, secondary, and tertiary levels of education.	Gray and Purser (2009)

significantly smaller for this region compared with the rest of the natural resource abundant regions and countries. This result is shown in Table 17.3, where we can see that the Latin America interaction coefficients are of the opposite sign and mostly significant. This indicates that for Latin America the positive effect of natural resources is relatively small and in some cases the total coefficient for the region is not significantly different from zero.

17.5 CONCLUSIONS

This chapter shows evidence against a natural resource curse on human development. We find evidence that changes of human development from 1970 to 2005, proxied by changes in the Human Development Index, are positively and significantly correlated with natural resource abundance. When we decompose the results for each HDI components, we find that natural resources could be positive for GDP growth but, most significantly, we find stronger evidence that natural resources are good for the non-income components of human development (especially literacy and life expectancy). These results contribute to a broader discussion of development by indicating that the positive effect of natural resource abundance is clearer for human development than for GDP growth, mainly through the education and health dimensions.

We have also studied the effect of resource abundance on progress in human development in the Latin America region. Results from the Latin America interactions show that the positive impact of natural resources on that region is significantly smaller than in the rest of the world. Since the average results are still positive and significant for the rest of the regions, this suggests the possible existence of institutional features in the region that interact with natural resources in a detrimental way. Nevertheless, even in Latin America's case there is no evidence that natural resources harm human development.

REFERENCES

ACEMOGLU, D., JOHNSON, S., and ROBINSON, J. (2001). 'The Colonial Origins of Comparative Development: An Empirical Investigation', *American Economic Review* 91.5.

—— —— —— (2003). 'An African Success Story: Botswana', in D. Rodrik (ed.), *In Search of Prosperity: Analytic Narratives on Economic Growth*, Princeton, NJ: Princeton University Press.

ARAGÓN, F., and RUD, J. (2009). 'The Blessing of Natural Resources: Evidence from a Peruvian Gold Mine', Working Papers 2009-014, Banco Central de Reserva del Perú, Lima.

BELSLEY, D., KUH, E., and WELSCH, R. (2004). *Regression Diagnostics Identifying Influential Data and Sources of Collinearity*, New York: Wiley-Interscience.

BINDER, M., and GEORGIADIS, G. (2010). 'Determinants of Human Development: Insights from State-Dependent Panel Models', Human Development Research Paper 24, UNDP-HDRO, New York.

BLOMSTRÖM, M., and KOKKO, A. (2007). 'From Natural Resources to High-Tech Production: The Evolution of Industrial Competitiveness in Sweden and Finland', in Lederman and Mahoney (2007c).

BRAVO-ORTEGA, C., and DE GREGORIO, J. (2007). 'The Relative Richness of the Poor? Natural Resources, Human Capital, and Economic Growth', in Lederman and Mahoney (2007c).

CASELLI, F., and MICHAELS, G. (2009). 'Do Oil Windfalls Improve Living Standards? Evidence from Brazil', CEPR Discussion Paper No. 7579, London.

COLLIER, P., and GUNNING, J. (1996). 'Policy Towards Commodity Shocks in Developing Countries', IMF Working Paper WP/96/84, Washington, DC.

COLLIER, S., and SATER, W. F. (1996). A History of Chile, 1808–1994. Cambridge: Cambridge University Press.

COOK, R. D., and WEISBERG, S. (1982). Residuals and Influence in Regression, London: Chapman & Hall.

CORDEN, W. M. (1984). 'Booming Sector and Dutch Disease Economics: Survey and Consolidation', Oxford Economic Papers 36.3.

CUDDINGTON, J., LUDEMA, R., and JAYASURIYA, S. (2007). 'Prebisch-Singer Redux', in Lederman and Mahoney (2007c).

DI JOHN, J. (2009). From Windfall to Curse? Oil and Industrialization in Venezuela, 1920 to the Present, University Park: Penn State University Press.

DUNNING, T. (2005). 'Resource Dependence, Economic Performance, and Political Stability', Journal of Conflict Resolution 49.4.

EASTERLY, W. (1999). 'Life During Growth', Journal of Economic Growth 4.3.

—— (2005). 'National Policies and Economic Growth: A Reappraisal', in P. Aghion and S. Durlauf (eds), Handbook of Economic Growth, Amsterdam: Elsevier.

GRAY, G., and PURSER, M. (2010). 'Human Development Trends Since 1970: A Social Convergence Story', New York: HDRO, UNDP.

HABER, S., and MENALDO, V. (2009). 'Do Natural Resources Fuel Authoritarianism? A Reappraisal of the Resource Curse', draft.

—— RAZO, A., and MAURER, N. (2003). The Politics of Property Rights: Political Instability, Credible Commitments, and Economic Growth in Mexico 1876-1929, Cambridge: Cambridge University Press.

HAUSMANN, R., HWANG, J., and RODRIK, D. (2007). 'What You Export Matters', Journal of Economic Growth 12.1.

—— and KLINGER, B. (2006). 'Structural Transformation and Patterns of Comparative Advantage in the Product Space', CID Working Paper No. 128 (August), Harvard University.

—— and RODRÍGUEZ, F. (eds) (2009). Venezuela: Anatomy of a Collapse, Cambridge, Mass.: Harvard University.

—— —— and WAGNER, R. (2007). 'Growth Collapses', in C. Reinhart, A. Velasco, and C. Végh (eds), Money, Crises, and Transition: Essays in Honor of Guillermo Calvo, Cambridge, Mass.: MIT Press.

HESTON, A., SUMMERS, R., and ATEN, B. (2002). 'Penn World Table Version 6.1', Center for International Comparisons at the University of Pennsylvania (CICUP).

HUMPHREYS, M., SACHS, J., and STIGLITZ, J. (2007). *Escaping the Resource Curse*, New York: Columbia University Press.

KARL, T. L. (1997). *The Paradox of Plenty: Oil Booms and Petro-States*, Berkeley and Los Angeles: University of California Press.

KOENKER, R., and HALLOCK, K. (2001). 'Quantile Regression', *Journal of Economic Perspectives* 15.4.

LEAMER, E., MAUL, H., RODRÍGUEZ, S., and SCHOTT, P. (1999). 'Does Natural Resource Abundance Increase Latin American Income Inequality?', *Journal of Development Economics* 59.

LEDERMAN, D., and XU, L.C. (2007). 'Comparative Advantage and Trade Intensity: Are Traditional Endowments Destiny?', in Lederman and Mahoney (2007c).

—— and MALONEY, W. (2007a). 'Neither Curse nor Destiny: Introduction to Natural Resources and Development', in Lederman and Mahoney (2007c).

—— —— (2007b). 'Trade Structure and Growth', in Lederman and Mahoney (2007c).

—— —— (eds) (2007c). *Natural Resources: Neither Curse nor Destiny*, Palo Alto: Stanford University Press and World Bank.

MAHON, Jr, J. (1992). 'Was Latin America Too Rich to Prosper? Structural and Political Obstacles to Export-Led Industrial Growth', *Journal of Development Studies* 28.2.

MALONEY, W. (2007). 'Missed Opportunities: Innovation and Resource-Based Growth in Latin America', in Lederman and Mahoney (2007c).

MANZANO, O., and RIGOBÓN, R. (2007). 'Resource Curse or Debt Overhang?', in Lederman and Mahoney (2007c).

MARTIN, W. (2007). 'Outgrowing Resource Dependence: Theory and Developments', in Lederman and Mahoney (2007c).

NUNN, N. (2008). 'The Long-Term Effects of Africa's Slave Trades', *Quarterly Journal of Economics* 123.1.

OCAMPO, J. A., and PARRA, M. A. (2003). 'The Terms of Trade for Commodities in the 20th Century', *CEPAL Review* 79.

PREBISCH, R. (1950). 'Crecimiento, desequilibrio y disparidades: interpretación del proceso de desarrollo', *Estudio económico de América Latina 1949*, Santiago, Chile: ECLAC.

RODRÍGUEZ, F. (2007). 'Cleaning Up the Kitchen Sink: Growth Empirics When the World is not Simple', Wesleyan Economics Working Paper No. 2006-004, Middletown, Conn.

—— (2009). 'What Does the Human Development Index Really Measure?', *New York Times* Freakonomics Blog, accessed April 29, 2010 at: http://freakonomics.blogs.nytimes.com/2009/06/01/another-perspective-on-the-human-development-index/

—— and GOMOLIN, A. (2009). 'Anarchy, State, and Dystopia: Venezuelan Economic Institutions before the Advent of Oil', *Bulletin of Latin American Research* 28.1.

—— and SACHS, J. (1999). 'Why Do Resource-Abundant Economies Grow More Slowly?', *Journal of Economic Growth* 4.3.

ROS, J. (2000). *Development Theory and The Economics of Growth*, Ann Arbor: University of Michigan Press.

SACHS, J., and WARNER, A. (1995a). 'Economic Reform and the Process of Global Integration', *Brookings Papers on Economic Activity* 1.

—— —— (1995b). 'Natural Resource Abundance and Economic Growth', NBER Working Paper No. 5398, Cambridge, Mass.

SALA-I-MARTIN, X., and SUBRAMANIAN, A. (2003). 'Addressing the Resource Curse: An Illustration from Nigeria', NBER Working Paper No. 9804, Cambridge, Mass.

——DOPPELHOFER, G., and MILLER, R. (2004). 'Determinants of Long-Term Growth: A Bayesian Averaging of Classical Estimates (BACE) Approach', *American Economic Review* 94.4.

SHAXSON, NICHOLAS. (2005). "New Approaches to Volatility: Dealing with the 'Resource Curse' in Sub-Saharan Africa," International Affairs 81, no. 2 (March): 311–24.

SINGER, H. W. (1950). 'US foreign investment in underdeveloped areas, the distribution of gains between investing and borrowing countries', *American Economic Review, Papers and Proceedings* 40.

STIGLITZ, J. (2007). 'Introduction: What Is the Problem with Natural Resource Wealth?', in Humphreys et al. (2007).

TORNELL, A., and LANE, P. (1999). 'The Voracity Effect', *American Economic Review* 89.1.

VAN WIJNBERGEN, S. (1984). 'The "Dutch Disease": A Disease After All?', *Economic Journal* 94.373.

VENABLES, A. (2007). 'Trade, Location, and Development: An Overview of Theory', in Lederman and Mahoney (2007c).

WANTCHEKON, L. (1999). 'Why do Resource Dependent Countries Have Authoritarian Governments?', working paper, Yale University.

WRIGHT, G., and CZELUSTA, J. (2007). 'Resource-Based Growth Past and Present', in Lederman and Mahoney (2007c).

CHAPTER 18

....

FOREIGN DIRECT INVESTMENT IN LATIN AMERICA

....

JOÃO CARLOS FERRAZ, MICHAEL MORTIMORE,
AND MÁRCIA TAVARES

> ...foreign private investment...shares to a very high degree the ambiguity
> of most human inventions and institutions: it has considerable potential
> for both good and evil.
>
> (Albert O. Hirschman 1969)

18.1 INTRODUCTION

....

Historically, foreign direct investment (FDI) has had an ambivalent role in terms of its contribution to development and especially how it shaped the productive sector in Latin America such that it became a recurrent theme in the region's economic literature. The debate on the impacts of FDI on local development has been inconclusive largely because of difficulties in analytically isolating FDI from prevailing business and institutional conditions, like local technological and entrepreneurial capabilities, and national regulatory frameworks, among other factors.

Yet FDI flows to Latin America have soared since the 1990s, converting it into an even more important variable. More recently, there has been a smaller but equally unprecedented rise in outward direct investment (OFDI) by Latin American foreign investors (see Figure 18.1). This creates new policy challenges for productive development in the region.

This chapter provides an overview of inward and outward FDI patterns in Latin America since the mid-1990s. Section 18.2 is dedicated to inward FDI and section 18.3 deals with outward FDI over this period. The fourth and final section briefly summarizes main findings and contemplates policy challenges.

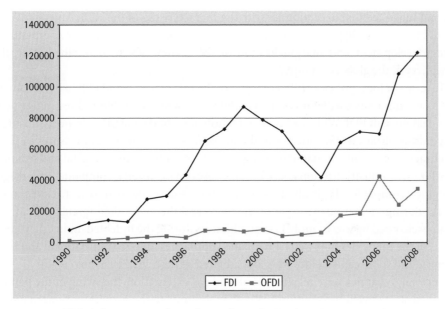

FIGURE 18.1 FDI inflows to and outflows from Latin American countries, 1990–2008 (US million)

Source: Elaborated by the authors based on official figures provided by the ECLAC.

18.2 INWARD FDI IN LATIN AMERICA

18.2.1 A love–hate relationship

The strong ideological debate surrounding FDI and the questioning of the behavior of transnational corporations (TNCs) in Latin America can be traced back to the region's early history as a source of natural resources within a colonial context, and more recent *causes celèbres* of illegal or otherwise wrong behavior by TNCs. However, it should be understood that most of the debate on the costs and benefits of contemporary FDI in the region relates to the performance of TNCs operating legally and in pursuit of legitimate goals. Tension exists between the priorities of these companies with regards to their global strategies and the limited host country (Latin American) institutional, technological, and economic capacities to ensure that expected national benefits materialize.

FDI has been a persistent topic in the works of development economists. Though the approaches and interpretations have evolved over time, there have been two consistent but apparently paradoxical perspectives. One held that the involvement of TNCs in national development strategies was necessary primarily to contribute to macroeconomic stability with regards to financial balance of payments considerations, and to assist with the upgrading of local industrial structures by way of new technologies. The second suggested that in economies with the characteristics of the Latin American ones, including a relatively poor industrial fabric, the presence of TNCs actually perpetuated underdevelopment and marginalization of the region, which maintained it on the periphery of the global economy.[1]

In terms of local policies, different views of the role of TNCs and FDI in development led to a continuous oscillation of the pendulum between favorable and restrictive policies dealing with FDI. With the implementation of second generation import-substituting industrialization (ISI) policies in the 1950s, several countries put measures in place to attract investments in manufacturing in order to ensure foreign capital and technology for their industrialization goals, in some cases giving foreign companies advantages over local companies. Typically, these measures were changed to more restrictive frameworks during the nationalistic era of the 1960s and the 1970s; then foreign capital was again welcomed by way of more liberal initiatives during the indebted-industrialization crisis of the 1980s (Jenkins 1991). Pragmatic approaches linking transnational and local (private and state) capital elites were also adopted, as described by Evans (1979).

Sectoral dynamics were relevant. In oil and gas exploration, the swing of the pendulum had started well before World War II, with limits to the activities of international petroleum companies in several countries, especially in the context of the Mexican Revolution, then ongoing, in a sequence of deregulation/nationalizations and back again cycles (Odell 1968). In public services and infrastructure, whereas foreign capital had been present, especially in electricity and transportation, since the beginning of the 20th century, state capital started taking over in the 1930s and 1940s, and by the 1980s most such services were provided by states and state-owned companies. In manufacturing, the 1970s witnessed several initiatives to "fade out" full foreign ownership, such as those in Mexico and the Andean countries.

The debt crisis of the 1980s and the collapse of the Berlin Wall truncated the existing debate to a very large extent, as aggressive market-friendly policies came to the fore. Attracting more FDI became one of the pillars of the reforms based on the Washington Consensus, both to finance imbalances in the balance of payments and because transnational corporations were considered key players to fill in for the crippled state by way of deregulation and privatization (Williamson 1990). The policy focus was on attracting high volumes of FDI, with less emphasis on the quality of FDI in terms of the linkages between local and foreign firms, and other impacts of FDI. In certain industries this led to costly competition between potential host countries and even between administrative regions within those countries, as was the case of the tax incentives war between Brazilian states for FDI in the automobile industry.

Later, when the time came to evaluate the results of the Washington Consensus reforms, FDI came under different kinds of criticism from a number of host countries. Bolivia and Venezuela and to a certain extent Ecuador, for example, imposed new restrictions on private participation (which had been almost exclusively foreign) in key

---

[1] For a review, see Kerner (2003). Key works include Cardoso and Faletto (1971), Sunkel (1972), Cardoso (1973), and Fajnzylber (1975).

industries, such oil and gas. More recently, new, state-owned foreign players started to invest in these countries. In Argentina, dissatisfaction with private (and mainly foreign) provision of basic services such as water and sanitation led to the return of concessions to public management as well as to a number of investor-state disputes. Nevertheless, in other countries, such as Mexico, Chile, Peru, Colombia, Central America, and the Dominican Republic, the determination to reinforce the FDI-assisted development was evident in the explosion of bilateral investment treaties and free trade agreements with investment chapters, particularly with the United States.

Against this background, the following section provides a closer look at recent FDI tendencies, and evaluates their contribution to development in the region.

18.2.2 Two waves of FDI flows to Latin America: 1994–2003 and 2004–8

Though liberalizing reforms began in the late 1980s, the explosive growth of FDI flows to the region became evident from 1994 onwards. The first wave of post-reform FDI peaked in 1999 at $87 billion before falling to $42 billion in 2003. Factors that triggered or contributed to this first recent wave of FDI include trade and financial liberalization, large-scale privatizations and deregulation of industries previously reserved to the state or to national companies, economic stabilization, and the entry into force of NAFTA and MERCOSUR. Moreover, the development of new industries such as mobile telephony created opportunities for TNCs in the region. This first wave came to an end in 2003 following the slowdown of the world economy and, within the region, with the deepening of the Argentine crisis and its impact on neighbors.

A second wave of FDI to Latin America began in 2004 as the world and regional economies recovered and as China's increased demand drove commodity prices upwards. Increased TNC profits drove a wave of mergers and acquisitions (M&As) that, in contrast to the previous wave, were not primarily associated with privatizations. FDI flows into Latin America peaked in 2008 at $115 billion before slowing down in 2009 as the global financial and economic crisis hit Latin American economies. During the 1994–2008 period FDI was concentrated in Brazil and Mexico—a little under 60% of total investment. Smaller countries generally had larger FDI/GDP ratios, with the exception of years in which FDI flows to the bigger countries were affected by exceptionally large acquisitions.

Comparing 1994–2003 to 2004–8, the distribution of FDI among Latin American countries varied, reflecting changes in policy and individual economic performances (see Table 18.1).

The United States has been the major investor country throughout both periods, followed by Spain and the Netherlands. Existing data (available more consistently starting in 1997) suggest a loss in the share of FDI originating in the United States, as well as greater diversification of the sources of such investment, although gaps in statistics make it impossible to confirm this. Spain, a strong player in privatizations of oil and gas and

Table 18.1 Distribution of FDI in Latin America, 1994–2003 and 2004–8 (Current US$ Million and %)

	1994–2003 (annual average)	1994–2003 Share of total	2004–08 (annual average)	2004–08 Share of total
Argentina	7,302	13	5,874	7
Bolivia	599	1	190	0
Brazil	18,124	32	26,328	30
Chile	4,493	8	10,552	12
Colombia	2,426	4	7,907	9
Costa Rica	481	1	1,372	2
Dominican Republic	673.8	1	1,605	2
Ecuador	747.5	1	554	1
El Salvador	247.8	0	684	1
Guatemala	205.6	0	422	0
Honduras	199.7	0	705	1
Mexico	15,665.20	27	22,974	26
Nicaragua	183.6	0	357	0
Panama	636.7	1	1,756	2
Paraguay	128.8	0	124	0
Peru	2,048.50	4	3,413	4
Uruguay	215.4	0	1,188	1
Venezuela	2,926.40	5	1,169	1
Total	57,304	100	87,172	100
Subregion 1: Central America, the Dominican Republic, and Mexico	18,293	32	29,875	34
Subregion 2: South America	39,011	68	57,297	66

Source: Elaborated by the authors based on official figures provided by ECLAC.

public utilities, lost ground to the Netherlands during the second phase, although, given the latter country's role as a financial center, the ultimate origin of a substantial share of those investments is likely to be a third country (see Figure 18.2). The announcement of acquisitions and greenfield investments by Chinese, Indian, and other developing country players particularly since 2006 suggest that this trend may become more significant and more clearly visible in the statistics in the years to come (ECLAC 2007; 2008).[2]

[2] It is, however, likely, that many of these foreign investments are and will continue to be underestimated by the statistics because of the use of financial centers or the undertaking of foreign investments through subsidiaries outside the ultimate home country.

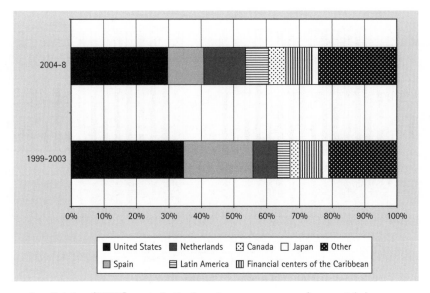

FIGURE 18.2 Origin of FDI flows to Latin America, 1999–2003 and 2004–8 (%)

Source: Elaborated by the authors based on official figures provided by the ECLAC.

FDI data registered in the balance of payments do not distinguish between greenfield investment and M&As. Information on M&As show that the FDI boom in the 1990s was strongly fueled by privatizations. In Brazil, privatizations accounted for 19% of total FDI flows received between 1996 and 2002. The surge in FDI since 2004 had to do with another M&A boom involving mostly mergers and acquisitions of privately held assets, but was accompanied by an increase in greenfield investment especially in 2007 and 2008, such that the ratio of known M&A volumes to FDI has fallen.

18.2.3 Types of FDI, trends, and impacts

FDI in primary activities has played a larger role in South America (subregion 2) than in Mexico, Central America, and the Caribbean (subregion 1), while the opposite is true for manufacturing (see Figure 18.3). This section explains the factors behind these patterns.

Nonetheless, aggregate FDI data provide little insight into the essential nature of FDI and its impact on host economies. A conceptual framework based on a taxonomy of motivations of TNCs undertaking FDI has guided the production of a series of flagship reports by the Economic Commission for Latin America and the Caribbean (ECLAC).[3] This framework considers four main types of investment motivations: natural resource-seeking; market-seeking; efficiency-seeking (or investment in low-cost export platforms

[3] This classification builds on Dunning (1993) and Dunning and Lundan (2008), which in turn build on an earlier taxonomy used by Jack Behrman in 1972.

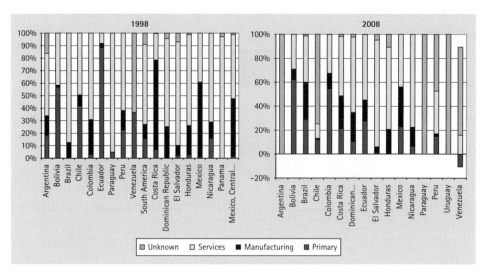

FIGURE 18.3 Sectoral distribution of inward FDI, 1998, 2007 (%)

Source: Elaborated by the authors based on official figures provided by the ECLAC.

Notes: The figure for Chile does not include estimates of reinvestments in mining, which account for a large share of investments in the country.

serving major markets); and strategic asset-seeking ("to augment the acquiring firm's global portfolio of physical assets and human competences, which they perceive will either sustain or strengthen ownership-specific advantages or weaken those of their competitors," Dunning and Lundan 2008).

Since the 1990s, efficiency-seeking investments have been concentrated in subregion 1, i.e. Mexico, Central America, and the Caribbean; natural resource-seeking investments have been concentrated in subregion 2, South America; and market-seeking investments have been widespread, although in manufacturing especially they have been concentrated in the largest markets. Strategic asset-seeking investments are quite scarce and mostly located close to electronics manufacturing clusters in Mexico and Brazil.

18.2.4 Natural resource-seeking investment

Most FDI in primary activities in Latin America is concentrated in hydrocarbons and in mining, with only a minor share going to agriculture and forestry. If one discounts the outlier value of foreign investment in oil and gas in 1999, which was attributable largely to the privatization of the oil and gas industry in only one country (Argentina), FDI in extractive industries has risen most significantly since 2004, in keeping with the global commodities boom.

FDI in hydrocarbons was larger than in mining in the 1990s, while mining became more important as of 2004. This is due to the fact that there was stronger participation of

TNCs in oil and gas privatizations than in mining, as a large share of state-owned mining assets remained in the hands of local private capital when privatizations took place (see Campodónico 2004; Lardé, Chaparro, and Parra 2008). Moreover the prices of minerals were not as conducive to new FDI in the 1990s as they came to be later on. Thirdly, regulatory changes and TNC/state disputes in Bolivia, Ecuador, and Venezuela, and the economic crisis in Argentina, led to a retraction of TNCs in oil and gas in what had previously been the major recipient countries, while Colombia has received an increasing and substantial share of new FDI following the implementation of more FDI-friendly policies (ECLAC 2007; 2008; 2009). The global boom in the mining industry, on the other hand, led to acquisitions and new and expanded projects by TNCs, particularly in Chile and Peru, and even in regions that had not been traditional recipients of these investments in recent history, such as Mexico and Central America. In the oil and gas industry, while traditional TNCs have more recently reduced their investments in the region, companies from the region and from other developing countries—many of which are state-owned—are playing an increasingly important role.

The analysis of impact of FDI in extractive industries has provoked a controversial debate. TNCs have been key agents in the expansion of the oil and gas and mining industries in the region, and their investments (along with those of local firms) have had both positive and negative impacts. The positive ones include increasing local exploration efforts and generating higher levels of production and exports, and thereby revenues for host states in accordance to tax and royalty policies. Exploration and production efforts by TNCs generated jobs in areas away from urban centers. FDI contributed to the development of infrastructure that enabled the export of primary goods (including oil and gas pipelines). There is, moreover, evidence of improvement in social and economic indicators in mining areas where adequate state programs are in place to channel resources, such as the Antofagasta region in Chile (Lardé et al. 2008) and in Peru (Santillana Santos 2006), where TNCs are important investors alongside local companies.

Nonetheless, as is demonstrated by the regulatory changes that occurred particularly in 2005–7, certain governments and social groups have complained that local economies and stakeholders have not had much access to the increasing wealth generated by the extraction of resources. Conflict has arisen between social groups (often representing poor and indigenous communities) and TNCs, with the state caught in the middle, over the environmental impacts of mining and drilling (including pollution of local water sources, harm to glaciers and biodiversity, harm done to migratory and mating patterns of game, and loss of arable land resulting from the infrastructure development) (Gordon and Webber 2008; Roncallo 2006). Many TNCs, while formally establishing corporate social responsibility (CSR) programs and practices, in many cases did not take this beyond rhetoric (Sawyer and Gomez 2008). Moreover, there has been tension between state goals of ensuring the development of energy sources and the profit-oriented goals of TNCs. For example, Repsol YPF's low levels of investment in exploration and the development of new oil reserves in Argentina in the face of an uncertain macroeconomic environment led to a critical situation in reserves starting in 2004 (Campodónico 2004).

Thus, natural resource-seeking FDI met some of the goals that governments had set out for it when further opening up these industries to private participation, and helped host countries to benefit from the commodities boom that took place between 2004 and 2008. At the same time, regulatory designs and governance structures seem not to have taken adequate account of the high economic, social, and environmental stakes involved in some of these activities, and were generally not capable of designing a policy model that would ensure mutually satisfactory terms to all stakeholders in the long run.

18.2.5 Market-seeking investment

While it is difficult to precisely separate in the statistics market-seeking FDI from the other classes of FDI, it is safe to assume that most FDI in services in all the region, and most FDI in manufacturing in South America, are market-seeking (ECLAC, several issues of the Foreign Investment Report; Laplane 2006).

Since the beginning of the 1990s, FDI flowed into services (banking, supermarkets, fuel distribution, public utilities) as a result of privatizations and public service deregulation, of the general liberalization of FDI policy, and of the elimination of restrictions on the participation of foreign capital in specific industries. In manufacturing, on one hand, the dismantling of ISI led to a decrease in the operations of TNCs where market size was incompatible with efficient scale. On the other hand, liberalization and improved macroeconomic performance increased the attractiveness of the region for foreign investment in several industries, including food and beverages, automobiles and electronics, leading to increased FDI particularly in the largest markets. Moreover, despite the end of ISI, incentives schemes and certain trade barriers were kept in place for key industries. Investments in market-seeking manufacturing in South America were again spurred by improved macroeconomic performance after 2003 and in the context of the international commodities boom.

FDI in services fell substantially from 2001 onwards, due to the end of the privatization and deregulation cycle and, as described below, to the withdrawal of a number of services companies from the region, often after selling their assets to local companies. Starting in 2004, a number of acquisitions increased the regional footprint of Latin American TNCs (or *translatinas*) in services such as telecommunications, retail, banking, and fuel distribution (ECLAC 2006; 2007; 2008).

As for the impact of market-seeking FDI, it is useful to look at two groups of FDI where governments had placed high expectations on the entry of expansion of TNCs: public utilities and infrastructure in all the region; and manufacturing in MERCOSUR.

18.2.5.1 *Utilities and infrastructure*

TNCs have invested in public utilities since the 19th century. The increasingly conflictive relation between TNCs and local users led, from the 1930s onwards, to increased state controls on public utilities and eventually nationalization (see e.g. Baer 2008 on the Brazilian experience). In the 1990s, TNCs came back into the picture particularly in the Southern Cone in the context of Washington Consensus reforms. TNCs took over previously state-owned utilities that had typically underinvested in infrastructure, and were in critical financial situations, among other reasons, because they had often been obliged by their own government to charge below cost in order to keep inflation down or for social reasons. By way of privatization and deregulation of electricity services, telecommunications, transportation infrastructure, and water and sewage services, the private sector was expected to overcome these deficiencies. Given relatively weak indigenous experience with the functioning of public utilities in a newly deregulated setting, TNCs were seen as key actors, more than local private capital.

The models adopted in privatizing and deregulating private services and infrastructure varied, but generally reforms unbundled vertically integrated segments, introduced competition in those that were not natural monopolies, and awarded concessions over natural monopolies to the highest bidder, regulating tariffs and conditions of service and often imposing performance requirements relating to efficiency, quality, and access. In many cases, reforms—where TNCs were key players—led to improved infrastructure, wider access to services, greater efficiency, and better quality (Chong and Lora 2007). In addition to generating income from concession fees and the payment for state-owned assets, they also freed state revenue for other functions. However, the results of TNC participation in these privatizations were far from uncontroversial.

The market- and competition-oriented reforms often involved the elimination of subsidies and the approximation of rates based on real operating and capital costs, which in some cases implied an initial tariff increase. Whereas in most cases changes in the rate structure did not lead to major conflicts, in a few emblematic cases, particularly in the water and sanitation industry, local communities found them to be unacceptable. Public outrage and political support for that outrage led to the annulment of concessions and the return of certain assets to the state, leading to investor/state disputes usually brought before the International Centre for Settlement of Investment Disputes (ICSID).

A second, and larger, source of investor/state disputes arose in Argentina, specifically, and related to the incompatibility of TNC interests with the social and economic needs of macroeconomic policy in a time of crisis. In its efforts to attract FDI in public services, the Argentine government had based the rate mechanism for public services on the convertibility regime (rates were in practice set in dollars and indexed to the United States wholesale price index). The country had also ratified a number of bilateral investment agreements that in practice—at least as sustained by companies that are parties to these disputes—transferred the business risk associated with the sustainability of the convertibility regime to the state. When the convertibility crumbled in 2001 and emergency measures were adopted, this combination generated huge liabilities, estimated at approximately $20 billion (Mortimore and Stanley 2006; Solanes and Jouravlev 2007; ECLAC 2009).

Third, though privatizations accounted for a large share of FDI received by Latin America in the 1990s, much of that foreign investment went into acquisitions rather than towards expanding and improving infrastructure and service provision (Mortimore 2009). The privatization models that had largely been based on the European experience were not conducive to certain types of foreign investment in a region that, in stark contrast to Europe, was gravely deficient in infrastructure and was still struggling with macroeconomic stability issues. The droughts in Brazil in 2002 exposed severe underinvestment in electricity generation despite large-scale privatization, and led to losses in the electricity distribution companies as well as to shortages, and to forced slowdowns in industrial production (ECLAC 2005).

In sum, while there were successful experiences of TNC participation in public services and infrastructure, the social and political sensitivity of these industries required carefully thought-out regulatory frameworks that could take into account the particularities of regional economies, including the need to generate incentives for foreign investment in new infrastructure and to consider social and economic structures, and macroeconomic instability. This was not always the case.

18.2.5.2 *Manufacturing in MERCOSUR*

FDI was seen in post-World War II Latin America as a means to accelerate the development of new industrial sectors, especially where modern technology or sufficient capital were not available locally. In the context of the second-generation ISI policies, countries attracted FDI with the goal of developing national companies in key industries. TNCs contributed with knowhow as well as organizational and administrative technology (Baer 2008). Though ISI policies were dismantled, post-ISI policies attracting FDI in manufacturing still followed much the same goals, based on potential static benefits of the presence of manufacturing operations (employment, revenues), more than dynamic ones (technology and knowledge spillovers, industrial upgrading, and improvement of local capacities through competition and demonstration effects) (Hiratuka 2008). In practice, dynamic benefits have seldom materialized to the extent hoped for. In fact, even some of the static benefits were questioned, as in some cases the import of capital-intensive technology by TNCs led their employment impact to be small or even negative (Amman and Baer 2002; Baer 2008).

Particularly after 1994, market-seeking manufacturing FDI was stimulated in MERCOSUR countries by the elimination of restrictions and by improved macroeconomic performance. New foreign investments were made in food and beverages, automobiles, machinery, white goods (domestic appliances), and electronics, among others. However, studies undertaken on Argentina, Brazil, and Uruguay show that the results of these investments in terms of dynamic spillovers—particularly the effect of FDI on the development of local industry—were mixed.

National companies competing with TNCs lost market shares to TNCs and thereby lost scale and efficiency. However, competition with TNCs has also led many local companies to invest more in innovation activities, particularly R&D.[4] Among the companies competing with TNCs, those with higher levels of knowledge capacity (resulting from organized and continuous innovation activities) were found to have had a higher

---

[4] Araujo (2004) finds evidence that domestic companies in Brazil started spending more on R&D when TNC market shares rose.

probability of taking advantage of the positive spillovers of TNCs (Gonçalves 2005; Laplane 2006). Positive spillovers have been stronger for local suppliers of TNCs than for their competitors, but this has depended on the type and strength of the linkages between suppliers and their transnational clients. These were found to be weaker in Uruguay than in Brazil and Argentina, leading to little evidence of vertical spillovers in that country. Generally, market-seeking strategies where companies import a large share of inputs and components tended to have negative horizontal impacts and weak vertical ones (Laplane 2006).

Even for Brazil, which underwent industrial restructuring starting out from a more complex and integrated industrial base than many other Latin American countries (Bielschowksy and Stumpo 1996) and was thus arguably better positioned to take advantage of TNC presence in the form of market-seeking FDI, the spillovers, particularly in high-technology industries, were not clear. In Brazil during the ISI period, most TNCs had to rely on local firms for much of their inputs, and transmitted some relevant technology and organizational practices to their suppliers (Baer 2008). However, when markets were opened in the 1990s, the changes in the global production systems of TNCs, which had led to an increase in the importance of scale and in intra-firm trade, hit the Brazilian industrial structure hard and led to the shake-out of many local suppliers of transnational corporations (as well as their competitors), particularly in industries categorized as "innovation carriers" (Ferraz, Kupfer, and Iootty 2004; Lacerda 2004). This led to a situation in which—in the automobile industry for instance—inputs and components that are technology intensive are imported by TNCs rather than sourced locally. This has impacted the relationship between exports and imports in terms of value and technological profile (Hiratuka and De Negri 2004). In the ICT hardware industry, Brazil has struggled, through a complex incentive scheme, to develop the industry upstream towards technology-intensive components, but encountered restrictions associated to the availability of a competitive components industry. The local components industry, or what was left of it, suffered from a widening technology gap, the incompatibility of the scale of the local market with minimum efficient scale requirements for the more technologically intensive components, resulting in the fact that the country could not compete internationally in these products because of high costs related to taxation, infrastructure, and exchange rate volatility (ECLAC 2008). These have also limited the attractiveness of Brazil for other TNC operations that could have combined local market- and export-oriented investment in other products and industries.

With the predominance of foreign companies and suppliers in higher-technology industries, technological development and innovation were driven out of the country and local operations remained dependent on foreign technology (Baer 2008). Although there is a global trend towards internationalizing R&D investment, Latin America is not a preferred destination of TNCs for R&D operations, with the exception of adaptation functions (UNCTAD 2005; Mortimore 2008).

In sum, though increased TNC presence in manufacturing has generated benefits for local economies, shortcomings in local capacity combined with global sourcing and technological strategies that do not favor local sourcing have limited the dynamic benefits of FDI in market-seeking manufacturing. The absorptive capacity of local firms is a prime determinant of the generation of spillovers from TNCs to local companies.

18.2.6 Efficiency-seeking

While most of the manufacturing FDI received by South America was directed at the local market, the surge in manufacturing FDI in Mexico, Central America, and the Caribbean since the 1990s was mainly directed at export platforms supplying the North American market. Export processing zones and other tax incentives stimulated the establishment of these export platforms in these countries in the context of NAFTA and other preferential trade agreements. Since 2001, changes in these agreements and the entrance of China into the WTO and its growth as a world supplier of low cost goods has created new challenges for Mexico, Central America, and the Caribbean—namely to find competitive advantages that go beyond cost, and to diversify markets. This has led to a restructuring of certain industries as well as a shift to export services (ECLAC 2009). The downturn of the North American economy starting in 2008 exposed the vulnerability of industries dedicated to feeding that market.

Generally, efficiency-seeking FDI has generated export earnings and has enabled the development of different industrial sectors in this subregion. However, competitiveness based on low cost and preferential trade agreements has limited much of the industry to assembly operations or to low-technology industries, dedicated almost exclusively to the North American market. This explains the fact that, while FDI flows to South America remained buoyant in 2008, in Mexico, Central America, and the Caribbean they fell substantially. The automobile industry in Mexico, the apparel industry in Central America and the Caribbean, and the ICT hardware cluster in Costa Rica illustrate the impacts of this type of investment in Latin America and the Caribbean.

18.2.6.1 *The automobile industry in Mexico*

The automobile industry was one of the principal sectors that motivated the negotiation of NAFTA. As of the 1990s FDI, mainly by US TNCs, converted an uncompetitive industry focused on the national market into a competitive export platform (two-thirds of production or more) aimed at the North American one. Although the industry generated strong increases in export earnings, much like the South American experience, it did not substantially transform Mexican industry due to the nature of the production process. Linkages between TNCs and local suppliers were weak due to the dependence of the assembly operations on imported components. Moreover, while US auto TNCs quickly set up operations in Mexico, the industry leaders from Japan (Toyota, Honda) and Korea (Hyundai) set up their new operations for the North American market in the US and Canada, and the country had difficulty jumping from assembly based on imported parts to the creation of a manufacturing center. This made the multiplier effect of FDI on the value added in the Mexican automotive industry small compared to what it represented in terms of exports. Weaknesses in the supplier base also kept Mexico from significantly increasing its share in markets outside North America, since to take advantage of other free trade agreements Mexico had signed, it would have to significantly increase the Mexican content of vehicles and auto parts and rely less on imports from the United States and Canada. Positive spillovers in Mexico have been identified between TNCs and local firms, but the effect is not generalized. Rather, it depended on the technological capacities of the local firms to absorb technology, operate it, and improve it (Mortimore and Barron 2005; Dussel Peters et al. 2007).

18.2.6.2 *The apparel industry in Central America and the Caribbean*

Particularly since the 1980s, the apparel industry has been the focus of FDI attraction policy in Central America and the Caribbean. Several export-processing zones (EPZs) were established specializing in apparel for the US market, benefiting from special access mechanisms and from the Multifiber Agreement and the Agreement on Textiles and Clothing, and later benefiting from the Caribbean Basin Trade Partnership Act. Large US apparel companies and smaller companies functioning as outsourcers established plants in these countries. Differently from Asia, however, where mostly indigenous firms gradually emerged through industrial and technological upgrading, the model in Central America and the Caribbean was bound by the production-sharing mechanism with the United States which locked these countries into assembly operations based on higher-cost US inputs, and even the relatively lower wages in those countries could not make those goods competitive in other markets. This led to what has been defined as illusory competitiveness, i.e. increased export values and rising import market shares but whose impact on the host economy was weak due to the focus on static advantages, the truncation of productive linkages, and the high dependence on imported inputs (Mortimore 2003). The tax revenue benefit of EPZs was minimized through competition between countries to attract these foreign investments. Finally, the Central American and Caribbean model lost some relative advantages to Mexico with NAFTA, and to Asia (and particularly China) with the end of the GATT/WTO Agreement on Textiles and Clothing (Mortimore 2008). While the CAFTA-DR integration scheme provided a boost to the apparel industry (encouraging FDI from third countries to take advantage of market access), it did not resolve the problems of the superior competitiveness associated with global vertical integration in the textile-clothing chain (Padilla et al. 2008).

18.2.6.3 *Intel in Costa Rica*

The establishment of Intel in Costa Rica in the late 1990s was a success story on many levels, and is hailed as an example of a well-focused FDI targeting process (Mortimore and Vergara 2006). It signified a major step in Costa Rica's strategy of attracting FDI to upgrade into more technology-intensive activities. Indeed, the establishment of Intel led to a huge increase of the country's exports and an improvement in its composition, and led to the formation of a significant electronics cluster, which that in turn created a mass of professionals that were later employed in associated services (ECLAC 2009). However the experience is not free from the limitations of other Latin American countries with manufacturing in high-technology industries. The ICT hardware cluster is still strongly focused on Intel, and did not expand or consolidate to the extent expected considering other, especially Asian experiences. Part of the reason for this was a slowdown of the hardware industry worldwide in the years following the establishment of Intel in Costa Rica. But part of the bottleneck was found to be in the development of local suppliers and in the weakness of linkages between suppliers and foreign investors (Ciarli and Giuliani 2005; World Bank 2006).

Although market- and efficiency-seeking FDI in manufacturing are different from the point of view of corporate strategies and have had different effects on host economies, the challenges are similar in making the two types of foreign investment work towards host country industrialization, diversification, and technological upgrading. In both cases, the competitiveness and scale of local providers has generally not enabled assembly operations to evolve into manufacturing centers for the final products exported and their more technologically intensive components. In essence, Latin America has not managed to link the attraction of quality FDI directly to core developmental priorities.

18.2.7 Strategic asset-seeking investment

This fourth category is often associated with foreign investments that seek human capital and technology. Latin America has not been, up to now, an important destination in technology- or human capability-seeking investments. FDI by TNCs in ICT design houses, in mechanical industry design, engineering, and R&D facilities are increasing as some international corporations revise their geographical strategies and identify potentially competitive locations—for instance in and around Santiago, Chile, Monterrey, Mexico, and São Paulo, Brazil. There are signs that much of the innovation-related activities undertaken by TNCs are linked to the adaptation of products to the regional market rather than to innovation and technological development within globally integrated research networks. Nonetheless, when this type of activity is present, the main motivation of the foreign investment is rarely strategic-asset seeking. Mostly, companies take advantage of infrastructure and human resources placed for market- and efficiency-seeking motives, and subsequently explore their strategic advantages.

18.3 INTERNATIONALIZATION OF LATIN AMERICAN COMPANIES

In parallel to the increase of FDI flows into Latin America, particularly from 2004 onwards, there has been a boom in outward direct investment (OFDI) from the region (see Figure 18.1). This occurred in a context of rising OFDI from other emerging markets as well (UNCTAD 2006). For Latin America, the boom in commodities markets strongly influenced this trend, as did the maturing of a number of regional companies that had survived the economic and competitive challenges of the 1990s and emerged with a more global outlook, stronger managerial capacities, and better access to financial markets.

Whereas in the second half of the 1990s, Argentina and Chile were the main Latin American investors abroad, since 2002 Brazil has been the largest, followed by Mexico (see Figure 18.4). Many of the Argentine companies that internationalized during the 1990s were subsequently acquired by foreign firms, often in the context of macroeco-

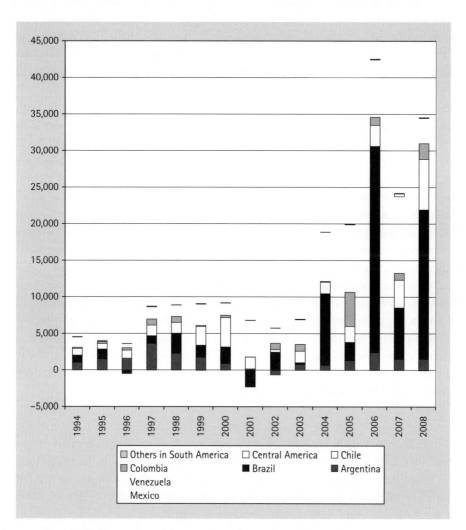

FIGURE 18.4 OFDI by investor countries, 1994–2008 (US million)

Source: Elaborated by the authors based on official figures provided by the ECLAC.

Notes: Data for Mexico between 1994 and 2000 are based on UNCTAD estimates.

nomic instability. This happened to a smaller extent with some of the Chilean outward investors, though Chilean OFDI grew in absolute values between the two periods, and has grown steadily and significantly since 2003 (ECLAC 2006; UNCTAD 2007). Brazil, on the other hand, had little outward investment in the 1990s relative to the size of its economy (Da Rocha 2003); but this began to change starting in 2002, when a number of domestic, regional and international changes (including changes in the corporate structures and ownership of some of the largest firms, opportunities in Argentina due to the 2001–2 crisis, and the commodities boom).

Latin American countries have demonstrated distinct foreign investment patterns. Although few countries publish statistics on the sectoral and country distribution of their OFDI, the contrast between Chile and Brazil illustrates the diversity of country-level internationalization patterns. In 2008, while 72% of Chilean investment abroad was directed at other Latin American countries, for Brazil this figure was only 12%, with the United States being the major recipient country. The diversity in patterns reflects the nature and OFDI motivations of the "trans-Latins" (or Latin American companies with significant investments abroad).

The largest Latin American global players are heavily concentrated in natural resources and natural resource-based manufactures, starting from a strong base in their home countries: oil and gas (PDVSA, Petrobras), mining (Vale), steel (Gerdau, Techint, CSN), cement (CEMEX), petrochemicals (Mexichem), and construction/engineering companies whose development was historically tied to these industries (Odebrecht, Camargo Correa, Impsa). The exception that confirms the rule is Brazilian airplane manufacturer Embraer. For the most part, the internationalization strategies of these companies (originating mainly in Argentina, Brazil, Mexico, and Venezuela) were geared to complementing the domestic resource base and ensuring markets for further growth. The fact that these companies were global providers of natural resource-based products, and that they went in search of resources where resources were known to exist, explains why their internationalization was not limited to Latin America, and did not follow a gradual expansion pattern. PDVSA and Vale invested in processing facilities in Europe and the United States to ensure refining and marketing of the oil and minerals, respectively, extracted in their home countries, Petrobras, which at the time had relatively small volumes of reserves in Brazil, invested in exploration outside the region to secure those resources.

Starting in 2004, a new phase of internationalization led to foreign investments at unprecedented levels by the large global players. The acquisition of Canadian nickel producer Inco by Vale in 2006 for over $16 billion, and of Australian cement producer Rinker by CEMEX in 2007 for over $14 billion, provide an idea of the magnitude of these investments. Having become international players, these companies needed to consolidate themselves as global players by aggressively expanding their international footprint. Among other motivations, by acquiring significant assets in developed markets, companies aimed to reduce the impact of country risk on their cost of capital. They also sought a balance between high-growth, high-risk and low-growth, low-risk markets. Vale was a leading iron ore producer and exporter, but to jump to the top ranks of global mining companies it needed to diversify in terms of the geographical position of its assets and in terms of its range of products. CEMEX, which has the largest share of assets, sales, and employment outside its home country among the trans-Latins (UNCTAD 2008) internationalized through FDI earlier and to a larger extent than the other large global players because of the nature of its product, which required local presence. CEMEX then took its global operations to a new scale, first with the acquisition of RMC, then with that of Rinker, also as a means to manage risk by balancing out markets with high risk and high profit margins (developing country markets) with less profitable but more stable markets operating in hard currency (developed country ones). Ironically, the US economic crisis hit CEMEX harder because of its acquisition of Rinker.

In medium-technology manufacturing industries (autoparts, white goods), production facilities were established to cater to specific transnational clients in those markets in which they had often developed long-lasting relationships in their own market. A small number of large companies in the food and beverages industry have moved beyond regional borders and been transformed into global players, either taking advantage of their knowhow on functioning in developing country settings (such as Peruvian low-cost soft drink producer Ajegroup, which has invested in Asia after conquering the Mexican market)[5] or taking regional products (such as Gruma's corn products) to global markets. Mexican bread producer Bimbo has established a leading position in the United States and other global markets. In spite of this progress, Latin American global players are still exceptions rather than the rule in consumer goods and services. In fact, some of the largest companies in these industries, such as beverage companies Bavaria (Colombia) and AmBev (Brazil), were acquired or merged into TNCs when they reached the apogee of their regional internationalization (ECLAC 2006). A different pattern has motivated the global expansion of Brazilian meat and poultry producers. These companies had competed globally through exports for a number of years before undertaking investments abroad, more significantly after 2005. The need to diversify the risk associated with phytosanitary and other trade barriers, exchange rate risk, the search for scale, and the attempt to move up the value chain led companies such as JBS Friboi, Sadia, and Perdigão (which merged in May 2009 to form Brasil Foods) to invest in the United States, Europe, Asia, Australia, and the Middle East, as well as in the Southern Cone.

Trans-Latins in the consumer goods and services industries have done well regionally. They are leading firms in telecommunications (Telmex and America Movil from Mexico), retail (Cencosud, Falabella from Chile), banking (Itaú from Brazil), fuel distribution (Terpel from Colombia, Petrobras from Brazil), food and beverages (Arcor from Argentina, Femsa from Mexico). In many cases these companies took the place of exiting TNCs, suggesting that there is value in knowhow on successfully operating in complex markets with institutional voids and macroeconomic uncertainties.

---

[5] Khanna and Palepu (2005) discuss institutional voids in developing countries as a source of advantages for firms from those countries.

18.4 Conclusions and policy implications

FDI flows to Latin America were multiplied by a factor of 10 in less than two decades; however, the quantity of inward FDI received says little about its impact on local development. The results have been mixed. TNCs have contributed to Latin American and Caribbean development by providing competitive products and services, by generating local competition and demonstration effects leading to improvements in the quality of goods and services provided by national companies, by creating jobs, by undertaking investment in infrastructure, and by enabling the extraction of natural resources thereby generating income for host countries. They have also helped countries diversify their industries and export structures. Despite its many benefits, FDI has been a frustration for Latin American host countries which had high expectations of FDI to solve local capital scarcity, industrial deepening, and technological upgrading. Although there are exceptions, the balance has generally not been found between the nature of regulation necessary to secure low-cost, reliable public services or sustainable extraction of natural resources with substantial feedback to local economies and communities and the TNCs' global profit-seeking goals. In manufacturing, poor absorptive capacities of local firms, and weakened national productive and innovation capacity in the context of global TNC sourcing networks, where the higher-technology functions are kept outside the region, has led to a relatively small multiplier effect of FDI and exports and weak technological externalities (Ocampo 2004; Laplane 2006).

The behavior of TNCs is the result of the combination of their legitimate profit-seeking global corporate goals and various aspects of the local institutional frameworks, including regulation and tax structures, and the innovation and technological capacity of the local industrial and entrepreneurial base. This combination has not always been pursued by government policy in Latin America and the Caribbean, which has not always succeeded in properly marrying these two elements. In short, the benefits of FDI are not automatic, and the experience of other regions, especially Asia, suggests that they depend on proactive industrial, innovation, and FDI-related policies as well as on improvements in local technological and entrepreneurial capacity (Narula and Lall 2006).

As regards OFDI, to the extent that many of the region's leading companies have moved towards world-class management and financial capacities, they can now take advantage of opportunities on an international—and no longer just national or even regional—basis. While hosting the headquarters of these emerging multinationals can have a number of advantages, the phenomenon also presents challenges for home countries which must now work not only on maintaining a competitive business environment to attract foreign capital but also on maximizing (in quantity but particularly in quality) the national component of its locally based companies' investment plans.

Latin America's experience with FDI and OFDI shows that neither is good or bad *per se*. Apart from extraordinary coincidences, there is no mechanism that will ensure that corporate and government goals and expectations will necessarily coincide with TNC strategic plans. TNCs and trans-Latins are profit-oriented commercial organizations that will act to maximize their interests within given regulatory and business settings. For TNCs to contribute to policy goals in fostering quality jobs and local technological development, developing natural resource industries, providing public services, building infrastructure, or upgrading the local industrial fabric, conditions have to be in place not only to attract FDI but to gear TNCs toward those goals. Likewise, for OFDI to contribute to local productive development, policies may be necessary to strengthen home country competitiveness in strategic operations and to take advantage of opportunities in regional and global markets, when these opportunities contribute to the achievement of well defined policy goals.

More than ever, FDI policy has to be integrated into broader policies for industrial restructuring and development and for technological upgrading. The Asian experience, while not always an appropriate comparison, is at least instructive in that active industrial and technology policies have been successfully used to develop locational advantages, and FDI policies have been used to channel foreign investments towards national priorities. The challenge ahead lies in fostering incentive and regulatory schemes adequate to increase the technology content of activities carried out by foreign affiliates, integrating operations between foreign affiliates and local firms and institutions, and eventually developing world-class TNCs of their own in industries that have enabled OFDI to feed positively back into local economies in an unambiguous manner.

REFERENCES

AMMAN, E., and BAER, W. (2002). 'Neoliberalism and its Consequences in Brazil', *Journal of Latin American Studies* 34.4.

ARAUJO, R. D. DE (2004). 'Desenvolvimento inovador brasileiro e comportamento tecnologico das firmas domesticas e transnacionais no final da decada de 90', master's thesis, Instituto de Economia, Universidade Estadual de Campinas.

BAER, W. (2008). *The Brazilian Economy: Growth and Development*, 6th edn, Boulder, Colo.: Rienner.

BEHRMAN, J. N. (1972). *The Role of International Companies in Latin America: Autos and Petrochemicals*, Lexington, MA: Lexington Books.

BIELSCHOWKSY, R., and STUMPO, G. (1996). 'Empresas transnacionales manufactureras en diferentes estilos de reestructuración en América Latina: los casos de Argentina, Brasil y México después de la sustitución de importaciones', in J. Katz (ed.), *Estabilización macroeconómica, reforma estructural y comportamiento industrial: estructura y funcionamiento del sector manufacturero latinoamericano en los años 90*, Buenos Aires: Alianza.

CAMPODÓNICO, H. (2004). 'Reformas e inversión en la industria de hidrocarburos de América Latina', Serie Recursos Naturales e Infraestructura No. 78, ECLAC, Santiago, Chile.

CARDOSO, F. H. (1973). 'Associated Dependent Development: Theoretical and Practical Implications', in A. Stepan (ed.), *Authoritarian Brazil: Origins, Policies and Future*, New Haven, Conn.: Yale University Press.

—— and FALETTO, E. (1971). *Dependencia y desarrollo en América Latina*, Mexico: Siglo XXI.

CHONG, A., and LORA, E. (2007). '¿Valieron a pena las privatizaciones?', *Nueva sociedad* 207.

CIARLI, T., and GIULIANI, E. (2005). 'Inversión extranjera directa y encadenamientos productivos en Costa Rica', in M. Cimoli (ed.), *Heterogeneidad estructural, asimetrías tecnológicas y crecimiento en América Latina*, Santiago, Chile: CEPAL-BID.

DA ROCHA, A. (ed.) (2003). 'Por que as empresas brasileiras não se internacionalizam?', in *As novas fronteiras: a multinacionalização das empresas Brasileiras*, Rio de Janeiro: Coppead/UFRJ.

DE ARAUJO, R. D. (2004). 'Desenvolvimento inovador brasileiro e comportamento tecnologico das firmas domesticas e transnacionais no final da decada de 90', master's thesis, Instituto de Economia, Universidade Estadual de Campinas.

DE LACERDA, A. C. (2004). *Globalização e investimento estrangeiro no Brasil*, São Paulo: Saraiva.

DUNNING, J. (ed.) (1993). 'Introduction: The Nature of Transnational Corporations and Their Activities', in *The Theory of Transnational Corporations*, London: Routledge.

—— and LUNDAN, S. (2008). *Multinational Enterprises and the Global Economy*, 2nd edn, Cheltenham: Elgar.

DUSSEL PETERS, E., GALINDO PALIZA, L. M., LORÍA, E., and MORTIMORE, M. (2007). *La inversión extranjera directa en México: desempeño y potencial—una perspectiva macro, meso, micro y territorial*, Mexico: Siglo XXI.

ECLAC (UN Economic Commission for Latin America and the Caribbean) (2005). *Foreign Investment in Latin America and the Caribbean 2004*, Santiago, Chile.

—— (2006). *Foreign Investment in Latin America and the Caribbean 2005*, Santiago, Chile.

—— (2007). *Foreign Investment in Latin America and the Caribbean 2006*, Santiago, Chile.

—— (2008). *Foreign Investment in Latin America and the Caribbean 2007*, Santiago, Chile.

—— (2009). *Foreign Investment in Latin America and the Caribbean 2008*, Santiago, Chile.

EVANS, P. (1979). *Dependent Development: The Alliance of Multinational, State, and Local Capital in Brazil*, Princeton, NJ: Princeton University Press.

FAJNZYLBER, F. (1975). 'Las empresas transnacionales', in *Expansión a nivel mundial y proyección en la industria mexicana*, Mexico: Fondo de Cultura Económica; reprinted in M. Torres Olivos (ed.), *Fernando Fajnzylber: una vision renovadora del desarrollo en América Latina*, Santiago, Chile: ECLAC/INTAL/IDB, 2006.

—— (2006). 'Las empresas transnacionales: expansión a nivel mundial y proyección en la industria mexicana', in M. Torres Olivos (ed.), *Fernando Fajnzylber: una vision renovadora del desarrollo en América Latina*, Santiago, Chile: ECLAC.

FERRAZ, J. C., and TAVARES, M. (2007) 'Translatinas: quem são, por onde avançam e que desafios enfrentam', in A. Fleury and M. T. Leme Fleury (eds), *Internacionalização e os países emergentes*, São Paulo: Editora Atlas.

—— KUPFER, D., and IOOTTY, M. (2004). 'Industrial Competitiveness in Brazil Ten Years after Economic Liberalization', *CEPAL Review* 82.

GONÇALVES, J. E. P. (2005). 'Empresas estrangeiras e transbordamentos de produtividade na indústria Brasileira: 1997–2000', 27° Prêmio BNDES de Economia, Rio de Janeiro.

GORDON, T., and WEBBER, J. (2008). 'Imperialism and Resistance: Canadian Mining Companies in Latin America', *Third World Quarterly* 29.1.

HIRATUKA, C. (2008). 'Foreign Direct Investment and Transnational Corporations in Brazil: Recent Trends and Impacts on Economic Development', Discussion Paper No. 10, Working Group on Development and Environment in the Americas, Medford, Mass.

—— and DE NEGRI, F. (2004). 'The Influence of Capital on Brazilian Foreign Trade Patterns', *CEPAL Review* 82.

HIRSCHMAN, A. (1969). 'How to Divest in Latin America and Why', *Essays in International Finance* 76.

JENKINS, R. (1991). 'The Political Economy of Industrialization', *Development and Change* 22.2.

KERNER, D. (2003). 'ECLAC, Transnational Corporations and the Quest for a Latin American Development Strategy', *CEPAL Review* 79.

KHANNA, T., and PALEPU, K. (2005). 'Emerging Giants: Building World-Class Companies in Emerging Markets', Harvard Business School Note No. 9-703-431, Cambridge, Mass.

LACERDA, A. C. DE (2004). *Globali zação e investemento estrangeiro no Brasil*, São Paulo: Saraiva.

LAPLANE, M. (2006). 'Transbordamentos de empresas transnacionais no Mercosul: evidências da indústria na Argentina, no Brasil e no Uruguai', in M. Laplane (ed.), *El desarrollo industrial del Mercosur ¿Qué impacto han tenido las empresas extranjeras?* Buenos Aires: Red de Investigaciones Económicas del Mercosur/Siglo XXI.

LARDÉ, J., CHAPARRO, E., and PARRA, C. (2008). 'El aporte del sector minero al desarrollo humano en Chile: el caso de la región de Antofagasta', Serie Recursos Naturales e Infraestructura No. 130, ECLAC, Santiago, Chile.

MORTIMORE, M. (2003). *Illusory Competitiveness: The Apparel Assembly Model of the Caribbean Basin*, Santiago, Chile: ECLAC.

—— (2008). 'The Transnationalization of Developing America: Trends, Challenges, and (Missed) Opportunities', in D. Sánchez-Ancochea and K. C. Shadlen (eds), *The Political Economy of Hemispheric Integration: Responding to Globalization in the Americas*, New York: Palgrave Macmillan.

—— (2009). 'Can Latin America Learn from Developing Asia's Focused FDI Policies?', *International Journal of Institutions and Economies*, Special Issue (vol. 1.1).

—— and BARRON, F. (2005). *Informe sobre la industria automotriz mexicana*, Santiago, Chile: ECLAC.

—— and STANLEY, L. (2006). 'Obsolescencia de la protección a los inversores extranjeros después de la crisis argentina', *CEPAL Review* 88.

—— and VERGARA, S. (2006). 'Targeting Winners: Can Foreign Direct Investment Policy Help Developing Countries Industrialise?', in Narula and Lall (2006).

NARULA, R., and LALL, S. (eds) (2006). *Understanding FDI-Assisted Economic Development*, London: Routledge.

OCAMPO, J. A. (2004). 'Globalisation and the Development Agenda', in J. J. Teunissen and A. Akkerman (eds), *Diversity in Development: Reconsidering the Washington Consensus*, The Hague: Fondad.

ODELL, P. R. (1968). 'The Oil Industry in Latin America', in E. Penrose (ed.), *The Large International Firm in Developing Countries: The International Petroleum Industry*, Cambridge, Mass.: MIT Press.

PADILLA, R., CORDERO, M., HERNÁNDEZ, R., and ROMERO, I. (2008). 'Evolución reciente y retos de la industria manufacturera de exportación en Centroamérica, México y la República Dominicana: una perspectiva regional y sectorial', Serie Estudios y Perspectivas No. 95, ECLAC, Santiago, Chile.

RONCALLO, A. (2006). 'Bolivia's Amayapampa and Capasirca Mines: Social Resistance and State Repression', in L. North, T. D. Clark, and V. Patroni (eds), *Community Rights and Corporate Responsibility: Canadian Mining and Oil Companies in Latin America*, Toronto: Between the Lines.

SANTILLANA SANTOS, M. (2006). 'La importancia de la actividad minera en la economía y sociedad peruana', Serie Recursos Naturales e Infraestrucutra No. 114, ECLAC, Santiago, Chile.

SAWYER, S., and GOMEZ, E. T. (2008). 'Transnational Governmentality and Resource Extraction: Indigenous Peoples, Multinational Corporations, Multilateral Institutions and the State, Identities, Conflict and Cohesion', UNRISD/IFAD Paper No. 13, Geneva and Rome.

SOLANES, M., and JOURAVLEV, A. (2007). 'Revisiting privatization, foreign investment, international arbitration, and water', Serie Recursos Naturales e Infraestructura No. 129, ECLAC, Santiago, Chile.

SUNKEL, O. (1972). 'Big Business and "Dependencia"', *Foreign Affairs* 50.

UNCTAD (UN Conference on Trade and Development) (2005). *World Investment Report 2005: Transnational Corporations and the Internationalization of R&D*, New York: United Nations.

—— (2006). *World Investment Report, 2006. FDI from Developing and Transition Economies: Implications for Development*, Geneva.

—— (2007). 'Global Players from Emerging Markets: Strengthening Enterprise Competitiveness through Outward Investment', Geneva.

—— (2008). *World Investment Report, 2008. Transnational Corporations and the Infrastructure Challenge*, Geneva.

WILLIAMSON, J. (ed.) (1990). 'What Washington Means by Policy Reform', in *Latin American Adjustment: How Much Has Happened?* Washington, DC: Institute for International Economics.

World Bank (2006). 'The Impact of Intel in Costa Rica: Nine Years after the Decision to Invest', Investing in Development Series, Washington, DC.

CHAPTER 19

CHINA AND THE FUTURE OF LATIN AMERICAN ECONOMIC DEVELOPMENT

KEVIN P. GALLAGHER AND ROBERTO PORZECANSKI

19.1 INTRODUCTION

In this chapter we analyze the extent to which China's unprecedented growth has improved the performance of the Latin American and Caribbean (LAC) economies in the period of economic boom that took place from the turn of the century until the run-up to the global financial crisis. It has been argued that China's rise has been a blessing for the region because Chinese demand boosted exports and in part caused a hike in commodities prices worldwide. Our critical examination of this research suggests otherwise. We find that the direct impact on the region's exports is much smaller than what was touted. What is more, we find that there are signs that Chinese demand is accentuating concerns about de-industrialization in the region.

The chapter is divided into three parts.

Section 19.2 analyzes the impacts of China's economic expansion on the pre-crisis commodity-driven boom in LAC. Section 19.3 examines the impact that China is having on the ability of LAC manufacturers to penetrate world manufacturing markets. And Section 19.4 summarizes our findings and outlines an agenda for policy and future research.

19.2 CHINA AND THE LATIN AMERICAN COMMODITIES BOOM

We start our analysis with a look at the extent to which Chinese demand enhanced the performance of Latin American economies. First, we calculate the fastest-growing and largest exports in LAC from the turn of the century to 2006. To approximate the extent to which China demand has propelled such exports, we then calculate the percentage of global export growth in those LAC export growth sectors that is taken by China. We then examine LAC's bilateral trade with China, analyzing the total amount and sectoral composition of such trade, and the major LAC countries involved in China–LAC trade. We find that China had a significant direct and indirect impact on LAC exports, but only in a handful of countries and sectors.

More specifically, we find that:

- for almost all of LAC's top commodities exports, China was responsible for a large part of global demand and affected price increases and exports for LAC; yet,
- 74% of all LAC exports to China were in primary commodities;
- Growth in LAC exports to China has been only 8% of all LAC export growth since the boom began in 2000;
- 10 sectors in 6 countries accounted for 74% of all LAC exports to China and 91% of all commodities exports to China;
- for the other LAC countries, the potential to trade with China was very low.

In sum, we find that China had a relatively small impact on trade in the region except in a small handful of countries and sectors. Moreover, as of 2009 and in the wake of the financial and economic crisis that started in 2008, the prices of most of those sectors declined.

For the majority of the calculations in this chapter, we use trade data from the United Nations Statistics Division's "Commodity Trade Statistics Database" (COMTRADE). We download data at the three-digit level (SITC Rev. 2) and classify it using Sanjaya Lall's "Technological Classification of Exports" (Lall 2000).

Before the crisis, Latin American growth was being fueled by a commodities export boom. On average, per capita GDP growth in LAC increased by more than 3.2% per annum for a total of 19% in real terms between 2000 and 2006. Exports grew almost 12% each year, and total export growth during the period was almost 90%, with commodities accounting for 70% of that export growth.

World exports to China increased tenfold in real terms from 1985 to 2006, starting at $34 billion and reaching $384 billion by 2006. One of the most marked changes, especially over the last decade, is the fact that developing countries became a significant factor in China trade. Developing countries accounted for only 14.3% of the $83 billion of global exports to China in 1995, but by 2006 were supplying China with 50.3% of China's $384 billion of imports. Whereas the developed world was once the chief exporter to China (85% in 1995), developed countries now supply just under half of all exports to China.

Developing countries have become, in turn, the largest commodity exporters to China, increasing their share from only 31.4% in 1995 to 61.2% in 2006. The majority of that change was captured by countries in the former Soviet nations (FS) (14.4 percentage point change, PPC), Sub Saharan Africa (SSA) (5.9 PPC), Latin America and the Caribbean (LAC) (5.6 PPC), and South Asia (SA) (4.9 PPC). East Asia and the Pacific

(EAP) continued to concentrate over 40% of all commodities exports to China. In the most recent period, between 2000 and 2006, LAC has captured the majority of gains.

China's unprecedented economic growth and its entry into the World Trade Organization (WTO) in 2001 have had direct and indirect effects on LAC's export and growth performance. Direct effects result from bilateral LAC–China trade. Indirect effects result from China's overall demand for LAC's top products and the extent to which that demand drove up prices for those products. We address each in turn.

19.2.1 Direct effects

Figure 19.1 exhibits LAC exports to China from 1985 to 2006. Between 2000 and 2006 LAC exports to China grew by 370%, dwarfing the overall LAC export growth of 62.5% during the period. This fact and figure have fueled the optimism described earlier in the literature, but is often not discussed in its full context. However, in 2006 exports to China were only 3.8% of all LAC exports. In turn, LAC's exports to China accounted for 5.8% of Chinese imports, the same level of LAC exports to China in the 1980s. Seventy-four percent of all LAC exports to China were in primary commodities. Finally, growth in LAC exports to China has been only 8% of all LAC export growth since the boom began in 2000.

There is no doubt that China had a positive effect on LAC export growth during the boom. In terms of bilateral trade, however, the fanfare should be tempered. The large increase in LAC exports to China barely held ground in terms of total Chinese import

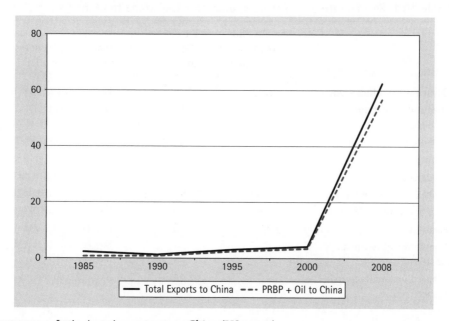

FIGURE 19.1 Latin American exports to China (US$ 2005)

Source: Authors' calculations, based on United Nations Statistics Division (2009).

shares, and trade to China represented a relatively small amount of total LAC exports. In addition, as we shall now see, only a small handful of countries and sectors accounted for almost all of the LAC export surge to China.

The benefits of LAC–China trade were highly concentrated in a few countries and sectors. Previous calculations by the authors showed that in 2006 just ten sectors in six countries accounted for 74% of all LAC exports to China and 91% of all commodity exports to China. Indeed, the top five sectors (ores and concentrates of base metals, largely copper ores; soybeans, iron, crude petroleum, and copper alloys) were 60% of all exports to China and 75% of commodities exports to China (Gallagher and Porzecanski 2010). As shown in Table 19.1, these trends accentuated through 2008. By 2008, these 10 sectors constituted 95% of all primary commodities (PRBP) exports to China, and 86% of all exports to China.

The third column of Table 19.1 shows the percentage of total LAC exports to China in a particular commodity from a particular country—for 2008. Looking at the first line, then, for soybeans, Brazil (59%) and Argentina (40%) account for 99% of all LAC soybean exports to China.

In 2006, a mere handful of countries accounted for LAC exports to China in these ten commodities. By 2008, as shown in Table 19.1, these trends had accentuated.

Four of the countries, Argentina, Brazil, Chile, and Peru, showed up as the dominant exporters to China. Mexico and Colombia accounted for the majority of exports of non-ferrous metal waste and scrap metal, but did not make a significant contribution to China exports in any other sector. Other research has compared the export basked of

Table 19.1 Five countries, ten sectors, dominate LAC trade to China (%)

Sector	Share of PRBP exports to China (2008)	Share of total LAC exports to China	Country (2008) (China share in total country exports in sector)
Soybeans and other seeds	24.4	22.0	Brazil (59), Argentina (40)
Ores and concentrates of base metals	16.3	14.7	Chile (49), Peru (38)
Iron ore and concentrates	15.3	13.8	Brazil (87), Peru (5)
Copper alloys	14.2	12.8	Chile (96)
Crude petroleum	7.9	7.2	Brazil (58), Argentina (25)
Soybean oil and other oils	6.5	5.8	Argentina (62), Brazil (35)
Pulp and waste paper	4.0	3.6	Chile (51), Brazil (47)
Feedstuff	2.8	2.5	Peru (72), Chile (24)
Non-ferrous base metal waste and scrap	2.3	2.1	Mexico (43), Chile (33)
Tobacco unmanufactured; tobacco refuse	1.1	1.0	Brazil (92), Argentina (8)
Total	94.9	85.6	

Source: Authors' calculations, based on United Nations Statistics Division (2009).

various LAC countries with the import potential of China, and found that for countries and sectors other than those on this list the potential to trade with China in the future is very low (Blázquez-Lidoy, Rodríguez, and Santiso 2006).

Finally, for the four major countries and sectors, we calculate in Table 19.2 the ratio of China exports in a sector to a country's total exports in that sector. For some sectors China exports were a very large part of a country's total exports in a sector and a large percentage of total LAC exports in that sector.

What stands out most is that 75% of all soybeans exported from Argentina were destined for China, and that 48% of all soybeans exported from Brazil went to China as well. 30% of all Brazil's iron exports went to China.

19.2.2 Indirect effects

Indirectly, during the boom increases in Chinese demand tightened supplies and raised global prices for many commodities, leading to a rise in exports. This drove

Table 19.2 Share of Chinese exports in selected countries and sectors, 2008

Country and sector	Exports to China in sector (US$ 2005)	Total country exports in sector (%)
Argentina		
Crude petroleum	656,569,941	43
Soybeans and other seeds	3,275,256,691	75
Soybean oil and other oils	1,333,737,904	22
Brazil		
Soybeans and other seeds	4,831,263,424	48
Iron ore and concentrates	4,433,865,636	30
Crude petroleum	1,544,880,273	12
Pulp and waste paper	626,789,897	18
Tobacco unmanufactured; tobacco refuse	333,316,952	14
Chile		
Ores and concentrates of base metals	2,668,990,686	19
Copper alloys	4,477,391,748	21
Pulp and waste paper	674,451,270	28
Non-ferrous base metal waste and scrap	260,112,161	44
Peru		
Ores and concentrates of base metals	2,093,555,535	29
Feedstuff	672,012,544	49

Source: Authors' calculations, based on United Nations Statistics Division (2009).

Table 19.3 Latin America's top commodity exports in context

Sector	2000 ($US 2005)	2006 ($US 2005)	2000–6 growth (%)	Chinese import growth/total world export growth (%)
Crude oil	48,987,186,770	112,575,599,155	129.8	5.5
Base metals	7,211,709,637	26,183,980,627	263.1	19.7
Copper	7,628,915,967	25,749,477,183	237.5	10.8
Refined Petroleum	16,620,782,467	18,806,398,334	13.1	5.2
Meat	3,535,083,967	11,070,973,817	213.2	−1.6
Iron ore and concentrates	3,811,562,912	9,425,950,165	147.3	54.8
Feedstuff	6,413,819,994	9,414,473,361	46.8	2.6
Fruit and nuts	6,609,994,529	9,214,179,325	39.4	0.1
Sugar and honey	3,293,727,533	8,358,410,784	153.8	1.8
Soybeans	4,155,155,048	8,209,199,475	97.6	57.8
Natural gas	1,422,921,528	8,053,331,973	466.0	1.8
Coffee and coffee substitutes	6,320,846,594	7,400,327,391	17.1	1.5
Oils, crude or refined	2,413,049,966	5,123,976,205	112.3	8.4
Aluminum	3,211,590,964	4,533,157,750	41.1	1.4
Fresh vegetables	3,322,155,825	4,531,071,548	36.4	4.2
Alcoholic beverages	2,757,791,184	4,188,139,047	51.9	2.5
Fish, fresh, chilled, or frozen	2,551,440,823	3,982,054,605	56.1	9.3
Pulp and waste paper	3,325,463,834	3,915,651,191	17.7	118.9
Average	7,421,844,419	15,596,463,996	110	17

Source: Authors' calculations, based on United Nations Statistics Division (2010)

up prices and increased overall demand for LAC goods (IMF 2008; World Bank 2009).

Table 19.3 lists LAC's top 17 commodity exports by their total exports (in dollars) through 2006, leading right up to the initial year of the financial crisis. These top exports were just shy of half of all LAC's exports during the period, and grew on average 110% over the period. Far and away the largest export was crude oil, which alone accounted for more than 18% of all LAC's exports.

The last column in Table 19.3 shows the share of Chinese import growth as a percentage of world export growth in a particular sector. For instance, Chinese imports accounted for 5.5% of the growth in crude petroleum exports between 2000 and 2006. In many sectors, Chinese demand accounted for well over 10% of total world export growth during the period, and on average it accounted for 17% of the rise in demand for

LAC's top exports. Base metals, copper, iron ore, soy, and pulp and paper are all high-lighted in bold because they are the core LAC exports to China that are discussed above. Chinese demand for global exports in these products was quite high, with 54.8% of the increase in world iron ore exports going to China, 57.8% of all soybeans, and more than 118.9% of pulp and paper.[1] In other words, indirectly through demand and subsequent price increases, China was indirectly responsible for much of Latin America's commodity export boom.

The analysis conducted in this part of the chapter has shown that China had and is probably still having a significant impact on LAC, but not necessarily in the ways portrayed by some. Many countries simply do not export the goods that China impacted directly through demand and price increases or through bilateral trade. In addition, we find that only ten sectors in six countries accounted for the majority of China–LAC trade during the boom. For those countries and sectors that were "winners," China both propped up world prices and accounted for a large part of the export increase in those countries. The boom came to a stop in 2008, but revived in 2009. Thus it is worth analyzing whether despite its obvious benefits, the boom also posed a development challenge to Latin America. To this question we now turn.

19.2.3 The future of Chinese demand and high commodity prices

These findings raise a number of concerns regarding China's impact in Latin America that run counter to the more euphoric tone about the LAC–China relationship that could be found in the popular press and some of the literature during the boom. Three key questions of concern need to be addressed by researchers and policymakers. For the small handful of LAC countries that are benefiting from China trade, how long can LAC depend on increasing Chinese demand for LAC commodities; similarly, to what extent—in the long term—will prices for such commodities remain high?

There are grounds for optimism. Estimates conducted before the outset of the financial crisis concluded that for the most important export sectors to China, Chinese demand would continue its rise for some time to come. Before the financial crisis hit, economic growth in China was expected to continue its unprecedented expansion for at least another decade. Estimates of Chinese economic growth have been corrected downward in light of the economic crisis, but they remain positive nonetheless. High prices for commodities are another matter however. Most forecasts estimate that the recent commodity boom was fairly unique and may last longer than those in the past—but not forever. Such projections, however, are pre-crisis, and in 2008 prices begun to push

---

[1] The reason why this percentage can exceed 100 is that Table 19.3 actually divides the *change* in Chinese import demand by the *change* in world exports. Even though Chinese imports could never exceed world exports, in some cases the growth in Chinese imports exceeds the growth in world exports, as a result of a reduction of imports in other markets.

downward (IMF 2008). However, it is important to point out that, although the historical trend for the price of foodstuff commodities is downwards (the same is true for minerals, albeit to a much lesser degree), in the immediate aftermath of the crisis some prices have begun to move up again. The future with respect to commodity prices, in other words, remains uncertain.

Forecasting future Chinese growth has become a small industry, but most conservative forecasts put annual growth rates for China between 7.1% and 8.6% to 2020 (Jianwu, Li, and Polaski 2007). In 2006 Deutsche Bank Research put together estimates of future Chinese demand in key commodities from Africa and South America. Deutsche Bank projections increased demand for all of the important sectors analyzed in the previous section (Deutsche Bank Research 2006).

Chinese growth may continue for the foreseeable future, but high prices for commodities in general may not. The International Monetary Fund (IMF) reminds us that although the prices for commodities are currently high they remain below their historical levels, are highly volatile, and over the long term are predicted to continue their downward trend. Since 1957 commodity prices have fallen relative to consumer prices at a rate of about 1.6% annually. However, volatility is more the norm than price decline— one standard deviation of annual price changes is close to 11%, compared to the 1.6% annual decline. The IMF attributes such falls to the productivity gains in agricultural and metals parts of the economy relative to others (IMF 2006). However, it should be noted that mineral prices are still very high by historical standards. And, in the long term, real mineral prices do not seem to show a downward trend, while agricultural prices do (Ocampo and Parra 2010).

The long-term deterioration of the terms of trade for commodities has been thoroughly documented for a longer period of time (see Ocampo and Parra 2003 for an analysis for the whole 20th century) and has been a core concern for long-term development in Latin America since the formulation of the Prebisch–Singer hypothesis (Prebisch 1951).

However, it is quite clear that both commodity prices and the terms of trade for Latin America increased from 2003 until before the crisis. The IMF and the World Bank acknowledge that the recent boom was one of the longest and largest in recorded history (IMF 2008; World Bank 2009). For the average country the boom lasted over four years and caused an improvement in the terms of trade by 9%, while past booms lasted on average two years and changed terms of trade by 3% (IMF 2008). Before the crisis, some analysts forecasted price increases through 2015. The International Food Policy Research Institute predicted that soy and soy oils would see significant increases until that year (International Food Policy Research Institute 2008).

What remains to be seen is how long the increase in commodity prices and the resulting improvement of terms of trade will actually last, and whether these improvements will reverse the downward trend observed since the beginning of the 20th century (Ocampo and Parra 2003). In fact, while the small range of estimates available disagree regarding how long price increases will last, even before the crisis there was consensus over the fact that they would eventually decline and that the commodity boom would not put LAC on the verge of long-term economic growth with current account surpluses (IMF 2006; Ocampo 2007). Moreover, despite the long-term trends, post-crisis estimates have begun to show a downward trend in 2009.

19.3 TAKING AWAY THE LADDER? CHINA AND THE COMPETITIVENESS OF LATIN AMERICAN MANUFACTURING

Another crucial issue is the extent to which LAC is competing with China in world and regional manufacturing markets. Based on measures of export similarity and market share, only a handful of countries presently compete with China: Argentina, Brazil, Chile, Colombia, Costa Rica, and Mexico. We calculate the extent to which manufactures exports in these countries are 'threatened" by China's rise. Astonishingly, we find that 94% of LAC's manufactures are threatened by China, representing 40% of all LAC exports. LAC manufactures are still growing, but at a slower pace and in sectors where China is rapidly increasing its global market share.

The analysis below first charts the growth of Chinese manufacturing with respect to world manufactures. It then outlines two complementary methodological approaches used to analyze the relative competitiveness among nations and the specific literature on China. This serves to discuss the relative competitiveness of China and LAC's export manufacturing in world markets. We finally look at the impact of China on regional and home LAC markets.

19.3.1 The growth of China and LAC manufacturing exports

Over the past 25 years there has been significant growth in the world economy, and that growth has been propelled by a surge in global manufacturing exports. The experiences of China and LAC did not deviate from that trend. Indeed they manifest it, and China's growth has been nothing short of extraordinary.

The right-hand scale of Figure 19.2 sets out the steep increase in world manufacturing exports from 1985 to 2006. The left-hand scale juxtaposes the experiences of China and LAC.

While in 1985 the size of the global manufacturing export market was approximately $952 billion, in 2006 the market grew to more than $7 trillion—a 674% increase. Within that growing market, both Chinese and Latin American manufacturing exports also grew significantly, albeit in a completely different order of magnitude. In terms of volume, Chinese manufacturing exports grew even faster than world manufactures exports, by a factor of 24 between 1985 and 2006. LAC exports also bucked the global trend by increasing by a factor of 13. Part of this difference, of course, is explained by the fact that

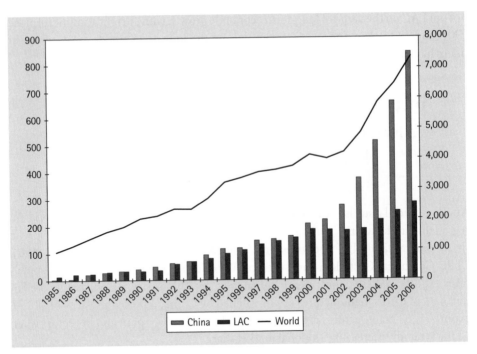

FIGURE 19.2 Manufacturing exports (current $ billion)

Source: Authors' calculations, based on United Nations Statistics Division (2009).

in 1985 Latin American manufacturing exports were significantly higher than Chinese exports. In 1985 Latin America exported more than $22 billion, but China only exported around $3.5 billion.

Between 2000 and 2006, among all developing countries it was China that captured the greatest share of world growth in manufacturing during the period. As Figure 19.3 shows, as a region, the EU 15 captured the greatest share of the growth with 33% (of which 14.02 percentage points is growth captured by Germany). China captured 19.7% of the more than $7 trillion in growth in manufacturing exports between 2000 and 2006. It was the largest growth captured by a single country, and represented more than all the growth captured by East Asia and the Pacific (including Japan), which captured 15.01%. The United States captured 4.76%. Latin America, as a whole, captured 3.02% of the growth, of which half was captured by Mexico (1.5%), while Brazil captured almost 1%.

China's unprecedented manufacturing expansion put it among world leaders in terms of export-led industrialization. In 1985, Chinese manufactures exports represented barely over 10% of total exports as the world average hovered just below 60%. By 2006 China's share became the largest in the world, just short of 90%. The world average is now around 63%. Mexico is the only nation in LAC at a similar level to China, and has itself had a fairly spectacular move from 40% to 72%. Interestingly, both China and Mexico now enjoy similar shares of manufacturing in total exports to export powerhouse Germany. The nature of these manufactures is very different in China and Mexico. China's level of value

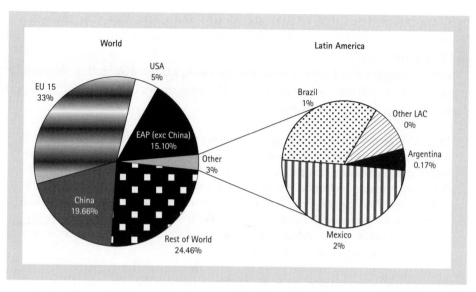

FIGURE 19.3 Share of total manufacturing export growth, 2000–6

Source: Authors' calculations, based on United Nations Statistics Division (2009).

added and technological sophistication is increasing rapidly, whereas Mexico is stagnating at relatively low levels. In Germany of course, the level of manufactures is a very high level of value-added production (Gallagher and Porzecanski 2010).

19.3.2 Estimating the competitiveness of LAC exports with China: previous work

China's impact on Latin American export competiveness is the subject of a burgeoning literature. Most early studies compared the export profiles of China and LAC's manufacturing to estimate the extent to which LAC might be threatened by China. With the exception of Mexico and some Central American countries, the majority of these studies took a rather optimistic view about the relative competitiveness of China and LAC in manufacturing. The nations of South America, it was held, exported a significantly different basket of goods to the world relative to China. Therefore the exports of China and LAC could be seen as complimentary rather than rival. However, more recent studies that use this approach have come to different conclusions.

The comparison of export structures entails examining "the statistical correlation between the export structures of China and LAC (higher correlation indicates greater potential for competition and rising correlations over time suggest that the potential is growing)" (Lall and Weiss 2005: 169). Lall and Weiss compare the export structures of countries in LAC with that of China. The only two countries whose export structure significantly correlates with China's are Mexico and Costa Rica (correlations are, respectively, 0.470 and 0.274.) All other countries' correlations are 0.068 or less (Lall and Weiss 2005: 187).

Again, comparisons of export structure are based on the assumption that similar export structures will suggest highest potential for competition. An earlier OECD report depicts the earlier consensus on this issue:

> In general terms, the results suggest that there is no trade competition between China and Latin America...[Moreover] this trade competition is even decreasing rather than increasing over the recent period of time. Not surprisingly, countries that export mainly commodities face lower competition...Paraguay, Venezuela, Bolivia, and Panama are those that exhibit the lowest figures among 34 selected economies, i.e. those are the countries that suffer less from Chinese trade competition. Brazil could be considered as an intermediate case between Mexico and Venezuela. (Blázquez-Lidoy et al. 2006)

However, a more recent IDB study was the first to predict that the export structures of China and LAC may run into each other at some point. The IDB found that over time the two areas' export profiles were beginning to converge and therefore fierce competition could ensue in the future: "As China and Latin America—and Mexico in particular—have converged toward increasingly similar export baskets, especially in manufacturing industries, direct competition has intensified" (Devlin, Estevadeordal, and Rodriguez-Clare 2006)

Recent work compiled by the World Bank suggests that the IDB's predictions have come true, at least for some countries. Hanson and Robertson (2009) find that in Argentina, Brazil, Chile, and Mexico (LAC's main manufactures exporters), export capabilities were strong where China's were also strong. This suggests that the majority of LAC manufactures exports could potentially be under threat from China in both world and home markets. In summary, as the decade after China's accession to the WTO went on, and empirical research followed, China's potential threat seemed to become a real one.

Most importantly, however, the approach of comparing the export profiles of China and LAC has been shown to have significant limitations. Comparing export structure has been recently criticized in the peer-reviewed literature. Jenkins (2008) has a comprehensive analysis of such methodologies. First, most analyses that compare export structures do not take into account China's accession to the WTO in 2001 nor the entrance into force of the WTO's agreement on textiles and clothing in 2005. Secondly, indexes that look at export structure normally only calculate export structure for a given year or one point in time, and therefore overlook changes in the competitive threat of a nation over time. Third, export structure indices are weighted measures of the significance of the fit between two countries' export baskets—thus the larger nation with more diversified export base will be underestimated by smaller countries.

For a more accurate picture, ample data are now available as a basis on which to examine actual levels of export penetration among China and LAC.

19.3.3 Actual impacts according to existing studies

Alternative measures have been deployed to look at actual changes in the competitiveness of China and LAC over time. Beyond merely comparing export structures, some authors have attempted to actually measure the observed impact of China's global export growth on Latin American manufacturing.

We do this in detail in the next section using Lall and Weiss's approach. Lall and Weiss look at the evolution of China and LAC export shares in both the world and US markets and look for evidence of increased Chinese competition in products that show increased penetration of Chinese exports in coincidence with decreased penetration of LAC exports.

As shown in Table 19.4, Lall and Weiss define a category in which China's market share is rising and LAC's decreasing for the US market as a category in which LAC is experiencing a "direct threat" from China. Similarly, they define a category of "partial threat" in which both China's and LAC's shares are increasing but China's share is increasing faster.

We call the difference in market shares between two periods of time the "dynamic revealed comparative position" or DRCP. We calculate market shares and DRCPs as a country's exports to the world for a given year and product divided by the sum of all the countries in the world's exports to the world for the same year and product (which we label "world exports"). In this, we depart from Lall and Weiss, as they calculate market shares in the US market and we do for the world market as a whole.

Table 19.4 Chinese export market shares

Other countries' export market shares	Rising	Falling
Rising	**A. No threat** Both countries have rising market shares and the latter is gaining more than China. **B. Partial threat** Both are gaining market share, but China is gaining faster than the other country.	**C. Reverse threat** No competitive threat from China. The threat is the reverse, from the other country to China.
Falling	**D. Direct threat** China gains market share and the other country loses; this may indicate causal connection unless the other country was losing market share in the absence of Chinese entry.	**E. Mutual withdrawal: no threat** Both parties loose market shares in export markets to other competitors.

Source: Lall and Weiss (2005).

Using their methodology, Lall and Weiss argue that "for the world market for all the LAC 18 countries [in their study], the average weighted share of 'threatened exports'—under direct plus partial threat—is surprisingly stable at 45.1% in 1990 and 39.4% in 2002." The authors also find the intensity of the Chinese threat to decrease significantly over time and find, in 2002, that only 11% of LAC exports are experiencing a "direct threat" (Lall and Weiss 2005).

Lall and Weiss, however, have not been alone in trying to analyze the observed impact of China's global export growth on Latin American manufacturing. Using a very similar methodology,[2] Mesquita Moreira finds that:

> LAC losses to China in the world markets in 1990–2004 were on the whole relatively small, reaching 1.7% of the region's total manufacturing exports in 2004 (US$5.5 billion). As expected, given the differences in factor endowments, the highest losses were in low-tech, labor-intensive goods, which responded for nearly 30% of the total losses."

However, argues Mesquita Moreira, "the losses seen in the other categories reinforce the earlier argument that LAC should be prepared to face competition from China on the whole factor-intensity spectrum, from high-tech to natural resource-based manufactured goods" (2007). Moreover, losses have been mounting in the last years of the period. In a previous version of the same paper which covered the 1990–2002 period, Mesquita Moreira (2004) had found that the equivalent of 0.7% of the region's exports was being lost to China. Adding two years to the analysis increased the figure to 1.7%.

Studies that use similar methodologies but with more recent data that reflect the post-WTO period come up with different findings than the earlier Lall and Weiss and Mesquita Moreira analyses. Jenkins (2009) deploys a "constant market share" method whereby countries gain from those nations where exports are growing more slowly, and lose to nations whose exports are growing faster. Analyzing the impact of China on LAC exports to the US, Jenkins finds that contrary to export structure analyses, only Nicaragua and Peru have not lost exports in the US to Chinese competition. Recent work by Dussel points to the grave concerns over Mexico (Dussel Peters 2005; 2007; 2008).

It must be underscored, however, that although these methods do a better job at taking a more dynamic view of relative competitiveness, they do not infer concrete evidence of causality between China's rise and LAC's corresponding decline. One study that takes a more dynamic approach and conducts statistical analyses to determine the causality between China's export expansion and Mexico's decline was conducted by World Bank economist Caroline Freund. Freund and Ozden (2009) estimate with econometric techniques whether exports from China are displacing LAC's exports. They find that China's rise has a statistically significant and negative impact on Mexico's

---

[2] Where "a market share loss for LAC (in any product or market) is understood as a reflection of the fact that its exports have grown less than world exports because its exports were (i) less dynamic than those of China and/or (ii) less dynamic than those of the rest of the world." Because he focuses on China, Mesquita Moreira's figures refer to "the losses due to (i), that is, market share losses that can be attributed directly to China, measured as a percentage of total exports in 2004" (2007).

penetration of the US market. Using data from 1985 to 2004, they also find that: "(a) China's export growth has had only small effects on overall LAC exports, (b) China's export growth is primarily affecting Mexican export growth in industrial goods in Western Hemisphere markets, and (c) China's export growth is negatively affecting LAC exports of relatively high-wage goods" (Freund and Ozden 2009: 203).

In sum, despite earlier studies to the contrary, regardless of the methodology used there is a growing concern of the extent to which China is outcompeting LAC in world markets.

19.3.4 Competition in world markets

As we have seen, in just over a quarter-century, China went from insignificance to becoming the most competitive manufactures exporter in the world. At the same time most LAC nations remained insignificant, and those that gained some ground have struggled to maintain it. Only Mexico seems to be (to some extent) holding on.

Table 19.5 ranks the most competitive manufactures nations as measured by their share of total world manufactures exports from 1980 to 2006. In terms of relative competitiveness, a quick look at the evolution of China's competitive position in comparative perspective highlights how dramatic its gains in manufacturing competitiveness have been. Chinese growth has driven China to the second position in terms of manufacturing exports (Table 19.5 also shows the evolution of manufacturing exports for the United States and Germany, the other major players in the manufacturing export market). If Hong Kong is counted (and China certainly counts it!), China has leapfrogged to become the most competitive manufacturer in the world.

Since 1980, China has steadily captured an ever-increasing share of world manufacturing exports. While in 1986 China's manufacturing exports represented only 0.4% of world manufacturing exports, by 2006 it had become second only to Germany as an exporter of manufactures, with 11.5% of world manufacturing exports. Argentina and Brazil have somewhat maintained a small share of world manufacturing exports (around 1% for Brazil, 0.2% for Argentina) but have fallen down the export ladder as other countries have gained market share. Mexico, on the other hand, succeeded in increasing its share and climbing up the export ladder (going from 0.5% of world manufacturing exports in 1990 to 3.3% in 2000). Since 2000, however, Mexico's share and position as a manufacturing exporter have begun to erode again (reaching 2.5% of world manufacturing exports in 2006.)

19.3.5 Threat analysis

How have Latin American countries fared in term of China's threat in the world, when unprotected by proximity and a web of preferential trade agreements? Not that well. Table 19.6 exhibits our calculations where we look at the percentage of all world exports

Table 19.5 China: taking away the (manufacturing) ladder? (percentage of world manufacturing exports)

1980	1985	1990	1995	2000	2006
Fmr Fed. Rep. of Germany — 17.0	Japan — 17.2	FFR Germany — 15.6	USA — 12.8	USA — 14.5	Germany — 11.8
USA — 15.4	FFR Germany — 14.8	USA — 13.0	Japan — 12.4	Japan — 10.4	**China** — 11.5
Japan — 13.8	USA — 14.2	Japan — 12.8	Germany — 12.2	Germany — 10.2	USA — 10.2
France — 8.4	France — 6.6	France — 6.9	France — 6.1	France — 5.3	Japan — 7.5
United Kingdom — 8.0	Italy — 6.4	Italy — 6.6	**China** — 5.8	**China** — 5.0	France — 4.7
Italy — 7.0	United Kingdom — 6.1	United Kingdom — 6.2	Italy — 5.2	Italy — 4.7	Italy — 4.4
Belgium, Luxembourg — 4.2	Canada — 4.5	China, Hong Kong SAR — 3.6	United Kingdom — 4.8	United Kingdom — 4.6	United Kingdom — 4.1
Netherlands — 3.6	Belgium, Luxembourg — 3.6	Belgium, Luxembourg — 3.2	China, Hong Kong SAR — 3.6	China, Hong Kong SAR — 4.5	China, Hong Kong SAR — 4.0
Canada — 2.8	Netherlands — 3.0	Netherlands — 3.0	Rep. of Korea — 3.2	Canada — 3.4	Rep. of Korea — 3.7
Switzerland — 2.5	Rep. of Korea — 2.8	Canada — 2.8	Belgium, Luxembourg — 3.0	Rep. of Korea — 3.2	Belgium — 3.2
Sweden — 2.4	China, Hong Kong SAR — 2.4	Rep. of Korea — 2.8	Canada — 2.8	**Mexico** — 3.1	Netherlands — 2.9
China, Hong Kong SAR — 2.0	Switzerland — 2.0	Switzerland — 2.2	Netherlands — 2.3	Belgium — 3.0	Singapore — 2.7
Rep. of Korea — 1.8	Sweden — 1.8	**China** — 2.1	Singapore — 2.0	Singapore — 2.9	Canada — 2.5
Austria — 1.5	Spain — 1.5	Sweden — 1.5	Switzerland — 1.9	Netherlands — 2.0	**Mexico** — 2.5
Spain — 1.5	Austria — 1.5	Spain — 1.3	Spain — 1.8	Spain — 1.9	Spain — 1.9
Poland — 1.2	Singapore — 1.2	Singapore — 1.1	**Mexico** — 1.7	Malaysia — 1.8	Switzerland — 1.6

Table 19.5 (contd.)

1980		1985		1990		1995		2000		2006	
Denmark	1.0	**Brazil**	1.0	Austria	1.0	Malaysia	1.6	Switzerland	1.6	Malaysia	1.5
Singapore	0.9	Denmark	0.9	Denmark	0.9	Sweden	0.9	Sweden	1.6	Sweden	1.4
Finland	0.7	Finland	0.7	Malaysia	0.7	Austria	0.7	Thailand	1.3	Austria	1.3
Norway	0.6	Czechoslovakia	0.7	**Brazil**	0.7	Thailand	0.7	Ireland	1.2	Thailand	1.2
Ireland	0.4	Poland	0.6	Finland	0.6	Denmark	0.7	Austria	0.8	Czech Rep.	1.0
India	0.4	Ireland	0.6	Ireland	0.6	Ireland	0.7	Philippines	0.8	Poland	1.0
Australia	0.4	Norway	0.5	Thailand	0.5	Finland	0.6	Denmark	0.7	Turkey	0.9
Portugal	0.3	Turkey	0.5	Portugal	0.5	**Brazil**	0.6	Indonesia	0.6	Ireland	0.9
S. African Customs Union	0.3	Malaysia	0.4	Czechoslovakia	0.4	Portugal	0.5	Finland	0.5	India	0.8
Malaysia	0.3	Portugal	0.4	**Mexico**	0.4	Indonesia	0.5	**Brazil**	0.5	**Brazil**	0.8
Greece	0.2	India	0.4	Fmr Yugoslavia	0.4	India	0.5	India	0.5	Hungary	0.8
Argentina	0.2	**China**	0.4	India	0.4	Czech Rep.	0.4	Hungary	0.5	Denmark	0.7
Thailand	0.2	Israel	0.3	Norway	0.3	Turkey	0.4	Czech Rep.	0.5	Finland	0.7
Philippines	0.1	Australia	0.3	Turkey	0.3	Poland	0.4	Poland	0.4	Russian Federation	0.6
New Zealand	0.1	Thailand	0.2	Poland	0.2	Australia	0.3	Turkey	0.4	Philippines	0.5
Hungary	0.1	Greece	0.2	Australia	0.2	Israel	0.3	Russian Federation	0.3	Indonesia	0.5
Saudi Arabia	0.1	Pakistan	0.2	Israel	0.2	Norway	0.3	Israel	0.3	Slovakia	0.4
Tunisia	0.1	**Argentina**	0.1	Indonesia	0.2	S. African Customs Union	0.3	Portugal	0.3	Portugal	0.4
China, Macao SAR	0.1	Venezuela	0.1	Pakistan	0.1	Hungary	0.2	Australia	0.2	Ukraine	0.3
Colombia	0.1	Philippines	0.1	Romania	0.1	Philippines	0.2	South Africa	0.2	Romania	0.3

(continued)

Table 19.5 (contd.)

1980		1985		1990		1995		2000		2006	
Bangladesh	0.1	Saudi Arabia	0.1	Greece	0.1	Pakistan	0.2	Norway	0.2	South Africa	0.3
Peru	0.1	Indonesia	0.1	Argentina	0.1	Slovenia	0.1	Slovakia	0.2	Israel	0.3
Indonesia	0.0	New Zealand	0.0	Philippines	0.1	Argentina	0.1	Ukraine	0.2	United Arab Emirates	0.3
Morocco	0.0	China, Macao SAR	0.0	Saudi Arabia	0.1	Slovakia	0.1	Pakistan	0.2	Australia	0.3
Cyprus	0.0	United Arab Emirates	0.0	United Arab Emirates	0.1	Romania	0.1	Argentina	0.2	Viet Nam	0.3
New Caledonia	0.0	Hungary	0.0	Tunisia	0.1	Greece	0.1	Romania	0.1	Norway	0.2
Kenya	0.0	Bangladesh	0.0	Morocco	0.1	Saudi Arabia	0.1	Slovenia	0.1	Saudi Arabia	0.2
Sri Lanka	0.0	Tunisia	0.0	New Zealand	0.1	Tunisia	0.1	United Arab Emirates	0.1	Slovenia	0.2
Syria	0.0	Morocco	0.0	China, Macao SAR	0.1	Croatia	0.1	Vietnam	0.1	Pakistan	0.2
Mauritius	0.0	Colombia	0.0	Venezuela	0.0	New Zealand	0.1	Luxembourg	0.1	Argentina	0.2

Source: Authors' calculations, based on United Nations Statistics Division (2009).

under threat from China by country. For LAC as a whole, we find that 62% of manufacturing exports fall under Lall's definition of a direct threat, and over 31% as a partial. Those manufacturing exports under threat represent 94% of all LAC's manufacturing exports and *40% of all LAC exports in 2006*, and add up to more than $260 billion.

For the largest manufacturers in the region, the threat level in world markets is significantly higher than the threat level in LAC markets, which we will look at in detail in the next section. Consistent with the literature on the subject, the situation for Mexico is the gravest (and thus discussed in depth in the next section). Ninety-nine percent of Mexico's manufacturing exports are under threat from China, representing 72% of Mexico's entire exports. Ninety-six percent of Costa Rica's exports are under threat, comprising 58% of all the country's exports. Brazil and Argentina also see over 90% of their manufactures exports under threat, but those exports under threat represent less than the LAC average with 39% and 27% respectively.

Though not shown in tabular form, we also looked at the composition of the top 20 Latin American manufacturing exports. Several aspects are noteworthy about these top

Table 19.6 Threatened exports to the world (%)

	Direct	Partial	Total
Argentina			
As % of manufacturing exports in 2006	37	59	96
As % of all exports in 2006	10	16	27
Brazil			
As % of manufacturing exports in 2006	20	70	91
As % of all exports in 2006	9	30	39
Chile			
As % of manufacturing exports in 2006	29	53	82
As % of all exports in 2006	2	4	5
Colombia			
As % of manufacturing exports in 2006	15	66	81
As % of all exports in 2006	5	20	25
Costa Rica			
As % of manufacturing exports in 2006	36	60	96
As % of all exports in 2006	22	36	58
Mexico			
As % of manufacturing exports in 2006	70	28	99
As % of all exports in 2006	52	21	72
LAC			
As % of manufacturing exports in 2006	62	31	94
As % of all exports in 2006	27	14	40

Source: Authors' calculations, based on United Nations Statistics Division (2009).

20 categories. First, they represent more than 60% of all Latin American manufacturing exports. Moreover, in all but two of these top 20 manufacturing exports (pig and sponge iron, spiegeleisen, etc., ferro-alloys, and polymerization and copolymerization products), Latin America is under threat from China. Of the top 20 Latin American manufacturing exports, the 18 that are under threat from China also represent more than 60% of all Latin American exports under threat. Finally, it is worth noting that for the top 20 Latin American manufacturing exports there is a heavy concentration in terms of suppliers. For most of these sectors, Mexico and Brazil are practically the only relevant players.

19.3.6 Competition in regional LAC and home markets

Relatively little attention has been given to the extent to which China is threatening the competitiveness of LAC exports in the LAC region, and even less regarding whether China is displacing LAC manufacturing firms in home markets. Initial analyses, including our own, suggest that the situation is not much better for LAC in this regard.

The relative lack of attention to these matters is a problematic oversight, though this is admittedly at least in part due to data constraints. The LAC region is an important anchor market for LAC manufacture exports. Moreover, like the world market, the LAC market has been growing as well. Between 1990 and 2006 LAC manufacturing import markets grew almost fivefold (497%, to be exact). More recently and specifically, between 2000 and 2006 the Latin American manufacturing import market grew 73%, while manufacturing imports from China grew 420%, capturing 21.5% of the total growth in Latin American manufacturing imports.

Indeed, the importance of looking at the impact of China's global export growth on Latin American manufacturing in Latin American markets stems from the fact that for Latin American exporters, regional markets absorb the largest share of their exports. This is particularly true in the case of manufacturing exports. As Table 19.7 shows, for Argentina, Brazil, Chile, and Colombia, regional markets capture a significant share of their manufacturing exports (in all cases around half).

Moreover, in the cases of Argentina, Brazil, and Colombia, this reliance on regional markets for manufacturing exports has become more accentuated with time. While Argentina sent 31% of is manufacturing exports to Latin America in 1985, in 2006 this figure had reached 69%. For Brazil, while in 1985 only 16% of manufacturing exports were destined for the region, by 2006 this figure was 42%. Colombia is in a similar situation.

The reality for Costa Rica and Mexico is different. Costa Rica's dependency on the region has decreased to below the LAC average, and Mexico has never had any significant manufacturing export flow to LAC. While LAC's aggregate dependency on LAC markets for manufacturing has been significant (around 20% for the whole period) it never reached the levels of dependency observed in Argentina, Brazil, Chile, and Colombia.

Table 19.7 Exports to Latin America: share of total (%)

	1985	1990	1995	2000	2006
Argentina					
Manufacturing	31	39	60	64	69
Total	19	26	47	48	42
Brazil					
Manufacturing	16	18	36	37	42
Total	10	11	23	25	26
Chile					
Manufacturing	63	45	67	64	52
Total	15	13	19	22	17
Colombia					
Manufacturing	45	44	62	61	59
Total	12	16	28	29	31
Costa Rica					
Manufacturing	58	46	62	19	19
Total	17	17	21	19	18
Mexico					
Manufacturing	6	9	5	3	5
Total	6	6	5	3	5
LAC					
Manufacturing	20	21	21	14	20
Total	12	14	19	16	17

Source: Authors' calculation, based on United Nations Statistics Division (2009).
Note: Data for 1985 was unavailable. 1985 calculation was performed with 1986 data.

How has, then, China's global export growth impacted Latin American manufacturing exports in Latin American markets? As we mentioned earlier, there are very few analyses on this subject. One exception is new work by Eva Paus. In methodology that resembles the comparison of export structures discussed above, Paus estimates the degree to which China's exports might compete with Latin American imports and domestic production in the future looking at a "domestic competition index" (DCI) which measures the degree of correspondence between China's export structure and a Latin American country's import structure. Looking at this index, Paus concludes: "What gives rise for concern is not the size of the DCI *per se*, but the fact that the DCI increased considerably in just four years. It suggests the potential for domestic market competition from China may be rising substantially further in the future" (2009).

As Table 19.8 shows, Chinese manufacturing exports are significantly threatening LAC manufacturing exports in LAC markets. The threat is particularly acute in the cases of Costa Rica and Mexico, albeit less important, given the relative minor importance of LAC's market for these two exporters. For Argentina, Brazil, Chile, and Colombia, the impact is significant. In 2006, 68% of what countries in Latin America imported in manufactures from Argentina was under threat from China (for the 2000–6 period, 40% was "direct threat," 28% "partial"). Moreover, threatened manufacturing imports from Argentina represented 29% of all LAC's imports from Argentina in 2006. For Brazil— the other manufacturing powerhouse with a significant regional export bias—the figures are not that high, but they are significant. Forty-five percent of what countries in Latin America imported in manufactures from Brazil was under threat from China, representing 32% of all LAC's imports from Brazil in 2006.

Table 19.9 provides more detailed information on the sectoral composition of Latin American manufacturing imports from China by listing the top 20 Latin American manufacturing imports from China, which account for 61.8% of all Latin American manufacturing imports from China. Several elements are noteworthy. Latin American manufacturing imports from China grew much more between 2000 and 2006 than manufacturing imports from the rest of the world. In fact, while the rate of growth on average for the top 20 Chinese imports was 570% for China, it was only 40% for the rest of the world. The strikingly different rates of growth were possible because imports from China captured a very significant share of the growth in LAC manufacturing imports in the period: an average of 67.3% for the top 20.

Table 19.8 Threatened exports to Latin America, 2006 (%)

	Direct	Partial	Total
Argentina			
As % of manufacturing imports	40	28	68
As % of all imports	17	12	29
Brazil			
As % of manufacturing imports	9	36	45
As % of all imports	7	26	32
Chile			
As % of manufacturing imports	28	64	91
As % of all imports	5	13	18
Colombia			
As % of manufacturing imports	21	47	67
As % of all imports	12	27	39
Costa Rica			
As % of manufacturing imports	27	69	95
As % of all imports	20	51	70
Mexico			
As % of manufacturing imports	32	46	78
As % of all imports	26	38	65

Source: Authors' calculations, based on United Nations Statistics Division (2009).

Table 19.9 Characteristics and dynamism of top 20 LAC manufacturing imports from China

	Imports from China	World growth (%)	Chinese growth (%)	China share of growth (%)
Telecommunication equipment; parts and accessories	2,296,494,568	70	970	38
Automatic data processing machines and units thereof	1,826,090,364	63	645	66
Parts and accessories for machines of headings 751 or 752	953,440,582	70	517	59
Baby carriages, toys, games, and sporting goods	940,620,178	52	112	87
Footwear	812,475,064	110	246	59
Gramophones, dictating machines, and other sound recorders	811,485,773	395	2,465	63
Cycles, scooters, motorized or not; invalid carriages	699,419,118	127	552	82
Electrical machinery and apparatus	688,932,328	31	350	63
Thermionic, microcircuits, transistors, valves, etc.	656,938,057	78	553	20
Household type equipment	613,519,749	68	294	54
Radio-broadcast receivers	479,564,317	79	187	77
Television receivers	401,909,859	188	1,757	32
Fabrics, woven, of man-made fibers (not narrow or special fabrics)	378,575,285	18	337	175
Heating and cooling equipment and parts thereof	370,179,667	31	701	52
Women's, girls', infants' outerwear, textile, not knitted or crocheted	361,694,713	83	322	74
Outerwear knitted or crocheted, not elastic or rubberized	344,251,827	61	176	82
Travel goods, handbags, etc., of leather, plastic, textile, others	330,437,864	111	185	76
Electrical apparatus for making and breaking electrical circuits	325,892,900	48	568	26
Men's and boys' outerwear, textile fabrics not knitted or crocheted	322,088,371	35	195	138
Articles, of plastic materials	318,834,369	57	277	24

Source: Authors' calculations, based on UN Statistics Division (2009).

Even less work has focused on the specific impact of Chinese export expansion on domestic production. This is largely due to the difficulty in merging global trade data with domestic production data. A recent paper by Jenkins (2009) summarizes work that looks at domestic markets in Argentina and Brazil. For Argentina, Jenkins finds that China represented only 2.5% of Argentine domestic manufacturing demand in 2006, yet the bulk of that demand was concentrated in a handful of industries. In seven manufacturing industries the share of domestic demand supplied by Chinese imports increased by five percentage points between 2001 and 2006, and the share provided by domestic producers fell in six of those sectors. In four of them, in the transport and electronics sectors, total demand increased (while China's increased and domestic producer share decreased), leading the authors to conclude that "China could be regarded as having had a negative impact on domestic production" (Jenkins 2009: 13). Jenkins also examines the impacts in Brazil, and finds that only two industries, lamps and lighting and basic electronics, saw domestic contraction due to Chinese import penetration. With respect to employment, López and Ramos conclude that increased imports from China have negatively affected employment levels in Argentina. Similar impacts on employment have been found in Chile (López and Ramos 2007; Álvarez and Claro 2009).

19.4 CONCLUSION

Numerous international institutions have hailed China's rise as the long-awaited remedy to the lackluster economic growth that has plagued the region in all but a handful of exceptions since the early 1990s. This chapter critically analyses such claims and finds that China's rise may be a double-edged sword for Latin America. On the one hand, China's growing demand for LAC products is creating demand for primary product exports in its bilateral trade relationship with LAC. This is a welcome and necessary development in the short term. However, China is simultaneously out-competing LAC manufacturing exporters across the globe. Jointly, these two dynamics are accentuating the bias toward primary product export production that the region has tried so hard for decades to rid itself from.

The findings in this chapter have sought to provide a more critical analysis of China's impact on the recent Latin American commodity boom. During this boom, Latin American export growth, which was considerably faster than GDP growth, was being driven by a commodities boom. Indeed, 70% of the growth in LAC exports has been due to growth in commodities exports, and commodities exports accounted for 74% of all LAC exports. China had both indirect and direct effects on this trend. Directly, LAC exports to China have increased by 370% since 2000. This has been the cause of much cheer, but should be analyzed with more scrutiny. Indirectly, Chinese consumption of global commodities was making them scarcer and boosting global prices, and therefore leading to more LAC exports.

LAC exports to China were only 3.8% of all LAC exports. LAC's exports to China comprised 5.8% of Chinese imports, the same level of LAC exports to China in the 1980s; 74% of all LAC exports to China were in primary commodities; growth in LAC exports to China was only 8% of all LAC export growth from the start of the boom in 2000; ten sectors in six countries accounted for 74% of all LAC exports to China and 91% of all commodities exports to China; for the other countries in LAC, the potential to trade with China is very low.

The analyses we conduct in this chapter also shows that LAC manufacturing industries are increasingly being out-competed in world and regional LAC markets. Recent work on export similarity indices shows that this may only be the beginning. Rather than aiding in the diversification of LAC production and exports, China seems to be accentuating the narrowing of LAC production that has been occurring since the 1980s in the region. China is increasingly threatening LAC manufacturing exports in world and regional export markets. Indeed, this chapter shows that over 94% of LAC manufactures exports are under some sort of threat from China, representing 40% of total exports. For Mexico the situation is even graver, with 99% of manufacturing exports under threat, constituting 72% of total exports.

What accounts for China's rapid increase in competitiveness? There is considerable debate in the literature and in the popular press concerning China's massive increase in competitiveness in general. Most studies argue that the changes are due in some part due to China's exchange rate, its productivity growth and wages, and the relative amount of industrial "policy space" that China has and is using relative to LAC.

China clearly treats export competitiveness seriously, and takes it into account when defining exchange rate policy. If one looks at the real exchange rate (local currency to the US$) in China and selected LAC countries from 1985 to 2006, it is clear that in the case of Mexico (where the greatest quantity of high-technology exports are under threat) the Chinese yuan is depreciating in real terms relative to the US$ and the Mexican peso is appreciating. For Costa Rica, Brazil, and Argentina, an exchange rate argument would be less clear.

In terms of productivity and wages, Mesquita Moreira finds that these are fairly even between China and Mexico for consumer electronics, and that Brazil's productivity is higher (Mesquita Moreira 2007). For personal computers, China lags behind both Brazil and Mexico in terms of productivity. However, productivity growth in the three countries tells a radically different story according to Mesquita Moreira. Since 1990, productivity in manufacturing as a whole in Brazil and Mexico has grown by a factor of approximately 1.4, but manufacturing productivity in China has leapt by a factor of almost 7. In terms of wages in manufacturing as a whole, China's wages are four (Brazil) to seven (Mexico) times lower than their LAC counterparts (Mesquita Moreira 2007).

Another explanation under debate is the shift in the orientation of industrial policies in LAC, away from development programs targeted to promote selected sectors. Up until 1984, LAC's industrial policy was geared to intervene strongly in specific sectors. Since then, the policy has been to let markets largely determine the profile of manufacturing and exports. As Mesquita Moreira puts it:

Whether or not these [Chinese] interventionist policies are behind China's takeoff or whether or not they guarantee or compromise China's long term growth is already the stuff of a prolific policy debate, which, as it happened to other East Asian tigers, is bound to be inconclusive, not least because economists have yet to find a satisfactory way of dealing with the counterfactual. Yet, from LAC manufacturer's point of view, the omnipresence and generosity of the Chinese state has a very practical and immediate implication, that is to heavily tilt the playing field in favor of their Chinese competitors, either local or foreign affiliates, in a scenario where they already face endowment, productivity and scale disadvantages. (Mesquita Moreira 2007: 15)

Further research is needed on the extent to which exchange rate policy, industrial policy, tariff liberalization and other policies have improved China's competitiveness vis-à-vis LAC. At this point, however, it is clear that China seems to be driving up demand for primary products from LAC on the one hand, and eroding LAC's ability to compete for manufacturing in world markets on the other. In the longer run, these twin trends could put LAC back to the 19th century.

REFERENCES

ÁLVAREZ, R., and CLARO, S. (2009). 'David *Versus* Goliath: The Impact of Chinese Competition on Developing Countries', *World Development* 37.3.

BLÁZQUEZ-LIDOY, J., RODRÍGUEZ, J., and SANTISO, J. (2006). 'Angel or Devil? China's Trade Impact on Latin American Emerging Markets', *CEPAL Review* 90.

Deutsche Bank Research (2006). *China's Commodity Hunger: Implications for Africa and Latin America*, Frankfurt.

DEVLIN, R., ESTEVADEORDAL, A., and RODRIGUEZ-CLARE, A. (eds) (2006). *The Emergence of China: Opportunities and Challenges for Latin America and the Caribbean*, Washington, DC: IDB.

DUSSEL PETERS, E. (2005). *Economic Opportunities and Challenges Posed by China for Mexico and Central America*, Bonn: German Development Institute.

—— (ed.) (2007). *Opportunidades en la relacion economica y commercial entre China y Mexico*, Santiago, Chile: CEPAL-UNAM.

—— (2008). 'The Mexico–China Economic Relationship in Electronics: A Case Study of the PC Industry in Jalisco', in R. Jenkins (ed.), *The Impact of China's Global Economic Expansion on Latin America*, Norwich: University of East Anglia.

FREUND, C., and OZDEN, C. (2009). 'The Effect of China's Exports on Latin American Trade with the World', in D. Lederman, M. Olarreaga, and G. E. Perry (eds), *China's and India's Challenge to Latin America: Opportunity or Threat?* Washington, DC: World Bank.

GALLAGHER, K., and PORZECANSKI, R. (2010). *The Dragon in the Room: China and the Future of Latin American Industrialization*, Palo Alto, Calif.: Stanford University Press.

HANSON, G., and ROBERTSON, R. (2009). 'China and the Recent Evolution of Latin America's Manufacturing Exports', in D. Lederman, M. Olarreaga, and G. E. Perry (eds), *China's and India's Challenge to Latin America: Opportunity or Threat?* Washington, DC: World Bank.

IMF (International Monetary Fund) (2006). *World Economic Outlook*, Washington, DC.

—— (2008). *World Economic Outlook*, Washington, DC.

International Food Policy Research Institute (2008). *The World Food Situation*, Washington, DC.

JENKINS, R. (2008). 'Measuring the Competitive Threat from China for Other Southern Exporters', *World Economy* 31.10.

—— (2009). 'The Economic Impacts of China's Global Expansion on Latin America', available online at: http://www.uea.ac.uk/dev/faculty/Jenkins/china-latinamerica

JIANWU, H., LI, S., and POLASKI, S. (2007). *China's Economic Prospects, 2006–2020*, Washington, DC: Carnegie Endowment for International Peace.

LALL, S. (2000). 'The Technological Structure and Performance of Developing Country Manufactured Exports, 1985–98', *Oxford Development Studies* 28.3.

—— and WEISS, J. (2005). 'People's Republic of China's Competitive Threat to Latin America: An Analysis for 1990–2002', *Oxford Development Studies* 33.2.

LÓPEZ, A., and RAMOS, D. (2007). 'A Study of the Impact of China's Global Expansion on Argentina', Working Paper No. 1, World Economy and Finance Research Programme, London.

MESQUITA MOREIRA, M. (2004). *Fear of China: Is There a Future for Manufacturing in Latin America?* Washington, DC: Latin America/Caribbean and Asia/Pacific Economics and Business Association.

—— (2007). 'Fear of China: Is There a Future for Manufacturing in Latin America?', *World Development* 35.3.

OCAMPO, J. A. (2007). 'The Macroeconomics of the Latin American Economic Boom', *CEPAL Review* 93.

—— and PARRA, M. A. (2003). 'The Terms of Trade for Commodities in the Twentieth Century', *CEPAL Review* 79.

—— —— (2010). 'The Terms of Trade for Commodities Since the Mid-Nineteenth Century', *Journal of Iberian and Latin American Economic History* 28.1.

PAUS, E. (2009). 'The Rise of China: Implications for Latin American Development', *Development Policy Review* 27.4.

PREBISCH, R. (1951). *Growth, Disequilibrium and Disparities: Interpretation of the Process of Economic Development (Economic Survey of Latin America 1949)*, Santiago, Chile: ECLAC.

World Bank (2009). *Global Economic Prospects 2009: Commodities at the Crossroads*, Washington, DC.

United Nations Statistics Division (2009). 'United Nations Commodity Trade Statistics Database (COMTRADE)', New York.

CHAPTER 20

....

LATIN AMERICA IN THE RECENT WAVE OF INTERNATIONAL MIGRATION

....

ALEJANDRO I. CANALES

20.1 INTRODUCTION

....

International migration is not a new phenomenon in Latin America, but we have seen it undergo substantial changes in recent years (Pellegrino 2003). As a region, Latin America showed some polarization in terms of its profile and type of participation in international migration. The first type related to international immigration, usually in the Southern Cone countries (Argentina, Chile, and Uruguay), southern Brazil, Venezuela, and Cuba; the second type, international emigration, applied to Mexico and to a lesser extent to some Caribbean countries (the Dominican Republic and Haiti). Also, although intraregional migration has always been of considerable magnitude, it has generally been considered as a phenomenon occurring in only some countries.

However, important changes have occurred in the region since the 1980s, which have resulted in new forms and migratory patterns. In contrast to past eras, international migration has not only intensified but "extensified:" migratory flows have diversified in their origins, destinations, and forms due to the cumulative processes we call globalization (Canales and Montiel 2007). In fact, the incorporation of these new Latin American immigrants into the labor market of the receiving countries is associated with and conditioned by the contractual deregulation and labor flexibility that reflect the new forms of social differentiation and labor segmentation in the era of globalization (Stalker 2000).

Accordingly, we can discuss five aspects which manifest the diversity and complexity of international migration in Latin America:

- Formerly a region which received immigrants, Latin America has become an important zone of emigration, especially to the developed nations—a great march from the South to the North. Although the USA has become the principal destination of Latin American emigration, there are also important flows towards Europe (principally Spain) and Japan.

- Intraregional migration has also diversified and increased (Martínez 2008). In additional traditional flows between neighboring countries (Bolivians to Argentina, Colombians to Venezuela, Brazilians to Paraguay, and Guatemalans to Mexico), new migratory flows have developed (Nicaraguans to Costa Rica, Haitians to the Dominican Republic, Peru to Chile, Colombia to Ecuador, the return of Brazilians to Paraguay, Ecuador to Chile, among others) while others are expanding their destinations (from Bolivia to Buenos Aires).

- We should also note the growing complexity and diversity of the different forms of migration. We need to add other types of definition to the classic ones of permanent and temporary migration: circular migration, cross-border migration, return migration, and undocumented migration, among others.

- We need to recognize the diversity of the participants that actually migrate (Pujadas and Massal 2005; Pedone 2006), such as the migration of women, indigenous populations, and family migration (primarily children and senior citizens). The participants who are part of the migratory flow have become more visible. This is true in the case of women, whose immigration for many years was invisible, subsumed into and associated with male migration (UNFPA 2006).

- Finally, the level that remittances have reached is not only a public opinion issue, but an emergent topic for politics and social sciences. In the case of Latin America, remittances currently amount to more than $60 billion annually, a figure that makes them one of the main items of current transfers in balance of payments (Martínez 2008). However, there is no consensus about the social effects and economic impacts of remittances. On one hand, international organizations for development have paid special attention to remittances as a tool that would contribute to the reduction of poverty and to the development of the regions of origin of international migration (OIM 2003; FOMIN 2004; Terry 2005). On the other hand, many academics are skeptical about it: they consider that remittances are just transferences between particulars, and thus do not take the place of the state's and the market's roles in the promotion of economic development and the population's welfare (Canales 2007b; de Haas 2007). In any case, the current economic crisis redefines the scope of this discussion. Without doubt, remittances are one of the areas where the economic crisis has had a more direct impact. However, although remittances are reduced, they have not collapsed. World Bank estimates for 2009 indicate a reduction by only 10% of remittances in Latin America (World Bank 2011).

All these changes make it necessary to revise and reformulate the framework for analysis, categorization, and understanding of this phenomenon. The objective of this text is to document, with recent statistical information, the characteristics of Latin American emigration to Spain and the USA and to record it into the great march from the South to the North. This will allow us to appreciate the diverse migratory forms and their participants.

We begin with an analysis which allows us to contextualize Latin American migration within the framework of the so-called new era of global migration (Castles and Miller 1993). Secondly, we will focus on a comparative analysis between Spain and the USA, both of which are currently the principal destinations for Latin American emigrants. This comparative analysis is based on migration volumes, as well as the sociodemographic profiles of the migrants and their insertion into the labor force.

20.2 INTERNATIONAL MIGRATION AND GLOBALIZATION

Without entering into the globalization debate, I would like to focus attention on the new patterns of incorporation of immigrant workers into the labor process and their connection with the transformation brought about by globalization in the organizational forms of work and labor relations. By making employment precarious, globalization sets in motion various mechanisms of social inclusion and exclusion that result in new patterns of social polarization and differentiation based on two different and complementary processes. One of these is the configuration of a labor system based on flexibility and deregulation—a system that Beck (2000) characterizes as a system of labor risk—that has replaced the labor system and social institutions associated with the welfare state. The other is the transformation of the employment system through increasing segmentation and accompanying social differentiation (Castells 1996).

The polarization of the employment structure is apparent in the expansion of executive, professional, and highly qualified technical positions based on information processing and a similar increase in the number of jobs requiring very low levels of technical training. Concentrated in the so-called personal service sector, these low-skilled jobs enhance the quality of life for others. The increase in their number is the necessary counterpoint to the expansion of high-level occupations that, with their increased purchasing power, generate a demand for personal services.

In addition to this job polarization, there are new flexible working conditions in various branches of industry and in construction. The outsourcing of services and of various phases of production through subcontracting contributes to the precariousness of unskilled work (Sassen 1998). This degradation of working conditions ends up driving the local labor force out of jobs that are flexible and deregulated, replacing them with migrant workers whose vulnerability makes them willing to accept a situation in which they have no possibility of unionizing, work without contracts, receive low wages, and are subject to very high levels of labor instability (Castles and Miller 1993). Precarious and undervalued jobs such as janitorial work, gardening, restaurant work, and domestic services are increasingly performed by migrant labor.

This segmentation of the labor market contributes to the division of the population into differentiated and unequal social and cultural strata. While the various occupational strata are configured by the economic logic of the market, the composition of these social and cultural strata results from extra economic social differentiation, especially cultural, ethnic, demographic, and gender, and the condition of being migrants (Canales and Montiel 2007). These factors of social differentiation are the origin of the new internal boundaries that have emerged in the course of globalization, contributing to the segmentation of the social structure in modern society.

On the basis of these factors of social differentiation and unequal incorporation into the labor market, particular population groups experience different levels of social vulnerability, a situation that is aggravated by the structural context in which the mechanisms of social and political negotiation that emerged in industrial society and achieved their highest form in the welfare state have ceased to exist for the most vulnerable groups (Beck 2000). This is the mechanism by which social and cultural minorities are created and re-created in global society. The socially constructed vulnerability of immigrants is transferred to the labor market in the form of a devaluation of the labor force, its life circumstances, and its social reproduction. In this context, the poverty and precarious existence of these workers are not the result of exclusion from the labor market but of the way in which they are incorporated into it. In the context of economic deregulation and labor flexibility, modernization generates and reproduces its own forms of poverty and precariousness. Individuals' social vulnerability as members of social, demographic, and cultural minorities based on gender, ethnicity, and migration ceases to be a factor that exposes them to possible economic exclusion and becomes a prerequisite for their inclusion.

20.3 LATIN AMERICAN MIGRATION IN THE CONTEMPORARY GLOBAL CONTEXT

The current view of Latin American[1] international migration is radically different from the one that prevailed 100 years ago in the region. At the beginning of the 20th century, some countries (Argentina, Venezuela, and to a lesser extent Chile and southern Brazil), together with North America (USA and Canada) and Australia, were the international immigrants' principal destinations (Tapinos and Delaunay 2000). In all these cases, the immigrants sought to benefit from expansion capitalism. On the other hand, at the dawn of the new millennium, Latin America is now one of the main regions of population

[1] I have used the ECLAC classification under which the countries comstituting Latin America are Argentina, Bolivia, Brazil, Colombia, Chile, Ecuador, Paraguay, Peru, Uruguay, Venezuela, Costa Rica, El Salvador Honduras, Guatemala, Nicaragua, Panama, Cuba, Haiti, the Dominican Republic, and Mexico.

emigration to the principal economies of the developed world (the USA, Europe, and to a lesser extent Japan) (Pellegrino 2003).

By the year 2000, there were 22.3 million Latin Americans residing in a country that was not the one of their birth (Table 20.1). Of these, 19.2 million lived in a country outside Latin America, while the other 3.1 million became intraregional migrants—i.e. they lived in Latin America, but not in their birth country. In contrast, in the same year, there were only 5.1 million international immigrants in all of Latin America. Of this group, only 2 million came from countries outside of the region, while the other 3.1 million belonged to the above-mention intraregional group.

We can identify and describe three basic aspects regarding Latin America's role and profile in the contemporary migratory situation at the international level.

20.3.1 Intraregional and extraregional emigrants

Globally, it is estimated that there were 175 million international emigrants around the year 2000. Of these, 48% were migrants that moved within their region of origin (intraregional migrants), and the other 52% were extraregional migrants (Table 20.1). This was the case in Oceania, Asia, the European Union, and to a lesser degree North America. Meanwhile in Africa and Eastern Europe, there was a greater prevalence of intraregional migration than extraregional movement. Specifically, while Africa and Eastern Europe are important emigratory population regions, extraregional emigration represents less than a third of the total emigration in those zones. In other words, more than two-thirds of their emigrants move to another country within the same region.

In contrast, Latin American migration presents a very different pattern. In this case, much like the Caribbean and the Persian Gulf, more than 85% of Latin American emigrants (19 million people) move to a country outside their region of origin. However, Latin America is the region with the second highest volume of extraregional emigrants—second only to Asia, which has 33 million migrants. In fact, Latin America generates 21% of extraregional emigration, while the Caribbean and the Persian Gulf supply only 2.8% and 1%, respectively.

In addition, although Asia generates the greatest volume of extraregional emigrants (34%), they represent less than 1% of the population of that continent. The 19 million Latin American emigrants, in contrast, represent 3.8% of the continent's population. This places Latin America as the second region with the highest rate of extraregional emigration in the world.

The data indicate that the emigratory pattern in Latin America is very different from that of the rest of the world. The predominance of extraregional movements in the region indicates Latin America's important role in contemporary international migration. This process can be understood more clearly within a globalization framework. In other world zones with higher internal and intraregional movement, factors such as environment, history, and regional powers appear to have a greater influence.

Table 20.1 Characteristics and composition of migrant population by major world region (c. 2000; 000)

	International emigrants			Extra regional migration			Migration rate (%)	
	Total	Intraregional	Extraregional	Immigration	Emigration	Net migration	Extra regional	Net migration
Latin America	22,303	3,105	19,197	2,005	19,197	−17,193	3.8	−3.4
North America	5,151	2,901	2,250	37,806	2,250	35,556	0.7	11.3
Caribbean	2,750	176	2,574	429	2,574	−2,145	6.8	−5.6
Europe Union	28,504	12,997	15,507	23,744	15,507	8,237	3.1	1.7
Eastern Europe	38,878	25,703	13,175	3,792	13,175	−9,382	3.5	−2.5
Asia	57,988	26,685	31,303	6,839	31,303	−24,464	0.9	−0.7
Persian Gulf	1,017	143	874	9,487	874	8,613	2.4	23.2
Africa	17,553	12,153	5,400	2,503	5,400	−2,897	0.7	−0.4
Oceania	1,565	731	834	4,511	834	3,676	2.7	12.1

Source: Author's estimates on the basis of Global Origin Data Base (updated March 2009), The Development Research Centre on Migration, Globalisation, and Poverty, University of Sussex.

20.3.2 From South to North: migratory patterns in the global economy

Net migration (NM) gives us another indication of contemporary international migration. As can be seeen in Table 20.1, net emigration regions can clearly be identified in oppositon to net immigration regions. The population emigration regions are part of the third world: Asia, Latin America, Eastern Europe, Africa, and the Caribbean. In contrast, the regions that attract population belong to the developed world: North America, the European Union, and to a lesser extent, Oceania. The Persian Gulf countries are the exception to this rule. This can be explained by the importance of petroleum in the region and its important strategic role in the global economy.

We can define contemporary international migration as a great march by the southern hemisphere workforce to the more developed north. Latin America not only participates in this great movement, but supplies almost one-third of the net interregional migrants. This places Latin America as the region with the second highest net global emigration, after Asia. Latin America has a negative net migration balance of about 17.2 million people. This means that the region has the second highest absolute population loss globally. The importance of Latin American international migration is especially clear when we look at net international migration rates. Latin America has the highest relative rate among regions that have high net emigration volumes. Latin America's NM represents 3.4% of its total population. In contrast, Asian and African NM represent only 0.7% and 0.4%, respectively. Eastern Europe is the only other region with a relatively important NM rate (2.5%). However, it is still lower than that of Latin America.

As a result of net international emigration, Latin America has a negative NM balance vis-à-vis all other regions in the world. Table 20.2 shows that there are more Latin Americans in all other regions of the world than there are immigrants from the same areas in Latin America. Along with the Caribbean countries, Latin America maintains a negative NM balance with the rest of the world.

20.3.3 New patterns of intraregional migration

In recent decades, intraregional migration in Latin America has become more complex and heterogeneous. As illustrated in Table 20.3, until 1990, Argentina and Venezuela were the two main destination countries for intraregional migration. Together, these countries attracted over 60% of this type of immigration in the region. In both cases, it was immigration from neighboring countries. In the case of Venezuela, it was essentially the migration of Colombians, which represented 22% of total intraregional migrants until that year.

In the case of Argentina, the immigrants came from Bolivia, Chile, Paraguay, and Uruguay, preferring to move to the respective areas bordering with Argentina: Bolivians to the provinces of Salta and Jujuy, Paraguayans to El Chaco and Formosa, Chileans to

Table 20.2 Latin America: immigrants, emigrants, and net migration, by major international region (c. 2000, in thousands)

	Total	North America	Caribbean	European Union	Eastern Europe	Asia	Persian Gulf	Africa	Oceania
Emigrants	19,197.4	15,511.8	218.2	1,805.7	245.8	980.3	155.3	197.1	83.2
Immigrants	2,004.7	479.2	36.1	1,129.5	56.6	270.0	2.4	24.9	6.1
Net migration	−17,192.7	−15,032.6	−182.2	−676.2	−189.2	−710.3	−153.0	−172.2	−77.1

Source: Author's estimates on the basis of Global Origin Data Base (updated March 2009), The Development Research Centre on Migration, Globalisation and Poverty, University of Sussex.

Table 20.3 Major intraregional gross migration flows in Latin America

Migratory flows until 1990			Migratory flows in the 1990s		
Country of origin	Destination country	%	Country of origin	Destination country	%
Colombia →	Venezuela	22.5	Nicaragua →	Costa Rica	15.6
Paraguay →	Argentina	10.7	Bolivia →	Argentina	10.0
Chile →	Argentina	9.3	Colombia →	Venezuela	8.9
Bolivia →	Argentina	6.1	Paraguay →	Argentina	8.1
Uruguay →	Argentina	5.7	Peru →	Argentina	7.2
Brazil →	Paraguay	4.6	Haiti →	Dominican Rep.	6.9
			Peru →	Chile	5.6
			Paraguay →	Brazil	3.3
			Colombia →	Ecuador	2.2
			Ecuador →	Chile	2.2

Source: Author's estimates on basis on IMILA, *Investigación de la Migración Internacional en Latinoamérica*, CELADE, Population Division of ECLAC.

Mendoza, Neuquén, and Río Negro, and Uruguayans to the metropolitan area of Buenos Aires.

In the 1990s, however, intraregional flows became more diversified, in relation both to countries of origin and to destination of migration within the region (see Table 20.3). Between 1990 and around 2000, it is estimated that over 900,000 people moved into Latin America. This represents about a third of the stock of intraregional migrants by 2000. The largest flow was that of Nicaraguans to Costa Rica. Between 1990 and 2000, it is estimated that that over 120,000 Nicaraguans immigrated to Costa Rica, representing 16% of total intraregional movement of the 1990s.

Although in recent years the migration of Chileans and Uruguayans to Argentina has ceased, Argentina maintains its importance as a center of intraregional migration. Bolivian and Paraguayan migration maintains its level of importance, contributing over 18% of total intraregional migrants. More recently, Peruvian migration to Argentina accounted for more than 7% of intraregional movement of the 1990s. It should be noted also that the Bolivian and Paraguayan migration is not only to border areas, but extends to the metropolitan area of Buenos Aires.

Also, the migration of Colombians to Venezuela, so important in the past, now represented only 9% of total intraregional migration. We should also mention the recent migration of Colombians to Ecuador. In this case, it is basically forced displacement as a result of social conflicts and political violence in Colombia.

Finally, we should mention two other migrations of some importance in this period: Haitians to the Dominican Republic, and Peruvians and Ecuadorians to Chile. In all these cases, the volume seems to have been minimally significant until the beginning of the

1990s. The Chilean case is particularly interesting, because it illustrates how this country ceases to be one of emigration to become an immigration country within the region.

20.4 USA AND SPAIN: CURRENT LATIN AMERICAN IMMIGRATION

Until the year 2000, the USA was without a doubt the main destination of Latin American extraregional emigrants (Martínez 2008; Pellegrino 2003). However, Europe, especially Spain, has become a second front for Latin American emigration in recent years. At the end of the 1990s, the USA received Latin American emigrants at a ratio 17 times greater than Spain (Figure 20.1). In other words, for every Latin American that migrated to Spain, another 17 moved to the USA. This began to change in 2000. Between 2000 and 2005, the ratio shifted to 3:1, i.e. for every three emigrants that moved to the USA, one migrated to Spain. Furthermore, this ratio was reduced to the point that by the year 2007, Latin American emigration to the USA was only 17% greater than that of Spain.

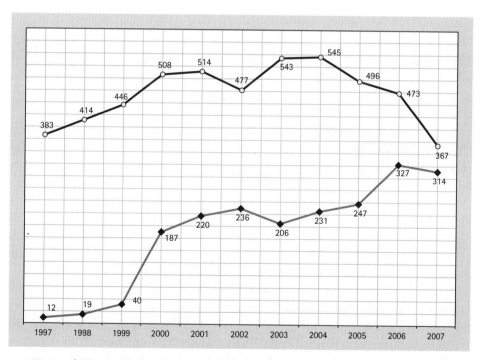

FIGURE 20.1 Latin America: gross annual migration flow to USA and Spain, 1997–2007 (000)

Source: Author's estimates on the basis of INE, Spain, *Padrón municipal de población*, 2001–8; US Census Bureau, *Current Population Survey*, March supplement, 2001–8.

These data indicate that Spain and the USA are the two principal destinations for Latin American migrants. This is mirrored by the fact that Latin Americans are the largest groups of migrants received by these countries. Between 2000 and 2006, 48% of all immigrants in the USA and 43% in Spain were from Latin America. However, in Latin America not all countries have the similar migratory patterns. We can identify markedly different migratory patterns for each region and country: Mexicans and Central Americans have a very strong tendency to immigrate to the USA, while South Americans show a strong preference for Spain.

In the first case, between 2001 and 2007, more than 96% of the emigrants from Haiti, Mexico, El Salvador, and Guatemala migrated to the USA (see Table 20.4). The population that emigrated from these countries to Spain or another European country is almost statistically insignificant. There was a similar situation in Honduras and Cuba for the same time period. In fact, 80% of Hondurans and 70% of Cuban went to the USA. The last case is particularly illustrative. Although Cuban immigration to Spain became more frequent, the ratio was still more than 2:1 in favor of the USA.

This situation is reversed in the case of South American emigrants. At the aggregate level, only 25% of South Americans migrate to the USA. Instead, they show a strong preference to emigrate to Spain (and Portugal in the case of Brazil). In Peru and Columbia, emigration to Spain was more than three times higher than to the USA during 2001–7, and double in Chile. The Colombian case is particularly striking, because until a few years ago, most Colombian emigration was to the USA and, to a lesser extent, Venezuela.

This preference for Spain is even more pronounced in the cases of Ecuador, Argentina, and Uruguay. In all these countries, emigration to Spain was more than four times greater than to the USA. Ecuador is the country that has had the greatest migratory flow to Spain: from 2001 to 2007, almost one in five Latin Americans who arrived in Spain was from Ecuador.

Uruguay and Bolivia are perhaps the most extremes case. Between 2001 and 2007, Uruguayan emigration to Spain was nine times greater than to the USA, and Bolivian emigration was fourteen times greater: more than 250,000 Bolivians immigrated to Spain while only 17,000 went to the USA.

Brazil, Venezuela, and the Dominican Republic have a more mixed immigration profile. There, emigration to Spain and the USA was proportionally similar and almost equally divided. Brazil is a special case, because emigration to Portugal is as important as Spain. At first glance, Brazilian emigration to the USA appears to be 40% more than that of Spain. But, if we consider Portugal, the situation is the opposite.

In summary, we can identify at least three large migratory regions. Mexico, El Salvador, Guatemala, Honduras, Cuba, and Haiti show a clear emigratory preference for the USA. In contrast, South American migrants, with the exceptions of Venezuela and Brazil, strongly prefer to move to Spain. There is also a third area where both migratory destinations are equally important: Brazil, the Dominican Republic, and Venezuela. Finally, there are the countries which have very low levels of emigration: Costa Rica, Panama, and Nicaragua.

Table 20.4 Gross immigration from Latin America, stock and flow by country of birth: USA and Spain

Country of birth	Migratory stock 2008		Gross migration flow, 2001–7	
	USA	Spain	USA	Spain
Latin America	18,949,144	2,295,899	3,415,012	1,765,251
Mexico	11,845,294	42,413	2,199,538	32,975
Central America	2,640,384	53,876	395,113	45,629
Costa Rica	88,775	2,883	19,010	2,182
El Salvador	956,557	7,120	115,512	5,178
Guatemala	724,009	5,861	129,661	4,361
Honduras	546,829	23,673	90,315	22,416
Nicaragua	206,759	10,098	17,929	8,804
Panama	117,455	4,241	22,686	2,688
Caribbean	2,270,021	207,290	294,373	128,597
Cuba	996,986	92,583	122,851	51,868
Haiti	397,209	–	87,329	242
Dominican Rep.	875,826	114,707	84,194	76,487
South America	2,193,445	1,992,320	525,988	1,558,050
Argentina	144,733	290,281	57,184	214,886
Bolivia	62,786	240,912	17,423	253,703
Brazil	393,563	142,149	155,394	131,698
Chile	58,543	66,874	29,180	51,237
Colombia	598,489	330,419	72,652	247,264
Ecuador	406,817	458,437	83,483	330,214
Paraguay	9,172	68,885	–	57,061
Peru	333,403	162,425	40,075	119,192
Uruguay	25,947	87,345	8,099	66,365
Venezuela	159,992	144,593	62,499	86,430

Source: Author's estimates on the basis of INE, Spain, *Padrón municipal de población*, 2001–8; US Census Bureau, *Current Population Survey*, March supplement, 2001–8.

20.5 SOCIODEMOGRAPHIC PROFILES OF LATIN AMERICAN MIGRANTS

The sociodemographic profile of Latin American immigrants in Spain and the USA shows quite a bit of heterogeneity, depending on the region and country of origin. In some cases the emigrants are primarily male and have a low level of education; in other

situations, there are a high proportion of female migrants; in others, we see the participation of senior citizens. The last case indicates that we are talking about a migration
which renews itself very slowly. In this section, I give a brief sociodemographic characterization of Latin American immigrants using three measures: age structure, gender,
and level of education.

20.5.1 Age structure

Generally, Latin American migration follows the classic age pattern in that the majority
of the emigrants are young, economically active adults. This is true in both the USA and
Spain. Figure 20.2 shows that the large majority of the migrants are between the ages of 20
and 49. In Spain, more than 71% fall into this category and approximately 65% in the USA.
This is true for men and women. This age structure reflects the fact that Latin American
migration to Spain and the USA is essentially labor-based. The absence of child migrants
reinforces this idea. Family migration is very low and statistically insignificant.

Since the majority of Latin American migrants are young, they have made a large contribution to the population dynamics of both Spain and the USA. Latin American immigrants between the ages of 25 and 35 constitute 10% and 12% of the resident populations
of the same age group in Spain and the USA, respectively. This means that in Spain, one
in ten people between these ages is a Latin American immigrant. In the USA, this figure
is approximately one in eight.

This highlights the large contribution that Latin American immigrants have made to
the growth of the populations of young people in Spain and the USA. Since the end of
the 20th century, both of these countries have experienced the final stages of the
Demographic Transition, a phenomenon that occurs primarily in the absolute and relative reduction of children and young people, as direct result of declines in fertility and
birth rates. In fact, Spain's birth rates actually fell below the population replacement level
(Cooke 2003; Lee 2003; Pérez Díaz 2003; Adsera 2006).

Without international immigration between 2002 and 2007, in both countries the
populations of people aged between 20 and 49 would have been reduced significantly.
Specifically, the native populations would have been reduced by almost 192,000 in Spain
and 242,000 in the USA if the immigrants had not arrived (see Figure 20.3). This is
important, because these are the people who are at the height of their productive and
reproductive capacities.

The immigration of young Latin Americans has not only compensated for the declining fertility and birth rates, but has also produced important growth in the populations
of this age group (United Nations 2001; Domingo i Valls 2006). Effectively, immigrants
between the ages of 20 and 49 increased the population by 2.7 million people in the USA
and by 1.8 million in Spain. Thus, between 2002 and 2005, the population of 20–49-year-
olds increased by 2% and 8.5% in the USA and Spain, respectively.

These data show that international immigration greatly contributes to the
demographic sustainability of the populations of the USA and Spain. The structural

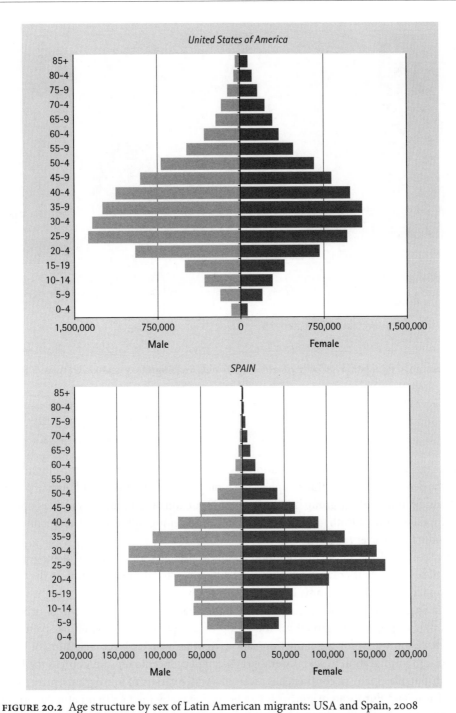

FIGURE 20.2 Age structure by sex of Latin American migrants: USA and Spain, 2008

Source: Author's estimates on the basis of INE, Spain, *Padrón municipal de población*, and US Census Bureau, *Current Population Survey*, March supplement.

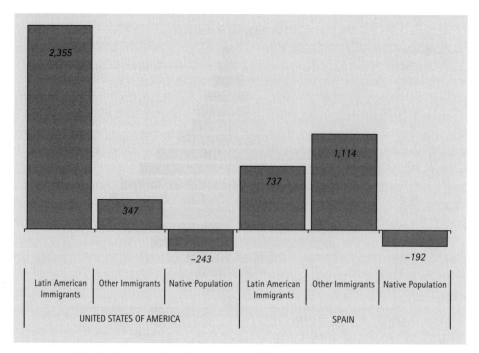

FIGURE 20.3 Population growth of 20–49-year-olds by migratory status: USA and Spain, 2002–7 (000)

Source: Author's estimates on the basis on INE, Spain, *Padrón municipal de población 2002–7*, and US Census Bureau, *Current Population Survey*, March supplement, 2002–7.

importance of this age group population rests in two complementary factors. First, they are the demographic base that supports the biological reproduction of all human populations. Second, this age group has the largest proportion of economically active population in each country. Both factors are the basis for the demographic, social, and economic reproduction of every society.

In Spain and the USA, immigration fulfills a similar transcendental demographic function. However, there are certain specific differences to take into account. In the USA, the contribution of immigrants is mainly those from Latin America. However, the situation in Spain is more balanced. In the USA, Latin American immigrants have contributed with 87% of population growth of the group of 20–49-year-olds, while in Spain that number is only 40% for the same population. In other words, the contribution of Latin American immigration to social, demographic, and economic reproduction in the USA is indisputable. Spain, in contrast, has received a wider variety of immigrants, principally of African and European origin. This can be explained by the fact that Latin American immigration to Spain is a relatively recent phenomenon compared to that of the USA.

Until the late 1980s, Spain was not a migratory attraction country. On the contrary, it was a country with high emigration to other countries, especially other European ones (Cabré 1999; Domingo i Valls 2006). Also, Latin American migration was concentrated in the USA until the beginning of the 1990s. In 1996, Latin American migrants represented less than 0.5% of the resident population of Spain. That figure reached almost 5% in 2008: the immigration rate of Latin American increased almost ten times in only twelve years.

20.5.2 Relation of gender to emigration

One demographic dimension which distinguishes and characterizes the migratory process is the varying participation that men and women have in each flow. Sometimes there are flows which are primarily female and at other times, principally male. There are also flows which are characterized by equal gender distribution. The difference in the gender composition of a migration is usually the result of the labor conditions and social integration in the destination country and how these conditions affect men and women. Controlling for gender helps us to understand how varying social conditions affect people, especially women, in every sphere of social life (in our case, migration). We can observe gender divisions in the case of Latin American migration.

Comparisons of sex ratios (number of males per 100 females) from the Latin American migrations to Spain and the USA give us an impression of the differences in their gender compositions. If we observe the accumulated stock or the recent flows (2001–7) of migrant residents in both countries, we can clearly see that there was a higher proportion of female migrants to Spain while in the USA there was a greater male proportion. Among the Latin American migratory stock in Spain, there were only 84 men for every 100 women, while in the USA, the situation was reversed: 115 men for every 100 women (see Table 20.5).

These differences are even more marked in the case of the recent migratory flow. In Spain, the ratio has not changed much, with fewer than 90 men for every 100 women. However, in the USA the gender difference has increased to more than 150 men for every 100 women.

Table 20.5 Latin American immigrants in USA and Spain, by sex and sex ratio (no. of men per 100 women)

| | Migratory stock 2008 | | Gross migration flow, 2001–7 | |
	US	Spain	US	Spain
Total	18,949,144	2,295,899	3,415,012	1,765,251
Men	10,142,620	1,051,038	2,078,778	827,499
Women	8,806,524	1,244,861	1,336,234	937,752
Sex ratio	115.2	84.4	155.6	88.2

Source: Author's estimates on the basis on INE, Spain, Padrón municipal de población 2001–8, and US Census Bureau, Current Population Survey, March supplement, 2001–8.

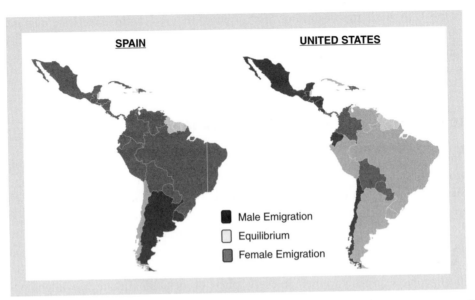

MAP 20.1 Gender composition of gross emigration flow to Spain and the USA by countries of origin, 2006–8

Source: Author's estimates on the basis on INE, Spain, *Padrón municipal de población 2006–2008*, and US Census Bureau, *Current Population Survey*, March supplement, 2006–8.

A specific analysis of gender differences in migration by origin/destination country offers us a regional view of these variations. In Map 20.1 we can see that in Spain there is a pattern of feminization, with the exceptions of Argentina, Uruguay, and to a lesser extent Chile. In the other countries, there is a clear domination of female emigration to Spain: in El Salvador and the Dominican Republic, women represented almost two-thirds of those countries' total emigration to Spain.

When we discuss Latin American emigration to the USA, we see a more heterogeneous situation. Along with countries that show a high masculine predominance, there are also countries which have a highly feminized migration. In the first category are countries which have a long-standing tradition of migration to the USA: Mexico, El Salvador, Honduras, Guatemala, and Ecuador. In the second category are countries which also have a long history of migration, such as Colombia, the Dominican Republic, and Haiti.

Finally, it is worth noting that over the long term, the sex ratio has been relatively stable, although there have been some cyclical variations which do not alter the structural pattern. In the USA, for example, the sex ratio has maintained itself at more than 115 men for every 100 women since the mid-1990s. It was only from 1999 to 2001 that the gender ratio dropped somewhat, but this never indicated a feminization of the migration pattern (see Figure 20.4). Something similar but in reverse has occurred in the case of Latin American emigration to Spain. Here, the sex ratio has always been fewer than 85 men for every 100 women, although it has changed somewhat in recent years.

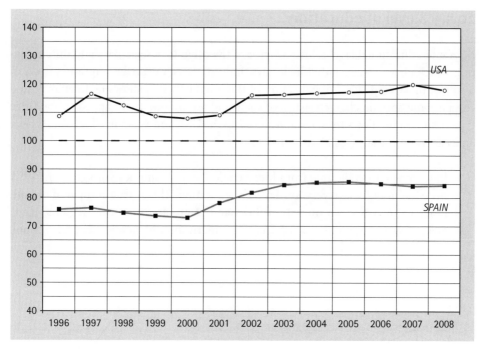

FIGURE 20.4 Sex ratio of Latin American immigrants in USA and Spain, 1996–2008 (no. of men per 100 women)

Source: Author's estimates on the basis on INE, Spain, *Padrón municipal de población* 1996–2008, and US Census Bureau, *Current Population Survey*, March supplement, 1996–2008.

The relative stability of the sex ratio indicates structural differences between Latin American emigration to the USA (more masculine) and emigration to Spain (more feminine). Furthermore, the stability of this pattern applies to almost all the countries in the region.[2] This greater presence of female migrants in Spain (and, in general, the rest of Europe) has been widely documented (Pedone 2006). This female predominance can be explained by Latin American women's incorporation into the service industry, especially caretaking (children, older people, and sick people, among others) and domestic service (house-cleaning). This incorporation has been dubbed the transnationalization of the maternal and care industry (Hondagneu-Sotelo 2001; Herrera 2005).

The predominance of male migrants in the USA can be explained by the long-standing migratory tradition of Mexicans and Central Americans who tend to work as agricultural or construction day-laborers—economic sectors which are traditionally and overwhelmingly male (Durand and Massey 2003; Canales 2007a).

[2] The only exception to this is Central American emigration to the USA. Here, emigration was markedly feminine in the mid-1990s, and has been markedly masculine in the last few years. From 1995 to 1996, the sex ratio was 90 men for every 100 women, while that same ratio has been more than 120 men per 100 women since 2006.

20.5.3 Level of education

Migrants' educational level is also a factor of the migratory selectivity and differentiation which characterizes individual flows. Indeed, we can describe migration flows in terms of the average level of education of the migrants. This allows us to analyze and compare the specific characteristics of each migration flow. There appear to be three types of migration flows from Latin America to the USA and Spain in which this type of analysis is appropriate (see Figure 20.5).

- In the first case, migrants from Mexico and Central America who go to the USA overwhelmingly have very low levels of education. This is true compared to both other Latin American migration flows and migrants from other regions. Here, 60% of Mexicans and 51% of Central Americans did not finish high school.

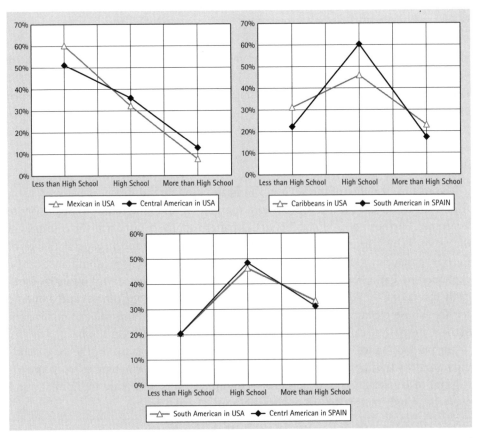

FIGURE 20.5 Latin American immigrants by level of education and region of origin: USA and Spain, 2007

Source: Author's estimates on the basis on INE, Spain, *Padrón municipal de población* 2007, and US Census Bureau, *Current Population Survey*, March supplement, 2007.

Furthemore, only 8% of Mexicans and 13% of Central Americans have some post-secondary education. The rest of immigrants have finished high school, but have no post-secondary education.

- In stark contrast, compared to other Latin American emigrants, South American migrants who immigrate to the USA and Central Americans who move to Spain tend to show higher than average levels of education. In both these cases, nearly one-third of the migrants have university or professional education (although not necessarily completed). At the same time, between 46% and 48% have finished high school. Furthermore, only 20% of these migrants have lower than high school education.
- Finally, South Americans who migrate to Spain and Caribbeans who go to the USA tend to have an intermediate level of education: their level of education is much higher than that of the Mexicans and Central Americans in the USA, but lower than the second group of South Americans and Caribbeans. Specifically, there are a high percentage of migrants who have finished high school but not a particularly large number of people who have professional or university studies.

It is particularly interesting to compare the educational profile of the South American migrants who go to the USA with those who go to Spain. While the immigrants in Spain demonstrate a high level of education, those who migrate to the USA have an even higher one. This difference is due to the different places of origin, in every country, of the South Americans who go to Spain as opposed to those who go to the USA. The Ecuadorian case illustrates this. Ecuadorian emigrants to the USA are predominantly from the Sierra region and rural areas.On the other hand, Ecuadorian emigrants who go to Spain are from the coastal region and urban areas, and have a higher level of education than those from the Sierra and rural areas.

20.6 LABOR PARTICIPATION OF LATIN AMERICAN IMMIGRANTS

The integration of Latin American immigrants into the US and Spanish economies is constrained by the contractual processes of deregulation and labor flexibility of markets, giving rise to new forms of labor differentiation and segregation in the current era of globalization (Stalker 2000). In this context, the Latin American immigrant faces similar working conditions, marked by social exclusion and vulnerability. In this regard, an analysis of the socioeconomic profile of migrants will allow us to illustrate the precarious economic and living conditions of many Latin American emigrants.

20.6.1 Economic participation

Latin American migration to Spain and the USA is essentially driven by labor and economic factors. This is the reason that we see very high levels of participation among economically active adults. It should be noted that this high level of economic activity occurs across all levels of education, as documented above. However, when we compare the labor situation of men and women, we see important differences.

Latin American male immigrants systematically demonstrate a higher than average level of participation in the labor market as compared to the native populations of Spain and the USA. In Spain, South American male migrants have a labor participation rate of 90% and Central Americans and Caribbeans have an 80% rate. Both these statistics are far higher than the 67% of the native Spanish population (see Figure 20.6). The situation is similar in the USA. Mexicans and Central and South Americans have an average participation rate which is between 13 and 19 percentage points higher than Anglo-American men. Only the Caribbean male immigrants (Cubans, Dominicans, and Haitians) have a rate which is closer to the average for Anglo-Americans. Even so, it is still 6 percentage points higher.

The situation is somewhat different for women, however. In Spain, there is a similarly high level of female immigrant participation in the labor force, while in the USA there is greater heterogeneity among the female migrants according to country and region of origin. In the Spanish case, all Latin American female immigrants maintain a high level of economic participation, generally above 70%. However, in contrast, only 47% of native Spanish women of working age actually participate in the labor force.

The situation is very different in the USA. Participation appears to be driven by region of origin. Female immigrants from Central and South America show a less than 5 percentage point higher level of economic participation than native Anglo-American women. In contrast, Caribbean women show levels of employment that are very similar to the native one. Mexican female immigrants have the lowest level of economic participation.

In both countries, gender differentiation applies to Latin American male and female immigrants' employment rates. The Spanish situation highlights the particular situation of female immigrants in that they have employment levels that are much higher than the national average. This is very relevant to the fact that Latin American migration to Spain is markedly female in nature, as previously discussed. This means that we are talking about a migration that is female and labor-based.

20.6.2 Employment

The previous data clearly illustrate the hypothesis that Latin American migration is essentially motivated by the labor factor. By the same token, the migrants are exposed to

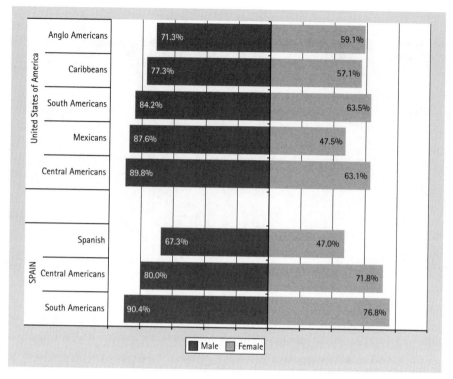

FIGURE 20.6 Economic activity rates by sex: USA and Spain, 2007

Source: Author's estimates on the basis on Ministerio del Trabajo, Spain, *Encuesta de Población Activa, Primer Trimestre, 2007*, and US Census Bureau, *Current Population Survey*, March supplement, 2007.

conditions of vulnerability and insecurity that characterize the changes in the labor market in the developed nations. These changes are due to processes of globalization and labor flexibility. They are marked by the segmentation and polarization of different occupations and the employment structure itself (Zlolniski 2006).

In both Spain and the USA, Latin American migrants tend to work in very specific employment sectors (Figure 20.7). The men work predominantly in the construction industry, which employs 31% of the male migrant work force in the USA and 39% in Spain. The labor situation for Latin American women is more heterogeneous. In the USA, almost 50% of them work in professional and social services. Another 18% work in the personal services industry. These are very different fields, especially in terms of remuneration and labor conditions. Without a doubt, professionals have better labor conditions than in the social and personal services. These differences are probably due to the fact that immigrants from South America tend to have higher levels of education than those from Mexico and Central America: South Americans are more likely to have a professional career, while Mexican and Central American women are more likely to work in the personal services.

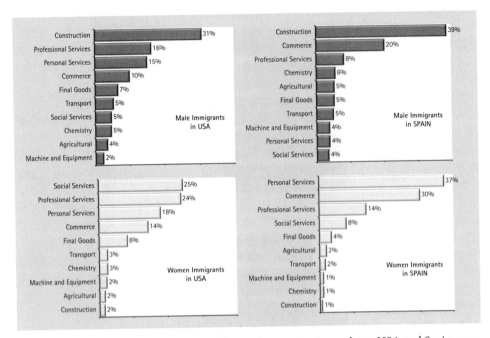

FIGURE 20.7 Latin American immigrants by employment sector and sex: USA and Spain, 2007

Source: Author's estimates on the basis on Ministerio del Trabajo, Spain, *Encuesta de Población Activa, Primer Trimestre, 2007*, and US Census Bureau, *Current Population Survey*, March supplement, 2007.

In Spain, on the other hand, only 14% of Latin American immigrant women work in professional services, 37% are employed in the personal services, and 30% work in the commercial sector. Compared to the USA, there is greater concentration in fewer labor sectors and there is also greater homogeneity in employment. This could be due to the fact that compared to the USA, Latin American immigration is more recent and come from a smaller group of countries, which could explain this greater homogeneity in employment.

In addition to these arguments, it is interesting to note the influence that Latin American immigration has on particular occupations in both Spain and the USA. In the case of the USA, for example, Latin American immigrants compose 37% of day-laborers in construction, 34% of domestic workers, 33% of agricultural workers, and 27% of all employees in the apparel and footwear industries (see Figure 20.8).

In Spain, Latin American immigrants constitute 32% of domestic service workers and 24% of day-laborers in the construction industry. These large contributions of workers illustrate the dependency on Latin American immigration of certain industries in both countries. The case of domestic service workers is especially important because it directly highlights not only migratory differentiation but also social class distinctions that limit and contextualize Latin American immigrants' social and economic integration into the societies of the developed world.

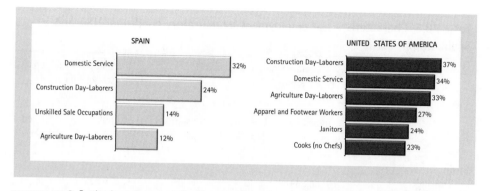

FIGURE 20.8 Latin American immigrants in selected occupations by sex: USA and Spain, 2007

Source: Author's estimates on the basis on Ministerio del Trabajo, Spain, *Encuesta de Población Activa, Primer Trimestre, 2007*, and US Census Bureau, *Current Population Survey*, March supplement, 2007.

These figures are important because these are the employment sectors which have high levels of job insecurity, which make the migrants more vulnerable economically. This pattern of labor participation of Latin American immigrants in both Spain and the USA illustrates the polarization of occupations and labor market segmentation that characterizes the new economy in developed countries. Indeed, different forms of labor flexibility directly affect the structure of occupations, employment levels, and wages, as well as labor relations. The international employment structure has been transformed to favor part-time jobs, working at home, and other forms of outsourcing. This inevitably leads to job insecurity and increased vulnerability of workers to these new labor market operating conditions (Castells 1996). To illustrate, we discuss three job characteristics of Latin Americans in the USA and Spain (see Table 20.6).

First, Latin Americans are inserted into lower skilled jobs. In Spain, 37% of South American migrants are employed in unskilled occupations, against only 12% of Spanish in these occupations. In the USA the situation is more complex. On the one hand, 40% of Mexicans and 37% of Central Americans are in unskilled jobs, a proportion much higher than that of Anglo and African Americans. Furthermore, although the Caribbean and South America seem to have better options, in both cases their jobs are also more precarious than those of Anglo and African American population.

Secondly, the insertion into unskilled jobs translates into greater job insecurity. In Spain, 52% of South Americans do not have a permanent contract, almost twice the rate prevailing among native workers. This situation also affects Latin Americans in the USA. Sixty-five percent of Mexican workers and 61% of Central Americans do not access employment benefits of any kind, a proportion more than twice that prevailing among the Anglo and African American population. Again, South American and Caribbean migrants are better off, but still far from the levels of employment protection that benefit native workers.

Third, job segregation affecting Latin American immigrants is also reflected in the difficulty in accessing positions of higher grade, even if you have the human capital and

Table 20.6 Characteristics of employment by migratory condition: USA and Spain, 2007

	Total employed population			Employed with high school education or above	
	Total	Unskilled jobs (%)	Precarious jobs (%)	Total	Unskilled jobs (%)
Spain					
Spanish	16,816,569	12	28	13,816,835	9
South Americans	1,416,420	37	52	1,122,322	32
Other migrants	1,744,332	31	52	1,311,732	27
USA					
Anglo-Americans	102,323,120	11	30	93,829,519	9
Afro-Americans	15,354,028	17	32	13,517,032	15
Mexican	7,639,690	40	65	3,315,143	33
Central Americans	1,918,946	37	61	962,497	26
Caribbeans	1,490,459	20	44	1,134,983	17
South Americans	1,578,500	23	48	1,330,026	21
Other migrants	12,468,804	12	32	11,245,469	9

Source: Author's estimates on basis of INE, Spain, Active Population Survey, First Quarter 2007, and US Bureau of Census, *Current Population Survey*, March supplement, 2007.

levels of schooling for that. In Spain, 32% of South American immigrants with high-school education or above are employed in unskilled jobs. By contrast, only 9% of Spanish with this level of schooling are in such jobs. In the USA the situation is very similar. Thirty-three percent of Mexicans and 26% of Central Americans with this level of schooling are employed in unskilled jobs—a proportion almost three times higher than that prevailing among Anglo Americans. Although the situation is somewhat better for South American and Caribbean immigrants, they too are affected by this situation of segregation, resulting from the processes of labor market segmentation that impedes and restricts access of Latin American immigrants to jobs in line with their qualifications and job training.

20.7 CONCLUSIONS

International migration is one of the best illustrations of structural inequalities between the countries and regions associated with globalization. Latin America is not immune to these processes. Actually, the mobility of its population has contributed to the diversity and ever-increasing complexity of migration patterns. One of the most relevant facts about Latin America is that it has changed from being an immigraton region to a region of emigration, contributing to the great march from the South to the North. This mirrors world population movements in this era of globalization.

Effectively, Latin American migration has not only intensified but "extensified." This is true in terms of its origins, destination countries, and migration forms. Until the 1970s, Latin American emigration was almost exclusively intraregional and was primarily among neighboring countries. Today, we can observe two important modifications. First, these intraregional movements have spread beyond cross-border flows. Secondly, emigration has increased exponentially towards the developed world, especially the US, and more recently Europe, Japan, and Australia (Martinez 2008).

In this chapter I have used recent statistical information to document the characteristics of Latin American emigration to the USA and Spain—the two countries that are the primary destinations of Latin American emigrants. We have seen that this new emigration is directly linked to changes in the production structure and labor markets in the developed economies. These changes are a result of the processes of employment polarization and segmentation in a globalized world.

This resulting heterogeneity is the basis for new forms of exclusion, discrimination, and social segregation which affect migrant workers, among others (Castells 1996). In particular, the strategies of flexibility and labor deregulation are the basis for new types of employment for the migrant population (Sassen 1998). Therefore, this situation has direct implications for the dynamics of migration and their changes in the last decade. The structural situation allows us to explain not only the growth of migration but also its new forms, sociodemographic profiles, and employment conditions, all of which are documented above.

In general, there has been an increase in emigration in all Latin American countries, though not in the same proportions. Without a doubt, Mexican migration is the largest, currently contributing more than 60% of Latin American emigrants to the USA. However, there are two facts we should take into account. First, emigration from even small countries is increasing. This is the case for El Salvador, which has the highest emigration rate to the USA in Latin America. Also, Ecuador has the largest volume of migrants to Spain. Secondly, in contrast to Mexican migration, which is almost exclusively to the USA, the situation in the rest of Latin America is more complex. Europe has become a destination which is equally or more important than the USA for Dominicans, Ecuadorians, Colombians, and more recently, Argentines. Similarly, Japan is now an important destination for Brazilians and to a lesser extent Peruvians.

The sociodemographic profile is complex and diverse. In general, Latin American emigration is labor-driven. It essentially involves young, economically active adults aged 15–39. However, there is wide diversity in the composition of migrant populations. Migration to Spain is principally female in nature, while in the USA, the situation is more heterogeneous. Mexican and Central American migrants in the USA are primarily male. In contrast, Dominican, Haitian, Colombian, Bolivian, and other South American emigrants to the USA tend to be female.

In terms of the employment of Latin American immigrants, the situation is not very diverse. In particular, we note that, with some exceptions, Latin Americans tend to be exposed to varying conditions of precarious employment and occupational segregation. In this regard, I have presented data which allow us to document three different aspects of this particularly vulnerable labor situation.

- First, Latin American immigrants have a systematically higher level of economic participation than the native populations of both Spain and the USA.
- Second, this high level of employment is frequently marked by job placement in positions which are unstable, precarious, and unskilled.
- Finally, this high level of employment insecurity and vulnerability means that Latin American migrants often have lower levels of social protection and more instability. They are strongly affected by deregulation and the precariousness of their working conditions, since they often find themselves employed in domestic service as well as in the agricultural and construction industries.

References

ADSERA, A. (2006). 'Marital Fertility and Religion in Spain, 1985 and 1999', *Population Studies* 60.2.

BECK, U. (2000). *The Brave New World of Work*, Cambridge: Polity Press and Malden, Mass.: Blackwell.

CABRÉ, A. (1999). *El sistema català de reproducció*, Barcelona: Proa.

CANALES, A. (2007a). 'Inclusion and Segregation: The Incorporation of Latin American Immigrants into the U.S. Labor Market', *Latin American Perspectives* 34.1.

—— (2007b). 'Migrant Remittances; Savings Funds or Wage Income', in G. Zárate-Hoyos (ed.), *New Perspectives on Remittances from Mexicans and Central Americans in the USA*, Kassel: Kassel University Press.

—— and MONTIEL, I. (2007). 'A World Without Borders? Mexican Immigration, Internal Borders and Transnationalism in the USA', in A. Pecoud and P. de Guchteneire (eds), *Migration Without Borders: Essays on the Free Movement of People*, Oxford and New York: Berghahn Books and UNESCO.

CASTELLS, M. (1996). *The Information Age: Economy, Society and Culture 1 (The Rise of the Network Society)*, Malden, Mass.: Blackwell.

CASTLES, S., and MILLER, M. (1993). *The Age of Migration: International Population Movements in the Modern World*, New York: Guilford Press.

COOKE, M. (2003). 'Population and Labour Force Ageing in Six Countries', Working Paper No. 4, Workforce Ageing in the New Economy Project, University of Western Ontario.

DE HAAS, H. (2007). 'Remittances, Migration and Social Development: A Conceptual Review of the Literature', Social Policy and Development Programme Paper No. 34, New York: United Nations.

DOMINGO I VALLS, A. (2006). 'Tras la retórica de la hispanidad: la migración latinoamericana en España. Entre la complementariedad y la exclusión', in A. Canales (ed.), *Panorama actual de las migraciones en América Latina*, Mexico: University of Guadalajara and Latin American Population Association.

DURAND, J., and MASSEY, D. (2003). *Clandestinos: migración México–Estados Unidos en los albores del siglo XXI*, Mexico: M. A. Porrúa and Universidad Autónoma de Zacatecas.

FOMIN (Fondo Multilateral de Inversiones/Multilateral Investment Fund) (2004). *Remittances to Latin America and the Caribbean: Goals and Recommendations*, Washington, DC: IDB.

HERRERA, G. (2005). 'Mujeres ecuatorianas en las cadenas globales del cuidado', in G. Herrera, M. C. Carrillo, and A. Torres (eds.). *La migración ecuatoriana: transnacionalismo, redes e identidades*, Ecuador: Facultad Latinoamericana de Ciencias Sociales.

HONDAGNEU-SOTELO, P. (2001). *Doméstica: Immigrant Workers Cleaning and Caring in the Shadows of Affluence*, Los Angeles: University of California Press.

LEE, R. (2003). 'The Demographic Transition: Three Centuries of Fundamental Change', *Journal of Economic Perspectives* 17.

MARTÍNEZ, J. (ed.) (2008). *América Latina y el Caribe: migración internacional, derechos humanos y desarrollo*, Santiago, Chile: ECLAC.

OIM (International Organization for Migration) (2003). *The Migration–Development Nexus: Evidence and Policy Options*, Geneva.

PEDONE, C. (2006). *Estrategias migratorias y poder: tú siempre jalas a los tuyos*, Ecuador: Ediciones ABYA-YALA.

PELLEGRINO, A. (2003). *La migración internacional en América Latina y El Caribe: tendencias y perfiles de los migrantes*, Santiago, Chile: ECLAC.

PÉREZ DÍAZ, J. (2003). *La madurez de masas*, Madrid: Imserso.

PUJADAS, J., and MASSAL, J. (2005). 'Migraciones ecuatorianas a España: procesos de inserción y claroscuros', *Iconos, Revista de ciencias sociales* 14.

RATHA, D. (2003). 'Worker's Remittances: An Important and Stable Source of External Development Finance', in *Global Development Finance 2003*, Washington, DC: World Bank.

SASSEN, S. (1998). *Globalization and its Discontents*, New York: New Press.

STALKER, P. (2000). *Workers Without Frontiers: The Impact of Globalization on International Migration*, Boulder, Colo.: Rienner.

TAPINOS, G., and DELAUNAY, D. (2000). 'Peut-on parler d'une mondialisation des migrations internationales?', in *Mondialisation, migrations et développement*, Paris: OECD.

TERRY, D. (2005). 'Remittances as a Development Tool', in D. F. Terry and S. R. Wilson (eds), *Beyond Small Change: Making Migrant Remittances Count*, Washington, DC: IDB.

UNFPA (United Nations Population Fund) (2006). *State of World Population: A Passage to Hope—Women and International Migration*, New York.

United Nations (2001). *Replacement Migration: Is It a Solution to Declining and Ageing Populations?* New York.

World Bank (2011). *Migration and Remittances Factbook 2011*, Washington, DC.

ZLOLNISKI, C. (2006). *Janitors, Street Vendors, and Activists: The Lives of Mexican Immigrants in Silicon Valley*, Berkeley: University of California Press.

PART IV

PRODUCTIVE SECTOR DEVELOPMENT

CHAPTER 21

....

STRUCTURAL TRANSFORMATION AND ECONOMIC GROWTH IN LATIN AMERICA

....

RICARDO HAUSMANN

21.1 LATIN AMERICAN GROWTH: NEO-CLASSICAL INTERPRETATIONS[1]

....

Latin American growth has picked up since 2003, and the region went through the Great Recession more resiliently than most expected. Per capita GDP growth in the 2003–8 period averaged 4.1% for the region, its best five-year growth rate since the late 1960s and early 1970s. Is Latin America's relative stagnation over? Has the region solved its growth problems? Is this the beginning of a new long, expansionary phase of Latin American growth?

Two observations about the recent growth performance suggest a less optimistic interpretation. First, the recent growth was not a unique Latin American phenomenon. World growth accelerated in this period making it easier for all regions to grow. Second, the region's terms of trade improved. Third, much of this growth was a cyclical recovery from the 1998–2002 recession. If we look at growth for the decade to 2008, Latin American growth underperformed growth in all the developing regions of the world and all middle- and lower-income groupings. If we look back for twenty years, the picture remains equally worrisome, with Latin America performing worse than all regions of the world except for Sub-Saharan Africa.

[1] I am thankful to Dani Rodrik, Bailey Klinger, and Jason Hwang with whom I have been working over the last years on the set of ideas I base this chapter on.

Yet this could have been a period of significantly higher growth, as falling fertility rates caused dependency ratios to decline and female labor force participation to increase. Hence, the number of workers per capita in a typical country in the region rose by 1.1% per year (Table 21.1). This dynamic, the so-called demographic window of opportunity, was the fastest rate of any region or country grouping. For any given rate of productivity growth, it should have led to a faster rate of growth of GDP per capita. However, what we observe instead is that GDP per worker in Latin America grew at 0.6% in the decade to 2007, the slowest rate of any region and country grouping.

And this does not control for the fact that the years of schooling of the labor force have been growing much faster in Latin America than in the US. Table 21.2 tries to make some calculations regarding this effect. We use estimates of years of schooling and returns to schooling using two household surveys separated by about a decade. We impute how much output per worker should have grown, assuming that schooling maintained the estimated rate of progress over the 1996–2006 decade and that the returns to schooling remained at the levels estimated in the later survey. While in the United States education accounts only for about 0.5% of the 1.9% increase in GDP per worker, in the typical Latin American country the increase in GDP per worker was 0.7% lower than what would have been expected from the education effect alone.

These facts are hard to square with what we may call the standard reading of the neoclassical growth model (Solow 1956; 1957) and its variants (Mankiw, Romer, and Weil 1992). According to it, differences in levels of per capita income across countries are affected by differences in the following four variables: investment/savings rate, human capital accumulation rate, population growth (driven by fertility and mortality), and total factor productivity levels.

In most of these dimensions, the gap between Latin America and the US has been narrowing. For example, the gap in life expectancy vis-à-vis the US declined, with many Latin American countries going from a gap of twelve years in the 1950s to within one or two years of the US level at present. The gaps in secondary and tertiary school enrollment are in a clear downward trend. The fertility rate in Latin America declined from 5.7 children per woman in the 1960s to 2.7 in the first decade of the current century. The equivalent numbers for the US are 3.0 and 2.0 respectively. So many of these gaps have narrowed dramatically, but the gap in income per capita between the US and Latin America has widened, not narrowed. One could make similar points about the gap in inflation rates, country risk, democracy, business environment, financial depth, etc.

This is the standard reading of the Solow model. An alternative reading would emphasize the fact that the bulk of the growth process is due to the so-called Solow residual, which some call total factor productivity, but which Abramovits aptly referred to as a measure of our ignorance. In essence, growth is driven by something other than the accumulation of physical and human capital in a constant-returns-to-scale environment. Exactly what it is that we are ignorant about is shrouded in mystery.

Table 21.1 Growth in GDP per capita and GDP per worker and workers per capita, 1997–2007 (%)

Country	GDP per capita	GDP per worker	Workers per capita
Argentina	1.6	0.6	0.9
Bolivia	1.3	0.3	1.0
Brazil	1.5	0.2	1.3
Chile	2.6	1.9	0.6
Colombia	1.8	0.1	1.6
Costa Rica	3.4	2.5	0.9
Dominican Republic	3.9	2.3	1.6
Ecuador	1.9	0.4	1.4
Guatemala	1.4	−1.3	2.7
Haiti	2.2	2.5	−0.3
Honduras	−0.9	−1.7	0.8
Mexico	2.1	1.5	0.5
Nicaragua	2.3	0.8	1.5
Panama	3.6	2.9	0.7
Paraguay	2.6	1.1	1.5
Peru	−0.1	−1.6	1.5
Uruguay	1.5	1.1	0.3
Venezuela	1.0	−0.6	1.7
Latin America & Caribbean	1.7	0.6	1.1
Other regions			
East Asia & Pacific	6.9	6.5	0.4
Europe & Central Asia	4.9	4.4	0.5
Middle East & North Africa	2.5	1.1	1.3
South Asia	4.9	4.3	0.5
Sub-Saharan Africa	1.7	1.4	0.3
Country groupings			
High income	1.8	1.6	0.2
High income: OECD	1.8	1.6	0.2
High income: non-OECD	2.9	1.8	1.0
Middle income	4.1	3.6	0.4
Upper middle income	2.7	1.8	0.8
Lower middle income	5.9	5.5	0.3
Low & middle income	3.9	3.5	0.5
Low income	2.9	2.4	0.6
Least developed countries: UN classification	3.3	2.8	0.5
Heavily indebted poor countries (HIPC)	1.7	1.4	0.3

Source: World Development Indicators, 2009.

Table 21.2 GDP per worker and contribution of increased schooling

Country	Returns to schooling (%)	Increase in schooling years per decade	Implied education effect (output per worker)	GDP per worker (growth 1996–2006)	Other factors
Argentina	9.1	1.1	0.9	1.1	0.2
Brazil	13.4	1.2	1.6	−0.7	−2.3
Chile	12.3	1.5	1.8	2.7	0.9
Costa Rica	9.8	1.0	1.1	0.9	−0.2
Honduras	9.3	1.2	1.8	0.7	−1.1
Mexico	12.6	1.6	1.9	1.3	−0.6
Panama	12.7	1.4	1.4	1.7	0.3
Peru	12.9	1.7	2.8	0.5	−2.3
Uruguay	8.4	1.2	1.1	1.3	0.2
Venezuela	8.7	1.3	1.3	−0.8	−2.1
Average	10.9	1.3	1.6	0.9	−0.7
Thailand	19.2	0.3	0.4	1.3	0.9
USA	12.0	0.5	0.5	1.9	1.4

Source: Data on education from Hausmann and Velasco (2005). GDP per worker from World Development Indicators.

21.2 THE LATIN AMERICAN GROWTH PUZZLE AND THE FATHERS OF DEVELOPMENT ECONOMICS

For the fathers of development economics, a world described by a well-behaved constant-returns-to-scale aggregate production function that depends only on the availability of a few well-known factors of production such as capital, land, and labor made little sense. Rosenstein-Rodan (1943) or Arthur Lewis (1954) start from a dichotomy between a traditional and a modern economy, and imagine different obstacles to the transformation of one into the other, such as insufficient market size to support a modern economy. If there is a traditional subsistence sector that is large, market size will be small, limiting the size of the modern sector. If there are economies of scale, there may be poverty traps. In this view, a big push would put economies on the right side of growth.

But in much of Latin America the non-market subsistence sector has pretty much disappeared. The region has become highly urbanized, and the market economy is pretty much the only game in town. One could potentially imagine a reinterpretation such that the traditional sector becomes the informal sector, and its large size prevents the modern sector from achieving the scale it needs to exploit economies of scale. But in a globalizing world it is unclear what aspect of market size would be a limit to growth. If something about market size were the obstacle, there should be enough global demand to make the growth of the modern sector profitable.

Raul Prebisch (1950) thought that there was a fundamental difference between natural resource-based activities and industrialization, with the former being subject to a secular decline in the terms of trade. The ensuing years have weakened the importance of the argument based on terms-of-trade trends, but the idea that different activities may have a differential impact on growth propensities seems persuasive. It is open to debate what the relevant dimensions of this difference are, and I shall argue below for a particular view. A modern restatement of the Prebisch distinction is the paper by Matsuyama (1991), who puts the emphasis not on the evolution of the terms of trade but on that of productivity. If the dichotomy is between a sector with high productivity growth—call it industry—versus a sector of lower productivity growth, say agriculture, then those that for static reasons of comparative advantage specialize in the low-productivity growth activity will end up growing more slowly and falling relatively behind. This sounds theoretically plausible, but empirically, agriculture, mining, and oil have seen very large increases in productivity, and it is hard to argue that this productivity differential, or the terms of trade, can be much of an explanation for the lack of Latin American convergence.

Albert Hirschman (1958) saw the growth process not as an equilibrium phenomenon but as one of disequilibrium. If a new industry develops, it will cause the appearance of other industries through forward and backward linkages. While Hirschman was never too clear as to what the essence of these linkages was, the literature interpreted them essentially as demand effects between one industry and another. So an exogenous decision to invest in some strategic industry—a development pole—will create a development process in which related industries will appear. It is important to be precise about the nature of the linkage between the original industry and those that are crowded in. In a globalizing world, many inputs can be traded internationally. The apparel industry uses cloth, but it need not buy it at home; it can and does import it. So if there are such inter-industry spillovers, it is important to understand their nature.

Mainstream economics has become much more sympathetic to this style of reasoning after the limitations of the neoclassical approach became clearer. Robert Lucas (1988) convinced the profession that without externalities, growth could not be explained. He suggested that these externalities might be related to human capital, but the empirical evidence in favor of this interpretation is weak (Acemoglu and Angrist 2000). Paul Romer (1990) developed a model where growth is related to economies of scale in innovation, through the creation of increased product variety. Aghion and Howitt (1992) created a model where the innovation is not about increasing variety but increasing quality within the same variety, causing creative destruction. In these models, the economies of scale are bounded by monopolistic competition among imperfectly substitutable goods. In general, in these models, elements that in the Solow model affect only the differences in the steady-state level of income of countries, such as population growth, investment effort, and education, will also affect their long-run growth. As such, this only increases the puzzle of Latin American growth: convergence in human capital and institutional quality, but diverging outcomes. Our challenge is to explain a widening income gap in spite of narrowing gaps in the observed underlying determinants.

These traditional and new growth models in the mainstream literature contrast with the Latin American tradition of trying to explain the level and dynamism of output by the composition of output (see Fajnzylber 1990; Katz 2000; Ocampo 2005). In these works, obstacles to productive transformation are key to understanding growth problems. This chapter will continue in this tradition.

21.3 STRUCTURAL TRANSFORMATION

One way forward is to start from a less aggregated description of the development process. Let us look not at the dichotomy between two sectors but at a more detailed composition of output. Imbs and Wacziarg (2003) have shown that in the process of development, countries become more diversified until they reach a level of income similar to that of Ireland or Spain in 1990. After that, countries seem to become more specialized. Hence, for the relevant Latin American range, development seems to be associated with diversification.

Said differently, rich countries do not just produce more per person. They also produce different kinds of goods. Since countries tend to export the things they do relatively better (i.e. the products in which they have comparative advantage), it is instructive to know what happens to the composition of exports at different levels of development. In Hausmann, Hwang, and Rodrik (2007) we developed a measure of the income level of exports, which we called EXPY. We constructed this in two steps. First, for each product traded internationally, we calculated the weighted average of the GDP per capita of countries that export that good, where the weights are the revealed comparative advantage in that good of the countries that export it. Hence we associate a certain income level to each product, which we call PRODY. Then, for each country we calculate EXPY as the weighted average of the PRODYs of the country's export basket, where the weights are the shares that each good has in the export basket of each country. Figure 21.1 shows a strong upward relationship between the level of income of a country and the level of income of its export basket.[2]

The idea that rich (poor) countries tend to export goods exported by other rich (poor) countries is obvious, and is compatible with many possible theories. For example, in conventional trade theory *à la* Heckscher–Ohlin, countries export products that are more intensive in the factors of production that are relatively abundant at home. As development takes place, physical, human, and institutional capital is accumulated and the products countries export become more intensive in these factors. While this is no doubt part of the story, I shall argue below that there are also other important processes at work behind the relationship captured in Figure 21.1.

One implication of this relationship is that, as the process of development takes place, countries change their export package, i.e. they must undergo structural transformation. Depending on one's view of the world, this may be easy or hard. In a Heckscher–Ohlin world, products have no major significance: they are a mechanism for countries to exchange the relative endowments of the underlying factors of production. Labor-abundant countries trade with land- or capital-abundant countries in order to acquire more efficiently the goods that are intensive in the factors they do not have. The transition between goods is of little significance: the products are the passive consequence of changing factor endowments.

However, if changing products is complicated, i.e. if there are important market failures in the process of structural transformation, then for any given level of development, countries that have a more advanced export package are likely to grow more rapidly in the future. Since they have already upgraded their export package, their income level can more easily catch up with this upgraded package. Those that have not yet gotten around to improving what they export, on the other hand, will be constrained by the low productivity associated with their export package, just as crustaceans cannot grow until they change their external shells. Hausmann et al. (2007) test this proposition. Controlling for other determinants of growth, a more sophisticated

---

[2] For ease of exposition, we will also refer to EXPY as the level of sophistication of exports.

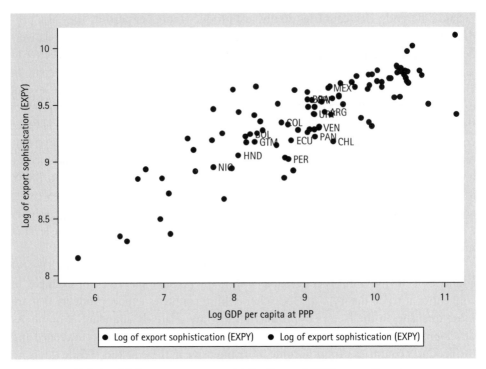

FIGURE 21.1 Relationship between export sophistication and GDP per capita, 2005

initial export package is predictive of growth over the following years. Countries converge to the level of income implied by their exports, or said differently: you become what you export.[3]

This is somewhat difficult to square with a strict interpretation in terms of conventional comparative advantage or Heckscher–Ohlin theory. Under received theory, a country with an export package that is significantly more sophisticated than that indicated by its current income level is one that has misallocated resources (by pushing them into areas where the country does not have a comparative advantage). Such a country should perform badly relative to countries whose export packages are more in line with current capabilities. That we observe the opposite suggests that the process of structural transformation is more rife with market failures than is implied by standard trade theory. What is the nature of those failures? We shall return to this question, but before we do this, let us look at Latin America in this dimension.

As noted, Figure 21.1 highlights the Latin American countries in a scatterplot relating EXPY to GDP per capita. Clearly, except for Mexico and Brazil, no other countries in the region have a level of sophistication of exports substantially above the expected level. In

---

[3] In Hausmann, Hwang, and Rodrik (2007) we perform 5-year and 10-year panel regressions using different estimation techniques and applying several robustness checks.

fact, most Latin American countries are well below the expected level. This indicates that lack of export sophistication acts as a drag on growth. In other words, most countries cannot adopt a strategy of producing more of the same as the current level of sophistication of exports would not support much higher incomes. Interestingly, Mexico and Brazil, the two countries with the best performance on this indicator, have also been serious laggards in the growth process, making the puzzle that much deeper.

One trivial implication of the preceding analysis is that countries should improve what they produce. But how? What obstacles may impede this process?

21.4 MARKET FAILURES THAT IMPEDE STRUCTURAL TRANSFORMATION

In general, two classes of problems may be involved: coordination failures and information spillovers. Coordination failures occur when markets are incomplete so that the return to one investment depends on whether some other investment is also made: building a hotel near a beautiful beach may be profitable if somebody builds an airport. However, there may not be a way for the market to coordinate both investments. A typical solution is for the government to provide a guarantee to both investors. If done well, this will be cost-free for the government ex post, as the investments will be profitable when they both take place. If the guarantee is not credible, then the government can just build the airport and the hotels will follow.

This problem is more pervasive than in the infrastructure example just described. As we will see below, new industries require specific human capital, inputs, infrastructure, and regulations, among other things. Let us refer to all these inputs as capabilities. Thus stated, the problem with productive transformation is that new products cannot be made because the requisite capabilities are not present. But in addition, there is no point in accumulating any of the requisite capabilities because there is no demand for them, since the industry that uses them does not exist, and it would not be expected to exist given the other missing capabilities. For example, soon after the development of the flower industry in Colombia in the 1970s, investors tried to mimic the same business model in Ecuador. However, the industry failed because air transport could not be adequately supplied. The flower industry did boom in the 1990s when logistical problems were ironed out.

Another source of market failure is information spillovers. In Hausmann and Rodrik (2003) we focus on spillovers in self-discovery, which we defined as the process of finding out the cost structure of an economy for the production of new goods.[4] The first

---

[4] Structural transformation is not really about inventing new products. It is about identifying which of the products that exist in the world a particular country can profitably produce. It is not a discovery of a product, but of a national capability: hence the term.

mover will find out whether something is profitable or not; if it is, she will be copied by other entrants. But if she fails, she bears the whole loss. Because of this, the private returns from engaging in this type of innovation are lower than the social benefits, and the market incentives for self-discovery are inefficiently low. The typical policy implication is to provide a subsidy in order to bring the private returns in line with the social returns.

One example of self-discovery externalities in Latin America is the case of Peru, studied by Klinger (2007). In this case, the development of asparagus, artichoke, and paprika in Peru required the pioneer to adapt the products to the context. Later, many new entrants followed into the business. However, the pioneers were able to internalize the externalities by moving into the seed supply and packing business. In instances where such internalization is not feasible, the problem is harder to address.

Labor training is another source of spillovers. A firm that trains its labor force provides a potential benefit to other firms that may poach its workers. This dampens the incentives to provide the optimal amount of training for fear of losing the investment. Clearly, labor mobility may not entail a social loss, as the worker can deploy his skills elsewhere, but the company cannot appropriate these benefits while incurring the training cost. The problem is inadequate investment in labor training; the solution is to subsidize training.

It is clear that coordination failures and spillovers are more acute for new activities than for established ones. In the first place, coordination is impeded by the proverbial chicken-and-egg problem: new activities are hard to develop unless their suppliers are present, but why would the suppliers exist if they have nobody to sell to? Secondly, by definition, new activities must incur self-discovery costs. And finally, they cannot find workers with experience in the new activity, since the activity has not been in existence and hence has not been hiring and training workers.

So how would structural change ever take place? One way forward is the development of new activities that can mostly use the factors and capabilities that an economy has already developed for other purposes.

21.5 IS THERE A STAIRWAY TO HEAVEN?

It is easy to imagine the difficulties that a new activity will face. Production of a particular good or service requires a set of rather specific inputs. By specificity, we mean that these inputs would be much less productive if deployed in some other activity. Hence, the degree of specificity can be approximated by how much less productive an input would be in its alternative use. These inputs include physical installations and machinery, workers with particular skills, a set of specific intermediate inputs, a logistic system to transport the inputs and deliver the outputs, a procurements and marketing system to acquire information about suppliers and customers, a system of property rights and contracts that society finds legitimate and is willing to respect, a set of standards and regulatory rules on product characteristics, labor norms, financial rights and consumer protection that affect the behavior of other stakeholders, etc.. These inputs or requirements are developed to solve the more or less particular needs of existing activities, but they may or may not be supportive of some other potential, not yet existing activities. Hence, development will be path-dependent on the opportunities opened by the assets and institutions bequeathed by previously existing activities.

The related markets may not yet exist, thus creating a serious coordination problem. The norms around transactions may yet need to be developed and agreed upon. Legal rules and standards may be missing, specific infrastructure needs remain unattended. Solutions to these problems have uncertain characteristics and costs.

For this reason, the new activities that do develop need to exploit existing capabilities, by which we mean the markets, physical and human assets, norms and institutions that were developed and accumulated for other pre-existing activities. These capabilities will be useful to the extent that they are similar to the needs of the new activity in question.

The degree of similarity of those needs may vary widely between any pair of activities. The export of garments requires an industrial zone with good access to workers and energy, a logistic system that allows for the import of required intermediate goods and the export of the final product with little cost or delay in customs and ports, market access rules that guarantee the right to sell in foreign markets, a labor code that facilitates the management of labor relations, a tax regime that is adequate, etc. These capabilities may be similar to those needed for car harnesses, or shoes, but quite different from those needed for the production of soybeans, fruit, steel, natural gas, or copper. Just think how different are the infrastructure requirements (dedicated train lines for mining, rural roads for soybeans, cold storage and transport systems for fruit, gas pipelines), the kind of trained labor force required (seamstresses, farmers, metallurgical workers, geologists, chemical engineers), the regulatory needs (phyto-sanitary, industrial standards), property rights (concessions for gas and mining, agricultural land property rights, rights for building roads, railroads and pipelines).

The view that capabilities are quite specific to each activity is consistent with a puzzle discussed in Hausmann and Rodrik (2003). There we pointed out that Korea exports many microwave ovens and almost no bicycles, while the opposite is true of Taiwan. Bangladesh exports hats but no soccer balls, while Pakistan does the opposite. Production seems to require something more specific than just broad asset categories. Otherwise, countries with similar endowments of these broad categories would export similar goods. Specificity is needed to explain what would otherwise look like a quite haphazard pattern of specialization.

It makes sense to think of products as being at some distance from each other in terms of the requisite capabilities. Hausmann and Klinger (2006) use the metaphor of a forest. Each product is a tree, and is placed at some distance from each other tree in the forest or product space. Some are nearby and others are farther away. Firms are like monkeys that live on a tree, off a tree, i.e. they exploit a certain product. The distance between the trees reflects the similarity of the requisite capabilities. It is a measure of how useful are the capabilities needed for the production of good A when deployed in the production of good B. This implies that it is easier for new activities to develop near the areas where monkeys already exist, because many of the requisite capabilities are already present. Producing at larger distances involves the need for capabilities that have not been previously accumulated. Trying to accumulate these capabilities in the process of self-discovery may create serious coordination problems, since the new capabilities need to be developed at the same time that the new activity is put in place. In this context, the market on its own will only jump short distances. The proverbial social planner could potentially coordinate the development of new activities with the new requisite capabilities.

In the context of our metaphor, the process of structural transformation can be described as follows. The Hausmann et al. (2007) finding implies that a part of the forest is rich (some goods have high PRODY) and a part of it is poor (others have low PRODY). Rich (poor) countries have their monkeys in the rich (poor) part of the forest. The process of structural transformation involves the monkeys jumping from the poor part to the richer part. The ability of firms to do so depends critically on the topography of the forest. If the forest is very regular in the sense that trees are at a similar distance from the next tree, then there is always a parsimonious way forward: a stairway to heaven. It is common to describe this ladder in the East Asian experience as starting with garments and toys and moving into electronics and autos. But is this really so? Is there always a stairway to heaven, or are there missing rungs in the stairway? And if the starting-off point *is* conducive to an uninterrupted ascent to heaven, what are the respective roles of natural forces and government action in its selection?

Hausmann and Klinger (2006) proceed by proposing first a measure of the distance between products. Instead of trying to identify commonality of inputs, which are unknown, they adopt an outcome-based measure. They base their measure of the distance between product A and product B on the conditional probability that countries that have comparative advantage in A also have comparative advantage in B.[5] In other words, if the capabilities needed to produce two different products are similar, this would be revealed in the fact that countries that are good at one are also good at the other.

With this measure, Hidalgo et al. (2007) document several characteristics of the product space. First, there is indeed an enormous heterogeneity in the forest. The space has a center–periphery structure. There are central parts that are very dense and peripheral parts that are sparse. This is not without consequence. The development of comparative advantage in new products is strongly affected by how far the products in which a country already has comparative advantage are from potential new ones. They show that indeed monkeys tend to jump short distances. Progress in the sparse part of the forest is much slower. They demonstrate this point in three different ways. First, the average distance to the trees that are eventually occupied is much smaller than the distance to a randomly chosen tree. Second, the probability of jumping to an individual tree is strongly affected by

---

[5] Hausmann and Klinger take the minimum of the conditional probability of A given B and of B given A. This creates a symmetric measure of distance that is less sensitive to spurious coincidences. To calculate these probabilities they use global trade data that is disaggregated by country and product at the 4-digit level, which includes over 120 countries and over 1,000 goods.

how far the occupied trees are from it. Finally, they develop an aggregate measure of the position of the country in the forest and show that it predicts how quickly a country upgrades its exports over time.

The nature of the product space can be analyzed econometrically (see Hausmann and Klinger 2006), yet it is much more revealing to illustrate this space graphically. Using the tools of network analysis an image of the product space can be constructed (Hidalgo et al. 2007). Considering the linkages as measured in the 1998–2000 period, Figure 21.2 shows the visual representation of the product space. Each node is a product, its size determined by its share of world trade. We can immediately see from Figure 21.2 that the product space is highly heterogeneous. There are peripheral products that are only weakly connected to other products. There are some groupings among these peripheral goods, such as petroleum products (the large nodes on the left side of the network), sea-food products (below petroleum products), garments (the very dense cluster at the bottom of the network), and raw materials (the upper left to upper periphery). Furthermore, there is a core of closely connected products in the center of the network, mainly of machinery, chemicals and other capital intensive goods.

This heterogeneous structure of the product space has important implications for structural transformation. If a country is producing goods in a dense part of the product space, then the process of structural transformation is much easier because the set of acquired capabilities can be easily redeployed to other nearby products. However, if a country is specialized in peripheral products, then this redeployment is more challenging as there is not a set of products requiring similar capabilities. The process of structural transformation can be impeded due to a country's orientation in this space.

To make this last point, Hausmann and Klinger (2007) develop a measure of how dense is the product space near the areas in which a country has comparative advantage (or occupied trees). The idea is that the denser the forest near the occupied trees, the easier it will be for firms to move to other products. They capture centrality by first calculating the centrality of each product and then averaging the average centrality of the products in which a country has comparative advantage.

Table 21.3 shows the ten most centrally connected products and the ten least connected, using the SITC four-digit code. Clearly, the most connected products are all manufactured goods, while the ten least connected are based on raw materials. This is an interesting point to make in relation to the emphasis put by Raul Prebisch and Albert Hirschman on the importance of industrialization. In our interpretation, parts of the manufacturing industry are indeed in a much more centrally located part of the product space, so that if capabilities are developed in products in those dense areas, further progress will be made easier, as those capabilities will be more easily redeployed into a broader class of products.

Hausmann and Klinger (2006) calculate the average centrality of the products in which a country has comparative advantage, controlling for how sophisticated the product is. They call this variable "open forest." Not surprisingly, "open forest" predicts the speed at which countries increase the level of sophistication of their exports (EXPY) and the rate of growth of the economy. This shows that not all roads lead to Rome—or,

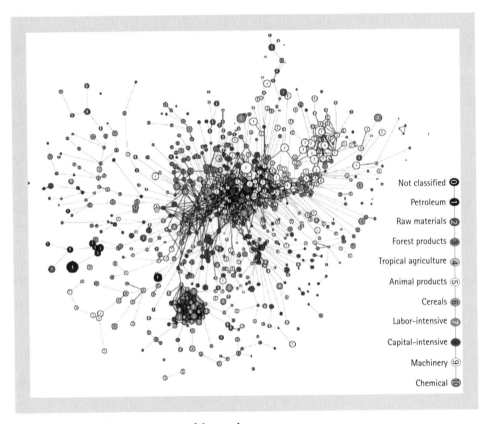

Not classified

Petroleum

Raw materials

Forest products

Tropical agriculture

Animal products

Cereals

Labor-intensive

Capital-intensive

Machinery

Chemical

FIGURE 21.2 Visual representation of the product space

Source: Hidalgo et. al. (2007).

Notes: For more information and graphics, go to http://www.chidalgo.com/productspace/.

alternatively, that the rungs in the stairway are very irregular and do not all lead to heaven. For some countries, there are indeed missing rungs in the stairway and it is often very difficult to make progress because there are no nearby trees, i.e. no easy ways to transfer existing capabilities towards the development of new products.

Figure 21.3 shows the value of "open forest" and GDP per capita. Two things are important to note. First, while in general there is a positive relationship between the level of development (as captured by GDP per capita) and "open forest," the relationship shows enormous heterogeneity. Some developing countries like China, India, Turkey, Poland, and the Czech Republic are in a very propitious part of the forest, while other countries at the same level of income are much less so.

So how does Latin America look in this space? In general, no Latin American country is in an exceptionally propitious part of the product space. The best-located countries are Brazil and Mexico. Quite a few countries are in a very poorly connected part of the product space, especially Venezuela, Ecuador, Bolivia, Nicaragua, and Panama.

Table 21.3 Centrality of goods in the product space

(a) The ten goods in the densest part of the product space, 2000		
Code	Product name	Paths
6785	Tube & pipe fittings (joints, elbows) of iron/steel	0.217
6996	Miscellaneous articles of base metal	0.209
6921	Reservoirs, tanks, vats and similar containers	0.208
6210	Materials of rubber (eg, pastes plates, sheets, etc)	0.207
7849	Other parts & accessories of motor vehicles	0.206
8935	Art of electric lighting of materials of div, 58	0.206
8939	Miscellaneous art of materials of div 58	0.205
7139	Parts of int comb piston engines of 713.2–/713.8	0.204
7492	Taps cocks, valves, etc, for pipes, tanks, vats, etc.	0.203
5822	Aminoplasts	0.202

(b) The ten goods in the sparsest part of the product space, 2000		
Code	Product name	Paths
9610	Coin other than gold, not being legal tender	0.02
6545	Fabrics woven of jute or of other textile bast fib	0.02
5723	Pyrotechnic articles (firework, railway fog, etc.)	0.03
1245	Castor oil	0.03
2440	Cork, natural, raw & waste (included in blocks/sheets)	0.04
2613	Raw silk (not thrown)	0.04
0721	Cocoa beans, whole or broken, raw or roasted	0.04
6812	Platinum and other metals of the platinum group	0.04
0573	Bananas fresh or dried	0.04
2876	Tin ores and concentrates	0.05

Source: Author's calculations restricted to goods with at least 8100M in world exports for illustrative purposes.

It is interesting to note how poorly connected are countries that export oil, such as Saudi Arabia, Algeria, Iran, and Venezuela. This suggests an alternative interpretation of the so-called "resource curse."[6] Oil and other natural resources require capabilities that are very specific. It is not just that the machinery and human skills are quite specialized; even the dedicated infrastructure such as pipelines and ports and the system of property rights, regulations, and taxes are also specific to the industry. It does not generate spillovers that are easily seized.

[6] There is an ample literature about the sources of the so-called "resource curse," including the Dutch Disease, rent-seeking, and inefficient specialization. For further discussion, see Hausmann and Rigobon (2003).

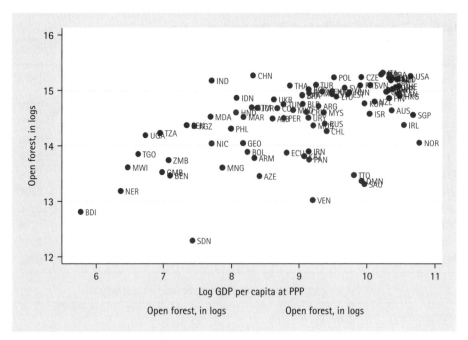

FIGURE 21.3 The "open forest" at different GDP levels

This idea has been applied by Hausmann, Rodriguez, and Wagner (2007) to explain the determinants of the duration of growth collapses. They find that while countries fall into crisis for many reasons such as export collapses, wars, sudden stops, and political transitions, most of these variables do not help predict the duration of the crisis episode. However, they find that the density of the product space around the areas of comparative advantage of a country at the time of the crisis has a very strong predictive power of the duration of a crisis. The interpretation is straightforward: when a country suffers a shock to its current exports, the speed of recovery depends on how easy it will be for the country to redeploy its capabilities into new products. This depends on how far alternative products are from current areas of comparative advantage.

21.6 UPGRADING WITHIN PRODUCT VS. BETWEEN PRODUCTS

Our view of the process of structural transformation and its co-evolution with the development of the requisite capabilities is reinforced by recent work on quality improvements in existing products. Jason Hwang (2007) has examined the within-product distance to the (quality) frontier by looking at US import unit values across highly disaggregated product categories from different exporting countries. As is typical in this literature (see Schott 2004), he defines distance to the frontier as the percentage difference in the unit price earned by a country on the export of a given product and the highest unit price observed among all exporters of that good.[7] Three findings are particularly significant for our discussion. First, once a good is exported, there appears to be unconditional convergence to the frontier within that good. By contrast, we know from the empirical literature on growth that economy-wide productivity does not exhibit unconditional convergence. Second, quality convergence at the product level takes place at a relatively fast rate, usually in excess of 5%. This contrasts with measured rates of (conditional) income convergence between countries of less than 2%. Hence, the process of learning and improving within product appears to be quite universal and fast. This means that countries that are farther from the quality frontier will tend to grow faster.

Figure 21.4 shows the distance to the frontier on existing export products for all regions of the world and a selected group of countries. Interestingly, Sub-Saharan Africa and Latin America have the smallest quality distance to the frontier in the products they are currently exporting.

Third, when a country moves to a new product it usually does so at a greater distance to the frontier than its average distance in the products it has already been exporting. Put differently, when monkeys jump to new trees, they land in the lower branches of the tree. But once established in the tree, it is easy for them to move up.

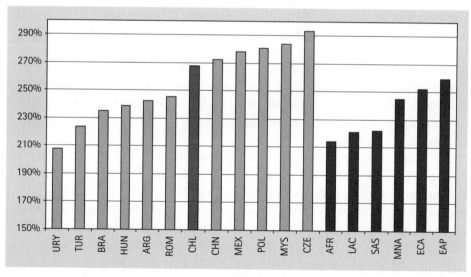

FIGURE 21.4 Distance to the quality frontier in existing export products

---

[7] To avoid potential measurement errors in looking at the highest price, he chooses instead the 90th percentile as the frontier.

These stylized facts are supportive of our story. Once an activity develops, it is much easier to work out the coordination failures and accumulate the specific capabilities that it requires. Within-product quality convergence is so fast that it cannot explain the lack of global income convergence. An important implication is that moving between products is more likely to become the binding constraint on development, since improvements within products seem to be much easier. In fact, the higher the frequency of jumps to new trees, the greater the distance to the quality frontier (as new products are produced far from the quality frontier), and hence the faster the subsequent growth.

So in our interpretation, many countries in Latin America are in a relatively sparse part of the product space. Hence, the distance to the top of the tree is short and the distance to the next tree is large, both effects limiting growth.

21.7 LATIN AMERICAN GROWTH REVISITED

Let us return to the Latin American growth puzzle. Can the considerations presented so far help explain the region's growth predicament? One way to address this question is to run growth regressions controlling for some of the new variables we are considering (Table 21.4). We look at growth in GDP per capita in the period 1985–2005. The first equation controls only for regional dummies. It shows that Latin America grew 0.8% slower than the industrial world. The second equation controls for initial GDP per capita and finds a similar result. The third equation controls for export sophistication, which is a strong predictor of future growth. With this variable the Latin American dummy falls to –0.5 and loses statistical significance. We next introduce open forest and initial population, both in logs. Since larger countries have, other things being equal, larger open forest, we control for this effect. The Latin American dummy falls to –0.47%. Finally, we introduce both export sophistication and open forest, and have the Latin American dummy fall below –0.3% and loose all statistical significance. This suggests that some of the Latin American predicament can be explained by the elements I have discussed in this chapter.

This interpretation of potential growth problems should not be seen as the only ailment countries may encounter, but instead as an additional dimension in which problems may arise. Clearly, in the recent past Brazil and Mexico have exhibited slow growth in spite of having a relatively propitious location in the product space, so other obstacles to growth are at work in those two countries. As argued in Hausmann, Rodrik, and Velasco (2008), the binding constraints on growth may be quite heterogeneous across countries, and obstacles to productive transformation represent just one more potential pitfall.

Much of the reform agenda of the 1990s was related to the presumption that government failures were at the center of poor growth performance. In a view summarized by Larry Summers (2003), growth was seen as the natural consequence of an environment in which the government provided sound money, openness to trade, and investment

Table 21.4 Growth regressions controlling for the product space

Variables	Growth	Growth	Growth	Growth	Growth
	1985–2005	1985–2005	1985–2005	1985–2005	1985–2005
Initial GDP pc (logs)	-0.00811*	-0.000446	-0.00635**	-0.00287	-0.00668***
	(-1.739)	(-0.241)	(-2.545)	(-1.464)	(-2.594)
Initial export sophistication (logs)			0.0201***		0.0156**
			(3.339)		(2.22)
Initial open forest (logs)				0.00654***	0.00438*
				(3.004)	(1.871)
Initial population (logs)				-0.000766	-0.00109
				(-0.767)	(-1.099)
Latin America		-0.00847*	-0.00508	-0.00472	-0.00296
		(-1.722)	(-1.062)	(-0.952)	(-0.602)
Sub-Saharan Africa	-0.0168***	-0.0178***	-0.0128**	-0.0103	-0.0087
	(-4.065)	(-3.012)	(-2.190)	(-1.647)	(-1.411)
South Asia	0.00654	0.00548	0.00511	0.0054	0.0066
	(0.892)	(0.638)	(0.626)	(0.63)	(0.784)
East Asia and Pacific	0.00968**	0.00936*	0.00910*	0.0106**	0.0104**
	(2.039)	(1.886)	(1.929)	(2.198)	(2.185)
Middle East and North Africa	-0.00664	-0.00681	-0.00416	0.00153	0.000921
	(-1.233)	(-1.248)	(-0.792)	(0.258)	(0.158)
Constant	0.0216***	0.0257	-0.103**	-0.0307	-0.103**
	(7.45)	(1.473)	(-2.455)	(-1.159)	(-2.475)
Observations	102	102	102	102	102
Adjusted R-squared	0.246	0.238	0.312	0.295	0.324

Source: Author's calculations. Expy is based on the definiton in Hausmann, Hwang, and Rodrik (2007). Open forest is calculated following Hausmann and Klinger (2007). Other data from World Development Indicators.

Notes: significant at 10%; ** significant at 5%; *** significant at 1%.

and property rights. The market would do the rest. A reform agenda focused on these three areas would deliver income convergence. It is clear that many Latin American countries improved quite dramatically in these three dimensions, but incomes continued to diverge. This is somewhat suggestive of the proposition that the obstacles to long-term growth may have lain elsewhere.

Obstacles to structural transformation may be an alternative explanation. The intensity of these obstacles is not constant across countries, but is dependent on their location in the highly irregular product space. China, India, Hungary, and the Czech Republic occupy a very dense part of the product space where obstacles to productive transformation are much smaller. Much of Latin America has a more peripheral location, as expressed in its low "average paths" score. This implies greater coordination problems that express themselves in three dimensions: lower average level of export sophistication (EXPY), fewer jumps,[8] and smaller distance to the quality frontier in current export products, all three factors adversely affecting long run growth.

The policy agenda to overcome pitfalls in productive transformation is necessarily quite distinct from the paradigm that inspired the reforms of the 1990s. The 1990s paradigm had implicit preferences for policies along particular sides of two dimension. First, policies would have to be horizontal, i.e. they should not be industry-specific, but relevant across sectors. Second, the policies should be relatively "low-dimensional." By low-dimensional we mean a process that ultimately depends on few goals. The circulatory system in the body has such characteristics: it is ultimately about pumping blood. The immune system, by contrast, is high-dimensional, as it must defend the body against a myriad of very different pathogens. In the policy arena a low-dimensional policy goal would be price or real exchange rate stability, while a high-dimensional goal is an environment appropriate for tourism, as it involves many elements including security, infrastructure, public attitudes, culture, and international law. To understand how limiting a focus on low dimensional horizontal policies is, it is convenient to imagine a two-by-two matrix of policies where we open these two dimensions to their alternatives (see Table 21.5).

The 1990s reform paradigm was focused on the upper left quadrant of Table 21.5. In recent years, the business policy agenda has moved in the direction of higher dimensionality. For example, the *Doing Business Survey* of the World Bank includes measures regarding business creation, dealing with licenses, moving product across borders, difficulties in hiring and firing workers, registering collateral, and closing a business. The areas of government performance are many more—hence the higher dimensionality—but the conception is horizontal: i.e. in principle they are about inputs that, in one form or another, all activities need. This has the advantage of not creating the need for governments to "pick winners." They can concentrate instead on providing an encouraging general business environment.

---

[8] Hausmann and Klinger (2006) find that the relatively low frequency of new exports in Latin America is not explained by national characteristics, after controlling for the position of the country in the product space. In other words, the problem is not that the monkeys are insufficiently agile, but that their location in the forest makes the distance to new trees very long.

Table 21.5 Typology of development policies

	Low dimensional	High dimensional
Horizontal	The 1990s paradigm Low inflation, stable RER	WB Doing business
Industry-specific		Structural transformation policy

However, as we have argued, the specificity of the business environment helps explain the structure of the product space. We argued that human capital, infrastructure, logistics, property rights, market access, certifications, licenses, regulatory requirements, contractual forms, etc. have in practice a highly specific character. This amplifies enormously the level of complexity, as the public inputs required are not just high-dimensional but also relatively specific. The list of requirements of existing and potential activities is not only enormous but unknowable ex ante.

How does the government organize the supply of the different inputs to each activity? How does it know when it is not supplying the right amount or the right design? How does it find out what is needed? How does it know if it is doing a good job?

21.8 ADDRESSING GOVERNMENT'S PERENNIAL PROBLEMS

Because the provision of publicly provided inputs and capabilities for productive activity cannot be supplied by markets, it faces serious problems of information and incentives. First, can government entities acquire the information about the characteristics and qualities of the demand for publicly provided inputs when market signals do not work? Second, how can these entities be structured to respond efficiently to the information, when the profit motive cannot be relied upon?

21.8.1 Eliciting information

It is clear from our arguments that the information required to address the efficient supply of publicly provided inputs is very diffuse and varied. Each activity has a demand for actual or potential inputs. Given the interactions between inputs, it may even be hard for those activities to figure out what potential new inputs are most valuable. After all, firms are in the business of finding solutions to the problems they face, taking some things as given. They are not in the business of asking what changes to their environment would be most beneficial to them. Having said this, it is clear that existing economic activities and potential investors have information that would be potentially very valuable and that the government cannot access on its own.

It is clear from this account that industrial policy cannot rely on an omniscient government. It must rely on mechanisms that reveal information, wherever it may be. There are many alternative ways of doing this. Firms lobby the government directly or through trade associations, thus revealing their preferences. They participate in the political process by funding elections and lobbying members of parliament and the administration. And they may attempt to influence the public bureaucracy directly in more or less legitimate ways. There is a long-standing tradition in economics, best represented in the work of George Stigler, that is suspicious of the motives behind public regulation of market activities. These motives are seen to emanate from rent-seeking, and involve the creation of barriers of entry to limit competition and protect incumbents.

Our argument provides important qualifications to this perspective. New economic activities need inputs—rules, organizations, infrastructure, labor training, etc.—that provide real value and that are win/win or Pareto-improving. However, there is a participation constraint: if these improvements are going to be shared by all existing and potential market participants, it is best to free-ride on the lobbying efforts of others. Hence, to address the participation constraint, there may indeed be the need to share part of the potential improvements with those who exert effort by providing information and engaging in the policy process to find and implement solutions. In this interpretation of the world, trade associations may be a cooperative solution to the free-rider problem among private participants. Their main motivation might be to secure the provision of the right publicly provided inputs, which is socially and privately productive. They need some sort of benefit to justify their efforts, but they may also stray into more negative forms of rent-seeking, i.e. activities that imply negative-sum transfers of resources.

Therefore, the relationship between the government and the lobby groups is potentially an excellent source of information but also of problems. How to create an environment that maximizes the informational benefits and limits the rent-seeking costs? In order to make the process legitimate vis-à-vis the rest of society, it is important to follow three principles: open architecture, self-organization, and transparency (Hausmann and Rodrik 2006).

Open architecture. It is important that whenever possible the government should not predetermine who it will deal with in terms of sectors or activities. Opportunities may exist in areas that were not under consideration when an organizational decision was made. It is important to let the potential areas of attention evolve with the appearance of opportunities and of agents willing to act on them. We may be doomed to choose, but we should only choose when the maximum amount of information has been revealed and when we are unable to do otherwise. Open architecture makes choices endogenous to an open process. Picks are weaned out of this process, not capriciously decided.

Self-organization. Inputs have a high and varying degree of specificity. Forcing groups to organize according to some predetermined criteria, e.g. by sector classifications, may create groups that have few specific needs in common. The fruit producers of a certain region may require a particular type of public good that may be quite different from cereal producers of a different region. A large single investor, whether foreign or domestic, may have highly specific requirements not shared by existing groups. Forcing them into a single channel of communication with other activities and regions, and explicitly or implicitly requiring them to all agree on their common requirements, may bias the requests towards the items they have most in common, like tax holidays, and away from the more specific and potentially most valuable requests, like particular infrastructure projects.

Transparency. It is important to create an environment where the requests that private-sector groups pose to the government are biased towards those that are socially productive. One way to facilitate this is to make the requests public knowledge, and to commit to performing an independent evaluation of the request from the point of view of the public interest. This evaluation should also be part of the public domain. This will force the petitioners to select, among their many potential demands, those that are socially most productive. Interventions that increase the size and profitability of certain activities are legitimate if they contribute to the rest of society through taxes and higher productivity jobs.

One way of setting up self-organizing, open-architecture, transparent entities is to create "windows." A window is an entity that receives requests. It has a set of predetermined rules as to what issues it hears and what kinds of instrument it is willing to deploy. Beyond that, what activities it deals with and who gets its attention and support is determined by the interaction between the design of the window and the realities of firms, private-sector organizations, and markets.

One element that may encourage the self-selection of socially productive initiatives and increase the legitimacy of the endeavor vis-à-vis society at large is to take some requests off the table ex ante. One principle is to focus only on requests that increase productivity, and not on interventions that compensate a sector financially for other inefficiencies in the system. Another is to focus only on new activities—defined as new products, processes, training, investments, and so on that are not currently taking place in similar form elsewhere in the economy—to ensure that policy serves the needs of structural transformation rather than simply enriching incumbents.

21.8.2 Overcoming the incentive problem

Governments are hierarchical organizations. As pointed out by the literature on complexity (Bar Yam et al. 2004), the amount of complexity that such a structure can handle is necessarily limited. The collision between the desire for clarity and simplicity and the inevitable complexity of the underlying issues often leads to permanent periodic reorganizations in search of simplicity followed by a gradual reversion back to a messier situation.

The World Bank is a good example of this problem. The Bank must deal with many different countries which face a variety of problems requiring highly context-specific solutions. There is a tendency for the Bank to get into a rapidly changing portfolio of activities that create increased complexity, followed by the desire to streamline operations and for the Bank to focus on a few things it does well. The Bank has toggled between organizing itself along areas of competency (e.g. economic policy, social policy, infrastructure) and organizing itself with a country focus. In its current structure, it has a matrix structure with small country departments that have the bulk of the budgetary resources and a small staff, and networks of experts that have the bulk of the personnel but that must "sell" their services to the country departments. This structure attempts to reproduce an internal market where many allocation decisions can be taken in a rather decentralized manner with greater information about country needs and institutional capabilities.

Governments face a similar problem. Each activity needs a myriad relatively specific inputs, but these inputs are the administrative responsibility of different agencies. Getting the whole system to work well is a highly complex function that requires many tasks to be performed well lest a few dysfunctional elements destroy a lot of value. The temptation is to centralize decisionmaking and control in a clear hierarchy. As with the case of the World Bank, sometimes this is done by function, while at other moments it is done by sector. But either solution is bound to bump against the inability of any hierarchy to deal with high complexity.[9]

Network-like arrangements may deliver what is required without any single node of the network being fully aware of all the things that are going on at any point in time. In this interpretation, many of the existing organizations, whether private or public, may be acting as part of an institutional tissue that identifies opportunities, creates the incentives to act, and coordinates the outcome. In this respect, trade associations may play a role akin to that of the account executive in a global bank, coordinating the relationship between a particular sector of activity and the myriad of public institutions it must deal with. Also, departments and ministries that deal with particular industries may also play the role of account executive, maintaining a conversation with particular industries and then trying to coordinate the different government agencies involved in implementing solutions. Development banks, beyond their financing function, may be in the role of identifying opportunities and obstacles. They regularly try to use their insider status in the public sector to raise awareness of factors impeding potential activities.

It seems useful to think of two classes of organizations: first, there are the instrument-based organizations that specialize in the management of a given policy instrument (e.g. labor training subsidies, transport infrastructure, industry regulation). Each one of these entities accumulates specific know-how in the management of a given policy instrument. Second, there are the coordinating entities that attempt to make sure that the right mix of policy instruments is deployed. These are organized by area of activity. The question then is how to assure that they have the capacity to coordinate the instrument-based organizations while respecting their autonomy. The World Bank solution

---

[9] One typical example of the attempt to limit complexity is the push towards a one-stop shop in government regulation.

involved placing budgetary discretion with the client-centered country divisions while creating an internal market for sector-specific talent. For governments, creating strong activity-based coordinators empowered with either political or budgetary discretion may be a way to create an institutional network that can better address the underlying complexity.

21.9 CONCLUDING REMARKS

Latin America is finally growing again. However, the weak underlying growth trends suggest that something else is amiss in much of the region. I have argued that obstacles to productive transformation may be a significant part of the growth problem in many countries. This means that the continuation of a low-dimensional horizontal policy stance is unlikely to help. Inevitably, policies will have to move back to a more activist role in terms of listening to and promoting economic activity. This may cause legitimate fears about the return to the mistakes of the dirigiste past.

In fact, the reform paradigm of the 1990s moved against sector-specific interventions and in favor of low-dimensional priorities in part as a reaction against the previous development strategy. It is important in this context to differentiate what I have been arguing for in terms of policy and some of the rationale behind the industrial policies of the past. First, the focus is on the provision of requisite public inputs, not on private goods or subsidies. Hence, while a subsidy may be called for to compensate for some externality, it is clearly better to increase the productivity of economic activity by providing the requisite public inputs than by compensating entrepreneurs for the lack of provision.

Second, the design of policies does not assume omniscience but instead supposes the organization of a social search process where obstacles and opportunities are identified and attention directed to them.

Third, special attention needs to be given to maintenance of legitimacy of the policy process. The standard critique of the industrial policies of the past is that they lead to rent-seeking and corruption. In the framework I have discussed, by concentrating on public inputs, the typical rent-seeking distortions are contained. Resources are present to fund public inputs, not private transfers. Private lobby groups organized in order to demand public inputs are more likely to self-select on the basis of the social productivity of those inputs than if the door were left open for transfers. Principles of transparency and accountability are key to maintaining broad social support for a more activist development policy.

Fourth, the strategy calls for partnerships between the public and the private sector in order to identify and co-produce solutions to the provision of public inputs. This again contrasts with the old state/market dichotomy. The problem is not where to put the border between the two entities, but how to create a rich connecting tissue between them.

The fathers of development economics saw productive transformation as central to the development process. They also considered it a process rife with market failures. While the precise understanding of the nature of those failures has evolved and will continue to evolve, part of that evolution will depend on the new experiences societies will have as they actively explore the set of new possibilities.

REFERENCES

ACEMOGLU, D., and ANGRIST, J. (2000). 'How Large Are Human Capital Externalities? Evidence from Compulsory Schooling Laws', *NBER Macroeconomics Annual* 15.

AGHION, P., and HOWITT, P. (1992). 'A Model of Growth through Creative Destruction', *Econometrica* 60. 2.

BAR-YAM, Y., RAMALINGAM, C., and BURLINGAME, L. (2004). *Making Things Work: Solving Complex Problems in a Complex World*, Cambridge, Mass.: NECSI Knowledge Press.

FAJNZYLBER, F. (1990). 'Industrialization in Latin America: From the "Black Box" to the "Empty Box"', *Cuadernos de la CEPAL* 60.

HAUSMANN, R., HWANG, J., and RODRIK, D. (2007). 'What You Export Matters', *Journal of Economic Growth* 12.1.

——and KLINGER, B. (2006). 'Structural Transformation and Patterns of Comparative Advantage in the Product Space', Working Paper No. 128, Center for International Development, Harvard University.

——— (2007). 'The Structure of the Product Space and the Evolution of Comparative Advantage', Working Paper No. 146, Center for International Development, Harvard University.

——and RIGOBON, R. (2003). 'An Alternative Interpretation of the "Resource Curse": Theory and Policy Implications', in J. M. Davis, R. Ossowski, and A. Fedelino (eds), *Fiscal Policy Formulation and Implementation in Oil-Producing Countries*, Washington, DC: IMF.

——and RODRIK, D. (2003). 'Doomed to Choose: Industrial Policy as Predicament', paper presented at the First Blue Sky Conference, Center for International Development, Harvard University.

——— (2006). 'Doomed to Choose: Industrial Policy as Predicament', mimeo Harvard University.

——and VELASCO, A. (2005). 'Slow Growth in Latin America: Common Outcomes, Common Causes?', Working Paper, Center for International Development, Harvard University.

——RODRIGUEZ, F., and WAGNER, R. (2007). 'Growth Collapses', in C. Reinhart, A. Velasco, and C. Végh (eds), *Money, Crises,and Transition: Essays in Honor of Guillermo Calvo*, Cambridge, Mass.: MIT Press.

——Rodrik, D., and VELASCO, A. (2008). 'Growth Diagnostics', in J. Stiglitz and N. Serra (eds), *The Washington Consensus Reconsidered: Towards a New Global Governance*, New York: Oxford University Press.

HIDALGO, C. A., KLINGER, B., BARABÁSI, A. L., and HAUSMANN, R. (2007). 'The Product Space Conditions the Development of Nations', *Science* 317.

HIRSCHMAN, A. (1958). *The Strategy of Economic Development*. New Haven, Conn.: Yale University Press.

HWANG, J. (2007). 'Introduction of New Goods, Convergence and Growth', mimeo, Department of Economics, Harvard University.

IMBS, J., and WACZIARG, R. (2003). 'Stages of Diversification', American Economic Review 93.1.

KATZ, J. (2000). Reformas estructurales, productividad y conducta tecnológica, Santiago, Chile: ECLAC/Fondo de Cultura Económica.

KLINGER, B. (2007). 'Uncertainty in the Search for New Exports', CID Working Paper No. 16, Harvard University.

LEWIS, W. A. (1954). 'Economic Development with Unlimited Supplies of Labor', The Manchester School (May).

LUCAS, R. E. (1988). 'On the Mechanics of Economic Development', Journal of Monetary Economics 22.1.

MANKIW, N. G., ROMER, D., and WEIL, D. N. (1992). 'A Contribution to the Empirics of Economic Growth', Quarterly Journal of Economics 107.2.

MATSUYAMA, K. (1991). 'Increasing Returns, Industrialization, and Indeterminacy of Equilibrium', Quarterly Journal of Economics 106.2.

OCAMPO, J. A. (2005), "The Quest for Dynamic Efficiency: Structural Dynamics and Economic Growth in Developing Countries', in J. A. Ocampo (ed.), Beyond Reforms: Structural Dynamics and Macroeconomic Vulnerability, Palo Alto, Calif: Stanford University Press, ECLAC, and World Bank.

PREBISCH, R. (1950). The Economic Development of Latin America and its Principal Problems, New York: United Nations.

ROMER, P. M. (1990). 'Endogenous Technical Change', Journal of Political Economy 98.5.

ROSENSTEIN-RODAN, P. 1943. 'Problems of Industrialization of Eastern and South-Eastern Europe', Economic Journal (June–September).

SCHOTT, P. K. (2004). "Across-Product versus Within-Product Specialization in International Trade', Quarterly Journal of Economics (May).

SOLOW, R. M. (1956). 'A Contribution to the Theory of Economic Growth', The Quarterly Journal of Economics 70.1.

—— (1957). 'Technical Change and the Aggregate Production Function', Review of Economics and Statistics 39.3.

SUMMERS, L. H. (2003). Godkin Lectures, John F. Kennedy School of Government, Harvard University (April).

World Development Indicators (n. d.). The World Bank. Available at: http://data.worldbank.org/data-catalog/world-development-indicators.

CHAPTER 22

....

LEARNING, TECHNOLOGICAL CAPABILITIES, AND STRUCTURAL DYNAMICS

....

MARIO CIMOLI AND GABRIEL PORCILE

22.1 INTRODUCTION[1]

....

Economic development is the process by which a country transforms its productive and employment structures based on learning and the accumulation of technological capabilities (TCs). It is by large a Schumpeterian process in which institutions, technology, and structural change interact to reduce the distance between a laggard economy and the international technological frontier. In the Latin American case, this approximation to the frontier has not occurred and the region tended to fall behind in the long run. This chapter discusses why this happened and compares the Latin American experience with that of other more successful catching up economies.

The chapter is organized in three sections besides the introduction and the concluding remarks. Section 22.2 briefly presents the structuralist center–periphery theory, which we believe it is still a useful device to discuss the features that distinguish the Latin American economies (the periphery) from the developed ones (the center). Structuralism provides a good account of the macrodynamics of technology, specialization, and relative economic growth. However, it lacks a theory of the microeconomics of learning and the accumulation of TCs supporting this macrodynamics. We argue that the Schumpeterian evolutionary school offers such micro-foundations and discuss the various channels linking the Schumpeterian micro with the structuralist macro.

Section 22.3 discusses the growth trajectory of Latin America in the postwar period from a structuralist-Schumpeterian perspective, relating the accumulation of TCs to

[1] The views expressed in this chapter are those of the authors, and do not necessarily reflect the views of the Economic Commission for Latin America and the Caribbean (ECLAC-UN).

different institutional arrangements and policies. We suggest that these arrangements were unfavorable to learning and structural change, and discuss why the region remained in a hysteresis state since the early 1980s. This represented a low-growth trap in which the technological and productivity gaps with the center could not be reduced. Empirical evidence on the relationship between structural change, the technology gap, and relative growth is presented, comparing the region with other regions in the international economy.

22.2 GROWTH IN THE INTERNATIONAL ECONOMY AND THE DYNAMICS OF LEARNING

22.2.1 Structuralism and the macrodynamics of growth

Structuralist theory regards asymmetries in the dynamics of learning as a central force explaining why two very different structures (center and periphery) emerge in the international economy (Prebisch 1949; 1963; 1976; Rodríguez 2007). The analysis begins with an undifferentiated international economy, where technological capabilities and productivity levels are fairly similar across regions. At a certain point in time technical change accelerates in one of the regions (that will become the center), gradually transforming its productive structure, which becomes diversified and homogeneous. As a result, technology-intensive sectors increase their share in total GDP. The emerging center economy is diversified because it comprises a large number of sectors and activities, and homogeneous because labor productivity is fairly similar across them. At the same time, technology diffuses very slowly at the international level and penetrates in a highly localized form in other regions. In these regions, which will form the periphery of the system, the economic structure is specialized and heterogeneous: there are fewer sectors and activities, and they exhibit major differences in labor productivity, as technical change leaves untouched large traits of the production system.

In an open economy, asymmetries in TCs and differences in the economic structure are related to the pattern of specialization (Dosi, Pavitt, and Soete 1990; Cimoli and Porcile 2009). To the extent that the periphery specializes in the production of commodities and low-tech goods, it tends to grow less than the center. In effect, this type of specialization implies a lower income elasticity of the demand for exports (ε_p) and a higher income elasticity of the demand for imports (ε_c). To keep the trade balance in equilibrium with constant relative prices, the relative growth of the periphery in relation to the center (y_p/y_c) should be equal to the income elasticity ratio ($\varepsilon_p/\varepsilon_c$) (Thirlwall 1979).

In the long run, the income elasticity ratio depends on the diversification of the periphery towards high-tech sectors. The relative growth of the periphery will thus depend on he relative weight of technology-intensive sectors in the periphery as compared to the center (S^p/S^c). Competitiveness based on abundant natural resources or raw labor cannot be sustained and is bound to decline. Only competitiveness based on TCs would allow the periphery to have a presence in markets whose demand grows at higher rates. A higher share of technology-intensive sectors gives rise to externalities and increasing returns, spillover effects, backward and forward linkages, and technological externalities which boost exports, capital accumulation, and growth (Rosenstein-Rodan 1943; Gerschenkron 1962; Hirschman 1977).

In other words, catching-up and convergence requires transformation of the production structure towards rents generated by knowledge and learning, rather than by the availability of natural resources or cheap labor (ECLAC 2010). In Latin America, as will be discussed below, sectors intensive in natural resources and raw labor have generally had a dominant position in exports. Structural change and diversification were remarkably slow compared to those countries that succeeded in catching up, particularly the Asian countries.

22.2.2 An evolutionary approach to learning paths, capabilities, and industrial dynamics

Both economic history and economic theory generally acknowledge a deep relationship between technical change and economic development. The opening of the technological black box by the Schumpeterian literature has produced new insights on how learning and technological capabilities co-evolve, and why technology gaps rise or fall across nations and time (Cimoli and Dosi 1995; Mytelka 2007; Cimoli, Dosi, and Stiglitz 2010). Since the mid-1980s, the Schumpeterian evolutionary literature has steadily developed new microeconomic tools for analyzing learning in catching-up economies.[2] Technological learning features a set of interrelated regularities that can be briefly summarized as follows:

- It requires real time.
- It is subject to path-dependency, i.e. the evolution of capabilities depends on previous experience and directions of past learning.
- There exists complementarity between sectors and capabilities, in such a way that externalities and increasing returns are crucial at both the industrial and economy wide levels.
- There is irreversibility in the building of certain (physical and technological) assets, and thus high costs if they are simply abandoned.
- It has a critical tacit component that could not be obtained from importing capital goods nor from reading manuals and other forms of codified information.

---

[2] See e.g. Lall (1982), Fransman and King (1984), Teitel (1984), Teubal (1984), Katz (1987), Bell (2006).

- Countries and firms that are closer to the technological frontier have an advantage in innovation and will tend to increase their distance with respect to the laggards. There exist cumulative processes leading to vicious or virtuous cycles that help to explain why some countries move to a path where learning, production capabilities, and institutions interact virtuously, while others remain in a hysteresis state within a low-growth (divergence) trap.

These properties suggest that there is no reason for naïve optimism about convergence. Path-dependency and cumulativeness lead to strong inertia in the patterns of learning and specialization. On the other hand, catching up may be possible under specific circumstances, when industrial policies and institutional building create a favorable environment for learning from imported technology.

In the process of catching up there is no clear-cut distinction between innovation and diffusion. The speed of diffusion is related to the capacity to acquire technology (in the form of capital goods, know-how, training, and so forth), adapt it to specific local conditions and—gradually—develop specific competitive advantages in the international economy by means of incremental innovations. A number of empirical studies describe how technological capabilities matured in the periphery from the 1950s to the early 1980s (Fransman and King 1984), allowing a small group of peripheral countries to gradually export medium- and high-tech goods and even become technology exporters. Reducing the technology gap required the sequential deployment of various forms of tacit and incremental learning, favored by the literacy and skill level of the workforce, the technical competence of engineers and designers of mechanical artifacts, and (increasingly) the existence of managers capable of efficiently running complex organizations.

Effective learning necessarily relies on active policies whose instruments and objectives change over time (Cimoli et al. 2010). Market signals alone are often not enough for fostering the accumulation of TCs, and in some case they compromise such accumulation. This occurs because learning takes place around existing technological capabilities, and investment concentrates in low-tech sectors that have already achieved comparative advantages and higher profitability. There are sound learning-related reasons that explain the historical evidence showing that just prior to industrial catching-up, average industrial import tariffs are relatively low, but they rise rapidly in the catching-up phase and eventually fall when mature industrialization has been attained. Indeed, it is during the catching-up phase that the requirement of distorting (international) market signals is more acute, precisely because learning-intensive industries are at this stage relatively fragile infants (Amsden 1989; Chang 2001).[3] In this process a key role is played by the management of rents to generate incentives and credible compulsions for learning (Khan and Blankenburg 2008).

---

[3] Safeguarding the possibility of learning was indeed the first basic pillar of the infant industry logic. In order to maintain an inefficient industry (or plant) in the market, some sort of "learning protection" must be by force introduced for a limited period of time (Lall 1982; Fransman and King 1984).

22.2.3 Combining the dynamics of growth and learning

The interrelated dynamics of growth and learning is illustrated in Figure 22.1, which puts together the evolution of labor productivity (π) and that of aggregate demand/production (Y). In the space π-Y points p and c indicate the prevailing levels of productivity and income in the periphery and the center, respectively. There is clearly a large difference in average labor productivity between the two poles, which reflects asymmetries in TCs. The challenge of the periphery is to move from p to c.

There are alternative paths towards c that define different levels of employment growth and productivity growth through time. A path which goes most of the time though B reflects policies that stress productivity growth, while a path that goes through A represents policies that emphasize employment. Still, in both cases a catching-up economy should be able to traverse until point c, which combines high levels of productivity and employment. Any possible convergence path leading to point c has to comply with some conditions:

- The accumulation of TCs is related to the transformation and diversification of the periphery's economic structure in such a way that growth in effective demand (and the ensuing demand for labor) increases the share of the modern sector in total employment.
- The traverse should be sustained by a virtuous cycle in which productivity growth, exports, effective demand, and learning reinforce each other—by means of the various Kaldor–Verdoorn increasing returns mechanisms, such as learning by investing, learning by doing, and learning by using.

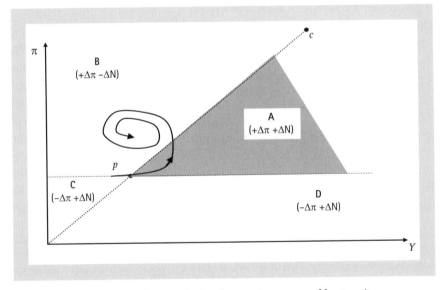

FIGURE 22.1 Traverse in development process and hysteresis

- For virtuous cycle to exist there must be in place an articulated institutional framework in which firms and non-profit organizations (particularly those directly related to education and R&D) are nested in a network of technological and productive flows which enhances the problem-solving capabilities of producers and stimulates the various forms of interactive learning—what has been called the National System of Innovation, NSI (Nelson 1993; Kim 1997; Lall 1997; Ocampo 2005; Cimoli and Porcile 2009).

In Latin America the accumulation of TCs has been deeply affected by macroeconomic and structural shocks and by weak institutions for science and technology that compromised the above conditions. This is illustrated in Figure 22.1 by a growth trajectory that has remained in region B without approaching point c.

In the next section we discuss different combinations of policies, institutions, and structural change in the postwar period that sustained different phases of growth. We therefore revisit the recent economic history of the region from the standpoint of the structuralist–Schumpeterian approach presented above.

22.3 PHASES OF ECONOMIC GROWTH IN LATIN AMERICA: FROM STATE-LED INDUSTRIALIZATION TO THE COMMODITY BOOM

Several phases in the evolution of GDP per capita in Latin America can be identified in the postwar period (see Table 22.1). First, there is the phase of state-led industrialization, which lasted until 1974. It was characterized by high rates of growth, slightly above the world average, led by the expansion of industrial production, particularly in the larger countries of the region (like Argentina, Brazil, and Mexico). A second phase is related to the first oil shock and the end of the Bretton Woods system of a fixed exchange rate. There was convergence (Latin America grew at a higher rate than the rest of the world), but at lower rates of GDP per capita growth than in the previous era.

Table 22.1 Phases of economic growth in Latin America (GDP per capita growth rates; %)

	1960–74	1974–82	1982–90	1990–2004	2005–8
Latin America and Caribbean	3.2	1.3	−0.4	1.4	4.1
World	3.0	1.0	1.9	1.3	2.1
LA/World	1.1	1.3	−0.2	1.0	2.0

Source: World Development Indicators, World Bank (2010).

Growth was based on a soaring external debt that brought about a major crisis in 1982, opening the lost decade of the 1980s. Growth only recovered in the 1990s with the return of foreign capital, but at rates that were just enough to avoid losing more ground in the international economy. Finally, after 2004 growth increased as a result of the bonanza created by the boom in commodity prices, which ended with the crisis of September 2008. Each of these phases had specific features regarding learning and the accumulation of TCs.

Since the 1930s, industrial protection served to build up the critical capabilities, skills and organization required to industrialize. In the second half of the 1950s some Latin American countries moved from the so-called "easy" import-substituting industrialization (textiles, food products) towards a more complex phase led by industries with higher intensity in scale, capital, and technology (chemical products, steel, and automobiles). This phase can be labeled as state-led industrialization to the extent that it was largely driven by public policies aimed at diversifying the industry (Cárdenas, Ocampo, and Thorp 2000). They had a major impact on the intensity and direction of technological learning.

In the new phase of industrialization, the state was in many cases the main producer of infrastructure and capital-intensive intermediate goods (telecommunications, energy, transport), while national producers dominated in low-tech sectors and foreign firms prevailed in durables. In this arrangement, foreign firms counted on high levels of protection and in many cases subsidized inputs (by state enterprises). The public sector not only played a key role as a producer of intermediate goods, but also made a significant (albeit clearly insufficient, if compared to the Asian experience) effort towards extending and improving education. In addition, several research institutions were created (particularly, but not exclusively, related to the agricultural sector) that sought to support the upgrading of productive capacities (Kosacoff et al. 1999; Katz and Stumpo 2001).

Each type of firm had a specific approach to learning. National firms could be small or large, public or private. In the case of the small private firms, frequently they began as workshops using second-hand equipment (or equipment produced by the firms themselves), relying on the experience and expertise of migrants (Katz 1987). Some firms would subsequently grow and became important players in their sectors (mainly textiles, food, leather, and metallurgy). As regards large domestic firms, the role of state enterprises in the building of TCs was crucial. These firms set up research departments which in some cases drew on abundant financial resources and qualified personnel, allowing them to accumulate TCs in sectors regarded as strategic (telecommunications, petrochemicals, and steel). Foreign firms prevailed in sectors of medium and high technology, such as engineering industries, pharmaceuticals, and petrochemicals (Stumpo 1998). Their technological strategy was to adapt the technology developed in their countries of origin, and in this they attained a degree of success, although confined to knowhow rather than to know-why.

As argued in the previous section, there is no passive diffusion of technology: this process is necessarily based on a stream of minor innovations, adaptations, and improvements that reflect the specific conditions in which innovations are adopted. Diffusion gives rise to specific, idiosyncratic technological trajectories in each country. The cumulative learning that accompanied industrialization was far from negligible, and gains in productivity were significant. It gradually redefined comparative advantages and the production structure, reshaping the industrial landscape in the largest economies of the region.

Thus, the postwar period witnessed a new phase of industrial growth in the largest economies of the region, spurred by active industrial policies and the efforts deployed mainly by state and foreign firms to adapt foreign technology and produce minor innovations. However, the National System of Innovation (NIS) of the region lacked the strength and articulation that can be found in the Asian economies, and catching up was limited (Chudnovsky, Nagao, and Jacobson 1984; Fajnzylber 1990; ECLAC 1990; Wade 1990). Industrialization depended on high levels of protection without parallel demands by the governments (and commitments by the firms) for achieving exports and/or technological targets. As a result, the region failed to fully exploit learning opportunities related to industrial growth and diversification, while problems of international competitiveness and external unbalances remained high.[4]

After the 1973 oil shock, and in a scenario of stagflation in the central economies, two different policy responses could be found in Latin America. In some countries, like Argentina, Chile, and Uruguay, the new military governments challenged the very existence of the industrial sector and adopted policies of rapid trade and financial liberalization that discontinued the previous path of accumulation in TCs. There were substantial losses in capabilities, as firms, research centers, and qualified personnel exited the industry—particularly in Argentina, which had accumulated significant capabilities in several sectors, like metal-mechanical and chemicals. Brazil followed a different path. This country opted to advance the ISI, extending the process of import substitution to new intermediate and capital goods, which represented a continuity of the industrialization project that began in the 1950s.

Two kinds of policy were encouraged by and based upon abundant foreign lending from international private banks. Still, the escalation of the external debt combined with rapidly rising international interest rates in the early 1980s made these policies unsustainable. The 1982 Mexican default triggered a major external crisis in almost all Latin American countries, giving rise to the phase of slow or negative growth, low investment, and high inflation labeled as the "lost decade." The need to export capital, the collapse of investment, and negative rates of growth of GDP per capita were the result of the combination of falling terms of trade and extremely high interest rates on the accumulated foreign debt of Latin America. To the extent that a large part of the debt became public (with few exceptions, such as Colombia), the debt crisis implied a fiscal crisis, as well as the loss of the capacity by the state to finance and implement development policies. It was a period of widespread disorganization at the institutional level. The lost

---

[4] The specific experience of each country is different, as some made a move towards export promotion earlier and in a more effective form; see Chapter 1 above by Ocampo and Ros.

decade of the 1980s was dominated by desperate efforts to pay the debt and tame the vey high levels of inflation that haunted the region.

Only from the early 1990s, when international conditions became more favorable, did these efforts begin to work. Latin American countries then applied major economic reforms, comprising trade liberalization, privatization of large domestic firms (particularly in the service sector), and deregulation of financial markets (Stallings and Péres 2000). Economic reforms succeeded in reducing inflation, in most cases with the parallel appreciation of domestic currencies, supported by the return of foreign lending. This in turn compromised industrial competitiveness, a problem compounded by the dismount of national institutions for fostering technological learning. The 1990s were a period of uncritical confidence in the capacity of market forces to deliver the best outcomes in all cases. Industrial and technological policies were seen mainly as barriers to market forces—and hence as sources of inefficiency. With the exception of Brazil, industrial policies were swept out of the region, to return slowly by the mid-2000s (Péres 2010). The momentum of technical change was confined to activities that rationalized the production processes and reduced costs, particularly in tradables, whose collateral effect was to raise unemployment (ECLAC 2008).

The new macroeconomic context modified the pattern of learning in many activities (Cimoli and Katz 2003; Teitel 2004). Relative prices and incentives to innovate were redefined. In technology-intensive fields there was a trend towards substituting domestically produced intermediate inputs with cheaper (and sometimes better) imported inputs. Firms also reorganized production on an assembly-type operations basis, with a much higher content of imported inputs. Market structures changed as well, as the share of large firms (either local subsidiaries of transnational corporations or domestically owned conglomerates) in gross domestic product (GDP) significantly increased during the adjustment process. There was an increase in the presence of foreign capital in production.

The combination of rapid trade liberalization, the appreciation of the domestic currency, and large inflows of foreign capital, along with the absence of active industrial and technology policies, had major implications for the competitive strategies of firms and the economic structure in Latin America. It should be stressed that they encouraged a process of modernization that paradoxically inhibited local TCs (Capdevielle 2005). Latin American firms emerged from three decades of protection and from the lost decade of the 1980s to face open competition in the international markets. Although in the 1990s investment modestly recovered from the collapse of the 1980s, it remained at lower levels than in the 1970s, and firms in the region were in a weak position to respond to the new challenge of international competitiveness (see Cimoli, Porcile, and Rovira 2010). On top of that, the positive shock in the terms of trade of the 2000s contributed to the disarticulation of local systems of innovation and production, the loss of institutions and personnel specialized in R&D, and the move towards a specialization concentrated in commodities.[5]

[5] Patterns of specialization vary significantly across the region, although the trend towards less technology-intensive sectors seems to be widespread. See also Mortimore and Péres (2001).

22.4 PRODUCTIVITY GROWTH, SPECIALIZATION, AND STRUCTURAL CHANGE IN LATIN AMERICA

21.4.1 Structural change

In this section we present some empirical evidence on the dynamics of the technology gap, structural change, and specialization in Latin America, and relate this evidence to the phases of growth discussed in the previous section. The analysis is undertaken in comparative terms, for which we divided the international economy into four groups of countries: Latin America (LA), Developing Asia (DA), developed economies whose exports exhibit a significant share (more than 40%) of goods intensive in natural resources[6] (DCNR), and mature, highly industrialized economies (ME), where natural resources play a minor role in exports. Some key indicators of TCs, specialization, and structural change are then compared across the four groups of countries (see Table 22.2). Clearly, there are very large differences within the LA group. Therefore, although in Table 22.2 we address the region as a single group, we will later present data for specific countries to take into account these differences.

The key point to be explained is why LA grew less than all the other groups of countries for the period considered. We do not present econometric evidence on this point,[7] but set forth some stylized facts that may contribute to explain why LA fell behind. In terms of Figure 22.1, we discuss why LA remained in area B, and was unable so far to move towards the virtuous traverse represented by area A.

First it is interesting to look at the pattern of specialization. We present in Table 22.2 the share of goods intensive in natural resources in total exports. In principle, the higher this share, the less dynamic will be the export structure, to the extent that the international demand for goods intensive in natural resources grew at lower rates than the demand for industrial goods, particularly those of medium and high technology (ECLAC 2008). Table 22.2 shows that this share is much higher in LA than in the other groups. This seems to point to the existence of some curse associated with natural resources. Yet the group of DCNR is formed by countries which achieved a high income per capita and nevertheless have a large share of natural resources in their total exports. Such a comparison suggests that the curse is far from inevitable. It also poses a challenge to the idea that the economic structure matters: if structural change is so important for growth, then the two groups (LA and DCNR), with such varied income per capita, should be expected to show very large differences in the export structure as well.

---

[6] This group is defined following TradeCan, and includes 45 basic products with a low degree of processing and 35 manufactured goods based on natural resources (agricultural, minerals except steel, oil products, glass, and cement).

[7] Econometric evidence can be found in ECLAC (2007) and Cimoli et al. (2010).

Table 22.2 Specialization, productive structure, TCs, and growth

Region	RP1	RP2	KI	AI	% NR	RD	Patents	Growth pc
LA	0.30	0.23	0.78	0.44	70	0.40	0.50	1.64
DENR	0.70	0.72	0.33	1.32	59	1.89	65.39	2.29
DA	0.80	0.99	0.39	2.33	30	1.21	30.45	4.77
ME	0.88	0.97	0.16	1.8	24	2.43	132.62	2.00

Source: Elaborated from ECLAC (2007), Trade Can, WDI, USPTO, and PADIWIN.
LA = Latin America, includes Argentina, Bolivia, Brazil, Chile, Colombia, Peru, Mexico, and Uruguay.
DENR = developed economies where more than 40% of total exports are based on natural resources; includes Australia, Canada, Denmark, Finland, Ireland, Norway, and New Zealand.
DA = developing Asia; includes South Korea, Philippines, India, Malaysia, Singapore, and Taiwan.
ME = mature economies; includes France, Italy, Japan, Sweden, UK, USA.
RP1 = relative participation of engineering industries in total manufacturing value added (ratio with respect to the participation in the USA), 1982–2002.
RP2 = relative participation of engineering industries in total manufacturing value added (ratio with respect to the participation in the USA), 2002–7 (UNIDO 2010—the last available year varies for each country).
KI = Krugman Index (benchmark US), 1982–2003.
IA = Adaptability Index, 1985–2000.
%NR = participation of exports based on natural resources in total exports (%).
RD = investment in research and development as % of GDP (average 1996–2007).
Patents = accumulated patents per million inhabitants, average, 1995–2008.
Growth pc = average growth rate of the GDP per capita, 1970–2008.

However, the proxy used in Table 22.2 (the share of goods intensive in natural resources in total exports) is a very poor indicator of structural change. In effect, a country which is an exporter of this type of goods, but which at the same time managed to use these exports as a basis for learning, linkage effects, technological learning, and moving down and up in the productive matrix (towards sectors which are more technology-intensive), will certainly have much a better performance than countries that just rely on the static rents provided by natural resources. In other words, more important than having or not having natural resources is to effectively use them as a basis for learning and structural upgrading. To have a correct idea of how each country used the rents from natural resources, one should look beyond specialization. It is necessary to look at the evolution of technological intensity of the industrial structure. We need a broader perspective, addressing how specialization and structural change in production patterns co-evolved through time. We used two indexes to obtain this broader perspective, the Krugman Index and the Index of Relative Participation.

The first proxy of technological intensity of a country's economic structure is the Krugman Index (KI), defined as:

$$KI_j = \sum_{i-1}^{i=n} |X_{ij} - X_{iR}|$$

where X_{ij} is the participation of sector i in the total manufacturing value added of country j while X_{iR} is the participation of the same sector in the total manufacturing value added of country R, which is the benchmark. R must be a country which features a high participation of technology-intensive sectors in its industrial structure and which has reached (or is very close to) the technological frontier. Thus, the assumption is that in a country with a high KI the technology-intensive sectors are poorly represented in manufacturing. The larger the "distance" KI of country j with respect to the reference country R (which is the technological leader), the less technologically intensive the manufacturing sector of country j is considered to be. In addition, if KI increases through time, then structural change in j goes in the "wrong" direction (the structure of j becomes increasingly different from that of the advanced economy). In other words, an increase in KI implies lagging behind in terms of structural change (in the sense that the structure is becoming more dissimilar to that of the benchmark country).

The sectors used to compute the KI are the 28 sectors of the International Standard Industrial Classification (ISIC) as provided by the UNIDO Databank. The country used as a reference is the United States, a mature economy very close to the international technological frontier. Although the USA is not the technological leader for every industry, it can nevertheless be considered a reasonable benchmark, to the extent that it is one of the main sources of technology and a leading market for exports from developing countries.

The other indicator of the technological intensity of the industrial structure is the Relative Participation (RP) index, defined as:

$$RP_i = \frac{S_i}{SA}$$

where Si is the participation of the engineering industries in the total manufacturing value added of country i, while SR is the average participation of these industries in the manufacturing value added of a sample of 25 countries (which includes developing and developed countries). A higher RP index (a higher share of engineering industries vis-à-vis that of the rest of the world) is assumed to be a proxy of the technological intensity of the manufacturing industry.

When we look at the productive structure using these indicators, it can be seen in Table 22.2 that LA has a higher KI and a lower RP index than the other regions, indicating that the process of structural change has been weaker. We also compared the *RP* index in two periods, 1982–2002 and 2002–7 (first and second columns in Table 22.2, respectively), in order to see if differences tended to fall with time. The comparison suggests that LA continued to fall behind, while the Asian developing economies were able to further the process of structural convergence.

The results for the whole LA region are confirmed when one considers individual countries (see Table 22.3). Argentina, for instance, has a much lower *RP* index than Australia, a country with which Argentina has been frequently compared as both are exporters of similar agricultural goods. In the same vein, Uruguay and Chile show indicators of structural change which are much lower than those of New Zealand. Moreover,

Table 22.3 Productive structure and technology: selected countries

Country	RP	IK	Patents	RD
Argentina	0.4	0.65	1.1	0.44
Brazil	0.61	0.38	0.5	0.9
Mexico	0.54	0.44	0.7	0.41
Uruguay	0.22	0.77	0.6	0.28
Chile	0.28	0.73	0.8	0.56
New Zealand	0.54	0.42	27.6	1.14
Australia	0.78	0.29	43.5	1.79

RP = relative participation of engineering industries in total manufacturing value added (ratio with respect to the participation in the USA), average, 1970–2003.
KI = Krugman Index (benchmark US), average, 1970–2003.
RD = investment in research and development as % of GDP (average, 1996–2007).
Patents = accumulated patents per million inhabitants, average, 1995–2008.

it is worth stressing that a very small country like NZ displays a manufacturing structure which is not so dissimilar to that of Brazil and Mexico, the two largest and most populated countries in LA.

The indicators clearly suggest that structural change was much more intense in the DCRN than in LA. Such a conclusion is reinforced by traditional indicators of technological efforts and technological intensity of the economy. In effect, the figures relating to patenting intensity and levels of investment in R&D in LA are much lower than in the DCRN. These indicators confirm that in the DCNR natural resources were used to foster learning, while this relation between natural resources and structural change was absent in the LA case. Forward and backward linkages, along with technological spillovers, were more intense in that group than in LA.

The different intensity of structural change has significant implications for competitiveness and long-run growth (last column of Table 22.2). A manufacturing structure which is more intensive in technology also has higher levels of R&D patenting and productivity, which implies a growth path going through region A in Figure 22.1, based on industrial diversification and demand growth, along with productivity growth. Aggregate demand and learning should go hand by hand, as argued in the structuralist–Schumpeterian perspective presented in section 22.2.

In sum, if development is a Schumpeterian process of creative destruction driven by innovation, then Schumpeterian traces (as Narula 2004 puts it) of learning and structural change towards high-tech sectors are to be found in the productive structure. The proxies for structural change and technological intensity we used in our comparative study offers evidence that corroborate this view.

22.4.2 Specialization and the demand for exports

So far we have addressed structural change focusing on the manufacturing sector. Now we will look more closely at the pattern of specialization. What counts in the long run for avoiding the external constraint is the capacity to change the export structure towards goods whose international demand grows faster. Recall that in Figure 22.1 the key to higher employment levels with productivity growth lies in a large impact of diversification and learning on effective demand. We therefore used a new proxy, which we called the Adaptability Index (AI), which aims at capturing the "Keynesian efficiency" of the specialization pattern (Dosi et al. 1990). We define this Index as follows:

$$AI = \frac{SD}{SND}$$

SD represents the share of dynamic exports in total exports, while SND represents the share of non-dynamic exports.

Dynamic exports are defined in Keynesian terms—as those exports whose demand grows at higher rates than the average growth rate of world exports. The third column of Table 22.2 shows that LA presents lower values of the AI than all the other groups considered. We have argued that international competitiveness depends on TCs which allows the country to react and adapt to changing demand patterns in the world economy. Thus, the AI gives more than a static picture of what the country is exporting at a certain moment; it also gives an idea of its capacity to have a continuous presence in the most dynamic markets, moving across sectors and reacting to demand shocks. As there is a strong positive association between high-tech industries, R&D, and the ability to specialize in sectors with high demand growth in the international markets, then the AI reflects the dynamics of structural change (although some space for the commodity lottery should be allowed).

Of course, causality among structural change, competitiveness, demand growth, and exports run in several directions. It is not possible to disentangle these relations in the context of this chapter. Still, the evidence strongly suggests that this dynamics is a key part of any explanation of why growth rates differ—and in particular of why LA failed to catch up. In turn, trends in structural change and specialization are the consequence of the absence of long-run policies in favor of learning and the weakness of the NSI in LA as compared to other regions (as discussed earlier).

22.4.3 The productivity gap

Another way of looking at the gap in TCs is to examine the evolution of the productivity gap. Latin American backwardness in relation to the developed world can be observed by comparing the productivity levels of manufacturing in the region with that of the USA. Since the 1980s the trend in the index of relative productivity between Latin America and the USA (the inverse of the productivity gap) has been negative (the productivity

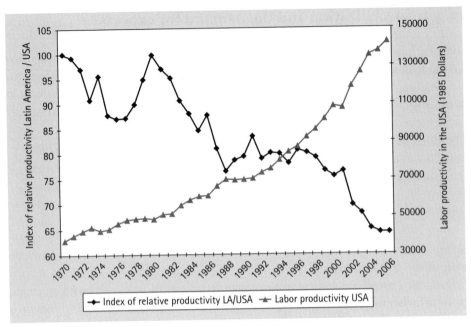

FIGURE 22.2 Productivity gap between Latin America and the technological frontier

Source: Based on data from ECLAC, PADIWIN (Programa para el Análisis de la Dinámica Industrial).

Notes: The relative productivity index of Latin America is calculated as the simple average of the relative productivity index of 4 countries (Argentina, Brazil, Chile and Mexico). Labor productivity is defined as value added per worker in the manufacturing sector.

gap increased) and this fall was especially intense in the last six years (Figure 22.2). In spite of a sustained recovering of growth during the "bonanza" years, between 2003 and 2008 (the year of the latest crisis), the performance of the region in terms of relative productivity was the worst of the last 36 years. It should be stressed that US productivity increased at a rate of 5% at year in this period—an acceleration mainly explained by the ongoing process of industrial transformation based on the incorporation of the ICTs. The rapid incorporation of the new paradigms in the US accounts for this favorable performance, while LA lagged behind.

The effects of successive external shocks on LA relative productivity can be seen Figure 22.2: a dramatic fall during the debt crisis, a moderate improvement during the 1990–7 expansion, and a new fall after the Asian crisis that continued through the 2000s. The workings of Kaldorian increasing returns are clearly visible in the cycles of expansion and contraction of GDP, which are associated with the evolution of labor productivity. In addition, hysteresis phenomenon is observed as well, as LA never recovered the relative productivity it had attained in the 1970s.

The key assumption that guided policymakers in the period of reforms in Latin America—that firms and sectors adapt and produce more efficiently when markets are liberalized and resources move freely—proved misguided. While capabilities in sectors with medium or high technological intensity were lost in this period, there was no symmetric construction of new capabilities in sectors based on natural resources—at least strong enough to avoid relative decline. The hysteresis forces at work implied the recovery following each crisis failed to lead the LA economies back to their previous relative position.

In Figure 22.1 the process of productivity growth based on the rationalization of production and lower levels of employment is represented by a trajectory within the B space—productivity increases $(+\Delta\pi)$ but employment does not follow suit $(-\Delta N)$. Hysteresis is illustrated by the loop in the growth trajectory that prevents the economy from moving towards point c.

22.4.4 Productivity growth and structural change

We will now focus on the interaction between structural change and productivity growth in the industrial sector. Figure 22.3 depicts the co-evolution of these two variables. The productivity levels (in chained dollars at 1985 prices) of three different groups of industries are represented in the horizontal axis. In the vertical axis are represented the accumulated shares of these groups in the total value added of the manufacturing sector. The groups are defined as engineering-intensive industries (triangle), labor-intensive indus-

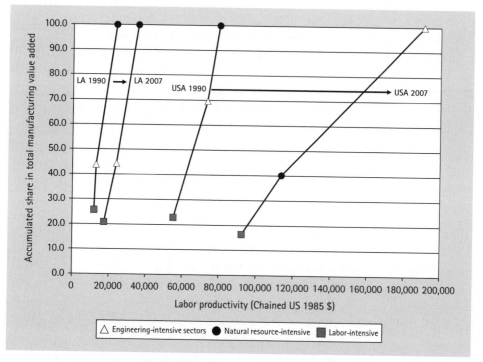

FIGURE 22.3 Productivity and structural change: Latin America and the USA, 1990–2007

Source: Elaborated from ECLAC, PADIWIN.

tries (square), and industries intensive in natural resources (circle). The sum of the accumulated share of the three groups of industries equals 100. Two regions are compared, Latin America and the United States, in two different points in time 1990 and 2007. Some interesting aspects emerge.

The first is the higher increase in productivity levels in *all* sectors in the US as compared to Latin America during 1990–2007. Secondly, the group that led such an increase in the US was the one intensive in engineering skills. The extremely sharp increase in productivity of this group seems to have pushed productivity growth in the whole US manufacturing sector. The engineering industries increased their share in total manufacturing value added from 46.7% in 1990 to 60% in 2007. Last but not least, note that the productivity of the engineering industries was lower in the US than that of the industries intensive in natural resources in 1990, a situation that was reversed in 2007.

On the other hand, in Latin America the shift of the curve to the right between 1990 and 2007 was a modest one—a clear expression of the increase in the productivity and technology gaps we mentioned above. Moreover, the industries that increased their share in total manufacturing value added were those intensive in natural resources, which also remained as leaders in terms of labor productivity. In the year 2007, the industries intensive in natural resources represented the highest share in total manufacturing (55.6% against 23.4% of engineering) and the highest productivity. This implies that—at variance with the US experience—the sectors which led growth and productivity in Latin America had a lower potential for generating a learning process with a significant impact on the productivity levels of the whole industrial sector.[8]

In sum, the interaction between productivity growth and structural change, and the weakness of the virtuous circle of learning in Latin America as compared to the USA, are illustrated by the different intensity of the rightward shift of the productivity curve and by the leadership (in both productivity levels and participation in manufacturing production) of the engineering sectors in the USA.

22.5 CONCLUDING REMARKS

The transformation of the productive and employment structures, driven by technological innovation, plays a central role in economic development. But innovation has strong cumulative features and tends to concentrate in a small group of developed (center) countries. The international diffusion of technology to the periphery occurs in a confined, limited form which produces a poorly diversified, less dense economic structure, incapable of fostering learning and productivity growth or of providing employment to

---

[8] In addition, these sectors show tended to show as well a lower rate of growth of demand: in this sense the less dynamic path from the technological point of view is matched by less dynamism from a demand point of view (which is why region A was unattainable for Latin America).

most of the workforce. This is the meaning of the structuralist perception of the periphery as an economy which is at the same time heterogeneous and specialized.

For the periphery, the challenge to correct asymmetries is to absorb, adapt, and improve foreign technology, moving up the technology ladder towards increasingly technology-intensive activities. This implies being able to traverse towards a virtuous cycle in which learning, productivity growth, and demand growth reinforce each other. Along with supply-side variables, the demand-side is crucial, as a rapidly rising demand for exports (and a higher income elasticity ratio) is required to increase employment in the modern sector and reduce that in the subsistence sector, while at the same time keeping the trade balance in equilibrium. There are various levels involved in this interaction between learning and growth, each part of a set of necessary conditions for development.

First, there is the micro level of learning: the efforts firms made to incorporate innovations, to reshape their organization and production processes, to adopt new routines, and to develop the tacit knowledge that are at the heart of productivity growth and quality improvements. This is also the force that builds up dynamic competitive advantages at the firm level. Secondly, there is the level of the productive structure: the complementarities that exist between sectors and different types of agents (e.g. firms and universities), the spillover of knowledge, and the various types of externalities that feed increasing returns. Finally, there are the macroeconomic determinants of demand growth—fiscal policy, income distribution, the exchange rate, the administration of protection and exports subsidies—that are a critical complement of technical change and which allow demand growth to move hand in hand with productivity growth. The concept of NSI as a set of formal and informal rules that govern and coordinate all these different levels points to the complex interrelations that exist between them, and to the necessity of active policies that channel the efforts of heterogeneous agents towards the objective of accumulating TCs.

The forces driving technological change are strongly cumulative, and market forces alone are bound to reproduce asymmetries through time. Path-dependence, localized technical change, and the various barriers to diffusion (either legal or those related to tacitness and experience in knowledge) produce a built-in trend towards divergence. But the empirical and theoretical literature based on evolutionary microeconomics points out that there is room for learning, and countries that succeeded in building articulated NSI succeeded as well in catching up. This has been the case of several Asian countries. The economic history of Latin America, on the other hand, shows a persistent failure to build a NSI with a focus on learning. While protection is a necessary step in all industrialization process, it remained at a very high level and for too many years in the Latin American cases, with no parallel demand of learning and export targets by local firms. In the same vein, the liberalization process completely neglected the previous path of learning and the need to move forward in terms of TCs. The result was feeble, localized technical change, regressive or very slow structural change, and high levels of uncertainty related to the external constraint and demand growth.

The slow rates of economic growth that the region displayed over the past twenty years, and the widening of the technology gap, reflect a hysteresis state which could only be overcome by means of a thorough redefinition of the industrial and technology policies in the coming years. These policies should challenge the various forces that hamper the accumulation of TCs.

On one hand, trade liberalization and the appreciation of the local currency favored sectors which are less technology-intensive. A similar effect is related to positive shocks in the terms of trade of commodity exports, as resources were reallocated to other, less technology-intensive activities. The commoditization of production made redundant part of the R&D activities and infrastructure that firms had created in the state-led industrialization period (Katz 2000; ECLAC 2002). There was less demand for adaptation to local conditions and less interaction between producers and users (reflecting a less integrated productive structure). As a result, these shocks produced more than short-term fluctuations. When relative prices returned to their pre-shock levels, the capabilities lost in the adjustment process were not easily recovered and the economy was less able to respond to new challenges, or to increase productivity at the same rate as before.

On the other hand, firms have become more closely integrated to global chains of value in which the stimulus to speed up indigenous learning was abandoned in favor of a focus on homogenization of inputs and goods within a hierarchical system of production. This occurred in parallel with the progressive commoditization of the production of goods and services in the region. These processes jointly resulted in a disarticulation of local production chains along with the marginalization of small and medium domestic firms. Rationalization based on the more intense use of imported inputs and equipment produced blanks in the production matrix, and had negative effects on the levels of employment and heterogeneity.

References

AMSDEN, A. (1989). *Asia's Next Giant: South Korea and Late Industrialization*, New York: Oxford University Press.

BELL, M. (2006). 'Time and Technological Learning in Industrialising Countries: How Long Does It Take? How Fast Is It Moving (if at all)?', *International Journal of Technology Management* 36.1–3.

BÉRTOLA, L., and PORCILE, G. (2006). 'Convergence, Trade and Industrial Policy: Argentina, Brazil and Uruguay in the International Economy, 1900–1980', *Journal of Iberian and Latin American Economic History* 24.

CAPDEVIELLE, M. (2005). 'Globalización, especialización y cambio estructural en América Latina', in M. Cimoli (ed.), *Heterogeneidad estructural, asimetrías tecnológicas y crecimiento en América Latina*, Santiago, Chile: BID-CEPAL.

CÁRDENAS, E., OCAMPO, J. A., and THORP, R. (eds) (2000). *Industrialization and the State in Latin America: The Post War Years*, Basingstoke and New York: Palgrave Press and St. Martin's Press.

CHANG, H.-J. (2001). 'Infant Industry Promotion in Historical Perspective: A Rope to Hang Oneself or a Ladder to Climb With?', prepared for 'Development Theory at the Threshold of the Twenty-First Century', ECLAC, August.

CHUDNOVSKY, D., NAGAO, M., and JACOBSON, S. (1984). *Capital Goods Production in the Third World: An Economic Study of Technical Acquisition*, London: Pinter.

CIMOLI, M., and DOSI, G. (1995). 'Technological Paradigms, Pattern of Learning and Development: An Introductory Roadmap', *Journal of Evolutionary Economics* 5.3.

—— and KATZ, J. (2003). 'Structural Reforms, Technological Gaps and Economic Development: A Latin American Perspective', *Industrial and Corporate Change* 12.

—— and PORCILE, G. (2009). 'Sources of Learning Paths and Technological Capabilities: An Introductory Roadmap of Development Processes', *Economics of Innovation and New Technology* 18.7.

—— DOSI, G., and STIGLITZ, J. (eds) (2010). *Industrial Policy and Development: The Political Economy of Capabilities Accumulation*, Oxford: Oxford University Press.

—— PORCILE, G., and ROVIRA, S. (2010). 'Structural Convergence and the Balance-of-Payments Constraint: Why Did Latin America Fail to Converge?', *Cambridge Journal of Economics* 34.2.

DOSI, G., PAVITT, K., and SOETE, L. (1990). *The Economic of Technical Change and International Trade*, London and New York: Harvester Wheatsheaf and New York University Press.

ECLAC (UN Economic Commission for Latin America and the Caribbean) (1990). *Changing Production Patterns with Social Equity: The Prime Task of Latin American and Caribbean Development in the 1990s*, Santiago, Chile.

—— (2002). *Globalization and Development*, Santiago, Chile.

—— (2007). *Progreso técnico y cambio estructural en América Latina*, Santiago, Chile.

—— (2008). *Structural Change and Productivity Growth, 20 Years Later: Old Problems, New Opportunities*, Santiago, Chile.

—— (2010). *Time for Equality: Closing Gaps, Opening Trails*, Santiago, Chile: ECLAC.

FAJNZYLBER, F. (1990). *De la caja negra al casillero cacío*, Santiago, Chile: ECLAC.

FRANSMAN, M., and KING, K. (1984). *Technological Capability in the Third World*, London: Macmillan.

FREEMAN, C. (1994). 'Technological Revolutions and Catching-Up: ICT and the NICs', in J. Fagerberg, N. von Tunzelman, and B. Verspagen (eds), *The Dynamics of Technology, Trade and Growth*, London: Edward Elgar.

GERSHENKRON, A. (1962). *Economic Backwardness in Historical Perspective*, Cambridge, Mass.: Belknap Press.

HIRSCHMAN, A. (1977). 'Generalized Linkage Approach to Development, with Special Reference to Staples', in M. Nash (ed.), *Essays on Economic Development and Cultural Change in Honor of B. F. Hoselitz*, Chicago: University of Chicago Press.

KATZ, J. (1987). *Technology Generation in Latin American Manufacturing Industries: Theory and Case-Studies Concerning its Nature, Magnitude and Consequences*, London: Macmillan.

—— (2000). *Reformas estructurales, productividad y conducta tecnológica*, Santiago, Chile: ECLAC.

—— and STUMPO, G. (2001). 'Regímenes sectoriales, productividad y competitividad internacional', *CEPAL Review* 75.

KHAN, M., and BLANKENBURG, S. (2010). 'The Political Economy of Industrial Policy in Asia and Latin America', in M. Cimoli, G. Dosi, and J. E. Stiglitz (eds), *Industrial Policy and*

Development. The Political Economy of Capabilities Accumulation, Oxford: Oxford University Press.

KIM, L. (1997). 'Korea's National Innovation System in Transition', presented at the STEPI International Symposium on Innovation and Competitiveness in NIEs, Seoul, Korea (May).

KOSACOFF, B. et al. (1999). 'Hacia un mejor entorno competitivo de la producción automotriz en Argentina', mimeograph, Proyecto ADEFA CEPAL, Buenos Aires.

LALL, S. (1982). 'The Emergence of Third World Multinationals: Indian Joint Ventures Overseas', *World Development* 10.2.

—— (1997). 'Technological Change and Industrialisation in the Asian NIEs: Achievements and Challenges', presented at the STEPI International Symposium on Innovation and Competitiveness in NIEs, Seoul, Korea (May).

MORTIMORE, M., and PERES, W. (2001). 'Competitividad empresarial en América Latina y el Caribe', *CEPAL Review* 74.

MYTELKA, L. (ed.) (2007). *Innovation and Economic Development*, Cheltenham: Elgar.

NELSON, R. (ed.) (1993). *National Systems of Innovation*, Oxford: Oxford University Press.

OCAMPO, J. A. (2005). 'The Quest for Dynamic Efficiency: Structural Dynamics and Economic Growth in Developing Countries', in J. A. Ocampo (ed.), *Beyond Reforms: Structural Dynamics and Macroeconomic Vulnerability*, Stanford, Calif.: Stanford University Press.

PÉRES, W. (2010). 'The (Slow) Return of Industrial Policies in Latin America and the Caribbean', in M. Cimoli, G. Dosi, and J. E. Stiglitz (eds), *The Political Economy of Capabilities Accumulation: The Past and Future of Policies for Industrial Development*, Oxford: Oxford University Press.

PINTO, A. (1976). 'Naturaleza e implicaciones de la heterogeneidad estructural de la América Latina', *El trimestre económico* 37.145.

PREBISCH, R. (1949). *El desarrollo económico de América Latina y su principales problemas*, New York: United Nations.

—— (1963). *Hacia una dinámica del desarrollo Latinoamericano*, Mexico: Fondo de Cultura Económica.

—— (1976). 'A Critique of Peripheral Capitalism', *CEPAL Review* 1.

RODRÍGUEZ, O. (2007). *El estructuralismo Latinoamericano*, México: Siglo XXI.

ROSENSTEIN-RODAN, P. (1943). 'Problems of Industrialization in Eastern and Southeastern Europe', *Economic Journal* 53.

STALLINGS, B., and PÉRES, W. (2000). *Growth, Employment and Equity: The Impact of Economic Reforms in Latin America and the Caribbean*, Washington, DC: Brookings Institution Press.

—— and WILSON, P. (2000). *Crecimiento, empleo y equidad: el impacto de las reformas económicas en América Latina y el Caribe*, Santiago, Chile: ECLAC.

STUMPO, G. (1998). *Empresas transnacionales, procesos de reestructuración industrial y políticas económicas en América Latina*, Santiago, Chile: ECLAC and Alianza Estudios.

SUNKEL, O. (1978). 'La dependencia y la heterogeneidad estructural', *El trimestre económico* 45.1.

TEITEL, S. (1984). 'Technology Creation in Semi-industrial Economies', *Journal of Development Economics* 16.1–2.

—— (2004). 'On Semi-industrialized Countries and the Acquisition of Technological Capabilities', ICER Working Paper No. 19-2004, Turin.

TEUBAL, M. (1984). 'The Role of Technological Learning in the Exports of Manufactured Goods: The Case of Selected Capital Goods in Brazil', *World Development* 12.8.

THIRLWALL, A. P. (1979). 'The Balance of Payments Constraint as an Explanation of International Growth Rates Differences', *Banca Nazionale del Lavoro Quarterly Review* (January).

UNIDO (United Nations Industrial Development Organization) (2010). *UNIDO Industrial Statistics Database*, Geneva.

WADE, R. (1990). *Governing the Market: Economic Theory and the Role of Government in East Asian Industrialisation*, Princeton, NJ: Princeton University Press.

World Bank (various years). World Development Indicators online: http://databank.worldbank.org/ddp/home.do

CHAPTER 23

WHY HAS PRODUCTIVITY GROWTH STAGNATED IN MOST LATIN AMERICAN COUNTRIES SINCE THE NEO-LIBERAL REFORMS?*

JOSÉ GABRIEL PALMA

23.1 INTRODUCTION

Except for commodities and a small number of other activities, Latin America's economic performance since the beginning of neo-liberal reforms has been poor. This not only contrasts with its own performance pre-1980, but also with what has happened in Asia since 1980. I shall argue that the weakness of the region's new paradigm is rooted as much in its intrinsic flaws as in the particular way it has been implemented. Keynes once said (discussing Say's Law) that Ricardo conquered England as completely as the Holy Inquisition conquered Spain; the same could be said for neo-liberalism in Latin America: it has conquered the region, including many in its left-wing intelligentsia, as completely (and fiercely) as the Inquisition conquered Spain. This process has been so successful that it has actually 'closed the imagination' to conceptualizing alternatives.

* I would like to thank Anish Acharya, Stephanie Blankenburg, Ha-Joon Chang, Antonio David, Jonathan Di John, Samer Frangie, Jayati Ghosh, Daniel Hahn, Geoff Harcourt, Andre Hofman, Edward Hogan, Jorge Katz, Mushtaq Khan, Jan Kregel, Javier Nuñez, José Antonio Ocampo, Isidoro Palma Matte, Guillermo Paraje, Carlota Pérez, Jonathan Pincus, Ignês Sodré, Lance Taylor, Damián Vergara, and participants at several conferences and seminars for their helpful comments. Acute shortage of space in the Handbook means I shall be unable to review some of the relevant literature. The usual caveats apply.

The genesis of the new development strategy can be located in a series of negative external and domestic shocks c. 1980, when the region was particularly vulnerable. As had happened in the 1930s, these laid the foundations for a radical ideological transformation that led to the new paradigm along the lines of Anglo-Saxon neo-liberalism and US neo-conservatism. This was quite distinct from what was happening in Asia, where reforms were implemented in a much more pragmatic way. Perhaps the main difference is that in Asia most actors in favor of the reforms (including local capitalist élites, the administrative classes, and most intellectuals—even many in the 'new' left) have a strong sense of reality, national identity and historical awareness. Nobody had to convince them that in the real world there are so many distortions, market failures, coordination failures (especially with investment) and financial fragilities that when it came to policy-making the Washington Consensus's set of 'first-best' policies belongs to a fantasy world. Perhaps they also were cynical enough to realize that the neo-liberal ideology is based mostly on recycled 19th-century ideas wrapped in a narcissistic 'end of history' aura. So, in Asia one often finds the parallel existence of a neo-liberal discourse (to appease the gods of the markets), with a more pragmatic, targeted and sometimes imaginative implementation of reforms. And a pro-growth macro is never far away. In LA, instead, policy makers (including those in the 'new' left) do not just aim at 'talking the talk' of the neo-liberal orthodoxy; for them—and often with the enthusiasm of the new convert—what really matters seems to be the 'walking the walk' of that orthodoxy!

In fact, I sometimes wonder whether the brand of neo-liberalism bought by so many Latin Americans is just shorthand for 'nothing left to decide'—and, of course, 'nothing left to think about *critically*' (Palma, 2009a). Indeed, in most of the region the attitude today towards neo-liberal economics and (in particular) policy-making resembles Lord Kelvin's attitude towards physics at the end of the 19th century (Kelvin, 1900), when he famously declared that in physics "there is nothing new to be discovered now. All that remains is more and more precise measurement."

What characterizes LA's economic reforms most is that they were undertaken primarily as a result of perceived economic weaknesses—i.e., there was an attitude of 'throwing in the towel' vis-à-vis the previous state-led import substituting industrialization strategy (ISI). Basically, most politicians and economists interpreted the 1982 crisis as conclusive evidence that ISI had led the region into a cul-de-sac. As Hirschman has argued (1982), policy-making has a strong component of 'path-dependency'. As a result, people often stick with policies well after they have achieved their aims, and those policies have become counterproductive. This leads to such frustration and disappointment with existing policies and institutions that is not uncommon to experience a 'rebound effect'. An extreme example of this 'backlash' (or 'reverse shift') phenomenon is post-1982 LA, where economic reforms were mostly about the reversal of the previous development strategy—which, in many aspects, had overstayed its welcome.

From this perspective, what most differentiated LA from Asia was not just the strength with which the new neo-liberal ideology was adopted, but also the form in which the previous one (ISI) was given up. Hirschman called this LA's tendency to 'fracasomania' (1982). So, perhaps it should not be surprising that the discourse of the reforms ended up resembling a compass whose 'magnetic north' was simply the reversal of the previous development strategy—as Gustavo Franco (when President of Brazil's Central Bank) explained, the main task of Cardoso's reforms was "...to undo forty years of stupidity [besteira]..." (Veja, 15/11/1996). With that 'reverse-gear' attitude, this experiment inevitably ended up as an exercise in 'not-very-creative-destruction'. This phenomenon was reinforced by the usual dynamic of idealization: when there is an unremitting need to sustain the idealization of something (in this case, the neo-liberal economic-reforms), what is needed is simultaneously to demonize something else (in this case, anything to do with 'the past', especially the previous development strategy of state-led industrialization). In fact, the more evident the flaws of what was idealized, the stronger the demonization of the past has to be. The mere idea that alternatives could exist met with contempt. Franco again: "[The alternative now] is to be neo-liberal or neo-idiotic [neo-burros]." Perhaps one reason why 'pure' ideology is so important in LA is because there is little else in the form of social cohesion. This helps to explain the peculiar set of priorities and the rigidity with which the reforms were implemented in LA, as well as their poor outcome, as distinct from many Asian countries—where reforms were implemented not as a messianic endeavor but (rightly or wrongly) as a more targeted and pragmatic mechanism to lift specific pressing economic and financial constraints in order to continue and strengthen their existing ambitious industrialization strategies.

LA is also a region whose critical social imagination has stalled. The emergence post-1950 of an intellectual tradition in the social sciences somehow runs against what one could call the 'Iberian tradition', which has been far more creative in painting, music, literature and film than in contributions to the social sciences. Basically, in the Iberian Peninsula social sciences have suffered due to a lack of 'enlightenment' beyond the arts and letters, and specifically the lack of sophistication in the state's exercise of power. Foucault's ideas can help understand this issue: knowledge and power are interrelated, one presupposing the other (Foucault, 2004). Foucault intended to show how the development of social sciences was interrelated with the deployment of more 'modern' forms of power (Frangie, 2008). But in the Iberian world, since states have often governed through 'un-modern' means, and at times via crudely mediated forms, they have not required much social knowledge, or sophistication in the forms of control. So, social sciences have been relegated to a relatively marginalized academic enterprise. In essence, what has became manifest in the implementation of economic reforms in LA is how its brand of neo-liberalism—with its Anglo-Saxon fundamentalism and its Iberian 'minimalism'—has fitted perfectly with its underlying power structure (and in particular with its perennial rent-seeking bias), and its lack of political need for more sophisticated forms of social imagination. Perhaps that also helps understand why this ideology was soon wrapped in an aura of superiority, 'specialness' and contempt, not just for possible alternatives but also for everything that happened before (the past, even the recent past, acquired a growing sense of unreality).[1] And (not unrelatedly) what became 'modern' in

[1] For Hobsbawm the business of historians is to remember what others forget. Today in LA this applies also especially to economists.

terms of economic thinking reminds us of Adorno's proposition: "[t]oday the appeal to newness, of no matter what kind, provided only that it is archaic enough, has become universal" (2006).

Ortega y Gasset once referred to LA's "…narcissistic tendency to use reality as a mirror for self-contemplation, rather than as a subject for critical analysis and progress." He also observed that in LA he found too many "self-satisfied individuals," reminding them that "…human history is the product of discontent" (1918). There's probably no better way to summarize what is wrong with LA's current ('Anglo-Iberian') neo-liberal paradigm and its political economy than Ortega's observations, as (for reasons beyond the scope of this chapter—see Palma, 2009a) these regional features have returned with a vengeance.

23.2 LATIN AMERICA'S POOR GROWTH PERFORMANCE POST-1980: TWO MAIN STYLISED FACTS

23.2.1 The collapse of Latin America's growth rate post-1980 is unique in the Third World

As is well-known, the beginning of neo-liberal reforms instituted by Reagan and Thatcher was followed by a slowdown of the world economy. This was also associated with the complex transition from the 'mass-production-for-mass-consumption' techno-economic paradigm to the age of information and telecommunications, with its more knowledge-intensive and flexible production techniques (Pérez, 2002). The average annual growth rate of the world economy fell from 4.5% (1950–1980) to 3.5% (1980–2008). The median rate fell even further—from 4.7% to 3.1% (GGDC, 2009). However, LA's collapse was extreme, even in this context (5.4% to 2.7%).

The exception to the general slowdown was the 'third-tier' NICs (China, India, and Vietnam). Elsewhere, the 'second-tier' NICs (Malaysia, Thailand, Indonesia) managed to keep their growth-rate despite 1997, while in the 'first-tier' NICs (Korea, Hong-Kong, Singapore, Taiwan), and in North Africa and Sub-Saharan Africa growth-rates declined, but by a relatively small margin. LA, meanwhile, saw its growth rate *halved* to 2.7%. For example, if one ranks all countries of the database (excluding oil-exporting Middle Eastern countries) by GDP growth-rate (97 countries), Brazil's growth-ranking collapses from 10 (1950–80) to 70 (1980–2008); in turn, Mexico's falls from 13 to 62. What a contrast with China (43 to 1), India (72 to 7), and Vietnam (84 to 2)—see Figure 23.1.

Although from a Gerschenkronian (or Kuznetsian) perspective one expects some catching-up, the extent of Asia's post-1980 gains is remarkable—and China's catching-

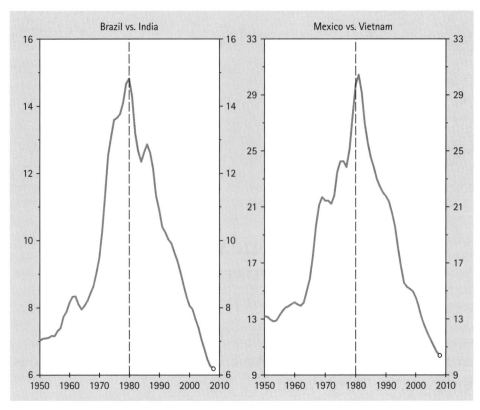

FIGURE 23.1 Brazil's GDP per capita as a multiple of India's GDP per capita, and Mexico's as a multiple of Vietnam's, 1950–2008

Source: WDI (2010, data in constant 2000-US$). The series were brought back to 1950 using GGDC (2009).

Notes: 3-year moving averages.

up is faster still. Figure 23.1 also confirms that LA's relative growth weakness is *not* confined to the 1980s. Moreover, LA's disappointing post-1980 performance is fairly homogenous—see Figure 23.2.

While between 1950 and 1980 the range of growth in LA was rather wide (from 2.1% (Uruguay) to 6.8% (Brazil)), in the latter period (1980–2008) 10 of the 13 countries of the database appear within a very narrow range—between 2.2% (Uruguay) and 2.9% (Guatemala). Furthermore, Colombia only emerged from this narrow range after 2004 (see 'co*'), leaving only Costa Rica and Chile properly outside (growth-rates of 4.3% and 4.5%, respectively).

Moreover, only Chile (and marginally Uruguay) managed to grow faster in the second period. In Chile, however, reforms began in 1973, so a more meaningful comparison would be between pre-1973-ISI and post-1973-reform periods. In this case, the growth rate is actually the same (4%; see 'ch*' in Figure 23.2). This Figure also confirms the remarkable growth-collapse of Brazil and Mexico—only Japan does worse.

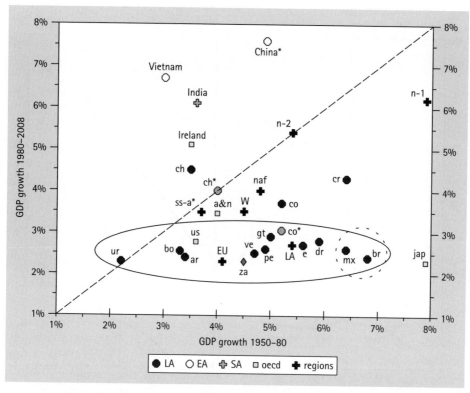

FIGURE 23.2 Latin America and other regions: GDP growth, 1950–80 and 1980–2008

Source: GGDC (2009, data in constant 1990-US$, converted at Geary Khamis PPPs). The GGDC dataset only provides information for 13 Latin American countries (all included in the graph). Unless otherwise stated, this will be the source of all data on GDP, employment and labor productivity in this chapter.

Regions: LA=Latin America; EA=East and South East Asia; EU=European Union (excluding Germany because of unification); n-1=first-tier NICs; n-2=second-tier NICs; naf=North Africa; SA=South Asia; ss-a*=Sub-Saharan Africa (excluding South Africa); and W=world (weighted average for the 97 countries of the source).

Countries: a&n=Australia and New Zealand; ar=Argentina; bo=Bolivia; br=Brazil; ch=Chile (ch*=Chile 1950–72 and 1972–2008; 1972 is chosen as a cutting year to avoid the distorting effect of 1973, the year of the military coup); China*, rate of growth 1980–2008=8.5%; co=Colombia (co*=Colombia, second period 1980–2004); cr=Costa Rica; dr=Dominican Republic e=Ecuador; gt=Guatemala; mx=Mexico; pe=Peru; us=United States; ur=Uruguay; ve=Venezuela; and za=South Africa (the rate of growth of the second period improves to 3.6% if restricted to 1994–2008). Unless otherwise stated, these acronyms will be used throughout the chapter.

23.2.2 In Latin America the decline in GDP growth after 1980 was entirely absorbed by productivity, leaving the employment growth practically unaffected

A comparison between Mexico and Thailand helps explain the second contrast between LA and Asia—how a decline in GDP growth is absorbed differently by employment and labor productivity (Figure 23.3).

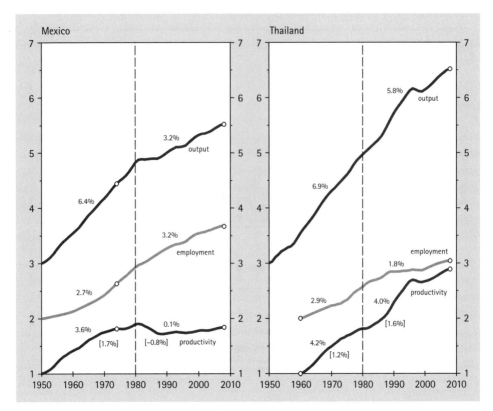

FIGURE 23.3 Mexico and Thailand: output, employment, and productivity, 1950–2008

Source: as Figure 23.1. For TFP growth, see Figure 23.5 below.

Notes: Log scales and 3-year moving averages. Percentages above the lines are average annual real rates of growth for respective periods (Mexico, 1950–74 and 1974–2008 due to its different productivity cycle); those in brackets below the productivity lines indicate factor productivity (TFP) growth rates (due to lack of data, throughout this chapter TFP rates are restricted to 1960–2004). For Thailand (and other Asian countries below), the first period in employment and productivity also starts in 1960 because the GGDC database only provides employment data from that date.

If one divides these six decades into two periods, during the first there is little difference between the two countries. This is clearly not the case afterwards: although both GDPs slowed, in Mexico this is *totally* absorbed by a decline in labor productivity (from 3.6% to 0.1%), and in Thailand by employment. So while Mexico's productivity growth collapses, employment creation actually accelerates. In contrast, Thailand's productivity growth continues at the same pace and employment absorbs the fall in GDP growth. Both countries have cycles and sectoral diversities, but the contrasting picture in terms of GDP-'shock-absorbers' is clear. And as Thailand has had little industrial policy, this asymmetry mostly reflects market outcomes. In fact, in Mexico, as the whole of GDP growth ends up being explained by additional employment, TFP growth becomes negative (and remains so after reforms; see Table 23.3). This contrast in terms of GDP-'shock-absorbers' also applies to the other countries of each region.

Pre-1980 only the 'first-tier' NICs (N-1) were doing better than LA in terms of GDP and employment. LA's pre-1980 productivity growth was also relatively energetic (2.5 %); i.e., productivity doubling every 28 years, with Brazil and Mexico needing less than 20. However, post-1980 things changed sharply: while LA's GDP growth rate fell by half (becoming among the worst), its employment creation remained basically stable. Consequently, its employment elasticity nearly doubles (from 0.49 to 0.92, a level about twice most other countries'), and its labor productivity sinks to the bottom of the league.

A further comparison (Brazil vs. Korea), helps illustrate the above phenomenon. In terms of productivity, Brazil was just about keeping up with Korea between 1960 and 1980 (3.6% and 4.8%, respectively). In fact, by 1980 Brazil's overall productivity level was still slightly higher (US$12,500 and 11,500, respectively). However, by 2008 Korea's productivity was over 3 *times* higher (US$41,000 and 12,900; data in constant 1990-US$). So, while Korea was closing the productivity gap with the US—up from 28% (1980) to 63% (2008)—Brazil was falling behind, (down from 30% to 20% of US productivity levels, respectively).

23.3 WHY IS IT SO DIFFICULT FOR LATIN AMERICA TO SUSTAIN PRODUCTIVITY GROWTH (AND TFP GROWTH) FOR ANY SIGNIFICANT LENGTH OF TIME?

23.3.1 Productivity growth in Latin American countries: an international perspective

Perhaps the most significant stylized fact emerging from the above is that while LA is perfectly capable of generating periods of dynamic productivity growth, it seems unable to *sustain* it long-term. Meanwhile, many in Asia mastered this technique quite nicely (Figure 23.4).

As mentioned above, Brazil (like most of LA) followed the same contrasting productivity pattern as Mexico: a dynamic annual rate of productivity growth pre-1980 (3.6%), followed by a long period of productivity-stagnation (-0.1% in 1980–2005). As has been widely reported, the Brazilian economy then entered a new growth-cycle in 2004 (led mostly by commodities, finance and real estate), which was quickly resumed in 2010 after the 2009 slowdown. As a result, productivity growth has accelerated to 2.3% (2005–2009). The other three Latin American countries of Figure 23.4 are included because (with Uruguay and some recent recoveries) they are the only ones in the region that also experienced at least some years of rapid productivity growth after 1980. However, productivity growth in them all stopped abruptly after a relatively short period—and TFP growth became negative after that point (see also Figure 23.5; the same happened to Uruguay). So, if pre-1980 many LA countries were at least good

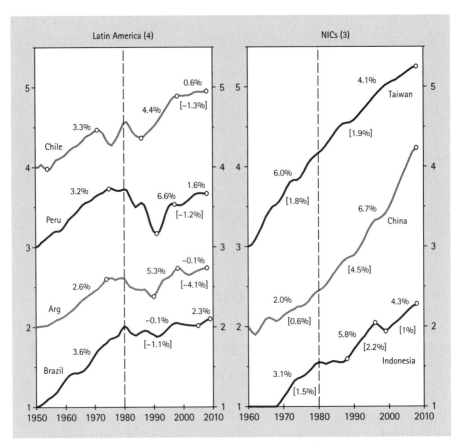

FIGURE 23.4 Productivity growth: Argentina, Brazil, Chile, and Peru vs. China, Indonesia, and Taiwan, 1950–2008

Notes: Log scales and 3-year moving averages. Percentages above the lines are average annual real rates of productivity-growth during respective cycles; those in brackets below the lines indicate TFP growth rates between the end of the respective growth period and 2004 (last year for which TFP-data are available). Employment data for Asian countries are only available since 1960. For Brazil data were extended to 2009 using an update of the GGDC database (so, the last rate of growth corresponds to 2005–9). Arg=Argentina.

middle-distance (productivity-)runners, post-1980 they became at best good sprinters… Meanwhile many Asian tigers became top marathon-runners (a skill that crucially includes the ability to hold one's nerve more effectively in both stages of the economic cycle).

The Chilean case is notable, in that its high productivity-growth period stopped abruptly in 1998 without a financial crisis (as in Argentina) or political crisis (Peru). Chile needed only a relatively minor contagion from Asia and Russia, and an over-reaction by its Central Bank. Subsequently productivity growth practically vanished (0.6% 1998–2008), becoming actually negative in 'per-hour-worked' terms (-0.4%)—and even more so in TFP terms (-1.3%).[2] How different from the three Asian countries of

---

[2] Referring to these two contrasting periods, Michael Porter once said that Chile was like a two-act play; by then Chile was well into the second act, but most Chileans were still giving the first a standing ovation…

Figure 23.4 (each representing one of the three NIC groups), or from other Asian countries that also managed rapid productivity growth during the three decades post-1980, such as Korea (4.7%), Vietnam (4.2%), Thailand (4%), India (3.8%), Hong-Kong (3.4%), Malaysia (3.3%), Singapore (3.1%), Sri Lanka (3.1%), Bangladesh (2.4%), or Pakistan (2.9%), among others. LA's average for this period (0.2%) seems to belong to a different world. Even if the 1980s are excluded and the period is restricted to the post-reform 1990–2008 one, LA's average (1.3%) is just a fraction of that of most Asian countries (China 8%, Vietnam 5%, India 4.2%, Taiwan 4%, Korea 3.9%, Malaysia 3.7%, Thailand 3.5%, and so on).

Indonesia is included in Figure 23.4 (even though it is the least dynamic of the N-2) because its experience is relevant for a comparison with LA. Not only was it the hardest hit by the 1997 crisis, but its whole post-independence history has been turbulent, plagued by natural disasters, separatism, poverty, genocide and corruption (the latter two especially during Suharto's three-decade-long presidency). Also, since the end of its oil-boom, Indonesia largely abandoned its (somewhat megalomaniac) industrial policy, and soon acquired a Latin-American-style proclivity for premature financialization and monetarist-macro. ('Financialization' is the rise in size and dominance of the financial

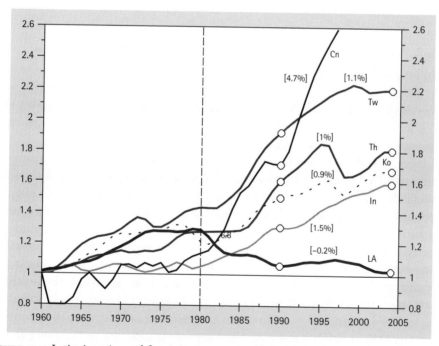

FIGURE 23.5 Latin America and five Asian economies: TFP, 1960–2004

Source: Calculations made by Anish Acharya and author, using the Hall and Jones (1999) methodology for decomposing output per worker; data were available only until 2004 (2003 for some countries). Acharya (2009), and Palma (2010).

Notes: 1960=1. Cn=China (2003=3.12); In=India; Ko=Korea; Th=Thailand; and Tw=Taiwan. Percentages shown in the graph are TFP growth rates between 1990 and 2004 (i.e., the period of full-blown neo-liberal economic reform throughout Latin America). Three-year moving averages.

sector, as well as the diversification towards financial activities in non-financial corpora-tions.) Yet, no country in LA has managed Indonesia's productivity growth-rate since 1990.

For those who consider TFP growth a more telling indicator of economic success (despite the problems associated with its concept and its measurement), Figure 23.5 shows that in LA the contrasting picture between the two periods is even more striking.

Much has been said regarding Krugman's 'TFP-critique' of East Asia (EA), as if factor accumulation could be dismissed as 'not the real thing'. However, Figure 23.5 and Table 23.1 show that even these more moderate Asian TFP-rates are well above LA's post-1980 performance. That was not the case pre-1980.

With the exception of Chile, all LA posted a negative TFP-rate during the 1980s, and in half of them TFP growth remained negative after 1990 (and in two others is zero, and in another two practically stagnant). As a result, both during the 1980s and the post-1990 reform-period LA's average is negative and well below everybody else's. That was clearly not the case between 1960 and 1980. So, for those who follow the Washington Consensus, the most challenging question must be how was it that in most of LA TFP growth became negative (or at best stagnant) well *after* full-blown economic reform? And the well-rehearsed answer that what is needed is yet more of the same neo-liberal reforms sounds increasingly hollow.

23.3.2 Latin America's remarkably poor investment effort and its political economy

There is little doubt that the core of LA's inability to sustain productivity growth after 1980 is its low rate of accumulation—poor even from the perspective of its relatively inadequate historical record (Figure 23.6).

In Panel A, while investment-rates in EA and South Asia (SA) are stationary around a positive trend, LA's rate is stationary around a (low) intercept.[3] It is fairly obvious that LA's capitalist élite has a preference for luxury consumption and for accumulating via mobile assets (financial ones and capital flight) rather than via 'fixed' capital formation.[4] And neo-liberal reforms—despite all their efforts towards defining and enforcing property rights, and many other 'market-friendly' policies—have had little impact on investment. Even the small increase during the surprisingly positive environment after 9/11 (particularly in terms of finance and terms of trade) is unremarkable vis-à-vis those of Asia (see Panel A). Basically, in LA (2002–7) while the ratio of the stock of financial assets to GDP jumped from 106% to 182%, the investment rate only improved from 19% to 22% (see IMF, 2009). Not much evidence here of the supposed revitalizing effects of 'financial-deepening' promised by McKinnon and Shaw.

Basically, no theory of investment seems to be able to explain LA's stationarity-around-a-low-intercept behavior, especially taking place during such a long period, such diverse domestic and international scenarios, and through such divergent develop-

---

[3] Due to space constraints, for relevant statistics, see Palma (2010).

[4] At least easy access to mobile assets help oligarchies become more democratic (Boix, 2003).

Table 23.1 TFP growth: Latin America, Asia, South Africa, and OECD, 1960–2004

	1960–80	1980s	1990–2004		1960–80	1980s	1990–2004
China	0.6	4.2	4.7	Chile	0.5	0.7	1.4
Ireland	1.9	2.0	2.6	D Republic	1.0	-1.8	1.0
India	0.2	2.5	1.5	Costa Rica	0.4	-1.6	0.8
Nordic	1.0	0.8	1.1	Argentina	0.1	-2.9	0.8
Taiwan	1.8	2.9	1.1	Peru	1.1	-3.7	0.3
Thailand	1.2	2.4	1.0	El Salvador	-0.7	-2.4	0.3
Australia	1.2	0.2	1.0	Brazil	2.2	-2.5	0.0
Korea	0.8	2.4	0.9	Guatemala	2.1	-1.6	0.0
Singapore	1.2	1.4	0.9	Uruguay	1.4	-1.5	-0.1
US	0.8	0.8	0.8	Nicaragua	-1.7	-4.6	-0.4
Malaysia	1.1	0.0	0.7	Ecuador	2.8	-1.3	-0.5
World (84)	1.2	0.7	0.7	Mexico	1.6	-2.4	-0.6
New Zealand	0.2	0.9	0.6	Colombia	1.9	-1.1	-0.6
EU	2.0	0.9	0.3	Honduras	0.6	-1.2	-1.1
South Africa*	1.7	-2.1	0.1	Paraguay	1.9	-1.8	-1.3
Latin America	1.4	-2.3	-0.2	Venezuela	-0.5	-1.6	-2.4

Source: as Figure 23.5.

Notes: Countries/regions are ranked according to their TFP growth rates between 1990 and 2004. Nordic=median Nordic country (Sweden); EU=median EU country excluding Nordic countries (Belgium); and South Africa*=later period 1994–2004 (to reflect the period since the beginning of democracy and end to sanctions).

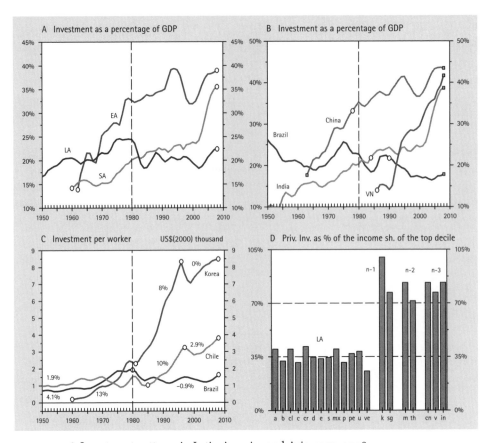

FIGURE 23.6 Investment patterns in Latin America and Asia, 1950–2008

Source: for investment, and for income distribution, WDI (2010); for investment before 1960 in LA, CEPAL (2010);
in India (http://mospi.gov.in/). For employment, GGDC (2009); for private investment, IMF (2010).

Notes: In Panel **B**, **VN**=Vietnam; white circles indicate the beginning of economic reform (for China, Deng Xiaoping's
1978 speech to the Third Plenary Session of the Party's Eleventh Central Committee; for India, 1980; for Vietnam,
1986—Doi moi; and for Brazil, 1990—Collor's 'New Brazil' Plan. In Panel **C**, percentages shown in the graph are growth
rates in the respective periods (for Brazil, 1950–80 and 1980–2008; for Chile, 1950–80, 1985–98 and 1998–2008; and for
Korea, 1960–80, 1981–97 and 1997–2008. Panel **D**, **n-3**=third-tier NICs (China, India, and Vietnam), and **a**=Argentina;
b=Brazil; **cl**=Chile; **c**=Colombia; **cr**=Costa Rica; **d**=Dominican Republic; **e**=Ecuador; **s**=El Salvador; **mx**=Mexico;
p=Paraguay; **pe**=Peru; **u**=Uruguay; **ve**=Venezuela; **k**=Korea; **sg**=Singapore; **m**=Malaysia; **th**=Thailand; **cn**=China;
v=Vietnam; **in**=India. Three-year moving averages.

ment strategies. In turn, Panel B shows that in Brazil (like the rest of LA) economic
reform seems to have unleashed more powerfully the predatory and rentier instincts of
the region's capitalist élites (the former especially during the privatization period) rather
than their Schumpeterian ones. In many Asian countries, meanwhile, reforms, especially
(partial) financial liberalization, may have brought complex challenges to the macro and
the inevitable financial fragilities (as well as 'flexible' labor markets, increased inequalities, and so on), but at least in these Asian countries the rate of accumulation increased

after their implementation. In LA, meanwhile, the cloud did not even have that silver lining. The contrast between Brazil and India in panel B is particularly telling.

Furthermore, in the very few cases in LA where investment actually increased after reforms, as in Chile, it is not obvious why it took so long for it to happen (over ten years after the beginning of reforms), let alone why it ran out of steam so easily afterwards (post-1998). Panel C indicates a similar difference in terms of investment per worker. While in Chile, at least for a time, this statistic show dynamic growth, in Brazil (despite the post-2003 recovery) by 2008 investment per worker was still 22% below that of 1980 (US\$1,634 and 2,106 respectively—data in constant 2000-US\$). On average, LA as a whole follows a pattern similar to Brazil's, with its 2008 level still *below* that of 1980. An extreme example is post-1980 Mexico: despite the highest level of FDI per worker in the world, by 2008 its investment per worker still had not recovered its 1980/1 level. By then, and despite 1997, Korea had a level 3.6 times higher, and Malaysia and Thailand 2.2 times higher. In turn, China's 2008 level was 12 times higher, India's 4.5 times higher, and Vietnam had more than trebled this statistic since 1994 (first year data are available).

Perhaps from this perspective the contrasting productivity growth performance of LA and many in Asia—and the inability of LA *to sustain* productivity growth—are not that difficult to explain after all. In Brazil, for example, when between 1965 and 1980 investment per worker grew at an annual rate of 6.8%, productivity grew at East Asian levels (4.3%). And when investment per worker subsequently collapsed, productivity stagnated. Finally, when investment per worker began to increase again (6.9% between 2004 and 2009), productivity growth improved to 2.3%. However, what is still unclear is why (despite the huge share of national income appropriated by the top earners, well-defined and enforced property-rights, and 'pro-market' reforms) every time private investment in LA manages to rise much above 15% of GDP its capitalist élite starts experiencing feelings of vertigo.

From this perspective, the most striking difference between LA and Asia is found in their contrasting relationships between investment and income distribution (see Figure 23.6, Panel D). It is often acknowledged that the historical legitimacy of capitalism—i.e., the legitimacy of a small élite to appropriate such a large proportion of the social product—rests on the capacity of its élite to develop society's productive forces. And they can do so mainly by reinvesting most of that huge share. So, no other statistic seems to reflect so neatly the difference in the nature of capitalism in LA and most of Asia than that of Panel D in Figure 23.6.[5]

---

[5] In South Africa (in this respect, LA's honorary middle-income country in Africa), and in The Philippines (the honorary one in Asia) similar low ratios for private investment as a proportion of the income share of the top decile indicate that their capitalist élites have the same Latin preference for having their cake and eating it... Also, as discussed in detail in Palma (2009c), with globalization there seems to be now more Latin-'contagion', as LA is now exporting its political economy to the US. In the latter country, private investment as a percentage of the income share of the top decile has fallen from about half (before 1980s' Reagan) to a more relaxed 'Latin' level of about a third. In other words, and as opposed to Marx's prediction, now it is the less developed countries that seem to be showing the more industrialized ones the image of their own future.

Figure 23.7 shows another key component of the poor investment effort in LA after neo-liberal reforms—the collapse of public investment.

One of the stated aims of neo-liberal reform in LA (but not in Asia) is tying the hands of governments in terms of their capacity to create so-called 'artificial' rents. In LA, however, neo-liberal reforms has only succeeded in tying government hands in terms of public investment—as it left its squeeze as the only mechanism to square public finances—while all sorts of 'growth-hindering' rents (e.g., from lack of proper competition policy) and corruption continued unabated. Basically, a low tax intake (on average, less than half the OECD level) and an emphasis on balanced budgets left little room for public investment (DiJohn, 2007). In some countries, especially Brazil, there was the added problem of servicing a huge public debt—a debt acquired mostly as a result of the mismanagement of financial reforms (Palma, 2006). Unsurprisingly, crumbling infrastructure and shortages of complementary capital became major constraints for growth.

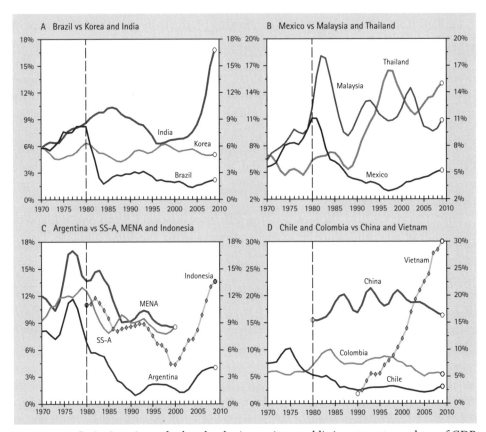

FIGURE 23.7 Latin America and other developing regions: public investment as a share of GDP, 1970–2008

Source: for countries, IMF (2010; data for China and Indonesia only available from 1980, and for Vietnam from 1990). For regions, WB (2002; data available only until 2000).

Notes: Panel C, MENA=Middle East and North Africa; SS-A=Sub-Saharan Africa. Three-year moving averages; current prices.

So, as Figure 23.7 indicates, the collapse in public investment took place as much in economies with high tax intake (Brazil) as in those where this was low (in Mexico just 12% of GDP for non-oil taxes). In fact, Colombia, with the lowest tax collection among the major economies, had a slightly higher rate of public investment. Chile at least invested in infrastructure via private 'concessions'.

23.3.3 The crucial relationship between investment and productivity growth: the economy's engine-room

The most robust statistical relationship between the growth of investment and productivity is found between non-residential investment per worker and productivity *per hour worked*. Not only is there a strong correlation between the two (stationary) series, but also (via an autoregressive distributed lag model that allows for more complex dynamics in the data) investment is found to have a large—and highly significant—impact multiplier (Palma, 2010).[6] Figure 23.8 summarizes the cycle in two economies with at least one period of (Asian-pace) growth: Brazil (1964–80) and Chile (1986–98).[7]

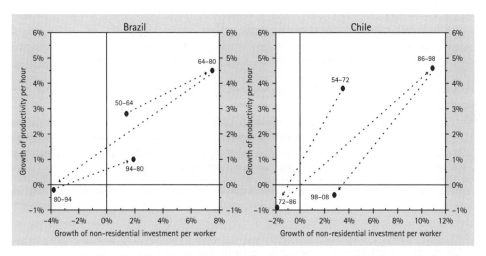

FIGURE 23.8 Brazil and Chile: growth of non-residential investment per worker and of productivity per hour, 1950–2008

Source: for productivity and employment, GGDC (2009); for investment, WDI (2010). To obtain the non-residential component of investment, I have multiplied the WDI data by the share of non-residential investment in total investment (from Hofman, 2000; this author provided the necessary updates).

Notes: Each observation indicates the average rate of growth for both variables during the respective period.

[6] In Brazil (1960–2008), for example, the R^2=68%, and the impact multiplier is 0.37 (with a 't' statistics=9).

[7] In Chile I have chosen 1986 as the starting date of the high growth period because after the 1982 crisis the economy only recovered its pre-1982 level of GDP in 1987.

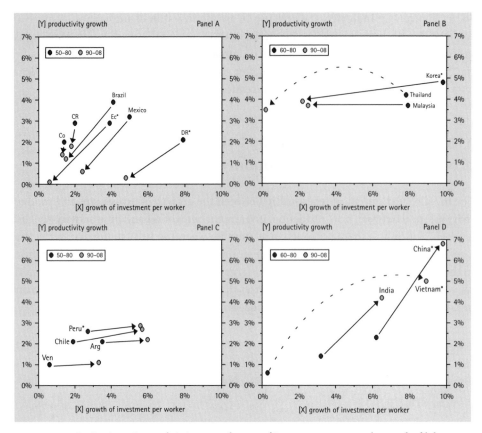

FIGURE 23.9 Latin America and Asia: growth rate of investment per worker and of labor productivity, 1950–80 and 1990–2008

> *Source*: as Figure 23.8 (due to lack of data for the residential component of Asia' investment, the horizontal axes
> represent the growth of overall investment per worker). Investment for Colombia, CEPAL (2010).

> *Notes*: [Y]=vertical axis; and [X]=horizontal axis. In Panel A and C, due to lack of data for Ec*, DR* and Peru* first
> observation is restricted to 1960–80; Korea*, investment growth rate for 1960–80=13%. China*, investment growth rate
> for 1990–2008=12.2%; Vietnam*, first observation is only a rough estimate (using information from Trần Văn Thọ, et al.,
> 2000);. Note that in all panels the second period is restricted to 1990–2008 in order to compare LA's post-1990 economic
> reform period with its pre-1980 ISI one.

Of the many intriguing issues arising from Figure 23.8, three are revealing: first,
unsurprisingly, the periods of rapid productivity growth are associated with high investment growth.[8] Second, when investment declined, productivity growth did not just
decline, it actually *collapsed*. Finally, although investment growth in the last period
resembles that in the first, productivity growth is significantly lower. Figure 23.9 shows
that in this respect the striking difference between LA and Asia is even more intriguing.

In Figure 23.9, LA is divided between those countries in which the investment per
worker growth-rate was lower in 1990–2008 than in 1950–80 (six countries, Panel A), and

---

[8] For Kaleckian growth-dynamics, see Ocampo, Rada, and Taylor (2009); and Taylor (2010).

those where it was higher (four, Panel C); Asia is divided along the same lines in Panels B and D. Starting with the top panels, the contrast between LA (Panel A) and three of the Asian countries affected by the 1997 crisis (Panel B) could not be starker: while in LA a declining investment rate is associated with a collapse of productivity growth, in Asia an extraordinary post-1997 fall in the investment rate leaves productivity growth practically unaffected. Aside from Asia's preference for absorbing shocks via employment rather than productivity, this comparison suggests a more solid productivity growth foundation in Asia due to higher levels *and* different sectoral distribution of investment. This helps hedge productivity growth against temporary drops in investment.

The contrast between the countries shown in Panels C and D is even more remarkable, indicating the opposite vertical and horizontal trajectories from those found in Panels A and B. In the four Latin countries of Panel C, an increased investment rate is associated with *constant* rates of productivity growth (in fact, Bolivia and Guatemala, not included in the graph, do not even travel horizontally: an increased investment rate was associated with *lower* productivity growth). In Asia (Panel D), enhanced investment rates are instead associated with hugely improved rates of productivity growth.

23.4 Latin America's unique post-reform combination of high employment elasticities and low productivity growth

As far as employment elasticities are concerned, post-1980 LA seems to live in a world of its own—see Figure 23.10, Panel B

As mentioned above, LA's post-1980 employment elasticities are about twice as high as anybody else's. A sectoral analysis of LA's high employment elasticities indicates that these levels are entirely due to services. For example, in Brazil (1980–2008) net-job creation reached 32 million, of which 30 were in (slow-growing) services—11 in trade/hotels/restaurants; 2 in transport/storage/communication; 2.5 in finance/insurance/real estate; and 14 in community/social/personal/government services. That is, while output in services was growing at just 1.9%, employment did so at 4.1%. Furthermore, there is no evidence that these are mainly government jobs—the overall employment elasticities of services was 2.2, while excluding the latter sub-sector this increases to 3.5.

At the same time, and going against the expectations of those in the Washington Consensus, other than in the 'maquila' industry (an industry that exists due to artificially-created preferential access to the US markets) there is little evidence that increased employment creation relates (in a Heckscher–Ohlin-Samuelson fashion) to trade liberalization. This is especially true in commodities. In fact, not only did employment in the primary sector decline in most countries (Brazil lost 2 million jobs), but there is no evidence that the jobs created in services are significantly associated with the commodity boom.

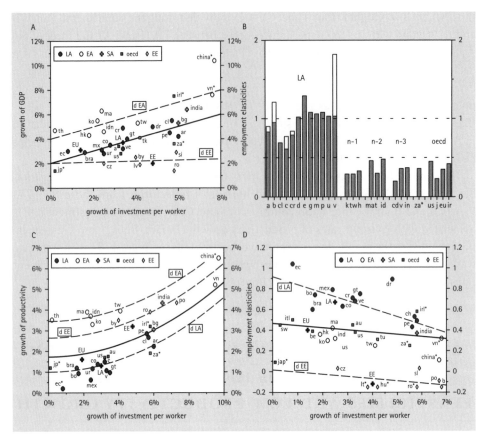

FIGURE 23.10 Latin America: the contrasting fortunes of employment and labor productivity in the post-reform period, 1990–2008

Full titles: Panel **A**, Growth of investment per worker and of GDP, 1990–2008. Panel **B**, Latin America and Asia: employment elasticities, 1980–2008. Panel **C**, Growth of Investment per worker and of labour productivity, 1990–2008. And Panel **D**, Growth of investment per worker and employment elasticities, 1990–2008.

Sources: for GDP and investment, WDI (2010, constant 2000-US$); for Taiwan (2010). For GDP in domestic currencies, GGDC (2007), and UN (2010); for employment GGDC (2009).

Notes: in Panels A, C, and D, acronyms as in Figure 23.2, and au=Australia; bg=Bangladesh; by=Belarus; cz=Czech Republic; EE=Eastern Europe; hk=Hong Kong; idn=Indonesia; irl*=Ireland (1993–2007, to reflect the high growth period); lv=Latvia; ro=Romania; si=Slovenia; tk=Turkey; tw=Taiwan; v=Venezuela; and za*=South Africa (1994–2008). china*=investment growth, 12.2%; ec*=productivity growth, -0.1; and jp*=-0.6%. 'd LA'=dummies for LA (intercept in Panel C, and intercept and slop in Panel D); 'd EA'=dummy intercept for EA (Panels A and C); 'd EE'=dummy slop for EE (Panel A), and intercepts for Panels C and D). In Panel B, employment elasticities as in Table 23.1 (African countries are excluded because the GGDC 2009 dataset does not provide data on employment, and the ILO database only provides econometric estimate; for South Africa, Quantec, 2009). White bars on top of grey ones are additional elasticity when ratio is calculated using GDP in domestic currencies. The employment elasticities for most EE are actually negative (see Figure 23.11). Acronyms as in Figure 23.6, and eu=European Union; ir=Ireland; h=Hong Kong; j=Japan; and t=Thailand. For regression statistics, Palma (2010); R² in Panel A=77%; in Panel B=86%; and in Panel D=82%; all variables are significant at the 1% level. In these and following regressions, 't' statistics are calculated using White's heteroscedasticity adjusted standard errors.

There are, of course, many political economy issues that emerge from LA's high employ-ment elasticities that cannot be analyzed here. However, I would like to mention at least one: the historical legacy of the 'new' left. Whatever one's views on the 'new' left, its emer-gence certainly helped reduce the capitalist élites' 'workers-paranoia' (Palma, 2009a). Basically, when the 'new' left became convinced that it could not get political power to implement its own political and economic agenda, it decided to gain power to implement someone else's agenda. In fact, Mrs. Thatcher was right when she proudly proclaimed that 'New' Labour was her greatest political achievement. Likewise, perhaps the greatest politi-cal achievement of Pinochet (and other similar dictators) is the Latin American 'new' left. So, as far as employment was concerned, there was not much point for the capitalist élites continuing with their anti-labor bias. Here a comparison between Brazil and South Africa is telling. Both countries started reforms simultaneously, and had similar growth rates post-1994 (i.e., the beginning of the ANC period, and the first election of Cardoso and the 'Real Plan'). However, in the following decade South Africa's GDP growth is almost entirely explained by productivity growth, Brazil's by employment. There are, of course, many dif-ferences between the two countries, but the fact that in Brazil the PT became the capitalist élite's best friend while in South Africa COSATU (one of the ANC dominant forces) remained a militant organization had a lot to do with this. From this perspective, South Africa's main problem is that it has East Asian levels of employment elasticities, but Latin levels of GDP growth, resulting in a quarter of its labor force being unemployed.

The main lesson from the contrast between these two countries indicates that even in this globalised world there are still significant degrees of freedom regarding the labor-intensity of output. And if LA has chosen a labor-intensive growth-path and South Africa the opposite, this has been for *endogenous* political economy reasons.

Panels C and D of Figure 23.10 indicate that in post-1990 LA there is a contrasting geometry between investment and productivity growth, on the one hand, and between investment and employment growth, on the other. While in panel C, LA is best represented by a highly significant *negative* (productivity) dummy, in Panel D it gener-ates a highly significant *positive* (employment) one. However, both dummies cancel each other out, and LA's relationship between investment and GDP growth (Panel A) ends up best represented by the base regression.[9]

The fundamental point here is whether LA's ability to generate high employment elas-ticities affects investment and GDP growth *negatively*. More specifically, the two crucial questions are: what is the nature of the relationship between LA's high employment elas-ticities and low productivity growth? And (crucially), if there is a fundamental relation-ship between the two, which is the direction of causality? See Figure 23.11.

[9] For a discussion of the important econometric issues raised by cross-section regressions like these, see Pesaran et al. (2000). In particular, one has to understand that these regressions are simply a cross-sectional *description* of cross-country differences, categorized by the explanatory variable. That is, they should *not* be interpreted in a 'predicting' way, because there are a number of difficulties with a curve estimated from a single cross-section—especially regarding the homogeneity restrictions that are required to hold.

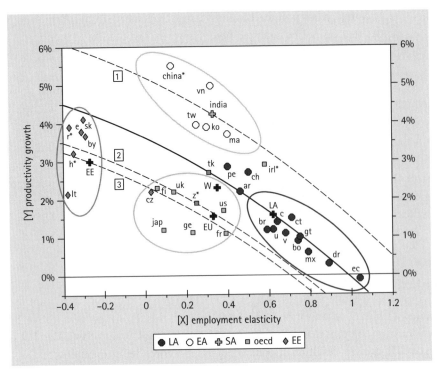

FIGURE 23.11 Latin America's "flexible" labor markets, 1990–2008

Notes: [Y]=vertical axis; and [X]=horizontal axis. Countries and regions as Figure 23.2 and 23.10, and c=Colombia; fi=Finland; sk=Slovak Republic; uk=United Kingdom; u=Uruguay; and v=Venezuela. Employment elasticity for h*, Hungary=-1.2; and for r*, Romania=-2. china*, productivity growth=8%. [1]=dummy intercept for EA; [2]=dummy intercept for OECD countries; and [3]=dummy intercept for EE. R^2=85%; all variables are significant at the 1% level (for regression statistics, see Palma, 2010).

Even though this is a difficult relationship to interpret as both variables have crucial elements in common, Figure 23.11 complements what we already know from Figures 23.3 and 23.10 above—this time for the shorter post-reform period 1990–2008. That is, most Latin American countries are uniquely positioned within the geography of this relationship during the post-reform period due to their remarkable labor market 'flexibility'—flexibility in the sense that they are able to generate single-digit unemployment rates despite such poor GDP growth.

As far as LA is concerned, there are at least two ways of understanding this intriguing relationship between employment, productivity, investment and growth. One is the (neo)structuralist view, postulating that in the absence of a binding foreign exchange constraint, output growth is largely driven by the demand. The emphasis here is in deficient demand leading to low GDP growth as the starting point for understanding overall low productivity growth. Sluggish output growth leads to modest labor absorption in the 'modern' (higher-productivity) sector, and to high absorption in the informal sector, resulting in low overall productivity growth (see Ocampo, 2004; and Ocampo, Rada, and Taylor, 2009). So, slow aggregate productivity growth is understood mostly as a low-effective-demand/low-GDP-growth problem leading to increased informality, rather than as a Kaleckian-low-investment phenomenon. On such 'Pasinetti grounds', a high employment elasticity is a *derived* measure.

There is an alternative perspective on the 'causality question', which is the one suggested here. Even though some of the above mechanisms may well also be at play, my view emphasizes a converse logic: there are analytical and statistical reasons for arguing that the starting-point is not low GDP growth (somehow determined somewhere else in the economy), but *the political economy of the labor market* (reinforced by that of public finance). High employment elasticities are not the end result but *the starting point* of the analysis. Here the dynamics run mostly from high employment elasticities to low productivity growth via an alternative 'Cambridge-connection'—especially those of Marshall, Kalecki, Joan Robinson, and Salter. In essence, I shall argue that what could be called 'excessive-labor-market-flexibility' is a key foundation for LA's poor productivity performance—mostly via its negative impact on both investment per worker, and efficiency wages.

From this perspective, two different dynamics (leading to structural heterogeneity) are at work. On the one hand, in many commodities and in a few industrial and service activities international competition has launched more interesting investment-productivity growth dynamics. However, in the (more protected) bulk of the economy there is a very different reality. In LA, unemployment rates may be relatively low, but this does not mean that labor markets are tight: the labor force still grows fast by new entrants; in most countries the primary sector and often also manufacturing keep shedding labor; and there is a large 'reserve army' in the informal sector. Consequently, this dominant part of the economy (typically more than two-thirds) can operate with a remarkably elastic supply of labor and little pressure on wages, investment per worker and productivity growth. In other words, this bulk of the economy can operate with few *compulsions* for productivity growth thanks to 'flexible' labor markets, natural protection, and a (typically) high degree of oligopolistic concentration. And if in the bulk of the economy output can grow mostly by additional employment, what would be the incentive (let alone the compulsion) to invest, particularly in terms of investment *per worker*; or what would generate upward pressure on wages to give a Marshallian efficiency-wage dynamics a chance? As Joan Robinson analyzed long ago in her criticism of the supposed 'exogeneity' of the variables making up the Harrod–Domar model, the incentives for investment and productivity growth would only really kick in when the labor market gets tight.

Furthermore, as labor-intensive techniques in manufacturing have been mastered in low-income Asia—where wages are even lower and labor is in abundance—LA cannot compete in low-wage labor-intensive manufacturing anymore (except when its geographical location and trade treaties favor 'maquila' activities). So in LA services are the employment-answer. At the same time (and very importantly), in relatively high middle-income countries there is also an insatiable (and often highly income-elastic) demand for low-cost low-productivity services—both formal *and* informal (although sometimes 'low-productivity' is due to the peculiar way in which output in services is measured in national accounts). In low-income Asia, meanwhile, more growth-enhancing labor-intensive manufacturing provides the higher employment-GDP-growth-outlet. Bangladesh is a good example of this, with its labor market more flexible than India's (and its minimum wages of less than US$2 a day). So, Bangladesh follows a typical Lewis-model (e.g., 2 million workers have been absorbed by the export-garment industry), but LA (in the bulk of the economy) follows an atypical one: there is high labor-absorption, but labor is being transferred to little or no productivity-growth-potential services (and often to 'informality')—sometimes even *from* manufacturing (due to de-industrialization; see Palma, 2005b and Section 23.7 below).

LA's abysmal rates of productivity growth in services between 1980 and 2008—either zero (Chile and Colombia) or negative (rest of the region)—are clearly not shared by the Asian countries discussed so far (India 4%, Taiwan 3.7%, Singapore 3.6%, Malaysia 3.5%, Indonesia 2.4%, Hong Kong 2.3%, Korea and Thailand 1%), where (among other factors) rapid growth in manufacturing helps by pulling services *à-la*-Hirschman (as was often the case in LA before 1980). This single factor goes a long way to explaining the differences in the *overall* productivity growth rates between both regions.

From this perspective, one piece of the puzzle that the structuralist analysis underestimates is that LA's low-productivity-growth in services is not just low effective demand/ informality-related, but also low-investment-related. An autoregressive distributed lag model indicates that in LA there is also a strong correlation in services between the growth of investment and of productivity—the former in terms of investment in infrastructure and business construction per worker employed in services (both series are stationary; see Palma, 2010). There is also a large and highly significant investment impact-multiplier. For example, in Brazil (1960–2008) the R^2=50%, the impact multiplier is 0.33, and its 't'=6.

From this perspective the squeeze of public investment (particularly in infrastructure) is, of course, a crucial component of LA's post-1980 abysmal rates of productivity growth in services. The investment boom in infrastructure and business construction in Chile between 1986 and 1998 is the exception that confirms that in LA, too, services can not only absorb labor (3.8% per annum), but also generate productivity growth (3.3%; see also Figure 23.12).[10]

In sum, low productivity growth in services is not just a low-effective-demand/low-GDP-growth phenomenon limiting the capacity of the 'modern' sector to absorb additional labor (with 'high-employment-absorption-informality' coming to the rescue, like the cavalry in every good old Western—the structuralist model). It is also the result of both the political economy of LA's labor markets, and low investment in business construction and (a mostly public-investment-squeeze-related one) in infrastructure endogenising sluggish output growth.[11] The resulting productivity growth rates may be poor, but there is a relatively stable low-intensity dynamic that the 'invisible hand' finds it difficult to break. This, together with peculiar politics (particularly when the 'new' left is involved), has led to political settlements characterized by 'low-intensity' Nash equilibria (Palma, 2009c). And where something different has been attempted, as in Venezuela, the results have been rather disastrous.

[10] On average, post-1973-Chile has seen no productivity growth in services either before or after the 1986–98 period of high investment in infrastructure and business construction.
[11] In most of LA net-investment in infrastructure and business construction was remarkably poor; see Hofman (2000).

So, in most of the region today investment per worker is below, or at best similar to 30 years ago, and the unintended consequence of tight monetary policy (making sure that labor markets never even begin to get tight) is to preserve this 'market failure.' Unless governments get serious with (East Asian-style) trade and industrial policies, increased public investment, more growth-enhancing macros, more effective market compulsions and other forms of 'disciplining' the capitalist élite, it is difficult to envisage a break-through. Unique specific circumstances may have helped some countries to break tem-porarily with this dynamic, but perhaps it is unsurprising that after a relatively short period they have returned to the fold, their burst of productivity growth having fizzled out. And despite a growing euphoria (and what Ortega y Gasset would have probably called an abundance of "self-satisfied individuals"), there is so far little evidence that Brazil's current growth-acceleration could prove to be the exception to this rule.

Within the context of the above-mentioned structural heterogeneity, LA has developed two types of successful 'modern-sector' regional oligopolies: those involved in large-scale capital-intensive commodity production for exports, and those that have mastered the technique of organizing low-value-added labor-intensive production chains—sometimes for exports (mostly agricultural products), and sometimes in services (eg. retail).[12] Ultimately, in LA, the commodity boom has lifted foreign exchange constraints; services have generated the precarious, low-productivity and low-wage employment (both formal and informal), while financial markets have provided all the fun.[13]

So, what is really wrong in post-reform LA is that neither the really 'modern' sector (usually associated with large-scale commodity production), nor the rest of the formal economy (mostly oriented towards the domestic market, although lately more region-ally oriented), or (unsurprisingly) the informal sector are able to generate much of what really matters for the complexities of economic growth—i.e., the externalities and the spill-over effects, and the processes of cumulative causation that take advantage of dynamic economies of scale, increasing returns, etc. That is, those issues which are cen-tral to the 'how-one-thing-leads-to-another' Hirschmanian growth-philosophy when dealing with such complex market structures as those that characterize developing countries (often with the added problem of size)—complexities that get even more intri-cate as developing countries move to middle and high/middle income levels.

Although neo-liberals were just about the only political group who really understood Kalecki's idea that capitalism cannot endure the political consequences of sustained periods of full employment, Latin American neo-liberals have overshot in the opposite direction: capitalism with clearly insufficient labor market compulsions seems not to work very effectively either. That is, as capitalists practically need not compete with each other in the labor market, there are few market pressures coming from this direction either forcing productivity growth, or the investment levels necessary to back this up.

---

[12] Their success has made the entry by foreign firms into the latter markets difficult; it is only when these regional oligopolies need new technologies that they get a foreign partner—see Robinson (2008).
[13] In LA (2002–7) the capitalization of the stock exchanges increased *annually* by 45% in real terms, bank assets by 21%, and private and public bonds by 22% and 25% (see IMF, 2009).

To perpetuate this, in most countries there is no collective bargaining, strike-breakers are legal, sub-contracting labor (as a mechanism to bypass even timid labor legislation) is widespread (even in the public sector), minimum wages are not just remarkably low but often ignored, (even in the formal sector many workers do not have a contract), and there are still activities in which workers do not even have a legal minimum wage or some other basic right—domestic servants in Chile, for example, an occupation that accounts for 12% of female employment, still do not have a minimum wage, and their legal working hours are 12 per day, and so on.[14] And at the first sign of labor markets getting tight, not just 'independent' Central Banks, but also governments are quick to react. For example, in Chile, when the market for domestic servants became slightly tight, and meager wages threatened to increase, the socialist government immediately opened up immigration from Peru—many things are possible in LA, but middle classes unable to afford domestic servants is not one of them.

23.5 SECTORAL DIVERSITIES AND THE "ONE-THING-AT-A-TIME" PROCESSES OF CATCHING-UP

Figure 23.12 measures the relative productivity gaps of four Latin American countries vis-à-vis the US. In Panel A, Brazil's productivity gaps throughout the whole 1950–2007 period show very clearly LA's 'one-thing-at-a-time' style of catching-up. While pre-1980 ISI succeeded in significantly closing the manufacturing productivity gap, this happened at the expense of commodities; the opposite was the case afterwards. One big difference, however, is that (as in EA) the pre-1980 manufacturing catching-up also managed to pull services à-la-Hirschman. This goes a long way to explain the differences in the aggregate productivity growth rates between the two periods (3.7% per annum in 1950–1980 and 0.4% in 1980–2008). Another one, of course, is the superior growth-enhancing characteristic of manufacturing due to its dynamic economies of scale, spill-over effects, and so on. And yet another is the fact that the post-1980 commodities' catching-up (except in Chile) was really only a mining phenomenon.[15] This does not mean that agriculture had not also gone through a major transformation as well. In fact, a technological revolution has been unfolding, which has altered the organization of production and the social relations in the rural sector of several Latin American countries. In many cases, the traditional farmer has been replaced by 'sowing pools' and 'cero tillage' production arrangements. And this technological and organizational change has not come about only because of the influence of multinationals;

[14] In Mexico, for example, in real terms, (i.e., when deflated by the consumer price index) in 2010 the minimum wage was worth just one-third of its 1976 value. (see http://www.inegi.org.mx). Latin American neo-liberals have not paid much attention to Churchill's views that low wages only subsidize inefficient producers, because "...the good employer is undercut by the bad, and the bad employer is undercut by the worst."

[15] Even in Argentina, and despite the boom in soya, the overall agriculture productivity gap with the US widened vis-à-vis 1980.

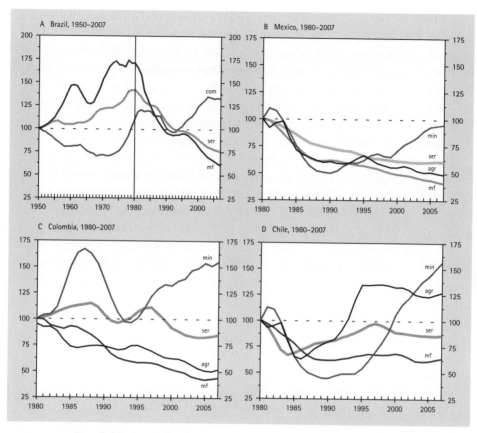

FIGURE 23.12 Brazil, Mexico, Colombia, and Chile: relative productivity gaps with the US

Source: GGDC (2007); ILO (2010); and UN (2010).

Notes: com=commodities (primary sector); agr=agriculture, forestry and fishing; min=mining and quarrying; mf=manufacturing; and serv=services. Each line is an index number (1950=100 for Brazil, 1980=100 for the rest) of the ratio of labor productivities between the respective country and the US (each in real terms and domestic currencies). An increase implies 'catching up' with the respective labor productivity in the US, and a decline a falling behind. Three-year moving averages; due to sharp fluctuations, Colombia's mining is a 5-year one.

it has also been the result of domestic technological efforts involving R&D carried out both by public institutes (such as Fiocruz or Embrapa in Brazil, INTA and Instituto Malbran in Argentina, INIA in Chile), and local companies. Furthermore, the primary commodities revitalization has had the added advantage of benefiting from the post 9/11 surge in commodity prices. Yet, as this phenomenon has been fuelled by massive speculation, it may well prove to be no more than a short term bubble; although it is possible that it could last for longer, while China and India continue to surge ahead. However, the key question here, as well as with the mining, timber and fisheries' revolution is why they have had such little capacity to pull the rest of the economy with them. Basically, what is happening is that while a few activities in the primary sector have succeed in forging ahead in their efforts to 'catch-up' with their counterparts in rich nations, the bulk of the economy (including, as Figure 23.12 shows, most of manufacturing) is being left behind. "Convergence", therefore, seems to be a more complex phenomenon than it is implicit in neo-classical models. This is a remarkable fact that (with few exceptions; see Katz, 2004) finds little emphasis in the literature.

Panel D synthesizes Chile's better 1986–98 GDP performance. What took place was mostly an investment-led burst of productivity growth in agriculture, forestry and fishing (10% p.a.), and increased productivity in services (3.3%), backed up by infrastructural investment and business construction. The growth of productivity in mining only started in the mid-1990s (when other sectors began to falter), reaching 11% p.a. in 1994–2003. Also, after falling behind in the 1980s, the productivity gap in manufacturing stabilized.

One phenomenon apparent from Panel B is Mexico's particularly poor performance. For reasons of space, I cannot analyze this here in detail (see Palma, 2005a) but, basically, an economy with FDI levels and access to the US markets that policy-makers in other developing countries can only (day)dream of, has performed particularly disappointingly in terms of productivity growth—falling behind the US in *all* sectors.

Regarding the remarkable neglect of manufacturing, as argued elsewhere (Palma, 2005b and 2008), there is plenty of evidence to suggest that the closer one gets to the productivity frontier, the need for industrial policy increases exponentially.[16] From this perspective, the sad irony is that LA abandoned industrial policy at the very moment it needed it most! So, for example, Brazil's 1980–2007 manufacturing productivity has fallen behind the US's by more than a factor of three (Panel A). As all three groups of NICs were instead catching up with the US in manufacturing, LA fell behind them by an even larger *relative* margin—for example, the collapse of Brazil's productivity in manufacturing relative to Korea's is truly remarkable: since 1980, manufacturing productivity in Korea has forged ahead of Brazil's by a factor of 7.5! (Palma, 2010).

23.6 EXPORTS AS A FALTERING ENGINE OF GROWTH : THE MIDDLE-INCOME 'EXPORT-TRAP'

As far as exports are concerned, LA moved from a situation in which pre-1980 exports and GDP were growing at roughly the same pace, to one where (on average) they grew about three times faster—3.5 in Mexico. As in the ISI period income elasticities for imports were certainly higher than one, there was an inevitable accumulation of foreign debt. Therefore, a pro-exports policy re-engineering was surely inevitable. However, the one chosen has not been the most effective: while the rate of growth of exports has increased on average by about half, that of GDP *fell* by half (excluding Venezuela, for the post-1990 economic reform period these rates are 8.1 percent and 2.6 percent, respectively). In this pro-exports policy re-engineering, the East Asian strategy of simultaneously insulating domestic markets and outwardly orienting manufacturing production was never even considered as an

[16] See also, Khan and Blankenburg (2009).

option. So, unsurprisingly, when comparing LA with the rest of the world the region generates a significant negative export-GDP dummy (Figure 23.13). The comparison between Mexico and Malaysia (or Thailand) in the middle of the figure is the most telling.

There is little doubt that one of the foundations of LA's negative export-GDP dummy is the fact that in an export-led model what matters is not only how much, but *what* one exports (and, of course, how one makes those exports—i.e., the 'maquila' issue). In addition, having a non-monetarist growth-enhancing macro-policy (able to deliver both a competitive exchange rate and a reasonable interest rate, as in most of fast-growing Asia) also helps. Figure 23.14 looks at this 'quality' of exports issue.

This figure shows that LA's remarkable increase in market shares (export-competitiveness)—i.e., the successful movement from quadrants 1 to 2—was not accompanied by an improvement in the 'quality' of its exports—an upward movement from '2' to '3'. It is well-known that LA's improved export-competitiveness did not include many 'high-tech' products, with their high-positive-externalities and spill-over-effects (Palma, 2009b).

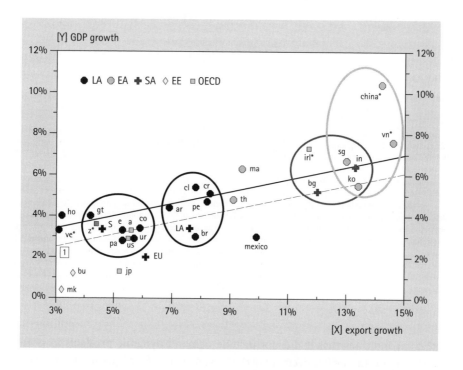

FIGURE 23.13 Exports and GDP growth in four developing regions, 1990–2008

Source: WDI (2010).

Notes: [Y]=vertical axis; and [X]=horizontal axis. As Figures 23.2 and 23.10, and a=Australia; bu=Bulgaria; china*, export growth=17.1%; e=Ecuador; mk=Macedonia; S=Sub-Saharan Africa excluding South Africa; v*=Venezuela (exports growth=0.2%); vn*=Vietnam (exports growth, 19.8%); and z*=South Africa (1994–2008). [1]=intercept dummy for LA; there are also negative intercept dummies for the EE and the OECD (not included in Figure). LA=Latin America excluding Venezuela (including Venezuela, average export growth=6.9%). R^2=79%, and all variables (including dummies) are significant at the 1% level (for regression statistics, see Palma, 2010).

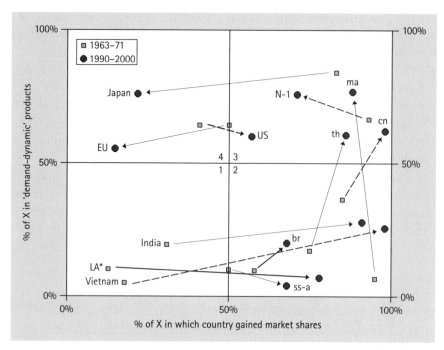

FIGURE 23.14 "Anti-clockwise" export trajectories between the 1960s and 1990s

Full title of axes: horizontal axis, Percentage of exports in which country/region gained market shares in OECD imports; vertical axis, Percentage of exports to OECD markets consisting of "demand dynamic" products.

Source: Trade-CAN (2009).

Notes: excludes oil. LA*=Argentina, Bolivia, Chile, Colombia, Ecuador, Paraguay, Peru and Uruguay (i.e., Latin America excluding Brazil, oil-exporting Venezuela, and Mexico and Central America due to maquila exports); N-1 excludes Hong Kong. Data for Taiwan correspond to those reported in the second edition of the Trade-CAN software. Regarding Vietnam, the first observation corresponds to the period 1973–84 (i.e., from the date when US combat troops left Vietnam until the beginning of economic reform; Trần Văn Thọ et al., 2000). First observation: export profile of a country or region between 1963 and 1971. Second observation: that between 1990 and 2000. In the vertical axis, 'demand-dynamic' products are products that increased their share in OECD imports during respective periods (due, for example, to their higher income elasticity). That is, the vertical axis refers to product 'quality', and the horizontal one to countries/regions' competitiveness. Therefore, if an observation is in Quadrant 1 this indicates an 'uncompetitive' country (i.e., less than half its exports have gained market shares) exporting 'non-demand-dynamic' products (i.e., less than half its exports are 'demand-dynamic' products); if it is in quadrant 2, it shows a 'competitive' country exporting 'non-demand-dynamic' products; if in quadrant 3, a 'competitive' country exporting 'demand-dynamic' products; and in quadrant 4, an 'uncompetitive' country exporting 'demand-dynamic' products. See Appendix 3 in Palma (2009b) for a more formal definition of the four quadrants.

Figure 23.14 indicates that it did not include demand-dynamic products in general.[17] Meanwhile in EA the swift movement of the N-2 and China from quadrants 2 to 3 is so fast that it even eats away some degree of export-competitiveness of the N-1. This process is much more acute vis-à-vis Japan (and the EU). With the exception of the US (mostly due to the Clinton years), the overall pattern that emerges is an anti-clockwise trajectory.

[17] In Palma (2009b) I show that the statistic used in Figure 23.14 to measure 'demand-dynamics' could also be considered a proxy for a product's technological content.

For LA and other countries moving into quadrant 2, the crucial trade and industrial policy issue is whether there are *endogenous* market forces that would lead them afterwards in an upward '2-to-3' trajectory. Or whether there are crucial (Ricardian) market failures that would trap them into being increasingly competitive in products that tend to be marginalized (in value terms) from world markets—except for temporary cycles such as those benefiting many commodities after 9/11, and after the 2008 global financial crisis. Furthermore, especially in commodity-markets, excessive competitive struggle for market shares often leads to a self-defeating fallacy of composition problems.

So far, there is little evidence of endogenous upward forces from '2-to-3'. Countries in quadrant 2 seem to need an East Asian-style 'exogenous push'. For these policies to be effective, however, what is also needed is an underlying power structure and institutional arrangements that would allow them to be successful (as was the case in most of Asia). These include a professional bureaucracy capable of devising a competent educational and training system that encourages the acquisition of productive capability, as well as being able to implement intelligent trade and industrial policies that generate rents as incentives for the transfer of resources towards more growth-enhancing activities (such as those with more long-term productivity growth potential), and, a state strong enough to be capable of imposing performance-related conditionalities to 'discipline' the capitalist élite to use them effectively—i.e., a state capable of threatening nonperforming companies credibly with withdrawal of subsidies.

If these policies—and the institutional arrangements necessary for their success—are not implemented in LA, the potential GDP-growth-enhancing effect of further increases in export-competitiveness would continue to be restricted by the generally low productivity growth *long-term* potential of its current export pattern, its modest positive externalities and spill-over effects, and its low capacity to induce productivity growth elsewhere in the economy (including services). In other words, as has become evident so far, without these policies LA's current export pattern has little capacity to generate growth-enhancing processes of cumulative causation.

Existing evidence for LA indicates that the (not-so-)invisible hand of globalised markets are only creating incentives leading towards further penetration into quadrant 2. This quadrant-2 'stickiness' is what I like to call the middle-income 'exporter trap'. This 'trap' seems to be equally relevant to those who export commodities (in terms of the difficulties to increase the share of manufacturing value added in their exports via the up and downstream manufacturing activities associated with commodity extraction and processing, as in the Nordic model), as to those who export 'maquila'-manufacturing (in terms of the difficulties to increasing the share of value added in the gross value of output). In fact, current Ricardian international comparative advantages, as Cimoli, Dosi, and Stiglitz (2009) state, "are a luxury that only technological and market leaders can afford (indeed a major asset that they can exploit)." One case in point is Chile, whose Ricardian comparative advantages led to a horizontal export trajectory (in fact, slightly downward) from quadrant 1 to 2. Its copper industry is a good example; while rapidly gaining market share, Chile has actually been *reducing* the share of manufacturing value-added in its copper exports, with the proportion of refined copper in total exports being drastically reduced in favor of the far more primitive copper 'concentrates' (Palma, 2009b). Not much evidence of a Hamilton-List-Akamatsu-style logic here. There is ample evidence, however, that the sharp slowdown in Chile's growth since the late 1990s is partly due to this under-investment in upward productive diversification (Moguillansky, 1999). Finally, the nature of regional trade agreements with the U.S. is likely to make the '2-to-3' transition even more intricate—as opposed to Asia's Japanese and Chinese 'upward pulling' powers.

In sum, export-led growth when based on relatively unprocessed primary commodities or 'thin' maquila exports has proved to be a poor engine of growth. The main lesson from post-reform LA is that if the region wants to insist on this export orientation, it should think about this model only as an export-'enabling' growth-strategy, not as an export-'led' one. That is, one in which dynamic (but not much growth-enhancing) exports can only be expected to provide the necessary foreign exchange to enable a fast rate of growth that is not balance-of-payments constrained. However, for this growth actually to take place there is still the need for a proper 'engine' to be found elsewhere in the economy. That is, other sectors or activities that would play the role of 'production frontier shifters', able to set in motion processes of cumulative causation—characterized by their positive feedback loops into the system, and capable of generating a momentum of change which is self-perpetuating (e.g., in the Veblen/Myrdal or Smith/Young/Kaldor manner). There is not much evidence from LA that unprocessed primary commodities or 'maquila' exports can play that role—nor that the countries of this region have made much effort toward export-upgrading or looking elsewhere for an effective engine of growth.

As Stiglitz has often said, even from the perspective of mainstream economics, in a world full of distortions the lifting of one (e.g., a trade barrier) does not necessarily lead to a superior (let alone optimal) equilibrium. Or, as Lipsey and Lancaster demonstrated half a century ago, "if one of the Paretian optimum conditions cannot be fulfilled, a second best optimum situation is achieved only by departing from *all* other optimum conditions" (1956, p. 12; emphasis added). For example, if policy makers in LA ignore distortions simply because they are out of bounds (such as Asian competitors with 'distorting', pro-growth macros, and 'distorting' trade and industrial policies) and design what they—from their mainstream perspective—consider to be 'first-best' policies (and apply, for example, flexible exchange rates, a low and flat import tariff, or abandon trade and industrial policies), then the likely outcome will not even be 'second-best'. Additionally, if policy makers in LA keep assuming they live in a world in which the 'efficient capital market theory' rules, and continue to implement sweeping financial deregulation and full opening of capital accounts (as if all that mattered in financial markets were market discipline and self-regulation), the likely outcome is even more financialisation, financial fragilities, overvalued exchange rates, and so on.

Surely it is time to realize that free trade, Ricardian comparative advantages, fully open capital accounts, 'flexible' exchange rates, 'independent' monetary policy, regressive taxation, liberalized finance, economies on automatic pilot with policy 'neutrality', and so on may be internally coherent in mainstream economic models, but do not lead to sustainable growth. Although there is little doubt that pro-growth macros, progressive taxation, strategic trade and industrial policies, coordination of investment, capital controls, a competent educational system, and so forth are challenges as big as they come, why should it be that only Asian countries are able to master this course of action effectively? Perhaps LA's 'purity of belief' is just an excuse for not even trying...

To summarize, perhaps the main problem with LA's neo-liberal economists (of all political denominations) is how a rigid ideology seems to constrain their core policy making from moving beyond a virtual world of 'first bests'. As a famous Chicago-trained economist said recently in Chile, the main problem with Latin American market fundamentalists is "...that [their] ideology... is blind to the common sense." (www.stanford. edu/dept/SUSE/ICE/pdfs/Chilepaper.pdf).

23.7 MANUFACTURING AS A FALTERING ENGINE OF GROWTH DUE TO LATIN AMERICA'S PREMATURE DE-INDUSTRIALIZATION

It's hard to believe today that during the 1960s LA was the undisputed manufacturing power-house of the South, responsible for nearly three of every four dollars of manufacturing value-added generated there (Panel A, Figure 23.15). Although its share began to fall in the 1970s due to some inevitable catching-up from late-starters, this process accelerated after 1980 in such a way that by 2008 LA's share represented just one-fourth of the total—and adding Taiwan, just one-fifth. As South Asia has kept its share almost intact, and as Sub-Saharan Africa represents a small proportion of the total, what was really going on was a switching of position between LA and EA. That is, when the inevitable catching-up from East Asian late-starters began to take place properly, LA, instead of putting up a fight, threw in the towel.

LA's relative decline is particularly acute in the case of Brazil. By the mid-1970s Brazil's manufacturing output was almost identical to the *combined* output of China, India, Korea, Malaysia and Thailand. By 2008 its manufacturing output was equivalent to less than 10 per-cent the combined output of these 5 Asian countries (WDI, 2010). This turnaround took place because while between 1965 and 1980 Brazil's manufacturing output was able to grow at roughly the same pace as the combined output of these Asian countries (9.2% and 9.5%, respectively), between 1980 and 2008 it did so at a rate which was just one-fifth the Asian one (1.9% and 9.8%, respectively—2.1% vs. 10.1% for the post-1990 economic reform period).

In turn, Panel B in Figure 23.15 shows that in manufacturing (unlike in exports) LA is best represented by the base regression: poor performance in manufacturing is linked to similarly poor performance in GDP. Also, the most robust specification for this relation-ship tends to confirm 'Kaldorian' dynamic increasing returns in manufacturing; that was not the case for the (linear) export regression.

Together with low rates of accumulation and lack of upward export capacity diversifi-cation, there is little doubt that the remarkable neglect of manufacturing lies at the heart of LA's productivity problem, especially its long-term sustainability.

Finally, Panels C and D build on my previous work on de-industrialization (Palma, 2005b and 2008), this time using an imaginative de-composition methodology (Tregenna, 2009), which disaggregates the changes in the share of manufacturing employment into its three

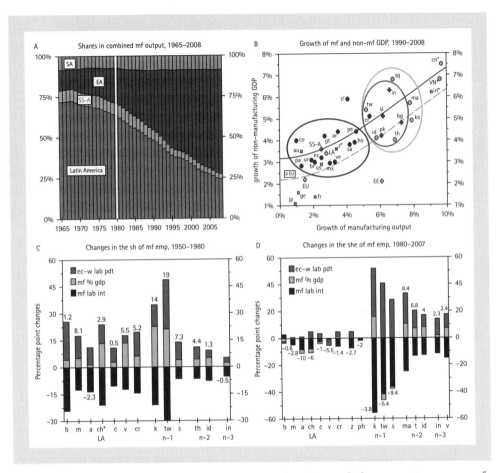

FIGURE 23.15 Latin America: the neglect of manufacturing and the post-1980 process of de-industrialization

Full titles: Panel A, Developing regions: shares in combined manufacturing output, 1965–2008; Panel B, Growth of manufacturing output and of non-manufacturing GDP, 1990–2008; Panel C, Changes in the share of manufacturing employment: a three-way decomposition analysis, 1950–80; and Panel D, 1980–2007

Source: for manufacturing output, WDI (2010; in Panel B, for some Eastern European countries data are only available from 1995). For manufacturing output in Ireland, UN (2010), and in Taiwan, Taiwan (2010). For manufacturing employment, GGDC (2007) and ILO (2010). In Panels C and D, Tregenna (2009) was used for the methodology in the 'three-way decomposition' analysis.

Notes: in panels C and D, 'ec-w lab pdt'=economy-wide labor productivity; 'mf % gdp'=the share of manufacturing in GDP; 'mf lab int'=labor intensity in manufacturing (the inverse of labor productivity). Percentages shown above each bar are the overall percentage change in the share of manufacturing in total employment (the net effect of the three processes at work); when the figure is negative, the percentage is shown below the bar. Regions: in Panel A according to WDI definitions; EA excludes Taiwan. In Panel B, SS-A=Sub-Saharan Africa (excluding South Africa); and EE=median country for EE (Hungary). Countries: in Panels B, acronyms as Figures 23.2 and 23.10; and cn*=China (manufacturing growth=12.3%); h=Honduras; fr=France; ge=Germany; m=Mexico; u=US; id=Indonesia; and pk=Pakistan. [d EU]=intercept dummy for the EU; there is also a negative intercept and slope dummy for EE, and a negative intercept dummy for SS-A not shown in the graph. In Panels C and D, acronyms for as Figures 23.2, 23.6, and 23.10, and ch*=Chile (1950–73); Malaysia and Vietnam are excluded from Panel C due to lack of data on manufacturing employment. R^2 in Panel B=71%; all variables are significant at the 1% level (for regression statistics, see Palma, 2010).

main components—the economy-wide labour productivity, the share of manufacturing in GDP, and the labour intensity in manufacturing (i.e., the inverse of labour productivity). The main findings are: first, with the exception of Argentina, between 1950 and 1980 (Panel C) changes in the share of employment in manufacturing were all positive, and were the outcome of large changes in its three components. Second, that LA's post-1980 decline in the share of manufacturing employment (Panel D) are similar to those of much more advanced, N-1 economies (rather than those at more similar level of development—the N-2). Third, that the post-1980 decline in the share of employment in manufacturing, although similar in size to those in the N-1 countries, was the result of forces of a *very* different nature. This suggests that after trade liberalization and neo-liberal reforms LA adopted a type of 'standing still' defensive strategy in this respect. And fourth, as the evidence of Panel D suggests, that rather than referring just to the 1980s as the 'lost decade,' as far as manufacturing is concerned, in LA the three post-1980 decades might well deserve that label.

ISI's legacy, of course, was not helped either by the distortions created by its rigid protection in highly-income-unequal domestic markets, as incentives inevitably led to horizontal diversification because there were more rewards for developing new products than for productivity 'deepening'. In this sense, despite its discourse, ISI did not really have an 'infant industry' agenda because its logic was not one of temporary protection to help—and push—firms to get to the frontier and become internationally competitive (Pérez, 2008; Díaz-Alejandro, 1989; and Fajnzylber, 1990). Rather, it was usually supposedly 'infant' corporations (eg. General Motors, ITT, General Electric, Bayer, or Nestlé) who were being protected with effective rates that sometimes reached four-digits. In fact, there was actually a 'double play': with big exceptions (eg. EMBRAER), the manufacturing industry that emerged from ISI may have been too fragile to adjust to the new open paradigm (especially at the speed taken by trade liberalization, and the unnecessary difficulties and distortions created by monetarist-macros). But what developed around ISI (including institutions, suppliers and skills) was considerable.[18]

On the supply side, after trade liberalization LA's manufacturing had to struggle against an Asian "double-squeeze". On the one hand (and as mentioned above), as low-income Asia had mastered labor-intensive techniques in manufacturing—where wages are even lower, labor is in abundance, and exchange rates and interest rates are kept at levels which are both stable and competitive—LA found it particularly difficult to compete in low-wage, labor-intensive, tiny-profit-margins manufacturing (except when its proximity to the US favored 'maquila' activities). On the other, LA's manufacturing also found it difficult to compete with technologically-advanced, rapid-product-evolving manufacturing production from high-middle income Asian countries, with their huge investment rates, effective trade and industrial polices, 'pro-growth' macros, and outstanding technological-absorbing capabilities. From this perspective, what is particularly difficult to understand is what little effort was made by Latin American countries to develop the obvious manufacturing niche available to them: the up and downstream manufacturing activities

---

[18] Unfortunately, ISI was not allowed to transform the region's political configuration either (as a normal process of industrialization would have done)—military regimes put a stop to that.

associated with commodity extraction and processing. Moreover, on the demand side, Latin American-style neo-liberal capitalism has been characterized by a chronic deficiency of effective demand for its non-commodities tradable sector, especially manufacturing. This has been the direct outcome of the 'deadly triad' of undervalued labor, overvalued exchange rates (backed up by high interest rates), and 'sterilized' governments. These are, respectively, the direct outcome of 'flexible' labor markets, open capital accounts with 'tough' macros, and governments with their hands (institutionally) tied in terms of implementing effective counter-cyclical action and pro-active public investment.

To summarize, in post-reform LA there is not much evidence in manufacturing of the characteristics that have been associated with a 'high-imagination-enabling-country'. Rather, evidence in Panel D points towards countries whose manufacturing sectors are (defensively) 'in hibernation'.

23.8 CONCLUSIONS

In the economic literature there are three different analytics of growth, but only in one is growth analyzed as a 'sector-specific' phenomenon (the structuralist/Post Keynesian/heterodox tradition; see Palma, 2005b, and 2008). From this perspective, LA's abysmal TFP-record well after economic reform should make those who believe otherwise think again. For example, how can those in the Washington Consensus—with their emphasis on 'getting the prices right' and 'getting the institutions right'—explain that well after putting into practice open capital accounts, free trade, balanced public accounts, well defined and enforced property rights on physical capital, independent central banks and so on (i.e., well after having set the Latin American economies on automatic pilot and policy neutrality), LA's TFP record can still only be described as appalling?[19] And the well-rehearsed argument that what is needed is yet more of the same sounds increasingly hollow. Perhaps the main lesson from LA's experiment with neo-liberal reforms is that the Washington Consensus is just one of the many heaps of ideological recipes still waiting for a theory relevant to the real world (or a bonfire…). How can it explain how so many in Asia do things 'wrong' (sometimes *very* 'wrong') but develop fast, while LA does almost everything 'right' (and with so much 'credibility', and scoring so high in the usual indices, such as those of 'economic freedom', 'competitiveness', and so on), but can only achieve a low-intensity growth dynamic—with all its difficulties in creating, let alone sustaining productivity growth—that the 'invisible hand' does not know how to break? When Keynes said that people usually prefer to fail through conventional means rather than to succeed through unconventional ones, he could not have guessed just how accurately his remarks would define LA today.

[19] Not much evidence, though, of 'getting the social capital right', but this was never part of the neo-liberal blueprint. As Mrs. Thatcher famously made it clear, from a neo-liberal perspective "there is no such a thing as society, just individuals."

So, most of Asia gets a capitalism that is pretty unsavory (with all its contradictions, unfairness and excuses), but at least capable of developing many of the productive forces of society.[20] LA, meanwhile, gets a neo-liberal brand of capitalism which is not even able to offer much productivity growth—i.e., LA gets the cloud without the silver lining. This is mostly due to an elite that does not want to know what capitalism is really about, and a bunch of highly-trained economists who still believe that when it comes to policy making the first commandment is that one has to stick to the 'first-best'. From the latter perspective, perhaps the key difference between LA and Asia is that policy-makers in the former still believe that the Washington Consensus is a set of ingenious tricks devised by Dumbledore, while the latter instinctively know that they actually are the work of Voldemort... Apparently, in LA market capitalism is a system in which only workers and small firms continuously have to struggle to improve their performance just to survive; for big capital the rules of the game are more agreeable. What the new neo-liberal paradigm seems not to grasp is that it is one thing to implement reforms to create market *opportunities*, but quite another to ensure that there are sufficient market *compulsions* to guarantee that these opportunities are taken up (Wood, 2002; and Khan, 2005). As a result, LA's brand of capitalism is characterized as much by its capacity to generate market opportunities as by its ability to waste them. What LA urgently needs today is new institutions to help create both the required capabilities and the necessary compulsions for productivity growth, especially those that would help to 'discipline' the capitalist elite *à-la* EA. It also needs a new structure of property rights—including well-defined and enforced rights on skills à la Japan or Germany (Pagano, 1991). And, of course, the ideology to back this up would also help—as Gramsci said, more often than not battles are won or lost on the terrain of ideology.

Added to this is the already mentioned phenomenon that Latin American-style capitalism has also been characterized by a chronic deficiency of effective demand from the 'deadly triad' of undervalued labor (due to 'flexible' labor markets), overvalued exchange rates with high interest rates (due to open capital accounts and monetarist macros), and 'sterilized' governments.

In summary, the region's growth performance since economic reform may be rather disappointing, but Latin American-style neo-liberal capitalism is unrivaled when offering world-class commodities, an abundance of (precarious, low-productivity and low-wage) jobs, stylish retail, lucrative finance, and the 'purity of belief'.

By now it should be obvious that 'flexible' labor markets do not transform an oligarchy into a proper capitalist class; even from a neo-liberal perspective surely one can have too much of a good thing. The same happens with the opening of capital accounts excessively reinforcing

---

[20] India, for example, is an extreme example of this. It has had 30 years of remarkably rapid GDP-growth, leading to a near six-fold increase in GDP, and three-fold boost in productivity. However, according to the Multidimensional Poverty Index (an index that measures the 'deprivations' in households—from education and health to assets and services), just eight Indian states currently account for more poor people than in the 26 poorest African countries combined (421 million). And the 'intensity' of the poverty in parts of India is often worse than that in Sub-Saharan Africa (see http://www.ophi.org.uk/policy/multidimensional-poverty-index/).

the domestic élite's 'high-appropriation-cum-little-accumulation' distributive strategies, and its long-standing biases for mobile assets. As discussed in detail elsewhere (Palma, 2009a and 2009c), neo-liberalism may well have become the most effective technology of power ever in terms of its capacity to get away with such remarkable inequalities and political settlements *within democracies*. That is, for its capacity to transform a particularly asymmetric set of distributive strategic choices, and the corresponding payoffs, into a Nash equilibrium by convincing the majority that there is no point trying to challenge these strategies while the all-too-powerful top income players keep theirs unchanged. What is particularly remarkable about neo-liberalism is its capacity to achieve this not by traditional forms of social conflict resolution, such as 'chicken' or 'hawk-dove' games, but mostly by ideological conviction. In other words, there is no longer any need for neo-liberals to threaten the majority with the idea that they have too much to lose and little chance of winning by challenging the top player's strategy. Now, by convincing the majority that this is the only workable game in town, they can get away with such a remarkably asymmetric distributional outcome through a spontaneous consensus type of hegemony (in the Gramscian sense). As a result, in most of LA military regimes—as a hedge against a distributional challenge by the majority—have become obsolete. The key point here is that there is a big difference between the great majority entering into such an unfavorable Nash equilibrium out of having 'thrown in the towel' when faced with overwhelming odds against the likelihood of succeeding in challenging the 'pure' distributional strategy of the capitalist élite, or entering into this Nash equilibrium simply out of ideological conviction. If the latter dominates, the game would then cease to be one of 'chicken'. The astounding aspect of this most unlikely of Nash equilibria (in which the great majority is now ideologically prepared to put up with such an unequal distributive outcome as if it was just their lot in life) is that it takes place despite the obvious 'collective action' conundrum by which the majority could clearly improve their payoffs if only they could somehow agree on a strategy different from the current one. This most unlikely of Nash equilibrium surely deserves an entry in the 'Guinness Book of Political Records.' However, with very few exceptions, from an economic perspective, this remarkable set of ('by ideological conviction') Nash equilibria in terms of political settlements and distributive outcomes seems only able to deliver nearly productivity-less growth and a huge process of financialisation. For example, in the five-year period before the global financial crisis the capitalization of LA's stock exchanges increased 10 times faster than GDP (IMF, 2009). So (as mentioned above), in Latin American style neo-liberal capitalism, commodities provide the foreign exchange, services the jobs, and financial markets the fun. So this is a rather good example of a Nash equilibrium that (although rather pleasant for the élite) is clearly not Pareto optimal. Perhaps, the very fact that this equilibrium has been unchallenged from within is a significant ingredient in the dynamic that leads to productivity-less growth. When Adam Smith said that 'without competition there is no progress', he was surely also referring to ideology. And as Ortega y Gasset explained, "human history is the product of discontent." The UNDP may well call this model 'pro-poor' because the alternative could be South African unemployment levels—but (despite all the current euphoria in Brazil) there is no emerging 'tiger' in sight.

Some economists, like Rodrik, have argued that in LA the contrast between the two periods is based on the fact that during ISI there were incentives to invest (industrial policies), but little market discipline due to lack of competition. In turn, during the reform period there was little incentive to invest, but a lot of market discipline. However, on the latter issue, I think the region is still waiting for the real thing—as the head of Chile's largest holding company and former President of the Confederation of Chilean Industry explains, "[t]his is a market economy in name only. Competition has disappeared; mergers and acquisitions have led to a huge degree of oligopolistic concentration." (http://www.atinachile.cl/node/4629). Moreover, one should never forget that in many countries in EA the 'market discipline' has had an added 'state discipline' component; i.e., the ability of the state to threaten non-performing companies credibly with withdrawal of subsidies.

Those in heterodox circles who like to look at the Anglophone periphery as models (i.e., Ireland and New Zealand rather than Korea or Malaysia), and argue that what LA needs to be able to replicate their pattern is an industrial policy that attracts FDI to fill the more challenging productivity gaps, create 'clusters', and so on, have something to explain: how will middle-income LA ever become a dynamic capitalist endeavor without a proper domestic capitalist class (like those found in some Asian countries)? In this respect, the weakness of post-reform FDI-intensive Mexico is particularly telling. And oddly enough, many pre-1980 structuralist thinkers made the same mistake, expecting (in vain) that FDI would be the force that would transform ISI into a more export-oriented endeavor. Despite its many contributions, FDI was actually part of ISI's main problem: its anti-learning bias (Pérez, 2008). In addition, even when it was the Latin American domestic firms that had contracts with foreign companies, they normally had to import the technology and use it rigidly as it came; whenever possible, they also had to import the machinery and parts. In the early 1970s Brazil may have produced more cars than the whole of developing Asia put together, but there was no *Hyundai* in sight…

Surely it is time to acknowledge that Latin American economies, some of them already well above the ten thousand dollar mark in per-capita PPP terms, should be perfectly capable of both relying on their own resources and capabilities, and dealing with their two main current challenges. The first is the one facing LA's neo-liberal economists of all political persuasions: when it comes to policy making, how to abandon their fantasy world of the 'first-best'. The second is the one facing LA's capitalist élites: how to change their long-standing addiction to 'low-intensity' economic life (currently so well nourished by the 'discreet charm' of a narcissistic ideology) for the Schumpeterian ambitions of some of their Asian counterparts—with their Canon-style motto: 'if anybody can, we can'.

Perhaps the key difference between the Latin American and many Asian oligarchies simply boils down to the fact that while the former have 'tenure', the latter have continuously to deliver if they want to go on enjoying their power and privileges (Palma, 2011).

Alexis de Tocqueville once said that he "[could not] help fearing that men may reach a point where they look on every new theory as a danger, every innovation as a toilsome trouble, every social advance as a first step toward revolution, and that they may absolutely refuse to move at all" (quoted in Judt, 2010). Neo-liberalism (despite all the flashy virtual realities and fickle-minded euphorias) may well be leading LA into that cul-de-sac…

REFERENCES

ACHARYA, A. (2009), 'The Impact of Globalisation on International Convergence and Growth,' BA dissertation, Cambridge University.

ADORNO, T. (2006), *Minima Moralia*, London: Verso.

BOIX, C. (2003), Democracy and Redistribution, New York: Cambridge University Press.

CEPAL (2010), 'Statistical Division,' Available online at: http://www.cepal.org

CIMOLI, M., DOSI, G. and STIGLITZ, J. (eds.) (2009), *The Political Economy of Capabilities Accumulation*, New York: Oxford University Press.

DÍAZ-ALEJANDRO, C. (1989), Collected Essays, (edited by A. Velasco), New York: Oxford University Press.

DI JOHN, J. (2007), 'The Political Economy of Taxation and Tax Reform in Developing Countries,' in H-J Chang Institutional Change and Economic Development, London: Anthem Press.

FAJNZYLBER, F. (1990), Unavoidable Industrial Restructuring in Latin America, New York: Macmillan.

FRANGIE, S. (2008), 'The Good Governance Agenda,' PhD thesis, Cambridge University.

FOUCAULT, M. (2004), *Naissance de la Biopolitique*, Paris: Gallimard Seuil.

GGDC (2007), '10-Sector Database,' Available online at: http://www.ggdc.net/

—— (2009), 'Total Economy Database,' Available online at: http://www.conference-board.org/economics/

Government of India (2010), 'Statistical Division.' Available online at: http://mospi.gov.in/

HALL, R. and JONES, C. (1999), 'Why Do Some Countries Produce So Much More Output Per Worker Than Others?' *Quarterly Journal of Economics*, Vol. 114, No. 1.

HIRSCHMAN, A. (1982), *Shifting Involvements*, Princeton: Princeton University Press.

HOFMAN, A.A. (2000), *The Economic Development of Latin America in the Twentieth Century*, Cheltenham: Edward Elgar.

ILO, (2010), 'KILM,' Available online at: http://www.ilo.org

IMF (2009), 'Global Financial Stability Database,' Available online at: http://www.imf.org

—— (2010), 'WEO Database,' Available online at: http://www.imf.org

JUDT, T (2010), *Ill Fares the Land*, London: Allen Lane.

KATZ, J. (2004), Market-oriented reforms, globalization and the recent transformation of Latin American innovation systems, Oxford Development Studies Vol. 32, No. 3.

KHAN, M.H. (2005), 'The Capitalist Transformation', in Jomo, K.S. and E.S. Reinert (eds.), *The Origins of Development Economics*, London: Zed.

—— and BLANKENBURG, S. (2009), 'The Political Economy of Industrial Policy in Asia and Latin America', in M. Cimoli, G. Dosi, and J. Stiglitz (eds.), *The Political Economy of Capabilities Accumulation*, New York: Oxford University Press.

KELVIN, LORD (W Thomson) (1900), Address to the British Association for the Advancement of Science: http://www.physics.gla.ac.uk/Physics3/Kelvin

MOGUILLANSKY, G. (1999), *La Inversión en Chile*, Santiago, Chile: BID-FCE.

OCAMPO, J.A. (2004), *Reconstruir el futuro: Globalización, desarrollo y democracia en América Latina*, ECLAC.

—— (2005), *Beyond Reforms, Structural Dynamics and Macroeconomic Vulnerability*, Palo Alto: Stanford University Press and World Bank.

—— RADA, C., and TAYLOR, L. (2009), *Growth and Policy in Developing Countries: A Structuralist Approach*, New York: Columbia University Press.

ORTEGA Y GASSET, J. (1918), 'Impresiones de un viajero,' Hebe, 5.

PAGANO, U. (1991), 'Property Rights, Asset Specificity, and the Division of Labour under Alternative Capitalist Relations', *Cambridge Journal of Economics*, Vol. 15, No. 3.

PALMA, J.G. (2005a), 'The Six Main Stylised Facts of the Mexican Economy Since Trade Liberalisation and NAFTA,' *Industrial and Corporate Change*, Vol. 14, No. 6.

—— (2005b), 'Four Sources of De-industrialisation and a New Concept of the Dutch Disease', in J.A. Ocampo (ed.), *Beyond Reforms: Structural Dynamics and Macroeconomic Vulnerability*, Palo Alto: Stanford University Press and World Bank.

—— (2006), 'The 1999 Financial Crisis in Brazil: "Macho-monetarism" in Action', *Economic and Political Weekly*, Vol. 41, No. 9.

—— (2008), 'De-industrialization, Premature De-industrialization and the Dutch Disease', in S. Durlauf and L. Blume (eds.), *The New Palgrave Dictionary of Economics*, 2nd ed., New York: Palgrave Macmillan.

—— (2009a). 'Why Did the Latin American Critical Tradition in the Social Sciences Become Practically Extinct?' in M. Blyth (ed.), *The Handbook of International Political Economy*, Abingdon: Routledge.

—— (2009b), 'Flying-geese and Waddling-ducks: The Different Capabilities of East Asia and Latin America to 'Demand-adapt' and 'Supply-upgrade' Their Export Productive Capacity', in M. Cimoli, G. Dosi, and J. Stiglitz (eds.), *The Political Economy of Capabilities Accumulation*, New York: Oxford University Press.

—— (2009c), 'The Revenge of the Market on the Rentiers: Why Neo-liberal Reports of the End of History Turned Out to Be Premature,' *Cambridge Journal of Economics*, Vol. 33, No. 4. An extended version can be found in http://www.econ.cam.ac.uk/dae/repec/cam/pdf/cwpe0927.pdf

—— (2010), 'The Latin American Economies since 1980', mimeo.

—— (2011), 'Homogenous Middles vs. Heterogeneous Tails, and the End of the "inverted U": it's all about the share of the rich,' *Development and Change*, Vol. 42, No. 1: 87–153. Also at http://www.econ.cam.ac.uk/dae/repec/cam/pdf/cwpe1111.pdf./

PÉREZ, C. (2002), *Technological Revolutions and Financial Capital*, Cheltenham: Edward Elgar.

—— (2008), 'A Vision for Latin America: A Resource-based Strategy for Technological Dynamism and Social Inclusion,' Globelics Working Paper No. WPG0804.

PESARAN, H., N.U. HAQUE, and S. SHARMA (2000), 'Neglected Heterogeneity and Dynamics in Cross-Country Savings Regressions', in J. Krishnakumar and E. Ronchetti (eds.), *Panel Data Econometrics—Future Direction*, Kidlington: Elsevier Science.

Quantec (2009), 'South African Standardised Industry Database'. Available online at: http://www.quantec.co.za/data/easydata-rsa-regional-indicators

ROBINSON, W.I. (2008), *Latin America and Global Capitalism*, Baltimore: Johns Hopkins University Press.

Taiwan (2010), 'National Statistics'. Available online at: http://eng.stat.gov.tw/mp.asp?mp=5

TAYLOR, L. (2010), *Maynard's Revenge: Keynesianism and the Collapse of Free Market Macroeconomics*, Cambridge, Mass.: Harvard University Press.

Trần Văn Thọ, (2000), *kinh tÕ viÖt nam 1955–2000*, Hanoi: Nhà xuất bản Thống Kê.

TREGENNA, F. (2009), 'Characterising Deindustrialization,' *Cambridge Journal of Economics*, Vol. 33, No. 3.

WOOD, E.M. (2002), *The Origins of Capitalism: A Longer View*, London: Verso.

World Bank (2002), 'Investment as a Share of GDP'. Available online at: http://www.world-bank.org

—— (2010), 'World Development Indicators.' Available online at: http://www.worldbank.org

CHAPTER 24

....

AGRICULTURAL AND RURAL DEVELOPMENT

....

SALOMÓN SALCEDO, FERNANDO SOTO-BAQUERO,
JOSÉ GRAZIANO DA SILVA, RODRIGO CASTAÑEDA
SEPÚLVEDA, AND SERGIO GÓMEZ ECHENIQUE

24.1 INTRODUCTION

Until the 1950s, the Latin American farm sector was characterized by relative self-sufficiency compared to the rest of the economy and was synonymous with rural life. The sector also maintained a relative autonomy in relation to urban and manufacturing activities, and comprised a true mosaic of activities (some productive, others not). The rise of the Green Revolution in the 1960s significantly increased the use of chemical inputs (fertilizers and pesticides), machinery, and various types of equipment as the region began a period of agricultural modernization. Key to this process was the way in which these "modern inputs" were financed using subsidized rural credit, a policy that assumed major importance at the beginning of the 1970s as a mechanism for modernizing the Latin American farm sector. As a result of this modernization process, the "old rural sector" began to break down into various "agro-industrial complexes," new productive chains that linked segments of urban/industrial style manufacturing production with a number of rural-based agricultural and livestock activities. Cases in point include the sugarcane industry (which in the case of Brazil also incorporated the production of alcohol for use as a fuel), the soy industry, and the poultry/corn industry, among many others (Graziano da Silva 1994).

This trend became more apparent and it was no longer possible to speak of the agricultural sector as being completely rural nor of the rural economy as being completely agricultural. First, an important part of the activities of these various agro-industrial complexes had been urbanized, as in the case of production of chemical inputs, cotton processing, and meat processing, among others. Secondly, the old rural world of *latifundia* and *minifundia* was giving way to a growing number of new social actors (technified family farmers, ecologists, seasonal farm workers, etc.) and new activities, including many of a non-agricultural nature.

Structural reforms implemented at both the macroeconomic and sector levels beginning in the 1980s played a fundamental role in the formation of Latin America's heterogeneous agricultural sector. Nearly all countries in the region embraced the same reform principles.[1] Typically, these reforms saw unilateral trade liberalization (later complemented by numerous intra- and extraregional free trade agreements), the elimination of subsidies (including production and input subsidies and the withdrawal of credit to farmers), the privatization or closure of state-owned firms, the dismantling of research and extension institutions or a significant curtailment of their activities, and the deregulation of markets for agricultural goods and services.

These reforms, when combined with the dynamics of national and international markets, technological developments, and the structural characteristics of each country, left lasting imprints on the agricultural sector, the productive structure, job creation, and rural wellbeing in the countries of the region. This chapter reviews these reforms, the challenges each country has faced in their implementation, and their impacts on the agriculture sectors of Latin American countries. It also considers the role of the state in agriculture and rural development.

24.2 MAJOR REFORMS OF THE 1980S AND 1990S

During the 1980s and 1990s, the countries of the region undertook a process of structural reform both of the economy in general and of the agricultural sector in particular. Informed by the recommendations of the Washington Consensus and the notion that the "best policy is an absence of policy," these processes were aimed at significantly reducing the role of the state in order to increase national efficiency and competitiveness. We will now provide a brief summary of the principal changes implemented during this time.

24.2.1 Trade policy

Most Latin American countries joined the General Agreement on Tariffs and Trade (GATT) in the 1980s and 1990s (though countries such as Brazil, Chile, and Cuba joined as early as the 1940s). During the 1980s and 1990s, Latin American members of GATT

---

[1] The timing and forms of their adoption, however, varied from country to country. For example, Chile and Mexico implemented a trade opening and both fiscal and agro-reforms roughly at the same time even as countries such as Brazil and Argentina retained strong trade protection and high tariffs as features of their macroeconomic stabilization plans (Spoor 2000).

embarked on a unilateral process of tariff reductions. However, this process of trade liberalization was at times frustrated by the broader macroeconomic context of exchange rate appreciation and low international prices. This context was linked to local market problems and sudden drops in farm profitability, and on many occasions, governments felt compelled to restore tariffs in an attempt to address these problems. Thus, producers were often given contradictory signals by their governments, signals which hindered their planning of long-term investments.

In addition to trade liberalization, work proceeded on the development of subregional trade blocs (the Andean Community, Central American Common Market, and the Southern Common Market). While there was a clear intention to achieve subregional trade integration (efforts that in some cases date back to the 1970s), economic, political, and social problems have complicated efforts to achieve this integration.

In part due to a failure to establish effective intra-regional trading blocs, the 1990s saw Latin America begin negotiating bi-regional trade agreements, a trend that has intensified in recent years. This process (led by Mexico and Chile) has seen most Latin American countries negotiate bi-regional trade agreements with regions in the North and Asia. Many governments in Latin America believe such agreements represent the most viable means of accessing lucrative agricultural markets, especially in the context of the continuing uncertainty surrounding the Doha Round multilateral negotiations (Valdés and Foster 2005).

Indeed, after agriculture was included for the first time as part of GATT negotiations in the 1994 Uruguay Round, which accepted the use of internal and export subsidies as well as the use of tariff-rate quotas (TRQs) and special safeguards, negotiations have been painfully slow in the Doha Round. As yet, there has been no progress on the stated goals of the negotiations: improving market access by lowering import tariffs, domestic support, and export subsidies.[2]

The policy of unilateral trade liberalization, the creation of subregional free trade zones, and the establishment of free trade agreements with countries outside the region pose great challenges for the countries of Latin America. These challenges include the need to:

- identify mechanisms needed to deal with price volatility, (which has been exacerbated in recent times by the extent to which agricultural and energy markets are now interrelated);

---

[2] Latin American countries have adopted somewhat differing positions. As part of the Cairns Group, Argentina, Bolivia, Brazil, Chile, Colombia, Costa Rica, Guatemala, Paraguay, and Uruguay push for the elimination of all forms of agricultural export subsides, and also argue for setting specific rules in relation to agricultural export credit as well as substantial lowering of all tariffs. Honduras, Nicaragua, and El Salvador, along with other developing countries of the Caribbean, Africa, and Asia, propose a special and differentiated treatment for developing countries. To that end, they recommend the establishment of development funds to protect and encourage domestic production of basic foods and improve food security.

- achieve effective management of the multiple FTAs currently operating in the region. This is especially important in terms of managing tariff-rate quotas, the implementation of safeguards (both those linked to FTAs and anti-dumping measures), technical contraband, and export promotion;
- encourage quality, traceability, and good agricultural practices as a means to achieve full access to increasingly demanding international markets;
- reduce transport and transaction costs; and
- apply sanitary policies that improve their phytosanitary and zoosanitary status as these are preconditions for successfully intervening in international markets (Salcedo 2006).

24.2.2 Price and direct support policies

Prior to reform, the countries of the region generally sustained both producer and consumer price controls. Some countries, including Argentina, Brazil, Colombia, and Mexico, operated major publicly owned agencies that engaged in direct interventions in the domestic and international trade in cereals, oil crops, legumes, and milk. However, in addition to distortions in the allocation of productive resources, in some instances there was a growing awareness of the lack of effectiveness and efficiency of these agencies. Furthermore, their massive budgets, which weighed heavily on public finances, primarily benefited the largest commercial producers and did little to improve small farmers' income.

The reforms of the 1980s and 1990s signaled the elimination of numerous price-setting mechanisms (which had already begun to lose importance as a result of the trade openings these countries were pursuing) and the closure of publicly owned distributors.[3]

However, the transition from markets with price controls to free markets was by no means easy for most Latin American countries. Agricultural profitability was significantly depressed by artificially low international crop prices (due largely to subsidized production in developed countries) and unfavorable changes in exchange rates. A continued lack of profitability in the agricultural sector sparked protests by organized producers, and as a result, governments turned to other types of price support mechanisms.

In Central America, the Andean Countries, and Chile, "price bands" were adopted for products regarded as basic and economically and socially sensitive. Under this mechanism, imported products attract a fixed tariff if their import price falls within certain price levels. A tariff premium is required if the product is priced below the bottom level of the band, but a tariff discount is applied if it is priced above the band's upper limit.

In addition, countries such as Colombia and Mexico implemented mechanisms such as *precios de concertación* (literally, agreed-upon prices) under which the government,

---

[3] Only a few countries maintained during the reform public companies that continue to regulate agricultural prices and that directly intervene into the purchase and sale of basic products, such as the Dominican Republic's Instituto Nacional de Regulación de Precios, INESPRE.

farmers, and agribusinesses jointly agree on sales prices for specific products. Mexico also introduced marketing support mechanisms that were initially provided to agro-industries as an incentive to purchase domestic production; later the support was distributed directly to farmers. Brazil, for its part, re-established minimum price-setting mechanisms for maize, soybeans, beans, and rice in 1991, assuring the purchase of these products through the state-owned Compañía Nacional de Abastecimiento (CONAB).

In 1996, Brazil created a system of auctions in which buyers agreed to a minimum price. Under this scheme, the government agreed to cover any difference between this minimum price and the market price. That same year, Brazil introduced a Government Sell Option Contract as a guarantee against falling agricultural prices. In 2003, CONAB introduced the Food Acquisition Program for purchasing the produce of family farms at market prices (OECD 2009).

Another mechanism introduced to cope with the elimination of price supports was direct payments such as those by Mexico's PROCAMPO program, which began operating in 1993 (Salcedo 1999). Once a producer enrolls in the program, he or she receives a fixed per-hectare payment regardless of what and how much that land produces.

Clearly, there has been no full liberalization of markets for agricultural products in the region. In addition to market prices, various other factors such as marketing support, insurance against falling prices, price bands, direct support, and minimum-price setting have influenced the decisionmaking of farmers. Nevertheless, the direct transmission of the structure of relative international prices to the agro-economies of the region has also raised doubts about the search for long-term economic efficiency in resource allocation. That is, given the subsidies and high levels of protection that the developed countries have traditionally provided their agricultural sectors, international prices have been artificially suppressed, sending distorted signals to Latin American producers.

24.2.3 Policies for input markets and agricultural credit

Until the late 1980s, governments played a fundamental role in both seed production and distribution, as well as subsidizing fertilizer purchase, whose use was encouraged as part of public farm extension systems. The reforms of the 1980s and 1990s brought about a liberalization of seed markets, the elimination of fertilizer-use subsidies, and the privatization of systems for seed import and distribution.

However, such measures did not lead to the emergence of private domestic seed producers, but rather saw increasing dependence on imports from major multinational firms. At the same time, little importance was assigned to initiatives aimed at the protection and reproduction of native genetic crop material that could help to improve the productivity of small producers.

In most Latin American countries, public banks were the major source of credit for agricultural producers until the 1980s. These specialized banks managed extensive networks of branch locations that covered most rural areas, and awarded loans at subsidized interest rates. Due to their vulnerability and the fact that many were employed for political purposes, a number of the farm banks experienced deep crises (Peru, Ecuador, Guatemala, El Salvador, Nicaragua, Honduras, Mexico). Frequently, much of the available credit was concentrated in the hands of politically powerful producers who often defaulted on these loans without legal consequences.

While it led directly to the closure of most agricultural development banks, the reform failed to achieve both the expected expansion of credit from private sources and the promised generalized improvement in the ability of debtors to repay their loans. The elimination of public banks (as in Peru, Ecuador, Bolivia, Nicaragua, El Salvador, and Honduras) had many negative effects, not least of which was the destruction of the social capital caused by the loss of financial institutions with an extensive institutional infrastructure for the provisioning of financial services in rural areas.

Some countries of the region, such as Brazil, Mexico, Costa Rica, Uruguay, Chile, and Guatemala, opted to transform their specialized public banks into multi-sector public banks employing commercial standards and solid indicators of financial and institutional sustainability. Almost twenty years after the reform, the formal financial system has achieved only minimal depth and coverage in rural areas. On average, a scant 8% of all credit granted by the financial system in the region in 2004–5 was placed in the agricultural sector—a percentage that for almost all countries falls below the sector's contribution to GDP (Trivelli and Venero 2007). There can be no doubt that this limited depth and coverage is not only the result of supply-side restrictions but is also due to limitations in the effective demand for loans. Most producers continue to lack access to assets, services, and markets, a weakness that manifests in their inability to access credit and continued low profitability.

Despite the reform, today there are thirty-two financial development institutions in the region which manage credit portfolios totaling US$87.50 billion, 26% (US$23 billion) of which is placed in agriculture. These institutions provide 34% of all agricultural credit issued each year in the region, or at least 50% in Argentina, Uruguay, Costa Rica, Brazil, and the Dominican Republic. In Peru, Honduras, and Venezuela, however, they account for less than 7% of all farm credit.

24.2.4 Research and technology transfer policies

Prior to the reform, many Latin American countries had created important bodies dedicated to agricultural research. Practically every country had set up a National Agricultural Research Institute (NARIs) staffed with foreign-trained technicians. While the NARIs made fundamental contributions to the region's agriculture by developing seed varieties of grains, oil crops, fruits, and vegetables as well as technical agricultural and livestock technological packages, etc., they were frequently criticized for running top-heavy bureaucracies that complicated the planning and management processes, and separating research from its beneficiaries in the productive sector (especially small producers).

The reform of the 1980s greatly reduced the role of NARIs, as shrinking research budgets limited their research capacities and contributed to a brain drain amongst trained staff. Brazil however, did not dismantle its main agricultural research institution (EMBRAPA), which has continued to introduce innovations based on the concept of "tropicalization" (adapting the technologies developed in the countries of the North to conditions prevailing in the Brazilian agro-frontier). Another of EMBRAPA's notable accomplishments is its sponsoring of a PhD studies program abroad for its technicians. In fact, Brazil's agricultural scientists are regarded as among the best-trained in the world (EMBRAPA 2008).

Other actors such as NGOs, universities, producer organizations, and the private sector have tried to fill the void left since governments scaled back their participation in research. As a result, there are growing concerns as to just how much this fragmentation erodes research efficiency. This process has been especially pronounced in Central America, where one study revealed that 40 out of 63 institutions employ fewer than 10 researchers (Stads et al. 2008).

Prior to the reform, the agricultural research conducted by NARIs was accompanied by public extension programs. Some major agro- or rural development programs also included technology transfer components. Once the reform got under way, public extension systems also experienced major cutbacks; some were decentralized to state and/or municipal governments (e.g. Colombia, Bolivia, Venezuela, and Mexico), the private sector and NGOs were encouraged to play a greater role in technology transfer, and producers were encouraged (initially with government support) to pay for extension services. The results of these measures have generally proven unsatisfactory, and the resulting gaps left in these areas have aggravated the technology gap separating the traditional and corporate agricultural sectors.

Research and extension services face great challenges, and remain a subject of debate among experts. Various NARIs continue to struggle to improve their administrative management and gain access to financial resources while trying to avoid a brain drain within their pools of researchers. The research priorities of these institutions often do not align with the goals of agricultural subsectors, key processors, or the demands of consumers, who have recently begun to demand products from greener agriculture, and even carbon-footprint information for each product. In short, the fragmentation of agricultural research in various countries of the region has impeded the establishment of national research systems capable of developing a comprehensive vision of productive chains in priority subsectors, as witnessed in countries such as New Zealand. While interesting new approaches to farm extension have been developed over time (e.g. the Municipal Units of Agricultural Technical Assistance (UMATAS) in Colombia), gaping holes remain in the mechanisms that can most effectively allow small-scale producers to access existing knowledge and technologies. De Janvry, Key, and Sadoulet (1997) point out that "market failures [in Latin America] create important roles for the government in the provisioning of research and extension."

24.2.5 Land and irrigation policies

Access to land and water resources has been a highly sensitive issue not only during the reform years but also in decades past, and figured as a central issue in social uprisings such as the Mexican Revolution of 1910–17, the Bolivian Revolution of 1952, the Cuban Revolution of 1959, and Nicaragua's Sandinista Revolution in the 1980s. The issue of land and water resources clearly goes beyond matters of agricultural production.

Up until the 1970s, agrarian policies in Latin American countries had favored land redistribution processes as part of a broader reformist vision. One proponent of these policies was the Alliance for Progress, which received support from the US government to reduce the risk of "agrarian revolutions" in the wake of the Cuban Revolution (Flores, in Delgado 1965). Some of these reform processes were the product of autonomous movements of *campesino* farmers such as the agrarian reforms of Mexico and Bolivia. In this way various countries of the region implemented agrarian reforms, redistributing idle land from large estates to landless farmers in an effort to help them engage in productive activities.

During the reform years, agrarian redistributive processes were replaced with property-titling programs as well as market-based land-access pilot programs, both supported by the World Bank. There were, however, exceptions to this trend. For example, El Salvador launched a broad process of agrarian reform in 1980. In 1985 Brazil approved a National Agrarian Reform Plan—New Republi—that for reasons of social justice expropriated land for landless farmers while compensating the previous landowners. The 1980s also saw the formal establishment of the Landless Workers Movement or MST in that country. In Colombia the 1980s witnessed a revival of the idea of redistributing land in conflict zones, and an unsuccessful effort in 1994 to adopt a new Agrarian Reform Law. In late 2001, Venezuela adopted a new Agrarian Reform Law to replace one that had operated since 1960. Similarly, in 2006 Bolivia launched a campaign to redistribute 2 million hectares of land to peasants and indigenous peoples.

Countries such as Ecuador, Guatemala, Colombia, and Brazil launched these sorts of pilot programs, but often encountered barriers to such redistribution. It also appears that land inventory, registry, and titling initiatives have proven inadequate even in the case of large scale programs such as Mexico's Certification and Titling Program for *Ejido* Lands and Urban Plots (PROCEDE) and Peru's Rural Land Titling and Registry Program. As a result, several countries of the region continue to suffer problems of insecurity in land ownership that limit access to credit and agricultural investment.

The reforms also greatly reduced public investment in projects aimed at bringing new lands under irrigation. Brazil, through its MODERINFRA credit line with subsidized interest rates, was one of the few countries that continued to invest heavily in farm irrigation even during the reform years—albeit at a lesser rate than in previous decades. Chile, for its part, resumed its public funding of medium-sized and small irrigation infrastructure projects beginning in 1990, and in 1992 implemented a Program for the Rehabilitation and Construction of Medium and Small Irrigation Projects, but achieved relatively insignificant growth in the amount of land under irrigation.

Due in part to its inefficient management, but above all because of reductions in public spending that made it increasingly difficult to sustain proper maintenance, irrigation management units were decentralized to their users. Colombia began this process in 1976 at the request of producers. Other countries followed, including Mexico, Argentina, Peru, Brazil, and the Dominican Republic. This decentralization signaled a substantial reduction in, or elimination of, the subsidies that the government had previously awarded for the operation and maintenance of irrigation districts. Following decades of government-subsidized irrigation, the 1980s and 1990s saw farmers begin paying the real cost of water, a move that assuredly helped to reduce the inefficient use and waste of such water.

Lastly, another important change in irrigation policy was the emergence of markets for the sale of water rights for farm irrigation. With its Law Decree 1122 of 1981, Chile became the first country in the region to generate a water rights market (Portilla 2000), followed by Mexico in 1992. In Mexico, where water rights transactions were already taking place before the relevant legislation was adopted, a number of complex problems meant that markets evolved through a process of trial and error. Garduño (2005) offers a series of lessons in the implementation of water rights markets based on the Mexican experience.[4]

Given the indispensable need for water, the number of sectors competing for access to it, and the magnitude of water scarcity, this would appear to be an area ripe for policy design that the countries of the region have yet to address. While there have been some examples of success in Chile and Mexico, in the context of declining public investment in irrigation works, there is still no ideal model of incentives with which to encourage private investment not only in new projects but also in the optimum maintenance of existing works. Lastly, small-scale irrigation, which has largely been overlooked by government policy and academic research alike, is a rich field for the design and implementation of irrigation policy.

24.3 CHANGES IN THE STRUCTURE OF AGRICULTURAL PRODUCTION

The agricultural sector in Latin America (LA) is heterogeneous. Modern agriculture exists alongside ancestral slash-and-burn technologies. Just as there are farms extending over thousands of hectares and with thousands of head of cattle, there are those with just a couple of rows and a pair of cows. The region's agricultural activity takes place in the

[4] Some of the suggestions posed by Garduño include the need: (a) to take a gradual approach to regulating existing users, (b) for water rights systems to never go beyond institutional and user capacity, (c) to make adjustments as a result of trial and error, (d) to strike a balance between administrative and ecological boundaries and the needs of water rights management, (e) to remove legal obstacles as they are encountered in practice, (f) to build and nurture a fruitful and dynamic bureaucratic–political relationship, (g) for communication as crucial to success registering existing users, and (h) for information systems that can provide formidable support for water rights management, provided they are kept simple and improved gradually.

most varied agro-ecological zones: from arid lands to forests; from sea level to regions more than 4,000 meters above the sea level. This agro-climatic diversity, which includes a range of varied production systems, makes possible the production of all varieties of vegetables and animals: from wheat to coffee; from cattle to alpaca; from quinoa to cashews; and a vast array of tropical fruits, tubers, grains and vegetables.

The importance of agriculture varies throughout the region from as much as 20.7% of GDP in Paraguay to as little as 3.4% in Venezuela. Farm exports can account for up to 80% of total exports in Panama, Nicaragua, and Paraguay and less than 4% in Venezuela.

However, a number of commonalities shared by some countries of the region help to explain the current map of subregional economic integration. It is possible to identify three major subregions: Mexico and Central America; the Andean Zone; and MERCOSUR countries. We will now describe the changes that have occurred in the productive agricultural structure of the three subregions of Latin America.[5]

24.3.1 Agriculture

In the past 25 years the amount of land under cultivation in Latin America has expanded from 100 to 132 million hectares. Most of that growth came from Brazil, Argentina, Bolivia, and Paraguay, countries that constitute a subregion called MERCOSUR (excluding Bolivia and including Uruguay) that contributed 27 of the additional 32 million hectares of crops in the region. Andean countries also achieved a notable expansion of harvested land, while Central America and Mexico achieved only moderate growth in this same period.

The main change in the productive structure of the region, generally speaking, was the dramatic boom in the production of oilseed crops, most notably soybeans in MERCOSUR countries. Today, as much land in the region is devoted to oilseeds as to cereals, crops whose share of land under cultivation fell in both relative (from 48.6% in 1979–80 to 36% in 2005–7) and absolute (1.3 million hectares) terms. In each subregion, however, productive structure performance has varied, as described below.

24.3.1.1 *Central America and Mexico*

In this subregion there has been a notable decline in the amount of land cultivated with oilseed crops (1 million hectares in Mexico and 260,000 hectares in Central America). This decrease occurred in response to the elimination of product price supports and input subsidies and the resulting loss of competitiveness relative to US imports, combined with the presence of pests (whitefly) that in the case of Mexico eliminated

---

[5] Table 24.1 lists the countries that constitute each subregion in this analysis; due to the changes we have noted in the section on trade policy and the availability of statistical information, these lists do not necessarily coincide with the current composition of subregional integration bodies.

soybeans from its main production region in the state of Sinaloa. In contrast, and motivated by increased access to export markets (especially to the US), the amount of land devoted to vegetables doubled and that used for fruit production grew 71%; the percentage of land devoted to agro-industrial crops was essentially unchanged at 34%. While the production of cereals also came under strong competition from US imports, their weight in the productive structure was almost constant (slipping by a mere percentage point but growing in absolute terms by almost 700,000 hectares), in response to government programs and exchange rate movement. Nevertheless, the amount of land on which dry legumes were harvested (mainly beans) fell by almost 10% in Mexico but soared 140% in Central America, thereby maintaining the position it occupied in the productive structure of the subregion at the beginning of the 1980s.

24.3.1.2 *Andean countries*

Over the past 25 years, slightly more than a million hectares were added to the total land cultivated for the production of cereals (mostly maize and rice), and the same amount was dedicated to the production of oilseed crops (mainly oil palm in Colombia and soybeans in Bolivia). The performance of these crops is explained to a large extent by the establishment of the Andean system of price bands, which made it possible to offset artificially depressed international prices for these crops, the rise in domestic demand, and the presence of agro-ecological conditions conducive to the production of oil palm. No less a factor was the incorporation of slightly more than 600,000 hectares to fruit production that is largely intended for export. Despite the importance of agro-industrial crops to this subregion (coffee, cacao, and sugar, to name a few), the amount of land used for such crops was practically stable, but its relative share of the production structure declined 7 percentage points.

24.3.1.3 *MERCOSUR*

The Southern Cone was unquestionably the subregion with the most dynamic agricultural sector. On average, slightly more than one million hectares were brought into production each year, with oilseed crops including soybeans the key growth drivers. This boom is explained by a number of factors: the existence of a vast agro-frontier, rising demand for food in developing countries, especially China and India, the development in the 1990s of genetically modified seeds, and foreign exchange policies that were favorable to the export sector[6] (FAO 2007). Cereals lost ground both in percentage and absolute terms, with 3.1 million of hectares removed from cereal production. Dry legumes also lost ground, with almost one million hectares taken out of production. While agro-industrial crops have kept their relative share almost intact, they added almost 4 million hectares to production. In Brazil, one of the drivers of this expansion was the production of bio-ethanol, which absorbed almost half of total sugarcane production during the 2008 harvest.

---

[6] Except for 1995–8, when the currency was overvalued (the real maintained parity with the dollar), Brazil kept the real undervalued, thereby contributing to the country's export boom.

Table 24.1 Changes to the agro-productive structure of Latin America, 1979/81–2005/7

Crop	Area harvested (millions of ha)				Variation 1980–2007			Value of production (US$ million)	Share of value of LA production (%)
	1979/81	Share (%)	2005/7	Share (%)	Absolute (ha)	Relative (%)	Share (% points)		
Latin America									
Cereals	48.9	48.6	47.6	36.0	-1,289,813	-2.6	-12.7	13,611	100.0
Oil seeds	22.0	21.9	47.6	35.9	25,596,992	116.5	14.1	11,895	100.0
Agro-industrial crops	11.5	11.5	16.1	12.2	4,561,130	39.5	0.7	10,059	100.0
Dry legumes	7.9	7.9	7.2	5.5	-711,755	-9.0	-2.4	2,227	100.0
Fruits	4.0	3.9	6.2	4.7	2,257,921	57.1	0.8	12,775	100.0
Roots and tubers	4.0	4.0	4.0	3.0	-15,714	-0.4	-1.0	4,310	100.0
Vegetables and melons	1.5	1.5	2.2	1.7	760,910	51.4	0.2	6,145	100.0
Other crops	0.8	0.8	1.4	1.1	632,100	79.4	0.3	n.d.	100.0
TOTAL	100.5	100.0	132.3	100.0	31,791,770	31.6		n.d.	
Central America and Mexico									
Cereals	11.5	59.0	12.2	57.9	697,400	6.1	-1.0	4,520	33.2
Agro-industrial crops	2.2	11.5	3.0	14.3	773,150	34.6	2.8	2,057	20.4
Dry legumes	2.1	10.8	2.4	11.3	280,060	13.3	0.5	928	41.7
Fruits	0.9	4.4	1.5	7.0	616,374	71.4	2.6	4,032	31.6
Vegetables and melons	0.4	2.2	0.9	4.2	449,927	105.7	2.0	2,741	44.6
Oil seeds	2.0	10.4	0.7	3.5	-1,288,928	-63.8	-6.9	540	4.5
Roots and tubers	0.1	0.7	0.2	0.7	28,556	22.5	0.1	672	15.6
Other crops	0.2	1.1	0.2	1.0	-447	-0.2	-0.1	n.d.	n.d.
TOTAL	19.5	100.0	21.0	100.0	1,556,092	8.0		n.d.	

Table 24.1 (contd.)

Crop	Area harvested (millions of ha)				Variation 1980–2007			Value of production (US$ million)	Share of value of LA production (%)
	1979/81	Share (%)	2005/7	Share (%)	Absolute (ha)	Relative (%)	Share (% points)		
Andean									
Cereals	3.9	37.1	5.0	36.9	1,140,939	29.4	-0.2	2,175	16.0
Agro-industrial crops	2.9	27.3	2.8	20.6	-45,917	-1.6	-6.6	2,396	23.8
Oil seeds	0.8	7.6	1.9	13.9	1,106,007	139.8	6.4	373	3.1
Fruits	1.0	10.0	1.6	12.1	608,066	58.4	2.2	2,980	23.3
Roots and tubers	1.0	9.9	1.1	8.2	73,477	7.1	-1.8	1,742	40.4
Vegetables and melons	0.3	2.8	0.6	4.2	271,808	92.6	1.3	987	16.1
Dry legumes	0.5	4.8	0.5	3.7	-4,658	-0.9	-1.1	181	8.1
Other crops	0.1	0.5	0.0	0.3	-4,731	-9.4	-0.1	n.d.	n.d.
TOTAL	10.5	100.0	13.6	100.0	3,144,992	30.1		n.d.	n.d.
Mercosur									
Oil seeds	19.2	27.1	44.9	46.0	25,779,913	134.6	18.9	10,982	92.3
Cereals	33.5	47.5	30.4	31.1	-3,128,153	-9.3	-16.4	6,917	50.8
Agro-industrial crops	6.4	9.1	10.3	10.5	3,833,897	59.5	1.4	5,606	55.7
Dry legumes	5.3	7.6	4.3	4.4	-987,157	-18.5	-3.1	1,118	50.2
Fruits	2.0	2.9	3.1	3.2	1,033,481	50.5	0.3	5,763	45.1
Roots and tubers	2.8	4.0	2.7	2.8	-117,747	-4.2	-1.2	1,896	44.0
Vegetables and melons	0.8	1.1	0.8	0.8	39,175	5.2	-0.3	2,418	39.3
Other crops	0.5	0.7	1.2	1.2	637,277	120.8	0.4	n.d.	n.d.
TOTAL	70.6	100.0	97.7	100.0	27,090,686	38.4		n.d.	n.d.

Source: FAO/RLC on FAOSTAT production reports.

Notes: 1. Agro-industrial crops include sugarcane, coffee, cacao, rubber, tobacco, and tea. Cotton is classified with oilseed crops rather than with fibers. Other crop classifications include fibers, nuts and others. 2. Central America: Costa Rica, El Salvador, Guatemala, Honduras, Nicaragua, Panama, and Mexico. Andean: Bolivia, Colombia, Ecuador, Peru, Venezuela. Mercosur: Argentina, Brazil, Chile, Paraguay, Uruguay. 3. Production value does not include countries such as Guatemala (Central America and Mexico) and Venezuela (Andean).

24.3.2 Livestock

Most of the Latin America region has experienced a substantial expansion of aviculture in response to technological innovation, economies of scale, and genetic improvements. The relatively short biological cycle of poultry makes it possible to lower prices, making both poultry meat and eggs more accessible to broad social layers. Cattle ranching and beekeeping have also experienced dramatic growth. The number of pigs in the region has been essentially flat (even as technological change has allowed for a significant rise in the production of pork), and there has been a clear decline in stocks of sheep and goats alongside only modest increases in productivity.

24.3.2.1 *Central America and Mexico*

Over the past 25 years there has been a significant decrease in the number of pigs in response to trade liberalization, declining producer prices, and the elimination of subsidies for key inputs such as sorghum. The production of bees has fallen due to the extent to which hives have been Africanized, their infestation by *Varroa jaco-bisini* parasites in Mexico beginning in 1992 (ASERCA 1993), and greater competition in export markets from countries such as Argentina, China, Thailand, and Vietnam. In contrast, the number of cattle has increased 5.8% in response to US exports of calves.

24.3.2.2 *Andean countries*

This subregion has witnessed the most significant expansion of poultry stocks, a rise powered by growing domestic demand and by developments in genetics, equipment and feed, and in Bolivia by the extent to which expanded soybean production has enhanced access to more affordable feed (FAO 2003). Pork stocks are essentially unchanged, while those of cattle have grown by almost 30%, the number of sheep and goats has risen 13.6%, and hives have declined 16.2%.

24.3.2.3 *MERCOSUR*

With the exception of sheep and goats, whose numbers have fallen by 33.8% as wool prices continue to recede, Southern Cone countries have greatly expanded their stocks of various types of livestock. In the past 25 years, as feed became more affordable and international demand continued to balloon, the number of cattle grew 45% and came to represent 72.2% of the Latin American total; poultry heads grew 128% and the number of hives jumped 146%. Only the number of pigs was essentially flat, a stagnation that can be explained at least in part by the tightening of regulatory controls over hog farm waste that have raised the production costs of farms located near cities.

Table 24.2 Variations in the stock and production value of the livestock sector, 1980–2005

Species	No. (millions of units) 1980	No. (millions of units) 2005	Variation (%), 1980–2005	Share of LA total (%), 2005	Value of production (US$ million)	Share of value of LA production (%)
Latin America						
Poultry	955.3	2,433.1	154.7	100.0	11,550.0	100.0
Pigs	71.3	70.2	–1.5	100.0	4,814.2	100.0
Hives	4.9	7.1	43.5	100.0	171.1	100.0
Cattle	280.6	384.2	36.9	100.0	16,381.5	100.0
Sheep and goats	137.1	112.0	–18.3	100.0	660.3	100.0
Central America and Mexico						
Poultry	231.6	622.9	168.9	25.6	3,574.0	30.9
Pigs	19.4	17.4	–10.6	24.7	1,970.7	40.9
Hives	2.8	2.0	–26.7	28.8	86.2	50.4
Cattle	38.8	41.0	5.8	10.7	3,659.2	22.3
Sheep and goats	16.7	17.0	1.5	15.1	233.1	35.3
Andean						
Poultry	166.0	537.3	223.8	22.1	2,324.7	20.1
Pigs	11.6	11.7	0.8	16.6	586.1	12.2
Hives	0.2	0.1	–16.2	1.8	3.8	2.2
Cattle	46.4	59.8	28.9	15.6	1,929.7	11.8
Sheep and goats	32.4	36.9	13.6	32.9	160.6	24.3

(continued)

Table 24.2 (contd.)

Species	No. (millions of units)		Variation (%), 1980–2005	Share of LA total (%), 2005	Value of production (US$ million)	Share of value of LA production (%)
	1980	2005				
MERCOSUR						
Poultry	557.7	1,273.0	128.2	52.3	5,651.3	48.9
Pigs	40.3	41.2	2.1	58.7	2,257.4	46.9
Hives	2.0	4.9	146.1	69.3	81.0	47.4
Cattle	195.4	283.3	45.0	73.7	10,792.5	65.9
Sheep and goats	87.9	58.2	–33.8	52.0	266.6	40.4

Source: FAO/RLC based on FAOSTAT production reports and the nominal exchange rate of countries as reported in World Development Indicators, World Bank.
Notes: 1. Poultry includes the number of chickens, ducks, turkeys, geese, and guineafowls. 2. Production value data does not include countries such as Guatemala (Central America and Mexico) and Venezuela (Andean). 3. The value of pork production is reported in terms of indigenous meat (by FAO classification) and natural honey in the case of apiculture.

24.3.3 Composition of international trade

The agricultural sector plays an important role in the foreign trade of the countries of the region. While the general trend has been for agro-food[7] products to occupy a shrinking share of the total export mix, in 2004–6 they continued to account for slightly more than 30% of exports from Southern Cone countries, and about 10% from the other subregions. Agro-food imports, for their part, accounted for roughly 8% of the mix in Andean Countries, in Central America and Mexico.

Latin America has tended to enjoy a surplus in agro-food trade, which has grown significantly in recent decades. But there are notable variations between subregions, including some significant trends in 1980–2006. In addition to bolstering their trade balances for primary agricultural products, Andean countries managed to reverse the deficit they were recording in the early 1980s on the level of processed products and to convert it into an average annual surplus of US$1.47 billion in 2004–6. The Central America and Mexico region managed to slightly more than double its trade surplus in the case of primary agricultural products, but the incipient deficit in processed products this region recorded in the early 1980s grew almost ten times over by 2004–6. MERCOSUR, for its part, managed to more than triple its agricultural trade surplus in both primary and processed products.

Of particular significance is the growing importance of processed agricultural products in Latin American trade. In each instance (exports and imports), the ratio of export value of processed products to that of primary products continues to grow, and this is perhaps one of the most promising characteristics of the region's agro-food trade.

In any event, the diversification of agro-food exports appears to have been insignificant in MERCOSUR,[8] a subregion in which the relative weight of the top 40 export products has shown little change in each of the past two decades (91% and 97% of total agro-food exports, respectively). In the Andean countries and in the Central America–Mexico subregion there has been some degree of export diversification: the leading 40 export products have seen their weight in total agro-food exports fall by 4 and 7 percentage points, respectively. Some of the products that have broken into the ranks of the main agro-food exports from Andean countries include oilseed paste, palm oil, and cattle, while in Central America and Mexico the newcomers include non-alcoholic beverages, some citrus fruits, and pork. In the case of Mexico, however, Taylor (2007) analyzed total exports (agricultural and non-agricultural), and concluded that NAFTA has stimulated trade growth but done little to alter the country's export structure.

---

[7] Agro-food exports are defined as all primary and processed products from the agricultural, livestock fishing, and fisheries sectors. They do not include the forest products sector.

[8] Many products in MERCOSUR have experienced a value-added process even though they share a common origin. The best example is meat products, which have incorporated much more of a processed component and are exported canned and refrigerated. The same cannot be said of grains or other processed products.

Table 24.3 Latin American trade in agro–food products, 1979/81 (A) to 2004/6 (B)

	Primary		Processed		Total	
	A	B	A	B	A	B
Exports (US$ bn)						
CAN*	3,140	5,871	779	5,730	3,919	11,602
MERCOSUR	7,871	24,523	8,353	39,088	16,224	63,611
Central America and Mexico	3,859	10,514	1,113	8,686	4,972	19,200
Imports (US$ bn)						
CAN*	1,216	2,763	1,598	4,093	2,813	6,856
MERCOSUR	2,587	3,074	1,236	4,423	3,822	7,497
Central America and Mexico	2,007	6,461	1,511	12,768	3,518	19,229
Trade balance (US$ bn)						
CAN*	1,924	3,108	−819	1,637	1,105	4,746
MERCOSUR	5,284	21,449	7,117	34,664	12,402	56,113
Central America and Mexico	1,852	4,013	−398	−4,205	1,454	−204

	Exports		Imports	
	A	B	A	B
Ratio processed products/primary products				
CAN*	0.2	1.0	1.3	1.5
MERCOSUR	1.1	1.6	0.5	1.4
Central America and Mexico	0.3	0.8	0.8	2.0

Source: The authors, based on UN COMTRADE (2009).
Note: Includes the fishing/fisheries industry and excludes the forest-products sector. Estimates based on SITC classifications rev. 1, rev 2. * Includes Venezuela.

There has, however, been significant diversification in some export markets, and interregional trade has acquired greater weight in Latin American trade activity. Over a period of 15 years, interregional trade as a percentage of total trade grew from 3.8% to 13.6% among Andean Countries, and from 4.7% to 7.7% in MERCOSUR. In Central America and Mexico it tripled as a percentage of total trade between 1986/8 and 2004/6.

Asia has emerged as an increasingly important destination for Latin American exports while Europe and North America have seen their relative importance diminish except for Central America and Mexico, where geographical proximity and preferential access have allowed these countries to further consolidate North America as the subregion's main export market.

Table 24.4 Destination of farm exports by subregion, 1982/4–2004/6 (%)

Andean

Destination	1982/4	2004/6
Andean	3.8	13.6
Latin America	3.4	5.3
North America	38.4	30.4
Europe	43.2	34.6
Asia	6.6	12.6
Rest of the world	4.7	3.5
Total	100.0	100.0

Central America and Mexico

Destination	1986/8	2004/6
Central America and Mexico	2.7	9.2
Latin America	0.8	1.6
North America	66.5	70.6
Europe	23.0	12.6
Asia	5.0	4.5
Rest of the world	1.9	1.5
Total	100.0	100.0

MERCOSUR

Destination	1983/5	2004/6
MERCOSUR	4.7	7.7
Latin America	3.2	5.4
North America	17.1	10.0
Europe	42.1	37.5
Asia	15.9	29.8
Rest of the world	16.9	9.6
Total	100.0	100.0

Source: Based on UN COMTRADE (2009).

24.4 SOCIAL AND ECONOMIC EFFECTS

24.4.1 Economic performance

Macroeconomic and sector reforms, combined with technological developments as well as the dynamics of both international and national markets, have had diverse effects on

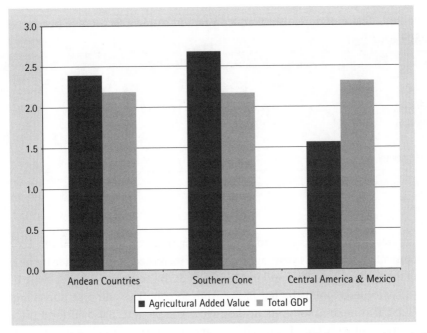

FIGURE 24.1 Average annual rate of growth in agricultural added value and total GDP, 1979/81–2005/7 (%)

Source: Authors, based on ECLACSTAT.

the agricultural economies of the region. During the 1980–2007 period, the Andean and MERCOSUR subregions posted the most significant agricultural growth relative to the overall economy. On average, agriculture grew half a percentage point more each year than did the general economy in the MERCOSUR countries, and by almost a fourth of a percentage point in the Andean Countries. In Central America and Mexico the general economy outpaced agriculture by three-fourths of a percentage point on average. In Central America, whose economies and agricultural sectors grew slightly faster than did those of Mexico, the gap separating growth in GDP and agricultural value added was also slightly more pronounced than in Mexico (0.78 vs. 0.65 percentage points, respectively).

The reforms appear to have greatly reduced the anti-agricultural bias that had marked macroeconomic and sector policies until the 1970s. Anderson and Valdés (2007) note that the relative rate of assistance (RRA) to the region's agriculture increased from −39.8% in the early 1970s to −0.6% in 2000–4. While RRA varies greatly between countries depending on the crop in question, there is an apparent growth trend in agricultural RRA that generally parallels similar developments in other regions of the world.[9]

---

[9] It is probable that if we were to adjust the RRA figures for exchange rate distortions, they would be lower. Furthermore, market failures apparent in the region presume lower RRAs for the segment of small producers.

Table 24.5 Share of agricultural added value in total GDP: average per decade, 1980–2007 (%)

Decade	Andean Countries	Southern Cone	Central America and Mexico
1980s (a)	6.6	4.8	5.8
1990s (b)	6.8	4.8	5.3
2000–7(c)	7.0	5.3	4.8
Difference (c)–(a)	0.4	0.5	−1.0

Source: Authors, based on ECLACSTAT data.

In contrast to what we came to expect under traditional approaches to economic development, in the past 25 years agriculture has increased in importance in the economies of the Andean countries and in MERCOSUR. By 2007, agriculture's share of GDP was 0.41 percentage points higher in the Andean countries and 0.54 points higher in MERCOSUR compared to levels in the 1980s. Volatile international food prices, the future outlook of global food and energy markets, and the agricultural potential of the region all suggest the need to reassess the role traditionally assigned to agriculture in Latin American economic development.

24.4.2 Population and rural employment

Today only 22% of the population in Latin America lives in areas regarded as rural, making the region excessively urban for its income level. Nevertheless, roughly 121 million people remain in the countryside. The Latin American process of urbanization was accelerated by the extent to which ownership of productive lands was concentrated in large estates, the dire conditions of farm employment, and the greater access to basic services that was to be found in the cities, thereby consolidating the process that had begun in decades past of migration away from the countryside to the cities.

Although the population of rural areas is in constant decline, the rural economically active population (EAP) grew between the 1990s and 2000. Three factors explain this apparent paradox: changes in the composition and structure of the rural population; the increased participation of women in the workforce; and a rise in non-agricultural activities in rural areas.

Latin America's rural population has grown both older and increasingly male in recent decades as a larger segment of the youth population migrates to other regions or countries and women seek a better life and greater income opportunities in the job market (Dirven and Ortega forthcoming). The incorporation of women into the labor force is perhaps one of the most important changes to occur in the rural labor market. Although the rate of women's employment remains much lower than that of men, it

Table 24.6 Population and employment in Latin America (millions of people)

	1980	1990	2000	2005	2010
Population total	354.6	433.6	511.6	546.5	582.4
Urban population	231.2	306.2	387.5	425.4	463.2
Rural population	123.3	127.4	124.1	121.2	119.3
Total EAP	121.3	163.3	222.0	248.9	276.5
Urban EAP	81.9	118.5	171.7	197.4	223.4
Rural EAP	39.5	44.9	50.2	51.4	53.1
Rate of employment among men (%)	82.0	80.8	80.1	80.1	80.0
Rate of employment among women (%)	31.9	38.2	48.1	50.6	52.8

Source: ECLAC (2008b) and the Centro Latinoamericano y Caribeño de Demografía (www.eclac.cl/celade). The 1980 EAP and rate of employment figures are from ECLAC (1999)

climbed by 13 percentage points between 1980 and 2005. A similar process has been taking place in urban sectors.

The rise in part-time employment and a drastic reduction in full-time jobs in agricultural enterprises is another significant development. This shift reflects the type of modernization implied by regional specialization in some crops whose consequences included a concentration of demand for labor to specific seasons of the year. Alongside this rise in seasonal employment, the labor market has been reshaped by the emergence of the intermediary institutions who supply temporary workers in keeping with the needs of employers.

Equally significant is the rise in rural non-farm employment (RNFE),[10] especially in Bolivia, Brazil, Chile, and Mexico. Over the course of the 1980s and 1990s, non-agricultural jobs came to represent up to 40% of the income of rural households, and more recently that figure has climbed as high as 65%. According to estimates, such activities have made it possible to avoid wild seasonal fluctuations in family income and for households to diversify their income sources, thereby diminishing the precarious conditions that accompany agriculture's inherent risks (IDB, FAO, and ECLAC 1999). The retail trade and services, especially those of a local nature, are the main sources of rural non-farm employment.

24.4.3 Rural poverty

At the beginning of the 1980s, 19% of people in the region lived in extreme poverty, a figure that continued to growth throughout that decade and into the early 1990s before

[10] The rise in RNFE explains why the rural EAP grew even as the agricultural EAP fell in response to the increasing mechanization of crops. Statistical information shows that agricultural employment in Latin America and the Caribbean narrowed from 45.3 million in 1991 to 42.7 million in 2001, but by 2007 had risen to 46.4 million, clear evidence that agriculture remains by far the main source of employment in the rural sector.

shrinking to 13% by 2007. In the "lost decade" of the 1980s, poverty grew amid the debt crisis. This occurred again in the late 1990s as we moved into a new century amid the foreign exchange crises that prompted significant contractions of GDP in most countries of the region. Between 1990 and 2007 extreme poverty in the region fell, largely due to an increase in non-working sources of income such as remittances, direct transfers, subsidies, and pensions as well as demographic and structural changes to households such as the number of family members employed. Remittances have had an especially pronounced impact on the household incomes of the poorest families.

As the region slowly emerged from crisis in the first years of the current decade and prior to 2008, most countries in the region embarked on sustained growth, especially beginning in 2003 with per capita GDP in the region expanding by more than 3% annually. This factor is a key reason for the poverty reduction recorded in those years. While that relative ebbing of poverty has unquestionably been a positive development, the percentage of people in need remains much higher in the countryside than in the cities.

As Table 24.7 shows, in the period under discussion, extreme poverty fell by 15% in rural areas and increased 27% in urban zones. By 2007, however, extreme poverty rates in rural areas were still three times higher than in urban areas. This suggests that extreme poverty is more difficult to eradicate in rural zones than in urban areas. The fact that minimum wages go widely unenforced in agricultural activities throughout various countries of the region is one of the factors that explain the levels of poverty and rural poverty.[11]

Table 24.7 Poverty and extreme poverty in Latin America, 1980–2007

	Poverty			Extreme Poverty		
	Total	Urban	Rural	Total	Urban	Rural
Millions of people						
1980	136	63	73	62	22	40
1990	200	122	78	93	45	48
2002	221	146	75	97	51	46
2007	184	121	63	68	34	34
Percentage of the population						
1980	40	30	60	19	11	33
1990	48	41	65	22	15	40
2002	44	38	62	19	14	38
2007	34	29	52	13	8	28

Source: Based on ECLAC (2008a).

[11] In Argentina, for example, out of every 10 full-time, wage-earning farm workers, 66 were paid less than the minimum wage. In Brazil this indicator varies greatly by region. Whereas a high percentage of

24.5 THE RECENT SHOCKS: A CALL BACK TO STATE-LED AGRICULTURAL DEVELOPMENT?

As we have already noted, since late in the past century pro-market reforms have led to a drastic downsizing of government structures dedicated to supporting the agricultural sector. Government roles were quite different from country to country depending on the internal play of domestic political forces. From the "foreign debt crisis" in the early 1980s until the "foreign exchange crisis" of the late 1990s, in general, Latin American governments implemented compensatory sector policies only for specific segments of agriculture and only in response to political pressure. In addition, there was a total loss of medium- and long-term planning capability in the agricultural sectors of these countries except for specific exporting segments. The segments dedicated to supplying food products to the internal market—especially for low-income strata of the population—were relegated to a secondary status and received only emergency aid. The prevalent idea was that the world was a giant supermarket replete with cheap food and agricultural inputs, especially subsidized products from developed countries.

Beginning in 2005, and intensifying from 2006/7 through mid-2008, a perfect storm of factors coalesced to send the prices of some agricultural commodities (such as maize, wheat, soybeans, and rice), minerals, and oil spiraling higher (Graziano da Silva 2008). These factors included:

- a surge in demand for basic foods within Asian countries such as China and India, due in part to increased incomes among the poorer segments of the population of these countries;
- a rapid rise in consumption of yellow corn in response to increased demand for poultry and pig feed, as well as the rise demand for biofuels within the US, the source of 3/4 of the world's corn exports;
- a series of climate disasters, especially the droughts in two of the world's leading wheat producers, Australia and Argentina; and
- financial speculation in futures and derivative markets in response to a plummeting US dollar, the currency in which commodities are traded globally.

The combined effects of food and oil price rises had a particularly strong impact on countries that were net importers of food and energy. These countries found their ability

---

sugarcane cutters in the northeast were paid less than the minimum wage, in Sao Paulo close to 90% were paid the minimum, though the percentage was higher among full-time than among temporary workers. A similar situation prevails in Honduras; nationwide 50% of workers earn less than the minimum wage, but that figure climbs to 66% in agriculture, forestry, and fishing, segments marked by significant violations of labor laws.

to respond to the food crisis as a nation greatly diminished, as they no longer had a public system for providing support to segments of agriculture dedicated to supplying the domestic market. For net food-importing countries, bottlenecks in the availability of seed supply frustrated the expansion of local production. In an effort to overcome these bottlenecks, Andean and Central American countries have tried to achieve greater public intervention to re-establish national seed production and distribution systems, with considerable participation on the part of producers. The countries of the region have steeped up regulation of the markets that import and distribute fertilizers and, in cases such as Ecuador, have implemented direct controls on fertilizer prices. For their part, Brazil, Venezuela and Ecuador have adopted public policies to encourage the domestic production of fertilizers linked to the petrochemical industry. Similarly, countries such as Costa Rica have invested in research and technology transfer directed at small-scale producers of basic crops.

As the financial crisis of 2008–9 affected the financial system of the Latin American region, international liquidity inflows ebbed and credit became increasingly scarce. One major factor in each country's ability to respond to the crisis and to reactive agricultural and productive credit in general is the role that the state plays in the financial system. Although the reform led many countries to significantly curtail or entirely eliminate state participation in the financial sector, the ones who made the deepest cuts were the same ones who found it most difficult to channel credit to agriculture. Indeed, several of them appeared to be locked in a race against time as they struggled to revive what little was left of development-oriented financial institutions and their public credit support instruments (Soto Baquero 2009).

As for the agrarian question, it appears that there is still a long road left to travel. In addition to matters of titling and land access, recently new issues have arisen such as armed conflicts, the concentration of landownership, the setting of limits on the extension of private land holdings, sustainable land use, the *minifundio*, normalization of indigenous community property, the aging and feminization of current landholders, and recently, the rise in foreign ownership of land.[12]

But Latin American governments have not confined their efforts toward re-exerting an important role in managing rural space to strictly productive and financial issues. Since the beginning of the 1990s, the countries of the region have significantly revised programs providing direct assistance to the poor to include the distribution of material assistance (usually through cash transfers) to assure basic levels of consumption in the face of either economic crises or persistent poverty. Today, conditional transfer programs have spread throughout the region, and have become one of the main poverty reduction factors in many countries of Latin America and the Caribbean between 2002

---

[12] It appears that the food crisis of 2007–8 sparked a wave of purchases of farm land in developing countries on the part of other countries looking to assure supplies of food and biofuels. Von Braun and Meinzen-Dick (2009) analyze various sides of the question, and while they deal with countries outside Latin America, it would come as no surprise to uncover the same trend in Latin American countries with vast tracts of farm land such as Brazil, Bolivia, and Argentina.

and 2008.[13] Some of these programs have been integrated into social protection systems, while others remain temporary aid programs for the poor in the absence of a social strategy that could assure their sustainability.

One of the most important changes in public policy is the degree to which major social programs place "social" issues at the heart of the policy agenda. Another factor that has emerged in the last decade consists of sweeping programs aimed at mobilizing resources with which to profoundly intervene into the issue of food security. One case in point is the Mexico "Living Better" strategy designed to build a broad network of support programs for the most vulnerable segments of the population and which includes the Opportunities program. Colombia's most notable initiatives are "Bogota Without Hunger," a plan in the Capital District with broad coverage, the Food Security Network (RESA) for displaced families, and the Ten-Year Plan for the Promotion, Protection and Support of Breastfeeding. In Bolivia, the government is implementing a "Zero Hunger Program," and Argentina is implementing the "Most Urgent Hunger National Plan." These programs have become centerpieces of strategies for alleviating rural poverty, which has become the region's "hard core" of social exclusion.[14]

In any event, if there is a lesson that needs to be learned with regard to the reforms of recent decades and from the food and financial crises of 2007–9, it is that food is too sensitive an issue to be left to the "invisible hand" of the free market or to a few agents that manage prices based on their own private interests. The future outlook for food and energy prices appears to hold out the promise of a reactivation of agricultural production in the countries of the Latin American region. However, there seems to be little chance that producers, especially small and medium-sized farms, will have much of an opportunity to take advantage of such an opening, especially considering their lack of access to technologies needed to improve their yields, and the scarcity of funds with which to obtain inputs.

In order to take advantage of this opportunity, farmers—especially the smallest ones—depend on the existence of proactive governmental policies for assuring access to credit, minimum prices for their products, and the functioning of formal markets. In other words, what is needed is effort to strengthen public and private institutions and to put in place public policies that allow for the development of small-scale agriculture.

The ability of governments to design institutional arrangements that can effectively tackle both old and new economic and social problems in the 21st century, especially those related to a lack of job opportunities and thus of household income, is a crucial issue today. This is especially true in the context of needing responses to a crisis that is shaping up to be the most severe crisis the world has seen since 1929. It is too soon to say whether governments will be successful in confronting these challenges.

---

[13] For 2009 we found that 17 programs include some form of conditionality for the dispensing of transfers that were based on the predetermined conduct of beneficiaries.

[14] In Brazil the Family Income Program, *Programa Bolsa Familia*, which has been inserted into the Zero Hunger Program, contains a series of activities that has had a significant effect on the incomes of the rural poor. On a lesser scale the same thing can be said of Chile's "Chile Solidarity" program.

REFERENCES

ANDERSON, K., and VALDÉS, A. (2007). 'Distortions to Agricultural Incentives in Latin America', Agricultural Distortions Working Paper No. 60, World Bank, Washington, DC.

ASERCA (Apoyos y Servicios a la Comercialización Agropecuaria/Support and Services for Agricultural Trading) (1993). *Claridades agropecuarias 4*, México: Secretaría de Agricultura y Recursos Hidráulicos.

DE JANVRY, A., KEY, N., and SADOULET, E. (1997). 'Agricultural and Rural Development Policy in Latin America: New Directions and New Challenges', Agricultural Policy and Economic Development Series No. 2, Rome: FAO.

DELGADO, O. (1965). *Reformas agrarias en la América Latina*, México: FCE.

DIRVEN, M., and ORTEGA, D. (forthcoming). *Políticas para la juventud rural*, Santiago, Chile: ECLAC.

ECLAC (UN Economic Commission for Latin America and the Caribbean) (1999). *América Latina: población económicamente activa 1980–2025*, Santiago, Chile.

—— (2006). *Cuatro temas centrales en torno a la migración internacional, derechos humanos y desarrollo*, Santiago, Chile.

—— (2008a). *Panorama social de América Latina 2008*, Santiago, Chile.

—— (2008b) *América Latina y el Caribe: fecundidad*, Santiago, Chile.

EMBRAPA (Empresa Brasileira de Pesquisa Agropecuária/Brazilian Agricultural Research Corporation) (2008). *Agricultura tropical: cuatro décadas de innovaciones tecnológicas, institucionales y políticas*, Brasilia: MAPA and EMBRAPA.

FAO (Food and Agriculture Organization) (2003). 'Livestock Sector Report', available online at: http://www.fao.org/Ag/AGAInfo/resources/en/publications/sector_reports/lsr_andean.pdf

—— (2007). *Expansión sutura de la Soja 2005–2014*, Santiago, Chile.

GARDUÑO, H. (2005). 'Lessons from Implementing Water Rights in Mexico', in B. R. Bruns, C. Ringler, and R. Meinzen-Dick (eds), *Water Rights Reform: Lessons for Institutional Design*, Washington, DC: IFPRI.

GÓMEZ, S. (2002). *La nueva realidad: ¿qué tan nueva?* Santiago, Chile: Ediciones LOM.

GRAZIANO DA SILVA, J. (1994). 'Complejos agroindustriales y otros complejos', *Revista agricultura y sociedad 72*.

—— (2008). 'Crisis de los alimentos: lecciones de la historia reciente', *Revista española de estudios agrosociales y pesqueros 218*.

IDB (Inter-American Development Bank), FAO (Food and Agriculture Organization), and ECLAC (UN Economic Commission for Latin America and the Caribbean) (1999). *Conclusiones y recomendaciones del seminario internacional sobre desarrollo del empleo rural no agrícola en América Latina*, Santiago, Chile.

OECD (2009). *Agricultural Policies in Emerging Economies: Monitoring and Evaluation*, Paris.

PORTILLA, B. (2000). *La política agrícola en Chile: lecciones de tres décadas*, Santiago, Chile: ECLAC.

SALCEDO, S. (1999). *Impactos diferenciados de las reformas sobre el agro Mexicano: productos, regiones y agentes*, Santiago, Chile: ECLAC.

—— (2006). *Comercio internacional agrícola: tendencias y retos de política*, Santiago, Chile: FAO.

SOTO-BAQUERO, F. (2009). *Crisis financiera y financiamiento agropecuario y rural en América Latina: una mirada más allá del corto plazo*, Santiago, Chile: FAO.

SPOOR, M. (2000). *Two Decades of Adjustment and Agricultural Development in Latin America and the Caribbean*, Santiago, Chile: ECLAC.

STADS, P.-J., HARTWICH, F., RODRÍGUEZ, D., and ENCISO, F. (2008). *I&D agropecuaria en América Central: políticas, inversiones y perfil institucional*, Washington, DC: IFPRI and IICA.

TAYLOR, T. (2007). 'Export Diversification in Latin America and the Caribbean', *Journal of the Caribbean Agro-Economic Society* 7.1.

TRIVELLI, C., and VENERO, H. (2007). *Banca de desarrollo para el agro: experiencias en curso en América Latina*, Lima: Instituto de Estudios Peruanos.

UN COMTRADE (2009). United Nations Commodity Trade Statistics Database, New York.

VALDÉS, A., and FOSTER, W. (2005). 'Agricultural Trade Liberalization and the Rural Economy in Latin America and the Caribbean', presented at the workshop 'Rural Development and Agricultural Trade', IDB, July 18.

VON BRAUN, J., and MEINZEN-DICK, R. (2009). '"Land Grabbing" by Foreign Investors in Developing Countries: Risks and Opportunities', IFPRI Policy Brief No. 13, Washington, DC.

World Bank (2008). *Informe sobre el desarrollo mundial: agricultura para el desarrollo*, Washington, DC.

....

CHAPTER 25

AN ENERGY PANORAMA
OF LATIN AMERICA

....

HUMBERTO CAMPODÓNICO

25.1 INTRODUCTION[1]

....

Latin America as a region is self-sufficient in energy and indeed a net exporter. Fossil fuels represented 71% of total energy supply and renewable energy 26% in 2007. Nevertheless, when countries are analyzed individually there are great disparities, as some are net importers, mainly of oil.

After looking at the regional energy matrix in section 25.2, section 25.3 examines the legal changes in the hydrocarbon sector in the 1990s, characterized by a trend to market openness and deregulation, and in the first decade of the 21st century by a strong desire by some countries to claim a greater share of oil revenues and to modernize state-owned enterprises (SOEs). Section 25.4 looks at investment patterns in this sector in recent years, where the weight of SOEs is very high.

Sections 25.5 and 25.6 examine the growing importance of two energy sources: natural gas, including liquefied natural gas, which has become more important for both domestic consumption and regional integration; and renewable energy, particularly biofuels, a recent addition to the region's energy matrix. This is followed by an analysis of regional integration initiatives (section 25.7). Section 25.8 presents an overall balance of the region's energy sector.

25.2 THE REGIONAL ENERGY MATRIX

....

The total supply of primary energy in Latin America and the Caribbean was of 5.331 billions barrels of oil equivalent (boe) in 2007, which represented 4.5% of total world

[1] I thank Armando Mendoza for his support.

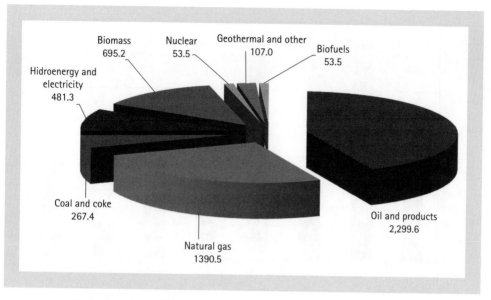

FIGURE 25.1 Latin America and the Caribbean: energy demand, 2007 (in millions boe)

Source: OLADE (2008).

Notes: Total energy demand: 5,348 million boe.

supply. Around 71% of this supply is provided by fossil fuels, while renewable energy makes up 26%, with biomass representing the dominant share of the latter. The most important changes over the last twenty years have been the replacement of oil by natural gas, the increase in hydroelectricity, and the increase, albeit small, of biofuels; Brazil's ethanol is the most important example in this regard.

The final demand for primary energy, which amounted to 5.348 billion boe in 2007, is also dominated by fossil fuels (74%), with the important participation of hydropower, biomass, and biofuels (Figure 25.1). One of the challenges for the region is to change the energy matrix by replacing hydrocarbons and coal, which emit greenhouse gases, with renewable energies, of which the region possesses ample resources.

The consumption of oil derivatives grew strongly from 1971–2005 above all in the industrial and transport sectors, where it increased threefold. The transport sector accounted for the largest increases in oil consumption between 1971 and 2005 (see Figure 25.2). Problems associated with climate change makes it imperative that countries in the region improve their energy efficiency policies, discussed elsewhere in this Handbook (see Chapter 6 by de Miguel and Sunkel).

The regional commercial energy balance was positive in 2007 at 1.741 billion boe.[2] This overall pictures hides, however, significant differences by subregions. The Andean

---

[2] Total production of primary energy in the region was 7.732 billion boe. To obtain the total supply of primary energy it is necessary to subtract energy exports and add energy imports. As total supply was less than total production, the region was a net exporter of energy.

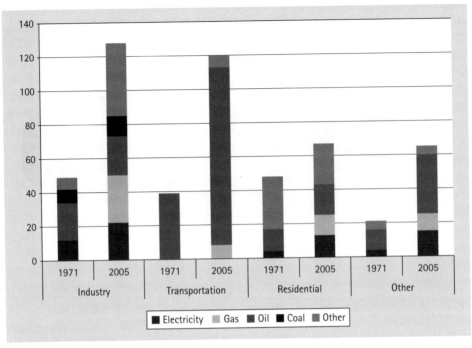

FIGURE 25.2 Latin America and the Caribbean, 1971 and 2005: total fuel consumption by sector (millions of tons oil equivalent)

Source: ECLAC (2009).

Notes: 1 ton boe is equivalent to 7.2 boe.

countries, Mexico, Trinidad, and Tobago show an energy surplus, whereas the subregions with the greatest deficits, in terms of their consumption, are the Caribbean and Central America, as they have limited oil and gas reserves. Brazil and the Southern Cone have smaller relative deficits (see Table 25.1).

This indicates that Latin America is in no way homogeneous. In the case of oil, by far the most important energy source, there are major exporters in the region but also entire subregions, like Central America, which import 100% of the oil they consume.

The country with the greatest oil reserves is Venezuela, with 99 billion barrels (68% of the regional total), followed by Brazil with 14 billion barrels (not including 10–12 billion of pre-salt layers, recently discovered in Santos Bay, which will double its reserves). They are followed by Argentina, Colombia, Ecuador, and further behind, Peru and Trinidad and Tobago. Venezuela also has the greatest reserves of natural gas, followed by Bolivia. Mexico, Argentina, and Trinidad and Tobago follow, each with around 6% of the regional total; Peru and Colombia are far behind.

Oil and gas production is of singular economic importance to the GDP, exports, and tax base of producing countries (Table 25.2). This is the case for Bolivia, Ecuador, Mexico, Trinidad, and Venezuela and to a lesser extent, Argentina, Brazil and Peru. It should be

Table 25.1 Latin America and the Caribbean: trade balance (TB), 2007 (million boe)

Countries/subregions	TB	TB/internal consumption
Mexico	458.7	0.35
Central America	−108.6	−0.49
Caribbean	−152.8	−0.67
Trinidad and Tobago	165.5	1.34
Andean area	1638	1.77
Southern Cone	−108.4	−0.13
Brazil	−151.3	−0.09
Total LAC	**1741.1**	**0.33**

Source: OLADE–SIEE.

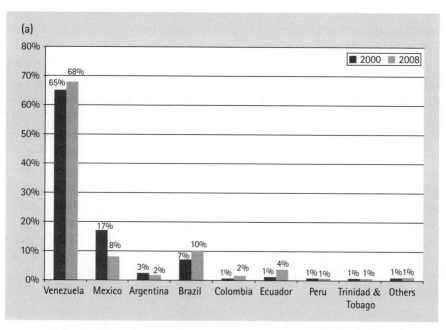

FIGURE 25.3(A) Oil reserves by country (% distribution), 2000 (118 billion barrels) and 2008 (136 billion barrels)

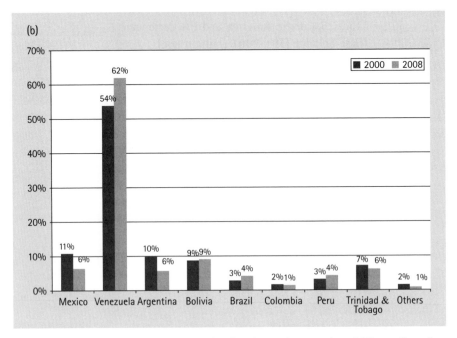

FIGURE 25.3(B) Gas reserves by country (% distribution), 2000 (7.71 billion m³) and 2008 (7.81 billion m³)

Source: British Petroleum (2009).

Table 25.2 Importance of the hydrocarbon sector in the economy, 2007 (%)

Country	GDP	Exports	Tax income	Energy matrix
Argentina	1.5	11.8	n.d.	80
Bolivia	6.9	48	34	72
Brazil	3.1	0	n.d.	55
Colombia	1.9	26	2.8	63
Ecuador	13	59.7	25	79
Peru	0.5	7.4	5.9	59
Mexico	8.64	15.8	37	87
Trinidad	46.3	87	54.5	94
Venezuela	16.2	53.3	84.6	76

Source: Official data by country.

noted that tax revenues reported in Table 25.2 do not take into account those raised through taxes on fuel consumption, including only those from the upstream collection.

The United States is the main market for Mexico and Venezuela, the region's most important exporters. Between 2000 and 2009 the proportion of US oil imports from Latin America was 27% of total imports.

25.3 REFORMS OF THE HYDROCARBON SECTOR IN THE 1990S AND THE NEW MILLENNIUM

25.3.1 The producing countries

Market reforms had an impact on the modernization of the hydrocarbon sector in the majority of the countries in the region, with new rules of the game for the "upstream" and "downstream" (particularly fuel prices in the domestic market). But these reforms (as opposed to what happened in other productive sectors) did not result in the privatization of state-owned enterprises (SOEs), because states expected to continue to appropriate a major share of oil and gas profits. SOEs were entirely or partially privatized only in Argentina, Bolivia and Peru. The reforms focused, therefore, on removing upstream and downstream entry barriers, new forms of oil contracts, different schemes of industry privatization, and strategic alliances and internationalization policies of the SOEs.

Within the upstream sector, there was an attempt to attract risk capital to help increase reserves and production, satisfy internal market demand, and expand exports, by allowing contracts to provide for longer time horizons. There were also explicit measures taken to reduce taxes on firms within the sector, granting open availability of crude oil and explicit guarantees to foreign investors. Restrictions were eliminated on foreign currency holding, trade, and financial discrimination, and in several cases, international arbitration was granted for the settlement of disputes.

In the downstream sector, in some countries there was a tendency to reduce the state monopolies of public enterprises in transport and refining by, for example, opening and deregulating retail markets.

The modernization of SOEs and the development of new business strategies took different forms. There were four major modernization models:

(a) exclusive state property in Mexico;
(b) state dominance with the encouragement of private investment in Brazil, Chile, and Venezuela;
(c) mixed management between state and private companies in Colombia and Ecuador; and

(d) the predominance of private ownership in Argentina, Bolivia, and Peru (Campodónico 2007b).

Beginning in 2000—when the region was suffering from its "half-lost decade" of 1998–2002—but above all after the sharp increase of international oil prices in the mid-2000s, there was a strong shift in several countries—particularly Bolivia, Ecuador, and Venezuela—to push reforms aimed at increasing the states' share in oil and gas profits.

In Ecuador, in 2006, Law 42 was promulgated, which re-established an economic balance for contracts signed with foreign oil companies. It states that when the average monthly sales price of oil exceeds the monthly average price of sale, stated at the date of signature of the contract, the state receives at least 50% of the additional revenue generated by the price difference. Later this share was increased to 99%. In 2009, a new constitution was approved together with a new hydrocarbons law establishing contracts for the provision of services, with the contractors now receiving a fee per barrel, but without the right to share the benefits of the deposits. The process of renegotiation of contracts is not yet completed.

Bolivia held a referendum in 2004 in which Bolivians declared themselves in favor of substantial changes to the hydrocarbon legal regime. A new hydrocarbons law was promulgated in 2005 which imposes a 32% direct tax, with royalties added, which now takes total royalties to 50%. In 2006 there was a sui generis nationalization of hydrocarbons, with the state becoming their owner at the wellhead, while foreign investors retain their corporate ownership. The refineries and oil fields (partially privatized in 1996) have been nationalized and taken over by the SOE, YPFB, whose functions have been expanded. In 2006 and 2007, the price of gas exported to Argentina and Brazil was renegotiated, with large gains for Bolivia.

In January 2002, Venezuela announced a new Organic Law of Hydrocarbons increasing state participation in primary activities and royalties. In 2006 the income tax was set at a uniform rate of 50%. This implies, in particular, that the strategic associations in the Orinoco Belt (*Faja del Orinoco*) pay a 50% tax from 2007, rather than a 34% tax as previously. The "operating agreements" transformed the firms doing the exploitation into mixed enterprises with at least 50% of shares held by the state. In the implementation of the law, it was established that the state would control operating agreements in the Orinoco Belt; mixed enterprises have been established between the old operators and the SOE, Petróleos de Venezuela S.A. (PDVSA), and will have a minimum of 60% of equity of the latter.

The other countries have continued the general direction of the 1990s hydrocarbon reforms, with a focus now on various ways to strengthen the sector's institutions. So, for example, Brazil, Colombia, and Peru have created government entities with the specific objective of negotiating contracts with hydrocarbon companies, a role previously performed by state enterprises. Brazil created the National Petroleum Agency (Agencia Nacional de Petróleo) in 1997, and Colombia the National Hydrocarbons Agency (Agencia Nacional de Hidrocarburos) in 2003, while Peru established PERUPETRO in 1993 as part of the hydrocarbons law.

In Colombia, the new hydrocarbon contract legislation provides for the reduction of royalties to promote foreign investment. The modernization and internationalization of ECOPETROL has also taken place. In 2006 the legal status of ECOPETROL was altered from that of a public company consisting of shares (Sociedad Pública por Acciones) entirely owned by the state to that of a mixed or joint stock company (Sociedad de Economía Mixta). The purpose was to obtain new investment for the company by registering it in the stock exchange, facilitating the issuance of new shares which would contribute to the US$60 billion investment plan for 2008–15. It was decreed that the nation would retain a minimum of 80% of shares in circulation and with equivalent voting rights. Ownership of the remaining 20% would be negotiated through the stock exchange and would include small individual investors.

Foreign investment also increased in Brazil (although PETROBRAS continues to be the largest investor). As in Colombia, the state company PETROBRAS is also registered in the stock market. Private investors hold more than 70% of preferential shares, while the state has more than 57.6% of ordinary shares, which give it control of the firm. PETROBRAS has revamped and strengthened its investment plan to around US$174 billion for the period 2009–13. In 2009 a new hydrocarbons law was proposed for the exploitation of the pre-salt layer which would create a new company to develop these reserves, either on their own or in alliance with other companies. The law will also establish more favorable conditions for the state in the distribution of profits. The law was appored in 2010.

In Argentina, the predominant management style in the hydrocarbon sector continues to be private. However, the state has created a new state enterprise, Energy Argentina (Energía Argentina, ENARSA) which has an important investment role in the sector's infrastructure and imports of hydrocarbons. Reforms were also aimed at improving mechanisms of tax collection, inspection, and regulation of the companies in the different phases of the industry. In 2002 the state imposed a tax on oil exports and at the same time set a maximum price of US$40 per barrel, a price which also applied in the domestic market.

In Mexico, Petróleos Mexicanos (PEMEX) continues to hold the monopoly on exploration and exploitation, although there have been recent moves by the company to reverse the decline of hydrocarbon production. In 2008, legislation introduced reforms such as the addition of new members to PEMEX's board representing other productive sectors, and the establishment of a new consultative committee designed to provide some independent coordination for long-term energy strategy. The reforms also allow PEMEX to write service contracts using incentives for private companies. The reforms grant the company greater autonomy, including the capacity to create new debt and to establish more flexible mechanisms for buying assets and property as well as making investments. It is too early to evaluate the impact of this reform.

The management style in Peru remains predominantly private. In 2006, however, Law 28440 was promulgated which excludes PETROPERU from privatization and permits it to participate in upstream activities. The modernization of the Talara refinery continues and the company has signed agreements of association with PETROBRAS, ECOPETROL, and PETROECUADOR. Legislative decree 1031 (2008) requires state enterprises to have a minimum 20% of their capital in the stock market. At the time of writing this chapter, such action has not been undertaken.

25.3.2 Reforms in energy deficit countries

The energy situation in Central America and the Caribbean is very different from the rest of the region, given that hydrocarbon reserves are modest and the countries highly dependent on imports (aside from Trinidad and Tobago, which is an important producer of natural gas).

As a result, the hydrocarbon sector, both private and government-owned, is of reduced dimension. However, in several of these countries, state participation is important in downstream activities (refining, distribution, and marketing). Given the strong dependence of these countries on fuel imports, the presence of the state has been perceived as a counterweight and guarantee against supply problems and market manipulation.

Given the above, the reforms of the 1990s did not have the same impact in Central America and the Caribbean as it did in other subregions. State participation in hydrocarbon activities not only continued but also expanded, as a response to requirements of local demand and the fuel supply.

In Costa Rica, since the 1970s, the importation, refining, and wholesaling of fuel has been under the state monopoly of RECOPE, which was reconfirmed explicitly in a 1993 law. At the end of this decade, RECOPE began an ambitious modernization and expansion, expanding its operations, including the refinery at Moin and the construction of a pipeline. This effort was continued in the new millennium with additional investments in the pipeline. Today, RECOPE has begun a project to triple Moin's refining capacity to 60,000 barrels a day, which will cover all domestic demand. RECOPE has requested funds from multilateral organizations, and is considering a joint venture with China's National Petroleum Corporation.

In Cuba, CUPET is the state monopoly for downstream and upstream activities in the domestic market. For decades, Cuba received significant help from the former USSR in energy supply, with abundant oil supplies under preferential conditions. The breakup of the Soviet Union was thus a traumatic event for Cuba. To face these new circumstances, the government applied draconian measures to ration fuel consumption, while at the same time investing huge amounts in petroleum exploration and the development of new oilfields. This led to a quadrupling of oil production between 1988 and 2008, to 52,000 barrels a day—which does not, however, cover domestic demand.

The agreements signed between the Cuban and Venezuelan governments at the end of the 1990s provided preferential and economic access to Venezuelan oil, and generated multiple opportunities for cooperation between the state enterprises of both countries. So, in association with PDVSA, the refinery complex at Cienfuegos has been modernized and expanded, to give it a refining capacity of 120,000 barrels per day. Additionally, the government has made intensive efforts to explore offshore oil, in association with Chinese, Brazilian, Spanish, Norwegian, and Venezuelan companies among others. Up to the present there have been no discoveries of commercial significance.

Guatemala produces a moderate amount of oil, insufficient for domestic demand. However, faced with the lack of sufficient refining capacity, the country exports most of its production, which has also been declining. As a result, Guatemala's commercial petroleum balance is negative. The presence of foreign firms is limited, and concentrated in downstream activities.

In Nicaragua, PETRONIC has operated since 1979 in the exploration, exploitation, and marketing of hydrocarbons. However, its activities were reduced during the 1990s as almost all its assets were privatized. This situation has been reversed in recent years, and PETRONIC has been modernized with a particular emphasis on the marketing of fuels, thanks to its collaboration with PDVSA. In 2007 ALBANISA, a mixed enterprise with participation from PDVSA (Caribbean) and PETRONIC, was formed to administer the supply of Venezuelan petroleum to Nicaragua.

In the Dominican Republic, the state acquired all of Shell's shares in the Dominican Petroleum Refinery (Refinería Dominicana de Petróleo, REFIDOMSA) in 2008. However, the private sector, through AES, a US firm, has constructed a regasification terminal for liquefied natural gas that supplies the major electricity-generating companies.

It is also important to mention PETROCARIBE, an initiative that supports energy integration and which was launched in 2005 by Venezuela to provide petroleum to sixteen Caribbean countries. By this agreement, signatories have the option of importing Venezuelan oil on credit with preferential credit conditions, and the option to repay the credits with products and services.

PETROCARIBE is also undertaking energy policy work in the region and has signed a dozen supply agreements, has established eight mixed enterprises for oil supply management, and has an ambitious portfolio of energy infrastructure projects, including the expansion of the Kingston (Jamaica) refinery and the construction of new refineries in Leon (Nicaragua), Dominica, and Belize. The global recession of 2008–9 put on hold the implementation of some of these projects.

25.4 STATE AND FOREIGN DIRECT INVESTMENT IN THE HYDROCARBONS SECTOR

25.4.1 The main state-owned and mixed enterprises

According to the magazine *América Economía*, the total sales (domestic and external) of the main private and public petroleum companies amounted to US$424.9 billion in 2007, of which 79% was accounted for by state companies and the remaining 21% by domestic or foreign private companies. It is worth pointing out that a great number of domestic sales by private firms (above all in the case of Brazil) are not in the upstream but only in the downstream.

The total value of accumulated investment in the oil sector in Latin America's most important countries reached US$329.5 billion between 2000 and 2008. State enterprise investment increased to US$282 billion, about 87% of the total, while foreign direct investment (FDI) was US$47.3 billion or 13%. SOE investments grew notably during this period, mostly after 2005 (see Figure 25.4).

The most important SOEs in the region are PETROBRAS, PEMEX, and PDVSA. In the period 2000–4, PEMEX exceeded PETROBRAS investments, but this situation was reversed in 2005–8. For its part, PDVSA continues to occupy third place, doubling its investments in each of these time periods.

ECOPETROL comes in at fourth place and has also doubled its investments. Significantly below is the Chilean state enterprise ENAP, which—without possessing important oil fields in Chile—has carried out important petroleum explorations outside its frontiers and modernized its refineries. Next is PETROECUADOR; it has important oil fields but has not undertaken the necessary investments, due above all to legal and administrative issues. The last state enterprise is PETROPERU, which was partially privatized between 1992 and 1996 (selling its producing fields and most important refinery).

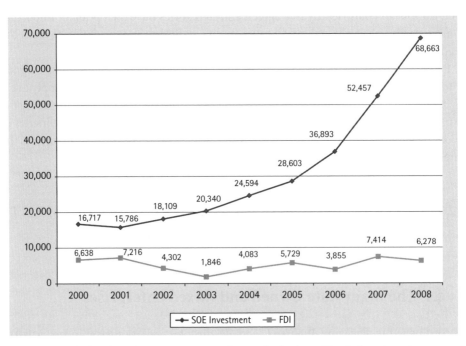

FIGURE 25.4 Latin America: state enterprise and foreign direct investments, 2000–8 ($ million)

Source: Official organizations by country.

Table 25.3 Investment by state-owned and mixed oil enterprises, 2000–8 ($ billion)

	2000	2005–8	Total	Share, (%) 2000–8
PEMEX	43.9	57.7	101.6	36
PETROBRAS	28.0	78.4	106.4	38
PDVSA	18.7	38.7	57.3	20
ECOPETROL	3.3	8.6	11.8	4
ENAP	1.1	1.3	2.4	1
PETROECUADOR	0.5	1.9	2.5	1
PETROPERU	0.1	0.1	0.1	0
Total	95.5	186.6	282.2	100

Source: State enterprises by country.

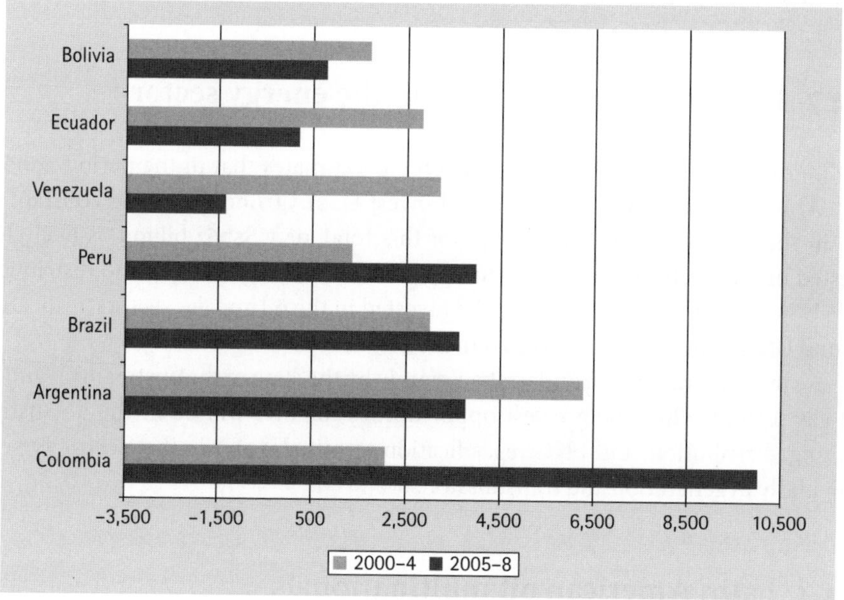

FIGURE 25.5 Latin America and the Caribbean: FDI in the oil sector ($ million)

Source: Official organizations by country.

25.4.2 Foreign direct investment

The value of foreign direct investment (FDI) grew in the hydrocarbons sector by US$47.3 billion in the period 2000–8, and its behavior is more or less stable. Colombia received the greatest portion, with FDI almost quintupling in the period 2005–8, followed by Argentina, where, to the contrary, FDI shrank between the two periods (Figure

25.5). Brazil comes second, with investments of US$3 billion in both periods. While FDI is small, it worth pointing out that there will be an important increase owing to the development of the recently discovered pre-salt oilfields (offshore).

In Ecuador and Bolivia, FDI fell in the period between 2005 and 2008 when compared to 2000–4 owing above all to the contract renegotiation process with foreign companies and the nationalizations of some firms, which led to disinvestment in the sector. The same happened in Venezuela, with an even greater impact, as the FDI balance was strongly negative. In Peru, FDI has grown mainly because of projects linked to the natural gas fields of Camisea, which includes a project to export liquefied natural gas (LNG).

Most FDI comes from US, UK, Spanish, and French companies that have a large presence in the region. Chinese firms are growing in importance and are represented in Peru, Ecuador, Venezuela, and Colombia by SINOPEC (China Petroleum and Chemical Corporation), CNPC (China National Petroleum Corporation), and CNOOC (China National Oil Offshore Corporation). In the first quarter of 2010, CNOOC bought 50% of the Argentine firm Bridas, and SINOPEC has signed an agreement with PETROBRAS that includes partnerships in two oil blocks.

25.4.3 Investment perspectives in the energy sector

The International Energy Agency of the OECD estimates that in the period 2006–30, Latin America and the Caribbean should invest US$1.5 trillion (in 2006 constant dollars) in the energy sector. Around 50% of this total, or US$762 billion, is likely to be invested in the electricity sector (including generation, transmission, and distribution) while US$432 and US$292 billion will be invested in the oil and gas sectors, respectively. Around US$10 billion will be invested in the coal sector.

These investments will be undertaken mainly by the state in the upstream oil and natural gas sectors, while the greatest opportunities for FDI will be in the downstream (refining, distribution, and LNG regasification terminals) and in the electricity sector, particularly in generation and transmission.

25.4.4 Latin American oil multinationals

Oil multinationals with a Latin American origin are mainly state or parastatal companies. As we have seen, this is the result of policies that have attempted in different ways to control and ensure access to a natural resource of great economic and strategic value. This explains why Latin American state-owned multinationals have emerged even in countries like Chile, which has no significant hydrocarbon reserves.

It is notable that the international expansion of Latin American oil multinationals has grown as a response to the extraordinary increases in oil prices from 2006 to 2008, and the growing global struggle for control of energy resources. This growth has been sustained by agreements and strategic alliances with other Latin American multinationals and local firms, both state and private. There is now an extensive regional network of corporate relations in this sector.

The internationalization of Latin American multinationals has also been character-ized by the development of integrated operations, with the parent company building a conglomerate of subsidiaries and affiliates, engaging in activities that range from explo-ration to marketing and related operations, resulting in the vertical integration of the business groups.

The main Latin American multinationals are state owned PETROBRAS, PDVSA, ECOPETROL, and ENAP, while the most important completely private Latin American multinational is PLUSPETROL, from Argentina.

25.5 THE GROWING IMPORTANCE OF NATURAL GAS AND LNG

Until the 1990s the use of natural gas was limited to domestic markets, particularly in Argentina and, to a lesser extent, Colombia, Venezuela, and Bolivia. The most notable changes over the last fifteen years have been associated with the construction of cross-border pipelines between various countries and with the construction of regasification terminals for LNG.

A small cross-border pipeline, via which Argentina supplied gas to Bolivia, was a pio-neering project opened in 1972. But it was not until the mid-1990s that the construction of cross-border pipelines really boomed. Here, the discovery of important natural gas reserves in Bolivia led to the construction of the Santa Cruz–São Paulo pipeline, 3,500 km in length, in which both state and private enterprises participated. From 1995 to 2000, four pipelines where built across the Andes to export gas from Argentina to Chile. At the end of the 1990s and above all at the beginning of the millennium, Bolivia began to export gas to Argentina. With this, the capacity of pipelines to transport natural gas in South America expanded, to reach 18–22 million m^3 per year (Table 25.4).

By mid-2004, the Argentine government announced that, owing to a decline in natu-ral gas reserves, it was no longer possible both to supply the domestic market and to meet its export obligations to Chile, which were therefore restricted. In 2005, the gov-ernments of Venezuela, Brazil, and Argentina began discussions about the construction of the Southern Gas Pipeline (*Gasoducto del Sur*), around 12,000 km, to export Venezuelan gas. More recently, the suggestion has been raised of an "energy ring" con-necting Peruvian gas from Camisea with the gas pipeline networks of Argentina, Chile, and Uruguay. There was also a proposal for a gas pipeline between Colombia and Venezuela as part of the Project for Mesoamerican Integration, which planned to build a gas pipeline between Mexico and Colombia, through Central America. Today it appears that only the pipeline between Colombia and Venezuela has been built. Various factors explain this situation. One is the geopolitical problem which impedes the export of

Table 25.4 Latin America: export capacity by gas pipeline, 2008 (billion m³)

Exporter importer	Brazil	Argentina	Chile	Venezuela	Total
Bolivia	8–11	1.5–2.5			9.5–13.5
Argentina			7.3		7.3
Colombia				1.56	1.56
Total	**8–11**	**1.5–2.5**	**7.3**	**1.56**	**18.3–22.3**

Source: Official organizations by country.

Bolivian gas to Chile. Another is the scarce gas reserves in Argentina and Peru. Finally, the Southern Gas Pipeline was discarded because of its high cost.

Even before these issues arose, countries had begun to look for alternatives, such as LNG. The main characteristic of this process is that natural gas is liquefied at origin, transported in an LNG carrier, and, upon arrival at its destination port, undergoes a process of regasification, which returns it to its original state.

Globally, the LNG market has demonstrated important growth rates in the last few years, overtaking the growth of export by gas pipeline. While transport costs by pipeline are less than by LNG carrier, trade in LNG has been increasing, not least because it allows links between isolated markets that cannot be connected by gas pipelines. Moreover, in recent years, both the cost of liquefaction and transport has fallen. In addition, the fact that the emission of greenhouse gases is lower from natural gas than from oil has been influential. Latin American imports of LNG have been given a strong momentum: in only a few years, regasification plants, in some cases along with regasification vessels, have been installed in different countries. Importing countries are Argentina, Brazil, Chile, the Dominican Republic, and Mexico.

In 2009 and at the beginning of 2010, two regasification plants were inaugurated in Chile: Quintero (with the participation of the state company ENAP) and Mejillones, (50% owned by CODELCO, the state mining company). In Mexico, apart from the existing plants in the Costa Azul and Altamira, two others will be in operation: a plant in Manzanillo (5.2 billion m³ supplied by Peruvian gas) and Puerto Libertad (10.4 billion m³). There are various additional regasification plants in different stages of progress, such as the one in Uruguay (2.2–3.6 billion m³ annually).

With an import capacity of 45.2 billion m³ of LNG in the region, the capacity of the interconnecting gas pipelines has duplicated among countries.

Trinidad and Tobago was the biggest producer and exporter of LNG in 2008, with exports of 17.3 billion m³. In 2010 Peru became an exporter of LNG, with an annual volume of 6.3 billion m³. Venezuela has plans to export LNG with the development of the Deltana Platform (4.2 billion m³), Mariscal Sucre (4.2 billion m³), and Blanquilla-Tortuga (capacity not yet known). These plans will be implemented on the basis of the successful exploration work carried out by different oil companies.

Table 25.5 Regasification terminal capacity (billion m³)

Argentina	3.00
Dominican Republic	2.32
Mexico	18.10
Brazil (Ceará)	2.19
Brazil (Rio)	5.11
Chile (Quintero) 2009	7.30
Chile (Mejillones) 2010	2.00
Mexico (Manzanillo) 2010	5.20
Total	**45.22**

Source: International Group of Liquefied Natural Gas Importers (2009) and official organizations.

25.6 RENEWABLE ENERGY AND BIOFUELS

Renewable energy is an alternative source to fossil fuels both in the world and the region and represents, on average, 25.7% of total primary energy supply (see Figure 25.1). Solar, wind, geothermal, and tidal power, hydropower, and biofuels make up renewable energy; biomass is also a part of renewables and consists of wood, agricultural and livestock residues. Of all renewable energies, apart from biomass, the most important are hydraulic energy and biofuels, even though these are in their initial development stage (see below).

In the 1970s, the proportion of hydroelectric energy passed from 4% to around 9% in the 1990s and up to a maximum of 11.5% by 2000. From then on its participation fell consistently, stabilizing at around 9%. This can be explained by structural reforms, in particular privatizations and the reduction in public investment in infrastructure in general and energy.

Investments in energy infrastructure (public and private but especially the former) fell from 1.95% of GDP in the period 1980–5 to 0.71 in 1996–2001, and to 0.47% in 2002–6 (Rozas, Guerra-García, and Bonifaz 2008). In addition, the investment dynamics of the electricity sector favored the development of power stations (largely natural gas) at the expense of hydropower plants (Altomonte et al. 2008).

However, there are possibilities of increasing the hydropower potential in LAC, estimated to be 728,591 MW, or approximately 22% of the global potential. However, the exploitation of these resources is still very limited, and by the end of the 21st century will reach only 15% of its present potential.

The proportion of solar, wind, geothermal, and tidal energy is quite small. Nevertheless, governments in the region have taken note of their importance as an alternative to fossil fuels, enacting laws and adopting different types of incentive to promote them.

An ECLAC study has analyzed the policies adopted by countries to promote renewable energy (excluding biofuels), and reached the conclusion that all the laws or body of norms used in countries in the region were adopted after 2002, i.e. at the historic point when the oil price started to experience a sharp upward trend to more than US$50 a barrel after a relative period of equilibrium (Altomonte et al. 2008).

One of the obstacles to the sustained development of these renewable energy resources is that whatever the increase in the price of hydrocarbons, these alternative forms of energy production continue to cost more than conventional energy. Indeed, the cost of electricity generated by most renewable energy sources continues to be greater than the wholesale cost of electricity produced from fossil fuels and hydropower.

From this it is possible to calculate, according to ECLAC, a series of relevant indicators about solar, wind, and geothermal energy. Small hydroelectric plants and biomass are now competitive in terms of costs with fossil fuel and large hydro plants in the energy wholesale market (large clients and networks, i.e. those that manage large electricity volumes). Wind and geothermal energy do not appear to be fully competitive, although it is possible that their technological "learning curve"—added to the continuing high oil prices—could allow them to reach this threshold over the medium or the short term. Solar energies (solar thermal and photovoltaic) are still far from competitive in the major energy markets.

However, it is interesting to note that, photovoltaic cells aside, all of these renewable energies could begin to compete on a cost/price basis if sold directly to the final client (e.g. in isolated rural electricity markets or small markets with regulated clients). All this confirms that governmental economic promotion remains the key element in allowing these types of source to flourish.

The most important development in this field is that of biofuels, which in recent years has begun to grow as an alternative energy source in the region, both as a domestic substitute for oil derivatives and as an alternative export to industrial country markets, primarily the US.

In 2008, the global production of biofuels reached volumes of 83 billion liters, four times the volume produced in 2000. The output is made up of 68 billion liters of ethanol and 15 billion liters of biodiesel. This quantity is about 1.5% of overall transport consumption. OECD's International Energy Agency projects a steady increase in demand in the coming years.

The US and Brazil are the main producers of ethanol, with around 90% of production in 2008, with Brazil representing 40%. Brazil produces its ethanol from sugarcane, while the US uses corn. It is worth noting that Colombia is also an important producer of sugarcane-based ethanol. The US and Brazil are also the main producers of biodiesel (Brazil with 10% of world production) made from vegetable oils (soybeans, palm oil, rapeseed) and animal grease. However, the combined European production is around 40% of world production. Argentina, Thailand, and Colombia are also important biodiesel producers. Although the US and the member countries of the European Union (EU) are major producers of ethanol and biodiesel, they are also net importers of both. This reached 600 million liters for both products to the EU, and is increasing.

One of the problems that face biofuels is that, in order to compete with fossil fuels, it requires government subsidies over normal price ranges. According to the International Monetary Fund (IMF), when the oil price is at US$80 per barrel, a gallon of gasoline in the United States costs 34 US cents. At this price, only Brazilian sugarcane-based ethanol is cheaper; all the other crops used to make ethanol cost more. On the other hand, no type of biodiesel can compete with oil at that price, independently of the raw material used—palm oil, soybeans, or rapeseed (IMF 2008).

The growing global awareness of the importance of reducing emissions of greenhouse gases from fossil fuels, together with the problems associated with the difficulties ensuring the supply of oil and derivatives, and the substantial rise in fuel prices in recent years, has led the US and the EU to adopt programs to promote the cultivation of biofuels products. These policies are also being applied in Latin America and the Caribbean, with producer incentives for biofuel production, both for the domestic market and for exports to industrial countries. These programs in the region face opportunities, challenges, and risks. One of the most serious issues is the criticism that lands are being used to produce, not food, but alternative energy resources.

Recent studies have estimated the potential hectares that could be used for biofuels. The countries with the greatest potential are Brazil, Argentina, Colombia, Peru, and Mexico, while Central America and the Caribbean (along with Chile) have the least potential. Cuba and Nicaragua are in an intermediate situation (Abreu 2008).

The development of biofuel production should be set within a national policy framework so that it can be considered simultaneously with economic growth, protection of natural capital, and social equity. These policies should not be adopted without careful and consistent prior examination of the impacts on development; on agriculture and the use of soils; on social development, particularly their effect on poverty reduction; and on the price of food. The introduction of biofuels should also encourage the sustainable diversification of energy consumption. It is recommended that the ministry of energy and mines becomes the competent central authority that monitors the joint intersectoral public policies involved.

Public biofuels policies should not neglect national objectives, which are a matter of promoting not only product specialization and agribusiness, but also greater energy access for the population and protection of natural capital. It follows that each country must define its own agenda, using the demand from developed countries to resolve its own issues and in doing so provide new opportunities for sustainable development. A number of countries in the region have already established a series of legal provisions to regulate mandatory biofuel blends in their domestic markets. These include Argentina, Brazil (a pioneer country, whose use of ethanol began more than twenty years ago), Colombia, Paraguay, Peru, and Uruguay (Table 25.6). In Bolivia, this policy mixture has been delayed by the present government, which is opposed to its use. Several governments in the region have established standards for the local biofuels market, and have promulgated legislation with a bias towards the development of this resource.

Table 25.6 Latin America: biofuel mix for gasoline and diesel

Country	Ethanol	Biodiesel
Argentina	E 5	B 5
Bolivia		B2.5 to B20 in 2015
Brazil	B5	E20
Colombia	E10	B5
Paraguay	E24	B1
Peru	E7.8	B5
Uruguay	E5 (from 2014)	B2 from 2011; B5 from 2012

Source: Altomonte et al. (2008).

The US imposes an import tax of 2.5% on ethanol, plus a surcharge of 54 cents a gallon with the objective of encouraging its national production (the US subsidizes production with internal transfers to farmers worth about 45 cents per gallon).

However, countries of Central America and the Caribbean, such as El Salvador, Jamaica, and Costa Rica (Caribbean Basin Initiative members), can access the US market without paying tariffs. These countries import ethanol from Brazil, which is dried and then re-exported to the US. It is a way in which Brazilian exports, which are almost half the global total, have access to the American market, the largest in the world (Furtado 2009). The other countries in the region that do not enjoy the benefits of the CBI have to pay the tariff and surcharge to enter the US market.

25.7 THE OUTLOOK FOR REGIONAL ENERGY INTEGRATION

Energy integration has always been among the objectives of the governments of the region. The most advanced projects are the bi-national hydroelectric plants of Salto Grande (Argentina–Uruguay), Yacyretá (Argentina–Paraguay), and one of the world's largest hydroelectric dams, Itaipu (Brazil–Paraguay). In the early 1970s the Andean Group proposed the integration of electrical grids, but there has been no further progress.

In the 1990s, in line with market reforms, energy integration took on a new urgency but with a new focus (liberalization, market deregulation, and private initiative) and a broader, continental scope, which included the United States and Canada (Ruiz Caro 2010).

This led to the Hemispheric Energy Initiative, launched in 1994 at the Summit of the Americas in Miami. The idea was simple enough: on the one hand Latin American countries have enormous hydrocarbon reserves but lack the investment to develop them; on the other, the US has to import hydrocarbons from "insecure" sources such as

Arab countries to satisfy consumption, a good reason to finance the expansion of Latin American production.

The vehicle to achieve this goal was the Free Trade Area of the Americas (FTAA), launched by the said Summit. Part of its agenda included measures to encourage deregulation, the privatization of state companies, and the free circulation of energy services.

As we have seen, however, privatization did not conquer the oil sector in the most important countries, which remained dominated by SOEs. For them, the Hemispheric Energy Initiative began to lose interest, and after 2001 the annual meetings of Ministers of Energy did not take place. In contrast, at the meeting of the South American Community of Nations in 2005, energy integration became a central objective, which was ratified in later meetings. Beyond the declarations, however, there are different criteria in terms of what should be done. The most ambitious proposal is that of Venezuela, which involves setting up PetroAmerica, a union of all SOEs. However, this initiative has not prospered.

It is also important to realize that one of the key actors promoting regional energy integration is Brazil, both for its volume of production and, above all, for its energy needs. As Brazil has not only achieved oil self-sufficiency but also has the possibility of becoming an oil and gas exporter following the discovery of the pre-salt layer, many of the decisions about energy integration must take this new reality into account. Brazil's priorities for energy integration could change (reduction of gas imports from Bolivia in the future; cancellation of the Southern Gas Pipeline), with an emphasis on the development of the biofuels market, mainly ethanol; and, at the South American level, by providing technology and machinery to encourage the development of energy integration and the possibility of exporting to the US.

LNG imports are another factor; these have replaced regional integration via gas pipelines, by opting for supply security (LNG can come from any country). Trinidad and Tobago is the only country in Latin America and Caribbean that exports LNG, although it will be joined by Peru this year when it exports gas from Camisea.

A number of initiatives that promote electrical integration are also in progress. In 2011 the System of Electricity Interconnections (*Sistema Interconectado de Electricidad*, SIEPAC) will be concluded, connecting all Central American countries. There have been negotiations between Brazil and Peru to sign a Peru–Brazil Energy Integration Treaty, which includes the construction of several hydroelectric plants in the Peruvian jungle.

In terms of outlook, regional energy integration still lacks regulatory frameworks, harmonization of price policy, and clear agreements between private and public, via public/private associations.

25.8 Conclusions: a balance of the energy sector

Latin America and the Caribbean continue to be a region with abundant energy resources, allowing a trade surplus in hydrocarbons. However, this surplus hides profound differences in the allocation of resources between countries. The greatest surpluses are those of Mexico, Venezuela, Brazil, Colombia, Ecuador, Argentina, and Bolivia, while the countries of Central America and the Caribbean have deficits, with the exception of Trinidad and Tobago, as do Paraguay, Uruguay, and Chile.

In the last twenty years Latin America and the Caribbean have gone through two reforms in the energy sector. The first, at the beginning of the 1990s, was characterized by liberalization and deregulation of markets and an emphasis on the modernization of SOEs in the oil sector. In contrast to the other sectors, the majority of the countries did not privatize these enterprises, with Argentina, Bolivia, and Peru as the exceptions.

At the beginning of the new millennium, which coincided with the increase of the international price of oil, various countries in the region took different measures to capture a greater proportion of petroleum profits, including renationalizations and changes to oil contracts (increased royalties and taxes). Other countries modernized their SOEs, created new agencies for oil contracts, and increased their investments. The value of such investment in hydrocarbons surpassed FDI, although the latter increased in some countries, especially Colombia. The United States continues to be the major market for producing countries.

Natural gas consumption has grown strongly in recent years in various countries in the region. In addition to Argentina, the pioneer, Colombia, Bolivia, and Peru now produce large quantities for the domestic market. Bolivia exports important quantities of natural gas to Brazil and Argentina (via gas pipeline), while five cross-Andean gas pipelines between Argentina and Chile were built at the end of the 1990s and the beginning of the millennium. Most recently, Colombia began to export small quantities of gas to Venezuela.

However, it is the imports of LNG that have experienced the fastest growth in the last decade, with regasification terminals installed in Mexico, Argentina, Brazil, Chile, and the Dominican Republic to meet domestic demand, and a proposed new terminal in Uruguay. LNG imports are attractive, as they provide reliable supply, in light of issues between Argentina and Chile (due to lack of reserves) and between Bolivia and Brazil (with respect to the export price). Trinidad and Tobago is the only LNG exporter, to be joined in 2010 by Peru.

In the field of renewable energy there has been little progress on the construction of hydroelectric plants, although the region has tremendous potential. Neither has there been much progress in production from other sources, such as wind and solar, while nuclear energy has remained stagnant (in Argentina and Brazil).

Biofuels (ethanol and biodiesel) have grown in the renewable energy area and are important in Brazil, followed by Colombia and Argentina. A significant number of countries have adopted laws to promote their domestic consumption and exports, while members of the Caribbean Basin Initiative export biofuels to the US originating in Brazil. Biofuel production has generated much debate, owing to the greater use of agricultural land for this purpose. A more comprehensive and integrated management of this resource is thus required.

As concerns energy integration, the countries in the region have passed through two distinct phases. The first was the initiative of a hemispheric energy integration focused on market liberalization with a continental dimension. This policy was influential until the beginning of the new millennium. The second, since the end of the 1990s, is more closely allied to the states in the framework of the South American Community of Nations. However, it lacks objectives and clear instruments by which to advance toward energy integration.

Finally, it should be noted that the region is involved in activities to combat global warming caused by greenhouse gases from fossil fuels (discussed by de Miguel and Sunkel in Chapter 6 in this Handbook). The major tasks are to prevent growing deforestation and to increase energy efficiency (the amount of energy consumed per unit of product). In both cases, regional progress has been meager.

REFERENCES

ABREU, F. (2008). *Biocombustibles y alimentos en América Latina y el Caribe*, Costa Rica: Instituto Interamericano de Cooperación para la Agricultura (IICA).

ALTOMONTE, H. et al. (2008). *América latina y el Caribe frente a la coyuntura energética internacional: oportunidades para una nueva agenda de políticas*, Santiago, Chile: ECLAC.

América Economía (2008). 'Las primeras 500 empresas de América Latina', available online at: http://www.americaeconomia.com

British Petroleum (2009). 'Statistical Review of World Energy', available online at: http://www.bp.com

CAMPODÓNICO, H. (2007a). 'La gestión de la industria de hidrocarburos con predominio de empresas del Estado', Natural Resources and Infrastructure Division Paper No. 121, ECLAC, Santiago, Chile.

—— (2007b). *Gestión mixta y privada en la industria de hidrocarburos*, Natural Resources and Infrastructure Division Paper No. 122, ECLAC, Santiago, Chile.

Comunidad Andina de Naciones (2008). *El cambio climático no tiene fronteras: impacto del cambio climático en la comunidad andina*, Lima.

ECLAC (UN Economic Commission for Latin America and the Caribbean) (2009). *Cambio climático y desarrollo en América Latina y el Caribe 2009*, ed. J. L. Samaniego, Santiago, Chile.

—— (several years). *Foreign Investment in Latin America and the Caribbean*, Santiago, Chile.

FURTADO, A. (2009). *Biocombustibles y comercio internacional: una perspectiva latinoamericana*, Santiago, Chile: ECLAC and GTZ.

Gas Energy Latin America (2009). 'Mercado mundial de GNL y reintegración LatinoAmericana', available online at: http://www.gasenergy.com.br

IMF (International Monetary Fund) (2008). *World Economic Outlook 2007, Trends 2008*, Washington, DC.

International Group of Liquefied Natural Gas Importers (2009). 'The LNG Industry 2008', available online at: http://www.giignl.org

OECD (Organisation for Economic Co-operation and Development) (2008). *World Energy Outlook 2007*, Paris: IEA.

OLADE (Organización Latinoamericana de Energía) (2008). *Informe de estadísticas energéticas 2007*, Quito.

OLADE (Organización Latinoamericana de Energía)–SIEE (Sistema de Información Económica-Energética/Energy-Economic Information System) (several years). *Sistema de información económica-energética*, Quito.

Renewable Energy Policy Network for the 21st Century (2009). 'Renewables Global Status Report 2009 Update', available online at http://www.ren21.net

ROZAS, P., GUERRA-GARCÍA, G., and BONIFAZ, J. L. (2008). 'El financiamiento de la infraestructura, opciones públicas y privadas', Santiago, Chile: ECLAC/MOP.

RUIZ CARO, A. (2010). 'Puntos de conflicto de la cooperación e integración energética en América Latina y el Caribe', Natural Resources and Infrastructure Division Paper No. 148, ECLAC, Santiago, Chile.

SÁNCHEZ ALBAVERA, F. (2007). 'Panorama de las energías sostenibles en América Latina y el Caribe', Natural Resources and Infrastructure Division, ECLAC, Santiago, Chile.

CHAPTER 26

....

INFRASTRUCTURE IN LATIN AMERICA

....

CÉSAR CALDERÓN AND LUIS SERVÉN

26.1 INTRODUCTION[1]

An adequate supply of infrastructure services has long been viewed as a key ingredient for economic development, by both academic economists and policymakers. Indeed, transport infrastructure played a central role in Adam Smith's vision of economic development. Over the last two decades, starting with the work of Aschauer (1989), academic research has devoted considerable effort to theoretical and empirical analyses of the contribution of infrastructure development to growth and productivity (see e.g. Sánchez-Robles 1998; Canning 1999; Demetriades and Mamuneas 2000; Röller and Waverman 2001; Esfahani and Ramirez 2003; Calderón and Servén 2004b; 2010a). More recently, increasing attention has been paid also to the impact of infrastructure on poverty and inequality (Estache, Foster, and Wodon 2002; Calderón and Chong 2004). While the empirical literature on these two topics is far from unanimous, on the whole a consensus has emerged that, under the right conditions, infrastructure development can play a major role in promoting growth and equity—and, through both channels, helping reduce poverty.

From the policy perspective, the renewed concern with infrastructure can be traced to two worldwide developments that took place over the last two decades. The first one was the retrenchment of the public sector since the mid-1980s, in most industrial and developing countries, from its dominant position in the provision of infrastructure, under the increasing pressures of fiscal adjustment and consolidation. The second was the opening up of infrastructure industries to private participation, part of a worldwide

[1] We thank José Antonio Ocampo and Jaime Ros for comments on an earlier draft, and Rei Odawara and Junko Sekine for able research assistance. The views expressed here are only ours and do not necessarily reflect those of the World Bank, its Executive Directors, or the countries they represent.

drive towards increasing reliance on markets and private sector activity, which has been reflected in widespread privatization of public utilities and multiplication of concessions and other forms of public–private partnership. While this process first gained momentum in industrial countries (notably the UK), over the 1990s it extended to most developing economies, with Latin America leading other developing regions in terms of both speed and scope of private involvement in infrastructure industries.

Against this background, there is a growing perception that poor infrastructure has become one of the key barriers to growth and development across Latin America. Such perception is found among policymakers as well as in surveys of infrastructure users in the region. The underlying concern is that private sector participation has not offset the decline in public infrastructure spending under the pressures of fiscal consolidation, thus resulting in an inadequate provision of infrastructure services, with potentially major adverse effects on growth and welfare. As a result, infrastructure has become a priority theme in Latin America's policy debate (see e.g. Fay and Morrison 2005; Corporación Andina de Fomento 2009).

This chapter revisits the theme of infrastructure development in Latin America from a macroeconomic standpoint. The focus is threefold. First, the chapter documents, in a comparative cross-regional perspective, the trends in Latin America's infrastructure development, as reflected in the quantity and quality of infrastructure services and the universality of their access. Overall, there is evidence that an "infrastructure gap" vis-à-vis other industrial and developing regions opened up in the 1980s and 1990s. Second, drawing from recent research, the chapter provides an empirical assessment of the contribution of infrastructure development to growth across Latin America, as well a quantitative illustration of the growth cost of the region's infrastructure gap. Third, we examine the changing roles of the public and private sector in Latin America's infrastructure, presenting updated information on the trends in the financing of infrastructure investment, and analyzing how they have been shaped by macroeconomic policy constraints. Finally, the chapter summarizes the lights and shadows from two decades of private sector participation in Latin America's infrastructure development.

26.2 Infrastructure trends in Latin America and the Caribbean

We begin by offering a comparative overview of the trends in availability, quality, and accessibility of infrastructure across Latin America and other world regions over the last 25 years. We work with a large sample of countries, but exclude very small economies (those with population smaller than 1 million in 2005) for which infrastructure may pose some special issues (such as indivisibilities). In the case of Latin America and the Caribbean (LAC), this leads to the exclusion of small-island economies and leaves us with 21 countries. However, some portions of our analysis may be restricted to a narrower set of countries as determined by data availability.

For the most part, our discussion focuses on three core infrastructure sectors: telecommunications, power, and land transportation, although we also review trends on access to water and sanitation. We compare their evolution in the Latin American region with that of two comparator groups: (i) the middle and high-income countries of East Asia (which we call EAP non-LICs) and (ii) the group of middle-income countries excluding LAC countries (non-LAC MICs). The first group comprises the seven "East Asian miracle" nations (Hong Kong, Indonesia, Korea, Malaysia, Singapore, Taiwan, and Thailand) and some of the region's fast-growing countries such as China, Cambodia, the Philippines, and Vietnam. The second group—after dealing with issues of data availability—includes a total of 70 countries.[2] Furthermore, we assess the progress of infrastructure development in these developing areas vis-à-vis 21 OECD economies.[3] Finally, for reasons of space we focus mostly on region-wide performance, but we should point out that there is great deal of heterogeneity in infrastructure development (availability, quality, and accessibility) across countries in each region.

26.2.1 Infrastructure quantity

The first three columns of Table 26.1 summarize the trends in the availability of telecommunications, electric power, and roads over the last quarter-century for the various comparator groups considered, as well as for the Latin America and the Caribbean region and its four subregions defined as (i) Central America: Costa Rica, Guatemala, Honduras, Mexico, Nicaragua, Panama, and El Salvador; (ii) the Caribbean: Bahamas, the Dominican Republic, Jamaica, and Trinidad and Tobago; (iii) the Andean countries: Bolivia, Colombia, Ecuador, Peru, and Venezuela; and (iv) the Southern Cone: Argentina, Brazil, Chile, Paraguay, and Uruguay. For each country group, the table reports the median of the country averages over the periods 1981–5, 1991–5, and 2001–5. The table also shows separately the trends in each of the seven major LAC countries (Argentina, Brazil, Chile, Colombia, Mexico, Peru, and Venezuela).

Telecommunications. Telephone density—as measured by the total number of phone lines (fixed and mobile) per 1000 workers—has risen sharply in all regions after 1990, due to the impressive growth in the number of mobile phones. The LAC region has consistently lagged behind other regions in terms of telephone density, but the gap has changed over time. In 1981–5, LAC trailed non-LAC MICs by a relatively small margin, whereas in EAP non-LICs, telephone density was three times as high as in LAC. By 2001–5, LAC had gained some ground relative to non-LAC MICs, but relative to EAP non-LICs the gap remained at levels similar to those of 1981–5—it widened during the

---

[2] We use middle-income economies rather than all developing countries because most Latin American countries belong to the former category.

[3] OECD is defined here excluding Korea and Mexico.

Table 26.1 Infrastructure quantity and quality: LAC vis-à-vis other regions (5-year period averages)

Region	Period	Infrastructure quantity			Infrastructure quality		
		Telecom	Electric power	Total roads	Telecom	Electric power	Total roads
Industrial countries	1981–5	774	2.83	0.992	0.998	0.929	0.811
	1991–5	1,095	3.48	1.031	1.000	0.938	0.915
	2001–5	2,778	3.96	1.363	1.000	0.936	0.919
East Asia	1981–5	298	0.71	0.528	0.912	0.917	0.831
	1991–5	796	1.14	0.602	1.000	0.919	0.870
	2001–5	2,437	2.36	0.961	1.000	0.943	0.958
Middle-income countries	1981–5	121	0.73	0.123	0.208	0.894	0.309
	1991–5	228	0.99	0.160	0.287	0.887	0.494
	2001–5	872	1.27	0.179	0.675	0.885	0.481
Latin America (LAC)	1981–5	93	0.56	0.118	0.293	0.881	0.145
	1991–5	186	0.77	0.136	0.329	0.865	0.183
	2001–5	758	1.02	0.144	0.821	0.856	0.234
Central America	1981–5	49	0.36	0.146	0.304	0.876	0.140
	1991–5	94	0.37	0.136	0.212	0.872	0.183
	2001–5	729	0.47	0.157	0.719	0.828	0.286
Caribbean	1981–5	61	0.56	0.602	0.168	0.791	0.300
	1991–5	186	0.65	0.763	0.379	0.837	0.585
	2001–5	972	1.25	0.833	0.570	0.836	0.608
Andean countries	1981–5	93	0.55	0.071	0.222	0.883	0.108
	1991–5	143	0.50	0.096	0.329	0.839	0.119
	2001–5	610	0.61	0.101	0.700	0.832	0.152
Southern Cone	1981–5	122	0.85	0.076	0.451	0.891	0.111
	1991–5	280	1.28	0.078	0.567	0.868	0.152
	2001–5	933	1.47	0.081	0.854	0.865	0.205

Selected LAC countries

Country	Period						
Argentina	1981–5	225	1.34	0.076	0.223	0.881	0.262
	1991–5	309	1.28	0.078	0.567	0.840	0.284
	2001–5	964	1.47	0.081	0.838	0.865	0.279
Brazil	1981–5	122	0.75	0.169	0.451	0.899	0.071
	1991–5	167	0.78	0.206	0.517	0.865	0.083
	2001–5	933	0.93	0.221	0.854	0.856	0.111
Chile	1981–5	110	0.85	0.109	0.283	0.885	0.111
	1991–5	280	1.00	0.105	0.524	0.901	0.152
	2001–5	1,656	1.69	0.106	0.883	0.941	0.205
Colombia	1981–5	134	0.55	0.086	0.314	0.864	0.102
	1991–5	207	0.65	0.096	0.339	0.825	0.119
	2001–5	657	0.64	0.101	0.467	0.832	0.152
Mexico	1981–5	144	0.83	0.111	0.051	0.894	0.327
	1991–5	240	0.90	0.136	0.284	0.881	0.338
	2001–5	1,075	1.04	0.176	0.569	0.871	0.335
Peru	1981–5	56	0.53	0.051	0.222	0.902	0.108
	1991–5	81	0.46	0.055	0.329	0.854	0.109
	2001–5	370	0.48	0.061	0.578	0.906	0.137
Venezuela	1981–5	180	2.02	0.071	0.203	0.883	0.368
	1991–5	278	2.39	0.101	0.136	0.839	0.344
	2001–5	864	1.81	0.105	0.174	0.799	0.336

Notes: The table reports the 5-year period averages of the different indicators of the quantity and quality of infrastructure. The quality indicators are: the number of telephone main lines and mobile phones per 1,000 workers, electricity generating capacity (in megawatts per 1,000 workers), and the length of the road network (in km. per sq. km. of surface area). The quality indicators are the waiting time for main telephone line installation, the share of transmission and distribution losses in electric energy production, and the share of paved roads in total roads. All these variables are normalized such that higher values indicate higher quality of services. The data is obtained from the International Telecommunications Union, the US Department of Energy's International Energy Annual, International Road Federation, and the World Bank's World Development Indicators.

Source: Data from International Telecommunications Union, US Department of Energy, International Road Federation, and World Bank.

1980s and then narrowed in the 1990s. Finally, the gap between the LAC region and industrial economies has narrowed over time: the ratio of industrial country telephone density to that of LAC has more than halved: it has declined from almost 8 in 1981–5 to 3.6 in 2001–5. Across LAC subregions, Central America has consistently shown the lowest telephone density over the last 25 years, while the Andean countries had the highest until they were overtaken by the Caribbean subregion in 2001–5.

Power. Electricity generation capacity (in megawatts per 1,000 workers) is our approximate measure of the availability of electric power. As with telecommunications, in this dimension the LAC region has fallen behind not only East Asia but also the rest of the middle-income countries. By 2001–5 the region had slightly reduced the gap vis-à-vis non-LAC MICs; however, it fell further behind EAP non-LICs. Across LAC subregions, Central America and the Andean countries have lagged consistently behind the regional average—in fact, they practically made no progress at all during the 1980s—while the Southern Cone countries have been ahead of the other subregions.

Land Transportation. Trends in the land transport network are captured by road density, measured by the total length of the road network relative to the country's total area. This is in contrast with our measures of the availability of power and telecommunications, which were normalized by the total labor force. We do this to adjust for the wide disparities in size across the countries in our sample.

Table 26.1 reveals a big gap between industrial and developing regions in terms of road density. Latin America and the non-LAC MICs have fallen further behind rich countries and East Asia since 1990. Moreover, while Latin America was roughly on par with non-LAC MICs in 1981–5, by 2001–5 its road density had barely grown, and as a consequence is now well below that of middle-income countries, and even further below East Asia's. Across subregions, road density is below the LAC-wide norm in the Andean countries and in the Southern Cone. In contrast, road density in the Caribbean is similar to that of East Asia.

26.2.2 Infrastructure quality

Broadly speaking, the quality of infrastructure services can be proxied by two types of information: officially recorded data on quantitative measures of the quality of infrastructure services; and surveys of experts or final users regarding the performance of infrastructure services—typically qualitative in nature.

The availability of officially recorded statistics on infrastructure quality is scarce relative to that on its quantity. This is particularly problematic in the case of telecommunications. Cross-country data on the telecommunications quality indicators that on conceptual grounds should be most informative—such as the frequency of telephone faults and unsuccessful calls—are extremely sparse. Thus, we complement this information showing data on the waiting time for installation of main lines, which in theory is a measure of excess demand, but in practice shows a significant correlation (see Calderón and Servén 2004b) with the theoretically preferable measures just cited, over the reduced sample for which the latter are available. Information on waiting times can be collected for a fairly large sample of country-years.

The situation is better for power and transport. There is fairly abundant data on two widely used (albeit far from perfect) measures of quality—the percentage of power losses and the share of paved in total roads, respectively.

It is worth noting that all these infrastructure quality indicators show a high correlation with their corresponding quantity indicators reviewed above. In a large panel data set, Calderón and Servén (2004b) find sector-wise correlation coefficients (e.g. between power generation capacity and power losses, or between road density and road quality) around 0.5 and significantly different from zero at any reasonable significance level. The implication is that more abundant infrastructure typically comes along with better infrastructure.

In view of the limitations of these indicators of infrastructure quality, increasing effort has been devoted in recent years to the compilation of survey-based assessments of infrastructure performance. Two leading sources of such kind of data are international surveys of business conditions that reflect the views of international experts, and firm-level surveys that capture the perceptions of infrastructure users. At present, however, the time-series dimension is in both cases very limited (virtually nil, in the case of firm surveys), and comparability over time and across countries is sometimes hampered by changes in the relevant survey questions.

26.2.3 Officially recorded statistics of infrastructure quality

Telecommunications. Table 26.1 reports the evolution of an indicator based on the waiting time (in years) for the installation of main telephone lines. This indicator has been rescaled such that it takes values between 0 and 1, with higher values indicating shorter wait times and, in this interpretation, higher quality of telecommunication services.

Along this dimension, LAC's progress over the last two decades was spectacular: the region's median waiting time was reduced from six months in 1981–5 to a few days by 2001–5, well below the norm of non-LAC middle-income countries. In rich countries, waiting time fell to zero in the early 1980s, while in East Asia the same happened by 1991–5 (see Table 26.1). The fast improvement in the reduction of waiting time for main telephone installation extended to all LAC subregions, with Central America and the Southern Cone showing the fastest pace of improvement in the quality of service.

Other quality indicators, whose availability is more limited, tell a similar story. Calderón and Servén (2009) show that telephone faults per 100 main lines declined considerably across Latin America—to a regional median of 5 in 2001–6 from 52 in 1991–6. In addition, not only did the number of phone faults decline, but the percentage of faults cleared next day rose considerably—from 55% in 1991–6 to approximately 87% in 2001–6.

Power. The percentage of transmission and distribution losses relative to total output offers a rough measure of the efficiency of the power sector. However, observed power losses include both "technical" losses, reflective of the quality of the power grid, and pilferage (i.e. power theft), and unfortunately it is virtually impossible to disentangle the relative importance of the two. The quality measure of power reported in Table 26.1 is based on these losses, rescaled to lie between 0 and 1, so that higher values indicate higher quality.

By this measure, the table shows that the quality of electric power services actually deteriorated in Latin America over the 1980s and 1990s. The same happened among middle-income countries. In contrast, quality showed a steady improvement in East Asia and industrial countries, so that Latin America's gap vis-à-vis these high-performing regions has widened over time.

Land transportation. The only quality indicator widely available for this sector is the percentage of paved roads in the total road network. Table 26.1 shows that, by this measure, the LAC region lags the other country groups by a huge margin. By 2001–5, less than a quarter of the road network (25%) was paved in the typical Latin American country, far behind the non-LAC MIC norm (close to 50%), and much further behind East Asia and the industrial-country norm, both close to 100%. Not only was the level of the indicator low in Latin America; it also grew at a very slow pace—from 15% in 1981–5 to 23% in 2001–5. Across LAC subregions, road quality is lowest in the Andean countries and the Southern Cone, and highest in the Caribbean.

26.2.4 Survey measures of infrastructure quality

We next summarize the information available from the surveys of international experts conducted for the World Economic Forum's *World Competitiveness Report*. Rather than quality alone, they tend to capture perceptions on both the quality of infrastructure services and their availability—which is likely to be closely related to the volume of infrastructure stocks. The coverage of these data is more limited than that of the official statistics reviewed so far. The time series dimension is short, so for the most part we show data for 2000 and 2006 only. Country coverage of Latin America, as well as other middle-income countries, is somewhat limited, and hence the regional medians shown below have to be taken with some caution.

Figure 26.1(a) summarizes perceptions regarding the overall quality of infrastructure across world regions, with higher bars denoting higher quality, within a range from 1 to 7. It is clear from the figure that Latin America lags behind East Asia and the group of middle-income countries—as well as industrial countries. Moreover, the gap has, if anything, increased since 2000.

Figure 26.1(b) reports perceptions of the reliability of power. In this case, we report data for 2002 and 2006. The subjective index shows a significant negative correlation with that on the percentage of power losses described earlier. Perceived quality is highest in industrial countries. Among developing regions, only East Asia shows a definite trend towards improving quality. In contrast, perceived quality seems to be on the decline among middle-income countries. Nevertheless, quality perceptions are still lowest in

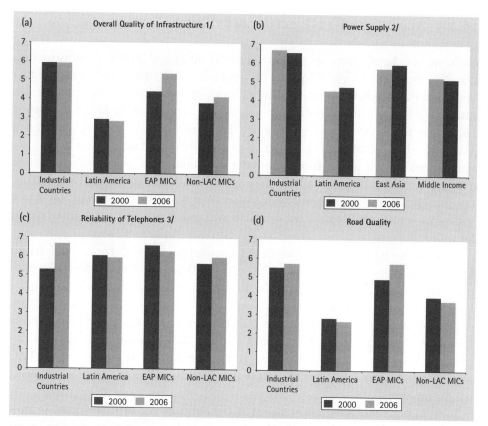

FIGURE 26.1 Survey measures of infrastructure quality

Source: The measures of perception of the quality of infrastructure reported here are surveyed by the World Economic Forum's World Competitiveness Review. It gives marks from 1 (strongly disagree) to 7 (strongly agree) to the following statements: 1. The quality of the infrastructure in your country is among the best in the world. 2. Your country has sufficient power generation capacity. 3. Telephone lines have ample capacity and are highly reliable. 4. Roads are extensive and well maintained.

Latin America. This is in agreement with results found earlier when using power losses as quality proxy: in both cases Latin America does worst among the country groups shown.

Figure 26.1 depicts the perceived reliability of telephones. The regional rankings for 2000 show a counterintuitive pattern, with industrial countries lagging behind all other country groups shown. In 2006, in turn, Latin America was on par with middle-income countries, and behind industrial and East Asian economies, although the differences across groups seem quite marginal.

Finally, Figure 26.1(d) shows the perceived quality of the road network. The cross-country correlation of the subjective index with the objective measure used above—the percentage of roads paved—is large and significantly positive. Unsurprisingly, therefore, the regional perspective is similar in both cases: Latin America lags behind the other country groups. In this case, it is also the only region not showing an improving trend.

26.2.5 Access to infrastructure services

So far we have been concerned with the overall quantity and quality of infrastructure. But from the point of view of equality of opportunity and poverty reduction, another important dimension is the universality of access to infrastructure services—i.e. the extent to which existing infrastructure assets yield services to the broad population rather than just a few. One way to measure this phenomenon is through access rates. Table 26.2 offers a comparative perspective on standard indicators of access to telecommunications, electric power, roads, and water and sanitation. Coverage of information on access rates is limited, especially in the time-series dimension, and therefore we confine ourselves to the cross-country dimension, except in the case of water, for which some time-series information is also available. We present median access rates by region for 2006.[4]

Table 26.2 shows that in Latin American countries typically 47% of households have a fixed telephone—well below the rate of access for EAP non-LICs and industrial economies (52% and 93%, respectively). On the other hand, the cellular network covers more than 90% of the population among industrial countries and East Asia (99% and 91%, respectively) whereas the coverage of mobile phones reaches 85% of the population in the LAC region—a figure similar to that of non-LAC MICs. Finally, there are wide disparities across regions in access to internet services. While East Asia leads the pack, LAC has the lowest access rate—typically less than 10% of the homes have access to internet in LAC countries.

Table 26.2 also shows the percentage of households with access to electricity, an indicator which is only available for developing countries. Latin America's median access rate equals 87%, short of the 90% of other middle-income countries, and far behind the 98% observed in the successful East Asian economies. Across countries in the region, Venezuela, Chile, and Costa Rica exhibit access rates on par with East Asia's. At the other end, less than two-thirds of the population enjoys access to electricity in Bolivia and Honduras.

Access to transport is approximated by the widely used rural access index (RAI), which measures the percentage of the rural population living within a short distance (2 km) of an all-season passable road. Table 26.2 shows that Latin America trails East Asia as well as other middle-income economies along this dimension. Among LAC countries, access to transport is particularly poor in Nicaragua, where it reaches just over one-fourth of the population.

Regarding access to safe water, we report the percentage of population with access to safe water, including treated surface water and untreated but uncontaminated water such as from springs, sanitary wells, and protected boreholes. Latin America ranks below the group of other middle-income countries. At just under 80%, its access rate is still far from the almost universal coverage observed among successful East Asian economies.

---

[4] Due to the lack of information for 2006 in some subgroups of countries, we report the averages of the percentage of people with telephone for the period 2004–6.

Table 26.2 Access to infrastructure (averages for the latest available year)

	Industrial countries	East Asia	Non–LAC MICs	Latin America
Access to fixed telephone[a]	92.5	51.8	50.9	46.6
Coverage of mobile cellular network[a]	99.0	90.9	85.7	84.8
Access to internet[a]	47.2	60.0	14.9	8.6
Rural road access (RAI)[b]	93.7	85.3	76.0	64.3
Access to electricity network[c]	–	98.4	90.2	86.7
Access to improved water sources[d]	100.0	95.0	83.5	79.0
Access to improved sanitation facilities[d]	100.0	98.5	94.5	93.0

Notes: [a] Access to telecommunication services is measures by the percentage of households with fixed telephones, the coverage mobile cellular network (population, in %), and the percentage of homes with internet. The data is obtained from the International Telecommunications Union (ITU) database.
[b] The rural access index (RAI) was constructed by Roberts et al. (2006) and is obtained from household survey results.
[c] The indicator reported is the percentage of households with access to electricity. The data is compiled from household surveys by Cieslikowski (2008), and refers to commercial sales of electricity (excluding unauthorized connections).
[d] We show the percentage of the population with improved water sources and sanitation facilities. Data collected from the World Health Organization and UN Children's Fund, Joint Monitoring Program.

Uruguay is the only Latin American country to have reached universal access. In Bolivia and Nicaragua, less than half of the population enjoys access to safe water.

Finally, regarding access to improved sanitation, Latin America has caught up with the norm of middle-income countries, reaching a median access rate of 93%. Both East Asia's successful economies as well as industrial countries enjoy universal access. In Latin America, a number of countries (notably Ecuador and Paraguay) have shown major progress since 1990, although at present few countries show access rates comparable to those of East Asia.

On the whole, Latin America has made major progress in infrastructure development. The availability, quality, and accessibility of infrastructure services have improved considerably in the last quarter century. Still, the region lags behind other middle-income countries, and even further behind East Asia, in almost all dimensions (quantity, quality, and accessibility of services) and infrastructure sectors (telecommunication, electric power, and roads). While details vary, overall much of the lag developed in the 1980s at the time of the public sector's retrenchment in the midst of macroeconomic instability. In some dimensions (particularly telecommunications), a partial catch-up has taken place since the mid-1990s, so that Latin America's gap vis-à-vis the other country groups has narrowed somewhat, but in most dimensions it remains considerable.

26.3 INFRASTRUCTURE, GROWTH, AND DEVELOPMENT

These trends in the quantity, quality, and accessibility of infrastructure are of interest because, as an extensive theoretical and empirical literature has argued, infrastructure is a key ingredient for growth and development. There is abundant theoretical work on the contribution of infrastructure to output, productivity, and welfare. Much of it is concerned with the effects of public capital expenditure on output and welfare under alternative financing schemes. Arrow and Kurz (1970) were the first to include public capital as an input in the economy's aggregate production function, in the context of a Ramsey model with long-run exogenous growth. Barro (1990), on the other hand, developed the endogenous growth version of this model where it was assumed that the government's productive expenditures drive their contribution to current production. Over the last fifteen years, this analytical literature has grown enormously.[5]

The empirical research, in turn, took off recently. It has boomed over the last fifteen years after the seminal work of Aschauer (1989). Literally hundreds of papers have been devoted to assessing the effects of infrastructure on growth, productivity, poverty, and other development outcomes, using a variety of data and empirical methodologies. Calderón and Servén (2010a) offer a partial account of the literature on the growth and inequality effects of infrastructure; more comprehensive surveys include Estache (2006), Romp and de Haan (2007), and Straub (2007).

The bulk of the empirical literature on the effects of infrastructure has focused on its long-run contribution to the level or growth rate of aggregate income or productivity. It all starts with Aschauer's (1989) finding that the stock of public infrastructure capital is a significant determinant of aggregate TFP in the US. However, his estimate (based on time-series data) of the marginal product of infrastructure capital—as much as 100% per year—was implausibly high.

The massive ensuing literature on the output effects of infrastructure has employed a variety of data, empirical methods, and infrastructure measures. The most popular approaches include the estimation of an aggregate production function (or its dual, the cost function) and empirical growth regressions. Infrastructure is variously measured in terms of physical stocks, spending flows, or capital stocks constructed by accumulating the latter. The majority of this literature finds a positive long-run effect of infrastructure on output, productivity, or their growth rate. This is mostly the case with the studies using physical indicators of infrastructure stocks, but results are more mixed among studies using measures of public capital stocks or infrastructure spending flows (Straub 2007).

Another strand of recent literature has examined the effects of infrastructure on income inequality. The rationale is that infrastructure provision may have a

---

[5] See e.g. Turnovsky (1997), Glomm and Ravikumar (1997), Baier and Glomm (2001), and Ghosh and Roy (2004).

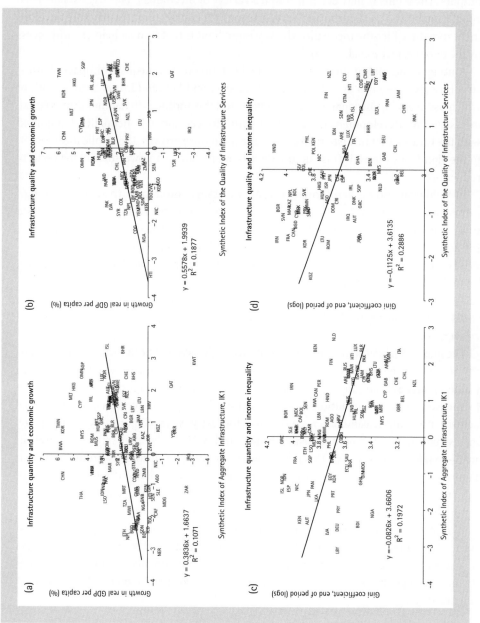

FIGURE 26.2 Infrastructure quantity, quality, growth, and inequality

disproportionate effect on the income and welfare of the poor by raising the value of the assets they hold (such as land or human capital), or by lowering the transaction costs (e.g. transport and logistical costs) they incur to access the markets for their inputs and outputs. These effects may occur through a variety of mechanism (see e.g. Estache et al. 2002; Estache 2003; Calderón and Servén 2010a). Of course, for infrastructure development to reduce income inequality, the key ingredient is that it must help expand access by the poor (Estache et al. 2000).[6]

Among the empirical studies that have tackled directly the inequality impact of infrastructure are those of López (2004) and Calderón and Servén (2010a; 2010b), both of which use cross-country panel data. In both cases, the finding is that, other things equal, infrastructure development is associated with reduced income inequality. Combined with the finding that infrastructure also appears to raise growth, the implication is that, in the right conditions, infrastructure development can be a powerful tool for poverty reduction.

In Calderon and Serven (2010a; 2010b), we assess empirically the contribution of infrastructure to growth by estimating a simple equation that relates growth per capita to a set of standard controls, augmented by measures of the quantity and quality of infrastructure. The set of standard control variables included in the regressions comprises measures of human capital (secondary enrollment, from Barro and Lee 2001), financial depth (from Beck, Demirguc-Kunt, and Levine 2000), trade openness, institutional quality, lack of price stability, government burden, and terms-of-trade shocks—in addition to the lagged level of GDP per worker, to capture conditional convergence.

The main conclusion that emerges from this analysis is that both infrastructure quantity and quality have a positive and strongly significant effect on growth. Drawing from Calderón and Servén (2010b), we can illustrate the economic significance of this effect by measuring the contribution of infrastructure development to growth performance across Latin America and other regions over the last 30 years (Figure 26.3). On average, infrastructure development increased growth in LAC by only 0.32 percentage points in 1986–90 relative to 1976–80. This is the lowest value among all country groups shown in Figure 26.3(a). It comprises growth of 0.51 percentage points due to the accumulation of infrastructure stocks, and a contraction in GDP growth of 0.19 percentage points due to lower quality of infrastructure services. Across comparator regions, the largest contribution of infrastructure development to growth during this period was achieved in East Asia, where it reached 1.93 percentage points per annum. Of this total, enlarged stocks increased growth by 1.32 percentage points per year, while enhanced infrastructure quality raised growth rates by 0.61 percentage points per year in 1986–90 relative to 1976–80 (Figure 26.3(a)).

---

[6] There may be two-way causality in this relationship, i.e. income inequality may prevent the access of poorer people to infrastructure services. For example, Estache, Manacorda, and Valletti (2002) show that income inequality adversely affects access to internet, while Alesina, Baqir, and Easterly (1999) argue that more unequal societies devote less effort to the provision of public goods, including infrastructure.

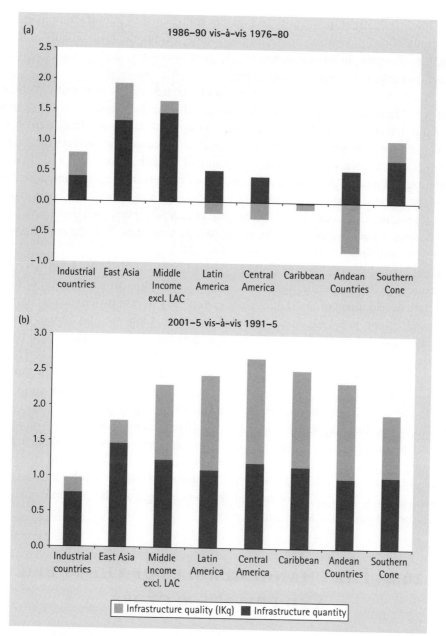

FIGURE 26.3 Growth changes across regions due to infrastructure development (change in average per capita growth)

Across LAC subregions, the Southern Cone achieved the largest contribution of infrastructure development to growth, with 1.03 percentage points per annum—of which 0.7 and 0.32 percentage points were respectively due to larger stocks and higher quality of infrastructure services. At the other end, infrastructure made a negative contribution to growth during this period in the Caribbean and the Southern Cone. While in the former subregion, both lower infrastructure quantity and quality contributed to a contraction in growth per capita of 0.11 percentage points, in the Southern Cone the lower quality of infrastructure offset the positive contribution of larger stocks—thus leading to a reduction in growth per capita of 0.28 percentage points.

Figure 26.3(b) reports a similar exercise, but based now on the comparison between 1991–5 and 2001–5. Interestingly, the LAC region is the one that achieved over this period the largest contribution of infrastructure development to growth (2.43 percentage points). Faster accumulation of infrastructure stocks accounts for a growth increase of 1.1 percentage points, whereas improved quality of infrastructure added a further 1.33 percentage points to the hike in growth. Across comparator regions, infrastructure development also contributed significantly to higher growth in middle-income economies (excluding LAC countries), by an average of 2.29 percentage points—of which 1.23 and 1.06 percentage points are attributed to faster accumulation of stocks and improved quality, respectively.

What kind of growth benefits could be derived from closing Latin America's infrastructure gap? To be specific, assume a counterfactual under which the level of infrastructure development of each Latin American country rises to match the average level observed among non-LAC middle income countries. Calderón and Servén (2010b) draw the implications for growth. On average, growth in Latin America would rise by approximately 2 percentage points per year—mostly attributed to an expansion in the infrastructure network (1.5 percentage points). The Andean countries would gain the most—3.1 percentage points of growth on average, with most of it (2.4 percentage points) due to the considerable improvement in infrastructure quality that catch-up would entail. Central America, on the other hand, would reap an increase in its growth rate of almost 3 percentage points—with the bulk (1.9 percentage points) due to enlarged infrastructure stocks acquired in the catch-up. Finally, the subregion that would collect the smallest benefits—because it is already ahead of the rest—is the Southern Cone (0.98 percentage points), with most of the contribution coming from the improved quality of infrastructure services (0.61 percentage points).

26.4 THE CHANGING ROLES OF THE PUBLIC AND PRIVATE SECTORS

Until the 1980s, the public sector had an almost exclusive role in the provision of infrastructure services in industrial and developing countries. But things started to change in the 1980s. Across the developing world, and in Latin America in particular, the debt crisis and the ensuing macroeconomic and financial turbulence forced governments to implement drastic expenditure cuts and tax increases to correct large fiscal imbalances, in a new global context of hardened budget constraints brought about by the evaporation of foreign financing. The drive to fiscal austerity of Latin American public sectors over the 1980s and much of the 1990s resulted, among other things, in a severe cut in their infrastructure expenditures.

This change in the global economic environment was accompanied by a similarly global change in the development paradigm. The pervasive government intervention in the economy, and the direct participation of the public sector in the production of goods and services that characterized the state-led development model—whose limitations had been exposed by the debt crisis—gave way to a new model in which free markets and private-sector initiative were expected to play the leading role.

These two forces were behind the retrenchment of developing-country governments across the world from some of their traditional activities, including involvement in the industrial and commercial sectors of their economies, with infrastructure prominently among them. Infrastructure industries, hitherto reserved to the public sector, were opened to various forms of private participation in many countries. Nowhere in the developing world was this opening up as fast and deep as in Latin America. The process was certainly uneven across the region, with some countries—notably Chile—moving ahead of the rest, but eventually it affected virtually all countries and all infrastructure sectors.[7]

These trends had important consequences for the development of infrastructure across Latin America over the last quarter-century. Their most immediate impact was on the level and composition of infrastructure spending in the region (Calderón, Easterly, and Servén 2003; Calderón and Servén 2004a; 2009). Figure 26.4 depicts the trends in infrastructure investment, as a ratio to GDP, in the six largest Latin American economies.[8] It is immediately apparent from the figure that total infrastructure investment collapsed in the second half of the 1980s, and the fall has not been reversed in the ensuing two decades.[9] As a result, by 2006 total infrastructure investment in the six countries considered represented under 2% of their total GDP, barely half of its value in the early 1980s, and well below the level that, according to various estimates, would be required for sustained growth in the region (e.g. Fay and Morrison 2005).

The decline in overall investment was a result of the sharp contraction in investment of the public sector, which fell by two-thirds between the early 1980s and the 2000s. Private investment did show a noticeable rise after 1990, but it peaked in 1998 and stagnated thereafter. In the 2000s its volume has been on par with that of public investment, around 1% of GDP. Overall, the private investment expansion was insufficient to offset the fall in public investment.

---

[7] Detailed chronologies of the opening up of Latin America's infrastructure industries to private initiative are given by Calderón, Easterly, and Servén (2003) and Andrés et al. (2008).

[8] Argentina, Brazil, Chile, Colombia, Mexico, and Peru. The figures shown are GDP-weighted averages. Comparable data for other Latin American economies is not available.

[9] For the purposes of this figure, as well as Table 26.3, total infrastructure investment is defined as comprising power, telecommunications, roads and railways, and water and sanitation. See Calderón and Servén (2009) for details.

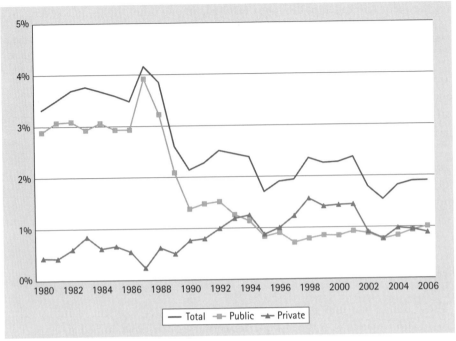

FIGURE 26.4 Total infrastructure investment in Latin America (% of GDP, GDP-weighted average)

Note: Total infrastructure investment includes investment outlays in telecommunications, electric power, land transportation (roads and railways), and water and sanitation. The regional figure is the GDP-weighted average of investment outlays in infrastructure for Argentina, Brazil, Chile, Colombia, Mexico, and Peru.

To complement these aggregate figures, Table 26.3 provides the details for each of the individual countries and infrastructure sectors considered. Total investment in telecommunications rose in all six countries shown. In contrast, investment in power fell everywhere except in Chile, and investment in land transportation fell in all countries except Chile (where it rose) and Peru (where it was roughly unchanged). In turn, the fall in public investment affected virtually all countries and sectors. Likewise, private investment rose virtually in all countries and sectors as well, but on the whole its volume has remained fairly modest. The exception is the telecommunications sector. Hence the presumption that private investment rises would offset the cuts in public investment—which was voiced by some observers as a reason why the public sector retrenchment should not be a concern—does not seem to be validated by the facts: there is no evidence that private investment rose the most in the sectors or countries in which public investment fell the most (Calderón et al. 2003).

26.4.1 The fiscal dimensions of public infrastructure

Comparing the scale of Latin America's fiscal adjustment of the 1980s and 1990s with the declining trend of public infrastructure investment reveals that the fiscal consolidation

Table 26.3 Investment in infrastructure in Latin America, 1981–2006 (% of GDP)

Country	Period	Electric power			Land transportation[a]			Telecommunications			Water and sanitation			Total Infrastructure[b]		
		Total	Public	Private	Total	Public	Private	Total	Public	Private	Total	Public	Private	Total	Public	Private
Argentina	1981–6	1.53	1.53	0.00	0.81	0.81	0.00	0.30	0.30	0.00	0.12	0.12	0.00	2.76	2.76	0.00
	2001–6	0.50	0.06	0.44	0.68	0.56	0.13	0.38	0.00	0.38	0.10	0.06	0.04	1.67	0.68	0.98
	Change	−1.02	−1.47	0.44	−0.13	−0.25	0.13	0.08	−0.30	0.38	−0.02	−0.06	0.04	−1.09	−2.08	0.98
Brazil	1981–6	3.30	2.44	0.86	0.82	0.51	0.31	0.72	0.36	0.37	0.30	0.30	0.00	5.15	3.60	1.54
	2001–6	0.63	0.36	0.28	0.41	0.24	0.17	0.78	0.29	0.50	0.28	0.26	0.02	2.11	1.15	0.97
	Change	−2.67	−2.08	−0.59	−0.41	−0.26	−0.14	0.06	−0.07	0.13	−0.02	−0.04	0.02	−3.03	−2.45	−0.58
Chile	1981–6	1.65	1.65	0.00	1.04	1.04	0.00	0.47	0.47	0.00	0.29	0.29	0.00	3.44	3.44	0.00
	2001–6	1.84	0.32	1.52	1.69	0.71	0.97	0.90	0.00	0.90	0.78	0.64	0.14	5.21	1.68	3.53
	Change	0.19	−1.33	1.52	0.65	−0.33	0.97	0.43	−0.47	0.90	0.49	0.36	0.14	1.77	−1.76	3.53
Colombia	1981–6	1.56	1.56	0.00	0.94	0.94	0.00	0.32	0.32	0.00	0.31	0.31	0.00	3.13	3.13	0.00
	2001–6	0.58	0.45	0.13	0.67	0.48	0.20	1.01	0.36	0.65	0.50	0.40	0.10	2.77	1.68	1.08
	Change	−0.98	−1.11	0.13	−0.27	−0.47	0.20	0.69	0.04	0.65	0.19	0.09	0.10	−0.37	−1.45	1.08
Mexico	1981–6	0.51	0.51	0.00	1.50	1.50	0.00	0.24	0.24	0.00	0.19	0.19	0.00	2.44	2.44	0.00
	2001–6	0.20	0.20	0.00	0.37	0.22	0.15	0.54	0.01	0.53	0.11	0.10	0.01	1.23	0.53	0.69
	Change	−0.31	−0.31	0.00	−1.12	−1.27	0.15	0.30	−0.24	0.53	−0.08	−0.09	0.01	−1.21	−1.91	0.69
Peru	1981–6	1.35	1.34	0.01	0.36	0.34	0.02	0.32	0.32	0.00	0.08	0.07	0.01	2.11	2.07	0.04
	2001–6	0.44	0.16	0.28	0.37	0.09	0.28	0.64	0.26	0.38	0.04	0.02	0.02	1.49	0.54	0.96
	Change	−0.92	−1.18	0.27	0.01	−0.25	0.26	0.32	−0.06	0.38	−0.04	−0.05	0.01	−0.62	−1.54	0.92
Weighted Avg. (by GDP)	1981–6	1.91	1.56	0.35	1.02	0.90	0.12	0.46	0.31	0.15	0.23	0.23	0.00	3.62	3.00	0.92
	2001–6	0.51	0.26	0.24	0.50	0.29	0.20	0.66	0.14	0.52	0.23	0.20	0.03	1.89	0.89	0.99
	Change	−1.40	−1.30	−0.10	−0.52	−0.60	0.08	0.20	−0.17	0.37	0.00	−0.03	0.03	−1.73	−2.11	0.38

[a] Land transportation includes investment in roads and railways.
[b] Total infrastructure consists of power, land transportation, telecommunications, and water.

had a strong bias against infrastructure. On average, the investment cuts accounted for some 40% of the observed improvement in the primary deficit in Latin America's major economies between the early 1980s and the late 1990s (Calderón et al. 2003). But the fiscal pattern of infrastructure compression was not limited to that period. Afonso (2005) documents the case of Brazil, where the bulk of fiscal adjustment occurred later than in the other large economies of the region. Between 1995 and 2003, the primary surplus of the non-financial public sector rose by close to 4% of GDP; the decline in infrastructure investment contributed around 1.5% of GDP to that rise—i.e. about 40% of the total adjustment.

This is remarkable because public infrastructure investment typically represents a fairly small fraction of GDP, and a relatively small part of overall public expenditure as well. To put it differently, in Latin America's fiscal adjustment, investment as a ratio to GDP fell much more abruptly than public consumption. Indeed, in a majority of the countries for which data is available, public consumption rose relative to GDP, while public infrastructure investment fell, implying that the public investment cuts partly financed an expansion of public consumption.

The anti-investment bias of fiscal discipline likely reflects several factors. Among them, political economy considerations are surely important: it is politically much harder to cut pensions or public sector wages than to cancel infrastructure projects. However, another key factor behind the bias is the fact that fiscal adjustment programs typically focus on the short-term path of the government's cash deficit and debt stock. These two magnitudes are closely scrutinized by multilateral institutions and private creditors and investors, and usually form the basis of loan conditions in the fiscal and macroeconomic dimensions.

However, debt and the cash deficit can be misleading as measures of solvency—which is the ultimate concern of fiscal adjustment programs. Solvency assessments based on debt and the cash deficit treat all public expenditures in the same way, since they all pose the same claim on today's fiscal resources. This blurs the distinction between expenditures that yield future fiscal benefits and those that do not—even though they may have radically different implications for tomorrow's public revenues, and therefore for solvency itself. Many infrastructure expenditures fall in the former category: they have a positive impact on growth, and hence on the future expansion of tax bases (or user fee collection) and, ultimately, future government revenues.

Infrastructure cuts set this mechanism in reverse motion: when fiscal adjustment disproportionately cuts infrastructure spending that enhances growth, it can lead to a vicious circle in which low growth generates lower future tax revenues and unsustainable debt dynamics, which force further fiscal adjustment implemented through investment cuts, which lowers growth further, and prompts additional fiscal retrenchment and investment cuts. In other words, if debt stabilization is pursued primarily by cutting productive spending, the result can instead be destabilization (Easterly, Irwin, and Servén 2008).

This begs the related question of whether infrastructure can pay for itself—i.e. whether public infrastructure projects can be "self-liquidating" (Mintz and Smart 2007).

Conceptually, the answer depends on three factors (Servén 2008). The first is the magnitude of the growth impact of infrastructure spending, given by the marginal productivity of infrastructure assets and the cost of acquiring them. Other things equal, the growth contribution is likely to be higher when the government has strong project-selection capabilities, when the initial endowment of infrastructure capital is low, and when budgetary institutions ensure that the acquisition of infrastructure assets is free from waste and corruption. The second factor is the government's ability to capture at least part of the marginal product of infrastructure, directly via user fees or indirectly through taxes—which, in the latter case, depends on the strength of the tax system and its administration. If these are weak—as happens in many Latin American countries—and fiscal revenues only capture a small fraction of the extra income, then even projects with high growth impact may weaken public finances. The third factor is the marginal cost of borrowing faced by the government, related to its level of debt and to investors' perceptions about the government's commitment to fiscal stability.

These ingredients involve a host of country-specific and even project-specific features, so it is not surprising that empirical assessments of the self-financing potential of infrastructure reach different conclusions for different countries. For Latin America, the only published empirical evaluation of this question is that of Ferreira and Araujo (2008) using Brazilian data in a framework very similar to that of Perotti (2004). Overall, their conclusion is that public infrastructure investment is generally self-financing in Brazil, although in their experiments it takes at least ten years for the government to collect sufficient tax revenues to recoup the initial investment expenses. Because of this long lag, their results are sensitive to the real interest rate used to discount future revenues.

26.4.2 The experience with private participation in infrastructure

Private sector participation (PPI) in Latin America's infrastructure surged in the 1990s. Following the opening up of infrastructure activities, private investment commitments rose from $10 billion in 1990 to over $70 billion in 1998.[10] After 1998, however, commitments declined sharply (Figure 26.5). In spite of an incipient recovery in the 2000s, in 2006–7 private investment commitments averaged less than half of their peak value.

This trend of boom and bust was observed also in East Asia, the other major destination of private infrastructure investment. The decline of the late 1990s can be traced to the retrenchment of global investors in the wake of the financial turmoil of the East Asia and Russia crises—as well as that of Argentina in the case of Latin America. Moreover, the near-completion of the utility privatization cycle in several Latin American countries—which had been a key ingredient in the earlier boom—was another contributing

---

[10] It is important to emphasize that these figures refer to announced investment intentions, which can (and typically do) differ substantially from actual investment.

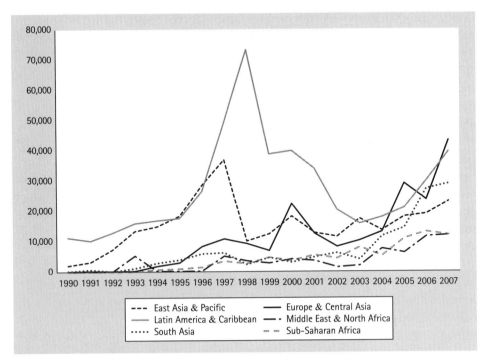

FIGURE 26.5 Private sector participation in infrastructure (investment commitments by region, US$ million)

Source: World Bank PPI Database.

factor to the deceleration of private sector activity. Nevertheless, Figure 26.5 clearly shows that the scale of private involvement in infrastructure was much larger in Latin America than anywhere else.

The PPI surge was unevenly distributed across sectors and countries in Latin America. As already noted, the telecommunications sector was the prime destination for private investment, in Latin America as well as the rest of the developing world. In Latin America, close to 50% of total private investment commitments over 1990–2007 went to telecommunications. In the rest of the world, the figure exceeded 60%. The power sector took second place, with some 30% of total private investment in Latin America (25% elsewhere). The leading role of telecommunications can be explained by its rapid demand growth potential, the relatively short payback period, and the limited social sensitivity and government interference relative to those of other infrastructure sectors. Across countries, Brazil took the lion's share of private infrastructure finance, followed by Argentina and Mexico. These three countries alone accounted for close to half of PPI investment worldwide over 1990–2005 (Andrés et al. 2008).[11]

---

[11] This refers to absolute investment figures. Relative to GDP, however, Bolivia stands out as the country attracting the largest PPI amounts.

Private participation is often mistakenly equated with privatization. In reality, there is a broad range of private participation modes in the provision of infrastructure services, depending on the degree of government involvement and the allocation of risk and investment responsibilities (see Guasch 2004 for a detailed typology). However, the most common forms are outright privatization, and concessions (also called public–private partnerships, or PPPs). Concessions involve long-term contracts between the government and a private investor that bundle investment and service provision. Unlike privatization, concessions do not entail sale or transfer of assets. They last for a limited period of time, and receive close government oversight.

Relative to other world regions, the frequency of outright privatization has been higher in Latin America—although it lost steam after 1998. Across sectors, privatization has been the preferred mode of private participation in telecommunications and, to a lesser extent, power generation. In roads and water, however, PPPs have been much more common, in large part owing to legal restrictions on the sale of public assets (Andrés et al. 2008).

Advocates of Latin America's shift to private financing of infrastructure offered two main arguments to justify its appeal. The first one was the superior efficiency of the private sector at managing and providing infrastructure services, relative to the inefficiency of state-owned enterprises, and the perception that the private sector would be better able than cash-strapped SOEs to expand access and improve the quality of services. The second argument was that delegation of investment and service provision to the private sector would alleviate the fiscal burden of infrastructure development and release public funds for other uses. The validity of this claim, however, depends on that of the previous one. In present value terms, privatization of public infrastructure assets (or the state enterprises that operate them) does not improve public finances unless the government is able to collect privatization proceeds in excess of the present value of the net returns it would have obtained from providing the infrastructure services. If investor myopia is ruled out, this can happen only if the private purchaser of the assets can operate them more efficiently, and hence obtain higher returns, than the government would have.

The same reasoning applies to PPPs, under which investment is done by the franchise holder in return for future service fees collected from the users (plus government subsidies in some cases). Resources saved by the government by not having to finance the upfront investment are offset one-for-one by ceding the future revenue flows to the private sector, so there is no net gain to the public sector in present value terms, regardless of whether or not raising public funds involves distortions (Engel, Fischer, and Galetovic 2007).

Yet resort to privatization and PPPs was often guided by fiscal considerations rather than by the search for efficiency. In effect, these arrangements offered a way to place investment projects beyond the reach of short-term deficit and debt targets—not unlike the off-budget vehicles for infrastructure investment to which some governments resorted in order to hide investment costs (and the associated liabilities) from public view. In the case of PPPs, these explicit liabilities were typically replaced with contingent liabilities in the form of minimum revenue, credit and/or foreign exchange guarantees granted to private investors—as in the cases of roads in Chile and Colombia (Irwin et al. 1997)—or long-term purchase obligations (such as "take or pay" agreements) under which the government commits to acquiring the service from the private provider.

In this fashion, the government may be left with essentially the same liabilities and risks that it would have acquired if the project had been undertaken directly by the public sector—except for the fact that the lack of clear standards for the budgetary accounting of contingent liabilities and long-term obligations allows them to go unnoticed. Because forecasts of the growth in demand for new services supplied by concessionaries at the time of contract negotiation tend to be overstated, minimum revenue and similar guarantees have been called for relatively frequently, often with major fiscal consequences. In the case of Colombia, for example, generous government guarantees eventually resulted in fiscal costs in excess of 50% of the total investment supplied by the private sector. In the case of power generation projects, the figure was as high as 90%. Even when guarantees were not formally offered ex ante, they were often provided ex post through renegotiation of concession agreements.[12] In the case of roads, the result of these ex ante and ex post guarantees is that, contrary to expectations, private financing of new highways freed up few government resources because large volumes of public funds were diverted to bailouts of franchise holders (Engel, Fischer, and Galetovic 2003).

Of course, PPP arrangements involving contingent government obligations can, and sometimes do, have efficiency-increasing effects (e.g. Martimort and Pouyet 2008), but they often leave the public sector—i.e. taxpayers—bearing most or all of the investment risk (Hemming et al. 2006; Irwin 2007). And they pose the danger that the selection and design of infrastructure projects may be guided more by their repercussions on fiscal accounting than by their efficiency-enhancing potential.

Finally, let us turn to the achievements of PPI in terms of the efficiency, quality, and coverage of infrastructure services. In the early 1990s, advocates of private participation held high hopes that the private sector would take the leading role and help quickly realize major gains along all these dimensions. Almost two decades later, the view is much more nuanced. Gains from PPI have been uneven and, after the boom-and-bust cycle of private investment, it is increasingly clear that the public sector will continue to play a key role in Latin America's infrastructure for years to come.

One of the key disappointments was the extremely high frequency of renegotiation of concessions, which has been thoroughly examined by Guasch (2004). Until 2001, renegotiation had affected over half the concessions in Latin America. Its incidence was particularly high in the water and transport sectors, in which the vast majority of contracts (81% and 65%, respectively) were renegotiated. Moreover, renegotiation of long-term contracts typically occurred soon after the concession agreement—around two years on average—which strongly suggests that renegotiation was not the response to events unforeseen in long-term incomplete contracts.

---

[12] For example, the bailout of the Mexican toll road program in 1997 cost between 1 and 1.7% of GDP (World Bank 2005; see also Guasch 2004).

In principle, renegotiation just implies a departure from the expected service improvements; in practice, its outcome has been almost always adverse for the users, in the form of delays, reduced investment obligations, and higher tariffs. Renegotiation has been singled out as the key reason why highway privatization failed to deliver its expected benefits (Engel et al. 2003). Like explicit guarantees, access to renegotiation weakens operators' incentives to assess accurately expected project profitability, limit risk-taking, and improve efficiency, which is the key rationale for private participation in the first place. Renegotiation in fact allowed operators to shift losses to taxpayers—a strategy facilitated by the lack of public scrutiny that characterized most renegotiation episodes.

Most observers attribute the incidence of renegotiation to the poor design and enforcement of PPP contracts. There were two main factors behind this. The first one was the weak regulatory framework under which concession agreements were reached—with the rush to private involvement taking priority over regulation. The lack of a clear contractual structure led to cost overruns and violation of the conditions of the original contracts. The fact that performance of the agency supervising the franchises was often measured by the scale of the concession program contributed to the regulator's lax enforcement of contract compliance. The second factor was the inadequate contractual allocation of risks, in large part due to the use of fixed-term contracts that in effect leave demand risk to the operator. This fueled operators' pressure for guarantees and renegotiation. Research suggests that it would have been preferable to design the concessions as variable-term franchises (Engel et al. 2007). But the main lesson is that, without credible hard budget constraints on franchise holders and independent regulatory and supervisory bodies, private provision may not be better than public provision of highways.

On the other hand, the lack of adequate accounting standards probably was another contributing factor to the ubiquitous renegotiation of concessions. In effect, it allowed governments to backload payments, by accepting low bids at the initial negotiation stage, and then compensating the concessionaries with additional payments after renegotiation. The reason is that, unlike the initially negotiated amounts, the additional expenditures and future commitments acquired by the government in the renegotiation are typically not recorded in the budget. Engel, Fischer, and Galetovic (2009) argue that this strategy offered governments the possibility of hiding part of their spending, and shift the burden of payments to future administrations.[13]

For sectors other than roads (i.e. telecommunications, power, and water), Andrés et al. (2008) offer the most comprehensive evaluation to date of the results of PPI in Latin America. While details vary across countries and sectors, overall the conclusion is that private participation did result in improved quality of service, higher technical efficiency—as measured by distributional losses and service reliability—and increased sector productivity. On the other hand, PPI had no discernible effects on output volume or

---

[13] The most obvious way to close this loophole would have been to ensure that infrastructure assets procured through PPPs are fully counted as public investment. Of course, this would have reduced considerably the appeal of PPPs.

service coverage trends, resulted in higher prices more often than not—although in many cases pre-privatization prices were highly subsidized and fell short of cost recovery—and led to reduced sector employment (which was the main mechanism behind the productivity increases).

The study also highlights key factors that limited the gains from private participation. They echo those mentioned above in the context of highway privatization. The weak regulatory framework and poor supervisory capacity were often unable to prevent public monopolies from becoming private ones—a deliberate strategy on the part of the government in some cases, in order to maximize the concession (or divestiture) price. In addition, the poor design of concession agreements and privatization programs led to continuous conflicts and ended up costing governments enormous sums. The lack of transparency of the whole process of privatization, contract award, and renegotiation contributed to fuel popular discontent with private participation.

26.5 CONCLUSIONS

Poor infrastructure is commonly viewed as a key obstacle to economic development. Across Latin America, there is an increasing perception that inadequate infrastructure is holding back growth and poverty reduction. As a result, infrastructure has become a major priority in the policy agenda. This chapter has offered an overview of the trends in Latin America's infrastructure sectors over the last quarter-century, and an evaluation of the potential contribution of improved infrastructure to growth in the region.

The chapter documents the evolution of infrastructure availability, quality, and accessibility across the region, in comparison with other benchmark regions. This is done for four basic infrastructure sectors: telecommunications, electricity, land transportation, and water and sanitation. In spite of the progress made in some specific cases, on the whole Latin America and the Caribbean still significantly lags other MICs and East Asian countries both in terms of quantity and quality of infrastructure. The same holds for the universality of infrastructure access in the region: it is still well behind that of East Asia and other MICs.

The chapter has also offered an illustration of the potential contribution of infrastructure to growth in the region. Overall, there is robust evidence that infrastructure development—measured by an increased volume of infrastructure stocks and an improved quality of infrastructure services—has a positive impact on long-run growth. Also, the evidence suggests that these effects are not different in Latin America vis-à-vis other regions. In short, given the gap in terms of infrastructure availability, quality, and accessibility between the region and comparable country groups, the conclusion is that infrastructure development offers a considerable potential to speed up the pace of growth and poverty reduction across Latin America.

Over the last quarter-century, the roles of the public and private sector in Latin America's infrastructure have undergone big changes. A substantial retrenchment of the public sector has been accompanied by a surge in private participation. The chapter has offered a detailed account of the trends in their respective contributions to infrastructure financing across the region, drilling down to the level of individual infrastructure subsectors.

The pressures of fiscal consolidation had a disproportionate adverse effect on public infrastructure spending. We have argued that much of this anti-investment bias can be traced to the use of cash deficit targets to guide fiscal adjustment, disregarding the future revenues that increased infrastructure can bring about through its effect on growth. Public infrastructure cuts achieve short-term fiscal adjustment at a potentially high cost in terms of growth.

Although private financing has increased, it has not come to play the dominant role in the provision of infrastructure services in Latin America and elsewhere that some observers expected. Private financing now dominates telecommunications, and has a significant presence in other infrastructure industries in some countries, but it still plays a small role in roads and water and sanitation. This is unlikely to change in the short term, and it is increasingly clear that the public sector will continue to play a major role in Latin America's infrastructure for years to come.

There is no question that private participation did deliver some efficiency and quality gains. But they were held back by weak regulatory and supervisory frameworks, and poorly designed concession and privatization agreements, which led to ubiquitous renegotiations and ended up costing governments enormous sums. In retrospect, the drive towards private sector participation was prompted by the governance difficulties and incentive problems posed by public-sector provision of infrastructure services. Twenty years later, the experience of Latin America shows that the governance and incentive problems posed by private participation are no less difficult.

References

Afonso, J. (2005). 'Fiscal Space and Public Sector Investment in Infrastructure', IPEA Texto para Discussao No. 1141, Rio de Janeiro.

Alesina, A., Baqir, R., and Easterly, W. (1999). 'Public Goods and Ethnic Divisions', Quarterly Journal of Economics 114.4.

Andrés, L., Guasch, J., Haven, T., and Foster, V. (2008). The Impact of Private Sector Participation in Infrastructure, Washington, DC: World Bank.

Arrow, K., and Kurz, M. (1970). Public Investment, the Rate of Return, and Optimal Fiscal Policy, Baltimore: Johns Hopkins University Press

Aschauer, D. (1989). 'Is Public Expenditure Productive?', Journal of Monetary Economics 23.

Baier, S. L., and Glomm, G. (2001). 'Long-Run Growth and Welfare Effects of Public Policies with Distortionary Taxation', Journal of Economic Dynamics and Control 25.

Barro, R. J. (1990). 'Government Spending in a Simple Model of Exogenous Growth', Journal of Political Economy 98.

——and Lee, J. (2001). 'International Data on Educational Attainment: Updates and Implications', Oxford Economic Papers 53.

BECK, T., DEMIRGUC-KUNT, A., and LEVINE, R. (2000). 'A New Database on the Structure and Development of the Financial Sector', *World Bank Economic Review* 14.3.

CALDERÓN, C., and CHONG, A. (2004). 'Volume and Quality of Infrastructure and the Distribution of Income: An Empirical Investigation', *Review of Income and Wealth* 50.

—— EASTERLY, W., and SERVÉN, L. (2003). 'Latin America's Infrastructure in the Era of Macroeconomic Crises', in W. Easterly and L. Servén (eds), *The Limits of Stabilization: Infrastructure, Public Deficits, and Growth in Latin America*, Palo Alto, Calif.: Stanford University Press.

—— and SERVÉN, L. (2004a). 'Trends in Infrastructure in Latin America', World Bank Policy Research Working Paper No. 3400, Washington, DC.

—— —— (2004b). 'The Effects of Infrastructure Development on Growth and Income Distribution', World Bank Policy Research Working Paper No. 3401, Washington, DC.

—— —— (2009). 'Infrastructure in Latin America: An Update 1980–2006', MS, World Bank, Washington, DC.

—— —— (2010a). 'Infrastructure and Economic Development in Sub-Saharan Africa', *Journal of African Economies* 19.

—— —— (2010b). 'Infrastructure in Latin America', World Bank Policy Research Working Paper, Washington, DC.

CANNING, D. (1999). 'The Contribution of Infrastructure to Aggregate Output', World Bank Policy Research Working Paper No. 2246, Washington, DC.

CIESLIKOWSKI, D. (2008). 'Focus on Results: The IDA 14 Results Measurement System and Directions for IDA 15', World Bank RMS Report.

CORPORACIÓN ANDINA DE FOMENTO (2009). *Caminos para el futuro*, Caracas.

DEMETRIADES, P., and MAMUNEAS, T. (2000). 'Intertemporal Output and Employment Effects of Public Infrastructure Capital: Evidence from 12 OECD Economies', *Economic Journal* 110.

EASTERLY, W., IRWIN, T., and SERVÉN, L. (2008). 'Walking Up the Down Escalator: Public Investment and Fiscal Stability', *World Bank Research Observer* 23.1.

ENGEL, E., FISCHER, R., and GALETOVIC, A. (2003). 'Privatizing Highways in Latin America: Fixing What Went Wrong', *Economia* 4.

—— —— —— (2007). 'The Basic Public Finance of Public–Private Partnerships: The Case of Toll Roads', NBER Working Paper No. 13284, Cambridge, Mass.

—— —— —— (2009). 'Soft Budgets and Renegotiations in Public–Private Partnerships', MS.

ESFAHANI, H., and RAMIREZ, M. (2003). 'Institutions, Infrastructure and Economic Growth', *Journal of Development Economics* 70.2.

ESTACHE, A. (2003). 'On Latin America's Infrastructure Privatization and its Distributional Effects', MS, World Bank, Washington, DC.

—— (2006). 'Infrastructure: A Survey of Recent and Upcoming Issues', MS, World Bank, Washington, DC.

—— FOSTER, V., and WODON, Q. (2002). *Accounting for Poverty in Infrastructure Reform: Learning from Latin America's Experience*, Washington, DC: World Bank.

—— GOMEZ-LOBO, A., and LEIPZIGER, D. (2000). 'Utility Privatization and the Needs of the Poor in Latin America', MS, World Bank, Washington, DC.

—— MANACORDA, M., and VALLETTI, T.M. (2002). 'Telecommunications Reform, Access Regulation and Internet Adoption in Latin America', *Economia* 2.2.

FAY, M., and MORRISON, M. (2005). *Infrastructure in Latin America and the Caribbean: Recent Developments and Key Challenges*, Washington, DC: World Bank.

Ferreira, P., and Araujo, C. (2008). 'Growth and Fiscal Effects of Infrastructure Investment in Brazil', in G. Perry, L. Servén, and R. Suescún (eds), *Fiscal Policy, Stabilization and Growth*, Washington, DC: World Bank.

Ghosh, S., and Roy, U. (2004). 'Fiscal Policy, Long-Run Growth, and Welfare in a Stock-Flow Model of Public Goods', *Canadian Journal of Economics* 37.3.

Glomm, G., and Ravikumar, B. (1997). 'Productive Government Expenditures and Long-Run Growth', *Journal of Economic Dynamics and Control* 21.1.

Guasch, J. (2004). *Granting and Renegotiating Infrastructure Concessions: Doing It Right*, Washington, DC: World Bank.

Hemming, R. et al. (2006). *Public–Private Partnerships, Government Guarantees, and Fiscal Risk*, Washington, DC: IMF.

Irwin, T. (2007). *Government Guarantees: Allocating and Valuing Risk in Privately Financed Infrastructure Projects*, Washington, DC: World Bank.

——Klein, M., Perry, G., and Thobani, M. (1997). *Dealing with Public Risk in Private Infrastructure*, Washington, DC: World Bank.

López, H. (2004). 'Macroeconomics and Inequality', presented at the World Bank Research Workshop 'Macroeconomic Challenges in Low Income Countries' (October).

Martimort, D., and Pouyet, J. (2008). 'To Build or Not to Build: Normative and Positive Theories of Public–Private Partnerships', *International Journal of Industrial Organization* 26.

Mintz, J., and Smart, M. (2007). 'Incentives for Public Investment Under Fiscal Rules', in G. Perry, L. Servén, and R. Suescún (eds), *Fiscal Policy, Stabilization and Growth*, Washington, DC: World Bank.

Perotti, R. (2004). 'Public Investment: Another (Different) Look', IGIER Working Paper No. 277, Milan.

Roberts, P., S. Kc, and C. Rastogi (2006). *Rural Access Index: A Key Development Indicator*, Washington, DC: World Bank.

Röller, L.-H., and Waverman, L. (2001). 'Telecommunications Infrastructure and Economic Development: A Simultaneous Approach', *American Economic Review* 91.

Romp, W., and De Haan, J. (2007). 'Public Capital and Economic Growth: A Critical Survey', *Perspektiven der Wirtschaftspolitik* 8.1.

Sanchez-Robles, B. (1998). 'Infrastructure Investment and Growth: Some Empirical Evidence', *Contemporary Economic Policy* 16.

Servén, L. (2008). 'Fiscal Discipline, Public Investment and Growth', in G. Perry, L. Servén, and R. Suescún (eds), *Fiscal Policy, Stabilization and Growth*, Washington, DC: World Bank.

Straub, S. (2007). 'Infrastructure: Recent Advances and Research Challenges', MS.

Turnovsky, S. (1997). 'Fiscal Policy in a Growing Economy with Public Capital', *Macroeconomic Dynamics* 1.

World Bank (2005). *Infrastructure in Latin America: Recent Developments and Key Challenges*, Washington, DC: World Bank.

PART V

SOCIAL
DEVELOPMENT

CHAPTER 27

··

THE RISE AND FALL OF INCOME INEQUALITY IN LATIN AMERICA

··

LEONARDO GASPARINI AND NORA LUSTIG

27.1 INTRODUCTION[1]

··

One of the most prominent features of Latin American countries is their high and persistent levels of socioeconomic inequalities. All nations in the region are characterized by large disparities among their citizens in income and consumption, access to education, land, basic services, and other socioeconomic variables. Inequality is a distinctive, pervasive characteristic of the region. In fact, it is often stated that Latin America is the world's most unequal region.[2] In this chapter we focus the analysis on inequality in the distribution of *income*, the proxy for wellbeing that is available in all national household surveys in the region. Although we also provide historical evidence and comparisons with other regions of the world, the chapter is mostly concerned with the income inequality patterns in Latin America since the 1980s.

The income distributions in Latin American countries experienced two distinct trends in the period 1980–2008. During the so-called "lost decade" of the 1980s, the structural reforms of the 1990s, and the crises at the turn of the century, income inequality increased in most countries for which comparable data are available. Starting in the late 1990s in a few countries and in the early 2000s for the rest, inequality began to decline. Between 2002 and 2008, income inequality went down significantly in most

[1] This chapter is partly based on the UNDP-sponsored project "Markets, the State and the Dynamics of Inequality in Latin America" coordinated by Nora Lustig and Luis Felipe López-Calva. We are thankful to Emmanuel Vázquez and Monserrat Serio for excellent research assistance. See Lopez-Calva and Lustig (2010).
    [2] See IDB (1998), Morley (2001), Bourguignon and Morrison (2002),World Bank (2004).

Latin American economies. This chapter documents this pattern of rise and fall of income inequality in the region and comments on some plausible explanatory factors. After an overview of the regional trends and comparisons with other regions of the world, it focuses on three countries for which substantial analysis is available: Argentina, Brazil, and Mexico.

The analysis suggests the following conclusions. The macroeconomic crises were unequalizing because the poor were less able to protect themselves from high and runaway inflation, and adjustment programs frequently hurt the poor and the middle ranges disproportionately. The unequalizing effects of the crises were compounded because safety nets for the vulnerable were conspicuously absent or ill-designed and insufficient.[3] Market-oriented reforms were associated with rising inequality, although this pattern had a notable exception in the case of Brazil. In most countries employment reallocations brought about by trade liberalization and the skilled-biased technical change associated with the modernization of the economy implied a sizeable reduction in the demand for unskilled labor, which led to higher inequality. In some countries adjustments that led to a contraction in the demand for labor affected unskilled workers disproportionately. All these changes took place in a framework of weak labor institutions and safety nets, and hence their consequences made a full impact on the social situation.

Since the early 2000s, the decline in inequality appears to be driven by a large set of factors, including the improved macroeconomic conditions that fostered employment, the petering out of the unequalizing effects of the reforms in the 1990s, the expansion of coverage in basic education, stronger labor institutions, the recovery of some countries from severe unequalizing crises, and a more progressive allocation of government spending, in particular monetary transfers. The empirical evidence on the driving factors of the recent fall in inequality is, however, still scarce and fragmentary.

The rest of the chapter is organized as follows. Section 27.2 is an overview of the main characteristics and patterns of Latin America's income distribution; section 27.3 discusses the plausible determinants of the inequality changes in the region; section 27.4 provides an in-depth analysis of the three country cases; and section 27.5 offers some concluding remarks.

27.2 LATIN AMERICA'S INCOME DISTRIBUTION

Although we are still far from having international, fully comparable inequality statistics, all pieces of evidence suggest that Latin America is, with Africa, one of the most unequal regions in the world (see Figure 27.1). From the fifteen most income-unequal countries in the UNU/WIDER World Income Inequality Database (WIDER 2007), ten

---

[3] See e.g. Lustig (1995).

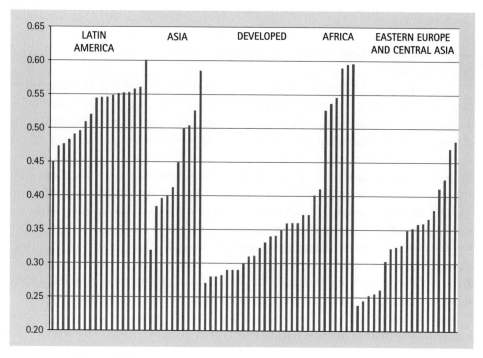

FIGURE 27.1 Gini coefficients: countries around the world

Source: Gasparini et al. (2011).

Notes: Each bar represents the Gini coefficient for the distribution of household per capita income in a given country (last available observation in period 1995–2005).

belong to Latin America. The average Gini coefficient[4] in that region is 0.525 (2004), a value exceeded only by the mean Gini of those few African countries in the WIDER income database.[5] The average income Gini in Latin America is 8 percentage points higher than in Asia, 18 points higher than in Eastern Europe and Central Asia, and 20 points higher than in the developed countries. When using consumption or expenditure as the base for the Gini inequality indicator, Latin American countries also rank among the most unequal in the world.[6]

Most empirical studies find that inequality in Latin America is higher than predicted according to its level of development. This "excess inequality" constitutes a pervasive

---

[4] Named after its proponent, the Gini coefficient is a very commonly used indicator to measure inequality. The Gini coefficient is an index that can take values between 0 and 1 (or between 0 and 100 if in %). The closer it is to 0 (1), the less (more) unequal the distribution. In practice, Ginis are usually never above 0.65 or below 0.20.

[5] It should be mentioned that even in the countries whose surveys collect information on non-wage income, there is every reason to believe that there are gross underestimations particularly with respect to property income. Hence, existing measures may underestimate the true levels of inequality in a non-trivial way.

[6] See also World Bank (2006) and Ferreira and Ravallion (2009).

characteristic of Latin American societies (Londoño and Székely 2000). Figure 27.2 illustrates this point: Latin American countries are all above the smoothed regression line; Ginis for Latin American countries are higher than expected according to their level of per capita GDP.

According to World Bank (1994), in the 1970s the income share of the bottom 20% in Latin America equaled 2.9% of total income, the lowest when compared with other developing regions. In contrast, the share of the richest 10% was 40.1%, the highest in the developing world. Psacharopoulos et al. (1992) report that at the end of the 1980s the average Gini coefficient was 0.50 compared with 0.39 for non-Latin American countries. According to estimates in Gasparini, Cruces, and Tornarolli (2010), the mean Gini across Latin American and Caribbean countries has been significantly higher than in Asia, the developed countries, and Eastern Europe in the last four decades. There are signs of a small reduction in the inequality gap with Asia and Eastern Europe, two regions that experienced strong and potentially unequalizing economic transformations in the 1990s. Interestingly, the characterization of Latin America as a highinequality region has been unchanged for decades, and probably for centuries, despite substantial changes in the demographic, economic, social, and political environment.

Figure 27.3 suggests that Latin American distributions are mainly characterized by a higher income share of the rich, relative to countries in other regions of the world. Who

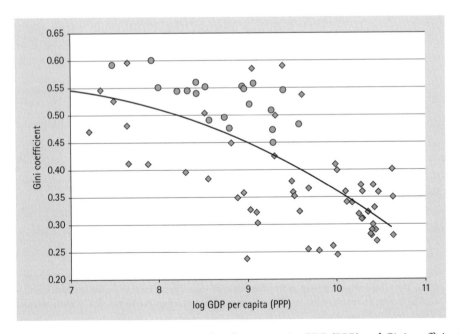

FIGURE 27.2 Latin American excess inequality (log per capita GDP (PPP) and Gini coefficient, c. 2003)

Source: Gasparini et al. (2011).

Notes: Latin American countries marked in circles.

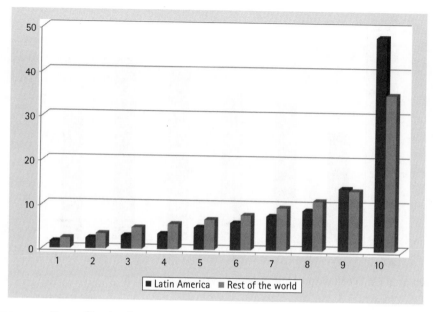

FIGURE 27.3 Inequality in Latin America and the world (share of deciles in income distribution)

Source: Gasparini (2004) based on Bourguignon and Morrison (2002).

are the losers from this "excess share"? The figure suggests that the eight bottom deciles have lower income shares in Latin America than in the rest of the world. In fact, if a typical Latin American distribution had to mimic a typical income distribution of the rest of the world, the income share of the top ventile (i.e. the richest 5% of the population) would have to be reduced to assign the proceeds to increase more or less evenly the shares of the poorest 80% of the population.

Modern inequality analysis is based on microdata from national household surveys that became consolidated in several Latin America countries only in the 1970s. The picture of income inequality from that decade on is hence much clearer than before.[7] During the 1970s, inequality went down or remained constant in most countries, with the exception of the Southern Cone (Argentina, Chile, and Uruguay), where income disparities widened. The 1980s were a "lost decade" also in distributional terms, as most countries in the region suffered significant increases in the level of income inequality. The 1990s were not successful on distributional grounds either, although experiences were more heterogeneous, as inequality increased in some countries and went down in others. The evidence indicates a small rise in the average inequality indicators for the region. Income inequality has declined since the late 1990s in a few countries, and since the early 2000s in

---

[7] ECLAC pioneered periodical reports depicting the level, structure, and trends of income inequality in the region, and promoting the study of its determinants. See e.g. Altimir (1987; 1996; 2008).

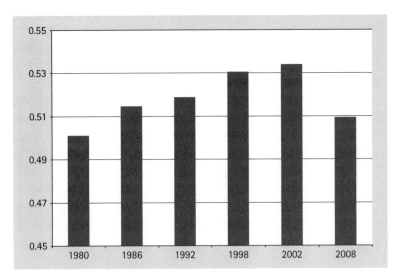

FIGURE 27.4 Gini coefficients: Latin America, 1980–2008

Source: Gasparini et al. (2011).

Notes: Data for all countries since 1992. Latin American Ginis projected from data for 14 countries in 1986 and 8 countries in 1980.

the rest. According to data from ECLAC (BADEINSO 2010), in the period 2002–8 inequality decreased in fourteen out of the seventeen continental Latin American countries, while on average the Gini coefficient dropped 2.3 points. The results are similar (slightly more positive) when using data from SEDLAC (2010): income inequality went down in sixteen countries, and the mean Gini fell by 2.9 points.[8] Figure 27.4 illustrates the rise and fall of income inequality in Latin America in the three decades between 1980 and 2008.[9] It is likely that the levels of income inequality in Latin America at the beginning of the second decade of this millennium are not very different from those prevailing in the 1970s.

27.3 ACCOUNTING FOR THE INEQUALITY PATTERNS

Which factors account for this pattern in Latin America's inequality dynamics? In the 1980s, growing domestic macroeconomic imbalances (in particular, large fiscal deficits which were financed with loans from foreign commercial banks) coupled with adverse

---

[8] SEDLAC is the Socioeconomic Database for Latin America and the Caribbean, a project carried out by CEDLAS and the World Bank. Based on SEDLAC data, Gasparini, Cruces, and Tornarolli (2010) and López-Calva and Lustig (2010) report falls in income inequality in the 2000s.

[9] See also Londoño and Székely (2000) and Altimir (2008).

world economic conditions (in particular, a sharp increase in US interest rates and the sudden halt in the availability of external credit) resulted in severe balance of payments crises and produced sharp economic downturns in most countries in the region. Between 1982 and 1989 the accumulated per capita GDP growth was negative for most Latin American countries. The crisis forced governments to undertake drastic adjustment programs and far-reaching reforms. The adjustment programs implied severe cuts in fiscal deficits (including social spending) and sharp devaluations of the domestic currencies. The market-oriented reforms, broadly speaking, comprised three main components: trade and (foreign direct) investment liberalization, privatization, and financial liberalization. In some countries, the bulk of the reforms were introduced in the 1980s, in others during the first half of the 1990s.

How did income distributions in Latin America change when many countries had to endure stagnant or negative growth, fiscal austerity, and profound economic restructuring? Although data limitations are substantial, the pattern of increasing inequality is clear. During the 1980s the Gini coefficient rose in most countries.[10] It was not always the poor whose share fell by more than that of the other groups. In several countries, it was the middle class that lost disproportionately. However, in country after country, while the bottom or the middle ranges shares shrank, the share of the top 10% increased, sometimes substantially.

Did the increase in inequality during the 1980s and 1990s result from the debt crisis and its inevitable aftermath? Or was it a result of the policies adopted by governments to restore economic stability and growth? It is always difficult to disentangle the contribution of certain policies to a particular outcome, and the distribution of income is no exception. This explains why there has been a lot of controversy and conflicting evidence regarding the impact of orthodox stabilization programs and market-oriented reforms on inequality. The difficulty is compounded because there are intertemporal (lower income today and higher income tomorrow vs. "flatter" income growth) and within-group (e.g. rural vs. urban poor) trade-offs. Broadly, the basic conclusion of the many studies available on the subject is that:

> the impact of adjustment depends largely on the country's initial conditions, on the nature of the shock and on the characteristics of the adjustment program. A second finding was that the "no policy" adjustment option was worse than any of the alternatives. A third finding was that different types of poor persons (rural vs. urban) could fare quite differently during the adjustment process. Conflicts can emerge between the interests of the poor and the non-poor, and among types of poor persons, when different policy combinations result in different distributive outcomes.[11]

There is evidence, however, that suggests orthodox adjustment policies often resulted in overkill (Taylor 1988). This caused poverty to increase beyond what was necessary to restore the macroeconomic equilibrium; and perhaps so did inequality.

---

[10] See Fiszbein and Psacharopoulos (1995), Lustig (1995), and Morley (1995), Altimir (2008).
[11] Lustig (2000).

Regarding the impact of market-oriented reforms on inequality, Morley (2001) concludes that "the recent reforms have had a negative but small regressive impact on inequality mainly because many of the individual reforms had offsetting effects. Trade and tax reform have been unambiguously regressive, but opening up the capital account is progressive." While the effect of capital liberalization is debatable, there seems to be some consensus on the (rather small) unequalizing impact of trade openness in most Latin American countries.[12]

A complementary explanation for the increase in inequality in some countries relies on skilled-biased technical change (SBTC) and capital incorporation. Technological and organizational changes that increase the relative productivity of skilled workers translate into wider wage gaps and, with labor market rigidities, also into lower employment for the unskilled.[13] In fact, some studies find a greater relevance of the capital/technology channel over the trade channel. Behrman et al. (2003) combine policy indices with household survey microdata on wage differentials by schooling levels for 18 Latin American countries for the period 1977–98. The authors fail to find a significant effect of trade reform on wage differentials in their panel of countries, but they do find an impact of the share of technology exports, which they use as a proxy to technology adoption. They conclude that "technological progress rather than trade has been the mechanism through which the unequalizing effects have been operating." Sánchez-Páramo and Schady (2003) reach a similar conclusion using repeated cross-sections of household surveys for a series of Latin American countries. They stress an important point: although the direct effect of trade on wage inequality may be small, trade is an important mechanism for technology transmission.[14]

An important point raised by some authors is that these economic changes took place in a framework of weak labor and social institutions, and hence their consequences made a full impact on the social situation. In most countries the role of unions and the minimum wage was weakened by authoritarian regimes and/or labor deregulations,[15] while social policies, although not absent, were not very active in ameliorating the impacts of the economic changes.

Several crises hit the region at the turn of the century. While some Latin American economies experienced stagnation, others suffered severe macroeconomic crises with substantial drops in GDP. Between 1999 and 2002 Argentina, Colombia, Ecuador, Paraguay, Uruguay, and Venezuela underwent episodes of serious economic downturns associated with significant increases in poverty and inequality.

The rising trend in inequality came to a halt in the early 2000s. Since then, there seems to be a declining trend. In fact, the forces driving inequality down might have started to

---

[12] See Morley (2001), Behrman, Birdsall, and Székely (2003), Vos et al. (2006), and Goldberg and Pavcnik (2007) as examples of a rich and growing literature.

[13] See e.g. Acemoglu (2002) and Card and DiNardo (2006).

[14] See also Acemoglu (2003), Yeaple (2005) and Atolia (2007).

[15] Before the mid-1980s many countries in the region were ruled by military dictatorships that restricted the functionings of labor institutions. Later, some democratic governments also limited the power of unions mainly through labor deregulations.

act in the late 1990s, but remained hidden in several countries by the highly unequalizing macroeconomic crises of the turn of the century. The decline in inequality in the 2000s has been significant in most countries, both in the statistical sense and in economic magnitude. Inequality has fallen in high-inequality countries (Brazil) and low-inequality (by Latin American standards) countries (Argentina); in countries governed by different political models (Bolivia/Venezuela; Brazil/Chile; Mexico/Peru); in countries with a universalistic social policy (Argentina and Chile); and in countries with a traditionally exclusionary state (Bolivia and El Salvador). This widespread decline in inequality is remarkable for a region that has traditionally witnessed high and persistent—and often rising—levels of inequality. Contrary to what some observers may think, it is not just the growth dividend from rapid economic growth in 2003–8, supported inter alia by a commodity price boom. Inequality has declined in both fast- and slow-growing countries, as well as countries recovering from crisis. In fact, the longest periods for which the decline could be documented correspond to Brazil and Mexico, two countries whose growth rates were rather slow.

Why did inequality decline in Latin America during the 2000s? The evidence, still preliminary, points out to several different factors.[16] First, in 2003–8 Latin America experienced a period of strong growth, accompanied by a surge in employment. A stronger labor market is associated with fewer jobless workers and higher wages, in particular for unskilled labor, which are both factors that tend to lower income inequality. Second, changes in the expansion of basic education over the last couple of decades reduced inequality in attainment and made the returns to education curve less steep, reducing wage premia. Third, the reduction in the earnings gap also results from the petering out of the unequalizing effects of some market-oriented reforms in the 1990s. Fourth, as mentioned above, several countries in the region suffered severe macroeconomic crises in the late 1990s and early 2000s associated with large jumps in inequality levels. However, their impact on inequality indicators is often short-lived: as economic relationships return to normality, inequality rapidly falls. Fifth, in several Latin American countries new administrations engaged in a more active role in the labor market, raising the minimum wage or taking a more pro-union stance, which at least in the short run is likely to have an equalizing impact on the labor market.[17] The last factor in this non-exhaustive list is more progressive social spending (monetary and in-kind transfers). After the successful experience of *Progresa* in Mexico, several Latin American countries adopted or expanded conditional cash transfer programs (CCTs), which according to the evidence are well targeted on the poor, and are thus

---

[16] In addition to the country studies discussed in the next section, see Eberhard and Engel (2008) for Chile, Ferreira et al. (2007) for Brazil, Gray Molina and Yañez (2010) for Bolivia, and Jaramillo and Saavedra (2010) for Peru. See Cornia (2009), Gasparini, Cruces, and Tornarolli (2010), and López-Calva and Lustig (2010) for discussions on trends for the whole region.

[17] In one of the few studies that provide empirical evidence on factors behind the drop in inequality, Cornia (2009) states that "in addition to an improved business cycle and favorable terms of trade, the new policy model of fiscally prudent social-democracy which is emerging in much of Latin America generated a favorable impact on the distribution of income."

highly progressive. But CCTs were not alone; expansions in the pension systems and increases in public spending in education and other social services were also very important.

The next section will examine the factors affecting inequality dynamics through an in-depth analysis of Argentina, Brazil, and Mexico.

27.4 THE RISE AND FALL OF INEQUALITY IN ARGENTINA, BRAZIL, AND MEXICO

Argentina, Brazil, and Mexico, the three largest Latin American economies, went through a period of rising inequality during the years of adjustment and reform, a trend which came to a halt around 2000 (earlier for Brazil and Mexico and later for Argentina), when inequality began to decline. We now turn to explore the determinants of this pattern in each country.

27.4.1 Argentina[18]

Argentina, a country well-known for its large middle class in the 1960s, has experienced a sharp increase in income inequality during the last thirty years. The Gini coefficient for the distribution of household per capita income in the Greater Buenos Aires area (GBA) soared from 0.345 in 1974 to 0.466 in 2008. Figure 27.5 shows the trends for inequality in that metropolitan area along with the evolution of per capita GDP.[19]

Gasparini and Cruces (2010) divide the last three decades into six episodes. The first episode covers the dictatorial military regime characterized by weak labor institutions, with almost no role for unions, by a sweeping trade liberalization reform, and by a sharp overall increase in inequality.[20] The second episode comprises most of the 1980s, and is characterized by the return to democratic rule, a substantially more closed economy, increased union activity, stronger labor institutions (minimum wage enforcement, collective bargaining), macroeconomic instability, and a rather stable income distribution. The third episode corresponds to the serious macroeconomic crisis of the late 1980s that included two hyperinflations, and is characterized first by a sharp increase and then by a

---

[18] Most of the section on Argentina draws from Gasparini and Cruces (2010). The data for inequality and poverty indicators come from Argentina's main official household survey (Encuesta Permanente de Hogares, EPH), which covers the main urban areas of the country.

[19] Beccaria and Carciofi (1995) and Altimir and Beccaria (2001) document income inequality in Argentina, finding similar patterns. Trends in inequality in urban Argentina—which can be traced to the early 1990s—are similar to those of the GBA area.

[20] The *coup d'état* that initiated the military regime took place in 1976. However, data are only available for 1974 and from 1980 on.

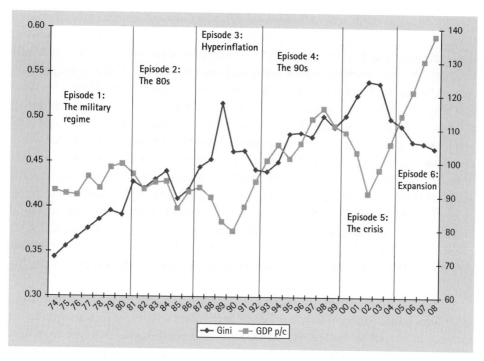

FIGURE 27.5 Inequality in Argentina (Gini coefficient of the distribution of household per capita income GBA, and per capita GDP (index mean 74–08=100))

Source: Gasparini and Cruces (2010).

Notes: The graph was expanded to consider the period 2006–8.

sudden fall in inequality after the successful stabilization in 1991.[21] The fourth episode includes most of the 1990s, and is characterized by relative macroeconomic stability, a currency board with an exchange rate fixed to the US dollar, and deep structural reforms which implied a much more open and flexible economy, with weaker labor institutions. The income distribution during the 1990s became substantially more unequal. The recession that hit the country in the late 1990s and the ensuing macroeconomic crisis in 2001–2, with an economic meltdown and the devaluation of the currency, mark the fifth episode, again characterized by first a sharp increase in inequality and then a substantial fall after the stabilization. The sixth episode started around 2004/5 with the rapid growth in the aftermath of the crisis. Its main characteristics include the adjustment of economic agents to the new relative prices introduced by the devaluation, stronger labor institutions, and a more extensive safety net. Inequality fell to pre-crisis levels over this period.

Due to data availability, most of the empirical research covers the fourth episode—the substantial increase in inequality during the 1990s in a context of reforms and economic

---

[21] See Beccaria and Carciofi (1995) for an analysis of income inequality in the 1980s.

growth. The Gini coefficient for household per capita income in urban areas increased from 0.45 in 1992 to 0.505 in 2000. Gasparini and Cruces (2010) apply a parametric decomposition and find that unskilled workers lost ground both in terms of hourly wages and hours of work during the 1990s, and that these changes had a very significant role in shaping the distribution of hourly wages, earnings, and household income. What was behind the sharp increase in the gap between skilled and unskilled workers during the 1990s? There is evidence that both the sectoral reallocation of production and employment and changes in the skill composition within sectors favored skilled workers, in particular college graduates. Research suggests that while the direct effect of trade liberalization on wage inequality was small, the indirect effect of trade and capital account liberalization through their impact on adoption of new skill-intensive technologies of production and organization might have been substantial.[22] The technological and organizational changes associated with economic openness implied a rapid decline in the demand for unskilled and semi-skilled workers who, in the absence of compensatory social protection programs and weak labor market institutions, suffered falling living standards.[23]

Although unemployment rose sharply in the 1990s, primarily driven by an increase in labor force participation of women and younger cohorts, its direct contribution to the increase in overall inequality was rather small. Unemployment, however, may have affected inequality because of its indirect (downward) effect on wages. Some authors have emphasized the role played by macroeconomic adjustments, the appreciation of the peso, and the resulting reduction in the aggregate demand for labor as central arguments for the increase in inequality in the 1990s.[24] They point to "credentialism"—the process by which economic activities traditionally carried out by unskilled and semi-skilled workers become increasingly performed by skilled workers. This downgrading of the employment structure may have lowered the incomes of the unskilled workers who became unemployed or were forced to work fewer hours.

The Argentine labor market has been characterized by the presence of strong, industry-wide unions, which played a significant role in shaping the country's social, economic, and political outlook. The decline in union activity during the 1990s coincided with a period of rising wage inequality, but unfortunately there is little empirical evidence on the factors behind this correlation, mainly due to data limitations.

As mentioned above, following the 2002 crisis and after experiencing a sharp increase, income inequality fell: the Gini coefficient dropped from 0.533 in 2002 to 0.474 in 2006 and to 0.458 in 2009 (according to preliminary estimates at the time of writing this chapter). This period was characterized by high GDP growth and a sharp fall in the unemployment rate from more than 20% to 8%. Gasparini and Cruces (2010) argue that the

---

[22] See Galiani and Sanguinetti (2003), Acosta and Gasparini (2007), and Galiani and Porto (2010) for evidence for Argentina, and de Hoyos and Lustig (2009) for a broad survey.

[23] Although the government had created *Plan Trabajar*, an employment program, the scale at which it operated was too small to make a noticeable difference.

[24] See Altimir and Beccaria (2001), Maurizio (2001), and Groisman and Marshall (2005).

fall in inequality could be accounted for by the employment generation associated with the recovery, the shift in favor of more low-skilled labor intensive sectors as a result of the devaluation in 2002, the recovery of real wages that followed the overshooting of the devaluation of the peso, a growing relevance of labor institutions (unions, collective bargaining, minimum wages), the fading out of the effect of the skill-biased technical change that occurred in the 1990s, and a significant increase in social spending, in particular due to the implementation of a large cash transfer program in 2002—*Programa Jefes y Jefas de Hogar*, which covered around 20% of poor households in Argentina. According to Gasparini and Cruces (2010) this program accounted for a reduction of around 1 Gini point in 2006. The estimated impact is larger when using other inequality indices that attach more weight to the poorest individuals.

27.4.2 Brazil[25]

Brazil has one of the highest levels of income inequality in the world. There were years when Brazil's Gini coefficient was equal to 0.63, almost a historical and worldwide record. During the years of crisis and adjustment in the 1980s, inequality rose significantly. In contrast to what occurred in other countries, inequality did not rise in the 1990s when some market-oriented reforms were introduced, and there are some indications that trade liberalization might have reduced wage inequality. After a few years with little change, the Gini coefficient has been falling steadily since 1998. The steepest decline occurred between 2001 and 2007 when Brazil's Gini coefficient fell 4.1 percentage points from 0.593 to 0.552 (see Figure 27.6). Extreme poverty and moderate poverty declined too, in spite of the fact that average GDP growth during the period was modest (around 2.5% per year).

Although Brazil fared relatively better than Argentina and Mexico in the 1980s, the debt crisis took its toll. Output growth declined from 8.6% per year for the period 1968–80 to 1.5% per year between 1980 and 1990. Inflation was very high through most of the period. The Gini coefficient rose from 0.58 in 1980 to 0.61 in 1990, and the share of the bottom 20% declined from 3.6% to 2.8% in the same period.[26]

Barros, Cardoso, and Urani (1993) show that the levels of unemployment and inflation were positively correlated with income inequality.[27] Ferreira, Leite, and Litchfield (2008) also show that inflation was positively and significantly correlated with inequality for the period 1981–93, which includes the years of high inflation and hyperinflation.

As mentioned in the previous section, available empirical studies suggest that in a number of countries trade liberalization was associated with an increase in (wage)

[25] Most of the section on Brazil draws from Barros et al. (2010). The inequality measures are estimated using Brazil's National Household Survey PNAD (*Pesquisa Nacional por Amostra de Domicilios*).

[26] Although slightly different in levels, the same change is recorded by Ferreira, Leite, and Litchfield (2008).

[27] See also Neri (1995).

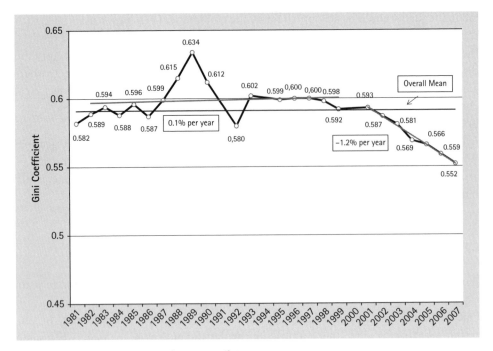

FIGURE 27.6 Inequality in Brazil: Gini coefficient, 1981–2007

Source: Barros et al. (2010).

inequality primarily because the wage skill premium increased. Ferreira, Leite, and Wai-Poi (2007) found that in the case of Brazil, trade liberalization produced the opposite result: the economy-wide skill-premium fell by 14.3% between 1988 and 1995. A factor that drove the skill premium up in other Latin American countries was that prior to liberalization, tariffs were generally higher for industries intensive in unskilled labor. That was not the case in Brazil, and thus the changes in relative prices caused by trade liberalization had an equalizing effect through the employment and occupational reallocation that took place in response.

After 2000, the decline in inequality in household per capita income started to accelerate. From 2001 to 2007, the per capita income of the poorest 10% grew 7% per year, a rate of growth nearly three times the national average (2.5%) while that of the richest 10% grew only 1.1%. Two-thirds of the decline in extreme poverty can be attributed to the reduction in inequality. For the same reduction in extreme poverty to be reached through growth, it would have been necessary for Brazil's overall per capita income to have grown an extra 4 percentage points per year.

Between 2001 and 2007, there were several changes in labor markets and public policy that one would expect to have affected the distribution of post-transfer household per capita income. During this period, the wage differentials between workers of different skills, living in different locations, and working in different sectors (formal/informal; primary/secondary) narrowed. Also during this period, public transfers rose (in terms both of average benefit and of coverage), and the real minimum wage increased. Barros, et al. (2010) estimate the role played by these factors by applying non-parametric decomposition methods in which actual Gini coefficients are compared with counterfactual ones generated by keeping some of the proximate determinants of income inequality or income sources unchanged (Barros, Foguel, and Ulyssea 2006; Barros, de Carvalho, and Franco 2006).

Between 40% and 50% of the decline in income inequality—depending on the inequality measure—was due to changes in the distribution of non-labor income per adult. Changes in the distribution of labor income per adult can account for 31–46% of the decline in inequality, due to a significant growth in labor income per adult and to a moderate decline in its inequality. The contribution of changes in the inequality of access to jobs was rather limited; workers from poor households were not among those that benefited the most from job creation during 2001–7.

The fall in labor income inequality is accounted for by several factors: a fall in the skill premium due to a combination of supply-side and demand-side factors, a reduction in spatial and sectoral labor market segmentation, and a reduction in the gaps in the access to education.[28] Regarding the latter factor, the 1990s was marked by an accelerated expansion of education in Brazil, more than twice as fast as the expansion that occurred in the 1980s, which resulted in a more equal distribution of educational attainment: the standard deviation in years of schooling fell from 4.51 in 2001 to 4.41 in 2007.

As mentioned above, the decline in non-labor income inequality can account for as much as 50% of the decline in household income inequality. Barros et al. (2010) find that the contribution of changes in the distribution of income from returns to assets (rents, interest, and dividends) and private transfers were unequalizing but limited. Most of the impact of non-labor income on the reduction of overall income inequality was due to changes in the distribution of public transfers: changes in size, coverage, and distribution of public transfers explain 49% of the total decline in inequality.

Public transfers represent over 80% of non-labor income and 29% of household income, and include pensions and other standard contributory social security benefits: *Benefício de Prestação Continuada* (a transfer to the elderly and disabled, BPC) and *Bolsa Família*.[29] The latter is Brazil's signature conditional cash transfer program which distributes cash to poor families on condition that the children and adolescents attend school and meet basic healthcare requirements. The program reaches 11 million families, a large proportion of the country's 50 million individuals living in poverty. On average, the post-transfer income of the poor is raised by around 12%.[30] Since 2001, the

---

[28] A number of additional factors which could account for the "unexplained" share in wage inequality, including changes in gender and ethnic discrimination and returns to other observable and unobservable characteristics, sectoral reallocations of production, and rural–urban migration.

[29] These two programs represent 1% of household income and 5% of the public transfers concept measured in the survey. Pensions and BPC are adjusted following the minimum wage. Since Lula became president of Brazil, the minimum wage has been raised significantly and therefore so have the contributory and noncontributory pension benefits.

[30] Fiszbein and Schady (2009).

government has increased the average amount of all transfers and broadened the coverage of well-targeted programs such as *Bolsa Familia*, whose coverage increased by close to 10 percentage points between 2001 and 2007, reaching 17% of households.

According to the decomposition results, while social security benefits account for almost 30% of the overall reduction in income inequality, changes in the BPC and *Bolsa Familia* each explain about 10% of the overall decline. In the case of social security transfers, the equalizing effect occurred primarily through an increase in the amount of the average benefit, while in the case of *Bolsa Familia* the predominant factor was the increase in coverage.

From 2001 to 2007 the minimum wage increased by 35% in real terms. Barros et al. (2010) acknowledge that raising the minimum wage must have contributed to the reduction in inequality through its impact both on wage inequality and on the evolution of social security benefits. However, the authors argue that the minimum wage is not the most effective of the available redistributive instruments.

27.4.3 Mexico[31]

The "debt crisis" was born in Mexico when the government announced in mid-1982 that it would not be able to meet its debt payments on time. In the next six years Mexico faced runaway inflation, while GDP and real wages declined at 1.8% and 8.6% a year, respectively. During the 1980s Mexico liberalized its trade and investment regimes, dismantled most of its industrial policy, and privatized many state-owned enterprises. Inequality rose sharply: the Gini coefficient for household per capita monetary income went from 0.489 in 1984 to 0.564 in 1994 (Figure 27.7).[32]

Since the mid-1990s, right after the implementation of the North American Free Trade Agreement (NAFTA) and the currency crisis in 1995, inequality has been on a downward path. In 2005 the Gini coefficient came back to more or less its 1984 level. Why did inequality rise so sharply during the period of crisis and structural reforms? How much were policy reforms responsible for such increase?

Between 1984 and 1994 there was a significant increase in the skill premium and changes in the structure of employment (towards wage employment) and labor supply (female participation rose by 8 percentage points). There was also an increase in average educational attainment and an equalization of its distribution: average years of schooling increased from 5.6 to 6.9 years, and the Gini coefficient for the distribution of years of education fell from 0.42 to 0.37. In 1984, 48% of the population had no education or had not completed primary school. That figure went down to 38% in 1994.

Legovini, Bouillon, and Lustig (2005) analyze the contribution of these changes to the increase in inequality by applying a microsimulation model. The results of the decom-

[31] Parts of this section come from Esquivel, Lustig, and Scott (2010). The indicators presented here are calculated using the Household Income Expenditure Surveys for various years.
[32] Lustig and Székely (1997).

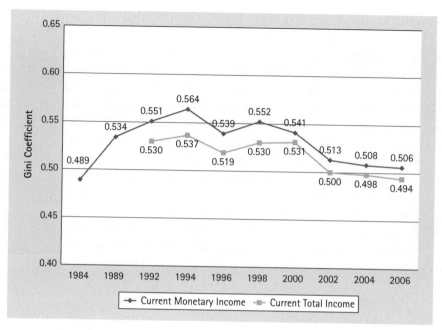

FIGURE 27.7 Inequality in Mexico: Gini coefficient, 1984–2006 (using alternative income definitions)

Source: Esquivel, Lustig, and Scott (2010).

position exercise at the household level reveals that the increase in (relative) returns to higher education accounted for close to 25% of the increase in the Gini for household per capita income observed between 1984 and 1994. Growing disparities in returns between rural and urban areas accounted for 19% of the change in the Gini coefficient. Paradoxically, a more equal distribution of years of schooling was unequalizing: according to the microsimulation exercise it accounted for 15% of the increase in the Gini. This effect, found in several other countries, has been called by Bourguignon et al. (2005) the "paradox of progress." It is a consequence of the fact that when returns to education are convex, the relationship between inequality of education and income inequality has the shape of an inverted U: as education inequality falls, income inequality rises initially and then starts to fall.[33]

Why did skill premia rise?[34] Hanson and Harrison (1995) found that trade liberalization had an unequalizing effect but its contribution was modest: around 23% of the increase in the wage gap by skill can be attributed to that factor. Revenga (1997) also found that trade liberalization in Mexico was unequalizing for labor earnings. One

---

[33] For the mathematical explanation of this property see Bourguignon et al. (2005: ch. 10, p. 396).
[34] Evidence of a rising skills gap has been established for Mexico by several other authors. See e.g. Cragg and Epelbaum (1996), Feenstra and Hanson (1996), Hanson and Harrison (1999), and Feliciano (2001).

explanation for this effect is that, unlike Brazil, the sectors that were protected the most prior to trade liberalization were intensive in low-skilled workers. Nicita (2004) found that when taking into account the impact on purchasing power because of lower prices for consumption goods, all income groups benefit from trade liberalization but the benefit rises with income. Other authors emphasize the role of an increase in the demand for skilled workers associated with the presence of foreign investment (Feenstra and Hanson 1996), a skill-biased technological change (Cragg and Epelbaum 1996; Esquivel and Rodríguez-López 2003), and a process of quality-upgrading due to an increase in exports (Verhoogen 2008). All these forces are not mutually exclusive, but it is difficult to establish which ones were predominant. Just as in the case of Argentina, the direct effect of trade liberalization was modest but the indirect effect of openness on skills upgrading appears to have been much more substantial.

The divergence in conditions between rural and urban areas was another factor which accounted for the increase in household per capita income inequality. Between 1984 and 1994 agricultural workers suffered a severe decline in real income—around 45%—as a result of terms-of-trade reversals in their principal crops, including coffee and cocoa, and the elimination of agricultural subsidies and price support schemes. Self-selection in migration also contributed to the fallout for rural economies: the most entrepreneurial workers may have moved to the city, leaving behind those least able to adjust to changing rural conditions.

After the period of rising inequality in the 1980s and early 1990s, Mexico's income inequality has been falling since the mid-1990s. Between 1994 and 2006, Mexico's Gini coefficient fell from 0.564 to 0.506.[35] The incomes of the bottom 20% grew more than twice the incomes of the top 10%. The faster growth of incomes at the bottom of the distribution happened during a period of lackluster aggregate economic growth. After the 1995 peso crisis, when GDP contracted by around 8%, the economy quickly recovered. Between 1996 and 2000 Mexico's per capita GDP grew at a rate of 4% per year. However, between 2000 and 2006, growth slowed significantly: per capita GDP grew at only 1% per year. Mexico experienced a period of slow pro-poor growth.

The decline in inequality coincided with the implementation of NAFTA in 1994 and with a shift in government spending patterns. Since the early 1990s, public spending on education, health, and nutrition has become more progressive. Also, in 1997 the Mexican government launched the conditional cash transfer program *Progresa* (later called *Oportunidades*), a large-scale anti-poverty program which reaches around 5 million poor households. These changes made the post-fiscal income distribution less unequal, reinforcing the trend followed by income inequality shown above.

Esquivel, Lustig, and Scott (2010) analyze the proximate determinants of the decline in income inequality between 1994 and 2006. Using non-parametric decomposition methods and standard benefit-incidence analysis, the authors examine the roles played

---

[35] This Gini coefficient reported here was calculated using current monetary household income per capita to make it comparable to the Ginis for Argentina and Brazil.

by changes in the distribution of labor income, demographics, and government transfers in accounting for the decline in inequality. The results suggest that the increase in the proportion of adults and of working adults was equalizing, but the impact was modest compared to the equalizing effects of changes in the distribution of labor and non-labor income.

What has caused the distribution of labor income per working adult to change from being an unequalizing factor in 1994 to an equalizing one thereafter? Hours worked changed very little; in fact, they fell slightly for the bottom quintiles, an inequality-increasing change. Changes in relative hourly wages, in contrast, caused the distribution of labor income per working adult to change from unequalizing to equalizing. The distribution of the stock of education in the labor force became more equal too. The combined effect of a fall in the returns to education and the decline in inequality in educational attainment[36] was a reduction in labor income inequality. It is not clear whether the fall in the skilled/unskilled wage gap was the result of demand-side or supply-side factors. Several studies have looked at the demand-side factors emphasizing, among other things, the increasing integration of manufacturing production between the United States and Mexico, and its resulting increase in demand for low-skilled workers in Mexico. However, an examination of the changes in the composition of the labor force by education and experience and the corresponding relative wages suggests that supply-side factors must have been important too.

The reduction in the relative supply of workers with low levels of skills (measured by school attainment) might be associated with changes in public spending on education combined with the effects of the conditional cash transfer program *Progresa/Oportunidades* which tied monetary transfers to keeping children of poor households in school. Public spending on education in the 1970s and 1980s was heavily biased towards higher education. This changed in the 1990s: the relative ratio of spending per student in tertiary vs. primary education in Mexico declined from a historical maximum of 12 in 1983–8 to less than 6 in 1994–2000 (by comparison, the average ratio for high-income OECD countries is close to 2). More resources on the supply-side and the implementation of demand-side subsidies for education through *Progresa/Oportunidades* changed the incidence of public spending on education from being slightly regressive in 1992 to being progressive in 2006. Hence, the fall in skill premia can be linked both to market factors, which affected the demand for labor by skill, and to state action in education spending.

As for the effects of non-labor income, the evidence suggests an increasing equalizing contribution of remittances and transfers over time. Transfers became more equalizing because their share in total income rose and because they became more pro-poor. Although *Procampo* had been expanding since its creation in 1994, the lion's share of the expansion in households receiving non-labor income was due to the implementation of *Progresa* in 1997, which reached 14.8% of households in 2006. While *Procampo* is not a

---

[36] The equalization of educational attainment at this point went beyond the turning point that had made it unequalizing in the 1980s; it had reached the downward sloping side of the inverted U.

pro-poor transfer; *Progresa/Oportunidades* is an example of "redistributive efficiency." With as little as 0.36% of GDP and 4% of total redistributive spending, *Progresa/ Oportunidades* accounts for 18% of the change in the post-transfer Gini.

27.5 CONCLUDING REMARKS

The income distributions in Latin American countries went through two distinct phases in the last three decades. During the 1980s and 1990s they became more concentrated. In several countries (though not in all), the increase in inequality during this period was associated with macroeconomic crises and market-oriented reforms in a context of weak labor institutions and social safety nets.

From the early 2000s, income inequality in Latin America has declined (from the late 1990s in a few countries). Several factors appear to be behind this phenomenon, including the improved macroeconomic conditions that fostered employment, the petering out of the one-time unequalizing effect in the labor market of some market-oriented reforms in the 1990s, the expansion of coverage in basic education during the last couple of decades, and stronger labor institutions. Probably due to the improved fiscal situation and the increased concern on social issues, most Latin American countries augmented social spending and adopted or expanded conditional cash transfers programs. The evidence suggests that these programs are well targeted on the poor, and are thus highly progressive.

In spite of this undeniable progress, Latin America still remains a region with very high income inequality, in which governments redistribute relatively little through taxes and transfers. Despite the evident progress in making public policy more pro-poor, a large share of government spending is neutral or regressive, and the collection of personal income and wealth taxes is relatively low. In order to continue on the path towards more equitable societies, it is crucial that public spending is made more progressive and that efforts are redoubled to improve access to quality services (education, in particular) for the poor.

REFERENCES

ACEMOGLU, D. (2002). 'Technical Change, Inequality, and the Labor Market', *Journal of Economic Literature* 40.

—— (2003). 'Patterns of Skill Premia', *Review of Economic Studies* 70.

ACOSTA, P., and GASPARINI, L. (2007). 'Capital Accumulation, Trade Liberalization, and Rising Wage Inequality: The Case of Argentina', *Economic Development and Cultural Change* 55.4.

ALTIMIR, O. (1987). 'Income Distribution Statistics in Latin America and Their Reliability', *Review of Income and Wealth* 33.2.

—— (1996). 'Cambios de la desigualdad y la pobreza en la América Latina', *El trimestre económico* 61.1.

—— (2008). 'Distribución del ingreso e incidencia de la pobreza a lo largo del ajuste', *CEPAL Review* 96.

—— and BECCARIA, L. (2001). 'El persistente deterioro de la distribución del ingreso en la Argentina', *Desarrollo económico* 40.160.

ATOLIA, M. (2007). 'Trade Liberalization and Rising Wage Inequality in Latin America: Reconciliation with HOS Theory', *Journal of International Economics* 71.

BADEINSO (Base de Estadísticas e Indicadores Sociales) (2010). *Base de Estadísticas e Indicadores Sociales*, Santiago, Chile: CEPAL/BADEINSO.

BARROS, R., CARDOSO, E., and URANI, A. (1993). 'Inflation and Unemployment as Determinants of Inequality in Brazil: The 1980s', Texto para Discussas No. 298, IPEA, Brasil.

—— DE CARVALHO, M., and FRANCO, S. (2006). 'O papel das transferências públicas na queda recente da desigualdade de renda Brasileira', mimeograph.

—— —— —— and MENDONÇA, R. (2010). 'Markets, the State and the Dynamics of Inequality: Brazil's Case Study', in L. López-Calva and N. Lustig (eds), *Declining Inequality in Latin America: A Decade of Progress?* Washington, DC: Brookings Institution.

—— FOGUEL, M., and ULYSSEA, G. (eds) (2006). *Desigualdade de renda no Brasil: uma análise da queda recente 1*, Brasil: IPEA.

BECCARIA, L., and CARCIOFI, R. (1995). 'Argentina: Social Policy and Adjustment during the 1980s', in N. Lustig (ed), *Coping with Austerity: Poverty and Inequality in Latin America*, Washington, DC: Brookings Institution.

BEHRMAN, J., BIRDSALL, N., and SZÉKELY, M. (2003). 'Economic Policy and Wage Differentials in Latin America', Center for Global Development Working Paper No. 29, Washington, DC.

BOURGUIGNON, F., and MORRISON, C. (2002). 'Inequality Among World Citizens: 1820–1992', *American Economic Review* 92.4.

—— FERREIRA, F., and LUSTIG, N. (eds) (2005). *The Microeconomics of Income Distribution Dynamics in East Asia and Latin America*, Washington, DC: World Bank and Oxford University Press.

CARD, D., and DINARDO, J. (2006). 'The Impact of Technological Change on Low-Wage Workers: A Review', in R. Blank, S. Danziger, and R. Schoeni (eds), *Working and Poor: How Economic and Policy Changes Are Affecting Low-Wage Workers*, New York: Russell Sage Foundation.

CORNIA, G. A. (2009). 'What Explains the Recent Decline of Income Inequality in Latin America?', mimeograph.

CRAGG, M., and EPELBAUM, M. (1996). 'Why Has Wage Dispersion Grown in Mexico? Is It the Incidence of Reforms or the Growing Demand for Skills?', *Journal of Development Economics* 51.1.

DEHOYOS, R., and LUSTIG, N. (2009). 'Liberalización comercial, pobreza y desigualdad: una reseña sobre enfoques metodológicos y la asignatura pendiente', *El trimestre económico* 76.1.

EBERHARD, J., and ENGEL, E. (2008). 'Decreasing Wage Inequality in Chile', in L. F. López-Calva and N. Lustig (eds), *Markets, the State and the Dynamics of Inequality: How to Advance Inclusive Growth*, UNDP. Available online at: http://undp.economiccluster-lac.org/

ESQUIVEL, G., LUSTIG, N., and SCOTT, J. (2010). 'A Decade of Falling Inequality in Mexico: Market Forces or State Action?', in L. López-Calva and N. Lustig (eds), *Declining Inequality in Latin America: A Decade of Progress?* Washington, DC: Brookings Institution.

—— and RODRÍGUEZ-LÓPEZ, J. (2003). 'Technology, Trade and Wage Inequality in Mexico before and after NAFTA', *Journal of Development Economics* 72.

—— and HANSON, G. (1996). 'Foreign Investment, Outsourcing and Relative Wages', in R. Feenstra, G. Grossman, and D. Irwin (eds), *The Political Economy of Trade Policy: Papers in Honor of Jagdish Bhagwati*, Cambridge, Mass.: MIT Press.

FELICIANO, Z. (2001). 'Workers and Trade Liberalisation: The Impact of Trade Reforms in Mexico on Wages and Employment', *Industrial and Labor Relations Review* 55.

FERREIRA, F., LEITE, P., and LITCHFIELD, J. (2008). 'The Rise and Fall of Brazilian Inequality: 1981–2004', *Macroeconomic Dynamics* 12.S2.

—— —— and WAI-POI, M. (2007). 'Trade Liberalization, Employment Flows, and Wage Inequality in Brazil', World Bank Policy Research Working Paper No. 4108, Washington, DC.

—— and RAVALLION, M. (2009). 'Poverty and Inequality: The Global Context', in W. Salverda, B. Nolvan, and T. Smeeding (eds), *The Oxford Handbook of Economic Inequality*, New York: Oxford University Press.

FISZBEIN, A., and PSACHAROPOULOS, G. (1995). 'Income Inequality Trends in Latin America in the 1980s', in N. Lustig (ed), *Coping with Austerity: Poverty and Inequality in Latin America*, Washington, DC: Brookings Institution..

—— and SCHADY, N. (2009). 'Conditional Cash Transfers: Reducing Present and Future Poverty', World Bank Policy Research Report, Washington, DC.

GALIANI, S., and PORTO, G. (2010). 'Trends in Tariff Reforms and Trends in the Wage Structure', *Review of Economics and Statistics* 92.3.

—— and SANGUINETTI, P. (2003). 'The Impact of Trade Liberalization on Wage Inequality: Evidence from Argentina', *Journal of Development Economics* 72.2.

GASPARINI, L. (2004). 'Different Lives: Inequality in Latin America and the Caribbean', in *Inequality in Latin America and the Caribbean: Breaking with History?* Washington, DC: World Bank.

—— and CRUCES, G. (2010). 'A Distribution in Motion: The Case of Argentina', in L. López-Calva and N. Lustig (eds), *Declining Inequality in Latin America: A Decade of Progress?* Washington, DC: Brookings Institution.

—— CICOWIEZ, M., and SOSA ESCUDERO, W. (2011). 'Pobreza y desigualdad en América Latina: conceptos, herramientas y aplicaciones', mimeograph, CEDLAS-UNLP, La Plata.

—— CRUCES, G., and TORNAROLLI, L. (2010). 'Recent Trends in Income Inequality in Latin America', *Economia* 10.2.

GOLDBERG, P., and PAVCNIK, N. (2007). 'Distributional Effects of Globalization in Developing Countries', *Journal of Economic Literature* 45.1.

GRAY MOLINA, G., and YAÑEZ, E. (2010). 'The Dynamics of Inequality in the Best and Worst Times, Bolivia 1997–2007', in L. López-Calva and N. Lustig (eds), *Declining Inequality in Latin America: A Decade of Progress?* Washington, DC: Brookings Institution.

GROISMAN, F., and MARSHALL, A. (2005). 'Determinantes del grado de desigualdad salarial en la Argentina: un estudio interurbano', *Desarrollo económico* 45.

HANSON, G., and HARRISON, A. (1995). 'Trade, Technology, and Wage Inequality in Mexico', NBER Working Paper No. 5110, Cambridge, Mass.

———— (1999). 'Who Gains from Trade Reform? Some Remaining Puzzles', *Journal of Development Economics* 59.1.

IDB (Inter-American Development Bank) (1998). *América Latina frente a la desigualdad*, Washington, DC.

JARAMILLO, M., and SAAVEDRA, J. (2010). 'Inequality in Post-Structural Reform Peru: The Role of Market and Policy Forces', in L. López-Calva and N. Lustig (eds), *Declining Inequality in Latin America: A Decade of Progress?* Washington, DC: Brookings Institution.

LEGOVINI, A., BOUILLON, C., and LUSTIG, N. (2005). 'Can Education Explain Changes in Income Inequality in Mexico?', in F. Bourguignon, F. Ferreira, and N. Lustig (eds), *The Microeconomics of Income Distribution Dynamics in East Asia and Latin America*, Washington, DC: World Bank and Oxford University Press.

LONDOÑO, J., and SZÉKELY, M. (2000). 'Persistent Poverty and Excess Inequality: Latin America 1970–1995', *Journal of Applied Economics* 3.

LÓPEZ-CALVA, L., and LUSTIG, N. (eds) (2010). *Declining Inequality in Latin America: A Decade of Progress?* Washington, DC: Brookings Institution.

LUSTIG, N. (ed.) (1995). *Coping with Austerity: Poverty and Inequality in Latin America*, Washington, DC: Brookings Institution.

—— (2000). 'Crises and the Poor: Socially Responsible Macroeconomics', *Economía* 1.1.

—— and SZÉKELY, M. (1997). 'México: evolución económica, pobreza y desigualdad', IDB Technical Study, Sustainable Development Department, Washington, DC.

MAURIZIO, R. (2001). 'Demanda de trabajo, sobreeducación y distribución del ingreso', presented at the V Congreso Nacional de Estudios del Trabajo, Argentina.

MORLEY, S. (1995). 'Structural Adjustment and Determinants of Poverty in Latin America', in N. Lustig (ed), *Coping with Austerity: Poverty and Inequality in Latin America*, Washington, DC: Brookings Institution.

NERI, M. (1995). 'Sobre a mensuração dos salários reais em alta inflação,' *Pesquisa e planejamento econômico* 25.3.

NICITA, A. (2004). 'Who Benefited from Trade Liberalization in Mexico? Measuring the Effects on Household Welfare', World Bank Policy Research Working Paper, Washington, DC.

PSACHAROPOULOS, G., et al. (1992). 'Poverty and Income Distribution in Latin America: The Story of the 1980s', LAC Regional Studies Program Report No. 27, World Bank, Washington, DC.

REVENGA, A. (1997). 'Employment and Wage Effects of Trade Liberalization: The Case of Mexican Manufacturing', *Journal of Labor Economics* 15.3.

SÁNCHEZ-PÁRAMO, C., and SCHADY, N. (2003). 'Off and Running? Technology, Trade and Rising Demand for Skilled Workers in Latin America', prepared for the World Bank report *Closing the Gap in Education and Technology in Latin America*, Washington, DC.

SEDLAC (Socio-Economic Database for Latin America and the Caribbean) (2010). 'Socioeconomic Database for Latin America and the Caribbean', CEDLAS and the World Bank website.

TAYLOR, L. (1988). *Varieties of Stabilization Experience*, Oxford: Clarendon Press.

VERHOOGEN, E. (2008). 'Trade, Quality Upgrading, and Wage Inequality in the Mexican Manufacturing Sector', *Quarterly Journal of Economics* 123.2.

VOS, R., GANUZA, E., MORLEY, S., and ROBINSON, S. (eds) (2006). *Who Gains from Free Trade? Export-Led Growth, Inequality and Poverty in Latin America*, London: Routledge.

WIDER (World Institute for Development Economics Research) (2007). 'UNU/WIDER World Income Inequality Database', Helsinki.

WILLIAMSON, J. (2010). 'Five Centuries of Latin American Inequality', *Journal of Iberian and Latin American Economic History* 28.2.

World Bank (1994). *Poverty Alleviation and Social Investment Funds: The Latin American Experience*, Washington, DC.

—— (2004). *Inequality in Latin America and the Caribbean: Breaking with History?* Washington, DC.

—— (2006). *World Development Report 2006: Equity and Development*, Washington, DC.

YEAPLE, S. (2005). 'A Simple Model of Firm Heterogeneity, International Trade and Wages', *Journal of International Economics* 65.

CHAPTER 28

....

MULTIDIMENSIONAL POVERTY IN LATIN AMERICA: CONCEPT, MEASUREMENT, AND POLICY

....

REBECA GRYNSPAN AND LUIS F. LÓPEZ-CALVA

28.1 INTRODUCTION[1]

....

Poverty has many faces and its measurement requires a multidimensional approach. There is a well-established view—both in academia and in policy circles—sustaining that a pure income-based approach to poverty is misleading. Yet, when it comes to the decision of which dimensions are relevant, how they should be measured, and what is the best way to aggregate them, opinions diverge in fundamental ways. As this chapter shows, despite the different views on these issues, there have been important advances in the last twenty years in terms of the methodologies used to measure poverty in a multidimensional setting, as well as in terms of establishing a general framework in which different visions may coexist.

In the policy realm, the need for a more comprehensive view of poverty has also permeated widely. On the one hand, poverty undoubtedly remains one of the main problems to be solved on the world governments' agenda, and the design of poverty reduction policies requires a clear understanding of both its magnitude and the

[1] The opinions expressed in this chapter are those of the authors, and do not necessarily represent the views of the United Nations Development Programme, or those of the Regional Bureau for Latin America and the Caribbean. The authors would like to thank Eduardo Ortiz-Juarez and Samantha Lach for excellent research assistance.

processes that cause it. Also, there is a conviction that the causes are multiple and usually associated to a situation in which a number of long- and short-term influences converge. Among the structural influences, not only economic but also political, social, and cultural contexts appear to be relevant. From an economic perspective, the difficulties in achieving sustained economic growth, the absence of equitable and efficient redistribution policies, the persistence of unequal opportunities, the difficulty in creating stable, "quality" jobs, and the absence of an integrated social protection strategy are some of the many conditions that prevent a country from effectively addressing the prevailing backwardness of important population groups. Thus, the challenge consists of designing the right mix of universal and targeted policies to tackle poverty and vulnerability, for which a consistent multidimensional notion of poverty is needed.

The design of better social policy requires the establishment of a comprehensive view of poverty, relying on a robust methodology to identify those who are poor, and setting up a way to evaluate policy interventions rigorously, in ways in which the evaluation feeds back into policy design. Multidimensionality is seen as the foundation for monitoring and evaluating the impacts of policies and programs. Yet impact evaluation exercises typically measure effects on areas such as health, education, or income, without using a multidimensional index of impact. Multidimensionality is more commonly used in the selection of beneficiaries of targeted social programs, such as Conditional Cash Transfers (CCT).[2] Though inequality and poverty remain two of the most important challenges faced by Latin American societies, there has been an improvement in the ways policies were designed and implemented in the last two decades.[3] Partly as a result of this, and combined with a reasonable record in terms of growth for most countries in the first years of this century, poverty went down in the majority of the Latin American countries. With the exception of Argentina and Uruguay, due to the 2001 macroeconomic crisis, and Paraguay, the decrease in poverty throughout the region was remarkable, with Ecuador, Venezuela, Brazil, and Chile among the countries displaying the greatest improvement (see Table 28.1).

As the following sections show, a multidimensional approach allows for a better understanding of the trends in poverty during these years, as well as a more nuanced policy response to address the challenges. A multidimensional perspective shows, for example, that in spite of the progress registered at an aggregate level, the results show persisting poverty in rural areas, with important disparities in relation to urban ones. Also, in the cases of Brazil, Chile, El Salvador, and Mexico the results suggest that people in rural areas are not only more likely to be poor, but also more likely to experience multiple deprivations at the same time.

This chapter summarizes the conceptual and methodological discussion on multidimensional measurement of poverty, and shows recent applications to Latin American

---

[2] A thorough discussion of CCT is Fiszbein and Schady (2009).
[3] For a discussion of the trends in inequality, which is not an issue addressed in this chapter, see López-Calva and Lustig (2010).

Table 28.1 Evolution of income poverty in Latin America (% of people)

Country	Mid-1990s	2008[a]
Latin America	45.7	33
Argentina[b]	16.1	21
Bolivia	62.1	54
Brazil	45.3	25.8
Chile	27.6	13.7
Colombia	52.5	46.8
Costa Rica	23.1	16.4
Ecuador[b]	57.9	39
El Salvador	54.2	47.5
Guatemala	61.1	54.8
Honduras	77.9	68.9
Mexico	45.1	34.8
Nicaragua	73.6	61.9
Panama[b]	25.3	17
Paraguay[b]	49.9	52.5
Peru	47.6	36.2
Uruguay[b]	9.7	14
Venezuela (RB)	48.7	27.6

Source: CEPALSTAT, ECLAC.

Notes: 'Mid-1990s' refers to 1993 in Brazil; 1994 in Argentina, Chile, Mexico, Uruguay, Colombia, Venezuela, and Latin America; and 1995 in El Salvador.
[a] 2007 data for Honduras and Bolivia; 2006 for Argentina, Chile, and Guatemala; 2005 for Colombia and Nicaragua; and 2004 for El Salvador.
[b] Urban areas.

countries. The chapter is organized as follows. Section 28.2 discusses the conceptual foundations of multidimensionality based on Amartya Sen's notion of functionings and capabilities. Section 28.3 provides a brief literature review on the existing approaches to measure multidimensional poverty, including the human development and the basic needs approaches. There follows a discussion of recent theoretical contributions on methods based on the axiomatic derivation of poverty indices for disaggregated data and generalizations of income-based methodologies, as well as subjective and participatory approaches. Section 28.4 includes empirical applications of multidimensional measures in Latin America, and discusses the evolution of poverty in the region from a multidimensional perspective. Before concluding with some views on avenues for further research, section 28.5 reviews the policy use of multidimensional measurement in specific anti-poverty programs.

28.2 POVERTY AS A MULTIDIMENSIONAL CONCEPT

28.2.1 Income, unsatisfied needs, and social exclusion

For many years, poverty has been analyzed and measured in the monetary space. This approach identifies a poverty condition as a shortfall in income—or consumption—from a certain threshold or "poverty line," determined, for instance, by equalizing a minimum level of nutritional requirements to the amount of money necessary to acquire the appropriate food bundle. This "absolute" poverty line has traditionally been the most used in empirical applications and has also been adopted by several governments as the official method of poverty measurement. Other instances consider "relative measures," for example by defining as poor all those individuals or households whose income is below one half of the median income of the distribution. The issue of identification under this approach, however, is not the only concern. In a seminal paper, Sen (1976) highlighted the importance of also selecting an aggregate index that reflects overall poverty. Thus, *identification* and *aggregation* have become the two relevant aspects to solve methodologically when measuring poverty. The most widely used measure, due to its properties and the fact that it is decomposable, is the class of indices proposed by Foster, Greer, and Thorbecke (1984).

This class of indices, known as the FGT or α-measure, computes the sum of all individual poverty gaps (measured by the average income or consumption shortfall from the poverty line), expressed as a fraction of the poverty line, and allowing the analysis of poverty aversion by raising the poverty gaps to an α power. The parameter α measures the aversion to poverty, with larger values giving greater emphasis to the poorest poor. When $\alpha = 0$, the FGT is the headcount measure, where all poor individuals are counted equally. When $\alpha = 1$, the measure is the poverty gap, where individuals' contribution to total poverty depends on how far away they are from the poverty line; and when $\alpha = 2$, the measure is the squared poverty gap, where individuals receive higher weight the larger their poverty gaps are. In other words, when $\alpha > 0$ the FGT is sensitive to the depth of poverty, and when $\alpha > 1$ it is sensitive to the distribution among the poor.[4]

In general, the monetary approach is justified given that income or consumption indicators are widely available and transparent. A more solid justification relies on the concept that individuals must have a minimum income for the purchasing power it entails, allowing the acquisition of goods or services and thus the achievement of a minimum level of wellbeing (Thorbecke 2008). Nevertheless, the monetary approach is criticized for several reasons. The most common criticisms are those related to the idea that certain attributes cannot be purchased because markets do not exist—as in the case of public goods—or that this approach overlooks heterogeneity among people, their personal requirements, and the inequalities in intra-household distribution of resources.

---

[4] Foster (2006) provides a recent survey of axioms in unidimensional poverty measurement.

Moreover, there are aspects of poverty that lie in the realm of the subjective, such as lack of self-respect, alienation, and lack of empowerment. The identification of all aspects of poverty could lead to better policy.

Indeed, the development of multidimensional notions and measures of poverty is not new. One of the main approaches is related to the idea of *basic needs* which is an absolute concept of poverty and defines as poor those people or households who cannot access the satisfaction of basic goods and services (discussed in Stewart 1985). The unsatisfied basic needs approach (UBN) suggests that an improvement in wellbeing is related not only to income growth, but to the satisfaction of fundamental needs like clothing, shelter, and access to education, health, and other public services. Analogous to the monetary approach, the identification of poor people requires the assessment of whether individuals can afford or access the "satisfaction" of needs, given a previously determined threshold. There is a vast tradition in the application of these methods in Latin America, as discussed in López-Calva and Rodriguez-Chamussy (2005) and Grynspan (2008).

A second approach that attempts to go beyond the income-shortfall manifestation of poverty relies on the concept of social exclusion. This approach was originally proposed in the context of advanced economies, and by definition is a relative concept. It relates to people excluded from observed living standards in a society due to social relationships that limit a full social participation (Townsend 1979; Atkinson 1998). This approach indeed involves a relative point of view: the analysis of poverty depends on a particular context, society, and current and future circumstances. The relative notion is key in the empirical implementation. For instance, in a society where an individual of working age is unemployed, it could be argued that such an individual suffers exclusion from a particular living pattern. The "relative notion" in this approach requires a clear definition of dimensions to be assessed and thresholds to be defined.

On the other hand, the World Bank (2001) has established three sets of characteristics to be considered when grouping the dimensions for poverty measurement. These three areas would be "resource deprivation," "lack of empowerment," and "vulnerability." Indeed, access to goods and services, and income itself, could be considered within the realm of resources. Social and political aspects, such as voice, participation, and autonomy, would be labeled as a lack of empowerment, while the exposure to asset losses and permanent reduction in wellbeing due to idiosyncratic and systemic shocks would be identified as vulnerability. This classification certainly points in the direction of identifying the many faces of poverty in a structured way, but lacks a conceptual framework within which to view poverty and its inherent multidimensionality in a comprehensive way.

28.2.2 Poverty as capability failure

Undoubtedly, one of the most influential approaches for the multidimensional analysis of poverty relates to the theory of functionings and capabilities. Sen (1980; 1985) has argued that wellbeing should be evaluated in the space of "beings and doings"—or functionings— to live a "valued" life. The achievement of functionings, however, is not the central element of this approach. Sen suggests that capabilities, or freedom, provide information on the array of feasible functionings that a person can achieve (Basu and López-Calva 2002).

For an intuitive explanation, assume that an individual owns a bicycle (access to a good or commodity). Such good has a vector of characteristics which make it useful for specific purposes. Since a function represents what the individual can do or be, the bicycle and its attributes open several possibilities, i.e. given the ability of the individual to ride it (transformation function), specific functionings become available: being healthy, being able to commute faster, socializing with other people, applying for a job as postman or delivery person, and so on. Those functionings are included in the whole set of options an individual is effectively able to choose from. The set of options available to that individual is his or her capability set.

The capability approach rejects monetary indicators as the measure of wellbeing, since these are considered only as means rather than ends. As mentioned earlier, access to monetary resources does not take account of the individual's differences in transforming resources into valuable achievement—differences which depend on personal characteristics or on the life context (imagine the case where an individual has access to a bicycle, but this individual suffers a physical disability or has never learned to ride a bycicle). Therefore, poverty in this framework is a capability failure, or a narrowing down of the set of available options, "beings and doings" basic to human life.

Despite its conceptual value, translating the capability approach into an empirical framework requires that several issues be addressed. First, identifying a capability failure—or differentiating the poor and non-poor—requires the definition of basic capabilities and thresholds.[5] Empirical applications generally address the capability failure as deprivation of basic needs—food, health, and education—which implies a measurement of functions rather than capabilities. Second, transforming the capability approach into an overall poverty index imposes some aggregation problems, one of which is related to the notion that different capabilities are valuable, rejecting the possibility of trade-offs between achievements. On this aggregation concern, the growing discussion of the multidimensionality of poverty has driven the development of measures that allows for varying rates of trade-off across dimensions. For targeting policies purposes, however, aggregation methods are commonly found in the field of composite indices.

28.3 EMPIRICS: THE MULTIDIMENSIONAL MEASUREMENT OF POVERTY

As previously noted, there is a vast and rich conceptual discussion of multidimensionality. Yet it is relatively recently that the multidimensional literature began offering some guidance on the empirical measurement in an axiomatic way. There is no clear consen-

---

[5] This issue has been subject to several attempts (see e.g. Alkire 2002; 2008).

sus, but several aggregation methods have been developed as an attempt to capture the multidimensionality of the social phenomenon in an overall measure.

It must be said that any multidimensional index of wellbeing must solve the following questions:

- Which dimensions should be considered?
- How should they be measured?
- Which weight should be given to each of them?
- How should they be aggregated?

28.3.1 The human development approach

The answers to the above questions define the characteristics of the indicator to be used. In terms of the weights, for example, normative weights would imply a justification of the relative importance of each dimension. Empirical weights may hinder comparability over time. The dimensions to be included are in many cases determined by the availability of data and thus by the answer to the second question. Linear aggregations may be insensitive to inequality among the poor, which could be a variable of interest. As an example, the traditional Human Development Index (HDI), published by UNDP since 1990, is an index estimated at the aggregate level (for groups, not for individuals). It contains three dimensions (income, education, and health), each dimension being measured by a very specific indicator (income by GDP per capita, education by literacy and enrollment, and health by life expectancy), and the weights are normative (one-third to each dimension). The dimensions are aggregated linearly, and thus the HDI is not sensitive to inequality, being an arithmetic average of the dimensions. Recently, there have been attempts to overcome some of the weaknesses implied by the above methodological constraints; (Foster, López-Calva, and Székely 2005; Grimm et al. 2009; Seth 2009).

It is important to note that the HDI was originally developed for international comparisons of achievements on the basis that human development is the process of enlarging people's choices and their level of achieved wellbeing (Anand and Sen 1994).[6] Thus, the HDI is not a measure of poverty, but rather the inverse: a measure of achievement. The inclusion of the achievements in the three dimensions of life considered (health, education, and economic resources) may be justified as being available and measurable data. The straightforward construction of the index requires, first, that the indicators used are normalized; and second, that the final value is calculated as the average of such indicators. This simplicity and policy content are probably the most important characteristics of the index, since it enables comparisons at different geographic levels. It is important to note, however, that several of the criticisms in the recent literature have focused precisely on such simplicity.

---

[6] An early attempt to produce multidimensional measures of wellbeing by combining several social indicators was the Physical Quality of Life Index developed by Morris (1979).

A first criticism relates to the narrow definition of human wellbeing, as the index does not include, for example, human and political rights (Dasgupta 1990).[7] Moreover, since income is regarded as a means in the human development approach, the index has also been criticized for including this indicator as one of its three relevant dimensions. A second criticism rests on the selection of weights and the redundancy between the HDI and its components.[8] Finally, a third criticism relates to the insensitivity of the HDI to inequality.

Despite these valid criticisms, the HDI has changed in many ways the manner in which the policy world judges advances in social conditions. The HDI was complemented by the development of a related index: the Human Poverty Index (HPI). The HPI provides a better understanding of the interconnections between different deprivations, and serves as an important targeting tool in the absence of disaggregated data. Distinguishing between the HPI-1 for developing countries and the HPI-2 for developed ones, the index comprises the same three dimensions as the HDI, where the monetary indicator is omitted. In the case of the HPI-1, the indicators include the probability of not surviving the age of 40, the adult literacy rate, and the equally weighted average of the percentage of population without access to piped water, as well as the percentage of children under weight for age.[9] The three dimensions are normalized to range between 0 and 1, and the aggregation uses generalized means. The value of the index is then calculated as the mean of the three averaged deprivations using a parameter that penalizes the dimensions with higher levels of deprivation.

Other methods are designed to be applied at either aggregate or household level, and rely on the specification of empirical weights by using specific statistical techniques, such as factor analysis (FA) and principal components (PC). The idea is to disentangle the elements that explain why a person belongs to the poor sector in a society, by associating a set of characteristics. Such techniques map different socioeconomic indicators by household, group, or region to an overall index or score. There are also innovative approaches based on information theory (Maasoumi 1993), efficiency analysis (Ramos and Silber 2005), non-axiomatic methods like fuzzy-set theory (Cerioli and Zani 1990), and participatory exercises (Narayan 2000).

The most extensive literature to address the multidimensionality is related to methods based on axiomatic derivations of poverty indices. In this field the recent contribution of Bourguignon and Chakravarty (2003) and Alkire and Foster (2007) stand out.[10]

---

[7] In addition to the already classic comment by a well-known economist (Nick Stern): "The HDI converts three numbers I understand into one number I don't understand", addressing the issue of the loss involved in aggregation.

[8] Several analyses have demonstrated how some rankings are fully robust to changes in weights. See e.g. the work by Cherchye, Ooghe, and Puyenbroeck (2008) and Foster, McGillivray, and Seth (2009).

[9] The HPI-2 includes the rate of long-term unemployment as a fourth dimension. See Anand and Sen (1997) and Technical Notes in UNDP's Human Development Reports for a formalization of the HPI.

[10] See also Tsui (2002) and Duclos, Sahn, and Younger (2006).

It is a fact, however, that aggregation into an overall index implies a loss. The choice of any of these methods involves a trade-off because information will be lost in the process. Yet such aggregation in an overall index may be useful for specific policy purposes, as discussed below.

28.3.2 Multidimensional measures for disaggregated data

Empirically, the multidimensionality of poverty may rely on quantitative, qualitative, and participatory data. As suggested within quantitative approaches, the developed measures range from those based on statistical techniques to dominance comparisons, counting methods, fuzzy-set theory, and others.

As mentioned above, principal components analysis (PCA), for instance, has been commonly used to construct an overall deprivation index composed by multiple deprivations that allow the design and targeting of public policies. The construction of this class of indices requires the transformation of a set of correlated dimensions into another uncorrelated one. This process ranks dimensions, so that the first explains the variability in the dataset to the greatest degree. Other techniques, such as discriminant analysis, have been applied to the selection of beneficiaries of public programs. This analysis implies the estimation of a discriminant function, and the correlation of different characteristics of the poor and non-poor. This function summarizes these characteristics into a single continuous variable—a score—that sorts individuals or households according to their level of poverty and, given a cut-off, selects them as beneficiaries of policies or not.

In dealing with the multidimensionality of poverty, there is a broad tradition of seeking to translate individual's deprivations into an overall measure. On this tradition, the previously mentioned UBN method constitutes an influential way for measuring poverty in terms of deprivations in specific needs. Under this approach, the measurement requires an initial definition of the basic needs and also a definition of a minimum standard where individuals or households satisfy their needs (being non-poor) or do not (being poor). In this process, the deprivation of a specific need of an individual or household is expressed as the normalized difference between the current satisfaction of the need and the minimum standard established.

Although this method is a turning point for deprivation measurement, the identification mechanism described has been identified in itself as its main weakness, as it does not reveal the magnitude of such deprivations. Moreover, if the objective is to obtain an overall measure of poverty, there is no aggregated index, but separate headcounts for each deprivation. Even in an attempt to obtain an overall measure, the number of deprivations required to be considered poor is arbitrary, as the approach identifies as equally poor those households that do not satisfy at least one or (for instance) five attributes. This deficiency carries important implications, although in some contexts the UBN measures may be useful for targeting policies on specific deprivations (imagine a geographical unit where the only available data comes from census). From this perspective, the UBN method provides at any rate an important tool to "characterize" some dimensions of poverty.

Given the aggregation failures of the UBN method, the literature on multidimensional poverty has evolved towards the development of more solid measures by imposing a number of axioms to be satisfied. This is the case of the framework of Bourguignon and Chakravarty (2003) (B&C from here onwards), who propose a measure that sets a threshold for each of the analyzed dimensions of poverty. As a multidimensional version of the traditional FGT family indices, the authors build a class of poverty measures by aggregating relative deprivations based on a constant elasticity of substitution (CES) function. This measure takes into account an elasticity of substitution between the attributes of an individual, the coefficient of aversion to poverty, and the weight given to each attribute. In the analysis of B&C the identification can take two forms: a union approach which considers as poor those individuals falling below the cutoff in some dimension, and an intersection approach which defines poverty if they experience shortfalls in all dimensions. A key feature of the B&C measures is the analysis of different degrees of substitutability—or complementarity—between attributes. In the case of two attributes this implies, for example, that a high level of deprivation in one attribute may be compensated by a lower level of deprivation in another.

A recent and innovative measure that addresses the aggregation deficiencies is the Alkire and Foster (2007) poverty measures (A&F hereafter). The A&F class of measures is a counting-based method (satisfying a set of desirable axioms) under which the poverty level is identified through a dual cut-off. In other words, there is a usual cut-off that classifies individuals as deprived in a certain dimension representing the headcount ratio, but there is also a cross-dimensional cutoff that indicates the minimum range of deprivations necessary before a person is considered to be poor. The aggregation method proposed by A&F follows the logic of the traditional FGT family of indices, and yields inter alia a measure that represents the percentage of the population identified as poor, multiplied by the share of the dimensions in which the multidimensionally poor individual is deprived.

The A&F class of indices has the advantage over previous measures of being sensitive to the number of deprivations experienced by the multidimensionally poor. For instance, suppose two regions, A and B, each with 50% of its population deprived in two or more dimensions. If the poor in A experience 2 of 6 deprivations, while the poor in B experience 4 of 6, then the A&F measure will be higher in B than in A. Although this approach is relatively new, it has growing empirical applications around the world, as shown below.

From a different perspective, part of the literature has argued that poverty is a concept that requires a continuous qualification, rather a binary one (poor vs. non-poor). A monetary approach implies that each individual is identified as poor (if her/his income is less than the poverty line) or non-poor (if his/her income is above the threshold) based on a threshold. Within a multidimensional framework an individual may be considered poor in some attributes but non-poor in others. This ambiguity has been analyzed through the notion of fuzzy-set theory which determines the degrees of membership—expressed by scores belonging to the interval $[0, 1]$—of an individual to the poor or non-poor groups. Originally applied to the analysis of poverty by Cerioli and Zani (1990), this approach has had strong resonance in the empirical literature of multidimensional poverty.[11]

28.3.3 The view from the poor: subjective and participatory approaches

All the poverty measures reviewed so far—including both monetary and multidimensional—have been criticized for not taking into account the views of poor people, the group who face the reality of poverty in their everyday life. There has been a recent growth in the literature on subjective wellbeing and the participatory approaches to poverty measurement, which are based on self-reported information on the conditions of poverty.

Although the first approach refers to individual's self-perception on multiple dimensions of their lives, the empirical analysis has focused mainly on the relationship between subjective and economic wellbeing. In principle, self-reported wellbeing and life satisfaction imply that individuals consider the several dimensions that are relevant for them, apply weights, and report an aggregate index of valuation. The literature shows no clear relation between subjective wellbeing ("happiness" and related notions) and income (Graham and Pettinato 2000; Layard 2006). Critiques of the subjective wellbeing approach question the policy relevance of the approach. The notion of subjective wellbeing and life satisfaction as "happiness" implies a return to the original interpretation of "utility" in Bentham, which brings back the "ex post" view of welfare, as opposed to the "ex ante" notions such as equality of opportunity and capabilities.[12] Recently, Sen (2008) has argued that "being happy" is an important function, like others (being well nourished, being healthy), though it is a function with a weak link to policy. Two individuals who are equally poor, but of whom one is happier than the other, cannot be judged equally without having a relevant implication for public action. Recent contributions to the subjective wellbeing literature include Teschl and Comim (2005) and McGillivray (2005).

Regarding the so-called participatory poverty assessments (PPA), it is clear that they constitute a growing field of analysis to address the multidimensionality of poverty, based on gathering information directly from the "voices of the poor" to inform development policy. Although the PPA method faces some important methodological

---

[11] A relevant example is the analyses carried out by Chiappero-Martinetti (1994).

[12] In the spring of 1776, following his first publication, *A Fragment on Government*, Jeremy Bentham invoked what he described as a "fundamental axiom", "it is the greatest happiness of the greatest number that is the measure of right and wrong" (see Burns 2005). Throughout his work, Bentham suggested the interpretation of "utility" as "happiness."

challenges, it represent a very valuable tool to supplement traditional poverty profiles (Thorbecke 2003). The exercises carried out by Narayan (2000) and Székely (2003) constitute good examples of this approach.

28.4 FROM THEORY TO PRACTICE: MULTIDIMENSIONAL MEASUREMENT IN LATIN AMERICA

This section briefly reviews applications of measurements in the Latin American and Caribbean region, including the Human Development Index, the Unsatisfied Basic Needs Approach, and more recent multidimensional measures.

28.4.1 The Human Development Index 1990–2007

The Latin American region has shown significant progress in the past two decades in terms of the evolution of the HDI (UNDP 2010). The annual rate of growth of the HDI has slowed down recently, from 0.8% in the 1990s to 0.6% in 2000–7—which is not surprising, given that this is an indicator that is bounded above. Comparatively, the performance of individual countries is fairly heterogeneous (see Table 28.2), although those that are relatively further behind have displayed significantly higher rates of growth than the countries with the highest HDI levels, thus allowing us to talk about a pattern of HDI convergence.

It is important to mention that, in spite of the overall trend, aggregate figures mask important inequalities, such as geographical inequality; inequality between groups, such as gender and ethnic inequality; and inequality among the different dimensions of human development. Regarding dimensions, the contribution of each component may differ, although all components hold the same weight in terms of the final result. It is possible for countries to display similar HDI values while having very different levels in terms of the indices that compose the final one. A country with a high health index and a low income index may display the same HDI as another country with a high income but low health index. The HDI in this case would reflect an equivalent level of human development for both countries, while the opportunities and capabilities of the vulnerable population in each country—and the priorities in terms of public policy—would differ.

From this perspective, the education index contributes the most to the HDI, explained by the decrease in illiteracy and increased attendance in school in the region, as a result of the expansion of access to education and coverage. The contribution of health is the most homogeneous of the three, while income is the component with the lowest contribution to the HDI. Figure 28.1 shows the regional trends of the HDI and its components, displaying the maximum, average, and minimum values for the years 1990, 2000, and

Table 28.2 Evolution of the Human Development Index in LAC countries (HDI values)

Country	1990	2000	2007-9
Latin America	0.717	0.765	0.795
Argentina	0.801	0.848	0.866
Bolivia	0.619	0.691	0.729
Brazil	0.72	0.784	0.813
Chile	0.79	0.845	0.878
Colombia	0.715	0.773	0.807
Costa Rica	0.788	0.822	0.854
Dominican Republic	0.686	0.747	0.777
El Salvador	0.653	0.721	0.747
Guatemala	0.591	0.661	0.704
Honduras	0.636	0.694	0.732
Mexico	0.779	0.822	0.854
Nicaragua	0.593	0.657	0.699
Panama	0.762	0.808	0.84
Paraguay	0.702	0.739	0.761
Peru	0.714	0.764	0.806
Uruguay	0.802	0.837	0.865
Venezuela (RB)	0.79	0.802	0.844

Source: Human Development Index, UNDP (2009); Gray and Purser (2010).

Notes: Data for Venezuela for years 1990 and 2000 from the United Nations Human Development Report.

2006. It is clear from the figure that the income dimension has displayed, on average, lower levels and growth than the health and education dimensions, suggesting that income remains one of the biggest challenges in the region. It is worth stressing that the HDI and its components are a measure of achievement with respect to a previously established maximum, indicating progress towards a desired level. In this sense, a low contribution in any dimension suggests that the progress achieved in such dimension is still far from the established target.

28.4.2 Unsatisfied Basic Needs (UBN) in Latin America and the Caribbean

The UBN method has been extensively used in Latin America. It has the advantage of making effective use of widely available census data, allowing the identification of situations of deprivation in several dimensions and geographical levels. The UBN method

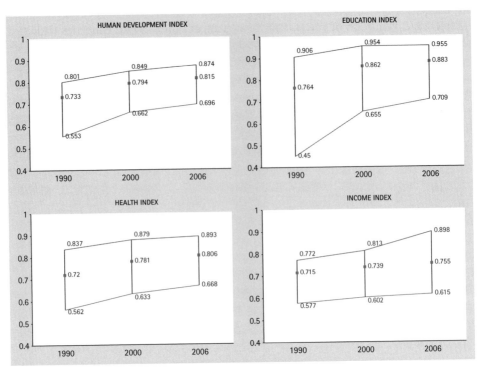

FIGURE 28.1 Human Development Index value trends in LAC, 1990, 2000, and 2006 (maximum, average, and minimum value trends by HDI and by component[a])

Source: UNDP (2010).

[a] Averages weighted by population; includes only countries for which there is available information.

thus represents a practical complement for indirect methods of measuring poverty (Feres and Mancero 2001). The approach was first introduced in the region in the early 1980s by the Economic Commission for Latin America and the Caribbean (ECLAC). Most Latin American countries adopted the method and used it with the census rounds of 1990 and 2000. In general, as suggested previously, the main contribution of the UBN method is related to its capacity to identify geographically the unsatisfied needs of the population, allowing for path-breaking poverty-map analysis.

Usually, UBN indices in Latin America focus on housing conditions, such as the quality of shelter and overcrowding; access to sanitary services, including availability of potable water and sanitation services; access to education, taking into account the enrollment and attendance of school-age children; and economic capacity, accounting for the probability of income sufficiency of the household—generally measured by the economic dependency rate and the education level of the household head (Hyman 2006).

The UBN approach has been used extensively throughout the region, exploiting the advantage of its potential use for geographic targeting. For example, in ECLAC (2005), sixteen countries in the region were analyzed using the traditional UBN approach,[13] comparing the measurement with that of extreme poverty. The preponderant unmet basic needs identified refer to overcrowding—close to 30% of the population in 9 countries lived in households with 3 or more people per bedroom; and lack of appropriate solid waste disposal systems—the same percentage of the population in 13 countries experienced lack of sewage services (or septic tanks in rural areas). Alternatively, one of the dimensions with the lowest rate of occurrence in the region related to school attendance. Only 5% of children or fewer did not attend an educational establishment in 13 countries, with Bolivia as the only country presenting a higher level of school-age children not attending an education facility (close to 41%).

Assuming that an individual having at least one unsatisfied need is poor, the rate of poverty found in this study ranges from 15% in the urban areas of Argentina to 84% in Nicaragua. One of the main inconveniences of this approach, however, lies in the variability of results according to the number and type of basic needs considered. For example, if the variable regarding overcrowding is dropped, the proportion of unmet needs in Mexico decreases from 36% to 14%, changing the position in which this country would be ranked.

In terms of evolution, the research found that unmet basic needs decreased between 1990 and 2002, for both rural and urban areas. The proportion of individuals who had critical lacks decreased across all analyzed dimensions in 2002, in relation to 1990. Although comparable information was not available for all countries, the trends observed were representative for most countries, as corroborated by the evolution of social indicators performed in the same study (ECLAC 2005).

In a more recent exercise, Hammill (2009) applies the UBN approach to Mexico, Costa Rica, El Salvador, Guatemala, Honduras, and Nicaragua, using data from country household surveys between 2004 and 2007, and the dimensions traditionally considered in the region.[14] The incidence of unmet needs in this subregion ranged from 5% of the population with unmet needs in terms of education and available electricity to well over 30% of the population not covering their basic needs in terms of overcrowding and consumption capacity. For the Central American countries alone, the incidence of UBNs in education increases to 11%.

Costa Rica was the best-performing country in this sample, with less than 3% of its population presenting unmet needs, with the sole exception of inadequate housing

---

[13] The UBN analysis employed the framework typically used in the region including: access to housing, determined by construction materials and an overcrowding indicator; access to basic services, particularly water and solid waste disposal; access to education, indicated by school attendance; and economic capacity, determined by years of education of the household head, and rate of demographic dependency (Feres and Mancero 2001). The thresholds utilized also correspond to those typically employed in previous applications of the UBN approach; differentiated thresholds were used for urban and rural areas. To see the satisfaction thresholds for each indicator and details on modifications to the framework, see ECLAC (2005).

[14] Quality of housing; household population density; access to water and sanitation; school attendance and level of education; availability of electricity; and a synthetic measure of household consumption capacity, defined by the dependency rate and education level of the household head.

quality (for 11% of the population). Overcrowding was the highest dimension for Mexico (with 35% of Mexicans living in households with 3 or more people), but in all other dimensions the incidence was low, between 1% and 5%. Guatemala presents a high incidence of inadequate housing (16%) and the highest incidence of inadequate household density (52%). In El Salvador, 25% of the population have unmet needs in terms of access to clean water, while this country and Honduras ranked the lowest regarding consumption capacity, with 35% and 34% of their population respectively. Nicaragua presents the highest UBN in terms of sanitation (39%), inadequate housing (17%), and access to electricity (28%, together with Honduras) (Hammill 2009). Thus, due to its census-based characteristics, the UBN approach provides a practical source of disaggregated data. In this sense, despite its limitations, it is a useful tool, particularly when looking for geographical disaggregation.

28.4.3 Beyond UBN: recent multidimensional measures

There have been other attempts to apply multidimensional measures, both at aggregate and household levels. Barros, De Carvalho, and Franco (2006) carried out an analysis in Brazil to examine the profile of poverty at the household level, by proposing the Index of Family Development (IDF, *Índice De Desenvolvimento Da Família*) as a measure for estimating the multidimensional level of poverty for each household. The IDF was designed to be estimated using data from the Brazilian household survey (PNAD); and it was composed of six dimensions (vulnerability, education, employment, income and assets, child development, and household characteristics), 26 components, and 48 indicators. The weighting is normalized so that the extent of poverty in each family can vary from 0 (for families without poverty) to 100 (for the absolutely poor families). The overall poverty measure results from the arithmetic mean of the synthetic indicators of the six dimensions.[15] In general, their results for Brazil as a whole suggest that between 1993 and 2003 the level of poverty of families declined by five percentage points, although the analysis shows a heterogeneous pattern of the reduction across dimensions.

Following the B&C approach, Arim and Vigorito (2007) explore how child poverty is related to lack of income and other, non-monetary indicators, for the case of Uruguay. Using data from the Uruguayan Household Survey (*Encuesta Continua de Hogares*) for 1991–2005, their results suggest divergences between the different dimensions analyzed, indicating that child poverty implies deprivations in non-economic indicators, mainly related to parents' education or to deficient conditions in housing. In another study for Uruguay, Amarante, Arim, and Vigorito (2008) compare the B&C measures, fuzzy-set theory, and the stochastic dominance approach. Their analysis is focused on children attending public schools in Montevideo, and the dimensions used refer to

---

[15] The synthetic indicator of each component is the arithmetic mean of its indicators, and the synthetic indicator of each dimension is the arithmetic mean of the synthetic indicators of its components.

nutritional status, social participation, educational attainment of parents, characteristics of their households, and income. For the three measures analyzed, their results show a similar poverty reduction trend between 2004 and 2006. However, when income is excluded from the analysis, the stochastic dominance yields different results, suggesting that poverty is practically stable over the period. An additional application of the B&C measures was carried out by Conconi and Ham (2007). The study measures poverty in Argentina, based on cross-sectional surveys for 1998–2002, assessing the dimensions related to employment, household characteristics, education, and income. Their results show that poverty increased during the period, mainly due to the 2001 crisis, employment and income being the dimensions that contributed most to a rise in the overall index.

Despite these previous and valuable attempts to measure poverty in a multidimensional perspective, cross-country analyses based on comparable data and methodology were not available until very recently. It was not until Battiston et al. (2009) that an attempt was carried out for six Latin American countries: Argentina, Brazil, Chile, El Salvador, Mexico, and Uruguay. By operationalizing the A&F method, the authors include six indicators for the period 1992–2006: income, education of the household head, school attendance, sanitation, connection to piped water, and shelter. Given the availability of information, for Argentina and Uruguay only data for urban areas were considered, while both urban and rural data were used for the rest of the countries.

The results in general suggest that aggregate multidimensional poverty has decreased during the analyzed period. As shown in Figure 28.2, El Salvador is the poorest country, followed by Mexico, Brazil, and Chile. However, these countries have experienced more significant reductions of poverty during the analyzed period than those achieved by the urban areas in Uruguay and Argentina. The decline of the multidimensional poverty levels between 1992 and 2006 suggests not only that people are less deprived, but that those deprived experience on average a smaller number of deprivations. This decrease is consistent with the trend shown in income poverty, as estimated in the region by ECLAC (2009). Yet it provides information that "qualifies" the simple, unidimensional trends.

In spite of the progress registered at an aggregate level, the results show persisting poverty in rural areas, with important disparities in relation to urban ones. The information available for Brazil, Chile, El Salvador, and Mexico suggests that people in rural areas are not only more prone to be poor, but also more likely to experience multiple deprivations at the same time. Figure 28.3 shows that in 2006 the measurement of poverty was higher in rural than in urban areas for all four countries—often at least twice as large—for all dimensions (k) chosen. Furthermore, with the exception of Chile, the proportion of individuals suffering multiple deprivations is still high. The pattern suggests that when people living outside cities do not reach the adequate level of achievement in a given indicator (i.e. education), they are more likely to be deprived in several other indicators as well (sanitation, shelter, etc.).

A final result from this study relates to how each dimension contributes to overall multidimensional poverty, as shown in Figure 28.4. In these results, a person is

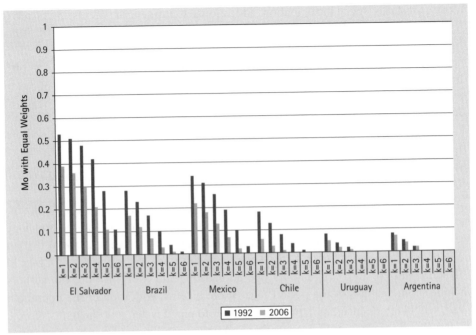

FIGURE 28.2 Evolution of multidimensional poverty in Latin America (six countries): M_o with different k values and equal weights, 1992–2006

Source: Battiston et al. (2009).

considered poor if she falls short of the adequate level in two or more dimensions ($k = 2$).[16] Looking at the contributions of each dimension to the multidimensional poverty measure (Mo), as well as the deprivation rates by dimension, the results show that access to proper sanitation and education of the household head are the highest contributors to overall multidimensional poverty, accounting for 20–30% of overall poverty. Other significant contributors to multidimensional deprivation are income in Argentina, Uruguay, and Brazil, and shelter in Chile and Mexico. Alternatively, deprivation arising from children being unable to attend school is among the lowest contributors in all countries, as a result of the high enrollment rates observed in the region. This last result suggests that future generations may enjoy better-educated household heads, as long as this trend remains.

As an input for the UNDP's 2010 Human Development Report, a recent analysis conducted by Alkire and Santos (2010) applies the AF class of indices to about 108 developing countries in order to construct an international multidimensional poverty index that reflects the distribution of deprivations, calculated from household surveys. The

---

[16] The authors chose this cut-off as it is the minimum k that requires an individual to be deprived in more than one dimension so as to be considered poor (i.e. it is "truly" multidimensional), while at the same time being meaningful for all countries.

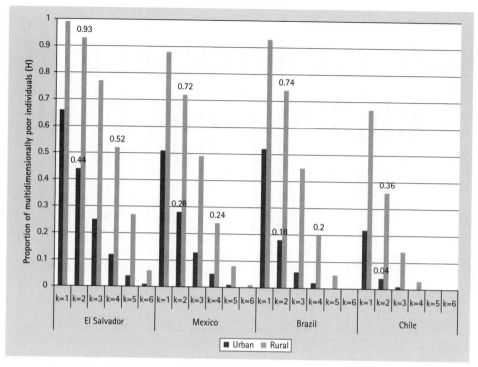

FIGURE 28.3 Multidimensional poverty in Latin America: urban vs. rural (four countries): proportion of individuals deprived (H) in k=1, 2 ... 6 dimensions and equal weights, 2006

Source: Battiston et al. (2009).

index shows disadvantages in very rudimentary services and core human capabilities, being composed by three dimensions (health, education, and standard of living) which are measured using 10 indicators (health through child mortality and nutrition; education by years of schooling and enrollment; and the standard of living by the availability of electricity, water, sanitation, flooring, the type of cooking fuel, and possession of basic assets).

In this analysis, a person is identified as multidimensionally poor if she "is deprived in any two health/education indicators, or if she is deprived in all 6 standard of living indicators, or if she is deprived in 1 health/education indicator plus 3 standard of living indicators" (Alkire and Santos 2010). The measurement for Latin America shows that poverty estimates are highly heterogeneous across countries. While Uruguay, Ecuador, Argentina, and Mexico range between 2% and 4% of the multidimensionally poor, in Haiti, Guatemala, Bolivia, and Honduras the incidence goes up to 33%–57% (see Table 28.3). In the case of the breadth of deprivations suffered by the poor, Latin Americans are deprived in about 44% of the indicators, on average, the Surinamese being the most deprived in 59% of the indicators.

In general, the proposed approaches to the multiple dimensions of poverty have provided valuable elements for the better design and targeting of public policies to different

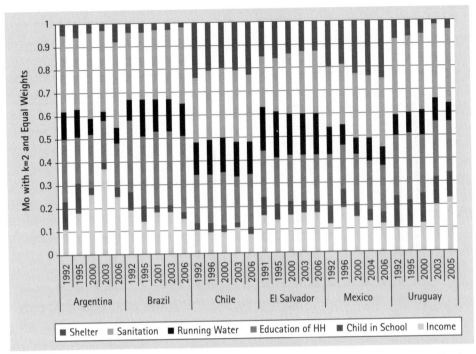

FIGURE 28.4 Evolution of poverty in Latin America by dimension (six countries; contribution of deprivation by dimension to M_0 with k=2 and equal weights), 1992–2006

Source: Battiston et al. (2009).

groups with specific deprivations. While in recent years a combination of positive economic growth with broader social programs has driven improvements in the poverty levels for several countries in the region, the effects of the recent global financial crisis will have a negative impact on these achievements. These effects will be reflected not only in the direct deterioration of purchasing power or through unemployment, but also in direct effects on indicators of health, nutrition, and education, with permanent impacts on long-run wellbeing. Poverty is multidimensional, and therefore the analytic tools for a better and more equitable public action must be equally multidimensional. The actual and potential policy relevance of the measures reviewed so far is discussed in the following section.

28.5 POLICY APPLICATIONS OF MULTIDIMENSIONAL MEASUREMENT

The multidimensional approaches have slowly gained attention in policy circles. For example, one of the most important applications of principal components techniques for public policy purposes is represented by Mexico's Marginality Index (*Índice de Marginación*), used as a criterion to redistribute resources from federal sources. On the

Table 28.3 Multidimensional poverty index in Latin America and the Caribbean (estimate for mid-2000s)

Country	% of poor	Contribution of each dimension			
		Breadth of poverty	Education	Health	Standard of living
Argentina	3	37.7	41.1	13.8	45.1
Belize	5.6	42.6	22.8	35.8	41.4
Bolivia	36.3	48.3	30.4	22.9	46.6
Brazil	10.8	45.2	71.1	8.8	20.1
Colombia	10.6	44.5	29.1	30.2	40.7
Dominican Republic	11.1	43.3	40.6	18.1	41.3
Ecuador	2.3	41.7	71.6	9.6	18.8
Guatemala	36.5	52	41.5	30.5	28
Guyana	12.9	39.6	3.8	77.2	19
Haiti	57.2	53.3	27.5	21.5	51
Honduras	33.2	48.9	37.5	17.5	45
Mexico	4.1	39	37.6	25.4	36.9
Nicaragua	18.4	43.7	28.4	18	53.6
Paraguay	17.1	49.8	40	15.7	44.4
Peru	19.8	43	15.3	19.1	65.6
Suriname	7.5	59.2	42.5	21.6	35.8
Trinidad and Tobago	5.6	35.1	1.3	94.3	4.4
Uruguay	2.2	34.5	96.6	0.5	2.9

Source: Alkire and Santos (2010).

basis of a multidimensional approach, this index summarizes nine socioeconomic indicators related to education, housing, geographical dispersion, and access to public services, aggregated at the geographical level.

The Marginality Index is also used as a first-step selection criterion in the Mexican CCT program, originally named *Progresa*, later *Oportunidades*. As discussed in Fiszbein and Schady (2009), in order to select beneficiaries, several CCT programs in Latin America typically employ geographical targeting, household targeting, or a mix of both. Household targeting is usually carried out through proxy means testing—although this may vary: for example, Brazil's CCT programs rely on means (not proxy means) tests. The formula for the proxy means test is generally obtained from household survey datasets, although the specifics also vary across countries.

Among the existing targeting approaches in CCT programs are Jamaica's Program of Advancement through Health and Education (PATH) and Ecuador's *Bono de Desarrollo Humano* (BDH) programs, which target households using proxy means testing. *Mi Familia Progresa* in Guatemala and *Red de Protección Social* (RPS) in Nicaragua draw on both geographical and household multidimensional targeting. Other programs use geographical targeting as a first stage, and then appeal to community-based selection of beneficiaries. Such is the case of Peru, *Juntos*, and the *Tarjeta de Asistencia Escolar/ Incentivo a la Asistencia Escolar* (TAE/ILAE) in the Dominican Republic. Examples of other approaches are Argentina's *Programa Familias* and the *Subsidio Unitario Familiar* (SUF) in Chile, which use indicators like whether the households are enrolled in the social security system, or whether the household head has completed secondary school.

The policy relevance of these identification systems goes beyond the CCTs themselves, and frequently the same system is used to target several different policy interventions. For example, the System of Beneficiaries (SISBEN), a proxy means test used in Colombia for the CCT program *Familias en Accion*, is also exploited to determine eligibility in training, workforce, and health programs. *Chile Solidario* employs a targeting system that is also used to select beneficiaries for older-established subsidies and allowances. The uses of a new proxy means test system in Jamaica also go beyond the CCT program, including determining eligibility for school lunches.

Although the design may vary across the region, it is clear that a multidimensional perspective is somehow embedded in these programs. Yet there is no clear recognition of the multidimensional nature of the phenomenon in the overall policy design. It can be fairly said that multidimensionality thus far has entered the policy world through the back door of targeting. An explicit multidimensional approach to poverty is needed. Those whose poverty is characterized by a shortfall of income benefit from social programs that complement their incomes, but such policies might not reach segments of the population that are deprived in other dimensions. Those that are poor in basic services (ie. education, health, etc.) require specific interventions, perhaps unrelated to targeted transfers of income.

Figure 28.5 portrays the various typologies of poverty that can be discerned through a multidimensional approach. For instance, those who are poor in terms of income, but also deprived in a certain number of dimensions—characterized as structurally

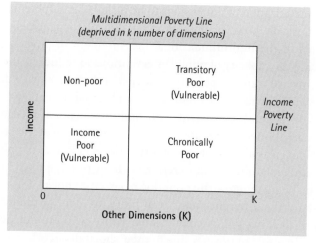

FIGURE 28.5 Multidimensional and income poverty

poor—benefit from programs that address the underlying causes of poverty such as structural unemployment. These policies, however, are not necessarily optimal for those who are not income-poor, but are deprived in a certain number of dimensions. This group, usually overlooked when targeting poverty reduction programs, is vulnerable to aggregate and idiosyncratic shocks, and requires social safety nets to prevent them from falling into structural poverty. Social policy is more effective and efficient if it customizes its programs to address the underlying characteristics of poverty in different groups. In this sense, multidimensional poverty measures provide policymakers with information to better target their poverty reduction strategies.

28.6 CONCLUDING REMARKS

Concepts and measurement of poverty have important implications for policy design. There is now a consensus in both academic and policy circles regarding the multidimensional nature of poverty. There are several methodological approaches to the issue, dealing in different ways with the selection of dimensions to be included, the way to measure them, and the weights that should be assigned to each. Empirical weights, obtained through statistical methods such as principal components and factor analysis, have been used in recent social programs to select beneficiaries, and have certainly reduced the distortions induced by unidimensional means-testing.

Conceptually, the capabilities approach developed originally by Amartya Sen constitutes a comprehensive way to tackle the problem. By differentiating between the access to resources and services, the process through which such resources are transformed into "beings" and "doings," and the evaluation function of individual states, allow for a thorough characterization of dimensions to be included and (potentially) weights to be assigned. Empirically, however, the approach is difficult to implement.

The final goal of the multidimensional measurement of poverty is to improve policy, enhancing the capacity of public interventions to reduce its incidence. There has been a downward trend in poverty incidence in Latin America during the first years of this century, when measured by the traditional monetary method. While the trends are, in general, consistent with multidimensional measures using the methodologies mentioned above, approaching the evolution of the phenomenon in a multidimensional way allows for an identification of key areas of policy. Moreover, it furthers the understanding of "different ways to be poor." Being chronically poor is different from being temporarily poor due to specific shocks, for example. A failure to understand the difference and, even more, to identify the different groups could lead to misleading policy conclusions. Those who are not poor in income terms but are vulnerable to poverty due to their shortfalls in other dimensions also require a good design of policy interventions. Indeed, a multidimensional approach to poverty helps understand the need for universal policies in several dimensions, going beyond targeted programs—which should complement rather than compose the foundation of social policy.

References

ALKIRE, S. (2002). 'Dimensions of Human Development', *World Development* 30.2.

—— (2008). 'Choosing Dimensions: The Capability Approach and Multidimensional Poverty', in N. Kakwani and J. Silber (eds), *The Many Dimensions of Poverty*, London: Palgrave Macmillan.

—— and FOSTER, J. (2007). 'Counting and Multidimensional Poverty Measurement', OPHI Working Paper No. 7, Oxford.

—— and SANTOS, M. E. (2010). 'Acute Multidimensional Poverty: A New Index for Developing Countries', UNDP-HDRO background paper, New York.

AMARANTE, V., ARIM, R., and VIGORITO, A. (2008). 'Multidimensional Poverty among Children in Uruguay 2004–2006: Evidence from Panel Data', presented at the Network on Inequality and Poverty, Santo Domingo (June).

ANAND, S., ARIM, R., and VIGORITO, A. (2007). 'Un análisis multidimensional de la pobreza en Uruguay: 1991–2005', Working Paper No. 10/06, Instituto de Economía, Universidad de la República, Uruguay.

—— and SEN, A. (1994). 'Human Development Index: Methodology and Measurement', UNDP-HDRO Occasional Paper No. 12, New York.

—— —— (1997). 'Concepts of Human Development and Poverty: A Multidimensional Perspective', UNDP Human Development Papers, New York.

ARIM, R. and VIGORITO, A. (2007). 'Un análisis multidimensional de la pobreza en Uruguay. 1991–2005', Documento de Trabajo DT10/06, Instituto de Economía, Universidad de la República.

ATKINSON, A. B. (1998). 'Social Exclusion, Poverty and Unemployment', in A. B. Atkinson and J. Hills (eds), *Exclusion, Employment and Opportunity*, London: LSE.

BARROS, R. P., DE CARVALHO, M., and FRANCO, S. (2006). 'Pobreza multidimensional no Brasil', Texto para discussão No. 1227, IPEA, Brasilia.

BASU, K., and LÓPEZ-CALVA, L. F. (2002). 'Functionings and Capabilities', in K. Arrow, A. Sen, and K. Suzumura (eds), *Handbook of Social Choice and Welfare*, London: Elsevier and North-Holland.

BATTISTON, D. et al. (2009). 'Income and Beyond: Multidimensional Poverty in Six Latin American Countries', OPHI Working Paper No. 17, Oxford.

BOURGUIGNON, F., and CHAKRAVARTY, S. R. (2003). 'The Measurement of Multidimensional Poverty', *Journal of Economic Inequality* 1.1.

BURNS, J. H. (2005). 'Happiness and Utility, Jeremy Bentham's Equation', *Utilitas* 17.1.

CERIOLI, A., and ZANI, S. (1990). 'A Fuzzy Approach to the Measurement of Poverty', in C. Dagum and M. Zenga (eds), *Income and Wealth Distribution, Inequality and Poverty*, Berlin: Springer.

CHERCHYE, L., OOGHE, E., and PUYENBROECK, T. V. (2008). 'Robust Human Development Rankings', *Journal of Economic Inequality* 6.4.

CHIAPPERO-MARTINETTI, E. (1994). 'A New Approach to the Evaluation of Well-Being and Poverty by Fuzzy Set Theory', *Giornale degli economisti e annali di economia* 53.

CONCONI, A., and HAM, A. (2007). 'Pobreza multidimensional relativa: una aplicación a la Argentina', CEDLAS Working Paper No. 57, Universidad Nacional de La Plata.

DASGUPTA, P. (1990). 'Well-Being in Poor Countries', *Economic and Political Weekly* 25.31.

DUCLOS, J.-Y., SAHN, D. E., and YOUNGER, S. D. (2006). 'Robust Multidimensional Poverty Comparisons', *Economic Journal* 116.

ECLAC (UN Economic Commission for Latin America and the Caribbean) (2005). *Panorama social de America Latina*, Santiago, Chile: ECLAC.

—— (2009). *Panorama Social de America Latina*, Santiago, Chile: ECLAC.

FERES, J. C., and MANCERO, X. (2001). *El método de las necesidades básicas insatisfechas (NBI) y sus aplicaciones a América Latina*, Santiago, Chile: ECLAC.

FISZBEIN, A., and SCHADY, N. (eds) (2009). *Conditional Cash Transfers: Reducing Present and Future Poverty*, Washington, DC: World Bank.

FOSTER, J. (2006). 'Poverty Indices', in A. De Janvry and R. Kanbur (eds), *Poverty, Inequality and Development: Essays in Honor of Erik Thorbecke*, New York: Springer.

—— GREER, J., and THORBECKE, E. (1984). 'A Class of Decomposable Poverty Measures', *Econometrica* 52.3.

—— LÓPEZ-CALVA, L. F., and SZÉKELY, M. (2005). 'Measuring the Distribution of Human Development: Methodology and an Application to Mexico', *Journal of Human Development* 6.1.

—— McGILLIVRAY, M., and SETH, S. (2009) 'Rank Robustness of Composite Indices', OPHI Working Paper 26.

GRAHAM, C., and PETTINATO, S. (2000). 'Frustrated Achievers: Winners, Losers and Subjective Wellbeing in New Market Economies', Working Paper Series 20, Centre on Social and Economic Dynamics, Brookings Institution, Washington, DC.

GRAY, G., and PURSER, M. (2010). 'Human Development Trends Since 1970: A Social Convergence Story', UNDP-HDRO background paper, New York.

GRIMM, M. et al. (2009). 'Inequality in Human Development: An Empirical Assessment of Thirty-Two Countries', Discussion Paper 6, Courant Research Centre PEG, Göttingen.

GRYNSPAN, R. (2008). *Introducción a las políticas de superación de la pobreza*, Santo Domingo: CEDAF.

HAMMILL, M. (2009). *Income Poverty and Unsatisfied Basic Needs*, Mexico: ECLAC.

HYMAN, G. (2006). 'Poverty Maps from Unsatisfied Basic Needs Indicators in Latin America', mimeograph, Columbia University.

LAYARD, R. (2006). 'Happiness and Public Policy: a Challenge to the Profession', *Economic Journal* 116.510.

LÓPEZ-CALVA, L. F., and LUSTIG, N. (eds) (2010). *Declining Inequality in Latin America: A Decade of Progress?* Washington, DC: Brookings Institution.

——and RODRIGUEZ-CHAMUSSY, L. (2005). 'Muchos rostros, un solo espejo: restricciones para la medición multidimensional de la pobreza en México', in M. Székely (ed.), *Números que mueven al mundo: la medición de la pobreza en México*, Mexico: Porrúa.

MAASOUMI, E. (1993). 'A Compendium to Information Theory in Economics and Econometrics', *Econometric Reviews* 12.

McGILLIVRAY, M. (2005). 'Measuring Non-Economic Well-Being Achievement', *Review of Income and Wealth* 51.2.

MORRIS, M. D. (1979). *Measuring the Condition of the World's Poor: The Physical Quality of Life Index*, New York: Pergamon.

NARAYAN, D. (2000). *Voices of the Poor: Can Anyone Hear Us?* Washington, DC: World Bank.

RAMOS, X., and SILBER, J. (2005). 'On the Application of Efficiency Analysis to the Study of the Dimensions of Human Development', *Review of Income and Wealth* 51.

SEN, A. (1976). 'Poverty: An Ordinal Approach to Measurement', *Econometrica* 44.2.

——(1980) 'Equality of What?', in *The Tanner Lectures on Human Values 1*, Cambridge: Cambridge University Press.

——(1985). *Commodities and Capabilities*, Amsterdam: North-Holland.

——(2008). *The Idea of Justice*, Cambridge, Mass.: Harvard University Press.

SETH, S. (2009). 'A Class of Association Sensitive Multidimensional Welfare Indices', OPHI Working Paper No. 27, Oxford.

STEWART, F. (1985). *Planning to Meet Basic Needs*, London: Macmillan.

SZÉKELY, M. (2003). 'Lo que dicen los pobres', Human Development Paper No. 13, Sedesol, Mexico.

TESCHL, M., and COMIM, F. (2005). 'Adaptive Preferences and Capabilities: Some Preliminary Conceptual Explorations', *Review of Social Economy* 63.

THORBECKE, E. (2003). 'Tensions, Complementarities and Possible Convergence between the Qualitative and Quantitative Approaches to Poverty Assessment', in R. Kanbur (ed.), *Q-Squared: Combining Qualitative and Quantitative Methods in Poverty Appraisal*, Delhi: Permanent Black.

——(2008). 'Multidimensional Poverty: Conceptual and Measurement Issues', in N. Kakwani and J. Silber (eds), *The Many Dimensions of Poverty*, London: Palgrave Macmillan.

TOWNSEND, P. (1979). *Poverty in the United Kingdom: A Survey of Household Resources and Standards of Living*, Harmondsworth: Penguin.

TSUI, K.-Y. (2002). 'Multidimensional Poverty Indices', *Social Choice and Welfare* 19.

UNDP (United Nations Development Program) (various years). *Human Development Report*. New York: Oxford University Press.

——(2010). *Regional Human Development Report for Latin America and the Caribbean*, RBLAC, New York.

World Bank (2001). *World Development Report 2000/2001: Attacking Poverty*, Washington, DC.

CHAPTER 29

····································

ECONOMIC INSECURITY AND DEVELOPMENT IN LATIN AMERICA AND THE CARIBBEAN

····································

ROB VOS

29.1 INTRODUCTION[1]

····································

When the Berlin Wall collapsed in 1989, the talk was of an emerging era of widespread peace, prosperity, and stability thanks to the spread of democratic values and market forces. A string of financial crises in emerging economies in the 1990s and early 2000s, the 2007–8 food and energy security crises, and the 2008–9 Great Recession were certainly not part of that future. Half of the population in Latin America saw economic problems as the number one concern in an opinion survey published at the end of 2009, amidst the global economic crisis. Yet this was not much different from before the crisis: in 2006, interviewees in 10 out of 18 countries mentioned unemployment as their key concern in life, and 67% of the people in the region were worried about losing their job.[2] Delinquency was perceived as the next important problem. Opinion survey evidence is no substitute for careful analysis. Still, it does highlight a growing sense of unease about the economic course that has been charted in recent years.

[1] This chapter has greatly benefited from research undertaken for the *World Economic and Social Survey 2008: Overcoming Economic Security* (United Nations 2008; see also Vos and Kozul-Wright) and I am grateful to Richard Kozul-Wright, Diana Alarcón, Nazrul Islam, Oliver Paddison, Alex Julca, Mariangela Parra-Lancourt, and Piergiuseppe Fortunato for their contributions to that research.
[2] Survey data are from Latinobarómetro, Annual Reports of 2007 and 2009. They can be consulted at http://www.latinobarometro.org

This unease has emerged strongly in advanced countries where increased economic insecurity has been associated with rising inequality and the squeezing of social provisioning. In middle-income countries, including most countries in Latin America and the Caribbean, economic shocks, accelerated trade liberalization, and premature de-industrialization have constrained economic diversification and formal job creation. In more than one case, this has been compounded by intractable poverty which has fed a vicious circle of economic insecurity and political instability and, on occasion, ferocious communal violence, such as food riots that broke out in Haiti in April of 2008 in response to steep rises in food prices.

These concerns have been compounded by new global threats. Climate change has become the defining generational challenge for the international community. Several increasingly destructive natural disasters have provided tangible evidence of the threat this carries for economic livelihoods, in rich and poor countries alike. Unstable financial markets and volatile capital flows have brought devastation to economic livelihoods across the world owing to their adverse impact on productive investment, economic growth and job creation.

This chapter will be mainly concerned with economic insecurity as emanating from global economic volatility; weaknesses in domestic policies and institutions in responding to this; and structural changes that have led to increasing employment insecurity and income uncertainty at the household level. Latin America, more than most other developing regions, suffers from high degrees of economic insecurity, which—though not unambiguously—has increased in recent decades with greater economic openness and a dismantling of traditional social protection systems. While societies and individuals will always have to live with a certain degree of economic uncertainty and insecurity, a high degree of this will be an impediment to development and poverty reduction. It is argued that much—but not all—economic insecurity can be mitigated through a proper integration of macroeconomic, industrial, labor market, and social policies.

29.2 Security matters

It is not easy to give a precise meaning to economic insecurity. This is in part because it often draws on comparisons with past experiences and practices, which have a tendency to be viewed through rose-tinted lenses. In part, it is because security has a large subjective or psychological component linked to feelings of anxiety and safety that draw heavily on personal circumstances. Still, in general terms, economic insecurity arises from the exposure of individuals, communities, and countries to adverse events, and their inability to cope with and recover from their costly consequences.

In trying to gauge the possible damage from these sources of insecurity, economists have distinguished between *idiosyncratic risks*, generated by individual and isolated events such as an illness, accident, or crime, and *covariant risks*, which are attached to events that hit a large number of people simultaneously, such as an economic shock or climatic hazard, and often involve multiple and compounding costs.

Finding the right mix of informal, market, and social measures to help citizens cope with and recover from these events is a longstanding policy challenge. This has essentially meant weighing up the advantages of pooling the risks against the offsetting administrative and behavioral costs (moral hazard) that this can produce. This is easier when the threat is small and reasonably predictable. Precautionary savings, or spreading the risk through insurance contracts, can often suffice, particularly in response to idiosyncratic threats. Covariant risks, which carry significant negative spillovers, are more difficult to manage in this way, leading to various forms of social insurance and assistance.

In most advanced countries, a mixture of public and private mechanisms has been used to ensure maximum coverage and protection. In poorer countries, the mix of options is much more limited, with greater reliance on informal mechanisms such as family support or moneylenders. Expanding those options of risk management has received greater attention from the policy community in recent years.

However, managing risk does not exhaust the insecurity challenge. This is because for many of the events that threaten downside losses, the causes are more systemic in nature, and the outcomes can be catastrophic. Such events are much more difficult to predict and to cope with. This, for example, is true of economic crises. But the same is mostly true for natural disasters and political conflicts.

Addressing these threats is primarily the responsibility of national governments by removing underlying vulnerabilities, greatly reducing the exposure of households and communities, and supporting their recovery if disaster does strike. This requires significant investment in prevention, preparation, and mitigation measures. But it also requires filling the public domain with a dense network of institutions—a social contract—that can secure spaces in which individuals, households, firms, and communities can pursue their day-to-day activities with a reasonable degree of predictability and stability, and with due regard for the aims and interests of others. This is particularly true in societies with an increasingly complex division of labor, where high levels of trust, long-term investments in physical, human, and social capital, and openness to innovation and change are key ingredients of long-term prosperity and stability.

29.3 Growth and macroeconomic instability

Defying popular beliefs, we seem to be living in an economically more secure world, at least by some macroeconomic measures. Leaving aside the impact of the Great Recession of 2008–9, macroeconomic volatility has decreased worldwide over the past decades as compared with the 1970s and 1980s. Fluctuations in output growth and inflation rates have fallen in developed and developing countries alike, including Latin America and the Caribbean (see Table 29.1). Economic volatility, however, remains much higher in developing than in developed countries. The standard deviation of output growth fell to less

Table 29.1   Macroeconomic volatility (standard deviations in %)

	1971–80	1981–90	1991–00	2001–8
Developed economies				
GDP growth	2.4	1.9	1.5	1.0
Gross fixed capital formation	6.0	5.4	4.4	3.4
Private consumption	7.2	5.6	4.9	5.6
Inflation[a]	9.2	6.1	2.4	2.0
Latin America and Caribbean				
GDP growth	3.3	4.6	3.4	3.1
Gross fixed capital formation	11.3	13.3	11.8	9.8
Private consumption	6.2	5.2	5.6	3.4
Inflation[b]	63.3	310.3	23.4	7.6
Africa				
GDP growth	5.2	4.7	3.2	2.2
Gross fixed capital formation	17.3	16.5	14.3	12.5
Private consumption	7.5	9.5	8.0	8.7
Inflation[c]	13.0	16.0	103.9	13.7
East and South Asia				
GDP growth	4.6	3.4	3.0	1.6
Gross fixed capital formation	11.3	9.3	11.0	6.0
Private consumption	4.9	3.9	3.7	1.6
Inflation[d]	9.9	9.0	9.4	5.4

Source: UN/DESA, based on United Nations Statistics Division, National Accounts Main Aggregates database; inflation estimates based on World Bank World Development Indicators Online database, Accessed 8 May 2008.

Notes: Volatility of GDP growth, investment, consumption is measured by the standard deviation of the annual change of GDP (%), investment and private consumption at constant prices of 2000 weighted by the relative share of countries' GDP at the beginning of the period. Inflation is defined as average change of annual consumer prices weighted by the share of countries' GDP at the beginning of the period. It was calculated by the subset of countries in each region with available data.

[a] "Developed countries" does not include economies in transition.

[b] Inflation rates for 16 Latin American countries and Barbados which represent around 55 % of regional GDP.

[c] Inflation for 28 African countries which represent almost 90 % of regional GDP.

[d] East and South Asia's inflation estimate includes 10 countries, which represent around 60 % of regional GDP.

than 1% in the developed countries in the pre-crisis period from 2001 to 2008, compared with more than 2% during the 1970s, as shown in Table 29.1. Including the 2009 crisis and subsequent recovery, however, the volatility measure was back up to that of the 1970s. In developing countries, the fluctuation around the average economic growth rate came down to 2.4 percentage points, less than half the degree of volatility in the 1970s or 1980s. This also holds when including the years of the Great Recession. Output volatility is generally lower in developing Asia than in other parts of the developing world. In Latin America and the Caribbean, growth volatility has fallen from highs during the lost decade of the 1980s, but remains similar to those of the 1970s with a standard deviation averaging 3 percentage points around the mean growth rate. Inflation rates have fallen worldwide, and with them, aggregate price volatility. In Latin America and the Caribbean, average inflation volatility dropped significantly in the 1990s and further in the present decade, in a clear break with the hyperinflation episodes of the 1980s.

Table 29.1 also shows that investment growth remains highly volatile in most developing-country regions. During the 2000s, investment volatility fell notably in East and South Asia, but much of it is explained by the robust economic growth context in China and India. Investment volatility has remained particularly high in Latin America and Africa.

The continued high investment volatility in Latin America results from a combination of factors. Even leaving aside the global crisis of 2008 and 2009, the frequency and depth of economic recessions have remained high since the 1970s (see Table 29.2). This remains a major source of business uncertainty, holding off long-term productive investment. Accelerated trade and capital market opening during the 1990s have been related sources of volatility and investment uncertainty. This has been reinforced by the mostly procyclical macroeconomic policy stance in many countries in response to downturns and recessions. As discussed further below, the emerging phenomenon described as "financialization" possibly has also tilted incentives against productive investment and job creation, and has presented itself as a new source of economic insecurity.

Reduced macroeconomic volatility has, by and large, come at the cost of lower average growth rates. In developed countries, growth of GDP per capita has been on a declining trend since the 1970s. For developing countries, trend growth has been up since the 1990s, but this is largely explained by fast growth in China and India. When these are left out, the trend level of per capita output growth over the past three decades is well below that of the 1970s, including for Latin America and the Caribbean (Figure 29.1). A few Latin American countries (like Argentina, Chile, and Costa Rica) managed to step up growth from levels achieved in the 1970s, in part because of crises suffered in that decade.

A predictable macroeconomic environment is an essential element of a strong investment climate. A volatile business climate can increase uncertainty, making investors reluctant to expand capacity, which in turn can slow productivity growth, increasing the potential for further uncertainty. In the absence of automatic stabilizers and because of the heavier reliance of investment on external financing and imported capital goods, the business cycle is expected to be more volatile in developing than in developed countries. This can make it all the more difficult to establish a long-term development path, given that the minimum scale of investment required to launch and sustain an industrialization drive has been steadily rising (United Nations 2006; Ocampo and Vos 2008).

Table 29.2 Incidence of recessions

	1971-80			1981-90			1991-2000			2001-6		
	No. of recessions	Avg. length in years	Avg. GDP shortfall	No. of recessions	Avg. length in years	Avg. GDP shortfall	No. of recessions	Avg length in years	Avg GDP shortfall	No. of recessions	Avg length in years	Avg GDP shortfall
Developed economies[a]	44	1.22	-2.52	44	1.38	-1.90	66	2.44	-8.78	17	1.46	-1.36
Developing economies	122	1.79	-4.18	134	2.36	-4.89	121	1.72	-3.77	47	1.54	-2.75
LAC	27	2.26	-2.74	50	2.52	-4.37	40	1.48	-2.79	19	1.25	-2.57
East Asia	12	1.29	-3.07	10	2.02	-3.82	14	2.10	-5.77	7	1.29	-1.72
South Asia	10	1.65	-4.72	3	2.00	-4.18	5	1.44	-1.70	1	1.00	-1.93
Africa	43	1.68	-3.83	41	2.34	-4.00	34	2.09	-3.45	10	2.06	-2.31
Least developed	85	2.24	-4.39	75	2.74	-4.13	70	2.47	-4.75	33	1.59	-3.37

Source: UN/DESA, based on United Nations Statistics Division, National Accounts Main Aggregates database.

Note: A recession is defined as episodes of negative growth. Average length is the average number of years of negative GDP growth. Average shortfall is the average decrease in GDP growth during a recession.

a "Developed economies" include countries from European Union (EU), other Europe, Commonwealth of Independent States, and other economies in transition.

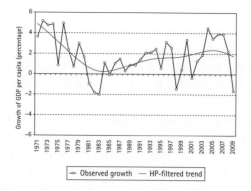

FIGURE 29.1(a) Growth of GDP per capita in developing countries, excluding China and India, 1970–2009

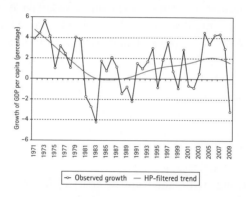

FIGURE 29.1(b) Growth of GDP per capita in Latin America and the Caribbean, 1970–2009

Source: UN/DESA, based on UN Statistics Division, National Accounts Main Aggregates database

Notes: The grey line is a smooth trend on the rate of growth of GDP per capita calculated with a Hodrick and Prescott Filter. It removes short-term fluctuations from longer-term trends. Following the literature, the long-term trend in the figure was calculated with a lag of 1 and μ = 100, as suggested for yearly data.

29.4 GLOBALIZATION AND ECONOMIC INSECURITY

29.4.1 Trade shocks

Trade volumes and terms-of-trade fluctuations have historically played a major role in the business cycles in developing countries, particularly in commodity-dependent economies. This is still the case, and has likely been accentuated by the widespread shift towards export-led strategies in the developing world.

The degree of diversification of countries and their insertion into world markets constitute an important factor explaining growth and economic instability. The steady diversification of economic activity has been identified as a common feature of a modern growth path and closely associated with industrial development (Imbs and Wacziarg 2003). The diversification of exports towards higher value added products increases the resilience of countries to trade shocks, and provides a stronger foundation for improving growth and stability over longer periods of time (Rodrik 2007).

Accordingly, trade shocks form a challenge in particular for countries reliant on more traditional export sectors, as remains the case for most countries in Latin America and the Caribbean. South and Central America still rely on primary products and simple manufactures (around 78% of exports in 2005, down from around 90% in 1983). In contrast, the share of primary products, resource-based, and low-technology manufacturing in the total exports of East Asia declined from 76% in 1980 to 35% in 2005. China alone reduced its share from 93% in 1985 to 44% in 2005.

For many Latin American countries, the overall impact of terms-of-trade shocks over the period 1980–2005 was negative, with a reversal in the late 1990s when some countries benefited from favorable movements, and again since 2003 up to the global crisis of 2008 and 2009 when commodity prices collapsed (Morley and Vos 2006).

International trade, in that sense, continues to be a major source of instability, especially in the less diversified economies in the region. Figure 29.2 highlights the stark difference in sensitivity to trade shocks (defined as changes in export volumes plus terms-of-trade effects) depending on whether economies are primary exporters or have moved up the ladder and become exporters of manufactures, or have diversified exports and related production structures.

However, while moving up the ladder and diversifying into manufactures may reduce an economy's vulnerability, it is no guarantee of insulation from external shocks. Lack of market diversification may constitute a further source of vulnerability. Mexico, for instance, diversified into more technologically advanced, assembly-made manufactures. The strong dependence (more than 80%) on United States markets made Mexico's economy particularly sensitive to the business cycle of its Northern neighbor, as reflected in the strong downturn of Mexico's economy in 2009.

New patterns of trade have also induced other forms of economic insecurity, especially for workers in export sectors that are part of global value chains. The "offshoring" of manufacturing and service activities of developed countries to lower-cost locations has created sizeable amounts of new jobs in developing countries. The process has its roots in the early 1970s, but its acceleration during the 1990s and 2000s has coincided with the coming on tap of vast new sources of labor in the developing world, particularly in China and India. While a source of employment creation, an important share involves low value added and unstable assembly jobs, like the *maquiladores* in Mexico and large parts of Central America and the Caribbean. When the job creation takes place in production enclaves with the shallowest of linkages with the surrounding economy, it still leaves workers and the economy at large exposed to unexpected shocks if firms decide to run down or shift the activity in response to shifts in perceived global market conditions and production cost differentials.

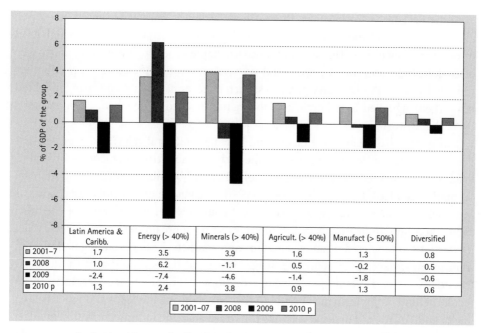

	Latin America & Caribb.	Energy (> 40%)	Minerals (> 40%)	Agricult. (> 40%)	Manufact (> 50%)	Diversified
2001–7	1.7	3.5	3.9	1.6	1.3	0.8
2008	1.0	6.2	-1.1	0.5	-0.2	0.5
2009	-2.4	-7.4	-4.6	-1.4	-1.8	-0.6
2010 p	1.3	2.4	3.8	0.9	1.3	0.6

☐ 2001–07 ■ 2008 ■ 2009 ■ 2010 p

FIGURE 29.2 Latin America: trade shocks of countries grouped by sector of export specialization, 2001–10 (% of GDP)

Source: UN/DESA, World Economic Vulnerability Monitor, No. 3 (January 2010).

Notes: "Trade shocks" are defined as changes in demand for merchandise exports in volume terms plus the change in the terms of trade, expressed as a percentage of GDP. Defining countries by sector of export specialization (based on current dollar values, 3-year average 2006–8). "Export diversified countries" are defined as those where the export sector with the highest concentration is no greater than 40% of the total or 50% of the total for manufactures since it covers a larger number of products. Otherwise, they are considered export-specialized in the sector of greater concentration. Thus: "Manufacture exporter" is when manufacture exports are greater than 50% of total exports. "Energy exporter" is when the main exports are energy and are greater than 40% of total exports. "Mineral exporter" is when the main exports are minerals and metals and are greater than 40% of total exports. "Agriculture exporter" is when the main exports are food and agriculture raw material and are greater than 40% of total exports.

Policymakers have long sought ways to manage international trade in order to maximize the benefits and limit the costs. Successful cases have never relied solely on trade liberalization.

29.4.2 Unleashing global finance

The weight and influence of financial markets, financial actors, and financial institutions have grown dramatically in recent years. This has been accompanied by a massive accumulation of financial assets and by a variety of institutional innovations that have supported growing levels of debt in the household, corporate, and public sectors. Domestic financial debt as a share of GDP has just about doubled in Latin America since the early 1980s. This process of "financialization" has, in turn, helped to entrench a singular macroeconomic policy focus on fighting inflationary threats.

In the decades following 1945, the business cycle was mainly driven by investment and export demand and underpinned by strong wage growth which fed into high levels of consumer spending. This was not always a stable process. Levels of volatility were often quite high, and wages, profits, and tax revenues would often outpace productivity growth, leading to inflationary pressures, current account deficits, and rising indebtedness. These signalled to policymakers that action needed to be taken, often ending in cyclical downturn.

This pattern has been changing as debt, leverage, collateral value, and expected asset prices have become dominant drivers of the cycle. The shift from an income-constrained to an asset-backed economy has been supported by the liberalization of international capital markets. Indeed, the links between domestic financial markets and capital flows are much stronger in developing countries. Most countries in Latin America opened their capital accounts prematurely in the 1990s, creating mutually reinforcing, pro-cyclical interactions among credit, capital, and currency markets. Under weak regulation, common to most developing countries, surges in capital flows exacerbated the tendency towards excessive risk-taking, creating the conditions for boom–bust cycles, and were key factors behind multiple financial crises in the region during the 1980s and 1990s (see e.g. Taylor and Vos 2002). Financial volatility thus translated into increased investment uncertainty and volatility, which were detrimental for long-term economic growth. This heightened volatility has resulted in average rates of capital formation still well below those enjoyed in the 1970s. Infrastructure investment and additional manufacturing capacity in Latin America appear hardest hit, both critical to improving the resilience of countries against external shocks. The decline in infrastructure investment is directly linked to pro-cyclical stabilization policies during the 1980s and 1990s, with fiscal consolidation being highly detrimental to public investment (Figure 29.3). In addition, as discussed below, losses of investment, employment, and income incurred during recessions are not fully recovered when the economy turns up, pulling down the long-term average.

29.5 FROM ECONOMIC VULNERABILITY TO ECONOMIC INSECURITY

The pro-cyclical behavior of finance and the vulnerability of countries to external shocks result in economic insecurity for individuals and households. The remaining high investment volatility and consequent lower growth has adversely affected growth of employment and household incomes. Episodes of exceptionally rapid economic expansion driven by financial bubbles can no doubt bring greater prosperity than expansions where finance plays a more passive role. However, there are serious questions about how far that prosperity spreads, and whether susceptibility to deeper recessions or longer periods of stagnation do not result in considerable waste of resources of both capital and labor.

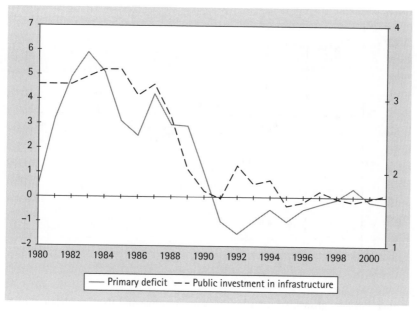

FIGURE 29.3 Latin America: primary deficit (left axis) and public infrastructure investment (right axis), 1980–2001 (% of GDP)

Source: United Nations (2006: fig. IV.9).

A basic lesson to be drawn from successful development experiences is that sustained poverty reduction depends on a fast pace of growth. However, the connection between growth and poverty is not a direct one. Some fast-growing economies have failed to tackle poverty, while some slower-growing economies have had a more successful record in this area (United Nations 2008). Also in Latin America, some countries, like Cuba and the Dominican Republic, that witnessed relatively fast growth of income per capita during the 1990s to mid-2000s, could not prevent the incidence of extreme poverty from rising (Figure 29.4). Those countries did witness increased volatility in per capita output growth during the 1990s and 2000s as compared with preceding decades. Inversely, some countries, including Honduras, managed substantial poverty reduction despite modest growth performance. While the poverty–growth link is not straightforward, it holds more generally that the poorest communities are often most at risk from financial crises, natural disasters, or civil conflicts. Indeed, more often than not, poverty acts to compound these threats, while for poorer people there is a dearth of effective mitigation, coping, and recovery mechanisms.

Insecurity is associated with being vulnerable to falling into poverty or falling into greater poverty. This "downside risk" is a combined function of the *exposure* and *response* to adverse pressures, which include idiosyncratic events such as illness, and workplace accidents and crime, as well as covariant events such as climatic shocks, harvest failure, and economic downturns. Exposure to these downward threats varies with the size, frequency, timing, and bunching of the particular shocks in question, as well as the spatial

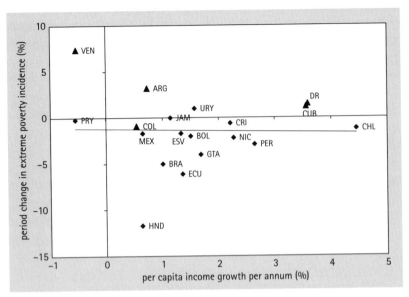

FIGURE 29.4 Poverty–growth relationship in Latin America and the Caribbean, 1990 to mid-2000s

Source: Sánchez et al. (2010: ch. 2); United Nations, Millennium Development Goals database; and United Nations, WESP database.

Notes: Countries marked with ▲ witnessed increased volatility in growth of GDP per capita during the 1990s and 2000s as compared with 1980s. Other countries witnessed less volatility.

proximity to them (and the threat of contagion), but is also linked to the systemic or more cumulative stresses determined by the pattern of relations among growth, distribution and employment.

Perry et al. (2006), reviving the language of Gunnar Myrdal, have suggested that the Latin American region in contrast is caught in a vicious circle of persistent poverty, insecurity, and unstable growth, which has been perpetuated by a persistent and widespread tendency to underinvest in productive assets and social capital.[3] The lack of adequate labor protection, low coverage of social security, and weak social safety nets are part of this vicious circle.

29.5.1 Labor market vulnerability

The expansion–recession–recovery cycles driven by international capital flows have hurt workers because of longer-lasting effects on the downside. In the labor market, booms generated by capital inflows typically would push up real wages, but employment effects would depend on several factors such as the labor intensity of non-tradable sectors relative to export sectors. During the downturns, however, real wages would fall and

---

[3] An earlier World Bank study (De Ferranti et al. 2000) reached the same conclusion.

unemployment would rise sharply, often to levels below those of the previous recession. Subsequent recoveries would be by and large "jobless" in the short run with unemployment rates remaining above pre-crisis levels for several years.[4]

Mexico's labor market adjustment after the "Tequila crisis" of 1994–5 is a case in point. Unemployment, relatively stable at around 3% before the crisis, started to increase during 1994 and reached 5.8% in 1995, almost twice the pre-crisis rate. However, these figures mask the actual loss of jobs, since the share of informal employment rose from 30% in 1993 to 35% in 1995 (ILO 2005). By 1997 Mexico had achieved its pre-crisis income level, with the unemployment rate lagging the economic recovery by one year. However, the share of informal employment remained above the pre-crisis level (van der Hoeven and Lübker 2006). Similarly, Brazil experienced a boom in foreign capital inflows from 1994 which turned to bust after investor sentiment swung suddenly after the Russian debt default of August 1998. In efforts to defend the exchange rate, the Brazilian government strongly raised interest rates. The policy failed to stem massive capital outflows, and a currency crisis emerged. During the economic recession that followed, the rate of unemployment increased from 7.7% in 1997 to 9.6% in 1999. Despite the subsequent economic recovery, unemployment rates stayed at or above 9% till 2005.

As discussed, countries with less diversified production and export structures tend to show greater investment volatility and are more vulnerable to external shocks. With the lack of adequate social protection systems, such volatility directly translates into more insecure employment conditions in most developing-country contexts. Further, specialization in primary export production and light manufacturing, typical in most offshore production zones, does not (in the absence of other policy measures) create strong employment multiplier effects. Much of the production of light manufactures for exports involves assembly operations (*maquiladoras*), which, while labor-intensive, are also characterized by a low share of value-added generation and limited spinoff effects to the rest of the economy, as production is highly reliant on imported inputs. A study of Mexico, for example, estimates that imports for processing constitute as much as one-half to two-thirds of total sales of affiliates of US-based transnational corporations in industries such as computers and transport equipment, while the growth in value added has been negligible (Hanson et al. 2002).

For the majority of urban workers in Latin America, the lack of employment generation in high-productivity activities continues to push vast numbers of workers into low-paid informal sector jobs, generally characterized by a high degree of job and income insecurity. The absence of universal social protection for most of these workers leaves them without proper access to healthcare services and pensions for old age. In 2005, 58.9% of the total urban employed in Latin America had health and/or pension coverage; the lowest coverage (33.4%) was in the informal economy, where 48.5% of workers are employed (Figure 29.5). A large share of informal employment is generally associated with lower levels of development, and this is no different in Latin America (Figure 29.6).

---

[4] On the evidence for jobs and wages in these cycles, see e.g. UNCTAD (2000); ILO (2004); and van der Hoeven and Lübker (2006).

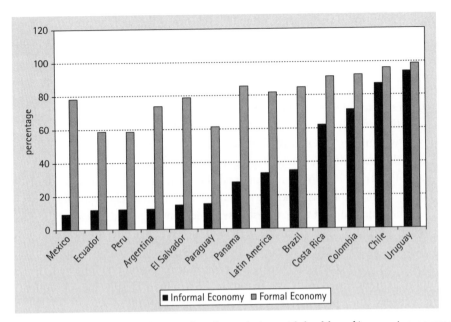

FIGURE 29.5 Latin America: urban employed population with health and/or pension coverage in selected Latin American countries

Source: ILO, 2006 Labour Overview: Latin America and the Caribbean (Lima, International Labour Office, Regional Office Caribbean).

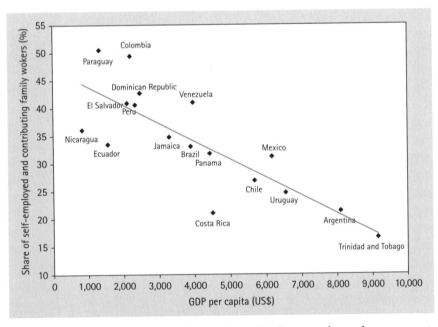

FIGURE 29.6 Latin America and Caribbean: relationship between share of own account and contributing family workers in employment and GDP per capita, mid-2000s

Source: ILO (2007), United Nations (2009).

Reducing the vulnerability of workers in the informal sector will require an expansion of social security coverage and social protection programs. As discussed below, in Latin America coverage of the former generally weakened over the past two decades, as the emphasis on social policies shifted to targeted social safety nets delinked from labor status. Evidence regarding the degree of protection given to the most vulnerable through this policy shift is mixed at best, but such measures will likely fall short if not at the same time backed by the adoption of policies designed to decrease macroeconomic instability, raise the level of productive investment, and, along with industrial policies, to increase the level of employment and productivity in the formal economy.

29.5.2 Social policies and social protection

Social policy in Latin America has gone through distinctively different stages. In the period between World War II and the late 1970s, social policy was seen as a fundamental part of the overall development strategy. An important element of social policy consisted of the widespread provision of subsidies for goods and services, from which the expanding urban middle-income groups benefited most. The subsidies provided income support, but also contributed to keeping wage costs low in support of industrial sector development. Urban workers in growing modern industrial sectors and in government services were also the main beneficiaries of expanding social security covering health risks and old-age income security (pensions), as well as from subsidized and state-provided education and health care services. Without offsetting the urban bias in social transfers, rural producers also received subsidies, and there were varied attempts at land reforms. For the most part, however, the needs of the structurally poor, especially in rural areas, were neglected as part of social policies. The industrial growth strategy and the subsidies relied heavily on public borrowing and were ultimately unsustainable.

With the debt crisis of the early 1980s and the fiscal consolidation as part of the new macroeconomic policy orthodoxy, social policy underwent substantial changes. Low growth and the pressure to reduce fiscal deficits combined to severely restrict new investments in health and education. Spending did not decline as a proportion of the budget in most countries, as the political pressure to sustain civil service jobs and wages, which take up the bulk of social spending, was considerable. However, in many countries in the region spending in absolute terms per child and per health client declined along with overall government spending. In addition, user fees were introduced to cover costs of complementary inputs—books, medicines, and so on—not only conceived to reduce the fiscal burden, but also believed to improve efficiency and quality in social service delivery. The remnants of the old policy provided limited but insecure job guarantees for that portion of generally urban workers in government services or large modern enterprises. The policy adjustments left most of the rural and urban poor with hardly any form of social protection. By the end of the 1980s, there was increasing evidence of growing inequality and substantial increases in poverty and vulnerability (Lustig 1995; Morley 1995).

This led to the recognition that macroeconomic stabilization and structural adjustment programs came at a high social cost, and new, targeted social programs were introduced to protect the poor. These included social emergency and social investment funds introduced with financial support by the multilateral banks. While targeted at the poor, in practice the programs turned out to be limited in coverage and too rigidly designed to adjust coverage and benefits in response to macroeconomic shocks (Lustig 1995). In fact, social policy and overall development and growth strategies of the Latin American countries became totally disconnected. At the same time, emphasis remained on fiscal consolidation and social sector reforms. Evidence of the impact of the pension reforms on coverage are mixed (Mesa-Lago 2007; Vos, Ocampo, and Cortez 2008), but generally did little to provide additional protection to the poorest.

Towards the end of the 1990s, a fourth phase of social policy had emerged. Many countries saw some recovery of growth, and had created greater fiscal space for real increases in public spending on broad social programs. Trade liberalization increased demand for more skilled workers and pressures to raise productivity in order to stay competitive in global markets. Continued high economic volatility and several financial and currency crises during the 1990s, together with the failure of social investment funds to provide effective protection, gave rise to a new form of social program that provided incentives to the poor and vulnerable populations to invest in human capital. Cash transfer programs, such as *Progresa* (later renamed as *Oportunidades*) in Mexico and *Bolsa Escola* in Brazil (later *Bolsa Familia*), were targeted at the poor and were not only designed to provide income support, but were aimed at keeping children in school and/or allowing mothers and children to visit health centres. Many evaluations show that (conditional) cash transfer programs have indeed helped to increase school enrollment and use of health services by the poor; this may help mitigate income insecurity both by investing in education and health and by providing income support (see e.g. Morley and Coady 2003; Coady, Grosh, and Hoddinott 2004; de Brauw and Hoddinott 2008; and Fiszbein and Schady 2009, for surveys). Such programs have now been implemented in a majority of Latin American countries, and include social pension schemes such as those in Argentina, Bolivia, Brazil, and Ecuador. An evident advantage of these programs is that they are relatively easy to implement, have immediate impact, and are affordable (typically costing a few percentage points of GDP). This makes them politically highly attractive.

There are also important drawbacks, however. The most important is that this approach to social policy does not effectively address the underlying causes of persistent high poverty and economic insecurity. For instance, increased spending on education may help increase schooling levels among poor children, but will not raise future income if broader economic policies fail to generate sufficient employment and there are no complementary policies which address idiosyncratic determinants of economic vulnerability, including ethnic, racial, and gender discrimination, and which keep wage returns low to some poor people. Nor will social investments raise incomes if the poor cannot accumulate physical and financial capital, or if recurrent economic downturns force periodic decumulating of their limited assets. Social policy alone, as currently conceived in most Latin American countries, cannot change the economic environment or the underlying elements in the structure of the economy that are contributing to poverty and volatile employment and income conditions for vast numbers of households.

29.6 Breaking through the vicious circle of poverty, insecurity, and unstable growth

It follows that in Latin America and the Caribbean, efforts to break the poverty–insecurity trap will require a policy framework that not only generates higher growth but also examines how investment strategies adopted by both the public and private sectors address the underlying vulnerabilities which expose households and communities to larger downside risks. The main operational objective is to devise long-term poverty reduction strategies for addressing these root causes of chronic poverty through a mixture of measures that not only target the vulnerabilities leading to economic security but also allow for better management of the risk through mitigation and coping measures (Table 29.3).

Table 29.3 Managing risks and vulnerabilities

Macro policies	Social security and social protection programs
Mitigation	Mitigation
Macroeconomic policies (growth-oriented, countercyclical and pro-poor)	Social security and pension mechanisms
Agricultural development policies	Structural cash transfer programs
Infrastructure investment	Targeted price subsidies
Financial regulation and supervision	
Adaptation	Adaptation
Asset transfers (land, credits)	Public health and education
Development of savings mechanisms for the poor and vulnerable	Access to microfinance schemes
	Minimum wage and labor market policies
Coping	Coping
Migration and remittances (policies)	Workfare programs (triggered when unemployment rises)
Credits, debt restructuring, debt relief	Disaster relief
Food subsidies	Cash transfers

Source: United Nations (2008).

Risk reduction measures are taken in advance of an emerging shock or stress, and aim to reduce the likelihood that the shock or stress will occur. The central aim is to make societies and people more resilient to shocks and insecurity by giving them the assets and means to better manage risks. Examples include macroeconomic policy measures to reduce the risk of financial crises, as well as labor market policies that improve employment standards. At the individual or community level, there are many informal mechanisms of risk mitigation including diversification of sources of income, producing large families for farm labor or for income generation, and adopting contractual arrangements, such as sharecropping, which trade off profits for insurance. Examples from a public policy perspective include extension of microfinance and provision of social insurance.

Coping measures are those that take effect only after a shock occurs. Such measures can include informal mechanisms for coping with risk such as selling assets, drawing on savings or stocks of grain, and obtaining help through remittances from family members abroad, along with more formal responses, whether through the market, (e.g. various insurance mechanisms) or in terms of public policy (through transfers under e.g. social assistance schemes and price subsidies). Many of these schemes are identical to those aimed at the chronic dependent poor.

Non-catastrophic events can be frequent but with non-severe effects (transitory illness, temporary unemployment) and households can cope with those mostly from their savings, loans, family transfers, or private insurance. For very poor households, however, such events may still be devastating and require "welfare" policy responses to prevent them from turning into personal and community disasters. Still, given resource constraints and depending on the nature of risks and exposures, a balance may have to be sought between policies that reduce or mitigate risks and make households more resilient towards shocks and capable of better managing risks—for example, through strengthening their assets (adaptation)—and those that provide support in alleviating the immediate distress caused by shocks (coping).[5]

Table 29.3 classifies a wide range of policy areas, which cannot be addressed in full here. In line with the preceding analysis, the focus here will be on forms to mitigate economic insecurity through pro-poor and countercyclical macroeconomic policies and improving resilience to economic insecurity through labor market and social policies.

29.6.1 Risk mitigation through countercyclical and pro-poor macroeconomic policies

Risk reduction (or mitigation) measures aim to lower the probability and severity of negative income shocks. Though there is much that can be done in this regard at the individual and community levels, a prominent role still belongs to the government,

[5] For an earlier discussion about links between poverty and insecurity, see World Bank (2001).

which can use various macroeconomic and other policies to reduce negative income shocks. Macroeconomic policies in support of reducing economic insecurity and poverty would need to be countercyclical, pro-investment, and aimed at greater social cohesion through strong job creation. In the Latin American context this will require—much more than has been the case in most countries—a better integration of macroeconomic and development policies, together with countercyclical fiscal and monetary policy frameworks, including stronger social safety nets which can mitigate the social impacts of economic downturns as well as mitigating the downturn itself.

From the 1980s, the predominant approach to macroeconomic policymaking in Latin America shifted to a narrow focus on controlling inflation, fiscal prudence, and promoting export growth. The debt crisis and the demise of the import-substitution industrialization "model" gave way for a belief that low inflation and deregulated markets would bring economic stability and growth. As discussed, this promise did not materialize. In contrast, the fast-growing East Asian economies embedded macroeconomic policies into a broader development strategy and did not substitute industrial policies for generalized trade liberalization. A broader, more developmental approach to macroeconomic policies could rest on the following pillars:

- Fiscal policies would give priority to development spending, including investment in education, health, and infrastructure. Such policies would also mean using fiscal instruments such as tax breaks, accelerated depreciation allowances, and subsidies to boost productive investment.
- Macroeconomic policies would be conducted on the basis of countercyclical rules.[6] These could consist of fiscal targets that are independent of short-term fluctuations in economic growth (so-called structural budget rules) as well as commodity stabilization funds,[7] such as those that Chile has effectively applied over the past two decades (Fiess 2002; Ffrench-Davis 2006).
- In Latin America, where countries have open capital accounts, conducting countercyclical monetary policies has become increasingly difficult. The space to do so can be increased by introducing measures to control and regulate international capital flows as well as the operations of the domestic financial sector, as again Chile and Colombia have managed for a certain time with some success.
- As with the East Asian experience, monetary policy would be coordinated with financial sector and industrial policies, including directed and subsidized credit

[6] See Ocampo (2008) and Ocampo and Vos (2008: ch. 4) for more elaborate discussions of this approach.

[7] It should be noted, however, that fiscal stabilization funds are by no means a panacea, and careful management of such funds is required. One complication is the difficulty of distinguishing cyclical price patterns from long-term trends. The usefulness of such funds as a form of self-insurance has been questioned on these grounds, given that prolonged commodity price booms or collapses risk either endlessly accumulating resources or rapidly exhausting them. Contingent, market-based insurance instruments are sometimes seen to be better mechanisms (Davis et al. 2001; Devlin and Titman 2004).

schemes and managed interest rates, so as to directly influence investment and savings. The right mix of these policies can be applied deliberately so as to promote investment in specific industries at specific times, but it should be especially promoted in sectors with the greatest potential for upgrading skills, reaping economies of scale and raising productivity growth, and thereby increasing the rates of return on investment.

- Such measures can further set the tone for a different kind of competition policy which, instead of promoting competition for its own sake, looks to utilize it to foster diversification and development.
- Maintaining competitive exchange rates is considered essential for encouraging export growth and diversification. A depreciated real exchange rate lowers labor costs and enhances the competitiveness of labor-intensive exports. The empirical evidence suggests, however, that this does not condemn countries to permanent specialization in low-tech exports; rather, with consistent policy direction, export diversification into higher-end products will be promoted (Rodrik 2005; Cornia 2007; Ocampo and Vos 2008). This contrasts with the policy practice in most Latin American countries of the past three decades, where inflation targeting often resulted in exchange rate overvaluation, undermining export growth and diversification (UNCTAD 2003).
- Agricultural development policies have been key to successful development strategies in East Asia, but relatively neglected in Latin America over the past decades. In the period from 1950 to the 1970s, many countries in the region attempted agrarian reforms mainly focused on land distribution, but resulting in small productivity gains and reduction in rural inequality (De Janvry 1981). What would be needed is a broader approach to agricultural development policies, focusing on access to land, extension services, improved inputs, credits, and rural infrastructure so as to secure greater and more predictable marketable surplus and income to farmers and inputs for agro-industrial development. Crop and weather insurance mechanisms which have also been introduced in developing countries recently, to provide income protection to farmers, have been analyzed as being more effective when embedded in a broader agricultural development strategy (Linnerooth-Bayer and Mechler 2007; United Nations 2008: ch. 3).

29.6.2 Risk adaptation and coping through labor protection and social policies

Despite efforts at the national, regional, community, and individual levels to reduce risks, it is difficult to expect that they can be completely eliminated. It is therefore important to take measures that can help people live with risks. As done in Table 29.3, these measures are classifiable into two types: ex ante or *risk adaptation* measures and ex post or *risk coping* measures, i.e. measures that can be taken when negative income shocks have already occurred. The focus here will be limited to three areas: the role of minimum wage policies as a form of labor protection; use of microcredit and micro-insurance as mechanisms for greater income security; and social welfare programs.

29.6.2.1 *Minimum wage policies*

Minimum wage legislation has been used in Latin America as a social policy ostensibly to protect workers from falling into poverty. The degree of protection provided depends on how many and which workers benefit from it as much as the indirect effects of minimum wages on earnings throughout the economy, employment, and inflation. The application of minimum wage policies varies widely across the region in terms of wage-setting mechanisms, coverage, and enforcement. By the early 2000s, the level of the minimum wage ranged from less than 20% of wages for low-skilled workers to 43% higher than the low-skilled wage, and from less than the poverty line to more than six times the poverty line. Up to 20% of the labor force earns the minimum in some countries and as few as 1% in other countries (Kristensen and Cunningham 2006). There is controversy whether expanding minimum wage coverage and levels would affect growth, employment generation, and inflation. A survey of empirical studies for Latin America suggests that minimum wage increases (a) compress wage disparities, though the degree to which and the spill-over effects to other sectors (including informal sectors) varies across countries in the region;[8] (b) tend to have mixed employment effects, either positive or negative but mostly small and clustered around zero; and (c) do not tend to be inflationary (Lemos 2007).

In some countries, such as in Paraguay, Ecuador, Nicaragua, Colombia, and Venezuela, over 40% of workers earned less than the minimum wage in the early 2000s. Expansion of minimum wage coverage would provide greater income protection to workers. If effectively enforced, minimum wages would also strengthen automatic stabilizers and as such dampen economic cycles during downturns. However, there remain serious enforcement problems, and many see it as, by itself, a particularly blunt instrument for providing more secure livelihoods (United Nations 2007).

29.6.2.2 *Assets and finance for the vulnerable*

Social policy is already well understood to include increasing the ability of the poor to acquire human capital by increasing public spending on health and education programs. Reference has already been made to the potential of using cash transfers to enhance household demand for schooling through cash transfers to mothers (in this case) tied to children's school attendance or visits of mothers and children to health centres. But

---

[8] A positive impact on wages in large enterprises in the formal sector due to minimum wage legislation is reported in most studies. Some have also reported a similar impact on wages in smaller enterprises in Latin America, including informal and rural sectors, with an accompanying positive effect on poverty reduction (Lustig and McLeod 1997; Gindling and Terrell 2005; Kristensen and Cunningham 2006), although others find this to be conditional on a strong growth performance (Morley 1992).

social policy should also embrace more explicit efforts to ensure access of economically vulnerable households and individuals to land and financial markets. Market-friendly land reform programs in Brazil and Colombia undertaken in the 1990s are examples of what can be done, but have remained small and under-funded. In other countries even less is being done.

The liberalization of the financial sector has not helped the poor attain more secure income conditions; those with other assets, including information, education, and land or physical capital to provide collateral, have been much better able to exploit the liberalized financial markets. To increase access to credit for the poor requires a long list of arcane, technical fixes in the system. Promoting institutions that make micro-loans is one step—but to date these institutions account for not even 1% of the credits provided by commercial banks in Latin America. As argued in United Nations (2005), expansion of micro-credit schemes critically depends on development of broader networks of institutions, including credit unions, savings banks, development banks, and special lending windows of commercial banks. Legal changes that allow using moveable assets as collateral and that allow leasing and factoring, creation of credit bureaus, and fiscal incentives that encourage group lending and more timely bankruptcy procedures would all contribute to increasing the supply of conventional bank credits to the poor. Emphasis on competition in the banking sector and (as noted above) on macro-policy to minimize recourse to high real interest rates should also be seen as fundamental to sensible social policy.

29.6.2.3 *Welfare programs and social protection*

Such strategies come in various forms. These range from workfare programs, long in place in many countries, to recently popular cash transfer programs, as discussed. While most of these programs were originally launched and used as ex post measures to help affected people cope with economic downturns, in more recent years they have increasingly been used as ex ante measures to reduce the exposure of the poor to insecurity.

Many countries in Latin America introduced workfare programs after going through spells of economic crisis, such as Chile's emergency employment program in the early 1980s, Bolivia's emergency social fund following its crisis of hyperinflation in the mid-1980s, and Argentina's *Trabajar* program of the early 2000s. Such programs would offer jobs to displaced workers though at wages below market average (typically around half of mean wage rates). In most instances, such programs have remained temporary and ex post responses, however. In contrast, India's Maharastra Employment Guarantee Scheme guarantees 100 days of employment in a year to all who wish to participate, and is an example of a workfare program that was transformed from a post-shock temporary arrangement into a semi-formal permanent employment scheme.

A similar transformation from ex post to ex ante arrangements can be seen with respect to cash transfer programs used to promote specific development objectives, such as school attendance by children and use of health services. Just as budgetary support has become a more popular form of providing aid at the macro-level, so has provision of cash become a more popular form of social protection at the household level.

A perennial issue with the design and implementation of such measures is whether these are best pitched as universal policies or specifically targeted at the poor. The trend in recent years has been towards the latter approach. This has not achieved the right balance. In general, universal systems have a better track record in eliminating poverty. This reflects a combination of a better income distribution (with potentially stronger growth dynamics), a broader political appeal, particularly with support from the middle classes, and some clear administrative and cost advantages.

29.7 CONCLUSIONS

Latin America's economic structures remain highly vulnerable to global economic shocks and macroeconomic volatility. Economy-wide, efficiency-enhancing economic reforms of the 1980s and 1990s have not lived up to their promise of bringing robust and stable growth, let alone dealing with widespread poverty and inequality. In several ways, structural reforms have led to new forms of job insecurity and pushed more people in vulnerable employment conditions. Social policies in Latin America have been subject to major changes in focus, with important consequences for households coping with conditions of economic insecurity. Most importantly, social policies have become increasingly delinked from economic development policies, and emphasis in past decades has been on providing some compensation for target population groups for their lack of access to markets, assets, and job opportunities. A more recent turn towards social transfers linked to human capital investments and credit schemes targeted at the poor put more emphasis on strengthening resilience of households to economic risks and uncertainty. Evidence regarding the degree of protection given to the most vulnerable through this policy shift is mixed at best, but are always likely to fall short if not at the same time backed by the adoption of policies designed to decrease macroeconomic instability and raise the level of productive investment and, along with industrial policies, to increase the level of employment and productivity in the formal economy.

The outline of a broader and integrated approach to macroeconomic and social policy illustrates a simple point: when we focus on assets and opportunities for the poor, we end up talking about the economic system as a whole. Dealing with economic insecurity in Latin America, as much as elsewhere, is not something which can be achieved through either narrowly defined macroeconomic stabilization policies or narrowly defined social welfare programs which temporarily increase welfare levels (or compensate for losses). Both need to be embedded in a broader developmentalist framework to mutually reinforce each other. Only then can the vicious circle of persistent poverty, insecurity and unstable growth be broken.

References

Coady, D., Grosh, M., and Hoddinott, J. (2004). *Targeting of Transfers in Developing Countries: Review of Lessons and Experiences*, Washington, DC: World Bank and International Food Policy Research Institute.

Cornia, G. A. (ed.) (2007). 'Potential and Limitations of Pro-Poor Macroeconomics: An Overview', in *Pro-Poor Macroeconomics: Potential and Limitations*, New York: Palgrave Macmillan.

Davis, J., et al. (2001). 'Stabilization and Savings Funds for Nonrenewable Resources: Experience and Fiscal Policy Implications', IMF Occasional Paper No. 205, Washington, DC.

de Brauw, A., and Hoddinott, J. (2008). 'Must Conditional Cash Transfers be Conditioned to be Effective? The Impact of Conditioning Transfers on School Enrollment in Mexico', IFPRI Discussion Paper No. 757, Washington, DC.

De Ferranti, D., et al. (2000). *Securing Our Future in a Global Economy*, Washington, DC: World Bank.

De Janvry, A. (1981). *The Agrarian Question and Reformism in Latin America*, Baltimore: Johns Hopkins University Press.

Devlin, J., and Titman, S. (2004). 'Managing Oil Price Risk in Developing Countries', *World Bank Research Observer* 19.1.

Ffrench-Davis, R. (2006). *Reforming Latin America's Economies: After Market Fundamentalism*, Basingstoke: Palgrave Macmillan.

Fiess, N. (2002). 'Chile's New Fiscal Rule', mimeograph, World Bank.

Fiszbein, A., and Schady, N. (2009). *Conditional Cash Transfers: Reducing Present and Future Poverty*, Washington, DC: World Bank.

Gindling, T. H., and Terrell, K. (2005). 'The Effect of Minimum Wages on Actual Wages in Formal and Informal Sectors in Costa Rica', *World Development* 33.11.

Hanson, G., et al. (2002). 'Expansion Strategies of U.S. Multinational Firms', in S. Collins and D. Rodrik (eds), *Brookings Trade Forum 2001*, Washington, DC: Brookings Institution.

Imbs, J., and Wacziarg, R. (2003). 'Stages of Diversification', *American Economic Review* 93.1.

ILO (International Labour Organization) (2004). *Economic Security for a Better World*, Geneva.

——(2005). *World Employment Report 2004–05: Employment, Productivity and Poverty Reduction*, Geneva.

——(2006). *Labour Overview: Latin America and the Caribbean*, Lima: International Labour Office, Regional Office Caribbean.

——(2007) *Global Employment Trends 2007*, Geneva.

Kaminsky, G., Reinhart, C., and Végh, C. (2004). 'When It Rains, It Pours: Procyclical Capital Flows and Macroeconomic Policies', NBER Working Paper No. 10780, Cambridge, Mass.

Kristensen, N., and Cunningham, W. (2006). 'Do Minimum Wages in Latin America and the Caribbean Matter? Evidence from 19 Countries', World Bank Working Paper Series No. 3870, Washington, DC.

Lemos, S. (2007). 'A Survey of the Effects of the Minimum Wage in Latin America', Department of Economics Working Paper No. 07/04, University of Leicester.

LINNEROOTH-BAYER, J., and MECHLER, R. (2007). 'Insurance Against Losses from Natural Disasters in Developing Countries', in *World Economic and Social Survey 2008*, New York: United Nations Department of Economic and Social Affairs.

LUSTIG, N. (ed.) (1995). *Coping With Austerity: Poverty and Inequality in Latin America*, Washington, DC: Brookings Institution.

—— and MCLEOD, D. (1997). 'Minimum Wages and Poverty in Developing Countries: Some Empirical Evidence', in S. Edwards and N. Lustig (eds), *Labour Markets in Latin America*, Washington, DC: Brookings Institution.

MESA-LAGO, C. (2007). 'Social Security in Latin America: Pension and Health Care Reforms in the Last Quarter Century', *Latin American Research Review* 42.2.

MORLEY, S. (1992). 'Structural Adjustment and the Determinants of Poverty in Latin America', prepared for the Conference on Confronting the Challenge of Poverty and Inequality in Latin America, Brookings Institution (July).

—— (1995). *Poverty and Inequality in Latin America: The Impact of Adjustment and Recovery in the 1980s*, Baltimore: Johns Hopkins University Press.

—— and COADY, D. (2003). *From Social Assistance to Social Development: Targeted Education Subsidies in Developing Countries*, Washington, DC: International Food Policy Research Institute.

—— and VOS, R. (2006). 'External Shocks, Domestic Adjustment and the Growth Slowdown', in R. Vos, E. Ganuza, S. Morley, and S. Robinson (eds), *Who Gains from Free Trade? Export-Led Growth, Inequality and Poverty in Latin America*, London: Routledge.

OCAMPO, J. A. (2008). 'A Broad View of Macroeconomic Stability', in N. Serra and J. Stiglitz (eds), *The Washington Consensus Reconsidered*, New York: Oxford University Press.

—— and VOS, R. (2008). *Uneven Economic Development*, New York: Zed Books.

PERRY, G., et al. (2006). *Poverty Reduction and Growth: Virtuous and Vicious Circles*, Washington, DC: World Bank.

RODRIK, D. (2005). 'Policies for Economic Diversification', *CEPAL Review* 87.

—— (2007). 'Industrial Development: Some Stylized Facts and Policy Directions', in *Industrial Development for the 21st Century: Sustainable Development Perspectives*, New York: United Nations Department of Economic and Social Affairs.

SÁNCHEZ, M. V., VOS, R., et al. (eds) (2010). *Public Policies for Human Development: Achieving the MDGs in Latin America and the Caribbean*, London: Palgrave Macmillan.

TAYLOR, L., and VOS, R. (2002). 'Balance of Payments Liberalization in Latin America: Effects on Growth, Distribution and Poverty', in R. Vos, L. Taylor, and R. Paes de Barros (eds), *Economic Liberalization, Distribution and Poverty: Latin America in the 1990s*, Cheltenham: Elgar.

UNCTAD (UN Conference on Trade and Development) (2000). *Trade and Development Report 2000: Global Economic Growth and Imbalances*, Geneva.

—— (2003). *Trade and Development Report 2003: Capital Accumulation, Growth and Structural Change*, Geneva.

United Nations (2005). *Building Inclusive Finance for Development*, New York.

—— (2006). *World Economic and Social Survey 2006: Diverging Growth and Development*, New York.

—— (2007). *Report on the World Social Situation 2007: The Employment Imperative*, New York.

—— (2008). *World Economic and Social Survey 2008: Overcoming Economic Insecurity*, New York.

United Nations (2009). *World Economic Situation and Prospects 2009*, New York.

VAN DER HOEVEN, R., and LÜBKER, M. (2006). 'External Openness and Employment: The Need for Coherent International and National Policies', presented at the 22nd G-24 Technical Group Meeting, Geneva (March).

Vos, R., and KOZUL-WRIGHT, R. (eds) (2010). *Economic Insecurity and Development*, New York: United Nations.

——OCAMPO, J. A., and CORTEZ, A. L. (eds) (2008). *Ageing and Development*, New York: Zed Books.

World Bank (2001). *World Development Report 2000/2001: Attacking Poverty*, New York: Oxford University Press.

CHAPTER 30

EMPLOYMENT: THE DOMINANCE OF THE INFORMAL ECONOMY

VICTOR E. TOKMAN

30.1 INTRODUCTION[1]

During almost four decades, the concept of informality has been the object of debate. Its increasing acceptance in the development literature constitutes proof of its relevance: few new concepts in this field introduced during the second half of the last century lasted so long.

The development literature contains diverse readings of the existence of informality. For a large number of development economists, the level of informality is a function of economic development and will tend to fall over time. It constitutes a temporary feature in developing countries. Although cross-country comparisons support this expected outcome, time series evidence for Latin America shows that it has expanded since the 1980s, reaching an average of 64% of non-agricultural employment at the beginning of this century. Its relevance is due to the capacity of the concept to capture some of the most significant employment problems affecting developing countries.

Additional factors contributed to the lasting interest in informality. There are strong links between informality, poverty, and underemployment, as well as a significant presence in the informal sector of vulnerable groups, particularly women and young people. There is increasing evidence that policies to promote better jobs and income for informal workers are feasible and require fewer resources. In addition, the concept of informality has been adapted to the outcomes of the ongoing discussion, and to the emerging

[1] This chapter draws upon several papers written by the author on this subject, esp. Tokman (2008a; 2008b).

factors associated with economic and social changes during the development process. This also constitutes its liability, since prescriptions tend to continuously change. However, the main policy guidelines have remained.

This chapter deals with informality and its transition to formality. This transition enables those working in the informal economy to improve their chances of being included, to become less vulnerable, and to improve their economic performance. The chapter starts (section 30.2) by reviewing briefly the main trends registered in labor markets and the increasing importance of informality. Section 30.3 analyzes the evolution of the concept of informality and in particular, the transit from the informal sector to the informal economy. Sections 30.4 to 30.6 analyze, on the basis of the data available, the size, characteristics, and evolution of the informal economy in Latin America. Section 30.7 briefly outlines the main components of a strategy to promote inclusion and opportunities for those working in the informal economy. The strategy is mostly based on the conceptual framework and on policies already introduced in many countries of the region.

30.2 Main trends in labor markets and emerging patterns

30.2.1 Demographic transition and increased participation of women

Two main processes affected the evolution of the supply of labor: demographic transition and increasing participation of women in the labor market. The demographic transition resulted from the decrease in mortality rates since the 1950s and in fertility rates from the 1960s.[2] As a result, the rate of growth of population slowed from 2.7% to 1.5% between 1950–5 and the present. This process took place in a diverse manner and in different stages among various countries. At the beginning of the 1960s most countries (88.5% of the population of the region) were in the early stages of transition; only Uruguay was in the advanced stage. Five decades later, only Guatemala is in the middle stage, while 97.8% of the population of the region is in the final two stages of the transition.

The demographic transition was accompanied by an increase in life expectancy, to a current average of 73 years, 7.4 years more than at the beginning of the 1980s. It affected

---

[2] The demographic transition is defined in the four stages of the evolution of both mortality and fertility rates. In the first stage, both rates are high and relatively stable. A second stage is characterized by a reduction of the former and the maintenance of the latter. In the third stage, the fertility rate decreases and the mortality rate remains stable. During the final stage, both rates are low and relatively stable. The rate of population growth moves from low to stable to lower and closer to nil respectively in each of the stages.

the growth of different age groups, resulting in an inverse pyramid—where the oldest group is at the top and the youngest at the bottom. It also resulted in a decrease of the dependency rate, since the reduction in the birth rate, affecting the younger population, has been faster than the increase of the oldest age group.

Women's participation in the labor market increased from 30.1% in 1990 to 50.5% in 2008, while the participation rates of men remained at 80%. The gap is decreasing, but remains at 30 percentage points. This trend is similar to that observed in developed countries, although the female rate of participation is higher, since the rates for OECD countries vary from 60% or less in Korea, Turkey, and the countries in southern Europe to more than 80% in the Nordic countries and in Central Europe.

Women's entry into the labor market contributes to increasing incomes in nuclear families by adding one income earner. It also contributes to improving the level of family welfare, and promoting equal opportunities. Households in the upper quintiles register more income recipients than those at the bottom, and women's participation in the labor market constitutes an effective way to escape from poverty. While women in non-poor households register a participation rate of 55%, in poor households the rate is only 43%. Women on average are subject to higher unemployment than men, and their wages are 35% lower than those earned by men for similar jobs.

In addition, a universal increase of education coverage is taking place in the region. The demographic transition reduces the rate of growth of the number of individuals at an early age, when the pressure for more schooling is higher, and hence the demand for additional resources diminish. However, human capital increases and potential income earned at the time of entering into the labor market can be higher, as well as productivity. In addition, participation rates at young ages are already falling because of the postponement of age of entry to the labor market, due to individuals remaining longer in school. This could also mean that, in spite of higher specific youth unemployment rates registered universally, the absolute number involved could be smaller.

30.2.2 Employment generation and informality under economic and labor reforms

From the mid-1980s, and particularly during the 1990s, the world economy registered fundamental changes. Globalization and technological change affected the growth model of developing countries. Successive crises, high financial liquidity, and liberalization of trade and finances transformed the international system, and a major change of the growth model became necessary, particularly in Latin America. Economic reforms were introduced from the 1980s, accompanied later by labor reforms aimed at increasing flexibility in the labor market, while decentralization of production and labor was promoted to improve competitiveness.

The region emerged from the reforms with economies more open, more price stability, and more integration into international markets. However, economic recovery was insufficient, and below the performance during the postwar period. The rate of post-reform growth reached only 2.6% per year, or 1% per capita. Both rates were less than half the rates of 5.2% and 2.7% registered between 1950 and 1980. In addition, growth of productivity per occupied person was almost nil during the 1990s, while it expanded at 2.7% per year during the reference period (Ocampo 2004).

A more integrated world economy, in a context of rapid development of information technology and increasing importance of financial aspects, accelerated the process of diffusion of benefits and costs. The macroeconomic regime changed, and employment was more closely linked with variations in foreign demand, while the expanding internal demand or increasing wages beyond productivity was constrained by the reduced possibility of transferring the impact to prices without affecting international competitiveness. As a consequence, the region became more unstable.

Volatility of output in Latin America was twice that registered in an industrialized countries, and higher than in countries of Southeast Asia. Consumption instability was even higher, three times that of the developed countries, only that of Sub-Saharan countries being lower. The variation of the output coefficient during the 1990s was lower than in the previous decade and higher than in the 1970s, but its level was still significantly higher than in developed countries (1.7 times) and differences in consumption instability increased (De Ferranti et al. 2000).

The scenario of increased volatility resulted in a greater vulnerability to unemployment. Adjustment to unstable growth was made by reducing the level of employment during crises. This option was reinforced by labor reforms geared towards flexibility, by easing the causes for firing, by introducing atypical labor contracts, and by reducing the costs involved. The positive outcome was to diminish the adjustment period. However, real wage volatility decreased due to lower inflation. The cost of adjustment was then absorbed mostly by increased unemployment.

There was also an asymmetric behavior of unemployment during the economic cycle. Unemployment increases during a recession, and takes longer to reduce during the recovery. Unemployment showed conventional behavior during the debt crisis of the early 1980s, but the performance between 1990 and the end of the first decade of this century was different (see Figure 30.1). The decade of the 1990s and the beginning of the following decade were a scenario of successive crisis: "Savings and Loans" in 1988–90, "Tequila" in 1994–5, the "Asian crisis" during 1998–9, Brazil and Argentina in 2001–2, and the more recent world financial crisis that began in 2008 (Tokman 2010). In all these crises, the unemployment rate increased, and except for the most recent one, in each the maximum unemployment level exceeded that of the previous crisis. The peak of unemployment in the S&L crisis was similar to the debt crisis (8.1%), while in subsequent crises unemployment peaked at 10–11% without the rate reducing significantly during the recovery. The only exception is found in the crisis that ended in 2003 and during the recovery reached a rate of 7.4% in 2008, a low level similar only to that reached almost two decades ago. The explanation for this fast recovery is to be found in the boom of commodity prices and high international liquidity that lasted until the first half of 2008. The 8.3% unemployment rate estimated for 2009 marks a reversal in the trend, but economic recovery in 2010 resulted in an unemployment decrease to 7.6%, returning to the level registered before the crisis.

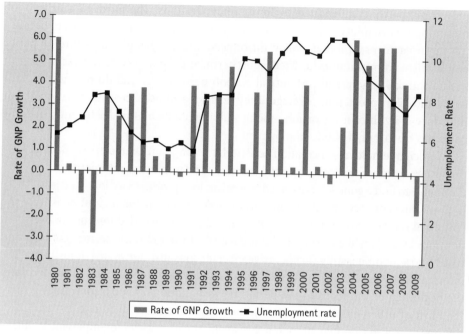

FIGURE 30.1 Unemployment rate and growth of GNP: Latin America and the Caribbean, 1980–2009

Source: ECLAC series of rates of GNP growth and unemployment.

It must also be noted that the levels of unemployment registered after 1980 are significantly higher than the 4% registered during 1950–70. Unemployment becomes then a new problem for the region, and a priority for employment policies in most countries. It is not, however, the only employment problem, nor in most countries the most important one, since changes in the employment structure also affected job quality. Economic and labor reforms affected the employment structure and contributed to the increase in job instability and decrease in protection for workers. Three processes, among others, were important: privatization, informalization, and precariousness. As a result, coverage of labor protection diminished.

Privatization was important in order to diminish fiscal deficits and to provide incentives for private, particularly foreign, investment. Adjustment of the public sector constituted a crucial component of the package, not only to balance the economy in the short run but also to shift the orientation of the long-run strategy mostly by opening up economies, increasing the flows of private foreign and national investment. One effect of the strategy was a restriction on wages and employment in the public sector. The contribution of the public sector to employment generation was 15% on average for Latin America during the 1980s. The percentage fell below 12% during the 1990s and to 9.6% by 2004; later on, it gradually recovered to around 10%. Employment in the public sector is associated with a statutory regime of contractual permanence and full social protection, partly compensated by lower remunerations. The move to a private job meant higher instability and lower protection, particularly for those unable to obtain a job in larger firms. Another policy introduced was to change the nature of public employment from statutory to fixed, short-term, and labor service contracts. Most of these contracts generate uncertainty about job permanence and do not fully include social and labor protection coverage. They help to keep fiscal costs under control, but introduce a significant distortion among public-sector employees affecting, in some countries, up to half of public employment.

Insufficient employment creation constituted a long-run characteristic from at least the 1950s; and given the total or partial absence of unemployment insurance, those who are unable to find a good job are forced to work in low-productivity, low-paid jobs. These jobs are concentrated in micro-enterprises and self-employment, and constitute the "informal sector." During 1950–80, the informal sector provided four out of every ten new jobs created, while during the "lost decade" of the 1980s the sector's contribution rose to 70%, compensating for the private-sector jobs lost during the adjustment. The informal sector accounted for 47% of urban employment in 1990, and expanded from the beginning of the 1990s to the period between 2000 and 2005, contributing more than half of urban employment during the period of structural adjustment and labor reforms. It served to soften, though not to avoid, the increase of unemployment during the period. The following recovery was accompanied by a decrease in the size of the sector.

Informal-sector jobs provide an income generated at low levels of productivity, usually in a non-regulated labor framework and without access to labor and social protection. However, this is neither exclusive of the informal firms nor of the self employed. Precarious labor can also affect individuals working, directly or indirectly, in larger firms. This results both from the decentralization of the process of production to gain competitiveness in more open economies and from introducing increased flexibility in the labor relation as promoted by the reforms, the main factor being the introduction of atypical labor contracts in an environment of weak labor inspections. According to CEPAL (2006a), in Latin America on average only 57.6% of workers in sectors with high or middle productivity were party to a labor contract in 1990, and the percentage decreased to 47.2% by 2005. In addition, the labor contract was permanent only for 26.6% of the workers under a formal contract in these sectors. More than 40% do not have a formal contract, and of these, in three-quarters of cases it is an atypical one. Hence, informality exists beyond the sector.

As a result, social protection deteriorated during the period of reform. Sixty-three per cent of those employed had access to social protection[3] in 1990, falling to around 57–53% in 2005. While access was wider in the case of those working in high- or middle-productivity enterprises, the trends were similar, showing a reduction from 93% to 74–70% during the same period (CEPAL 2006b). The ILO also found a reduction in pension coverage between 2000 and 2005, and a recovery between 2005 and 2008 (ILO

---

[3] Measured as the percentage of workers that contribute to an old age pension.

2009). When health protection is added to the contributions for old age pensions, the percentage of workers covered increase in the ILO study from 50.1% to 54.5% in 2000, and there is a continuous increase in coverage, reaching 61.2% in 2008.

30.3 FROM THE INFORMAL SECTOR TO THE INFORMAL ECONOMY: A CONCEPTUAL TRAJECTORY

The notion of the informal sector was brought to the international discussion on development by the ILO (1972) in an employment report on Kenya.[4] The main contribution was to highlight that the problem of employment in a less developed country was not one of unemployment but rather of employed people who did not earn enough money to make a living. They were "working poor," and economic informality was defined "as a way of doing things." They worked in small units, produce or sell goods and services, employ members of the family and, eventually, wage earners. They were concentrated in urban areas and used little capital, while the division of labor was limited. The key conditions were ease of entry and the operation in unregulated or competitive markets. The outcome was low productivity and a reduced potential for growth. As a result, incomes are low and they constitute most of the poor population. The conceptual interpretation was made in opposition to formality, and on the basis of their lack of access to markets and productive resources.

The conceptualization was also based on the logic of survival, since employment created in the formal sector was not enough to absorb the increasing population, and the only option available was to create their own jobs under conditions of lack of access to resources and markets.[5] The logic of survival was not equivalent to a dualistic approach, since early in the 1970s it was recognized that informality was connected to the rest of the economy, while the issue was to determine the nature of those interrelationships (Tokman 1978). The main question was not whether the informal sector would grow— that was evident, given the rapidly growing labor force and the insufficient creation of new jobs—but rather, as noted by Emmerij (1974), whether the expansion would be accompanied by higher or lower average incomes for those employed in the sector.

Like all new concepts, the informal sector definition was questioned by many authors, inside and outside the ILO, on the basis that informal workers constituted a reserve of labor functional to the accumulation process of modern enterprises, since they were

---

[4] The mission was headed by Richard Jolly and Hans Singer, both from the IDS at the University of Sussex. A previous paper on the subject was written by Hart (1970), who also became a member of the ILO mission and had a strong influence on the Report.

[5] In Latin America this perspective was further developed (Tokman 1978), introducing informality within the employment analysis in a structural framework as developed by e.g. Pinto (1965) and Prebisch (1970).

many and available as needed at lower wage levels (Gerry 1974; Bromley 1978). Linkages were recognized and subcontracting relations were identified, although less intensive than in countries at a more advanced stage of industrialization.[6] A more recent conceptual development was linked to the increasing productive decentralization associated with globalization and changes in technology that made it possible.[7] To deal with an increasing demand, modern enterprises adapt to the new environment by introducing more flexible productive systems and decentralizing production and labor processes, which reduce costs, externalize demand fluctuations, and weaken the bargaining power of unions. The typical employment relationship between an employer and his workers within an enterprise was partly displaced by another employment relationship, not always visible or clearly defined, that could also mean multi-firm involvement. Obligations and responsibilities became diffused, resulting in higher flexibility and lower labor costs, but for the workers reduced wages and loss of protection.

Another research approach allocated a growing importance to the informal sector's operation beyond the prevailing legal and institutional frameworks.[8] This coincided with the reform period guided by the Washington Consensus, which emphasized the need to liberalize the economy and to reduce government intervention, in particular regulations and bureaucracy. Heavy regulations and inefficient processing introduce barriers for business development of micro-enterprises, forcing them to operate informally. As argued by De Soto, Ghersi, and Ghibellini (1986), inadequate regulations designed for formal enterprises affect the legal recognition of the assets of the poor and result in exclusion from property, while "paper walls" and long processing times conspire against formalization. Furthermore, according to a recent interpretation by the World Bank, this results in exit rather than exclusion, since the "voluntary" informal workers avoid formality given the existing barriers. We will come back to this issue in the next section. At the same time, labor reforms in search of flexibility, including decentralization of labor processes, were included as part of the second-generation reforms of the Consensus. The introduction of atypical contracts increased job precariousness and instability, affecting mostly (though not exclusively) workers in formal firms (Tokman 2007).

Thirty years later the ILO revised the definition of informality, expanding the concept from the sector to the economy. The informal economy was defined as "all economic activities by workers and economic units that are—in law or in practice—not covered or insufficiently covered by formal arrangements."[9] It includes both enterprise and work relationships, and rather than eliminating the informal sector it expands it to include all workers that are not sufficiently covered even if they are employed in formal units of

---

[6] Lubell (1991) arrives at this conclusion based on the research undertaken under the World Employment Programme of the ILO in Africa, Asia, and Latin America. His survey of studies and policies undertaken at the OECD Development Center constitutes an important contribution.

[7] Portes, Castells, and Benton (1989). See also Chen, Vanek, and Carr (2004).

[8] De Soto et al. (1986).

[9] ILO (2002).

production. It provides a framework within which to capture the spurious decentralization that is associated with externalization or even subcontracting inside formal units of production.

Beyond the debates and different analytical perspectives, the concept of informality has helped to understand employment and development problems and to identify strategies and priorities. The debate will surely continue, but it is an appropriate time to capture the milestones of an evolving concept. It started as an issue related to urban problems and urban planning, and was upgraded by the World Employment Programme of the ILO which placed it in the context of employment, poverty, and development in developing economies around the world. In the 1970s and up to the mid-80s, informality was crucial to understanding the employment problem in developing countries, and to learning why it adopted less visible forms—particularly, why growth was not ensuring a convergence path to the situation prevailing in developed countries. The informal sector debate served to advance the understanding of the dynamics of growth and employment creation from multiple perspectives, capturing the most relevant structural features of underdevelopment and, particularly, the determinants of poverty and the mechanisms of survival that people were forced to create.

The fundamental changes introduced since the mid-1980s, instead of shifting the debate away from informality, introduced new perspectives into a concept that by then was beyond academic discussion and was becoming an accepted political and policy instrument. Protection in the formal sector was eroded and jobs became more unstable. This was increasingly visible, affecting not only the structurally excluded in the informal sector but also those working in small and medium-size enterprises participating in decentralized production chains, who were becoming more vulnerable to economic fluctuations and emerging risks, while the expected upward mobility to more stable and protected jobs weakened. The recognition of the workers in this situation as informal, but beyond the sector, was captured by expanding the definition of informality to the economy (ILO 2002). This revised concept includes the informal sector, but adds all those workers without protection, even if they are employed in formal activities.

The introduction of the informal economy contributed to a focus on jobs and workers' rights associated with the employment relation. Lack of compliance with regulations is subject to sanctions. However, this hybrid definition can still give place to a less uniform approach. This is the case, for instance, in relation to the self-employed or micro-entrepreneurs who are not subject to a labor relation but are directly affected by government regulations. Another situation prevails even in relation to those working in micro-enterprises that fail to fully comply with labor regulations because of the inability of these units to absorb the cost involved. The informal-sector units in general comply with labor obligations—although not with all and particularly not with contributions to old age pensions (Tokman 1992). Lack of protection is the result rather than a characteristic of the post. Contributions to social security can only be afforded if those working in the sector are able to evolve out of the low productivity/low surplus trap.

30.4 THE INFORMAL ECONOMY IN LATIN AMERICA

30.4.1 Dimensions, structure, and country diversity

The informal economy in Latin America accounted for 64% of non-agricultural employment in 2008.[10] The informal sector accounted for 48.5.7%, while 15.5% were unprotected waged workers occupied in formal enterprises.[11]

The informal economy expanded from 58.8% to 64% of non-agricultural employment between 1990 and 2008, as a result of increases in the informal sector and precarious workers in formal enterprises. Although they both contributed to the expansion of the informal economy, the rate of growth of the latter was almost five times that of those employed in the informal sector (Table 30.1).

The situation among countries is diverse. Three groups of countries can be distinguished. The informal economy exceeds 65% in Andean and Central American countries (El Salvador, Guatemala, Honduras, Nicaragua, Ecuador, Paraguay, Peru, and Bolivia). In Brazil, Mexico, and Argentina the informal economy reached between 55% and 65%. The remaining group of countries, Uruguay, Panama, Costa Rica, and Chile, registers an informal economy below 50%.

The differences in size of the informal economy are also observed in relation to the informal sector with the exception of the intermediate group, which includes the three

Table 30.1 Informal economy in Latin America, 1990–2008 (% of urban employment)

	1990	2008
Informal economy	58.8	64.0
Informal sector	47.8	48.5
Precarious formal workers	11.0	15.5

Source: ECLAC on the basis of households' surveys and Tokman (2007).

Note: Includes 17 countries in 2008 and in 1990 for the informal sector. "Precarious formal workers" in 1990 refers to 10 countries. Arithmetic means.

---

[10] "Informal economy" is defined as all those workers without an employment relation subject to the standards established by the labor legislation, independently of where they work (ILO 2002). In this chapter it is measured as the sum of those workers in the informal sector (self-employed, employers, and workers in micro-enterprises and domestic services) plus all other wage earners without a labor contract or without protection. It refers only to non-agricultural employment.

[11] Protection is measured by contribution to a pension system.

largest economies of the region. The first group, with the highest levels of informal economies, also has the highest informal sector and precarious labor in formal enterprises.
At the other end, the group of more formalized countries register the smallest informal
sectors and, in particular, a high degree of formality among wage workers in formal
enterprises. On average, around 93% of workers in formal enterprises have a recognized
employment relation and access to social and labor protection. The intermediate group
(Argentina, Brazil, and Mexico) register a lower informal sector, but around 15% of the
workers in formal enterprises were unprotected (see Figure 30.2).

Differences among countries can be explained by the evolution of the modernization
process. Countries that register lower informality are those that today are the most
urbanized and where the majority of workers are wage earners fully covered by labor
regulations. In countries with an informal economy of low or medium size, the urban
population reaches between 80% and 90% of total population, and wage earners account
for 70–80% of non agricultural occupations, while in countries with the highest informality, 40–50% of the population still lives in rural areas and between 40% and 50% of
employment in urban areas consists of self-employed or domestic services. This also
helps to explain differences in access to labor and social protection, which in the case of
the former group of countries is on average four times higher when related to national
coverage and 2.5 times in relation to employment in urban areas.

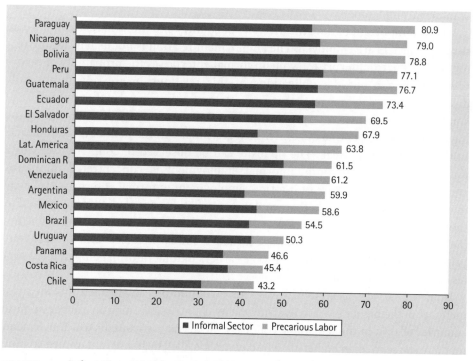

FIGURE 30.2 Informal economy by country, 2008

Source: Based on data on the informal sector from ECLAC, Social Panorama, 2009, and precarious labor from
unpublished household surveys processed by ECLAC for each country around 2008.

30.4.2 Employment structure in the informal economy

Differences in size and structure of the informal economy among countries are high, but in addition labor insertion by employment category adds a new dimension to diversity. Wage earners accounted for 43.8% of informal employment in 2008, thus constituting the largest proportion, closely followed by self-employment that amount to 42%, while 8.3% were in domestic services and the remainder were micro-entrepreneurs.

Wage earners are less homogeneous than the percentage figures suggest, since more than half of them are employed in formal establishments in a precarious situation and 42% are occupied in micro-enterprises. The data available suggests that the share of self-employment has decreased between 1990 and 2008, as a result of a decrease in self-employment and of an expansion of informal wage workers.

The averages hide different country situations. The self-employed account for more than half of the occupations in the informal economy in Central American countries and Peru, Bolivia, Dominican Republic, and Venezuela, while they constitute less than one-third in Argentina, Chile, Costa Rica, Mexico, Panama, and Uruguay. This suggests that the larger the informal economy, and particularly the informal sector, the more significant is the existence of self-employment. The share of wage earners in the largest countries of the region (Brazil, Mexico, and Argentina) is above average and, in the case of the latter two countries, represents more than half of informal employment.

It is also important to note the diversity of country situations in relation to where the wage earners are employed. The employment relation is not usually legally recognized in micro-enterprises, while in formal enterprises the probability of recognition is higher, but the obligations of this relationship are not always fully discharged. The data suggests that in the largest countries, the share of informal employment in formal enterprises significantly exceeds the average, reaching the highest value in Argentina (32%). This suggests that enforcement of labor contracts in those countries is weak. The opposite can be observed in countries like Costa Rica and Uruguay. In both, informal employment is concentrated in micro-enterprises, while the share of informal employment in formal enterprises is below 18%. This confirms not only that employment relations are explicitly recognized in those enterprises but also that they are largely enforced. In the remaining countries, the data suggest that the share of wage earners is similar in micro- and formal enterprises, although the importance of wage earners in total informal employment varies according to countries.

Domestic services account on average for 9% of informal employment, but the share increases in the higher income/less informality countries, reaching an average in those countries of 14%. In the remaining countries, the average is around 5.6%. The demand for domestic services in higher-income countries is filled by immigrant women coming from the lower-income countries. Micro-entrepreneurs represent between 5% and 6% of informal employment in most countries, with the exception of Costa Rica, where the proportion is around 13%.

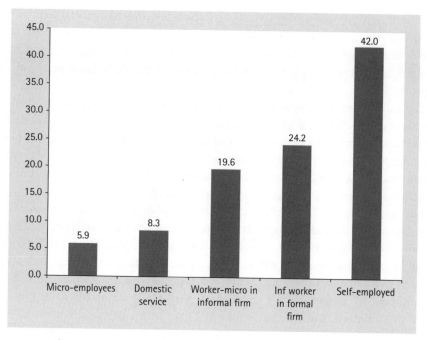

FIGURE 30.3 Informal economy: employment structure in Latin America, 2008

Source: ECLAC, Social Panorama (2009).

30.5 INFORMALITY: LABOR INSERTION AND RESTRICTED ACCESS TO SOCIAL PROTECTION

Labor insertion constitutes a major determinant of access to social security. Contributory coverage reproduces the labor market features, since workers with more experience or more educated and inserted under a labor-dependent relation in larger-size enterprises, or in sectors with greater job stability, have a higher probability of contributing. Only 13.5% of the non-professional self-employed in the informal sector are covered by contributory social security. When wage earners in informal firms are included, the coverage increases to 21.7%. This coverage is still far below the 68.2% registered by those working in private formal enterprises and the 83% coverage of those working in the public sector (Tokman 2007).[12] Labor insertion, type of employer, and size of the enterprise are important.

The legal recognition of the existence of an employment relation is also a major determinant of access to social security coverage. The type of labor contract is also significant.

---

[12] A multivariate analysis also confirms that the probability of coverage falls significantly for the self-employed, domestic services, and workers in informal firms. A positive influence is observed for public employees, workers in formal firms, and professional or technical work (CEPAL 2006b).

On average, only 19.3% of workers without contracts are covered by social security, while the coverage increases to 80.4% when they work under a written labor contract. Of those with contracts, 74% have permanent ones and their coverage reaches near 85% of the workers in these conditions. For the rest, working under other type of contracts, the protection coverage decreases to 61%.

Chile and Panama achieve almost universal social security coverage for workers with permanent contracts (96–97%), and coverage for workers on other contracts is also high (92 and 82%, respectively). By contrast, in Argentina, only 82% of workers under permanent contracts are covered, and only 18% of those who work under atypical contracts. Working without contract in Argentina amounts to working without any sort of social protection, since only 8% of such employees are covered.

Contracts can have different effects depending on where the job is performed, whether it is public or private, and whether it is a micro-enterprise or a formal firm. While a permanent contract for workers in formal firms means coverage of 89%, a similar contract in a micro-enterprise results in 63% coverage. A similar situation happens with atypical contracts that can ensure coverage of 65% if it is performed in a formal firm, or reduce the coverage to almost half if applied to workers in informal enterprises (see Figure 30.4). Indeed, a worker in an informal firm with a permanent contract would

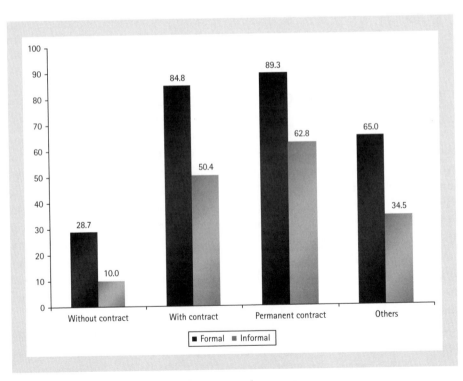

FIGURE 30.4 Social security coverage by sector and contract

Source: Tokman (2006), based on tabulations from household surveys processed by ECLAC.
Notes: Average for 7 countries. Coverage refers to % contributing to a pension system by contractual situation.

gain coverage by moving to a formal enterprise, even with an atypical contract (62.8–65%). On the other hand, it is also clear that coverage with atypical contracts in formal firms is lower than coverage when working under a permanent contract. Workers in this situation do not enjoy full protection or stable jobs. In fact, these contractual arrangements have increased due to the labor reforms and the strategic adaptation to competitive markets under globalization. As a result, a new feature has emerged in labor markets: that of informal workers performing in formal enterprises, even if the employment relation is legally recognized by a written contract.

30.6 EXIT OR EXCLUSION?

A study on informality in Latin America by the World Bank (Perry et al. 2007) introduced an additional factor to the conceptual framework analyzed previously. The study argues that independent workers voluntarily work informally because the income earned is higher than what they could obtain by working formally. It claims that this is particularly the case in countries where access to social protection benefits in formality is limited, and there are universal alternatives or non-contributory programs that can compensate for the lack of coverage.[13] Exit would be then a rational decision in an environment of inadequate and costly regulations, and could coexist with exclusion resulting from labor market segmentation and constraints on doing business at a small scale.

Income differences between independent workers and informal micro-entrepreneurs are significant. A non-professional independent worker could, on average, triple his income if he became a micro-entrepreneur. However, his income is on average 16% higher than the wage of an informal worker. There are no incentives for an independent worker to move to that job, but it could be attractive to move to a wage earner post in a formal firm that would allow him to increase his income by 36%. Exit is not supported by the income data, except in relation to workers in informal firms. In general, independent workers would have incentives to move to a wage earner position in formal enterprises that would allow them to increase their income by one-third, or to an entrepreneur position—whether in micro-enterprises, where income will triple, or in formal firms, where income will multiply by seven.[14]

The voluntary option for self-employment is also argued on the basis of employment profiles during the working life. Although the prevailing insertion at an early age is as wage earner in the informal economy, with ageing (after the 19–23 cohort), self-employment and formal wage work become predominant.[15] When this hypothesis was tested using data available for seventeen Latin American countries (Tokman

[13] This point has been also raised for Mexico by Levy (2008).
[14] See Tokman (2008a) for income differences between independent and wage earners for 17 Latin American countries. The ratio mentioned in the text refers to arithmetic averages of the region. The direction of the differences is observed in all countries with a few exceptions.
[15] The argument of the report by Perry et al. (2007) is based on employment profiles for Argentina, Brazil, and Mexico.

2008a), on average the pattern of mobility found was different.[16] Both informal workers and self-employed, as percentages of the occupied population, decrease as age increases. The former presents a continuous decreasing trend, while the latter registers a significant decrease of around 11 percentage points when they reach the 20–4 years cohort. The level registered when entering the labor market is only regained at the 40–4 years cohort. The decreasing trend observed for both job categories at early ages is consistent with the increasing availability of formal wage work, and suggests exclusion rather than exit.

Formal wage work reaches its higher levels in the cohorts with the most active participation rates (25–5 years) and then starts to decrease. Informal wage work shows a continuous decrease after entry to the market, while self-employment increases after reaching 30 years of age. Although exclusion prevails at early ages, as insufficient availability of good jobs continues, exit could constitute an option for self-employment at later ages. This could be reinforced by the fact that those in self-employment register the lowest level of education, since around 70% of those in the 25–9 cohorts have not completed secondary education. However, experience could contribute to increasing human capital, and after a decade, incentives to remain in self-employment could be greater.

An alternative mobility pattern for the self-employed is to become a micro-entrepreneur, but this option is restricted to those who have that ability, higher education, and access to capital. Micro-entrepreneurship constitutes an increasing source of employment with ageing, but only reaches 6% of the total occupation at end of the working life.

The analysis above, as well as labor histories available for other countries,[17] supports the conclusion that self-employed workers are mainly waiting for an opportunity as wage earner in formal firms to become available. It is highly unlikely that they will evolve to become owners of larger enterprises, while the majority among them can be considered as wage workers rather than entrepreneurs. Only a minority among them has characteristics similar to owners, but they are still significant.

30.7 A STRATEGY FOR INCLUSION AND OPPORTUNITIES FOR THE INFORMAL ECONOMY

A strategy focused on recognition of rights and empowerment of those in the informal economy can provide an integrated framework. People have to be recognized as citizens, and to be able to ensure the exercise of rights, not only political but also economic and social. This recognition needs to be accompanied by access to justice and freedom of

---

[16] Data available from household surveys around 2005. Only a few exceptions to the average behavior were found.

[17] See e.g. de Mel, McKenzie, and Woodruff (2008).

organization. Latin American countries have made progress on civil and political rights. The present challenge is to advance in economic and (particularly) social citizenship, since these advances provide the necessary conditions to diminish inequality. The informal economy includes two main forms of exclusion. First is the existence of a significant informal sector where most of the jobs are held by the poor. They are entrepreneurs and workers and many are both; they belong to the excluded, with unprotected and unstable jobs in addition to low incomes. The second form is labor inserted in formal enterprises or in productive chains under different subcontracting arrangements, with neither job security nor full protection.

A strategy for inclusion and opportunities should be focused both on micro-entrepreneurs and on informal workers, including self-employed.[18] This section concentrates on changes needed in regulations affecting activities, and mostly on those relevant to improving earnings and social protection for people working in the informal economy.

30.7.1 Micro-enterprise regulations to promote business

In Latin America, there are 2.6 times as many business regulations as in OECD countries and more than there are in Asian countries; only in Africa and in the Middle East are such regulations more numerous (Loayza, Oviedo, and Servén 2006). There have been marked improvements in trade opening and financial sector modernization, but the largest backlog is found in the regulations governing business licenses.

Regulations designed with larger enterprises and more organized sectors in mind are inadequate for the needs and conditions of micro-enterprises. There is a need for adjustment and simplification to facilitate compliance. Bureaucratic difficulties hold up requests to open or close informal business activities because of the numerous laws and regulations involved and bureaucratic inefficiency. These regulations apply to all enterprises, but the smaller ones are disproportionately affected as they do not have the means to overcome the obstacles to doing business. Improving the situation for small businesses constitute a precondition to improving the wages and working conditions of informal workers.

Simplifying bureaucratic procedures contributes to lowering access barriers, and also registration regimes, by unifying registries and reducing administrative steps. The introduction of single registry/single window regimes reduces the cost of formalization. Creating a single authority avoids overlapping and contradictory regulations, administrative procedures, and oversight efforts. The recognition of property rights by simplified methods, as suggested by De Soto, can also facilitate access to credit.

The analysis in relation to informal wage earners needs to differentiate between two groups: those occupied in micro-enterprises and those working directly or indirectly in formal firms.

---

[18] For an expanded analysis of this strategy and specific policies introduced in Latin American countries, see Tokman (2001a; 2001b; 2008a).

30.7.2 Labor rights in informal enterprises

Labor law does not fully apply to a significant percentage of workers in the informal sector, and few productive units are able to meet the obligations arising from the establishment of an employment relationship.

The share of workers without a contract or on atypical contracts is over 90% in Bolivia and Guatemala, and reaches about 85% in Mexico and Ecuador. Pensions coverage extends to only 18% of those occupied in the informal sector, compared with 68% in the formal sector (Tokman 2006). Most workers in the informal sector are not entitled to employment protection because their employment relationship is not legally recognized. On average for Latin America, 78% of wage earners in micro-enterprises do not have a written labor contract.[19]

In addition, micro-enterprises are less able to absorb the costs of employing their workers on a formal basis. Surveys of micro-enterprises in Colombia and Peru showed that around 76% could not pay total labor costs (Gómez, Huertas, and Olea 1998; Yañez 1998).

Recognition of the employment relationship helps to improve labor and social protection. This could be achieved with proof of the existence of unwritten contracts by registration of regular hours and periodic wage payments into the accounts, or by witnesses. This would provide workers with the necessary credentials to be entitled to protection, and would encourage micro-entrepreneurs to acquire the necessary skills to do business on a proper basis. This first step could, however, not be sufficient because of the enterprises' inability to absorb the costs of compliance. Some adjustment to the existing legislation may be necessary to facilitate enforcement, but this should avoid a deterioration of existing labor conditions. Alternatively, systems especially designed for the informal sector could be introduced. This would imply dual or preferential systems, as practiced in various countries, such as Argentina, Brazil, and Peru. However, this could mean different treatments among workers. For this reason, a single regulatory system is preferable with regard to labor aspects (ILO 1991).

The reality should be recognized, but this does not necessarily mean refraining from intervening. A possible approach should be to introduce a compulsory minimum threshold on labor issues. An initial component could include fundamental labor rights such as those included in the ILO Declaration of 1998 (freedom of association and collective bargaining, elimination of forced and child labor, and discrimination with respect to employment and occupation). This amounts to human rights transferred to the labor sphere. In addition, related aspects of working conditions could also be included, such as minimum wage, hours of work, and work-related accidents and illnesses.[20] This minimum should be enforced for all workers in the informal sector independently of the size

---

[19] It includes 11 countries. In 6 of them this percentage is higher than 90% (CEPAL 2006b).

[20] This broader minimum threshold has been incorporated into the free trade agreements signed by the US and various countries, including Mexico, Chile, all the countries of Central America and the Dominican Republic, Panama, Peru, and Colombia (the latter 2 still awaiting definitive adoption).

or form of the unit in which they work. This is not at odds with the notion of operating with a margin of tolerance, which allows for the constraints encountered by informal-sector production units.

Introducing a minimum threshold does not mean accepting that workers in the informal sector have access to only some of the rights enshrined in existing labor laws. On the contrary, the proposal is to recognize the need to make progress in the labor sphere by improving informal-sector enterprises' ability to comply, and committing them to follow this path.

30.7.3 Insecurity, vulnerability, and atypical employment contracts

Insecurity and vulnerability are linked to the absence of legally and explicitly recognized employment relations, but also to situations governed by contracts other than the permanent employment contract. This must be distinguished from the situation of workers whose employment relationships are ill-defined or not properly recognized by the labor legislation.

Both have increased in recent decades to adapt to the new economic conditions under globalization. Decentralization of production and labor processes has emerged as an instrument to decrease costs, particularly labor costs, as well as to increase efficiency given the availability of new technology and the explosive introduction of information technology. This has happened both within and between countries, as illustrated by the expansion of multinational investment flows worldwide. This contributed to a spurious decentralization in order to erode compliance with labor regulations or even to dilute the employment relation definition. At the same time, there was a need to adapt to a more open and volatile international economic environment. Adjustments were needed, and the search for flexibility to diminish the costs involved became a priority. Several Latin American countries introduced labor reforms during the first half of the 1990s, among them Argentina, Colombia, and Peru, the labor reform of Spain in 1981 being the most relevant precedent.

Labor reforms in Latin America introduced alternative contracts to the permanent employment with this objective.[21] A strategy of "flexibility at the margin" was followed by introducing atypical contracts for new hires and reducing the cost of dismissals. Employment relationships without contracts are concentrated in the informal sector, while atypical contracts tend to concentrate in formal enterprises and even in the public sector. However, given that they are associated with insecurity, they are considered a natural component of the informal economy. In general, they do not affect social protection as long as workers remain employed; nor are they illegal, as they were introduced by

[21] For the analysis of the labor reforms, see Chapter 31 below, by Murillo, Ronconi, and Schrank. See also Tokman (2004; 2007).

labor reforms. This insecurity affects workers and their families as well as productivity, because of the loss of incentives to innovate and to upgrade skills. For this reason, while recognizing that these contracts are necessary, particularly to promote employment for women and the youth, limits on their use should be introduced and efforts should focus on ways of making long-term contracts more flexible. This is, in fact, the orientation introduced in the second generation of labor reforms.

Spain, a pioneer country in 1981, and Argentina in 1991 and 1995 introduced labor reforms searching for flexibility at the margin. Spain introduced twelve modalities of special contracts that involved a reduction in firing costs and in contributions to social security. Argentina followed the same orientation, creating a fixed-term contract for multiple purposes. All of them contained partial or total exemptions of the employer contributions to social security.

Recognizing the negative effects of the reforms, both countries have changed the orientation of their reforms since the mid-1990s. Spain restricted the use of fixed-term contracts to collective bargaining, and transferred the search for flexibility to the permanent contract, facilitating the judicial process of firing and reducing the costs involved. A new tripartite agreement was reached in 2006 reinforcing this orientation. Argentina followed the same path in the reforms of 1998 and 2000, constraining the use of fixed-term contracts, reducing indemnities in permanent contracts, and extending trial periods.

30.7.4 Ill-defined employment relationships and their regulation

Ill-defined employment relationships are those that are difficult to establish, or are disguised or unprotected owing to gaps in the labor regulation or compliance control. The rights and obligations of both parties are often unclear, which may result in loss of worker protection. Such cases are growing in number in the context of globalization and decentralization of production, making it necessary to identify workers' rights and to determine who the responsible employer is. Most of the enterprises involved in these relations are formal, but workers' rights in subordinated firms are not necessarily fully complied with. They are part of the informal economy.

A law of subcontracting adopted in Chile in 2004 advances in this direction. The responsibility lies with the subcontractor, but the law also places responsibilities on the main contractor. It transformed the present subsidiary responsibility of the main contractor into a joint responsibility for these obligations. However, the main enterprise may exercise its right to require certification of compliance by the subcontractor, and may withhold payments due in case of non-compliance. While recognizing that this subcontracting model has the advantage of being more flexible, the law requires a proof of compliance from the enforcement authority involved, and makes the main enterprise an indirect control agent to ensure that the subcontractor complies with his legal obligations.

30.7.5 Expanded access to social security for informal workers

Coverage extension of social protection (health and pensions as well as maternity) for informal workers requires a strategy that considers different options, from expanding coverage of existing systems to the development of new mechanisms by the excluded through pooling of resources or insurances. These rights should be granted to the people as citizens rather than as workers, and awarded on universality principles. This has been a major change in the redesigning of the "traditional model" in Latin America, as well as completing the private defined contribution pension systems by adding a solidarity pillar funded from public resources. Perry et al. (2007) fully supports this change for the cases both of health and of pensions coverage. In the case of healthcare, it is recognized that shocks that go uncovered impose significant costs to society, there is a case for providing minimum essential direct cover, delinked from the labor contract and financed through general taxation. Similarly, in the case of insufficient income in old age, there are social costs involved that justify a minimum income support not associated with the labor contract.

Bolivia is the only country in Latin America that introduced a universal non-contributory pension (BONOSOL), and Brazil has a similar system for rural workers (FUNRURAL). Chile, a pioneer country in introducing the privatization of the pension and health systems, introduced a non-contributory measure that guarantees a solidarity pension to all citizens older than 65 years on a universal basis. Health is covered to a larger extent than pensions, and achieves universality by a combination of different systems: social insurance in Costa Rica that covers contributors and non-contributors, a public funded system in Cuba, and a mix of public institutions, social security, and private insurances in Uruguay, Brazil, and Chile, among others.

References

BROMLEY, R. (1978). 'Organization, Regulation and Exploitation in the so-called Urban Informal Sector', *World Development* 6.9–10.

CEPAL (Comisión Económica para América Latina) (2006a). *Panorama social de América Latina*, Santiago, Chile.

—— (2006b). *La protección social de cara al futuro: acceso, financiamiento y solidaridad*, Santiago, Chile.

—— (2009). *Panorama Social, 2009*, Santiago, Chile.

CHEN, M., VANEK, J., and CARR, M. (2004). *Mainstreaming Informal Employment and Gender in Poverty Reduction*, London and Ottawa: Secretary of the Commonwealth and IDRC.

DE FERRANTI, D., et al. (2000). *Asegurando el futuro en una economia globalizada*, Washington, DC: World Bank.

DE MEL, S., McKENZIE, D., and WOODRUFF, C. (2008). 'Who Are the Micro-enterprise Owners? Evidence from Sri Lanka on Tokman v. De Soto', World Bank Policy Research Paper No. 4635, Washington, DC.

DE SOTO, H., GHERSI, E., and GHIBELLINI, M. (1986). *El otro sendero: la revolución informa*, Lima: El Barranco.

EMMERIJ, L. (1974). 'A New Look at Some Strategies for Increasing Productive Employment in Africa', *International Labour Review* 110.3.

GERRY, C. (1974). 'Petty Producers and the Urban Economy: A Case Study of Dakar', WEP Urbanization and Employment Research Programme Working Paper No. 8, ILO, Geneva.

GÓMEZ, L. R., HUERTAS, G., and OLEA, D. (1998). 'Desafíos de la modernización y el sector informal urbano: el caso de Colombia', ILO Working Paper No. 87, Geneva.

HART, K. (1970). 'Small Scale Entrepreneurs in Ghana and Development Planning', *Journal of Development Studies* 6.4.

ILO (International Labour Organization) (1972). *Employment, Incomes and Equality: A Strategy for Increasing Productive Employment in Kenya*, Geneva.

—— (1991). 'The Dilemma of the Informal Sector', Report of the Director General submitted to the 78th International Labor Conference, Geneva.

—— (2002). 'Decent Work and the Informal Economy', Report of the Director-General presented at the International Labor Conference, Geneva.

—— (2009). *Labor Overview 2008: Latin American and the Caribbean*, Lima: ILO.

LEVY, S. (2008). *Good Intentions, Bad Outcomes: Social Policy, Informality and Economic Growth in Mexico*, Washington, DC: Brookings Institution.

LOAYZA, N., OVIEDO, A. M., and SERVÉN, L. (2006). 'The Impact of Regulation on Growth and Informality: Cross Country Evidence', in B. Guha-Khasnobis, R. Kanbur, and E. Orstrom (eds), *Linking the Formal and Informal Economy: Concepts and Policies*, Oxford: Oxford University Press.

LUBELL, H. (1991). *The Informal Sector in the 1980s and 1990s*, Paris: OECD.

OCAMPO, J. A. (2004). 'Latin America's Growth and Equity Frustrations During Structural Reforms', *Journal of Economic Perspectives* 18.2.

PERRY, G., et al. (2007). *Informality: Exit and Exclusion*, Washington, DC: World Bank.

PINTO, A. (1965). 'Naturaleza e implicaciones de la heterogeneidad estructural de la América Latina', *El trimestre económico* 37.145.

PORTES, A., CASTELLS, M., and BENTON, L. (1989). *The Informal Economy: Studies in Advanced and Less Developed Countries*, Baltimore: Johns Hopkins University Press.

PREBISCH, R. (1970). *Transformación y desarrollo: la gran tarea de América Latina*, Santiago, Chile: CEPAL.

TOKMAN, V. E. (1978). 'An Exploration into the Nature of Informal–Formal Interrelationships', *World Development* 6.9–10.

—— (1992). *Beyond Regulations: The Informal Sector in Latin America*, Boulder, Colo.: Rienner.

—— (2001a). 'Integrating the Informal Sector in the Modernization Process', *SAIS Review* 11.1.

—— (2001b). *De la informalidad a la modernidad*, Santiago, Chile: ILO.

—— (2004). *Las dimensiones laborales de la transformación productiva con equidad*, Santiago, Chile: CEPAL.

—— (2006). *Insercion laboral, mercados de trabajo y proteccion social*, Santiago, Chile: CEPAL.

—— (2007). 'The Informal Economy, Insecurity and Social Cohesion in Latin America', *International Labour Review* 146.1–2.

—— (2008a). *Informality in Latin America: Facts and Opportunities*, Stockholm: Sida. Available online at: http://www.wiego.org/publications/SIDA_regional_Reviews/Informality_in_Latin_America_Tokman_2008.pdf

—— (2008b). 'The Informal Sector', in A. K. Dutt and J. Ros (eds), *International Handbook of Development Economics*, Cheltenham: Elgar.

—— (2010). *El empleo en la crisis: efectos y politicas*, Santiago, Chile: CEPAL.

YAÑEZ, A. M. (1998). 'La legislación laboral y su impacto en la microempresa: costos y desafíos', in E. Chavez et al. (eds), *El sector informal frente al reto de la modernización*, Peru: ILO.

CHAPTER 31

....

LATIN AMERICAN LABOR REFORMS: EVALUATING RISK AND SECURITY

....

MARÍA VICTORIA MURILLO, LUCAS RONCONI, AND ANDREW SCHRANK

31.1 INTRODUCTION

....

This chapter addresses procedural and substantive changes to Latin American employment law in the late 20th and early 21st centuries. It covers eighteen Latin American market economies between 1985 and 2009 and pays particularly careful attention to reforms undertaken in the 2000s in light of their variegated—and somewhat anomalous—predecessors. While Latin American policymakers responded to the debt crisis by liberalizing their trade regimes, credit markets, and capital accounts in the 1980s and 1990s, they were reluctant to deregulate their labor markets—and in a number of well-known cases actually adopted *new* regulations designed to protect workers or appease their political representatives (Lora and Panizza 2003: 127; Pagés 2004: 67; Singh et al. 2005: 17–18). The existing literature therefore holds that the relationship between international competition and labor market reform is mediated by domestic politics, in general, and by the partisan loyalties of governing parties, in particular (Madrid 2003; Murillo and Schrank 2005; Cook 2007). In fact, Murillo (2005) concludes that traditionally populist or labor-backed parties and politicians who courted big business with promises of "pro-market" trade, investment, and commercial policies in the late 20th century simultaneously mollified their core constituents in the labor movement by *rededicating* themselves to labor market regulation.

Are her findings relevant today? Do partisan loyalties continue to influence the region's labor and employment laws? And, if so, how? We begin to address these questions by documenting and accounting for the principal reforms to the laws and practices that were designed to protect Latin American workers from the risks incurred by unemployment in the late 20th and early 21st centuries. We begin by assessing recent reforms to: (i) laws that are designed to reduce the *likelihood* of job loss by limiting the employer's authority to dismiss his or her workers (i.e. "external flexibility"); and (ii) laws that are designed to influence the *compensation* workers receive in case of job loss by creating or reinforcing either (a) unemployment insurance programs or (b) severance payments.[1] We proceed to address the question of enforcement by examining the evolution of resources devoted to labor inspection across the region. And we conclude by discussing the theoretical implications of our findings.

31.2 HISTORICAL ANALYSIS

The canonical western European literature on labor market regulation assumes the existence of income replacement schemes that pool the risk of unemployment across workers. Neither the Iberian countries (Bonoli 2003) nor their New World offspring (Schrank 2009a) adopted risk pooling, however, and the Western European literature is therefore broadly inapplicable to Latin America. Instead, Latin American labor codes obliged employers to compensate their former employees with experience-rated severance payments—and thereby limited risk pooling to the level of the enterprise.[2] The implications are decidedly important. While severance payments are designed to mitigate the cost of job loss, and thereby provide an alternative to social insurance in theory, they tend to raise the cost of hiring and firing for individual employers and have ambiguous results in practice—especially with regard to coverage of informal workers.

Experts have recently advised Latin American policymakers to abandon their "labor market-based" (Bonoli 2003: 1008) systems of social protection for a northern European alternative. They are particularly enthusiastic about the Danish "flexicurity" model (Haagh 2006; Tokman 2007a; Cohen and Sabel 2009) which allegedly reconciles efficiency with social protection by combining a low level of employment protection (i.e. flexibility) with a high level of unemployment insurance (i.e. security). But they nonetheless worry that flexicurity presupposes levels of taxation, formalization, and social dialogue that are at best unusual—and at worst unavailable—in Latin America (Tokman 2007a: 102; CEPAL 2008: 54–5).

[1] We ignore labor reforms that do not directly modify the cost of hiring, employing, or firing a worker, or the benefits workers receive in case of unemployment. This restriction implies that we do not analyze reforms affecting collective bargaining, union rights, or labor inspection. Certainly, these reforms can affect working conditions, e.g. via collective agreements. However, whether they produce more or less flexibility/security depends on several factors such as the degree of union democracy and labor's political alignments. We also ignore social policies that provide non-contributory benefits to unemployed workers such as Progresa/Oportunidades in Mexico, or Jefes de Hogar in Argentina.

[2] A number of scholars have attributed the limited redistribution of the risk of unemployment to the weakness of Latin American states and their inability to provide more comprehensive social insurance schemes. See e.g. Mares (2005) and Schrank (2009a).

Are Latin American policymakers defending labor market-based systems of social protection, moving toward flexicurity, or pursuing alternative strategies? We address these questions by defining three different indicators of the character of labor market regulation in the region: external flexibility; unemployment insurance; and personal compensation for the risk of job loss.

- Our indicator of "external flexibility" assesses the extent to which the regulation of the individual employment contract—and severance payments in particular—increases the cost of hiring and firing. A decrease in the value of severance payments (or limits on their use) is assumed to increase external flexibility and vice versa.
- Our indicator of "unemployment insurance" assesses the extent to which the government pools the cost of income replacement by means of taxation that redistributes income across work categories (or even the general budget) and thereby mitigates the cost of job loss without increasing the cost of hiring and firing. The initiation or augmentation of a social insurance scheme constitutes an increase in unemployment insurance and vice versa.
- Our indicator of "personal compensation" is a composite variable that increases when individual compensation for the risk of job loss increases either due to increased severance payments or expanded unemployment insurance. The indicator therefore recognizes that both schemes provide employed workers compensation for the risk of job loss, and in so doing affect their propensity to invest in skills that may affect the productivity of their firms.

We will eventually create and deploy ordinal variables that code increases in each indicator as "1," decreases as "–1," and stasis as "0." But first we will discuss the historical underpinnings of the three indicators and their evolution in the region over time.

31.3.1 External flexibility

Latin American labor codes are notoriously complicated pieces of legislation. According to Heckman and Pagés (2003: 10), the region's "labor codes determine the types of contracts, the lengths of trial periods, and the conditions of part-time work" available. They tend to give full-time, indefinite contracts pride of place over part-time, temporary contracts. They frequently stipulate when and how an employer can dismiss his or her workers. And they almost invariably mandate the payment of severance upon the dismissal of workers on standard contracts. In short, Latin American labor codes have traditionally substituted a labor-market based system of social protection for northern European-style social insurance.

31.3.1.1 *Normative changes 1985–99*

By the time Heckman and Pagés had published their analysis of Latin American labor and employment law, however, the region's labor codes had been subject to a number of different reform campaigns. Labor market reform was part of a larger reform agenda that included trade, price, and capital account liberalization, deregulation, privatization, and similar reforms designed to foster market competition and the exploitation of globalization. While the international financial institutions and their local supporters portrayed labor market regulation as a threat to the region's competitive advantage, and therefore joined forces in support of deregulation in the 1980s and 1990s, they were ultimately disappointed by reforms that fell short of their expectations in terms of pace, scope, and content (Weller 2001; Heckman and Pagés 2003)—and at times actually increased, rather than decreased, the scope of worker protection (Pagés 2004: 67). The first wave of labor market reform nevertheless provides a necessary introduction to the wave that would follow in the post-2000 period, and we therefore describe it briefly in Table 31.1 by country, year of the reform, and outcome, i.e. whether the reform increased or decreased external flexibility for hiring and firing.[3]

Labor market reforms have frequently been invoked to demonstrate the continued importance of partisan politics in late 20th-century Latin America. After all, the aforementioned reforms occurred during the halcyon days of the Washington Consensus (1985–99), when the external constraints imposed by the debt crisis of the 1980s were apparently at their peak, and were nonetheless limited in scope, inconsistent in direction, and better predicted by the ideologies of their political architects than by the presence or intensity of external constraints (Murillo 2005).

31.3.1.2 *Normative changes since 2000*

Did the same logic hold in the first decade of the new millennium? The incentives to adopt pro-market reforms have, if anything, declined since the turn of the century, when the net transfer of resources from Latin America to the rest of the world once again turned negative in 1999 and 2000 and the bloom wore off the free market rose more generally. While Latin American policymakers were by no means invulnerable to the influence of international markets and creditors in the first decade of the 21st century, they were in all likelihood more autonomous—and more likely to impose limits on external flexibility—than they were in the free market 1990s, and we therefore expect our review of normative changes to Latin American labor regulation in the new millennium to expose policy reversals and the revival of labor market-based systems of social protection.

In short, Latin American labor reforms have been inconsistent in nature. The region's policymakers not only increased but at times decreased external flexibility in both the late 20th and the early 21st centuries. While policymakers apparently had a slight preference for flexibility in the former period, they exhibited a modest tendency toward policy reversal in the latter. The big story, however, is that cross-country variation in labor market reform is greater within than between periods—a finding that would appear to distinguish labor market reform from reform in other issue areas.

---

[3] See Vega Ruiz (2005) for a more extensive analysis of the first wave of labor market reform.

Table 31.1 Reforms to procedures affecting external flexibility, 1985–99

Country	Year	External flexibility	Effect
Argentina	1991	Reduction in severance pay. CDD (Contrato de duración determinada) (part-time contracts and apprenticeship contracts) for new activities and youth; duration up to 5 years with union agreement through collective bargaining.	↑
	1995	CDD for small and medium companies.	↑
	1998	Cancelled CDD, limited apprenticeships, and reduced probationary period.	↓
Brazil	1988	Increased severance payments.	↓
	1998	CDD 2 years; no warning period for dismissal.	↑
Chile	1990	Employers must show cause to dismiss employees or pay higher severance.	↓
Colombia	1990	CDD 3 years + conditions to end CDI (Contrato de duración indeterminada). Reduction in severance payment.	↑
Dom. Rep.	1992	Increased compensation for dismissal.	↓
Ecuador	1991	CDD 1 year minimum except for occasional employment. But increased severance.	↑
El Salvador	1994	Increased severance pay; but eliminated women's right to return to same job after pregnancy; allowed hiring of 12-year-olds if it did not affect school or health.	↓
Guatemala	1992	Abolished the reinstatement of workers fired without just cause.	↑
Nicaragua	1990a	Dismissal only under a list of just causes.	↓
	1990b	New firing procedures reversing prior reform.	↑
	1996	Increased severance pay; allowed collective dismissal for economic reasons; and allowed reinstatement or higher severance for unjust individual dismissal—mixed but overall reduction in flexibility (Heckman and Pages 2003; Gamboa et al. 2007).	↓
Panama	1986	Increased duration of the probationary period (2 weeks to 3 months) with lower dismissal cost.	↑
	1995	CDD 2 years, collective dismissal for reduction in economic activity.	↑
Peru	1986	Reduction in probationary period (3 years to 3 months).	↓
	1991	Apprenticeships allowed until 25 years of age; CDD up to 5 years for up to 10% of payroll; dismissal without reason; mass layoffs with economic and technological objectives.	↑
	1994	Allowed subcontracting for up to 30% of company employees.	↑
	1996	Increased severance payment.	↓
Venezuela	1990	Limited firing and increased compensation for dismissal.	↓
	1997	Reduced severance payments and established private accounts for capitalization of severance payments.	↑

Table 31.2 Reforms to procedures affecting external flexibility, 2000–10

Country	Year	External flexibility	Effect
Argentina	2000	Increased length of the probationary period.	↑
	2002	Eliminated "unjustified firing"; transitional increase of severance payment to two times their value.	↓
	2004	Extended the transitory increase in severance payments as long as unemployment is above 10%.	↓
	2004	Reduced length of probationary period; increased minimum severance payment.	↓
Bolivia	2006	Established the right of workers to continue working rather than accept dismissal in case of "unjustified firing."	↓
	2009	Granted severance payment to all employees with more than 90 days tenure.	↓
Chile	2002	Increase severance payments.	↓
Colombia	2002	Reduced severance payments; eased use of apprenticeship contracts.	↑
Ecuador	2000	No severance payment in new category of work by the hour (*Trole* 1).	↑
	2000	Reduced severance payments and introduced temporary contacts (*Trole* 2).	↑
	2000	Declared *Trole* 2 unconstitutional.	↓
	2008	Eliminated *Trole* 1 and eliminated subcontracting.	↓
Panama	2002	Established lower cost of dismissal if firms hired young workers.	↑
Paraguay	2002	Established lower cost of dismissal if firms hired young workers.	↑

31.3.1.3 *Unemployment insurance*

The aforementioned reforms addressed external flexibility. Advocates of flexibility maintained that reforms would foster the growth of formal-sector employment by lowering the cost of job creation, unleashing comparative advantage, and undercutting the basis of informality. While their primary goal was to minimize the likelihood or *risk* of unemployment, they simultaneously altered the size and availability of severance payments and thereby influenced the perceived *cost* of job loss as well. We therefore compliment our analysis of external flexibility by examining normative changes that influence income security: first, by examining policies that provide an alternative to labor marked-based systems of social protection by pooling risks in the form of unemployment insurance; and second, by exploring the combined effects of reforms that affect external flexibility and the level or availability of unemployment insurance to see whether the flexicurity model—or something like it—has taken hold in Latin America. That is, by focusing on the compensation for unemployment risk that workers receive from different sources, we can assess the impact of such compensation on workers' incentives.

31.3.1.4 *Normative changes 1985–2000*

Only seven Latin American countries have established unemployment insurance as a form of social insurance to pool the risk of unemployment across different types of workers: Argentina, Brazil, Chile, Colombia, Ecuador, Uruguay, and Venezuela. In all seven countries, these systems are characterized by:

- Low recipiency rates. Because benefits are largely limited to workers who were employed in the formal sector, only 5–15% of the unemployed population in the aforementioned seven countries actually receive benefits (Jaramillo and Saavedra 2005).
- Low benefit replacement rates. Benefits are usually between 40% and 60% of a worker's former wage, and in some cases (i.e. pre-reform Chile and Colombia) they are lower than that level (IDB 2000).
- Poor monitoring. Benefits often go to persons who are currently employed or not actively seeking work (Vroman and Brusentsev 2005).

How did these systems evolve in the late 20th century? Did unemployment insurance compensate workers for diminished employment protection in liberalizing countries? Or did it follow a different logic?

In Brazil, the *Decreto-ley* No. 2283 (1986) introduced unemployment insurance in addition to advanced notice procedures, access to the *Fundo de Garantia de Tempo de Serviço* (FGTS), and a 40% (of the worker's individual account) fine for unfair dismissal. A major reform took place in 1990, when a large development fund called the *Fundo do Amparo ao Trabalhador* (FAT) was created. The program was placed on a more secure financial basis, underwent broader administrative and operational changes, and expanded eligibility to a wider range of workers (Mazza 1999). The unemployment compensation program offers partial coverage for up to four months of unemployment—extended to five months after 1996 (Amadeo, Gill, and Neri 2000).

In 1991, unemployment insurance was introduced in Argentina. To qualify for benefits, a worker must have contributed social security payments for at least twelve months during the three years prior to the termination of employment and must be legally unemployed, i.e. as a result of being fired without just cause or the expiration of an employment contract. The term of insurance ranges from four to twelve months, depending on the length of the contribution period, and the benefit depends on the duration of unemployment and on the monthly salary during the prior period of employment (Hopenhayn and Nicolini 1997).

In 1989, Venezuela enacted an unemployment insurance system similar to the one described in Argentina (Decree No. 449). But according to the IDB (2004) it was never implemented. The system was reformed in 1999, but again it was never implemented.

In short, Latin America has recently played host to a series of tentative experiments with the creation of European-style systems of social insurance that pool the risk of unemployment across—rather than within—firms. While the new insurance schemes differ markedly from the labor market-based systems of social protection that emerged in the postwar period, they cover a relatively small percentage of the workforce in a minority of the region's polities, and therefore fail to constitute a decisive break with the past. In fact, Latin American policymakers may have unintentionally bolstered support for the pre-existing personal insurance systems based on severance payments by implementing unemployment insurance in a timid manner in the late 20th century. If reasonable levels of unemployment insurance had instead been made available to the bulk of the Latin American workforce, European-style social protection would in all likelihood have been a more attractive alternative to the segmented welfare states that continue to dominate the region.

31.3.1.5 *Normative changes since 2000*

Latin American policymakers allegedly adopted their original (and timid) unemployment insurance (UI) schemes in an effort to compensate for the decrease in personal security engendered by the growth of external flexibility in the 1980s and 1990s. We might therefore expect either (i) the retrenchment of UI and the revival of severance payments or (ii) the expansion of UI in conjunction with other types of social provision (e.g. social security, conditional cash transfers) in the aftermath of the free market revolution, and we are therefore agnostic with regard to the direction of UI reform in the new millennium.

We ultimately observe little reform to unemployment insurance since 2000. Only Chile and Colombia have made meaningful reforms in this area. Chilean Law 19,728 (2001) creates a new UI system. It was implemented in October 2002 and created a mixed program with two types of funding mechanisms: an individual savings account for each worker, and a contingency fund called the "Solidarity Fund." Contributing workers are entitled to one monthly payment for every twelve months of contributions to the fund, and the amount of the payment is a function of the accumulated funds. If the accumulated savings in the individual account are insufficient, however, the worker has the right to receive a subsidy from the Solidarity Fund (IDB 2004).

The previous system was non-contributory with low benefits (between $12 and $25 per month) for twelve months (Acevedo, Eskenazi, and Pagés 2006). By way of contrast, the new program is financed by the government, employers, and employees; and the government has agreed to spend the equivalent of its expenditure on the previous unemployment subsidy on the Solidarity Fund. The employer pays 0.8% of each employee's monthly wage into this fund as well as 1.6% of wages into an individual account set up for each employee (similar to a pension account). The worker contributes 0.6% of his or her monthly wage to his or her individual account (Sehnbruch 2004), and a single private firm administers all of the individual accounts. Contributions are compulsory for all permanent jobs that started after 2002, and voluntary for holders of previous jobs. Workers with temporary jobs do not participate in the system.

Law No. 789 (2002) creates *auxilios al desempleo* (unemployment aid) in Colombia. This program gives unemployed workers 25% of the minimum wage for six months. The program is primarily financed by formal workers' contributions, and part of the funding is used to provide transitory assistance to informal workers (Gaviria and del Mar Palau 2006). This program is considered "timid" (Reyes Posada 2007), and the government is currently attempting a major change.

31.3.2 Reforms in Latin America and "flexicurity"

We have already established that Latin America took rather modest steps toward the provision of unemployment insurance between 1985 and 2009, and that all but two of the experiments with UI were established in the 1990s. We are agnostic, however, on the rationale for UI provision. Were Latin American policymakers trying to establish a variant of the flexicurity model by increasing external flexibility and UI more or less simultaneously? Or were different motivations in action? We begin to address the question by adopting a composite indicator that tracks reductions in the *cost* of job loss attributable to either (i) the establishment of unemployment insurance systems that pool risks across firms or (ii) the reinforcement of traditional severance payment schemes that pool risks within firms. Reforms that augment the benefits workers receive upon dismissal—whether by means of UI or severance payments—are categorized as increasing "personal compensation." While reforms that increase external flexibility and personal security simultaneously are compatible with flexicurity in theory, reforms that increase external flexibility and decrease personal security underscore Louise Haagh's sense that "security and flexibility are considered bed-fellows in Europe and trade-offs in emergent economies" (Haagh 2006: 389).

Our composite indicator of "personal security" is more than simply the inverse of our indicator of external flexibility for two reasons. First, not all reforms that increase external flexibility have a negative effect on "personal security." Regulatory changes that affect the ease of hiring and firing but leave severance payments untouched (e.g. the reform that imposed limits on unfair dismissal in Nicaragua in 1990) constitute the primary exceptions. Second, "personal compensation" is influenced by the extent and level of benefits derived from *either* unemployment insurance *or* severance payments. Although reforms that reduce severance payments but establish unemployment insurance payments have mixed effects, we have coded them as reductions in "personal compensation," because severance payments provided larger benefits and covered a broader section of the workforce than unemployment insurance in all of the cases we examined. In fact, we have not found a single country that has successfully compensated for the decline in severance payments by increasing the scale and scope of unemployment insurance, thereby reflecting a movement in the direction of flexicurity. Although the reforms in Argentina in 1991 and in Colombia in 2002 reduced severance payments and increased unemployment insurance, in neither case was the UI able to compensate for the decline in severance.

31.4 PATTERNS OF LABOR REFORM

The following figures summarize the general patterns of reform associated with the three indicators between 1985 and 2009. We lack confidence in cross-national comparisons of interval measures, and the analysis is therefore based on the direction of the reforms alone (i.e. whether they increase or decrease external flexibility, unemployment insurance, and personal compensation). Figures 31.1(a) and (b) describe the number of

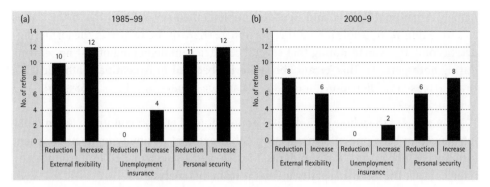

FIGURE 31.1 Number of reforms: Latin America, 1985–2009

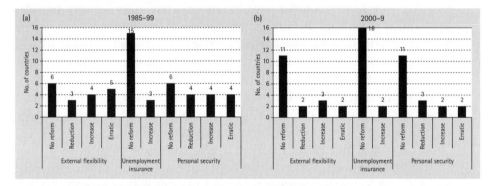

FIGURE 31.2 Number of countries implementing reforms: Latin America, 1985–2009

reforms implemented in Latin America that affected external flexibility, UI, and personal compensation in each of two sub-periods (1985–99 and 2000–9). The size of the column reflects the number of reforms. For example, the first column in Figure 31.1(a) is equal to 10, meaning that ten reforms reducing external flexibility were implemented in Latin America between 1985 and 1999.

While the total number of reforms was slightly smaller in the second sub-period, the second sub-period was also shorter, and the overall probability of reform therefore remained more or less unchanged over time. Nor do we observe a large change in the direction of reforms. We observe more reforms aimed at reducing external flexibility in the 2000s while the opposite occurred in the 1980s and 1990s, but the differences are again quite small and therefore difficult to interpret. Most reforms affect external flexibility (employment law), and very few affect unemployment insurance in either subperiod.

Figures 31.2(a) and 31.2(b) compare both periods using the country as a unit of analysis. Some interesting facts emerge. First, we observe that while most countries in the region implemented reforms affecting external flexibility between 1985 and 1999 (12 out of 18 countries), only 7 countries implemented reforms in this area in the 2000s. The difference between Figures 31.1(b) and 31.2(b) is due to the fact that a few countries, namely Argentina, Bolivia, and Ecuador, implemented several reforms in the 2000s and were thus responsible for a disproportionate share of the reform in the former figure. Second, it is worth noting that several countries implemented offsetting reforms during both periods. This "erratic" behavior is observed in Argentina (both periods), Brazil (1985–99), Ecuador (2000–8), Nicaragua (1985–99), Peru (1985–99), and Venezuela (1985–99).

An analysis of the whole period (1985–2009) shows that most countries (14 out of 18) introduced at least one reform affecting either external flexibility or unemployment insurance. Only Costa Rica, Honduras, Mexico, and Uruguay failed to introduce any reforms at all. The following patterns emerge from this analysis:

- There are clearly more reforms to employment law than to unemployment insurance (i.e. only seven countries have insurance, while every country provides employment protection). Reforms adopted in the 1980s and 1990s were slightly more likely to increase external flexibility, while reforms adopted during 2000–9 were slightly more likely to reduce flexibility. However, since 2002 all employment law reforms have been aimed at reducing external flexibility.
- Several countries that adopted pro-flexibility reforms in the 1990s did not reverse those laws (e.g. Brazil, Colombia, Guatemala, and Panama); however, Ecuador and Peru recently introduced employment protection reforms.
- Chile, Colombia, and Panama present a very consistent behavior over time. Chile introduced several reforms that bolstered employment protection, while the other two countries consistently moved towards greater external flexibility. By contrast, Argentina, Ecuador, Peru, and Venezuela exhibit very erratic behavior.
- Argentina (1991) and Colombia (2002) are the only countries to increase external flexibility and UI simultaneously. But it is hard to argue that they are getting closer to the Danish model given the limited coverage of their UI systems. Nor are they alone. Very few Latin American countries provide unemployment insurance, and those that have established UI limit benefits to about 10% of the unemployed population. Considering the extent of coverage in northern European countries, it is worth underscoring the fact that no country in Latin America is even close to embracing the flexicurity model.

31.4.1 Political and economic determinants of labor reforms

What accounts for the pattern of labor law reform in Latin America between 1985 and 2009? While the literature on economic reform underscores the role of external financial pressures, and would therefore have predicted divergence between the late 20th and the early 21st centuries, we find only small differences between the two subperiods. More generally, we find that variation across countries—and even contradictory patterns within countries—trump longitudinal variation between periods in

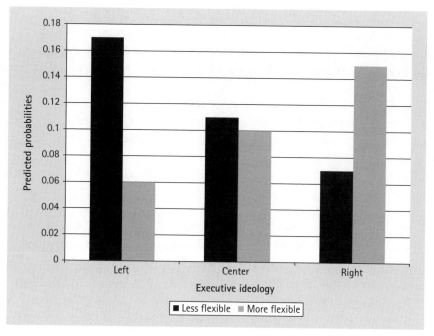

FIGURE 31.3 External flexibility by executive ideology

Notes: The unit of analysis is a presidential administration. The sample includes the 108 administrations found in Latin America since 1985; however, administrations that failed to pursue reform (i.e, "no net change") are excluded from the figure. Codings by authors. Ordered logistic regression coefficient = .48; robust standard error = .27; z = 1.81 (p = .071); full results available from authors on request.

size and importance. In order to explain these patterns, we follow the prior work of Murillo (2005), who finds that the partisan ideology of the executive is a decidedly more powerful predictor of reform than economic variables like openness to trade and inflation.

31.4.2 The politics of employment protection

We initially extend Murillo's findings by examining the relationship between executive ideology and patterns of employment law reform across the 108 presidential administrations found in Latin America since 1985. We expect that right-of-center governments are more likely to liberalize their labor markets and left-of-center governments are more likely to augment employment protection. The administrations that constitute our units of analysis are therefore coded on: (i) an ordinal scale from "left" (–1) to "right" (1), with "center" in between (based on an updated version of Coppedge's codings); and (ii) a similar scale from "less flexible" (–1), if their labor markets were less (externally) flexible when they came to a close than when they began, to "more flexible" (1), if their labor markets were more (externally) flexible when they came to a close than when they began, with "no net change" (o) in between (based on our own analysis of data described in section 31.3). We then analyzed the impact of government ideology on the predicted probability of reform in either direction, derived from an ordered logistic regression of the reform scale on the executive ideology scale. Figure 31.3 provides a graphical representation of our findings.

The results indicate that partisan ideology is indeed a powerful predictor of reform. Right of center governments are substantially more likely to liberalize, and less likely to regulate, their labor markets than their left-of-center counterparts. Non-reform is the modal category and is left off the figure.

Furthermore, the results become, if anything, more powerful when we limit our analysis to the post-1999 period—perhaps due in part to the decline of external pressures, improvement in the region's terms of trade, and the corresponding growth of policy autonomy (Murillo, Oliveros, and Vaishnav 2008). Only eight administrations made net changes to external flexibility in the current decade: flexibility was augmented by the right-leaning governments of Noboa in Ecuador, Moscoso in Panama, González Macchi in Paraguay, and Uribe in Colombia; and flexibility was limited by the left-leaning administrations of Nestor Kirchner in Argentina, Morales in Bolivia, Lagos in Chile, and Correa in Ecuador. Thus, executive ideology all but perfectly predicts the direction of reform in the post-1999 period.

31.4.3 The politics of unemployment insurance

The politics of unemployment insurance are much harder to discern. Only five countries—Argentina, Brazil, Chile, Colombia, and Venezuela—have undertaken reforms in this area since 1985, and most were at best restricted in nature. While Argentina and Brazil implemented their unemployment insurance schemes in response to the macroeconomic shocks on the 1980s, they did so in decidedly different political environments. In Argentina, a modest unemployment insurance scheme was part of the price the Menem administration paid for organized labor's acquiescence to other painful reforms (Mazza 1999: 15) including increases in external flexibility. In Brazil, by way of contrast, workers defended their traditional prerogatives—including employment protection—while playing an active part in the formulation of a new unemployment insurance scheme in the mid-1980s (Sarney 1986: 112). Similarly, the labor-backed Lagos administration implemented an unemployment insurance scheme without compromising employment protection in Chile in 2001 (Sandbrook et al. 2007: 252; see also Weyland 1997: 46–7 on organized labor's support for unemployment insurance). And the right-of-center Uribe administration implemented unemployment insurance while liberalizing labor markets in Colombia. Consequently, the institution of unemployment insurance was accompanied by growing personal security in Brazil and Chile and declining personal security in Argentina and Colombia.

A no less important question concerns the relative absence or poverty of unemployment insurance in most of Latin America. Why is the region allergic to

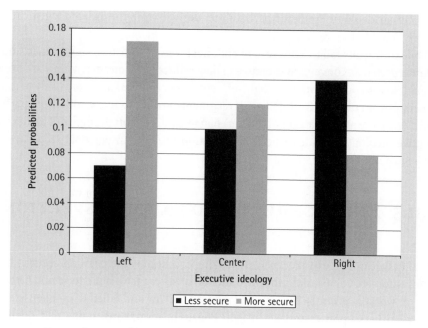

FIGURE 31.4 Personal security by executive ideology

Notes: The unit of analysis is a presidential administration. The sample includes the 108 administrations found in Latin America since 1985; however, administrations that failed to pursue reform (i.e., "no net change") are excluded from the figure. Codings by authors. Ordered logistic regression coefficient = -.41; robust standard error = .27; z = 1.59 (p = .11); full results available from authors on request.

European-style social insurance? A substantial body of literature traces the answer to the region's inability to raise the revenue needed to fund more ambitious UI systems (Schrank 2009a) and the concomitant consolidation of a vicious circle of segmentation and informality. Latin American governments have therefore addressed their social spending less to UI than to conditional cash transfers targeted at the unemployed and underemployed. By targeting the unemployed and the underemployed in the informal sector, these programs may further increase the incentive to sustain the status quo in terms of labor regulation.

31.4.4 The politics of personal compensation

What, then, accounts for variation in personal security? While our indicator of personal security is a composite variable, it is by no means random in nature. On the contrary, we would expect executive ideology to influence personal security as well as flexibility, and we therefore code our 108 presidential administrations on an ordered scale that tracks whether workers were "less secure" (–1) at the end of the administration, "more secure" (1) at the end of the administration, or experienced "no net change" (0) in security over the course of the administration, and regress the resultant indicator on executive ideology. Predicted probabilities derived from the ordered logistic regression are found in Figure 31.4.

While the results fail to achieve conventional levels of statistical significance, and are best interpreted as convenient exercises in data reduction in any event, they are broadly compatible with our hypotheses. Right-of-center governments are more likely to undercut personal security. Left-of-center governments are more likely to bolster personal security. And the modal category is no net change (and is left off the figure). Furthermore, executive ideology provides a perfect prediction of shifts in personal security in the post-1999 period.

31.5 ENFORCEMENT AND LABOR INSPECTION

Labor laws are unlikely to affect wages, working conditions, and personal security if they are not enforced. For example, the introduction of severance payments would have little effect on workers' security if employers ignored the law and failed to compensate their former workers upon dismissal. In fact, Bensusán (2007) maintains that regulatory agencies can foster flexibility in the absence of legal reform by reducing the vigor of their enforcement efforts. Cook agrees that non-enforcement of labor law frequently fosters a form of "de facto flexibility" that renders de jure reform unnecessary (2007: 193). And Tokman admits that "haphazard compliance with labor law is commonplace" not only in the so-called informal economy but in "modern activities, particularly in countries where fiscal discipline is poor and inspection capabilities are limited" (2007b: 261). In order to provide a better picture of the worker protection in the region, therefore, it is necessary to analyze the evolution of labor law enforcement over time.

In this section, we address the question of enforcement in two steps: first, by examining trends in enforcement resources and practices; and second, by exploring their political sources. We focus on labor inspectorates rather than labor courts because the former constitute the first line of defense against noncompliance and abuse. That is, we focus on "enforcement" based on the resources for monitoring the application of the law rather than the sanctioning of infractions—in part, because the legal process is usually started after the employment relationship has been ended rather than being remedial.

31.5.1 Enforcement trends

We begin with a variant of the International Labour Organization's standard enforcement indicator: the ratio of labor inspectors to the economically active population (EAP) in millions (i.e. the "enforcement ratio"). While the ratio of inspectors to workers "is currently the only internationally comparable indicator available" (ILO 2006: 4), it is not made available on a systematic basis, and we have therefore compiled data and statistics from ministry websites, academic papers, newspapers, country reports produced by ILO, the US Department of Labor, and the US State Department, and our own survey of country experts in an effort to build the most comprehensive dataset possible.

Table 31.1 includes data on the absolute number of inspectors and the enforcement ratio for four potentially overlapping years: the first and last years for which we have been able to find reliable data; and the years in which the enforcement ratio took on its highest and lowest values respectively. The data suggest the following:

- Between the first and the last observed years, enforcement efforts have expanded in nine countries (Argentina, Chile, Colombia, the Dominican Republic, El Salvador, Guatemala, Panama, Peru, and Uruguay) and declined in eight countries (Bolivia, Brazil, Costa Rica, Ecuador, Honduras, Mexico, Nicaragua, and Paraguay). Data for Venezuela are inconclusive.
- Enforcement expansion has rarely been consistent over time. While Chile and El Salvador appear to have undertaken more or less continuous expansions in the absolute number of inspectors since 1990 and 2002, respectively, most countries have experienced volatility. For instance, the enforcement ratio initially fell and later recovered in Argentina, Colombia, Panama, Peru, and Uruguay and, by way of contrast, initially expanded and then contracted in the Dominican Republic and Guatemala.
- Over the last few years not only El Salvador, Nicaragua, and Panama but a number of the region's largest economies—including Argentina, Colombia, Mexico, and Peru—appear to have undertaken meaningful expansions in their inspectorates. The broad pattern would therefore seem to be one of increasing enforcement.

31.5.2 The role of trade agreements

In short, the region's labor inspection agencies have been subject to more change than the laws they are designed to enforce. What accounts for the difference? Regional and bilateral trade agreements (RBTA) are one potential source of longitudinal and cross-sectional variation. After all, the United States has signed RBTAs with eleven Latin American countries since the early 1990s, and all but the North American Free Trade Agreement—which relegates labor standards to a controversial "side agreement" between the US, Canada, and Mexico—treat labor law enforcement as a condition of membership. For example, the US–Chile Free Trade Agreement stipulated that member countries had to enforce their own labor laws (Martin 2005: 203). And similar language was inserted into subsequent agreements with Panama, Peru, Colombia, and the so-called CAFTA countries (Costa Rica, El Salvador, Guatemala, Honduras, Nicaragua, and the Dominican Republic; see Schrank and Piore 2007).

Do RBTAs between Latin American countries and the US foster enforcement efforts among their participants? Unfortunately, the answer is difficult to discern for at least three reasons. First, the causal order of the relationship between the agreements and the enforcement efforts is inverted. While statistical methods assume that causes produce

Table 31.3 Enforcement resources in Latin America, 1985–2009

Country	First observed year			Last observed year			High year			Low year		
	No.	Ratio	Year	No.	Ratio	Year	No.	Ratio	Year	No.	Ratio	Year
Argentina	212	17.27	1988	475	24.77	2007	475	25.32	2006	71	5.03	1994
Bolivia	37	14.74	1990	19	4.18	2008	73	27.54	1992	15	3.72	2004
Brazil	3285	52.62	1990	3021	31.18	2009	3285	52.62	1990	2873	30.93	2006
Chile	80	14.22	1990	357	52.05	2009	357	52.05	2009	80	14.22	1990
Colombia	260	14.28	1998	746	30.99	2008	746	30.99	2008	248	12.38	2001
Costa Rica	61	44.95	1995	90	41.78	2008	117	86.22	1996	90	41.78	2008
Dom. Rep.	70	25.93	1991	203	50.12	2007	212	73.03	1994	70	25.93	1991
Ecuador	74	17.53	1993	61	9.07	2007	74	17.53	1993	61	9.07	2007
El Salvador	40	15.41	2002	159	53.77	2008	159	53.77	2008	40	15.41	2002
Guatemala	98	30.97	1995	238	51.76	2009	292	77.80	2002	98	30.97	1995
Honduras	125	56.82	1997	120	33.98	2008	125	56.82	1997	80	32.57	1999
Mexico	801	23.91	1993	616	13.58	2007	801	23.91	1993	568	13.16	2004
Nicaragua	84	46.98	2001	98	42.26	2009	84	46.98	2001	57	28.02	2005
Panama	80	64.57	1999	185	114.27	2009	185	114.27	2009	78	50.58	2007
Paraguay	38	18.56	1996	41	12.48	2009	103	48.54	1997	41	12.48	2009
Peru	158	14.10	1999	480	33.98	2007	480	33.98	2007	150	12.94	2000
Uruguay	80	59.13	1989	142	76.55	2009	142	76.55	2009	74	52.59	1991
Venezuela	97	7.78	2004	97	7.78	2004	97	7.78	2004	97	7.78	2004

Notes: The enforcement ratio is defined as the ratio of labor inspectors to the economically active population (EAP) in millions.

effects over time, US policymakers ask their trading partners to make the necessary changes to their enforcement efforts pre-emptively—so that enforcement efforts anticipate, rather than follow, the approval of the trade agreements that ostensibly cause the outcome in question. Second, indicators of the *desire* to forge an RBTA are unavailable. While enforcement efforts are perhaps best seen as products not of the trade agreements themselves but of the desire to forge trade agreements with countries like the US that impose conditions on their trading partners, we lack data on the origins of those desires and are therefore unable to trace changes in the level of enforcement to changes in the desire to forge an RBTA over time. And, finally, there are ceiling and floor effects. Nobody would expect an RBTA to foster increased enforcement in a country that is already doing an adequate job of enforcing its labor laws or meeting with US approval. And nobody would expect the absence of an RBTA to foster diminished enforcement in a country that was already lagging behind. As a result, the most compelling explanation for the growth of enforcement in recent years is not readily subject to systematic multivariate analysis.

We therefore pursue an alternative approach by (i) simply comparing the enforcement ratios of RBTA negotiators and non-negotiators and (ii) drawing upon qualitative data to explain any differences in their efforts. Table 31.4 includes descriptive statistics and significance tests and reveals that RBTA negotiators are on average twice as aggressive on the enforcement front as non-negotiators.

The mean differences between negotiators and non-negotiators are broadly significant under either a standard t-test ($t = 1.92$; $p = .07$) or a non-parametric alternative ($z = 2.31$; $p = .02$). The between-group differences in the median values of the enforcement ratio are even higher ($X^2 = 4.2$; $p = .04$). And the estimated probability that the enforcement ratio is higher for negotiators than for non-negotiators (derived from the non-parametric Mann-Whitney test) is .83.

The US did not, however, "cherry pick" trading partners with exemplary labor records. On the contrary, many RBTA members have regrettable enforcement histories (e.g. the Dominican Republic, El Salvador, Guatemala, and Colombia), and qualitative data therefore suggest that trade considerations are linked to enforcement efforts in a number of different ways. For example, the Dominican Republic and Guatemala increased their

Table 31.4 Enforcement resources by RBTA negotiating status

RBTA status	Mean	Median	Minimum	Maximum	Countries
Negotiator	47.1	42.3	13.58	114.27	Chile, Colombia, Costa Rica, Dominican Republic, EL Salvador, Honduras, Guatemala, Mexico, Nicaragua, Panama, Peru
Non-negotiator	23.7	12.5	4.18	76.55	Argentina, Bolivia, Brazil, Ecuador, Paraguay, Uruguay, Venezuela

Notes: The enforcement ratio is defined as the ratio of labor inspectors to the EAP in millions. Significance tests: $t_{enforcement\ ratio} = 1.92$ ($p = .07$); Mann-Whitney's $U = 64$ ($z = 2.31$; $p = .02$).

enforcement efforts in response to unilateral US pressure in the 1990s and early 2000s, and were thus well positioned to meet US demands when negotiations over CAFTA began a few years later (see e.g. Fuentes 2007; Schrank and Piore 2007; Schrank 2009b). El Salvador and Peru dragged their feet in the earlier epoch and were thus forced to expand their efforts more rapidly in the mid-2000s (Alliance for Labor Rights-Peru 2007: 21; Rogowsky and Chyn 2008: 130). Chile and Costa Rica have for the most part been at the forefront of regional enforcement efforts, and thus had little to worry about when their respective trade negotiations began at more or less the same time. And Colombia and Panama have recently tripled the sizes of their respective inspectorates in an effort to convince the US Congress to ratify their recently negotiated agreements (see e.g. Ministerio de Trabajo and Desarollo Laboral 2008; Ministerio de la Protección Social 2008).

The point, therefore, is not to posit a simple cause-and-effect relationship between RBTAs and labor law enforcement, but to describe a multi-player game in which an evolving array of US trade conditions alter the incentives of Latin American policymakers over time. Some Latin American governments accepted increasing enforcement as the price to be paid for preferential access to the US market in the 1990s. Others were forced to follow their lead or risk losing market share to their more compliant competitors. And the competition merely intensified when unilateral preferences were replaced by regional and bilateral trade agreements in the 2000s.

The North American Free Trade Agreement not only constitutes the hemisphere's first RBTA but provides the exception that proves the rule. After all, NAFTA's negotiators initially overlooked the labor question and wound up relegating the issue of labor standards to a politically controversial and legally ineffective "side agreement." While the negotiators of subsequent trade agreements would learn from their predecessors' mistakes, and would therefore include labor standards in the core of their agreements, their efforts would make little difference in Mexico—which still boasts the lowest enforcement ratio of any RBTA member by a fairly substantial margin.

In short, the pattern of labor reforms seems to respond to the ideological incentives of policymakers and their ties to organized labor. By contrast, differences in enforcement—measured as resources dedicated to monitoring those same laws—are more related to the efforts of Latin American countries to gain access to the US market. This is to be expected in a world in which left-leaning political parties in Latin America look for visible legislative victories that will appease their allies in the labor movement and left-leaning politicians in the US look for enforcement commitments that will appease their allies in organized labor as well—and thus condition preferential market access on the enforcement, rather than the character, of Latin American labor law.

31.6 CONCLUSION

We find that Latin American countries have not experimented with flexicurity in any meaningful way. After all, the provision of unemployment insurance has been limited to a relatively small population of formal-sector workers in a small number of countries. And Latin American workers and unions have therefore focused their efforts on the defense of the region's pre-existing model of risk reduction through severance payments and employment protection.

The defense of the traditional model simultaneously constitutes a rational response to the state's inability or unwillingness to provide effective unemployment insurance, and underscores the validity of Mares' account of the politics of social insurance in the context of state weakness (2005). But Latin American informality provides a further obstacle to the emergence of broad-based risk pooling. And the growth of non-contributory cash transfer programs that are designed to deal with unemployment and poverty are likely to further complicate the politics of social provision in the future, especially if their beneficiaries organize to defend their survival rather than to defend or reinforce regulations that address formal employment.

Our analysis is anything but a brief in defense of labor-market based systems of social protection. Employment protection laws and severance payments pool risks at the level of the enterprise rather than the economy, and thereby elevate labor costs, undercut redistribution, and give firms and workers an incentive to enter the informal economy. Informality further enervates the state's ability to mitigate risks and protect workers. And policymakers therefore respond to the growth of poverty, informality, and popular political opposition in accordance with the incentives derived from their partisan preferences, especially since labor reforms in dualistic economies are insufficiently salient to drive national electoral outcomes. The precise balance between liberalization and regulation tends to depend on the ideology of the governing party and the nature of its core constituency, and executive ideology and union influence are therefore more important predictors of labor law reform than "economic" variables like debt and unemployment.

They are by no means the only relevant variables, however, for the failure to develop more thoroughgoing systems of social insurance may well be explained by fiscal constraints. In fact, Victor Tokman worries that the northern European experience is rendered all but inapplicable to Latin America by structural differences including not only pervasive informality in the latter region but an almost chronic inability to generate "sufficient fiscal resources to fund a system of social and labour protection sufficiently broad and generous to provide security for the whole population" (2007b: 102). Latin American governments therefore continue to defend a low-cost welfare state that gives core workers security through statutory labor law and leaves peripheral workers to fend for themselves. In turn, these institutions reinforce the policy preferences of both formal and informal workers who are simultaneously unable to extract redistributive social insurance schemes and unwilling to pool their own resources through a state mechanism that they have little capacity to monitor.

Efforts to gain or consolidate preferential access to the US market may well constitute a shock to the system—if not necessarily a threat to the equilibrium as a whole. While policymakers in North America are inclined to condition their trade agreements and preferences on the nature of labor standards in Latin America, they are understandably reluctant to expose their own labor and employment laws to international scrutiny, and they have therefore focused their efforts on the enforcement—rather than the over-haul—of existing laws and the protection of the most "universal" of labor rights (e.g. freedom of association). Latin American governments have responded by augmenting their enforcement efforts. The potential consequences for informality, employment, and personal security are by no means obvious.

References

ACEVEDO, G., ESKENAZI, P., and PAGÉS, C. (2006). 'Seguro de desempleo en Chile: un nuevo modelo de ayuda al ingreso para trabajadores desempleados', *Bienestar y política social* 2.1.

Alliance for Labor Rights-Peru (2007). *Labor Standards and Levels of Implementation and Compliance by Peru in the Context of Free Trade Agreements*, Lima: Red Peruana por una Globalización con Equidad.

AMADEO, E., GILL, I., and NERI, M. (2000). 'Brazil: The Pressure Points in Labor Legislation', Economics Working Paper No. 395, Graduate School of Economics, Getulio Vargas Foundation, Rio de Janeiro.

BENSUSÁN, G. (2007). *La efectividad de la legislaciónn laboral en América Latina*, Geneva: Instituto Internacional de Estudios Laborales.

BONOLI, G. (2003). 'Social Policy through Labor Markets: Understanding National Differences in the Provision of Economic Security to Wage Earners', *Comparative Political Studies* 36.9.

CEPAL (Comisión Económica para América Latina) (2008). *Los mercados de trabajo, la protección de los trabajadores y el aprendizaje de por vida en una economía global*, Santiago, Chile.

COHEN, J., and SABEL, C. (2009). 'Flexicurity', *Pathways* (Spring).

COOK, M. L. (2007). *The Politics of Labor Reform in Latin America: Between Flexibility and Rights*, University Park: Pennsylvania State University Press.

FUENTES, A. (2007). 'A Light in the Dark: Labor Reform in Guatemala during the FRG Administration, 2000–2004', thesis, Department of Urban Studies and Planning, MIT.

GAMBOA, M., D'ANGELO, A., and KRIES, S. (2007). *Flexibilización del mercado laboral en Nicaragua*, UNIFEM, New York.

GAVIRIA, A., and DEL MAR PALAU, M. (2006). 'Evolución reciente del mercado laboral urbano y alternativas de política', *Coyuntura social* 34.

HAAGH, L. (2006). 'Equality and Income Security in Market Economies: What's Wrong with Insurance?', *Social Policy and Administration* 40.4.

HECKMAN, J., and PAGÉS, C. (2003). 'Law and Employment: Lessons from Latin America and the Caribbean', NBER Working Paper No. 10129, Cambridge, Mass.

HOPENHAYN, H., and NICOLINI, J. P. (1997). 'Designing an Optimal Unemployment Insurance Program', in S. Edwards and N. Lustig (eds), *Labor Markets in Latin America: Combining Social Protection with Market Flexibility*, Washington, DC: Brookings Institution.

IDB (Inter-American Development Bank) (2000). *Social Protection for Equity and Growth*, Washington, DC.

—— (2004). *Good Jobs Wanted*, Washington, DC.

ILO (International Labour Organization) (2006). *Strategies and Practice for Labour Inspection*, Geneva.

JARAMILLO, M., and SAAVEDRA, J. (2005). 'Severance Payment Programs in Latin America', *Empirica* 32.

LORA, E., and PANIZZA, U. (2003). 'The Future of Structural Reform', *Journal of Democracy* 14.2.

MADRID, R. (2003). 'Labouring Against Neoliberalism: Unions and Patterns of Reform in Latin America', *Journal of Latin American Studies* 35.1.

MARES, I. (2005). 'Social Protection Around the World: External Insecurity, State Capacity and Domestic Political Cleavages', *Political Studies* 38.6.

MARTIN, S. (2005). 'Labor Obligations in the US–Chile Free Trade Agreement', *Comparative Labor Law and Policy Journal* 25.

MAZZA, J. (1999). *Unemployment Insurance: Case Studies and Lessons for Latin America and the Caribbean*, Washington, DC: IDB.

Ministerio de la Protección Social (Colombia) (2008). 'Sistema de inspección, vigilancia y control se moderniza: 207 nuevos funcionarios ingresarán al Ministerio de la Protección Social', Accessed October 9, 2009 at: http://www.minproteccionsocial.gov.co/vbecontent/NewsDetail.asp?ID=17279&IDCompany=3

Ministerio de Trabajo y Desarollo Laboral (Panama) (2008). *Informe de Gestión, 2003–2008*, Panama.

MURILLO, M. V. (2005). 'Partisanship Amidst Convergence: The Politics of Labor Reform in Latin America', *Comparative Politics* 37.4.

—— and SCHRANK, A. (2005). 'With a Little Help from My Friends: Partisan Politics, Transnational Alliances, and Labor Rights in Latin America', *Comparative Political Studies* 38.8.

—— OLIVEROS, V., and VAISHNAV, M. (2008). 'Voting for the Left or Governing on the Left?', prepared for the conference 'Latin America's Left Turn: Causes and Implications', Harvard University (April).

PAGÉS, C. (2004). 'A Cost–Benefit Analysis to Labor Market Reform', *Federal Reserve Bank of Atlanta Economic Review*, 2nd quarter.

REYES POSADA, A. (2007). *Viabilidad de un seguro de desempleo para Colombia: Algunas reflexiones y cálculos preliminares*, Colombia: Departamento Nacional de Planeación.

ROGOWSKY, R., and CHYN, E. (2008). 'US Trade Law and FTAs: A Survey of Labor Requirements', *Journal of International Commerce and Economics* 1.

SANDBROOK, R., et al. (2007). *Social Democracy in the Global Periphery*, New York: Cambridge University Press.

SARNEY, J. (1986). 'Brazil: A President's Story', *Foreign Affairs* 65.1.

SCHNEIDER, B. R., and SOSKICE, D. (2009). 'Inequality in Developed Countries and Latin America: Coordinated, Liberal and Hierarchical Systems', *Economy and Society* 38.10.

SCHRANK, A. (2009a). 'Understanding Latin American Political Economy: Varieties of Capitalism or Fiscal Sociology?', *Economy and Society* 38.1.

—— (2009b). 'Professionalization and Probity in a Patrimonial State: Labor Law Enforcement in the Dominican Republic', *Latin American Politics and Society* 51.2.

—— and PIORE, M. (2007). *Norms, Regulations and Labor Standards in Central America*, Mexico City: CEPAL.

SEHNBRUCH, K. (2004). 'Privatized Unemployment Insurance: Can Chile's New Unemployment Insurance Scheme Serve as a Model for Other Developing Countries?', CLAS Working Paper No. 12, University of California, Berkeley.

SINGH, A., et al. (2005). *Stabilization and Reform in Latin America: A Macroeconomic Perspective on the Experience since the early 1990s*, Washington, DC: IMF.

Tokman, V. (2007a). 'The Informal Economy, Insecurity and Social Cohesion in Latin America', *International Labour Review* 146.1–2.

—— (2007b). 'Modernizing the Informal Economy', in J. A. Ocampo and K. S. Jomo (eds), *Towards Full and Decent Employment*, London: Zed Books.

Vega Ruiz, M. (2005). *La reforma laboral en América Latina, 15 años después: un análisis comparado*, Lima: OIT.

Vroman, W., and Brusentsev, V. (2005). *Unemployment Compensation Throughout the World: A Comparative Analysis*, Kalamazoo, Mich.: Upjohn Institute.

Weller, J. (2001). *Economic Reforms, Growth, and Employment: Labour Markets in Latin America and the Caribbean*, Santiago, Chile: CEPAL.

Weyland, K. (1997). 'Growth with Equity in Chile's New Democracy?', *Latin American Research Review* 32.1.

CHAPTER 32

....

EDUCATION

....

MIGUEL URQUIOLA

32.1 INTRODUCTION

Improving education is a recurrent policy goal in Latin America, which reflects the fact that education is considered to have a causal and beneficial effect on outcomes ranging from labor income to civic participation.

Further, in analyzing education, the literature often makes a distinction between quantity and quality. Quantity captures the extent to which individuals have contact with or make progress through the educational system, and is generally measured by enrollment rates or years of schooling. Quality generally refers to the skills students actually gain while in school, and is generally measured using standardized tests.

This chapter reviews the progress and remaining challenges in terms of raising educational quantity and quality in Latin America. The chapter focuses on primary and secondary ("K-12") schooling, setting aside issues related to higher education or early childhood development. It makes the case that in terms of quantity, the region has made substantial strides. The remaining challenges revolve around reducing delayed entry, repetition, and dropout rates. The policy outlook in this area provides some grounds for optimism, as many governments are already implementing interventions (e.g. conditional cash transfers) that have been credibly evaluated and shown to be effective at tackling these issues (see Schady 2006 for a review).

Regarding quality, a first fact is that there is clear evidence that learning levels in Latin America are quite low. In the few cases in which data permit an assessment, there is also little evidence that countries have achieved significant improvements in this dimension (Hanushek and Woessman 2007; McEwan, Urquiola, and Vegas 2008; Vegas and Petrow 2008).

Beyond this, the policy outlook in this area offers less to be optimistic about, as little is known regarding how to raise educational quality (not just in Latin America), and this knowledge base is likely to improve only slowly. The latter reflects three aspects. First, although Latin America is by no means a laggard in terms of trying out innovative, quality-oriented educational interventions, these are rarely implemented in ways that facilitate rigorous evaluation. Second, improving quality may ultimately have more to do with changing incentives than increasing particular inputs, and here again designing—let alone implementing—reform is difficult (MacLeod and Urquiola 2009). Third, in many countries policy continues to emphasize educational quantity rather than quality. For example, in some countries conditional cash transfer programs are the main focus of educational policy, but there is reason to believe that these address quality at best tangentially (Reimers, DeShano da Silva, and Trevino 2006).

32.2 QUANTITY

Along a quantity dimension, Latin American educational systems have delivered substantial and sustained progress. To illustrate this, Figure 32.1 draws on Duryea and Székely (2000) to show the average years of schooling achieved by males from the 1938–40 and 1968–70 birth cohorts. While there is heterogeneity in the gains observed, the overall picture is one of significant progress—average schooling increased by between 2 and 4.5 years in the countries pictured. Further, the processes that have produced these gains appear to be quite resilient, continuing even during significant recessions (Schady 2004).

To get a sense of the remaining policy challenges, it is useful to have a more detailed view of what is happening to younger cohorts in terms of enrollment and completion.

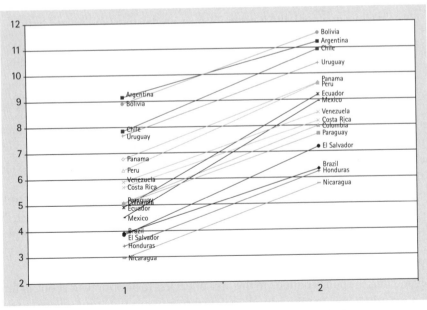

FIGURE 32.1 Average years of schooling for 1938–40 and 1968–70 birth cohorts

Source: Duryea and Székely (2000).

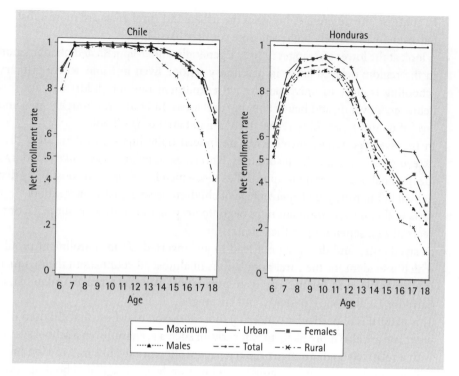

FIGURE 32.2 Age-enrollment profiles for Chile and Honduras

Source: Urquiola and Calderón (2006).

Urquiola and Calderón (2006) provide a sense of this for most countries in the region by analyzing household survey data for each of them, which allows them to produce comparable information.

To illustrate the type of heterogeneity that arises, Figure 32.2 graphs age-specific net enrollment rates for Chile and Honduras, two fairly extreme cases in the region. The figure presents the national enrollment rates as well as those observed for males, females, the rural area, and the urban area.[1]

There are several observations regarding this first set of results:

- As is well known, in most Latin American countries and for most age ranges, there are few differences between males and females' aggregate enrollment outcomes. As for Honduras in Figure 32.2, when differences emerge, they are often slightly in favor of females.

---

[1] This discussion draws on Urquiola and Calderón (2006). The specific data for Figure 32.2 can be found in that paper, along with notes on many technical considerations. A relevant note is that Figure 32.2 considers only individuals enrolled in grades 1–12. This matters only in the upper age ranges (17 and 18) where some high-school graduates are enrolled in postsecondary education.

- In contrast, the differences between the urban and rural areas are more substantial, even in a relatively higher income country like Chile.[2]
- A look at the lower age ranges reflects a generally under-appreciated phenomenon in the region: delayed entry into primary school. Even in Chile, where primary schooling is close to universal, the net enrollment rate for children of age 6 is below 90% overall, and below 80% in rural areas. In Honduras, roughly 40% and 20% of 6- and 7-year-olds, respectively, are not attending school.
- In the 8–13 age range, enrollments are indeed quite high—in urban areas they exceed 90% in essentially all countries. Nevertheless, in some cases like Honduras, the national rate never quite approaches 100, which leaves open the possibility that a small but non-negligible percentage of children never actually enter school.
- As is well known, enrollment rates begin to drop significantly at about 13, 14, or 15 years of age, depending on the country.
- Delayed entry and dropping out lead to an "inverted-U" age enrollment profile, which is evident for the rural populations in almost all countries in the region. It is also visible even for the aggregate population in Bolivia, Brazil, Colombia, El Salvador, Guatemala, Honduras, and Nicaragua.
- This pattern is of particular concern *if* there is reason to believe that children who enter late are also more likely to exit early. In such a scenario, even a school system with a relatively high average primary net enrollment rate, like that in Honduras, will be producing many "graduates" with 5 or fewer years of schooling, even assuming no repetition.

In terms of considering a broader sample of countries, these observations suggest that one should analyze how thoroughly different educational systems serve three populations: (i) children aged 6–7, those in the range in which delayed entry can be a problem, (ii) ages 8–13, the range in which most children are actually in school in virtually every country, and (iii) ages 14–18, the range in which net enrollment rates fall.[3]

32.2.1 Urban enrollment

Urquiola and Calderón (2006) explore these aspects in the context of urban enrollments. This is a useful benchmark because several countries have surveys representative of only their urban populations. As a first exercise, Table 32.1 presents a ranking of countries according to urban net enrollment ratios as well as according to those observed in each of the three age ranges cited.

---

[2] An important caveat is that these calculations make no attempt to define the rural area consistently across countries, but rather simply take the definition that comes with each household survey (see Urquiola and Calderón 2006 for further discussion).

[3] It is important to note that two characteristics that vary across countries: normative starting ages, and the number of grades in the formal primary and secondary educational system. In most countries, the normative start age is 6 and the whole primary and secondary sequence consists of 12 grades. In a few, however, the start age is 7 (e.g. Guatemala), or the system has only 11 grades (e.g. Colombia).

Table 32.1 Country rankings by urban enrollment rates in specific age ranges

Ranking 1: ages 6–18		Ranking 2: ages 6–7		Ranking 3: ages 8–13		Ranking 4: ages 14–18	
Country (1)	Rate (2)	Country (3)	Rate (4)	Country (5)	Rate (6)	Country (7)	Rate (8)
Chile	94.3	Argentina	98.8	Chile	99.0	Chile	88.7
Argentina	93.2	Uruguay	97.6	Argentina	99.0	Bolivia	87.0
Bolivia	92.0	Mexico	97.5	Panama	98.5	Argentina	84.0
Panama	92.4	Peru	97.3	Paraguay	98.1	Panama	82.0
Brazil	92.0	Panama	97.2	Peru	98.1	Brazil	79.7
Peru	89.0	Venezuela	97.2	Uruguay	97.9	Paraguay	75.2
Paraguay	88.6	Costa Rica	96.6	Venezuela	97.6	Peru	74.7
Uruguay	87.8	Ecuador	94.4	Brazil	97.2	Ecuador	73.5
Venezuela	87.8	Paraguay	94.0	Bolivia	97.0	El Salvador	72.8
Costa Rica	86.9	Chile	94.0	Costa Rica	96.8	Colombia	72.4
Mexico	86.1	Colombia	93.5	Mexico	96.0	Venezuela	72.2
Ecuador	85.7	Bolivia	92.1	El Salvador	94.4	Uruguay	71.6
Colombia	85.7	Brazil	90.2	Colombia	94.2	Costa Rica	71.2
El Salvador	84.4	El Salvador	83.5	Nicaragua	93.9	Nicaragua	70.2
Nicaragua	82.9	Guatemala¹	82.7	Ecuador	93.0	Mexico	69.7
Guatemala	77.2	Nicaragua	81.5	Honduras	91.4	Guatemala	60.9
Honduras	75.8	Honduras	76.3	Guatemala	90.0	Honduras	56.8

Source: Urquiola and Calderón (2006).

Columns 1 and 2 present what the authors label Ranking 1, which is based on the entire 6–18 age range. Chile and Argentina are placed at the top, as one might expect given their per capita income. Perhaps more surprisingly, Bolivia and Panama are ranked next. El Salvador, Nicaragua, Guatemala, and Honduras place at the bottom of this sample, as will be the case in many of the comparisons below.

The following columns break down the results into more specific age ranges, and show that Ranking 1 conceals interesting variation. For instance, Chile ranks highest in both the 8–13 and 14–18 age ranges (rankings 3 and 4). The latter in particular is expected given this country's pioneering (in the region) efforts to make secondary schooling universal. In contrast, it ranks much lower, 15th, in the 6–7 age range (Ranking 2). Uruguay illustrates the opposite pattern—it is close to the median in the highest age ranges, but is at the top of Ranking 2 because it manages to get almost all young children into school.

One possibility this raises is that countries that manage to incorporate children on time may end up with higher average years of schooling. One must be careful about such an inference, however. To see this, suppose households have a target set of skills or grades that they want their children to achieve. For instance, assume they want them to learn basic reading and writing skills, but not much beyond that (say because they consider those skills sufficient in the type of labor market they envision their children will enter). Assume also that this set of skills is mastered upon completion of the 3rd or 4th grade. If this is the case, then the age at entry might indeed affect the age at which children leave school, but perhaps not the years of schooling they eventually complete. In one country, a child might enter at 6 and leave at age 12, after repeating two grades. In another, she might enter at 7 and leave at 13, also after repeating two years. In the extreme, in such a scenario, implementing policies to lower the age at entry might have no effect on years of schooling.[4]

This type of reasoning also suggests that there might be a trade-off in how well countries do in the three age ranges in Table 32.1. For a final illustration, consider Bolivia and Uruguay. Bolivia is ranked 12th in the earliest range, 9th in the second, and 2nd in the last. As the above implies, this might reflect children remaining in school trying to achieve the skills they have not mastered, either because they entered late or repeated a lot (or because standards are low). In contrast, Uruguay does well (2nd) in the earliest range, but its relative performance goes down thereafter (12th in the final range), which might reflect achievement of a target set of skills or grades at a younger age.

Table 32.1 yields interesting comparisons, but these must be made with care and realizing that implicit in many of them is a model of how people decide on the number of years of schooling they desire; i.e. these numbers always reflect the interaction of supply and demand, and hence drawing policy implications from them is complicated.

---

[4] Glewwe and Jacoby (1995) refer to this issue using evidence from Ghana. They suggest that delayed entry might indeed be optimal if children's readiness for school is cumulative due to nutritional reasons. From this point of view, reducing it might even be counterproductive.

32.2.2 Years in school and years of schooling

Net enrollment rates display the interaction of demand and supply: the state and the private sector make slots in school available (at given direct and indirect costs), and households decide to use them or not. Thinking of the situation this way suggests another useful measure: average years *in school* (not to be confused with average years *of schooling*, to which we turn below), obtained by cumulatively adding age-specific net enrollment rates like those in Table 32.1.

This summation yields the expected or average number of years that an individual will spend in school by a given age, given the enrollment patterns currently observed in his or her country. In some sense this measure contains no new information relative to that already conveyed by the age-specific net enrollment rates. Nonetheless, we introduce it both because it provides a convenient summary of the resources (if only in time) expended by states and households to keep children in school, and because it provides a useful benchmark against which to compare countries' performance in terms of producing years of schooling—i.e. actual grades completed.

To illustrate, columns 2 and 5 in Table 32.2 present this measure for Chile and Honduras. For age 6, it is simply equal to the net enrollment rate expressed as a proportion (0.88 in Chile, and 0.57 in Honduras). This entry indicates that, on average, by the time they are 6 years old, children will have spent 0.88 years in school in Chile, and 0.57 in Honduras. Columns 2 and 5 then cumulate the entries in columns 1 and 4, showing, for instance, that by age 15 Chilean children will have spent an average of 9.7 years in school, while Honduran children will have spent 7.5; by age 18, these figures are 12.1 and 8.6, respectively.

Figure 32.3 begins to illustrate why this measure is useful. For each country, the top segment graphs the maximum feasible attainment (measured in years of schooling) that an individual of a given age could have if she started at age 6 and had a "normal" progression through the educational system. For example, this person could have completed a maximum of one year of schooling by age 6, two by age 7, and so on, up to 12 by age 17.

The middle line is the average years *in school* measure. Focusing first on Honduras, note that at age 6 the gap between these two segments is relatively small. A gap is clearly visible, nonetheless, because of the non-trivial delayed entry observed in this country. The two series then run roughly parallel up to about age 10, reflecting the high net enrollment rates in this age range. After that, the two lines diverge markedly, as dropout rates increase.

In the case of Chile, the average years in school segment begins very slightly below the maximum, which reflects the non-zero delayed entry observed even in this country. The gap then essentially does not grow until about age 14; after that, some divergence is again observed as enrollment rates drop for secondary schooling.

In short, the middle segment captures the *expected* number of years a child in each country will spend in school. Finally, columns 3 and 6 in Table 32.2, as well as the third segment in Figure 32.3, present the average years *of schooling* reported by individuals in each of these countries—that is, the grades they claim they have actually passed.

Table 32.2 Net enrollment rate, years of school, and years of schooling: Chile and Honduras

Age	Chile			Honduras		
	Net enrollment rate (1)	Average years in school (2)	Average years of schooling (3)	Net enrollment rate (4)	Average years in school (5)	Average years of schooling (6)
6	87.7	0.88	0.2	56.8	0.57	0.0
7	98.9	1.87	0.8	82.8	1.40	0.2
8	98.9	2.86	1.8	90.1	2.3	0.9
9	99.2	3.85	2.7	91.3	3.2	1.7
10	99.0	4.84	3.7	91.9	4.1	2.4
11	99.2	5.83	4.7	89.3	5.0	3.2
12	98.5	6.81	5.5	82.0	5.8	3.9
13	98.3	7.80	6.4	68.0	6.5	4.6
14	96.6	8.76	7.3	54.7	7.1	5.0
15	94.4	9.71	8.2	47.2	7.5	5.5
16	89.3	10.6	9.0	38.7	7.9	5.9
17	84.0	11.4	9.8	36.6	8.3	6.2
18	66.3	12.1	10.4	26.7	8.6	6.2

Source: Urquiola and Calderón (2006).

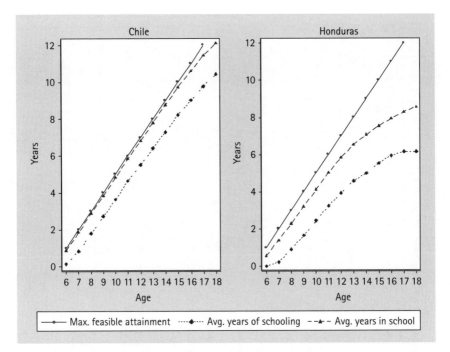

FIGURE 32.3 Maximum schooling, average years in school, and average years of schooling in Chile and Honduras

Source: Urquiola and Calderón (2006).

Comparing the second and third segments in Figure 32.3 gives an indication as to how effectively an educational system turns average years *in school* into average years *of schooling*. Put otherwise, considering the three segments in Figure 32.2 provides an answer to the question: "Why doesn't every 18-year-old in Honduras achieve 12 years of schooling?" The figure makes clear that this is due to two distinct problems: the lack of universal attendance (the gap between the first and the second segment) and the failure to turn years in school into years of schooling (the gap between the second and the third), largely but not exclusively due to repetition.

The growth in the gap between the middle and bottom segments as one moves to the right in these graphs reflects the increasing failure of systems to turn years in school into years of schooling. The figure for Chile indicates, for instance, that this gap has grown to about one year by the time children reach age 18. In the case of Honduras, the gap at this age exceeds two years.

For further detail, Table 32.3 presents rankings according to these two measures. Ranking 5 orders countries according to the average years *in school* observed at age 18 What is clear from this is that Latin American countries devote a lot of resources to education, at least as measured by the time households declare children are in contact with the schooling system—in all but four countries, the average time spent in school exceeds 10 years by age 18.

Table 32.3 Ranking by average years of schooling accumulated in the formal '1–12' system

Ranking 5: Average years in school at age 18		Ranking 6: Average years of schooling at age 18		Ranking 7: Average years of schooling at age 8		Ranking 8: Average years of schooling at age 13	
Country (1)	Years (2)	Country (3)	Years (4)	Country (5)	Years (6)	Country (5)	Years (6)
Argentina	12.1	Chile	10.4	Ecuador	2.5	Argentina	6.5
Chile	12.1	Argentina	9.8	Uruguay	2.0	Chile	6.4
Panama	11.5	Panama	9.5	Venezuela	1.9	Uruguay	6.3
Brazil	11.4	Peru	9.0	Mexico	1.8	Ecuador	6.3
Uruguay	11.4	Bolivia	8.9	Chile	1.8	Mexico	6.2
Bolivia	11.2	Uruguay	8.7	El Salvador	1.8	Venezuela	6.1
Peru	11.1	Ecuador	8.7	Brazil	1.7	Bolivia	6.0
Venezuela	11.0	Mexico	8.7	Bolivia	1.7	Panama	6.0
Paraguay	10.7	Venezuela	8.6	Argentina	1.7	El Salvador	5.6
Mexico	10.6	Colombia	8.4	Panama	1.5	Peru	5.6
Colombia	10.5	Paraguay	8.4	Peru	1.5	Costa Rica	5.4
Costa Rica	10.5	El Salvador	8.0	Paraguay	1.5	Colombia	5.3
Ecuador	10.4	Costa Rica	7.8	Colombia	1.3	Brazil	5.3
El Salvador	10.0	Brazil	7.3	Nicaragua	1.2	Paraguay	5.0
Nicaragua	9.7	Honduras	6.2	Costa Rica	1.1	Honduras	4.6
Honduras	8.6	Nicaragua	5.9	Honduras	0.9	Nicaragua	4.4
Guatemala	8.2	Guatemala	5.5	Guatemala	0.7	Guatemala	3.8

Source: Urquiola and Calderón (2006).

Rankings 6, 7, and 8 are based on the average years *of schooling* children have accumulated at three ages: 18, 8, and 13, respectively.[5]

Ranking 6 (columns 3 and 4) refers to age 18. The country with the best performance in this "final" outcome is Chile, which achieved an average of more than 10 years of schooling among 18-year-olds in 2000. Argentina and Panama place close behind. There is then a large number of countries (more than half the sample) with between 8 and 9 years of schooling, and a smaller number producing less than 8. The latter group contains some of the usual suspects but also, perhaps more surprisingly, Brazil and Costa Rica. At the extreme, Guatemalan 18-year-olds in 2000 had only 5.5 years of schooling on average.

As above, the rankings that result at earlier ages are substantially different. For instance, Chile is much closer to the median in terms of attainment at age 8, partially reflecting its underperformance in the delayed entry-related rankings above. In contrast, Ecuador starts out very strongly, but then factors like repetition or high drop-out rates drive its position down substantially.

The fact that the variance in Ranking 6 is greater than that in 5 suggests considerable variation on how effective different systems are at turning attendance into years of schooling—countries that do well in rankings 1–5 but not in rankings 6–8 are underperformers in this regard. Brazil is a notable example.

Because this "failure" is an interesting outcome *per se*, we present a final set of rankings based on the following measure:

Effectiveness gap = (average yrs in school – average yrs of schooling) –
  (average yrs in school at age 6 – average yrs of schooling
  at age 6)

where the last term is meant to capture that a constant difference might exist between these two measures, as mentioned above, perhaps due to the month at which the survey was collected (and how it interacts with the school calendar).[6]

Table 32.4 presents rankings based on the values this measure takes at ages 8, 13, and 18. As expected, the average level of this gap grows with age, although more so in some countries. Because these rankings take countries' enrollment performances as given, its results are somewhat different from those seen above. For instance, Guatemala and Honduras no longer come at the bottom, but closer to the median of the distribution. In other words, abstracting from their relative poor performance in getting kids in school, these two countries perform adequately in terms of turning attendance into years of schooling. Chile is at the top of the ranking, showing that its first place in "final"

[5] One issue here is that Table 32.3 stops making the distinction between urban and rural areas despite the fact that the latter are not represented in the surveys of Argentina and Uruguay. See Urquiola and Calderón (2006) for a technical discussion.

[6] In other words, this is a blunt way to control for the fact that the interaction between factors such as the school calendar, school-starting cutoff months of birth, and the month in which the survey is taken, will introduce constant differences between these two measures across all age ranges.

Table 32.4 Ranking by effectiveness gap

Ranking 9: age 8		Ranking 10: age 13		Ranking 11: age 18	
Country (1)	Gap (2)	Country (3)	Rate (4)	Country (5)	Rate (6)
Uruguay	0.2	Argentina	0.5	Chile	0.9
Mexico	0.2	Mexico	0.6	Panama	1.1
El Salvador	0.5	Chile	0.7	Mexico	1.1
Venezuela	0.3	Uruguay	0.7	Colombia	1.3
Chile	0.3	Panama	0.9	Peru	1.3
Ecuador	0.3	Venezuela	0.9	Argentina	1.4
Argentina	0.4	El Salvador	1.0	Paraguay	1.5
Guatemala	0.4	Ecuador	1.0	El Salvador	1.7
Panama	0.5	Bolivia	1.1	Ecuador	1.7
Paraguay	0.5	Colombia	1.2	Guatemala	1.8
Peru	0.6	Costa Rica	1.3	Venezuela	1.8
Bolivia	0.6	Peru	1.3	Costa Rica	1.8
Brazil	0.6	Honduras	1.4	Honduras	1.8
Nicaragua	0.6	Guatemala	1.4	Bolivia	1.9
Colombia	0.6	Paraguay	1.6	Uruguay	1.9
Costa Rica	0.8	Nicaragua	1.8	Nicaragua	3.2
Honduras	0.8	Brazil	1.9	Brazil	3.7

Source: Urquiola and Calderón (2006).

outcomes does not come only from high enrollment. In contrast, Brazil, with well-known repetition problems, ranks at the bottom by age 18.

As in all cases above, the results also illustrate that countries' performance is not static along the age range. Colombia is a good example of rapid improvement, i.e. it seems to start with substantial repetition problems, which seem to get mitigated as children move on in school. Venezuela is an example of the opposite pattern.

32.2.3 Summarizing country-level performance along quantity dimensions

From a policy point of view, the results presented essentially highlight countries' performance along two dimensions: (i) getting children into school in time and keeping them there, and (ii) turning their contact with the school system into years of schooling.

Urquiola and Calderón (2006) also present a "bottom line" classification of countries, one that summarizes countries' outcomes along the above two dimensions: enrollment and their measure of "effectiveness." More specifically, they create four groups of countries according to their enrollment performance. These are presented in the four rows of

Table 32.5 A "bottom line" ordering of countries by attendance and effectiveness

Enrollment group	Effectiveness group			
	1 (Best performance)	2	3	4 (Worst performance)
1 (Best performance)	Argentina Chile Panama Uruguay			
2		Bolivia Peru Venezuela	Paraguay	Brazil
3	Mexico	Colombia Ecuador	Costa Rica Paraguay	
4 (Worst performance)	El Salvador	Guatemala	Honduras	Nicaragua

Source: Urquiola and Calderón (2006).

Table 32.5. As one moves down these rows one finds countries which have generally made less progress in terms of getting children into school.

The four columns in turn order countries by their relative performance in the effectiveness measure introduced above—the gap between average years in school and average years of schooling—where those in the leftmost column are the best performers. Within each cell, countries are presented in alphabetical order.

The rows indicate that the best performers in terms of enrollment are Argentina, Chile, Panama, and Uruguay. The next group is composed of Bolivia, Brazil, Peru, Venezuela, and Paraguay. The columns suggest, however, that within this group, Paraguay and particularly Brazil perform much worse in turning children's contact with the school system into years of schooling.

At the opposite extreme, El Salvador, Guatemala, Honduras, and Nicaragua do worst in enrollment. But again there is variance in their "effectiveness": El Salvador does as well as Argentina, Chile, Panama, or Uruguay in this regard, given the attendance patterns it starts with. Nicaragua, in contrast, does as poorly as Brazil.

The countries in the two middle rows are somewhat more similar in that minor changes in the weighting schemes can result in countries crossing from the second to the third group, and vice versa, i.e. the countries in these two rows are not as clearly differentiated—although they are rather more clearly differentiated from the best and worst performers (rows 1 and 4).

32.2.4 Quantity: prospects for progress

Taken together, the above results make clear that in terms of quantity, Latin America has displayed sustained gains. That said, essentially all countries must deal with some combination of three challenges: delayed entry, dropping out, and repetition.

The outlook regarding the feasibility of doing this, particularly in terms of the first two, is generally positive. Specifically, conditional cash transfer initiatives and fee reduction programs may tackle at least the demand-related components of these challenges. Conditional cash transfers further stand out among regional education interventions in that several of them have benefited from random assignment—those for Ecuador, Honduras, Nicaragua, and Mexico, for instance—allowing for unusually clear impact evaluations.[7]

More specifically, the design of many of these programs equips them to deal with delayed entry. The programs in Ecuador, Guatemala, Honduras, Mexico, and Nicaragua, for example, cover either 6-year-olds or else children in 1st grade. Even when these ages or grades are not explicitly targeted (e.g. in Brazil and Colombia), one might imagine that households would send their children to school promptly in the expectation of eventually receiving the cash subsidies.

Most of these programs also deal with enrollment deficits in the 8–13 and 14–18 age range—with the latter receiving more attention, as they are extended to cover secondary grades as well (e.g. the Argentinean program focused on secondary from its inception, whereas the Mexican was extended to this level). Finally, in a few cases conditional cash transfers are also geared towards dealing with problems of repetition. For example, *Progresa/Oportunidades* cuts benefits for children who fail a grade more than once, but in most cases repetition-related interventions are not part of the design.

32.3 QUALITY

We now turn to the outlook regarding educational quality. A starting point in this discussion is that by both absolute and relative measures, educational quality in Latin America is low. Figure 32.4 begins to provide a sense of this, showing that, as is well known, there are substantial deficits in terms of testing performance.[8]

Panels A, B, and C draw on *Laboratorio latinoamericano de evaluación de la calidad de la educación* (2001) to consider the percentage of public and private school children that attain different levels of reading readiness. Roughly, Level 1 (Panel A) refers to a basic literal understanding of texts—being able to identify the actors in a simple plot, for instance. Level 2 (Panel B) considers the ability not only to understand a text but to express its basic elements in words different from those used in the original. Level 3 (Panel C) explores whether children can "fill in the blanks" in a text, regarding aspects like assumptions and causation.

[7] For Mexico, see Schultz (2004), Behrman and Skoufias (2006), Berhman et al. (2006), and Todd and Wolpin (2007); for Nicaragua, see Maluccio and Flores (2005); for Ecuador, Schady and Araujo (2006). See also Barrera, Linden, and Urquiola (2007) for work on fee reductions.

[8] For a recent review on quality deficits in Latin American education, see Vegas and Petrow (2008).

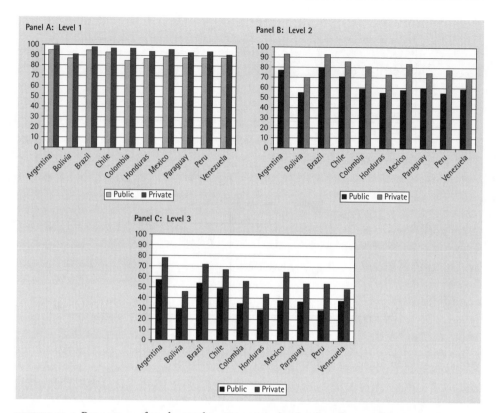

FIGURE 32.4 Percentage of students who attain given levels of reading proficiency

Source: Laboratorio latinoamericano de evaluación de la calidad de la educación (2001).

As the figure shows, the majority of 3rd and 4th graders in the region have attained proficiency at level one. Still, more than one in ten children is unable to fulfill this benchmark in all countries save Argentina, Brazil, and Chile. By level 3, more than 1 out of 2 children fail to attend proficiency in all countries but Argentina and Chile.

Thus, by this objective standard, educational quality in Latin American is rather low. Pritchett (2004) provides a broader comparison by looking at how countries that have participated in international samples perform relative to OECD countries. Figure 32.5 reproduces a figure from his paper, showing countries' average scores in reading, mathematics and science, scaled by the standard deviation of scores in the OECD sample. The figure therefore gives a sense of how many OECD standard deviations each country is below the OECD median performer. The box in the figure presents the region wide average, and the 10th, 25th, 75th and 90th percentiles.

The exercise places the Latin American average 4.8 OECD standard deviations below the OECD median. Even children at the 90th percentile in Latin America, are almost 2 standard deviations below the OECD median. For a concrete example, Pritchett suggests that only about 3% of Brazilian students would outperform the average Danish student, while the average Brazilian student would find himself at the level of only 2% of

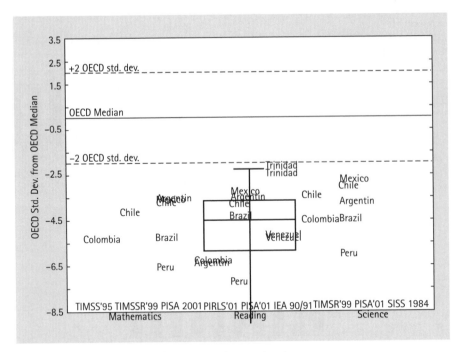

FIGURE 32.5 Latin American performance in international tests

Source: Pritchett (2004).

Danish students. These results might even understate the difference in achievement, since a larger proportion of children are tested in the OECD than in Latin America.

In short, by both absolute and relative measures, educational quality in Latin America is low. To our knowledge, there is much less of a sense of how it has evolved historically—most countries simply do not have test score time series long enough to allow us to say much in this regard (although there is a clear upward trend in self-reported literacy). To cite one example, Chile has been testing students since the 1980s, and has also participated in international tests since the 1970s. Although comparability issues are important over such long periods, there is widespread perception that its outcomes have not improved much, particularly over the last decade when more test score observations are available (see Hsieh and Urquiola 2006; McEwan et al. 2008; Gallego 2008).

All this implies that coming up with strategies to effectively improve quality would seem to be a clear priority for educational policy in the region. The remainder of this section elaborates on three obstacles that suggest this is unlikely to happen quickly.

32.3.1 Obstacle 1: little knowledge regarding effective inputs

Expenditure policies have historically had a prominent place in efforts to improve educational quality. This reflects the possibility that schools might underperform simply because they do not have sufficient inputs. Policies that increase spending across the board, however, have generally met with limited success. Specifically, the picture is one in which most countries have seen their educational expenditures climb substantially over recent decades, often with scant testing gains to show for it. This has led Pritchett (2003) and others to argue that there has been a generalized decline in school productivity across the OECD; in the same spirit, Hoxby (2002) suggests that US school productivity has declined by 50% since the 1970s. Though there is less information on the issue, the general sense is that the Latin American experience is consistent with this.

One response to disappointment with generalized expenditure policies has been to conjecture that it might reflect that policymakers have simply not discovered, and are therefore not prioritizing, the "correct" inputs. A fairly recent and significant body of research therefore tries to credibly identify specific inputs (e.g. class size reductions, textbooks, computers) that might raise learning; namely, there is large-scale effort among US academics in this regard—see Banerjee, Cole, and Linden (2007) for an example of such research; see Banerjee and Duflo (2009) for a review.

This body of research is still some way from providing a clear and complete sense of how policymakers might go about raising learning. Further, at least so far it is partially bypassing Latin America in two important respects. First, the educational experiments being carried out by US-based academics are largely focused on Africa and Southern Asia, although they nevertheless have relevance for Latin America,[9] and there are exceptions to this—see for example work on Colombia by Barrera-Osorio and Linden (2009). There is also some quasi-experimental work in the region, for example, the regression discontinuity-based analyses of class size effects by Urquiola (2006) in Bolivia, and Urquiola and Verhoogen (2009) in Chile.

Second, Latin American ministries of education are not compensating for this by rigorous evaluation of their own. This is somewhat surprising, since they have in fact produced many notable examples of innovative quality-related interventions; they simply seem reluctant to credibly evaluate them.

This is illustrated by Chile, which is among the leading innovators in educational policy in the world, and has the technical capabilities of at least a middle income country. One of its policy initiatives in the 1990s was the introduction of interventions targeted on the lowest-performing schools. Specifically, the P-900 program sought to improve learning in the 900 schools testing lowest in 4th grade achievement. An ex post regression-discontinuity evaluation by Chay, McEwan, and Urquiola (2005) suggests the program had a significant impact, if less than previously estimated, but could not speak to the precise components that generated this impact. Chile has continued to experiment with such compensatory programs (e.g. the *Escuelas críticas* and *Liceos prioritarios* programs), but has not done it in a manner that would facilitate credible evaluation, making it hard to discern which components work or not.

---

[9] See Damon and Glewwe (2007) and Urquiola (2007) for a discussion of applicability.

This situation is representative of much of the region—Latin American governments are not lacking in terms of generating interesting quality-related educational interventions, but are not nearly as effective in implementing them in ways that will allow clear evaluation. Pritchett (2008) raises interesting considerations as to whether this reflects an oversight or broader political economy issues.

Regardless, the bottom line is that if much greater efforts toward evaluation are not developed in the region, there is likely to be a rather limited supply of tried and tested innovations that could be directed at improving learning.

32.3.2 Obstacle 2: maximizing student effort and school productivity

As discussed in the previous section, one possible explanation for the fact that substantial increases in spending often do not result in greater learning is that there is insufficient knowledge regarding the causal effect of specific inputs.

Another possibility, however, is that educational systems are not structured to provide incentives for effort on the part of schools, and that therefore spending might be ineffective. Specifically, economists since at least Friedman (1962) have emphasized the possibility that what is wrong with the educational sector is that schools do not face enough competitive pressures. The argument has been that, as long as parents value schools with good reputations for quality, then a free market should ensure the efficient provision of educational services.

There has also been disappointment with initiatives in this area, however. For example, in 1981 Chile essentially implemented an unrestricted voucher scheme similar to that called for by Friedman, but widespread disappointment still surrounds the evolution of its educational quality (see Hsieh and Urquiola 2006; McEwan et al. 2008).

MacLeod and Urquiola (2009) present a model that suggests that promoting competition may indeed not be enough, and that an element of market design may be necessary for school choice to successfully increase school productivity and student effort. An analysis of their model suggests that reaching such a design is a work in progress, and that many of its elements would be difficult to implement in Latin America (and elsewhere).

Specifically, the model produces three key findings:

- When schools cannot select students based on ability, competition raises school productivity. Further, consistent with Friedman's (1962) intuition, in this case distributing vouchers clearly promotes equality, as it: (i) increases educational consumption on the part of lower income students, (ii) raises the probability that high-productivity schools enter the market to serve lower-income children.
- In contrast, when schools can use measures of innate ability to select students, competition lowers student effort and, in some cases, skill accumulation; it also raises inequality. When a selective and a non-selective sector coexist (for example,

a private selective sector might coexist with a non-selective public sector, as happens in much of Latin America), expansions in the size of selective sector adversely affect those left behind in the non-selective segment. These conclusions hold even abstracting from peer effects.

• These results suggest that, aside from reducing stratification, one way to improve learning outcomes is by introducing (or increasing the precision of) graduation tests, and tying performance in them to outcomes that students and parents care about. The more precise these exams are, the easier it will be for students to transmit their skill and the greater the incentive they will have to exert effort.

In short, this model leaves open the possibility that the levels of learning that different countries display will not be independent of (i) how much selection/stratification exists in their schools systems or (ii) whether they provide clear individual specific measures of learning. These characteristics will determine to what extent students exert effort and to what extent schools have to compete in terms of value-added rather than student composition. Further, the results suggest that both resource and choice policies (in the form in which the latter are usually implemented) are likely to disappoint, consistent with results observed in the region.

One question is then to what extent Latin American school systems display the two characteristics mentioned. Regarding sorting or stratification, to our knowledge there is no centralized source of information that would permit definitive statements, but the general perception is that Latin American school systems tend to be fairly stratified. School admissions policies are common in private schools, and implicit or explicit selection takes place even in the public sector. In part this reflects the fact that the region displays high levels of income inequality as well as substantial residential segregation.

These facts suggest that in Latin America, policies that facilitate sorting will likely have a large impact on observed stratification, and this may reduce their impact on learning. For an example, consider again the introduction of vouchers in Chile, where private voucher schools were allowed to implement a wide range of admissions policies. The model in MacLeod and Urquiola (2009) predicts that these measures would result in substantial entry, with the private sector skimming the best students from the public sector, and itself becoming stratified. The evidence is consistent with this. First, mainly for-profit private schools presently account for most enrollments, up from about a 10% share at the time of the reform. Second, Hsieh and Urquiola (2006) suggest that this growth was associated with the middle class largely following upper-income households into the private sector, with the lowest-income students remaining in public schools. Third, at present one observes clear hierarchies of schools by income.

Further, the model in MacLeod and Urquiola (2009) predicts that (while perhaps not raising average learning, consistent with evidence) the growth of the private sector would have very different consequences for those transferring into it and for those left behind. On the one hand, students attending selective private voucher schools might experience an increase in wages, as Bravo, Mukhopadhyay, and Todd (2008) suggest in fact happened. On the other hand, the growth of the selective sector would generally lower the welfare of individuals remaining in the public sector. Consistent with this, over the past few years Chilean public high-school students, despite having access to schools that have improved substantially at least in terms of amenities, have taken to (at times violently) demanding changes in the laws that govern the school sector (PREAL 2006). In short, the model suggests that the Chilean voucher system was perhaps structured in a way that led schools to compete on selectivity (or amenities) rather than productivity in the generation of skill.

These considerations are policy-relevant because initiatives that promote competition between schools need not be implemented in a manner that increases sorting. Consider the case of Sweden. In the early 1990s, Sweden allowed independent schools to begin receiving per-student subsidies equal to about 80% of those given to public schools. Independent schools can have explicit religious affiliations, and can be operated for profit. In relevant dimensions, therefore, the Swedish system is quite similar to Chile's. However, Swedish private schools must be operated on a first-come, first-served basis, and cannot select students based on ability, income, or ethnicity. MacLeod and Urquiola (2009) suggest that this design would produce less stratification and greater effects on learning. The literature is broadly consistent with Swedish private schools on average not being that different from public schools in terms of socioeconomic composition, in stark contrast with the outcome in Chile.

MacLeod and Urquiola (2009) also suggest that national testing can be useful in motivating students—the claim is that educational systems that provide individual-specific measures of learning tied to outcomes parents care about will tend to develop school systems geared toward higher achievement. Consistent with this, Woessmann (2007) suggests that countries with standardized graduation or college admissions exams perform better than expected in international tests. For instance, Romania and South Korea display extensive private tutoring industries that parents use to supplement their children's learning at school.

At the opposite extreme, consider cases in which there is nothing resembling a graduation test, and in which students' family wealth and connections determine access to higher education (a perhaps not too distant characterization of some settings in Latin America). In this case, the system will provide few incentives for student effort, and if this is an important ingredient for learning, educational interventions that do not address it may prove disappointing.

The educational market is very complicated, and improving its outcomes in terms of learning may require elements of market design, as opposed to the introduction of unfettered competition or research on which inputs are most effective. Here again, the research is far from producing a clear policy roadmap. Further, even if it were, its elements might be hard to implement in the region. For example, restricting the types of admissions policy allowed, or the manner in which slots at the top universities are allocated, might well be controversial.

32.3.3 Obstacle 3: the continuing policy emphasis on quantity

A final obstacle to improvements in quality arises from the continued policy emphasis on educational quantity. For example, the use of conditional cash transfer programs has increased in the region but, as argued by Reimers et al. (2006), these interventions do not directly target quality, and may ultimately compete for educational funding with policy options that would more directly address it.

Unfortunately it is difficult to move very clearly beyond speculation in this area, in part because there is little evidence on the effects of conditional cash transfers on learning. Nevertheless, one of the few studies on the subject, Berhman, Parker, and Todd (2006), finds evidence consistent with Mexico's *Progresa/Oportunidades* not having had a positive effect on students' test scores. This might not be completely surprising, since in the extreme conditional cash transfers can, through congestion effects, actually lower the quality of instruction.

32.4 CONCLUSION

This chapter has reviewed the outlook in terms of improving educational quantity and quality in Latin America. It has made the case that as far as quantity is concerned, the region has displayed sustained gains in the past decades. That said, substantial cross-country variation is still observed in the degree to which school systems must deal with three challenges: delayed entry, dropping out, and repetition. The outlook regarding the feasibility of such progress is generally positive.

First, economic growth and development alone will likely allow some countries to move their performance closer to that displayed by their higher-income counterparts. Second, policy tools aimed at some of these challenges are available, primarily in the form of conditional cash transfers and fee reductions. Second, quite unusually for social-sector interventions in the region, these have been rigorously evaluated and shown to be effective. In this context, it would seem that the key remaining challenge is to look for better interventions to address repetition, particularly in a handful of countries like Brazil and the Dominican Republic.

In terms of quality, the prospects for progress are much more uncertain, which is disturbing given that the region would seem to begin from a very low level. A first aspect to note is that in this area Latin America is not alone—the lack of sound knowledge on how to improve learning extends even to developed countries.

For the region, however, the key obstacles are threefold. First, one avenue to improve education may be to undertake a massive experimentation effort, essentially testing which school inputs or practices might most effectively raise learning. Unfortunately, there is not much of this going on in the region. In particular, regional ministries of education produce many interesting interventions, but are clearly less aggressive when it comes to rigorous evaluation. Second, it may be that the binding constraint actually consists of coming up with market designs which provide schools and students with the optimal incentives for effort. Figuring this out is difficult as well, and even if this were possible, the issue of implementation remains, in part due to political economy constraints that may prove formidable in the region. Third, in many cases regional governments and even multilateral agencies continue to remain focused on the quantity aspect of educational performance.

References

Banerjee, A. V., and Duflo, E. (2009). 'The Experimental Approach to Development Economics', *Annual Review of Economics* 1: 151–78.

———Cole, S., and Linden, L. (2007). 'Remedying Education: Evidence from Two Randomized Experiments in India', *Quarterly Journal of Economics* 122.3.

Barrera-Osorio, F., and Linden, L. (2009). 'The Use and Misuse of Computers in Education: Evidence from a Randomized Controlled Trial of a Language Arts Program', mimeograph, Columbia University.

———and Urquiola, M. (2007). 'The Effect of User Fee Reductions on Enrollment: Evidence From a Quasi-Experiment', mimeograph, Columbia University.

Behrman, J., Parker, S., and Todd, P. (2006). 'Do School Subsidy Programs Generate Lasting Benefits? A Five Year Follow-Up of *Oportunidades* Participants', mimeograph, University of Pennsylvania.

———and Skoufias, E. (2006). 'Mitigating Myths about Policy Effectiveness: Evaluation of Mexico's Antipoverty and Human Resource Investment Program', *Annals of the American Academy* 606.1.

Bravo, D., Mukhopadhyay, S., and Todd, P. (2008). 'Effects of a Universal School Voucher System on Educational and Labor Market Outcomes', mimeograph, University of Pennsylvania.

Chay, K., McEwan, P., and Urquiola, M. (2005). 'The Central Role of Noise in Evaluating Interventions that Use Test Scores to Rank Schools', *American Economic Review* 95.4.

Damon, A., and Glewwe, P. (2007). 'Three Proposals to Improve Education in Latin America and the Caribbean', report to the Copenhagen Consensus Center and IDB.

Duryea, S., and Székely, M. (2000). 'Labor Markets in Latin America: A Look at the Supply Side', *Emerging Markets Review* 1.

Friedman, M. (1962). *Capitalism and Freedom*, Chicago: University of Chicago Press.

Gallego, F. (2008). Comment on McEwan et al. (2008), *Economia* 8.2.

Hanushek, E., and Woessman, L. (2007). 'The Role of School Improvement in Economic Development', NBER Working Paper No. 12382, Cambridge, Mass.

Hoxby, C. (2002). 'School Choice and School Productivity (or Could School Choice be a Tide That Lifts All Boats)?', NBER Working Paper No. 8873, Cambridge, Mass.

Hsieh, C.-T., and Urquiola, M. (2006). 'The Effects of Generalized School Choice on Achievement and Stratification: Evidence from Chile's School Voucher Program', *Journal of Public Economics* 90.

Laboratorio Latinoamericano de Evaluación de la Calidad de la Educación (2001). 'Primer studio internacional comparative sobre lenguaje, matemática y factores asociados, para alumnus del tercer y cuarto grado de la educación básica', Paris: UNESCO.

MacLeod, B., and Urquiola, M. (2009). 'Anti-lemons: School Reputation and Educational Quality', NBER Working Paper No. 15112, Cambridge, Mass. http://www.nber.org/papers/15112

Maluccio, R., and Flores, R. (2005). 'Impact Evaluation of a Conditional Cash Transfer Program: The Nicaraguan *Red de Protección Social*', Research Report No. 141, International Food Policy Research Institute, Washington, DC.

McEwan, P., Urquiola, M., and Vegas, E. (2008). 'School Choice, Stratification, and Information on School Performance: Lessons from Chile', *Economia* 8.2.

PREAL (Programa de Promoción de la Reforma Educativa de América Latina y el Caribe) (2006). 'El conflicto de los secundarios en Chile', Executive Summary No. 25, Santiago, Chile.

Pritchett, L. (2003). 'Educational Quality and Costs: A Big Puzzle and Five Possible Pieces', mimeograph, Harvard University.

—— (2004). 'Towards a New Consensus for Addressing the Global Challenge of the Lack of Education', Copenhagen Consensus Challenge Paper.

—— (2008). 'The Policy Irrelevance of the Economics of Education: Is "Normative as Positive" Just Useless or Worse?', mimeograph, Harvard University.

Reimers, F., DeShano da Silva, C., and Trevino, E. (2006). 'Where is the "Education" in Conditional Cash Transfers in Education?', mimeograph, UNESCO Institute for Statistics, Montreal.

Schady, N. (2004). 'Do Macroeconomic Crises Always Slow Human Capital Accumulation?', *World Bank Economic Review* 18.2.

—— (2006). 'The Impact of Conditional Cash Transfer Programs on Schooling Outcomes', mimeograph, World Bank, Washington, DC.

—— and Araujo, M. (2006). 'Cash Transfers, Conditions, School Enrollment, and Child Work: Evidence from a Randomized Experiment in Ecuador', World Bank Policy Research Working Paper No. 3930, Washington, DC.

Schultz, T. P. (2004). 'School Subsidies for the Poor: Evaluating the Mexican PROGRESA Poverty Program', *Journal of Development Economics* 74.1.

Todd, P., and Wolpin, K. (2007). 'Using a Social Experiment to Validate a Dynamic Behavioral Model of Child Schooling and Fertility: Assessing the Impact of a School Subsidy Program in Mexico', mimeograph, University of Pennsylvania.

Urquiola, M. (2006). 'Identifying Class Size Effects in Developing Countries: Evidence from Rural Bolivia', *Review of Economics and Statistics* 88.1.

—— (2007). Comment on Damon and Glewwe (2007), alternative view paper for the *Consulta de San José*.

—— and Calderón, V. (2006). 'Apples and Oranges: Educational Enrollment and Attainment across Countries in Latin America and the Caribbean', *International Journal of Educational Development* 26.

—— and Verhoogen, E. (2009). 'Class-Size Caps, Sorting, and the Regression Discontinuity Design', *American Economic Review* 99.1.

Vegas, E., and Petrow, J. (2008). *Raising Student Learning in Latin America: The Challenge for the 21st Century*, Washington, DC: World Bank.

Woessmann, L. (2007). 'International Evidence on School Competition, Autonomy, and Accountability: A Review', *Peabody Journal of Education* 82.2–3.

....

CHAPTER 33

SOCIAL PROTECTION IN LATIN AMERICA: ACHIEVEMENTS AND LIMITATIONS

....

FRANCISCO H. G. FERREIRA AND DAVID A. ROBALINO

33.1 INTRODUCTION[1]

....

Governments make transfers to households, either in cash or in kind, for two basic reasons. The first reason is the management of risk. Individuals in all countries are exposed to uncertainty and risk in various dimensions, including health (arising from possible illness or disability), longevity (arising from uncertainty about the time of one's death), and income (arising from unemployment or other sources of unexpected fluctuation in the income stream, such as weather shocks for farmers). If insurance markets were perfect, there might be little role for the state to intervene in the management of such risks, or to promote consumption smoothing. But well-known problems of adverse selection and moral hazard cause insurance markets to be far from perfect and, in many cases, to be missing altogether. This leads to insufficient levels of risk-pooling in the private market. Ever since the birth of European social security in Otto von Bismarck's Germany, governments have stepped in to address these insurance market failures, by means of various *social insurance* mechanisms, including old age and disability pensions, unemployment insurance, and public health insurance.

[1] We are grateful to José Antonio Ocampo and Jaime Ros, and to Emanuela Galasso, Margaret Grosh, Santiago Levy, Helena Ribe, Norbert Schady, and Ian Walker for comments on an earlier version of the chapter, and to Carlos Prada for excellent research assistance. We would also like to thank Helena Ribe and Ian Walker for permission to draw on their recent joint work with Robalino (Ribe, Robalino, and Walker 2010). The views expressed here are those of the authors, and should not be attributed to the World Bank, its Executive Directors, or the countries they represent.

The second basic reason why governments make transfers to households is to help reduce poverty. This motive originates not from individuals' aversion to risk, but from society's aversion to poverty or inequity: if the primary distribution of income is too unequal, or includes too much deprivation for the taste of decisionmakers (whether one thinks of them as social planners or as the median voter), governments can redistribute by taxing some people and transferring resources to others. Transfers made for this purpose are generally grouped under the rubric of *social assistance*. Together, social assistance and social insurance make up a country's *social protection* system.[2]

Although the conceptual distinction between social insurance and social assistance—the former intended for consumption smoothing and the latter for redistribution in permanent incomes—is important for clarity in policy design, it often blurs in practice—for two reasons. First is the very fact that people's income streams are volatile: unexpected unemployment is a negative shock, and public unemployment insurance mitigates it, but it may also prevent the victim of the shock from falling into poverty. Conversely, a cash transfer intended primarily to alleviate long-term poverty may help smooth consumption for poor recipients during a recession. Free health care provided in kind as an insurance against negative health shocks may prevent a beneficiary from falling into poverty which could, in its absence, have become a long-term state. In short: the existence of a social insurance system designed to address risk will often act so as to reduce poverty—or prevent it from increasing; while the existence of a social assistance system designed to reduce poverty will often protect the poor from at least some negative effects from shocks. Such "mission overlap" may well be for the best, if properly understood and adequately managed.

The second factor blurring the distinction between social insurance and social assistance arises from the social preference, in many countries, to redistribute for equity purposes over and above the poverty line. While such redistribution is conceptually distinct from the risk-management and insurance functions we identify as the central *raison d'être* of social insurance, and could in principle be accomplished entirely through the tax system, it does in practice also take place through implicit or explicit transfers within the social insurance system. Many pension and health insurance schemes therefore involve systematic cross-subsidies among contributors, with the result that some people contribute more than they receive in expectation, while the converse is true for others. In addition, social insurance is sometimes partly financed by general tax revenues, often because there is a deficit between payouts and contribution incomes. Reliance on general taxation also entails a systematic redistribution, in this instance quite possibly from people outside the social insurance system altogether—including future generations who will bear the cost of the unfunded liabilities of some of today's social insurance systems.

---

[2] Some classifications add a third component in social protection: policies that aim to reduce risks ex ante, rather than to insure against them, include active labor market programs that seek to improve matches in the labor market and thereby reduce the frequency and duration of unemployment spells. See e.g. Holzmann and Jorgensen (2001).

Added to the mix is the notion, now widely accepted, that social insurance systems are not justified exclusively on the basis of imperfect insurance markets and the need for more risk-pooling. They are also in part motivated by the empirical observation, from behavioral economics, that human beings generally tend to "over-discount" the distant future, and to procrastinate in making even basic investments with large long-term returns. Known as myopia, "hyperbolic discounting," and by various other names, these departures from standard rationality appear to be quite common.[3] They provide an additional theoretical justification for mandatory savings for retirement, through contributory old age pensions.

The combination of mandating long-term savings (even for expected retirement periods) and insuring against uncertainty (say, that a person's retirement period may be unexpectedly long) would already make devising a good social insurance system a complex mechanism design problem. Adding systematic interpersonal redistribution complicates things even more, because of the obvious tension between the redistribution motive and the needed incentives for saving for one's own retirement. Finally, the nature of both social insurance and social assistance instruments affects the consequences of various individual decisions on the margin—in areas as diverse as labor supply, job search intensity, propensity for private savings, and family formation. The optimal design of these instruments should in principle take into account not only their likely benefits in terms of reduced income volatility, inequality, and poverty but also the likely efficiency costs.[4] Understanding the interactions between the two components of the social protection system, even while distinguishing between them conceptually, is an important part of this complex public action design problem.

This chapter focuses on *social assistance* programs in Latin America and the Caribbean (LAC): those designed primarily to reduce poverty and deprivation. We look briefly at the evolution of these programs since their inception, about a century ago, but concentrate primarily on the dramatic expansion in and transformation of Latin America's social assistance portfolio in the last two decades. In so doing, we pay special attention to four basic types of programs:

(i) in-kind transfers (particularly food programs);
(ii) workfare programs;
(iii) noncontributory social insurance schemes (such as social pensions); and
(iv) conditional cash transfers (CCTs).[5]

---

[3] See O'Donoghue and Rabin (1999), and Thaler and Sunstein (2009).

[4] Some social protection policies may also lead to efficiency *gains*. One example is their possible protective effect on the human capital of the poor (World Bank 2006).

[5] Two of these program types are good examples of the blurred boundaries between social assistance and social insurance. Workfare is typically intended as a temporary source of income for workers hit by negative employment shocks, and is thus very close to a social insurance motive, but is generally designed to self-target to the poorest among the unemployed. "Non-contributory social insurance" is intended as a social insurance substitute for those excluded from the mainstream, contributory system.

The chapter summarizes how each of these programs works, their achievements, and their limitations. While a number of programs do share similarities across countries, the considerable heterogeneity of social and economic conditions throughout Latin America implies that there are also important differences among them. Building on the above discussion about the tensions and complementarities between the insurance, redistribution, and savings motives, we also discuss two alternative options for better integrating social assistance and social insurance programs (including the large old age and disability pension systems, and the health insurance systems) in Latin America.

Beyond this introduction, the chapter is organized in four sections. Section 33.2 provides a brief historical overview of social protection systems in Latin America and the Caribbean (LAC), including the roots of social insurance but emphasizing the gradual shift in policy priorities that has increased the prominence of social assistance programs and led to the development of large-scale anti-poverty programs. Section 33.3 provides a snapshot of the state of social assistance programs in LAC today, for each of the four types of programs listed above. Section 33.4 takes a broader view, and considers how the various pieces of the recent "social assistance revolution" in Latin America fit together. The section reports both on important achievement and gaping limitations, and briefly discusses elements of the current debate on strategies to expand the coverage and improve the coherence and effectiveness of social protection systems in LAC. Section 33.5 summarizes and concludes.

33.2 A BRIEF HISTORY OF SOCIAL PROTECTION IN LATIN AMERICA

Social protection systems in LAC date back to the early years of the 20th century, and the introduction of insurance schemes for civil servants (including teachers), employees in public enterprises, members of the military, and urban private-sector workers in certain industries. Countries in the Southern Cone—Argentina, Brazil, Chile, and Uruguay—were the first to introduce occupational schemes in the early 1920s, inspired by the Bismarckian approach. These occupational plans offered disability pensions, survivorships, old age pensions and in some cases health insurance. Broader social insurance availability to part of the private sector labor force came later, influenced by the Beveridge report of 1942 in the United Kingdom. Under its influence, Latin America saw a second wave of social insurance adoption in the 1940s, in countries such as Colombia, Costa Rica, Mexico, Paraguay, Peru, and Venezuela. Countries in Central America and the Caribbean followed in the mid-1950s and 1960s respectively.

Throughout this early period, social protection in LAC was essentially synonymous with social insurance. The systems introduced in the two decades after World War II consisted largely of old age, disability, and survivorship pensions and, in some cases, elements of health insurance. They generally extended to private-sector workers the

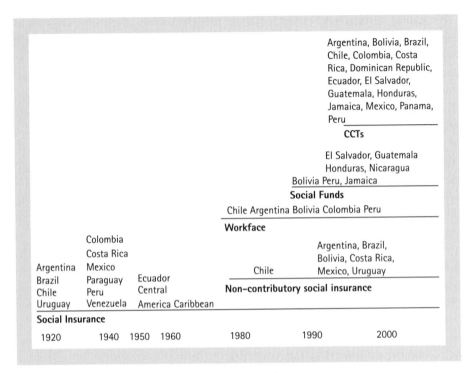

FIGURE 33.1 Chronology of major innovations in social protection in LAC

pioneering schemes introduced earlier for civil servants and the military. But coverage remained limited, in virtually all cases, to formal-sector workers in urban areas, and thus excluded the majority of workers in most Latin American countries, who worked in rural areas, or in the urban informal sector. Figure 33.1 provides a schematic summary description of the evolution of Latin America social protection systems.

Until the early 1980s, social assistance in Latin America consisted almost exclusively of various forms of commodity subsidies, primarily applied to food (e.g. bread, sugar, milk, rice) and energy commodities (e.g. gas and kerosene). There were a few direct feeding programs, or small transfer programs for narrowly-defined vulnerable groups such as the disabled. Examples of feeding programs included the Brazilian *Programa Nacional de Alimentação e Nutrição* (PRONAN) or the feeding program for young children in Guatemala and Costa Rica (Beaton and Ghassemi 1982). It was only after the debt crisis of the 1980s that a number of Latin American governments started to consider broader "safety nets," aimed at "poverty alleviation" more generally. Chile was a pioneer, introducing a workfare program known as *Programa de Empleo Mínimo* to provide temporary employment for low-income/unskilled workers in the early 1980s. At its peak, the various public work sub-programs within *Programa de Empleo Mínimo* employed no less than 13% of the Chilean labor force (see Lustig 2000). Workfare programs were also adopted by Argentina, Bolivia, and Colombia in the 1990s, and more recently in Peru.

During the early 1990s, as the continent sought to recover from the prolonged recessions of the 1980s, several countries also instituted a new set of programs that became known as social investment funds. These funds typically involved setting aside discretionary budget under a purpose-built, administratively autonomous central government agency, such as the *Fondo de Inversion Social de Emergencia* (FISE) in Ecuador, which then funded an array of small infrastructure or income-generating projects proposed by local communities in poor areas. Two aspects made these funds rather innovative in the relatively staid context of Latin American social assistance: the degree of decentralization of decisionmaking, and the reliance on community-level participation to propose, apply for, and implement the projects. The projects themselves generally aimed to create or upgrade small-scale social and economic infrastructure, while simultaneously generating employment at the local level.

Social investment funds are now seen as Latin American precursors to a wave of "community-driven development" (CDD) projects that have swept the developing world. Evaluations of these funds have generally found that they were successful in targeting poor communities, and that they did contribute to building needed basic infrastructure (see Paxson and Schady 2002 on Peru's FONCODES; and Newman et al. 2002 on Bolivia's social investment fund). Their success implied that, although initially intended as temporary instruments for crisis relief, some of these funds eventually became permanent fixtures in their countries. In most cases, as crises receded and other transfer instruments were introduced, their role gradually evolved from a social assistance and public works function towards a local or municipal development rationale.

Social investment funds notwithstanding, social protection systems in Latin America in the mid-1990s were still best described as a dual system, providing rather generous (and often subsidized) social insurance benefits to a minority of the labor force—civil servants and the predominantly urban formal sector—while leaving the majority of the population, and almost all of the poor, uncovered. Even among the relatively restricted group of participants, benefit amounts varied considerably, and were seldom horizontally equitable. From their inception, the continent's Bismarckian social insurance systems were implemented with the (often implicit) expectation that, as economies developed and income per capita grew, a majority of the labor force would end up in salaried jobs in the formal sector. This expectation remains unfulfilled. Even today, over half of LAC's workforce is employed in the informal sector; the lowest level of informality is observed in Chile (near 40%) and the highest in Bolivia (close to 75%). (See Chapters 30 by Tokman and 34 by Uthoff in this Handbook.)

This "truncated welfare state"—where income redistribution took place primarily among the better-off, to the exclusion of those most in need—coexisted with persistent poverty and inequality in Latin America (see Chapters 27 by Gasparini and Lustig and 28 by Grynspan and López-Calva in this Handbook).[6] In fact, the evidence suggests that, in some countries, the truncated welfare state was more a part of the problem than a part of the solution. Regressive commodity subsidies and the type of *implicit* redistribution

---

[6] See De Ferranti et al. (2004) for an early discussion of the "truncated welfare state."

generated by social insurance systems often aggravated instead of alleviating the problem. In large part, the regressivity of many contributory pension systems in Latin America arises from the fact that the value of benefits paid out exceeds the value of contributions received (plus interest), with the financing gap filled from general revenues. Since the poor do pay taxes (primarily on expenditures) but seldom participate in the contributory social insurance systems, these subsidies end up being regressive (see e.g. Lindert, Skoufias, and Shapiro et al. 2006).

It was against this background that a quiet revolution in Latin America's social assistance systems began in the early 1990s. Democratic congresses and administrations proved more averse to high levels of poverty and inequality than their dictatorial predecessors had been, and in many countries, these new governments sought to extend the redistributive role of the state towards those most in need of its support.[7] The desired expansion of social assistance was implemented through two main types of programs: non-contributory social insurance (pensions and health insurance) and conditional cash transfers (CCTs).

Non-contributory social insurance (NCSI) schemes were targeted at low-income workers not covered by the social insurance system. Chile, Brazil, and Bolivia, for instance, implemented social pensions: flat benefits provided to individuals older than a certain age that can be either universal or conditional on an income test.[8] Similarly, Colombia and Mexico developed non-contributory health insurance programs targeted to low-income informal sector workers and the poor. Conditional Cash Transfers (CCTs) were introduced in the mid-1990s, sometimes as replacements for inefficient and regressive subsidies. These programs offer cash assistance to poor families, provided that members—usually children—meet certain conditions related to school attendance and health care use. Conditional cash transfers are now the prevalent model for income support in LAC. CCT programs (in several designs) have been established in Argentina, Bolivia, Brazil, Chile, Colombia, Costa Rica, the Dominican Republic, Ecuador, El Salvador, Guatemala, Honduras, Jamaica, Mexico, Panama, and Peru, and many of these are large-scale. Both NCSIs and CCTs are discussed in more detail in the next section.

Despite these innovations, expenditures in social assistance as a share of GDP remain low in Latin America relative to most other regions of the world. Calculations from Weigand and Grosh (2008) suggest that, whereas LAC countries spend on average 1.3% of GDP on social assistance (and 3.8% on social insurance), African countries spend 3.1%, the Middle East and North Africa spend 3.6%, Europe and Central Asia spend 2.0%, and OECD countries spend 2.5%. The ratio of social assistance expenditure to GDP is smaller than LAC only in Asia, where the average in both East and South Asia is 0.9%. Nevertheless, the introduction of non-contributory social pensions and CCTs in the last two decades has dramatically altered the coverage and incidence of the combined system in Latin America. Figure 33.2 illustrates the impact of non-contributory

[7] A classic example is the "welfarist" tone of the 1988 Brazilian Constitution, which introduced the "Organic Social Assistance Law" (LOAS) and a number of the social pensions we discuss below.
[8] See Holzmann, Robalino, and Takayama (2009).

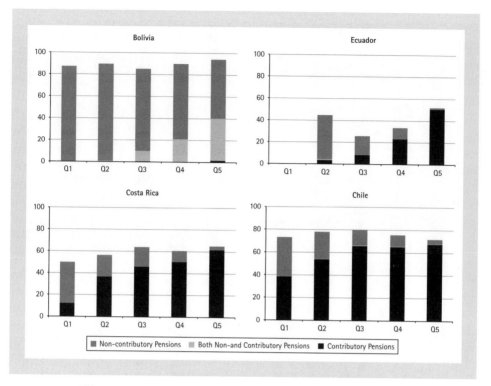

FIGURE 33.2 Old age pension coverage: contributory and non-contributory

Source: Ribe et al. (2010).

pensions on the distribution of old age pension coverage by quintile in four countries: Bolivia, Chile, Costa Rica, and Ecuador. Whereas contributory systems hardly reached the poor in Bolivia and Ecuador, the new social pensions have succeeded in substantially increasing coverage in the bottom quintiles.

Benefit amounts for social pensions are generally—but not always—smaller than for contributory pensions, so social insurance (including both social security and public health expenditures) continues to account for the bulk of social protection expenditures in the region. Table 33.1 reports social spending figures for health, social security, and other items in Latin America, around 2005 and 2006, both in dollars per capita and as a share of GDP.[9] There is considerable cross-country variation, as one would expect, with annual social assistance expenditures ranging from $1 per capita in Honduras and Peru, to $118 in Argentina and Trinidad and Tobago. As a share of GDP, social assistance ranges from 0.1% (in Peru) to 3.4% (in Bolivia).

[9] In terms of the terminology in this chapter, "social insurance" corresponds to the combination of health and social security. Most of the expenditure under "other" would correspond to social assistance, although in some countries some active labor market programs are also included. Because countries and international agencies classify programs differently, caution is always needed when making international comparisons as in Table 33.1.

Table 33.1 Social expenditures in LAC (per capita and as a share of GDP)

Country	As a share of GDP (%)				Dollars per capita (US$ constant 2000)			
	Health	Social security	Social assistance and other	Total	Health	Social security	Social assistance and other	Total
El Salvador	1.69	0.04	1.2	2.9	34	1	26	61
Honduras	3.44	0.26	0.1	3.8	36	3	1	40
Ecuador	1.28	2.36	0.2	3.8	19	36	4	59
Guatemala	1.09	0.98	2.0	4.1	16	14	33	63
Jamaica	2.78	0.46	1.2	4.5	81	13	37	131
T&T	2.18	1.44	1.3	4.9	203	134	118	455
Peru	1.52	3.65	0.0	5.2	37	101	1	139
Paraguay	1.7	2.39	1.2	5.3	16	34	7	57
Dom. Rep.	1.54	1.28	2.6	5.4	46	38	76	160
Nicaragua	3.47	–	2.9	6.3	29	0	25	54
Mexico	2.67	2.11	1.8	6.6	163	129	108	400
Venezuela	1.82	4.64	1.6	8.1	82	197	67	346
Chile	2.79	5.86	0.2	8.9	158	365	12	535
Colombia	2.2	7.21	0.6	10.0	49	166	14	229
Bolivia	3.4	4.39	3.4	11.2	35	45	35	115
Costa Rica	4.95	5.24	1.7	11.9	220	237	74	531
Panama	5.69	6.02	1.2	12.9	240	254	49	543
Uruguay	1.75	12.47	0.3	14.6	111	791	21	923
Argentina	4.58	9.47	1.7	15.7	366	739	118	1223
Cuba	6.46	8.52	2.6	17.6	218	270	93	581
Brazil	4.92	12.98	1.1	19.0	180	476	35	691

Source: Social database, ECLAC.

Table 33.2 Trends in social assistance expenditures in LAC countries

	1990	1995	2000	2001	2002	2003	2004	2005	2006	Trend[a]
Argentina	0.9	1	1.3	1.3	1.2	1.4	1.5	1.7	1.9	++
Bolivia[b]		1.3	1.4	1.4	1.4	1.2	1.1			–
Brazil			1	1	1.2	1.2	1.4	1.5		++
Chile	1.4	1.6	1.7	1.8	1.7	1.7	1.5	1.6	1.5	NT
Costa Rica	0.9	0.7	1.7	1.6	1.6	1.5	1.5	2.8		++
Dominican Rep.		0.4	1.1	1	0.3	0.5	1.7	1.3		++
Jamaica			0.8	0.8	0.8	0.6	0.8	0.8	0.7	NT
Mexico[c]	0.1	0.4	0.2	0.2	0.2	0.3	0.3	0.3	0.4	+
Nicaragua		1	1.2	0.8						–
Paraguay		0.2	0.4	1.5	1.3	1	1	0.7		++
Peru			0.8	0.8	0.8	0.7	0.8		0.7	NT
Venezuela	0.98	1.41	0.78	0.87	0.82	1.04	1.17			NT

Source: Ribe, Robalino, and Walker (2010: ch. 6), based on national accounts and using United Nations definitions for social assistance.

[a] ++ = strong increase; + = increase; NT = No trend, – = Decline.
[b] Data in 1995 column for Bolivia are from 1997.
[c] Data for Mexico are only for *Progresa/Oportunidades*.

Although spending on social assistance typically remains low, both in absolute terms and relative to health and social security expenditures, the available data suggest that most countries have been increasing those expenditures over the last decade. Table 33.2 shows the evolution of social assistance expenditures for twelve countries for which data are available between 1990 and 2006. Only in Bolivia and Nicaragua did expenditures decline somewhat. In the other countries they either remained constant (Chile, Jamaica, Peru, and Venezuela) or increased (Argentina, Brazil, Costa Rica, the Dominican Republic, Mexico, and Paraguay).

But the transformation of Latin America's social assistance system over the last two decades or so goes beyond the increase in the monetary value of its expenditures. From a situation twenty-five years ago, when social insurance was only available to a minority of workers in urban areas and social assistance was limited to a few untargeted food and fuel subsidies, many countries in the region have now created systems that distribute resources to large numbers of poor people, including in rural areas. In that sense, the system's effectiveness has increased more markedly that its costs.[10] In the next section, we examine the four main components of the contemporary social assistance system in LAC: food subsidies and in-kind transfers; workfare programs; non-contributory social insurance; and conditional cash transfers.

33.3 THE MODERN SOCIAL ASSISTANCE SYSTEM IN LATIN AMERICA

Modern social assistance systems comprise three core program types: cash transfers; in-kind transfers; and workfare. Cash transfers can be further sub-divided into those that seek to mimic the benefits of social insurance systems in the absence of private contributions, and those that seek to promote certain positive behaviors by conditioning the transfers. The former category of transfers is dominated by non-contributory social insurance programs that include social pensions (universal or targeted), disability pensions, non-contributory health insurance, and unemployment assistance. The latter category involves mainly CCTs, which aim to promote investments in human capital.[11]

---

[10] The increased effectiveness of LAC's social protection system includes the enhanced capacity to cushion the poor from the effects of negative aggregate economic shocks, such as recessions, as indicated by the experience of Mexico and Colombia during the "great recession" of 2008–9 (Ferreira and Schady 2009).

[11] It also includes a more recent type of program, Matching Defined Contributions (MDCs), which are being considered by countries like Colombia and Mexico. MDCs are transfers to low-income workers outside the urban formal sector designed to promote adherence to various insurance schemes (e.g. pensions, health, or unemployment insurance), with the aim of reducing long-term expenditures on anti-poverty programs (see Palacios and Robalino 2009).

33.3.1 In-kind transfers (food-based programs)

As discussed above, food-based programs were one of the main forms of social assistance in Latin America until the 1970s. With somewhat more efficient designs, many countries still have them. Ribe, Robalino, and Walker (2010—henceforth RRW) identify two broad types of food-based programs, as defined by their target group. The first type targets poor households and includes soup kitchens, the distribution of basic staples or nutritional supplements (e.g. *papillas*, *maicena*, or *atoles*) to mothers and babies, as well as food-for-work programs for which participants self-select on willingness to work for low compensation (as in workfare). The second type comprises categorical programs that target specific demographic groups, rather than the poor. Most of these programs focus on school children, and are common in countries like Haiti, Honduras, Peru, Ecuador, Bolivia, Colombia, Brazil, and Jamaica. Since many of these programs operate through public schools, and because the rich in Latin America tend to select out of the public school system and into private alternatives, school feeding programs end up having a largely progressive incidence, despite their de jure categorical nature.

There is considerable diversity in design among food programs targeted to the poor: they range from in-kind food rations that household members can collect in certain shops (such as in the *Tortivale* program in Mexico) or in public clinics (as in the *Programa Nacional de Alimentación Complementaria* in Chile), to food stamps targeted at the poorest households (the Food Stamp Program in Jamaica or the *Bono Escolar* and the *Bono Materno Infantil* in Honduras). Although school feeding programs, like the *School Cafeterias Program* of Costa Rica or Peru's *Desayunos Escolares*, are in principle less heterogeneous, there are nevertheless substantial differences in both practice and effectiveness. Grosh et al. (2008: ch. 7.2 and table B.2) describe a variety of examples from around the world, including LAC.

There are few rigorous impact evaluations of school feeding programs in LAC, and the evidence that emerges is mixed. On the one hand, these programs can increase enrollment and attendance, and when food is given at the start of the day, children can get an energy boost that improves concentration and learning. In rural primary schools in Jamaica, a randomized experiment showed that school breakfasts increased attendance rates, particularly among undernourished children (Powell et al. 1998). A breakfast program in Huaráz (Peru) increased the attendance rates of fourth- and fifth-grade students (Jacoby, Cueto, and Pollitt 1996). On the other hand, the evidence on long-term learning achievement, even when it is positive, is often based on efficacy trials, and is difficult to generalize (Adelman, Gilligan, and Lehrer 2008). In addition, some in-kind transfer programs, such as Peru's *Vaso de Leche*, do not appear to reach their nutritional objectives (Stifel and Alderman 2006).

As discussed by RRW, perhaps the most promising development in this area takes the form of a set of new programs that move beyond pure "food distribution" and focus on the final outcome of improving nutrition. These programs recognize that food is sometimes only one missing input into the "nutrition production function." Accordingly, they seek to address informational gaps, influence entrenched behaviors, and assist with child weight and height monitoring, as well as supplying nutritious foods. These programs include the *Programa Nacional de Alimentación y Nutrición* (PNAN, 2000) in Ecuador, and the *Atención Integral a la Niñez–Comunitaria* (AIN–C) model in Central America. As in the case of cash transfers, food is used as an incentive to promote participation in the programs. Some countries have also used in-kind transfers to motivate enrollment in early childhood development (ECD) programs such as PAININ in Nicaragua, which also promote hygiene and early stimulation, in addition to improved nutrition. There is some evidence that children who participate in these programs have higher levels of cognitive development and school readiness (e.g. Cueto and Díaz 1999), although more empirical work is needed.

33.3.2 Workfare

The rationale for workfare programs arises from an acknowledgement that traditional unemployment insurance programs, which are part of contributory social insurance in Latin America, largely exclude the poorest workers in these countries. Workfare aims to provide a cushion against unemployment risk for those workers, by offering some monetary compensation for "emergency" or "short-term" work, typically in the maintenance, upgrading, or construction of local infrastructure. In theory, wages should be set at a level such that it can assist participants and their households in avoiding hunger and extreme deprivation, but which is otherwise low enough that the program will not attract other low-productivity workers from their main occupations. Because it is targeted at workers without formal employment links or documents, budget sustainability is attained either by quotas or by self-selection, i.e. by attracting only workers who are sufficiently destitute to accept the program's low wages in return for 30–40 weekly hours of often very hard work. The latter is clearly more desirable in terms of allocating placements to those most in need.

Although workfare programs have a long tradition in other parts of the developing world, they became more widespread in LAC only in the 1990s. As discussed above, Chile was an early adopter of the program. Mexico followed years later with the *Programa de Empleo Temporal* introduced in 1995, as part of the government's response to the severe economic downturn associated with the "Tequila crisis". Unlike many other LAC programs, the PET was aimed primarily at poor rural areas, where it sought to create labor-intensive jobs in the rehabilitation and improvement of local infrastructure. Since 2002, the reach of the program has been broadened, and it has become more permanent (World Bank 2009).[12]

In 1996, it was Argentina's turn to introduce a workfare program in response to a sharp rise in unemployment and a contemporaneous increase in poverty. The first

---

[12] The use of workfare programs is now widespread. Workfare has been a well-studied component of India's social protection system, with a number of studies of e.g. the Maharashtra Employment Guarantee scheme (see e.g. Ravallion, Datt, and Chaudhuri 1993).

objective of *Trabajar* was to provide short-term work opportunities to the unemployed poor, subject to a strictly enforced work requirement of 30–40 hours per week. The program tried to locate socially useful projects in poor areas that involved maintaining and building local infrastructure. The main targeting mechanism was the low wage rate, supplemented by a project selection process that geographically targeted poor areas. Despite positive evaluation results in terms of targeting, *Trabajar* evoked considerable political opposition. Because the wage rate was not set low enough, there was excess demand for spots in the program, and their allocation was often perceived as being captured by local political agents.

As a result, *Trabajar* was replaced by a new workfare program in Argentina in 2002, known as *Jefes y Jefas de Hogar*. The program transferred Arg$150 (about US$48) per month to beneficiaries who met the following criteria: (1) unemployed; (2) head of a household; (3) live in a household with at least one minor below the age of 18, a pregnant woman, or a handicapped person of any age; and (4) work or participate in training or education activities for 4–6 hours a day (no less than 20 hours a week) in exchange for the payment. The transfer amount was set at a level slightly below the going wage for full-time work for unskilled workers. This was a larger program than *Trabajar*: by 2003 it had nearly 2 million beneficiaries, or some 11% of the economically active population. As the Argentine economy recovered, however, participation in the program declined.[13] Since 2004, the emphasis has shifted towards promoting the reinsertion of the unemployed in the labor market through skill upgrading and job search support, implemented by the *Seguro de Capacitación y Empleo*, an ancillary active labor market component targeted to *Jefes y Jefas* beneficiaries.

Workfare programs were also implemented in Bolivia, Colombia and Peru in the 2000s. Bolivia's *Plan Nacional de Empleo de Emergencia* was set up in 2001, and benefited some 4.5% of the economically active population, before being folded into the *Red de Protección Social* in 2004. Peru's *A Trabajar Urbano* was a smaller program, set up in 2002 to provide support to poor victims of the 1998-2001 recession. By 2003, it provided some 77,000 jobs, each lasting for four months, at a total cost of US$50 million, or 0.08% of GDP. Colombia's *Empleo en Acción*, launched in 2001, was integrated into a broader social assistance system from the outset.[14] Alongside *Familias en Acción* (a CCT) and *Jóvenes en Acción* (a youth program), it formed the *Red de Apoyo Social*, an integrated social support network. Despite this laudable attempt at an integrated design, *Empleo en Acción* is subject to the national minimum wage, which constrains the program's targeting based on self-selection.

Given the low coverage of unemployment benefit systems in the continent, workfare programs have provided a useful mechanism to assist the most vulnerable among the unemployed—particularly during macroeconomic crises. Some of these programs, such as the *Programa de Empleo Temporario* (PET) in Mexico, played an important role

---

[13] See Galasso and Ravallion (2004) and Almeida and Galasso (2007).
[14] Colombia also had an earlier experience with workfare as part of the *Red de Solidaridad Social*, between 1994 and 1998.

during the recent 2008–9 financial crisis. Many workfare programs, however, have not yet been properly evaluated and many are still affected by design problems, both in terms of targeting the most vulnerable workers and in the selection of investment projects and public works to which the labor is applied.

33.3.3 Non-contributory social insurance programs

With informality rates generally upwards of 40% of the labor force, unemployment benefits were not the only component of the contributory social insurance system that was unavailable to most poor people in Latin America. The vast majority of them had no old age or disability pensions either. Similarly, only a minority had access to health insurance. In principle they could receive health care through national health services (i.e. where health insurance is provided by universal in-kind access to services), but benefits are often inadequate in both quantity and quality. Even if they could land themselves a workfare spot during a recession, or after having lost a job for idiosyncratic reasons, their old age security or insurance against disability and sickness were not guaranteed. The problem was aggravated by the fact that even those covered by social insurance programs are not covered all the time. In Argentina, Chile, and Uruguay, for instance, median contribution densities are below 50% (see Forteza et al. 2009). This is not surprising, since most poor people in Latin America are not consigned permanently to the urban formal sector. They change jobs frequently, sometimes into and out of formal employment.

A natural response to this (large) coverage gap has been to develop non-contributory or subsidized insurance programs—mainly for pensions and health insurance. In the case of pensions the programs are of one of two variants: so-called social pensions; and matching defined contributions (MDCs). Social pensions are effectively entitlements, financed entirely out of general revenues (or earmarked taxes, which is much the same in this context, only more distortionary), and paid out to certain predetermined categories of individuals. These categories can be defined by age alone, as in Bolivia's *Bono Solidario*, which makes a universal fixed cash transfer to all Bolivian citizens aged 65 or more. Or they may be defined by some combination of age and previous employment history, as in the case of Brazil's *Previdência Rural*, which since 1991 has extended old age, disability, and survivor pensions to men aged 60 or older, and women aged 55 or older, who previously worked in subsistence activities in agriculture, fishing, and mining, and to those in informal employment. Some programs, like Chile's social pension, also have an income test.

These are not small programs. In the late 1990s, while they were still relatively young, they cost about 1% of GDP, both in Bolivia and Brazil (see Barrientos and Lloyd-Sherlock 2002). They probably account for larger expenditures and reach more people now. There is some evidence that they have made non-negligible contributions to poverty reduction, although it is often pointed out that they do so relatively inefficiently, since they are less well targeted than alternative programs (see Barros, Foguel, and Ulyssea 2006).

The other programs that have been considered (mainly in Colombia, Mexico, and Peru) are MDC systems, which target individuals in the informal sector with some (albeit limited) savings capacity. Such schemes consist of individual accounts and benefit from varying degrees of state subsidization (where the government matches individual contributions, much as a private-sector employer usually does in a contributory scheme). None of these programs has been rigorously evaluated, but the Mexican experience so far indicates that take-up rates have been low.[15]

33.3.4 Conditional cash transfers

The program type that has been credited with contributing to poverty reduction as much as, if not more than, NCSIs, and which is argued to do so more effectively, because of better targeting, is the conditional cash transfer (CCT). Conditional cash transfers consist of periodic payments targeted to poor households (and usually delivered to women), which are made only if household members meet certain conditions, such as attending school (for children) or visiting health clinics for hygiene lectures and check-ups (for parents and children). The objective is to alleviate current poverty (by targeting transfers to the very poor) while simultaneously seeking to break the intergenerational transmission of poverty by encouraging investment in the human capital of poor children.

Originally proposed by two Brazilian economists, CCTs were first implemented in practice in Brazil's Federal District and in the city of Campinas in 1995.[16] Their rise to prominence began when they were adopted by the Mexican government in 1997, and deployed in a set of poor rural areas by means of an experimental design which permitted careful evaluation of its impacts. CCTs now exist in fifteen LAC countries and benefit an estimated 22 million households (over 90 million people or 16% of the region's population).

Where CCTs exist, they have absorbed a significant share of social assistance expenditures, with budgets ranging between 0.1% of GDP (Chile and Peru) and 0.6% of GDP (Ecuador). There are nonetheless important variations across countries in terms of coverage and the level of benefits. For instance, coverage rates vary between 1.5% of the population (in El Salvador) and 54% of the population (Bolivia). Benefits range between 0.25% of GDP per capita (Costa Rica) and 20% (El Salvador). There are also differences regarding the enforcement of conditionalities. Unlike in Mexico's *Oportunidades*, for example, in Ecuador's *Bono de Desarrollo Humano* benefits are paid without monitoring conditionalities (see RRW). In the remainder of this section, we summarize what is known about the effects of CCTs on three different types of outcomes they seek to affect:

---

[15] For a discussion of the systems and their potential see Palacios and Robalino (2009).

[16] See Camargo (1993) and Almeida and Camargo (1994) for the original proposals. Camargo and Ferreira (2001) review the early Brazilian experiences, and propose the consolidation that led to the *Bolsa Família* program.

present income or consumption poverty; educational outcomes; and health and nutrition outcomes.

Poverty reduction. Recent studies argue that CCTs have made important contributions to poverty reduction in at least some of the countries where they have been implemented. Using a micro-simulation technique, Fiszbein and Schady (2009) estimate that CCTs have reduced the national headcount poverty rate by 8% in Ecuador (BDH) and Mexico (*Oportunidades*), by 4.5% in Jamaica (PATH), and by 3% in Brazil (*Bolsa Família*) (see Table 33.3). These reductions arise essentially because CCT benefits have been unusually well-targeted, and not substantively offset by labor supply disincentives. The combination of geographical targeting and proxy means-testing that many (but not all) CCTs have used to identify beneficiary households has proved to be one of the main sources of their success. Mexico's *Oportunidades* delivers 45% of all benefits to the poorest 10% of its population, while programs in Chile and Jamaica achieve equally impressive shares of 35–40% to the bottom decile (see Fiszbein and Schady 2009: ch. 3).

Educational outcomes. The evidence on the educational impacts of CCTs is both of higher quality (because it often relies on the internal comparison of outcomes for children randomly allocated to treatment or control groups) and more mixed. There is considerable evidence that the programs increased school enrollment and attendance, and lowered school drop-out rates (Behrman, Sengupta, and Todd 2000; Britto 2004; 2007, Rawlings 2005). This effect was particularly pronounced at the secondary school level—where enrollment rates are lower—and, in some countries, for girls. But there is much less evidence that the programs helped improve final educational outcomes—such as learning as measured by achievements in standardized examinations. It would thus appear that the behavioral impacts of CCTs are stronger on (if not limited to) the immediate behaviors on which the transfers are conditioned, such as enrollment and attendance at schools. It has been hypothesized that further improvement in actual learning requires additional measures, including investments in the supply side of the educational system.[17] Such investments are all the more needed in that the children being attracted to—or retained in—school as a result of CCTs are typically from poorer family backgrounds, and may require additional support to achieve even the learning levels of their new peers.

Health outcomes and nutrition. CCTs also appear to have increased the demand for health services (on which they are conditioned). For instance, the evidence reviewed in Lomelí (2008) suggests that, as a result of the programs, take-up of prenatal, natal, and postnatal care has increased in Peru, Honduras, Mexico, and El Salvador. Take-up of child growth monitoring increased in Colombia, Honduras, Mexico, Nicaragua, and Peru, while vaccination rates increased in Colombia, Honduras, Nicaragua, and Peru. It is less clear, however, whether the programs have had long-term impacts on health outcomes. Although positive effects on maternal mortality rates (in Mexico) and morbidity rates (Mexico and Colombia)

---

[17] The original and highly successful *PROGRESA* program in Mexico, which was the precursor to *Oportunidades*, did in fact implement such complementary supply-side interventions. But they would appear to have been overlooked in most subsequent, large-scale CCT programs.

Table 33.3 The impact of CCT programs on national poverty indices

	Headcount poverty rate			Poverty gap			Squared poverty gap		
	Pre-transfer	Post-transfer	Relative reduction (%)	Pre-transfer	Post-transfer	Relative reduction (%)	Pre-transfer	Post-transfer	Relative reduction (%)
Brazil	0.245	0.237	−3.3	0.100	0.090	−9.7	0.06	0.05	−16.30
Mexico	0.241	0.222	−7.6	0.085	0.068	−19.3	0.04	0.03	−29.40
Ecuador	0.244	0.224	−8	0.070	0.061	−13.8	0.03	0.02	−18.70
Jamaica	0.244	0.233	−4.5	0.066	0.060	−8.6	0.03	0.02	−13.20

Source: Fiszbein and Schady (2009: 110, table 4.3).

have been reported in the literature, methodological and data shortcomings mean that the evidence remains less than conclusive.[18] There is nonetheless some robust evidence that *PROGRESA* has caused a substantial (17%) reduction in infant—although not in neonatal—mortality rates in rural Mexico (see Barham forthcoming).

On balance, CCTs have transformed the social assistance landscape in (and, increasingly, beyond) Latin America in large part because they greatly enhanced the state's capacity to target resources effectively to the poorest people in society. As we saw above, the bottom fifth of the income distribution had been effectively excluded from any serious state assistance throughout Latin America's history, and this only started to change with the introduction of NCSIs and CCTs in the 1990s. Furthermore, this appears to have been the case under very different targeting systems, ranging from the careful, multi-layered geographical-cum-proxy-means approach of *PROGRESA*—rural *Oportunidades*—to the enormously decentralized and much less rigorous approach of *Bolsa Família*. The fact that the latter program also appears to be very well targeted would seem to warrant further research on the determinants of CCT targeting.[19]

33.4 THE FUTURE OF SOCIAL ASSISTANCE WITHIN LAC's SOCIAL PROTECTION SYSTEMS

As argued in the previous two sections, social assistance has come a long way in Latin America in the last two decades. In the 1980s, the continent's "social assistance system" was really no more than a disparate collection of food and fuel subsidies, a few direct feeding programs and the odd workfare scheme. It channeled limited resources, and only a small share of those ever reached the poor, since most subsidized commodities were normal goods. Alongside this "non-system" stood a truncated social insurance system that provided some incentives for mandated savings for retirement for civil servants and formal-sector workers, as well as health and some unemployment insurance—often through severance pay schemes.

By 2010, social assistance expenditures had risen and a sizeable fraction of the continent's truly destitute people had received or continued to receive direct cash transfers from the government. In some countries, like Brazil, Chile, and Mexico, it is now possible to claim that a majority of the poor are in receipt of one or more government programs created with the specific purpose of redistributing income or opportunities. And it seems to be working: a number of recent studies claim that part of Brazil's success in reducing poverty and inequality since 2001 is directly attributable to social assistance programs in general, and to *Bolsa Família* in particular.[20] The region pioneered

---

[18] See Fiszbein and Schady (2009: ch. 5).

[19] For a more detailed discussion of CCTs, see Ferreira and Robalino (2010).

[20] See Barros, Foguel, and Ulyssea (2006), Ferreira, Leite and Litchfield (2008), and Ferreira, Leite, and Ravallion (forthcoming).

conditional cash transfers—arguably *the* social policy innovation of the last two decades—and succeeded in scaling them up from small municipal programs with relatively limited impact to large, nationwide systems that actually make a dent on poverty, and even on the previously impervious level of inequality. It introduced non-contributory social insurance systems that have contributed substantially to closing the coverage gap. It experimented with social investment funds, devolving project selection and investment decisions to poor communities in remote Andean and Amazonian villages. Is it time to uncork the champagne?

While much has been achieved, the very fact that social assistance programs in LAC have grown "organically," without much planning or thought given to how the various pieces of the puzzle fit together, has given rise to considerable inefficiency, and to a whole new generation of challenges. We consider two such challenges to be of first-order importance: first, the disconnect between the social assistance and social insurance "halves" of social protection; second, the incompleteness of policies aimed at promoting greater opportunity for durable poverty reduction.

The disconnect between social assistance and social insurance arises fundamentally from the fact that the two systems remain separate, and social insurance remains contingent on labor market status. Formal-sector workers qualify for social insurance, funded primarily by mandatory contributions and payroll taxes. Many, and in some cases most, of those who do not, are now eligible for other sorts of "replacement" benefits, under the rubric of social assistance. If a worker does not qualify for a contributory old age pension, she may qualify for a non-contributory one. If another has no right to unemployment insurance, he may still earn some income from a workfare scheme—or receive cash for keeping his children in school. Although the levels of the formal benefits remain on average much higher, the financing mechanisms that have been set in place may reduce incentives for formal employment coupled with a subsidy on the informal sector. The payroll taxes or other social security contributions that fund formal social insurance introduce a wedge between labor costs paid by formal-sector firms and wages received by their workers. This distorts decisions on two fronts: it makes labor expensive vis-à-vis capital in the formal sector, relative to the non-intervention prices. And, on the margin, it makes formal sector employment less attractive than informal employment for a worker of given productivity. This latter effect is compounded by subsidies he or she may receive in the informal sector, from social assistance programs.

This inefficiency was described, both theoretically and empirically (for the case of Mexico), by Levy (2008); and although disagreements remain about the quantitative estimates of the efficiency cost, there is little dispute that it is a problem. At least two alternative solutions have recently been proposed. Levy (2008) suggests a simple—but radical—solution: basic old age pensions and health insurance should become universal entitlements, funded out of general revenues, raised by a tax on consumption expenditures. Additional coverage might be purchased privately, of course. Taxing people "at the door of the store" rather than workers "at the factory gates" (as he puts is) would eliminate the distortionary wedge between labor costs and wages in the formal and informal sectors.

Levy's proposals are grounded in undeniably good economics, and have the beauty of simplicity. Politically, the package may be difficult to implement in countries that have already adopted social insurance systems (old age and disability pensions, health insurance, and unemployment insurance) with mandates that go beyond a basic package of social security benefits. An alternative proposal has been put forward by RRW. As in Levy (2008), RRW recognize that non-contributory programs can discourage formal work and that social security contributions have a large tax component that distorts labor markets. They emphasize that a large share of the tax arises from implicit redistributive arrangements within the system, and argue that the focus of reform should be on eliminating this implicit redistribution. This could be accomplished, for instance, by moving from defined benefits to defined contribution pensions, from unemployment insurance to unemployment savings accounts, and from earnings-based health insurance to premiums-based health insurance. The programs could then be open to workers outside the formal sector under the same rules. To cover individuals with limited or no savings capacity, there would be an integrated system of subsidies that top up contributions and/or benefits. These subsidies would be allocated on the basis of means (not on where individuals work) and would be financed through general revenues. The proposal also calls for reviewing (and harmonizing) the mandates of the various insurance schemes in order to make them more affordable and reduce the implicit taxes associated with excessive precautionary savings. In essence, their proposal separates the insurance and redistributive function of the various programs, and makes the latter more transparent and less distortionary.

Whichever one of these approaches one prefers, or indeed whether or not one has an alternative proposal, these recent contributions to the debate have the great merit of pointing out that, even as it represented a success in terms of reaching the poor, the rise of social assistance in Latin America in the last two decades has been incoherent and, therefore, inefficient. One challenge that faces the system as it moves forward is the need to integrate the contributory and non-contributory "halves" in a way that is fair, that preserves social gains to the poor, but also that is less distortionary and restores the right economic incentives for firms and workers —both in terms of static resource allocation and in terms of long-term savings.

The second challenge for Latin America's social protection system is that, despite having finally reached the poor, it remains remarkably timid in the kinds of support it offers them in their quest to leave poverty behind permanently. Non-contributory social insurance programs, including social pensions, are now a mainstay of modern social assistance in Latin America, but they are effectively social insurance substitutes, which prevent people from falling deeper into poverty when they become unemployed or too old to work. Programs that move—to paraphrase a recent title—from protection to promotion, are rarer.[21] CCTs obviously claim a spot, since they are designed specifically to break the intergenerational transmission of poverty, by investing in the human capital of

---

[21] *For Protection and Promotion* (Grosh et al. 2008).

poor children. Some of the investments in social and economic infrastructure made under the aegis of social investment funds at the local level also count as efforts to promote greater opportunity for a sustainable exit from poverty. Similarly, recent programs that promote "competency certification" (in Argentina) or lifelong learning skills (in Chile) are steps in the right direction.

Perhaps the most promising recent initiatives that qualify as "opportunity rope" policies, rather than merely "safety nets", are programs to promote early childhood development. It has long been known that performance in certain cognitive tests at early ages (e.g. 3–6) are powerful predictors of future achievements in education, labor market attachment, and earnings (see e.g. Currie 2001). It has also long been understood that those early childhood skills (both cognitive and non-cognitive) that appear to have such persistence are responsive to relatively simple interventions. Child weight, height, and cognitive skills respond to nutritional supplementation. Psychosocial stimulation also enhances cognitive and non-cognitive skills. This was documented in LAC as early as 1991, in the influential *Lancet* study by Grantham-McGregor et al. (1991).

Longer-term longitudinal studies in the United States have shown that some of the effects of early-childhood interventions persist well into adulthood. Recent work by James Heckman and various collaborators has further documented that the economic returns to early childhood interventions tend to be very high.[22] Because the impacts of these interventions also tend to be higher among children from disadvantaged social backgrounds, they are a rare example of policy interventions with no equity-efficiency trade-off (World Bank 2006).

There are now a number of interventions targeted at improving health, nutrition and skills for young children, aged 0–6, in Latin America. They include *Hogares Comunitarios* in Colombia, *Educación Inicial no Escolarizada* in Mexico, *Programa de Atención Integral a Niños y Niñas Menores de Seis Anos de la Sierra Rural* (PAIN) in Peru, and many others. In Chile, where there had been a few smaller pilot interventions early on, the government has recently launched a large national program with a wide range of interventions aimed at this age group, *Chile Crece Contigo*. This program is much larger than most of its predecessors in Latin America in terms of coverage, budgetary resources, and scope of interventions, and much should be learned from it in the next few years.[23]

There have also been substantial "downward extensions" of the educational system in Latin America, by expanding the coverage of pre-school enrollment. Credible evidence from Uruguay suggests that pre-school attendance increases the likelihood of subsequent school attendance at age 15 by 27 percentage points (Berlinski, Galiani, and Manacorda 2008). At even younger ages, there have also been substantial increases in coverage rates for day care and similar center-based programs, but there is much less evidence on their long-term effects, particularly when compared to the counterfactual of care by a child's parents.

---

[22] See Carneiro and Heckman (2003), Cunha et al. (2005), and Cunha and Heckman (2007).

[23] Schady (2006) and Vegas and Santibañez (2010) review the literature and programs on ECD in Latin America.

Although the mix of conditional cash transfers, early childhood development interventions, and a new breed of active labor market programs is exciting, and contains many promising elements, it certainly does not yet represent a coherent strategy. It has been suggested that public policy against poverty should move beyond (while continuing to incorporate) safety nets; that there is a legitimate role for public action to seek to level the playing field, by promoting greater opportunities for the poor and disadvantaged.[24] Though many countries in Latin America have recently begun to experiment with such active promotion policies, none has yet developed an integrated strategy for this. Chile comes closest, with the combination of *Chile Solidario* and *Chile Crece Contigo*. Elsewhere, coherence in a set of policies aimed explicitly at promoting opportunity for the disadvantaged remains lacking. Therein lies the second great challenge to the social protection system in LAC.

33.5 Conclusions

This chapter has reviewed the achievements and limitations of social protection in Latin America in the last couple of decades, and considered some of the challenges that face it in the immediate future. In doing so, it has sought to take into account the multiple layers of interdependence between social assistance and social insurance. We introduced their distinct objectives as risk-pooling and consumption-smoothing for social insurance, and poverty reduction for social assistance. But the interdependence between the two systems, arising from the variability of income streams, overlapping sources of finance, and the incentives they set for individuals, was also noted.

These interrelationships were a common thread in our brief review of social assistance in LAC since World War II. Because mandatory and contributory social insurance schemes were Bismarckian in inspiration, and thus contingent on formal employment, they excluded the bulk of workers, and almost all of the poor in the region. Since the late 1980s, democratic governments have sought to complement this "truncated welfare state" by extending non-contributory social assistance benefits to those previously excluded. This has led to mixed results. On the one hand, states in Latin America have succeeded in reaching their poor. A variety of non-contributory social pensions, such as Brazil's *Benefício de Prestação Continuada* (BPC), now do make relatively large transfers to people formerly excluded from any social protection. Unemployed and informal-sector workers in Argentina can now receive the *Asignación Universal por Hijo*. Most prominently, conditional cash transfers—a homegrown invention—have mushroomed throughout the region, with a remarkably good track record in targeting, and proven impact on school enrollment (at least).

On the other hand, the system of benefits that arose from this "organic expansion" remains dualistic and divided. Because social insurance is (largely) financed by taxing

---

[24] See World Bank (2006) and Bourguignon, Ferreira, and Walton (2007).

formal-sector employment, while social assistance is financed out of general revenues and subsidizes (primarily) informal-sector workers, the net effect is a labor market distortion that generates an inefficient allocation of resources across the economy.

In addition to pursuing a more efficient (and equitable) integration of the two "halves" of the social protection system, we have argued that the other great challenge facing Latin American policymakers in this area is the creation of a more holistic and coherent set of policies aimed at promoting sustained poverty reduction. Such policies would not restrict themselves to serve as "safety nets." They should also provide the means by which those who would otherwise be likely to spend most of their lives in poverty might escape that fate by accumulating assets and accessing opportunities. Although early childhood development interventions, CCTs, and some active labor market programs are promising elements of such a system of "opportunity ropes," much more is needed.

In the early 2000s, the incidence of absolute poverty at the $2.50-a-day international poverty line was a quarter of the population or more in 15 of 23 countries for which data was available (Ferreira and Robalino 2010). If there is as much progress in social protection in Latin America in the next two decades as there was in the last two, a chapter similar to this written in 2030 may well have a hard time finding a single country with over a quarter of the population in extreme poverty.

References

ADELMAN, S.W., GILLIGAN, D. O., and LEHRER, K. (2008). *How Effective Are Food for Education Programs? A Critical Assessment of the Evidence from Developing Countries*, Washington, DC: International Food Policy Research Institute.

ALMEIDA, H., and CAMARGO, J. M. (1994). 'Human Capital Investment and Poverty', Department of Economics Working Paper No. 319, Pontificia Universidade Católica, Rio de Janeiro.

ALMEIDA, R., and GALASSO, E. (2007). 'Jump-Starting Self-Employment? Evidence among Welfare Participants in Argentina', World Bank Policy Research Working Paper No. 4270, Washington, DC.

BARHAM, T. (forthcoming). 'A Healthier Start: The Effect of Conditional Cash Transfers on Neonatal and Infant Mortality in Rural Mexico', *Journal of Development Economics*.

BARRIENTOS, A., and LLOYD-SHERLOCK, P. (2002). 'Policy Forum on Ageing and Poverty', *Journal of International Development* 14.8.

BARROS, R., FOGUEL, M., and ULYSSEA, G. (2006). *Desigualdade de renda no Brasil: uma análise da queda recente*, Rio de Janeiro: Instituto de Pesquisa e Economia Aplicada.

BEATON, G. H., and GHASSEMI, H. (1982). 'Supplementary Feeding Programs for Young Children in Developing Countries', *American Journal of Clinical Nutrition* 35.

BEHRMAN, J. R., SENGUPTA, P., and TODD, P. (2000). 'The Impact of PROGRESA on Achievement Test Scores in the First Year', MS, International Food Policy Research Institute, Washington, DC.

BERLINSKI, S., GALIANI, S., and MANACORDA, M. (2008). 'Giving Children a Better Start: Preschool Attendance and School-Age Profiles', *Journal of Public Economics* 92.

BOURGUIGNON, F., FERREIRA, F., and WALTON, M. (2007). 'Equity, Efficiency and Inequality Traps: A Research Agenda', *Journal of Economic Inequality* 5.

BRITTO, T. F. (2004). 'Conditional Cash Transfers: Why Have They Become so Prominent in Recent Poverty Reduction Strategies in Latin America?', Institute of Social Studies Working Paper No. 390, The Hague.

——(2007). 'The Challenges of El Salvador's Conditional Cash Transfer Program, Red Solidaria', Country Study 9, International Policy Centre for Inclusive Growth, Brasilia.

CAMARGO, J. M. (1993). 'Os miseráveis', Folha de SãoPaulo (March).

——and FERREIRA, F. (2001). 'O benefício social único: uma proposta de reforma da política social do Brasil', Department of Economics Working Paper No. 443, Pontificia Universidade Católica, Rio de Janeiro.

CARNEIRO, P., and HECKMAN, J. (2003). 'Human Capital Policy', in J. Heckman and A. Krueger (eds), Inequality in America: What Role for Human Capital Policy? Cambridge, Mass.: Massachusetts Institute of Technology Press.

CUETO, S., and DÍAZ, J. (1999). 'Impacto de la educación inicial en el rendimiento en primer grado de primaria en escuelas públicas urbanas de Lima', Revista de psicología 17.

CUNHA, F. and HECKMAN, J. (2007). 'The Technology of Skill Formation', American Economic Review 97.2.

—— —— LOCHNER, L., and MASTEROV, D. (2005). 'Interpreting the Evidence on Life-Cycle Skill Formation', National Bureau of Economic Research Working Paper No. 11331, Cambridge, Mass.

CURRIE, J. (2001). 'Early Childhood Education Programs', Journal of Economic Perspectives 15.2.

DE FERRANTI, D., PERRY, G., FERREIRA, F., and WALTON, M. (2004). Inequality in Latin America: Breaking with History? Washington, DC: World Bank.

FERREIRA, F., LEITE P., and RAVALLION, M. (forthcoming). 'Poverty Reduction without Economic Growth? Explaining Brazil's Poverty Dynamics, 1985–2004', Journal of Development Economics.

——and ROBALINO, D. (2010). 'Social Protection in Latin America: Achievements and Limitations', World Bank Policy Research Working Paper No. 5304, Washington, DC.

——and SCHADY, N. (2009). 'Social Consequences of the Global Financial Crisis in Latin America: Some Preliminary, and Surprisingly Optimistic, Conjectures', World Bank Latin America and the Caribbean Region Crisis Brief, Washington, DC.

——LEITE, P., and LITCHFIELD, J. (2008). 'The Rise and Fall of Brazilian Inequality: 1981–2004', Macroeconomic Dynamics 12.S2.

FISZBEIN, A., and SCHADY, N. (2009). Conditional Cash Transfers: Reducing Present and Future Poverty, Washington, DC: World Bank.

FORTEZA, A., APELLA, I., FAJNZYLBER, E., et al. (2009). 'Work Histories and Pension Entitlements in Argentina, Chile and Uruguay', World Bank Social Protection Discussion Paper 0926, Washington, DC.

GALASSO, E., and RAVALLION, M. (2004). 'Social Protection in a Crisis: Argentina's Plan Jefes y Jefas', World Bank Economic Review 18.3.

GRANTHAM-MCGREGOR, S. M., CHANG, S. M., WALKER, S. P., and HIMES, J. H. (1991). 'Nutritional Supplementation, Psychosocial Stimulation, and Mental Development of Stunted Children: The Jamaican Study', Lancet 338.8758.

GROSH, M., DEL NINNO, C., TESLIUC, E., and OUERGHI, A. (2008). For Protection and Promotion, Washington, DC: World Bank.

HOLZMANN, R., and JORGENSEN, S. (2001). Social Protection Sector Strategy: From Safety Net to Springboard, Washington, DC: World Bank.

—— ROBALINO, D., and TAKAYAMA, N. (eds) (2009). *Closing the Coverage Gap: Role of Social Pensions and Other Retirement Income Transfers*, Washington, DC: World Bank.

JACOBY, H., CUETO, S., and POLLITT, E. (1996). 'Benefits of a School Breakfast Program among Andean Children in Huaraz, Peru', in *Food Nutrition Bulletin 1996*, Tokyo: United Nations University.

LEVY, S. (2008). *Good Intentions, Bad Outcomes: Social Policy, Informality, and Economic Growth in Mexico*, Washington, DC: Brookings Institution.

LINDERT, K., SKOUFIAS, E., and SHAPIRO, J. (2006). *Redistributing Income to the Poor and the Rich: Public Transfers in Latin America and the Caribbean*, Washington, DC: World Bank.

LOMELÍ, E. (2008). 'Conditional Cash Transfers as Social Policy in Latin America: An Assessment of their Contributions and Limitations', *Annual Review of Sociology* 34.

LUSTIG, N. (2000). 'Crises and the Poor: Socially Responsible Macroeconomics', *Economía* 1.1.

NEWMAN, J., PRADHAN, M., RAWLINGS, L. B. et al. (2002). 'An Impact Evaluation of Education, Health, and Water Supply Investments by the Bolivian Social Investment Fund', *World Bank Economic Review* 16.

O'DONOGHUE, T., and RABIN, M. (1999). 'Doing It Now or Later', *American Economic Review* 89.1.

PALACIOS, R., and ROBALINO, D. (2009). 'Matching Contributions as a Way to Increase Pension Coverage', in R. Holzmann, D. Robalino, and N. Takayama (eds), *Closing the Coverage Gap: The Role of Social Pensions and Other Retirement Income Transfers*, Washington, DC: World Bank.

PAXSON, C., and SCHADY, N. (2002). 'The Allocation and Impact of Social Funds: Spending on School Infrastructure in Peru', *World Bank Economic Review* 16.2.

POWELL, C. A., WALKER, S. P., CHANG, S. M., and GRANTHAM-MCGREGOR, S. (1998). 'Nutrition and Education: A Randomized Trial of the Effects of Breakfast in Rural Primary School Children', *American Journal of Clinical Nutrition* 68.4.

RAVALLION, M., DATT, G., and CHAUDHURI, S. (1993). 'Does Maharashtra's "Employment Guarantee Scheme" Guarantee Employment? Effects of the 1998 Wage Increase', *Economic Development and Cultural Change* 41.

RAWLINGS, L. B. (2005). 'A New Approach to Social Assistance: Latin America's Experience with Conditional Cash Transfer Programs', *International Social Security Review* 58.

RIBE, H., ROBALINO, D., and WALKER, I. (2010). *From Right to Reality: Achieving Effective Social Protection for all in Latin America*, Washington, DC: World Bank.

SCHADY, N. (2006). 'Early Childhood Development in Latin America and the Caribbean', *Economía* 6.2.

STIFEL, D., and ALDERMAN, H. (2006). 'The "Glass of Milk" Subsidy Program and Malnutrition in Peru', *World Bank Economic Review* 20.3.

THALER, R. H., and SUNSTEIN, C. R. (2009). *Nudge: Improving Decisions About Health, Wealth, and Happiness*, New Haven, Conn.: Yale University Press.

VEGAS, E., and SANTIBÁÑEZ, L. (2010). *The Promise of Early Childhood Development in Latin America and the Caribbean*, Washington, DC: World Bank.

WEIGAND, C., and GROSH, M. (2008). 'Levels and Patterns of Safety Net Spending in Developing and Transition Countries', World Bank Social Protection and Labor Discussion Paper No. 0817, Washington, DC.

World Bank (2006). *World Development Report 2006: Equity and Development*, Washington, DC: World Bank and Oxford University Press.

—— (2009). 'Containing Unemployment in Mexico: Role of Labor Policies in Response to the Financial Crisis', Labor Primer Note, Social Protection and Labor, World Bank, Washington, DC.

CHAPTER 34

SOCIAL SECURITY REFORMS IN LATIN AMERICA

ANDRAS UTHOFF

34.1 INTRODUCTION

The development of social security systems in Latin America has been, both historically and by country, strongly influenced by different views of the role of government. Nevertheless, it is the combined forces of the late demographic transition, persistent informality, and relatively low tax burdens that have limited these countries' capacity as welfare providers.

In analyzing reforms to social security programs, various reports (CEPAL 2006; ILO 2008; World Bank 2009 (draft); AISS 2010) have shown that their coverage in Latin America and Caribbean (LAC) has improved only slowly. These reports advocate a new social contract which comprehends and responds to the realities of labor markets, especially the prevalence of informality and frequent changes of employment.

Among countries the present social security systems are highly unequal, with the lowest-income countries failing to raise the fiscal and contributory resources to meet the costs of protection against social risks. The informal labor market acts as an important income provider, to a greater or lesser extent, in all countries in the region. Given the contractual nature of informal workers, their relative importance has an impact on social security systems by inversely affecting the coverage of their contributive components.

In the following section, social security coverage levels are compared across countries, income groups, and the social protection sectors for which there are comparable data, using household data and studies by ECLAC (2006), the ILO (2008), and Rofman, Lucchetti, and Ourens (2008). The comparison shows that, first, coverage of social insurance systems varies by type of risk, but it is generally low throughout the region and falls well short of the goal of universal coverage; second, the poorest have the lowest levels of coverage, distribution outreach is highly unequal, and even though there has been some improvement in equity by using non-contributory benefits these are limited by budget constraints. Finally, many countries in the region complemented their poverty reduction strategies with income support programs targeted to compensate for stagnant coverage among low-income groups, sticky poverty rates, and persistently skewed income distribution. This has resulted in broader population coverage but with a mix of instruments that are fragmented and often result in unintended outcomes (World Bank 2009).

This chapter reviews the history of social security in the Latin American region and the failure of market reforms to improve their performance; it analyzes their outreach in different specific contexts and provides a profile of the new generation of reforms. It ends with a series of recommendations with particular reference to health care, retirement income, and unemployment benefits.

34.2 SOCIAL SECURITY IN LATIN AMERICA

Latin America's social security models have evolved from the Bismarckian model, and aim to protect workers from loss of income due to illness, disability, ageing, and death, under social insurance financed out of contributions from the wage bill; and from the Beveridge model, which includes the use of social assistance to prevent and mitigate poverty and is funded from non-contributory sources. A new generation of reforms is evolving, providing benefits under the criteria of citizens rights not directly linked to labor conditions or contributory records. These changes are the outcome of the alternative ways in which policymakers take into consideration the cultural, political, economic, social, and institutional contextual factors that largely determine both the profile of risks that the population faces and individual citizens' opportunities to access the social security systems to protect themselves and their families.

34.2.1 The social security debate

Bismarckian social security systems assume a society where all workers have long-term, steady job opportunities and live in stable, single-headed extended family households, with one main breadwinner. It follows that all family members are protected if the head of the household is working. Thus, under contributory insurance schemes workers should provide protection for all, and the system should be financed by a specific labor tax based on the wage bill, with benefits estimated actuarially. The model was adopted in different Latin American countries in four waves: Argentina, Brazil, Costa Rica, Chile, Cuba, and Uruguay in the 1920s; Bolivia and Ecuador in the 1930s; Venezuela, Panama, Costa Rica, Mexico, Colombia, and Paraguay in the 1940s; and El Salvador, Guatemala, Honduras, Nicaragua, and the Dominican Republic as latecomers. Despite these advances, the system failed to achieve universal coverage. The reliance on contributions has been criticized because of: (i) low and segmented coverage; (ii) insufficient and poor-quality benefits; and (iii) increasing dependence on fiscal resources. These outcomes are the product of current Latin American labor markets, which offer few stable job opportunities with persistent incidences of underemployment and poverty, and which results in a very low contributory base from which to protect all citizens. In addition, not all families are extended and stable, with a range of family compositions—single women as heads of households, two breadwinners, etc.—which challenge how reforms are designed.

It was in the US in the mid-1930s that the challenge to social protection from the impact of high levels of poverty, underemployment, and diverse family structures led to the explicit idea of social security using non-contributory financing schemes to increase coverage and protect workers against other risks. It used transfers from government and internal solidarity schemes. Poverty alleviation was incorporate into social security by Beveridge in the mid-1940s in England. In fact, the International Labor Organization in its Philadelphia Declaration (1944) raised the concept of social security, and called on members to expand their coverage and integrate its design into economic and social policies, later enshrined in the 1948 United Nations Declaration of Human Rights, which proclaimed that all human beings had rights to social security.

The difficulties in meeting the internationally agreed norms have proven to be harsh in Latin America, mainly because authorities permanently need to deal with large inequalities and budget constraints. Although parametric[1] reforms had been introduced to improve the solvency of contributory systems—by for example increasing contributory rates, and reducing replacement rates and/or increasing age of retirement—it was in the mid-1990s that a series of structural reforms heralded key changes to the benefit rules (from defined benefits to defined contributions); the financing mechanism (from pay-as-you-go to fully funded); and the role of the state (from manager and provider to regulator). More recent reforms propose the integration of contributive and non-contributive systems in order to improve coverage in an integrated single system.

In fact, non-contributive financing has become an essential feature of social security and its operations. Public funds and policies are expected to perform a threefold role: (i) secure stable macro-economies by following stabilization fiscal rules; (ii) ensure stable social security finance by creating reserve funds in anticipation of future demographic and labor market changes, and (iii) promote social institutional developments. It is these issues that have encouraged international financial organizations to include social security system reforms into their stabilization and structural adjustment policy recommendations in Latin America.

---

[1] These reforms refer to changes in the factors (parameters) that secure medium-term sustainable funding in social security contracts that operate under pay-as-you-go regimes. They do so by actuarially linking actual and future affiliates' contributions to actual and future beneficiaries' benefits. They include eligibility conditions and quality of benefits.

34.2.2 The World Bank-led wave of reforms

The World Bank has played a leading role, particularly in pension system reforms in Latin America, following the options set out in "Social Protection Strategy: From Safety Net to Springboard" (2001), the only Board-approved document which followed other influential reports, in particular the Bank's earlier publication "Averting the Old Age Crisis" (1994). For instance, in the area of old age income protection programs the Bank recommends the establishment of flexible multi-pillar pension systems, consisting of three pillars with different forms of income support, as long as the appropriate initial conditions prevail. The first pillar consists of a publicly managed, directly unfunded plan; the second is a mandatory privately funded plan; and the third is a voluntary, privately funded plan. It also recommends complementary retirement income provision for uncovered workers and the poor.

The Bank has recognized that fiscal imbalances were the main cause for countries to undertake pension reform. Nevertheless it was not until after allocating $5.4 billion for pension-specific lending around the world, with Latin America as a dominant recipient,[2] that they recognized, in their draft document "Building an Effective and Inclusive Social Protection System in Latin America" (2009), the failure to provide country-specific guidance for project development. The main weaknesses are the lack of a detailed profile of the living conditions of the aged; underestimating the key role of the growth of coverage; and not emphasizing the importance of better administration of existing public pension systems, the correct design of disability and survivor's pensions, and political aspects of reforms.

The World Bank lending operations show a bias in Latin America towards supporting and developing multi-pillar pension systems rather than reforming publicly managed ones. The Bank allowed for different ways of implementing transitions from pay-as-you-go to fully funded systems, by either promoting a total substitution, as in (Chile, El Salvador, Dominican Republic, Mexico, Bolivia), complementary multi-pillar (Argentina, Uruguay), or competing pillars (Colombia and Peru).

The World Bank-led wave of pension reforms gave priority to additional objectives such as greater worker choice, higher economic growth through increased savings, and the promotion of capital market development. The primary objectives of pension reform, such as reducing old age poverty and smoothing lifetime consumption, became secondary. Unsurprisingly, the subsequent debate about pension systems concentrated on macroeconomic preconditions, including sustainable macroeconomic policies, a sound financial sector, and sufficient implementation capacity. In terms of social security, the debate emphasized system efficiency rather than universality and solidarity,

---

[2] During the 1990s and following the Chilean model (1981), 8 countries (Argentina, Bolivia, Colombia, the Dominican Republic, El Salvador, Mexico, Peru, and Uruguay) have moved from their original pay-as-you-go system to a partially or fully funded individual accounts managed pension system. Lately, Costa Rica, Ecuador, and Panama have partially incorporated some elements of the World Bank proposal, while largely maintaining their original schemes.

largely ignoring polices to protect the vulnerable elderly and the large number of informal-sector workers who, in practice, are either ineligible or cannot fulfill the public pension systems requirements.

The reformed systems erroneously focused on secondary objectives and missed the basic outcomes. The results in the region showed large gaps between the number of affiliates and the number of contributors to the funded pillars (AIOS several years; ECLAC 2006), difficulties in financing transition costs (ECLAC 1998; Bravo and Uthoff 1999), and serious problems of conflict of interests and governance that required better regulation of funded pillars (Government of Chile 2006). In addition to failing to increasing pension coverage in most reforming countries, and in contrast with the stated reform objectives, there is little evidence that privately funded schemes have succeeded in increasing national savings or in developing capital markets (Barr and Diamond 2009).[3] Preconditions were never met.

34.3 STRUCTURAL PRECONDITIONS
FOR SOCIAL SECURITY REFORMS

The World Bank's operational approach was based on two incorrect assumptions: first that all individual workers have the capacity to save and engage in intra-generational transfers; and second that the state has the financial capacity to provide for the neediest.

These assumptions were at the center of social security reforms that promoted affiliated workers' choice when systems changed from a reliance on defined benefit schemes to defined contributions and allowing competition among pension fund and insurance managers. Under the extreme cases of reforms that promoted individual health insurance and savings accounts, affiliates were expected to choose among the best health insurance and pension fund managers on the basis of getting the most out of their contributions. This reasoning led to two simple but strongly incomplete policy recommendations: (1) promoting a competitive health insurance and pension fund management industry, with employee choice, while at the same time (2) providing basic benefits for the neediest.

In practice, weak employment and precarious income conditions constrained individual's budgets and limited the affiliates' capacity to choose. The lack of permanent employment limited continued affiliation to the contributory system, which has an impact on the density of contributions. For the individual contributory health insurance subsystem, this implies long periods of exclusion and therefore increases the demand for public health services. For the individual saving accounts pension subsystem, it implies reduced saving and thus poorer pension benefits, leading to a higher demand

---

[3] An outstanding survey of the Chilean experience can be found in the Marcel Commission Report to the Chilean President Michelle Bachelet (2006).

for public assistance with disability, old age, and subsistence benefits. In sum, a large number of affiliates to the system and their families would end up demanding public assistance programs, also subject to budget constraints.

This vicious cycle is the result of relying on individual choice within very unequal societies. Whenever access to social security is conditioned by individual contributions, a large number of workers will be excluded from the system as a consequence of two constraints: (i) because of their individual budget limitations, they might have never affiliated; (ii) because of their unstable job conditions, although they might have once been affiliated, they may not necessarily fulfill the continuous contributory record. The lesson learned from these cases is that non-regulated contributory systems, operating under defined contributions benefits, lead to a collision between two principles—those of equivalence[4] and solidarity.[5] The profile of insurance system coverage ends up by reproducing the same deficiencies arising from labor market inequalities.

Below, I discuss how countries face this challenge, and the implications for coverage.

34.3.1 Demography, employment, and public finance: the structural preconditions

The debate over and planning of pension systems should return to the primary objectives of social security, and reanalyze the preconditions, including labor market structures and policies, demographic profiles, and fiscal capacity. Social security analysis should attempt to reconcile the efficiency principle with those of universality and solidarity by developing a single integrated system, which both provides insurance and protects the vulnerable elderly and the large proportion of informal-sector workers.

But countries differ in their capacity to reach these goals. A useful indicator by which to group countries according to preconditions is the formal employment dependency ratio (Uthoff and Vera 2008), which summarizes several structural restrictions to individual workers choices. The employment dependency ratio expands the more common demographic dependency ratio (D, which reflects past fertility and mortality trends) with the addition of three components.

If we define:

- (n) the share of the working age population that does not seek market opportunities, either because they face strong restrictions such as school attendance, disability, and household work, or do not have sufficient incentives or do not need to do so;
- (u) the share of the working-age population that is looking for employment opportunities and has not found them; and

---

[4] Under which each contract is self-financed.
[5] Under which the higher-income (healthier) persons may pay for the poorer (sick) persons.

- (i) the share of the working-age population that works in the informal segment of the labor market.

The expanded demographic dependency ratio becomes:

$$D' = (D + n + u + i) \tag{1}$$

Where

D' = enhanced demographic dependency ratio

D = demographic dependency ratio = population aged 0–14 plus population aged 65 and above over population aged 15–64

n = inactive dependency ratio = number of inactive persons aged 15–64 over total population aged 15–64

u = unemployment demographic dependency ratio = number of persons aged 15–64 looking for employment and not obtaining it over total population aged 15–64

i = informal demographic dependency ratio = number of persons aged 15–64 employed in the informal market over total population aged 15–64

Dividing the enhanced demographic dependency ratio by the share of population aged 15–64 that are formally employed, we obtain the formal dependency ratio, which shows the number of dependents per formal worker.

$$F = D/(form) \tag{2}$$

Where

F = formal dependency ratio

form = formal demographic dependency ratio = number of persons aged 15–64 working in the formal market economy over total population aged 15–64

The upper curve in Figure 34.1 shows that this indicator (D′) is inversely related to the level of development measured by income per capita.

The lower curve in Figure 34.1 simulates the number of dependents per formal worker that could be eligible for benefits in terms of income per capita[6] and financed exclusively out of the current level of resources that governments have allocated to public social expenditure. This number increases as the labor market formalizes and tax burdens increase; thus it is positively related to income per capita. However, there is a gap between the effective number of dependents per formal worker and the hypothetical dependents that could receive benefits, associated with the level of development.

By using these gaps we can identify three groups of countries with the following characteristics:

---

[6] The benefit is measured against income per capita (see Uthoff and Vera 2008).

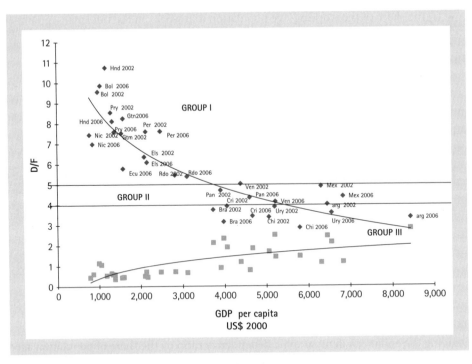

FIGURE 34.1 Number of dependents per formal worker

Source: ECLAC, Social Panorama (2008); Uthoff and Vera (2008).

- Countries with a large gap (i.e. weak state capacity/public administration and characterized by large informal labor markets). They include Bolivia, Ecuador, El Salvador, Guatemala, Honduras, Nicaragua, Peru, and Paraguay. They have a population with a relatively young age structure and a large number of young population and informal workers' dependents. They have an average per capita income of US$2,500 (2,000 PPP[7]), poverty incidence above 45% of the population, and social security coverage below 30% of persons employed.
- Countries with a moderate gap (i.e. a stronger state capacity and characterized by more developed labor markets where the state and employers complement the role of the informal sector as welfare providers). These include Colombia, Mexico, the Dominican Republic, Panama, and Venezuela. Their populations have experienced a fall in fertility during the last decades, show rapid changes to their age structure and school enrollment, and are characterized by a large share of young and inactive dependents. Average income is above US$5,500 (2,000 PPP), poverty incidences between 30 and 40% of the population; and social security coverage close to 50% of all employed persons.

---

[7] Purchasing Power Parity.

- Countries that have a small gap (i.e. with a relatively strong state capacity and have the potential to become welfare states). These are Argentina, Brazil, Chile, Costa Rica and Uruguay. They are only a few decades away from the initial stages of an ageing society, with the aged, the young, and the economically inactive being the largest shares of dependents. Income per capita is above US$7,000 (2,000 PPP), poverty incidence below 25% of the population, and social security coverage above 60% of all employed persons.

34.3.2 Coverage by preconditions

When comparing coverage levels across countries, income groups, and social protection sectors (ECLAC 2006; ILO 2008; Rofman et al. 2008), there are three general patterns and challenges.

- Coverage of social insurance systems varies by type of risk; it is low throughout the region and falls well short of the goal of universal coverage.
- Current outreach is highly unequal, with the poorest having the lowest levels of coverage. Several countries in the region have introduced reforms to make the system more equitable by providing non-contributory programs for specific risks. While there have been important advances in equity as a result of these programs, there are many policy issues yet to be resolved, such as further extensions of coverage and adequacy of current benefits.
- Many countries in the region complement their poverty reduction strategies with targeted income support programs to overcome stagnant coverage among low-income groups, sticky poverty rates, and persistently skewed income distribution. While serving a broader population, the mix of instruments is fragmented and has caused unintended outcomes.

Figure 34.2 and Table 34.1 show that overall coverage is not only low but also varies significantly across rural—urban contexts, formal and informal labor markets, income strata, and gender. In short, contributory schemes reproduce the underlying inequality found in labor contracts.

Coverage, as a proportion of total population, increases with the level of development and state capacity, although the sector profile of coverage remains relatively constant. Coverage is always greatest for formal urban workers, and lowest for rural and informal urban workers. Total coverage is below 30% in El Salvador, the largest in the first group, increasing to 60% in Dominican Republic in the second group; and Chile in the third group has the highest coverage at 67%. For Latin America average coverage is around 37%. Disparities by gender are not too significant among workers but are more extensive for men, when considering total working age population. This last is due to lower female participation rates.

These figures represent coverage at the contributory stage in contributory social security systems. Alternative measures of beneficiaries of social benefits, based on

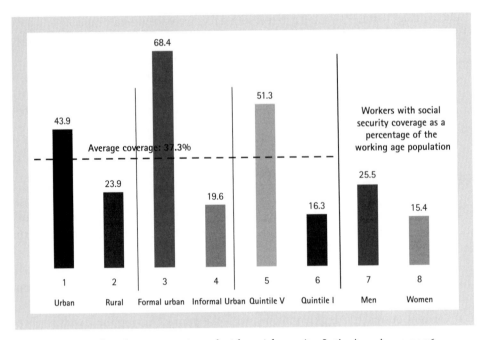

FIGURE 34.2 Employed persons registered with social security: Latin America, c. 2006

Source: ECLAC, on the basis of household surveys conducted in the respective countries.

Notes: Employed workers aged 15 and above who declared labor income. In Argentina and Venezuela, refers to wage earners in general. Simple average.

administrative records, could show different results. Overall, however, these figures show a historical failure of social security systems to provide coverage in the urban informal and rural sectors, where most of the poor find employment. It is no surprise that the low coverage is to be found in the lowest quintile (see Figure 34.2).

The challenge to expand social security coverage does not depend solely on having sustainable macroeconomic policies, sound financial sectors, and sufficient implementation capacity. It depends to a larger extend on identifying and overcoming the underlying limitations that arise from its demography, underdeveloped labor market structures, and weak fiscal capacities; then on designing a system that will overcome these limitations, and on getting the bill through the parliament.

34.4 POLICY OPTIONS FOR THE DESIGN OF SOCIAL SECURITY SYSTEMS

Latin America is undergoing a new wave of social security reforms, with the common aim of making current systems more responsive to the particular contexts in which they operate. Although these contexts differ by country and state, the main objective is

Table 34.1 Social security coverage: Latin America (17 countries), c. 1990, 2002, and 2006 (%)

Country	Year	Total national	Total urban areas	Total rural areas	Formal[a] urban sector	Informal-sector wage earners[b]	Total women	Total men
GROUP I WEAK STATE CAPACITY								
Bolivia	1989[f]	...	28,5	...	56,0	11,4	27,6	29,2
	2002	15,1	21,9	5,7	42,7	7,2	15,7	14,7
	2004	15,6	20,2	9,0	44,4	6,0	16,6	14,8
Ecuador	1990	...	37.5	...	67.8	17.6	35.8	38.4
	2002	...	32.1	...	57.5	13.0	31.4	32.6
	2006	28.7	33.1	20.4	59.6	14.9	30.4	27.6
El Salvador	1995	25.3	35.3	10.0	68.1	6.5	25.2	25.4
	2001	29.3	39.1	12.5	77.3	9.0	30.0	28.9
	2004	28.9	37.2	13.8	75.8	8.2	28.4	29.2
Guatemala	2002	17.1	30.2	8.2	63.4	9.9	15.9	17.8
	2004	17.7	27.1	7.9	61.2	7.5	16.3	18.4
Honduras	2006	19.8	32.6	7.4	65.6	5.7	25.8	16.6
Nicaragua	1993	25.3	35.7	11.2	58.7	14.5	30.0	22.8
	2001	17.6	24.3	7.2	53.2	7.2	21.1	15.6
	2005	17.4	25.7	5.7	58.6	3.2	22.0	14.8
Paraguay	2000	13.0	19.7	4.7	45.9	4.0	13.6	12.7
	2005	14.1	20.0	6.0	46.5	4.4	15.3	13.4
Peru	2001	12.9	18.8	2.7	44.0	4.1	10.1	15.0
	2003	13.7	20.1	3.4	46.2	4.7	9.8	16.8

(Continued)

Table 34.1 (contd.)

Country	Year	Total national	Total urban areas	Total rural areas	Formal[a] urban sector	Informal-sector wage earners[b]	Total women	Total men
Group II. Intermediate State Capacity								
Mexico	1989	50.4	56.4	39.4	61.9	67.6	58.9	47.0
	2002[c]	54.8	64.5	31.2	81.7	25.5	59.2	52.5
	2006	52.1	61.3	29.1	78.1	23.4	54.6	50.6
Panama	2002	53.4	66.8	29.4	88.3	37.0	63.4	48.3
	2007	47.8	60.2	24.3	85.3	27.6	49.9	46.5
Dominican Rep.	2006	58.4	61.6	49.5	70.2	8.5	59.3	63.6
Venezuela[c][g]	2002	61.5	...	...	75.6	19.8	67.1	58.0
	2006	60.9	...	...	68.6	16.1	65.0	58.2
Group III. Strong State Capacity								
Argentina[c]	1990[d]	...	94.6	...	88.9	89.8	92.3	96.0
	2002[e]	...	55.8	...	68.4	22.8	52.2	58.9
	2006[e]	...	60.0	...	68.8	22.3	55.0	64.1
Brazil	1990	53.3	62.8	20.0	97.7	29.0	51.0	54.5
	2001	46.7	53.4	16.5	78.0	34.2	45.9	47.2
	2006	49.5	56.0	20.5	78.7	35.1	48.3	50.4
Chile	1990	65.9	69.6	46.9	86.2	59.0	64.5	66.6
	2000	63.5	66.1	45.0	80.4	52.8	61.8	64.5
	2006	66.7	68.1	55.7	82.6	51.6	62.9	69.0
Costa Rica	1990	69.3	72.9	66.2	88.7	50.9	64.4	71.2
	2002	64.4	67.4	59.6	87.2	43.0	59.0	67.3
	2006	65.2	67.1	62.0	86.4	39.7	58.8	68.8

Table 34.1 (contd.)

Country	Year	Total national	Total urban areas	Total rural areas	Formal[a] urban sector	Informal-sector wage earners[b]	Total women	Total men
Uruguay	2002	...	63.0	...	84.9	44.3	63.1	63.0
	2005	...	61.1	...	82.7	40.5	60.7	61.5
Latin America[h]	2002	37.4	44.5	21.3	67.6	21.8	41.1	40.3
	2006	37.4	44.1	23.9	68.4	19.6	40.8	41.7

Source: ECLAC, based on household surveys of the respective countries.

Note: The variables used to define social security contributions by occupied workers of 15 years of age and more that declare labor income (excluding unpaid labor) vary by national survey; contribution or affiliation to a pension or health system (Argentina, Bolivia, Brazil, Chile, Colombia, Mexico, Paraguay, Peru, Dominican Republic, Uruguay); to national social security system (Costa Rica, Ecuador, El Salvador, Guatemala, Nicaragua, Panama) and the right to social benefits (Venezuela). Totals for men and women refer to national or urban totals, according to the national survey.

[a] Formal sector: salaried workers in the public sector and firms with more than five employees; professional and technical self-employed; owners of firms with 5 or more employees.

[b] Informal salaried sector; salaried workers in firms with fewer than 5 employees and domestic service workers.

[c] The rate corresponds to various social benefits (vacations, allowances, bonuses, pension contributions, or other legislated rights) of salaried employees excluding the self-employed, unpaid family workers, and firm proprietors.

[d] Greater Buenos Aires.

[e] Urban areas.

[f] Eight principal cities and El Alto.

[g] National total.

[h] Unweighted average for countries with information for around 2002 and 2006.

nevertheless the same: to make the principle of equivalence under social insurance contracts compatible with those of solidarity and universality needed in social security schemes. Four strategies are identified from a survey of current experiences. They involve different degrees of state capacity to simultaneously secure the conditions for efficient resource allocation; stable financing of social protection; and the provision of guidelines for institutional development. Solutions vary by subregion and by country, and for different components of insurance according to the socioeconomic and political characteristics of the countries (Ocampo 2008). A variety of approaches have been tested that depend on the state's capacity, and involve redesigning financing mechanisms for greater complementarity; improving insurance industry regulation; restructuring the benefits provided; and making affiliation mechanisms more labor market-friendly.

The ability of democratic governments to ensure that citizens' rights have a role in the design of social protection systems is both an opportunity and a challenge. In Latin America, this is complicated by the variety and heterogeneity that characterize these societies. In sections above this has been illustrated simply by taking particular aspects of the demographic transition, the development of the labor market, and the fiscal capacity of each country.

There are four main findings from the survey of social security analyses. They relate to the nature of its funding; the necessary mix between that state and the private sector; the need to be context-specific; and the importance of social dialogue.

34.4.1 Social security systems designed on the basis of individual contributions are exclusive, and ignore distributive issues such as reducing age-related poverty and securing access to health care

For this reason, it is necessary to develop integrated systems that include both contributory and non-contributory components, in order to overcome the obstacles rooted in a lack of equality which do not allow many citizens to claim their rights.[8]

34.4.1.1 *In the exercise of designing a social security system, fiscal viability cannot be ignored*

Pensions and health care must be compatible with the national capacity to finance pensions and health care, with investment for future growth, and with the ability of the state to raise funds. In Latin America the experience of introducing individual savings accounts and health insurance has been critical, particularly in those countries that underestimated the fiscal costs of the substitution on pension system financial schemes and/or the loss of social security contributions to private insurance.

---

[8] For pensions, see Barr and Diamond (2009).

34.4.1.2 *The government is a key participant in each and every social security system*

The technical capacity of the public sector is vital for the collection of social security contributions for it has to:

(i) keep track of many years of workers' contributions;
(ii) identify the problems associated with low density of contributions and which demonstrate the vulnerabilities linked to labor market;
(iii) ensure the efficiency and effectiveness of those markets that interact with the system (input and benefits suppliers, administrators of insurance and savings services); and
(iv) expend funds under the criteria of universality (Ocampo 2008).

The government should be prepared to guarantee both macroeconomic stability and consistent funding for the social security system. At the microeconomic level, the government has to be able to enforce compliance in relation to contributions, to guarantee effective regulation, and to supervise those markets with which it interacts, while protecting people for redistributive reasons.

Given the state's limited capacity to provide welfare, the private enterprise market and families have operated independently. The explicit inclusion of the private sector in social security systems harnesses market capacity with social security goals. In particular it is necessary to integrate the behavior of private agents under the principles that apply to social security. Individual decisions, in an unregulated market, can lead to a conflict between the principle of solidarity and that of equivalence.

34.4.1.3 *Social security systems should be administered in three distinct areas: management financing, benefit provision, and regulatory oversight*

Management financing involves the ability to collect contributions, to follow individual histories over a long time, to inform the individuals insured about their accumulated rights and future benefits in order to determine the amount and payment of benefits, and to manage considerable resources across time and generations. Benefit provision means offering benefits either in kind or in cash, effectively and efficiently. And regulation requires the establishment of standards and the ensuring of compliance with the principles of competition and social security. Traditionally, one institution manages the three functions, and thus conditions of perfect competition cannot be assured. In order to comply with the principles of social security, it is possible for the private sector to undertake the first two functions, but never that of regulation.

34.4.1.4 *Social security systems should be designed to maintain a careful balance between contributions and benefits*

The inclusion of the private sector as part of the social security system led to a bias towards individual contracts that required a link between entitlements and contributions. When there is a one-to-one relationship between contributions and inputs at each individual level, the system loses an important mechanism to establish solidarity. Solutions require complex systems which incorporate an adequate incentive structure with a combination of performance benefits based on defined contributions and guaranteed benefits based on solidarity funding. In the case of both pensions and health care, this leads to multi-tier systems that integrate contributory and non-contributory payments.

34.4.1.5 *Choice is important*

Participants should be educated in what to expect from social security systems, and be able to choose among the available alternatives. Many Latin American families have no choice, owing to their exclusion from exclusive contributive systems. For them, a rights-based component can be incorporated and individuals can be informed how to access non-contributory benefits. For those with the ability to choose, regulation should be implemented to improve information and overcome problems associated with decisionmaking.

There is no model that adjusts to all contexts. It is not possible to design a unique social protection system that meets all the different specificities of development within the region.

When compared to the rest of the world, Latin America qualifies as one of median income but with high diversity between countries.[9] One group of countries is found in the early stages of the demographic transition (young population) with underdeveloped labor markets (high informality) and a low tax burden (informal/family economies), and displays severe gaps in the capacity of its social security systems; other countries have advanced further in terms of each of these processes, and have more moderate gaps and a comparatively small welfare state, with important consequences for the social security system they might develop.

34.4.1.6 *In those countries with severe welfare gaps, the capacity of the state and market is limited and family capacity should be strengthened*

Such countries' options are very restricted, and often depend on funds from official development aid (ODA), as they are incapable of funding or establishing a national system for poverty alleviation. They depend on the family, non-governmental organizations, and local governments. Some use general taxes and ODA for their poverty alleviations strategies by transfers to local governments or by a national system targeted at certain age groups. However, these programs are insufficient to maintain income, and have to rely on local governments. They administer very segmented health and pensions systems separately, both tied to incomes. The principal reforms have been parametric, and three countries—Bolivia, El Salvador, and Peru—have unsuccessfully attempted to expand their pension coverage using individual capitalization schemes. Bolivia created a program to assist with ill health in old age (BONOSOL) as a method of reforming the contributions

---

[9] They all experience high levels of internal inequality between the haves and the have-nots.

pillar, but underestimated the institutional development necessary for its implementation; while Peru established a program to complement pension benefits for those with low contributions who are likely to be poor in their old age (Willmore 2005). All these systems should be improved as the state funding capacity and formal market develops. At present, private market solutions only operate for high-income sectors; they are not being formally integrated into the system, and are not sufficiently regulated.

34.4.1.7 *In those countries with moderate gaps, the state's capacity is greater, but high levels of informality and poverty continue to limit the coverage of contributive systems*

Three countries formally include the private sector in the administration of their pension system. Colombia attempted without success to maintain two competitive regimes with an intersystem solidarity fund. The Dominican Republic legislated a solidarity component, but without specifying the amount of funding. Mexico has to take account of different state regimes and implements compensatory measures to alleviate poverty among its elderly. Panama and Venezuela have mainly followed the path of parametric reforms, and of moving toward regimes with defined contributions. In all these cases interdependence with public finance persists, as the great challenge is to expand coverage. Regarding health care, in these countries, and especially in Colombia, there have been moves to integrate contributive and non-contributive funding and to regulate the system by establishing guaranteed health care benefit packages as well as solidarity funds. In all these countries, significant pockets of poverty have led to the development of complementary but not fully integrated programs of conditional transfers; they are criticized for creating perverse incentives in comparison to participation in the formal systems of social security. The pending challenge is to integrate these different programs into one social protection system.

34.4.1.8 *In those countries with comparatively very small gaps, there are two opposed options with respect to the strengthening of state capacity*

One option is to continue strengthening the state's and federal sector managed capacity to provide welfare services (Brazil and more recently Argentina); the other is to complement state capacity by the private sector, as in Chile and, less strongly, in Uruguay and, more recently, Costa Rica. Two examples of the latest generation of reforms are to be found in this group. The Chilean system is seeking to take back the distributive role of the state in providing benefits, but without eliminating the role of the private sector in the financing and provision of benefits. For both contributory and non-contributory components, there are guarantees provided under a basic package of health services to be funded by public and private resources. Another example, developed most recently in Chile, integrated a basic solidarity component into the pensions system by way of aligning incentives. Argentina, instead, has strengthened its state capacity by nationalizing funds for social security previously administered by the private sector. There are intermediate attempts in Costa Rica to complement the National Social Security fund

(*Caja Costarricense de Seguridad Social*) using public funds to alleviate the needs of the poorest. In Uruguay, incentives have been institutionalized to capture the contributions of micro-entrepreneurs, expand coverage, and improve efficiency by integrating health care and its funding but separating the system's functions. Brazil has strengthened state supplies with radical changes in funding, adding more resources to a unique health system and guaranteeing the rights of elder adults in rural areas, through greater taxation of commercial agriculture.

The design of a social security system constitutes part of a state policy that goes beyond particular governments and is the basis for an important social dialogue. Particular attention should be paid to the way the state is strengthened to create the necessary institutions to overcome; first, the limitations imposed by inequality; second, the budgetary constraints that prevent the provision of a guarantee of benefits to all citizens in terms of their social protection rights; and third, the likely lack of completion in the private providers industry.

This "social dialogue" should:

- evaluate the prerequisites for effective reform;
- develop the necessary administrative and financial institutions;
- provide regulators and supervisors for markets in which the system operates;
- make available records and undertake appropriate statistical analysis;
- train technical groups capable of reconciling funding and service provision in the way that is needed when linking the state, the private sector, and families;
- ensure appropriate criteria and methods for targeted programs;
- avoid moral hazard implicit in guarantees;
- ensure fair regulation so that workers have adequate protection without supplier disincentives;
- allow voluntary complementary insurance for the differences in preferences and individual restrictions;
- combine the redistributive function (principally to alleviate poverty) and those that protect income in the way that is most appropriate for the country, given its administrative capacity and fiscal limits;
- move toward unique and portable systems;
- undertake actuarial evaluations in terms of the parameters (such as the amount of benefits and conditions of eligibility) to make them consistent with fiscal sustainability; and
- integrate a solidarity component which is subject to verification of beneficiaries' income (Barr and Diamond 2009).

This dialogue should be multidisciplinary, open, and respectful of diversity. It should recognize that the social security systems' financial problems are long-term and not a short-term crisis, and should adjust to many national priorities and institutional contexts—specifically cultural, political, and economic—in order to develop a tailor-made system. It should also choose between simple alternatives based on real national capacity, based on principles that ensure viable taxation and avoid unsustainable solutions.

34.5 CONCLUSIONS

In unequal societies with strong macro and familial budgetary constraints, the design and planning of social security systems offer an unique opportunity to discuss the role of the state, the market, and families in the provision of welfare. It allows the examination of how to strengthen its capacities and to transfer resources that support democracy, guaranteeing the rights of citizens to overcome inequalities through solidarity, universalism, and fiscal responsibility.

Implementing purely contributory insurance/savings schemes for workers employed in underdeveloped labor markets has generated new forms of exclusion in Latin America. Demographic and epidemiological pressures, costly technological innovations, and financially constrained systems further aggravated the situation. New social security systems need to be built which take account of specific budgetary, labor market, demographic, and familial structures, and to adapt the system to them.

It has been demonstrated that all countries in Latin America have gaps in social security coverage, regardless of the state's capacity and labor market development. Recent evaluations have shown how contributory histories have been influenced by labor market outcomes. Rising unemployment and informality have limited the density of contributions for males and females. The 1990s reforms that sought to provide incentives for affiliation, by setting up defined contribution schemes for fully funded pension systems and individual savings accounts, have proved to be insufficient: neither changing family structure nor increasing employment vulnerability was then considered.

A new generation of reforms is being tried, with different outcomes in a number of countries.[10] Four strategies attempt to overcome the limitations of higher contributions. The first strategy is to reinforce solidarity by integrating financing sources from alternative schemes of social protection. Total integration is to be found in Brazil's health insurance system, while Costa Rica has integrated its social security fund; there is a partial integration of public health care and insurance in Chile. With some minor exceptions, all other countries continue providing health care protection with segmented schemes.

A second strategy is to reinforce regulation and surveillance in health insurance and pension fund administrations industries, in order to reconcile the principle of equivalence with that of solidarity. This can be done by overcoming market barriers that limit access. Such solutions involve designing an explicit, credible, and guaranteed social benefit package, complemented by a solidarity fund to ensure access to benefits for all. Such

---

[10] In Argentina, the authorities merged all affiliates back into defined benefit pay-as-you-go schemes to reinforce intra-solidarity in the national system. In Chile, the authorities reinforced the defined-contribution fully funded pillar, but complemented it with a defined-benefit solidarity pillar.

solutions can be partially found in Chile, Colombia, Mexico, and most recently in Brazil and Uruguay.

A third strategy is to make funds available to integrate social security benefits and social assistance together with income support programs, originally created for emergency situations and the neediest. In fact these programs are being transformed into permanent conditional cash transfer programs, with the aim of linking cash transfers to human capital development of the poor. These programs, in a wide range of designs, are found in the poorest, middle-income, and upper-income countries in the Americas. Non-contributory pension schemes have been established in Chile, Ecuador, and rural Brazil. Mexico and Peru have such schemes for the neediest elderly, and Bolivia for all citizens born before a certain date related to the fully funded reform there. Totally aligned incentives can be found only in Chile.

The fourth strategy is to experiment with demand and supply subsidies to make the social security system more accessible to all types of work in Latin American labor markets and households. Health insurance demand subsidies are implemented in Costa Rica, Colombia, and the Dominican Republic. Alternative incentives are being designed for pension affiliation by migrant workers' status in El Salvador, by housing need in Ecuador, and for the self-employed in Costa Rica and Panama.

The capacity of LA countries to follow the alternative strategies varies according to their implementation capacity. This capacity is to a large extent conditioned by demographic pressures, labor market developments, the strength of public finance, and institutional developments. The poorest countries are characterized by a late demographic transition, weak labor markets, low tax burdens, and weak institutional developments, young populations, large informal sectors, weak state capacity, and very vulnerable institutions, and should emphasize strategies three and four.

Middle-income countries are at more advanced stages of demographic transition, with more developed labor markets, higher tax burdens and/or rents from natural resources, and institutional improvements. Their populations are at the earlier stage of ageing, they still possess large informal labor market segments, a more competent state, and better institutional developments, and thus are able to follow all four strategies.

Finally, the upper-income countries in the region face the final stages of demographic transition, relatively more developed labor markets, larger tax burdens, and complex institutional challenges. They are experiencing the initial stages of an ageing society, but with substantial employment vulnerability, have greater state capacity and broader institutional developments, and should emphasize the first and second strategies.

Social security system design in Latin America should also take advantage of demographic characteristics. Support ratios of potential producers to consumers will continue a favorable trend in low- and medium-income countries, but will soon fall in high-income countries. Demographic dependency will then move from a young dependent population into an older one. For subsistence of the former, transfers have been predominantly familial, while for the latter they have been largely public. This change should be monitored and managed in the design of future reforms. For the next three decades the richer countries in the Americas will need to face lower support ratios and come to terms with older dependent populations. One or two decades later. a similar pattern will emerge in middle income and poorer countries (Miller et al. 2008).

The design of social security system reforms needs to specify the funding conditions to face the challenge of universal coverage. There is no doubt from the above analysis that, in order to secure access to social security for all, the systems will increasingly need to integrate contributive and non-contributive funding, and to invest much thought into how incentives are managed.

References

AIOS (Asociación Internacional de Organismos de Supervisión de Fondos de Pensiones) (several years), Informe Estadístico.

AISS (Asociación Internacional de la Seguridad Social) (2010). *Una seguridad social dinámica para las Américas: cohesión social y diversidad institucional: evolución y tendencias*, Geneva.

ARENAS DE MESA, A. (2005). 'Fiscal and Institutional Considerations of Pension Reform Lessons Learned from Chile', in C. Crabbe (ed.), *A Quarter Century of Pension Reform in Latin America and the Caribbean: Lessons Learned and Next Steps*, Washington, DC: World Bank.

BARR, N. (2004). *The Economics of The Welfare State*, 4th edn, New York: Oxford University Press.

——and DIAMOND, P. (2009). 'reforma de las pensiones: principios, errores analíticos y orientaciones políticas', *revista internacional de seguridad social* 62.

BERNSTEIN, S., LARRAIN, G., and PINO COBERTURA, F. (2005). 'Densidad y pensiones en Chile: proyecciones a 20 años plazo', SAFP Working Paper, Chile.

BPS (Banco de Previsión Social) (2008). *Monotributo*, Montevideo.

BRAVO, JORGE, and UTHOFF, ANDRAS (1999). 'Transitional Fiscal Costs and Demographic Factors in Shifting from Unfunded to Funded Pension in Latin America', Santiago, Chile: CEPAL.

CEPAL (Comisión Económica para América Latina) (2006). 'La protección social de cara al futuro: acceso, financiamiento y solidaridad', presented at the 31st session of the Economic Commission for Latin America and the Caribbean, Montevideo (March).

——(2007 and 2008). *Panorama social*, Santiago, Chile.

——(2008). *Objetivos del milenio: la progresión hacia el derecho a la salud en América Latina y el Caribe*, Santiago, Chile.

Consejo Asesor Presidencial (2006). *El derecho a una vida digna en la vejeza: hacia un contrato con la previsión en Chile I: diagnóstico y propuestas de reforma*, Santiago, Chile.

DINIZ COTTA, E. (2006). 'La experiencia de Brasil: reformas y desafíos (2003–2006)', Documento MPAS Brasil en el seminario 'Sistemas públicos de pensiones: situación actual y perspectivas', Guadalajara, Comisión Nacional Hacendaria México.

DRAIBE, S. M. (2006). 'Brasil: Bolsa-Escola y Bolsa Familia', in E. Cohen and R. Franco (eds), *Transferencias com corresponsabilidad: una mirada latinoamericana*, Mexico: SEDESOL.

DURÁN VALVERDE, F. (2008). 'La cobertura de los trabajadores independientes en la seguridad social de Costa Rica', Borrador, Oficina Subregional de OIT para los Países Andinos.

ECLAC (UN Economic Committee for Latin America and the Caribbean) (1998). The Fiscal Covenant: Strengths, Weaknesses and Challenges, Santiago, Chile.

ECLAC (UN Economic Committee for Latin Amercia and the Caribbean (2006). 'Shaping the Future of Social Protection: Access, Financing and Solidarity', presented at Trigesimo primer periodo de sesiones de la Comisión Económica para America Latina (Montevideo, March).

—— (2008). *Social Panorama of Latin America 2008*, Santiago, Chile.

GERTLER, P. J., NEUFIELD, L., and FERNALD, L. (2008). 'Role of Cash in Conditional Cash Transfer Programmes for Child Health, Growth, and Development: An Analysis of Mexico's *Oportunidades*', *Lancet* 371.

Gobierno de Colombia (2008). 'Transferencias condicionadas de dinero en centros urbanos', síntesis sobre seminario, Familias en Acción.

Government of Chile (2006). 'Reforma previsional', Santiago, Chile: Presidencia de la Republica.

HOLZMANN, R. (2005). 'Reforming Severance Pay: Toward an Understanding of Program Rationale, Economic Impact and Reform Options', *Empirica* 32.

—— PALMER, E., and UTHOFF, A. (2008). *Fortalecer los sistemas de pensiones latinoamericanos: cuentas individuales por reparto*, Colombia: MAYOL, Forsakrinngskassan, CEPAL, and World Bank.

IDB (Inter-American Development Bank) (2008). 'Entendiendo las barreras a la acumulación del capital humano en zonas urbanas: una agenda de ajustes al programa oportunidades'.

ILO, ITC (International Labour Organization, International Training Centre) (2008). *Quatrain News*, various reports, Geneva.

—— (2008). 'Can Low-Income Countries Afford Basic Social Security?', Social Security Policy Briefings Paper No. 3, Geneva.

LEVY, S. (2008). *Good Intentions, Bad Outcomes*, Washington, DC: Brookings Institution.

LOAYZA, N., and RIGOLINI, J. (2006). 'Informality Trends and Cycles', World Bank Policy Research Working Paper No. 4078, Washington, DC.

MACHINEA, J. L. (2006). 'Prólogo', presented at the 31st session of the Economic Commission for Latin America and the Caribbean, Montevideo, Uruguay (March).

MADSEN, P. K. (2002a). 'The Danish Model of Flexicurity: A Paradise with Some Snakes', in H. Sarfati and G. Bonori (eds), *Labor, Markets and Social Protection Reforms in International Perspective: Parallel or Converging Traces?* Aldershot: Ashgate.

—— (2002b). 'Security and Flexibility: Friends or Foes? Some Observations from the Case of Denmark', in P. Auer and B. Gazier (eds), *The Future of Work, Employment and Social Protection: The Dynamics of Change and the Protection of Workers*, Geneva: ILO and IILS.

Marcel Commission Report: Consejo Asesor Previsional para la Reforma Previsional (2006). *El derecho a una vids a digna en la vejez: hacia un contrato social con la previsión en Chile*, Santiago de Chile (July).

MARCEL, M., and RIVERA, E. (2008). 'Regímenes de bienestar en América Latina', in E. Tironi (ed.), *Redes estado y mercado: soportes de la cohesión social Latinoamericana*, Santiago, Chile: Uqbar.

MESA-LAGO, C. (2004). *Las reformas de salud en América Latina y su impacto en los principios de la seguridad social*, Santiago, Chile: CEPAL.

—— (2005) 'Las reformas de salud en América Latina y su impacto en los principios de la seguridad social', CEPAL Working Paper, Santiago, Chile.

MILLER, T., MARTINEZ, C., SAAD, P., and HOLZ, M. (2008). 'The Impact of the Demographic Dividend on Three Key Support Systems: Education, Health Care and Pensions', draft, CELADE, Santiago, Chile.

OCAMPO, J. A. (2004). *Reconstruir el futuro: globalización, desarrollo y democracia en América Latina*, Bogotá: Grupo Editorial Norma and CEPAL.

—— (2008). 'Las concepciones de la política social: universalismo versus focalización', *Nueva sociedad* 215.

OIT (Organización de Trabajo) (several years). *Panorama laboral: América Latina y el Caribe*, Lima: Oficina Regional.

PADDISON, O. (2005). *Social Security in the English Speaking Caribbean*, Santiago, Chile: ECLAC.

PAES-SOUSA, R., and PACHECO SANTOS, L. M. (2008). 'Measuring the Impact of *Bolsa Familia* Program Based on Data from Health and Nutrition Days', presented at the 3rd Seminario Internacional Transferencia Condicionadas, Erradicación del Hambre y la Desnutrición (Brazil, December).

PAREDES, R., and IGLESIAS, A. (2004). 'Análisis de propuestas para aumentar la cobertura de trabajadores independientes en el sistema de AFP', presented at the Seminar 'Competencia y Cobertura', Centro de Estudios Públicos y Superintendencia de Administradoras de Fondos de Pensiones, Santiago, Chile (November).

PERRY, G., et al. (2006). *Poverty Reduction Informality: Exit and Exclusion*, Washington, DC: World Bank.

ROFMAN, R. (2005). 'Social Security Coverage in Latin America', World Bank Social Protection Discussion Paper No. 0523, Washington, DC.

—— and LUCCHETTI, L. (2007). *Social Security in Latin America*, Washington, DC: World Bank.

—— —— and OURENS, G. (2008). 'A Cross-Country Comparison of Coverage Using Household Survey Data from 18 Countries', Washington, DC: World Bank.

Secretaría Ejecutiva Sistema de Protección Social Chile Solidario (2007). *Chile Solidario, Modelo de Gestión en Centros Urbanos*, Santiago, Chile.

TOKMAN, V. (2005). *Inserción laboral, mercados de trabajo y protección social*, Santiago, Chile: CEPAL.

UTHOFF, A., and VERA, C. (2008). 'Una nota sobre las políticas activas y el estado de bienestar', Santiago, Chile: CEPAL.

VILLATORO, P. (2005a). 'Estrategias y programas de reducción de la pobreza en América Latina y el Caribe', presented at XXXI Reunion Ordinar. Cons. Latinoam., Sistema Econ. Latinoam., Caracas.

—— (2005b). 'Los programas de proteccion social asistencial en America Latina y sus impactos en las familias: algunas reflexiones', presented at Reunión de expertos, 'Políticas hacia las familias, protección e inclusión sociales', CEPAL, Santiago, Chile (June).

WILLMORE, L. (2005). 'Non Contributory Pensions: Bolivia and Antigua in an International Context', Santiago, Chile: CEPAL.

WHO (World Health Organization) (2005). *World Health Report*, Geneva.

World Bank (1994). *Averting the Old Age Crisis: Policies to Protect the Old and Promote Growth*, Oxford: Oxford University Press for the World Bank.

—— (2001). *Social Protection Sector Strategy: From Safety Net to Springboard*, Washington, DC.

—— (2009). 'Building an Effective and Inclusive Social Protection System in Latin America: Diagnosis and Policy Directions', draft, Washington, DC.

Index

account surpluses, management 120
Acemoglu, D. and Robinson, J.
  on colonial heritage 36
  on institutions 33
Acemoglu, D., Johnson, S., and Robinson, J.,
    on Botswana, resource-based
    growth 422
Adaptability Index (*AI*) 559
adaptability of policies 58, *60–1*
Adaptation Fund 151
adjusted savings rates 143–*4*
adjustment policies, effect on income
    inequality 697
aggregate demand
  impact of external shocks *175*
  regulation of expansion 177–8
  relationship to GDP 175–6
aggregate demand management 119–20
aggregate employment, effect of trade
    liberalization 378–9
aggregation level, business groups 71–2
Aghion, P. and Howitt, P., model of
    growth 524
Agosin, M., on Chilean RER volatility 202
agrarian reform 8, 615, 632
agricultural added value
  average annual rate of growth *627*
  share in total GDP *628*
agricultural commodities, price rises 631–2
agricultural development banks 612–13
agricultural employment, effect of trade
    liberalization 381
agricultural policies 633, 760
  land and irrigation 615–16
  prices and direct support 611–12
  research and technology transfer 613–14
agricultural production, growth 131, *132*, 133
agricultural subsidies 336

agriculture 608–9
  challenges of free trade agreements
    610–11
  changes in land cultivation 617–18,
    619–20
  changes in livestock 621, 622–3
  composition of international trade 624–5
  credit access 612–13
  dependence on imports 612
  effects of structural reforms, economic
    performance 627–8
  heterogeneity 616–17
  productivity gaps with US *594*
  state intervention 7
agro-industrial complexes 608
air pollution 141–2
  PM10 emissions, selected cities *141*
Aizenman, J.
  on financial crises 257
  on financial opening 247
Ajegroup 455
ALBANISA 645
Alkire, S. and Foster, J., poverty
    measures 724
Alkire, S. and Santos, M.E., multidimensional
    poverty index 732–3, *735*
Amarante, V., Arim, R., and Vigorito, A.,
    on child poverty 736
AmBev 455
American Institutionalist School 122
Andean Community
  challenges 362
  intra-industry trade *357*
Andean Pact 323, 327, 346–7
  institutional structure 353
Anderson, K. and Valdés, A., on RRA *627*
Andrés, L. et al., evaluation of infrastructure
    PPI 683–4

apparel industry, efficiency-seeking FDI 451
appreciation bias, FIT arrangements 201–2
aquaculture, environmental
       consequences 142
Aragón, F. and Rud, J., on Peru 421
Argentina
  budget balance, 1990s 86
  CCT program 736
  civil service capacity 69
  "convertibility" regime 58, 195–6, 197
  crawling peg regimes 189, 190, 191
  crisis, 2001–2 197–8
  decentralization 282, 284
  dollarization 225
  domestic production, competition from
    China 484
  economic growth
    1997–2007 521
    in crisis periods 217
    state-led industrialization period 10
  economic liberalization 163
  education
    average years of schooling 822
    ranking by attendance and
      effectiveness 825
    ranking by effectiveness gap 824
    reading proficiency 827
    urban enrollment 817
  exchange rates, crisis periods 219, 220
  export shares by main destination, 2000
    and 2007 332
  exports 395
    to China 464, 465
    to Latin America 481
  factors in economic success 45
  FDI
    hydrocarbon sector 647
    inward 442
    outward 453
    public services 447
  fiscal policy 228–9
  food security program 633
  government expenditure 272
  heterodox stabilization program 194
  Human Development Index 727
  hydrocarbon sector reforms 643
  imports and exports, trends 370

income inequality 700–3, 701
indexation to the dollar 224
inflation rates 14, 216
  1980s 194
  1990s 85
infrastructure
  investment as percentage of GDP 677
  trends 663
interest rates, crisis periods 218
intraregional immigration 494, 496
judicial independence 68
labor laws, enforcement 806
labor market 13–14
  reforms 786, 794, 795, 796, 800, 802
legislature capabilities 66
manufactured exports, threat from
    China 479, 480, 482
migration to USA and Spain 499
natural gas reserves 640
natural resource use 420
natural resources 400–2, 408
oil production, economic importance 640
oil reserves 639
party system institutionalization (PSI) 71
per capita GDP
  1820–2003 32
  1950 and 1980 13
per capita income, growth, 1950–2006 112
personal income taxes 268
Policy Index 62
political regime 54
poverty levels 717, 731–2
  evolution by dimension 734
  multidimensional poverty index 735
productivity growth 578, 581
public balance as a percentage of GDP 280
public debt 287
  1990s 86
public investment 584
public policies 61
real exchange rates, 1980–2008 207
  SCRER strategy 202–3, 205
  volatility 201
redistribution of income 306
relative growth performance,
    1990–2008 21
RP and *KI* indices 558

size of financial system 245
social expenditure 273, 844
   trends 845
social security coverage 780, 874
social security reforms 879, 881
stock market turnover ratios 254
tariff rates, trends 321, 369
tax revenue
   from natural resources 144
   as a percentage of GDP 269
wage gaps 385
weighted average growth rates 11
workfare programs 848-9
Argentine–Brazil accord, 1986 324
Arida, P. and Lara-Resende, A., Larida
      proposal 196
Aschauer, D., on public infrastructure
      capital 670
Asian countries
   free trade agreements 331–2, 333
   reforms 569
Asian crisis 197, 198
Australia
   resource-based growth 421–2
   RP and *KI* indices 558
   TFP growth 581
authoritarianism, relationship to resource
      abundance 417
automobile industry
   Mexico, efficiency-seeking FDI 450–1
automobile use 140

backlash phenomenon 569–70
Baker, A., on popularity of free trade 372, 373
balance of payments, effect of trade
      liberalization 322
Bangladesh, labor market flexibility 591
bank-based financial systems 250
banking crises, as source of public debt 287
banking systems
   regulatory changes 246–8
   size 244–6
   small size 252–3
banks
   effect on liquidity 254
   market making function 261

Barbosa-Filho, N., on Brazilian RER
      appreciation 202
Barros, R., Cardoso, E., and Urani, A., on
      Brazilian income inequality 703
Barros, R., De Carvalho, M., and Franco, S.,
      Index of Family Development 730
Barros, R. et al., on Brazilian income
      inequality 705
Basel Convention on the Control of
      Transboundary Movements of
      Hazardous Wastes and their Disposal,
      signatories 154–5
Basel Core Principles for Effective Banking
      Supervision, compliance 246
Basel II 172
basic needs 719
Battiston, D. et al, multidimensional
      measurement of poverty 731, 733
Battle of Seattle 337
Bavaria (beverage company) 455
Beck, U., on labor risk 490
Behrman, J., Birdsall, N., and Székely, M. 387
   study of Consensus-style reforms 94
   on wage gaps 387
Behrman, J. et al., on wage differentials 698
Belize
   conservation efforts 139
   poverty levels, multidimensional poverty
      index 735
Belsley, D., Kuh, E., and Welsch, R., DFBETA
      measure 423
benefit provision 877
Bentham, J., on "utility" 725
Beveridge model of social security 864, 865
*Beyond the Washington Consensus:
      Institutions Matter*, World Bank,
      1998 101
Bielschowsky, R., on mass consumption 114
bilateral trade agreements 328, 346, 610
Bimbo 455
bindings, agricultural subsidies 336
biodiversity 137–8
   Cartagena Protocol 155–6
   causes of loss 138
   United Nations Convention on Biological
      Diversity 154–5
biofuels 652–4, 656

Birdsall, N. et al., on Washington
     Consensus 103–4
Bismarckian social security systems 864–5
"blue box" 336
Bolivarian Alternative for the People of the
     Americas (ALBA) 363, 364
Bolivia
    adjusted savings rate 143
    civil service capacity 68, 69
    decentralization 282
    economic growth, 1997–2007 521
    education
        average years of schooling 822
        ranking by attendance and
            effectiveness 825
        ranking by effectiveness gap 824
        reading proficiency 827
        urban enrollment 817
    energy consumption 137
    export shares by main destination, 2000
        and 2007 332
    FDI
        hydrocarbon sector 647, 648
        inward 442
    Human Development Index 727
    hydrocarbon sector reforms 642
    imports and exports, trends 370
    judicial independence 68
    labor laws, enforcement 806
    labor market reforms 795, 800
    legislature capabilities 66
    migration to USA and Spain 499
    natural gas reserves 640
    oil production, economic importance 640
    party system institutionalization (PSI) 71
    pension coverage 787
    per capita income, growth, 1950–2006 112
    Policy Index 62
    poverty levels 717
        multidimensional poverty index 735
    public policies 61
    relative growth performance,
        1990–2008 21
    social expenditure 273, 844
        trends 845
    social pensions 850
    social security coverage 873

    social security reforms 878–9
    tariff rates, trends 321, 369
    tax revenue
        from natural resources 144
        as a percentage of GDP 269
    wage gaps 385
    weighted average growth rates 11
    workfare program 849
bond markets 248
boom management 175, 183
    pro-cyclic behavior 278
Borio, C. and Packer, F., on debt
        intolerance 226
Botswana, resource-based growth 422
Bourbon reforms 39, 46
Bourguignon, F. and Chakravarty, S.R.,
        poverty measures 724
Brady bonds 169
Brady Plan 84, 195, 242
Brahmbhatt, M. and Canuto, O., on
        commodity price boom 399
Bravo-Ortega, C. and de Gregorio, J., on
        growth of disparities 420
Brazil
    agrarian reform 615
    budget balance, 1990s 86
    civil service capacity 68, 69
    conditional cash transfers (CCTs) 851,
        852, 853
    conservation efforts 138, 139
    crawling peg regimes 189, 190
    decentralization 282, 283, 284
    diesel sulfur content 141
    domestic production, competition from
        China 484
    economic growth
        1997–2007 521
        in crisis periods 217
        state-led industrialization period 10,
            12–13
    education
        average years of schooling 822
        ranking by attendance and
            effectiveness 825
        ranking by effectiveness gap 824
        reading proficiency 827
        urban enrollment 817

EMBRAPA 614
energy integration promotion 655
energy intensity 136, 137
exchange rates, crisis periods 219
export shares by main destination, 2000
    and 2007 332
exports 396
    to China 464, 465
    to Latin America 481
    promotion policies 72, 319
FDI
    hydrocarbon sector 647, 648
    inward 442
    outward 453, 454
FIT regime 199
floatation of Real 197
FX market interventions 199
GDP per capita, comparison with
    India 572
government spending 272, 308
growth of per capita income, 1950–2006 112
heterodox stabilization program 194
Human Development Index 727
hydrocarbon sector reforms 642, 643
impact of 1973 oil shock 191
imports and exports, trends 370
income inequality 703–6, 704
industrial policy 407
inflation rates 14, 216
    1980s 194
    1990s 85
inflation targeting 223
infrastructure
    investment as percentage of GDP 677
    trends 663
interest rates, crisis periods 218
investment rates 582, 583
irrigation policies 615
judicial independence 68
labor laws, enforcement 806
labor market 13
    reforms 794, 796, 800, 802
legislature capabilities 66
manufactured exports, threat from
    China 479, 480, 482
manufacturing decline 600
manufacturing FDI 449

meat and poultry production, global
    expansion 455
migration to USA and Spain 499
minimum price-setting 612
multiple equilibria 232
natural gas reserves 640
natural resource use 421
natural resources 406–7, 408
oil production, economic importance 640
oil reserves 407, 638, 639
party system institutionalization (PSI) 71
pension coverage 787
per capita GDP, 1820–2003 32
personal income taxes 268
Plan Real 229–30
Policy Index 62
political regime referendum 54
poverty levels 717, 731–2
    evolution by dimension 734
    multidimensional measurement 733
    multidimensional poverty index 735
privatization of electricity generation 448
productivity, comparison with Korea 577
productivity gaps with US 594
productivity growth 577, 578
public balance as a percentage of GDP 280
public debt, 1990s 86
public investment 584
public policies 61
real exchange rates, 1980–2008 208
    volatility 201, 202
Real Plan 196
redistribution of income 306
relationship between investment and
    productivity growth 585
relative growth performance,
    1990–2008 21
reserve accumulation 200
RP and KI indices 558
size of financial system 245
social assistance 854–5
social expenditure 273, 844
    trends 845
social security coverage 874
    pensions 850
social security reforms 880
stock market turnover ratios 254

Brazil (*cont.*)
   tariff rates, trends *321, 369*
   tax policy 271
   tax revenue
     from natural resources 144
     as a percentage of GDP *269*
   taxation of portfolio inflows 167
   TFP growth *581*
   under-5 mortality *141*
   wage gaps 385, 386
   weighted average growth rates *11*
"Brazilian miracle" 205–6
Brenner, R., on capitalist development 37
Bretton Woods rules 188
bubbles, regulatory measures 236
budget balances, 1990s *86*
budget deficits, comparison with OECD
     countries *296–7, 298*
bureaucracies 68
bureaucratic authoritarian governments 52
business groups, role in policy
     cooperation 71–2

Cairns Group of Fair Traders 335–6
Calderón, C. and Schmidt-Hebbel, K.,
     exchange rate regime
     classifications 220
Calderón, C. and Servén, L., on contribution
     of infrastructure to growth 672
Calvo, G, multiple equilibrium approach 232
Calvo, G. and Reinhart, C., on fear of
     floating 199
Calvo, G., Izquierdo, A., and Mejía, L., on
     banking crises 247
Canada, FDI *443*
Canitrot, A., on exchange rate populism 115
capabilities, specificity to activities 529–30,
     533
capability failure approach to poverty 719–20
capital account
   case for regulation 163–5
   management for development 182–3
capital account liberalization 161, 163, 180–1,
     183, 247
   crises as a result 161
   sequencing 164–5

capital account reforms 181–2
capital account regulations
   experience 166–7
   objectives 165–6
capital accumulation 33, 44
capital controls 125–6, 181
capital expenditures, comparison with OECD
     countries *301–2, 302*
capital flows
   association with crises 256
   composition, 1977–2008 *170–1*
   factors influencing dynamics 178–9
   impact on fiscal balance 180
   impact on public investment 180
   links with economic growth 174–80
   preconditions for sustained growth 179
   volatile nature 180
capital inflows, relationship to real exchange
     rate *177*
capital markets reform implementation,
     1990–2002 *90*
capitalism, peripheral 38–9
Caracazo, Venezuela 404
carbon dioxide emissions 132
   relationship to GDP *151*
Cardoso, C.F.S. and Pérez Brignoli, H.,
     Historia económica de América
     Latina 37–9, 41–2
Caribbean
   export shares by main destination, 2000
     and 2007 *333*
   PETROCARIBE 645
   proportion of land covered by forest *138*
   soil degradation 139
   under-5 mortality *141*
Caribbean Basin Initiative 324
Caribbean Community (CARICOM) 328
   total exports, 1990–2007 *326*
Caribbean Free Trade Area (CARIFTA) 323
Cartagena Agreement 323, 346
Cartagena Protocol on Biosafety to the
     Convention on Biological Diversity,
     signatories *155–6*
Caselli, F. and Michaels, G., on Brazil 421
cash transfer programs 699–700, 756, 762–3,
     846, 882
   Argentina 703

Brazil 705–6
  Mexico 708, 709–10
  see also conditional cash transfers (CCTs)
catching-up 549, 563
  Asian countries 571
  'one-thing-at-a-time' processes 594–5
cattle stocks *132*
CEMEX, OFDI 454–5
"center" of world economy 4
center–periphery model 16, 39–40, 110,
      547–8, *550*
Central American Common Market
      (CACM) 323, 328, 345–6, 363
  institutional structure 353
  intra-industry trade *357*
  total exports, 1990–2007 325–6
Central American Free Trade Agreement
      (CAFTA) 328
central banks
  autonomy 230–1
  instruments, comparison of new
      developmentalism and conventional
      orthodoxy *123*, 125–6
  mandate, comparison of new
      developmentalism and conventional
      orthodoxy *123*, 124
  role in fiscal policy 228–9
CEPAL (United Nations Economic
      Commission for Latin America) 6, 345
  *Changing Production Patterns with Social
      Equity* 18
Cerioli, A. and Zani, S., poverty
      measurement 725
Céspedes, L.F. and Valdés, R., on central bank
      autonomy 231
Céspedes, L.F., Chang, R., and Velasco, A., on
      dollar-denominated assets 224
Chang, R., on FX market interventions 199
*Changing Production Patterns with Social
      Equity*, CEPAL 18
Chávez, Hugo 404–5
Chay, K., McEwan, P., and Urquiola, M., on
      Chilean P-900 program 829
'Chicago Boys', Chile 402
child poverty, Uruguay 730–1
childhood interventions 856–7
  feeding programs 847–8

Chile
  adjusted savings rate 143
  budget balance, 1990s *86*
  CCT program 736
  Chicago school offensive 16
  childhood interventions 857
  civil service capacity 68, *69*
  Copper Stabilization Fund 279, 280, 411
  crawling bands 206
  crawling peg regimes 189, 190, 191, *193*
  decentralization 282
  diesel sulfur content 141
  dollarization 225–6
  economic growth
      1997–2007 *521*
      in crisis periods *217*
      state-led industrialization period 10
  economic liberalization 163
  education
      age-enrollment profiles *815*
      average years of schooling *822*
      policy initiatives 829, 831
      quantity *820–1*
      ranking by attendance and
          effectiveness *825*
      ranking by effectiveness gap *824*
      reading proficiency *827*
      urban enrollment *817*
  electoral volatility 70
  energy efficiency 150
  exchange rates, crisis periods *219*
  export policy 72, 395–6
  export shares by main destination, 2000
      and 2007 *332*
  export trajectory 598
  exports
      to China *464, 465*
      to Latin America *481*
      threat from China *479, 482*
  FDI
      inward *442*
      outward 453, 454
  features of public policies *61*
  fiscal policy 303
  FIT regime 199
  free trade agreements 330, 403
      with Asian countries *331*

Chile (*cont.*)
  FX market interventions 199
  GDP growth, 1990s 92
  government expenditure 272
  growth of per capita income,
      1950–2006 112
  Human Development Index 727
  imports and exports, trends 370
  inflation rates 14, 216
    1980s 193
    1990s 85
  infrastructure
    investment as percentage of GDP 677
    trends 663
  interest rates, crisis periods 218
  irrigation policies 615
  judicial independence 68
  labor laws, enforcement 806
  labor market reforms 794, 795, 797, 800, 802
  legislature capabilities 66
  liquidity 254
  macroeconomic policy, 1990s 196–7
  migration to USA and Spain 499
  monetary policy 232
  natural resource use 421
  natural resources 402–3, 408
  over-optimism 235
  party system institutionalization (PSI) 71
  pension reforms 88
  per capita GDP
    1820–2003 32
    1950 and 1980 13
  Policy Index 62
  poverty levels 717, 731–2
    evolution by dimension 734
    multidimensional measurement 733
  poverty reduction, 1990s 92–3
  productivity gaps with US 594, 595
  productivity growth 577–8, 581
  public balance as a percentage of GDP 280
  public debt, 1990s 86
  public investment 584
  real exchange rates, 1980–2008 208
    volatility 201, 202
  redistribution of income 306
  relationship between investment and
      productivity growth 585
  relative growth performance,
      1990–2008 21
  reserve accumulation 200
  RP and *KI* indices 558
  shift to export-led model 118
  size of financial system 245
  social expenditure 273, 844
    trends 845
  social protection 787
  social security coverage 780, 874
  social security reforms 879, 881
  sterilized interventions 206–7
  stock market turnover ratios 254
  Structural Surplus Rule (SSR) 280–1
  subcontracting law 786
  tariff rates, trends 321, 369
  tax revenue
    from natural resources 144
    as a percentage of GDP 269
  wage gaps 385, 387
  weighted average growth rates 11
China
  competition with LAC 469, 485
  economic growth predictions 467, 468
  as export destination 332–3
  impact on commodity price boom 484–5
  impact on LAC exports 462–3
    direct effects 463–5
    indirect effects 465–7
  increasing share in world trade 337, 339
  LAC exports
    1985–2008 463
    by sector and country 464, 465
  LAC manufacturing imports,
      characteristics and dynamism 483
  manufactured exports
    competition in regional LAC and home
      markets 480–4
    competition in world markets 475
    competitiveness with LAC 471–5
    growth 469–71, 470
  productivity growth 578
  TFP growth 581
  threat analysis 475, 479–80
Christiano, L.J. et al. 232–3
Cifuentes, L. et al., on particulate
      exposure 142

Cimoli, M., Dosi, G., and Stiglitz, J., on international comparative advantages 598
CITES (Convention on the International Trade in Endangered Species), signatories 153–4
civil rights 33
civil service capacity 64, 67–8, 69
clearing and settlement process reform implementation, 1990–2002 90
clientelist linkages, political parties 70
climate change 148–52, 153, 657
   adaptation costs 151–2
   contribution of Latin America and Caribbean 150, 151
   estimated costs 149–50
   impact on ecosystems 149
   increasing frequency of hydro-meteorological events 149
   mitigation opportunities 150
   United Nations Framework Convention 154–5
Closing the Gap in Education and Technology, World Bank, 2003 102
CMS (Convention on the Conservation of Migratory Species), signatories 153–4
CNOOC (China National Oil Offshore Corporation) 648
CNPC (China National Petroleum Corporation) 648
coalitions 337–8
coastal ecosystem degradation 142
Coatsworth, J.
   on end of nineteenth century 43
   on inequality 44
   on institutional modernization 42
   on missed opportunities 40–1
coffee production, Brazil 406
coherence of policies 58
collective action clauses 172
Collier, P. and Goderis, B., on natural resource curse 399
Collier, P. and Gunning, J., on natural resource curse 418
Colombia
   agrarian reform 615
   budget balance, 1990s 86

CCT program 736
childhood interventions 857
civil service capacity 69
conservation efforts 139
crawling peg regimes 189, 190
decentralization 282
dollarization 225
economic growth
   1997–2007 521
   in crisis periods 217
education
   average years of schooling 822
   ranking by attendance and effectiveness 825
   ranking by effectiveness gap 824
   reading proficiency 827
   urban enrollment 817
exchange rates, crisis periods 219
export shares by main destination, 2000 and 2007 332
exports, threat from China 479, 480, 482
exports to Latin America 481
FDI
   hydrocarbon sector 647
   inward 442
   outward 453
features of public policies 61
FIT regime 199
food security programs 633
GDP growth rates, 1980s 193
government expenditure 272
growth of per capita income, 1950–2006 112
Human Development Index 727
hydrocarbon sector reforms 642, 643
imports and exports, trends 370
inflation rates
   1980s 193
   1990s 85
inflation targeting 223
infrastructure
   investment as percentage of GDP 677
   trends 663
interest rates, crisis periods 218
intraregional migration 494, 496
judicial independence 68
labor laws, enforcement 806

Colombia (*cont.*)
  labor market reforms *794, 795, 797,* 800, 802
  legislature capabilities *66*
  macroeconomic policy, 1990s 196–7
  migration to USA and Spain *499*
  natural gas reserves *640*
  oil production, economic importance *640*
  oil reserves *639*
  party system institutionalization (PSI) *71*
  per capita GDP, 1820–2003 *32*
  personal income taxes *268*
  Policy Index *62*
  poverty levels *717*
    multidimensional poverty index *735*
  productivity gaps with US *594*
  public balance as a percentage of GDP *280*
  public debt, 1990s *86*
  public investment *584*
  real exchange rates, 1980–2008 *209*
    volatility *201,* 202
  redistribution of income *306*
  relative growth performance,
      1990–2008 *21*
  reserve accumulation *200*
  sector composition of employment *380*
  size of financial system *245*
  social expenditure *273, 844*
  social security reforms *879*
  stabilization funds *279–80*
  stock market turnover ratios *254*
  tariff rates, trends *321, 369*
  tax policy *270–1*
  tax revenue
    from natural resources *144*
    as a percentage of GDP *269*
  TFP growth *581*
  trade liberalization, effect on wage levels *383*
  wage gaps *385*
  weighted average growth rates *11*
  workfare program *849*
colonial heritage *32,* 39
  Marxist and structuralist approaches 36–8
  neo-institutional approaches 34–6, 45–6
commodities
  exports to China *462–3, 464–7*
  productivity gaps with US *594*
  top exports *466*

commodity boom 394–5, 552
  Brazil as beneficiary *406*
  China's impact 461–3, 484–5
    direct effects 463–5
    indirect effects 465–7
  future predictions 467–8
  trade policies *408*
commodity lottery 31
commodity power *337*
commodity subsidies *840*
Common Agricultural Policy (CAP) 335
common external tariffs (CETs) 346, 347, 363
  old and new regionalism *351, 352*
community-driven development (CDD)
      projects *841*
compensatory fiscal policy, Chile *403*
competition, in education *830*
competitiveness, exchange rates *181*
Competitiveness, IDB, 1997 102–3
Competitiveness and Growth, Andean
      Development Corporation
      (CAF) 102–3
complexity of organizations 541–3
components of colonial societies 37
COMTRADE (Commodity Trade Statistics
      Database) 462
CONAB (Compañía Nacional de
      Abastecimiento) 612
Concertación, Chile 402–3
concessions, infrastructure industries 681–2
  renegotiation 682–3
Conconi, A. and Ham, A., on poverty in
      Argentina 731
conditional cash transfers (CCTs) 699–700,
      716, 736, 756, 762–3, 842, 851
  as an educational intervention 826
  effects 852–4
    poverty reduction *853,* 856–7
  Mexico 708, 709–10
Congress, re-election rates 65
Congress Capability Indices *66*
congressional policymaking capabilities 64–5
competitive liberalization 361
Consensus-style reforms
  implementation 83–9
  outcomes 89–90
  conclusion 95

counterfactual overview 93–4
factual overview 91–3
see also Washington Consensus
conservation efforts 138–9
contributory social security systems 881
lack of universal coverage 865, 867–8
link between entitlements and
contributions 877–8
Convention Concerning the Protection of the
World Cultural and Natural Heritage,
signatories 153–4
conventional orthodoxy
comparison with new
developmentalism 120–6
defining propositions 112–13
failure 111–12
convergence 31, 45
"convertibility" regime, Argentina 58, 195–6, 197
coordination failures 527
coordination of policies 58, 261–2
copper production, Chile 402, 403, 421, 598
Copper Stabilization Fund, Chile 411
coral reef loss 142
Corden, W.M., on Dutch Disease 414
corporate bonds/GDP ratio 251
Costa Rica
adjusted savings rate 143–4
civil service capacity 68, 69
decentralization 282
economic growth 1997–2007 521
state-led industrialization period 10
education
average years of schooling 822
ranking by attendance and
effectiveness 825
ranking by effectiveness gap 824
urban enrollment 817
export shares by main destination, 2000
and 2007 332
exports
to Latin America 481
threat from China 479, 480
FDI, inward 442
features of public policies 61
government expenditure 272
growth of per capita income,
1950–2006 112

Human Development Index 727
hydrocarbon sector reforms 644
imports and exports, trends 370
Intel 451–2
judicial independence 68
labor laws, enforcement 806
legislature capabilities 66
migration to USA and Spain 499
party system institutionalization (PSI) 71
Policy Index 62
poverty levels 717
relative growth performance,
1990–2008 21
size of financial system 245
social expenditure 273, 844
trends 845
social security coverage 874
social security reforms 879–80
tariff rates, trends 321, 369
tax revenue as a percentage of GDP 269
TFP growth 581
unsatisfied basic needs (UBN) 729–30
wage gaps 385
weighted average growth rates 11
countercyclical regulation 162, 165, 178–80,
260, 759–60
country risk, relationship to stock exchange
prices 169
covariant risks 742, 743
crawling bands 193, 197
Chile 206
crawling peg regimes 7, 14, 203–4
1960s 189–90
1960s–1970s 206
1970s 191–2
1980s 193, 194
credentialism 702
credibility, in management of crises 237
credit, agricultural 612–13
credit access 762
credit rating 287
credit/GDP ratios 248, 249
creditors
dangers of 120
over-optimism 178
creeping threat, as driver of regional
integration 365–6

crises 237–8, 242, 698
    causes and effects 256–7
    as driver of change 259
    duration, relationship to product space
            density 534
    effect on employment 770–1
    emerging economies 178
    IMF lending 281
    link to booms 175, 183
    macroeconomic performance 215–16
    mistaken hypotheses 183
    monetary policy and exchange rate
            response 217–20
    relationship to financial
            development 243–4
    role of banking regulations 247
    role of pro-cyclical fiscal policies 278
    unequalizing effects 692, 697, 699, 700–1
cross-section regressions 588, 589
Cuba
    growth of per capita income,
            1981–2006 112
    hydrocarbon sector reforms 644
    migration to USA and Spain 499
    social expenditure 844
Cukierman, A., on central bank
            autonomy 230–1
CUPET 644
currency mismatches, control 165
current account deficits 168
custody arrangements, 1990–2002 90
customs unions 334
cyclical components of net capital inflows and
            real GDP, country correlations 279
cyclical conditions, discretionary fiscal policy
            response 275, 276
cyclicality of capital flows 165

De Gregorio, J., 216
De Gregorio, J., Tokman, A., and Valdés, R.,
            on FX market interventions 199
De Soto, H., Ghersi, E., and Ghibellini, M., on
            informal sector 774
de-dollarization 225–6
de-industrialization 601, 602
    see also Dutch disease
debt crisis 53, 80, 161, 553–4

1980s 15–16
    responses 193–5
    Mexico 706
    see also crises
debt cycle, virtuous 179
debt defaults, after decentralization 284
debt intolerance 226–7
debt profile improvement 165–6
debt reduction agreements 84
debts, public debt, 1990s 86
decentralization 281–2, 289, 774, 785
    accountability and efficiency 284
    bankruptcies and debt defaults 284
    effect on service delivery 282, 284
    revisions 285
    shortcomings 285
    of taxation 282–3
    transfers to subnational governments 283–4
Deepthi, F., on financial development 251
deforestation 131, 138
delegation of policy 63
delegative democracies 64
democracies 294
    association with decentralization 281
    instability 51, 52, 54
    regional integration 343
    relationship to fiscal policy 303–6
democratic legitimacy, improvement 310–12
democratization 56
demographic dependency ratio 868–9, 870
demographic transition 500, 768–9
    impact on social security systems 882–3
demographic window of opportunity 520
dependency school 39, 52
depletion effect, natural resources 415
deregulation 259, 554
    Washington Consensus 81, 82
derivatives, as source of instability 173
derivatives markets 248
    growth 168
desertification 138
devaluation
    1950s–1960s 189–90
    gradual 7, 14
development banks 247
development economics 523–4
development performance, state-led
            industrialization period 9–14

development policies 538–9
    government problems, eliciting
        information 539–41
development process
    changes in export composition 525
    diversification 524
development stage, differences between
        countries 109
development strategies 7–8
developmentalism
    national 108, 110, 111
    new 113–16
        comparison with conventional
            orthodoxy 120–6
        comparison with national
            developmentalism 116–20, 119
        conclusion 126
DFBETA measure 423
Di John, J., on Venezuela 420
Diana, G. and Sidiropoulos, M., on central
        bank autonomy 231
Díaz, Porfirio 417
Diaz-Alejandro, C.,
    on Crises 161
    on financial reforms 182
    on liberalization 242
diesel
    price 146–7
    sulfur content 141–2
diffusion 552–3, 562
    catching-up 549
directed credit 7
discretionary fiscal policy response 275, 276
discriminant analysis, in measurement of
        poverty 723
dispute settlement, old and new
        regionalism 351, 353
distance between products 529–30
distortions 599
diversification 398
    association with development 524
    benefits 747–8
    private capital flows 167–72
diversity 31, 42
Doha Declaration of Public Health 338
dollar-denominated liabilities 224
dollarization 221, 222, 236
    Ecuador and El Salvador 198

effect on liquidity provision 256
partial 223–6
Peru 200
domestic competition index (DCI) 481
domestic forces, study of 39–40
domestic investment ratio 168
domestic production, competition from
        China 484
domestic savings 87
    1970–2008 89
domestic services, informal
        employment 778, 779
Dominican Republic
    CCT program 736
    central bank dominance of fiscal
        policy 228
    civil service capacity 69
    economic growth, 1997–2007 521
    FDI, inward 442
    financial crisis 242, 246
    Human Development Index 727
    hydrocarbon sector reforms 645
    imports and exports, trends 370
    judicial independence 68
    labor laws, enforcement 806
    labor market reforms 794
    legislature capabilities 66
    migration to USA and Spain 499
    party system institutionalization
        (PSI) 71
    Policy Index 62
    poverty levels, multidimensional poverty
        index 735
    public policies 61
    relative growth performance,
        1990–2008 21
    size of financial system 245
    social expenditure 844
        trends 845
    social security coverage 874
    social security reforms 879
    tariff rates, trends 321, 369
    tax revenue
        from natural resources 144
        as a percentage of GDP 269
    TFP growth 581
    wage gaps 385
    weighted average growth rates 11

Donghi, H., "great delay" 39
DR-CAFTA 328, 363
drinking water supplies 142, 146
drought, increasing frequency *149*
dual divergence 112
dual economies 114
Duryea, S. and Székely, M., on quantity of
    education 814
Dutch disease (deindustrialization) 114, 116,
    395, 399–400, 414, *601*, *602*
  and Brazil 406
  neutralization 117, 118, 125, 418
dynamic exports 559
dysfunctions 252, 263
  relationship to financial structure 262
  relationships to structural features
    259–60, 262

Earth Summit (Rio, 1992) 145
East Asian crisis 161, 162
Easterly, W., Loayza, N., and Montiel, P., on
    trade liberalization 375
ECLAC (Economic Commission for Latin
    America and Caribbean) 110, 345
  Equity, Development, and Citizenship 104
  Productive Transformation with Equity 104
  *Structural Change and Productivity
    Growth* 102
econometric studies, Consensus-style
    reforms 93–4
Economic Complementarity Agreements 346
economic cycles, impact on political
    systems 52
economic development 546
economic growth 293, 523–4
  1980s onwards 20–1
  1997–2007 *521*
  China, future predictions 467, 468
  comparison of new developmentalism and
    conventional orthodoxy *123*
  contribution of increased schooling *522*
  difference from human development 412
  effect of "bad" institutions 43
  effect of Consensus-style reforms 91–2, 94, 95
  effect of crawling pegs 190
  effect of financial crisis 216, *217*

effect of inequality 44–5
effect of trade liberalization 374, *375*, 388
evolutionary approach 548–9
failure of conventional orthodoxy 111–12
growth rates of population and per capita
    GDP, 1500–1820 and 2001 *30*
growth strategies 99
international 27, 30–1
Latin American puzzle 523–4
  explanations 536–9
link to financial development 241, 243
links with capital flows 174–80
neo-classical interpretations 519–22
per capita GDP
  1500–2001 *28*
  1820–2003 *32*
population and GDP, 1500–2001 *29*
postwar phases *551–4*
pre-state-led industrialization 8–9
primary-product exporters 397–8
relationship to infrastructure 670, *671*,
    672–4, 684
relationship to learning 550–1, 563–4
relationship to macroeconomic
    volatility 745
relationship to natural resources 411–12,
    425, *426*, 427–8
relationship to poverty 751–2
relationship to trade policy 318
relative growth performances,
    1990–2008 *21*
as source of uncertainty *747*
state-led industrialization period 9–14
structuralist approach 547–8
unequal distribution 42
economic insecurity 741–2
  challenges 742–3
  conclusions 763
  financial volatility 749–50
  labor market vulnerability 752–5
  macroeconomic volatility 743–5
  poverty reduction strategies *757*
    labor protection and social
      policies 760–3
    risk mitigation 758–60
  poverty risk 751–2
  role of trade shocks 747–9

economic integration 23
economic orthodoxy 15
economic slowdown, effect on
       productivity 573–7
economies of scale 524
ECOPETROL 646, 647, 649
   modernization 643
Ecuador
   adjusted savings rate 143
   adoption of US dollar 198
   CCT program 736
   civil service capacity 68, 69
   conditional cash transfers (CCTs) 852, 853
   conservation efforts 138–9
   decentralization 282
   economic growth
       1997–2007 521
       state-led industrialization period 10
   education
       average years of schooling 822
       ranking by attendance and
          effectiveness 825
       ranking by effectiveness gap 824
       urban enrollment 817
   energy intensity 136, 137
   export shares by main destination, 2000
       and 2007 332
   FDI
       hydrocarbon sector 647, 648
       inward 442
   financial crisis 242
   government expenditure 272
   hydrocarbon sector reforms, Law 42 642
   imports and exports, trends 370
   judicial independence 68
   labor laws, enforcement 806
   labor market reforms 794, 795, 800
   legislature capabilities 66
   migration to USA and Spain 499
   oil production, economic importance 640
   oil reserves 639
   oil stabilization fund 279
   party system institutionalization (PSI) 71
   per capita income, growth, 1950–2006 112
   Policy Index 62
   poverty levels 717
       multidimensional poverty index 735

   public policies 61
   relative growth performance,
       1990–2008 21
   size of financial system 245
   social expenditure 273, 844
   social security coverage 873
   tariff rates, trends 321, 369
   tax revenue as a percentage of GDP 269
   TFP growth 581
   wage gaps 385
   weighted average growth rates 11
education 813–14
   conclusions 833–4
   effect of conditional cash transfers 852
   effect of decentralization 284
   international expenditure, 2006 102
   pre-school enrollment 857
   quality 273, 826–8
       expenditure inputs 828–30
       student effort and school
          productivity 830–2
   quantity
       age-enrollment profiles 815–16
       average years of schooling 814
       policy emphasis 833
       prospects for progress 825–6
       summary of country-level
          performance 824–5
       urban enrollment 816–18, 817
       years in school and years of
          schooling 819–24
Education Index 12
education spending 307
   relationship to performance 308
educational levels
   improvement 520, 769
       contribution to growth 522
   international migrants 506–7
   relationship to income inequality
       699, 707
   wage gaps 384, 385
effectiveness gap, education 823–4
efficiency of policies 58–9, 60–1
efficiency-seeking FDI 450
   apparel industry 451
   automobile industry in Mexico 450–1
   Intel in Costa Rica 451–2

El Salvador
  adoption of US dollar 198
  civil service capacity 69
  decentralization 282
  education
    average years of schooling 822
    ranking by attendance and effectiveness 825
    ranking by effectiveness gap 824
    urban enrollment 817
  electoral volatility 70
  emigration 513
  export shares by main destination, 2000
      and 2007 332
  FDI 442
  government expenditure 272
  Human Development Index 727
  imports and exports, trends 370
  judicial independence 68
  labor laws, enforcement 806
  labor market reforms 794
  legislature capabilities 66
  migration to USA and Spain 499
  party system institutionalization (PSI) 71
  Policy Index 62
  poverty levels 717
    evolution by dimension 734
    multidimensional measurement 731–2, 733
  public policies 61
  relative growth performance,
      1990–2008 21
  size of financial system 245
  social expenditure 273, 844
  social security coverage 873
  tariff rates, trends 321, 369
  tax revenue as a percentage of GDP 269
  TFP growth 581
  unsatisfied basic needs (UBN) 730
  wage gaps 385
  weighted average growth rates 11
  electoral rules 65
  electoral volatility 69–70
  electric power
    access to services 662–3, 668, 669
    generation capacity, trends 662–3, 664
    investment as percentage of GDP 677
    service quality, trends 662–3, 665–7
  elites, lack of power 40, 41

EMBRAPA 614
emerging economies (EEs)
  crises 178
  supply of funds 172
emigration 488–9
  see also international migration;
      intraregional migration; migrants to
      USA and Spain
employment
  1950–2008 575–6
  impact of Chinese imports 484
  effect of demographic transition 768–9
  effect of economic slowdown 573
  impact of globalization 490–1
  effect of reforms 769–73
  effect of trade liberalization 377–82, 388
  informal 753–5, 767–8, 772, 773–5
  see also informal sector
  instability 752–3, 775
  migrants to USA and Spain 508–12, 514
  rural, effects of structural reforms 628–9
  vulnerability 785–6
  women's participation 628–9, 769
  workfare programs 848–50
  see also labor market reforms
employment dependency ratio 868
employment elasticities 604
  1950–2008 575–6
  excessive labor market flexibility 590–1
  political economy issues 587, 589
  relationship to investment growth 588, 589–92
  sectoral analysis 587
employment protection, relationship to
      political ideology 801–2
employment relationships, ill-defined 786
ENAP 646, 647, 649
ENARSA 643
encaje, Colombia 223
energy balance, heterogeneity 637–8, 639
energy demand 636–7
energy integration 654–5, 657
energy intensity 136–7
energy sector, investment perspectives 648
energy sources 134, 136, 146–7
  renewable 651–2, 656
    biofuels 652–4
    see also hydrocarbon sector

energy use by sector *638*
enforcement of policies 58, *60–1*, 63
enforcement ratio, labor laws 804–5, *806*
Engerman, S. and Sokoloff, K., on colonial
    heritage 35
enhanced demographic dependency
    ratio 869, *870*
environment
  adjusted savings rates 143–4
  biodiversity 137–8
  climate change 148–52
  consequences of natural resource-driven
    development 134
  conservation efforts 138–9
  fertilizer and pesticide use 139–40
  greenhouse gas emissions 139
  land use changes 138
  multilateral agreements 153–6
  soil degradation 139
  urban 140–2
environmental conflicts 145
environmental expenditures 145
environmental policies 144–5
  Global Green New Deal 147–8
  implicit 146
  loss of impetus 145–6
  urgent activities 146
environmental sustainability 100, 130
  conclusions 152–3
equilibrium, determining variables 231–2
equity, absence from Washington
    Consensus 103–4
Equity, Development, and Citizenship,
    ECLAC, 2000 104
equity investment, volatility risks 169, 172
Escaith, H. and Morley, S.
  study of Consensus-style reforms 94
  on trade liberalization 372, 374, *375*
Esquivel, G., Lustig, N., and Scott, J., on
    Mexican income inequality 708–9
Estevadeordal, A., Freund, C., and Ornelas, E.,
    on regional integration 358
ethanol
  biofuel mix for gasoline and diesel *654*
  production as biofuel 652–3
Ethier, W., on new regionalism 348
Euro-African societies 37–8

Euro-American societies 38
Euro-Indian societies 37
European countries, redistribution of
    income 306
European Economic Community (EEC) 323, 335
European Union
  free trade agreements 332, 334
  TFP growth *581*
evolutionary approach to economic
    development 548–9
exchange controls 5, 14
exchange rate-based stabilization programs,
    trade-offs 204
exchange rate instability, effects 181
exchange rate populism 115
exchange rates 187, 220–3, *221*, 760
  1970s 190–2
  1980s 192–5
  1990s 195–8
  2000s 198–203
  comparison of new developmentalism and
    conventional orthodoxy *123*, 125
  crawling pegs 203–4
  crisis periods 217–20, *219*, *220*
  floating 204–5
  FX market interventions 205
  historical overview, 1950s and
    1960s 188–90
  as instrument of growth 125
  new developmentalism 117
  overvaluation 179, 180
  relationship to financial flows 168
  relationship to net capital inflows *177*
  stability, importance 181
  tendency towards overvaluation 114–15,
    116, 126
  Washington Consensus 81, 83
  see also real exchange rates
expansion to new areas 39, 46
export-enabling growth strategy 599
export-led growth 43
  advantages 118
  collapse 4–6
export pessimism 118
export-processing zones (EPZs) 451
export products, distance to quality
    frontier 535–6

export promotion policies 7, 14, 72, 319–20
export quality 596–7
export sophistication
   relationship to economic growth 537
   relationship to GDP 525–7, 526
"export subsidization," Rodrik's study 55
export trajectories 597–8
exports
   Adaptability Index (*AI*) 559
   agro-food products 624, 625
     destinations 626
   to China
     1985–2008 463
     by sector and country 464, 465
   composition by category,
     1990–2006 135
   destinations, 2000 and 2007 332–3
   geographical structure 357
   impact of Chinese demand 462–3
     direct effects 463–5
     indirect effects 465–7
   product structure 356
   relationship to GDP growth 595–6
   top commodities 466
   total value by subregional integration
     scheme 325–6
   trends 319, 322, 370, 371
   see also manufactured exports
external flexibility
   labor market reforms 792–3, 794–5
   relationship to executive ideology *801*
external shocks 23
   impact on aggregate demand *175*
external vulnerabilities 226–7
externalities 524
   self-discovery 528

Facing up to Inequality in Latin America,
   IDB, 1998 104
Fanelli, J.M., on financial crises 257
fear of floating 199
Federal Reserve 222
feeding programs 840, 847–8
Fernández-Arias, E. and Montiel, P.
   study of Consensus-style reforms 94
   on trade liberalization 375

Ferreira, F. et al., on Brazilian income
   inequality 703, 704
fertility rate 520
fertilizer production 632
fertilizer use 132, 139–40
fertilizer-use subsidies 612
Ffrench-Davis, R., on gap between actual and
   potential GDP 179
Ffrench-Davis, R. and Griffith-Jones, S., on
   preconditions for capital flows 179
Ffrench-Davis, R. and Ocampo, J.A., on
   volatility 101
FGT index (α-measure of poverty) 718
financial crises 23, 161, 162
   growth outcomes 216
   implications of resulting regulations 172
   inflation rates and volatility 215–16
   see also crises
financial development 241–2
   cluster analysis 248
   coordination of policies 261–2
   determinants 243
   drivers of change 259
   functional approach 258, 260
   institution-building 262–3
   institutional change 259–60
   legal and judicial framework 261
   link to economic growth 243
   macroeconomic policy 260–1
   relationship to crises and international
     financial integration 243–4
   role of dysfunctionalities 259
financial intermediation 182
financial liberalization 17–18, 87, 111
financial liberalization index, 1973–2002 *88*
financial reforms 181–2
   advance 1989–1999 *91*
financial sector, state participation 632
financial stability, trade-off with price stability 223
financial structure, relationship to
   dysfunctions and regulations 262
financial systems, stylized facts
   banks and markets 248–51
   regulatory changes 246–8
   size 244–6, *245*
financial volatility 749–50
financialization 745, 749

financierism 182
financieristic bias 181–2
financieristic trap 163
firewood production *132*, 133
'first-best' policies 569, 599, 603, 605
fiscal balance, impact of capital flows 180
fiscal capacity 266–7
    expenditures 271–4
    taxation 267–71
fiscal decentralization 267
fiscal discipline 84
    Washington Consensus 81
fiscal equilibrium, new
        developmentalism 120
fiscal legitimacy 304–5
    improvement 310–12
fiscal pacts 304
fiscal policy 266, 289, 294
    decentralization 281–5
    improvement 306–9
    interactions with monetary policy 227–30
    pro-poor policies 759
    relationship to democratic
        legitimacy 303–6
    stabilization 274–81
    sustainability of public finance 285–9
fiscal policy measures, comparison with
        OECD countries 296
fiscal reforms 303, 307
fiscal revenues, comparison with OECD
        countries 296
fiscal spending, pledges for progressivity 295
fiscal standards, comparison of new
        developmentalism and conventional
        orthodoxy *123*, *125*
fiscal systems, comparison with OECD
        countries 295–303
fiscal vulnerabilities 226–7
fish production *132*, 133
Fiszbein, A. and Schady, N., on conditional
        cash transfers 736, 852
flexible exchange rate regimes 220–2, 223
flexicurity model 791–2, 795, 798, 808
"flight capital" taxation 87
floating and inflation targeting (FIT)
        regimes 198–200
    RER volatility *201–2*

floating exchange rates 190–1, 204–5
floods, increasing frequency *149*
food crisis 632
food security programs 633, 840, 847–8
foreign banks 247
foreign countries constraint, developing
        countries 115
foreign direct investment (FDI) 438, 552,
        605, *646*
    conclusions 456–7
    environmental consequences 134
    growth 168
    hydrocarbon sector *647–8*
    inflows and outflows, 1990–2008 *439*
    inward
        classification 443–4
        costs and benefits 439–41
        distribution in Latin America *442*
        efficiency-seeking 450–2
        market-seeking investment 446–50
        natural resource-seeking
            investment 444–6
        origin of flows *443*
        sectoral distribution *444*
        strategic asset-seeking 451–2
    old and new regionalism *351*, 353
    outward 452–5
    policy implications 457
    two waves (1994–2003 and
        2004–2008) 441–3
    volatility 168–9
    Washington Consensus 81
foreign exchange (FX) market
        interventions 199–200, 205, 232
foreign exchange policy 180–1
    see also exchange rates
foreign exchange reserves *170*, 173
foreign investment 8
    comparison of new developmentalism and
        conventional orthodoxy *123*, *124*
forest, as proportion of land area *138*
forest fires, increasing frequency *149*
forest loss 131
forestry 133
formal dependency ratio 869, *870*
formal institutions 33
fossil fuel use 134–5, 136, 637

Foucault, M., on development of social
      sciences 570
fracasomania 569
fragmentation of business groups 72
free trade agreements 7, 17, 323–31, 349,
      359–61, 610–11
   bilateral 328, 346, 610
   Chile 403
   dates of implementation 348
   institutional structure 353
   North–South agreements 364–5
   proliferation in the Americas 365
   role in labor laws enforcement 805, 807–8,
      809–10
   trans-continentalism 331–4
Free Trade Area of the Americas (FTAA) 327,
      333–4, 337, 349, 359–61
   negotiations structure 360
   role in energy integration 655
Freund, C. and Ozden, C., on impact of
      Chinese export growth 474–5
Frieden, J. 53
fuel prices 146–7, 148
functional view of financial development 243
funding liquidity 253, 254
Furtado, C., *Plano Trienal* 120
fuzzy-set theory, poverty measurement 725

G-₁₁ 338
G-₂₀ 337
G-₃₃ 338
Galindo, L. and Ros, J., on Mexican FIT
      regime 202
garbage disposal 142
García Herrero, A. et al.
   on banking system 252
   cluster analysis of financial
      development 248
Garduño, H., on water rights markets 616
gas pipelines 649, 656
   export capacity 650
gas production, FDI 444–6
Gasparini, L. and Cruces, G., on Argentinean
      income inequality 700–3
GATT (General Agreement on Tariffs and
      Trade) 319, 320, 322, 334, 345, 609–10
   Uruguay Round 335, 336

Gavin, M. and Perotti, R., analysis of
      1970–1995 period 298
GDP
   1500–2001 29
   1950–2008 575–6
   accumulated increase 132
   growth rates
      effect of financial crisis 216, 217
      see also economic growth
   instability 174
   relationship to aggregate demand 175–6
Geddes, B. 53
gender differentiation
   economic activity of migrants to Spain and
      USA 508, 509
   emigration 503–5
   employment sectors of migrants to Spain
      and USA 509–10
   social security coverage 872–5
*General Theory of Employment, Interest and
      Money, The*, John Maynard Keynes 5
geothermal energy 652
German Historical School 122
"getting the prices right" 17
Gini coefficients 93, 693
   see also income inequality
Global Environment Facility 151
Global Environmental Outlook (GEO-4),
      UNEP 2007 137–8
Global Green New Deal 147–8
global warming *see* climate change
globalization 131, 358–9
   first boom 43, 44
   international migration 490–1
   second wave 190–1
globalization studies 46
gold standard, abandonment 5
Goni, E., López, H., and Servén, L., on
      personal income taxes 268
government expenditures 271–4
   comparison with OECD countries 296,
      298, 299, 301–2, 302
   effect of pro-cyclical fiscal policies 276
   pro-cyclicality 275
   reforms 307–9, 310, 311
government revenues
   comparison with OECD countries 298, 299
   composition 300–1

governments
    eliciting information 539–41
    participation in social security reforms 877
    problems handling complexity 541–3
    size
        comparison with OECD countries 297
        stabilizing role 277
gradual devaluation policies 7, 14
"great delay" 39
Great Depression 3, 4–5
"great divergence," international relative
        growth rates 27
Greece, per capita GDP, 1950 and 1980 13
greenhouse gas emissions 139, 150
    relationship to GDP 151
Griffith-Jones, S. and Ocampo, J.A., on
        international financial reform 161–2
gross enrollment ratio, relationship to natural
        resources 426, 430
growth collapses, duration, relationship to
        product space density 534
Growth Commission Report, 2008 101
growth strategies 99
growth volatility 744, 745
Guasch, J., on renegotiation of
        concessions 682–3
Guatemala
    CCT program 736
    civil service capacity 69
    conservation efforts 139
    decentralization 282
    economic growth, 1997–2007 521
    education
        average years of schooling 822
        ranking by attendance and
            effectiveness 825
        ranking by effectiveness gap 824
        urban enrollment 817
    electoral volatility 70
    export shares by main destination, 2000
        and 2007 333
    FDI 442
    government expenditure 272
    Human Development Index 727
    imports and exports, trends 370
    judicial independence 68
    labor laws, enforcement 806
    labor market reforms 794

legislature capabilities 66
migration to USA and Spain 499
oil production 645
party system institutionalization (PSI) 71
Policy Index 62
poverty levels 717
    multidimensional poverty index 735
public policies 61
relative growth performance,
        1990–2008 21
size of financial system 245
social expenditure 273, 844
social security coverage 873
tariff rates, trends 321, 369
tax policy 271
tax revenue
    from natural resources 144
    as a percentage of GDP 269
TFP growth 581
unsatisfied basic needs (UBN) 730
wage gaps 385
weighted average growth rates 11
Guyana, multidimensional poverty index 735

Haber, S., on Mexican banking system 252
Haber, S., Razo, A., and Maurer, N., on
        Mexican property rights 417–18
hacienda system 38
Haiti
    economic growth, 1997–2007 521
    energy consumption 137
    migration to USA and Spain 499
    multidimensional poverty index 735
Haltiwanger, J. et al., on effects of trade
        liberalization 382
Hammill, M., on UBN 729
Hammond, G., on inflation targeting 231
Hanson, G. and Harrison, A., on Mexican
        income inequality 707
Hanson, G. and Robertson, R.,, on export
        capabilities 472
Hausmann, R. and Klinger, B., on product
        space 529–31
Hausmann, R. and Powell, A., on liquidity
        provision 222
Hausmann, R. and Rodríguez, F., on
        Venezuela 419

Hausmann, R. and Rodrik, D.
   on information spillovers 527–8
   on specificity of capabilities 529
Hausmann, R. et al., on growth
      accelerations 206
Hausmann, R. , Hwang, and Rodrik, on
      income level of exports 525, 526
Hausmann, R., Rodríguez, F., and Wagner, R.
   on crisis duration 534
   on natural resource curse 415–16
Hausmann, R., Rodrik, D., and Velasco, A.,
      on outcome of reforms 98
health, effect of conditional cash
      transfers 852, 854
health care spending 307
health coverage 753–4, 755, 850
   access for informal workers 787
   effect of reforms 773
   see also social protection
Heckman, J. and Pagés, C., on labor market
      regulation 792
Heckman, J. et al., on returns to childhood
      interventions 857
Hemispheric Energy Initiative 654–5
hemispheric integration 366
Herrera, L.O. and Valdés, R., on
      dollarization 225–6
heterodox stabilization programs 194
hierarchies, problems with complexity 541–2
Hirschman, A. 523–4
   on industrialization 6, 15
   on "les trente glorieuses" 10
Historia económica de América Latina,
      Cardoso, C.F.S and Pérez Brignoli, H.
      37–9, 41–2
Honduras
   adjusted savings rate 143–4
   civil service capacity 69
   decentralization 282
   economic growth, 1997–2007 521
   education
      age-enrollment profiles 815
      average years of schooling 822
      quantity 820–1
      ranking by attendance and
         effectiveness 825
      ranking by effectiveness gap 824

reading proficiency 827
urban enrollment 817
energy consumption 137
export shares by main destination, 2000
      and 2007 333
FDI 442
features of public policies 61
government expenditure 272
Human Development Index 727
imports and exports, trends 370
judicial independence 68
labor laws, enforcement 806
legislature capabilities 66
migration to USA and Spain 499
party system institutionalization (PSI) 71
poverty levels 717
   multidimensional poverty index 735
relative growth performance,
      1990–2008 21
social expenditure 273, 844
social security coverage 873
tariff rates, trends 321, 369
tax revenue as a percentage of GDP 269
TFP growth 581
unsatisfied basic needs (UBN) 730
wage gaps 385
weighted average growth rates 11
Honohan, P., on deposit dollarization 224
Hoxby, C., on school productivity 829
Human Development Index (HDI) 12, 721–2
   correlation with natural resource
      abundance 412, 413
   relationship to natural resources 426, 427,
      432, 433
      data and empirical methodology 422–3
      results 423–5
      regional interactions 425, 432
      variable definitions 434
   trends 728
human development indicators, lack of
      correlation with economic
      growth 412
Human Poverty Index (HPI) 722
Humphreys, M., Sachs, J., and Stiglitz, J., on
      natural resource curse 415
Hwang, J., on within-product distance to
      quality frontier 534–5

hydrocarbon sector
  economic importance 638, *640*, 641
  foreign direct investment 647–8
  investment perspectives 648
  natural gas and LNG markets 649–50, 656
  oil multinationals 648–9
  reforms 656
    energy deficient countries 644–5
    producing countries 641–4
  state-owned and mixed enterprises 645–7
  see also natural gas reserves; oil
    production
hydroelectricity use 136, 651, 652
  energy integration 654
hyperbolic discounting 838
hyperpresidentialism 64
hysteresis phenomenon *550*, 560–1, 564

Iberian tradition 570
ICT hardware industry
  Brazil 449
  Intel, Costa Rica 451–2
idiosyncratic risks 742
igniting growth 99
Ilzetski, E. and Végh, C., on pro-cyclicality of
    public expenditures 275
Imbs, J. and Wacziarg, R., on development
    process 524
immigration, international 488
implementation of policies 58, *60–1*
implementation problems, Washington
    Consensus 96–7
implicit environmental policies 145, 146
Import Substitution Industrialization (ISI) 3,
    51, 53, 117, 317, 345, 395, 552, 553
  Argentina 400, 401
  effects 602
  foreign direct investment 440
  rationalization 6–7
  shift away 80, 569
  Venezuela 404
imports
  agro-food products 624, *625*
  composition by category, 1990–2006 *135*
  geographical structure *357*
  manufactured, from China *483*

  product structure *356*
  trends *370*, 371
Impossibilism 294
in-kind transfers 840, 847–8
income, relationship to social security
    coverage *872*
income distributions 694–5
income elasticity ratio 547
income inequality 691–2, 710
  Argentina 700–3, *701*
  Brazil 703–6, *704*
  'excessive' 693–4
  Gini coefficients 693
  influencing factors 696–700
  Mexico 706–10, *707*
  relationship to infrastructure 670, *671*, 672
  trends 695–6, 698–9
income policy, comparison of new
    developmentalism and conventional
    orthodoxy *123*, 126
increasing returns, technological
    capabilities 550–1
independence 39
Index of Family Development 730
indexation 224
India
  poverty levels 603
  TFP growth *581*
indirect taxation, comparison with OECD
    countries 299–301
Indonesia, productivity growth *578*, 579
industrial emissions 142
industrial employment, effect of trade
    liberalization 379–80
industrial planning, old and new
    regionalism *351*, 352
industrial policies 17
  absence in 1990s 554
  new developmentalism 119
Industrial Revolution 40, 41, 46
industrialization 5–7
  differences from resource-based
    activities 523
  macroeconomic policies in the
    periphery 4–5
  new paradigm 16–18
  as source of inequality 40

industrialization (*cont.*)
    state intervention 7–9 *see also* state-led
        industrialization
    technological learning 552–3
industry, fuel consumption 638
inequality 33, 41, 46, 59, 305, 309, 691
    in education 830–1
    effect of Consensus-style reforms 93, 94
    impact on growth 44–5
    in late nineteenth century 43–4
    political effects 53
    reduction 294, 295
    relationship to infrastructure 670, *671, 672*
    as result of globalization 491
    as result of industrialization 40
    role of tax policy 268
    in social expenditure 273–4
    wage gaps 384–7, 388–9
    Washington Consensus 103–4 *see also*
        income inequality
*Inequality in Latin America and the
    Caribbean*, World Bank, 2004 104
inflation rates 14, 236
    1980s 193–4
    1981–2009 *215–16*
    1990s 84, *85*
    effect of crawling pegs 190
    new developmentalism 120
    relationship to income inequality 703
inflation targeting 223, 231, 232, 255
inflation volatility *744, 745*
information acquisition, governments 539–41
informal employment 767–8
informal institutions 33
informal sector 772
    access to social protection 779–81
    conceptualization 773–5
    dimensions, structure and country
        diversity 776–7
    employment structure 778–9
    social security coverage 872–5
    strategy for inclusion and
        opportunities 782–3
        ill-defined employment
            relationships 786
        insecurity, vulnerability, and atypical
            contracts 785–6

labor rights 784–5
micro-enterprise regulations 783
social security access 787
    as a voluntary option 781–2
information spillovers 527–8
infrastructure 659–60
    access to services 668–9
    conclusions 684–5
    coordination failures 527
    fiscal dimensions 678–9
    foreign direct investment 440, 446–8
    investment as percentage of GDP *676, 677*
    private sector participation 679–84
    role in growth and development 670–4
    roles of public and private sectors 674–6
    trends 660–1
        availability 661–4
        quality 664–7
infrastructure development 8
infrastructure gap 660, 669
infrastructure investment, decline *750, 751*
infrastructure spending 274
    effect of pro-cyclical fiscal policies 276
Initiative for a Green Economy 147
Initiative for the Integration of the Regional
    Infrastructure of South America
    (IIRSA) 363–4
innovation 456, 562
    absence from Washington
        Consensus 101–3
    catching-up 549
    economies of scale 524
    in models of growth 524
    NSI 551, 553, 563
    self-discovery 527–8
insider trading laws, establishment
    1990–2002 90
institution-building 262–3
institutional analysis, New Institutional
    Economics 33–4
institutional change 258, 259–60
institutional modernization 42–3
institutional weakness, resource dependent
    states 416–17
institutions
    absence from Washington Consensus 101
    distrust of 294–5

in new developmentalism 122
old and new regionalism *351, 353*
instrument-based organizations 542
integrated social security systems 879, 880, 881
Intel, establishment in Costa Rica 451–2
intellectual property rights 336–7, 338
Inter-American Development Bank (IDB)
  Competitiveness 102–3
  on dollarization 224–5
  Facing up to Inequality in Latin
    America 104
  Latin America after a Decade of
    Reforms 101
  Overcoming Volatility 100
inter-temporal adjustment,
  destabilizing 175–7
interest payments, comparison with OECD
  countries 301–2
interest rate spreads 252
interest rates 124
  crisis periods 217, *218*
  in management of bubbles 236
  Washington Consensus 81, 83
international capital markets, growth 162
international financial institutions, liquidity
  provision 256
international financial reform 162
international migration 488–90, 491–2
  age structure 500–3
  characteristics of migrant populations *493*
  conclusions 513–14
  in context of globalization 490–1
  emigration 492
  gender differences 503–5
  immigrants, emigrants and net migration *495*
  net migration 494
  USA and Spain as destinations *497–8, 499*
    sociodemographic profiles of migrants
    499–507
  see also migrants to Spain and USA
International Monetary Fund (IMF)
  control of exchange rate
    adjustments 188–9
  liquidity provision 256
  role in avoidance of pro-cyclical fiscal
    policies 281
  role in paradigm shift 16

international relations, and New Institutional
  Economics 34
intertemporal pattern, political
  interactions 63
intertemporal transactions 57
intra-household pollution 140
intra-industry trade *357*
intraregional migration 489, 492
  patterns *494, 496–7*
investment
  energy sector 648
  role of state, comparison of new
    developmentalism and conventional
    orthodoxy *123*, 124
investment growth
  relationship to employment
    elasticities *588*, 589–92
  relationship to productivity growth 585–7, *588*
investment patterns, comparison with Asian
  economies *582*
investment rates, comparison with Asian
  economies 579–84
investment volatility *744, 745, 753*
inward FDI
  1990–2008 *439*
  classification 443–4
  conclusions 456–7
  costs and benefits 439–41
  distribution in Latin America *442*
  efficiency-seeking 450–2
  market-seeking investment 446–50
  natural resource-seeking
    investment 444–6
  origin of flows *443*
  sectoral distribution *444*
  strategic asset-seeking 451–2
  two waves (1994–2003 and
    2004–2008) 441–3
inward-looking phase 318
Ireland, TFP growth *581*
irrigation policies 615–16
ISEB (Instituto Superior de Estudos
  Brasilieros) 110
Isham, J. et al., on point source resources 398
issue-specific trade alliances 338–9
Italy
  per capita GDP, 1950 and 1980 *13*

Ize, A. and Levy-Yeyati, E., on
  dollarization 224–5
Izquierdo, A. and Talvi, E., on current
  account and fiscal surpluses 227

Jâcome, L. and Vásquez, F., on central bank
  autonomy 231
Jamaica
  conditional cash transfers 736, 853
  imports and exports, trends 370
  social expenditure 844
    trends 845
  tariff rates, trends 369
Japan
  FDI 443
  per capita GDP, 1950 and 1980 13
Jenkins, R.
  on Chinese impact on domestic market 484
  on manufactured exports 472, 474
job creation, 1990s 93
judicial activism 67
judicial framework 261
judicial independence 67, 68

Kaminsky, G. and Reinhart, C., on twin banking
  and credit crises 256–7
Kaminsky, G. and Schmukler, S., financial
  liberalization index 87
Kaminsky, G., Reinhart, C., and Végh, C.,, on
  pro-cyclical behavior 178
Karl, T.L., on natural resource curse 416–17, 418
Kelvin, Lord 569
Keynes, John Maynard
  The General Theory of Employment, Interest
    and Money 5
  on public deficits 119
Klinger, B., on Peruvian self-discovery
  externalities 528
knowledge, absence from Washington
  Consensus 101–3
Korea, TFP growth 581
Krueger, A.O. 15
Krugman Index (KI) 556–7, 558
Kyoto Protocol 151, 152
  signatories 155–6

labor contracts 772, 778
  atypical 785–6
  social security coverage 779–81, 780
labor deregulations 698
labor insertion 779
labor legislation 593, 775
  enforcement 804
    role of trade agreements 805, 807–8
    trends 804–5, 806
  historical analysis 791–2
labor market
  effect of economic instability 752–5
  effect of trade liberalization 371, 376–7
    aggregate employment 378–9
    employment mobility, stability, and
      informality 381–2
    sector composition of
      employment 379–81
    unemployment 377–8
    wage gaps 384–7
    wage levels 383–4
  flexibility 589, 590–1, 604
  liberalization 18
  strength, effect on income inequality 699,
    700
  women's participation 628–9, 769
labor market reforms 790
  1989–1999 91
  conclusions 808–10
  external flexibility 792–3, 794–5
  flexicurity 798
  patterns 798–800, 799
  political and economic
    determinants 800–1
    politics of employment
      protection 801–2
    politics of personal compensation 803–4
    politics of unemployment
      insurance 802–3
  unemployment insurance 795–7
labor productivity, 1950–2008 575–6
labor protection policies 760–3
labor rights, informal sector 784–5
labor supply, developing countries 114
labor training, spillovers 528
Laeven, L. and Valencia, F., on crises 257
Lall, S. and Weiss, J.

on Chinese export market shares *473–4*
on export structures *471–2*
land, foreign ownership 632
land cultivation, changes 617–18, *619–20*
land redistribution processes 615, 632
land reform programs 762
landslides, increasing frequency *149*
land use changes 138, 139
  biofuel production 653
Landes, D.
  on institutions 34
  on natural resource curse 396
Landless Workers Movement 615
Larida proposal 196
Latin America after a Decade of Reforms, IDB,
  1997 101
Latin American Economic Outlook 2009,
  OECD 2008 293–4
Latin American Free Trade Association
  (LAFTA) 323, 346
Latin American Integration Association
  (LAIA) 323, 346
  total exports, 1990–2007 325
"Latin American Manifesto," CEPAL (1949) 6
Law of the Sea, signatories *153–4*
learning protection 549
Lederman, D. and Maloney, W., on natural
  resources 399, 412, 415, 418–19, 422
legal framework 261
legislature capabilities 66
legislatures 64–5
Legovini, A., Bouillon, C., and Lustig, N., on
  Mexican income inequality 706–7
Levine, R., on financial development 243
Levy, S., on social insurance 855–6
Lewis, A. 523
Lewis-type economy 114
liberal reforms 39, 41–2, 46
liberalization 241–2
  association with crises 257
  see also trade liberalization
life expectancy 520
  demographic transition 768
  relationship to natural resources *426, 431*
Life-Expectancy Index *12*
Lindauer, D. and Pritchett, L. 15
linkages between industries 523–4

Linz, J., on presidentialism 54
liquefied natural gas (LNG) market 650, 655, 656
liquidity provision 222, 254, 255–6
literacy ratio changes, relationship to natural
  resources *426, 429*
Little, I., Scitovsky, T., and Scott, M. 15
"little divergence," international relative
  growth rates 27
livestock production, changes 621, *622–3*
Loayza, N. et al., study of Consensus-style
  reforms 94
Loayza, N., Fajnzylber, P., and Calderón, C.,
  on trade liberalization *374, 375*
lobby groups 540–1
López, A. and Ramos, D., on employment
  impact of Chinese imports 484
Lora, E., structural reform index 83, 88–9
Lora, E. and Barrera, F.
  study of Consensus-style reforms 94
  on trade liberalization *372, 375*
Lora, E. and Panizza, U.
  study of Consensus-style reforms 94
  on trade liberalization *374, 375*
lost decade 80, 320, 553–4
  income inequality 691
  poverty levels 630
lost half-decade 19
Love, J.L., on industrialization 6
low-dimensional policies 538
low financial development trap 250–1
Lubell, H., on informal sector 774
Lucas, R., model of growth 524
Lustig, N., on impact of adjustment policies 697

*MacLeod, B. and Urquiola, M., on school
  productivity and student effort* 830–2
macroeconomic policy 260–1
  comparison of new developmentalism and
    conventional orthodoxy *123*, 124–6
  countercyclical 759
  new developmentalism 119
macroeconomic populism 53
macroeconomic stabilization 104
  1990s 84
  econometric studies 94
  Washington Consensus 82

macroeconomic volatility 743–5
Magaldi de Sousa, M., on judicial activism 67
Mainwaring, S. and Scully, T.R., on party
        system institutionalization 69
Malaysia
    quantitative type regulations 166
    TFP growth *581*
Maloney, W.
    on Argentina 420
    on natural resource curse 417
managed floating 204–5, 206
management financing, social security
        systems 877
mangrove swamp loss 142
manufactured exports
        regional LAC and home markets
            480–4
    competitiveness of LAC with China 471–5
    growth
        comparison of LAC and China 469–71
        LAC share *471*
        threat from China 469–75, 479–80, 485
        trends 319
        world market competition 475, 476–8
    see also exports
manufacturing
    FDI 440, 446
        MERCOSUR 448–50
        outward 455
    productivity gaps with US 594–5
manufacturing decline 600–2, *601*
maquiladora plants 7, 319–20, 587
    as source of uncertainty 748, 753
    wage gaps 386
Marfán, M.
    on fiscal policy and monetary policy
        interactions 227
    on private sector exuberance 233, 235
Marfán, M., Medina, J.P., and Soto, C.,
        micro-founded DSGE model 233
Marginality Index, Mexico 734, 736
marine ecosystem degradation 142
market-based financial systems 250
market discipline 605
market diversification 748
market failures 527–8
market liquidity 253–5

market making function of banks 252–3, 261
market-oriented reforms, impact on
        inequality 698, 699
market reforms 16–18, 104–5
    policy diversity 18–19
market-seeking FDI 446
    manufacturing in MERCOSUR 448–50
    public utilities and infrastructure 446–8
market segmentation 253–4
Márques, G. and Pagés, C., on effects of trade
        liberalization 377, 378, 380
Marshall Plan 4
Martin, W., on natural resource curse 418
Marxism
    approach to colonial heritage 36–8
    comparison with New Institutional
        Economics 34
mass consumption 114
matching defined contributions (MDC)
        programs 846, 850, 851
Matsuyama, K., emphasis on productivity 523
maturity structure of debt 287
Menem, Carlos 401
MERCOSUR 324, 327, 328, 347, 348, *357*
    agro-food products 624, *625*
    challenges 362
    changes in land cultivation 618, *620*
    changes in livestock 621, *623*
    FTAA negotiations 361
    institutional structure 353
    market-seeking manufacturing
        FDI 448–50
    total exports, 1990–2007 *325*
    trans-continental agreements 332
mergers and acquisitions (M&A) 168–9
Meso-American Biological Corridor 138
Meso-American Integration and
        Development Project (PM) 363, 364
Mesquita Moreira, M., on competitiveness
        with China 474, 485–6
Mexico
    automobile industry, efficiency-seeking
        FDI 450–1
    bilateral trade agreements 328
    budget balance, 1990s 86
    childhood interventions 857
    civil service capacity 69

conditional cash transfers (CCTs) 852, 853, 854
conservation efforts 139
currency crisis, 1994 197, 198
decentralization 282, 283
dependence on US market 748
diesel sulfur content 141
dollarization 225
economic growth
   1997–2007 521
   in crisis periods 217
   state-led industrialization period 10, 12–13
education
   average years of schooling 822
   ranking by attendance and effectiveness 825
   ranking by effectiveness gap 824
   reading proficiency 827
   urban enrollment 817
educational spending 308
emigration 513
energy consumption 137
energy intensity 136–7, 137
environmental degradation, costs 143
exchange rate regime , late 1970s 192
exchange rates, crisis periods 219, 220
export promotion policies 72, 319–20
exports 470–1
   to China 464
   to Latin America 481
   shares by main destination, 2000 and 2007 333
   threat from China 475, 479, 480, 482, 485–6
external accounts, 1990–2002 234
FDI 442
   outward 453
free trade agreements 330, 349
government expenditure 272
Human Development Index 727
hydrocarbon sector reforms 643
imports and exports, trends 370
income inequality 706–10, 707
inflation rates 14, 216
   1980s 193–4, 194
   1990s 85
inflation targeting 223

infrastructure
   investment as percentage of GDP 677
   trends 663
interest rates, crisis periods 218
investment rates 583
judicial independence 68
labor laws, enforcement 806
land cultivation changes 617–18, 619
legislature capabilities 66
livestock, changes 621, 622
"Living Better" strategy 633
maquiladora plants 7
Marginality Index 734, 736
migration to USA and Spain 499
mortality, under-5 141
natural gas reserves 640
natural resource use 419–20
oil production, economic importance 640
oil reserves 639
output, relationship to productivity and employment 573–4
Pacto de Solidaridad Económica 194–5
party system institutionalization (PSI) 71
per capita GDP
   1820–2003 32
   comparison with Vietnam 572
per capita income, growth, 1950–2006 112
peso crisis 161
Policy Index 62
poverty levels 717, 731–2
   evolution by dimension 734
   multidimensional measurement 733
   multidimensional poverty index 735
price policies 611–12
private expenditure excess, 1990s 233
PROCAMPO program 612
productivity gaps with US 594, 595
proportion of land covered by forest 138
public balance as a percentage of GDP 280
public debt, 1990s 86
public investment 584
public policies 61
real exchange rates
   1980–2008 209
   1990–2002 234
   volatility 201
redistribution of income 306

Mexico (*cont.*)
  relative growth performance, 1990–2008 *21*
  reserve accumulation *200*
  RP and *KI* indices *558*
  sector composition of employment *379–80*
  selective property rights *417–18*
  size of financial system *245*
  social expenditure *273, 844*
    trends *845*
  social security coverage *874*
  social security reforms *879*
  stock market turnover ratios *254*
  tariff rates, trends *321, 369*
  tax collection capacity *307*
  tax revenue as a percentage of GDP *269*
  Tequila crisis, labor market effects *753*
  TFP growth *581*
  trade liberalization *320–1*
    effect on wage levels *383*
  unsatisfied basic needs (UBN) *730*
  wage gaps *385, 386–7*
  weighted average growth rates *11*
  workfare program *848*
Mexico–Japan Economic Partnership
      Agreement *331*
micro-enterprises
  informal employment *778, 779*
  labor costs *784*
  regulations *783*
micro-entrepreneurship *782*
micro-loans *762*
middle-income countries, suitability of new
      developmentalism *113*
migrants to Spain and USA
  labor participation *507*
    economic participation *508*
    employment *508–12*
    sociodemographic profiles *499–500*
      age structure *500–3, 501*
      educational levels *506–7*
migration *see* international migration;
      intraregional migration
milagre econômico, Brazil *190*
mineral royalties allocation *284*
minimum wage policies *761*
  Brazil *705, 706*
  lack of enforcement *630*

mining
  FDI *444–6*
  productivity gaps with US *594*
mining production *132, 133–4*
mixed economy model *8–9, 13*
mixed models of industrialization *6–7*
monetary policy
  crisis periods *217–20*
  interactions with fiscal policy *227–30*
  multiple equilibrium approach *232*
  tackling exuberance *235, 237*
Montreal Protocol, signatories *154–5*
Morley, S.
  on impact of market-oriented reforms *698*
  study of Consensus-style reforms *94*
Morris, M.D., Physical Quality of Life
      Index *721*
multidimensional poverty index *732–3, 735*
multilateral environmental agreements *153–6*
multilateral trade agreements *344*
multiple equilibrium approach *232, 237*
multiple exchange rates *5*
Murillo, M.V., on labor reforms *790, 801*

Naím, M., on Washington Consensus *79*
Nash equilibria *604*
National Agricultural Research Institutes
      (NARIs) *613–14*
national developmentalism *108, 110, 111*
  comparison with new
      developmentalism *116–20, 119*
national states *41*
National System of Innovation (NSI) *551, 553,*
      563
nations, economic role *122, 123*
natural gas
  cross-border pipelines *649*
  LNG market *650*
natural gas reserves *638, 640*
  see also hydrocarbon sector
natural gas use *637, 656*
natural resource curse *396–9, 555*
  alleviation *418*
  Argentina *400–2*
  and Brazil *406–7*
  Chile, absence *402–3*

Dutch Disease 414
    institutional weakness 416–17
    relationship to specificity of
        capabilities 533
    terms of trade deterioration 414–15
    Venezuela 403–6
    volatility 415
    vulnerability to external shocks 415–16
natural resource-driven development 131–4
    environmental consequences 134
natural resource-seeking FDI 444–6
natural resource uses 419–22
natural resource wealth measurement 422
natural resources 152
    compensation for loss 144
    export share as indicator of structural
        change 556
    OFDI 454–5
    relationship to economic growth 411–12,
        425, 426, 427–8
    relationship to gross enrollment ratio 430
    relationship to human development 412,
        413, 432, 433
        data and empirical methodology 422–3
        results 423–5, 426, 427
        regional interactions 425, 432
    relationship to life expectancy 431
    relationship to literacy ratio changes 429
    sustainability 143
neo-classical economics 121, 520
neo-liberalism 568–71, 603–6
    Chile 118
    economic slowdown 571
neo-mercantilism 200
neo-structuralism 18–19
net migration (NM) 494
Netherlands, FDI 442, 443
network-like organizations 542
new activities
    challenges 528–9
    use of existing capabilities 529
new developmentalism 113–16
    comparison with conventional
        orthodoxy 120–6
    comparison with national
        developmentalism 116–20, 119
    conclusion 126

New Institutional Economics (neo-
        institutionalism) 32, 33–4, 45, 45–6,
        122
    approach to colonial heritage 34–6
    comparison with Marxism 34
    focus on domestic forces 39–40
'new' left 587, 589
new regionalism 341, 347
    as complement to structural
        reforms 347–9
    Free Trade Area of the Americas
        (FTAA) 359–61
    MERCOSUR 362
    policy instruments 351–3
    policy objectives 349–50
    structure of trade flows 355
    trade openness 354
New Zealand
    RP and KI indices 558
    TFP growth 581
Nicaragua
    CCT program 736
    civil service capacity 69
    conservation efforts 139
    decentralization 282
    economic growth, 1997–2007 521
    education
        average years of schooling 822
        ranking by attendance and
            effectiveness 825
        ranking by effectiveness gap 824
        urban enrollment 817
    energy consumption 137
    export shares by main destination, 2000
        and 2007 333
    FDI 442
    government expenditure 272
    Human Development Index 727
    hydrocarbon sector reforms 645
    imports and exports, trends 370
    intraregional migration 496
    judicial independence 68
    labor laws, enforcement 806
    labor market reforms 794, 800
    legislature capabilities 66
    migration to USA and Spain 499
    Policy Index 62

Nicaragua (*cont.*)
  poverty levels *717*
    multidimensional poverty index *735*
  public policies *61*
  relative growth performance,
    1990–2008 *21*
  social expenditure *273, 844*
    trends *845*
  social security coverage *873*
  tariff rates, trends *321, 369*
  tax revenue as a percentage of GDP *269*
  TFP growth *581*
  unsatisfied basic needs (UBN) *730*
  wage gaps *385*
  weighted average growth rates *11*
Nicita, A., on Mexican income inequality *708*
nominal exchange rate (NER) *187*
non-contributory pension schemes *882*
non-contributory social insurance (NCSI)
    schemes *842, 850–1*
non-contributory social security *865*
non-labor income inequality
  Brazil *705*
  Mexico *709–10*
non-tax revenues *300, 301*
North, D., on institutions *33, 34, 36–7*
North American Free Trade Area
    (NAFTA) *324, 347, 349, 359, 708, 808*
  effect on agricultural employment *381*
  institutional structure *353*
  intra-industry trade *357*
North–South free trade agreements *364–5*
    see also Free Trade Area of the Americas
    (FTAA)
North–South struggle *334–5*

Ocampo, J.
  on capital account deregulation *247*
  on coordination of policies and
    regulations *261*
  on current account and fiscal surpluses *227*
  study of Consensus-style reforms *94*
Ocampo, J. and Parra, M., on terms of trade
    deterioration *414*
Ocampo, J. and Vos, R., on technological
    innovation *117*

O'Donnell, G., on instability of
    democracies *52*
OECD countries
  fiscal policy measures *296*
  fiscal systems *296–303*
off-equilibrium paths *232*
official development aid (ODA) *878*
"offshoring," as source of uncertainty *748*
oil boom *191, 421, 631–2*
oil exploration, foreign direct investment *440*
oil multinationals *648–9*
oil production
  economic importance *638, 640, 641*
  FDI *444–6*
  natural resource curse *416–17*
  Venezuela *403–6, 419, 420*
  see also hydrocarbon sector
oil reserves *638, 639*
  Brazil *407*
oil royalties allocation *284*
oil shocks *551*
  impact *320*
old regionalism *341, 344–5*
  Andean Pact (Community of Andean
    Nations) *346–7*
  Central American Common Market *345–6*
  Latin American Free Trade Association
    (LAFTA) *346*
  policy instruments *351*
  trade openness *354*
open architecture, lobby groups *540*
open forest *531–2*
  relationship to economic growth *536*
  relationship to GDP *532, 534*
  Venezuela *419*
"opportunity ropes" *857, 859*
Ortega y Gasset, J. *570–1*
output volatility *745*
outward FDI *452–5*
  1990–2008 *439*
  conclusions *456–7*
  by investor countries, 1994–2008 *453*
outward oriented growth strategy,
    Washington Consensus *82*
over-optimism *178, 235*
Overcoming Volatility, IDB 1995 *100*
overcrowding *729, 730*

ozone layer
  Montreal Protocol 154–5
  Vienna Convention 154–5

P-900 *program, Chile* 829
Pacto de Solidaridad Económica, Mexico 194–5
Panama
  adjusted savings rate 143–4
  civil service capacity 69
  decentralization 282
  economic growth
    1997–2007 521
    state-led industrialization period 10
  education
    average years of schooling 822
    ranking by attendance and
      effectiveness 825
    ranking by effectiveness gap 824
    urban enrollment 817
  export shares by main destination, 2000
    and 2007 333
  FDI 442
  government expenditure 272
  Human Development Index 727
  judicial independence 68
  labor laws, enforcement 806
  labor market reforms 794, 800
  legislature capabilities 66
  migration to USA and Spain 499
  party system institutionalization (PSI) 71
  per capita income, growth, 1950–2006 112
  poverty levels 717
  public policies 61
  relative growth performance, 1990–2008 21
  size of financial system 245
  social expenditure 273, 844
  social security coverage 780, 874
  social security reforms 879
  tax revenue
    from natural resources 144
    as a percentage of GDP 269
  wage gaps 385
  weighted average growth rates 11
Paraguay
  civil service capacity 68, 69
  decentralization 282

  economic growth, 1997–2007 521
  education
    average years of schooling 822
    ranking by attendance and effectiveness 825
    ranking by effectiveness gap 824
    reading proficiency 827
    urban enrollment 817
  export shares by main destination, 2000
    and 2007 332
  FDI 442
  government expenditure 272
  Human Development Index 727
  imports and exports, trends 370
  inflation rates 14
  judicial independence 68
  labor laws, enforcement 806
  labor market reforms 795
  legislature capabilities 66
  migration to USA and Spain 499
  party system institutionalization (PSI) 71
  per capita income, growth, 1950–2006 112
  Policy Index 62
  poverty levels 717
    multidimensional poverty index 735
  public policies 61
  relative growth performance,
    1990–2008 21
  social expenditure 273, 844
    trends 845
  social security coverage 873
  tariff rates, trends 321, 369
  tax revenue as a percentage of GDP 269
  TFP growth 581
  wage gaps 385
  weighted average growth rates 11
parametric social security reforms 865
parliamentary forms of government 54
participatory poverty assessments (PPA) 725–6
partisan politics *see* political ideology
party system institutionalization (PSI)
    69–70, 71
path-dependency 529, 569
Paus, E., domestic competition index
    (DCI) 481
PDVSA 644, 645, 646, 647, 649
  OFDI 454
peasants, as workforce 41

PEMEX 643, 646, 647
pension coverage 753–4, 755, 843
    access for informal workers 787
    effect of reforms 772
    individual savings schemes 18
    informal sector 784
    non-contributory schemes 882
    see also social protection
pension funds, effect on liquidity 253
pension reforms 88
    role of World Bank 866–7
per capita GDP 27
    1500–2001 28
    effect of Consensus-style reforms 91–2
    relationship to CO$_2$ emissions 151
    relative, Latin America and East Asia,
        1980–2006 92
per capita income, growth, 1950–2006 112
Pérez, Carlos Andrés 404
peripheral capitalism 38–9
"periphery" of world economy 4
Perón, J. 400–1
Perry, G. et al.
    study of informal sector 781
    on vicious circles 752
personal compensation for risk of job
        loss 792, 797, 798
personal income taxes 268
    comparison with OECD countries 300, 301
    decentralization 283
personal security 798
    relationship to political ideology 803–4
Peru
    adjusted savings rate 143
    budget balance, 1990s 86
    CCT program 736
    childhood interventions 857
    civil service capacity 68, 69
    decentralization 282
    dollarization 200, 225
    economic growth
        1997–2007 521
        in crisis periods 217
    education
        average years of schooling 822
        ranking by attendance and
            effectiveness 825
    ranking by effectiveness gap 824
    reading proficiency 827
    urban enrollment 817
    electoral volatility 70
    exchange rates, crisis periods 219
    exports
        to China 464, 465
        shares by main destination, 2000 and
            2007 332
    FDI 442
        hydrocarbon sector 647, 648
    FIT regime 199–200
    government expenditure 272
    Human Development Index 727
    hydrocarbon sector reforms 642, 643
    imports and exports, trends 370
    inflation rates, 1990s 85
    inflation targeting 223
    infrastructure
        investment as percentage of GDP 677
        trends 663
    interest rates, crisis periods 218
    judicial independence 68
    labor laws, enforcement 806
    labor market reforms 794, 800
    legislature capabilities 66
    macroeconomic policy, 1990s 197
    migration to USA and Spain 499
    natural gas reserves 640
    natural resource use 421
    oil production, economic importance 640
    oil reserves 639
    party system institutionalization (PSI) 71
    per capita income, growth, 1950–2006 112
    Policy Index 62
    poverty levels 717
        multidimensional poverty index 735
    productivity growth 578, 581
    public balance as a percentage of GDP 280
    public debt, 1990s 86
    public policies 61
    real exchange rates, 1980–2008 210
        volatility 201
    redistribution of income 306
    relative growth performance,
        1990–2008 21
    reserve accumulation 200

self-discovery externalities 528
size of financial system 245
social expenditure 273, 844
 trends 845
social security coverage 873
social security reforms 879
stock market turnover ratios 254
tariff rates, trends 321, 369
tax reforms 310
tax revenue
 from natural resources 144
 as a percentage of GDP 269
wage gaps 385
weighted average growth rates 11
workfare program 849
peso crisis 161
pesticide use 139-40
 Rotterdam Convention 155-6
PETROBRAS 646, 647, 649
 modernization 643
 OFDI 454
PETROCARIBE 645
PETROECUADOR 646, 647
petroleum, price 146-7
PETRONIC 645
PETROPERU 643, 646, 647
pharmaceutical industry, intellectual property
 rights 336-7
Philippines, private investment 583
Physical Quality of Life Index 721
PINE 143
Piñera, Sebastian 403
Pinochet, Augusto 402
Plan Real, Brazil 196, 229-30
Plano Trienal, Celso Furtado 120
plantations 38
PLUSPETROL 649
point source resources 398
polarization of employment 490, 509-12
policies
 characteristics 55-6, 58-9, 60-1, 74
 price controls 611-12
policy cooperation 56, 59
 influencing factors 63-4
  civil service capacity 67-8
  congressional capabilities 64-5
  judicial independence 67

party system characteristics 69-70, 71
 policymaking arenas 72-3
 socioeconomic interest groups 71-2
Policy Index 59, 62
policy recommendations 73-4
policy trends 317-18
policymaking 50, 543
 applications of multidimensional poverty
  measurement 734, 736-8
 countercyclical and pro-poor
  policies 759-60
 education expenditure 828-30, 831-2
 eliciting information 539-41
 labor protection and social policies 760-3
 regional integration 343
 social security reforms 872, 876
  fiscal viability 876
policymaking arenas, institutionalization
 levels 72-3
policymaking process (PMP) 55
 cooperation 56
 country level information 73
 as an intertemporal game 57
 spatial dimension 57
political economy 51-4
political ideology
 relationship to employment
  protection 801-2
 relationship to external flexibility 801
 relationship to personal
  compensation 803-4
 relationship to unemployment
  insurance 802-3
 role in labor reform 793
political incentives, role in pro-cyclical fiscal
 policies 278-9
political institutions 56
political parties
 linkages with voters 70
 party system institutionalization (PSI)
  69-70, 71
political regimes 54
political transparency 310-11
pollution
 intra-household 140
 PM10 emissions, selected cities 141
Pombalian reforms 39, 46

population growth *132*
  1500–1820 and 1820–2001 *30*
  1500–2001 29
populist cycles 53
Portugal, per capita GDP, 1950 and 1980 *13*
postwar period 3, 319
  development performance 9–14
  phases of economic growth *551–4*
poverty 736–8
  as capability failure 719–20
  measurement 718
  monetary approach 718
  multidimensional measurement 720–1
    disaggregated data 723–5
    human development approach 721–3
    Human Development Index
      (HDI) 726–7
    policy applications 734, 736–8
    recent measures 730–4
    subjective and participatory
      approaches 725–6
    unsatisfied basic needs (UBN) 727–30
  multidimensionality 715–16, 718–19
  relationship to growth 751–2
  targeted social policies 756
  typologies 736–7
  working poor 773
poverty–insecurity trap 751–2
poverty levels 22, 273, 294, 295, 305
  1980s onwards 21–2
  Brazil 704
  effect of Consensus-style reforms 92–3, 94, 95
  India 603
  rural populations, effects of structural
    reforms 629–30
  trends 716, *717*
poverty line 718
poverty reduction 632–3, *757*, 837, 859
  challenges 856–8
  conditional cash transfers (CCTs) 852, *853*
  labor protection and social policies 760–3
  risk mitigation 758–60
Prasad, E. et al., on volatility of FDI 168
pre-school enrollment 857
Prebisch, R. 395, 523
  on environmental sustainability 130
Prebisch–Singer thesis 396

precios de concertación 611–12
precipitation, changing patterns 148
preferential trade agreements 329–30, 344,
  355, 357
presidential democracies, instability 54
presidents, visits to Wall Street 182
price bands 337, 611
price-based regulations 166
price controls 611
price stability 236
  trade-off with financial stability 223
price volatility 610
primary exports 7
primary-product exporters, growth
  performance 397–8
primary surpluses 286
principal components analysis (PCA), in
  measurement of poverty 723
Pritchett, L., on education quality 827–8, 829
private bond markets 248
private capital flows
  diversification 167–72
  global influences 172
  new policy strength and challenges 173–4
  origins of surges 167
  risks of derivatives 173
private credit/ GDP ratio *251*
private investment 583
private-sector exuberance 233, 235, 236–7
privatization 17–18, 247, 248, 554
  1990s 87–8
  advance 1989–1999 *91*
  effect on employment 771–2
  effect on inequality 94
  FDI 447–8
  hydrocarbon sector 641
  infrastructure industries 659–60, 675–6,
    679–82, 685
    achievements 682–4
  Washington Consensus 81, 82, 83
pro-cyclicality of fiscal policy 267, 274–5
  avoidance 279–80
  causes 278–9
  consequences 275–8
'pro-poor' model 604–5
PROCAMPO program 612
processed agricultural products 624

product distance to quality frontier 535–6
product space 529–32, 538
  centrality of goods 533
  position of LACs 532–3
  relationship to crisis duration 534
product structure, trade flows 356
production sector policies 23
productive transformation 543–4
  obstacles 527, 536, 538
Productive Transformation with Equity,
      ECLAC, 1990 104
productivity gaps 594
  with US 559–61, 560
productivity growth 523, 550, 563, 603
  effect of Consensus-style reforms 91
  effect of economic slowdown 573
  effect of trade liberalization 374, 376, 388
  interaction with structural change 561–2
  international perspective 577–9, 580
  relationship to investment growth 585–7, 588
  sustainability 577
  TFP growth 603
    comparison with Asian economies 579,
    580, 581
programmatic linkages, political parties 70, 71
Progresa, Mexico 709–10, 736, 852, 854
property rights 33
  comparison of new developmentalism and
      conventional orthodoxy 123
  effect of crises 257
  intellectual 336–7, 338
  selective 417–18
  Washington Consensus 81
protectionist policies 5–6, 552–4, 563
prudential framework 260–1
Psacharopoulos, G. et al., on income
      inequality 694
public deficits 119–20
public balances as a percentage of GDP 280
public bonds/GDP ratios 248, 251
public debt
  1990s 86
  domestic component 287, 288, 289
  interest payments 301–2
  maturity structure 287
  relationship to sovereign rating 288
  unexplained changes in stock of debt 286–7

public debt management 267, 285–6
public expenditure re-prioritization,
      Washington Consensus 81, 82, 83, 88–9
public finance restructuring 1990s 17
public finance sustainability 285–9
public goods provision 271–4
public investment
  1970–2008 583–4
  impact of capital flows 180
public sector balance sheet, effect of
      crises 257
public services, foreign direct
      investment 440, 446–8
public spending 266
  effect of pro-cyclical fiscal policies 276
  pro-cyclicality 275
  reforms 307–9, 310, 311
public–private partnerships (PPPs),
      infrastructure industries 681–2
  renegotiation 682–3
public-regardedness of policies 59, 60–1
Puebla–Panama Plan *see* Mesoamerican
      Integration and Development Project

quality frontier, product distances 535–6
quantitative type regulations 166

Rajan, R., on financial development 258
Rama, M., on trade liberalization, effect on
      wage levels 383
Ramsar Convention on Wetlands of
      International Importance,
      signatories 153–4
re-centralization 285
re-election rates, Congress 65
reading proficiency 826–7
real exchange rate (RER)
  Argentina 207
  Brazil 208
  Chile 208
  Colombia 209
  influence on macroeconomic
      performance 203
  Mexico 209
  Peru 210

real exchange rate (*cont.*)
　relationship to net capital inflows *177*
　stable and competitive (SCRER) 190,
　　202–3, 205–7
　volatility, FIT countries *201–2*
　see also exchange rates
Real Plan, Brazil 196
reallocation of labor 382
rebound effects 569–70
recessions
　incidence *746*
　as source of uncertainty 745
RECOPE 644
rediscount loans 255
redistribution of income 305, *306*, 837
REFIDOMSA 645
reform fatigue 242
reforms 54, 321
　comparison of new developmentalism and
　　conventional orthodoxy 123–4
　effects on social protection 772–3
　employment generation and
　　informality 769–73
　foreign direct investment 440
　market-oriented 55
　neo-liberalism 568–9
　see also labor market reforms; social
　　security reforms; tax reforms;
　　Washington Consensus
regasification plants 650, *651*
regional integration 323–31
　conclusion 365–6
　efficiency and welfare effects 358
　Free Trade Area of the Americas
　　(FTAA) 359–61
　future perspectives 358–9
　intra-industry trade *357*
　new developmentalism, as complement to
　　structural reforms 347–9
　new regionalism 347
　　policy objectives 349–50
　old regionalism 344–5
　　Andean Pact (Community of Andean
　　　Nations) 346–7
　　Central American Common
　　　Market 345–6
　　Latin American Free Trade Association
　　　(LAFTA) 346

performance, trade openness 353–4
policy instruments *351–3*
preferential trade agreements 355, 357
rationale
　economic welfare 342
　policy signaling 343
　systemic strategies 343–4
structure of trade flows 355, *356–7*
subregional agreements 362–4
regional markets, competition from
　　China 480–2
regional oligopolies 593
regionalism 318
regulation of markets 121
　case for 163–5
　experience 166–7
　objectives 165–6
regulation of social security systems 877, 881
regulations, relationship to financial
　　structure 262
regulatory changes 260
　banking systems 246–8
Reinhart, C. and Rogoff, K., on banking
　　crises 247, 257
relative backwardness 31, 45
　dependency school approach 52
　link to colonial heritage 26, 32, 34,
　　36, 45
Relative Participation (*RP*) index 557, *558*
relative per capita GDP *9*
relative rate of assistance (RRA) 627
remittances 489
renewable energy use 136, 146, 637, 651–2, 656
　biofuels 652–4
　Uruguay 148
rent-seeking 416
repo transactions 253
research policies 613–14
reserve accumulation 205
　2000s 200
resource-based activities, differences from
　　industrialization 523
resource endowments 35, 44
　see also natural resources
Revenga, A., on Mexican income
　　inequality 707–8
"reversal of fortune" argument 36
reversibility of financial flows 168, 174

Ribe, H., Robalino, D., and Walker, I.
　on food-based programs 847–8
　on social insurance 856
risk adaptation 760
risk coping 760–1
risk management 743, 836
risks from economic insecurity 742
road density, trends 662–3, 664
road networks, investment as percentage of
　　GDP 677
road quality, trends 662–3, 666, 667
Roca Runciman Treaty 400
Rodríguez, F. and Gomolin, A., on
　　Venezuela 419
Rodríguez, F. and Hausmann, R., on
　　Venezuela 419
Rodríguez, F. and Sachs, J., on natural
　　resource curse 415
Rodrik, D.
　on effects of trade liberalization 382
　on growth strategies 99
　study of "export subsidization" 55
Romer, P., model of growth 524
Ros, J., on benefits of natural resources 416
Rosenstein-Rodan, P. 523
Rotterdam Convention, signatories 155–6
roundwood production 132
rules of origin, old and new regionalism 351, 352
rural access index (RAI) 668, 669
rural development 608–9
rural non-farm employment (RNFE) 629
rural populations, effects of structural
　　reforms 628–9
rural poverty 22
　effects of structural reforms 629–30
rural–urban inequality
　income 708
　social security coverage 872–5
Russian crisis 197, 198
　monetary policy 217

Sachs, J., on income inequality 53
Sachs, J. and Warner, A., on natural resource
　　curse 414–15
Saiegh, S.M., comparison of legislatures 65
Sala-i-Martin, X. and Subramanian, A., on
　　natural resource curse 417

Sánchez-Páramo, C. and Schady, N., on wage
　　differentials 698
sanitation 142, 146, 729
　access to facilities 669
　investment as percentage of GDP 677
savings constraint, developing
　　countries 115–16
Scandinavian countries, natural resource
　　use 420
Scartascini, C. et al., on civil service
　　capacities 68
Scartascini, C., Stein, E., and Tommasi, M.,
　　on judicial independence 67
Schmidt-Hebbel, K., on inflation
　　targeting 231
Schmidt-Hebbel, K. and Werner, A., on
　　policy reaction to exchange rates 223
Schmukler, S. and de la Torre, A., on financial
　　development 251
Schneider, B.R., on role of business groups in
　　PMP 72
school attendance 729, 814–16
　effect of conditional cash transfers 852
　urban enrollment 816–18, 817
　years in school and years of schooling
　　819–24, 820
school feeding programs 847
school productivity 829, 830–2
SCRER-targeting policies 205–6
　Argentina 202–3
sea levels, rise 148
"second conquest" 39
sector composition of employment, effect of
　　trade liberalization 379–81
Securing our Future in the Global Economy,
　　World Bank, 2000 101
Seddon, J. and Wacziarg, R., on effects of
　　trade liberalization 381–2
SEDLAC (Socioeconomic Database
　　for Latin America and the
　　Caribbean) 696
seed production 612, 632
segmented welfare states 8
selective education 830–2
selectivity of capital account
　　liberalization 164
self-contemplation 570
self-discovery externalities 527–8

self-employment
    access to social protection 779
    informal sector 778, 779
    as a voluntary option 781–2
self-financing, infrastructure 678–9
self-insurance strategy 242, 261
self-organization, lobby groups 540–1
Sen, A.
    on aggregate index of poverty 718
    on "being happy" 725
    on wellbeing evaluation 719–20
sequencing of reforms 97–8, 164
service provision, effect of
        decentralization 282–3, 284
services
    employment elasticities 591
    foreign direct investment 446
    low-productivity growth 591–2
    productivity gaps with US 594
settlement procedures, old and new
        regionalism 351, 353
settler economies, success 45
silver standard 5
Singapore, TFP growth 581
Singer, H. 395
SINOPEC 648
size of financial systems 244–6, 245
    small size of banking system 252–3
skill gap, contribution to income inequality 702
skilled-biased technical change (SBTC),
        impact on inequality 698
slavery, abolition 39, 46
Smoot–Hawley tariff 5–6
social assistance 837–8, 846
    challenges
        disconnection from social
            insurance 855–6
        poverty reduction 856–8
    conditional cash transfers (CCTs) 851–4
    in-kind transfers 847–8
    non-contributory social insurance (NCSI)
        schemes 850–1
    outcomes 854–5
    workfare programs 848–50
    see also social protection
social contract 743
social development, 1980s onwards 21–2

social exclusion approach to poverty 719
social expenditure 272–3
social insurance 310, 836–8, 843
    disconnection from social assistance
        855–6, 858–9
    NCSI 842, 850–1
social investment funds 841
social pensions 850, 856, 858
social policies 755–7, 761–3
    impact on inequality 699–700
social programs 633
social protection 809, 836–8
    access for informal workers 779–81, 787
    conclusions 858–9
    effect of reforms 772–3
    expenditure 842, 844
        trends 845–6
    history 839–42, 840
    pension coverage 843
    reforms 791–2
    see also social assistance
social sciences, marginalization 570
social security debate 864–5
social security reforms 863, 881–3
    administrative areas 877
    fiscal viability 876
    implementation capacity 878–80
    importance of choice 878
    link between entitlements and
        contributions 877–8
    policy options 872, 876
    role of World Bank 866–7
    social dialogue 880
    structural preconditions 867–71
social security systems
    coverage by preconditions 871–2, 872–5
    development 8
social vulnerability, as result of globalization 491
socioeconomic interest groups, role in policy
        cooperation 71–2
soil degradation 138, 139
soil usage changes 133
Sokoloff, K. and Robinson, J., on colonial
        heritage 35
Sokoloff, K. and Zolt, E., on tax policy 268
solar energy 652
Solidarity Fund, Chile 797

Solow residual 520
South Africa
    employment elasticities 589
    private investment 583
South to North migration 494
sovereign wealth funds 397
Spain
    FDI 441–2, 443
    labor reforms 786
    Latin American migrants 497–8, 499
        age structure 500–3, 501
        characteristics of employment 512
        economic activity by sex 509
        educational levels 506–7
        labor participation 507–12
        sex ratios 503–5
    per capita GDP, 1950 and 1980 13
    population growth of 20–49 year old by
        migratory status 502
special and differential treatment (S&D), old
        and new regionalism 351, 352–3
specialization
    correlation with growth 398
    specificity of capabilities 529, 533
specialization patterns 554, 555–6, 559
spillovers of TNCs 449, 451
spot transactions 57
structure, Marxist view 34
stability of policies 58, 60–1
stabilization 274–81
    relationship to government size 277
stabilization funds 279–80
stable and competitive real exchange rates
        (SCRER) 190, 202–3, 205–7
Stallings, B. and Peres, W., study of
        Consensus-style reforms 94
state development banks 7
state growth 121
state-led growth 46–7
state-led industrialization 3, 7–9, 118–19, 345,
        551, 552
    development performance 9–14
    paradigm shift 14–16
    shift away from 80
state-owned enterprises (SOEs) 646
    hydrocarbon sector 641, 645–7
sterilized interventions 206–7

Stiglitz, J., on Washington Consensus 83
stock exchange prices, relationship to country
        risk 169
stock market capitalization/GDP ratios 248,
        249, 250
stock market turnover ratios 254
stock of debt, unexplained changes 286–7
Stockholm Convention on Persistent Organic
        Pollutants, signatories 155–6
stop-and-go dynamics, 1950s–1960s 189
storms, increasing frequency 149
strategic asset-seeking FDI 452
stratification, educational systems 830–2
strong sustainability 143
structural change 555–8
    interaction with productivity
        growth 561–2
Structural Change and Productivity Growth,
        ECLAC, 2008 102
structural fiscal balance 275
structural reform index 83–4, 88–9
structural reforms
    econometric studies 94
    effect on income inequality 701
    effect on rural populations and
        employment 628–9
    effects on agricultural economies 627–8
    effects on rural poverty 629–30
    impact on agricultural sector 609
    income inequality 691
    land and irrigation policies 615–16
    new regionalism 347–9
    policies for input markets and agricultural
        credit 612–13
    price and direct support policies 611–12
    research and technology transfer
        policies 613–14
    trade policy 609–11
structural socioeconomic factors 52
Structural Surplus Rule (SSR), Chile 280–1
structural tendencies, comparison of new
        developmentalism and conventional
        orthodoxy 123, 124
structural transformation 525–7
    impedance by market failures 527–8
    new activities 528–30
    obstacles 538

policy agenda 538
product space 529–32
structuralism 110–11, 114–16, 547–8
subcontracting law, Chile 786
subregional integration 362–4
Suescún, R., structural fiscal balance 275
sugar exports, decline in 1980s 320
Summers, Larry, on economic growth 536, 538
Summit of the Americas, 1994 359
super-structure, Marxist view 34
supervisory agency creation, 1990–2002 90
surges in private capital 183
    diversification toward volatility 167–72
    origins 167
    preconditions for sustained growth 179
Suriname
    conservation efforts 139
    poverty levels, multidimensional poverty
        index 735
sustainability 143, 267, 285–9
sustaining growth 99
Sweden, education expenditure 832
System of Electricity Interconnections 655
systemic risk 255–6

tablitas 191
Taiwan
    productivity growth 578
    TFP growth 581
tariff rates
    biofuels 654
    trends 321, 369–70
tariff reduction 17, 87, 117, 269–70, 321–2, 336
    effect of free trade agreements 331
tax morale 304
tax reforms 88, 307, 310, 311
    advance 1989–1999 91
    Washington Consensus 81, 82
tax revenues
    comparison with OECD
        countries 298–301
    as a percentage of GDP 269
    trends 270
taxation 267–71
    decentralization 282–3
    for extraction and export of natural
        resources 144

fuels 146–7, 148
funding of social insurance 855–6
hydrocarbon sector 642, 643
technological capabilities, structuralist
        approach 547–8
technological innovation 117
    absence from Washington
        Consensus 101–3
technological learning 548–9, 552–3
    relationship to economic growth 550–1,
        563–4
technological policies 17, 23
    absence in 1990s 554
technological progress, impact on
        inequality 698
technological stagnation 38
technology gap 43, 548–9, 555, 557–8
technology transfer policies 613–14
telecommunications
    access to services 668–9, 669
    investment as percentage of GDP 677
    quality 664–5
    trends 662–3, 664–5, 667
telephone density, trends 661–4
temperatures, extreme, increasing
        frequency 149
Tequila crisis 233
    inflation rates 217
    labor market effects 753
    see also crises
"tequila effect" 197
terms of trade deterioration, as result of
        natural resource abundance 414–15
Thailand
    output, relationship to productivity and
        employment 573–4
    TFP growth 581
threshold effects, reforms 98
tin agreement, collapse 320
Tirole, J., on liquidity 254
Torgler, B., on tax morale 304
Tornell, A. and Lane, P.
    on natural resource curse 416
    voracity effect 398
total factor productivity (TFP) growth 603
    comparison with Asian economies 579,
        580, 581
tourism, environmental consequences 134

trade blocs 331, 610
trade coverage, old and new
        regionalism 351
trade flows
    geographical structure 357
    product structure 356
    structure 355, 356–7
trade liberalization 17, 87, 117, 180–1, 318,
        320–1, 369–71, 554, 609–11
    effects 368, 372, 374–6, 376–7, 388–9
        on aggregate employment 378–9
        on balance of payments 322
        on employment mobility, stability, and
            informality 381–2
        on income inequality 700, 707–8
        on sector composition of
            employment 379–81
        on unemployment 377–8
        on wage gaps 384–7
        on wage levels 383–4
    employment generation and
        informality 769–73
    expected results 371–2
    old and new regionalism 351, 352
    public opinion 371–2, 373
    regional integration 323–31, 343–4
    relationship to income inequality 703–4
    sequencing 98
    unequalizing effects 692
    Washington Consensus 81, 82–3
trade openness 353–4
trade policy
    relationship to growth 318
    structural reforms 609–11
trade reforms, advance 1989–1999 91
trade shocks 747–9
trade taxes 300, 301
trading systems reform implementation,
        1990–2002 90
trans-continentalism 331–4
trans-Latins 454–5
transfers
    comparison with OECD countries 302
    to subnational governments 283–4
transnational corporations (TNCs) 439–41
    spillovers 449, 451
    see also foreign direct investment (FDI)
transnational development style 131

transparency, lobby groups 541
transportation 140
    fuel consumption 638
    as source of pollution 141–2
Trinidad & Tobago
    energy consumption 137
    imports and exports, trends 370
    natural gas reserves 640
    oil production, economic importance 640
    oil reserves 639
    poverty levels, multidimensional poverty
        index 735
    social expenditure 844
    tariff rates, trends 369
"tropicalization" 613–14
truncated convergence 31
truncated welfare state 841–2
twin banking and credit crises 256–7
two-gap model 115–16

under-5 mortality rates 141, 142
unemployment
    effect of trade liberalization 377–8
    personal compensation 792
    relationship to income inequality
        702, 703
    as result of economic instability 752–3,
        770–1
unemployment insurance 791, 792, 809
    flexicurity 798
    reforms 795–7
    relationship to political ideology 802–3
union activity, decline, relationship to income
        inequality 702
union affiliation, Argentina 400
Union of South American Nations
        (UNASUR) 363, 364
union power, relationship to wage
        gaps 386
Unit of Real Value (URV), Brazil 196
United Nations Convention on Biological
        Diversity, signatories 154–5
United Nations Convention to Combat
        Desertification (UNCCD),
        signatories 155–6
United Nations Framework Convention on
        Climate Change, signatories 154–5

United States
  as destination of Latin American
    migration 499
  FDI 441, 443
  free trade agreements 324, 328
    role in labor laws enforcement 805,
      807–8, 809–10
  gap between LAC and US 520
  Latin American migrants 497–8
    age structure 500–3, 501
    characteristics of employment 512
    economic activity by sex 509
    educational levels 506–7
    labor participation 507–12
    sex ratios 503–5
  natural resource use 421
  population growth of 20–49 year old by
    migratory status 502
  TFP growth 581
unremunerated reserve requirements
    (URR) 166
unsatisfied basic needs (UBN) 719, 723–4,
    727–30
urban environment 140–2, 146
urban poverty 22
urbanization 628
Urquiola, M. and Calderón, V., on
    education 815, 816–18
Uruguay
  child poverty 730–1
  civil service capacity 69
  crawling peg regimes 191
  decentralization 282
  economic growth
    1997–2007 521
    state-led industrialization period 10
  economic liberalization 163
  education
    average years of schooling 822
    ranking by attendance and
      effectiveness 825
    ranking by effectiveness gap 824
    urban enrollment 817
  export shares by main destination, 2000
    and 2007 332
  factors in economic success 45

  FDI 442
  government expenditure 272
  Human Development Index 727
  imports and exports, trends 370
  inflation rates 14
  judicial independence 68
  labor laws, enforcement 806
  legislature capabilities 66
  migration to USA and Spain 499
  party system institutionalization (PSI) 71
  per capita GDP
    1820–2003 32
    1950 and 1980 13
  per capita income, growth, 1950–2006 112
  Policy Index 62
  poverty levels 717, 731–2
    evolution by dimension 734
    multidimensional poverty index 735
  public policies 61
  relative growth performance,
    1990–2008 21
  renewable energy use 148
  RP and KI indices 558
  sector composition of employment 380
  size of financial system 245
  social expenditure 273, 844
  social security coverage 875
  tariff rates, trends 321, 370
  tax revenue
    from natural resources 144
    as a percentage of GDP 269
  TFP growth 581
  wage gaps 385, 386
  weighted average growth rates 11
Uruguay Round (UR), GATT 335, 336, 610

Vale, OFDI 454–5
value added taxes (VAT) 270
  decentralization 283
Van Wijnbergen, S., on protection from
    Dutch Disease 418
Vargas, Getúlio 110
Venezuela
  adjusted savings rate 143
  agrarian reform 615

budget balance, 1990s 86
civil service capacity 69
conservation efforts 139
decentralization 282
dollarization 225
economic growth
    1997–2007 521
    in crisis periods 217
    state-led industrialization period 10
education
    average years of schooling 822
    ranking by attendance and effectiveness 825
    ranking by effectiveness gap 824
    reading proficiency 827
    urban enrollment 817
electoral volatility 70
energy consumption 137
energy intensity 136, 137
exchange rates, crisis periods 219, 220
exports 396
    shares by main destination, 2000 and
        2007 332
FDI
    hydrocarbon sector 647, 648
    inward 442
    outward 453
government expenditure 272
Human Development Index 727
hydrocarbon sector reforms 642
impact of 1973 oil shock 192
imports and exports, trends 370
inflation rates 14, 216
    1990s 85
infrastructure, trends 663
interest rates, crisis periods 218
intraregional immigration 494, 496
judicial independence 68
labor laws, enforcement 806
labor market reforms 794, 796, 800
legislature capabilities 66
migration to USA and Spain 499
natural gas reserves 640
natural resource use 419, 420
natural resources 403–6, 408
oil production, economic importance 640
oil reserves 638, 639

oil stabilization fund 279
party system institutionalization (PSI) 71
per capita GDP
    1820–2003 32
    1950 and 1980 13
per capita income, growth, 1950–2006 112
Policy Index 62
poverty levels 717
public balance as a percentage of GDP 280
public debt, 1990s 86
public policies 61
relative growth performance,
        1990–2008 21
size of financial system 245
social expenditure 273, 844
    trends 845
social security coverage 874
social security reforms 879
stock market turnover ratios 254
tariff rates, trends 321, 370
tax revenue
    from natural resources 144
    as a percentage of GDP 269
TFP growth 581
wage gaps 385
weighted average growth rates 11
Vienna Convention for the Protection of the
        Ozone Layer, signatories 154–5
Vinerian free traders 348
virtuous cycles 550–1, 563
volatility
    absence from Washington
        Consensus 100–1
    capital flows 164–5, 180
    effect on employment 770–1
    macroeconomic variables, effect on
        investment levels 179
    as result of natural resource abundance 415
    see also macroeconomic volatility
Von Braun, J. and Meinzen-Dick, R., on
        foreign ownership of land 632
voracity effect 398, 416
Vos, R. et al., on trade liberalization, effect on
        wage gaps 384
vulnerability zones 162–3
    improvement of debt profiles 165–6

wage earners, informal sector 778, *779*
wage gaps, effect of trade liberalization
      384–7, 388–9
wages
   effect of trade liberalization 376, 383–4, 388
   tendency to increase less than
      productivity 114, 121, 126
Wall Street, presidential visits 182
Wantchekon, L., on natural resource
      curse 417, 418
Washington Consensus 16, 53, 79–83, 111–12,
      121, 242, 321
   conclusion 104–5
   Consensus-style reforms
      implementation 83–9
      outcomes 89–95
   costs of reforms 97
   decalogue of polices 81
   foreign direct investment 440
   reaction to failure 113
   what went wrong 95–6
      faulty implementation and impatience
         view 96–7
      fundamental flaws view 97–9
      incomplete agenda view 100–4
water
   access to safe supplies 668–9
   investment as percentage of GDP *677*
water rights 616
weak sustainability 143
Weigand, C. and Grosh, M., on social
      assistance expenditure 842
welfare programs 762–3
welfare states, segmented 8
wellbeing
   self-reported 725 *see also* poverty,
         multidimensional measurement
Wicksel, K., on fiscal legitimacy 304–5

Williamson, J.
   on inequality 44
   Washington Consensus 16, 79–83, 111, 121
wind energy 652
windows 541
women, incorporation into labor force
      628–9, 769
workfare programs 762, 840, 848–50
World Bank
   adjusted saving measure 143
   *Beyond the Washington Consensus:
      Institutions Matter* 101
   *Closing the Gap in Education and
      Technology* 102
   contribution to industrialization
      process 15
   *Inequality in Latin America and the
      Caribbean* 104
   matrix structure 541–2
   on poverty measurement 719
   reform proposals 16, 18
   role in social security reforms 866–7
   *Securing our Future in the Global
      Economy* 101
World Income Inequality Database 692–3
World Trade Organization (WTO)
   asymmetries 337
   China's entry 339
   membership 322
Wright, G. and Czelusta, J., on United States,
      resource-based growth 421

Yasuni-ITT 138–9

Zuvanic, L. and Iacoviello, M.
   on bureaucracies 68